SOCIAL COGNITION

Understanding People and Events

DAVID L. HAMILTON &
STEVEN J. STROESSNER

Los Angeles | London | New Delhi
Singapore | Washington DC | Melbourne

Los Angeles | London | New Delhi
Singapore | Washington DC | Melbourne

SAGE Publications Ltd
1 Oliver's Yard
55 City Road
London EC1Y 1SP

SAGE Publications Inc.
2455 Teller Road
Thousand Oaks, California 91320

SAGE Publications India Pvt Ltd
B 1/I 1 Mohan Cooperative Industrial Area
Mathura Road
New Delhi 110 044

SAGE Publications Asia-Pacific Pte Ltd
3 Church Street
#10–04 Samsung Hub
Singapore 049483

Editor: Amy Maher
Editorial assistant: Marc Barnard
Production editor: Rachel Burrows
Marketing manager: Camille Richmond
Cover design: Wendy Scott
Typeset by: C&M Digitals (P) Ltd, Chennai, India
Printed in the UK

Library of Congress Control Number: 2020936956

British Library Cataloguing in Publication data

A catalogue record for this book is available from
the British Library

ISBN 978-1-4129-3553-1
ISBN 978-1-4129-3554-8 (pbk)

CONTENTS

ABOUT THE
AUTHORS

David L. Hamilton received his Ph.D. from the University of Illinois. He was on the faculty at Yale University for eight years before moving to the University of California, Santa Barbara. He has published extensively on topics in social perception, including stereotyping, impression formation, person memory, and perceptions of groups. He has served on numerous committees in professional organizations, including the Executive Committees of the Society of Personality and Social Psychology and the Society of Experimental Social Psychology, and for 25 years was co-organizer of the annual Person Memory Interest Group meetings. He has been associate editor of two journals and has served on several editorial boards. He received the MERIT Award from the National Institute of Mental Health in 1987. He has been awarded honorary degrees from two European universities, the University of Lisbon, Portugal (1997) and Eotvos Lorand University in Budapest, Hungary (2000). In 2000 he received the Thomas M. Ostrom Award, presented by the Person Memory Interest Group, for "outstanding contributions to social cognition," and in 2008 received the Jean-Claude Codol Award from the European Association of Social Psychology for "contributions to the advancement of social psychology in Europe." In 2014 he received the Distinguished Alumni Award from his alma mater, Gettysburg College.

Steven J. Stroessner is a Professor of Communication at the University of California, Los Angeles. Before this position, he was a Professor of Psychology and an award-winning instructor at Barnard College, Columbia University. He also served as a Senior Research Scientist at Disney Research. His research examines cognitive and motivational aspects of stereotyping and prejudice, and he has published extensively on social categorization and the utilization of stereotypes in judgment. More recently, his research has examined social categorization processes in judgments of non-social entities ranging from shapes to robots. He is a Fellow of the American Psychological Society and a Fellow and Executive Officer of the Society for Experimental Social Psychology. He co-edited a recent book, *Social Perception from Individuals to Groups*, and is an Associate Editor of the journal, *Social Cognition*. He holds B.A.s in Psychology and Social Work from Hope College in Holland, Michigan, and a Ph.D. in Social/ Personality Psychology from the University of California, Santa Barbara.

PREFACE

Neither of us thought we would ever write a textbook. However, for years an energetic and persistent editor regularly would visit Dave's office, asking him repeatedly if he were interested in writing a text on social cognition. Dave invariably resisted, announcing so clearly and forcefully, "I will never write a textbook," that the editor wrote it down verbatim in his notebook. There were shared smiles when Dave and his writing partner, Steve, were shown this note by the editor a few months later during a dinner celebrating that they had decided to embark on this project.

So, what changed? Dave had just finished some projects and was at a transition point, so time would be available. Also, he was annually teaching graduate and undergraduate courses on social cognition, and he had already edited a book of readings on the topic. It seemed these experiences would provide a valuable foundation for developing a full textbook. "It shouldn't be that difficult," he thought. (Wrong!) He knew, though, that if he were to do it, he wouldn't want to do it alone. Therefore, the next step was to find someone who would agree to work on it with him. Steve had been Dave's graduate student years before, and they had stayed close over the years. Here is where memories begin to differ. Dave has insisted for years that, as he made an early-morning exit from a shared conference hotel room, he asked a groggy Steve to co-author the book. Steve remembers being approached during a poster session the previous night, and, after agreeing on the spot, the brief morning discussion was just confirming what had already been decided. This would not be the last of our disagreements about this project.

We then had to start giving serious thought to what we wanted to do with this text. Dave flew from Santa Barbara to New York to see Steve, who was then a faculty member at Barnard, and also to visit his daughter and son-in-law, who then lived in New Jersey. Meeting in New York allowed us to get some work done while Dave was on the East Coast, but it also allowed us to enjoy some excellent New York restaurants and more than a few bottles of red wine. Many such trips to each coast happened over the next few years.

At our first meeting about the book, Dave asked, "What do we want to do with this project?" Steve responded, "There are several good textbooks on social cognition out there. Let's not do this unless we can do something distinctive." Dave liked this idea, and we chatted about what we thought a social cognition text should look like. We asked ourselves, "What should a social cognition text focus on?" and "How should it be structured?" We talked about our shared views of social cognition and decided that, if we could write a text reflecting those views, it would make our book unique. We determined to write a textbook with several crucial but related characteristics:

- Social cognition is an *approach* to understanding how people think about people and events. Social life entails a continuous flow of information that is critical in adapting to ever-changing social contexts. The essential characteristic of social cognition is its focus on the *cognitive processes* involved in social thought and behavior. We agreed that our text should reflect that defining characteristic. The book's organization would emphasize different aspects of information processing (e.g., attention, inference, memory) rather than focus on topics typically associated with social cognition (e.g., the self, impression formation, stereotyping). The text would present research findings from various content areas, but they would be embedded within and informed by discussions of process.

The next day, as he flew home to Santa Barbara, Dave was excited about organizing the text in terms of important processes underlying information processing. But suddenly, at about 35,000 feet, he realized that there may be a good reason that books often focus on topics like impression formation, stereotyping, and the self: for both instructors and students, these are inherently interesting topics. We need to retain and contribute to those interests. Therefore, we decided that each chapter, focusing on a different process, will end with a discussion of research relating that process to our understanding of the self, of persons, and of groups.

- As an *approach* rather than a *content area*, a social cognitive analysis can be applied to any topic. This analysis would focus on the mental structures and processes involved in any phenomenon relating to social thought and action. Social cognition has historically been used to advance our understanding of person perception, attitudes, and stereotyping. Still, we view its primary value as providing a conceptual framework and associated set of methods that can be used to gain a deeper understanding of a variety of topics. As such, our book should go beyond traditional topics in social cognition and incorporate a broad spectrum of issues in social psychology (e.g., false memories, counterfactual thinking, medical decision making). Hopefully, we can show that these topics can beneficially be considered from a social cognitive perspective.
- Social cognition is a research approach that now has a *rich intellectual history*. Nearly 50 years ago, the first studies focused on social information processing began to appear. Many exciting developments have emerged over subsequent decades, and it is crucial to convey new developments and discoveries that will continue to be explored in the coming years. However, we also believe that readers benefit from understanding the historical antecedents and influences on current research. Our field is sufficiently mature that we should discuss research findings based on their significance and not just their newness. Novel findings should be recognized, but not at the risk of de-emphasizing important discoveries that preceded them.
- Social cognition is *integral* to myriad consequential aspects of life. In its early years, social cognition was sometimes accused of offering a cold, mechanistic understanding of information processing with little relevance to real life. In retrospect, one can see that this criticism contained a kernel of truth. However, the field has developed considerably since its inception. Research demonstrating the critical importance of automatic processes, emotional considerations, and motivational factors in social information processing have revolutionized the field. Given the increased breadth of the social cognitive approach to understanding mental processes, it seemed apparent that many important aspects of life can benefit from a social cognitive analysis. We decided we would highlight many aspects of life that can be understood through a social cognitive lens. Research on real-world topics such as eyewitness identification, using cell phones while driving, and suicide risks should be included in the book.

These were our primary goals in writing this book. You will have to decide whether we have met them. As we mentioned earlier, we have not always agreed ourselves on how to achieve these aims – we suppose such is to be expected in a relationship between a former advisor and advisee. Nonetheless, we have enjoyed working together on this project, and our friendship has strengthened and deepened over this time. In the course of writing this book, we have also benefitted from conversations with and advice from numerous colleagues, including Don Carlston, Russ Fazio, Leonel Garcia-Marques, Jamin Halberstadt, John Holmes, Kerri Johnson, Gordon Moskowitz, Kyle Ratner, Jeff Sherman, John Skowronski, and Andrew Todd. We also thank Molly Ball for her contributions to the book.

We hope you find this text to be a useful, relevant, and engaging overview of social cognition as a fruitful and influential area of research.

ACKNOWLEDGEMENTS

Table 2.1 – Macrae, C.N., Milne, A.B., & Bodenhausen, G.V. (1994). Stereotypes as energy-saving devices: A peek inside the cognitive toolbox. *Journal of Personality and Social Psychology*, *66*(1), 37–47, APA, adapted with permission.

Figure 2.5 – Srull, T.K., & Wyer, R.S., Jr. (1979). The role of category accessibility in the interpretation of information about persons: Some determinants and implications. *Journal of Personality and Social Psychology*, *37*(10), 1660–1672, APA, adapted with permission.

Figure 2.9 – Ratner, K.G., Dotsch, R., Wigboldus, D.H.J., van Knippenberg, A., & Amodio, D.M. (2014). Visualizing minimal ingroup and outgroup faces: Implications for impressions, attitudes, and behavior. *Journal of Personality and Social Psychology*, *106*(6), 897–911, APA, reproduced with permission.

Table 3.2 – Bargh, J.A., & Pietromonaco, P. (1982). Automatic information processing and social perception: The influence of trait information presented outside of conscious awareness on impression formation. *Journal of Personality and Social Psychology*, *43*(3), 437–449, APA, adapted with permission.

Table 3.3 – Dijksterhuis, A., & van Knippenberg, A. (1998). The relation between perception and behavior, or how to win a game of Trivial Pursuit. *Journal of Personality and Social Psychology*, *74*(4), 865–877, APA, adapted with permission.

Table 4.1 – Lord, C.G., & Saenz, D.S. (1985). Memory deficits and memory surfeits: Differential cognitive consequences of tokenism for tokens and observers. *Journal of Personality and Social Psychology*, *49*, 918–926, APA, adapted with permission.

Table 4.5 – Taylor, S.E., & Fiske, S.T. (1975). Point of view and perceptions of causality. *Journal of Personality and Social Psychology*, *32*(3), 439–445, APA, adapted with permission.

Figure 4.4 – Pauker, K., Weisbuch, M., Ambady, N., Sommers, S.R., Adams, R.B., & Ivcevic, Z. (2009). Not so black and white: Memory for ambiguous group members. *Journal of Personality and Social Psychology*, *96*, 795–810, APA, adapted with permission.

Figure 4.6 – Eberhardt, J.L., Goff, P.A., Purdie, V.J., & Davies, P.G. (2004). Seeing black: Race, crime, and visual processing. *Journal of Personality and Social Psychology*, *87*, 876–893, APA, adapted with permission.

Table 5.1 – Semin, G.R., & Fiedler, K. (1988). The cognitive functions of linguistic categories in describing persons: Social cognition and language. *Journal of Personality and Social Psychology*, *54*, 558–568, APA, adapted with permission.

Table 5.3 – Balcetis, E., & Dunning, D. (2006). See what you want to see: Motivational influences on visual perception. *Journal of Personality and Social Psychology*, *91*, 612–625, APA, adapted with permission.

Figure 5.1 – Libby, L.K., Shaeffer, E.M., & Eibach, R.P. (2009). Seeing meaning in action: A bidirectional link between visual perspective and action identification level. *Journal of Experimental Psychology: General*, *138*, 503–516, APA, reproduced with permission.

Figure 5.3 – Mende-Siedlecki, P., Qu-Lee, J., Backer, R., & Van Bavel, J.J. (2019). Perceptual contributions to racial bias in pain recognition. *Journal of Experimental Psychology: General*, *148*, 863–889, APA, reproduced with permission.

Figure 5.4 – Balcetis, E., & Dunning, D. (2006). See what you want to see: Motivational influences on visual perception. *Journal of Personality and Social Psychology*, *91*, 612–625, APA, reproduced with permission.

Figure 5.7 – Cloutier, J., Mason, M.F., & Macrae, C.N. (2005). The perceptual determinants of person construal: Reopening the social-cognitive toolbox. *Journal of Personality and Social Psychology*, *88*, 885–894, APA, reproduced with permission.

Figure 5.8 – Cloutier, J., Mason, M.F., & Macrae, C.N. (2005). The perceptual determinants of person construal: Reopening the social-cognitive toolbox. *Journal of Personality and Social Psychology*, *88*, 885–894, APA, adapted with permission.

Table 6.2 – Amodio, D.M., & Devine, P.G. (2006). Stereotyping and evaluation in implicit race bias: Evidence for independent constructs and unique effects on behavior. *Journal of Personality and Social Psychology*, *91*, 652–661, APA, adapted with permission.

Figure 6.1 – Murphy, S.T., & Zajonc, R.B. (1993). Affect, cognition, and awareness: Affective priming with optimal and suboptimal stimulus exposures. *Journal of Personality and Social Psychology*, *64*, 723–739, APA, adapted with permission.

Figure 6.3 – Stout, J.G., Dasgupta, N., Hunsinger, M., & McManus, M. (2011). STEMing the tide: Using ingroup experts to inoculate women's self-concept and professional goals in science, technology, engineering, and mathematics (STEM). *Journal of Personality and Social Psychology*, *100*, 255–270, APA, adapted with permission.

Figure 6.5 – Sedikides, C., & Green, J.D. (2000). On the self-protective nature of inconsistency-negativity management: Using the person memory paradigm to examine self-referent memory. *Journal of Personality and Social Psychology*, *79*, 906–922, APA, adapted with permission.

Figure 6.6 – Rosenberg, S., Nelson, C., & Vivekananthan, P.S. (1968). A multidimensional approach to the structure of personality impressions. *Journal of Personality and Social Psychology*, *9*, 283–294, APA, reproduced with permission.

Figure 6.7 – Scherer, C.R., Heider, J.D., Skowronski, J.J., & Edlund, J.E. (2012). Trait expectancies and stereotype expectancies affect person memory similarly in a jury context. *The Journal of Social Psychology*, *152*, 613–622, APA, adapted with permission.

Table 7.2 – Blair, I.V., Judd, C.M., Sadler, M.S., & Jenkins, C. (2002). The role of Afrocentric features in person perception: Judging by features and categories. *Journal of Personality and Social Psychology*, *83*, 5–25, APA, reproduced with permission.

Table 7.3 – Smith, E.R., & Miller, F.D. (1983). Mediation among attributional inferences and comprehension processes: Initial findings and a general method. *Journal of Personality and Social Psychology*, *44*, 492–505, APA, adapted with permission.

Table 7.4 – Smith, E.R., & Miller, F.D. (1983). Mediation among attributional inferences and comprehension processes: Initial findings and a general method. *Journal of Personality and Social Psychology*, *44*, 492–505, APA, adapted with permission.

Table 7.7 – Andersen, S.M., & Ross, L. (1984). Self-knowledge and social inference: I. The impact of cognitive/affective and behavioral data. *Journal of Personality and Social Psychology*, *46*, 280–293, APA, adapted with permission.

Table 7.8 – Allison, S.T., & Messick, D.M. (1985). The group attribution error. *Journal of Experimental Social Psychology*, *21*, 563–579, APA, adapted with permission.

Figure 7.2 – Fein, S., Hilton, J.L., & Miller, D.T. (1990). Suspicion of ulterior motivation and correspondence bias. *Journal of Personality and Social Psychology*, *58*, 753–764, APA, adapted with permission.

Figure 7.5 – Blair, I.V., Judd, C.M., Sadler, M.S., & Jenkins, C. (2002). The role of Afrocentric features in person perception: Judging by features and categories. *Journal of Personality and Social Psychology*, *83*, 5–25, APA, reproduced with permission.

Figure 8.5 – Sherman, J.W., Stroessner, S.J., Conrey, F.R., & Azam, O.A. (2005). Prejudice and stereotype maintenance processes: Attention, attribution, and individuation. *Journal of Personality and Social Psychology*, *89*, 607–622, APA, adapted with permission.

Table 9.1 – Kahneman, D. (2003). A perspective on judgment and choice: Mapping bounded rationality. *American Psychologist*, *58*, 697–720, APA, adapted with permission.

Table 9.2 – Hastie, R., & Park, B. (1986). The relationship between memory and judgment depends on whether the judgment task is memory-based or on-line. *Psychological Review*, *93*, 258–268, APA, adapted with permission.

Figure 9.5 – Ames, D.R. (2004). Inside the mind-reader's toolkit: Projection and stereotyping in mental state inference. *Journal of Personality and Social Psychology*, *87*, 340–353, APA, adapted with permission.

Table 10.2 – Loftus, E.F., & Palmer, J.C. (1974). Reconstruction of automobile destruction: An example of the interaction between language and memory. *Journal of Verbal Learning and Verbal Behavior*, *13*, 585–589, APA, adapted with permission.

Table 10.4 – Srull, T.K. (1981). Person memory: Some tests of associative storage and retrieval models. *Journal of Experimental Psychology: Human Learning & Memory*, *7*, 440–463, APA, adapted with permission.

Table 10.6 – Garcia-Marques, L., & Hamilton, D.L. (1996). Resolving the apparent discrepancy between the incongruency effect and the expectancy-based illusory correlation effect: The TRAP model. *Journal of Personality and Social Psychology*, *71*, 845–860, APA, adapted with permission.

Figure 10.2 – Garcia-Marques, L., Garrido, M.V., Hamilton, D.L., & Ferreira, M.B. (2012). Effects of correspondence between encoding and retrieval organization in social memory. *Journal of Experimental Social Psychology*, *48*, 200–206, APA, adapted with permission.

Figure 10.3 – Wegner, D.M., Erber, R., & Raymond, P. (1991). Transactive memory in close relationships. *Journal of Personality and Social Psychology*, *61*, 923–929, APA, adapted with permission.

Table 11.1 – Kane, J., Van Boven, L., & McGraw, A.P. (2012). Prototypical prospection: Future events are more prototypically represented and simulated than past events. *European Journal of Social Psychology*, *42*, 354–362, APA, adapted with permission.

Table 11.2 – Burns, Z.C., Caruso, E.M., & Bartels, D.M. (2012). Predicting premeditation: Future behavior is seen as more intentional than past behavior. *Journal of Experimental Psychology: General*, *141*, 227–232, APA, adapted with permission.

Table 11.4 – Wilson, A.E., & Ross, M. (2001). From chump to champ: People's appraisals of their earlier and present selves. *Journal of Personality and Social Psychology*, *80*, 572–584, APA, adapted with permission.

Table 11.5 – Fischhoff, B. (1975). Hindsight is not equal to foresight: The effect of outcome knowledge on judgment under uncertainty. *Journal of Experimental Psychology: Human Perception and Performance*, *1*, 288–299, APA, adapted with permission.

Table 11.6 – Arkes, H.R., Faust, D., Guilmette, T.J., & Hart, K. (1988). Eliminating the hindsight bias. *Journal of Applied Psychology*, *73*, 305–307, APA, adapted with permission.

Figure 11.2 – Silka, L. (1981). Effects of limited recall of variability on intuitive judgments of change. *Journal of Personality and Social Psychology*, *40*, 1010–1016, APA, adapted with permission.

Figure 11.3 – Mallett, R.K., Wilson, T.D., & Gilbert, D.T. (2008). Expect the unexpected: Failure to anticipate similarities leads to an intergroup forecasting error. *Journal of Personality and Social Psychology*, *94*, 265–277, APA, adapted with permission.

Table 12.1 – Shoda, Y., Mischel, W., & Wright, J.C. (1994). Intraindividual stability in the organization and patterning of behavior: Incorporating psychological situations into the idiographic analysis of personality. *Journal of Personality and Social Psychology*, *67*, 674–687, APA, adapted with permission.

Table 12.2 – Davidson, A.R., & Jaccard, J.J. (1979). Variables that moderate the attitude-behavior relation: Results of a longitudinal survey. *Journal of Personality and Social Psychology*, *37*, 1364–1376, APA, adapted with permission.

1

PROCESSING SOCIAL INFORMATION

A Conceptual Framework

Social Cognition is the study of how people think about the people and events in their social world. Whether focused on a single person, a group, or even themselves, people invest a tremendous amount of time and energy in thinking about human beings, their behaviors, and their interactions. We form impressions of individuals we are meeting for the first time. We attend to people's appearance and behavior, trying to assess the traits, characteristics, and motives of others. We notice the social groups to which people belong, and our understanding of their behavior can be affected (often without our awareness) by our beliefs about their gender, ethnicity, age, nationality, or sexual orientation. We listen to others' opinions and arguments, identifying where we agree and disagree and considering if we should change our minds in response. We replay social interactions from memory, wondering why an exchange went as it did or how it might have been altered had our words or actions been different.

Social thinking is so central to the life of the mind that we rarely, if ever, stop engaging in social cognitive processes. Some have speculated that humans possess a neural network specifically dedicated to social cognition that is continuously active, available to dominate thinking whenever the mind begins to wander. Lieberman (2013) argued that the *social cognition network* "comes on like a reflex and it directs us to think about other people's minds, their thoughts, feelings and goals." Social cognitive processes are both ubiquitous and of paramount importance in navigating the social environment. They are the basis of our perceptions, interpretations, and reactions to the events we experience, and the manner in which we process information is the foundation of subsequent judgments and behavior. They are involved in all aspects of human social behavior, ranging from the genuinely mundane to the most important events of our lives.

This book presents current knowledge from the field of social cognition, an approach to studying how information from the social world is processed, stored, and used. It offers a particular focus on identifying processes that are involved in diverse aspects of social thought and behavior. We show how a set of core cognitive processes underlies and affects social thinking and action across a broad spectrum of situations and topics that previously have been studied in isolation. This approach will, we hope, promote greater integration of findings from research literatures that have traditionally adopted different assumptions, methods, and levels of analysis.

In attempting to cut across and integrate distinct content areas, it is important to highlight our view that social cognition is an *approach* rather than a separate *content area* in social psychology. Historically, it was quite common for social psychology textbooks to have a subsection on social cognition, typically focusing on findings in the literatures on impression formation, stereotyping, or, more recently, the self. As we will soon discuss, these were some of the research areas in which the social cognition approach in its earliest years provided numerous clear and novel insights. However, it is a mistake to limit social cognition to the analysis of these phenomena. Our view is that the social cognitive approach – the focus on identifying social information processes and an associated set of methods appropriate for probing those processes – can and should be used to study social phenomena that have not traditionally been examined through this lens. Indeed, social cognitive frameworks and methods are increasingly appearing in a variety of research literatures in psychology, including consumer behavior, relationships, health behavior, and procedural justice. Moreover, social cognition has influenced research in fields outside of psychology, such as medicine, law, and public policy. We provide a discussion of the field of social cognition that uses social information processes as the foundations of our framework, allowing recognition of similar findings across diverse bodies of knowledge and opportunities for the development of new knowledge.

THE CENTRALITY OF INFORMATION IN SOCIAL COGNITION

The central focus of social cognition is on the processing of social information. Therefore, it is crucial to make clear what constitutes "information" within the social cognitive approach. Information refers to all of the stimuli in the environment that impinge on an individual's sensory systems. "Stimuli" is, of course, a general term that characterizes both non-social and social aspects of the environment. If you think even briefly about all the non-social information that surrounds us at any given moment, it quickly becomes apparent that people cannot adequately attend to all of it with equal thoroughness. Consider entering a lecture hall for the first class of the semester. Most of the physical features in the room would likely receive little of your attention. You probably would not think much about the physical structure of the room, the placement of furniture, the lighting, or the color of the walls. This information would be available in virtually any classroom. However, these features do not typically grab our attention unless essential objects are absent (no chairs in a lecture hall?) or they are particularly unusual (new, comfortable chairs have replaced the old, dilapidated ones!).

What if we limit our analysis to just the *social* information available in the environment – the people entering the room, their behavior, the interactions among them, the groups that cluster together, and the apparent responses of these people to you? All of this is happening simultaneously. If we consider just these social aspects, situations are still so incredibly rich in information that our sensory, perceptual, and cognitive systems cannot keep up with all that is transpiring. As a consequence, we focus on a limited amount of information that is available, allocating attentional and cognitive resources to processing information that is particularly important, informative, surprising, or relevant to our goals. To return to our earlier example, upon entering the classroom, you might immediately see a friend with whom you took a class the previous semester. You also catch a glance at a couple of students talking quietly but intensely. You notice an older man who appears out of place and a woman who seems inexplicably anxious. You find your attention drawn to the nervous woman because you are puzzled by the cause of her anxiety. So you approach her with the intent of engaging in conversation, hoping you could perhaps assist in reducing her apparent anxiety. As you walk up to her, you see that her hairstyle, her clothing, and her shoes are all somewhat unusual compared with other students. You initiate a conversation with a simple "Hi," which prompts a response in what sounds like a foreign accent. "Aha," you might think to yourself, "I'll bet she's an exchange student."

A few things become apparent even in this brief analysis. In entering an environment, people often grab our notice. Some individuals become the focus of our attention, but many others do not. The people you do notice are those who are highly relevant to the self (the friend), are in some way unusual in the context (the middle-aged student), or are behaving in a manner that draws attention (the couple talking intensely and the anxious woman). We also rely on social categories to parse this social information, classifying people as "my friend," "colleagues," "a middle-aged man," and "a nervous person." These categories provide us with information about where we should allocate further attentional resources ("I wonder why that woman is nervous?") and how to act. You decide to approach the woman to gather more information, focusing on information that might be particularly useful or informative (her clothing and behavior). You seek to learn more by initiating a conversation that might help you understand, explain, and predict what the person is like. As you interact with her, additional information allows you to form a more detailed impression of what she is like and an explanation for her behavior.

This example barely hints at the actual richness of information available in the social environment. However, it does illustrate how an individual must selectively focus on a subset of that information to navigate even a simple social situation. It also highlights many of the processes that are of central interest in social cognition. These processes include attention (noticing the woman who is acting strangely), inference (inferring from her behavior that she is anxious), social categorization (deciding that she may be an exchange student), attribution (deciding that her behavior is likely caused by the unfamiliarity of the environment), and behavior regulation (deciding to approach her to gather additional information). All of these processes are central to social functioning, and each has received extensive research attention within social cognition.

A central goal of social cognition is to identify and characterize core cognitive processes that underlie social thought and behavior. It also tries to answer questions regarding the nature of these processes: How and when do they operate? What factors influence their operation? What are the benefits and costs of these processes? To what degree are these processes involuntary or operate under our control? Are we even aware of these processes? Research on these questions is explored throughout this text. Although not all issues have been fully resolved, our goal is to offer the current understanding of these issues from the perspective of social cognition.

Before launching this exploration, we begin with a brief history of the field of social cognition. Although by no means exhaustive, this history will provide an understanding of the philosophical roots of the social cognitive approach, the discoveries that promoted its emergence, and the features that differentiate social cognition from alternative approaches to understanding social thought and behavior. For another discussion of this history and background, see Hamilton and Carlston (2013).

HISTORICAL ROOTS OF SOCIAL COGNITION

Social cognition emerged as a distinct approach to understanding social behavior in the mid-1970s. The questions that social cognition attempts to address, however, have a much lengthier heritage, often reaching back millennia. For example, social cognition tries to account for the influence of social context on social thought, but philosophers dating back to Plato speculated about the influence of crowds on individuals' thought processes (McClelland, 1989). Much later, Gabriel Tarde's (1898, 1903) theories of social interaction emphasized the influence of aggregates of persons on single individuals and interpersonal processes. Fellow Frenchman Gustave Le Bon (1897) argued that crowds weaken rational thought and self-awareness, leading to the phenomenon of "contagion" in which private beliefs and values are replaced with primitive and savage instinctual urges. Social cognition also attempts to account for the processes involved in attitude change, but Aristotle speculated about the roles of "ethos" (speaker characteristics), "logos" (argument strength), and "pathos" (emotional and other audience characteristics) in persuasion. Social cognition also tries to identify the roles of conscious and unconscious processes in human thought and behavior. These questions were, of course, of paramount interest to Sigmund Freud in the early decades of the 20th century. So the *questions* of interest to social cognition are often not new.

Given that these questions have a long history, what *is* new about the social cognitive approach to these questions? The social cognitive approach differs from these previous attempts in its use of *scientific methods* to answer questions about *psychological processes*. Two characteristics of social cognition – the use of experimental methods to study social behavior and the emergence of research tools that allowed the direct investigation of underlying processes – did not emerge simultaneously. In fact, they were developed nearly a century apart. The use of experimental methods for studying thought and behavior began in the late 19th century, and the application to social phenomena began around the beginning of the 20th century. The development of sound scientific methods for examining cognition did not emerge until the 1950s and 1960s, however. Both developments were necessary precursors to the advent of social cognition as a distinct area of research in the 1970s.

The Development of Experimental Social Psychology

For many centuries, questions involving human thought and behavior were viewed as phenomena best explained by philosophy and sociology. Some mid-19th century philosophers such as John Stuart Mill and Auguste Comte had advocated the scientific study of human behavior, but this did not begin until Wilhelm Wundt founded an experimental psychology laboratory in 1879 at the University of Leipzig, Germany. Wundt was the first person to refer to himself as a "psychologist," and he is often considered "the father of experimental psychology." Under Wundt's leadership, the lab conducted investigations of human sensory experience. Although the research often relied on introspection, a method we now know to be fraught with problems, the establishment of the lab was an important landmark because it brought scientific methods to bear on psychological questions.

Research soon began to explore the role of social factors in psychological functioning and behavior. Max Ringelmann, a French agricultural engineer, showed in a series of experiments that workers exerted less force in a rope-pulling task when they were together than when alone. (Although this work was conducted in the 1880s, it was not published until 1913; see Kravitz & Martin, 1986.) Two psychologists, Binet and Henri, published a paper in 1894 showing that children's recollection of lines they had previously viewed could be biased by the comments of an adult (see Nicolas, Collins, Gounden, & Roediger, 2011). Despite these early examples, Norman Triplett (1898) is often credited with conducting the first social psychological studies when he showed that the presence of other individuals could improve performance on motor tasks.

These pioneering studies generally focused on the influence of social factors on observable behavior. Other work began to investigate more directly what was going on "inside the head" of social perceivers. Thurstone (1928), for example, initiated a program of scientific research on attitudes, which he defined as "the sum total of a man's inclinations and feelings, prejudice or bias, preconceived notions, ideas, fears, threats, and convictions about any specified topic" (p. 531). He focused on developing a means for measuring the distribution of attitudes within a given social group at a given time while recognizing that attitudes were susceptible to change over time through the persuasion. Sherif (1935) asked whether basic sensory experiences also might be amenable to social influence. In his studies, individuals reported their judgments of the distance that a light moved in a darkened room. Even though the light was stationary, judgments of how much it moved tended to converge within a social group, and these influences were internalized so that individuals continued to make judgments similar to their group norm even when they later judged the stimulus alone. These studies demonstrated that internal cognitive structures and processes, and the influence that others could exert on these processes, could be systematically studied.

The possibility that internal processes could be scientifically investigated stood in stark contrast to one of the central tenets of behaviorism, a movement that dominated American experimental psychology during the mid-20th century. Behaviorists, inspired initially by John Watson (1913), argued that psychology should be concerned only with observable phenomena. Internal thought processes relating to knowledge, beliefs, or even consciousness were not viewed as amenable to scientific investigation because they could not be observed and verified. Therefore, behaviorists gave no causal role to cognitive processes in determining behavior. Watson (1928) went so far as to argue, "He then who would introduce consciousness, either as an epiphenomenon or as an active force interjecting itself into the chemical and physical happenings of the body, does so because of spiritualistic and vitalistic leanings." As it evolved, behaviorism encompassed a range of theoretical views. Skinner (1938) recognized the existence of thoughts and feelings as legitimate phenomena, but he gave them no causal force. For him, internal processes exist within a "black box" that could not be investigated scientifically. Hull (1943) recognized a role for internal states but wanted them to be defined in terms of external operations, for example, defining drive strength in terms of the hours of deprivation and habit strength in terms of the amount of previous conditioning experience. Although the proponents of behaviorism varied in the degree to which they dismissed the study of cognition, social psychology's focus on cognitive processes and the structures responsible for these processes meant that it remained out of touch with mainstream American psychology for a lengthy period.

One consequence of this gap was that social psychology existed for a long time as a small and isolated enterprise within psychology. Although the study of internal, unobservable cognitive structures and processes was out of vogue, social psychology continued to focus intensely on the internal thoughts, beliefs, and feelings of individuals. It did so because it assumed that these processes were integral to human experience and played causal roles in accounting for human judgment and behavior (Zajonc, 1980a). Several theories emerged during this era that exemplify the importance of cognitive processes in human experience. Each of these theories played essential roles in the development of the field of social psychology and, later, social cognition. They each continue to be influential to this day.

Lewin's Field Theory

Kurt Lewin (1935) introduced *Field Theory*, reflecting the emphasis of Gestalt psychology on conscious experience as a construction of the mind rather than a direct reflection of "objective" reality. Field Theory argued that behavior (B) is the product of both the person (P) and the psychological environment (E), expressed symbolically as $B = f(P, E)$. This formulation viewed behavior as a product of both an individual's characteristics, including traits, motives, and desires, and the individual's perception of the existing social context. Person and situation variables are interdependent and dynamic, and, when combined as a unit, they constitute a *life space* that represents the complete psychological environment of the individual at any point in time.

Also central to Field Theory are notions about the dynamic interplay between person and situation elements over time. Motivation is derived from the relation between the perceived needs of the individual and the beliefs about the ability of those needs to be met within a given social context. As individuals navigate life spaces such as family, work, or school, behavior results from the perceived ability of the field (situational context) to facilitate or hinder meeting underlying psychological needs. In contrast to Freudian notions that behavior reflects manifestations of stable, unconscious drives, Field Theory conceived of motives as goal-directed forces that vary across psychological fields. Also, in contrast with behaviorism, Field Theory provided a causal role for thoughts, feelings, goals, and attitudes of the individual in dynamic interplay with subjective perceptions of social environments.

Heider's Balance Theory

Another theory that highlights the importance of cognitive elements and the dynamic relations among them is Fritz Heider's (1946) *Balance Theory*. Balance Theory assumed that the preferred psychological state of affairs is consistency among cognitive elements. Heider was interested in the implications of this assumption for social relationships. He focused on the relation between an individual (P), another individual (O), and a third element (X) that might be an object, attitude, or even another person. The links connecting these elements are either positive (+) or negative (−) in valence, and the relative satisfaction with the state of those relations can be determined by multiplying the valence of the three links. If the product of this multiplication process is positive, then the system is "balanced," and the individual (P) is satisfied with the state of relations with the other (O). If the product is negative, however, this produces an imbalance, and the person is motivated to reduce it. Imbalance can be reduced by modifying the valence of one of the links between elements, restoring balance and satisfaction.

For example, on a first date, it is quite common to discuss a variety of interests and tastes to gauge the degree of similarity and shared interests between the two of you. Assuming that the date has begun well, it is likely that the link between yourself and your date is positive in valence (i.e., you like the person). To the degree that you discover mutually shared interests, all links are positively valenced, and balance is maintained (+ * + * + = +). Even if you find that there is a shared *dis*like (neither of you like foreign films), balance is assured (+ * – * – = +). However, you might discover that your date has an attitude toward an object that you do not share, let's say, your date loves violent action movies, which you dislike. In that case, relations would be unbalanced (+ * – * + = –), and you will be motivated to modify the valence of the links to restore balance. You might change your belief about action movies, modifying your opinion to bring it in line with your date. Alternately, you might change the valence of the P-O link, liking your date less, so that your attitude toward the date is more consistent with your evaluation of movies. People who find their cognitive elements in a state of imbalance tend to modify whichever link is easiest to change (to change your movie preferences if your attitude was not strong or important to you, or to change your view of your date if the relationship began casually and other dating relationships are available). Balance Theory is important both because of its ability to account for a large variety of phenomena such as interpersonal and intergroup evaluation and because of its emphasis on the motivation to maintain consistency among cognitive elements.

Festinger's Theory of Cognitive Dissonance

A related but broader theory in which the maintenance of consistency is a fundamental motive is Leon Festinger's *Cognitive Dissonance Theory*. According to Festinger (1957), inconsistency between two cognitive elements or between a cognitive element and behavior produces an aversive psychological state termed *dissonance*. As in Balance Theory, individuals are motivated to eliminate the unpleasant state of dissonance and can do so in several ways. Consider, for example, a man who has a history of heart disease in his family and knows that he should exercise regularly but remains inactive. The discrepancy between what he knows he should be doing and his actual practices produces a state of discomfort (dissonance), which motivates him to reduce the discrepancy between these elements (and the associated discomfort). He may, for example, try changing his *behavior*. If he were to begin a program of regular exercise, the man would no longer feel anxiety because his behavior would no longer be discordant with his beliefs. Alternately, the man might attempt to reduce dissonance by changing his *beliefs* while maintaining his sedentary lifestyle. He might, for example, convince himself that heart disease is more likely to be triggered by stress than by inactivity. If he were successful in doing so, it might seem wiser to him to avoid strenuous physical activity and instead seek out activities that he enjoys to minimize the anxiety and tension. As a third alternative, he might pay particular attention to research suggesting a somewhat tenuous link between lack of exercise and heart disease, providing another means by which the perceived discrepancy between thought and action can be reduced.

Cognitive Dissonance Theory generated an enormous amount of research during the 1960s, which continues today. The historical importance of this theory for the development of social cognition is in the centrality it placed on cognition, on the interconnected relations between thought and behavior, and on the motivating nature of the affective state of dissonance in producing changes in thought and action.

Heider on Attribution

In addition to introducing Balance Theory, Heider (1944, 1958) was also responsible for inspiring several decades of research on *attribution* in social psychology. (In fact, Heider saw Balance and Attribution theories as being closely related, although research on these topics proceeded independently; Crandall, Silvia, N'Gbala, Tsang, & Dawson, 2007.) Attribution is concerned with the explanations that people generate to explain occurrences in their environment. In the example discussed earlier about the perceiver noticing a young woman's apparent anxiety, the decision to approach her represented an attempt to gather information that would explain her behavior. Heider proposed that people do this quite naturally but also follow intuitive rules, acting like "intuitive scientists" (Ross, 1977), to explain actions by seeking out and combining available information until arriving at a reasonable causal explanation.

Heider argued that people distinguish between internal and external causes of behavior. An internal cause locates the origin of the behavior in the actor, whereas an external cause is located in the context in which the behavior occurs. The woman's anxiety might be attributed to an external cause if the situation in which she is observed would likely produce nervousness in anyone (being in a room full of strangers with whom she did not share a language). Alternatively, it might be attributed to an internal cause if the woman was about to be interviewed for a job she strongly desired. Heider recognized that people tend to favor internal over external explanations because they offer the possibility of establishing predictability of action. In other words, if behavior can be attributed to the underlying characteristics of the actor, then we can gain a sense of how that person would behave in the future. Why would we seek to have such a "sense" of the other person? Effective social interaction requires mutual coordination between people. If we can anticipate others' responses, then we can guide our own behavior accordingly to achieve mutually positive outcomes in our interactions. The focus on the use of traits to explain people's actions inspired a great deal of research on attribution. Heider's theory, however, also recognized the role of individuals' motives and intentions as characteristics that are internal to the actor that can be used to understand and explain behavior (Malle, 2004).

Asch's Research on Impression Formation

Another important line of research that laid the groundwork for social cognition also focused on how people infer others' dispositions. However, it focused on the processes that occur as a perceiver attempts to gain a sense of another person's character per se, rather than to explain his or her behavior. This research on *impression formation* was begun by Solomon Asch (1946), and it directly foreshadowed the development of the field of social cognition with its focus on internal cognitive processes and mental representations. Asch argued that perceivers play an active role in forming impressions. People do not passively accumulate bits of information about an individual, but instead they actively construct impressions by integrating information into an ever-evolving impression as new information is received. As individuals learn about others, they organize the information as it is received and compare new information with the impression that has already been formed.

Reflecting his training in Gestalt psychology, Asch argued that the meaning of any single personality trait depended upon the totality of traits ascribed to a person. For example, he demonstrated that the intelligence of a person who is "intelligent" and "cold" was viewed as being quite different from the intelligence of a person who is both "intelligent" and "warm." Through the active use of dynamic processes, individuals attempt to discover underlying consistencies or "themes" that provide an accurate and relatively rich characterization of the person as a unique individual. Asch's work emphasized the central and vigorous role of perceivers' cognitive processes in integrating the information provided by the social environment.

The Emergence of Cognitive Psychology

Although these examples illustrate a continuing focus on cognitive structures and processes in social psychology as it developed as a distinct subdiscipline, social cognition would not have emerged from social psychology without some critical developments in other areas of the field (Gardner, 1985). First, in the 1960s, behaviorism began to wane as a dominant force in psychology. During this time, several discoveries were emerging that were difficult to explain through reinforcement contingencies alone. Noam Chomsky (1959), for example, argued that Skinner's account of verbal learning was inadequate, noting that children show an enormous capacity to learn and modify language. Reinforcement alone would have difficulty explaining how language develops so quickly or why children regularly demonstrate plasticity in their speaking. Latent learning (Stevenson, 1954), in which learning occurs in the absence of any obvious reinforcement contingencies, was also difficult to explain without recourse to cognition. Observational learning, in which people learned behavior by merely watching others, also was shown to arise without conditioning (Bandura, Ross, & Ross, 1961). As such, there arose widespread recognition that behaviorism could not easily account for many emerging phenomena.

Second, during World War II, a new field of research arose, rooted in Engineering and Mathematics, that focused on the quantification and communication of information. *Information Theory* (Miller, 1951; Miller & Frick, 1949) attempted to measure the effectiveness of the communication of information without resorting to its content. In the language of Information Theory, communication occurs when a source translates information into a code (or "encoded") that then is transmitted through a medium or channel to a receiver where it is "decoded." Information reduces uncertainty, but the transmission of information is not without error. As information is transmitted, entropy or decay occurs through the introduction of noise in the channel. Moreover, the amount of information that can be communicated simultaneously is constrained by the bandwidth of the channel.

Information Theory profoundly influenced theorizing in psychology. It provided a metaphor suggesting that people and machines can be viewed as components of communication systems. It characterized humans as information processors that function in ways similar to computers. It brought the term "information" into regular use in psychology (amazingly, William James's (1890) opus *Principles of Psychology* does not contain the word; Collins, 2007) and also terms such as "channel," "encoding," "decoding," and "noise" that are still used today. Most fundamental, perhaps, was the theory's emphasis on the role of processes involved in communication, providing a portrait of the individual as an active processor of information, in contrast to behavioristic approaches that de-emphasized cognitive processes.

Third, inspired in large part by Information Theory, the field of *artificial intelligence* emerged to model and replicate human cognitive abilities using machines such as computers (see Newell & Simon, 1972). To create machines that mimicked human intelligence, programmers embraced highly mentalistic views of cognition. Computer programs were written that could solve word problems in algebra, prove logical theorems, and generate language, and they did so by mimicking people's conscious, incremental reasoning abilities. These abilities pointed to a central and causal role of thought processes in accounting for human behavior. Moreover, artificial intelligence firmly established the computer as the primary metaphor for human cognitive functioning, involving, for example, "storage" and "retrieval" of information into short- and long-term memory stores.

These innovations in psychology and related fields led to the emergence of a new subfield in psychology – *cognitive psychology* (Neisser, 1967) – that examined the roles of mental structures and processes in human behavior. It portrayed humans as active information processors, utilizing stored knowledge to interpret, understand, elaborate on, and guide responses to new information and new experiences. It embraced an information processing approach, assuming that human cognitive processes and their products could be decomposed and traced as a sequence of mental operations with appropriate methods.

The early years of the field of cognitive psychology produced many critical discoveries, theories, and methodological innovations. For example, work by Broadbent (1958) and Treisman (1969) shed light on the nature of attention and functioning of attention. Theories and research by Bruner (Bruner, Goodnow, & Austin, 1956), Rosch (1973; Rosch & Lloyd, 1978), and Posner and Keele (1968, 1970) provided insight into the nature of categories and categorization processes. The limits and capacities of short-term memory were explored (Miller, 1956; Phillips & Baddeley, 1971), and research demonstrated the development and functioning of automatic processes (Shiffrin & Schneider, 1977). Schema theories (Bransford & Franks, 1971; Mandler, 1984; Rumelhart, 1984) helped elucidate the impact of stored knowledge on subsequent information processing.

Although this early research showed that mental systems and processes often allow the efficient processing of complex information, new work emerged demonstrating that information processing can fall short of ideal. A series of ground-breaking papers by Tversky and Kahneman (Kahneman & Tversky, 1971, 1973; Tversky & Kahneman, 1971, 1973, 1974), for example, showed that some efficiency derives from the use of nonoptimal mental procedures, called *heuristics*, that are shortcuts used for making quick and easy judgments and decisions. Heuristic use facilitates decision making, saving time and mental resources and producing reasonably accurate outcomes. However, the use of heuristics leaves us susceptible to error. Importantly, this work inspired a great deal of research exploring the limitations and biases inherent in the cognitive processing of social information (Gilovich, 1991; Nisbett & Ross, 1980). The early years of cognitive psychology provided impressive demonstrations of how humans generally function effectively within an overwhelmingly complicated world of information but also highlighted potential pitfalls in human reasoning and judgment.

THE RISE OF SOCIAL COGNITION

Soon, these discoveries inspired several psychologists to consider the ways that a cognitive approach could be used to further understand the processing of social information. The influential theories offered by mid-century social psychologists (Lewin, Heider, Asch, and Festinger) were already couched in terms of mental processes, so social psychology seemed particularly well-positioned to benefit from developments in cognitive psychology. Many of the discoveries emerging from cognitive psychology seemed highly relevant for understanding essential questions in the social domain. Doing so allowed novel insights into social phenomena but also promised potential integration across distinct research questions. If a set of common cognitive processes were involved in the variety of phenomena of interest to social psychologists, perhaps identification of those processes could allow the derivation of a set of principles for explaining social thought and behavior. Also, to the degree that the processes involved in social cognition could be identified, interventions for modifying those processes when they produce undesired consequences might become more readily apparent. These possibilities spurred an intellectual climate perhaps unprecedented in social psychology, as a generation of researchers began to explore the benefits of an approach that recognized cognitive processes as being central to social functioning and behavior (Ostrom, 1984).

It was not long before research using the theories and methodological tools of cognitive psychology were beginning to fulfill this promise. By the mid-1970s, several landmark studies provided dramatic evidence that cognitive theories and methods could provide fruitful insights regarding social phenomena (see Hamilton & Carlston, 2013).

Tajfel's Minimal Group Paradigm

Tajfel and his colleagues (Tajfel, 1970; Tajfel, Billig, Bundy, & Flament, 1971), using what they referred to as the "minimal group paradigm," demonstrated the power of categorization processes in creating bias in the perception and treatment of groups. In these studies, individuals were assigned to membership in one of two social groups on an arbitrary basis (e.g., based on their supposed preference for one painter over another).

Despite there being no actual differences between the groups (because group membership actually was randomly assigned), individuals revealed several manifestations of group bias in their judgments and behavior. They expressed more positive attitudes towards members of the ingroup, they saw outgroup members as more homogeneous than and different from the ingroup, and they were more likely to distribute rewards to ingroup than to outgroup members, even when allocating more resources to the ingroup could not provide any benefit for themselves. Thus, the mere cognitive differentiation of the social world into categories of "us" and "them" was sufficiently powerful to produce different responses to and behavior towards members of ingroups and outgroups.

Higgins, Rholes, and Jones' Research on Priming

A central tenet of cognitive psychology was that information that is *accessible* in memory could influence how subsequent information is processed. As information is encountered, the task of the perceiver is to link the information with knowledge that is already stored in memory. This allows the perceiver to use prior experience to guide responses to a particular piece of input that is encountered ("That red, shiny object in the bowl looks like an apple…I think I'll eat it!"). Information that happens to be accessible in memory, even if irrelevant or persisting from a prior task, can determine what knowledge is brought to bear to understand new input. This phenomenon is called *priming*.

Higgins, Rholes, and Jones (1977) provided an important demonstration of the consequences of this phenomenon in the domain of social judgment. In their experiment, participants initially completed a task in which they were asked to hold in memory trait words that were either positive ("adventurous," "self-confident," "independent," "persistent") or negative ("reckless," "conceited," "aloof," "stubborn") in nature. In what was described as a separate study, participants then read a story describing some actions performed by a man named "Donald" that were ambiguous, able to be interpreted either positively or negatively. The story said, in part:

> He was thinking, perhaps, he would do some skydiving or maybe cross the Atlantic in a sailboat (adventurous/reckless). By the way he acted, one could readily guess that Donald was well aware of his ability to do many things well (self-confident/ conceited). Other than business engagements, Donald's contacts with people were rather limited. He felt he did not really need to rely on anyone (independent/aloof). Once Donald made up his mind to do something, it was as good as done no matter how long it might take or how difficult the going might be. Only rarely did he change his mind even when it might well have been better if he had (persistent/stubborn).

Participants then were asked to characterize Donald's behavior verbally and to rate how desirable they considered him to be, both immediately and after a nearly 2-week delay. Donald's behavior was generally characterized consistently with the trait words to which participants had been exposed in the preliminary task. For example, Donald's desire to cross the Atlantic was described as being either "adventurous" or "reckless," depending on what had been primed in the first task. Participants also judged Donald's desirability consistent with the valence of these trait terms, particularly after a delay. Those participants who had been primed with negative traits saw Donald as being less desirable compared with those who had been primed with the favorable trait terms. These results showed that reasoning about people is influenced both by the information they provide and by whatever else happens to be accessible in memory when that information is processed.

Hamilton and Gifford's Research on Illusory Correlation

Historically, stereotypes had been viewed as reflecting the history of conflict between groups or the exaggeration of small but real group differences. In contrast with these earlier accounts, Hamilton and Gifford (1976) proposed that ordinary cognitive processes might play a central role in the formation of stereotypes. Research in cognitive psychology had shown that people tend to notice unusual information in their environment, and Hamilton and Gifford argued that similar processes could occur when individuals encounter information describing social groups of differing sizes. If people tend to notice the co-occurrence of unusual, infrequent events, then they might be especially likely to notice negative behavior performed by members of small groups.

To test this idea, Hamilton and Gifford presented individuals with a set of sentences describing desirable and undesirable behaviors performed by members of two hypothetical groups, referred to simply as Group A and Group B. Although the ratio of desirable to undesirable behavior was identical for both groups, participants' judgments reflected that an erroneous perception of an association – an *illusory correlation* – had formed between membership in the smaller group and performance of the infrequent, undesirable behaviors. The members of the numerically smaller group were disproportionately and erroneously associated with performing undesirable behavior to a greater degree than the members of the numerical majority group. This research showed that an information processing bias alone could contribute to the development of inaccurate stereotypes.

Associative Network Models in Person Memory

A model for understanding how information acquired about a person is represented in memory was first introduced by Hastie (1980; Hastie & Kumar, 1979) and later developed by Srull and Wyer (Srull, 1981; Srull & Wyer, 1989). In this model, a person is represented by a particular location in memory, metaphorically referred to as a "person node." All information learned about the person becomes attached to the person node and, as additional information is learned, associations can form between items to create an *associative network* containing one's knowledge and beliefs about the person. Associations between items of information are particularly likely to form if they are compared with one another. An item that violates a pre-existing impression or is inconsistent with what is already known about the person is especially likely to be compared with other items, creating numerous associations within the network. This model made clear predictions that could not be derived without a clear delineation of the relations among elements. For example, the model was able to predict the amount, order, and speed with which different kinds of information could later be recalled. (We discuss these findings in greater detail in the next chapter.) This work demonstrated the potential utility of models that specified the nature of social information processing for generating novel and counterintuitive predictions.

These early studies testified to the usefulness of social cognition for studying issues of longstanding interest to social psychologists. This research, and subsequent work stimulated by it, has demonstrated that the application of a cognitive approach to social phenomena can produce a much deeper, more detailed, and more nuanced portrait of the social information processor than had previously been possible. In addition, many discoveries have been made that would not have been possible without a social cognitive approach because they are rooted in the characteristics of human information processing systems themselves. Numerous important findings have emerged as it has become apparent that the *manner by which* individuals process information can affect interpretations, inferences, judgments, and attributions, and, ultimately, behavior in significant ways. Social cognition has proved to be a novel and fruitful lens for examining social thought and action.

WHY *SOCIAL* COGNITION?

Although social cognition has developed rapidly, one might question the need for the separate fields of social cognition and cognitive psychology. If social cognition represents the mere application of cognitive theories and methods to social stimuli, do we need separate sub-disciplines with their own texts, journals, college classes, and faculty? In fact, there are several good reasons (aside from maintaining your professor's job!) for maintaining distinct yet interconnected fields of cognitive and social cognitive psychology. Although cognitive and social psychologists are both concerned with the processing of sensory input, they focus on different kinds of input. Whereas cognitive psychology is interested in how people process information about all kinds of stimuli (such as objects, symbols, and language), social cognition focuses on the perception of *people* (including the self, other individuals, and groups of people), their behaviors, and their interrelations.

People are, of course, different from the stimuli studied by cognitive psychologists in many respects, and a brief discussion of some of these differences highlights the utility of maintaining the distinction between social cognition from the broader field of cognitive psychology. First, unlike inanimate objects, people are alive and active. Because of that fact, they differ in many *quantitative* respects from objects. People do more, and they change more than do objects. As Heider (1958) states, persons "are usually perceived as action centers" (p. 21). Compare, for example, your best friend with a rock. A rock might appear to change over long periods of time due to erosion or acid rain. In general, though, we would probably all agree that rocks do not show much variability over time. People, in contrast, show a high degree of variability over time. Your friend might move through multiple environments within even a single day as she wakes up in her apartment, attends a lecture, reads in the library, and has dinner with friends in a restaurant before attending a movie in the evening. She might vary her appearance as well, changing from a casual dress and appearance in the morning to smarter attire if she had to go to work in the afternoon. Her manner of behavior also might change quite dramatically, from being quite relaxed and friendly as she hangs out with her friends to being passive but formal as she sits in a classroom to being energetic and spontaneous as she dances in a club. People can also change dramatically over long periods as they age, develop new ideas and habits, and assume different social roles in the course of their lives (infant, child, student, spouse, parent).

People differ *qualitatively* from objects as well. External factors generally determine the "actions" of objects, but the actions of people often reflect their internal states. People, unlike objects, have thoughts, motives, intentions, goals, and emotions that can play essential roles in determining how they act. Steven King's novel, *Christine*, tells the story of a car that is intent on murdering its owner's friends and family because of jealousy – an unusual premise in that we do not normally endow an automobile with feelings, goals, and intentions. The intrigue of the story, though, perhaps lies in its ability to make us wonder how objects might behave and how we might think about them differently if they *did* have human thoughts and feelings.

However, because we know they do not, we seek out different information about people than about objects, and we engage in different processes to explain their actions. For people, we are interested in gaining information about people's actions over time and across social contexts. Doing so allows us to learn about and to test hypotheses about their internal states and attributes, their abilities, their personalities, their motives, and their goals. Because we recognize that individuals' internal states play a causal role in determining their actions, we spend much time and energy thinking about the behavior of others, attempting to understand people by interpreting and explaining their actions so we can gain a sense of what they are like.

Cognitive processes related to social perception can also be distinguished from more general cognition because of the nature of *perceivers as social beings*. Because of our social nature, people are particularly attuned to social information in the environment. Infants, for example, tend to pay particular attention to others' faces within hours after birth, and they will visually track the location of a drawing resembling a human face (Goren, Sarty, & Wu, 1975). Adults also show a proclivity to encode and process social information, selectively allocating attention to focus on people (and, interestingly, to animals) rather than inanimate objects when viewing complex, realistic scenes (New, Cosmides, & Tooby, 2007). Finally, thinking about the relation between semantic concepts and people versus objects activates different areas of the brain, suggesting that different neural circuitry can underlie social versus non-social perception (Mitchell, Heatherton, & Macrae, 2002).

Another difference between our perceptions of people and objects lies in the fact that the persons with whom we interact (but not the physical objects we perceive) are themselves active agents. That is, when we *act* toward them, they are likely to *react* (positively or negatively) to us. Moreover, we know that about them! Therefore, effective social interaction requires an ability to anticipate the response of others to our own actions. In this sense, social interaction is like a "dance" – effective interaction requires coordination among the participants, and the ability to understand, anticipate, and respond accordingly is crucial for its success.

Not only are we more likely to notice and pay attention to people, but we also think differently about people than about objects because we are socially interconnected and interdependent with other individuals and groups. Because people are interconnected, thinking about other individuals typically also involves thinking about the self. As we think about our family members, our friends, or our enemies, we tend to do so in terms that implicate the self, including our histories, beliefs, attitudes, and emotions intertwined with those individuals. We also think about ourselves and others in terms of group memberships, being conscious of our own and other people's groups and (generally) valuing groups to which we belong.

In sum, social cognition and cognitive psychology will never be wholly separated, nor should they be. Numerous essential insights have been and continue to be generated by applying the approaches of cognitive psychology to the study of social phenomena. Cognitive psychology has, in turn, also benefitted from developments in social cognition. Nonetheless, although the processes and structures underlying social and non-social cognition may be similar, social interactions involve perceivers and targets who are active, intentional, emotional, and motivated. Unlike objects, people can act as causal agents and can attempt to control events and outcomes intentionally. In short, people are more complex than objects or concepts.

A SOCIAL COGNITIVE FRAMEWORK

Before beginning our detailed discussion of research in social cognition, it is useful to delineate our general approach to the field and the framework we use for organizing the variety of topics covered in the chapters of this book. In doing so, we highlight some of the ways our text differs from alternate approaches that have tended to dominate the field historically. It is our view that social cognition is an *approach* rather than a *content area* in social psychology (see Carlston, 2013, for an alternate perspective). This approach focuses on the mental structures and processes underlying social phenomena, and we believe that the most significant contribution of social cognition to the field of social psychology, more broadly, is its emphasis on cognitive processes. Accordingly, our discussion of social cognition will not be organized by content areas, as is often the case (e.g., with separate chapters on attitudes, impressions, prejudice), but by fundamental processes that underlie social information processing. This text will characterize social cognition in terms of a process model recognizing the operation of cognitive systems as information is processed over time, allowing us to examine structures and processes that are common across content areas.

We believe there are several advantages to adopting this framework. One advantage is that it encourages the integration of research findings across different content areas in social cognition. Research on impression formation and stereotyping, for example, largely developed separately, utilizing different assumptions, methods, and terms. An approach that focuses on the role of structures and processes when people encounter information describing a single individual versus multiple members of a group would allow us to discover the specific ways in which impression formation versus stereotyping differ and are the same (Hamilton & Sherman, 1996). Consistencies across research areas can be identified, and gaps in our knowledge can more easily be recognized. Second, this approach allows social cognition to be applied to virtually *any* content area in social psychology. After all, in virtually any topic in social psychology (relationships, persuasion and social influence, decision making, health psychology), people are actively engaged in processing information. Understanding the processes involved and the biases resulting from their use are important for our knowledge of those topics.

The fact that our approach allows the possibility that it can be used to understand any content area certainly broadens the topics that can be studied from a social cognitive perspective to include attitudes, intergroup conflict, helping behavior, and relationships, to name a few. There are already large bodies of research on each of these topics, but research using a social cognitive approach can add unique value to these literatures, as already has been demonstrated. Finally, this approach promises to allow greater integration between psychology and other disciplines. The theories and methods of social cognition can be used to investigate a tremendous variety of issues involved in social thought and behavior from diverse disciplines such as economics, law, and medicine. The fact that this has already been occurring suggests that other communities have recognized the value of the social cognitive approach. Providing a framework that explicitly reflects the view of social cognition as an approach should, we hope, encourage these developments even further.

A Model of Social Information Processing

The chapters in this book focus on the role of mental structures and processes in social thinking. We begin the book by discussing in Chapters 2 and 3 the nature of mental representations and the importance of distinguishing relatively effortless from effortful information processing. Chapters 4–10 explore different aspects of social information processing, discussing in detail how information enters into and is used by the cognitive system. We examine how perceivers *attend* to some but not all information, and how they play an active role in *interpreting* encoded information, using it to form *evaluations*, draw *inferences*, and make *attributional judgments*. We explore how information is organized, stored, and retrieved from *memory* and how people use information to form *judgments* and make decisions. Chapters 11 and 12 examine the role of social cognitive processes in thinking about *time* and the relation between social cognition and action, asking how (and when) thought affects *behavior*. Throughout these chapters, several fundamental factors that must be considered at each phase of information processing will regularly reappear. These motifs will reinforce connections between processes, illustrating how all aspects of social information processing must be viewed in light of a set of common and influential factors. We begin by providing a brief preview of the topics that will unfold in these chapters.

Cognitive Representations and the Effortfulness of Processing

It is difficult to overestimate the importance of cognitive representations in social cognition. Cognitive representations contain the totality of our stored knowledge, reflecting experience as well as the beliefs and expectancies that we have formed as a result of those experiences. These representations might be formed either from direct experience (from events we have experienced first-hand) or based on indirect experience (from social norms or observing other people). Once formed, cognitive representations are available to be used when they are relevant to a situation or become activated in memory by an event or stimulus cue encountered in the environment.

Although this language implies that cognitive representations are either activated or not activated in binary terms, their relative activation levels can vary along a continuum. The activation level of a cognitive representation is termed its *accessibility*, and the accessibility of any representation can vary across contexts and between persons. Structures that are activated recently or frequently (either because external factors invoke them or because they are chronically accessible for a particular person) are more likely to become accessible in the future. It is essential to consider what representation will become activated in any given context since accessible cognitive structures guide and direct all aspects of information processing. The representations that are accessible in any given moment influence what information we notice, how we interpret it, and the nature of inferences and attributions that we make in response.

A second foundational chapter focuses on the role of effort and resources involved in social information processing. Thought processes vary in the degree to which they require deliberation and effort. Although thinking about ourselves and others often involves conscious attention and effort, much social information is processed spontaneously or "automatically." Information that does not receive our deliberate attention can be (and often is) processed quite thoroughly and is stored in memory for later use. We may not even be aware that our cognitive systems have processed information, but that information can nevertheless produce "automatic" effects on our judgments, feelings, and behaviors. With the relatively recent discovery of automatic effects on behavior, it appears that automatic processes influence people to a far greater extent than was previously recognized. Social information processing involves the interplay between both controlled and automatic processes. The influence of each – as well as the relation between them – will be a continuing focus as we discuss various aspects of processing.

Aspects of Information Processing

The information available in our social world is not just taken in and recorded in our memories. As we discussed earlier, only a portion of available information enters our cognitive system. Once there, it is embellished, expanded, and transformed by an active mind. Across several chapters, we discuss several distinct aspects of social information processing that reflect the role of an active information processor.

Attention

Any environment tends to offer information that is nearly infinite in quantity and complexity, and our sensory and cognitive systems cannot absorb all the information available in even a relatively simple context. Accordingly, out of necessity, we must selectively attend to certain aspects of the stimulus environment while not noticing or even actively ignoring other aspects. The focus of attention is not randomly determined, however, and our cognitive systems are adept at directing attention to information that is particularly important, self-relevant, or unusual.

Interpretation

From the moment information is encoded through selective attention, our cognitive systems must interpret it. Information, even if it gets our attention, has no inherent meaning; meaning is achieved through interpretation. Importantly, social information is often ambiguous and can be construed in multiple ways. We impose meaning on that information through the process of interpretation.

Evaluation

Interpretation typically (and perhaps inevitably) produces evaluative responses to social stimuli. The human tendency to evaluate elements of the social environment seems primary, pervasive, and inevitable. It is difficult to imagine, for example, how meeting and forming an impression of a new person could ever result in a genuinely neutral response. We typically like or dislike individuals (at least to some degree), tend to like some groups more than others, and even evaluate individual behaviors as good or bad. Of course, information is itself inherently devoid of evaluative content, and it is the person processing that information who imposes some evaluation on it. The complexity of this simple statement becomes clear when we recognize that different individuals can have very different and occasionally opposed evaluative reactions to the same social information or that the same individual can respond inconsistently at different times or on different occasions.

Inference

Typically, we elaborate further on information by making inferences about the behavior observed, the actor who performed the behavior, or the actor's social group. Traits and other attributes are inferred to characterize both the actor and the actor's behavior accurately, or inferences are made about the actor's motives or goals. Inference processes aid in comprehending new information being processed, they broaden one's understanding of social entities, and they provide a sense of predictability and control. However, like all other processes, they are also subject to bias and are heavily influenced by *a priori* beliefs and expectancies contained in our cognitive structures. Moreover, many inferences are made spontaneously, without deliberative thought or intent, and even without awareness of their occurrence.

Attribution

One type of inference is of particular importance, attributional inference. Attributions are inferences about causality, most commonly regarding the causes for one's own or another person's behavior. Social behavior is often ambiguous or overdetermined, inviting many possible conclusions about its causes. Nonetheless, we engage in attributional processing when we are motivated to understand why a person behaved in a particular way. Ultimately, we determine the most appropriate and compelling explanation for behavior, even though relevant information that explains behavior might be missing or biases might produce an inaccurate causal conclusion. Regardless of their accuracy, attributions, once formed, can have significant consequences in their own right. They both explain why events occur and can provide a basis for future judgments and behavior.

Judgment

We are often confronted with situations in which we must make a decision or render a judgment. In making a judgment or decision, we must identify the information that is most relevant, disregard information that should not be considered, and combine information in a manner that produces a decision that is (at least somewhat) rational and provides a "good" outcome for the decision-maker. To what degree is this possible? Can we effectively differentiate useful from useless information, and can information be combined in a fashion that produces a rational judgment? In addition, can we determine whether a judgment is good or poor based on its rationality?

Storage and Retrieval from Memory

Once elaborated, information from the social world is stored in memory. It is important to recognize that the processes of interpretation, evaluation, inference, and attribution have transformed the initially-encountered information such that the ultimate representation in memory can differ in significant ways from the stimulus events on which the representation is based. Nevertheless, it is this representation that is the basis for all subsequent usage. Moreover, information is not merely "dumped" into some memory receptacle, but instead is represented and stored according to certain principles that lend organization and structure to the representation.

This representation is available for later retrieval to serve as the basis of judgments and behavior. Retrieving information from memory is not a random process but rather is a guided search that involves the reconstruction of memory. Nonetheless, the retrieval process itself is flexible and open to influence by many factors. For example, our immediate goals or purposes in retrieving memories will guide how memory is searched and, consequently, the information that is successfully retrieved. Recent experiences or mood states can also affect what is remembered. Retrieval can also be influenced by numerous factors that influence the actual content of our "memories." Because memory retrieval is itself a constructive process, it is quite common for memories to contain inaccuracies or, in some cases, to be entirely erroneous.

Dynamic Factors Influencing Aspects of Processing

So far, we have highlighted a set of fundamental processes that play a central role in social cognition, and each process is discussed separately in one chapter of the book. However, these processes do not occur in a vacuum. All aspects of information processing are also affected by dynamic factors that can change from situation to situation, moment to moment, and person to person. These factors include motives, goals, affective states, and cognitive capacities. Any detailed consideration of social information processing must consider these factors as well, even though their consideration is woven into our discussion of basic processes rather than considered separately.

Motives relate to the desire to reduce the discrepancy between an individual's current state and a desired state, and motivational states can dramatically influence the way information is processed and used. Motives can affect all aspects of information processing, including attention, interpretation, elaboration, and inference. Large research literatures now testify to the power of motives based on affiliation and self-esteem needs to influence the processing of social information. Although some motives can be stable, different motives might become more apparent or accessible in different social contexts, and motives can increase and decrease in intensity based on recent experience.

Goals pertain to end-states that are desired by individuals, pursued in the interest of meeting some need or motive. An affiliation motive, for example, might lead an individual to have the goal of being admitted to a college fraternity or social club. Goals, like motives, can influence all aspects of social cognition. For example, individuals might selectively notice or seek out, with particular deliberation, information that will allow a goal to be met or information suggesting that progress toward a goal might be hindered. The specific goal might alter how one interprets and approaches a situation, such as when a student might either approach a learning situation with a goal to learn or a goal to exhibit excellent performance to others. Finally, goals might pertain to the desired result of information processing itself, such as when a person has the goal to either memorize information describing an individual or to form an impression of that person. These different goals alter the processing of available information, producing different representations of that target in memory.

Affect includes emotions and moods that can vary over time and across situations, able to influence both the content and processes involved in thinking. Mood and emotions can arise in response to information encountered in the environment, but pre-existing affective states can also influence how newly-encountered information is interpreted and processed. Affective factors can change the cognitive representations that become accessible during information processing, and they can also influence the degree and nature of the interpretation and elaboration of new information. Affect can also serve as a signal, for example, alerting individuals to attend to threatening stimuli or, by signaling safety and security, implying that deliberative processing is unnecessary.

Cognitive capacity pertains to the quantity and nature of cognitive resources available to engage in a specific process. Many cognitive processes require deliberative effort, attention, and executive resources for successful completion. However, cognitive capacity is dynamic and can vary as a function of moods, competing tasks, and even circadian rhythms. When an individual's capacity is low (as when in an experiment a person is assigned to complete two demanding tasks simultaneously), deliberative processing is undermined, reliance on shortcuts such as heuristics tends to increase, and attention is allocated in a way to maximize efficiency rather than thoroughness. Variations in available capacity have been shown to affect numerous critical cognitive processes involved in attention, inference, attribution, and memory.

Implications of Information Processing

We discuss the role of cognitive representations, cognitive processes, and dynamic considerations in social cognition. However, it is essential to note that cognition is not important in and of itself. Instead, social information processing helps people adapt to and manage their social environments. Social cognitive processes allow for successful navigation of experience over time and contribute to determining our actions. Our last two chapters focus on these uses of social knowledge.

We use stored knowledge in *understanding the past* and *anticipating the future*. Much of what we have discussed focuses on aspects of information processing in dealing with what is happening at a particular time. We form an impression of a person we are meeting for the first time; we need to understand the positions advocated by a political candidate; we try to gauge the goals and objectives of a group; we want to understand why an intergroup conflict has exploded into a near-riot. However, the persons, groups, and events we witness also have histories, and our knowledge of those histories is stored in our cognitive representations. Sometimes contemporary events can lead to a reconstruction of past events and experiences. How and when does that happen? Understanding how knowledge of the past can be reconstructed, and thereby take on new meaning, becomes essential for understanding how the past can shape and guide our current and future experiences.

Social cognition has historically focused on understanding the important endproducts of social information processing, including memory, judgments, inferences, and attributions. However, there has long been interest in the relation between social thought and *action*. Although individuals can act in ways consistent with their thought processes, there are also many situations in which thought and action are quite unrelated. Social cognition processes can also produce behavioral manifestations that are undesired, counterproductive, and opposed to the explicit desires and goals of the perceiver. Also, there is growing evidence that unconscious thought can affect behavior while invoking little more than minimal cognitive involvement. Understanding the consequences of thought on behavior and the conditions under which thought affects behavior and behavior affects thought are important research questions that are beginning to be answered.

One Important Caveat

Although we present a set of chapters examining a range of core cognitive processes ranging from those viewed as basic (e.g., attention) to those quite complicated (e.g., judgment and decision making), the sequence in which we consider each aspect should not be viewed as a statement about their temporal sequence. Historically, many process theories that rested on the assumption of processing "stages" have collapsed when evidence showed that the presumed invariant sequence of processes could occur in a different order, were iterative, or were recursive. We wish to avoid that mistake at the outset by emphasizing explicitly that the cognitive processes implicated in any social situation are fixed neither in number nor order. Not all information is affected by each process, and processes can be re-initiated and strategies revised as the person elaborates on available social information. With these caveats in mind, we do think that the order in which we discuss different aspects of processing builds naturally and reflects increasing complexity and elaboration.

A Process Approach

Characterizing and analyzing the field of social cognition as a set of common processes affected by a set of common factors will, we hope, illustrate that social cognition is an approach that can be used to investigate any content area involving social thought and behavior. Although we intend to provide an "open architecture" that can be used by a broad audience of researchers and individuals interested in social information processing in diverse domains, we also recognize the benefit of showing illustrative findings across a set of core content areas that have benefitted from the social cognition approach. Accordingly, we begin each chapter by discussing the nature and importance of the cognitive process under consideration in that chapter, providing examples from research. We then conclude each chapter by discussing illustrative research findings regarding the nature and function of that particular process as applied to the study of three distinct content areas that have long been of central interest within social cognition: understanding the self, understanding persons, and understanding groups. By highlighting the importance of each process for understanding each content area, we aim to provide thematic consistency while also providing a useful and novel approach to the field.

Understanding and Evaluating Research

Throughout this book, we will be discussing research investigating issues and processes in social cognition. Psychology is a science, and knowledge in any science is based on research for which there are clear and important standards by which that research can be evaluated. The credibility of research findings does not rest on whether they fit with our pre-existing beliefs, with appealing philosophies (historic or contemporary), with current public opinion, with the views of prominent authorities, or with what our friends think. Instead, the credibility of those findings depends on the extent to which the research meets specific criteria by which we evaluate the adequacy of that research and therefore the believability of its findings.

We expect that most readers already have learned about essential aspects of experimentation in psychology and some new vocabulary that came with it – experimental and correlational methods, independent and dependent variables, experimental design, the threat of confounds, the importance of control groups, and the reliability and validity of measures. All of these concepts refer to very important features that are crucial in evaluating the quality of research. In all cases, the goal is to determine the effect that one variable (the independent variable) has on another variable (the dependent variable).

When researchers complete a study and successfully publish it in the scientific literature, that is not the end of the evaluation process. Once that article is published, other researchers can conduct the same experiment, testing the same hypotheses using the same methods, procedures, and measures. This "re-doing" of the experiment is called a *replication* which, if the same methodology is used, should produce the same results. Replications provide evidence of the reliability of the finding.

In the natural sciences, this is typically a straightforward exercise. If a procedure involves adding 300 ml of Chemical A to 500 ml of Chemical B to form a precipitate, then the same result should occur regardless of the time of day it was done, the researcher performing the technique, the lab room being used, or the number of people present. By following precisely the same procedures on another occasion, one can determine whether the original finding has replicated.

In social psychology (and indeed, in the social sciences more generally), things often are more complicated. Suppose we wanted to test a hypothesis that achievement motivation increases one's persistence on a task. The procedures and measures to be used in testing this hypothesis are not obvious, and choices must be made as to how to operationalize both independent and dependent variables. Specifically, one must decide how to manipulate and measure the theoretical constructs of interest to examine the hypothesized relationships between them. One might decide to test this hypothesis with a correlational method, using an existing questionnaire to measure individual differences in achievement motivation. One then must also determine how to measure persistence. One will need to identify or develop a task that is not too easy or too challenging so that performance would be expected to vary based on differences in the independent variable. Even in this straightforward example, many specific choices must be made to test the hypothesis, guided by theory and previous research. Once these decisions are made and the study has produced some interesting results, one might want to know if the outcome of the experiment replicates.

This brings us to an important distinction. There are two kinds of replication, known as direct replications and conceptual replications. In a *direct replication*, the goal is to conduct the experiment in precisely the same manner as the original study, following the identical procedures, manipulations, measures, and participant population used previously. For example, if a questionnaire measure of achievement motivation correlated with the amount of time participants persisted in completing a series of challenging crossword puzzles, a direct replication of that study would follow exactly that procedure using those same measures. Alternatively, a *conceptual replication* attempts to test the same hypothesis between the same variables but using different operationalizations and measures of the independent and dependent variables. For example, one might want to test the same research question experimentally, manipulating achievement motivation by providing participants with false feedback that they had performed either very well or rather poorly on a test comprised of difficult SAT questions. These groups could then be compared on the time they spent generating creative uses for everyday objects. The theoretical question being tested is identical, but the method being used to test it is very different. If the conceptual variables are actually related as one theorizes, then variations in operationalizations should not substantially alter the findings that are obtained.

Direct replications and conceptual replications are both important, but they serve different purposes. Direct replication focuses on a specific result obtained under specific conditions and tests the *reproducibility* of that finding. In contrast, conceptual replication tests the same hypothesis – the same predicted relationship between the same conceptual variables – but does so using different methods of manipulating and measuring independent variables, different procedures, and different measures of the effect. Conceptual replication provides evidence of the *generalizability* of the findings, demonstrating that the original result is not limited to a specific means of testing a general conceptual hypothesis.

Although both kinds of replication contribute to scientific knowledge in these ways, scholars differ (and debate) which type of replication is more important. For example, direct replications are focused on a specific effect. Successful replication provides evidence that the effect can be reproduced under the same conditions. Failure to replicate the previously-obtained effect would raise questions about whether the effect is real. On the other hand, conceptual replications are more theory-oriented, focusing on testing hypotheses about relations between conceptual variables operationalized in multiple ways. They are less concerned with a specific effect operationalized in a particular manner and instead are more concerned with advancing theory by establishing, using multiple procedures, the relationships among theoretical variables.

In recent years the question of replication has become an important issue in social psychology and other sciences (Molden, 2014; Shrout & Rodgers, 2018). The catalyst for this concern is that some articles have appeared in which the results of some well-known experiments have failed to replicate. These surprising outcomes raised broader questions about the replicability of social science findings in general, and much debate has ensued regarding how this problem should be addressed (e.g., Cesario, 2014; Doyen, Klein, Simons, & Cleeremans, 2014; Pashler & Harris, 2012; Pashler & Wagenmakers, 2012; Stroebe, 2016; Stroebe & Strack, 2014). How can this problem be addressed? Several different approaches have been suggested, each having potential benefits and costs.

One approach is simply to make replication a more regular aspect of the scientific process. Historically, replication studies have been infrequently conducted and published. Encouraging replications to be conducted more frequently would provide more information about the reproducibility of results, and several scholars have embraced this initiative (e.g., Greenwald, 1976; Mummendey, 2012; Nosek & Lakens, 2014). Indeed, journals have become more open to publishing replications (both successful and unsuccessful), and an increasing number of such studies have been published in recent years.

Several large-scale efforts have been undertaken to study further the extent to which published findings are replicable. These include the Reproducibility Project (Open Science Collaboration, 2012, 2015), the "Many Labs" Replication Project (Klein et al., 2014), and the Pipeline Project (Schweinsberg et al., 2016). Under these initiatives, researchers enlist and coordinate many experimenters in diverse locations to conduct direct replications of a number of published studies. Results can then be examined to determine the extent to which the studies' findings replicated.

Another approach focuses on a single published experiment. In a Registered Replication Report, researchers from many labs all attempt to replicate the same study, using procedures that faithfully (as much as possible) reproduce the methods of the original study. Across these studies, one can then determine the frequency with which the original study's results have been replicated.

Regardless of the approach, the same pattern of results has emerged. Some findings have been replicated with relatively high regularity, whereas others have shown discouragingly low rates of replication (e.g., Alogna et al., 2014; Doyen, Klein, Pichon, & Cleeremans, 2012; Gibson, Losee, & Vitiello, 2014; Johnson, Cheung, & Donnellan, 2014; Klein et al., 2014; McCarthy et al., 2018; O'Donnell et al., 2018; Open Science Collaboration, 2015; Schweinsberg et al., 2016; Shanks et al., 2013; Wagenmakers et al., 2016).

Some general comments about these matters are useful at this point. First, regarding the strategy of encouraging that more replication studies be undertaken, it seems that sustaining regular replication efforts might be difficult from a practical point of view. Researchers quite naturally are more intrigued by testing new ideas than by re-testing already published work, and reward structures typically encourage the former over the latter efforts. Thus, it may be challenging to incentivize and maintain regular replication initiatives over time.

Second, most replication efforts have focused on direct replication rather than on conceptual replication. Scholars differ sharply in their opinions as to which type of replication is more important and valuable. Some argue that direct replication is crucial for establishing the reproducibility of a specific effect (Doyen et al., 2012, 2014; Open Science Collaboration, 2012; Pashler & Wagenmakers, 2012; Simons, 2014) whereas others argue that conceptual replication is more valuable for its ability to develop and expand theoretical knowledge on a topic (Cesario, 2014; Crandall & Sherman, 2016; Dijksterhuis, 2014; Fabrigar & Wegener, 2016; Stroebe, 2016; Stroebe & Strack, 2014).

Third, the original and replication studies are usually conducted by different experimenters. As in any domain, researchers vary in their knowledge, experience, and expertise in conducting experiments, which suggests that in replication studies the same hypothesis may be being tested by experimenters with varying skill and qualifications. This may be particularly true in large-scale studies where a replication is tested in multiple labs. Unfortunately, the qualifications of the researcher (a variable that should be irrelevant in assessing replicability) can influence whether an effect is replicated. A recent analysis showed that highly-qualified experimenters were more likely to produce successful replications of previous findings than were less well-qualified experimenters (Bench, Rivera, Schlegel, Hicks, & Lench, 2017).

Fourth, failures to replicate are not always informative (Fabrigar & Wegener, 2016; Maxwell, Lau, & Howard, 2015; Stroebe & Strack, 2014). Typically, a failure to replicate means that a statistically significant result from a previous study was not significant in the replication. Such a result is often interpreted as meaning that the previous result is not "real" or "true," and that the null hypothesis should be accepted. However, it is important to recognize that "the failure to replicate an effect does not conclusively indicate that the original effect was false" (Open Science Collaboration, 2012, p. 658).

There are many reasons for any nonsignificant finding (Maxwell et al., 2015): (a) The replication study may not have enough participants to provide an adequate test of the hypothesis. When the sample size is insufficient to produce statistically significant results even when a hypothesis is true, the study is considered *underpowered* (Maxwell, 2004; Szucs & Ioannidis, 2017). (b) The means of implementing an independent variable (the manipulation) may not be sufficiently strong to have a causal effect on the dependent measure. Measures designed to measure the effectiveness of manipulations (i.e., *manipulation checks*) are often used in research (Ejelöv & Luke, 2020), although concerns have been raised about their universal use (Fayant, Sigall, Lemonnier, Retsin, & Alexopoulos, 2017). (c) In most experiments, the primary interest is in whether Conceptual Variable A has a causal effect on Conceptual Variable B. To test that relationship, those variables must be operationalized (manipulated or measured) in some way. An important concern is how well a particular operationalization accurately reflects the concept being tested. Differences between original and replication studies in the operationalization of variables may introduce differences that might be responsible for a replication failure. In such a case, the failure would arise from a shortcoming in operationalizing a variable rather than from the absence of the hypothesized relationship. With careful pilot testing and manipulation checks to ensure that similar concepts are being studied, failed conceptual replications can be useful for identifying variables that reveal the conditions under which a theory does and does not hold (Crandall & Sherman, 2016). (d) Often a period of time has passed between the original study and the replication study. Over time, some experimental materials can become outdated. For example, materials that were quite useful for studying attitudes toward same-sex marriage 15 years ago would likely be outdated and inappropriate for conducting a replication of that study today (whether for manipulations or dependent measures). If the original study used materials that are no longer valid, then a failure to replicate a reported effect would not be surprising. It would not, however, mean that the original effect was not true. Fabrigar and Wegener (2016) and Stroebe and Strack (2014) provide excellent examples of how this problem can influence attempts to replicate past findings. (e) Differing results between original and replication studies can occur for several reasons, only one of which is that the original effect is invalid. Such outcomes may have more significance than simply questioning the reproducibility of an effect. They raise the question as to why this difference has occurred. That is, what moderates the effect? What are its boundary conditions? What other (as yet unknown) third variables influence whether or not the original effect replicates? Even in direct replications, a seemingly innocuous variation can change the results in ways that are psychologically interesting and worthy of further investigation. For example, one study (Noah, Schul, & Mayo, 2018) followed up on a failed replication of a well-known effect involving the tendency to infer emotional responses from facial expressions. In the replication attempts, cameras were focused on participants' faces to ensure that they were complying with experimenter instructions. However, this seemingly minor alteration also appeared to change the psychological processes underlying the original finding. In a condition where the camera was absent (as in the original study), the original finding again emerged. Therefore, just as we should not uncritically accept as true an effect based on a single demonstration, we should also resist concluding that an effect is false based on a single failed replication. (f) The variation in results across replication attempts could itself be informative. Such variation is inevitable and can be due to many factors. "Studies are conducted in different locations, with different experimenters, in different historical moments, and with different randomly selected participants. All of these…lead to heterogeneity. And this heterogeneity leads to concerns about the utility of any single study" (Kenny & Judd, 2019, p. 587). Such heterogeneity challenges the assumption of one "true" effect and suggests focusing instead on the complexities that underlie the heterogeneity of these effects.

In sum, questions of the extent to which research findings are reproducible (direct replication) and generalizable (conceptual replication) are of central concern in establishing the knowledge base of the discipline. As this brief introduction reveals, it is not a simple topic, and its complexities present a challenge. Scientists devote their time and their careers to the pursuit of knowledge. As one well-known scholar quipped, "I love my job. Every week I can choose which 60 hours I want to work." These scientists care deeply about their work and, therefore, about the quality of its findings. Standards guide both the conduct of research and the evaluation of its findings. When the results of a study do not replicate, it is a serious concern. In social psychology (as well as in other sciences), findings of nonreplication have made this an important issue. In this section, we have provided a brief summary of some of the issues that are at the heart of the matter. The debate surrounding these issues is ongoing, and, at the time of this writing, clear solutions have not been identified. However, this state of affairs is neither unusual nor alarming because this is how science proceeds. Recognizing, confronting, and debating the issues is how scientific progress is achieved.

SUMMARY

Social cognition is the study of how people process, store, and use the information they encounter as they observe, participate in, and adapt to social life. In all domains of life, people are continually acquiring new information, elaborating on it, representing it in memory, and using it to guide their behavior. This book explores how this is achieved. This chapter summarizes the historical roots of social cognition, exploring its relations with other traditions and with important antecedents in social psychology. Social cognition emerged in the 1970s and 1980s with significant advances that established it as an important new development. Unlike other topic areas in social psychology (e.g., attitude change, group dynamics, aggression, relationships), social cognition is an approach to studying any topic area by investigating the cognitive underpinnings of those subjects and examining the intersections of those cognitive processes with other mechanisms (motives, goals) that also guide behavior. Within the last three decades, the contributions of social cognition have been extensive, enhancing our understanding of the mechanisms underlying social thought and action.

FURTHER READING

Hamilton, D.L., & Carlston, D.E. (2013) The emergence of social cognition. In D.E. Carlston (Ed.), *The Oxford handbook of social cognition* (pp. 16–32). New York, NY: Oxford University Press.

Monteith, M.J., Woodcock, A., & Gulker, J.E. (2013). Automaticity and control in stereotyping and prejudice: The revolutionary role of social cognition across three decades of research. In D.E. Carlston (Ed.), *The Oxford handbook of social cognition* (pp. 74–94). New York, NY: Oxford University Press.

Payne, B.K., & Gawronski, B. (2010). A history of implicit social cognition: Where is it coming from? Where is it now? Where is it going? In B. Gawronski & B.K. Payne (Eds.), *Handbook of implicit social cognition: Measurement, theory, and applications* (pp. 1–15). New York, NY: Guilford Press.

Stroebe, W., & Strack, F. (2014). The alleged crisis and the illusion of exact replication. *Perspectives on Psychological Science, 9*, 59–71.

2
COGNITIVE REPRESENTATIONS
Structures of the Mind

Heaven is where…

the police are British,

the cooks are French,

the mechanics are German,

the lovers are Italian,

and it's all organized by the Swiss.

Hell is where…

the police are German,

the cooks are British,

the mechanics are French,

the lovers are Swiss,

and it's all organized by the Italians.

This modest bit of humor might bring a smile, a chuckle, or an eye-roll. We use it here not for its amusement but because it illustrates an important point. We wouldn't "get the joke" (or roll our eyes) if we did not already have some beliefs about what people from these countries are like and how they (supposedly) differ from each other. We, of course, have knowledge and beliefs about ourselves, other persons, and social groups. This chapter focuses on how we form and represent that knowledge and those beliefs and how they influence the way we think about and interact with the people and events in our social world.

In Chapter 1, we introduced several cognitive processes that perceivers use in comprehending, storing, and using the information they encounter in the social world. In later chapters, we will analyze each of these processes in more detail. All of this processing occurs in a person who, no matter how young or old, has had an abundance of prior experience living in and adapting to a complex stimulus world. That experience is represented and stored in our minds in what are called *cognitive or mental representations*.

Representations are the product of learning. As we navigate our world, experiencing both novel and familiar events, succeeding and failing in a variety of endeavors, we develop extensive knowledge about persons, places, and things. The information we acquire is represented in memory, and this knowledge can be retrieved and used when we encounter new situations to which that knowledge applies. Cognitive representations, then, contain the accumulated knowledge from our past experiences. More formally, *cognitive representations* can be defined as *the knowledge, beliefs, and expectancies that pertain to some domain of content*. These representations can then be used in comprehending new events, new experiences, and new people, and they can guide our use of new information. In fact, they influence every aspect of the information processing model we introduced in Chapter 1.

Representations play a vital role in normal human functioning. Without the ability to bring to mind, or *activate*, appropriate stored representations, each object and event that we encounter would seem unique and almost impossible to understand. By using our stored knowledge, however, the events we encounter can be interpreted and understood through the lens of experience. We usually take for granted the ease with which cognitive representations are activated and their usefulness for processing new information. For example, when we look at a metal frame with handlebars, supported by two large wheels, we immediately categorize the object as a bicycle, and our accumulated knowledge about bicycles quickly comes to mind. We might think of its attributes (how to use the handlebars to steer and apply the brakes), its uses (riding to school), or even experiences we have had with the object in the past (remembering a particularly enjoyable ride on a beautiful country road). Although we might not be able to verbalize all the content contained in our cognitive representations, the availability of such information helps us understand and interact with the object.

Given the ease with which we use cognitive representations, it is interesting to consider the difficulties we would experience if they could not be brought to bear as we process new information. One intriguing phenomenon that involves such a deficit is *associative visual agnosia*, a rare disorder in which individuals (typically with damage to the occipital and temporal lobes of the brain) cannot access relevant cognitive representations from memory (Behrmann & Nishimura, 2010; Gainotti, 2007). People with this disorder have intact visual systems so they can, for example, copy or draw pictures of an object or a face, even though they cannot identify the object or person they have drawn. Individuals with this disorder can generate information about a person when given the person's name, but they cannot access such information from viewing an image of the person's face.

Fortunately, such conditions are quite uncommon, and most of us retain the ability to rapidly access our stored representations, allowing us to efficiently process information in our environment based on prior experience. This chapter is concerned with understanding how that experience is retained in memory, activated, and subsequently used.

The term *cognitive representation* is a general term for knowledge stored in memory, but several other terms are used to refer to specific kinds of cognitive representations. A *concept* represents our stored understanding of the meaning and referent of a term. When someone refers to a book she read, the actual object may not be present, but your concept of a "book" enables you to understand what she is talking about. Concepts can also represent the meaning of abstract terms that extend beyond any specific referent, such as freedom, fear, and peace. A *category* is a cognitive representation that represents a class of objects. Assigning objects to membership in categories is referred to as *categorization*, a fundamental, pervasive process that permeates much of our mental life. We group objects into categories, whether they be physical objects (cars, cats, calendars) or humans (Caucasians, Catholics, Californians). A *script* (Abelson, 1981; Loucks, Mutschler, & Meltzoff, 2017; Schank & Abelson, 1977; Van Overwalle et al., 2019) is a cognitive representation that represents our knowledge of the sequence of events that transpires in commonly-recurring situations. We know what typically happens when we go to a restaurant, a party, a movie. Scripts represent in generalized form the information we have extracted from past experiences in particular settings. They help us to anticipate what will happen in similar situations in the future. Because we have scripts, we can engage in routine but complex behaviors such as dining at a restaurant, introducing one friend to another, or attending a movie with minimal confusion and awkwardness. Within social cognition, more specific structures are particularly crucial for the processing of social information. Three very familiar ones that we will repeatedly be talking about throughout this book are *traits*, *self-concepts*, and *stereotypes*.

To understand the nature and functions of cognitive representations, we will explore several important questions. What are cognitive representations, and how are they formed? How are they represented in memory? How are they used, and what do they do for us? What effects do they have? If we can answer these questions, we will have a good grasp of what cognitive representations are and how they function. In fact, we will come to see that cognitive representations are of central importance in our perceiving, comprehending, and adapting to the social world in which we live.

WHAT ARE COGNITIVE REPRESENTATIONS?

Cognitive representations are the accumulated knowledge, beliefs, and expectancies about some domain, based on experience. Similar objects, events, and experiences are recognized as recurrences of the same type of thing, and from that recognition we develop a concept. For example, we recognize elms, oaks, and maples as trees. We learn that planes, trains, and automobiles are all forms of transportation. We come to understand that staying abreast of news, voting in elections, and marching in protest are different forms of political behavior, all being different manifestations of the same concept. Through these experiences, we form concepts such as trees, vehicles, and political activism, and the different forms that each of these concepts can take. These examples also illustrate an important point, namely, that *each cognitive representation pertains to a particular domain of content*. The concept of being politically active might help us understand a person who practices the various behaviors described above, but it will not enlighten us very much about that person's religious views, sense of humor, or ability to balance a checkbook. Similarly, stereotypes are cognitive representations that contain knowledge, beliefs, and expectancies about particular social groups. The "heaven and hell" joke at the beginning of this chapter can only be amusing if people share a set of beliefs about those national groups and their differences.

A concept summarizes a large number of specific instances that are examples of that concept. The specific instances that we experience – the elm tree across the street, the blue car parked in the driveway, my father speaking on behalf of a candidate – are referred to as *exemplars*, and those exemplars become associated with a concept, which is an *abstraction* based on numerous exemplars. These two terms are important for understanding how information – the people, objects, and events that we experience – become represented and stored in memory. Each experience (my father advocating for a politician) can be stored as an exemplar, and each experience (exemplar) of that type can be represented as one instance of a more abstract concept (politically involved). Understanding specific experiences in terms of abstractions (concepts) provides those experiences with new meaning as they are comprehended in relation to other exemplars of that concept. In this way, very different specific behaviors – going to a particular building (a school) to vote, giving money to a political party, volunteering to gather signatures on a petition – can be understood as instances of a broader class of actions that have the same or similar meaning.

BASES OF REPRESENTATION IN MEMORY

Given that we have these experiences and store them in memory, the next question becomes *how* cognitive representations are formed and the principles that guide their formation. Several different theories have been proposed to answer these questions. The basic building blocks have already been introduced: exemplars and concepts. But how do exemplars become associated with a particular concept? And how do different concepts become associated with each other?

Similarity

One fundamental basis for developing concepts and categories is the *similarity* among stimulus elements. In perceiving the world, we notice similarities and differences, and we group stimuli based on this information. One of the authors used to have Irish Setters, which he loved. If you saw those Irish Setters, you would immediately know they were the same breed: fairly tall dogs with long red hair and floppy ears. You would also know that they are different from other breeds (beagles, poodles, etc.), none of which have the same configuration of features that Irish Setters share (and each of those breeds has its own set of features that are shared by its members). By noticing similarities and differences among dogs, we can identify different breeds. All of our concepts and categories depend on this process of detecting similarities and differences. We have already cited several examples – not only breeds of dogs but also types of trees, means of transportation, and varieties of religious behavior.

The same principle applies to our perceptions of people. We believe that males have certain attributes and that females have some other attributes, and we use these beliefs to identify those genders and the differences between them. Similarly, we rely on attributes to help us classify people by race, age, nationality, religion, and many other bases for grouping people into categories. Sometimes these distinctions are fairly obvious ("Don't you love her Italian accent?"), but others are more challenging ("Is he in his 60s or 70s? Hard to tell…I'm not sure."), and the stimulus cues we rely on may or may not be valid. Nevertheless, the perception of similarities and differences is the foundation for all of these distinctions.

Prototypes

Although exemplars of a given concept or category are often viewed as interchangeable, some exemplars are seen as *better* examples of the category than are others. For example, although ostriches and robins are both members of the category "bird," a robin is typically seen as a better example of a bird (Smith, Shoben, & Rips, 1974). This example illustrates the crucial point that category membership is *graded* (Douven, 2016; Verheyen & Égré, 2018; Zadeh, 1965), with exemplars arrayed at varying distances around the "best" example of the concept or category. That best representative of a concept is commonly referred to as a *prototype* (Cantor & Mischel, 1979; Rosch, 1978; see for a review Minda & Smith, 2011). The prototype may be a specific exemplar that becomes strongly associated with the concept. For example, your prototype of a "car" may be the blue four-door Honda Accord that your family had for many years. Your long association and experience with that car may have resulted in it becoming the best representative of the very general and broadly inclusive set of objects known as "cars." Alternatively, the prototype may be an abstraction representing the typical features of the concept. What comes to your mind, for example, when you think of the concept "apple"? You probably imagine an object that is round, red, perfectly symmetrical, shiny, and without a blemish on it. Of course, you will likely never see such a perfect apple in the grocery store (many of which have irregular bumps, brown bruises, or are even green), but that image can serve as a prototype of what apples look like.

Whether the prototype is a specific well-known exemplar or is an average or idealized representation, the prototype becomes the mental representation of that concept and serves essential functions in comprehending new information. Specifically, when new exemplars are encountered, the observer will comprehend that exemplar by associating it with some concept or category. This is accomplished by comparing this specific exemplar with the prototypes of relevant concepts. A juicy red apple matches your prototype of an apple and therefore is categorized (i.e., comprehended) as being an apple. However, suppose I hand you a Granny Smith apple, and you've never seen one before. You might be puzzled. "Based on its shape, it sure looks like an apple, but it can't be – it's the wrong color!" In such a case, you might compare this exemplar to prototypes of other categories – "Well, limes are green, but this thing is a bit large for a lime, and besides, the skin is smooth, unlike the rough exterior of a lime." Through this process, you finally decide that the Granny Smith has more similarity to your prototype of an apple than to the prototypes of other categories, so it is therefore included in the category of apples. Again, similarity – this time between a new exemplar and a prototypic representation of a concept – is the principle on which the decision is made.

Prototypes tend to share many features in common with other category members (Rosch & Mervis, 1975), are close to the "average" member (Posner & Keele, 1968), or have features that are viewed as ideal for the category (Burnett, Medin, Ross, & Blok, 2005). Compared with exemplars that are seen as atypical for the category, exemplars similar to the prototype are more quickly identified as category members (Rosch, Simpson, & Miller, 1976), are judged to be more typical of the category (Malt & Smith, 1984), are more likely to be spontaneously thought about and mentioned when considering the category (Barsalou, 1985; Rosch, 1977), and are more likely to serve as the basis of extrapolations to other category members (Rips, 1975).

Because category membership is graded, most categories do not have sharp demarcations separating members from non-members. Instead, they typically have *fuzzy boundaries* that are vague and involve overlapping features. The concepts "cup" and "bowl," for example, are very similar. Both concepts relate to concave dishes that hold liquids. Typically, bowls are deeper and broader than cups, and cups have handles whereas bowls do not. However, some bowls have handles and are shallow, and some cups have no handles. Although typical bowls and cups differ in appearance, they often share similar characteristics and features (both could be made of porcelain). The consequence is that the two concepts are similar enough that the vague boundaries separating them can make them difficult to differentiate (Labov, 1973).

Hierarchical Structures

Abstractions do not exist in isolation from one another; there are also associations between different concepts and categories. These associations are often arranged *hierarchically*, with broad, *superordinate* categories that have nested within them narrower subordinate *subtypes* that can themselves be differentiated. People tend to use one level to think and converse about concepts, referred to as a *basic-level category* (Mack, Wong, Gauthier, Tanaka, & Palmeri, 2009; Rosch, Mervis, Gray, Johnson, & Boyes-Braem, 1976; Tanaka & Taylor, 1991; see for a review Hajibayova, 2013). Basic-level categories are useful because they strike a balance between breadth and specificity. That is, they are broad enough to include a reasonably large number of members to be useful, yet they are specific enough to make meaningful distinctions between different subtypes.

A simplified model of a hierarchical structure is displayed in Figure 2.1, depicting how people might represent information about various animals. The category "animal" is a superordinate category with several subtypes (e.g., horses, dogs, cats). If this is the level that people typically use to think about and describe various animals, this would represent the basic level of categorization. Within these categories are additional subordinate categories for different subtypes of each animal. For dogs, there would be different representations for each breed (e.g., Hounds, Pugs, Akitas), each containing its own set of features that is the basis for its grouping and for distinguishing it from other breeds. However, each subtype also shares specific features with all members of the broader or superordinate category. All these representations are arranged in a hierarchy that represents a system of classifying diverse but related objects.

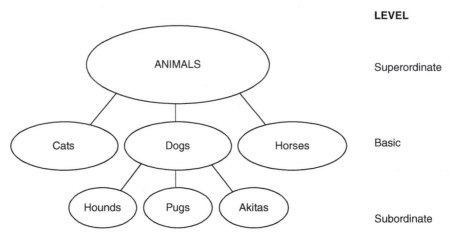

Figure 2.1 A simplified hierarchical representation of animals

The same processes underlie our perceptions of people. Perhaps the most fundamental distinction we make among people is between men and women, but this is far too broad a cut. The category of women includes a diversity of roles, including government leaders, store clerks, homemakers, business executives, welfare moms, successful lawyers, nurses, politicians, and professors. Each of these (and many other) subtypes has its own set of attributes that describe members of the subcategory, yet they are all women. The same point can be made for many other groups, including men and women (Carpenter & Trentham, 1998; Vonk &

Ashmore, 2003), African Americans (Devine & Baker, 1991; Hinzman & Maddox, 2017), gay men and lesbians (Clausell & Fiske, 2005; Geiger, Harwood, & Hummert, 2006), and the elderly (Brewer, Dull, & Lui, 1981; Neugarten, 1974; Schmidt & Boland, 1986). As we develop knowledge, beliefs, and expectancies about each subtype, each becomes its own cognitive representation embedded within a more extensive, superordinate structure. In this way, our increasingly varied experiences result in the development of more complex mental representations.

Even though similar processes underlie our categorization of objects in the social and nonsocial world, there are some significant implications when they are applied to social stimuli (individual people and groups). Physical objects do not care if they are excluded from their category, if they are seen as typical or atypical of their group, or if members of the same category are seen as relatively interchangeable. People, however, often care passionately about these things. Consider the uproar that can arise when information is revealed (often inadvertently) about the content of one's representation of a social group. The writer Byron York (York, 2009) once opined about President Obama, "The president and some of his policies are significantly less popular with White Americans than with Black Americans, and his sky-high ratings among African Americans make some of his positions appear a bit more popular overall than they actually are." This comment – which produced extensive criticism – suggests that Black Americans are poor representatives of the category "American" and that their views should be underweighted due to their low prototypicality.

The issue of fuzzy boundaries also can present some challenges when applied to categories of people. Consider another example involving Barack Obama, whose father was from Kenya and whose mother was from Kansas and was of English and Irish heritage. When he began his campaign for president in 2008, some commentators thought he was unelectable because he was Black, but others suggested that he (being mixed-race) might not be "Black enough." Yet others suggested that his biracial background was simply "too exotic." Consider, as well, the difficulties inherent in distinguishing the categories necessary for dealing effectively with people's problems. Clinical psychologists, for example, might have to decide which of three very different diagnoses – schizophrenia, schizoaffective disorder, or mood disorder – should be applied to a person exhibiting similar symptoms (Millon, Krueger, & Simonsen, 2011). Similarly, medical doctors must often quickly decide whether a set of symptoms characterizes a heart attack or merely heartburn (Weinstock & Neides, 2009). In each of these cases, perceivers must decide which of two or more highly overlapping and poorly differentiated categories should be used in understanding others.

Multiple Bases of Similarity

Although similarity is a fundamental basis for creating mental representations, it is itself not a simple concept. One challenge is that the number of different features (and hence criteria) that potentially could be used as a basis for categorizing similarities and differences is infinitely large. This was demonstrated in a famous episode of the TV program *Cheers* when the character Cliff Clavin loses all his winnings on the final question on the game show *Jeopardy!* The host provides the answer as "Archibald Leach, Bernard Schwartz, and Lucille LeSueurn," and Cliff responds, "Who are three people who have never been in my kitchen?" (The correct answer was "What were the real names of actors Cary Grant, Tony Curtis, and Joan Crawford?"). Of course, these individuals had never been in his kitchen but, to Cliff's frustration, similarity on that dimension alone was not enough to convince the judges that his answer was correct.

Also, focusing on different sets of features while comparing different exemplars can yield different category judgments. We can illustrate this point by borrowing an example from Schneider (2004, p. 73):

> If…I say that Sylvester Stallone is more like Arnold Schwarzenegger than like Woody Allen, there are likely to be several features I use (body build, height, weight, types of movies they appear in, whether they employ weapons in their movie roles, whether they are likely to drive fast cars, etc.). This seems reasonable enough. What is the problem?… In judging Sly as more similar to Arnie than to Woody, we are clearly privileging some features over others. There are…other features on which Sly and Woody are more similar. For example, both were born in the United States; both grew up on the East Coast; neither has been a professional body builder; neither has been married to a close relative of a U.S. President; and so forth. Obviously, if we used these criteria, Sly and Woody would be seen as more similar.

Similarity may play an important role in categorizing others, but these examples indicate that there is more to the story.

In some cases, objects are members of the same category not because they are highly similar in appearance but because they serve similar *functions*. For example, planes, trains, and automobiles do not look very similar to each other, but they are all means of transportation. In still other cases, exemplars become associated because they have some connection to each other based on some higher *meaning*. Attending church, donating money to a faith-based charity, and bowing one's head before meals are very different specific behavioral acts (low similarity), and it is not immediately apparent that they serve the same function. All of them, though, are excellent exemplars that reflect the individual's religiosity. The concept of religiosity provides a meaning structure that ties these behaviors together in a single category simply because they are different manifestations of the same underlying concept. Thus, categories need to have some explanatory function (Medin, 1989). A category is more than a set of elements that are grouped based merely on perceived similarities and differences; a category is also a *theory* that gives some account for *why* these elements, but not other elements, are included in the category. This explanation provides the "glue" that holds the category together.

Essentialism

There are several examples in social psychology in which categories are viewed as explanatory frameworks (e.g., Jost & Banaji, 1994; Sidanius & Pratto, 1999; Wittenbrink, Gist, & Hilton, 1997). One interesting principle is *essentialism* (Gelman, 2003; Haslam, 2017; Rangel & Keller, 2011; Rhodes, Leslie, Saunders, Dunham, & Cimpian, 2018; Rothbart & Taylor, 1992). This perspective rests on a distinction between two kinds of categories: *artifactual categories* and *natural kinds*. Artifactual categories are categories of objects that were created by humans, typically to serve some *function*. For example, chairs and bicycles were invented by smart people so they could sit down and relax and could get from one place to another with ease. Natural kinds, in contrast, are categories of objects that contain – and their category membership is defined by – some innate, biological, or chemical element, an *essence* possessed by all category members. For example, gold is defined by its chemical makeup; a tiger has some defining biological properties that are true of all tigers. Those underlying properties define the essence that makes the category what it is.

Several crucial features differentiate natural kinds from artifactual categories (Rothbart & Taylor, 1992; Sloman & Malt, 2003). One is *inductive potential*, the extent to which inferences can be made about category members. Natural kind categories have higher inductive potential than artifactual categories (Waxman & Gelman, 2009). If you know (or perceive) that an object is a member of a natural kind category, you should be able to infer many other features because they are true of all members of that category. If you know an animal is a cow, you can infer that it is large, four-legged, slow-moving, eats grass, and produces milk. All cows have these features. In contrast, artifactual categories do not have an underlying essence that generates similarities (features, behaviors) among all category members. A chair may be made of wood, metal, or plastic, it may have four legs, three legs (a stool), or even no legs (a bean-bag), and still be considered a chair.

The second property distinguishing the two types of categories is *inalterability*, the degree to which an object can change category membership. A natural kind is inalterable (Medin & Ortony, 1989). It has a basic nature – an essence – that cannot be changed. You can paint black and white stripes on a horse, but that will not make it into a zebra. Even young children grasp this concept at an early age (Gelman, 2003). Members of artifactual categories, in contrast, are defined not by their internal essence but instead by their function. While the primary function of a chair is to sit on it, it can also be used as something to stand on to reach a high shelf, as an object to defend oneself with against an intruder, or as firewood if needed.

Rothbart and Taylor (1992) applied this distinction to the perception of social groups. They argued that, although human groups generally do not have the properties that define natural kinds, people routinely perceive certain groups *as if* they are natural kinds. That is, people regularly endow groups (and their members) with an essence that is not really there. One might perceive Germans, Jews, African Americans, and other groups as possessing some inner essence that defines their category members, some fundamental disposition that is shared by all group members that will always be a part of them. The tendency to essentialize race occurs despite the view of scientists that race has little to no biological basis (Yudell, Roberts, DeSalle, & Tishkoff, 2016).

When perceivers essentialize a group, then specific consequences follow based on the assumptions of inductive potential and inalterability. That is, if a racial, religious, or national group is perceived as if it were a natural kind, then the perceiver is likely to infer that all members of the group share certain properties (fostering stereotypes) and group membership will be seen as inalterable ("Once an X, always an X"). Several negative implications flow directly from these beliefs (Haslam, Rothschild, & Ernst, 2002; Holtz & Wagner, 2009). Rothbart and Taylor's (1992) analysis has generated considerable interest and has been developed and extended by other writers (e.g., Dar-Nimrod & Heine, 2011; Hamilton, 2007; Haslam, Rothschild, & Ernst, 2000, 2004; Miller & Prentice, 1999; Tsukamoto, Enright, & Karasawa, 2013; Yzerbyt, Corneille, & Estrada, 2001; Yzerbyt, Rocher, & Schadron, 1997).

Association

Once information is categorized, an important subsequent principle regarding the mental representation of this information is *association*. Items of information that share similarities – whether features, functions, meanings – become associated with one another and therefore are linked in memory. If your concept of Irish Setters includes red hair and floppy ears, when you see a red dog with floppy ears, you can immediately classify it as an Irish Setter. This example illustrates how information is stored in terms of concepts, and properties associated with those concepts are linked to the concept in memory.

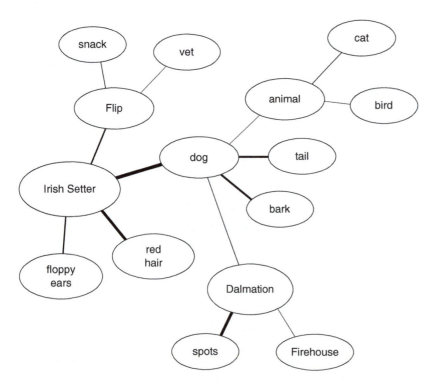

Figure 2.2   Example of an associative network

There are different ways of conceptualizing the nature of this mental representation in memory. We have already discussed one possibility, a *hierarchical* representation (Figure 2.1). This type of representation is really a classification system for organizing stimulus objects based on similarities and differences.

Another way to represent the storage of information in memory is through the use of *associative network models*. These models represent a concept by locating what is termed a *node* in memory, and features associated with that concept are linked to the node through *pathways*. Thus, Irish setters would be a node in memory, and each item of our knowledge of and beliefs about these dogs is connected to that node by a pathway. Physical features (red hair, floppy ears), typical behaviors (barking), associated beliefs (lovable), or anything else that has been associated with the concept become part of a network in memory organized around that concept. The node for Irish Setters can also be associated with other nodes representing, for example, other breeds of dogs (German Shepherds, pugs) or a specific Irish Setter exemplar (childhood pet Flip). Moreover, the node for Flip might also be associated with concrete memories attached to that exemplar (walking her in the woods, taking her to the veterinarian). As you can imagine, it does not take long to develop a rather elaborate network of associations within and between concepts. An example of a small portion of an associative network is depicted in Figure 2.2.

Spreading Activation

The associative pathways in a network are of crucial importance in understanding the retrieval of information from memory through the principle of *spreading activation*. When an instance of the node is encountered (you see an Irish Setter), then that node is activated or energized, and the activation of that node then spreads through the pathways associated with it, thereby activating other nodes, bringing those features, memories, and other associations easily to mind (floppy ears, wagging tail, walking in the woods, etc.). While connected nodes are energized through spreading activation, there is a parallel process of *spreading inhibition* that suppresses the activation of information that might compete with the relevant information. Inhibitory processes act to constrain activation so that an overwhelming quantity of knowledge is not activated when searching memory.

The strength of association varies within a network. You will notice in Figure 2.2 that the pathways differ in thickness and length. The thickness represents the strength of the association between nodes (floppy ears are definitely associated with Irish Setters). Features that are close to the node are more likely to be activated than are more remote features; yes, Irish Setters do bark, but it is not as closely associated as their floppy ears. Both strength and closeness of association are related to the spreading activation from the node. Activation can spread more easily to associates that are strongly connected and have short pathways from the node. Those associations will come to mind easily and quickly, compared to less strong or more remote associates. The same principle applies to retrieving information from memory. If you are asked to recall what you know about Irish Setters, then you will be more likely to generate (recall) those associates that have strong pathways and close proximity to the node.

REPRESENTATIONAL MODELS IN SOCIAL COGNITION

From its inception, social cognition has recognized the importance of representation. The way information is represented in memory affects what and how people think about any social entity – whether the self, a person, or a group – and how information about that entity is processed. As a consequence, there are numerous influential models of social representations ranging from those involving the self-concept (e.g., McConnell, 2011) to attitudes (e.g., Conrey & Smith, 2007; Fazio, 1986, 2007) to faces (e.g., Oosterhof & Todorov, 2008; Stolier, Hehman, Keller, Walker, & Freeman, 2018) to stereotypes (e.g., Fiske, Cuddy, Glick, & Xu, 2002; Sherman, 1996). All of these models incorporate, to varying degrees, the basic principles that we have discussed. Although we will not review all existing representational models that have emerged from a social cognitive perspective, we now consider several models that have been important in shaping how we think about mental representation. Each reflects some of the basic principles we have discussed while adding nuance and complexity.

An Associative Network Model of Person Impressions

One historically significant model (briefly introduced in Chapter 1) has been used to portray how information about a person is represented in an associative network (Hastie, 1980; Hastie & Kumar, 1979; Srull, 1981; Srull, Lichtenstein, & Rothbart, 1985; Srull & Wyer, 1989). Here, we elaborate on this model to demonstrate how it was able to generate numerous novel predictions based on principles of association and activation. This model is shown in Figure 2.3. In this conception, a person – let's call him Mark – is represented by his own *person node* in memory. All information learned about Mark (e.g., behaviors he enacts) becomes attached to

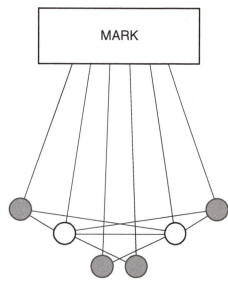

Figure 2.3 A person memory associative network
Source: Adapted from Hastie (1980), Srull (1981)

his person node; those associations are represented by the vertical lines connecting dots (items of information) with the "Mark" person node. Also, suppose you have an impression of Mark as a friendly, outgoing, sociable person. Some of the things you learn about Mark are quite compatible with that impression (e.g., he invites friends over for dinner, gives directions to the strangers who are lost, consoles a friend who has experienced a loss). These expectancy-congruent behaviors are represented in Figure 2.3 by the black dots. But you also might learn some things about Mark that are quite contrary to your impression of him (e.g., that he insulted someone without provocation). These behaviors, represented by the white dots in Figure 2.3, make it challenging to develop a consistent representation of Mark because they violate your existing impression of him. The model states that when you encounter such a fact, you think about it in relation to other things you have learned about Mark, including both behaviors consistent and inconsistent with your impression. You might try to reconcile this seemingly inconsistent behavior with the other information you have about him ("perhaps he is typically kind to people, but only so he can get his way") or you might explain away the inconsistent behavior by attributing it to other conditions ("perhaps he lost his temper because he has been coping with his parents' divorce"). Nonetheless, by thinking about those behaviors in relation to each other and trying to grasp the meaning of it all, associations are formed that directly connect those items. Those connections are portrayed by the horizontal links between items in Figure 2.3.

What we have discussed so far pertains to how information is represented in memory as it is encoded. The model posits that people devote more time and effort to processing information that violates a pre-existing impression than to information that confirms that impression. In doing so, they think about the relation of this inconsistent information in relation to other, already-acquired items. These predictions have been supported by research findings (Bargh & Thein, 1985; Sherman & Hamilton, 1994; Stern, Marrs, Millar, & Cole, 1984). The consequence is that the horizontal pathways, connecting items directly to each other, are formed when – and only when – expectancy-*incongruent* information is acquired and processed.

This model makes several predictions that might not be obvious without it. The model states that in retrieving information from memory, one would enter the network at the person node and proceed down a pathway to a particular item, which would then be recalled. From there, the model assumes that one would move to recall another item by traversing a horizontal (interitem) pathway, if possible, rather than returning to the person node and starting over again. Because more pathways are leading to incongruent than congruent items (because these pathways were formed in encoding the former), people will be able to recall more incongruent than congruent items. This outcome has been documented in numerous studies (see Srull & Wyer, 1989).

The model also makes some nonintuitive predictions about the likely sequence of recall of different types of items. For example, if you recall a congruent item, what is likely to be recalled next? Because all interitem pathways are formed during encoding of incongruent items, all such pathways are connected to incongruent items. For this reason, there never is a pathway directly connecting two congruent items. This leads to the predictions that (a) recall of a congruent item will be followed by recall of an incongruent item, (b) recall of an incongruent item will be followed by recall of either a congruent or an incongruent item, and (c) recall of a congruent item should *not* be followed by recall of another congruent item. As is displayed in Figure 2.4, this is precisely the pattern of free recall sequences that has been obtained in several experiments (Srull, 1981; Srull et al., 1985; Hamilton, Driscoll, & Worth, 1989).

This model, then, provides a straightforward account of how information is processed, stored in memory, and retrieved. In fact, it incorporates three aspects of information processing that we introduced in Chapter 1. First, it specifies how information is encoded, and it specifically indicates differences in the encoding of information that is congruent and incongruent with a prior impression. Second, it describes a framework – an associative network – whereby those items of information are represented in memory, forming a new cognitive representation that pertains to the target person. And third, it delineates a process by which that information is retrieved from memory. The research generated from this model would not have been possible without a deep appre-

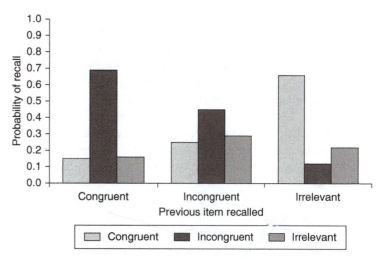

Figure 2.4 Probability of recall as a function of item type and previous item recalled

Source: Based on data from Srull & Wyer (1989)

ciation of the importance of mental representation. Understanding the processes by which information is represented in and retrieved from memory can be valuable in understanding the nature and functioning of mental representations.

Dual Structures

So far, we have discussed cognitive representations as if people have a single, unitary structure about any given entity that is activated in its entirety following categorization. Historically, that was implicitly assumed to be true. However, it became clear over time that this assumption is an oversimplification. People often have more than one cognitive representation about a domain, and evidence accrued over time reflecting the existence of two distinct memory systems for representation.

Why would this be? Some have speculated that separate memory systems have developed to allow people to address separate, incompatible demands (Smith & DeCoster, 2000). On the one hand, we need to develop a body of knowledge and beliefs based on a large sample of information, presumably so our representations will accurately reflect the average and typical experiences we have had. This need for stable, accurate information relies on the slow aggregation of information over time. On the other hand, we need to be able to respond effectively to novel information that has recently been encountered. This demand requires the ability to rapidly modify our representations in light of the new information. However, because the need to slowly accrue information (to maintain stability) is incompatible with the need to modify representations quickly (to reflect new information), separate memory systems have evolved.

This recognition allows us to understand how our representations might change over time, as new experiences occur. Consider, for example, the multiple cognitive representations that might be available to a White man who grew up in a racist family but who later embraced racial equality. He presumably grew up in a culture that routinely emphasized racial differences in characteristics and abilities, and he would have been exposed to a steady stream of representations in his surroundings that would have emphasized the supposed inferiority of African Americans. When he later had experiences that led him to reject this belief, would he be able to replace his original negative representation with an alternative, positive one? Several lines of research suggest that prior beliefs, in fact, are not replaced. Instead, beliefs learned early in life are augmented with alternate views that coexist alongside the original cognitive representation (Baumeister & Bushman, 2008; Greenwald & Banaji, 1995; Petty, Tormala, Briñol, & Jarvis, 2006; Wilson, Lindsey, & Schooler, 2000).

Although old and new cognitive representations can coexist, they tend to differ in several important ways. Structures developed earlier in life are more likely to be activated without intention or effort. Original structures are also relatively resistant to change, and they change only slowly in response to new information. In contrast, structures developed later in life require intention and effort to be activated, and perceivers are typically aware when they have been. Individuals can more readily report the contents of these structures and control their use. These structures can be modified more easily than their original counterparts, sometimes changing quickly and dramatically in response to new information.

What occurs when both early- and later-learned structures are available in a given domain? And since the expression of newer structures can be more easily controlled, do they override the expression of old attitudes? These questions were the focus of several studies by Rudman and her colleagues (Rudman, Phelan, & Heppen, 2007). In one study, participants' attitudes towards overweight people were assessed with both self-report and indirect measures where attitudinal expression is difficult to control. Of particular interest were the attitudes of adults who had been raised by an overweight mother whom they loved. It was hypothesized that these individuals might have dual attitudes about obesity. On the one hand, as children they might have formed positive attitudes toward obesity if their mother was viewed as overweight. On the other hand, as adults they might have developed more negative attitudes if they had become cognizant of the negative health implications of obesity or struggled themselves with being overweight. If this is the case, then these individuals might be expected to express negative attitudes on self-report measures but more positive attitudes on measures where control of expression is difficult. This is precisely what was found. People who were raised by a loved overweight mother showed more positive attitudes toward overweight than toward slim people on an indirect measure of attitudes. However, attitudes towards their mother's weight did not correlate with responses to self-report measures of attitudes towards obesity.

These results show that attitudes developed early in life can continue to affect responses, especially those responses that are difficult to control (Dunham, Baron, & Banaji, 2008; Rudman, 2004). Attitudes that are developed later tend to affect the explicit expression of attitudes, but their influence on subsequent responses is more sporadic since they must be intentionally activated.

Distributed Connectionist Models

Over time, and influenced by new developments in cognitive psychology, representational models in social cognition have incorporated even greater complexity. One recent development has been the idea that information about a social entity is not organized around a singular "node," but instead arises from patterns of activation within a set of richly interconnected nodes (Conrey & Smith, 2007; Freeman, Stolier, & Brooks, 2020; McClelland, 1991; Smith, 1996). Within such *distributed connectionist models*, any given input is assumed to activate a pattern of nodes based on both the pattern of associations connecting nodes and the strength of any given association. The nodes that are activated in response to input also depend upon the specific features of that input and the context in which it is encountered. The pattern of nodes that respond to input can vary quite dramatically depending on these variations, and, over time, the strength of association linking different nodes can also change to reflect learning. As such, mental representations are not "things" to be accessed so much as mental states that are created dynamically in response to inputs encountered in social contexts.

How might such an approach allow us to predict responses to an event in the environment? Let us say we want to account for a person's attitude towards a dog. We might start by determining the person's typical evaluations of dogs (Does he generally like or dislike dogs? Are there any breeds that he particularly likes or dislikes?). We would not expect that the person would respond identically to every dog that is encountered, however, because the features of any two dogs will likely differ, even within the same breed. So, an Irish Setter who barks incessantly will activate not only nodes in memory typically associated with Irish Setters (e.g., red hair, floppy ears) but also nodes associated with dogs that bark a lot. Presumably, dogs that bark continuously are less well-liked than quiet dogs, especially if they are encountered in contexts where barking is inappropriate or undesired. Accordingly, we would expect that the attitude generated toward an Irish Setter barking endlessly during an outdoor garden party will be quite unfavorable because the pattern of activated associations from memory will contain more negatively-toned concepts.

This simple example illustrates several important points. First, it shows that cognitive structures such as attitudes are context-sensitive reconstructions that inevitably vary across time and social contexts. In other words, no *single* cognitive representation is activated every time we encounter a category member. Instead, for every given experience, we generate a pattern of responses to the category, but these responses are also influenced by the particular features of the individual target and the context in which it is encountered. Second, it highlights how the current states of the perceiver (e.g., moods, goals, or material in memory from previous experience) can alter the nature of representations that are activated in response to a target. If I am currently in a happy mood, then nodes associated with "happiness" might be incidentally co-active with nodes associated with a category, allowing for a more positive evaluative response than would typically occur. Third, it helps account for changes in representations over time. If you repeatedly encounter a category member in a similar context (e.g., you regularly see the barking Setter playing with his owner in the park), then patterns of responses tend to change over time through the modification of associative strength between informational nodes (e.g., you associate barking Setters with happy play rather than embarrassment).

These points are well illustrated in research on stereotypic representations of groups (Garcia-Marques, Santos, & Mackie, 2006). In one study, participants indicated the traits that best described each of several stereotyped groups (e.g., gay men, African immigrants). In another study, participants were shown several members of each group and rated how typical each person was of their group. In a third study, participants were asked to think of five members of each group and to generate descriptions of each member. In each study, participants completed the same task in two sessions separated by 2–4 weeks, which permitted determining the stability over time of each person's responses. Results showed within-person *instability* in the traits selected as stereotypic of the groups, in the typicality ratings of group members, and in the attributes used to describe group members.

We often think of group stereotypes as stable, enduring cognitive representations, as belief systems about target groups that are resistant to change. The results of these studies convey a different picture, revealing the extent to which stereotypes can change over time, even within the same person. Such findings are compatible with a connectionist account of cognitive representations.

INTERIM SUMMARY To recapitulate, we have discussed several important points regarding the mental representation of information in memory, and these principles help us understand the nature of cognitive representations. Based on our exposure to numerous exemplars, we form concepts and categories that summarize, at an abstract level, the recurring aspects of our experiences. These concepts and categories are formed by noticing similarities and differences among the exemplars we encounter. We develop hierarchical representations of the relations among these concepts and categories, and these cognitive representations lend organization to the multitude of objects, persons, and events that we experience. We also develop network representations in which concepts are represented as nodes to which features, experiences, exemplars, and other nodes are attached by associative pathways. When a concept is activated, that activation spreads through the pathways to the associated features and other nodes, making them accessible in memory and possibly available for conscious awareness. Also, nodes and associative networks can become interconnected in intricate patterns, such that stimulus input can activate multiple nodes and a pattern of associations linked to each as well as associations connecting them. In all of these ways, the knowledge we have gained from experience is stored in memory and is accessible for use in the future.

ACTIVATION OF COGNITIVE REPRESENTATIONS

When a concept becomes accessible in memory, it can then be used in a variety of generally helpful ways. It can help us disambiguate information, can bring relevant beliefs and knowledge to bear, and can assist in "filling in the gaps" when information is incomplete or vague. However, before concepts can be used, they must be activated from memory. As we have just discussed, modern models of cognitive representation emphasize that both the nature of encountered information and the state of the perceiver at the time play crucial roles in determining the exact nature of representations that become accessible to influence subsequent information processing. Several factors deserve further elaboration.

Task Engagement
Stimulus objects can activate concepts directly merely by being observed, but concepts can also be activated by the activities we initiate. At any given time, we are typically trying to get something done, whether it be studying for an exam, planning a party for the weekend, or even something as mundane as deciding which TV programs we should watch tonight. When we are engaged in such activities, task demands can increase the accessibility of task-relevant information. If I am preparing a spaghetti dinner for some friends tonight, then the ingredients and utensils necessary for cooking become task-relevant. Consequently, those concepts, and the knowledge and beliefs associated with them, will be activated in my mind.

Goals and Motivations
Similarly, one's current goals and motivations, both short-term and long-term, can make certain cognitive representations relevant and, therefore, can result in their activation. If Sarah is a college sophomore whose long-term goal is to work in the information technology field, she will need to follow a path of preparation that will increase the likelihood of achieving that goal. This may entail planning what courses to take, how to acquire relevant experience and other aspects

of preparation for the time when she graduates and seeks the job of her dreams. Implementing plans for such long-term goals can result in the recurring activation of cognitive representations relevant to achieving that goal.

Priming

Another important way that cognitive representations can become activated is when a category has recently been used, a phenomenon called *priming* (Collins & Loftus, 1975; Higgins et al., 1977). If a concept has been activated (primed), then that concept is more readily available for use in processing new information. Other concepts linked to the primed concept are activated as well through spreading activation. Moreover, this activation persists for some period, which means that the primed concept and its associates continue to be accessible to influence subsequent processing. Thus, priming occurs when exposure to some event (the prime) increases the accessibility of related information already stored in memory.

These effects can be quite subtle. For example, Mandel and Johnson (2002) showed that material displayed on a web-page background can influence consumer choices. They created advertisements for a sofa with two contrasting backgrounds, designed to prime different desirable attributes. One background was blue with fluffy clouds, intended to prime the concept of *comfort.* The other background was green with pennies scattered in it, designed to prime concerns with *the price.* Participants were shown one of the web pages and were asked to list the most important features to consider when buying a sofa. Those who saw the ad with the "clouds" background were much more likely to list comfort as an essential attribute, whereas those who saw the "pennies" background were more likely to cite price as an important criterion. These data established that the web backgrounds did, in fact, prime (and make accessible) different features relevant to purchasing a sofa. A follow-up study showed that primes also affected actual product choices. Among those who were primed with the clouds background, a majority chose the comfortable (though expensive) sofa, whereas, among those primed with the pennies background, a majority chose the cheaper (though less comfortable) sofa. Thus, a relatively subtle form of priming (web-page backgrounds) made different features accessible that, in turn, influenced purchase choices.

This seemingly simple point has far-reaching implications, for it means that a cognitive representation that has been activated (primed) in one context can remain activated to influence processing for some period, even in another context that is entirely unrelated to the initial priming context. This effect was demonstrated quite clearly in the experiment by Higgins et al. (1977) that we discussed in Chapter 1, the study in which participants learned about the activities of a man named "Donald" after having been exposed to desirable and undesirable traits in a supposedly unrelated task. As you will recall, people who were primed with the positive terms (adventurous, confident, persistent) relevant to Donald's activities formed more favorable impressions of Donald than did participants primed with the negative trait words (reckless, conceited, stubborn), even though they read the same paragraph describing Donald.

These results demonstrate that a concept that is primed in one context continues to be accessible for use in processing subsequent information in another context. But does this always happen? Are our mental processes always driven by whatever concept has just been primed? And does it always work in the same way?

Applicability

Primed information must be *relevant* to a subsequently encountered stimulus or judgment for it to affect mental processes about that subsequent experience. In other words, if there is no overlap in the features of an accessible concept and an encountered stimulus, there likely will be little influence of the primed information on processing about the stimulus (Higgins, 1996).

This fundamental principle was also illustrated in the Donald study we just referred to (Higgins et al., 1977). There were actually two other conditions in the study that we have not discussed until now. In those conditions, participants also were provided with either four positive ("obedient," "neat," "satirical," "grateful") or four negative traits ("disrespectful," "listless," "clumsy," "sly") before they read the subsequent paragraph describing Donald's activities. However, these traits have little relevance to the behaviors performed by Donald. In other words, these primes did not apply to the subsequent information. As predicted, and in contrast with the applicable primes, these inapplicable traits did not affect evaluative judgments of Donald.

Recency and Frequency of Activation

Srull and Wyer (1979) wondered whether the temporal distance between the prime and the subsequent information might also determine whether primes exert any influence. They reasoned that a concept that has been *recently activated* would be more likely to influence processing than would a concept that has not been recently primed. They also wondered whether the number of times a concept has been primed would influence its effectiveness, hypothesizing that a concept that had *frequently been activated* would have more significant effects on processing than would less-frequently activated concepts.

To study these effects, they conducted an experiment similar to that of Higgins et al. (1977). Participants again thought they were participating in two separate studies. In the first, they were shown a series of sets of four words, and their task was to select three of the words and use them to make a sentence. For example, for the word set "leg break arm his" one would select three words ("break his arm") to form a sentence. For some word groups (such as this example), the sentences would almost certainly have to imply some degree of hostility; you cannot make a complete sentence from those words that does not suggest an aggressive act. If so, then the concept of hostility would be activated by constructing such sentences from those word sets. Participants completed either 30 or 60 of these problems, and either 20% or 80% of them led to the generation of hostility-related sentences. In this way, the *frequency* of activation of the trait "hostile" was implemented.

In the second part of the study, participants were again asked to form an impression of Donald, based on a one-page description of his activities during a day. Some of those events, while ambiguous in their meaning, could be interpreted as reflecting a hostile manner (e.g., refusing to talk to a salesperson, lying to avoid giving blood). The participants' task was to rate their impression of Donald on several traits,

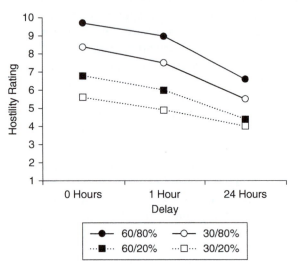

Figure 2.5 Ratings of target hostility as a function of frequency and recency of activation (number of trials/% hostile behaviors)

Source: Adapted from Srull & Wyer (1979)

some of which were related to hostility (e.g., hostile, unfriendly). This second task was administered either immediately after the first phase, one hour later, or 24 hours later. In this way, Srull and Wyer could test the effects of *recency* of activation on the interpretation of Donald's behavior, as reflected in the trait ratings.

The results, shown in Figure 2.5, showed that both the frequency and the recency of activation of the trait hostility had an impact on participants' impressions of Donald. The difference in the height of the lines shows the effect of frequency: the more frequently the concept was primed in the word task, the more hostile the participants' impressions of Donald. The downward slope of the lines reflects the decrease in this effect over time: priming had its greatest effect when the impression phase followed immediately, but that effect dissipated slowly such that it was still evident even when the impression formation phase of the study was not administered until 24 hours later.

Thus, priming a concept can affect the way subsequent information is processed, and the magnitude of this effect is strongly a function of both the recency and the frequency of that activation (Buchsbaum, Lemire-Rodger, Bondad, & Chepesiuk, 2015; DeCoster & Claypool, 2004; see Higgins, 2012).

Chronically Accessible Constructs

Concepts that are frequently activated are readily accessible for use in processing information (interpreting events, construing others). Consider the implications of that finding for real-life experiences. Suppose you grew up in a family in which you were repeatedly and openly rewarded for good performance in school ("That's really a good job, Kamal!"). Or you were routinely criticized for not being more sociable ("Lily, can't you be more friendly to people?"). In more general terms, what if we consider a lifetime of frequent (and therefore also recent) activation of certain constructs? Such constructs could become *chronically accessible*. That is, they would always be readily accessible to guide the way one construes the people and events one encounters in everyday life.

Of course, each person has his or her own unique history, and therefore people have different experiences in what concepts are frequently and recently activated in this way. It follows that people will, therefore, differ in which concepts become chronically accessible. What we have, then, is a cognitive mechanism (frequency and recency of priming) that would produce *individual differences* in the concepts that are chronically accessible in different people. The consequence is that people would differ in the way they "see" the world, in how they interpret events, and in how they evaluate persons.

This possibility was the focus of research done by Higgins, King, and Mavin (1982). This study involved two sessions. In the first session, the researchers assessed people's chronically accessible traits by having participants write down traits that described two male friends, two female friends, and themselves. It was assumed that chronically accessible traits would be the first ones that would come to mind when describing well-known target persons. In the second session, occurring two weeks later, people were asked to read a passage describing a variety of behaviors supposedly performed by a stranger. The passages had been written to include several desirable and several undesirable behaviors, and some of the traits exemplified in those behaviors were those that people had listed in the first session. Later, participants were asked (a) to reproduce the passage as accurately as they could and (b) to write about their impression of the person described in the passage. Both of these dependent measures were coded for how often each participant's own chronically accessible traits were used. These analyses showed that when people reproduced the passage, they were more likely to include the behaviors exemplifying their own chronically accessible traits. Also, when they wrote about their impressions, aspects reflecting their own chronically accessible traits were very likely to be included. In contrast, aspects of the stimulus information that were not, for them, chronically accessible were much more likely to be omitted.

These results are significant because they show that individual differences in the concepts that, through one's own experiences, are frequently (and therefore, recently) activated are readily accessible for use in processing novel information. Thus, different persons, presented with the same stimulus information, may view that information – interpret it, process it – in different ways. In other words, the same experience can take on different meanings for different people.

We have now reviewed in some detail the nature of cognitive representations, the way our knowledge from past experience is represented in memory in terms of these structures, and how those structures are activated for use in processing information. You might be wondering, then, what difference does it make? *How* does a structure influence processing? What effects does it have?

EFFECTS OF COGNITIVE REPRESENTATIONS ON INFORMATION PROCESSING

We defined cognitive representations as containing knowledge, beliefs, and expectancies about some domain developed from experience. Because they reflect our experiences, representations are activated and used when we encounter new instances and new situations that appear similar to those past experiences. The activation of cognitive representations can influence the processing of new information in many ways. Some of those effects are highly beneficial; unfortunately, some can cause problems.

How do cognitive representations help us? The knowledge learned through experience can be used to facilitate the *comprehension* of new information. This can be particularly beneficial when the stored knowledge is used to make sense of information that is otherwise confusing. Consider the following paragraph (Bransford & Johnson, 1972) and try to identify what it refers to:

> The procedure is actually quite simple. First you arrange things into different groups. Of course, one pile may be sufficient depending on how much there is to do. If you have to go somewhere else due to lack of facilities that is the next step, otherwise you are pretty well set. It is important not to overdo things. That is, it is better to do too few things at once than too many. In the short run this may not seem important but complications can easily arise. A mistake can be expensive as well. At first the whole procedure will seem complicated. Soon, however, it will become just another facet of life. It is difficult to foresee any end to the necessity for this task in the immediate future, but then one can never tell. After the procedure is completed, one arranges the materials into different groups again. Then they can be put into their appropriate places. Eventually they will be used once more and the whole cycle will then have to be repeated. However, that is part of life.

By itself, this description seems quite puzzling. However, if you knew in advance that it described the steps involved in "doing the laundry," then it is quite easily understood. Cognitive representations can help us comprehend the seemingly incomprehensible. In Chapters 4 (on attention) and 5 (on interpretation), we will offer numerous examples of how cognitive representations guide our understanding of objects and events in our experience.

Another important function of cognitive representations is that they provide bases for the *categorization* of objects that we encounter. Categorization is a fundamental process that pervades all that we do and enables us to group objects that are similar or functionally equivalent into categories. Just as we group trees, bicycles, dogs, and violins in categories, we also categorize the people we see into different human groups. We see persons as individuals, but we simultaneously see them as women, Latinos, Catholics, teachers, and so on. In doing so, individual members of each category are grouped and seen as relatively interchangeable with other category members. Categorizing a person as a teacher serves to equate that person with all other teachers. Since we have existing beliefs about teachers, the person so categorized becomes endowed with those qualities.

Some significant consequences follow from this categorization process. We can think of these effects as involving both *information gain* and *information loss*. When we encounter a new stimulus (a bicycle, a teacher), the knowledge and beliefs associated with that category can be applied to this new instance. Thus, until we know otherwise, an object identified as a bicycle and a person categorized as a teacher are assumed to have all the qualities possessed by other members of the category. To the extent that the knowledge and beliefs contained in one's cognitive representation are accurate, then the perceiver has gained a considerable amount of information about that object. In this way, the use of cognitive representations provides information gain.

However, if the beliefs and expectancies in the cognitive representation are erroneous, then the target will be falsely endowed with those attributes, and information is lost rather than gained. If, for example, one believes that teachers are trustworthy but they, in fact, are not, then use of the cognitive representation would lead a perceiver into erroneous perceptions and possibly risky behavior.

Moreover, it is important to recognize that even if the beliefs associated with a category are *generally* accurate, they are not likely accurate regarding *all* group members. Most teachers may be trustworthy, but it is possible to encounter a specific teacher who is not. If we apply our beliefs indiscriminately to all group members, we might fail to detect exceptions to the general rule. Also, even if the attributes associated with the category are valid, categorization focuses one's attention on those attributes, and hence on ways that, for example, teachers are all the same. What gets overlooked are characteristics of the teacher that are not stereotypic, ways that he or she differs from the typical teacher. In other words, one does not attend to the person as an individual, and hence potentially essential and useful information is ignored. In all of these ways, the use of cognitive representations can result in information loss, producing inaccuracies in judgments and beliefs.

In addition to representing accumulated knowledge, cognitive representations carry expectancies that can influence the processing of new information. Human behavior is often ambiguous, and the perceiver must impose some *interpretation* on it to understand its meaning. Those expectancies can guide one's attention to aspects of the information, often focusing on expectancy-consistent aspects and shaping one's interpretation of it. In many cases, this is extremely useful, but it can also result in biased interpretations that can lead to incorrect judgments and decisions.

In addition to comprehending and interpreting available information, cognitive representations also enable the perceiver to go beyond that information by making *inferences* from it. The expectancies carried by cognitive representations allow us to elaborate on the information we encounter, leading us to inferences that provide new "knowledge" (beliefs) about the object or person that goes beyond the information available.

In all of the ways we have just elaborated, cognitive representations facilitate and guide the processing of new information. Because we have and can use these cognitive representations, we can "flesh out" our understanding of persons and events, and by doing so, we can develop more thorough and elaborated mental representations for guiding our thinking, our judgments, and our behavior.

There is one additional benefit provided by these structures. Specifically, using cognitive representations can free up cognitive resources that are then available for a variety of other tasks that require attention and diligence. Many processes require some *cognitive resources* to enact them. Whether trying to remember a name during a noisy party or focusing on a lecture while hungry, it can be challenging to keep attentional resources on the task at hand. Interference from other stimulation at any stage can disrupt our focus. Similarly, when we process information about the persons and events in our social environment, these kinds of cognitive resources are, to varying degrees, required. It is why multi-tasking is often a challenge.

However, using cognitive representations can assist in freeing up cognitive resources, allowing perceivers to allocate these resources more efficiently. Macrae, Milne, and Bodenhausen (1994) showed this by having participants perform two tasks simultaneously. One task involved forming impressions of four individuals, each of whom was described by a set of 10 attributes provided by the experimenter. In one condition, each target person was also identified by his occupation (doctor, artist), whereas in the other condition, occupation labels were not provided. For each target person, half of the attributes were stereotypic of the person's occupational group; the other half were neutral concerning the occupation. It was hypothesized that participants who were given the occupational labels should benefit in processing the information, particularly for attributes stereotypic of the person's group. Of course, participants in the no-label condition would not have this benefit.

While they were reading these person descriptions and forming impressions of the persons described, all participants were asked to perform a second task simultaneously. Specifically, they were given headphones and asked to listen to a tape recording presenting information about the geography and economy of Indonesia. Participants were told that the two tasks were equally important and that they would be asked questions both about their impressions of the target persons and the information on the audiotape. Upon completing this procedure, participants were (a) asked to recall as many of the ten attributes describing each of the four persons as they could, and (b) were given several multiple-choice questions assessing their knowledge of the information about Indonesia presented on the tape.

The results of this study are shown in Table 2.1. Looking first at participants' recall of the trait attributes describing the target persons, it is clear that knowledge of the person's occupation did indeed facilitate participants' remembering those traits. Participants in the "stereotype present" condition recalled significantly more of the stereotypic attributes than did participants who had not been provided with the occupation information. Note that this better recall was specific to the traits consistent with the stereotype; there was no difference between conditions in their recall of the neutral traits. In other words, the occupation information did not merely make the task more interesting and therefore enhance the recall of all information. From these results, we know that the activation of the stereotypes aided performance in one of the two tasks.

Importantly, participants in the stereotype-present condition also performed better on the quiz testing their knowledge of the tape-recorded information about Indonesia.

Table 2.1 Recall of stereotype consistent and inconsistent information and performance on a multiple-choice exam as a function of the presence or absence of a stereotype

Task	Stereotype	
	Present	Absent
Trait Recall		
Consistent	4.4	2.1
Inconsistent	1.8	1.3
Multiple-Choice Questionnaire	8.8	6.7

Source: Adapted from Macrae, Milne, & Bodenhausen (1994)

Their scores were significantly higher than those of participants in the no-label condition. How can we explain this finding? Indeed, the knowledge of people's stereotypes did not, by itself, lead to better retention of information about Indonesia. Instead, the occupation information activated stereotypes that aided in processing the trait descriptions (particularly those attributes stereotypic of the occupations) so that performing the impression formation task required fewer cognitive resources. Consequently, those participants had more resources available to process the information about Indonesia, thereby enhancing their quiz performance (relative to those in the no-label condition). Thus, cognitive representations can facilitate some processing tasks, freeing up resources to more effectively engage in processing information on a different task at the same time.

ARBITRARY CATEGORIZATION AND ITS CONSEQUENCES

Categorization is an essential process employed by all of us in all aspects of life. It can be an extremely effective and useful tool for coping with the amount and complexity of information that people encounter in their social worlds. However, categorization can, at times, be arbitrary and, as demonstrated impressively by Tajfel's minimal group paradigm (Tajfel, 1970; Tajfel et al., 1971), can create biased judgments and adverse outcomes.

One such case stems from the fact that our cognitive systems seem disposed to think in terms of categories, even when the available information is not categorical in nature. Many different kinds of information in our environment involve continuous rather than categorical variables. Information regarding commonplace variables such as time, temperature, distance, height, weight, age, and even intelligence all exist on continua. However, we tend to think of and talk about these variables in categorical terms (e.g., the decades of the 80s vs. the 90s, "warm" vs. "cool" days, "gifted" vs. "average"). In each case, we are using categorical terms to divide a continuous variable into segments. Imposing categories on continuous variables facilitates communication, but it can also introduce bias and distortion (Krueger & Clement, 1994a). If a person from a cold climate (say, Norway) visits a friend who lives in a warm climate (say, Spain) in February, the Norwegian might comment on how warm it is while the Spaniard simultaneously complains about the chill in the air. For an example of perhaps more considerable social significance, consider the following. We routinely refer to people and categorize them as either "Black" or "White," as if it were a dichotomy. Yet there is enormous variation in skin tone among African Americans and White Americans alike. Again, we chunk a continuum into categories. As a result, people whose skin tones are quite different from each other are grouped as if they were all the same.

Arbitrarily grouping diverse individuals into categories can simplify social information processing for the perceiver, but it can also create difficulties and unanticipated consequences for the people being grouped. Consider the real-world example of the partitioning of India. After World War II, it was clear that India was about to be granted its long-sought independence from the British Empire. Establishing a new nation with a new government is not an easy task. It was further complicated, in some people's minds, by the heterogeneity of the population, especially in light of the various religious groups – Muslims, Sikhs, and Hindus. In 1947, in preparation for granting independence, Britain sent an official to India whose task it was to establish boundaries such that people of different religious faiths would live in different regions. Although many

Indians did not want such demarcation and preferred to have all religious groups within a single nation, the boundaries became established.

> Suddenly, hundreds of millions of people were categorized and forced to define themselves by religion – which heretofore had been a largely private and incidental matter for most of the people of India. People who had no religious belief at all suddenly found themselves defined entirely by a faith they did not hold. (Saunders, 2007)

From this period of Partition was born not only the nation of India but also of Pakistan. Ever since then, the relations between the two countries have been strained (with periods of open conflict). Arbitrary categorization can have unforeseen consequences.

Experimental research provides evidence illustrating some other consequences arising from the use of arbitrary categories (Foroni & Rothbart, 2011, 2013; Rothbart, Davis-Stitt, & Hill, 1997). In one study (Rothbart et al., 1997), participants read several folders of applicants for a managerial job. Each file included a summary sheet that provided the applicant's composite score summarizing performance on job-related skills. Each file also contained a continuum of possible composite scores, with lines indicating specific categories with labels (Ideal, Acceptable, Marginal, Reject) associated with each interval of scores. There were two conditions in the experiment, the only difference being where the "cuts" were placed (see Figure 2.6). For example, in one condition, the Ideal category required very high scores (upper 12%) compared to the other condition (upper 18%) – differences that could easily occur under different market conditions and the need to fill positions. Participants were asked to rate the similarity of various pairs of applications in job performance. The pairs of applicants presented were selected to include pairs whose composite scores (e.g., 840, 750) were within the same cat-

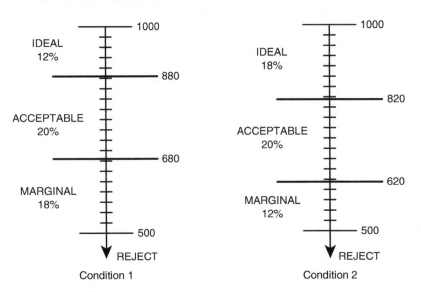

Figure 2.6 Relation of composite scores to category labels, as presented to participants

Source: From Rothbart et al. (1997)

egory in one condition but (due to different "cut" intervals) in different categories in the other condition. The results showed that within-category pairs were rated as more similar than the identical pair of applicants when they were in different categories. Thus, the arbitrary placement of category boundaries not only influenced which category an applicant might be in but also influenced participants' judgments of the similarity of a pair of applicants with comparable scores who happened to fall in the same or different categories.

MULTIPLE CATEGORY MEMBERSHIPS

Another instance of arbitrary categorization stems from the fact that people are members of many groups, and as perceivers we, therefore, have options for categorizing others. Suppose, for example, you know someone who is White, American, Jewish, a lawyer, and has an income that places him in the upper-middle class. He (like all of us) belongs to multiple categories. How do you categorize him? You could do so based on any single dimension of race, nationality, religion, profession, or social class standing, and any such categorization could influence your perceptions of him. If you are contemplating going to law school, you might think of him as a lawyer who could be a useful resource. If you are a Protestant, his Jewish heritage may be salient to you. If you happen to encounter him while you are on a vacation trip in London, you may think of him as an American in ways that never entered your mind when you have been with him at home in the States. Any of these ways of construing him would be legitimate and accurate. Whatever categorization is made, your beliefs and attitudes associated with that category (but not the alternative categories) would then become accessible to influence your perceptions and thoughts about him. In other words, any person can be construed in multiple ways. Two crucial questions then arise. First, what determines which category is used in construing the person? Second, what downstream consequences follow from using one versus another category?

Categorization processes can be influenced by our willingness to include another person as a member of our ingroup. If we want to benefit from an association with a respected individual, we might emphasize a category that makes that individual a member of a group to which we belong. Conversely, we might activate a category to which we do not belong if we hoped to distance ourselves from an undesired person. A particularly compelling illustration of the selective use of alternate categories was shown in an experiment focused on views of the sprinter, Ben Johnson (Stelzl, Janes, & Seligman, 2008). Johnson was born in Jamaica but moved to Canada when he was a teenager. In 1988 he qualified to be a member of the Canadian Olympic team that competed in Seoul, South Korea. In the 100-meter dash, Johnson smashed the existing world record and took the gold medal, instantly becoming a Canadian hero. Unfortunately, a few days later, a doping test revealed that he had been using performance-enhancing drugs. Johnson was stripped of his gold medal and now disgraced. How would this Jamaican-born Canadian athlete be seen during this period of highs and lows? Furthermore, most interestingly, did his salient group membership change as a function of his achievement and subsequent disgrace?

To answer these questions, the researchers gathered every article in several major Canadian newspapers that mentioned Johnson during the three weeks before and the three weeks following his disqualification, and they recorded every instance in which a nationality (Canadian or Jamaican) was mentioned. Before his disqualification, 64% of those citations referred to him as Canadian, whereas only 14% mentioned him as a Jamaican. Following his disqualification, however, references to his Canadian nationality dropped by half (to 32%), while references to his Jamaican identification doubled (28%). Thus, one's category group membership (in this case, one's nationality) can be used strategically to include or exclude a person from the ingroup (Canadians, for these Canadian journalists) as a function of the person's success or failure.

As we discussed in Chapter 1, one's motives can play a critical role in social information processing. Specifically, our categorizations of others can be driven in part by motivations to see ourselves – and the groups to which we belong – in a favorable light. When an ingroup member commits a highly undesirable act, we might both devalue him as a person (known as the *Black Sheep effect*; Kutlaca, Becker, & Radke, 2020; Marques & Paez, 1994; Marques &

Yzerbyt, 1988; Marques, Yzerbyt, & Leyens, 1988; Zouhri & Rateau, 2015) and construe him as a member of an entirely different category.

Other research, using the Implicit Association Test (IAT; Greenwald, McGhee, & Schwartz, 1998), has shown similar effects at the level of group perceptions. The IAT is a categorization task in which stimuli representing two different categories (e.g., faces of White or Black persons, and pictures of American or non-American symbols, such as the Statue of Liberty or a dollar bill versus the Eiffel Tower or a Euro) are presented. As is depicted in Figure 2.7, on some trials, the participant responds by pressing one key if the stimulus is, for example, "either a White American or an American symbol" and by pressing another key if the stimulus is "either an African American or a Foreign symbol." This arrangement is compared with another instruction in which "African American or American" are paired and "White American or Foreign" are paired. The amount of time to complete these responses to a series of such stimuli is recorded.

Response Key Pairings for Stereotypically Compatible Trials:

| WHITE AMERICAN | AFRICAN AMERICAN |
| AMERICAN | FOREIGN |

Response Key Pairings for Stereotypically Incompatible Trials:

| WHITE AMERICAN | AFRICAN AMERICAN |
| FOREIGN | AMERICAN |

Stimuli:

Facial images

National symbols

Figure 2.7 Critical trials in Implicit Association Test (IAT) asssessing the American = White hypothesis (Devos & Banaji, 2005). Facial images reprinted with permission from the Chicago Face Database (Ma, Correll, & Wittenbrink, 2015)

Devos and Banaji (2005) used such an IAT to demonstrate what they called the *American = White effect*. Specifically, responses to the first pairing were more natural (and hence quicker) than to the second pairing, indicating that "White American" and "American symbols" are implicitly associated in memory to a greater extent than are "African American" and "American symbols." Several studies have demonstrated this effect, documenting that White Americans, as a group, are implicitly conceived of as being more "American" than are Asian Americans, African Americans, and Native Americans (Devos & Banaji, 2005; Devos & Ma, 2008; Nosek et al., 2007).

Research has shown that such associations are not fixed in our minds but, in fact, can be quite malleable (Devos & Mohamed, 2014; Rydell, Hamilton, & Devos, 2010). Rydell et al. (2010), for example, primed positive or negative stereotypes of African Americans before the IAT task by showing pictures of several highly respected African Americans (e.g., Martin Luther King, Jr.) or negatively-valued African Americans (e.g., Mike Tyson). Their results showed that presenting positive African American exemplars decreased the American = White effect (as manifested on the IAT), whereas presenting negative African American exemplars increased it. Moreover, and paralleling Stelzl et al.'s (2008) findings, the valence of the presented exemplars influenced the inclusion or exclusion of African Americans from participants' category for "Americans" and also altered ratings of African Americans (in positive or negative directions) on traits stereotypic of that group.

Alternate categorization is not merely a matter of classifying persons according to one group membership or another. Macrae, Bodenhausen, and Milne (1995) argued that categorizing a person according to one group membership not only *activates* associations of that category but also actually *inhibits* the accessibility of associations to an alternate group membership. In a study testing this idea, participants watched a videotape of an Asian woman. In one version of the tape, she was seen eating noodles from a bowl with a pair of chopsticks – a scene emphasizing her category membership as an Asian. In the other version, she was seen putting on makeup in front of a mirror, a portrayal intended to highlight her category membership as a woman. A control tape was also shown in which no stereotype-relevant behaviors were included. The question investigated was what effect these alternate categorizations would have on the accessibility of the two (Asian and female) stereotypes.

A lexical decision task (LDT) was used to measure stereotype accessibility. In an LDT, letter strings are presented on a computer screen, and the participants' task is to indicate (with a key press), as quickly as possible, whether the letters do or do not form a word. The computer records the amount of time (in milliseconds) taken to respond "yes" when the letters form a word. Of particular interest in this experiment, some of the words were stereotypic of females (e.g., romantic, emotional), whereas other words were stereotypic of Asians (e.g., calm, gracious). If certain words are accessible because a stereotype has been activated, the response times (RTs) to those words should be quite fast. Alternatively, if words are inaccessible (due to inhibition),

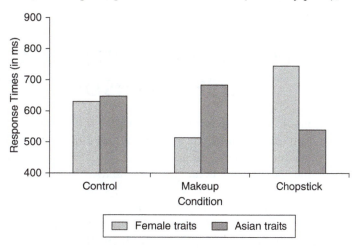

Figure 2.8 Mean RTs for traits stereotypic of females and Asians by experimental condition

Source: Based on data from Macrae et al. (1995)

then RTs to those words should be slow. It was expected that when participants saw the Asian woman eating noodles with chopsticks, the Asian stereotype would be activated. Hence, Asian-stereotypic words would be highly accessible, producing fast RTs on Asian LDT words. Similarly, when the woman was putting on makeup, activation of the female stereotype should produce fast RTs to the female LDT words. But what happens to the unprimed category (female when Asian was primed, and Asian when female was primed)? Macrae et al. argued that when one stereotype is activated, the alternate category is not merely inactive but is, in fact, inhibited (made less accessible than baseline). This inhibition would slow RTs for words associated with the stereotype associated with the alternative categorization.

The results are shown in Figure 2.8. RTs to the control tape (in which neither stereotype was explicitly activated by the woman's behavior) provide a baseline against which the other conditions can be evaluated. It can be seen that, in relation to these baseline RTs, priming the female stereotype reduced RTs for traits stereotypic of females *and* slowed response speed for traits stereotypic of Asians. Similarly, priming the Asian stereotype facilitated RTs to Asian-stereotypic words *and* slowed RTs for traits stereotypic of females. Thus, the categorization of persons into groups activates associated stereotypes and also inhibits stereotypes associated with alternate categories.

Although this research shows that multiple categories can compete for attention, research shows that some social categories tend to be perceived in combination, a phenomenon called *intersectionality* (Nicolas, de la Fuente, & Fiske, 2017; Purdie-Vaughns & Eibach, 2008; Remedios & Snyder, 2018). Consider, for example, a study by Stroessner (1996) showing that Black women tend to be categorized in terms of both their race and gender. In this experiment, photos of Black and White men and women were presented to participants. Before each photo, a label combining one of four possible race and gender category labels (e.g., "black male") was presented, and participants had to indicate as quickly as they could if the label described the person in the photo. It was expected that Black women because they reflect membership in unusual categories (i.e., they are both Black and female) would be categorized most quickly, and that hypothesis was confirmed. Other research (Carpinella, Chen, Hamilton, & Johnson, 2015; Goff, Thomas, & Jackson, 2008; Johnson, Freeman, & Pauker, 2012) confirms the notion that some social categories are not processed either in isolation or in competition, but instead are intertwined throughout social categorization and judgment processes.

COGNITIVE REPRESENTATIONS ABOUT THE SELF, PERSONS, AND GROUPS

As we indicated in the introductory chapter, our goal in this book is to inform you about social cognition as a way of understanding a broad range of phenomena in social psychology. Our organization is to focus in each chapter on a new aspect of the information processing system, to define and describe it, and to illustrate its role and function as we comprehend and adapt to a complex social world. As we do so, we will include some recurring themes. Specifically, we consider the relevance of the topic of each chapter for understanding three distinct and significant domains of social life: understanding the self, understanding persons, and understanding groups. For this chapter, then, the question is: What is the nature and role of cognitive representations in understanding the self, other persons, and social groups?

Cognitive Representations in Understanding the Self

We often think of the self as something that is deep inside each individual, at the core of his or her being, and what makes that person a unique individual. My self is the very essence of my being, the epitome of all that is good (and bad) about me, the home base of my feelings, my joys and my fears, my private thoughts, my goals, and aspirations. When we think of it this way, it hardly seems related to the concepts we have discussed in this chapter. However, in this section, we want to invite you to consider how the self, as an organized set of knowledge, beliefs, and expectancies about ourselves, in fact, constitutes a cognitive representation.

Self Schemas

If the self is a cognitive representation, then certain consequences should follow. For example, aspects of the self that are central to that representation – for example, the traits that really, genuinely describe me – should be very accessible. To test that idea, Markus (1977) identified people who were and were not *schematic* for a particular trait and then measured the speed with which they responded to traits that do or do not fit that schema. In a preliminary session, participants completed a personality questionnaire from which it could be determined which people thought of themselves as independent, as not independent, or as neither. In this way, three groups of participants were formed – independents, dependents, and aschematics (neither independent nor dependent).

In a second session a few weeks later, participants were presented 60 trait words on a computer screen. Fifteen of those traits reflected independence, 15 were synonyms of dependence, and 30 were traits unrelated to this dimension. When each trait word appeared on the screen, participants were to indicate (by pressing different keys on the keyboard) "Me" or "Not Me" to indicate whether the trait is or is not self-descriptive. The computer recorded both the participant's response (Me, Not Me) as well as the response latency (amount of time, in milliseconds) to respond to the trait word.

Analyses of these RTs showed that people responded faster in making "Me" responses for traits that corresponded to their self-schemas. Thus, people who thought of themselves as independent had faster RTs for independence-related traits than did people who had earlier described themselves as dependents.

These results show that the traits that define the way we think of ourselves are highly accessible in a cognitive representation representing our self-concept. These traits are very abstract, generalized characterizations that summarize much diverse information. Consider, for example, the variety of ways and the variety of contexts in which one can manifest behavior that could be called "independent." This feature, of course, is one of the benefits that derive from having cognitive representations: they capture much diverse information in a concise, meaningful form.

Multiple Selves

We often think of our self-concept as being highly stable. After all, I am basically the same person I was last week, a month ago, a year ago. This view assumes considerable stability in the self-structure. However, is this really true? Or do we think about ourselves differently at different times and in different contexts? If so, then there could be considerable variability in our self-concepts.

It is easy to imagine that the cognitive representation used to think about and describe the self could change dramatically from one situation to the next. The traits and characteristics you would choose to describe yourself would be very different when you are taking a difficult exam than when you are tanning on the beach. And your accessible self-description would likely differ substantially depending on to whom you were comparing yourself. If you were judging your intelligence, you would probably see yourself quite differently if comparing yourself with Einstein rather than a supermodel (Dijksterhuis et al., 1998). This situational variability in one's cognitive representation of the self is captured in the notion of the *working self-concept*, which Markus and Wurf (1987) defined as "a temporary structure consisting of elements from the collection of self-conceptions, organized in a configuration determined by ongoing social events."

Markus and Kunda (1986) demonstrated the malleability of the working self-concept by varying the degree to which a person believed that the self was similar to or different from others. People tend to resist views of themselves as too similar to others because it threatens their sense of uniqueness or too different from others because it threatens their sense of normalcy. Markus and Kunda reasoned that encouraging either an extreme sense of similarity or uniqueness would prompt people to react to that characterization by activating self-characteristics demonstrating their uniqueness and similarity, respectively. To test this idea, experimenters asked participants to respond to several questions about themselves before they were given feedback suggesting that they were either remarkably similar or extremely different from the other participants who completed the same experiment. After receiving this feedback, participants had to indicate whether a set of attributes indicating uniqueness (e.g., original, independent) or similarity (e.g., average, follower) were self-descriptive (Me, Not Me). Concerning the self-judgments, participants were unaffected by the experimental manipulation; their endorsement of which traits were self-descriptive was unaffected by whether they were told they were highly similar or different from others. However, the *accessibility* of traits reflecting similarity and uniqueness were profoundly affected by this manipulation. Participants were, for example, faster to indicate that uniqueness rather than similarity words described themselves when they had been led to believe they were highly similar to others.

This finding demonstrates that the social context can modify the cognitive representation of the self that is recruited from memory. This study also demonstrates that the self can be experienced both as stable (in that participants endorsed the same traits as self-descriptive, regardless of the context) and malleable (because the working self-concept can change based on the context).

Explicit and Implicit Self-Knowledge

Another model of self-representation (Greenwald, Banaji, Rudman, Farnham, Nosek, & Mellot, 2002; see also Asendorpf, Banse, & Mücke, 2002) proposes that the self is both stable and variable because people have differential access to self-knowledge that is held *explicitly* (available for self-report) versus *implicitly* (not readily reportable). More generally, the model represents the self as a node within an associative network, linked to behavioral information and traits (as in Hastie, 1980; Srull, 1981, discussed earlier) and also to social roles (e.g., student, sister). Moreover, both traits and roles have evaluative connotations based on one's attitudes and social stereotypes. Therefore, through these associations of the self with attributes and social roles, an individual can derive both her self-identity (through links to traits and roles) and self-esteem (through their evaluative connotations).

A critical aspect of the model is its assumption that individuals have limited ability to report the strength of associations within the network accurately and that associative strength can most accurately be assessed with implicit measures, such as the IAT. By using both the IAT and explicit measures of association between the self-identity, self-esteem, and attitudes about gender, Greenwald and his colleagues have demonstrated that women show a high degree of consistency in their implicit, but not their explicit, self-representations. Specifically, responses to implicit measures of gender identity (the association between the self and the social category of women), gender attitudes (the association between women and pleasantness), and self-esteem (the association between the self and pleasantness) were all positively correlated. In contrast, when measured through self-report, the correlations among these three variables were inconsistent and even reversed in some cases. An important implication of this finding is that explicit and implicit representations of the self can become dissociated. One might consistently report beliefs about one's characteristics that do not reflect or correspond with one's implicit beliefs about oneself. When this occurs, one might have the sense of self-stability by the consistent affirmation of explicit beliefs that may be wholly unrelated to changes in one's implicit self-representation.

Relational Selves

Another basis of variability in self-representations pertains to the fact that the self is also defined in important respects through one's relationships with others (Andersen & Chen, 2002; Andersen, Tuskeviciute, Przybylinski, Ahn, & Xu, 2016; Chen, Boucher, & Kraus, 2011). That is, the self is linked in memory with other individuals whom we view as significant in our lives. We have strong links between our self-concept and our representations of parents, siblings, children, or good friends. Not all aspects of the self will be consistently represented in these self-other associations. For example, there might be a strong emphasis on pursuing enjoyable activities in my link with my best friend, but my link with my parents might focus on our shared heritage or our duties to one another. These differing associations will serve to activate different aspects of an individual's self-concept. Moreover, these significant persons need not be physically present to influence the activated self-concept. Instead, one needs only to think about or be reminded of a significant other to activate the subset of beliefs about the self that are relevant to one's experiences in that relationship. Thus, the varieties of relationships we have with other people can also contribute to dynamic variability in the nature of the self-structure that is accessible at the moment.

Regulatory Focus

Another significant influence on a person's self-conception is the individual's motives and goals in a given situation. One's activated self-concept can be influenced by what one desires in a situation. For example, a person might be motivated to win an academic prize, and focusing on this goal will make certain aspects of the self highly accessible (e.g., beliefs that one is studious, serious, and hard-working) while inhibiting the accessibility of others (e.g., knowledge that you like to party on the weekends and sometimes skip studying to catch a movie). More chronically accessible motives can also influence the nature of self-representation. Higgins's (1998; Scholer & Higgins, 2010, 2011) *Regulatory Focus Theory*, for example, argues that individuals tend to be chronically motivated to either maximize growth (a *promotion focus* centered on achieving gains and avoiding non-gains) or to maximize safety (a *prevention focus* centered on maintaining security and avoiding failure). For individuals thinking of goal pursuit in promotion terms, the *ideal self*, highlighting the individual's hopes, dreams, and aspirations, tends to dominate. Individuals tend to exhibit eagerness in their behavior as they strive to maximize gains. Success in doing so produces elation, whereas failure induces dejection. In contrast, an individual who thinks in terms of prevention activates an *ought self*, emphasizing one's duties, obligations, and responsibilities. Individuals under a prevention focus usually manifest thoroughness in their behavior as they seek to ensure against losses. Success within this regulatory state produces relief, but failure yields agitation and anxiety.

> **INTERIM SUMMARY** Research on the cognitive representation of the self demonstrates that people possess a wealth of knowledge about the self that is selectively activated and combined in response to various situational and motivational needs. Certain aspects of the self are seen as central and valuable across contexts, and individuals tend to be self-schematic for this subset of information about the self. Accompanying this consistency is the variability that arises from environmental cues, personal relationships, and one's own needs and goals.

Cognitive Representations in Understanding Persons

Earlier in this chapter, we reviewed research on associative network models of memory representation applied to person memory and impression formation. At the core of these models was the assumption that new behavioral information is actively integrated into an impression of a person through association with a person node. Associations between items of behavioral information can also form depending on the consistency of an item with the other information already represented in the network or with a pre-existing trait expectancy for the person. This research focused on the associations between specific items of behavioral information, and it demonstrated the value of representational models for generating novel predictions.

In presenting this research, we did not address the nature of the representation that would serve as the basis of subsequent cognitions about the person once an impression was formed. We earlier introduced a distinction between two types of representations in memory: exemplars – specific stimuli, events, experiences we have encountered (that first kiss with a special person; the time you spilled a cup of coffee on a friend's beige carpet), and abstractions – generalized concepts that represent and give meaning to numerous exemplars (romantic, clumsy). What is the relation between exemplars and abstractions in mental representations of individuals? For example, the network representation we described was useful in understanding how specific items of information (behavioral exemplars) one learns about another person are processed and represented in memory while forming an impression of that person. Clearly, though, an essential aspect of impressions is the more general conceptions (trait abstractions) that we come to associate with the person. There is little doubt that impressions include both memories of specific experiences and generalized conceptions (traits, attitudes, goals) that characterize the person. Together, these different aspects provide us with an understanding of "what makes him tick."

How are those general concepts incorporated, and what is their relation to the behavioral exemplar information we acquire about a person? How are the two kinds of information used when we make judgments of a person? Do I judge Toby to be honest because I can retrieve from memory several instances when he has behaved honestly? Or does my memory representation of Toby (i.e., my impression) include the abstract concept "honest" so that I can rely on this generalized trait concept rather than having to retrieve exemplar information from memory? How would the process differ if he were to behave dishonestly? There are perhaps several approaches to addressing these questions, both conceptually and empirically. In this section, we summarize one such approach.

Research by Klein and his colleagues has provided insights into the workings of this system. To understand their approach, consider the following priming paradigm, developed by Klein and Loftus (1993). Participants are asked to think about a person and then to perform certain tasks. In the first task, the participants are given a stimulus trait ("honest") and are asked either (a) to generate a definition of the term (Define task) or (b) if the trait is consistent with their impression of the person (Describe task). All participants are then asked to retrieve from memory a specific behavioral incident in which the person behaved in an honest manner (Recall task), and the amount of time required to generate such a memory is measured.

The logic of this two-step paradigm is quite straightforward. If a mental process required for the second task occurs within the first task, the performance of the second task should be facilitated. Suppose, for example, that I judge Toby to be honest because I have retrieved from memory a time that he clearly behaved honestly. In the language of the paradigm, in "describing" Toby, I have recalled an instance when he behaved in that way. Having retrieved that memory to describe Toby, I now have available a specific behavioral exemplar that can be used to perform the "recall" task. Since that exemplar was generated during the "describe" task, I can answer the "recall" question more quickly than if I had not generated a behavioral exemplar during the first phase. In contrast, a memory of such a specific behavior would not be generated in completing the "define" task (we do not typically define concepts by citing examples). In this case, then, completing the "recall" task would require generating (for the first time) a memory of Brad's honest behavior, which means that the "recall" task would take longer than when the "describe" task had preceded it. Thus, that difference in the time required to recall a behavior exemplar consistent with the trait is an indicator that a behavior was, in fact, retrieved from memory while completing the task of deciding if the trait "honest" describes Brad. In this case, then, a trait judgment rests upon the retrieval of an exemplar from memory.

Consider, alternatively, that my judgment that Toby is honest is based simply on my already-formed abstract conception of him as an honest person. That is, answering the "describe" question does not require retrieval of his honest behavior. In this case, performance of the "recall" task would *not* be facilitated by having already performed the "describe" (compared to performing the "define") task; the memory would need to be generated at the time the "recall" question is posed, just as it is following the "define" task. The *lack* of such facilitation is an indicator that the judgment (during the "describe" task) did not require retrieval of an "honest" exemplar from memory.

This model, then, provides a method for diagnosing the mental processes that transpire (or do not transpire) when a specific judgment is made. That is, it pinpoints whether the judgment is based on retrieval of exemplar information or rests on already formed abstractions (trait concepts). Some studies have provided support for this model and, in doing so, have generated evidence indicating conditions when people rely on exemplar information versus abstractions in making judgments. For example, Sherman and Klein (1994) showed that, when learning about a previously-unknown target person, the amount of exemplar information available has a substantial impact. Initially, when first learning about a person, people necessarily rely on exemplar information as the basis for their judgments. However, the accumulation of increasing exemplar information allows the formation of generalized summary concepts. Once they have formed, judgments can be based on those trait concepts, and retrieval of relevant exemplar information would not be necessary. For a target person that is well known to the perceiver (mother, a close friend) such generalized concepts would likely have been formed and, in such cases, there was no facilitation in recall time as a result of having completed the "describe" (compared to the "define") task, indicating that people made the "describe" judgment based on an abstract trait concept and not on retrieved exemplar information (Klein, Loftus, Trafton, & Furhman, 1992).

The argument advanced in this research is that our cognitive representations of persons include both exemplar information based on direct experience and abstract representations formed from those exemplars. Interestingly, this principle also appears to apply to representation of self-knowledge. Klein, Chan, and Loftus (1999) studied an autistic adult who had very poor memory for specific events from his personal past experiences but was quite capable of describing his general personality characteristics. In fact, his self-ratings on personality scales agreed remarkably well with ratings of him made by a very close relative or friend. Thus, the individual had lost much of his knowledge of his past at the exemplar level but had retained an accurate generalized, trait-level representation of himself. The disjunction between these two sets of data is consistent with the argument that the two types of knowledge about oneself and other individuals are represented in memory independently, such that external events and circumstances (e.g., autism) can dramatically influence one type of representation in memory without severely affecting the other.

Cognitive Representations in Understanding Groups

It is appropriate that we begin our consideration of stereotypes in a chapter on cognitive representations. We have defined a cognitive representation as a person's "knowledge, beliefs, and expectancies about some domain." When that domain is a particular social group, then our knowledge, beliefs, and expectancies about that group are what we call a stereotype. As such, it is represented and stored in memory, it has structure, and it influences information processing in numerous ways, some that are highly beneficial and effective, some that are less admirable. Nevertheless, as a cognitive representation, it functions like other cognitive representations, operating by the same principles and reflecting the same biases. The social cognition approach has stimulated an impressive amount of research on stereotyping that has, in many respects, transformed our thinking on the topic (for reviews, see Dovidio, Hewstone, Glick, & Esses, 2010; Hamilton, 1981; Hamilton & Sherman, 1994; Hamilton, Stroessner, & Driscoll, 1994; Nelson, 2016; Schneider, 2004).

Before the emergence of the social cognitive approach, a large amount of research had attempted to measure the content of stereotypes. What are the specific beliefs that people associate with various social groups? One approach to answering this question involved asking university students to select five personality traits, from a list of 84, that they believed best described each of 10 different national and ethnic groups (Katz & Braly, 1933). This study was repeated at least four different times over nearly 70 years (Devine & Elliot, 1995; Gilbert, 1951; Karlins, Coffman, & Walters, 1969; Madon et al., 2001), allowing identification of both the degree of consensus and changes over time in prevailing stereotypes.

More recently, research examining the content of gender stereotypes shows that men often hold ambivalent beliefs about women (Glick & Fiske, 1996, 1997, 2011; Lee, Fiske, & Glick, 2010). Antagonistic beliefs about women (termed *hostile sexism*) are reflected in agreement with statements such as "Most women interpret innocent remarks or acts as being sexist," and such views are often accompanied by more chivalrous beliefs (termed *benevolent sexism*), captured by agreeing with items like "Women should be cherished and protected by men." Men with strong hostile sexist beliefs show a tendency to harass women because they are motivated to dominate them. Men with benevolent sexist beliefs, however, tend to harass women because they view them as weak and vulnerable (Fiske & Glick, 1995; Pryor, Geidd, & Williams, 1995). Furthermore, they tend to blame rape victims for behaving "inappropriately" (Abrams, Vicky, Masser, & Bohner, 2003).

Although these two examples attest to a longstanding interest in identifying the content of our cognitive representations of groups (i.e., stereotypes), the advent of social cognition changed the understanding of the structure and organization contained within stereotypes. Rather than viewing stereotypes only as a set of traits seen as descriptive of a group, stereotypes are now more likely to be understood as a network of associations, with the various facts, features, beliefs, typical behaviors, etc., represented via pathways to that group. Activation of the group concept then, through spreading activation, makes these associated beliefs more accessible.

Also, some stereotypes can usefully be considered belief structures that are hierarchically organized. Imagine that you are a White American, and as you grew up, you learned the traditional American stereotype of African Americans. Historically, this view has consistently been dominated by negative traits like lazy, unintelligent, aggressive, poor, along with some positive traits, such as musical, athletic, and religious (Devine, 1989; Devine & Elliot, 1995; Gilbert, 1951; Karlins et al., 1969; Katz & Braly, 1933). The stereotype you would have learned would include these elements. Over time, however, you encounter (either personally, through media exposure, or by other means) an increasing number of African Americans who quite clearly do not fit that stereotype. You know about basketball superstar LeBron James, actor Denzel Washington, former Secretary of State Colin Powell, former President Barack Obama, and others, and these negative attributes certainly do not apply to them. Moreover, in your personal experience, you have come to know members of that racial group who do not fit the stereotype and, in fact, are, in virtually all respects, indistinguishable from members of your own racial group. Somehow this mental representation of the racial category isn't working! Some kind of change needs to be made. What kind of changes?

One possibility would be to decide that the stereotype is fundamentally wrong and therefore is no longer valid. Throw it out and build a new belief system about what African Americans are like, what their attributes are, etc. Although that might be desirable, and even appropriate, it regrettably does not happen easily or often. A more common response to encountering people who disconfirm the stereotype is to elaborate the structure of the stereotyped group into more differentiated subtypes (Richards & Hewstone, 2001; Rothbart & John, 1985; Weber & Crocker, 1983). That is, one begins with an all-encompassing category of African Americans who, it is believed, have a common set of features and attributes – this constitutes the traditional stereotype. As individuals (exemplars) who do not fit that stereotype are encountered, they are separated from the predominant group into a subtype that has different features and attributes. For example, a subtype of Black athletes might be formed, individuals who are not viewed as lazy and unintelligent but rather as very talented, hard-working, and, in many cases, wealthy. When confronted with very successful political and business leaders, they are represented in another subtype of Black persons who are very intelligent, possess leadership ability, and have achieved great success and influence.

Through this process, the mental representation of African Americans has become more differentiated, and there may be quite different conceptions (stereotypes) of the subtypes than what was initially believed to characterize the entire group. As was mentioned earlier, this kind of differentiation of a cognitive representation into subtypes has been shown for several stereotyped groups, including women (Ashmore, 1981), Black people (Devine & Baker, 1991), mental patients (Ramsey, Lord, Wallace, & Pugh, 1994), and the elderly (Brewer et al., 1981).

To illustrate how such a hierarchical structure can be manifested, consider the work done on stereotypes of the elderly by Brewer et al. (1981). Stereotypes of the elderly are generally vague and imprecise. The elderly are old, and a few attributes go with that life condition, for example, moving slowly and having traditional values. However, Brewer at al. thought that people have much richer conceptions of specific subgroups of older people, and they set out to determine if people stereotype at the level of these subgroups. In one study, participants sorted a set of 30 photos of older adults into different piles, or categories, as they thought appropriate. The researchers determined how often each picture was sorted into the same pile as each other picture and hence identified which photos were consistently placed in the same categories. The analysis showed that there were three primary subtypes. From their perusal of the photos, the researchers named these three types "grandmother type," "elder statesmen," and "senior citizens."

These sorting data substantiate that participants differentiated among the different types of photos, sufficient to generate these distinct subcategories. However, do they have different beliefs about those subtypes? Brewer et al. advanced the argument that people's stereotypes are more strongly associated with subtypes than with the overarching, superordinate category (elderly people). This question was tested in a subsequent study where participants were presented with sets of photos of three people, each set of three representing one subtype (grandmother subtype, elder statesmen subtype, senior citizen subtype). Two subsets of each subtype were included. Another set consisted of one photo from each of the three subtypes, thereby representing the superordinate category of older adults as a whole. Participants were given a list of trait attributes and were instructed to check off any trait that all three people in the photo set had in common. The researchers then determined those attributes for which there was high agreement in participants' responses. The traits for which there was the highest consensus for each subtype are shown in Table 2.2. It is clear that (a) for each subtype, participants had a reasonably well-articulated conception of what the people shown in the photos were like, (b) there was very high agreement in these attributes for the

Table 2.2 Consensus stereotypes for elderly subtypes

Subtypes					
Grandmother		Elder Statesman		Senior Citizen	
Subset 1	Subset 2	Subset 3	Subset 4	Subset 5	Subset 6
Accepting	Accepting	Aggressive	Aggressive	Lonely	Lonely
Helpful	Helpful	Intelligent	Intelligent	Old-fashioned	Old-fashioned
Trustworthy	Trustworthy	Conservative	Conservative	Traditional	Weak
Traditional	Traditional	Dignified	Dignified		Worried
Serene	Serene	Neat	Neat		
Kindly	Kindly	Authoritarian	Authoritarian		
Optimistic	Optimistic	Traditional	Intolerant		
Calm	Calm		Competitive		
Cheerful	Cheerful		Strong-Willed		
Old-fashioned	Old-fashioned		Active		
Neat	Neat		Aware		
Emotional	Dignified				
Mixed Sets					
Subset 1	Subset 2	Subset 3	Subset 4	Subset 5	Subset 6
Traditional	Kindly	Traditional	--------	Traditional	Traditional
Conservative		Conservative		Intelligent	Conservative
				Active	Intelligent
					Dignified
					Neat

Source: Adapted from Brewer et al. (1981)

two subsets of the same subtype, and (c) the terms associated with the different subtypes convey distinct images. These data, then, show that participants had different "knowledge, beliefs, and expectancies" (stereotypes) about the different subtypes.

How do these subtype stereotypes compare to participants' stereotypes of older people in general? To answer that question, one can compare the subtype results to those for the sets comprising one photo from each subtype. As can be seen, there were very few attributes that participants agreed would characterize all three of the photos representing the broader category of older adults.

Brewer's method of having participants respond to visual representations of actual group members has been a very common approach in social cognition. Hundreds of studies have used the general technique of soliciting responses to pictorial representations of group members to assess mental representations of social categories. A more recent technique allows a more direct assessment of visual aspects of mental representation, "getting inside the head" of the social perceiver to determine how group members are imagined in terms of their physical features. This technique is called *reverse correlation image classification*. In a study using reverse correlation, participants view a series of pairs of visual stimuli (usually a face or body) and for each pair make a classification decision about some attribute (e.g., "Which face is more trustworthy?," "Which face belongs to an ingroup member?"). The two stimuli that are presented are each distortions of a "base image" upon which a random noise pattern has been superimposed that makes each stimulus appear slightly different from the other (see Figure 2.9a). After participants make hundreds of these classification judgments, the stimuli that were selected can be averaged to assess the semantic features that differentiate the groups in the perceivers' minds.

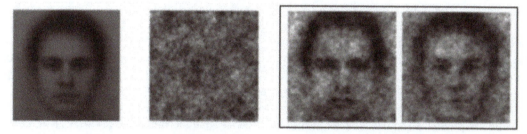

Figure 2.9a   Base image, noise pattern, and example of classification options in reverse correlation

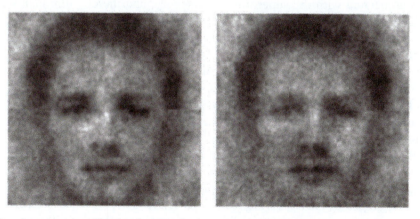

Figure 2.9b   Average classification images for ingroup versus outgroup member

Source: From Ratner, Dotsch, Wigboldus, van Knippenberg, & Amodio (2014)

Ratner, Dotsch, Wigboldus, van Knippenberg, and Amodio (2014) used this *reverse correlation method* to determine how visual representations of ingroup and outgroup members might differ. Using one of Tajfel's et al.'s (1971) procedures, participants were asked to judge the number of dots in a series of patterns that appeared rapidly on a computer screen. They were then given feedback about whether they tended to overestimate or underestimate the number of dots that had appeared. Of course, this feedback was determined randomly and served as the critical manipulation in the study. After being told they were over- or under-estimators, participants were then presented with 450 pairs of faces and were asked to indicate which was an ingroup or outgroup member (someone who supposedly shared or differed from them regarding their dot estimation tendencies). The selected choices were then averaged, and the resulting images for the ingroup and outgroup can be seen in Figure 2.9b.

A second set of participants who were unaware of how these two images were derived then made trait judgments of the two averaged images. The face represented on the ingroup image was seen as more attractive, intelligent, responsible, confident, trustworthy, caring, emotionally stable, and sociable than the outgroup face. The outgroup face was judged to be "weirder" than the ingroup face. These results show that our mental representations of group members can reveal distortions that tend to associate physical features linked to positive traits to ingroup members and features associated with negative attributes to outgroup members. Although Ratner et al. (2014) focused on distortions in minimal groups where real group differences are absent, reverse correlation techniques also have been used to explore representations of existing groups involving actual differences and how biases in representation are influenced by intergroup attitudes (Brown-Iannuzzi, Dotsch, Cooley, & Payne, 2017; Dotsch, Wigboldus, Langner, & van Knippenberg, 2008).

Whether we are considering semantic or visual representation, one fundamental question that is not yet clear pertains to the level at which stereotyping occurs. Do we stereotype at the superordinate level (i.e., using stereotypes of women, African Americans, elderly), or do we stereotype primarily at the level of subtypes, as Brewer et al. have argued? The issue remains unresolved, and it seems likely that the answer will depend in part on the degree of overlap between conceptions represented in the subtypes and the overall conception of the superordinate category. For example, in Brewer at al.'s findings, there was minimal overlap between the concepts associated with any given subtype and the attributes found in the superordinate representation. This outcome suggests that subtyping may weaken the stereotypes associated with the superordinate category, and thereby diminish stereotyping at that inclusive level. In other studies (e.g., Devine & Baker, 1991), the research has again identified subtypes within a larger class (in this case race) but some subtypes overlapped considerably with the broader conception of African Americans as a whole. This pattern of results implies that stereotypes at the superordinate level may remain "alive and well" (and in use), even when we recognize subgroups that do not "fit" the overall conception of the group and hence include them as subtypes within the overall structure. As these examples imply, the question of how subtyping influences the nature and use of stereotypes about the group(s) needs further research investigation.

Obviously, the hierarchical models we have presented are very simple examples of the cognitive representations that could be developed when one has extensive experience in some domain. These differentiations could proceed further. For example, one of Devine and Baker's subtypes of African Americans was Black athletes. This subcategory could be further differentiated into athletes in different sports (basketball, football), as they have quite different characteristics. Furthermore, these subtypes could be differentiated in terms of more specific subtypes (e.g., football players who are huge interior linemen versus speedy wide receivers). With more and more experience with group members, and hence encountering more "exceptions" to any of the subgroups represented in the typology, new subtypes could be added endlessly, as needed.

The extent to which categories can be divided (and how evaluations can change in those differentiations) was humorously portrayed in a sketch by comedian Emo Philips, in which he describes talking with a man threatening to jump off a bridge:

> I said, "Are you a Christian or a Jew?" He said, "A Christian." I said, "Me too. Protestant or Catholic?" He said, "Protestant." I said, "Me too. What franchise?" He says, "Baptist." I said, "Me too. Northern Baptist or Southern Baptist?" He says, "Northern Baptist." I said, "Me too. Northern Conservative Baptist or Northern Liberal Baptist?" He says, "Northern Conservative Baptist." I said, "Me too. Northern Conservative Fundamentalist Baptist or Northern Conservative Reformed Baptist?" He says, "Northern Conservative Fundamentalist Baptist." I said, "Me too. Northern Conservative Fundamentalist Baptist, Great Lakes Region or Northern Conservative Fundamentalist Baptist, Eastern Region?" He says, "Northern Conservative Fundamentalist Baptist, Great Lakes Region." I said, "Me too. Northern Conservative Fundamentalist Baptist, Great Lakes Region, Council of 1879 or Northern Conservative Fundamentalist Baptist, Great Lakes Region, Council of 1912?" He says, Northern Conservative Fundamentalist Baptist, Great Lakes Region, Council of 1912." I said, "Die, heretic!" and I pushed him over.

Fortunately, not all of our cognitive representations get so extensively articulated as this example, or with such dire consequences! Nevertheless, our conceptions of ethnic, national, and religious groups provide convincing demonstrations of people's capacity to both make and maintain distinctions among subtypes at numerous levels of differentiation.

SUMMARY

Cognitive representations contain the knowledge accumulated from past experiences and are used in comprehending and anticipating new events that we encounter. They organize that knowledge in meaningful ways and include the beliefs we form from those experiences. As such, they provide expectancies about people and future events, they help us to anticipate and guide our interactions, and thereby help us to adapt to a complex social world filled with people, groups, and events. Cognitive representations are organized in terms of associations formed among their elements and may be represented in memory hierarchically or in terms of a network of associations. Cognitive representations may be activated by stimulus events, task demands, goals, and priming by recent experiences. Once activated, cognitive representations can influence all subsequent aspects of information processing and can shape our conceptions of ourselves, other persons, and groups that we encounter.

FURTHER READING

McConnell, A.R., Brown, C.M., & Shoda, T.M. (2013). The social cognition of the self. In D.E. Carlston (Ed.), *The Oxford handbook of social cognition* (pp. 497–516). New York, NY: Oxford University Press.

Payne, B.K., & Cameron, C.D. (2013). Implicit social cognition and cognitive representation. In D.E. Carlston (Ed.), *The Oxford handbook of social cognition* (pp. 220–238). New York, NY: Oxford University Press.

Ratner, K.G., Dotsch, R., Wigboldus, D.H.J., van Knippenberg, A., & Amodio, D.M. (2014). Visualizing minimal ingroup and outgroup faces: Implications for impressions, attitudes, and behavior. *Journal of Personality and Social Psychology, 106*, 897–911.

Sherman, S.J., Sherman, J.W., Percy, E.J., & Soderberg, C.K. (2013). Stereotype development and formation. In D.E. Carlston (Ed.), *The Oxford handbook of social cognition* (pp. 548–574). New York, NY: Oxford University Press.

3
AUTOMATIC PROCESSING

Doing More Than We Know

Michael Larson kept winning. Mr. Larson, an unemployed ice cream truck driver, was competing on the game show *Press Your Luck* on May 19, 1984. To win, contestants had to press a button to stop a rapidly-moving light on squares containing prizes while avoiding squares that eliminated a player's winnings. The game was designed so that players would typically lose their winnings after an average of 6 turns. Michael overcame those odds, winning prizes on 47 straight turns. By the time he voluntarily ended the game, he had earned over $110,000 in cash and prizes. This was more than anyone had ever won in a single day on a game show in television history. How did he do it? Michael had videotaped previous episodes at his home and, after repeated viewings, determined that the light moved rapidly but not randomly. Through study, he discovered that the light followed one of five patterns. Michael memorized these patterns by viewing his videotapes for hours, often in slow motion, and learned, using the pause button on his video recorder, that he could consistently stop the light on squares containing prizes. As Michael accrued his winnings, the show producers realized to their dismay that he had mastered the game. However, they were powerless to stop him since he had done nothing illegal. Their mistake, they recognized, was in not appreciating people's ability to master even complex tasks through extensive repetition.

In our everyday lives, we typically feel that we know what we are doing and why. We see a movie because we want some entertainment and relaxation at the end of a busy day. We go to a store and buy some new jeans because the old ones are worn out. We choose to study psychology because several courses have seemed inherently interesting. In all of these (and many other) cases, we make decisions that guide the course of our lives (both short-term and long-term) by considering relevant information and weighing our options.

In this chapter, however, we consider an alternative possibility that also characterizes much of what we do. In fact, it is virtually the opposite of what was described in the previous paragraph. Specifically, we will explore ways in which people often are *not* aware of the factors that influence their judgments, decisions, and behaviors. We will see that often those judgments and actions are guided by external factors of which people are not cognizant. One of the most critical discoveries in psychology over the last several decades is the fact that people regularly perceive and behave without consciously deciding to do so and for reasons of which they are unaware. Strange as that may seem, this kind of processing is quite common and is routinely manifested in our judgments and behaviors.

UNCONSCIOUS PROCESSES?

For a long time, scholars have recognized the possibility that everyday behavior can occur without intent or awareness of underlying causes. The most familiar proponent of this view was Sigmund Freud, whose psychodynamic theory emphasized the critical role of unconscious processes in governing behavior. Is this what we are talking about here? No, not really (Greenwald & Banaji, 1995; Hassin, Uleman, & Bargh, 2005; Wilson, 2002). Because much has changed between Freud's theories and modern social cognition in the characterization of unconscious processes, it is important to contrast the "old" with the "new" conceptions of the unconscious.

In Freud's theory, mental life was partitioned into different segments or domains. The Conscious domain referred to those aspects of mental life of which we are aware. It includes rational, sophisticated thinking, but in Freud's view is the mere "tip of the iceberg." The Preconscious segment consisted of thoughts of which we are not currently aware but that can easily be made conscious by focusing attention on them. Most important for Freud's theory, the Unconscious domain contained thoughts and feelings that are actively kept out of consciousness because they are stressful, anxiety-arousing, threatening, or otherwise unacceptable to the person. Aspects of the self that are located in the Unconscious are actively repressed and therefore are not easily accessible.

Freud proposed that three mental structures – the id, the ego, and the superego – govern the relations among these aspects of mental life. The id is the source of basic drives that the organism seeks to satisfy, including sex and aggression, which often have their roots in internal conflicts about the self. These mechanisms thereby generate primitive desires that can be unacceptable to conscious thought and must be prevented from entering consciousness. The superego, the moral arm of the personality structure, wants these thoughts and urges suppressed because of their unacceptable nature. The ego is the CEO of the system, negotiating between the other two segments and using a variety of defense mechanisms – repression, projection, displacement, and others – to prevent unwanted material from emerging from the Unconscious into conscious thought. Together, the three components of personality allow individuals to adapt to the demands of intrapsychic drives, the conflicts among them, and the interface with the external world.

In Freud's conception, the Unconscious referred to a segment of the mind that contained repressed material. In contrast, cognitive and social psychology use the term "unconscious" to refer to processes having particular characteristics and functions. Like Freud, unconscious processes are believed to occur outside a person's awareness. Also, like Freud, this kind of processing is seen as pervasive, more widespread in everyday cognitive functioning than most of us realize, and it has significant effects on daily functioning.

However, the contemporary view differs dramatically from Freud's in several important respects (Wilson, 2002). Although unconscious processes typically occur outside of awareness, they do so not because they are repressed or deal with material that is threatening or traumatic. They also do not usually arise from internal conflicts over unacceptable drives and conflicts. Instead, unconscious processes commonly result from the repetition of mental processes that, over time, become so routinized or automatic that they occur without conscious awareness. Like Freud, they are often highly adaptive and beneficial to the person, but for entirely different reasons. From a contemporary perspective, unconscious processes allow us to engage in everyday behavior without being overwhelmed. Because these processes are vital to effective functioning, they have been called the *adaptive unconscious* (Hofmann & Wilson, 2010; Wilson, 2002, 2003).

In sum, despite some similarities, the origins, nature, and functions of unconscious processes are dramatically different in psychodynamic and social psychological approaches. We turn now to develop in greater detail the concept of automaticity from a social information processing perspective.

AUTOMATICITY

In much of the work in social psychology before the mid-1970s, it was assumed that people have insight into the mental processes underlying their judgments, preferences, decisions, and behaviors. People generally were assumed to know what they were thinking at any given moment, they could report these thoughts, and they usually knew why they were thinking about what they were. Beginning in the mid-1970s, research in both social psychology and cognitive psychology began to challenge these assumptions.

Development of Automaticity Research

One line of research focused on *mindlessness*, behavior that occurs with minimal attention or thought (Langer, 1978, 2014; Langer, Blank, & Chanowitz, 1978; Langer & Imber, 1980; Langer, Pirson, & Delizonna, 2010). An example of mindless behavior is when people follow routines or scripts. As we described in Chapter 2, people have well-learned scripts (Abelson, 1976, 1981) about the kinds of behavior sequences that typically occur in frequently-experienced settings (e.g., a movie theater, a restaurant, a classroom). These scripts, when activated, can guide behavior without the person consciously attending to either the stimulus that triggered them or the reasons for enacting the scripted behaviors. Such behaviors are, then, "mindless." As such, people at times may engage in behaviors under surprising conditions, seemingly without rational justification, just because it fits a script.

Langer et al. (1978) provided a compelling demonstration of this principle. In this experiment, an assistant approached a copy machine that was already being used and asked to use it. Such a request for a person to stop in the middle of a task and to let the assistant go ahead presumably would require some reason, some justification. In one condition, the person said, "I have five pages. May I use the Xerox machine because I'm in a rush?" providing a rationale for the interruption. And in fact, 94% of people agreed in this condition. In contrast, the request "I have five pages. May I use the Xerox machine?" would seem less reasonable because it provides little justification. Only 60% agreed to the request in this condition. The most interesting case was the third condition in which the person said, "I have five pages. May I use the Xerox machine because I have to make some copies?" The person's request has the general form of providing a reason, but it offers little to no justification. Yet because it fit the script (the form of an appropriate request), 93% of the people let the person use the copy machine when confronted with this request. These people acted mindlessly, agreeing to comply with the request without thinking about the information provided. Langer's mindlessness concept raised the specter that we are not always cognizant of why we do what we do.

To understand why we do what we do, we would need to be aware of both the mental processes that govern our choices, preferences, and decisions and the situational influences on these processes. Nisbett and Wilson (1977a) showed that neither assumption is tenable, proposing that we often have little access to the nature of our mental processes and do not recognize many of the factors that influence our thinking. They showed across numerous studies that people cannot accurately identify the influence of stimuli and events on their mental processes (inference, evaluation, choice). When they do describe those influences, they often are wrong.

Consider the following examples: (a) In the well-known research on bystander intervention (Latane & Darley, 1970), it has consistently been shown that the likelihood of helping is a function of the number of people (potential helpers) present. However, people repeatedly assert that their willingness to provide help was not influenced by the number of other people present. (b) Shoppers were asked to select the highest quality nylon pantyhose from a set of four options and to explain why they had chosen the pair they did. Unbeknownst to the shoppers, all of the pantyhose were identical. Nonetheless, there was a consistent bias such that the rightmost pair in the display was most frequently chosen, but no one ever mentioned position as a factor influencing their choice. (c) Participants were shown a short documentary film and later were asked to rate the movie on several properties (how interesting, impactful, etc.). In one condition, there was distracting noise of power tools from renovations being done in the hallway, and, in another condition, there was no distracting noise. After they made their ratings, participants were asked how much the sound had influenced their ratings. Most participants indicated that the noise had resulted in lower ratings, whereas there was no difference between these conditions.

These and other studies document that people both (a) fail to recognize the impact of influential stimuli (persons present, position effects) and (b) erroneously report the impact of stimulus factors (noise) that did not affect their behavior. These studies testify to the fact that people are generally ineffective in reporting on their cognitive processes. Indeed, they appear to have limited access to those processes and show little understanding of the factors that influence them and, through them, their behavior.

Independently, but at about the same time, research in cognitive psychology was laying important groundwork for new thinking about cognitive processes (e.g., Posner & Snyder, 1975; Shiffrin & Schneider, 1977). This work was demonstrating some of the benefits derived from unconscious processes. It was shown that with practice, some mental processes could be performed with minimal attention, required few cognitive resources such as time and effort, could occur very quickly, and did not need to be voluntarily initiated. Other research revealed new effects in studies of memory, showing that memories could form that could not be self-reported even though they affected performance on subsequent tasks. These memories were termed *implicit memories*, and they were distinguished from *explicit memories* which can be verbally recalled (e.g., Graf & Schacter, 1985; Schacter, 1987). Again, this appeared to reflect a qualitative difference in thinking about the unconscious that needed to be recognized (Hassin & Sklar, 2014; Payne, 2012; Payne & Gawronski, 2010).

All of these accumulating findings produced a glaring need for new ways of thinking about cognitive processing. Specifically, they led to the development of a critical distinction between two kinds of processing, *automatic* and *controlled. Controlled processing* is what we usually think of when we consider how we process and use information, make plans, judgments, decisions, and the like. It is thoughtful processing in which we intentionally engage for a specific purpose, and we are typically cognizant of the mental work we are doing. *Automatic processing* is processing that occurs without intention or effort. It requires few resources and often happens without our awareness.

Bargh (1994) argued that controlled and automatic processes differed in four critical features, which he referred to as "the four horsemen of automaticity." He argued that any given cognitive process could be characterized on the dimensions of *intentionality, awareness, efficiency, and control*. In their most extreme form, automatic processes:

1. Arise *unintentionally*, that is, without conscious initiation. They are triggered by an external stimulus of which the person may or may not be aware. Controlled processes, in contrast, are initiated intentionally (i.e., with *volition*).
2. Occur *outside of awareness*. The person might be unaware of the stimulus that initiated the processes and will have no insight into the cognitive processes underlying the experience triggered by it. In contrast, in controlled processing, people typically are quite aware of the cognitive processes they are engaging in as they plan, choose, judge, and evaluate.
3. Are *efficient*. They require minimal cognitive resources or effort. They do not interfere with other ongoing mental activity, and other simultaneous tasks will not affect their completion. Controlled processes, in contrast, require focused attention. Engaging in multiple controlled processes is challenging since one process will consume resources needed by other tasks, producing between-task interference.
4. Are *uncontrollable*. Once initiated, an automatic process cannot be halted and continues through to completion. In contrast, controlled processes can be influenced, altered, and even stopped.

Any given cognitive process exists along a continuum between highly automatic and highly controlled. Few (and perhaps none) of the processes involved in social cognition can be characterized as high on all four of these features (Sherman, Gawronski, & Trope, 2014). Instead, almost all processes reflect a mix of more automatic and more controlled features (Bargh, 1994; Dijksterhuis, 2013; Moors, 2016; Moors & De Houwer, 2007; Payne, 2012). Consider, for example, the processes involved in reading a sentence. On the one hand, once you read a familiar word, you cannot help but comprehend it. Seeing the word "apple" will trigger the activation of relevant semantic content, mental images, and your beliefs, evaluations, and memories associated with the concept. You could not stop these processes even if you tried. All of this seems entirely automatic. On the other hand, you will undoubtedly be aware that you have read the word (after all, that is why we read) and probably are aware that the image of an apple has come into consciousness, even if we might be unaware of many of the related processes that have been triggered (e.g., the greater accessibility of apple-related words through spreading activation). Those features seem more controlled. So, this simple task can be characterized as relatively high in unintentionality, efficiency, and uncontrollability, but more middling in terms of awareness.

Things become even more complicated when we consider a task that involves multiple processes differing in automaticity. In the Stroop (1935) task, people are required to name aloud the color of words while ignoring the words themselves. Sometimes, the words are compatible with the color with which they are printed (e.g., "red" printed with red ink). In other conditions, the words are incompatible with their color (e.g., "red" printed in blue). People usually complete this task more slowly in incompatible than compatible conditions. On incompatible trials, people do not intend to respond to the meaning of the word (the task is to name the ink color, not the word), but they typically become aware that it is easier said than done. They realize their attention is being drawn to the content of the words, despite its irrelevance to the task at hand and their intention to ignore it. To overcome this automatic draw on attention, people must assert control to report a judgment that has been made challenging by a competing automatic process. So, in this case, people are aware of an automatic process, but they cannot stop it and have difficulty correcting its influence.

In other cases, we might be successful in exerting control over processes of which we become aware, even if they were triggered automatically. For example, we might intentionally resist the impulse to enter a bakery while dieting, even though an urge to go in the store was automatically triggered by glimpsing a delicious array of breads and cookies in a window display (Sherman, Gawronski, Gonsalkorale, Hugenberg, Allen, & Groom, 2008). These examples show that the four features of automaticity may relate to one another in different ways and to differing degrees, and these relationships can change in various tasks and contexts.

In sum, automaticity is a graded phenomenon, with any given process exhibiting each characteristic to varying degrees. Each characteristic also may be thought of as existing along a continuum rather than acting in an all-or-none fashion; processes are more-or-less intentional and more-or-less controllable (Moors, 2016; Moors & De Houwer, 2007). Moreover, few processes occur in isolation. Most processes co-occur and mutually interact with other processes that also differ in their characteristics. Because of these complexities, it can be challenging to disentangle all of the contributions to performance on even a simple task (Conrey, Sherman, Gawronski, Hugenberg, & Groom, 2005; Ito et al., 2015; Sherman, Klauer, & Allen, 2010).

Roots of Automaticity

The syndicated cartoon, Pickles (Crane, 2010), once depicted a conversation between a young boy and his grandmother. The boy is intently staring at his grandmother's hands as she effortlessly knits a scarf. The boy says, "Grandma, do you know that when you fall asleep knitting, your fingers keep knitting without you?" The grandmother responds with surprise, "Really? I guess I've been knitting so long my fingers know how to do it themselves...it's like they have their own little brains telling them what to do." The boy wonders aloud, "Does anyone find that creepy but me?"

This example raises numerous questions about the origins and nature of automatic processes. How do automatic processes come about? Are we born with these processing capacities? Can they develop over time? If so, how do they develop? Research shows that some automatic processes are innate – with us since we were born – and other processes become automatic through experience. Innate processes require no learning, and they can be observed in newborn infants. For example, many motor reflexes, such as blinking in response to a puff of air, are present at birth, require no initiation or effort, cannot be controlled, and persist throughout life. Other automatic behaviors, called *primitive reflexes*, are present in healthy newborns but eventually disappear as the central nervous system matures and volitional control of behavior increases (Berne, 2006; Zafeiriou, 2004). These reflexes include behaviors related to eating (sucking and rooting reflexes), grasping, falling, and swimming, all of which would provide a survival advantage in evolutionary terms. As they age, infants quickly develop various capabilities in the social domain that cannot easily be explained by their levels of experience, suggesting that these abilities are, at least in part, innate (Bargh, Schwader, Hailey, Dyer, & Boothby, 2012). Among these is the ability to distinguish faces based on social categories including gender and race (Pascalis et al., 2011), to understand that people (but not objects) have and pursue goals (Woodward, 2009), and to prefer prosocial over antisocial individuals (Van de Vondervoort & Hamlin, 2018).

Both children and adults have hard-wired abilities to notice some potential threats. For example, infants as young as five months visually fixate on images of spiders compared with non-threatening stimuli (Rakison & Derringer, 2008). Adults show automatic visual attention to snakes and angry faces (Langeslag & van Strien, 2018). The automatic detection of threatening information should provide an evolutionary advantage and is likely selected for through natural selection. Some higher-level cognitive processes also show features of automaticity. People automatically notice stimuli that differ from others in the environment in color, size, or motion (Shiffrin & Schneider, 1984). Information regarding the frequency, location, and time of events is also encoded automatically (Hasher & Zachs, 1979, 1984). These categories of information are learned just as well when people are trying to remember them as when they are focused elsewhere, one of the key characteristics of automatic processes.

Other processes only become automatic with learning and extensive practice. These processes initially require initiative and effort, but, with many repetitions, become effortless. Many physical skills fit this description. Think back to when you were young and were learning to ride a bicycle. There you were, perched on the seat of this unstable piece of machinery, your parent holding the handlebars as you slowly moved, wobbling side to side, down a sidewalk. As you progressed, your attention was focused on every little thing you were doing: How much should I turn the wheel? How quickly should I pedal? How hard should I apply the brakes? Gradually, as your skills developed, your parent held on less tightly. Eventually (after a few falls and some scraped knees) you became capable of managing these challenges on your own.

Today, of course, you are an expert at performing this once-imposing task. You can guide your bike with one hand, can think about what you're going to do when you arrive at your destination and what you might want for dinner. Little of your attention is allocated to thinking about how much to turn the wheel or how hard to engage the brakes. The mechanical aspects of this behavior have become automatic – you can perform these actions without much thought and without them interfering with other tasks. This marvelous achievement has come about due to performing the same task many, many times – repetition has made it automatic. As the legendary UCLA basketball coach, John Wooden, once observed, "The importance of repetition until automaticity cannot be overstated. Repetition is the key to learning" (Wooden, 1997, p. 52).

The same points apply to *mental processes*. There are many mental processes we engage in repeatedly, like categorizing objects, evaluating products, and reading words. When the same mental operation is performed many times, we become proficient at it (Smith, 1990; Smith & Lerner, 1986). Schneider and Shiffrin (1977; Shiffrin & Schneider, 1977) conducted some of the earliest experiments demonstrating the development of automatic mental processes. In these studies, participants had to detect stimuli they had been told to remember on a series of judgment trials. Participants in one condition had to remember four letters (e.g., J K T & L) and to indicate as rapidly as they could whether any of those letters appeared in subsequent letter sets varying in number (1–4). The critical variable in the study was whether the memorized letter(s) stayed consistent or were variable through the study. In some conditions, the letter(s) participants were searching for remained consistent over hundreds of trials. For these participants, they might be asked to memorize J K T & L and had to search for these letters repeatedly.

In other conditions, the letter(s) that had to be remembered (and detected) were occasionally varied. For these participants, they might have first been asked to detect J K T & L, but, after a few trials, were then asked to detect A O S & M.

The results showed that the consistency of the letter set affected the speed with which letters could be detected. As is shown in Figure 3.1, when the remembered letters were consistent across the experiment, participants were more quickly able to judge whether any of the memorized stimuli appeared in a judgment trial. In this condition, judgments were equally fast when a letter appeared alone or with other letters that served as distractors. In contrast, when the to-be-memorized letters were variable over the experiment, participants were slower overall to detect their presence on a judgment trial. Judgments were particularly slow when these letters had to be detected among four letters.

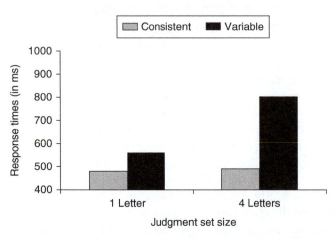

Figure 3.1 Judgments speeds as a function of consistent versus variable memorization sets and judgment set size

Source: Based on data from Schneider & Shiffrin (1977)

These results show that repetition of a mental process allows it to become automatic. With practice in searching for a consistent set of stimuli, participants could detect them efficiently and effortlessly. It took them little time to detect letters, even when they appeared amidst several distractors. Many of the participants in this condition reported that the letters they were seeking would "pop out" of the display – almost no attention was needed to detect their presence. The *pop-out effect* is now viewed as a signature of automatic processing (e.g., Berggren, Koster, & Derakshan, 2012; Hershler & Hochstein, 2005; Treisman & Gormican, 1988). In contrast, when the memorized stimuli were varied over the study, this skill did not become automatic. Instead, participants had to engage in effortful processes to determine whether any given letter later appeared, and the speed to do so decreased with the number of stimuli that need to be processed.

Subsequent research demonstrated that once stimulus detection becomes automatic, it also becomes resistant to interference from other attention-demanding tasks and is minimally affected by factors such as stress or fatigue. However, once a skill becomes automatic, it can be triggered without the perceiver's intention, it can be difficult to control, and cannot easily be stopped (Kahneman & Treisman, 1984; Posner & Snyder, 1975; Schneider & Chein, 2003).

Although this early work focused on the automatic processing of information involving letters and objects, the same principles characterize many aspects of *social* information processing. When we repeatedly engage in mental processes about people over time – determining a person's traits, inferring the causes of a person's behavior, or judging a group – these processes require less attention and time to complete. Eventually, they can be performed unintentionally, without our awareness, unaffected by other mental tasks we are performing, and difficult to halt. These are, of course, the features of automaticity.

EVIDENCE OF AUTOMATIC PROCESSING

We opened this chapter with the observation that people typically feel that they know what they are doing and why. The existence of automatic processes suggests that people may be misguided in that assumption, at least some of the time (which, in fact, was the focus of Nisbett and Wilson's (1977a) analysis). What evidence is there that processing information from the social world operates automatically? Are such effects limited to certain phenomena or domains? Do they influence perceptions and judgments? Evaluations? Goals? Social interaction? Intergroup behavior? The answer to all of these questions is "Yes." In the next several subsections, we present some evidence supporting these conclusions. Other examples will be provided later in the chapter when we discuss the implications of automatic processing for understanding the self, other persons, and groups.

Automaticity and Attention

Attention is a crucial initial step in information processing because it determines what aspects of the stimulus environment are encoded and available for further processing and use. Research evidence indicates that attention can automatically become focused on certain kinds of social stimuli.

In Chapter 2, we discussed that people have certain constructs that are *chronically accessible*. These are trait concepts, attitudes, and values that individuals regularly prioritize in social information processing. They require minimal if any external stimulation to activate them and, hence, are readily available to be used in attending to and comprehending the social environment (Higgins et al., 1982). Consequently, one would expect that these constructs might automatically influence how social information is processed.

This effect was demonstrated in a study (Bargh & Pratto, 1986) using a variant of the Stroop color naming task described earlier. In this task, participants are shown words printed in different colors and told to name the color in which the word is printed. Because naming the color can conflict with the natural tendency to read the word, the task can be difficult and slow. In this study, some of the words presented were known (from pretesting) to be traits that, for the participant, were *chronically accessible*. Other words were not. It took significantly longer to name the color of words representing chronically accessible traits than for traits relating to less accessible constructs. Another study using the Stroop task (Pratto & John, 1991) showed that naming the color of words of negative valence or that conveyed threat also was slowed compared with positively valued and non-threatening content. This research documents the role of automatic processing in attention to stimuli.

Automaticity and Evaluation

We routinely evaluate people, objects, and events that we encounter in everyday life. Evaluative reactions are pervasive, ranging from thinking how much we like a person we just met to discovering that we detest a new food. Because mental processes that are repeatedly engaged can become automatic, the regularity of evaluative judgments means we come to make them with minimal intention or effort. The degree that we are aware of our evaluative responses, however, can vary substantially. Sometimes we are fully aware of our evaluations, happy to share our opinions quite freely with others. Evaluative judgments that are accessible to conscious awareness are referred to as *explicit evaluations*. Other times, we form evaluative judgments without

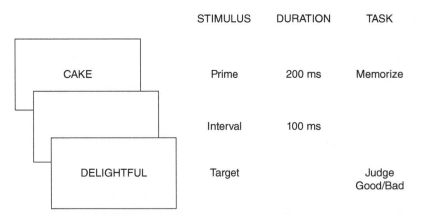

	STIMULUS	DURATION	TASK
CAKE	Prime	200 ms	Memorize
	Interval	100 ms	
DELIGHTFUL	Target		Judge Good/Bad

Figure 3.2 Typical sequential evaluative priming trial

Source: Based on Fazio et al. (1986)

recognizing we have done so, and we might have limited ability to identify or to verbalize our evaluations. These responses are referred to as *implicit evaluations*.

We will discuss in greater detail the relationship between automatic and controlled processes later in the chapter. For now, however, we raise a question that arises from the possibility that evaluative responses can happen automatically. If we form evaluative responses without intention, can we control those responses? Can they be constrained so that they are tied only to the entity that produced the response? If not, might these evaluations function like primes, able to color subsequent unrelated judgments?

These kinds of questions were pursued by Fazio and his colleagues (Fazio, Sanbonmatsu, Powell, & Kardes, 1986) using a *serial evaluative priming paradigm*. As depicted in Figure 3.2, participants in this paradigm complete a series of trials, each one consisting of a prime stimulus word they are to memorize followed, after a brief interval, by a target stimulus word. Some of the target words are clearly positive (e.g., appealing, delightful), and some are negative (e.g., repulsive, awful). On each trial, the participant's task is to press one of two response keys to indicate whether the target word is either positive or negative. The speed of their response is recorded, and automatic evaluative responses to the prime words can be inferred from the speed of categorizing the target words. If the prime words automatically activate a positive or negative evaluative response, then the speed with which participants judge the valence of the target word should be affected. When the prime and target are compatible (i.e., both negative or both positive), response times to the target word should be facilitated (faster); when they differ in valence, response times should be inhibited (slower).

That is what Fazio et al. (1986) and many others have found, at least under many conditions (see Herring et al., 2013). Valenced primes can affect the processing of subsequent information, a phenomenon called *evaluative priming*. Evaluative priming depends on the interval between the prime and the target words. In Fazio's et al.'s (1986) original research, the valence of the primes affected the speed of target judgments only when the interval between the words was small (only 100 ms). When the interval was increased to 800 ms, evaluative priming did not occur. Other research supports the notion that evaluative priming dissipates quickly and can be eliminated when participants are given time between primes and evaluative judgments (Hermans, De Houwer, & Eelen, 2001). In addition, evaluative priming is reduced when primes are irrelevant to current goals (Spruyt, Tibboel, De Schryver, & De Houwer, 2018) and when people are motivated to engage in controlled processing (Degner, 2009). However, evaluative priming often occurs quite automatically.

On what basis can we say that this is an automatic effect? First, participants are never asked to evaluate the prime words, so their evaluations occur spontaneously, without prompting. And second, similar effects occur in studies where primes have been presented subliminally

(Murphy & Zajonc, 1993; Niedenthal, 1990). Therefore, automatic evaluation does not rest on participants' awareness of the primes or an intentional strategy to engage in evaluation. In sum, the serial evaluative priming paradigm has been used in numerous experiments, the results of which clearly document the automatic evaluation of stimuli (see Fazio, 2001; Ferguson, 2007; Ferguson & Mann, 2014; Ferguson & Zayas, 2009). More broadly, research on evaluative priming is consistent with the idea that people regularly, naturally, and effortlessly evaluate information in their social world (Ferguson & Mann, 2014).

Goals

The fact that the outputs of simple cognitive tasks, such as those summarized in the two preceding subsections, can become automatized may not seem too surprising. One might question, however, the extent to which such automaticity could play a role in more consequential and complex domains. Consider, for example, our pursuit of important goals. In fact, for many years social scientists considered goal pursuit to be strictly a function of conscious choice.

Much of our behavior is oriented toward the achievement of goals: there are tasks to be accomplished, relationships to be maintained, and needs to be satisfied. When we are motivated to attain a goal, we think about and plan how that goal can be achieved, and those plans guide our behavior. If easily accomplished, fine. However, if goal attainment is difficult, we persist; if it is blocked, we return to it later in a further effort to achieve our objectives. In fact, these behaviors – persistence toward one's objectives and, if progress is blocked, returning to further pursuit – are two of the behavioral hallmarks of the motivational effects of goal activation, as revealed in past research. All of this processing seems to be well considered, even analytic, as we pursue some of life's essential tasks.

Much research, however, has demonstrated that both the activation and the pursuit of goals can occur automatically (Aarts et al., 2005; Custers & Aarts, 2010; Hassin, Bargh, & Zimerman, 2009; Parks-Stamm, Oettingen, & Gollwitzer, 2010). Goals are mental representations, just like the nouns and trait adjectives used in the studies described earlier (Bargh, 1982; Fazio et al., 1986). They include information about desired end-states as well as the plans and strategies that can be used to achieve those end-states. If they are indeed mental representations, then goal constructs presumably can be activated without awareness. Moreover, for goals that have frequently been engaged in the past, the mental processes that are functional to their attainment could become, through such repetition, automatic processes. If that were so, would we see similar kinds of effects for conscious and nonconscious goals?

A series of experiments by Bargh, Gollwitzer, Lee-Chai, Barndollar, and Trötschel (2001) provided evidence relevant to this question. One study showed that nonconsciously priming a goal to perform well resulted in better performance on a cognitive task. In the first part of the experiment, participants completed a word search task (finding specific words in a matrix of letters). For some participants, these words pertained to high performance (*succeed, achieve, win*) whereas in the control condition they were goal-neutral (*carpet, river, window*). This manipulation was intended to automatically activate a high-performance goal in one condition, but not the other. In the second phase, all participants were given new puzzles and were told simply to find as many words as they could. Participants who had been primed with the achievement goal in the first phase identified significantly more words than did participants in the control condition. A very indirect, unobtrusive priming of a goal translated into performance differences on a subsequent cognitive task.

One prominent feature of conscious goal pursuit is that people persist on a task, even in the face of difficulties. Would the same persistence occur following the nonconscious activation of a goal? To answer this question, Bargh et al. (2001) again induced (or not) a goal for high performance by giving people the word search task. Participants were then given a set of five consonants and five vowels, and their task was to generate and write down as many words as they could construct from those letters. Participants were unobtrusively videotaped during this task. Not much time was allotted for this task, and, at some point, participants were told over an intercom to stop working on it. The question was whether high-performance goal participants would continue working beyond this instruction. Researchers determined from the videotapes that 22% of the neutral prime participants continued to work after being told to stop. In contrast, 57% of the participants in the high-performance goal condition continued to construct words after they had been told to stop. Thus, given a high-performance goal, goal-relevant behavior persisted toward task completion even in violation of instructions.

In this study, participants were instructed to stop but could surreptitiously continue if they desired. However, what if their performance were truly interrupted, preventing completion of the task? A well-known finding in the goal pursuit literature is that when a person cannot pursue a task to completion, she is motivated to return to it later. Unfulfilled goals tend to instigate rumination (Syrek, Weigelt, Peifer, & Antoni, 2017), produce intrusive thoughts (Masicampo & Baumeister, 2011), and persist in memory (Zeigarnik, 1927), all of which drive the person back to goal-relevant tasks when opportunities later arise. Again, Bargh et al. (2001) asked if this effect would also occur in response to goal states that are activated nonconsciously. Participants were again exposed to the high-performance goal or neutral primes and then told they would perform two more tasks. For the first, they were to generate words, as in the previous experiment. In this case, however, an equipment malfunction (rigged as part of the experiment) interrupted the procedure. After the equipment was fixed, there was insufficient time to complete both tasks. Participants were asked to choose whether they would prefer to complete the word generation task or instead to judge the humor of a set of cartoons – the latter task being much more appealing to most people than the challenging word generation task. Results showed that 66% of high-performance goal participants chose to continue working on the word generation task, whereas only 32% of nonprimed participants made that choice. Persons primed with a high-performance goal and then blocked were motivated to complete the interrupted task.

The results of these experiments and many others provide compelling evidence that nonconscious goals produce similar effects as conscious, deliberative goals (Ferguson & Bargh, 2004; Marien, Custers, Hassin, & Aarts, 2012; McCulloch, Ferguson, Kawada, & Bargh, 2008). The demonstrations of persistence beyond a time limit and the return to a less-desired task following an interruption, in particular, indicate that nonconscious goal activation can generate the same motivational properties that are familiar in research on motivation and goal pursuit. As Bargh et al. (2001, p. 1025) stated, "using achievement as a prime activates not only related concepts such as success, effort, pride, and so on, but also the intention to do well, to find solutions to problems, and to overcome obstacles in the way."

Social Interaction

In the work we have discussed, the focus has been on the existence and functioning of these processes in the individual person. Research shows that automatic processes also affect social interactions between people. To be effective, social interaction requires the coordination of behavior. Coordination is necessary to establish rapport between participants in an interaction and to facilitate empathy between persons. As part of that process, people often subtly mirror another person's behaviors. People may adopt another's mannerisms during an interaction, and may even accommodate to another's speech patterns, accent, and manner of speaking (Gallois, Ogay, & Giles, 2005). On some occasions, we might imitate or copy another's behavior to please the person (as the saying goes, "Imitation is the highest form of flattery"). But that is ingratiation, and it is deliberate, intentional, and self-serving. The question posed in research by Chartrand and her colleagues (Chartrand & Bargh, 1999; Chartrand, Maddux, & Lakin, 2005; Chartrand & van Baaren, 2009; Larkin & Chartrand, 2003) was whether this phenomenon – which they called *behavioral mimicry* – can happen spontaneously, automatically, without the participant's intention or awareness. If so, how would it affect the relationship?

One study (Chartrand & Bargh, 1999) involved two people interacting on a task (looking at an album of photographs and describing them). One person was an experimental confederate who had been trained to enact certain specific nonverbal mannerisms – rubbing her face, shaking her foot – during the interaction. The question was whether the other person (the actual participant in the study) would manifest these same mannerisms. Analyses of video recordings of these interactions showed evidence of such mimicry. As is shown in Table 3.1, in the condition where the confederate frequently rubbed her face, so did the participant. If, however, the confederate tended to shake her foot a lot, so did the participant.

Table 3.1   Proportion of times participants mimicked confederate (c) per minute

	P's behavior	
C's mannerism	Rub face	Shake foot
Rub face	.57	.35
Shake foot	.45	.73

Source: Based on data from Chartrand & Bargh (1999)

In a second study, the same researchers demonstrated the adaptive function of such mimicry. The procedure was much the same as in the first study, except that rather than enacting certain mannerisms, the confederate either (a) mimicked whatever mannerisms the participant was doing or (b) performed other mannerisms. When the interaction was over, the participants rated how much they liked their partner (the confederate) and how smoothly the interaction had gone. As shown in Figure 3.3 (where higher values indicate greater liking and perceived smoothness), mimicry had beneficial effects on the relationship. When the confederate copied and mimicked the mannerisms of the participants, participants liked the confederate more and felt the interaction had been very effective. In both of these studies, post-experimental debriefing verified that the participants had no awareness of the confederates' specific behavioral enactments or of their mimicry of those actions.

Together these studies show that people automatically imitate another's behavior during social interactions and that such mimicry can have beneficial effects not only on the liking felt for one's partner but also on one's satisfaction and enjoyment

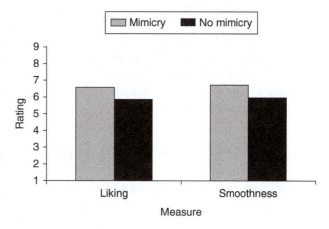

Figure 3.3   Mean ratings of liking of confederate and interaction smoothness based on mimicry or non-mimicry of confederate

Source: Based on data from Chartrand & Bargh (1999)

of the interaction. These effects also extend beyond the immediate interaction in which mimicry occurs. People who have been mimicked not only like the person who mimicked them but also engage in more prosocial behavior (helping, donating money) to others after the interaction has ended (van Baaren, Holland, Kawakami, & van Knippenberg, 2004).

Medical Decisions

There are many interpersonal contexts in which automatic attitudes can significantly impact the nature and outcomes of social interaction. As an example, consider the doctor-patient relationship and the question of whether that relationship differs as a function of the racial composition of the dyad. In particular, are there differences in the ways (perhaps subtle ways) that doctors deliver medical care to Black and White patients? If they do, do those differences reflect overt prejudicial attitudes or biases about which the physicians may not even be aware? Evidence of such biases would be of concern not only to the medical profession but also to the public at large (Blair et al., 2014; Fiscella & Sanders, 2016; van Ryn & Fu, 2003).

Research investigating these questions is not extensive, and more is needed. Nevertheless, some findings suggest there are reasons for concern. There is evidence, for example, that at least in some cases, physicians are less likely to prescribe medical procedures for Black than for White patients with similar conditions (Chapman, Kaatz, & Carnes, 2013; Dovidio, Penner, Albrecht, Norton, Gaertner, & Shelton, 2008; Lin & Kressin, 2015) and to assume that Black patients will be less likely to adhere to treatment guidelines (Bogart, Catz, Kelly, & Benotsch, 2001). The question of interest for our purposes in this section is whether such differences are overt prejudicial responses or are manifestations of subconscious, automatic bias.

In one study (Green et al., 2007), doctors were given a case study of a patient with symptoms of a heart condition that might warrant treatment by thrombolysis, a procedure to dissolve dangerous clots in blood vessels, improve blood flow, and prevent damage to tissues and organs. After reading the case summary, the physicians were asked to indicate whether they would give the patient thrombolysis. They then completed measures of racial attitudes. Explicit measures included ratings of whether they preferred White or Black Americans and how warmly they felt toward each racial group, and the implicit measure was an IAT designed to assess race bias. Results showed that, overall, physicians were equally likely to recommend thrombolysis for Black and White patients, and their explicit attitudes did not influence this decision. However, physicians' performance on the implicit IAT measures were related to their medical decisions. As anti-Black bias on the IAT increased, recommendations for the medical treatment for Black patients decreased. For White patients, the opposite finding was obtained. This evidence indicates that physicians' unconscious race biases may influence their decisions about critical medical interventions.

THE PERCEPTION-BEHAVIOR LINK

In the preceding section, we have highlighted the central role of automatic, unconscious processes in a wide array of important domains of social thought and behavior. In each case, we have described an illustrative experiment reporting data that demonstrate these outcomes, and numerous other studies provide similar documentation. In all of these cases, people's functioning has been guided in important ways by processes of which they are unaware, sometimes leading to judgments, behaviors, and outcomes that were not consciously intended.

In understanding these findings, we need to explore further the psychological mechanisms by which they occur. As we described earlier, automaticity can develop through the frequent and consistent pairing of some external stimulus (a trait concept) and some response (judgment, evaluation, behavior). Let us break this process down a bit more. You see a magazine advertisement showing a delicious-looking bowl of chocolate ice cream. The perception of that object is so well established in your mind that the actual perception of that stimulus requires no thought. It's automatic, and you would have difficulty perceiving that object as a banana or a tree or a library book. You have seen many bowls of ice cream in your life, and your perception of this one is quick and automatic. In many of those past experiences, perception of a picture of ice cream has (a) brought to mind many wonderful features of chocolate ice cream (delicious!), (b) made you think, "Do I really want some now?," all of which led you to (c) decide to go to the refrigerator in search of some. Given that this sequence has happened many times in your life, these steps become closely linked such that now, seeing that picture automatically triggers your movement toward the kitchen. This automaticity is known as a *perception-behavior link* (Bargh & Chartrand, 1999; Dijksterhuis & Bargh, 2001).

AUTOMATIC AND CONTROLLED PROCESSES

In this chapter, we have described myriad landmark experiments demonstrating that much of our mental life occurs outside our conscious awareness. These demonstrations of automatic effects stimulated a tremendous amount of research investigating unconscious processes, research that has further supported the conclusion that they play a central role in our lives. The accumulated evidence has led to the widespread belief that "most of human cognition occurs outside of conscious awareness or conscious control" (Nosek, Hawkins, & Frazier, 2011, p. 152) and that unconscious processes constitute "the majority of causes of behavior" (Baumeister & Bargh, 2014, p. 37).

While we recognize that we cannot always know what we are thinking or why, we also know that some of our mental activities are readily accessible to conscious awareness. We can think about what we want to eat for dinner, decide whether to vacation in the mountains or at the beach, or determine what we want to work on as we sit down at our desk. All of these thoughts are quite obvious to us, and we can reflect upon and report to others about the content of these cognitions.

What, then, are we to make of the co-existence of conscious, explicit processes and automatic, implicit processes? Are they completely independent modes of thinking, proceeding on parallel, independent tracks? Are conscious and unconscious thoughts consistent and compatible? Can they diverge? What ultimately determines what we think? As evidence of unconscious, implicit social cognition emerged, research addressing these questions has answered some of these questions about the nature of implicit and explicit systems and the relation between them. Several critical issues are yet unresolved, awaiting further research.

Automaticity, Awareness, and Measurement

So far in this chapter, the words "implicit" and "unconscious," and "explicit" and "conscious," have been used interchangeably. This has historically been common and continues through today (Corneille & Hütter, 2020). However, to investigate the nature and relationships between processes, terms must be clearly defined and distinguished. This task has proved surprisingly challenging (Greenwald & Lai, 2020). Memory researchers first coined the term *implicit memories* to describe effects that appeared on indirect measures (e.g., judgments of familiarity) but not on direct measures (e.g., free recall and recognition) (Graf & Schacter, 1985). As evidence of memory effects on indirect measures grew, many cognitive psychologists equated implicit with unconscious memories, despite warnings not to conflate these constructs (Jacoby, 1991).

When social cognition researchers first began to explore implicit processes, they also tended to equate implicit and unconscious processes: "the signature of implicit cognition is that traces of past experience affect some performance, even though the influential earlier experience is not remembered in the usual sense – that is, it is unavailable to self-report or introspection" (Greenwald & Banaji, 1995, p. 4). However, the situation became confused as terms expanded beyond process distinctions to include methodological considerations and blends of process and measurement issues (Corneille & Hütter, 2020). Recent recommendations advocate that the terms "implicit" and "explicit" be tied to issues of measurement (indirect versus direct, respectively), de-emphasizing issues of conscious involvement (De Houwer, Teige-Mocigemba, Spruyt, & Moors, 2009; Greenwald & Banaji, 2017; Hahn & Gawronski, 2018).

Although these definitions do help clarify matters, the question of conscious involvement in responding to implicit and explicit measures is still a central issue. It is important to recognize that there exists an asymmetry between the role of awareness in responding to direct measures (i.e., self-report) and indirect measures (i.e., where constructs are inferred from behavior not involving direct report). Whereas direct measures always involve some level of conscious awareness (after all, direct measures involve self-report), responses to indirect measures are influenced by unconscious processes, conscious processes, and usually both. Therefore, it is impossible to conclude that a judgment or response was made unconsciously simply because it was measured indirectly. That is because no measure is "process pure," that is, capturing only a single cognitive process (Jacoby, 1991; Sherman, 2006, 2008).

For example, several processes underlie performance on the IAT, the most commonly used implicit measure of racial attitudes. As we discussed in Chapter 2, the IAT is a task in which participants are presented with a series of stimuli representing two different categories (e.g., faces of White or Black persons and positive or negative words). Participants are asked to indicate using one of two letters on a keyboard whether it is a "White face or a positive word" or a "Black face or a negative word." The speed of these judgments is then compared with the speed of completing the opposing pairing ("Black or positive" vs. "White or negative"). To the degree people have more automatic positive associations with White than with Black people (as is the typical finding with White participants), the speed of completing the former trials should be faster than for the latter trials.

However, performance on this task can be affected by several other processes, some of which clearly involve conscious control and effort. You might, for example, be motivated to reject automatically activated negative evaluations of Black people and engage in controlled efforts to override this bias (Calanchini, Sherman, Klauer, & Lai, 2014; Sherman et al., 2008). You might also, in an attempt to appear non-prejudiced, intentionally slow your responses when they otherwise would occur quickly. These effortful processes, if successful, would make it appear as if you are unbiased when in fact you do have negative, automatically activated associations (Fiedler & Bluemka, 2005; Kim, 2003; Röhner & Thoss, 2018).

This example highlights the benefit of using multiple implicit measures to study unconscious processes. Each specific measure will have strengths and weaknesses and will implicate different underlying processes. The IAT has generally replaced self-report measures of racial attitudes, on the assumption that it can "reveal attitudes and other automatic associations even for subjects who prefer not to express those attitudes" (Greenwald et al., 1998, p. 1465). Other indirect measures can be used to provide additional evidence regarding any given phenomenon (see for reviews Brownstein, Madva, & Gawronski, 2019; De Houwer et al., 2009; Gawronski & Hahn, 2019). For example, another common implicit measure for assessing automatic evaluation is the Affect Misattribution Procedure (AMP; Payne, Cheng, Govorun, & Stewart, 2005). In the AMP, participants make evaluative judgments of ambiguous target images (e.g., Chinese pictographs) after brief exposure to stimuli (e.g., images of faces) they are told to ignore. The logic of the AMP is consistent with evaluative priming; automatic responses to a stimulus are expected to color the evaluative judgment of the subsequent Chinese character. Therefore, a participant's automatic evaluation of a person can be inferred from the pleasantness judgments following the presentation of the person's picture.

The Relationship Between Implicit and Explicit Attitudes

One might wonder the extent to which responses captured by implicit and explicit measures about a given issue tend to covary. In many circumstances, implicit and explicit judgments might be expected to correspond quite highly. As we briefly discussed, responses to implicit measures can be affected by controlled processes (at least in some situations), so a complete dissociation would be surprising. However, responses to implicit measures are also influenced by various processes of which people are unaware and cannot control. As such, there might also be contexts where responses to implicit and explicit measures do diverge. Consequently, research has not only addressed *whether* implicit and explicit responses diverge but also *when* they do and *when* they do not. Furthermore, some research has provided a basis for understanding *why* the strength of the relationship can vary in different domains.

Nosek (2005, 2007; Hofmann, Gschwendner, Nosek, & Schmitt, 2005; Nosek & Smyth, 2007) has shown that the degree of correspondence between responses to implicit and explicit measures can vary considerably. In this research, participants completed both evaluative IATs and self-report measures for one of more than 50 widely-varying topics (e.g., liking of famous actors, political attitudes, evaluations of body types). The median correlation of responses to implicit and explicit measures across all topics was +.48. However, the magnitude of correlation differed markedly across content domains. Some correlations were quite weak (e.g., a near-zero correlation between explicit and implicit measures of attitudes towards Asians versus Whites), whereas others were highly correlated (e.g., a +.78 correlation between implicitly and explicitly measured Pro-life versus Pro-choice beliefs).

The degree of correspondence between implicit and explicit responses depends on several moderating variables. The *strength* of people's beliefs and attitudes affects the degree that they respond similarly to implicit and explicit measures. Extensive experience in thinking about or acting upon one's beliefs in a domain increases the consistency in responding to implicit and explicit measures. This fits with the idea that well-practiced responses are more likely to become proceduralized, automatically coming into conscious awareness to guide and influence effortful processes. A second moderator is the *social sensitivity* of the topic. Responses to implicit and explicit measures may not correspond when people are concerned about expressing negativity toward a group because of potential social disapproval or because they would prefer not to have such attitudes (Olson, Fazio, & Hermann, 2007). Implicit measures are often better indicators of such socially sensitive attitudes than self-report (Dasgupta, McGhee, Greenwald, & Banaji, 2000; Greenwald, Poehlman, Uhlmann, & Banaji, 2009). The *distinctiveness* of one's beliefs can also moderate implicit-explicit consistency. Beliefs that are seen as differing in strength compared with others (e.g., feeling more strongly about an issue than most people) generally produces higher consistency in responding to implicit and explicit measures. Finally, the *dimensionality* of an issue (where being for something (Pro-Life) means being against something else (Pro-Choice)) also strengthens this relationship. In sum, people tend to show similar responses to implicit and explicit measures when attitudes and beliefs are strong, noncontroversial, unusual, and involve polarized issues.

Dual Process Models

We now turn to a discussion of *dual process models* that consider the involvement of multiple processes, some more automatic and some more controlled, in social cognition. The emergence of these models has been described as "one of the most significant theoretical developments in the history of social psychology" (Sherman et al., 2014, p. 3). However, despite (and perhaps because of) their importance, there has been much disagreement about the specific nature of automatic and controlled influences on how people think, evaluate, and behave.

Dual process accounts involve two distinct systems or processes with unique characteristics (see for reviews Deutsch & Strack, 2006; Evans & Frankish, 2009; Gawronski & Creighton, 2013; Sherman et al., 2014; Smith & DeCoster, 2000). Such models have been used to explain social cognitive processes in diverse domains, including attitudes and persuasion (Chaiken, Liberman, & Eagly, 1989; Gawronski & Bodenhausen, 2006; Petty & Cacioppo, 1986), attribution (Gilbert, 1989; Trope, 1986a), decision-making and judgment (Evans, 1984; Kahneman, 2003; Rolison, Evans, Dennis, & Walsh, 2012), moral reasoning (Haidt, 2001; Paxton, Ungar, & Greene, 2012), person perception (Brewer, 1988; Fiske & Neuberg, 1990), self-regulation (Hofmann, Friese, & Strack, 2009; Strack & Deutsch, 2004), and stereotyping and prejudice (Devine, 1989; Gaertner & Dovidio, 1986). The majority of these accounts focus on automatic and controlled processes in the domain for which they were developed. Consequently, they differ in many respects, and more detailed discussion of these specific dual process models will appear later in this chapter and throughout this text.

We will now discuss in detail two influential dual process models that characterize automatic and controlled processes at the system level. That is, they offer general considerations of the nature and functioning of conscious and unconscious processes, independent of specific content areas. Comparing these models can clarify some of the ways that dual process models are similar and dissimilar in critical respects. After describing each model, we will then highlight some of the differences between them that reflect broad areas of disagreement between various dual process approaches in social cognition. The general models we consider here are the *Systems of Evaluation Model* (SEM; McConnell & Rydell, 2014; McConnell, Rydell, Strain, & Mackie, 2008; Rydell, McConnell, Mackie, & Strain, 2006; Shoda, McConnell, & Rydell, 2014) and the *Associative-Propositional Evaluative Model* (APE; Gawronski & Bodenhausen, 2006, 2007, 2011, 2014a).

The SEM

This model assumes that people possess two partially independent cognitive *systems*, each with unique properties and characteristics. One system, the *associative system*, involves the formation and utilization of associations in memory to process social and attitudinal information. Evaluative responses can be generated by relying on valenced associations that are activated from cognitive representations in memory. Evaluations can be derived through the pairing of inputs and representations in memory based on similarity ("This new guy is a lot like my friend!") or contiguity (e.g., if the new person is observed socializing with a close friend). According to this model, evaluations derived from the associative system are slow to form and change because they reflect accumulated pairings of objects and evaluation over time.

A second system is *rule-based*, and it generates evaluations by applying logic and deductive reasoning to knowledge (stored in semantic cognitive representations) relevant to the entity being processed. Upon meeting a new person, you might take note of his interests, sense of humor, and apparent attitude toward yourself. This information can then be used to determine whether you think you will like him or not. Logic can be deployed intentionally to process information following one's needs and goals. Consequently, these evaluations often form and can be changed relatively quickly.

The evaluations produced by these distinct systems, one based on associations and the other on logical rules, are referred to as *implicit evaluations* and *explicit evaluations*, respectively. Implicit evaluations affect responding to measures designed to detect the existence of associations in memory (such as the IAT and the AMP). Explicit evaluations, being primarily based on the application of logical rules to semantic information, primarily affect how one responds to language-based measures such as questionnaires and rating scales.

The reliance on each system to guide judgments and behavior will depend on the availability of motivation and cognitive resources. When resources are diminished, behavior is less deliberate, and actions are influenced more strongly by implicit evaluations. Furthermore, because different systems underlie implicit and explicit evaluation, a person can produce discrepant responses on different attitudinal measures. Such discrepancies reflect both that implicit and explicit evaluations can differ, sometimes dramatically, and that most measures typically are better able to capture one aspect of one's evaluative response than the other.

The APE Model

The APE model distinguishes two sets of *processes* that operate based on different principles. One set of processes is *associative*, arising from conditioning and learning processes that link mental representations to one another or to inputs based on principles of similarity and contiguity. Activation through association is generally unintentional, though not always (Peters & Gawronski, 2011). Regardless of how they are activated, associations are often the basis of evaluation. For example, you might automatically decide that you like a new person based on his physical resemblance to a friend (Gawronski & Quinn, 2013). Importantly, such associations are independent of truth-value; associated concepts can be activated and used whether they are subjectively seen as valid or invalid, true or false.

The second set of processes is *propositional*, focused on the subjective validity (i.e., perceived truth) of activated information. That is, propositional processes monitor the output of the associative system, determining whether activated associations are accepted as accurate or rejected as false. If the activated content resonates with propositional beliefs ("I am having a negative response to this person, and I know I don't like her"), then this content will be used to make judgments and guide behavior. However, if activated associations are inconsistent with propositional beliefs ("I am having a negative response to this person, but it might be because of her race. Negative views based on race are wrong"), then propositional processes can be used to reason about or to override subjectively invalid associations. Usually, these processes are consciously accessible and can be verbally reported.

These two sets of processes produce distinct evaluations: "whereas implicit evaluations are assumed to be the behavioral outcome of associative processes, explicit evaluations are conceptualized as the behavioral outcome of propositional processes" (Gawronski & Bodenhausen, 2014b, p. 188). Therefore, differences in responding to implicit and explicit measures can reflect differences in associations and propositional beliefs.

Unresolved Issues

Although these models are similar in several respects, there are also striking differences between them (and among other dual process models, more broadly). We highlight here several broad issues that differentiate dual process models. These differences could have important implications for accounting for automatic and controlled processes across content domains. However, the resolution of these issues will require further research.

One way that these models differ regards whether distinct *systems* or *processes* underlie automatic and controlled processing. Like the SEM, some dual process models argue that two distinct systems underlie these respective modes of thinking (e.g., Kahneman, 2003; Lieberman, 2003; Wilson, Lindsey, et al. 2000). Consistent with this view is some neuroscientific evidence suggesting that different neural networks support automatic and controlled processes (Hikosaka & Isoda, 2010; Satpute & Lieberman, 2006; Spunt & Lieberman, 2013; Yu et al., 2014). These approaches suggest that there might be little interplay between controlled and automatic systems, given that each system might dominate processing under different conditions. In contrast, other dual process models agree with the APE model that two general sets of processes, one more controlled and one more automatic, underlie social information processing (Fiske & Neuberg, 1990; Trope, 1986a). Because these theories do not assume distinct systems, there would be an expectation of regular interplay between processes.

Second, models differ regarding the overlap between what processes do (*operating principles*) and when they do it (*operating conditions*). The SEM tends to equate these two factors, suggesting that associative processes are used when people are thinking automatically (and to respond to implicit measures), and rule-based processes are used to think effortfully (and to respond to explicit measures). Conditional factors (e.g., cognitive load) will moderate the reliance on associative or rule-based systems. The APE model views these issues as separable. In terms of operating principles, associative processes involve the activation of mental associations, and propositional processes involve the validation of activated information based on reasoning. In terms of operating conditions, the APE does not equate associative processes with automatic and propositional processes with controlled processing. Both associative and propositional processes have automatic and controlled aspects. For example, any association can be turned into a proposition if it is assigned a truth-value. Conversely, any propositional reasoning depends on activated associations. In sum, the APE model clearly distinguishes operating principles and operating conditions.

The Interplay Between Automatic and Controlled Cognition

Dual process models agree that information processing rests on contributions from systems or processes that differ in the degree that they are automatic. Much research has focused on how these systems might interact, particularly in cases where automatic and controlled components of our mental systems produce discrepant responses. Payne (2001; Bishara & Payne, 2009; Payne, Shimizu, & Jacoby, 2005) used a *weapon identification task* to disentangle the relative contribution of controlled and automatic processes to participants' judgment of whether an object, shown briefly in a picture, was a gun or a tool. Participants had to make that judgment as quickly as possible. Before the presentation of a given object, a picture of a White or Black male face appeared briefly (200 ms). Guns are categorized more quickly when they are preceded by a Black than a White Face. Also, when participants were given a narrow time frame to respond, they are more likely to mistakenly categorize tools as guns following a Black face. Both of these findings reveal that people tend to associate Black people with guns.

Payne used algebraic *process dissociation procedures* (PDP) to estimate the relative contribution of controlled and automatic processes to these effects. These estimates are achieved by contrasting trials in which automatic (reflecting stereotype-based associations) and controlled processes act in concert with trials in which they operate in opposition. When a correct response is congruent with a presumed automatic tendency (e.g., responding "gun" following a Black prime), automatic and controlled processes act together to produce the response. In contrast, when a correct response is incongruent with an automatic tendency (e.g., responding "tool" following a Black face), automatic and controlled processes act in opposition (i.e., the correct answer requires overriding the automatic association between Black people and guns). Payne calculated separate estimates of automatic and controlled processes by examining the accuracy of participants' performance across congruent (Black-gun) and incongruent (Black-tool) trials. The results showed that racial primes influenced automatic processing but not controlled processing. In other words, performance on the weapons identification task was based on the degree to which people automatically associated Black people with guns, and motivational or other controlled factors could not overcome this effect.

Sherman and his colleagues (Clerkin, Fisher, Sherman, & Teachman, 2014; Conrey et al., 2005; Sherman et al., 2008) have used sophisticated multinomial modeling procedures (Batchelder & Riefer, 1999; Erdfelder, Auer, Hilbig, Assfalg, Moshagen, & Nadarevic, 2009) to further decompose automatic and controlled processes into several interdependent but distinct components. As is depicted in Figure 3.4, Sherman et al.'s *Quad model* identifies four processes that vary in their controllability: activation (AC), detection (D), overcoming bias (OB), and guessing (G).

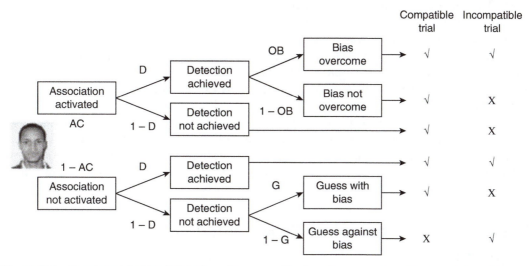

Figure 3.4 Quad model of implicit task performance. Each path represents a likelihood of predicting correct (√) and incorrect (X) responses on compatible and incompatible trials. Parameters reflect activation of biased associations (AC), detection (D), overcoming bias (OB), and guessing (G)

Source: From Allen & Sherman (2011)

Activation (AC) pertains to the degree that an association becomes active in memory upon exposure to a stimulus, and it is typically quite automatic. All else being equal, the stronger the AC component, the more likely the association will influence behavior. Detection (D) represents a more controlled process involving the detection of correct and incorrect responses. As a controlled process, D is affected by motivation and cognitive capacity. However, with consistent practice on a given task, D can become routinized and have features of more automatic processes. Overcoming Bias (OB) is a controlled process representing the likelihood that an activated association or behavioral impulse is overcome and replaced by a contextually appropriate or accurate response. OB comes into play only when an AC is incompatible with an appropriate response based upon D. Like D, OB can become automated with extensive practice. Finally, Guessing (G) describes a general bias to respond when no association is activated and a correct response cannot be identified. This parameter can be meaningless when people guess randomly. However, it can be informative when guessing tendencies are strategically shifted to appear unbiased (e.g., "when I'm unsure, I'll guess 'tool' to avoid stereotypical responding in case the target is Black").

This approach can be used to model performance on any tasks where there exist both compatible trials (where automatic and controlled processes work in coordination) and incompatible trials (where automatic and controlled processes work in opposition). The IAT and the weapon identification task are two such tasks. In Payne's task, AC would describe the degree to which a participant automatically associates guns with Black people. D pertains to the ability to correctly identify the to-be-judged object as being a gun or a tool. OB would be involved when a participant correctly categorizes a tool when it follows a Black face or a gun when it follows a White face. Gonsalkorale, Sherman, Allen, Klauer, and Amodio (2011) showed that the Quad model could be used to understand the role of motivation in performance on the weapon identification task. They analyzed the performance of participants on the task who, based on a previously-completed questionnaire, were known to vary in terms of their motivation to avoid prejudice. Whereas some participants were high in motivation to be unbiased for personal reasons others were not, and Gonsalkorale et al. showed that this difference influenced the degree of AC. Participants who were unmotivated to avoid bias showed stronger Black-gun associations than did motivated participants. The ability to detect a correct response (D) also differed between the groups, with motivated participants having better detection abilities than unmotivated participants. People who were motivated to avoid bias were skilled in monitoring their responses for accuracy. These people presumably have extensive experience at differentiating appropriate from inappropriate responses in situations involving possible race bias, helping them avoid the expression of bias.

Both process dissociation techniques and Quad modeling have proved invaluable in identifying how information processing is affected by controlled and automatic processes in tightly controlled laboratory experiments. We now turn to a question that might resonate more clearly with your daily experience: How do these processes interact within me to determine how I think and resolve inconsistencies?

Automatic and Controlled Processing in Intrapersonal Cognition

There are times when our automatic and controlled processes produce opposing responses. You know you should eat kale because it is nutritious but are put off by its tough texture. You embrace egalitarian values but find yourself fearing a Black man on the subway late at night.

Our automatic and controlled reactions are not always aligned. In particular, automatically activated thoughts often provide content we would rather avoid. What do we do in such cases?

Many dual process models emphasize the use of controlled processes to override, regulate, and redirect undesired cognitions (Baumeister & Bargh, 2014). Fazio's (Fazio & Olson, 2014; Fazio & Towles-Schwen, 1999) MODE model of attitudes, for example, differentiates between *spontaneous* attitudes reflecting immediate, effortless, reflexive evaluations and *deliberate*, reflective attitudes involving the systematic, conscious, and effortful consideration of an object or issue. When an undesired attitude is activated spontaneously, it can be replaced with a more deliberative, desired attitude. However, the process of replacement itself requires both motivation and opportunity to engage in controlled deliberative processes. If a person is fatigued, cognitively overwhelmed, or rushed for time, then judgments will be guided by the automatically-activated attitude, regardless of motivational levels.

Gawronski and Bodenhausen's APE Model (2006, 2007, 2011, 2014a) discusses in detail how associative and propositional processes interact when they produce inconsistent responses. If automatic associations are inconsistent with one another or with activated propositional beliefs, then inconsistencies will have to be resolved to minimize aversive feelings of cognitive dissonance. Consistency can be restored by using propositional logic to identify that an association is invalid (i.e., by deciding that an activated belief is wrong) or by searching for an additional proposition that resolves the inconsistency (Gawronski & Strack, 2004). Interestingly, if dissonance is reduced by intentionally negating the automatic association ("I should NOT associate Arabs with terrorism"), the association has not been eliminated. Implicit assessments will likely continue to reveal the association unless and until it is eliminated or replaced with an alternate positive association (Gawronski, Deutsch, Mbirkou, Seibt, & Strack, 2008). Until that occurs, there likely will exist a dissociation between implicit and explicit judgments (Gawronski, Peters, Brochu, & Strack, 2008).

In McConnell et al.'s SEM (McConnell & Rydell, 2014), inconsistent implicit and explicit evaluations often go unrecognized, at least consciously. Ambivalence can arise if perceivers become aware of the inconsistency, but, if they do not, they often experience a vague sense of unease. These aversive affective responses tend to trigger greater scrutiny of any information that is relevant to the inconsistency. However, because information scrutiny is a conscious, effort-based process, inconsistency-resolution will be guided more strongly by rule-based than associative processes. As a consequence, people will tend to reduce these negative feelings with an overreliance on logic and underutilization of associative inputs.

In sum, a large body of research attests to the contribution of both automatic and controlled processes that contribute to thought and behavior. For a long time, social psychology focused exclusively on the importance of conscious thought. We now know, however, that automatic effects are pervasive. They affect behavior both directly, guiding behavior without our awareness, and indirectly, by guiding, constraining, and interacting with more effortful processes to determine our judgments and actions. These automatic effects govern many aspects of our lives, big and small. We have come a long way from Freud's conceptions of the role of the unconscious. The role of unconscious effects influencing behavior is as prevalent in contemporary thought as it was in Freud's theory, but the characterization of why and how we function automatically is radically different.

The prominence of automatic processes in directing our thoughts and behavior does raise several disturbing questions. First, if behavior can automatically follow from exposure to stimuli, does that imply that our behavior is fixed? Can automatic responses – those perception-behavior links we discussed earlier – be changed? Is automatic behavior at all malleable?

Most fundamentally, do humans have free will? We consider these questions in the following sections.

THE ROLE OF CONSCIOUSNESS

> The list of psychological processes carried out [unconsciously] is so extensive that it raises two questions: What, if anything, cannot be done without awareness? What is consciousness for? (Uleman, 2005, p. 6)

The research we have described in this chapter provides ample documentation that the mind functions in ways of which we are unaware, triggered by events we do not know we are responding to. Our responses are often not the product of intentional, motivated choices. These findings portray the human being as reacting automatically to external stimuli to the extent that behavior seems not to be under the person's volitional control but rather as reflexive and involuntary. Does this suggest that people are mere robots at the mercy of environmental stimuli and that people have minimal ability to exert influence on the course of their behavior and activities?

To draw such a conclusion would be a serious misreading of this research. Recall that automatic responses (perception-behavior links) form as a result of frequent and repeated associations in our past experience. In this way, automaticity represents the mind's efficiency in streamlining the process of getting from perception to behavior, by relying on associations that have formed from past experiences, and in facilitating one's adaptation to a large and complex world. Such behavior can proceed without extensive thought and analysis, thereby preserving cognitive resources for other tasks. In that sense, automaticity is an essential adaptive mechanism of the mind.

Still, the two questions posed by Uleman (2005) in the above quote are important considerations. How pervasive in our thinking, judgment, and behavior are the automatic effects demonstrated in these studies? Furthermore, if these automatic (unintended, nonconscious) influences are pervasive, what role does consciousness play in our functioning? In fact, experts in this domain of work are divided in their thinking and their answers to these questions (Bargh, 2005; Baumeister & Bargh, 2014; Baumeister & Masicampo, 2010; Baumeister, Masicampo, & Vohs, 2011; Custers & Aarts, 2010; Dijksterhuis, 2013; Ferguson & Cone, 2013; Hassin, 2013; Hofmann & Wilson, 2010; Schooler, Mrazek, Baird, & Winkielman, 2015; Wegner, 2005).

As we have seen, research demonstrates that many responses we typically think of as products of conscious thought can be produced automatically, outside of awareness (e.g., Bargh & Pietromonaco, 1982; Bargh, Chen, & Burrows, 1996; Bargh et al., 2001; Chartrand & Bargh, 1996; Chen & Bargh, 1997; Devine, 1989; Dijksterhuis & van Knippenberg, 1998; Levy, 1996; McCulloch et al., 2008). These demonstrations of automatic functioning document that nonconscious effects *can* directly influence behavior. What the research has not yet adequately addressed is the question of *how much* behavior is driven by automatic processes. That is, the outcomes we have described – trait effects on judgments, effects of goal activation on the pursuit of goal achievement, effects of stereotypes on judgment and behavior – can occur either automatically or as a result of conscious, deliberative processing. So, in fact, there are two potential routes to the same outcome. The issue posed here is, which of these routes is more prevalent in our everyday functioning? Also, what determines which course is operative and more impactful at any given time?

The answers to these questions simply are not fully known at present. This has not prevented some writers from making bold statements on the matter. On the one hand, Bargh (1997) has stated that "there is ultimately no future for conscious processing accounts of the mind, in the sense of free will and choice" (p. 52). On the other hand, Kihlstrom (2008) has argued that "the irony in the popularity of automaticity is that there is no empirical evidence to support the proposition that social behavior is exclusively, or even predominantly, determined by automatic processes" (p. 596). At the moment, we can only be sure of one thing: the debate will continue and will constitute an important item on the agenda for future research.

Uleman's second question concerns the role of consciousness in cognitive functioning. The extensive literature on automaticity seems to suggest that much of our behavior is driven by nonconscious processing. In this view of human cognition, important questions arise regarding the extent to which conscious thought is necessary for and controls human action. Some have questioned the role of conscious motivation in directing the flow of one's behavior (e.g., Bargh, 2005; Dijksterhuis, 2013; Dijksterhuis & Nordgren, 2006; Ferguson & Cone, 2013; Hassin, 2013; Wegner, 2005). Other writers (e.g., Baumeister & Masicampo, 2010; Baumeister et al., 2011) have proposed that conscious thought serves important functions that automatic responses cannot. For example, although Baumeister and Masicampo (2010) do not question the importance of unconscious processes in guiding immediate behavior, they argue that consciousness uses the products of automatic processing for uniquely human activity, suggesting an interplay between automatic and conscious processing (as we discussed in a previous section). In their view, consciousness is crucially involved in generating sequences of thoughts (some of which may have been automatically activated), in producing simulations of possible outcomes (both future outcomes and alternative past outcomes) that play important roles in planning and reasoning, and in communicating the products of these mental activities with others as a basis for social life and the development of culture. Moreover, if unconscious (automatic) responses are the product of well-learned associations that develop through repeated activations, then processing new information, creating novel sequences of thoughts, prioritizing multiple goals, and planning an unknown future would seem to require conscious thought and analysis. The emphasis here is not on whether behavior is driven by unconscious or conscious processing but rather on the *mutual and intersecting roles* of these two modes of functioning (Baumeister & Bargh, 2014).

These are complex yet fundamental issues regarding the relations between conscious and nonconscious experience and the role of each type of process in human cognition. Current research is providing insights into the complexities of and the relations between the automatic and the deliberative aspects of cognitive functioning, offering a better understanding of the roles of the conscious and nonconscious aspects of human experience.

AUTOMATIC PROCESSES IN UNDERSTANDING THE SELF, PERSONS, AND GROUPS

In this chapter, we have summarized research demonstrating the role and impact of automatic processes in a variety of social contexts. In this section, we explore the implications of nonconscious processing in three important domains: understanding the self, understanding persons, and understanding groups.

Automatic Processes in Understanding the Self

One of the first studies showing automatic effects in social information processing (Bargh, 1982) demonstrated that people automatically attend to *self-relevant* information. Participants in this experiment were given a task in which different words were fed to different ears through headphones. In one ear, they heard a series of nouns spoken at constant intervals; in the other ear, the words were adjectives. Importantly, based on earlier pretesting, some of those adjectives were known to be self-descriptive. Participants were instructed to attend to one ear and to ignore the other, such that half of them attended to the nouns and the other half to the adjectives. Their task was to orally repeat each word presented to the attended ear (called "shadowing"). Later, they were given a test in which words were presented on a computer screen, and their task was to indicate whether they had heard that word or not. Their response times to these probes were recorded.

The idea guiding the study was that self-relevant traits might automatically capture one's attention. How would that affect performance in this study? Consider each condition of the experiment. If one's attention is focused on the ear receiving adjectives, including self-descriptive traits, then automatic attention to that information would facilitate performance, resulting in fast reaction times to indicate that a word had been presented. Now consider people who focused on the ear receiving nouns. Although that was supposed to be their primary focus, the adjectives were still being presented to the other ear, and some of those adjectives were self-descriptive traits. Automatic attention to those traits would draw attention away from the focus on the nouns, and this disruption would have the effect of slowing one's response times to noun words. This is, in fact, what the results showed. Attention was automatically drawn to the self-descriptive information, harming performance on the primary task in that condition. Other studies using different methodologies have also shown that self-relevant information receives advantaged processing (Alexopoulos, Muller, Ric, & Marendaz, 2012; Gray, Ambady, Lowenthal, & Deldin, 2004; Pfister, Pohl, Kiesel, & Kunde, 2012).

Being automatically attentive to self-relevant information is important, but do such effects extend to other aspects of self-perception? A person's sense of self – of who she is, of her self-worth – is an integral part of any person's individuality, and as we all have experienced, it can fluctuate in response to events that happen in our daily lives. Sometimes events occur that make us feel great; other times, we experience real disappointments. Often, we are acutely aware of those effects on how we feel about ourselves. Research has shown, however, that events can nevertheless automatically influence our own self-concepts even when we do not consciously experience them.

Baldwin, Carrell, and Lopez (1990) conducted two studies demonstrating this effect. Participants in the first study were graduate students in social psychology at the University of Michigan. Their first task was to write down the three most important ideas they were currently pursuing in their research (there are few things in life more important to grad students than their research ideas!). The next part of the experiment consisted of a series of trials. On each trial, one of those research ideas was presented on a computer screen, and participants evaluated the idea by marking a scale. Unbeknownst to them, each trial was preceded by a subliminal presentation of a picture of a face. On one trial, the picture showed the scowling, disapproving face of Robert Zajonc, an influential and highly esteemed social psychologist who was also the head of the students' graduate program. On another trial, the picture showed the smiling face of a postdoctoral fellow. These pictures were exposed for a very brief time (2 ms), so participants never had any conscious awareness of what was being presented. The question investigated in this study was whether the subliminal presentation of the frowning face of an influential figure in the participants' lives would affect their evaluations of their own research ideas. In fact, participants rated the research idea preceded by Zajonc's disapproving face more negatively than the idea that followed the smiling face of the postdoctoral student. Thus, stimuli that were not consciously experienced but that conveyed disapproval from an important authority figure significantly influenced participants' own self-evaluations.

There are a couple of possible explanations of this effect. One possibility was that the impact of the frowning face was due to an overall evaluation effect, in that people do not like being exposed to negative information that can, in turn, color their overall affective state and sense of self-worth. A second possibility was that the effect was more specific, occurring because the disapproving face was that of an immensely influential figure in the students' lives. To disentangle these two possibilities, Baldwin et al. (1990) conducted a second study.

Participants in this study were female students at a Roman Catholic college who were given passages from some stories to read, one of which described a sexual dream with enough detail to convey a permissive attitude toward sexuality. They then were exposed to some very fast flashes on a screen and, after that, completed a questionnaire measuring their self-concept and self-evaluations. The critical manipulation in the study regards those flashes. They were, in fact, either the frowning face of the Pope (a very significant figure to these Catholic students) or the frowning face of Robert Zajonc, who was an unfamiliar person of no particular personal significance for these students. If the results of the first study were due to an overall evaluative effect, both of these stimuli should have the same impact on students' self-evaluations. In contrast, if the effect was due to the personal relevance of the frowning authority figure, then only those exposed to the Pope's disapproving face should have lowered self-evaluations. The results showed that the Pope's face indeed had a more significant impact, and this effect was most substantial among those students who indicated (on a questionnaire) that they were practicing Catholics, for whom the Pope would therefore clearly be a prominent figure. *Self-evaluation* was affected by the unconscious activation of self-relevant, significant others.

Automatic processes also play a central role in *self-regulation*. All of us, at one time or another, have had concerns about our own difficult behavior patterns and of having to cope with their adverse effects. Conscious awareness of bad dietary practices, problems completing schoolwork, or dependence on a substance all can inexorably lead to heightened self-evaluation (Duval & Wicklund, 1972; Silvia & Duval, 2001; Silvia & Phillips, 2013). Focusing attention on the self can have cognitive, motivational, and affective consequences, including producing a determination to overcome the problems that are at the source of our difficulties. The issue then is whether we can make our thoughts, feelings, and behaviors conform to our standards.

Traditionally, self-regulation was considered to operate under conscious control and through effortful processes. Attaining self-regulation was viewed as requiring setting and achieving goals, and accordingly, many programs for training self-management strategies have been established. Contemporary research has shown, however, that many aspects of goal setting and attainment can operate automatically (Bargh & Chartrand, 1999; Bargh & Ferguson, 2000; Forster & Jostmann, 2012; Palfai, 2004).

Earlier in this chapter, we presented research demonstrating that the primary characteristics of goals and their functioning can be activated and implemented at an automatic level (Bargh et al., 2001). A series of studies showed that subliminally priming a performance goal improved performance, enhanced persistence toward task completion, and increased motivation to complete an interrupted task. Thus, the major aspects of achieving a goal can operate without effort, intention, or awareness. However, overcoming harmful and destructive habits typically involves not merely pursuing a goal but also contending with competing goals, distractions, and conflicting goals (e.g., going to the refrigerator too often or succumbing to addiction). Evidence indicates, however, that automatic processes can inhibit competing goals. For example, one study (Shah, Friedman, & Kruglanski, 2002) found that subliminally priming words representing goals people intended to pursue slowed reaction times to a task involving a competing goal. Thus, the mere activation of a goal can automatically suppress the accessibility of potentially interfering goals.

Likely, many of the strategies for achieving goals and contending with goal conflicts involve a combination of controlled and automatic effects (Forster & Jostmann, 2012). However, this evidence documents a potentially important role of automatic processes in efforts to self-regulate behavior under challenging circumstances (Palfai, 2004).

Automatic Processes in Understanding Persons

In Chapter 2, we described research on priming by Srull and Wyer (1979) in which the concept of hostility was either frequently or infrequently primed. This frequency of priming manipulation influenced participants' later interpretations of a paragraph describing a stimulus person, such that the person was rated as being more hostile in the high than in the low-frequency condition. The results showed that the frequency of activation of a concept (hostility) can influence impressions on a subsequent, totally unrelated task.

Bargh and Pietromonaco (1982) tested whether similar effects would occur when primes were presented subliminally, outside of conscious awareness. Participants were instructed to watch for flashes on a screen and to press a button as soon as they saw one. Those flashes were words, presented too fast to be detected as words, but either few or most of those words reflected hostility (*hostile, unkind, inconsiderate, hurt, punch*). Participants then read the same passage used by Srull and Wyer, describing a stimulus person that included ambiguous information that could be interpreted as hostile. They then rated the person on a series of trait scales, some of which pertained to hostility. The results (displayed in Table 3.2) showed that the higher the proportion of hostile words to which participants were exposed, the more negatively they rated the stimulus person. These findings indicate that priming effects – the effects of recent experience on subsequent processing – can occur automatically, outside of the perceiver's awareness.

Table 3.2 Mean hostility ratings as a function of percentage of hostile words presented in vigilance task

Trait type	Hostile primes		
	0%	20%	80%
Hostile-unrelated	4.95	5.77	5.94
Hostile-related	6.99	6.78	7.47

Source: Adapted from Bargh & Pietromonaco (1982)

Primes can also affect the automatic organization of information. Hamilton et al. (1980) had participants read a series of behavior-descriptive sentences to either form an impression of a person described in those sentences or to remember as many of the sentences as they could. They found that impression condition participants recalled more of those behaviors than did memory condition participants. Furthermore, participants in the impression condition organized information about different traits into clusters for storage in memory, whereas memory condition participants did not. Later research (Chartrand & Bargh, 1996) demonstrated that similar effects can occur automatically, without participants being consciously engaged in a processing task. Participants in this study were subliminally primed with either an impression formation goal (using stimulus words like *personality, evaluate, impression, opinion*) or a memorization goal (stimulus words included *absorb, remember, retain, memory*). As in Hamilton et al.'s experiment, participants in these two processing goal conditions read a series of behavior-descriptive sentences and were later asked to recall as many of those sentences as they could. Recall protocols were scored for the amount recalled and for the extent of trait-based clustering. Chartrand and Bargh's results closely replicated Hamilton et al.'s findings, using a nonconscious priming procedure to activate processing goals.

Just as we have processing goals that can be activated without awareness, we also hold goals relevant to relationships with romantic partners, family members, close friends, and room-mates. Those interpersonal goals might include intentions to help the partner, to maintain the relationship, and to avoid its dissolution (e.g., caring for, supporting, communicating with, and having fun with the relationship partner). When those goals are activated, they can influence the person's perceptions and behaviors within the relationship. Moreover, they might extend into perceptions and behaviors in other contexts not involving the relationship partner.

Fitzsimons and Bargh (2003; see also Kraus & Chen, 2009; Shah, 2003) proposed that relationship goals also can be activated and pursued automatically, outside of the person's awareness. In a series of studies, these researchers primed a meaningful relationship (with a close friend or mother) or another relationship (with a co-worker or stranger) to determine the subsequent influence of this activation on a range of perceptions and behaviors unrelated to the priming context. For example, in one study, those who had a "friend" primed were more likely to volunteer to help on an additional task after the conclusion of the experiment than were par-ticipants in a "co-worker" prime condition. The "friend" prime activated the goal of helping (which is part of the relationship schema), which in turn resulted in greater willingness to help in a context unrelated to the relationship.

In another study, the first part of the procedure involved priming either one's mother or best friend. Fitzsimons and Bargh (2003) reasoned that the "mother" prime would activate the goal of making one's mother proud by one's success. Would the activation of this goal carry over to influence processing in another situation? To test this possibility, all participants read a vignette describing a college student whose school performance was somewhat mixed, doing very well in some courses and more poorly in others. Those in the "mother" prime condition rated the student as being more motivated to succeed and do well in school, compared to participants in the "best friend" condition. Thus, nonconsciously activating a goal associated with a close relationship (mother) influenced participants' perceptions of the fictional character's motivation and effort to succeed in college.

These studies show that automatic processes influence how we form impressions and make judgments of individuals. A related issue is whether and how automatic processes are involved in *changing* impressions, particularly if they are *implicit impressions*, formed and held without awareness (Uleman, Blader, & Todorov, 2005). As we have already discussed, such impressions might be difficult to change in response to new information, given that they reflect associations that have accumulated slowly over time (McConnell & Rydell, 2014; Rydell & McConnell, 2006). Prevailing views of implicit cognition suggest that if an implicit impression is not cor-rected through effortful rule-based (McConnell & Rydell, 2014) or propositional (Gawronski & Bodenhausen, 2014b) processes, it might continue to guide interpersonal judgment and behav-ior even when new information indicates it is wrong.

However, several lines of research show that implicit impressions can be changed rapidly, at least in some circumstances. One way that implicit impressions can change in response to new information is when the perceiver is prompted to *reinterpret* existing beliefs. In Wyer (2010), participants were asked to form an impression of a man based on a photograph and information provided about him. There were four phases in the experiment. In phase one, par-ticipants viewed a photograph of a bald man named Edward, who was described as being either a "skinhead" or a cancer patient undergoing chemotherapy. In phase two, half of the partici-pants received no additional information (control condition), whereas the other participants were given behavioral information that was vague (evidence condition). For example, they were told he was inattentive when interacting with others. This could be interpreted as indicating rudeness (consistent with the skinhead stereotype) or as evidence that he was not feeling well (consistent with his status as a cancer patient). In phase three, all participants were told to imagine that they later met a friend who informed them that the man was undergoing cancer treatment, causing him to lose his hair. This was a change in category information for half of the participants (i.e., those who had been told he was a skinhead). Finally, in phase four, half of the participants who had been provided evidence about Edward were asked to re-read all of the information they had previously received. All participants then completed an implicit (an IAT assessing the strength of association between Edward and hostility) and an explicit (self-report trait ratings of Edward's hostility) measure to assess their impressions of Edward (who was believed by all participants at this point to be a cancer patient).

The central focus of this study was whether implicit and explicit evaluations would shift equivalently in response to information that should have changed initial impressions of Edward (i.e., among participants originally told that he was a skinhead but later learned he was also undergoing cancer treatments). The manipulation in phase four was to determine whether this new information alone would cause a shift in impressions or whether participants would have to re-engage with previously presented information to reinterpret it.

There were several notable findings. First, explicit impressions did not differ based on whether beliefs about Edward's social category had changed or remained constant. They appeared to judge Edward based on what was currently known about him. Second, a different pattern emerged on the implicit measure. Edward continued to be strongly associated implicitly with hostility among participants who had initially been told he was a skinhead and then were given behavioral evidence. Third, having participants review the behavioral evidence attenuated this effect. Being allowed to reinterpret Edward's behavior in light of new information reduced the implicit impression that he was hostile.

Other studies have confirmed the importance of reinterpretation in changing implicit impressions (Mann & Ferguson, 2015, 2017). In addition to reinterpretation, two other factors have been shown to support the rapid updating of implicit impressions (Ferguson, Mann, Cone, & Shen, 2019). Highly diagnostic information about a person can instantly change both implicit and explicit impressions. Participants who had been given 100 descriptions of a man's desirable behaviors and then told that he had been "convicted for mutilating a small, defenseless animal" dramatically shifted impressions assessed with both implicit and implicit measures (Cone & Ferguson, 2015; see also Shen, Mann, & Ferguson, 2020). Highly believable information is also more likely to produce a change in implicit evaluations (Cone, Flaharty, & Ferguson, 2019; Cone, Mann, & Ferguson, 2017).

In sum, research in social cognition traditionally focused on explicit judgments of individuals under the assumption that effortful processes are integral in dynamic impression formation processes. Although evidence of the dynamic nature of impression formation has continued to accumulate, it has also become clear that many processes involved in understanding others are automatically triggered by features of situations and produce impressions of which we are unaware. Many of our thoughts and evaluations about other people are inaccessible to conscious awareness.

Automatic Processes in Understanding Groups

Automatic processes can also play an essential role in processing information about groups and about group members. Paralleling the effects of activation of trait and goal concepts, activation of a stereotype has automatic effects on judgment and behavior. In fact, the role of automaticity in stereotyping and intergroup perception has been extensively investigated. We now explore several aspects of that research.

Automatic Associations

Stereotypes contain a person's "knowledge, beliefs, and expectancies about a social group" (Hamilton & Trolier, 1986, p. 133). For many years, researchers studied stereotypes as consisting of those attributes most commonly associated with a particular group, that is, the attributes that typically "come to mind" when thinking about or perceiving a group or group members (Brigham, 1971; Hamilton et al., 1994). In the language we have been using, those attributes are associations, and in this chapter, we have seen that associations can become automatically activated under certain conditions. The same principle applies to stereotypic associations.

In one study demonstrating this finding (Dovidio, Evans, & Tyler, 1986), a priming paradigm was used where, on each trial, a racial category prime (Black, White) was paired with a trait adjective. The trait adjectives were positive and negative traits that were stereotypic of Black or White people. For each category-trait pair, participants had to indicate if the trait could "ever be true" of the group or if it was "always false" of the group. Their response times were recorded. Participants responded faster when Black primes were paired with negative traits and when White primes were paired with positive traits. Also, Black primes produced faster responses to stereotypically Black traits, whereas White primes facilitated responses to stereotypically White traits. These fast response times reflect instances in which the race primes automatically activated the trait content. Other studies have demonstrated similar automatic effects in stereotyping, including race (Gaertner & McLaughlin, 1983), gender (Banaji & Hardin, 1996; Banaji, Hardin, & Rothman, 1993), and age (Perdue & Gurtman, 1990) categories.

The theoretical catalyst for much of this work was an important paper by Devine (1989), who was among the first to propose that stereotypes of African Americans are automatically activated. She argued that White Americans, because of the culture in which they have been socialized, have frequently and continuously been exposed to the traditional American stereotype of Black people. These pernicious stereotypes characterize Blacks as lazy, unintelligent, aggressive, athletic, and musical (Devine & Elliot, 1995; Gilbert, 1951; Karlins et al., 1969; Katz & Braly, 1933). As we have seen, concepts that are frequently and repetitively associated can become linked and automatically activated. Therefore, Devine (1989) argued that, once this link has been formed, the mere exposure to Black people in any way (interaction with, reference to them as a group, portrayal of Black people in the media) is sufficient to automatically and subconsciously bring to mind attributes that are stereotypically associated with this group.

In support of these ideas, Devine (1989) showed that subliminal priming of stereotype-related terms influenced participants' evaluations of an unknown person, of unspecified race, in a subsequent and seemingly unrelated study. In one condition of the study, words such as lazy, dirty, and ghetto were flashed on a screen at speeds too fast to be consciously detected. In another condition, such words were not presented. Later, in what was described as a separate study on impression formation, participants read an ambiguous passage about a man named Donald, whose race was not mentioned. The information describing Donald suggested (but did not state) that he might have hostile tendencies, and participants rated Donald on a series of attributes, some of which were related to hostility. Those whose stereotypes had been subliminally primed rated Donald as more hostile than did participants in the condition that had not been primed with the stereotype-related words. These results showed that stereotypes can be automatically activated, able to influence perceptions on a subsequent task.

Devine (1989) further proposed that, because of their shared cultural experience, this automatic activation was true of persons both high and low in prejudice. In fact, participants in this experiment completed a questionnaire measure of racial attitudes, and analyses showed that both those who were high and those who were low in prejudice showed the same automatic priming effect. What differentiated these two groups was a second, personal belief system about Black people. Whereas high prejudice persons might subscribe to the cultural stereotype of Black, low prejudice persons do not. Therefore, low prejudice persons must overcome the automatic activation of the cultural stereotype and use their more egalitarian beliefs in their judgments of persons. They need to override the automatically-activated stereotypical associations, which Devine argued is comparable to breaking a bad habit. This latter process, however, is a conscious, intentional, controlled, effortful process.

Devine's (1989) theory was intriguing, provocative, and well-grounded in research. It was also controversial. For example, not everyone accepted her proposal that all White Americans, because they have lived in the same culture, share a common stereotype of Black Americans based on traditional views of that group. Also, the notion that because of people's frequent exposure to that cultural stereotype, it becomes automatically activated in both high and low prejudiced persons, was not widely accepted. Finally, others were not convinced by the idea that the difference between high and low prejudiced persons resides not in their automatic stereotypes but in their personal beliefs and in their motivation to control the automatic activation of the stereotype.

Not surprisingly, the theory stimulated a great deal of research pursuing her ideas, some of which showed that some aspects of Devine's theory needed to be qualified. For example, the idea that automatic stereotype activation is equally likely for high and low prejudice persons has not been supported (Blair, 2002; Fazio, Jackson, Dunton, & Williams, 1995). Also, the extent and nature of stereotype activation can vary depending on the social context in which Black people are seen (e.g., in a church vs. on an urban street corner; Barden, Maddux, Petty, & Brewer, 2004; Casper, Rothermund, & Wentura, 2010; Wittenbrink, Judd, & Park 2001), and stereotype activation may not always translate into stereotype use (Fein & Spencer, 1997; Gilbert & Hixon, 1991; Krieglmeyer & Sherman, 2012). Nevertheless, a considerable body of research has supported Devine's primary proposal that stereotypes can be automatically activated and, through that activation, can influence later processing on seemingly unrelated tasks (Devine & Sharp, 2009).

Earlier, we described an evaluative priming paradigm (Fazio et al., 1986) that can assess the automatic effects of priming on evaluation. Fazio et al. (1995) applied this method to detect individual differences in automatically activated racial attitudes. In the study, priming stimuli (Black or White faces) were immediately followed by positive adjectives (*wonderful, attractive*) or negative adjectives (*disgusting, annoying*). Participants had to indicate, as quickly as possible, whether each adjective was positive or negative. Faster response times reflect the automatic effect of the prime on the evaluative response. Results showed that responses to negative (compared to positive) adjectives were faster when they were preceded by Black than by White faces, demonstrating the automatic effect of negative attitudes toward Black people. Differences among participants in the strength of this effect were correlated with indicators of prejudicial responding to other measures. This variation among participants called into question Devine's (1989) assumption that all people share an automatically activated cultural stereotype of Black people.

The automatic activation of stereotypes can function in more subtle ways, as well. Bargh et al. (1996) had college-age participants come to a laboratory and had them complete a "language test" that required them to create sentences from sets of words. They were given five words, and their task was to select four of those words that make a sentence. In one condition, a high proportion of the word sets included words such as retired, forgetful, Florida, or old. Using these words necessarily resulted in sentences that pertained to the elderly. In the other condition, the words did not relate to this group. This sentence construction task was designed to activate the stereotype of the elderly in one condition but not in the other. When they had completed this task, the experiment presumably was over, so participants exited the lab room and walked to the elevator. In the hallway was an experimental assistant who unobtrusively used a stopwatch to record the number of seconds it took the participants to walk from the lab room to the elevator. Those who had had the elderly stereotype activated took significantly longer to walk that distance than people in the control condition. In other words, unobtrusive activation of the stereotype of older people significantly influenced the walking speed (slower) of the participants as they left the experiment. Thus, the automatic activation of a stereotype not only can influence judgments and evaluations but also can directly affect simple motor behavior, such as walking speed, in a manner consistent with the content of the stereotype. Although this study is not without its critics (Doyen et al., 2012), several successful conceptual replications have been reported (Aarts & Dijksterhuis, 2002; Cesario, Plaks, & Higgins, 2006; Dijksterhuis, Spears, & Lépinasse, 2001; Kawakami, Young, & Dovidio, 2002; Ku, Wang, & Galinsky, 2010; Payne, Brown-Iannuzzi, & Loersch, 2016).

Can such priming automatically influence more complex behaviors as well? This question was investigated by Dijksterhuis and van Knippenberg (1998; see Bry, Follenfant, & Meyer, 2008; Galinsky, Wang, & Ku, 2008; Hansen & Wänke, 2009; Lowery, Eisenberger, Hardin, & Sinclair, 2007; Nussinson, Seibt, Häfner, & Strack, 2010; but also see O'Donnell et al., 2018). Their experiment comprised two parts. The first part was a priming phase, during which participants were asked to think about a typical professor or a typical secretary and to list their typical behaviors, lifestyle, and attributes. This phase was designed to activate one stereotype or the other. In a third condition, participants did not complete any such materials. When they had concluded that task, participants were given a general knowledge test, consisting of 42 difficult items from the game Trivial Pursuit. As can be seen in Table 3.3, people who had spent time listing the typical attributes of a professor got more of the Trivial Pursuit items correct than did people for whom the stereotype of secretaries had been activated. The subtle activation of a stereotype influenced participants' performance on a challenging cognitive task.

Table 3.3 Percent correct answers on Trivial Pursuit task

Condition	Mean % correct
No prime	49.9
Professor	59.5
Secretary	46.4

Source: Adapted from Dijksterhuis & van Knippenberg (1998)

Other research demonstrates that these gains in intellectual performance from priming effects are not limited to bright young college students. Levy and her colleagues (Levy, 1996; Levy, Ashman, & Dror, 2000) studied the effects of activating self-stereotypes, some of which are not flattering, on performance. *Self-stereotyping* is when a person accepts beliefs associated with the stereotype of his or her own group as being true of the self. Levy (1996) examined whether positive and negative self-stereotypes could be activated without awareness, and if so, would those stereotypes influence behavior. Specifically, she tested these ideas as manifested in the relation between aging and memory. It is widely believed (even among the elderly) that memory deteriorates with advanced age. What would be the effect of subliminally priming different concepts related to age on people's performance on difficult memory tasks? Levy's participants were men and women ranging in age from 60 to 90 years (mean age = 73). Participants were subliminally primed with a set of words that conveyed a positive or negative stereotype of the elderly (e.g., for the negative condition, *old, senile, forgets, confused*; for the positive condition, *wise, senior, learned, insightful*). These words were flashed on a computer screen so quickly that participants merely saw a blurred spot on the screen; their task was to indicate whether the flash appeared in the top or bottom half of the screen.

Both before and after this priming task, all participants completed a series of challenging memory tests. Levy (1996) found that people who were given the negative prime words (e.g., *senile*) produced lower performance after, compared to before, the primes. In contrast, those who were presented with the positive prime words (e.g., *wise*) produced higher memory scores after, compared to before, the prime presentation. Thus, self-stereotypes associated with old age can be subliminally primed in older adults without their awareness and, once activated, these stereotypes can influence actual memory performance on a variety of memory tasks. In other studies, priming of positive age stereotypes resulted in reduced cardiovascular response to stress and enhanced physical performance that improved over an 8-week period (Levy, Hausdorff, Hencke, & Wei, 2000; Levy, Pilver, Chung, & Slade, 2014).

Automaticity and Control

Given all of the evidence for automatic responding we have reviewed in this chapter, the question naturally arises whether such automatic effects are inevitable. More specifically for our concerns in this subsection, are stereotypic beliefs and prejudicial attitudes *always* activated by group stimuli, leading to stereotypic and prejudicial responses to those groups and their members? Is there no way of contending with these automatic effects on intergroup perceptions and evaluations? Are there ways these effects can be prevented or overcome? Several possible avenues of avoiding or overriding automatic effects have been investigated (Blair, 2002; Dasgupta, 2009).

Replacement

Devine's (1989) original theory included a mechanism specifically for this purpose. Recall that her theory argued that all persons, regardless of their prejudice level, have acquired through social learning the cultural stereotype of Black people, and, due to its frequent use, that stereotype is automatically activated. Responding in accord with that stereotype is unacceptable to low-prejudice persons, so they consciously and intentionally activate their more egalitarian personal belief system to guide their responses. Overriding an automatically activated association would seem to be challenging, and research has shown that it is. For example, one strategy (Kawakami, Dovidio, Moll, Hermsen, & Russin, 2000) involved extensive training in which participants were shown faces of members of a stereotyped group accompanied by descriptors. Their task was to respond "No" if the descriptor was stereotypic or "Yes" if it was a non-stereotypic descriptor. The training did reduce automatic bias, although such training may not be practical in everyday life contexts.

Monteith and her colleagues (Devine & Monteith, 1993; Monteith, 1993; Monteith & Mark, 2005; Monteith & Voils, 1998; Monteith, Ashburn-Nardo, Voils, & Czopp, 2002; Monteith, Woodcock, & Gulker, 2013) have systematically investigated the processes involved in overcoming automatic activation of prejudicial tendencies. Following from Devine's (1989) model, Monteith's Self-Regulation of Prejudice Model has focused on people low in prejudice who would be motivated to override automatically activated thoughts. These people would be aware of the discrepancies between their "natural" biased inclination and their egalitarian standards, and these discrepancies would induce feelings of discomfort, self-disappointment, and guilt. Those affective reactions then activate an inhibition system that increases attention and arousal, which leads to the formation of associations between one's prejudicial response and resulting negative affect with external stimuli for the prejudicial response. Those associations can then provide "cues for control" that, in future contexts, would signal situations in which prejudicial responses might occur. Given those cues, the person can then engage processes for controlling and limiting potentially biased responses in new contexts.

Research has provided support for many aspects of this model (Devine, Forscher, Austin, & Cox, 2012; Monteith & Mark, 2005; Monteith et al., 2013). This approach is limited by its focus on people who are low in prejudice and who are motivated to avoid or override automatically activated prejudicial responses. These factors would not, of course, be true of all people (e.g., those who are high in prejudice). Also, the processes at the core of the model require conscious attention to overcome responses that do not require attention (because they are automatic), a potential limitation on the generalizability of this approach.

Positive Exemplars

Other research has taken a different approach to testing the malleability of automatic attitudes. In one study (Dasgupta & Greenwald, 2001), participants were shown photos of several well-known Black and White individuals, and their first task was to identify the person seen in each picture. One group of the participants (pro-Black condition) was shown photos of admired Black persons (e.g., Denzel Washington, Colin Powell) and disliked White persons (e.g., serial killer Charles Manson, gangster Al Capone); a second group (pro-White condition) was shown pictures of disliked Black persons (e.g., Nation of Islam leader and anti-Semitist Louis Farrakhan, suspended boxer Mike Tyson) and admired White figures (Tom Hanks, Robert Redford). A third (control) group was shown nonracial stimuli. After finishing this task, all participants completed measures of racial attitudes, both an implicit measure that assesses automatic associations (the race IAT; Greenwald et al., 1998) and explicit measures of those attitudes, rating each racial group on rating scales (e.g., good–bad, honest–dishonest, pleasant–unpleasant).

The question of interest was whether the exposure to admired or disliked Black and White persons would influence the favorability of their attitudes toward these groups. Results showed that it did. On the IAT, the magnitude of White preference was significantly smaller after exposure to pro-Black exemplars compared to when they had seen the pro-White exemplars. Thus, being shown several examples of well-known figures that contradicted stereotypic expectations reduced the amount of automatic prejudice manifested on the IAT. The participants returned 24 hours later, and their attitudes were assessed again to investigate the stability of these differences. Results from this second session were the same as those from the first assessment, demonstrating that the effect of the manipulation persisted in the second session. These beneficial effects of exposure to positive exemplars have been demonstrated in other studies as well (Blair, Ma, & Lenton, 2001; Dasgupta & Asgari, 2004; Dasgupta & Rivera, 2008).

Suppression

It may occur to you that people could simply monitor their reactions to outgroup stimuli and suppress any inherent desire or inclination to respond in a stereotypical or prejudicial manner. If Nike advertisements can advocate "Just do it," maybe the mind can say "Just don't." Exercise mind control, and don't let yourself think that that member of Group G is "Xish." As plausible as that plan may seem, it usually does not work. You may be able to suppress that thought initially, but research shows that it has unexpected downstream consequences. In essence, the suppressed thought becomes even more accessible than if it had not previously been suppressed! This outcome became known as a *rebound effect* (Wegner, 1994; Wegner & Erber, 1992; Wegner, Schneider, Carter, & White, 1987).

The importance of this rebound effect for stereotyping has been demonstrated in several studies (Macrae, Bodenhausen, Milne, & Jetten, 1994). Participants were told they would write a story about a day in the life of a person shown in a photograph they would be given. Half of the participants were forewarned that impressions can be biased by stereotypes and were instructed not to use stereotypes about the person's group in their story. The other half were not given that instruction. All participants were then handed a photograph of a skinhead. The passages participants wrote were coded for how much stereotype content was included in them. Participants were then shown a photo of a different skinhead and were again asked to write a passage about a day in the life of this person. This time neither group received any instructions about avoiding the use of stereotypes. Again, their passages were coded for stereotype content. Analyses of the coded content were revealing. For the first passage, the group told to suppress their stereotypes were able to avoid stereotyping; they included far less stereotypic content in their stories about the skinhead than did those who did not receive that instruction. In the second story, however, the outcome was quite different. Those in the suppress condition included *significantly more* stereotypic descriptors than did those in the no instruction condition. In other words, suppressing the stereotype on the first story produced a rebound effect: participants not only used the stereotype in the second story but actually exceeded the other group in the amount of stereotypic content in their passages. Intentionally suppressing stereotype use had the effect of making the stereotype more accessible. Another study (Macrae, Bodenhausen, Milne, & Jetten, 1994) showed that people in a suppression condition (compared to a no-suppression control group) kept a greater interpersonal distance from the skinhead, again suggesting that suppression can have counterproductive effects.

Why does this rebound effect occur? One possible explanation is that during suppression, one would distract oneself from unwanted thoughts (the stereotype of skinheads) by focusing on distracting stimuli. In doing so, associations may form between these distractors and the unwanted content. When encountered later after suppression effort has ceased, these distractors then serve as retrieval cues for the unwanted thoughts, thereby producing the rebound effect. Follow-up studies (Macrae, Milne, & Bodenhausen, 1994), in fact, showed that the suppression task makes stereotypic information more accessible in memory (easier to retrieve quickly).

In everyday life, it is not often that someone explicitly instructs another person to suppress any inclination to use a stereotype. However, there may be social contexts in which the use of certain stereotypes is not appropriate. For example, social norms may inhibit the use of some stereotypes. In England, where the Macrae, Milne and Bodenhausen (1994) research was done, the use of the skinhead stereotype was acceptable and openly employed in conversations. In contemporary American culture, stereotyping of African Americans is usually met with disapproval, so people avoid its use. That is, persons spontaneously suppress the stereotype. Would such spontaneous suppression be effective, and would it persist longer than explicit suppression, thereby eliminating the rebound effect?

To answer these questions, Wyer, Sherman, and Stroessner (1998, 2000) implemented some modifications to Macrae et al.'s paradigm. Participants were told they would write about a typical day in the life of a person whose photo they would be shown. The target person was a Black male. Participants in the directed suppression condition were instructed to avoid using the stereotype of African Americans in writing their stories. Those in the spontaneous suppression condition were told that the study was being conducted by a political group called African Americans for Intercultural Understanding. This title was designed to make race salient and to induce participants to suppress the use of the stereotype spontaneously. Those in the control condition were not given either of these instructions. After completing this phase, participants were given a different task, forming an impression of a target person described in a passage that included several ambiguous behaviors that could be interpreted as hostile, a trait associated with the African American stereotype. Participants then rated this person on a series of attributes, some of which were related to hostility (e.g., hostile, unfriendly, dislikable).

Analyses showed that participants in both the direct suppression and the spontaneous suppression conditions (but not those in the control condition) did suppress the use of the stereotype in their stories about a day in the life of the Black male shown in the photograph. So, the suppression of stereotype use can be induced when social norms are salient. The critical question was whether spontaneous suppression would also lead to a rebound effect, which would be evident in ratings of the target person they read about. Participants' ratings of the person on hostility-related traits were significantly higher in both suppression conditions (compared to the control condition), indicating that even spontaneous suppression can make the stereotype more accessible and produce rebound effects.

In sum, efforts to suppress stereotype use can be effective in the short-term and can be induced either by direct instruction or by normative influences. Moreover, the effectiveness of these efforts can be a function of pre-existing prejudice levels and one's motivations to control prejudicial responses (Monteith, Sherman, & Devine, 1998; Wyer, 2007). However, such suppression usually heightens the accessibility of the stereotype and therefore leads to rebound effects and greater use of the stereotype once suppression efforts have been reduced.

Perspective Taking

Another approach to this problem is quite different from suppression, and in fact seems to take the opposite tack. We often hear comments that if you genuinely want to understand someone, you must "see the world through his eyes" or "walk a mile in his moccasins." This is the essence of perspective-taking. Rather than controlling stereotypic content from entering consciousness, perspective taking focuses on that content by adopting the perspective of a group member. Is this strategy effective in overcoming the implications of automatically activated stereotypes?

To answer this question, one study (Galinsky & Moskowitz, 2000) adapted the methodology of suppression studies. Participants were given a photo of an old man and were asked to write a passage about a day in his life. There were three conditions in the study. In one, participants were given suppression instructions to avoid using stereotypes in preparing their essays. In the second, they were instructed to adopt the perspective of the man and to imagine and write about a day in his life. Participants in the third (control) group were not given any instructions.

After completing their stories, participants were given a lexical decision task in which strings of letters were presented on a computer screen, and the task was to indicate if the letters formed a word or not. Some of the words were relevant to the stereotype of the elderly (*dependent, forgetful, lonely*), and others were irrelevant to the stereotype.

The essays written by participants were coded for the use of stereotypic content, as in Macrae, Bodenhausen, et al.'s (1994) study, and both suppressors and perspective takers used less stereotypic content that did control group participants. On the lexical decision task, however, suppressors had very fast response times to stereotype consistent words, reflecting the greater accessibility of this content following suppression. In contrast, for those in the perspective-taking condition response times to stereotype-consistent words were slower than in the suppression condition, indicating that perspective taking did not make the stereotype more accessible.

Many other studies have documented the positive effects of perspective taking on intergroup evaluations (see Todd & Galinsky, 2014). Several possible mechanisms underlie these effects. Perspective taking has been shown to increase empathy for the outgroup and individual outgroup members (Batson et al., 1997; Dovidio et al., 2004). Also, perspective taking can induce changes in attributional patterns. For example, when asked to explain inequalities between Blacks and Whites, participants in a perspective-taking condition provided more non-dispositional, situation-based explanations, and weaker dispositional attributions (Todd, Bodenhausen, & Galinsky, 2012). Finally, perspective taking induces more considerable overlap in mental representations of self and the target of perspective taking, a merging of self and outgroup (Davis, Conklin, Smith, & Luce, 1996; Galinsky & Moskowitz, 2000; Todd & Burgmer, 2013).

Egalitarian Goals

The mechanisms we have discussed so far have all been focused, in one way or another, on overriding automatically activated thoughts associated with a particular target group. Whether the strategy is to replace, suppress, or bypass through perspective taking, in every case the automatic activation of traditional stereotypic thoughts is assumed to occur and must be dealt with (at least among low prejudice persons). All of these techniques involve effortful processing (replacing the activated thought, thinking of distractors while suppressing, imagining a day in the life of a target person). The goal of another approach is to control the automatic activation of the stereotype itself (Moskowitz & Ignarri, 2009; Moskowitz, Gollwitzer, Wasel, & Schaal, 1999; Moskowitz, Salomon, & Taylor, 2000).

All of us have goals that direct and guide our thoughts and behaviors, and in some cases, these goals can become very important such that we virtually live by those goals. For example, the goal to be egalitarian, to treat people fairly and in an unbiased manner, and to promote equality can become central to one's life. These goals probably start as conscious goal intentions. However, over time, with repeated experiences in which one consciously confronts equality issues in observing and interacting with members of a certain outgroup, the egalitarian response can become automatic, just as other responses become automatic through repetition. If that were to happen, then encountering, for example, a minority group member may automatically instigate fair and unbiased thoughts and responding, circumventing any automatic activation of stereotypic thoughts or behaviors about that group.

An experiment testing this idea (Moskowitz et al., 1999) was based on the stereotype of women. Participants were males who, from pretesting, were known to have reliable and chronic egalitarian views toward women (chronics) or who were low in those values (nonchronics). Faces of women were presented as primes, and stimulus words followed each photo.

Both of them were presented very quickly (specifically, 200 ms) – too fast to allow conscious, controlled processing to occur. Some of the stimulus words were attributes that were stereotypical of females (*sensitive, dependent*), whereas others were nonstereotypical attributes (*colorful, arrogant*). Participants' task was to pronounce those words out loud as quickly as possible, and their response times in doing so were recorded. The reasoning behind this study was as follows. If the primes (women's faces) activate the stereotype of women, then responses to stereotypical words should be facilitated, and response times should be faster than for nonstereotypical words. This would be the typical automatic activation effect seen in many other studies, and, in this study, it should occur for nonchronics. If, however, chronically egalitarian goals are activated by the women's faces, and if that activation precludes triggering the stereotype, then responses for chronics to stereotypic words should be no faster than to nonstereotypical words. As shown in Figure 3.5, the results fit this pattern precisely.

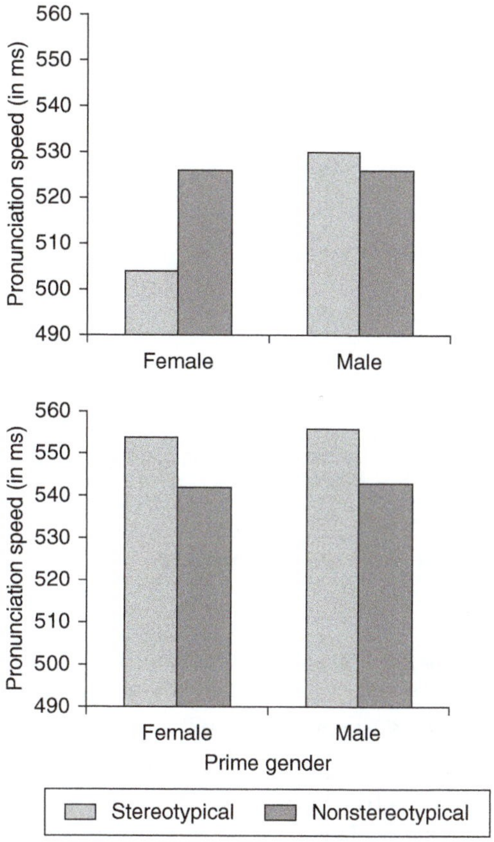

A Multi-faceted Intervention

Each of the research efforts we have discussed focused on a single mechanism or strategy that was proposed as a means of reducing automatic bias in intergroup perception and behavior. Although some of these efforts have been successful, most of these effects, while statistically significant, have not been substantial. It has become clear that reducing or eliminating automatic biases is not easy, and even when change is successfully induced, such change

Figure 3.5 Pronunciation speed for stereotypical and nonstereotypical words following male and female faces for nonchronic egalitarians (top panel) and chronic egalitarians (bottom panel) at short delay (200 ms)

Source: Based on data from Moskowitz et al. (1999)

may not be long-lasting. Of course, the fact that people are not even aware that they have these biases makes the task more challenging.

Perhaps the most extensively used measure of implicit bias is the IAT. There is evidence showing that the IAT effect is stable across time and has meaningful effects on downstream judgments and behaviors (Greenwald, Poehlman et al., 2009; Nosek, Greenwald, & Banaji, 2007). However, efforts to reduce the IAT bias have not had impressive success (Lai et al., 2014, 2016).

In contrast to previous studies that have tested the effectiveness of a single variable on bias reduction, some recent research has adopted a different approach. Devine et al. (2012) designed an intervention that incorporated several different strategies aimed at reducing bias. It was a multi-week longitudinal study of implicit race bias in college students at a major university. The intervention consisted of a 45-minute training session that introduced five strategies, some of which we have already discussed (e.g., replacement, perspective taking) as well as others (imagining examples of outgroup members behaving in ways that

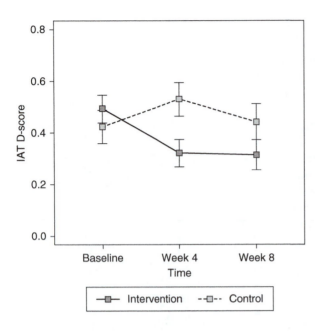

Figure 3.6 Mean IAT bias scores for intervention and control conditions at three points in time

Source: From Devine et al. (2012)

contradict the stereotype, thinking of others as individuals rather than as group members, increasing contact with outgroup members). Each of these strategies was explained and discussed with participants, who were then instructed to use these strategies during the next several weeks. Participants completed the race IAT at three points in time: before introducing the intervention, four weeks after the intervention, and eight weeks after the intervention. Participants in a control condition completed the same measures at the same time but did not receive the training intervention.

Results showed (Figure 3.6) that before the intervention, the two conditions did not differ in IAT bias. After four weeks, participants in the intervention condition had lower IAT scores than did those in the control group. Importantly, this difference persisted over time as the intervention group's IAT scores remained low after eight weeks. This multi-faceted intervention was effective in reducing implicit bias, a reduction that was still evident when re-assessed eight weeks later.

Comment on Automaticity

In the preceding paragraphs, we have reviewed research exploring several mechanisms that might be effective in diminishing, undermining, or overriding the automatic effects of stereotype activation on subsequent processing, judgments, and behaviors. There are two messages we can glean from this research. First, the good news is that automatic effects – those perception-behavior links discussed earlier – can be influenced, maybe even prevented or overridden. We are not robots; automatic responses are malleable. Second, the bad news is that achieving control over automatic responding is not easy. Some of these strategies (replacement, suppression, perspective taking) require that the person is motivated toward change and devote conscious effort in implementing the strategy. Some efforts have only been shown to have short-term effects, and one of them (suppression) has the ironic consequence of making the suppressed material more accessible for later use when the suppression has ceased. These constraints are not surprising, given that automaticity – the perception-behavior links – are the product of persistent associations and use in the past. Despite these limitations, it is sure that research will continue to pursue these topics and explore new avenues toward a greater understanding of the malleability of automatic responding.

SUMMARY

When we learn a new skill, our mind is focused on what must be done, how it is done, and the steps to be taken before completion. This is true for simple tasks (making scrambled eggs) and for more complex and challenging tasks (mastering a new camera). With repeated experience, these tasks become routine and can often be performed while our attention is simultaneously engaged in other activities (conversation, a TV program). The same is true for mental responding. Mental processes that occur very frequently can become routine and automatic. They can be triggered by an external event of which we may not be cognizant, occur without intention and awareness, and consume few if any cognitive resources and therefore can be performed without interfering with other ongoing mental processes. Processes vary in the extent to which they are automatic and hence have these properties. However, research has documented that automatic responding is pervasive in many different aspects of our lives, including our social lives. Given their wide-ranging use and effects, it becomes unclear when and how conscious and intentional processes play a role in everyday functioning. However, research has shown that automatic processes are (at least under some conditions) malleable and can be controlled.

FURTHER READING

Custers, R., & Aarts, H. (2010). The unconscious will: How the pursuit of goals operates outside of conscious awareness. *Science, 329*, 47–50.

Dijksterhuis, A. (2013). Automaticity. In D.E. Carlston (Ed.), *The Oxford handbook of social cognition* (pp. 239–256). New York, NY: Oxford University Press.

Ferguson, M., & Cone, J. (2013). The mind in motivation: A social cognitive perspective on the role of consciousness in goal pursuit. In D.E. Carlston (Ed.), *The Oxford handbook of social cognition* (pp. 476–496). New York, NY: Oxford University Press.

Gawronski, B., & Creighton, L.A. (2013). Dual process theories. In D.E. Carlston (Ed.), *The Oxford handbook of social cognition* (pp. 282–312). New York, NY: Oxford University Press.

4
ATTENTION
The Mind's Eye Meets
The Social World

On the evening of February 11, 2007, Katy Hadwin stopped at a gas station in Montgomery County, Texas, to fill her tank. As she was standing next to her car, a man approached her brandishing a black revolver. He demanded her purse and pointed the gun at her face. During the subsequent 20-second encounter, she found herself staring intently at the robber's weapon. Katy later told police that she had "a good look at his gun." Her description of the robber, however, was not particularly detailed. On the day of her robbery, she described her assailant as a "White male, about 5′9″ or 5′11″ tall." A man was later arrested and convicted of the robbery. However, the court never considered the possibility that Katy's impoverished description of the suspect might have resulted from her fixation on the gun. An appeal based on this very issue argued that expert testimony should have been allowed attesting to biases that arise when attention is focused on a criminal's weapon. The appeal was denied, and the man's conviction based only on her vague eyewitness testimony was allowed to stand.

One crucial aspect of a social cognition approach is the recognition that our daily life rests on continually processing various types of information. To understand the plot of a mystery movie, you must track various actions, characters, and events as they occur. In deciding for whom you will vote in an election, you process (in fact, are inundated with) information about the candidates, consider their positions on issues, weigh their backgrounds and qualifications, and evaluate their styles. In all of these cases, you are processing information with significant implications for your adaptation to and enjoyment of the world where you live.

We also must continually attend to information as we navigate our social world. When meeting someone for the first time, we quickly develop an impression of the person, based on the information acquired during even a brief interaction. When we are sitting in a seminar, as we observe the instructor and other class members during the discussion, we gain a sense of how the group functions, who participates and who does not, and who are the prominent members of the group. Our social environment is extremely rich in information, and our use of that information dictates how we function in those contexts.

SETTING THE CONTEXT

In Chapter 1, we provided an overview of how information is processed and used. This chapter focuses on when the perceiver meets the social context and how he or she responds to the information available in it. The technical term used to characterize the initial processing of information is *encoding* – how the mind "takes in" the information available in the social environment. The processes we discuss here are general and pertain to all information processing. Our focus is on how those processes play out in social domains and our perceptions of people – ourselves, other individuals, and groups.

Sources of Information

Our statement that there is much information in the social environment should not be too surprising. Imagine a situation in which you meet a person for the first time. Consider all the kinds of information around you that might influence your perceptions of the person. Some things are immediately evident upon seeing the person: it is virtually impossible to look at someone without knowing the person's gender, race, and age group. Other aspects may also be immediately conveyed – clothing and other possessions can signal the person's socioeconomic status, an accent may suggest nationality, a uniform may reveal the person's occupation. Specific physical characteristics also may draw your attention – the person is unusually tall or is somewhat overweight.

As you interact, other information becomes available. Indeed, what the person says conveys a great deal and guides the impressions formed. In addition to *what* is said, *how* it is said is also influential. Is the person smiling or frowning? Animated or bland? Using many gestures or standing stoically? Maintaining or avoiding eye contact? All of these questions refer to facial expressions and nonverbal gestures that perceivers routinely use to infer things about the person. As your acquaintance with the person develops, you observe the person's behavior, both alone and in interaction with others, and this behavioral information becomes a fruitful basis for further developing your impression. The variety of *sources* of information is impressive. Moreover, all of these sources are used to judge the person's characteristics, values, attitudes, goals, interests, and emotional reactions. Sometimes those judgments are accurate, sometimes not, and when not, they can produce insights into biases in the ways we process and use information.

Beyond the appearance and behavior of the person, several other crucial factors must be considered. Whatever you are learning about a person, it is happening in a particular *social context*, and the nature of that context is important. The setting can make some aspects of the person prominent, which can relate directly to the importance of that information in your perceptions. Moreover, the same behavior can mean entirely different things in different situations so that the context can guide your interpretation of any given comment, action, or expression.

We have briefly surveyed just some of the sources of information that we use to form an impression of a person we have just met. The same things apply in any context where we are perceiving and interacting with others – individuals and groups – and the behaviors we observe them enacting. In all of social perception, the sources of information are plentiful and diverse.

Two Components of Encoding

To understand how this information is encoded, it is essential to distinguish between two distinct processes: *attention* and *interpretation*. *Attention* plays a crucial role in focusing our cognitive resources on specific aspects of that information, while other aspects go mostly unnoticed. Given the richness and variety of the information available, the perceiver could quickly be overwhelmed by the demands of processing it all. The selectivity of attention in focusing on aspects of the social environment has significant ramifications.

Interpretation becomes vital because many of the behaviors, comments, and nonverbal expressions that we observe in others are ambiguous or vague, requiring additional processing to be understood. The perceiver not only observes but also imposes some interpretation on the information being processed. Only then does the information have meaning for the perceiver. In Chapter 2, we introduced the critical role of cognitive representations in guiding information processing. Our concepts, beliefs, and stereotypes are used to disambiguate the uncertainties of experience and to clarify the meaning of what we witness. In other words, the information we acquire in social interaction has its impact only after the observer has interpreted it.

One additional point to be made at the outset is that encoding processes happen very quickly. We do not spend our lives considering what to pay attention to and contemplating the meaning and implications of everything we observe. Through a lifetime of interacting with others, the processes of attention and interpretation can become highly routinized. In Chapter 3, we highlighted the importance of automatic processes, and our attention to and interpretation of information is, to a considerable extent, done automatically, without intention or awareness that we are doing so.

In sum, *attention* pertains to the question of what information enters into the cognitive processing system. *Interpretation* relates to the meaning that information acquires as we comprehend it. This chapter is concerned with attention and its role in processing information about others. Chapter 5 discusses the nature and function of interpretation in understanding our social world.

IMPORTANT PROPERTIES OF ATTENTION

Several essential aspects of our attentional systems need to be recognized. As we have already argued, the social environment provides more stimulus input than we can attend to at any given time. Our attention might be focused on what we need to do to achieve our goals at the moment, but numerous other aspects of the situation can command attention as well. In other words, there is a constant risk of *stimulus overload*. Given our inability to attend to everything around us, our attention focuses on certain kinds of information. Aspects of the environment that are unusual, unexpected, and surprising tend to draw our attention instinctively. The shifting of our focus to such events shows that *elements of the social context* can command attention, at least momentarily. Nevertheless, attention is, at least to some extent, under our control. People can and do, at times, focus their attention on aspects of the environment while blocking out other stimuli in the immediate social context. In other words, *attention is selective*.

Studying attention and its effects can be challenging because often it is difficult to know whether the outcomes assessed in a study reflect attention or some other process or combination of processes. For example, although we have just made a distinction between attention and interpretation, some frequently-used measures cannot clearly differentiate between registering a stimulus (attention) and imposing meaning on it (interpretation). A similar ambiguity arises in studies that measure recall of presented information on the assumption that greater attention to stimulus information facilitates recall of it. Although this assumption is plausible, there are many variables (in addition to attention) that influence recall performance, creating a degree of interpretive uncertainty. Fortunately, other strategies provide more "pure" measures of attention, such as recording eye movements and measuring the amount of time looking at a stimulus. The point here is that care must be taken in both the selection of measures and the interpretation of data.

Attention is a critical process that is integrally involved with almost all other subsequent processes. The importance of attention can be seen by considering the place of attention in the information processing framework we introduced in Chapter 1. Attention regulates the initial input of information from the environment into the cognitive processing system. All subsequent processes in our framework (considered in later chapters) build upon the information that is encoded. Thus, attention serves an essential gate-keeping function. Specifically, the information we encode from the social environment becomes the basis of all subsequent processing (e.g., evaluations, inferences, judgments, decisions, behaviors). Although some elements of encoding can indeed occur subliminally, outside of conscious attention to information, typically information that we do not attend to is lost or substantially diminished and, therefore, cannot influence later processing.

SELECTIVE ATTENTION: HOW DOES IT WORK?

Given the points we have just made, several essential questions quickly arise. How does the attentional system work? What determines where our attention is focused? What drives the selective nature of attention? What happens to "unattended" information? Cognitive psychologists provided some of the earliest answers to these questions, and we begin our consideration of this topic by reviewing some of their work and the theoretical ideas that guided them. In doing so, we can establish a foundation for understanding the attention process in social perception.

Filtering Attention

We begin with a famous experiment by Cherry (1953), who developed a *dichotic listening task* in which different speech elements (words, phrases) were presented simultaneously through headphones to each of the participants' ears. Cherry instructed participants to "shadow" one ear, that is, to repeat aloud what they heard in one ear while ignoring what they heard in the other ear. Later, their memory for the content of the unattended ear was tested. Participants had virtually no memory for that information, and, in one study, they even failed to notice when the message in that ear was changed to a different language. These results indicated that selectively focusing attention on one source of input can result in the complete loss of other information being presented. In fact, in one study (Moray, 1959), people had no memory for a word list that was presented to the unattended ear 35 times. Findings such as these led Broadbent (1958) to propose a *filter theory* in which unattended information is filtered out of the incoming stimuli, such that it never is processed. This filtering mechanism would explain why Cherry's participants had such poor memory for the information presented to the unattended ear.

Later studies showed that these claims were too broad (Wood & Cowan, 1995a). For example, if the participant's name was presented to the unattended ear, approximately one-third of the participants noticed it (Moray, 1959; Wood & Cowan, 1995b). This became known as the *cocktail party effect*, as when hearing your name mentioned in a nearby conversation during a noisy party immediately grabs your attention. Similarly, Cherry's (1953) original research showed that if the voice delivering the message to the unattended ear changed from a male to a female voice, a sizeable portion of the participants noticed it. This means that the unattended ear is not entirely "turned off" by the filter and that at least some aspects of that information are processed.

Allocating Attention

If unattended information is not entirely ignored, what do we extract from it? Treisman (1964) proposed an *attenuation theory* of attention to account for the processing of unattended information. She argued that unattended information is not ignored but instead is processed merely less extensively, allowing for some incomplete extraction of information from stimuli that are not the primary focus of attention. Selective attention allows for the extraction of information that can lead to a refocusing on material that perceivers are attempting to ignore. The appearance of one's name or a swear word, for example, might draw attention despite one's intention to ignore a stimulus stream.

Kahneman (1973) furthered this analysis by recognizing the ability to allocate attentional resources intentionally. In this view, attention can be directed according to the needs of and demands being placed upon an individual at any given moment. Thus, attention becomes selective through a process of allocating capacity to attend to one stimulus input versus another. This view has more flexibility in that attention allocation can change over time (even within a limited time frame; for example, in a dichotic listening task, shifting attention from one channel to the other) and it provides a mechanism for understanding the simultaneous allocation of attention to two (or more) tasks. It also gives the individual some control over how attentional capacity is allocated, rather than relying on a built-in filtering device.

Allocating Attention in Dual Tasking

In Chapter 3, we discussed the automatic processing of information, and we noted that such automaticity comes about through repetition and practice. As a child, you learned to tie your shoelaces. Initially, this seemed like an impossible skill to master, and every little step in the process required your full attention. With practice, it became a natural process that you could do with minimal thought. Once a task becomes automatic, it requires less attention. A consequence, then, is that more attentional capacity is available for focusing on other information or tasks.

These considerations raise the question of our ability to adequately attend to two tasks at the same time. Whereas the filter model would result in selective attention being focused on one, and only one, task or type of information, we now recognize that people have capacities that can, under some conditions (i.e., an abundance of available cognitive resources), allow us to multitask. We all perform multiple tasks simultaneously, allocating attention to both of them: sorting laundry while talking with one's partner; analyzing a friend's romantic crisis while picking things off the shelves in a grocery store. However, not all such combinations are successful. One of the authors enjoys listening to music while he is reading and working...but not all music. If it is soft-and-smooth instrumental music, he is fine; but vocal music? Cannot do; it becomes a distraction and completely disrupts his other task (reading). Generally speaking, we can devote attention simultaneously to two tasks when those tasks do not interfere with each other. However, if the two tasks demand the same resources, effective performance is disrupted.

Cell Phones and Driving

There is one all-too-common behavior involving attentional competition that gives rise to a severe societal concern: using a cell phone (mobile phone) when driving. As one driver describes his behavior:

> "It's convenient," a young man said when asked about texting while driving.
> "I put my phone on top of the steering wheel and text with both thumbs," he said,
> adding that he often has exchanges of 10 messages or more. Sometimes "I'll look
> up and realize there's a car sitting there and swerve around it." (Richtel, 2009)

Many people talk and text on their phones while driving and feel quite comfortable doing so as a way to save time. Unfortunately, doing so is also very dangerous. Research has consistently found that accidents are four times more likely when drivers are using cell phones than when they are not (McEvoy et al., 2005; Redelmeier & Tibshirani, 1997), and the accident rate for cell phone talkers approaches rates for drivers who are legally drunk (Strayer, Drews, & Crouch, 2006). Why is this so dangerous?

Figure 4.1 Driving simulator
Source: From Strayer & Drews (2007)

Much research that has tried to answer that question indicates that attentional processes play a critical role (Strayer & Drews, 2007). These studies use a variety of methods and measures. Some studies involve assessing driving performance in a simulator (see Figure 4.1) as one "drives" the car in a scene projected on a screen (the windshield). In other studies, a person drives an actual vehicle equipped with specialized instrumentation to record driving practices. Various measures of driving performance are recorded, including reaction times in braking, average driving speeds, following distance, moving in and out of lanes, and the number of collisions.

Numerous studies have provided evidence that cell phone use is dangerous and that attentional processes are integrally involved in diminishing performance. The reactions of cell phone users are negatively affected in several ways. Cell phone drivers react more slowly to unexpected traffic hazards (e.g., responding to brake lights in front of them, approaching an intersection with pedestrian crosswalk; Strayer & Johnson, 2001; Strayer et al., 2006). They show more changes in driving speed and acceleration (Strayer et al., 2006), and drift out of their lanes more than nonusers (Drews, Pasupathi, & Strayer, 2008). Safe driving often requires frequently glancing from side to side to see pedestrians, cars approaching intersections, people getting out of parked cars, and the like. Measures of eye movements show that cell phone users engage in fewer of these anticipatory glances of the environment than nonusers (Biondi, Turrill, Coleman, Cooper, & Strayer, 2015). They also show evidence of being distracted. They are more likely to entirely miss a Stop sign and have worse memory for landmarks (Strayer & Drews, 2007). This can lead to navigation errors, as demonstrated in one study where cell phone users were four times more likely to completely miss an exit they had been instructed to take compared with drivers who were conversing with a passenger (Drews et al., 2008). Comparison of driving while phoning with driving (in a simulator) while legally intoxicated show that both cell phone use and alcohol impair driving performance, but they do so in different ways – cell phone users had slower reaction times and more collisions, whereas intoxicated drivers applied brakes harder and followed more closely. The data suggest that the impairment experienced while driving during cell phone use may be as great as that due to alcohol, and both conditions were inferior to baseline performance.

There are, of course, many things that can distract a driver. All of them are distractions, but they differ in the demands they place on cognitive resources. Studies have compared several distracting elements to determine the extent of cognitive distraction and their interference with driving (Strayer, Turrill, Cooper, Coleman, Medeiros-Ward, & Biondi, 2015). Listening to a radio or a book on tape was moderately distracting, whereas conversing via cell phone – handheld or hands-free – was meaningfully more distracting. Conversations with a fellow passenger also can be a distraction, but they differ from cell phone use in critical respects. When something happens on the highway that poses a threat, both driver and passenger see it, and their conversation stops. This is not true with cell phones, so the conversation partner continues talking, providing a distraction at the very time when it can be most harmful. Moreover, the passenger, seeing the same driving conditions as the driver, can assist, for example, alerting the driver to a potential hazard or providing critical information (which, of course, cannot happen in a cell phone conversation). This research has clearly shown that cell phone use is particularly problematic.

When people are asked their opinions about cell phone use when driving, they acknowledge that there are risks but downplay the danger involved in using cell phones while driving. Most people believe they can drive safely while using a cell phone and think they are better at it than are others (Sanbonmatsu, Strayer, Behrends, Ward, & Watson, 2016). However, when placed in a driving simulator that records aspects of their driving performance, this high confidence proves to be unwarranted. Cell phone users made significantly more severe errors than nonusers, but they did not remember making more mistakes than nonusers. In other words, they drove unsafely but were unaware they were doing so (Sanbonmatsu, Strayer, Biondi, Behrends, & Moore, 2016).

People vary considerably in the extent to which they use cell phones while driving. One might expect, then, that those who are more experienced at this dual tasking would show better driving performance. This is not the case. Analyses showed that such experience did not alter the evidence of dual-task interference on the various measures of driving performance (Strayer et al., 2006).

In light of the increasing evidence that cell phone use while driving is associated with higher accident rates, several U.S. states and countries around the globe have adopted laws banning the use of hand-held cell phones but allowing the use of hands-free phones. Indeed, having one's hands free is useful in driving, but these laws do not address the primary cause of the problem. The primary problem with cell phone use while driving is not the hands;

it is *attention*. There have been many studies comparing hand-held versus hands-free conditions, using a variety of driving performance measures. In study after study, the results of these comparisons are quite consistent: *there is no difference between hand-held and hands-free cell phone use* (e.g., Horrey & Wickens, 2006; Ishigami & Klein, 2009; Patten, Kircher, Östlund, & Nilsson, 2004; Strayer et al., 2006, 2015; Strayer & Johnson, 2001; Törnros & Bolling, 2006). These results demonstrate that it is not the use of hand-held phones, per se, that harms driving. Instead, it is the *attention* required by conversing over cell phones, an activity that draws critical resources away from the task of driving, which makes cell phone use dangerous. As Strayer and Drews (2007, p. 129) observed, "The cell-phone conversation disrupts performance by diverting attention from the external environment associated with the driving task to an engaging context associated with the cell-phone conversation."

The evidence is even more disturbing for drivers who text while driving. On September 12, 2008, a commuter train crashed into a freight train in Chatsworth, California, killing 25 people and injuring 135 others. The engineer of the commuter train had failed to notice a red signal, and subsequent analyses uncovered the reason: at the time the commuter train approached the red signal, the engineer was sending a text message. A study of long-haul truckers whose cabs were outfitted with video cameras provides another disturbing demonstration. When these experienced truckers were texting while driving, the risk of a collision was 23 times greater than when they were not texting (Richtel, 2009). Moreover, when there was an accident or crash involving texting, videos showed that drivers' attention was focused on their phones for an average of 5 seconds before the incidents. Think about that. Suppose I asked you to close your eyes for 5 seconds while you are driving. Would you agree to do it? Undoubtedly not! However, by focusing on the cell phone, that in effect is what happens when people text while driving.

Cell phones are incredible inventions that serve us well in many ways. However, using them to communicate with others while driving is unsafe in ways that many people do not recognize. The research evidence clearly indicates that they should not be used while driving. Moreover, the research also makes clear that their ability to distract our attention is the reason they are so dangerous.

Inattention Blindness

One of the surprising findings reported in the research on cell phone use was that cell phone drivers fail to "see" certain things along the highway that are clearly in view. They miss stop signs, do not remember seeing billboards, and fail to get off at the desired exit. Other research on attention indicates that such failures can occur in other circumstances as well. The critical ingredient is that when attention is actively invested in one task, the person may fail to see a stimulus that one would think could not be missed. This is called *inattention blindness*.

One remarkable demonstration of this phenomenon is provided by a study (Simons & Chabris, 1999) in which participants watched a video depicting two teams of three persons moving around a room and passing a basketball to one another. One team wore black T-shirts, and the other wore white T-shirts. The participants' task was to pay attention to one team (say, the black shirts) and to count the number of times a person on that team threw the ball. Midway through the video, a person dressed in a gorilla costume walked through the action for a total of 5 seconds while the players continued passing the ball, as shown in Figure 4.2. After viewing the videotape and performing the monitoring task, participants reported their answers to the count question. They then were asked a series of probe questions about what they saw: Did you notice anything unusual on the video? Did you notice anything other than the six players? Did

Figure 4.2 Gorilla walking through (top picture) and acting conspicuously (bottom picture) during a pass-the-basketball game

Source: From Simons & Chabris (1999)

you see anyone else on the video? Did you see a gorilla walk across the screen? Responses to these questions were quite consistent: they either did or did not notice the unexpected event. The surprising result was that almost half of the participants failed to notice the gorilla at all. To make this unexpected event even more salient, the researchers ran another condition in which the gorilla stopped in the middle of the players as they passed the ball, turned toward the camera, conspicuously thumped its chest, and then resumed walking across the screen. Again, only 50% of participants noticed the gorilla. Participants were shown the video a second time, except this time without instructions to focus their attention on counting the number of ball throws. Without having to perform that monitoring task, participants saw the gorilla, were surprised to see it, and often remarked, "I missed that?!"

These results provide convincing evidence demonstrating inattentional blindness (Simons, 2000; Simons & Levin, 1998). When attention is heavily invested in one task, people can fail to see stimuli that are extremely obvious to them under other conditions. This phenomenon helps us understand why cell phone users have poor recognition memory for readily apparent aspects of their visual field while driving. It also demonstrates some of the capabilities and weaknesses of our limited attentional system.

FACTORS INFLUENCING ATTENTION

Given the importance and the selective nature of attention, it becomes crucial to understand what factors influence this process. Some of those influences originate within the individual, some reflect properties of stimulus information, and others reflect aspects of the social context. Some of them are highly adaptive and functional, and others reflect biases that can lead to less-than-optimal outcomes. In this section, we discuss several important influences on attention.

Person-based Influences on Attention

Immediate Goals

What we attend to is at least partially under our control. We often direct our attention to the task at hand, guided by our immediate goals. A student concerned about performing well on an upcoming final exam will concentrate on what the professor is saying. When the refrigerator is empty, one focuses on going to the grocery store to replenish supplies. Their immediate goals drive people's behavior, and their attention is focused on aspects of the environment that facilitate achieving those ends. Other person-based factors that influence attention may be less directly relevant to those tasks.

Expectancies

The cognitive representations discussed in Chapter 2 guide all aspects of information processing, and attention is no exception. The belief that a person is politically liberal will lead the observer to notice the person advocating for increased government support for social programs and gun control legislation but less likely to notice his opposition to an increase in gasoline taxes. A perceiver holding a traditional stereotype of African Americans may be particularly attentive to any behavior by a Black male that suggests hostility or aggressiveness but may be less likely to notice the hours each week that he devotes to tutoring children.

What happens, however, when a person's behavior blatantly violates the perceiver's expectancy about that person? Are we more or less likely to "see" something that contradicts what we already believe? Or do our prior beliefs (expectancies) lead us to overlook such contradictory information?

Because of these questions and their seemingly contrasting implications, a great deal of research has investigated how information *consistent* and *inconsistent* with prior expectancies is processed (Olson, Roese, & Zanna, 1996; Stangor & McMillan, 1992). Indeed, these questions arise when we consider almost all aspects of the information processing framework, so we will revisit them in subsequent chapters. For our purposes in this chapter, we focus on how expectancies influence the perceiver's attention to information that is consistent and inconsistent with expectancies.

Cognitive structures (such as beliefs, person impressions, and stereotypes) provide the basis of expectancies that influence attention to aspects of available information. We have all heard the old saying about encountering some unexpected outcome, "I wouldn't have believed it if I hadn't seen it." Some findings suggest a variation on that saying, namely, "I wouldn't have seen it if I hadn't believed it." That is, we "see" (attend to) evidence that is consistent with what we already believe (as represented in cognitive structures). What happens, however, when we encounter information that clearly contradicts prior beliefs? Research has shown that such information often captures attention simply because it does not fit with what we believe to be true. We now consider some relevant evidence.

One study addressing this question (Hilton, Klein, & von Hippel, 1991) had participants role-play a teacher evaluating the performance of two upper elementary level school children by listening to them orally answer questions (analogies, math, vocabulary, reasoning). The participants' expectations about the students were manipulated at the outset by information provided about the students, establishing that one of them was an excellent student and that the other was a poor student. Participants then heard both students being asked questions simultaneously on headphones, one student to one ear, the other to the other ear. So at any given moment, they could listen to one or the other student's performance. Following each answer by each student, the participant responded "correct" or "incorrect" by pressing one or another computer key. This allowed the researchers to know to which student their attention was directed. When the bright (poor) student answered correctly (incorrectly), the performance was consistent with expectations; the reverse constituted performance inconsistent with expectations. Analyses showed that participants spent a higher proportion of time attending to the child's performance when the initial information they received was inconsistent with their expectations than when it was consistent with those expectancies.

Another study (White & Carlston, 1983) used a different approach to measuring shifting attention. Participants listened to a stereophonic audiotape of two actors engaged in a series of simultaneous but separate conversations. On one channel (to one ear), participants could hear one of the actors engage in a sequence of three different conversations with other people; in the other ear, they simultaneously heard the other actor converse with three other people in sequence. The participants had a toggle switch that allowed them to switch back and forth between the two actors. In each ear, while listening to one actor's conversation, the other actor's discussion was in the background. Participants could switch to the other channel any time they wished, and the equipment recorded which channel they selected as they listened. Before listening to the tape, participants were told that one of the actors was a very honest person who would not take advantage of another individual. Participants received no information about the other actor.

As the tape proceeded through the first two conversations, participants heard somewhat neutral casual conversations in both ears. At the beginning of the third conversation, however, participants heard the "honest" actor admit that he had stolen a textbook from a classmate. The question of interest is what effect this expectancy-inconsistent information had on participants' attention to the two actors, as measured by their control of the toggle switch. Results showed that during the first two (neutral) conversations, they devoted essentially equal amounts of attention to each actor. However, when they overheard the comment about the stolen textbook, they immediately switched their focus to the supposedly honest actor. That is, when the actor revealed that he had behaved in an expectancy-inconsistent manner, their attention to that person increased dramatically. This shows that attention is selective, and perceivers focused their attention on the source of information that violated their prior expectancies.

In sum, cognitive structures and the expectancies they bring with them can influence attention in two different ways. First, they can guide attention to expectancy-consistent information, meaning that perceivers are oriented to attending to information that "fits" with what they already believe. Second, when something happens that contradicts such expectancies, attention is immediately refocused on that information. Expectancy inconsistent information receives more attention and more processing than consistent information as the perceiver tries to understand why the person engaged in expectancy-violating behavior and how to incorporate it into the existing impression (Bargh & Thein, 1985; Belmore, 1987; Hastie, 1984; Sherman & Hamilton, 1994; Stern et al., 1984; Susskind, Maurer, Thakkar, Hamilton, & Sherman, 1999).

Cognitive Load

Selective attention is particularly important when a task is cognitively demanding. If a task is new or is particularly challenging, then attention will have to be purposely directed to it for it to be interpreted and comprehended. However, what happens if our cognitive systems are operating at less than full capacity? What if our cognitive resources are temporarily depleted because we are tired or distracted? What if we are multi-tasking, such as when we surf the web while sitting in a lecture? Or what if we are trying to listen to the lecture but are repeatedly distracted by an ongoing whispered conversation in the row behind us or by thinking about an argument we had with a friend the previous night?

When external demands or internal pressures are operating at the same time we are processing new information, we are operating under what is called a *cognitive load*. A cognitive load substantially reduces the cognitive capacity that is available for performing a primary task. As you might expect, decreasing a person's available cognitive resources diminishes her ability to pay attention, and people struggle to maintain focus when they are cognitively taxed. In one classic study, Mackworth (1948) had participants monitor the movement of a hand on a clock and to indicate whenever it moved unexpectedly. Virtually all unexpected movements were reported near the beginning of the study. After a half hour, as participants became fatigued and attentional resources waned, over one-quarter of the movements went unreported. A highly complex task can place a high demand on attentional resources, leading us to experience cognitive load even if our capacity and motivation are high. For example, finding a particular stimulus in a stimulus display is more challenging and takes longer if it is surrounded by a large (compared to a small) number of similar-looking stimuli (Treisman, 1991).

However, people do have the ability to strategically allocate attention when they experience cognitive load. Sherman and his colleagues (Sherman, 2001; Sherman, Lee, Bessenoff, & Frost, 1998) argue, in their *Encoding Flexibility Model*, that people direct their attention towards some information and away from other types of information, particularly when their cognitive capacity is temporarily reduced. Specifically, they shift their focus away from information that is already known to information that is novel, unique, or surprising. Why? Sherman (2001) argues that it would make little sense for a perceiver to waste her cognitive resources on pursuing information that she already possesses. Such information would be redundant with what is already known, so devoting attention to this kind of information would be an inefficient use of a scarce cognitive resource. Instead, when resources are limited, the perceiver selectively attends to information that adds new information. By doing so, people allocate their attentional resources "in a way that maximizes the amount of information gained for the effort expended" (Sherman et al., 1998, p. 591).

This prediction has been tested in several studies (Allen, Sherman, Conrey, & Stroessner, 2009; Sherman, Conrey, & Groom, 2004; Sherman & Frost, 2000; Sherman et al., 1998) where participants were given information that confirms or disconfirms stereotype-based expectations (e.g., kind versus aggressive behaviors performed by an African American male). Also, cognitive load was manipulated by having some of the participants perform a task that reduces their available capacity (e.g., having them remember an eight-digit number) while they process the information. Several experiments, using a variety of measures, have shown that participants typically devote equal attention to stereotype-inconsistent and stereotype-consistent information when cognitive resources are ample. In contrast, they show a preference for stereotype-inconsistent over stereotype-consistent information when they are operating under a cognitive load. Participants under a cognitive load look longer at and are more likely to later recognize stereotype-inconsistent compared with stereotype-consistent information. They are also slower to respond to an unexpected event when they are processing stereotype-inconsistent compared with stereotype-consistent information, due to their greater attentional engagement with information that contradicts stereotypical expectations. These results show that attentional resources can be selectively allocated when cognitive resources are limited.

These findings also converge nicely with the research discussed earlier in which people had to simultaneously monitor two conversations that were presented in two audio channels presented to separate ears. In that study, participants switched their attention to a channel when they heard information inconsistent with a trait-based expectation regarding a person. Similarly, in the studies examining encoding flexibility, people under a cognitive load were more likely to attend to information that contradicted stereotype-based expectations regarding the members of a group. In both cases, people allocated their attentional resources strategically to maximize the efficient extraction of new information when their cognitive resources were limited.

Motives

All of us routinely experience a variety of needs, motives, and goals, and when aroused, these motivational states have a significant bearing on all aspects of cognitive processing. Indeed, our motives and needs can strongly influence attention to specific aspects of the information available.

Humans are social beings, and one of the most fundamental of our social needs is belongingness (Baumeister & Leary, 1995; Lieberman, 2013). People have a fundamental need to feel a part of something larger than themselves, to be valued and appreciated by others. Like other needs, the need to belong can vary in strength as a function of recent experience (Brewer, 1991). At times we need to be alone or with a few others, and at other times we need to feel a part of something much more significant. When the need to belong is aroused, we become attentive to social relations and the opportunities they afford.

Based on this reasoning, Gardner, Pickett, and Brewer (2000) proposed that when people's need to belong is frustrated, they will be highly attentive to available information regarding belonging. Their experiment had two parts. First, each participant interacted with other people in a chat room; in actuality, their conversation partners were confederates whose behavior was intended to vary the participant's social experience systematically. In one condition, confeder-ates conveyed feedback signaling acceptance, agreement, and approval. In the other condition, the confederates "discovered" common interests among themselves, which became the focus of the chat room interaction, thereby excluding the participant. This social exclusion would induce in the participant a high need for belongingness. In the second phase, the participant was asked to read material from the diary of another individual describing several experiences, some of which were experienced individually and some of which occurred with other people in social settings. People in whom the need for belongingness had been aroused should be particularly attentive to information about the more social events in the diary and hence, on a later recall task, should have better memory for them compared with the individual experiences. This is precisely what the results showed. When people had a heightened need to belong, information compatible with satisfying that motivation grabbed attention and was better retained in memory.

Information that signals acceptance also draws visual attention, particularly when one is made to feel lonely or excluded. In a series of studies (DeWall, Maner, & Rouby, 2009), par-ticipants were either led to believe that they would have a rich or impoverished social life in the future. For example, participants were given feedback from a supposed "personality test" indicating either that they could expect many positive and meaningful social relationships in their lives or that they would likely end up alone in the future. In a subsequent task, those par-ticipants who had been made to feel low in belonging were faster to identify a smiling face in a set of sad and angry faces. Participants who were made to feel socially connected did not differ in the speed with which they could find smiling, angry, or sad faces. In another exper-iment, participants' eye movements were tracked. Low belonging participants were more likely to look at smiling compared with angry, sad, and neutral faces, and they were slower to disengage their visual attention from smiling faces. These results show that the threat of social exclusion can lead people to direct their attention toward sources signaling acceptance.

Belongingness is only one of several social motives that can influence our functioning. Of course, we also have motives reflecting our biological needs, and they too can affect our attention to aspects of the stimulus environment. When we are hungry, our focus is drawn to anything related to food. For example, we pay more attention to a TV commercial promoting some delicious delicacy when we are hungry. In contrast, when we are not hungry, we might merely notice the actor in the commercial or our minds may drift off to think about something completely unrelated to food.

Hormonal variations can also influence attentional processes over time. Attentional biases correlate with hormonal levels both in men (primarily with variations in testosterone) and in women (primarily with variations in estrogens and progesterone) (Haselton, 2018). One body of research has studied the effect of hormones on attention by examining women at different stages of their menstrual cycle. It has been hypothesized that women during ovulation should be more sensitive to markers of masculinity than at other phases of the menstrual cycle (Penton-Voak & Perrett, 2000; Penton-Voak et al., 1999).

To investigate this hypothesis, researchers (Johnston, Arden, Macrae, & Grace, 2003; Macrae, Alnwick, Milne, & Schloerscheidt, 2002) had female participants at two different stages of the menstrual cycle – on days nearest to ovulation (high-conception-risk) or at the beginning of the menstrual cycle (low-conception-risk) – perform tasks involving attention measured in terms of judgment speed. In one task, participants had to judge the gender of a series of photographs of males and females. Presumably, if participants were attending to the masculinity of male faces during this task, then they should make gender categorization judgments more quickly than if they were attending to other gender-irrelevant characteristics. Consistent with this interpretation, women near ovulation categorized male faces faster than did women not ovulating. There were no such differences for female faces. The second task assessed the accessibility of male and female stereotypic content for these two groups of participants. Stereotypically masculine or feminine words were presented on a computer screen, and participants had to indicate whether each word was characteristically masculine or feminine. Each word was preceded by a brief presentation of a male face, a female face, or a gender-neutral stimulus pattern. Presentation of a face should make traits associated with that person's gender readily accessible, facilitating response to the word classification task (assessed by response times). The results showed that, when male faces preceded words, women near ovulation classified male-stereotypic words faster than female-stereotypic words, compared with women not ovulating. When words were primed with female faces, no such differences were obtained.

Why would females at the ovulatory stage of the menstrual cycle have heightened accessibility of gender stereotypes after seeing male faces? One explanation, drawing on evolutionary theory, emphasizes that females are especially attuned to information about potential reproductive partners during ovulation when the likelihood of conception is highest. Alternatively, Brinsmead-Stockham, Johnston, Miles, and Macrae (2008) reasoned that ovulation is not only a period when the possibility of conception is high; it is also a period of strong sexual desire. Either (or both) of these hormonally-based motivations would produce the results noted above.

To tease these mechanisms apart, Brinsmead-Stockham et al. (2008) investigated the effect of sexual orientation on attention. They presented the same sexual categorization task described above to a sample of (self-identified) lesbians, again at two stages of the menstrual cycle, differing in hormonal levels. The likelihood of conception account would predict that, at high compared to low fertility levels, these women, like heterosexual women, would be more sensitive to male faces, and hence have shorter categorization response times, than to female faces. On the other hand, the explanation based on sexual desire would predict that lesbian females would have heightened sensitivity, and hence faster response times, to female faces than to male faces during ovulation. The results provided strong support for the latter explanation. These participants had speedier categorization response times for female faces during high compared to low fertility. In contrast, there was no difference in categorization times for male faces during these two periods.

Variations in attention across menstrual cycles can also affect the nature and quality of relationships over time. For example, researchers (Gangestad & Haselton, 2015; Haselton & Gangestad, 2006) assessed daily diary reports from a set of heterosexual women to gauge variations in their judgments of their own attractiveness, their attention to new men, and the degree they received attention from their partner (if they were in a relationship). These self-reports were then collated with their menstrual cycles. The results showed that women nearing ovulation felt most attractive and had the most interest in meeting new men. These effects were consistent across women who had partners and those who were single. For those women with partners, they reported receiving the highest levels of attention from their partner around their peak of fertility. These effects were reduced for women who felt that their partners were high in attractiveness, suggesting that attention to extra-relational opportunities (and consequent attention from partners) reflected a lack of satisfaction with aspects of their relationship.

Together, these studies indicate that hormonal fluctuations that influence sexual desire can affect perceivers' attention to sexually relevant stimuli, with consequent effects on categorization processes, the accessibility of stereotypic content in judgment tasks, and the receptivity to novel sexual partners.

Stimulus Properties Influencing Attention

The findings described so far show that the selective nature of attention can be guided by a person's immediate goals, prior expectancies, and motives. Also, aspects of the information itself can influence how attention is allocated.

Negative and Threatening Information

Certain kinds of information may automatically capture attention. One technique for studying automatic effects on attention is the Stroop task (Stroop, 1935) that we described in Chapter 3. This task requires participants to name the ink colors with which different words have been printed while ignoring the meaning of the words themselves. Although performance on this task is optimized by not processing the meaning of the words, it is tough to avoid doing so. One must inhibit the natural inclination to say the word in order to make the appropriate response (name the color). In the Stroop task, the amount of time it takes the person to name the color is measured, and not surprisingly, it takes longer to name the colors when there is no relation between the word and the color (when "friendly" appears in blue ink). Responses are even slower when the two elements conflict (when "yellow" appears in red ink). In other words, our attention is automatically drawn to the meaning of words rather than their color, and the degree of conflict between the color and the semantic content will affect performance speed.

The Stroop task also serves as a good measure of attentional capture. Pratto and John (1991) adapted this technique to test the hypothesis that people are automatically attentive to negative or threatening content. Participants were presented with a series of personality trait adjectives that varied in valence. Whereas some of the words were positive (e.g., curious, happy), others were more negative (e.g., rude, wicked). These words were typed in different colors, and the participants' task was to name the color of ink in which each word was shown. The latencies for color naming were substantially longer for the negative, undesirable traits than for the positively-valued traits. Thus, the evaluative meaning of the words was automatically recognized, drawing attention from the primary task (naming colors), slowing response times, and this was particularly true for negative, undesirable traits.

This finding and many others show that one reason that negative information grabs attention is that it suggests a threat to well-being (Öhman & Mineka, 2001, 2003). Consider how quickly you respond when a large dog barks angrily at you, or when you see a snake while walking in the woods. One's attention is focused instantly on the negative and potentially harmful stimulus, and attending to it can be valuable, adaptive, and functional.

Similar attentional biases can occur in processing social information, often with unfortunate and even disastrous consequences. For instance, stereotypes often contain beliefs suggesting that a group's members might represent a threat to one's safety or security. For example, a common element in the stereotype of African Americans is that they are aggressive and threatening (Devine, 1989), and people tend to judge Black men as larger and more threatening than White men of identical size (Wilson, Hugenberg, & Rule, 2017). How might this association affect attention? It has repeatedly been shown that angry faces draw attention more quickly than do happy or neutral faces (Cooper & Langton, 2006; Fox, Russo, & Dutton, 2002; Hansen & Hansen, 1988). If this effect generalizes to interracial perceptions, is it possible that, for White perceivers, an African American person may spontaneously capture one's attention even in a benign context, merely because the person is associated with threat?

Research (Correll, Guillermo, & Vogt, 2014; Donders, Correll, & Wittenbrink, 2008; Trawalter, Todd, Baird, & Richeson, 2008) indicates that this, in fact, happens. In one study

(Trawalter et al., 2008), the experimenters used a *dot-probe detection paradigm*, which is useful in studying selective attention. In this paradigm, White participants were shown a series of images, each presenting two male faces. A dot was located behind one of the faces, and it was revealed when the faces disappeared from the screen. The participants' task was to press a button as soon as they saw the dot. On the trials of interest, one face was a Black male and the other a White male. The question of interest was how long it took to press the button when the faces disappeared and the dot was revealed. The logic of the paradigm is that if the participant is already looking at the face obscuring the dot, it should take very little time to press the button; the dot would be immediately apparent. If, however, the person is looking at the other face, then seeing the dot will take slightly longer. Thus, a faster response time for one race than the other can be used as an indicator of selective attention (because it indicates a preference to attend to that race). Response times were faster when the dot was behind the Black face than behind the White face. This research is consistent with the idea that negative and emotionally threatening stimuli capture attention, even when the perception of threat arises from stereotypes.

Stimulus Salience

Some stimuli capture our attention because they are highly salient, noticeable, or prominent. Stimulus salience may derive from the intensity of the stimulus (e.g., a sudden loud noise) or it may arise due to the context (e.g., for many observers, seeing a White person would not draw particular attention, but seeing the same person in a group of African Americans would considerably enhance the person's salience). Stimuli that are salient draw attention, and, as a consequence, that information is more likely to be encoded and to play a role in subsequent processes (e.g., judgments) (Taylor & Fiske, 1978). Of course, when attention is drawn to a salient stimulus, other aspects of the stimulus environment, including potentially important aspects, might be ignored, also biasing those subsequent processes.

These points were nicely illustrated in a series of studies by McArthur and Post (1977). In each study, participants watched a videotape of a discussion among several persons and, at the end of the tape, were asked to judge how much each person had contributed to and influenced the group discussion. One of those persons seen on the tape was made salient, and the studies differed in how that salience was achieved through a variety of techniques. In one study, for example, one of the persons was situated under a bright light, whereas the others were not. In another case, one person was seated in a rocking chair, whereas the others were not, and his movement in the rocking chair made him salient. In a third case, one person wore a brightly colored shirt, whereas the others wore plain shirts. None of these variables would logically be essential factors influencing the perceived contributions of various individuals to the group discussion. Nevertheless, participants rated the salient person – the one under the light, in the rocking chair, and wearing the bright shirt – as having been more active in the conversation and as having had more influence on the group discussion. Moreover, those salient features guided attention, as observers spent more time looking at the salient persons (McArthur & Ginsburg, 1981). Thus, even incidental variables that influence salience can guide attention, which can then affect subsequent judgments (McArthur, 1981).

The Weapon Focus Effect

When a salient stimulus captures our attention, we might not process other relevant information effectively. This principle underlies what is known as the *weapon focus effect*, the phenomenon at the center of the story that began this chapter. When someone witnesses a crime in which an assailant is using a weapon, the witness often will notice and remember the weapon very well but might remember less information about the perpetrator than if that person had not carried a weapon. The weapon draws the observer's attention and, as a consequence, details about the assailant do not receive attention, are poorly encoded, and hence are not remembered well later. This weapon focus effect has been demonstrated in numerous experiments (e.g., Fawcett, Peace, & Greve, 2016; Loftus, Loftus, & Messo, 1987; Pickel, 1998, 1999; Pickel, French, & Betts, 2003; Steblay, 1992).

What is it about a weapon that causes this effect? Two possible mechanisms draw on processes we have just discussed. One explanation that tended to dominate initial accounts (e.g., Maass & Kohnken, 1989) focused on the narrowing effects of threat on attention. According to this account, weapons draw attention because they inherently represent danger. However, studies that have manipulated the threat value of stimulus conditions have consistently failed to find support for the threat hypothesis (Erickson, Lampinen, & Leding, 2014; Kramer, Buckhout, & Eugenio, 1990; Pickel, 1998, 1999). A second explanation is that a weapon draws attention because it is a highly unusual and novel stimulus. Several studies (Loftus et al., 1987; Pickel, 1998, 1999) have tested the "unusualness" hypothesis directly by varying the conditions under which a weapon is observed. For example, seeing someone with a gun at a baseball field is highly unusual, whereas seeing someone with a gun at a shooting range is not. Similarly, seeing a priest with a gun is unexpected, but seeing a policeman with one is not.

Pickel (1999) found that participants had poorer memory about the gun-wielding person in the "unusual" conditions but not under conditions when the presence of a gun would be expected. Also, the weapon focus effect is more substantial when the weapon is stereotypically inconsistent (e.g., a woman holding a weapon; Pickel, 2009), and the presence of surprising non-weapons (e.g., someone brandishing a stalk of celery; Mitchell, Livosky, & Mather, 1998) produces similar effects. Together, these findings support the view that the weapon focus effect derives primarily from the fact that a highly unusual, novel, or distinctive stimulus draws attention, thereby decreasing attention devoted to other available information.

Social and Contextual Influences on Attention

The Role of Context-based Salience

Aspects of the social context can make some stimulus elements more evident to the observer, drawing attention to information that might typically go unnoticed. For example, suppose you see a group of seven men and one woman. Your attention will likely focus on the single woman because of her novelty in that social group. Research has shown that attentional biases favoring contextually unusual information can have significant consequences for subsequent judgments.

In one study (Taylor, Fiske, Etcoff, & Ruderman, 1978), participants listened to an audiotaped discussion involving six people. As each person spoke, a picture of that person was shown on a screen. In one condition, the group consisted of three men and three women, while in other conditions, the gender ratio was unbalanced (e.g., 1 man, 5 women or 1 woman, 5 men). The researchers reasoned that in these latter conditions, the "solo" male or female would be made salient by the social context and hence would draw more attention as participants listened to the group discussion. The conversation on the audiotape was the same in all cases. Nevertheless, as predicted, participants rated the "solo" person as having been more assertive, more confident, having a more forceful personality, and creating a stronger impression than when that same person was part of a gender-balanced group. The social context served to make the solo more noticeable and an object of attention, with consequent effects on perceptions of him or her.

However, how does a solo person see him or herself? Lord and Saenz (1985) reasoned that, in a parallel manner, the solo would be aware of his or her unique status and would therefore become an object of his or her own attention. These researchers wondered whether this awareness might harm the degree that the solo was engaged in the conversation. This might occur if preoccupations with one's "differentness" detract the solo's attention from the ongoing interaction, undermining his or her retention of the information that was exchanged. If so, solo persons (being self-focused) would pay less attention to the group discussion and would have poorer recall for the opinions expressed during the discussion. In their study, participants in 4-person groups discussed their views on a series of topics. The group was either balanced (4 males or 4 females) or unbalanced (3 males and 1 female, or 3 females and 1 male). Other participants observed the 4-person discussions but did not participate. Later, the memory of all participants for the opinions expressed in the discussion was assessed. Importantly, the design of the study included both the perceptions of solos by observers and self-perceptions by the solos themselves.

Directly opposite predictions were made in these two cases, and (as shown in Table 4.1) the results supported those predictions. Of course, participants had better memory for their own expressed opinions (the "Solo" row of the table) than they had for views expressed by others. More interesting are the differences in relative memory for the solo's comments by others and by the solos themselves. Specifically, due to their self-focused preoccupations, solo participants had poorer memory (86%) for their own comments than they had for opinions expressed by non-solo members of their groups (94%). They also had poorer memory for views of the other group members when they were solos (35%) than when they were not (47%). Solo status disrupted their processing of information in the discussion. What about the comparable data for observers? In contrast, because of the salience of a solo person to others (as in Taylor et al., 1978), observers' attention was drawn to the solo and thereby led to better memory for the opinions expressed by the solos (55%) than by the non-solo members of the groups (42%); in the balanced conditions, these observers had equivalent performance (39%) for the two cases.

Table 4.1 Mean percentage of opinions correctly recalled

Participants	Group Composition Condition	
	Solo	Balanced
Solo (self)	86	94
Other	35	47
Observers	**Solo**	**Balanced**
Solo	55	39
Other	42	39

Source: Adapted from Lord & Saenz (1985)

The common element in these studies is that, due to the gender composition of the group, one group member becomes highly salient and hence a focus of attention. For an observer, that attention leads to better memory for what the solo said and to stronger perceptions of the solo's personality. In contrast, for the solo, being aware of and attentive to his or her own solo status results in poorer memory for what transpired in the discussion. These differing outcomes occurred even though all participants witnessed the same conversation by the same people. In sum, the same principle regarding information processing can produce opposite effects in these two cases.

Illusory Correlation Due to Distinctiveness

The research we have just summarized shows that a *person* can become salient due to the social structure of the setting (e.g., the solo status of the person). A parallel idea underlies another line of research in which some *information* becomes distinctive because of its relative infrequency of occurrence within a more extensive set of information. Pairs of items, each of which occur infrequently, are particularly distinctive, they therefore draw attention, and they become associated with each other. Because of this attentional bias, that information gets particularly well represented in memory and therefore is highly accessible for retrieval at a later time, for example, when judgments are made. In other words, participants believe that the pairing of two distinctive stimuli occurred more frequently than was the case. This is known as a *distinctiveness-based illusory correlation* (Chapman, 1967; Hamilton & Gifford, 1976).

Hamilton and Gifford (1976) reasoned that this effect – the differential attention to and processing of the co-occurrence of distinctive (infrequent) stimuli – may contribute to stereotype formation. Consider, for example, a person who lives in a predominantly White suburban neighborhood. That person's exposure to African Americans is considerably less frequent than his exposure to White Americans, making Black people distinctive. Similarly, in everyday life, undesirable behaviors occur less frequently than desirable behaviors, so they also become distinctive by their relative infrequency. Therefore, when a Black person commits an undesirable behavior, it constitutes the co-occurrence of two distinctive events. If an illusory correlation forms, then the implication is that, even if Black and White people manifest undesirable behavior with comparable relative frequencies, our observer will overestimate how often Black, relative to White, people have committed such acts.

To test this idea, participants read a set of stimulus sentences, each one describing a member of Group A or Group B as having performed either a moderately desirable or undesirable behavior (e.g., "John, a member of Group A, visited a sick friend in the hospital"; "Dave, a member of Group B, always talks about himself and his problems"). There were 26 sentences about Group A and 13 about Group B. Also, 27 of the sentences described desirable behaviors, and 12 described undesirable behaviors (see Table 4.2a). Thus, both Group B and undesirable behaviors were distinctive by their relative infrequency. Note, however, that the frequencies of desirable and undesirable behaviors for Group A are precisely double the numbers for Group B, so there was no actual correlation between group membership and the desirability of the behaviors performed. However, if a distinctiveness-based illusory correlation formed, participants would estimate that members of Group B had performed proportionally more undesirable behaviors than had members of Group A. As can be seen in Table 4.2b, this is precisely what happened: participants overestimated the frequency of Group B members performing undesirable behaviors.

Table 4.2a Distribution of stimulus items for Experiment 1 in Hamilton and Gifford (1976)

Attributes	Group A	Group B	
Desirable	18	9	27
Undesirable	8	4	12
	26	13	39

Table 4.2b Mean frequency estimates

Attributes	Group A	Group B	
Desirable	17.1	7.3	27
Undesirable	8.9	5.7	12
	26	13	39

Source: Adapted from Hamilton & Gifford (1976)

Does this attentional bias have consequences for group perceptions? Participants also rated their impressions of Group A and Group B on several attributes that varied in desirability. Group A was rated significantly more favorably, reflecting the differential impact of the distinctive (Group B, undesirable) behaviors on subsequent judgments of the groups.

However, is this effect really due to the co-occurrence of rare stimulus events? As is often the case, alternative explanations were viable. For example, there is a well-known tendency for people to make more favorable evaluations of stimuli they have often seen, known as the *mere exposure effect* (Zajonc, 1968), and Group A occurred twice as often as Group B. Also, because Group B was small, participants may have surmised that it was a minority group. If they assumed that minority groups are generally less valued than majority groups, it might have biased their evaluative judgments in the same manner. Both of these possibilities would generate the same outcome, that is, more favorable evaluations of Group A than of Group B.

Therefore, a second study was conducted to test these various possibilities (Hamilton & Gifford, 1976). Participants again read sentences describing the members of Group A or Group B, each of whom was described as performing either a moderately desirable or undesirable behavior. The critical change in this study was that desirable (instead of undesirable) behaviors were infrequent: 12 sentences described desirable behaviors, 24 described undesirable behaviors (see Table 4.3a). This change means that both Group B and *desirable* behaviors were distinctive by their relative frequency. Again, however, the numbers for Group A were precisely double those for Group B, so there was no actual correlation between group membership and behavior desirability. In this case, if people formed an illusory correlation, they would overestimate the frequency of Group B performing *desirable* behaviors, and Group B would be rated more favorably than would Group A. On the other hand, both of the alternative explanations (mere exposure, assumptions about minority groups) would still predict more favorable evaluations of Group A. The results supported the distinctiveness explanation. Participants overestimated the frequency with which Group B/desirable behaviors occurred (Table 4.3b), and they rated Group B more favorably than Group A.

Table 4.3a Distribution of stimulus items for Experiment 2 in Hamilton and Gifford (1976)

Attributes	Group A	Group B	
Desirable	8	4	12
Undesirable	16	8	24
	24	12	36

Table 4.3b Average estimated frequencies from Hamilton and Gifford (1976)

Attributes	Group A	Group B	
Desirable	8.2	6.6	12
Undesirable	15.8	5.4	24
	24	12	36

The illusory correlation effect has been replicated many times (Acorn, Hamilton, & Sherman, 1988; Berndsen, McGarty, van-der-Pligt, & Spears, 2001; Chun & Lee, 1999; Hamilton, Dugan & Trolier, 1985; Johnson & Mullen, 1994; Johnson, Mullen, Carlson, & Southwick, 2001; Primi & Agnoli, 2002; Sanbonmatsu, Sherman, & Hamilton, 1987; Stroessner & Heuer, 1996). Alternative interpretations for why it occurs have been proposed (Fiedler, 1991; McGarty, Haslam, Turner, & Oakes, 1993; Rothbart, 1981; Shavitt, Sanbonmatsu, Smittipatana, & Posavac, 1999; Sherman, Kruschke, Sherman, Percy, Petrocelli, & Conrey, 2009; Smith, 1991). The illusory correlation is a robust phenomenon, and research suggests that there may be multiple cognitive processes that contribute to it (Stroessner & Plaks, 2001). Moreover, several variables, such as perceiver's mood state (Stroessner, Hamilton, & Mackie, 1992) and membership in one of the groups (Schaller & Maass, 1989), influence the magnitude of this effect. In all of these cases, however, infrequently co-occurring information captures attention, thereby biasing processing and judgments on subsequent tasks.

Deviation from a White Male Norm

All of us belong to multiple groups. For example, both authors are White males, American, social psychologists, fathers, and lovers of good wine. We have a friend who is an African

American woman, also a social psychologist, who does not drink alcoholic beverages, and is not a father (although she is a mother). In Chapter 2, we discussed how perceivers categorize others into groups, but the examples just described present new levels of complexity. That is, given that any person has multiple group memberships, which of those options will the perceiver use in categorizing such persons? Would the co-authors be perceived as White? Males? Fathers? Would their friend be categorized as a woman? An African American? A social psychologist? Or would some combination of these categories be used (e.g., Black female)? All of these alternative categorizations are available, and any of them would be accurate. However, they would imply different qualities and foster different impressions because they would activate different stereotypic expectations.

Research in the United States has shown that perceivers are attentive to categories that distinguish people from the *perceived norm*, emphasizing a categorization that identifies some way that a target person is different from the predominant expectation of others. This work indicates that perceivers operate based on a *White male norm* (Stroessner, 1996; Zárate & Smith, 1990). That is, because White people constitute much larger numbers than Black people in the U.S. population, being Black would be perceived as "different from" the norm. Similarly, although the numbers of males and females are roughly the same, women historically have been less prominent in American culture, politics, and media, and therefore might also be seen as deviating from the White male norm. These considerations imply that Black people and women would be likely to be categorized by race and gender, respectively, more than would White men, who fit the White male norm. Does this mean that perceivers attend to those alternate categorizations in their perceptions of others? Furthermore, if a perceiver's attention is drawn to one categorization, then is the other category simply ignored or is it actively inhibited, as suggested by research discussed in Chapter 2 (Dijksterhuis & van Knippenberg, 1996; Macrae et al., 1995)? Studies have used response time measures to assess the accessibility of various categorizations, given some stimulus input (Stroessner, 1996; Zárate & Smith, 1990). By determining what categorizations are made, we can understand more about people's attention to the various stimulus cues provided by the complexities of person perception.

Stroessner (1996) presented the following task to participants. Photographs of Black and White males and females were shown, each of them preceded by a cue word or label (e.g., "race," "gender") identifying a dimension of categorization. The participant's task was to respond as quickly as possible by saying the category membership of the person shown in the photo ("Black," "White," "Male," "Female"[1]). The response time in making each identification was recorded. Analyses of these response times showed systematic differences as a function of the person and the dimension being judged. For example, race identifications were made faster for Black men than for White men, and race judgments for Black men were faster than were gender judgments. Both of these results are consistent with the White male norm hypothesis: Black men differ from that norm regarding race, and hence attention to race facilitates race judgments, but inhibits gender judgments, in comparison to responses for White men.

The case of categorizing Black women was especially intriguing, as such women differ from the White male norm on both judgment dimensions. How would they be categorized? As we discussed in Chapter 2, Black women might be viewed as an *intersectional* category, where race and gender information are both salient. If so, then *both* "deviations from the norm" draw attention.

To test this hypothesis, photos of Black and White men and women were again presented but were preceded by cues combining race and gender dimensions ("black female"). Participants had to respond "yes" or "no" for each stimulus, depending on whether the label matched or did not match the person shown in the photo. Because this task requires attention to both race and gender, judgments of Black women should be facilitated if they are seen in intersectional terms (i.e., as being *both* Black *and* female). This is precisely what was obtained in this study. In this task requiring attention to both race and gender, Black women's category membership in a combined category was judged most quickly.

These studies demonstrate systematic differences in the way people are categorized based on their multiple group memberships and perceivers' attention to one or another of those group categories. These categorizations are important because, once activated, the category can provide a basis for subsequent inferences, evaluations, and judgments based on stereotypes associated with those categories. Zárate and Smith (1990) have demonstrated that the categorization used predicts which stereotype will be applied in making judgments of the person. They used a procedure similar to Stroessner's, but, in addition to making category identifications, participants also rated the stimulus persons on a series of traits reflecting race and gender stereotypes. They then tested the hypothesis that the speed of categorization by race or gender would predict which stereotype is applied in judgments of those persons. Their results supported this hypothesis. Participants who were fast in categorizing by race, and slow in categorizing by gender, rated the stimulus persons higher in racially stereotypic attributes. (A similar pattern did not occur for gender stereotyping, perhaps because people spontaneously emphasize gender and hence tend to apply gender stereotypes more generally.)

Power

It seems intuitively reasonable that people in positions of power would attend to different aspects of the social environment than would people who lack power. Precisely what are those differences between powerful and powerless persons in the nature and focus of their attention? And why?

An old proverb nicely presents one possible account of differences in attention for the powerful versus the powerless:

> An elephant and a mouse lived in the same part of a zoo. As the elephant spent his time lumbering about, he knew that the mouse was scampering around the area but never seemed to know (or care) exactly where he was. The mouse, however, was always, at some level, aware of where the elephant was about to step.

In this account, the elephant can freely trudge around, not paying much attention to the mouse, whereas the mouse must always be vigilant to where the elephant's next step will be. This suggests that powerful persons may not devote much attention to their underlings. Alternatively, people in positions of power have responsibilities and, therefore, must use their power and influence to achieve essential goals. A failure to attend to essential aspects of their social environment could be counterproductive. In fact, the research literature on the relationship between social power and attention reflects both of these perspectives.

Some research begins with the recognition that powerful persons' outcomes are not dependent on the powerless, so there would be little incentive to attend to them (Fiske, 1993). One consequence of this bias would be that powerful persons would perceive others not as individuals but more in terms of their group memberships. It follows from this analysis that powerful people would be more likely to stereotype the less powerful and to individuate them less (Fiske & Depret, 1996; Goodwin, Gubin, Fiske, & Yzerbyt, 2000).

Other research indicates that powerful people are more flexible, compared to their powerless counterparts, in shifting their focus of attention depending on the context and task demands. For example, the powerful are better able to focus on the central aspects of information and are more effective in inhibiting attention to peripheral aspects of the information. In contrast, powerless persons are less able to ignore peripheral stimulus cues, even when the task requires such inhibition (Guinote, 2007). Similarly, powerful persons are effective in orienting their attention to stimuli that are instrumental in achieving their goals, whereas powerless people do so less well (Overbeck & Park, 2001, 2006).

Smith and Trope (2006; Smith, Jostmann, Galinsky, & van Dijk, 2008) argued that these effects are generated through the effects of power differences on several aspects of cognitive functioning. Specifically, they have shown consistent differences between powerful and powerless in the level of abstractness with which information is perceived and processed. High power people process more abstractly, and this has implications for several cognitive processes. For example, powerful participants categorize information at a higher level of generality, they perceive more coherence and structure in stimuli, they focus attention on extracting the "gist" of the information, and they more effectively inhibit irrelevant (to them) details. In contrast, people low in power tend to focus on details and have difficulty ignoring irrelevant information. In short, the powerful tend to see a "forest" where the powerless see "trees."

Thus, differences in social power between persons can influence attention to different aspects of the available information and can guide subsequent processing of and use of that information.

INTERIM SUMMARY This section has reviewed research evidence documenting a variety of variables and conditions that influence the amount, direction, and effectiveness of attention, and we have identified some variables that can interfere with effective attentional processing. First, some of those factors are things the *individual* brings to the social context – the person's immediate task goals, prior expectancies, and current motives, as well as the amount of cognitive capacity available to devote to attending to the social context. Second, other factors are properties inherent in the *observed stimuli*, such that negative information and salient information can capture one's attention and divert it from other elements of the perceptual field. Finally, aspects of the *social context* – the relative infrequency of certain events, the deviation of some people from a "White male norm," and the relative power between persons in an interpersonal context – can influence the direction and extent of one's attention.

One important implication of this discussion is that while attention might seem relatively effortless, simple, and straightforward, it is, in fact, quite complicated. We like to think that what we pay attention to is under our control (and sometimes it is) and that we notice the most critical and functionally useful aspects of the social situation we are in (and sometimes we do). However, the research reviewed in this section also makes clear that attention – both the direction of attention and the amount of energy invested in it – is variable and can be influenced by a variety of factors. Some of these influences on attention can be highly functional, whereas others can divert attention and diminish its capacity from its optimal usefulness.

ATTENTIONAL PROCESSES IN UNDERSTANDING THE SELF, PERSONS, AND GROUPS

We have discussed a variety of aspects of the way information we encounter in the social world is encoded. We now consider some specific manifestations of these processes in the way we come to understand ourselves, others, and groups.

Attention in Processing Information About the Self

To state that people focus attention on themselves seems almost trite, and it is not in dispute that the self is the focus of much of our attention and cognitive energy. For our purposes in understanding how the mind works in this domain, the question becomes not "Do people focus their attention on themselves?" but rather "When are people most self-focused and with what consequences?" Research exploring these questions has revealed a lot about the nature of self-focused attention and its ramifications. In this section, we provide a sampling of this work that illustrates the complexity of these processes and reveals that the simple comment that people focus attention on themselves is far from inconsequential.

Automatic Self-relevant Attention

Self-relevant information is preferentially and efficiently processed. In Chapter 3, we summarized research showing that, on a dichotic listening task, people automatically attended to self-relevant words (Bargh, 1982). When words related to the self were presented to the attended ear, people could speak those words quickly. In contrast, when words were presented to the unattended ear, the automatic attention directed to those words interfered with speaking words presented to the attended ear. This demonstrates that self-relevant material automatically draws attention and hence is processed very efficiently. This conclusion is also supported by studies showing that self-relevant information (e.g., one's name) presented to an unattended channel automatically captures attention, as discussed earlier in work on the cocktail party effect (Cherry, 1953; Moray, 1959).

Other research has taken a different methodological approach to documenting automatic attention to personal information. Gray et al. (2004) tested the same ideas using psychophysiological recordings of ongoing brain activity, specifically, event-related potentials (ERPs). ERPs are segments of brain wave activity from EEG recordings that are sensitive to the allocation of attention to incoming stimuli. In particular, an ERP component known as P300 is a large positive wave that occurs approximately 300 ms after the presentation of a stimulus. Research has shown that P300 is proportional to the amount of attention invested in processing a given stimulus and is therefore useful as an indirect measure of attention allocation. Gray et al. reasoned that if people automatically process self-relevant information and if the magnitude of P300 reflects attention allocation, then P300 should be large for such cases.

Participants were presented sets of words sequentially on a computer screen. Each set of words represented one category of information, such as first names, hometowns, and religions. In some cases, one of the words was highly self-relevant (e.g., the person's first name, hometown, religion). For example, a list of towns might be Grand Rapids, Long Beach, New Haven, Phoenix, and Charleston. If the participant was, in fact, from, say, New Haven, then one of the towns was self-relevant and should, according to prediction, show a more significant

P300 response. This condition was compared to two others. In one (a baseline control condition), none of the towns was the participant's home, so none of them would be self-relevant. In another condition, one town was printed in red ink, whereas the others were printed in black (and none of them was the participant's hometown). This case was included because it is known from past research that a novel stimulus also draws attention and induces a larger P300 response. Comparing these three conditions showed that the P300 to self-relevant terms was significantly larger than that in the control condition, consistent with prediction, and similar to the large amplitude evoked by novel stimuli known to grab attention. Gray et al.'s results, using an on-line measure of attention allocation, confirmed that people spontaneously attend to information that has direct relevance to themselves.

Self-referent Encoding

The research just described shows that the self is a frequent object of our attention. The self is also a mental representation containing our knowledge and beliefs about ourselves. As with any mental representation, this self-concept can then influence the processing of information about the self.

Invoking the self-concept can influence encoding strategies used in information processing. For example, suppose you are presented the following series of words, one at a time:

Funny

LAZY

Popular

Intelligent

HONEST

Table 4.4 Encoding task questions used by Rogers, Kuiper, & Kirker (1977)

Encoding task	Question
Structural	Is the word typed all in capital letters?
Phonemic	Does the word rhyme with XXX?
Semantic	Does the word mean the same as XXX?
Self-reference	Does the word describe you?

As you read (encode) these words, you are asked a question about each one and are to answer "Yes" or "No." In fact, the different tasks induced by the questions can create various forms of encoding, as they focus attention on different aspects of the stimulus words. These tasks, with their corresponding questions, are shown in Table 4.4. Research has shown that, as one progresses from structural encoding through phonemic to semantic encoding, then people can recall more of the stimulus words on a subsequent memory test. The idea is that semantic encoding provides a richer context for encoding the information, which in turn makes it more easily remembered.

Rogers, Kuiper, and Kirker (1977) hypothesized that the self provides a particularly rich context for encoding information, so they conducted a study in which they added the self-reference encoding task and compared it to the others. Participants read 40 trait adjectives, one at a time, and for each item, they responded "Yes" or "No" to one of the four questions. Later they were asked to recall as many of the stimulus words as they could. If the various encoding strategies influence attention to and processing of information, then they should facilitate later recall of those words. Results showed that the various encoding tasks had a significant effect, and the self-reference task led to the best recall performance.

These results show that the self is a useful context for processing and retaining self-relevant information, but the reason it does so is a matter of debate. Competing explanations for this effect differ in their assumptions about the nature and role of various processes in encoding information: (a) *Self as special mental representation.* These data might suggest that the self is a special kind of mental representation that provides a beneficial framework for processing, storing, and retrieving information. Although there are reasons to believe that the self is an important representation and is used extensively in processing self-relevant information, the implication that the self, by itself, provides some advantage in encoding information requires scrutiny. It may be, for example, that self-referent encoding engages other processes that are known to facilitate encoding and thereby enhance recall. Two such processes are relevant here. (b) *Organization.* As a mental representation, the self provides an organized framework for comprehending and storing information. Therefore, when encoded according to self-reference, the stimulus items would be stored in an organized and meaningful way. Such organization can facilitate later recall of the information. (c) *Elaboration.* The self is a storehouse of self-knowledge. This knowledge base permits making inferences about new bits of information, such as the self-descriptive trait words in the stimulus list, associating them with other self-descriptive attributes. These associations can then provide retrieval cues for recall of the self-descriptive stimulus items.

Research by Klein (Klein & Loftus, 1988; Klein, Loftus, & Burton, 1989) investigated these two possible mechanisms underlying the self-reference effect. They created lists of stimulus items that were related to each other or not. Participants were given one of three tasks: to organize the items into categories (organization), to think of an item's meaning and associates (elaboration), or to indicate whether the item brought to mind a personal experience (self-reference). Their results showed that self-referent processing can involve both organizational and elaborative processes, and the relative importance of the two depends on the nature of the stimulus material being processed.

The Spotlight Effect

Our pervasive tendency to be sensitive to and attend to self-relevant information has some interesting ripple effects. One is known as the *spotlight effect* (Gilovich, Medvec, & Savitsky, 2000; Gilovich & Savitsky, 1999). Not only do we focus attention on ourselves, but we also assume that others are attending to us as well. In fact, we assume they are doing so more than they are! The spotlight effect, then, is an egocentric bias in our assumptions about the attention of others.

Gilovich et al. (2000) asked participants to put on a T-shirt with the picture of a famous person – singer Barry Manilow, whose popularity had peaked decades earlier – and then escorted the person (whom we will call the "target person") to a room where several other participants (whom we will call "observers") had already arrived and were working on completing a questionnaire. The target person took a seat and was about to begin the questionnaire when the experimenter interrupted and took the participant back out of the room, where he asked some questions about what the person noticed while in the room. One question asked the person to estimate how many of the persons in the room had noticed the Barry Manilow T-shirt. Simultaneously, another experimenter in the observers' room asked those participants if they could remember the person whose face was on the target person's T-shirt. A comparison of the target persons' estimates with the percentage of observers who actually could name

Barry Manilow as the person on the T-shirt showed that target participants greatly overestimated the extent to which the observers attended to and remembered the Barry Manilow T-shirt. Apparently, then, the target participants believed they were the focus of the observers' attention ("in the spotlight") to a greater extent than was true.

Based on pretesting, the researchers knew that Barry Manilow was not a popular figure among students at the college, so target participants may have been embarrassed to be seen wearing his image on their clothing. This raises the question as to whether the spotlight effect occurs only when our behavior could be embarrassing or make us look bad. To answer that question, in another study (Gilovich et al., 2000) the target persons wore T-shirts depicting persons whom they admired and with whom they would want to be associated. The procedure was otherwise the same, and again, target participants significantly overestimated the extent to which observers would notice and remember the persons adorning their T-shirts. An additional study showed that this effect is not limited to aspects of one's appearance but also pertains to one's behavior. For example, following a group discussion, people overestimated the extent to which other group members had noticed both the number of their contributions to the discussion as well as the number of comments that were critically received. Finally, the spotlight effect occurs even when people are only imagining how many people would notice if they were wearing an embarrassing T-shirt (Macrae et al., 2016). In sum, people not only are the focus of their own attention but also (mis)assume that they are (and would be) the focus of other people's attention as well.

Although it is quite natural for people to attend to themselves, people vary in the extent to which their attention is focused on themselves – individual differences that can be assessed by the Self-Consciousness Scale (Fenigstein, Scheier, & Buss, 1975). People also differ in their ability to shift their focus of attention away from themselves when tasks require their attention. Research has shown that people who (a) are high in self-focused attention and (b) do not easily shift their attention away from themselves to focus on another task are more likely to have high scores on measures of generalized anxiety and dysphoria (symptoms of depression) (Muraven, 2005). Whereas being cognizant of ourselves and attending to self-relevant information is common in all of us, being chronically self-focused, combined with an inability to shift attention away from ourselves easily, can have negative implications for one's emotional experience.

Attention in Processing Information About Persons

We have already discussed several ways that attentional processes affect the perception of persons. To review, we know that:

- A person's negative behaviors automatically capture the observer's attention.
- Features that make the person salient also capture attention, generating stronger, more extreme impressions of the salient (compared to a less salient) person.
- Perceivers attribute more influence to and remember more information about the salient person in an interaction.
- The co-occurrence of distinctive information draws attention, resulting in the overestimation of the frequency of those occurrences.
- If a person deviates from a "White male norm," he or she is likely to be categorized on that basis, rather than by other features.
- Attention to person information is affected by the perceiver's prior expectancies.

All of these findings reveal aspects of attentional processes that guide and influence perceptions of persons. In this section, we explore more thoroughly some ways that attention influences perceptions of a person.

Attention to Faces

Face processing is central to interpersonal perception. It has been argued that "faces are probably the most biologically and socially significant visual stimuli in the human environment" (Palermo & Rhodes, 2007, p. 75). Our attention is continually drawn to people's faces, allowing us to extract a plethora of valuable information. Faces are abundant in the information they provide. Faces almost immediately tell us a person's gender, race, and age group. Facial expressions convey the person's emotional state, perhaps suggesting the person's goals and intentions. Maintaining eye contact, or not, provides approach versus avoidance cues, and being stared at induces discomfort. We find some faces to be very attractive and others less so. All of these effects influence the nature of social interactions and, at the group level, intergroup relations. Thus, even before any actual interaction occurs, the face can set the tone for the ease or difficulty of interpersonal interaction.

Perceiving faces is also the launching pad for several other processes that influence person perception. Face stimuli are often ambiguous and therefore require interpretation. They invoke evaluative reactions. They stimulate inferences about the person's attributes. They may trigger attributional thinking to explain a person's facial expression (e.g., if angry or appears puzzled). These are processes we explore in subsequent chapters. In this chapter, we are concerned with attention, and therefore are focused on the extent to which the face captures and holds attention – when, how quickly, and for what purposes (Hugenberg & Wilson, 2013; Palermo & Rhodes, 2007). Attention seems to be inherently oriented to faces, and facial configurations can be recognized very quickly. Brain recordings show quick responses to face stimuli (roughly 100 ms), faster than for categorizations of objects and words (Pegna, Khateb, Michel, & Landis, 2004). In fact, the higher allocation of attention to faces begins immediately in life. Infants right after birth track faces and face-like schematic representations better than they track nonface-like stimuli (Goren et al., 1975; Johnson, Dziurawiec, Ellis, & Morton, 1991; Morton & Johnson, 1991).

The actual identification of a specific individual in a face requires additional attention (Itier & Taylor, 2004; Liu, Ioannides, & Streit, 1999). Also, lower thresholds are needed to detect faces when they are expressing emotions, particularly negative emotions such as threat and anger (Calvo & Esteves, 2005; Mogg & Bradley, 1999; Palermo & Rhodes, 2007; van Honk, Tuiten, de Haan, van den Hout, & Stam, 2001). Attention is particularly drawn to and focuses on the eyes, compared to other parts of the face (Henderson, Williams, & Falk, 2005). Moreover, this focus on eyes is at least partially automatic and not entirely under volitional control (Laidlaw, Risko, & Kingstone, 2012). People preferentially attend to ingroup more than outgroup members (Moradi, Najlerahim, Macrae, & Humphreys, 2020), and this bias is particularly strong regarding attention to eyes. For example, several studies have shown that White participants attend more to the eyes of White compared to Black target faces (Kawakami et al., 2014).

There is one crucial feature of face processing that differentiates it from most other object perception. Perceiving facial identity relies on the encoding of configural information (relations among features) and integrating those features into a meaningful whole, as opposed to relying on specific features (nose, eyes) (Calder, Young, Keane, & Dean, 2000; Maurer, Le Grand, & Mondloch, 2002; Palermo & Rhodes, 2002; Tanaka & Sengco, 1997; Yin, 1969; Young &

Hugenberg, 2010). Without the ability to process faces configurally, the perceiver is unable to extract identities from facial features, a disability known as *prosopagnosia*. Prosopagnosics often do not have other cognitive impairments, but this condition means that they cannot recognize faces.

The process of attention is inherently involved in all of these effects. They all attest that attention is immediately and continuously drawn to face stimuli.

Salience Effects

Certain kinds of person information are more informative than others, and what is informative will be salient, will attract attention, and hence will be given more weight in interpersonal judgments (Fiske, 1980). Specifically, negative information about a person reveals a way that the person deviates from the mildly positive expectations we generally have about others. Similarly, evaluatively extreme information – e.g., very positive and very negative behaviors – reveal ways in which the person has unusual characteristics. These properties make this information more informative about the target person, and therefore they become the focus of our attention. Judgments of a person should be based on information that is informative about that person's qualities and characteristics. Therefore, negative and extreme information about a person will have increased importance, or weight, in our judgments.

Fiske (1980) showed participants photos with captions portraying a person engaged in behaviors that varied in both valence (positive or negative) and extremity (mild or high) from a neutral point. Participants could look at each photo as long as they wanted, and the amount of looking time for each picture was recorded. They also rated how likable each person was. Fiske was able to determine how much weight was given to both valence and extremity information in participants' judgments of how much they liked the target person. As predicted, both negatively-valued and extreme information were weighted more heavily. Moreover, looking times for each photo directly corresponded to these weights, establishing that informative stimuli drew observers' attention in the course of making judgments.

Earlier, we reviewed studies showing that seemingly innocuous stimulus features (being under a bright light; rocking in a rocking chair; wearing a brightly-patterned shirt) influenced observers' visual attention. Do these salient cues affect more than gaze behavior? Do they impact judgments of persons as well? McArthur and Solomon (1978) showed that such effects influence perceptions in a more meaningful social interaction. Participants saw a videotape of two persons interacting, during which one person got quite angry and insulting. The critical manipulation of the study was the salience of the target of this aggressive behavior. When the recipient of this verbal abuse was salient – either by wearing a leg brace or merely by having red hair – participants rated that person as more responsible for the other actor's aggressive behavior. They also rated her more negatively on relevant attributes.

This finding is counterintuitive and has significant implications. Research described earlier (McArthur & Post, 1977; Taylor et al., 1978) showed that a salient person, by attracting attention, is perceived as having been more active and influential in a group discussion. In McArthur and Solomon's (1978) study, the salient person was not the active aggressor but was the *target* or victim of aggressive behavior by another person. If that person wore a leg brace or had red hair, she was blamed for the aggressor's behavior more than if she were not salient in those respects. In other words, victim salience has increased victim-blaming for another person's (mild) aggression. Victim blaming is not an uncommon phenomenon in today's society. Members of ethnic minorities and women frequently are blamed for injustices visited on them. McArthur and Solomon's (1978) study highlights the potential role of a basic underlying attentional mechanism in at least partially understanding how and why victim-blaming occurs.

Another factor that can influence salience, and therefore can guide attention, is the context in which a person is perceived. Imagine, for example, that you are in a social setting and you observe a person directly, and therefore seeing her face as she converses with someone else. Now compare that to another person you watch, but in this case, you view him from behind and

therefore see not his face but instead view the back of his head. Which person is more salient in your visual environment? Will this difference influence your perceptions of those persons?

Taylor and Fiske (1975) created an experimental situation to answer these questions. Six participants observed a conversation between two people (whom they thought were also participants but, in fact, were confederates who had learned a script). The six participants were seated around the two interactants, as shown in Figure 4.3. Two of the participants were directly viewing Confederate A (and saw Confederate B from behind). From their perspective, Confederate A was highly salient. Two other participants were directly seeing Confederate B (and saw Confederate A from behind),

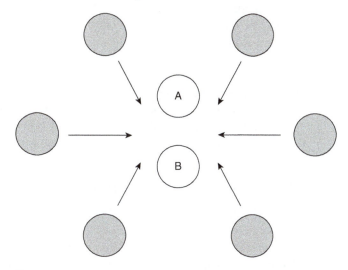

Figure 4.3 Arrangement of participants (grey circles) and confederates (clear circles) in Taylor & Fiske's (1975) experiment

so for them, Confederate B was highly prominent. The final two participants were seated to the side of the confederates and therefore had equal visual access to each of them, making them equally prominent. After viewing the conversation, participants rated each of the confederates with regard to their perceived influence on the conversation. The results are shown in Table 4.5. Those for whom Confederate A was salient perceived him as having been more influential; those for whom Confederate B was salient saw him as being more influential; those with equal visual access to each confederate saw them as being equally influential in their contributions to the conversation. This shows that the nature of the social context – a seemingly incidental difference in seating position, creating differences in the effect of visual perspective on what becomes salient for the observer – influenced not only participants' differential attention to the two conversing people but also their judgments of how active and influential they had been in the conversation.

These effects extend beyond the case of observing two people having a get-acquainted conversation. Research by Lassiter and his colleagues (Lassiter, 2002; Lassiter, Geers, Handley, Weiland, & Munhall, 2002; Lassiter, Geers, Munhall, Handley, & Beers, 2001; Lassiter, Geers, Munhall, Ploutz-Snyder, & Breitenbecher, 2002) has demonstrated comparable effects in a legal context. A recurring issue in the legal profession concerns the

Table 4.5 Effects of salience on perceived influence in discussion

	Confederate A	Confederate B
Orientation		
Facing A	20.3	15.5
Facing B	12.0	20.1
Facing both	17.5	16.8

Source: Adapted from Taylor & Fiske (1975)

nature of police interrogations of suspects and the validity of obtained confessions. One solution to these concerns was to videotape those interrogations, providing a record of the interrogation and an opportunity to evaluate how voluntary and reliable those confessions are. However, Lassiter and colleagues noted that these sessions were almost always recorded with the camera focused on the suspect. This makes intuitive sense, given that what the suspect says and how he says it are of primary interest. However, the focus of the camera also makes the suspect highly salient. Could the results reported by Taylor and Fiske (1975) also apply in this situation?

Studies were conducted in which participants watched videotapes of interrogations recorded from different angles: the camera focused on the suspect, on the interrogator, or equally on both (paralleling Taylor and Fiske's method). Participants' evaluations of suspects' confessions when the camera was focused directly on the suspects were judged to be more voluntary, the suspects were perceived as more likely to be guilty, and participants recommended stiffer sentences for them, compared to the other camera angles. Again, seemingly-minor variations in the context of observing others can influence the observer's attention to them and can thereby have significant consequences for how those persons are perceived.

Attention in Processing Information About Groups
Attention and Intergroup Differentiation

We routinely encounter members of different social groups in the course of everyday life. These groups differ in important (and some unimportant) ways and, therefore, it can be highly adaptive for perceivers to learn the features and characteristics that differentiate those groups. Recent research on attention indicates that a simple mechanism guiding attention can contribute to that process.

Attention Theory (Kruschke, 1996, 2003, 2011) posits that, in learning about categories, people preferentially attend to information that differentiates between those categories. Specifically, the theory argues that in learning about categories, people initially attend to features of the category learned first and then, when confronted with a second category, shift their attention not to all features of this group but specifically to features that distinguish the second category from the first. In this way, they form a stronger impression of the second than of the first category.

Although Attention Theory is a general theory of attention, recent research has shown that it can account for some well-established effects in social categorization, with implications for intergroup perceptions and stereotyping. In an intergroup context, Attention Theory states that majority group traits would be learned before minority group traits because perceivers encounter majority group members much more frequently. When they later learn about minority group members, the theory says that attention will shift to traits that distinguish the minority from the majority group. Those distinguishing traits then become more firmly attached to the minority than do traits that are equally shared by both groups. Also, they would form stronger associations between the minority group and its distinctive traits than between the majority group and its distinctive traits. The consequence of these attention differences is that people form stronger minority group stereotypes (Huang & Sherman, 2018; Sherman, Huang, & Sacchi, 2015).

These principles have been applied to how people learn about majority and minority groups (Sherman et al., 2009). They have generated new attention-based accounts of two robust findings in the intergroup perception research: the accentuation of actual differences between majority and minority groups (Corneille & Judd, 1999; Krueger & Clement, 1994a; Krueger &

Rothbart, 1990; Tajfel & Wilkes, 1963) and the distinctiveness-based illusory correlation (discussed earlier) in which people perceive a relation between distinctive groups and distinctive behaviors when, in fact, no such relation exists (Hamilton & Gifford, 1976; Johnson & Mullen, 1994; Johnson et al., 2001; Smith, 1991; Stroessner & Plaks, 2001). Thus, a simple tendency in how attention is allocated can have downstream effects on perceptions of majority and minority groups.

The Own Race Effect

Given that we continually perceive others, we should be experts at face perception. We spend our lives interacting with others, our attention is drawn to their faces much of the time, so we should be very good at it! And, in fact, we are. We have all had the experience of encountering a person, and we cannot remember much about her – exactly who she is, what her name is, when and where we saw her – but we *know* her face, and we know we have seen it before. We are, then, experts at perceiving faces.

Nevertheless, there are times when we are "less good" at face recognition than at other times. Among these is the common finding that people have higher recognition accuracy for faces of their own race than of other races (Hugenberg & Wilson, 2013; Malpass & Kravitz, 1969; Meissner & Brigham, 2001; Mondloch et al., 2010). This is known as the *Own Race Effect* (ORE) (Hugenberg, Young, Bernstein, & Sacco, 2010). It is a highly robust effect, and parallel ingroup-outgroup effects have been shown for many intergroup distinctions, including age, nationality, status, and even for arbitrary in- and outgroups established in a lab study. However, the vast majority of studies on the ORE have studied recognition of own and other races.

There have been many studies in which participants are shown photos of faces, some of their race (e.g., White) and others of a different race (e.g., Black). Later, they are given a recognition test in which these faces are shown again along with an equal number of "new" faces (both Black and White). Participants' task is to indicate, for each one, whether it was shown before or not. In these studies, perceivers consistently have higher recognition accuracy for faces of their race than of the other race (see Hugenberg & Wilson, 2013; Meissner & Brigham, 2001).

One plausible explanation rests on the fact that most of us have more experience interacting with (and therefore perceiving) members of our own race than of other races. Given that races differ in the facial features that are characteristic of them, through experience we should become more "expert" in learning to differentiate among own-race faces than among other-race faces. This is known as the *perceptual expertise explanation*, and some evidence supports this view. For example, some studies have found that people with more other-race contact show less cross-race recognition deficit (Brigham, Maass, Snyder, & Spaulding, 1982; Chiroro & Valentine, 1995) suggesting that greater contact with other-race faces can overcome, or at least diminish, the cross-race recognition deficit. Also, providing participants with training in the individuation of other-race faces can improve recognition accuracy in other-race perception. These participants manifested less of an own-race effect than they did on a similar test completed before training (Lebrecht, Pierce, Tarr, & Tanaka, 2009). The problem with this argument is that other studies have found no effect of living in integrated neighborhoods or attending racially-mixed schools on the accuracy of recognition of other-race faces (Brigham & Barkowitz, 1978; Ng & Lindsay, 1994). The literature, then, provides only inconsistent support for the perceptual expertise account (Meissner & Brigham, 2001).

Other accounts emphasize the importance of motivational and cognitive processes in producing the cross-race recognition deficit. For example, some people may cognitively disregard outgroup members to conserve cognitive resources for other processing (Rodin, 1987). Similarly, people may use different encoding strategies for ingroup and outgroup faces (e.g., category-based vs. individuated) (Bernstein, Young, & Hugenberg, 2007; Corneille, Huart, Becquart, & Bredart, 2004; Huart, Corneille, & Becquart, 2005; MacLin & Malpass, 2001; Rule, Ambady, Adams, & Macrae, 2007; Young, Hugenberg, Bernstein, & Sacco, 2012).

The *Categorization-Individuation Model* (CIM; Hugenberg et al., 2010) rests on the distinction between two modes of attention in face processing: categorization and individuation. *Categorization*, based on attending to features such as skin tone shared by members of a category, is immediate and fast. It produces perceptual assimilation among members, leading to the perception of within-group homogeneity, reduced differentiation among members, and poorer face memory. Category activation is typically stronger for perceptions of other-race than for own-race faces (Levin, 2000), which is one cause of the own-race advantage in face recognition.

Individuation involves attending to features of the face, especially to features that help identify the person as an individual. Moreover, identifying a particular individual requires recognizing the *configuration* of facial features (eyes, nose, mouth) in this individual face. Accurate face perception, therefore, requires perceiving the individuating characteristics of a person's face and how they are configured. Performance on a face recognition task would require that the perceiver knows the individuating features that distinguish one face from another. This would increase face memory and facilitate differentiation among the faces of group members. The CIM posits that people are typically more motivated to attend to, differentiate among, and learn more about ingroup than outgroup members. This motivational effect would serve to enhance the own-race effect on recognition memory for faces. This model has generated many experiments that have provided support for its basic principles and their implications (Bernstein et al., 2007; Hugenberg, Miller, & Claypool, 2007; Shriver, Young, Hugenberg, Bernstein, & Lanter, 2008; Young, Hugenberg, Bernstein, & Sacco, 2009).

Although all of these explanations are viable possibilities and have some support in the literature, none of them seem to provide an entirely adequate explanation for the consistency and pervasiveness of the ORE. It may be that all of them contribute to some degree to the ORE. One thing is clear, however. The categorization of others into own-race and other-race groups is fundamental and is an important catalyst for this effect (Hugenberg & Wilson, 2013).

In one crucial respect, however, the nature of interracial perception is changing. The number of multiracial persons in the United States has increased dramatically, so the simple distinction between own race (e.g., White) and another race (e.g., African American) is no longer so simple. How are multiracial persons categorized – as ingroup members or outgroup members? Moreover, what does that mean for face recognition?

Research has shown that the categorization of racially ambiguous persons is affected by motivational variables. One motivational force, known as *ingroup overexclusion* (Leyens & Yzerbyt, 1992), posits that individuals with ambiguous features (e.g., a person who could be either White, African American, or Latino) are likely to be categorized as outgroup members to protect the ingroup from "contamination" (Castano, Yzerbyt, Bourgignon, & Seron, 2002). Based on this motivation, some researchers predicted that racially ambiguous faces would be recognized less well than same-race faces and comparable to their recognition of other-race faces (Pauker et al., 2009). In their study, African American and White participants were shown a series of 10 White, 10 Black, and 10 mixed-race faces created by 50–50 morphing of Black and White faces. Later they were shown those 30 faces again, randomly intermixed with 30 new faces (10 Black, 10 White, 10 mixed-race) and, for each one, they were instructed to indicate if the face had been presented in the first phase. As can be seen in Figure 4.4 (with higher scores reflecting greater accuracy), both White and African American participants were more accurate in recognizing own-race than other-race faces, with ambiguous, mixed-race faces in between.

To explore the effects of intergroup motivations in accounting for these results, Pauker et al. (2009) conducted another study, using only White participants, in which participants' motivations were manipulated. Half of the participants were given instructions emphasizing accuracy ("Do your best to remember the faces accurately"). The other half were given inclusion instructions intended to counteract the ingroup overexclusion motivation ("people who are prejudiced tend to exclude biracial individuals from their group. Pay attention to how you view biracial faces to avoid appearing prejudiced"). Figure 4.5 shows that the motivation manipulation substantially influenced the recognition of mixed-race faces. Inclusion motivation improved memory for ambiguous faces, but not for White faces. Moreover, participants had better memory for white faces than ambiguous faces in the accuracy condition, but not in the inclusion condition. These results support the role of inclusion motivation in memory for ambiguous (mixed-race) faces (Pauker et al., 2009).

Attention in an Interracial Context

Imagine you are a participant in the following experiment (Eberhardt, Goff, Purdie, & Davies, 2004). The experimenter explains that you will be completing two different tasks in this study. The first task is an attentional vigilance task. You are seated in front of a computer, with a dot showing in the center of the screen. The experimenter instructs you to focus on the dot and indicates that periodically a flash will appear above or below and to the left or right of the dot. When you

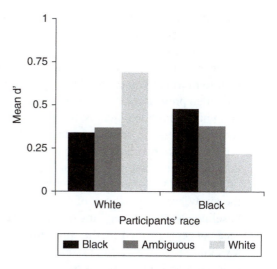

Figure 4.4 Accuracy (in d') of White and Black participants' face recognition for Black, Ambiguous, and White faces

Source: Adapted from Pauker, Weisbuch, Ambady, Sommers, Adams, & Ivcevic (2009)

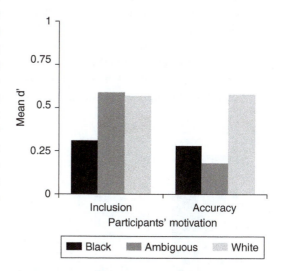

Figure 4.5 Effects of inclusion and accuracy motivation on White participants' recognition of Black, Ambiguous, and White faces

Source: Adapted from Pauker et al. (2009)

see the flash, you are to press a response key as quickly as possible. There are then 100 trials of this sequence. After completion of this sequence, the experimenter explains that the second task concerns people's ability to detect ambiguous objects. You will see a series of short video sequences. In each sequence, an object will first appear in a very degraded form, a "snowy" picture in which you cannot identify what the object is. The image gradually becomes clearer as the video progresses (through a series of 41 frames), and your task is to press a key as soon as you know what the object is. Some of those objects are crime-related objects (e.g., gun, knife), whereas others are not (e.g., camera, telephone).

That is the procedure of the study, as you experience it. What you were not aware of was that in the first task, each "flash" on the screen was a picture that was displayed so quickly (30 ms) that you could not even see it. Those pictures, depending on the three conditions of the study, were (a) photos of Black faces, (b) photos of White faces, or (c) in a no prime or baseline condition, were abstract line drawings. The question being investigated was whether race concepts primed by the subliminally-shown faces would (automatically and without your awareness) influence your ability to detect crime-related (compared to non-crime-related) objects. Specifically, the researchers measured how many of the 41 frames were required before participants could recognize each object. Eberhardt et al. (2004) predicted that exposure to Black faces would produce a *visual tuning* effect, facilitating attention to race-associated stimuli, such that the threshold for recognizing race-relevant objects would be reduced. As shown in Figure 4.6, that is exactly what they found. Exposure to the Black primes dramatically reduced the number of frames needed to identify crime-related (compared to crime-irrelevant) objects. In contrast, exposure to White primes diminished people's ability to detect crime-related objects. These results show that activation of race concepts influences attention to ambiguous stimuli. Subliminal priming with Black faces lowered the threshold for "seeing" objects (weapons) associated with race.

Eberhardt et al. (2004) also showed that the association of African Americans with crime is a bidirectional link. That is, just as priming race facilitated recognizing crime-related objects, activating concepts of criminality can influence perceptions of African Americans. Participants were subliminally shown images of weapons, activating concepts of criminality. They then were shown two faces, side by side, one Black male, one White male, for 450 ms. The dot-probe technique (which we described earlier) was used to study the effect of attention on responses. When the faces disappeared, a dot was in the location where one of the faces had been. The participants' task was to indicate whether the dot had been on the left or the right side. The amount of time taken to make that response was measured. If one of the two faces draws more attention and if the dot is behind that face, then when that face disappears as participants have been looking at it, the dot would still be there and it would take less time to respond. Results were consistent with this prediction: when the dot appeared in the place the Black face had been, participants who had been primed with crime-related objects were faster to find the dot.

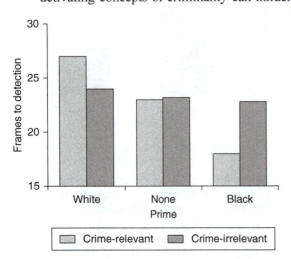

Figure 4.6 Mean frame number at which object could be detected as a function of race prime and object type

Source: Adapted from Eberhardt et al. (2004)

In another study, the researchers studied whether experience influences this attentional effect. For example, police officers receive extensive training and experience in dealing with crime-related issues. Perhaps they would not manifest the attentional bias shown in the previous study. On the other hand, the association on which the bias rests is derived from stereotypic associations, which police officers (and most other people) would have as well. In fact, Eberhardt et al. (2004) conducted the same study with police officers and obtained the same pattern of bias as obtained with college students. Taken together, the results of these studies demonstrate the strength of these stereotypic associations, such that not only are Black people thought of as criminals but also crime is thought of as black.

Is this effect limited to negative conceptions associated with African Americans? There are, after all, positively-valenced aspects of our stereotypes as well. For example, African Americans are stereotypically seen as being very athletic, a highly valued ability. Therefore, Eberhardt et al. (2004) conducted a similar study, again using the dot-probe method. In this case, they subliminally primed words associated with basketball (e.g., basket, dribble, dunk, rebound). Participants again saw two faces, one Black, one White, and when the faces disappeared, the dot appeared where one of the faces had been. Participants' latencies in detecting the location of the dot (left or right side) were measured. Priming participants with basketball-related terms produced faster responses when the dot was behind a Black face than behind a White face (but not when no prime was administered). Again, a race-related prime biased participants' attention to the Black face, making it easier to indicate the dot location when it appeared in the same spot where the Black face had been.

SUMMARY

The visual system is capacity-limited so that not all stimuli can be thoroughly analyzed simultaneously. Visual attention selects some stimuli for further processing and allows others to be ignored…Bottom-up factors, such as stimulus salience and top-down factors, such as expectations and current goals interact, forming a "salience map" that controls where, how, and what is attended. (Palermo & Rhodes, 2007, p. 85)

The human mind is a remarkable piece of equipment for processing information, a theme that will echo throughout this book. That processing of information begins when the individual perceives and attends to aspects of the social environment. This "interface between the mind's eye and the social world" determines what information is (and is not) encoded. The encoded information will be interpreted and elaborated in various ways (to be covered in subsequent chapters) and, having entered into the cognitive system, can influence various downstream consequences, including judgments, feelings, decisions, and behavior. On the other hand, information that is not encoded and does not enter the cognitive processing system cannot have such consequences. It is in this sense that attention plays a crucial gate-keeping role in the individual's attempts to understand the people, the events, and the social settings she encounters and with which she interacts.

Although we rarely stop to think about what it is we are attending to and why, this chapter has shown that the attention processes are complex and subject to a variety of influences that can influence subsequent processing. Attention is limited in capacity and, therefore, must function selectively, and that selectivity is open to several influences. Cognitive representations guide our attention in various ways such that we often "see" what we expect to see unless what we see contradicts our expectancies, in which case that expectancy-inconsistent information grabs our attention. Several critical variables – properties of the person, of the stimulus information, and of the social context – influence what grabs our attention. Finally, we have explored how the attention process is an essential aspect of the way we come to know and understand ourselves, persons, and groups.

FURTHER READING

Correll, J., Guillermo, S., & Vogt, J. (2014). On the flexibility of attention to race. *Journal of Experimental Social Psychology*, 55, 74–79.

Huang, L.M, & Sherman, J.W. (2018). Attentional processes in social perception. In J.M. Olson (Ed.), *Advances in experimental social psychology* (Vol. 58, pp. 199–241). New York, NY: Academic Press.

Hugenberg, K., & Wilson, J.P. (2013). Faces are central to social cognition. In D.E. Carlston (Ed.), *The Oxford handbook of social cognition* (pp. 167–193). New York, NY: Oxford University Press.

Palermo, R., & Rhodes, G. (2007). Are you always on my mind? A review of how face perception and attention interact. *Neuropsychologia*, 45, 75–92.

5
INTERPRETATION
Making Meaning

On September 24, 2014, an American National Football League game between the Green Bay Packers and the Seattle Seahawks was broadcast nationally on ESPN's *Monday Night Football*. The game was tightly contested, with the score favoring the Packers 12–7 as the host Seattle team gained possession of the ball with only minutes remaining in the game. After driving down the field, the Seahawks faced a fourth down at Green Bay's 24-yard line with 8 seconds left on the clock. The game would be decided on the final play. The Seahawk quarterback received the ball and eluded several defenders as he scanned the field for open receivers. In desperation and as time expired, he threw a "Hail Mary" pass toward a group of players from both teams clustered in the end zone. Seven players jumped for the ball, and a Packer appeared to grab it in midair, securing an interception and sealing the victory. As the gang of players fell to the ground, a Seahawk reached around the Packer and placed his hand on the ball. The home crowd anxiously awaited a signal from a referee. What had happened? Who had the ball? While one referee motioned that the pass had been intercepted, a second referee simultaneously raised his arms indicating a touchdown. A video review of the play led the officials to decide that the players had "simultaneous possession," awarding the touchdown (and the win) to the Seahawks. Public opinion showed that – with the notable exception of viewers in the Seattle area – the majority of viewers thought that the touchdown had been awarded in error. The controversy surrounding what became known as the "Fail Mary" game revolved around a difference in interpretation.

The attentional processes discussed in Chapter 4 document the gate-keeping function that occurs as information is encountered. Information is filtered regarding its fit with existing beliefs, in terms of implications for the self, and for relevance to the observer. In these ways, the observer copes with the task of selectively processing information from a complex and information-rich environment. These processes determine "what gets in" the cognitive processing system.

Information that enters the cognitive system is generally bereft of meaning. There is nothing inherently meaningful about a person's smile, his clenched fist, or his slow gait. All of these actions might draw our attention; however, "actions do not have inherent meaning but rather can be interpreted in many ways. The interpretation a person adopts has important effects on a range of higher-order cognitive processes" (Libby, Shaeffer, & Eibach, 2009, p. 503). To understand and to respond appropriately to the information we notice "out there," it must be internalized (attended to) and given meaning. To put it simply, we need to interpret what is happening. Although interpretive processes are always active, allowing us to adapt smoothly and effortlessly as we navigate the world, there are times when our need to interpret information becomes particularly acute. Interpretation is particularly critical when information is ambiguous and unclear, when it is vague and open to several different interpretations, or when it is novel and unexpected. In these circumstances, people are compelled to embellish information with meaning, and they often must do so by engaging in effortful and resource-demanding interpretive processes. Like all of the processes we discuss, how information is interpreted is influenced by several factors, including our knowledge and experiences stored in memory, our available cognitive capacity, and our current goals.

Consider an example of interpretation from the political domain. In an election year, we see candidates engage in debates on the issues of the day, and voters who view those debates (as well as political pundits) routinely make judgments of "who won" the debate. Of course, in any debate each candidate makes some points effectively, does less well on other topics, and also conveys a range of nonverbal cues as the debate transpires. All of this provides an ambiguous set of information that is open to alternative interpretations. Our view of who performed better can be influenced not only by their positions on issues but also by our desires, our preferences, and our identities. People are motivated to see their preferred candidate do well, and, as a result, there can be dramatic differences in people's interpretations of what occurred. Consider, for example, how partisans reacted very differently to a 2004 debate between Republican President George W. Bush and his Democratic challenger Senator John Kerry. In a post-debate poll of registered voters who watched the debate (Langer, 2004), 44% felt that Kerry had won the debate, whereas 41% said that Bush had won – essentially an even draw. However, when considered in light of people's preferences for one or the other candidate, things looked entirely different. Of those viewers who supported Kerry, 85% thought that Kerry had won, whereas 84% of Bush supporters declared him the winner. These people, who had watched the very same debate, interpreted what they saw very differently with dramatically different judgments of the result.

Although we usually feel quite sure about what we have just witnessed, much of the information we process is ambiguous and open to interpretation. When Kevin said he liked my new clothes, was that a genuine compliment or was he just saying the nice thing? Was Lana's sarcastic remark nothing more than poking fun at me, or did it reflect some real underlying bitterness? Sometimes it is challenging to answer these questions, but effective relations with others depend on our answers to them. And of course, when our interpretation is wrong – when we decide that Kevin was just polite or that Lana was aggressive – then our relations with others can suffer, all due to biased (and perhaps inaccurate) interpretation of another person's behavior.

We can carry this analysis to another level of generality. In addition to the ambiguity in people's actions, the words we use to describe people – their traits, motives, attitudes – can themselves be ambiguous and open to different meanings (Asch, 1946; Asch & Zukier, 1984; Hamilton & Zanna, 1974; Higgins et al., 1977; Zanna & Hamilton, 1977). If I describe someone to you as "proud," do you interpret that to mean "confident" or "conceited"? Does being "unde-cided" imply that the person is "open-minded" or "wishy-washy"? These examples illustrate that the same trait can be interpreted in very different ways, conveying very different meanings. In fact, in each of these examples, the stimulus word (e.g., proud, undecided) is paired with two possible meanings, one of which is quite favorable (confident, open-minded) and the other quite unfavorable (conceited, wishy-washy). Which interpretation is chosen can lead to extremely different impressions of a person or group (Hamilton & Zanna, 1974; Higgins et al., 1977).

As these examples illustrate, interpretation is an act of the observer, who imposes an inter-pretation and gives meaning to the behaviors, comments, traits, emotional expressions, etc., that he or she witnesses. These interpretations can be shared with others through communication, exerting social influence through the development of shared understanding. As such, the per-ceiver is actively contributing to the perception of the social world. This chapter explores how this happens.

DEALING WITH AMBIGUITY

Interpretation is an essential process because so much of the information we encounter is ambig-uous in its meaning. Coping with this ambiguity requires an effective system for interpreting and deriving meaning from this information.

Unitizing the Stream of Behavior

As perceivers, people see a continuous stream of behavior – people going about their activi-ties and interacting with each other. How do we encode the information from that continuous stream? It may seem that the mind acts as a video recorder that registers this ongoing flow as it occurs, stores it in memory, and then when we need to access that information, we essentially push the "Play" button on our mental DVR and – voila! – that stream of activity comes back to mind. Although intuitively plausible, research indicates that a quite different process occurs.

As observers witness the steady flow of behavior, they can gain information from what they see by chunking, or *unitizing*, that stream into segments or packets of information. How do we know this? In one study examining this process (Newtson, 1973), participants were shown a 5-minute video in which a man is seen filling out a questionnaire, getting up to get a cigarette from his jacket, throwing something in a wastebasket (which he misses so goes and retrieves it), returning to the desk and sitting down, and then looking through a book. As participants watched the video, they were instructed to push a button whenever one meaningful action had ended and a new one began. In this way, the participant is unitizing a continuous stream of behavior into useful segments. Newtson instructed some participants to use the smallest units that seemed natural, whereas others were told to use the largest units that seemed reasonable. Later, participants rated the man in the video on several traits and indicated how confident they were in those ratings. Analysis of these judgments showed that participants made more differ-entiated ratings and were more confident in those ratings when they had used smaller, more numerous units.

Why would fine-grained unitizing increase people's confidence in their impressions? Unitization is a means by which people extract information from behavior (Newtson, 1976), and by using smaller units, these people gained more knowledge from the behavior sequence they viewed. The use of more and smaller units means that the person is extracting additional information from the behavior stream. Consistent with this interpretation is the finding that, as people are unitizing the behavior on a videotape, the number of units increases (size of unit decreases) when an unusual behavior occurs amid an otherwise mundane behavior sequence (Newtson, 1973). Presumably, this happens because the unexpected incident spurs a need for more information to comprehend precisely what has happened (Zacks, 2004).

As perceivers are unitizing, these "chunks" are organized into hierarchies, such that smaller, fine-grained units are organized into more substantial, coarser units (Zacks, Tversky, & Iyer, 2001). The nature of the unitization and its organization has implications both for one's memory for what has been observed and for learning new activities (Zacks & Swallow, 2007). Greater unitization also occurs when people watch a video with no particular processing goal, as they need to extract much information to figure out what the person is doing and what it means. In contrast, when participants are given instructions to form an impression of the person (Lassiter, Geers, Apple, & Beers, 2000) or when people have a well-established expectancy about the target (Markus, Smith, & Moreland, 1985) – conditions where prior knowledge reduces the need for new information – observers use fewer and larger segments in unitizing a behavior stream. Person variables can also influence this process, as people who are sad or happy are less motivated to process information and hence use fewer units when processing neutral scenes compared with people in a neutral mood (Handley & Lassiter, 2002). Consistent with the view that unitization is a means of gaining information from the observed behavior sequence, studies have found that fine-grained, small unit segmentations result in better memory for information (Zacks & Swallow, 2007), especially for information that occurs at the breakpoints between successive units (Newtson & Enquist, 1976).

In sum, people are not passive observers of behaviors but instead are actively processing that information in ways that influence later judgments.

Identifying **What Occurred**

Any given behavior can be understood in different ways, and different characterizations of behavior can be equally accurate. At a very low or specific level, an action can be construed as a series of motor movements; at a higher level, it can be construed as goal-directed, driven by the actor's intentions. Differences in the initial interpretation of behavior emerge during a process called *action identification* (Vallacher & Wegner, 1987, 1989). Imagine watching someone pick an apple from a tree. This action can be described as "pulling an apple off a branch" or as "getting something to eat." Both action identifications are accurate characterizations of the behavior. They differ, however, in the richness of meaning extracted from that behavior. Low-level identifications focus on the literal movements involved in enacting the behavior – extending one's arm, grasping the apple, pulling until it is released from the branch. These characterizations tell you little about the person who engaged in the action. In contrast, higher-level identifications interpret the behavior as reflecting some internal state (hunger) or goal (eating to satisfy hunger) of the actor. The latter interpretation may include assumptions about the actor's motives and the causal relations required to achieve that goal. As such, higher-level identifications endow much more meaning to the interpretation of the behavior, although they can also invite speculation about unobserved properties of the actor.

Action identification is typically measured using a Behavior Identification Form developed by Vallacher and Wegner (1989). This form consists of 25 actions (e.g., tooth brushing). Participants are asked to consider each activity and to characterize it by choosing between two options, a high-level, mentalistic description ("preventing tooth decay") or a low-level, mechanistic description ("moving a brush over one's teeth").

Research has established that several factors influence the level of action identification (Kozak, Marsh, & Wegner, 2006). For example, perceivers make higher-level identifications for actions performed by liked compared to disliked persons. In one study participants first read vignettes describing a very likable person (e.g., he "likes to go to parties, hang out with friends and spend time with his family who live nearby" and "devotes a great deal of time helping to raise money for local animal shelters") or an unlikable person (e.g., he "has few friends and prefers to spend most of his time by himself" and "stole a classmate's lab report and turned it in as his own"). They then were given the Behavioral Identification Form containing a set of descriptions of behaviors supposedly performed by the person along with two possible identifications, one low level and one high level. Participants were asked to choose the identification that they felt best described each action. Participants made more high-level identifications for the likable than for the unlikable person, and this was especially true for positive compared with negative behaviors. For disliked persons, negative acts were more likely than positive acts to produce high-level identifications. Another study showed that lower-level action identifications were more likely for people enduring hardships (lost a job, was unable to pay bills). Thus, people we like and behaviors that are desirable acts engage our interest and lead us to think about the motives and goals implied by that description. In contrast, learning about a person who is disliked or is suffering some of life's hardships does not engage the same type of mental activity.

Subsequent research focused on the role of brain regions in action identification (Marsh, Kozak, Wegner, Reid, Yu, & Blair, 2010). It was hypothesized that areas of the brain that are integral in thinking about others' intentions and mental states might underlie high-level identification. If so, this would suggest that different neural resources are used when one is motivated to understand rather than merely to characterize the actions of another person. To test this possibility, participants completed a Behavior Identification Form while in an fMRI scanner. Each participant performed three different fMRI sessions, once when thinking about a likable person, once when imagining a person described neutrally, and once when thinking about an unlikable person.

Action identification results replicated those of Kozak et al. (2006), with high-level identifications most common for the likable person and least common for the unlikable person. Overall, the evidence from the fMRI showed that the inferior parietal lobule was more active when participants were identifying the actions of likable compared with unlikable targets. This is a brain region that, among other functions, is involved in the perception of emotions in others. The activity of several other brain areas depended on the likability of the target and the identification level chosen. For likable targets, the middle temporal gyrus near the extrastriate body area and the amygdala were particularly active during high-level identifications. Among other functions, these areas are involved in judging the social meanings of actions and in making valenced trait inferences, respectively. In contrast, high-level identifications of unlikable actors' behaviors were associated with activity in the ventral premotor cortex. This is a region that is involved in processing information about actions and their implied goals, but it is quite insensitive to the individual performing the action. Thus, high-level identifications were more common for liked targets, and these judgments appeared to reflect an interest in understanding the intentions and emotions of others. High-level identifications of unlikable targets, when they did occur, indicated an interest in understanding the motives and goals underlying the actions themselves rather than the person.

Trait Ambiguity

As already noted, the trait terms we use in describing others have varied meanings and connotations that can guide perceptions in very different directions. Consider learning that someone is "aggressive." The range and variety of behaviors that could be included under that umbrella are quite broad. They might include punching someone in a heated argument, being short-tempered with one's kids, or yelling insults at someone. Any of these behaviors might be labeled aggressive, so when you hear that term applied to someone, how do you interpret it? Is this someone who is volatile and potentially threatening, or does it mean this person is a reliable and outspoken advocate for what he believes? What "aggressiveness" means is ambiguous and open to interpretation.

Several variables can influence what interpretation is made. One factor that we know can guide interpretation is expectancies based on group stereotypes. For example, in one study (Kunda, Sinclair & Griffin, 1997), participants were asked to imagine a man – either a car salesman or an actor – who friends would describe as "very extraverted" and to write down behaviors that would describe him. The two lists were so different that the same term (very extraverted) had very different meanings. The extraverted salesman was viewed as pushy ("loud speaking," "monopolized conversation") whereas the extraverted actor was seen as socially adept ("life of the party," "makes others feel comfortable"). A parallel study asked participants to think about either a construction worker or a lawyer, to rate how aggressive he is, and then to generate behaviors likely to be performed by him. The construction worker and lawyer were both rated as equally aggressive, but quite different behaviors were listed as illustrating his aggressiveness. Behaviors listed for the construction worker included "beating up on people who make him angry" and "catcalls at women," whereas those for lawyers were more refined verbal behaviors ("forcing his opinion on others to prove a point," "would not stand by when some injustice was done to him"). In sum, even the same term used to characterize a person can have different meanings in different contexts.

Interpreting What Occurred

Once an action has been identified, other processes expand on this initial interpretation. Interestingly, several different research programs have built upon and further developed the importance of the general versus specific distinction introduced earlier. The research generated in these programs reveals several different ways in which that distinction is fundamental in the interpretation process.

Visual Perspective

Imagine that you are asked to make a brief oral presentation in a class. In preparing your talk, you will likely try to imagine what it will be like. You might picture the group seated in front of you, their faces staring intently at you. You find yourself periodically looking down at your notes as you speak, and you ready yourself to respond when someone's hand goes up to ask a question. Alternatively, you might imagine yourself giving your talk as if you were an audience member. You picture yourself in front of the class, speaking, smiling, and gesturing, moving from side to side in the front of the room as you talk. Both of these mental simulations are accurate, but they differ in the perspective represented in them. These different "imaginings" are referred to as a *first-person perspective* and a *third-person perspective*, respectively, and these two perspectives can result in dramatically different interpretations of the same event (Libby & Eibach, 2011; Nigro & Neisser, 1983; Sutin & Robins, 2008).

The perspective one adopts can influence the focus of one's attention and, consequently, the meaning derived from the action. Libby and Eibach (2011) argue that imagery perspective determines whether the perceiver understands the observed event in a bottom-up fashion, focusing on concrete features, motions, and details (via a first-person perspective), or in a top-down, abstract manner, integrating the event with the broader context in which it is observed (via a third-person perspective). One's perspective influences whether events are perceived concretely or abstractly, and this difference can alter the nature of one's mental representation of the event as well as the processes engaged in developing it.

These researchers (Libby & Eibach, 2011; Libby et al., 2009) tested their ideas using the Behavior Identification Form (Vallacher & Wegner, 1985) described earlier. This form consists of 25 actions (e.g., locking a door) that can be identified in either concrete and specific terms (inserting key in lock) or in abstract and general terms (securing the house). Participants were told to picture themselves doing each of these actions from either a first-person perspective ("see the scene as if you were actually performing the action; looking through your own eyes at the situation as you perform it") or a third-person perspective ("see the scene from the visual perspective an observer would have if you were actually performing the action; you can see yourself performing the action, as well as aspects of the situation"). When participants imagined performing these actions from the third-person rather than a first-person perspective, they were more likely to be described with the high-level, abstract rather than the low-level, concrete alternative. In other studies (Libby et al., 2009), different perspectives were induced by showing participants pictures of an action, for example, wiping a counter with a sponge,

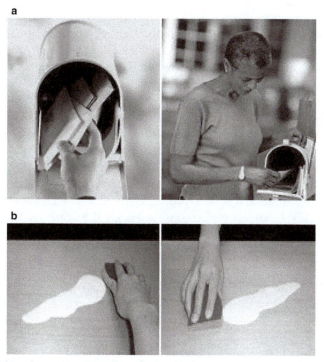

Figure 5.1 First-person and third-person perspectives for (a) getting the mail and (b) wiping the counter

Source: From Libby et al. (2009)

from two angles providing different visual views corresponding to first-person vs. third-person perspectives (see Figure 5.1). Again, actions were more likely to be characterized with high-level abstract descriptors when the photo represented a third-person rather than a first-person visual perspective.

Another study (Libby et al., 2009) explored the benefits associated with these different perspectives. The first-person perspective, by focusing on concrete details of the action and its components, would be oriented toward understanding *how* an action is performed. However, a third-person perspective, by focusing on abstract qualities and the fit with the behavior in a broader context, provides information about *why* an action is performed. The instructions provided to participants explained that photos often accompany text material to enhance communication. They were also told that sometimes the goal is to communicate *how* a particular action is performed, and other times it concerns *why* the action is performed. Participants were then shown 11 pairs of photos (as in Figure 5.1) and had to indicate which one would better succeed with each communication goal. Consistent with predictions, third-person images were commonly chosen to communicate why actions would be performed. In contrast, first-person images were more likely selected to illustrate how the action is performed.

This series of experiments shows that the perceivers' visual perspectives causally influence the meaning derived from actions.

Linguistic Category Model

The general-specific distinction is also central in a model that integrates the level of thought abstraction with the role of language in construing the behaviors of others (Semin & Fiedler, 1988, 1992). This model, called the *Linguistic Category Model* (LCM), differentiates four levels or categories at which any given behavior can be construed, understood, and described. These levels are described in Table 5.1, where it is evident that the same behavioral act can be encoded, interpreted, and communicated in different ways that convey different interpretations and meanings of the same information. A central property of this system is that the categories vary in their levels of abstraction. At the lowest level, a behavior can be encoded with *Descriptive Action Verbs* (DAVs) that refer to specific discrete actions in very literal, context-specific terms and do not include interpretation of the action. At the next level of abstraction, *Interpretive Action Verbs* (IAVs) construe a behavior in terms of a class of behaviors that also have clear beginnings and endings but also carry evaluative connotations regarding their consequences and convey interpretive meaning. *State Verbs* (SVs) construe an event in terms of the psychological state of the actor. The statement is not constrained to a specific episode or situation but is more abstract and is clearly interpretive, reflecting enduring mental or emotional states of the actor. Finally, behaviors can be construed using *Adjectives* (ADJ) that characterize the actor. This highest level of abstraction encodes the action in terms of abstract dispositions of the actor that generalize across specific events and situations.

Table 5.1   Linguistic category model levels of classification

Category	Criteria	Example
Descriptive Action Verbs (DAV)	Refer to one specific action, neutral description	Alan hit Bob
Interpretive Action Verbs (IAV)	Refer to a class of behaviors, positive or negative semantic connotations	Alan hurt Bob
State Verbs (SV)	Refer to mental or affective state of actor	Alan hates Bob
Adjectives (ADJ)	Refer to properties of the actor, not to specific actions or events	Alan is aggressive

Source: Adapted from Semin & Fiedler (1988)

What difference does it make how behavior is linguistically encoded? The levels of LCM increase in the abstraction with which the behavior is interpreted, moving from a limited description of a single act through various levels of encoding that carry extra meaning and generality. DAVs and IAVs provide useful but limited interpretations of specific actions in specific situations. SVs carry assumptions about affective and mental states and the actor's intentions, but these assumptions may not be expected to generalize across time and context. Finally, ascribing adjectives is an interpretation that implies both stability and generality of the actor, not constrained to the specific context of the behavior. Of course, the higher the generality, the more pervasive the mental conception of the event, the more it will be seen as typical of the actor and the more one will expect similar behaviors in the future.

Although adjectives are the highest, most general level in Semin and Fiedler's (1988, 1992) LCM framework, some have argued that nouns might represent an even higher linguistic category (Carnaghi, Maass, Gresta, Bianchi, Cadinu, & Arcuri, 2008; Hamilton, Gibbons, Stroessner, & Sherman, 1992). To describe Juan as *an intellect* conveys much more than saying that he is *intelligent*. Similarly, in group perception, encoding Deborah as *a Jew* is a broader, more pervasive, more all-encompassing construal than is referring to her as *Jewish*. In a series of studies (Carnaghi et al., 2008), target persons were described either by an adjective (athletic) or the corresponding noun (athlete). This research showed that, compared with adjectives, nouns facilitate inferences consistent with the descriptor and inhibit inconsistent inferences, and they more strongly inhibit classifying the person into alternate categories. Persons described by nouns were rated as being more stable through time and more resilient than persons described by adjectives. The higher the level of abstraction, the more general the characterization and hence the more stable, permanent, and unchangeable the quality seems to be.

Linguistic Intergroup Bias

The LCM has also been applied toward understanding how language is used in intergroup contexts (Dragojevic, Sink, & Mastro, 2017; Maass, 1999; Maass & Arcuri, 1992, 1996; Maass, Salvi, Arcuri, & Semin, 1989; Rubin, Paolini, & Crisp, 2013). This is an interesting domain in which to study how subtle differences in language can play essential roles in creating and perpetuating differences in the interpretation of groups and their members. One phenomenon that can be propagated through language use is *ingroup bias*, the tendency for people to routinely favor groups to which they belong (ingroups) compared to groups of which they are not members (outgroups). Maass et al. (1989) demonstrated the role of language in ingroup bias by examining behavioral interpretations during a time of intergroup strife. They did so by assessing linguistic descriptions of ingroup and outgroup members' actions during an annual Italian horse racing competition that pits residents of different neighborhoods against one another. Participants in the study were shown cartoon-like portrayals of a member of their own group (a fellow resident of their neighborhood) or of a competing group (a resident of a neighborhood with which they compete) engaging in either desirable (e.g., helping) or undesirable (e.g., littering) behaviors. For each one, the participants' task was to select one of four descriptions that best described the behavior.

Table 5.2   Mean level of abstraction as a function of group membership and social desirability

Group	Desirability of behavior	
	Desirable	Undesirable
Ingroup	2.69	2.51
Outgroup	2.47	2.82

Source: Adapted from Maass et al. (1989)

The four options were worded according to the four levels of the LCM, and participants' choices were scored regarding the level of abstraction of their choice (1–4, with higher scores representing higher abstraction). The results are shown in Table 5.2. When members of the ingroup performed desirable acts, participants on average chose a higher, more abstract descriptor than when the outgroup performed desirable behaviors. Just the opposite pattern occurred when undesirable behavior was displayed: higher generality was used in describing behaviors of outgroup compared with ingroup members. Maass et al. (1989) called this the *Linguistic Intergroup Bias* (LIB). It is based on motivation to protect the ingroup, portraying the ingroup more favorably than the outgroup through subtle differences in language use (Maass, Ceccarelli, & Rudin, 1996). It occurs in competitive intergroup contexts, particularly when the ingroup is threatened (Maass et al., 1996).

This difference in the level of abstraction in characterizing ingroups vs. outgroups is important because greater generality implies greater stability and typicality of the characterization. The fact that favorable ingroup behaviors and unfavorable outgroup behaviors are coded and interpreted at higher levels of abstraction suggests a bias in the interpretation of behavior that is communicated linguistically, contributing to the persistence of group stereotypes (Maass, 1999).

Maass et al.'s (1989) findings are based mainly on analyses of verb use in categorizing group behaviors. However, similar principles might apply to adjectives, which of course have always been of central interest to social psychologists, given their historical interest in impression formation and stereotyping. Because we often convey beliefs about social groups with adjectives, is it possible that different kinds of trait adjectives might underlie and perpetuate intergroup bias? Although Semin and Fiedler's (1988, 1992) LCM views adjectives as equally (and highly) abstract, there are, in fact, established differences in the inductive potential of different adjectives based upon their "breadth" (Hampson, John, & Goldberg, 1986). Broad trait adjectives allow easy generation of behaviors that exemplify the trait, whereas narrow traits are more tightly tethered to specific behaviors. For example, a person who regularly arrives on time for meetings might either be labeled as "responsible" or "punctual." The former description implies that the person is probably conscientious in many different ways and various aspects of life, whereas the latter suggests only that he or she appears on time for appointments. Interpreting the same behavior with traits differing in breadth is another way that language can subtly convey information about the stability and typicality of behavior.

Hamilton et al. (1992) used these insights to examine differences in the breadth of traits that comprise consensual stereotypes of different national groups. These researchers re-analyzed data that had been reported originally by Eagly and Kite (1987) involving American undergraduates' ratings of 28 different nationalities on 41 different traits. These traits were known to vary in desirability and breadth, based upon Hampson et al.'s (1986) research. Participants had also rated the degree that they thought each nationality was likable, and these judgments were used to identify nationalities that were generally liked and those that were generally disliked. Overall, and not surprisingly, liked nationalities were rated high on desirable traits and disliked nationalities were rated high on unfavorable traits, regardless of trait breadth. However, trait breadth played an important role in ratings on traits that were inconsistent with overall group evaluations. Specifically, liked groups were rated as having more narrow than broad undesirable traits, whereas disliked nationalities were seen as having more narrow than broad desirable traits. In other words, liked groups appear to have been "given the benefit of the doubt," being labeled with narrow adjectives for negative attributes. In contrast, disliked groups were "cut no slack" by being labeled with narrow positive attributes. Broad traits not only imply greater stability and generality but also are more difficult to disconfirm. Therefore, these differences in ascribing broad and narrow traits to liked and disliked groups serve to perpetuate intergroup evaluations and to make pre-existing differences resistant to change.

These biases have significant consequences not only for intergroup perceptions but also for the interpersonal transmission of beliefs. In fact, these biases can affect print media coverage of groups that are disliked and marginalized. For example, content analyses of articles about immigration issues in newspapers from four southwestern American states showed that comments about the positive ingroup (U.S.) used more abstract language than did positive comments about the outgroup (undocumented immigrants) and negative ingroup comments. In contrast, negative comments about the outgroup used more abstract language than both positive comments about the outgroup and negative comments about the ingroup (Dragojevic et al., 2017). Moreover, this pattern of language use in these articles resulted in more unfavorable attitudes toward Latinos (Mastro, Tukachinsky, Behm-Morawitz, & Blecha, 2014). Thus, aspects of language use can shape interpretations of behavior and intergroup attitudes.

Construal Level Theory

Another important approach to interpretation is *Construal Level Theory* (CLT; Trope & Liberman, 2010). "Construal" is a broad term that pertains to the ways that people perceive, comprehend, and interpret the world around them. The central concept in CLT is *psychological distance*. People construe people and events in a variety of contexts. They may interpret events occurring not only in the immediate present but also in the past and the future; in close physical proximity and the far distance; performed by persons similar to or different from oneself; by ingroup and outgroup members; and even imagined events that are not real. "Psychological distance" refers to how close or far away a person, object, or event is from the self, where distance can be defined in terms of time, space, social distance, and hypotheticality.

The overarching principle in CLT is that as psychological distance increases, so does the level of abstraction of construals. Psychologically distant persons and events are construed more abstractly, whereas psychologically near persons and events are construed in more specific, concrete terms. This same principle applies to all four ways in which distance may be experienced – temporal, spatial, social, and hypothetical. High-level, abstract construals are schematic portrayals that capture the gist of the current information. As such, they impose order and structure on that information, lending unity and coherence to it. In contrast, low-level, concrete construals are less structured and often are rich in details, offering more context-specific interpretations.

Why is greater distance associated with more abstract construals? If you think about an event that will not occur until sometime in the future or see a person or group that is at some physical distance or is quite different from yourself or your group, you typically have little knowledge and information about that event or person. Consequently, you can only form generic, abstract representations of them. In contrast, perceiving persons and events that are much closer in time or space or are more similar to oneself typically allows access to more detailed information that provides the basis for more concrete construals. According to CLT, this association between distance and abstractness becomes overgeneralized and comes to characterize a general relationship between distance and abstractness of construals. This relationship holds for all of the bases of psychological distance, providing a common basis for attaining meaning across dimensions of temporal, spatial, social, and hypothetical distance. Numerous studies have found support for these ideas, documenting differences in the level of construal as a function of temporal distance (Eyal, Hoover, Fujita, & Nussbaum, 2011; Eyal, Liberman, Trope, & Walther, 2004; Ledgerwood, Wakslak, & Wang, 2010; Nussbaum, Liberman, & Trope, 2006; Nussbaum, Trope, & Liberman, 2003; Rim, Uleman, & Trope, 2009; Wakslak, Nussbaum, Liberman, & Trope, 2008), spatial distance (Fujita, Henderson, Eng, Trope, & Liberman, 2006; Henderson, Fujita, Trope, & Liberman, 2006; Rim et al., 2009), and social distance (Liviatan, Trope, & Liberman, 2008; Stephan, Liberman, & Trope, 2010).

> **INTERIM SUMMARY** The research programs described in the last several paragraphs have a common theme that underlies them all. Whether it be the terms used in identifying individual actions (Vallacher & Wegner, 1987, 1989), the perspective adopted in perceiving behavior (Libby & Eibach, 2011), the linguistic categories used in categorizing observed behavior (Semin & Fiedler, 1988, 1992), the characterization of ingroup versus outgroup behaviors (Maass, 1999; Maass & Arcuri, 1996), or the psychological distance of a stimulus from the self (Trope & Liberman, 2010), the conceptual analyses have all identified variables that influence interpretations varying along an important continuum of very concrete, specific interpretations to very abstract, generic interpretations. The common theme is that, in a variety of ways, the level of abstraction of an interpretation makes a difference in the meaning of the behavioral information being processed.

VARIETIES OF AMBIGUITY

So far, we have discussed a series of examples and theoretical accounts primarily focused on how people interpret everyday, regular, often mundane events. These interpretational processes typically occur with minimal intention, effort, and awareness. Usually, we are unaware that we have engaged in interpretive processes at all in reacting to these kinds of behavior – it might never dawn on us that we could have interpreted the man we saw taking a drink as anything but a person quenching his thirst (rather than as a person who was swallowing liquid).

In some circumstances, however, the need to interpret information becomes much more apparent to us. We occasionally encounter information that is unclear and sometimes downright puzzling. We might see a person who looks or behaves in a manner that does not allow easy or quick interpretation. Alternatively, we might encounter information that violates our beliefs, our assumptions, or our expectations. In these cases, we will likely initiate efforts to process information carefully so we can come to at least some conclusion about what we are experiencing. We now turn to several examples of research focusing on such situations.

Perceiving Social Categories

It may often seem that information regarding a person's social category memberships is apparent and easy to discern. As we have already discussed, categorizations of people along race, age, and gender lines are typically characterized as automatic processes that occur without intention or effort. That is undoubtedly true when category cues are clear. For example, it is often the case that men and women wear gender-typical clothing, exhibit different hairstyles, and differ in visible physical characteristics. That is not always the case, however. People often exhibit gender-atypical characteristics and behavior, and this has become particularly true as people increasingly resist binary sex categories and embrace fluid gender identities. When signals regarding such social category memberships are absent, vague, or contradictory, then intentional interpretational processes are activated to aid in disambiguation.

Thus even everyday, routine aspects of social perception can, at times, present an interpretive challenge. The question then arises as to how, and on what bases, perceivers identify gender under conditions when the usually clear and obvious cues are not so clear and obvious.

Interpreting Gender: Morphology and Motion

When we encounter ambiguous or incomplete information about gender, we utilize cues from body shape (i.e., morphology) and motion to make sex categorization determinations. Men and women differ in body shape in numerous respects, but one key differentiator is reflected in average waist-to-hip ratios (WHRs). A small WHR reflects an "hourglass" figure, more characteristic of females, whereas larger WHR values ("tubular" figures) are more characteristic of men. Also, men and women walk differently. Males typically manifest more shoulder twist while walking (swagger), whereas females typically manifest more hip movement (sway). We observe these characteristic patterns all the time and presumably use both kinds of information in judging persons. How do perceivers use a person's morphology and his or her "swagger" and "sway" to judge the gender of a person?

Research (Johnson & Freeman, 2010; Johnson & Tassinary, 2005; Johnson, Gill, Reichman, & Tassinary, 2007; Johnson, Pollick, & McKay, 2010) has studied such questions by presenting computer-based degraded animations of humans (e.g., figural outlines and point-light displays in which all observable gender characteristics, such as facial hair, breasts, genitals, etc., have been removed) walking in place. The animations were constructed such that the figures themselves had five different WHRs and included five levels of swagger (shoulder motion) and sway (hip motion). Participants' eye movements as they watched the presentations were recorded to determine their focus of attention, and their binary gender category judgments were collected. These studies produced several important findings. First, sex category judgments were more strongly influenced by morphology than by motion. Not surprisingly, hourglass figures were perceived to be females. Body motion also influenced sex categorizations (with swaying walkers judged as females), although not as strongly as body shape. Second, eye tracking measured attention to four body areas – head, chest, waist-hips, and legs. Participants looked more at the waist-hip area than any other area, and this was true for both male and female observers. However, when the sex of the stimulus person was known, this focus on waist-hips information was significantly reduced. Third, analyses were conducted to determine the combined and interactive influence of morphology and motion on sex identification. As already noted, body shape is a primary basis for recognizing a person's gender. When information about body shape was controlled (or when cues to shape were diminished), swagger versus sway significantly influenced sex perception. Results also showed that body motion (swagger, sway) is perceived to be either masculine or feminine, and the individual's sex (male, female) is then inferred.

Interpreting Sexual Orientation: Cues from Gendered Characteristics

Other studies (Johnson et al., 2007; Lick, Johnson, & Gill, 2013) have focused on how body shape and motion affect perceptions of sexual orientation. The researchers reasoned that walkers manifesting *atypical* patterns – an hourglass body shape that moves with shoulder swagger, or a high WHR person walking with hip sway – would influence the interpretation of sexual orientation. Again, participants viewed walkers that systematically varied in morphology and motion.

Consistent with hypotheses, walkers manifesting *gender-atypical* patterns were rated as more likely to be lesbians and gay men than were those manifesting *gender-typical* patterns. These results show how observers interpret behavioral displays to draw inferences about the traits and group memberships of persons, by merely observing the way they walk.

We often have much more information than morphology and movement, and it probably is not a surprise that the face alone provides much valuable information regarding social categories such as gender, age, and race. What perhaps might be surprising is that facial details alone can also convey information about sexual orientation and other perceptually ambiguous categories. Several studies have shown that a person's sexual orientation can be judged from very brief exposures to the person's face or even facial features in isolation (Rule, 2017; Tskhay & Rule, 2013). Participants can detect gay (versus straight) male faces (Rule & Ambady, 2008; Rule, Ambady, Adams, & Macrae, 2008; Rule, Macrae, & Ambady, 2009) and lesbian (versus straight) female faces (Rule, Ambady, & Hallett, 2009) at above-chance accuracy, even when they were shown for as little as 40 ms. Accurate performance at these speeds suggests that sexual orientation is automatically detected from faces.

What facial cues are being utilized to interpret sexual orientation? Research indicates that gender-typicality plays an important role, as it did in the studies examining gender categorization we described above. In one series of studies investigating this factor (Freeman, Johnson, Ambady, & Rule, 2010), participants were shown both computer-generated and real faces in which two facial dimensions (shape and texture) became more gender-inverted. Men tend to have lower eyebrows, more clearly defined jawbones, hollower cheeks, and a squarer face overall. In contrast, women typically have higher eyebrows, less defined jawbones, round cheeks, and a rounder face overall. Texture involves darker coloring, more facial hair, and thicker eyebrows for men compared with women. For both artificial and real faces, results showed that the degree to which these gendered facial characteristics conflicted with one another (e.g., a masculine shape with a feminine texture), the probability of that face being perceived as gay or lesbian increased. Also, perceivers' use of gender-inverted cues increased the accuracy of sexual orientation categorizations when judging real faces. These results show that perceivers exploit gender-inverted cues to interpret sexual orientation and that their use of these cues increased the accuracy of their judgments.

Perceiving Behavior

Sometimes, but not always, we expend effort to interpret the behavior of others. We typically do not spend much time or energy interpreting a single commonplace behavior that we encounter with regularity. When we encounter a smile from a classmate, it seems pretty evident to us without giving it much thought that the person is friendly. In fact, it is both fortunate and adaptive that we can make such assumptions. If we were not able to interpret behavior automatically, it would be nearly impossible to walk down a city sidewalk or go grocery shopping without spending all of our cognitive resources interpreting routine occurrences. However, there are situations where our behavioral observations trigger effortful interpretive processes. Sometimes these efforts allow us to understand others more deeply, but these efforts can also lead to bias and error.

Interpreting Behavioral Variability

Although we often encounter others only briefly and momentarily (one of the authors, when he lived in New York City, used to see over a thousand people every morning when he took the subway to work), we sometimes get the opportunity to observe people over time and in different contexts. Doing so allows us to notice *patterns* in a person's behavior. Danielle got high scores on several (though not all) Math quizzes this term. Does this mean that Danielle has good Math ability? Several times recently, Luca has been pretty irritable. Does this indicate that Luca has a nasty streak or a low threshold for anger reactions? These cases are a bit more complicated than our earlier examples because they involve integrating multiple observations rather than interpreting single instances of behavior. As we "take in" multiple pieces of information about others, the meaning of the behavioral pattern – what it tells us about the person – must be determined by us as observers. That "meaning" depends on our interpretation of that information.

Sometimes the meaning of a pattern is evident. One friend, Felix, is always friendly and invariably upbeat. It is not difficult to surmise from this pattern that he has a positive and optimistic personality. A different friend, Noah, is usually kind, but he has been a bit of a jerk a few times recently, which others have noticed, such that one might wonder if he really is an irritable and moody sort of person. However, he's not that way all the time, and certainly all of us have a bad day now and then, which can make any of us temporarily irritable. What can we interpret about a person from such an erratic pattern of evidence? Major theories have been developed to explain what people do in such situations, and we delve into these accounts in detail later in the book. Nevertheless, we offer brief descriptions of them here to make the point that people *notice* such variations in behavior and attempt to *interpret* what they suggest about the actor.

One approach to understanding variability across time and context is provided in Mischel's account of personality. As we describe in detail in Chapter 12, Mischel and his colleagues (Mischel, 1968, 1973, 2004; Shoda, LeeTiernan, & Mischel, 2002; Shoda, Mischel, & Wright, 1989, 1994) have argued that we interpret ourselves and others by examining precisely how behavior varies across social contexts. In doing so, we consider how people act across different situations to create complex representations of a person's nature. Mischel calls this representation a "behavioral signature," and it incorporates information regarding the person, the situation, and the interaction between the person and situation. For example, we might at first be puzzled that our new boss is sometimes quite friendly but other times very rude and short-tempered. If we can observe his behavior for long enough and across enough social situations, we might discover that his behavior is more predictable than we thought. The observed differences begin to make sense when we see that he is almost always kind when interacting with or in the presence of his supervisors, but that he tends to demean the people who work under him. Rather than being unable to interpret our boss, we conclude that he has a "kiss up, kick down" personality (Vonk, 1998).

A second explanation for how behavioral variability is interpreted is provided by Attribution Theory (the focus of Chapter 8). Attribution Theory is actually a set of theories that describe how people form causal explanations of people's behavior. Most attribution theories agree that causal analysis is not conducted for all behavior we observe but is instigated in certain circumstances. One such case is when there is variability in behavior across time and contexts. When we see such variation, it often makes us ask, "Why did that person act that way?" and we engage in an attributional analysis to generate an answer. According to one highly influential theory (Kelley, 1967, 1973; Kelley & Michela, 1980), people examine three main factors to make causal attributions: consistency ("Does this person always do this to this person and in this situation ?"), distinctiveness ("Does this person do this to other persons and in different situations?"), and consensus ("How do other people act toward this person or in this situation?"). By answering these questions, we can often make sense of variability in the behavior of others as well as ourselves.

Interpreting Randomness

So far, we have provided examples and research evidence attesting to the fundamental human interest in interpretation. Whether it is effortless or effortful, people strive to find and maintain meaning in what they observe and experience (Heine, Proulx, & Vohs, 2006). Due to the need to understand what they witness, when meaning is threatened, people are motivated to restore it. However, this need to interpret can be so strong that it can often lead people to accept unwarranted conclusions.

One human pitfall is that we tend to see meaningful patterns or signals where there are none. We might believe that our daily horoscope provides unique insights into our life, even though on any given day thousands of people are reading the same one (Forer, 1949). We might believe we can predict accurately whether a parole candidate will again commit a crime based on a personal interview, even though intuitive judgments rarely, if ever, improve on purely evidence-based decisions (Dawes, Faust, & Meehl, 1993). Furthermore, once formed, beliefs about patterns can be difficult to dispel. An example illustrating this point comes from the world of sports, specifically, from basketball, where people often talk about a player who gets a *hot hand*. The notion is that certain players "get a hot hand" that results in streak shooting, in which the player will make several shots in a row. Having made a couple of shots, the player becomes more confident and feels "in a groove," "on fire," or "in the zone," increasing the odds of further success. On the other hand, sometimes a player will miss a few shots in a row, seemingly has "gone cold" and becomes hesitant, thereby extending his period of poor shooting. These examples reflect interpretations of *patterns* of behavior in which clusters of success (or failure) produce interpretations that the shooter has a hot hand (or has gone cold). Do these patterns really occur? Do they have meaning?

Gilovich, Vallone, and Tversky (1985) studied this question empirically. They obtained the shooting performance of every player of the Philadelphia 76ers (a professional American basketball team) for an entire basketball season. These records included every shot in sequence taken by each player and whether it was made or missed. Using these data, Gilovich et al. could determine the likelihood, given what happened on one shot, that the person would or would not make the next shot. For a shooter with a hot hand, the record should reveal streaks of "hits" in which baskets were made on several successive shots. However, Gilovich et al.'s statistical analyses of these data showed no such evidence for streak shooting. Instead, the evident patterns could be more easily and parsimoniously explained by chance.

The basis for our belief in systematically clustered shooting is that "chance" performance can include many patterns across time. For example, we believe that flipping a fair coin should have an equal probability of being a head or a tail. In the long run, that will be true; if you flip a coin 100 times, the results will be something close to 50–50 heads vs. tails. Within that sequence of 100 coin flips, however, there will be some "runs" of several heads (or tails) in a row that give the appearance of being something systematic (flip a coin 100 times and write down the result each time – there will be some clusters of identical outcomes). Nevertheless, it is not systematic. And this is why people (including players, coaches, and fans) believe basketball players can have a hot hand or be streak shooters. Players do score in some streaks, but those clusters of scoring are neither longer nor more frequent than would be expected by chance. As observers, however, we see order even in randomness. In fact, we may need to see meaningful patterns when none exist.

The limited ability of people to detect randomness in patterns of outcomes occurs not only in coin-flipping and basketball shooting. It can also appear in medicine. For centuries people (including doctors) have believed that the weather influences arthritic pain. The pain is felt more in cold and damp weather than in warm and dry weather. The puzzle is that, despite this widespread and long-held belief, the research literature reveals no relationship between these variables. As Redelmeier and Tversky (1996, p. 2895) observed, "Both laypeople and experts can sometimes detect patterns where none exist." They assessed the pain experienced by rheumatoid arthritis patients by several measures (both self-assessments and more objective measures) twice a month for 15 months. On those days, they also recorded weather reports of barometric pressure, temperature, and humidity. The patients fully believed that their pain was related to weather, but when correlations between pain measures and weather indices were calculated, the mean correlation was 0.016. The authors concluded that "people's beliefs about arthritis pain and the weather may tell us more about the workings of the mind than of the body" (p. 2896).

Similar phenomena can occur in the realm of social judgment. In Chapter 4, we presented research on *distinctiveness-based illusory correlations* (Hamilton & Gifford, 1976) in which a relation is perceived between two variables that does not exist in the data based on their infrequency. Another basis for seeing a nonexistent association is a pre-existing belief. An erroneous belief arising from prior expectancies is called an *expectancy-based illusory correlation* (Chapman & Chapman, 1967, 1969; Hamilton & Rose, 1980). In one study on this phenomenon (Hamilton & Rose, 1980), participants read a series of sentences in which individual persons were described by first name, occupation, and two trait-descriptive adjectives. Members of three professions (accountants, doctors, salesperson) were described, with eight members of each one. For each person, one of the traits was stereotypic of the person's profession (e.g., salesperson – talkative; accountant – perfectionistic) while the other trait was neutral concerning all three professions. In the stimulus set, each profession occurred the same number of times, and each stereotypic trait described each group the same number of times. Therefore, there was no actual relation between group membership and these trait attributes.

After reading all the sentences, participants were asked how many times each of the traits had described each group. The question was whether *a priori* stereotypic expectancies would bias their responses. They did. For each group, the traits stereotypic of that group were judged as having described that group more often than the other groups, even though each attribute was paired with each occupation the same number of times. Again, participants "saw" a relation between characteristics and groups that did not exist in the information they had read. They saw a pattern that did not exist. Note that in this case, the bias has significant implications for the maintenance of stereotypes. The stimulus information did not confirm stereotypic expectancies (each attribute described each group equally often). Yet, participants reported that the stereotype-consistent qualities (talkative salesperson) occurred more often than they did, apparently providing evidence that would subjectively reinforce and maintain the stereotypic beliefs.

The research we have just reviewed demonstrates that there are biases in the way people interpret information such that they "see" patterns in that information that do not exist. We have said that interpretation helps us make meaning from the information we acquire. In these cases, we are making a "meaning" (seeing a pattern) that is not there, and, of course, it becomes important to recognize and understand the biases that can distort our interpretations.

The same point applies to the everyday behaviors of people we observe and with whom we interact. Some people seem more intelligent than others, and some seem moodier than others, and we may be quick to characterize them in these ways. However, we need to be cautious about interpreting variations and apparent patterns in people's behaviors. Sometimes those can be real and valid patterns of variation – some people are smarter than others, and some people are bipolar and alternate regularly between positive and negative mood states, even to the point of needing medical treatment. In other cases, however, as we have seen in this section, what we observe is a normal variation in people's behavior patterns, and we need to be sensitive to the fact that apparent patterns may reflect randomness.

VARIABLES INFLUENCING INTERPRETATION

Several factors influence the way people interpret the information they encounter. In this section, we highlight the importance of two classes of factors: cognitive influences and motivational influences.

Cognitive Influences on the Interpretation Process

All of us have the benefit of a great deal of experience in perceiving and interacting with people in a very social world. Fortunately, this accumulated experience is represented in our mental representations. In Chapter 2, we considered various ways our experiences are represented in memory. A critical function of these representations is that they provide a basis for interpreting ambiguous information. When we encounter a new situation and it is not clear what we should make of it, we can use relevant stored knowledge to disambiguate the situation and thereby grasp some understanding of it. This seems entirely reasonable – the new experiences we have are often "reproductions" of similar past experiences (going to the grocery store is not a novel experience), so the representations of past events should be useful in understanding new events, new people, and new situations. Unfortunately, there is a downside to this story as well. The expectations provided by those representations may not always be accurate and, even if accurate, may not apply in a new context. Thus, while the use of mental representations can be quite functional, they can also lead to biased and incorrect interpretations of new settings.

Effects of Concept Activation on Interpretation

In Chapter 1, we described research by Higgins et al. (1977) in which trait concepts that were primed on a "perception" task later influenced the interpretation of information on a judgment task. Recall that participants were first exposed to a series of desirable or undesirable trait words reflecting different meanings of the same underlying concept (e.g., adventurous vs. reckless, persistent vs. stubborn). Later, in a supposedly separate experiment, they read a passage about a man named Donald whose behavior was ambiguous concerning the same concepts primed in the perception task. Those concepts, having been activated, were used to interpret the ambiguous behaviors manifested by Donald. If participants had read the terms "adventurous" and "persistent," they formed more favorable impressions of Donald than if they had read the terms "reckless" and "stubborn." Those concepts, having been made accessible by prior exposure during the perception task, guided the interpretation of ambiguous behaviors manifested by Donald in a different, independent experiment.

This priming effect is a fundamental mechanism by which information (concepts) stored in memory can become accessible for use in interpreting new information. Both the recency and the frequency with which a concept has been activated affect the strength of priming effects on subsequent interpretations (see Srull & Wyer, 1979, presented in Chapter 2). The applicability of the primed traits to the ambiguous behavior is also an essential factor. For example, manipulation of the terms "adventurous" vs. "reckless" would have a substantial effect on the interpretation of one's plans to ride rapidly-moving, treacherous river rapids in a one-person kayak. In contrast, the concepts "persistent" vs. "stubborn" would not (but would likely affect the interpretation of behavior during a heated argument, to which the latter concepts are relevant). Primed constructs do, however, influence interpretations beyond that constraint. For example, generalization of such effects can extend to evaluatively similar traits, even though they were not descriptively relevant to the priming traits. In addition, the size of priming effects can differ as a function of the breadth (e.g., extraverted) vs. narrowness (e.g., talkative) of the priming trait and the evaluative extremity of the prime trait (Bargh & Pietromonaco, 1982; Bargh, Bond, Lombardi, & Tota, 1986; Erdley & D'Agostino, 1988; Srull & Wyer, 1979). Priming effects also tend to be stronger under conditions of high than low arousal (Stangor, 1990). Finally, the fact that these priming effects occur when the priming traits are presented before, but not after, the descriptive passage indicates that these effects occur during the interpretation of stimulus information during encoding, not retrospectively during retrieval.

Effects of Concept Associations on Interpretation

The concepts stored in memory carry a range of associations, and (through spreading activation) those associations can also guide the analysis of events. One intriguing example of such an effect was demonstrated in research by Frank and Gilovich (1988). The color black has always been associated with negativity, including aggression, evil, and death, and these associations occur in many cultures (Adams & Osgood, 1973; Williams & McMurty, 1970). Can associations with the color black influence the interpretation of events? These researchers tested this idea in the realm of sports. Several sports involve extensive physical contact between members of opposing teams, and overly aggressive acts are penalized. Action in sports often happens very quickly, and in many cases, the question of whether a player's behavior "crossed the line" and should be penalized is open to interpretation. The referee, however, must decide quickly whether a penalty must be called.

Frank and Gilovich (1988) took advantage of the fact that some professional American football teams (Oakland Raiders, Pittsburgh Steelers) and hockey teams (Philadelphia Flyers, Boston Bruins) wear black uniforms, as do the New Zealand national rugby union team, the All Blacks. The researchers wondered if the color of their uniforms might play a causal role in interpreting the aggressiveness of their play. Specifically, might black uniforms influence the referees' interpretation of ambiguous plays and thereby result in a higher likelihood of being penalized? To answer this question, they analyzed the penalty data for all professional football and hockey teams over 15 years and determined the number of yards penalized by each football team and the number of penalty minutes by each hockey team. They then compared these data for teams wearing black uniforms or not wearing black. In both sports, the teams wearing black were penalized significantly more than teams not wearing black. These results suggest that connotations of the color black may influence the instantaneous interpretation of fast-occurring actions.

One alternate possibility is that teams who wear black in fact act more aggressively, providing a self-fulfilling prophecy supportive of the link between the color black and aggression. To rule out this possible interpretation, Frank and Gilovich (1988) created and filmed two "staged" football plays, using former high school and college football players. In each play, the actions of the defensive team could be interpreted as penalty-worthy violations, but they were not flagrant violations. Two versions of each play, well-rehearsed so that they would be as identical as possible, were videotaped. In one tape, the defensive team wore black uniforms, and in the other version, they wore white (the opposing team wore red in both cases). Participants watched each play and indicated whether they would penalize the defensive team's actions and rated the degree of aggression manifested in each play. Two sets of judges were used – a sample of football-knowledgeable college students and a sample of actual referees of high school and college games. For both of the plays, both the students and the referees indicated a higher likelihood of penalty for the team wearing black and rated that team as more aggressive than the team wearing white uniforms. Even when holding the aggression of the action itself constant, wearing black affected the interpretation of aggression.

The color black is not only tied to perceptions of aggression. Unfortunately, numerous studies show that in the social domain, black is also associated with *dehumanization*. Several lines of research indicate that, disturbingly, many Americans do not consider African Americans to be fully human, endowed with the same range of sensations, cognitions, and emotions as White Americans. For example, one set of studies (Goff, Eberhardt, Williams, & Jackson, 2008) showed that participants regularly associate African Americans with apes. This association affected how participants allocated their attention, processed visual information, and made criminal justice decisions. Another study conducted in the aftermath of Hurricane Katrina (Cuddy, Rock, & Norton, 2007) showed that White participants attributed fewer uniquely human emotions (i.e., *secondary emotions* such as anguish, mourning, and remorse) to Black than to White hurricane victims. A third set of studies (Mekawi, Bresin, & Hunter, 2016) showed that dehumanization affected actions directed toward Black individuals in simulated shooting scenarios (where men with weapons should be shot but men without weapons should not; Correll, Park, Judd, & Wittenbrink, 2002). Participants who were highest in fear of racial minorities and showed implicit associations linking Black with dehumanization showed a racial bias in decisions to shoot. In contrast, participants with low levels of implicit dehumanizing beliefs showed no racial bias in shooting, regardless of their fear levels.

How might a tendency to dehumanize African Americans affect how information about them is interpreted? Recent studies show that the interpretation of information regarding experiences of pain is affected in a manner consistent with the dehumanization of Black individuals (Hoffman, Trawalter, Axt, & Oliver, 2016; Trawalter & Hoffman, 2015; Trawalter, Hoffman, & Waytz, 2012). Deska et al. (2020), for example, reported an experiment where participants were shown pictures of White and Black individuals' faces and asked to judge how much social pain they would experience following a variety of distressing incidents (e.g., "This person's best friend gossips about them behind their back," "This person realizes after walking around all day that a pair of underwear was stuck to the back of their shirt"). The results (shown in Figure 5.2) indicate that both White and Black participants judged that the Black individuals would experience less severe levels of social pain in response to these events. Perhaps surprisingly, Black participants showed an even greater racial difference than did White participants in their ratings of anticipated pain.

Another set of experiments (Mende-Siedlecki, Qu-Lee, Backer, & Van Bavel, 2019) show that the interpretation of signals of physical pain is also affected by targets' race. In one of these experiments,

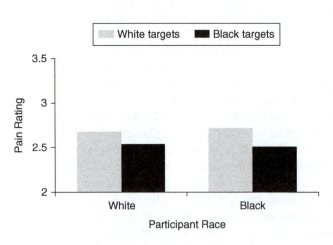

Figure 5.2 Judgments of social pain as a function of participant race and target race
Source: Adapted from Deska et al. (2020)

White participants were shown a series of images of faces of Black and White men who supposedly had been in a study in which they had received "painful burning stimulations on their forearms." The facial expressions were morphed to vary from neutral to displaying extreme levels of pain (see Figure 5.3). Participants were shown each morphed image and asked to indicate whether the man depicted was experiencing pain. After completing these pain judgments, participants were then told that an "experimental non-narcotic analgesic cream" could be provided to reduce the men's pain. They were again shown the same series of morphs and asked, for each one, "how many grams of the experimental analgesic cream should they be given?"

Figure 5.3   Images of Black and White men displaying neutral, medium levels of pain, or high levels of pain

Source: From Mende-Siedlecki et al. (2019)

Results showed that participants had more stringent thresholds for judging pain displayed in Black compared with White faces. In other words, the facial displays of pain needed to be, on average, more extreme before the participants interpreted a Black individual as experiencing the same level of pain as a White person. Furthermore, judgments of pain predicted the amount of analgesic that participants recommended. Because participants were less likely to perceive that the Black men were in pain given equivalent facial expressions, the consequence of this relationship was that Black men were less likely to be recommended for treatment that would alleviate their suffering. These data indicate the existence of disparities in interpreting cues of pain based on race. Such interpretational differences might contribute to and help explain existing racial disparities in the medical treatment of pain (Anderson, Green, & Payne, 2009; Mossey, 2011; Tait & Chibnall, 2014).

Motivational Influences on the Interpretation Process

We encode information from our social world to comprehend what we observe and experience, to understand its meaning, and to anticipate similar occurrences in the future. As we have described it thus far, it all sounds very rational: conscientious human beings trying their best to do it all well. Those human beings, however, are not entirely rational. They are driven by motives of all kinds that can play havoc with "rational" processes. Primary among those motives is self-interest. People like to think well of themselves, their performance, their outcomes, their popularity, and their prospects for the future. How do these motives influence the cognitive processing of information? This same question will recur as we progress through the various sections of this book. In this chapter, the query takes a specific form: How do these motives influence the interpretation of information as it is encoded?

Motives and Differing Interpretations of the Same Event

People with different needs, motives, and goals can witness the same event and come away with dramatically different interpretations of what they have just seen, as illustrated by the reactions of Seattle Seahawk fans to the "Fail Mary" play described at the beginning of this chapter. This phenomenon was studied empirically by Hastorf and Cantril (1954), who gauged reactions to an important football game between two rival universities, Dartmouth and Princeton. It had been a hard-fought very rough game, with many penalties for foul play and with several players being injured. Over the following weeks, there was considerable debate about the way the game was played and who was at fault for the ugliness, with people at each university blaming the other school's team. During this controversy, Hastorf and Cantril showed a film of the game to a sample of students at each university. As they watched the film, the students indicated each time they saw an infraction of the rules, and also whether it was a "mild" or "flagrant" foul. Not surprisingly, students from the two universities disagreed on these points. Princeton students "saw" Dartmouth players commit twice as many penalties as Princeton players, and the fouls committed by Dartmouth players were judged to be flagrant. In contrast, those by Princeton players were seen as mild. In contrast, when Dartmouth students viewed the same film, they identified an equal number of penalties committed by both teams, with approximately equal numbers of flagrant and mild fouls on both sides.

Figure 5.4 Ambiguous B–13 figure used in experiment by Balcetis & Dunning

Source: From Balcetis & Dunning (2006)

Although these differences may not seem surprising (we suspect those of you who are football fans can recall similar experiences of your own), it is important to realize that these data do not merely reflect the influence of motives on overall evaluative judgments ("They played dirtier than we did!") but rather on the *interpretation of specific acts* (infraction or not? mild or flagrant?) by the players in the game. The same film was shown to both groups, but the results suggest that they "saw" somewhat different games. The students' motives, based on their group loyalties, influenced the way the same behaviors were interpreted.

Other research has provided a more detailed analysis of the mechanisms underlying these effects and how personal motives can influence them. Balcetis and Dunning (2006) investigated the effect of desires and motives on fundamental perceptual processes. In an experiment presumably concerned with taste-testing, participants were given two glasses containing beverages. One glass contained fresh-squeezed orange juice whereas the other held a much less desirable "gelatinous, chunky, green, foul-smelling…concoction" described as an "organic veggie smoothie." Participants were told that they would have to drink 8 ounces of one of these beverages, which would be determined by whether a letter or a number appeared on the computer screen. Half of the participants were told that if the stimulus were a letter, they would drink the orange juice, but if it were a number, they would drink the veggie smoothie. The other participants were told the opposite. Thus, half of the participants were hoping to see a letter, and half were wishing for a number. Participants then saw a figure appear briefly (400 ms) that could be interpreted as either the letter B or the number 13 (see Figure 5.4) and were asked to report what they saw. The data in Table 5.3 show that participants' desires and motives influenced their interpretation of the ambiguous stimulus. Most participants hoping to see a letter reported that they saw the letter B, whereas those wanting to see a number reported seeing the number 13. Thus, people's motivational states can directly influence their interpretation of stimuli in their environment.

Table 5.3 Percentage of participants reporting seeing a letter (B) or number (13) in an ambiguous stimulus as a function of motivation

Motivated to see:	Reported by participants (%)	
	Letter	Number
Letter	72.0	0.0
Number	23.7	60.5

Source: Adapted from Balcetis & Dunning (2006)

Of course, it may be that people simply lied; they were highly motivated to drink the orange juice rather than the veggie sludge, so they may have just reported the letter or number that would fulfill their wish. Balcetis and Dunning did several follow-up experiments to rule out this possibility. Results from their five experiments document that people actually "saw" the figure they wished to see, and they were not even aware of the alternative interpretation of the ambiguous figure.

Biased Interpretation in Service of Self-protection

We want to believe that our opinions and the decisions we make are correct and well-justified. Consequently, when we hear someone offering views compatible with our own, we accept them without much thought and feel good about this confirmation of what we think. In contrast, we critically evaluate and challenge the arguments offered by someone holding views contrary to our own. In other words, we devote more time and effort to interpreting information that does not fit with our beliefs and desires. Moreover, we are not objective, impartial participants in this process. The extended effort at interpretation is biased by self-interest, seeking and accepting an interpretation that is compatible with self-views.

Several studies have provided evidence supporting this point. One study (Kunda, 1987) demonstrated that motives can bias the way people interpret and evaluate evidence relating to their preferred intuitions. Participants read a newspaper article reporting new scientific findings regarding the adverse effects of caffeine on health. People who were light coffee drinkers were more persuaded by the article's arguments than were people who drank much coffee. Those who were most threatened by the new evidence (heavy coffee drinkers) were more likely to interpret it in a way that doubted its validity.

Other research (Ditto & Lopez, 1992; Ditto, Munro, Apanovitch, Scepansky, & Lockhart, 2003; Ditto, Scepansky, Munro, Apanovitch, & Lockhart, 1998; Lench & Ditto, 2008) sheds light on the processes underlying the biasing effect of self-interest on interpretation. Specifically, there is an asymmetry in the extent to which information gets processed depending on the compatibility of the information with our interests. Information consistent with self-interest or a favored opinion is less likely to trigger analytic thinking as it is encoded, whereas information that challenges a cherished view or desire will be critically examined as its meaning is interpreted. People may actively try to refute opposing views, whereas they make little or no effort to determine the veracity of messages that are consistent with their opinions or desired outcomes.

In one study showing such an effect (Ditto & Lopez, 1992), participants learned about an enzyme (TAA), a deficiency of which purportedly could cause disorders of the pancreas. They then took a bogus saliva test that presumably would measure their TAA level. Through an experimental manipulation, some participants learned that they had TAA deficiency, whereas others learned that they did not (participants were actually randomly assigned to these outcomes). Participants who believed they were TAA deficient studied the results of the saliva test longer and often would retake the test before accepting the interpretation of the result. In contrast, participants whose test results showed they were not TAA deficient accepted the result without question or effort to verify it.

Both Kunda's (1987) and Ditto and Lopez's (1992) results show that people's motives and personal interests can drive the amount of thought and analysis that goes into interpreting information. In both cases, the feedback provided to participants involved a single, clear message about a particular health-related condition. What happens if the information received is more ambiguous, including mixed, conflicting, or inconclusive evidence? One possibility is that one should be cautious in making any interpretation or drawing any firm conclusions, given evidence that is mixed on an issue. A second possibility is that perceivers might take advantage of the ambiguity of information to embrace a desired conclusion selectively. Research shows that this latter possibility tends to characterize how ambiguous information is processed by people with pre-existing opinions on the topic. For example, one set of researchers (Lord, Ross, & Lepper, 1979) had participants read about two studies dealing with the issue of capital punishment and its effectiveness as a deterrent to murder. People had been recruited to participate in the study based upon their responses to an earlier questionnaire regarding their attitudes towards capital punishment, with a consequence that each participant read one study that confirmed their initial beliefs and another study that disconfirmed their beliefs. In each case, participants then rated, based on their reading of that article, any changes in their attitudes toward capital punishment and its deterrent value, as well as the impact of every single piece of evidence cited in the article and their cumulative impact on their attitudes. Consistent with Kundas (1987) and Ditto and Lopez's (1992) results, participants rated the article compatible with their positions to be more convincing than the article that advocated the opposing view.

Given this evidence of biased interpretation of the same materials by pro- and anti-believers, the question becomes, "what effect does this have on participants' attitudes?" Because they had read about the research supporting both sides of the issue, one might think that this information would moderate their opinions; that is, the two groups would move closer together. However, when asked about their final attitudes compared to what they were at the start of the study, proponents of capital punishment said they were more in favor of capital punishment, and opponents said they were less in favor of capital punishment. That is, the two groups became more polarized. Moreover, both proponents and opponents of capital punishment interpreted the specific pieces of information from the research (e.g., procedures used, results) as validating their initial attitudes.

The effect of being presented with identical information, providing the same level of support or disconfirmation, was to increase the gap between the views of proponents and opponents of capital punishment. As the authors observed, "Subjects' decisions about whether to accept a study's findings at face value or to search for flaws and entertain alternative interpretations seemed to depend far less on the particular procedure employed than on whether the study's results coincided with their existing beliefs" (Lord et al., 1979, p. 2106).

One's personal ideology (e.g., attitude regarding capital punishment) can not only influence the interpretation of information but also can change what we literally "see" in another person. This can affect even how people interpret a person's face. The face is a primary target of attention when one encounters another person (Palermo & Rhodes, 2007). However, the richness of information provided by a face can create ambiguity and hence an important opportunity for motives to affect interpretation.

One interesting example of interpretation in face processes is the demonstration that a person's political orientation can influence how she interprets facial stimuli, with significant downstream consequences. In a study conducted before the 2008 presidential election (Caruso, Mead, & Balcetis, 2009), participants who had earlier completed scales assessing their liberal versus conservative orientation were shown pictures of Barack Obama. Each photo was altered such that in one version, Obama's skin tone was lighter than in the original, and, in the other version, it was darker. Participants then rated how accurately each photograph depicted Obama. Results showed that liberal participants were more likely to see the lightened photo of Obama as most representative of him. In contrast, conservatives judged the darkened photo as more representative of Obama. Immediately following the election, participants were asked for whom they had voted. Even when controlling for political liberalism-conservatism, as well as for measured prejudice, the extent to which participants saw the lightened version of the photograph as more representative of Obama, the more likely they were to have voted for him.

In subsequent research (Stern, Balcetis, Cole, West, & Caruso, 2016), participants evaluated a job candidate whose application included three photos showing different poses of a racially ambiguous (mixed-race Black-White) man: the original photo, one in which skin tone was lightened, and one in which it was darkened. The extent to which the candidate and the participants had similar views on issues was manipulated through feedback. Participants viewed all three photos of the candidate and rated how well each one represented the target person. When participants and the candidate held similar views, White participants rated the lightened photo as more representative of the person, and Black participants rated the darkened photo as more representative. These skin-tone differences also predicted the participants' intentions to vote to hire the candidate. Together, these studies (Caruso et al., 2009; Stern et al., 2016) show that people's group memberships and their motivation to enhance their ingroup affected not only their interpretation of the representativeness of faces differing in skin tone but also their behavior in important decisions such as presidential voting and hiring decisions.

In this section, we have described a variety of studies that indicate that one's personal goals, desires, and attitudes can directly and importantly influence the interpretation of information being processed. The basic process of comprehending the meaning of information is subject to bias from personal positions and interests.

INTERPRETATION PROCESSES IN UNDERSTANDING THE SELF, PERSONS, AND GROUPS

We have discussed a variety of aspects of the way information we encounter in the social world is interpreted and some factors that guide those interpretations. We now consider some specific manifestations of these processes in the way we come to understand ourselves, others, and groups.

Interpretation Processes in Understanding the Self

We engage in interpretive processes because the information we encounter is inherently absent of meaning. We must use our knowledge based on a lifetime of experience to "go beyond the information given" (Bruner, 1957) to make it meaningful and useful. Information can often be ambiguous. Most social information – even seemingly clear and straightforward information – is open to alternative meanings and hence requires interpretation.

Of course, social information can vary in its ambiguity. Some of the behaviors we observe, events we witness, statements we hear seem very clear in their meaning, requiring little interpretive analysis. Presumably, the people, events, and social contexts that we know well should not need much interpretive thought; because of our familiarity with them, we know and understand the meaning of their actions. Carrying that thought one step further, certainly the person in the entire world that we know best, that we understand most well because of our extensive – and, in fact, continual – association with him or her, is ourselves. This suggests that we know who we are and what we are all about, so we do not need to spend much time interpreting the self-relevant information we encounter.

Much evidence questions this assumption. Several lines of research make it clear that we interpret information about ourselves just as much as we do information about other people. Self-relevant information that is amenable to interpretation is vast in variety and scope. Take, for example, knowledge about your own appearance. If there is one thing you might think you know very well, it would be your face. After all, we see our face in the mirror multiple times every day. This would seem to be one domain in which self-serving biases do not apply. Nevertheless, they do. Consider an experiment (Epley & Whitchurch, 2008) in which participants came into a lab to have their portrait photograph taken. They returned two weeks later for the second part of the experiment. In the interim, the researchers had morphed each participant's face with a very attractive face and with an unattractive face, producing a continuum of faces in which the actual photo of the participant was in the center. This continuum of 11 photos was shown to the participant (for an example of one such display, see Figure 5.5). The participant's task was to rate the likelihood that each photo was the picture taken of her in the first session. Were participants able to correctly choose their faces? Not really. Participants systematically selected a face that was (on average) two steps away from their own – in the more attractive direction (see Figure 5.6). Apparently, people are motivated to see themselves as more attractive than they actually are and therefore selected a face other than their own.

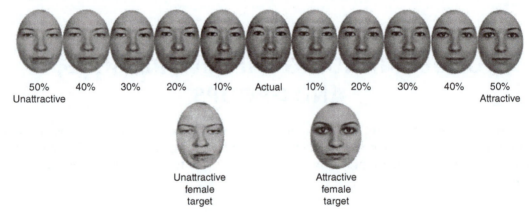

Figure 5.5 Example of face display presented to participants
Source: From Epley & Whitchurch (2008)

Earlier in this chapter, we talked about research showing that people's motives can influence the way they interpret the information they encounter. When it comes to the self, people have a persistent and robust motivation to perceive themselves in a very favorable light. We are motivated to think highly of ourselves as persons and to have favorable evaluations of our qualities and behaviors. Furthermore, we tend to believe we are a bit morally better than others.

For example, in advance of a fundraising event in which daffodils were being sold to raise money for a charity, Epley and Dunning (2000) asked people whether they were likely to buy a daffodil and if so, how many. They then made similar predictions about their peers. Three days after the event, people were asked whether they had purchased flowers and, if so, how many. Before the event, 83% of participants predicted they would buy at least one daffodil, but they expected that only 56% of their peers would do so. They also predicted they would buy more flowers than their peers. However, only 43% of the participants actually purchased flowers. People substantially overestimated the likelihood of their buying, whereas their predictions of their peers were considerably more accurate. This became known as the *better than average* (Alicke, Klotz, Breitenbecher, Yurak, & Vredenburg, 1995) or the *holier than thou* (Epley & Dunning, 2000) effect.

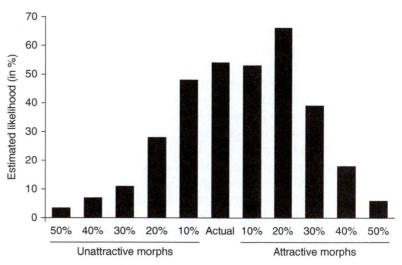

Figure 5.6   Average estimated likelihood that each image is the self
Source: Adapted from Epley & Whitchurch (2008)

This basic effect has been replicated in numerous experiments, using different paradigms. It is quite general and applies to a variety of judgments and behaviors. People believe they are more likely to act more altruistically, to donate money, to give blood, and to behave more fairly than others. In self-assessments, they rate themselves more favorably on a variety of traits than they rate others (Alicke et al., 1995; Allison, Messick, & Goethals, 1989; Balcetis & Dunning, 2008; Brown, 2012; Epley & Dunning, 2000; Goethals, 1986; Goethals, Messick, & Allison, 1991; Klein & Epley, 2016; Messick, Bloom, Boldizar, & Samuelson, 1985; Van Lange, 1991). We are most likely to judge ourselves as better than average on traits we consider to be important (Brown, 2012).

There are many possible explanations for these effects. It is possible, for example, that a minority of individuals are simply egotistical and make unreasonably glowing self-evaluations. If so, then people might appear to be egocentric on average because of these individuals. However, the data are not consistent with this interpretation. Instead, it appears that all of us engage selectively in self-enhancement, doing so in ways that avoid conveying the impression (to ourselves and others) that we think we are better than everyone else at everything. A self-view that one is better in some but not in all respects is not only more credible, but it also signals to others that our self-evaluations are discriminating and objective. Therefore, the tendency to view ourselves as better than others is constrained. One constraint is the dimension of judgment. The better-than-average effect consistently appears in judgments that are heavily evaluative, such as judgments on a general good–bad dimension (Allison et al., 1989) or fair–unfair dimension (Messick et al., 1985).

In contrast, the effect is much weaker (and perhaps does not occur) for intelligence judgments (Allison et al., 1989; Goethals, 1986). Why would this difference happen? If one is to maintain the self-view of being better than others in some way, it must be credible. As we have observed, behavior is often ambiguous and open to interpretation, but behaviors vary in their ambiguity. An intelligent behavior requires the presence of underlying ability and, therefore, quickly leads to the interpretation that the person is smart. Moral behavior, however, does not necessarily require moral character in the same way (moral people engage in ethical actions, but so do immoral people). The tighter correspondence between acts and inferred attributes for intelligence than for morality means that there is less interpretational ambiguity for intelligence than for morality. There is less room for motivated holier-than-thou conclusions in the intelligence domain. Thus, self-enhancement occurs for some dimensions of judgment more than for others.

A second constraint on the effect involves the target to whom the self is compared. In most studies, the judgments are made between the self and a generic, abstract other, such as "others," "people in general," or "peers." Some research has shown that self-enhancement is reduced when the comparison target is a specific individual (Alicke et al., 1995). Comparing ourselves with another specific person appears to reduce reliance on the assumption that "I am better than others" and forces us to engage in more specific and detailed comparisons.

A third constraint on self-enhancement concerns the evaluative dimension. A *better than average* comparison may be due to believing that one is more likely to do good things than others, less likely to do bad things than others, or both. In several studies, Klein and Epley (2016) gave participants a list of moral and immoral behaviors. They had participants rate, for each one, whether they or others were more likely to engage in the behavior. People rated themselves as less likely than others to engage in immoral behaviors, but there were no differences in judging the likelihood of moral behaviors. These authors concluded that people are less inclined to believe that they are "holier than thou" than to think they are "less evil than thou."

A fourth and final constraint on self-enhancement appears to involve issues of general mental health. Individuals who are chronically anxious, depressed, unhappy, or dissatisfied with themselves or their lives (Marshall & Brown, 2007; Taylor, Lerner, Sherman, Sage, & McDowell, 2003a) are less likely to self-enhance than others. This suggests that self-enhancement is one way that people maintain positive feelings about themselves. People who do not feel good about themselves tend not to think they are better than other people, possibly reinforcing their negative self-views (Brown, 2012).

In sum, information is often ambiguous, not only our and others' behaviors but even our facial appearance. The research summarized here shows that our interpretations are often, but not always, influenced by strong tendencies to favor interpretations that tend to enhance the self.

Interpretation Processes in Understanding Persons

Already in this chapter, we have described numerous instances in which interpretive processes play a crucial role in influencing our perceptions and understanding of individuals we encounter. In this section, we add two more bodies of research that illustrate, in different ways, the critical role of the interpretation process as we make meaning from the information we process about others.

Interpreting Behavior from Thin Slices

We have referred to a variety of sources from which we glean information about a person – for example, from his or her appearance, behaviors, facial expressions, nonverbal behaviors, and conversations. Given this range and diversity of information, the task of encoding information to gain some sense of what the person is like might seem to be a daunting challenge. For many years research has examined the perceiver's integration of trait and behavioral information into an impression of an individual or a clinician's integration of information about symptoms and clinical cues in making a diagnosis of a person. These processes require an abundance of information, as well as a perceiver who is motivated to consider a range of information and has the attentional resources required to do so. However, recent research has offered a much different portrait of the judgment process. This research shows that person judgments can be based on even brief exposure to information about a person. In fact, research on judgments from *thin slices* of behavior indicates that much useful knowledge about people can be gained from relatively small samples of behavior. These judgments are surprisingly consistent across different observers and are predictive of important social outcomes.

A thin slice of behavior is "a brief excerpt of expressive behavior sampled from the behavioral stream" (Ambady, Bernieri, & Richeson, 2000, p. 203). Imagine, for example, that on the first day of class, you are sitting in a lecture hall waiting for the professor to arrive. She walks in and begins talking about the course. What if we made you stop observing her after one minute and asked you some questions about her and the class? Will she be a good teacher? Will you enjoy the class? How confident would you be in these judgments made from only a single minute of observation? How accurate are such snap judgments? The stimuli used in these studies typically offer participants the opportunity to passively observe people by themselves or interacting with others for anywhere from a few seconds to a few minutes (Ambady & Rosenthal, 1992; Holleran, Mehl, & Levitt, 2009; Zebrowitz & Collins, 1997). These judgments of people based on such brief observations can be surprisingly accurate.

Consider the following study (Ambady & Rosenthal, 1993) in which participants were shown a series of brief (10 seconds each) videotapes of 13 college teachers (6 female, 7 male) teaching in class. There were three videotapes for each teacher, obtained early, in the middle, and late in the class period. The videos were silent; no sound was provided. After seeing the three tapes for a given teacher, the participants – complete strangers, not students in the courses – rated that teacher on several attributes, such as how accepting, active, competent, enthusiastic, and warm she seemed to be. These ratings were then correlated with the end-of-semester evaluations of the teachers from the students that had taken their classes. These analyses showed that teacher evaluations made by students who had taken these courses for an entire semester were significantly predicted by the participants' ratings, even though their ratings were based on observing only 30 seconds of a silent videotape.

In a follow-up study, the same analyses were done after showing even smaller slices of behavior – 5 seconds or 2 seconds. Again, participants' ratings of the teacher were effective in predicting end-of-semester teacher evaluations made by actual students in the courses. Thus, very brief exposures to expressive behaviors were substantially correlated with judgments of people who were much more familiar with the target persons. Although these findings may seem surprising, they are not unique. Similar effects have been found in a variety of judgment contexts, and research has further documented the accuracy of judgments based on thin slices. One study (Ambady, Hallahan, & Conner, 1999), for example, showed that participants could accurately judge a person's sexual orientation 70% of the time from observing ten seconds of a silent video clip of a person merely sitting in a chair.

Judgments of physical therapists' behaviors, based on three 20-second videotapes, have been shown to correlate not only with their clients' perceptions of them but also with the clients' physical and psychological improvement over time (Ambady, Koo, Rosenthal, & Winograd, 2002). Differences in communication style during social interaction can also be detected very quickly, and sometimes with severe consequences. In one study (Ambady, LaPlante, Nguyen, Rosenthal, Chaumeton, & Levinson, 2002), conversations between patients and surgeons during routine medical visits were recorded. Brief 10-second segments were extracted from the tapes and were coded for the tone of voice (with content removed). Half of the surgeons had previously had malpractice claims, whereas the other half had not. Analyses of the 10-second tapes showed that surgeons who sounded more dominant and less concerned were more likely to have been sued for malpractice than surgeons whose voice tone conveyed less dominance.

The accuracy of judgments based on thin slices can vary depending on the length of the observation and the attribute being judged. Both effects were shown in a study (Carney, Colvin, & Hall, 2007) in which participants observed a videotape of a person interacting with a stranger for differing lengths of time. Participants then made judgments of the person's intelligence, affective state, and various personality traits, and these judgments were then compared with external criteria (e.g., ratings of experts based on the entire interaction, results from an intelligence test). Table 5.4 shows the correlations between judgments and external criteria for the different attributes based on the length of observation. Several findings are notable from the pattern of correlations. First, several attributes, such as intelligence, extraversion, and negative affect, could be readily judged after very brief exposure. Second, the amount of exposure tended to increase the accuracy of judgments. Third, although some attributes could be judged quite accurately, others (e.g., agreeableness and neuroticism) were difficult to judge even with lengthy exposure. These results showed that at least some attributes could be readily judged from brief exposure to the behavior of an unknown person.

A related line of research shows that accurate judgments do not even require that behavioral information be available. Judgments based on merely seeing a person's face can be made quite quickly and can be surprisingly accurate in predicting a variety of social outcomes (Bjornsdottir & Rule, 2017; Freeman & Johnson, 2016; Jones, Tree, & Ward, 2019; Todorov, Olivola, Dotsch, & Mende-Siedlecki, 2015). In a series of studies, Willis and Todorov (2006) presented participants with images of unfamiliar faces for 100, 500, or 1,000 ms or with no time constraints. Judgments of the person's likability, competence, trustworthiness, and aggressiveness were then solicited. Judgments collected at brief exposure correlated highly with judgments collected under no time constraint (ranging from +.52 to +.74), and they did not differ significantly between conditions. Thus, people can very quickly infer attributes based on extremely brief exposure only to faces. How accurate are these judgments? Todorov and his colleagues (Todorov, Mandisodza, Goren, & Hall, 2005; Ballew and Todorov, 2007) have pursued this question by asking participants in several studies to judge various attributes of two unfamiliar political candidates running for the same office after only a brief exposure to their faces. Participants readily provided judgments of these attributes, and judgments of one attribute – competence – successfully predicted the election outcomes above chance with the person judged as more competent winning approximately 70% of the contests. Thus, person attributes can be readily inferred from facial characteristics that can have important implications for social judgments and phenomena.

Findings from these studies reveal that interpretation processes are engaged even by small segments of behavior. People need to make sense of what they witness, to find the meaning

Table 5.4 Judgment accuracy (correlation between judgment and external criteria) at different observation lengths.

	Observation length		
	1 mins	3 mins	5 mins
Attribute			
Positive affect	.11	.21	.26
Negative affect	.24	.31	.42
Neuroticism	.19	.18	.22
Extraversion	.29	.51	.41
Openness	.16	.23	.12
Agreeableness	.08	.12	.12
Conscientiousness	.20	.28	.34
Intelligence	.11	.30	.26

Source: Adapted from Carney et al. (2007)

of the transactions they observe. They do not merely attend and record in memory verbatim the literal events that occur. They go beyond that information to impose interpretation on it to uncover its meaning.

What's in a Face?

When we initially meet someone, the first thing we see is the person's face. Indeed, the face may be the only information we have about a person in a photo, whether it be in a magazine or on Instagram.

The face is a rich source of information. For example, a face immediately conveys information about gender, race, and age (Stroessner, 1996) – three categories about which most people have well-developed stereotypes that can then guide subsequent processing. We also automatically judge the physical attractiveness of people we encounter (Ritchie, Palermo, & Rhodes, 2017), a judgment that obviously can influence later perceptions and behaviors. Facial expressions (smiling, frowning) convey information about the person's current affective state (Du, Tow, & Martinez, 2014).

All of these judgments are important in understanding another person. However, a variety of judgments of other individuals rely on two different aspects of perceiving faces (Bruce & Young, 1986). On the one hand, although all faces have specific properties in common (eyes, nose, mouth), those features take a different form in different persons. Skin color, the shape of the mouth, and the size of the nose are among the essential features that differentiate faces. Encoding this type of information is called *featural* processing. On the other hand, it is the relations among those features that define each individual face, and encoding those relations is called *holistic* or *configural* processing (Maurer et al., 2002). All faces have two eyes, but those eyes can be close together or far apart, and the distance between those eyes and the nose can be minimal or relatively large. Perceiving the relations among features – patterning, distances, etc. – is configural processing. Both featural and configural processing are essential aspects of face perception, but they refer to different mechanisms by which we extract information from faces.

In the present context, featural and configural processing may be useful for different aspects of perceiving others (Cloutier, Mason, & Macrae, 2005). In any face, certain immediately obvious and easily perceived features indicate the person's membership in specific group *categories* (female, White, thirty-something). However, attention to the configuration among elements is necessary to identify the person. Therefore, whereas category membership may be based on featural processing, person perception and identification may be based on configural processing. If so, then identifying a person's category membership based on the presence of features (e.g., gender) may be easier, quicker, and less demanding than what is required to identify a person based on the configuration of features.

How can these questions be investigated? The strategy used in some research (Cloutier et al., 2005) was to compare participants' performance on two face judgment tasks – naming the gender of a person vs. naming whether a person is familiar (a well-known celebrity) or unfamiliar, a judgment that requires recognizing not only gender but the individual's identity. In the gender judgment condition, participants were to indicate whether the person was male or female. In the identification condition, photos were either celebrities (actors, singers) or not, and the participants' task was to indicate whether each person was familiar or unfamiliar. Also, these tasks were performed for faces shown under normal or challenging conditions, a distinction implemented by showing the photos in either normal position or inverted (upside down; see Figure 5.7, top). Why change the face orientation in this way? Whereas people can quickly and effortlessly recognize *features* of a face when it is upright or inverted, *configural* processing is severely disrupted (slower, less accurate) for inverted faces (Maurer et al., 2002). The accuracy of participants' responses and their response latencies in making their judgments were recorded and analyzed. Overall, people were more accurate and quicker in judging gender than individual identity and also were quicker and more accurate when faces were presented in upright rather than inverted position. Most importantly, however, the difference between judgments of upright and inverted faces was true only when making identification judgments; when judging whether a person is male or female, participants were equally quick and accurate, regardless of whether the photo was presented upright or inverted (Figure 5.8). Apparently, then, a category judgment (a person's sex) is more straightforward and can be made even when the face is inverted, whereas determining the person's identity (necessary for a familiar/unfamiliar decision) is more difficult, especially under inverted conditions.

Figure 5.7   Examples of upright and inverted faces and normal and blurred faces used in Cloutier, Mason, & Macrae (2005) experiments

Source: From Cloutier et al. (2005)

In follow-up experiments, Cloutier et al. (2005) tested the same hypothesis using different methods for making the photo judgment task demanding. In one case, rather than being inverted, photos were made blurry in half of the cases (see Figure 5.7, bottom). In another instance, pictures were shown for either 200 ms or only 20 ms. In both cases, the latter conditions made face perception more challenging. The results exactly replicated those reported above, such that naming the gender of the person was not affected by the blurring or speeded exposure. In contrast, these manipulations significantly interfered with determining the identity of the person.

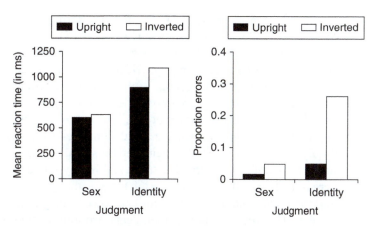

Figure 5.8   Mean reaction times (left panel) and error rates (right panel) for judgments of sex and identity for upright and inverted faces

Source: From Cloutier et al. (2005)

Interpretation Processes in Understanding Groups

Interpretive processes play an essential role in various aspects of information processing in intergroup contexts. In this section, we examine aspects of how we gain meaning in perceiving groups and how beliefs about the nature of groups can influence our interpretations of group members' behaviors.

Entitativity: Perceiving the Groupness of Groups

Before we explore how groups and group memberships can influence the way we interpret behaviors, we start with a more fundamental question: How and when do we perceive a group to be a group?

At its minimum, a group is a collection of persons, but not all collections of persons are groups. As perceivers, when we see a collection of people, we typically can determine not only *whether* those people constitute a group but also *what kind* of group they may be. In doing so, we are engaging in interpretation ("Those people definitely are a group"), and we are imposing meaning on what we see ("Those guys are a group of surfers"). How do we arrive at those perceptions? There are several stimulus cues that perceivers use in inferring that a collection of persons is a group (Campbell, 1958). For example, if the persons interact with each other a lot, and if their interactions appear to be coordinated, as if in pursuit of some common goal, then they are more likely to be perceived as a group. If the persons all share the same outcome from their activity (e.g., in team sports all members of a team win or all lose), they will appear to be a group, and if they share similarities (physical appearance, language, clothing such as a uniform), it will increase their apparent "groupness." All of these cues increase the perception of *entitativity* (Campbell, 1958), that is, the perception that this collection of persons constitutes a single entity (Hamilton, Sherman, & Rodgers, 2004; Lickel, Hamilton, Wieczorkowska, Lewis, Sherman, & Uhles, 2000). Once entitativity is perceived, those groups are seen to possess unity and coherence. This then facilitates drawing inferences about the nature of the group and its members, increases assumed consistency in the group across time, and promotes forming organized impressions of the group (Hamilton & Sherman, 1996). Given this perceived unity, several consequences follow regarding how the group and its behavior are interpreted (Brewer, 2015; Brewer & Harasty, 1996;

Hamilton, Chen, & Way, 2011; Hamilton, Sherman, & Castelli, 2002; Hamilton, Sherman, Way, & Percy, 2015; Stroessner & Dweck, 2015).

The number and variety of groups to which we belong, which we perceive, and with which we interact is enormous. Family, friendships, sports teams, racial and ethnic groups, males and females, occupational groups – all of these are groups, yet they vary considerably in their properties. Are there any commonalities in these groups? Are there different types of groups with differing features? Lickel et al. (2000) showed that perceivers differentiate among four major types of groups. *Intimacy groups* (family, close friends, support groups, gangs) are small, closely interactive, valued by their members, and stable over time. *Task groups* (committees, a jury, the cast of a play) are also small and highly interactive, but they exist primarily because there is a job to be done. When the job is done, the group may dissolve. *Social categories* (based on gender, race, nationality, religion) are very large groups that may be very important to some members (but less so to other members), are long-lasting groups, and for which it is difficult to change one's membership. Finally, *loose associations* (residents of a neighborhood, people attending a concert) are low in most of the features discussed except that joining or leaving them is comparatively easy.

These are four distinct types of groups and, in the sequence presented, have decreasing levels of entitativity. That is, your family is probably a highly entitative group, whereas the group of people in a large lecture hall has low entitativity. Moreover, these group types are more than convenient classifications. Research has shown that these group types are used spontaneously as people categorize others and store information about them (Sherman, Castelli, & Hamilton, 2002) and their use can serve different functions in meeting human needs (Johnson et al., 2006). Other research has shown that, across several groups, perceptions of group entitativity play a central role in stereotyping of those groups (Spencer-Rodgers, Hamilton, & Sherman, 2007). That is, people do not develop and use stereotypes about groups unless and until they are perceived as being entitative groups.

In sum, the perception of group entitativity is a building block that provides the foundation for many other processes. How we interpret the nature and function of groups gives meaning to our perceptions of them.

Effects of Stereotypes on Interpretation

Like concepts, stereotypes are cognitive representations that contain one's expectancies about a particular group. When a stereotype is activated, those stereotypic expectancies can guide the interpretation of group-relevant information. Those effects are particularly likely when the behaviors are open to alternative interpretations, as is very often the case.

In a study demonstrating this effect (Duncan, 1976), participants watched on a video screen an interaction between two men having a discussion and, whenever a signal light went on, their task was to code the behavior that just occurred. A sheet of paper provided several behavior categories they could use (e.g., "asked a question," "gave an opinion," "was assertive") whenever the light came on. As the discussion progressed, the two men increasingly disagreed, and the conversation became heated. At one point, one of the men reached over and gave the other a mild shove, and at that point, the light went on. The question of the study was, how was that shove interpreted?

In reality, the participants were not watching a live interaction but rather a videotape of two actors playing out a specific sequence. Four such tapes differed in the race of the two men: two Whites, two Blacks, or one White and one Black. In this way, the race of the "shover" and the "shovee" could be varied. The key factor determining how the shove was coded was the race of the man who made the shove (regardless of the race of the shovee) and led to dramatically different interpretations. If the shover was White, the shove was most often coded as a *dramatic gesture* emphasizing his point or as *playing around*. In contrast, if the shover was Black, the shove was coded as either an *aggressive act* or a *violent act*. Thus, the prevalent stereotype of African Americans, which includes concepts of aggression and hostility, strongly influenced the way the same action – an ambiguous shove – was interpreted.

But was it really the same act? After all, participants in the different conditions saw different actors enact the shove. Could it be that the Black actor shoved the other man a bit more enthusiastically than did the White actor? If so, the different codings could reflect accurate perceptions of qualitatively different acts, not biased interpretations of the same act. To explore this possibility, another study tested the same hypothesis using a different methodology that controlled for this concern (Sagar & Schofield, 1980). This study was conducted with 6th-grade children. Each child was shown a series of cartoon-like drawings showing an interaction between two children in a school setting (classroom, cafeteria), with a caption below. For example, one picture showed two students in a class, one seated behind the other, with the following caption:

> Mark was sitting at his desk, working on his social studies assignment, when
> David started poking him in the back with the eraser end of his pencil. Mark just
> kept working. David kept poking him for a while, and finally he stopped.

For each drawing, participants rated the extent to which the protagonist's behavior was mean, threatening, playful, and friendly.

With these drawings as stimuli, the researchers could manipulate the race of the protagonist (as well as the recipient of the behavior) by simply coloring the heads of the stick-figure actors differently. Consistent with Duncan's findings, participants in this study rated the Black protagonist's behavior as more aggressive and threatening and less playful and friendly than the White protagonist's behavior. Again, stereotypic expectancies influenced the interpretation of the same ambiguous behavior.

Stereotypic expectancies can bias the interpretation process such that the same behavior will be interpreted differently when performed by members of different groups. This point is illustrated in a controversy that arose in the during-game behavior of football players. Some players, having scored a touchdown (e.g., wide receivers after catching a pass in the end zone), perform elaborate and well-choreographed routines to celebrate their play. Some fans and officials considered these enactments to be arrogant showmanship, whereas others thought it merely an act of celebration after scoring. In 2006 the American National Football League adopted a "celebration penalty" in which the player was called for unsportsmanlike conduct. There also was the perception that such routines were more commonly enacted by Black than by White players. Hall and Livingston (2012) investigated this question by presenting participants written vignettes describing a player, whose name suggested he was Black or White, who scored on a touchdown pass and either did or did not engage in a celebration routine (consisting of spiking the football next to the defender, doing his "signature dance," and then waiting for the crowd's enthusiastic cheering). After reading their vignette, participants rated the arrogance of the player and the extent of the penalty that should be assessed against him. Analyses showed that the celebratory act was responded to negatively when performed by the Black player but not by the White player. Thus, the same behavior was interpreted differently when performed by Black versus White players.

Another aspect of the effect of stereotypes on interpretation was demonstrated by Dunning and Sherman (1997). Participants read a series of statements describing a behavior performed by a person who was identified only by membership in a particular group (e.g., occupation). Two versions of each sentence were presented, differing only in the group membership of the actor. For example, one pair of stimulus sentences was: "The nun (or rock musician) was unhappy about the amount of liquor being served at the party." Participants read a series of such sentences, presenting one or the other version of each pair. Later, participants were given a recognition test in which they were shown a list of sentences and were asked to indicate, for each one, whether it had been included in the stimulus list. For each stimulus sentence, two versions were presented that included minor changes to the original form. For the above example, the two versions were:

The nun was unhappy about the large amount of liquor being served at the party.

The rock musician was unhappy about the small amount of liquor being served at the party.

In one case, the recognition sentence was stereotypically consistent with the stimulus version (e.g., for the "nun" version, being unhappy about the *large* amount of liquor was stereotypically consistent). Participants' responses revealed that they mistakenly "recognized" more of the stereotypically-consistent interpretations than stereotypically-inconsistent versions. Thus, the stereotype that was activated (nun, rock musician) guided the interpretation of the stimulus sentence and, consequently, the participants falsely recognized the stereotype-based version as having been the item they initially saw.

Our conclusion in the previous sentence is a reasonable take-away message from this experiment. However, as is often the case, the results of any single study can be open to alternative interpretations. This experiment raises an important question that applies to many studies. Specifically, one might ask: does this bias happen during the encoding and interpretation of the information, as we have suggested, or does it happen later, at the time participants make their responses? In other words, do the results reflect biased encoding or biased retrieval?

There are a couple of possibilities that fit the latter interpretation, and neither of them would require that stereotypes are influencing initial interpretations. One possibility is that there is no bias in the initial processing of information, but later, when asked to recall or make recognition responses, the stereotype guides and distorts the information that is retrieved from memory. A second possibility is that participants' errors are a product of stereotype-guided guessing at the time they complete the recall or recognition test. Both of these alternative possibilities would produce the same results reported by Dunning and Sherman (1997), but those outcomes would not be the result of biased interpretation as information was encoded. However, knowing whether it occurs during encoding or retrieval is critical for understanding the processes underlying that outcome.

One way of testing whether an effect occurs at encoding or retrieval is to provide the same information in two conditions in which the same prime (trait, stereotype) is presented either before or after the information is provided. For example, the text may describe a person going through a house, noticing the floor plan, the nice furnishings, and valuable decorative objects. Either before or after reading that passage, participants would be told that the person is either a prospective buyer of the home or is a burglar casing out the place for future theft. Participants would later be asked to recall as many of the objects in the room as they can. The participants' differential recall of information that would be consistent with the buyer perspective (e.g., the leaky roof) or the burglar interpretation (expensive vase) would be determined. The difference in recall performance as a function of whether the prime was presented before or after reading the text would provide a test of whether those effects occurred during encoding or retrieval.

Several studies that have used this experimental strategy have shown that, although such effects at retrieval can occur, the biasing effects of concepts, goals, and stereotypes are stronger at encoding than at retrieval (Anderson & Pichert, 1978; Baillet & Keenen, 1986; Bodenhausen, 1988; Dunning & Sherman, 1997; Pichert & Anderson, 1977; Zadny & Gerard, 1974). These findings show that such priming influences the interpretation of subsequently acquired information.

Ambiguity in Race Perception

In the United States, race perception has traditionally been viewed as a simple matter of Black and White. Some people are Black, some people are White, and historically a great deal of effort has been exerted to create cultural norms and laws at all levels of government to preserve that distinction. Many state laws relied on what became known as the "one-drop rule," stating that a person that had any "Negro" blood was to be regarded as Black. It was only after World War II that things began to (slowly) change as a result of new laws and court decisions. The most famous of these was the *Brown v. Board of Education* decision in 1954 by the Supreme Court that declared segregated schools to be unconstitutional. Gradually (but not easily), changes began to appear in other life areas, including employment, residential patterns, access to hotels and restaurants, entertainment, and social institutions. In 1947 Jackie Robinson became the first African American to play baseball for a major league team, a change which itself was fraught with controversy. It was not until 1967 that the Supreme Court, in *Loving v. Virginia*, invalidated state laws prohibiting interracial marriage.

As these changes evolved, it became more evident that race should not be viewed as a Black/White dichotomy but instead as existing along a continuum. Consider, for example, skin color (Maddox, 2004). African Americans vary considerably in the darkness or lightness of their skin tone, from deep Black to very light (in which "passing" as White was viable). With a higher frequency of interracial marriage, people of mixed-race origin have become a sizeable (and increasing) segment of the population, and they identify themselves as mixed-race rather than of one race or another. Most of us have had the experience of seeing a multiracial person and wondering, "Is he Black or White?" Asking that question reveals that the observer thinks of racial categorization as dichotomous. Typically, the ambiguity posed in the question is resolved by regarding the multiracial person as Black. Thus, in their social judgments, people have often informally abided by, and therefore perpetuated, the one-drop rule. Known in this context as *hypodescent*, it is the tendency to assign a mixed-race person to the category lower in social class of the two social groups of origin.

Several different experimental paradigms have been used to explore this phenomenon. In some studies, participants are presented a series of photos of monoracial Black, monoracial White, and Black-White biracial persons, and the participants' task is to indicate whether the person in the photo is White or Black. Judgments of the monoracial White and Black persons are almost always correct, but the interesting question is how biracial persons would be categorized. In several studies, biracial target persons have been predominantly categorized as Black (Chen, Pauker, Gaither, Hamilton, & Sherman, 2018; Ho, Roberts, & Gelman, 2015; Ho, Sidanius, Cuddy, & Banaji, 2013; Ho, Sidanius, Levin, & Banaji, 2011; Peery &

Bodenhausen, 2008). In another paradigm, participants are shown many faces ranging along a continuum from 100% White to 100% Black, with many intermediate steps showing faces of varying degrees of Blackness and Whiteness (achieved by morphing a White face with a Black face to varying degrees). Participants' task is to judge each face as White or Black, and the place along the continuum where participants' judgments change from one category to the other is recorded. The logical place for that to occur would be at the 50–50 point along the continuum. According to hypodescent, however, it should take a lower degree of "Blackness" for the person to be considered Black. This outcome has been observed in numerous experiments (Halberstadt, Sherman, & Sherman, 2011; Ho et al., 2011; Krosch & Amodio, 2014; Krosch, Berntsen, Amodio, Jost, & Van Bavel, 2013).

As one might expect, judgments of racially ambiguous faces are affected by several factors. One set of studies (Kang, Plaks, & Remedios, 2015) focused on perceivers' beliefs regarding the nature of group differences. Some people tend to believe that racial groups are highly genetically distinct, whereas others believe that racial groups are very similar at a genetic level. In a first study examining how these beliefs affect responses to racially ambiguous individuals, participants' neural electrical activity was recorded via electroencephalography (EEG). While these data were collected, participants viewed a series of 15 videos depicting faces morphing from Black to White over 60 seconds. After watching these videos, participants completed questionnaires containing two crucial questions: (1) If you were to choose two people at random from the entire world, what percentage of genetic material would they have in common?; and (2) If you were to choose two people at random who happened to be from the same racial background, what percentage of genetic material would they have in common? Responses to these questions were used to assess the degree that people believe that racial groups are distinct or share a high degree of genetic overlap.

Results showed that a belief in lower genetic overlap was associated with stronger neural avoidance responses in the middle of the video displays. In other words, participants with the view that races are genetically distinct wanted to avoid biracial compared to monoracial targets. In a subsequent study in which participants made racial categorization judgments, stronger beliefs in low genetic overlap predicted slower response times to classify biracial (vs. monoracial) faces. In a final study where information about racial genetic differences was manipulated, participants who were told that racial groups are genetically distinct rated biracial targets more negatively than did participants who were told that racial groups differ minimally at a genetic level. These results show that beliefs about the nature of racial differences can affect processing fluency and evaluation of racially ambiguous people.

Another set of studies (Gaither, Pauker, Slepian, & Sommers, 2016) examined motivational variables that influence judgments of racially ambiguous faces. In all studies, participants made speeded White/Black categorization judgments for 20 computer-generated racially ambiguous faces. Depending on the study, participants either completed questionnaires to assess individual differences in motivation or underwent manipulations to affect motivational states. Results showed that higher needs to belong and stronger racial identification predicted more categorizations of racially ambiguous faces as Black for both White and Black participants. The same results occurred when these factors were manipulated (i.e., when participants were made to feel socially excluded or their racial identity was threatened). Note that these effects might represent meaningfully different responses for White and Black participants. For White participants, these results represent the *exclusion* of racially ambiguous individuals from the ingroup in people who had high belonging needs or strong levels of racial identification. For Black participants, the same pattern reflects a higher *inclusion* of ambiguous targets into the ingroup when belonging needs and racial identity were high. Therefore, motivational factors can interact with the social perceivers' race to affect the likelihood and meaning of hypodescent.

Of course, posing the question, "Is he White or Black?" (whether in an informal conversation or as the judgment to be made in an experimental task) forces the respondent to consider only two alternatives. However, as we have observed, the faces we perceive in everyday life vary along a continuum, suggesting that perceivers may judge those faces using more differentiated categories. Some studies (Chen & Hamilton, 2012; Chen, Moons, Gaither, Hamilton, & Sherman, 2014) have shown that providing a "multiracial" option in addition to "Black" and "White" categories makes a considerable difference. Participants were shown photos of White, Black, and multiracial faces. The mixed-race faces were either 50–50 morphs of White and Black faces or were photos of actual persons who had one Black and one White parent. Participants' task was to categorize these persons according to three categories: White, Black, and multiracial. Not surprisingly, there was a high consensus in judging the monoracial faces to be White and Black. The multiracial faces were judged to be multiracial more frequently than the other categories, although agreement was not as high as for the monoracial faces. Also, the amount of time required to make those judgments was recorded and showed that categorizing a face as multiracial took significantly longer than did the monoracial judgments. The categorization results indicate that perceivers do have and use a "multiracial" category in judging faces. However, the lower consensus and longer response times suggest that this category is not as well developed and is not as accessible as the monoracial categories, perhaps because of some lingering ambiguity in these perceptions. Also, people who are motivated to control prejudicial responses were more likely to use the multiracial category than were persons not so motivated (Chen et al., 2014).

Chen and Hamilton (2012) further examined participants' judgments of multiracial faces and reported findings that question the pervasiveness of hypodescent. As noted, participants often categorized biracial faces as multiracial, but not uniformly. When they did not categorize them as multiracial, what category option did they use? Hypodescent would predict that multiracial persons would be categorized as Black. In contrast, in several experiments, participants were more likely to classify multiracial individuals as White than Black. This finding suggests that the principle of hypodescent may not be used as pervasively as some studies have suggested. Extending this line of thinking, other research (Chen et al., 2018) has shown that multiracial faces are not necessarily seen as Black but may be categorized into various minority groups (Latino, Middle Eastern, Indian, Asian). Participants were also faster to exclude multiracial faces from the category "White" than from other racial categories. These results suggest the influence of a more general "minority bias" whereby multiracial faces are excluded from the category "White" more readily than categorized as "Black."

All of these findings must also be considered in light of changing conditions in society (Chen, 2019). The number of multiracial persons in American culture has been increasing rapidly in recent decades, with expectations that this trend will continue. One consequence will be that the social world will become more diverse and complex, increasingly multiracial. This change would seemingly make racial, ethnic, and other distinctions less prevalent, such that well-worn dichotomies may become less useful. In that case, interpretations of "What race is that person?" will have less bearing, and the meaning of race might have a diminished role in our understanding of the people we perceive.

SUMMARY

The events we experience, as well as the persons and groups that enact them, exist in reality, in the real world. They have no inherent meaning until we, as observers, impose some interpretation on them. Interpretation, then, is an act of the observer, and, once it happens, those events take on meaning for the observer. Understanding the process of interpretation is fundamentally critical because most events and behaviors have a considerable degree of ambiguity and therefore are open to alternative interpretations. These interpretations are not predetermined, but once they are made, the meaning gained from them can influence the way new information is processed and hence can guide ultimate emotional reactions, decisions, and behaviors.

Interpretation is a subjective process that can be influenced by many variables, as we have seen in this chapter. The act of identifying what happened and of unitizing a sequence of actions into units can guide the interpretation of those actions. These identifications can occur at various levels of abstraction, thereby expanding or constraining the meaning of those events. The perspective from which the event is viewed, physically or mentally, can guide the interpretation imposed. The ideas activated in this process can stimulate new associations that can further enhance the interpretation process. Moreover, the observer's pre-existing expectancies and current motives can affect the process of making sense out of the ambiguity encountered in observed behavior.

All of these factors play essential roles in guiding the interpretation process in dynamic and interactive ways as observers strive to make meaning in the events they encounter.

FURTHER READING

Balcetis, E., & Cole, S. (2013). On misers, managers, and monsters: The social cognition of visual perception. In D.E. Carlston (Ed.), *The Oxford handbook of social cognition* (pp. 329–351). New York, NY: Oxford University Press.

Caruso, E.M., Mead, N.L., & Balcetis, E. (2009). Political partisanship influences perception of biracial candidates' skin tone. *Proceedings of the National Academy of Sciences*, *106*, 20168–20173.

Libby, L.K., & Eibach, R.P. (2013). The role of visual imagery in social cognition. In D.E. Carlston (Ed.), *The Oxford handbook of social cognition* (pp. 147–166). New York, NY: Oxford University Press.

6

EVALUATION

Judging Good and Bad

On October 3, 2000, Presidential candidates Al Gore and George W. Bush met in Boston for the first of three debates. A year into the campaign, voters were eager to see a face-to-face interaction between candidates who were locked in a close race. When questioned later about who won the debate, some voters mentioned the policy positions and the quality of the arguments offered by the two candidates. Many voters, however, commented on the men's behavior and appearance. Gore appeared to be wearing substantial eerie orange makeup and audibly sighed and rolled his eyes during some of Bush's comments. According to one CNN commentator, Gore "looked and sounded about as appealing as a case of the flu." Bush, in contrast, was "relaxed and authentic, and he seemed at ease." When polls asked about the issues that were debated, they showed that Gore had won. However, when they asked about likability, Bush was preferred. This pattern persisted throughout the campaign. Bush was selected in a poll as the candidate with whom most people would want to share a beer. Gore, in contrast, was regularly described as arrogant, programmed, and unlikable. Polls on election day showed that "While Gore had an edge on issues, Bush had the advantage on candidate qualities" (Kenski, Aylor, & Kenski, 2002, p. 256). Given that Gore lost the Electoral College by 537 disputed votes in Florida, Al Gore likely lost the Presidency simply because people liked him less than George Bush.

In Chapter 5, we highlighted the importance of interpretation in social information processing: information must be understood before it can be used effectively. We discussed how people make use of their prior knowledge and beliefs as well as contextual information to categorize events and to disambiguate vague information. Interpretive processes allow people to understand people and events and to respond to information they receive from the social world effectively.

When we make sense of the world through interpretive processes, we simultaneously engage in *evaluative* processes. These processes distinguish good from bad, positive from negative, safe from dangerous, and right from wrong. Evaluative processes help us determine what gives us pleasure and pain, what we approach and avoid, and what we love and hate. These are some of the most fundamental and consequential assessments in our lives.

Survival itself can depend on the ability to evaluate; evaluative processes allow people to approach things that are safe while avoiding those things that pose a threat. *Attitudes*, chronic evaluative preferences, also help us organize, understand, and navigate our social environments. We see movies starring actors we admire, eat foods we like, and hang out with friends we enjoy. We avoid eye contact with people we fear and vote against politicians we despise.

We have emphasized in this text that the information we receive is devoid of meaning until our cognitive structures are brought to bear. By relying on our knowledge, beliefs, and expectations, we can interpret and understand people and events. The same is true of evaluation. Although it might seem obvious to us that flowers and ice cream are good and that dead bodies and mold are bad, those responses arise from and reflect our experiences. There is nothing inherent in objects themselves denoting how they should be evaluated. Instead, encountering these objects activates cognitive (knowledge or beliefs) and affective (feelings or emotions) information from memory associated with them. Shakespeare's character Hamlet reflected this idea when he proclaimed, "There is nothing either good or bad, but thinking makes it so."

THE PRIMACY OF EVALUATION?

Evaluative processes reflect both our stored knowledge and the feelings and emotions that arise when an object is encountered. Therefore, evaluative responses might be expected to temporally follow processes such as categorization and interpretation. After all, how can we decide that we dislike a stimulus (feeling fear upon glimpsing an ambiguous silhouette in an alley) unless and until we determine what it is (A friend? A mugger?). The ordering of these processes appears on its face quite straightforward. The categorization and interpretation of a stimulus seem logically to precede the activation of relevant emotional responses.

That is not necessarily the case, however. The temporal relation of evaluative responses and other processes such as interpretation and inference has been a matter of extensive debate. Zajonc (1980b, 1984) offered the provocative idea that "preferences need no inferences," suggesting that affective and cognitive systems can operate independently because they are distinct. In this view, affective response to a stimulus can arise even *before* extensive cognitive processing can occur. Zajonc argued that evaluative reactions can be elicited with minimal input, involving minimal cognitive processing or conscious awareness. He referred to this idea as the *affective primacy hypothesis*. Three kinds of studies provide support for this hypothesis.

Affective Priming

One set of studies shows that subliminally presented primes that are strongly valenced (associated with "good" or "bad") affect evaluations of subsequent stimuli (Murphy and Zajonc, 1993; Niedenthal, 1990; Paul, Pope, Fennell, & Mendl, 2012). For example, in one study (Murphy & Zajonc, 1993) participants were shown images of smiling or scowling faces presented either so briefly (4 ms) that they could not be detected (i.e., subliminal presentation) or for a duration (1000 ms) where they could easily be seen (i.e., supraliminally). The faces were then immediately followed by Chinese ideographs which, because they were unfamiliar to American participants, were neutral stimuli. There were also two types of control trials in the study when no images appeared before the ideographs (no prime control) and when the ideographs were preceded by one of several polygon shapes (polygon control). On each trial, participants had to indicate how much they liked the presented ideograph.

As depicted in Figure 6.1, results showed that the valence of the subliminally presented primes influenced participants' liking of

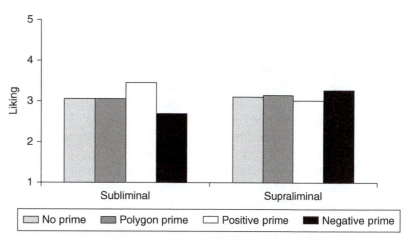

Figure 6.1 Average liking of Chinese ideographs as a function of prime condition and prime presentation speed (Subliminal vs. Supraliminal)

Source: Adapted from Murphy & Zajonc (1993)

the ideographs. The smiling facial expression elicited more favorable evaluations than did either of the control conditions, whereas the scowling expression led to more negative evaluations compared with the neutral controls. These effects only occurred when faces could not be seen, suggesting that the affective information presented subliminally was operating independently of conscious processes.

Evaluative Priming

Other supportive evidence is provided by studies examining the speed of evaluative judgments as a function of the consistency in valence between primes and targets (Fazio et al., 1986). This *evaluative priming paradigm* (initially described in Chapter 3; see Figure 3.2) has been used in dozens of studies (see Herring et al., 2013). In the original study, participants completed numerous trials where a prime word (that they were told to memorize) preceded a target word. The participant's task was to indicate by pressing a key whether the target word was positive (e.g., appealing, delightful) or negative (e.g., repulsive, awful). For both prime and target words, some were positive and some were negative. Results typically show that when the prime and target words are compatible in valence, response times to the target word are facilitated. When they differ in valence, response times are slowed. Interestingly, this occurs even when stimuli are presented in the perceiver's peripheral vision, showing that direct visual attention is not necessary to extract valence information from primes (Calvo & Nummenmaa, 2007). These results indicate that people can extract evaluative information from stimuli, even when that is not their primary goal.

Neuroscientific Evidence

The third line of supportive evidence shows that valenced information, specifically threatening information, is processed by two distinct systems in the brain. Threatening information, whether social or non-social, triggers processes centered in the amygdala and associated subcortical structures, often referred to as the "fear circuit" (Davis & Whalen, 2001; Suslow et al., 2013; Whalen, Rauch, Etcoff, McInerney, Lee, & Jenike, 1998). LeDoux and colleagues

(LeDoux, 1995, 1996, 2000; LeDoux & Pine, 2016) argued that amygdala-centered processes are responsible for controlling behavioral and physiological responses to threats and unconscious feelings of fear. In contrast, subjective feelings of fear and anxiety are regulated by circuits responsible for higher-order processes such as attention and working memory, mainly involving regions in the lateral and medial prefrontal cortex and also the parietal neocortex. In other words, distinct systems control behavioral and bodily fear responses compared with conscious interpretational responses.

Studies consistent with this view have shown that people with amygdala damage often fail to exhibit bodily reactions to threatening information (Adolphs, 2008; Phelps, 2006). Also, threatening information presented subliminally triggers amygdala activity and physiological responses even though participants lack conscious feelings of fear (Mineka & Öhman, 2002; Whalen et al., 2004). Thus, evaluative responses may arise even before an individual can identify an object or perceive it consciously. This system supporting rapid responding to valenced stimuli facilitates efficient actions to events that may be life-threatening.

Taken together, these separate lines of research all point to the potential importance of evaluative processes. Perceivers can have rapid evaluative responses to stimuli even when they are unaware of having seen them and when their task is not to evaluate them. The independence of physiological and cognitive responses to negative stimuli provides an understanding of why evaluations can produce behavioral effects with minimal awareness and conscious involvement. Although the idea that evaluative responses can occur before cognitive processing remains controversial (Fanselow & Pennington, 2017; Storbeck & Clore, 2007), it is clear that evaluations can arise exceptionally early in the processing of information.

INTEGRATION OF INFORMATION IN JUDGMENT

Even though some stimuli produce rapid evaluative responses based on a single characteristic, many stimuli involve multiple features and properties with evaluative implications. Information regarding these characteristics must be integrated to form evaluative and other judgments. How this integration is achieved is complex, and several models for this process have been proposed. Here we provide a brief introduction to the topic.

Each element in a given piece of stimulus information has some value associated with it. That is, we like some features and characteristics better than others. As a simple example, suppose you learn about several behaviors that have been performed by a new acquaintance named Aaron. For instance, you might learn the following:

> Aaron bought a new wheelchair for a disabled friend.
>
> Aaron carried some grocery bags for an older woman.
>
> Aaron put some bottles and cardboard boxes in the garbage rather than in the recycling bin.
>
> Aaron used a racial slur in describing a person.

Each of these behaviors performed by Aaron can be placed along a continuum representing how good or bad you value it, say, ranging from +5 to −5. Thus, each "fact" you have learned has its own value. Your overall evaluation of Aaron could then be calculated by somehow combining these values (e.g., by adding or averaging them together). It is also clear, however, that some of Aaron's behaviors are more important to your evaluation than are others. It's nice that he helped the lady and bad that he didn't recycle, but they are less critical to your evaluation than his use of a racial slur. These differences in importance are represented in the weight given to each item (say, between 1 and 5) as they are integrated. In sum, each item has its own *value* and its corresponding *weight*. For example, Table 6.1 shows hypothetical values and weights in your thinking about Aaron. In your integration rule, you might multiply each value by its weight and then average the resulting products to determine your overall evaluation of Aaron.

Table 6.1 Integrating information in judgment: hypothetical values and weights

Behavior	Value	Weight	V × W
Bought wheelchair	+5	4	20
Carried grocery bags	+2	2	4
Bottles and boxes in garbage	−3	4	−12
Used racial slur	−5	5	−25
Weighted average			−3.6

This example may seem rather trite, but, in fact, it represents in microcosm a process people engage in all the time in virtually every context of life. It is difficult to imagine encountering a person, group, event, or situation about which one is totally neutral (i.e., when one is devoid of evaluative reaction). This kind of integration process must occur in some way in all of these cases, from the mundane to the most important. Last night I had dinner at a restaurant. You might ask me, "How did you like your meal?" The question calls for an overall evaluation, but there were several elements to the meal, some better than others. The salad was mediocre, the halibut was quite good, the wine was ordinary, and the chocolate dessert was sublime. Clearly, I had different values for these elements, and the question then becomes how I weighted them. The same process applies when we evaluate candidates for political office. Ms. Henderson seeks your vote. What do you know about her? She is strongly in favor of greater controls on the availability of handguns, advocates more government support for health care, supports increased spending for defense, wants lower taxation, and opposes legislation imposing constraints on fossil fuel industries. What value do you place on each of those positions, and how important (weight) is each one to you? These (and many other) elements will become integrated into an overall evaluative judgment that will guide your vote.

Some essential points can be noted about the integration process and its elements. First, in any given situation people will differ in both their values and their weighting of stimulus elements. Those differences in the political domain are what make politics. Second, the weights associated with any given feature will differ in different contexts. For example, if you are judging Aaron as a possible co-worker on an important project at work, his intelligence and motivation will be weighted more heavily than if you are considering him as a drinking buddy. Nevertheless, the integration process itself is the same and underlies all evaluative judgments.

A NEGATIVITY BIAS IN EVALUATION?

The research we have reviewed suggests the existence of a *negativity bias* in evaluation. That is, although social perceivers benefit from being able to respond both to things they dislike (to avoid adverse outcomes) and to things they like (to achieve positive outcomes), there is substantial evidence that "bad is stronger than good" (Baumeister, Bratslavsky, Finkenauer, & Vohs, 2001). There is an advantage for detecting, responding to, and learning about information that is negative rather than positive in valence (Cacioppo, Gardner, & Berntson, 1997; Ledgerwood & Boydstun, 2014; Rozin & Royzman, 2001), and this tendency exists in both humans and other mammals (Abdai & Miklosi, 2016). The finding that negative information tends to dominate positive information is now seen as one of the most robust findings in psychology (see Baumeister et al., 2001; Peeters & Czapinski, 1990; Rozin & Royzman, 2001).

Negative information draws attention. In one study demonstrating the quick detection of negative stimuli (Öhman, Flykt, & Esteves, 2001), participants scanned a series of images of threatening (snakes and spiders) and non-threatening (flowers and mushrooms) stimuli to determine whether they showed a single category (e.g., only flowers) or contained a deviant image (e.g., a snake among flowers). Participants were faster to detect snakes and spiders among flowers and mushrooms than vice versa, and the detection of threatening (but not benign) targets was unaffected by the number of distractors in the display. Similar effects have been shown in the social domain. In Chapter 2, we described research by Pratto and John (1991) in which participants were consistently slower to name the colors in which undesirable (e.g., sadistic) compared with desirable (e.g., honest) trait words were printed. These slowed naming times indicate that participants had difficulty ignoring the negative valence of the undesirable traits even though it was irrelevant to the task at hand. Attentional biases to negativity emerge early in life. Infants aged 8–14 months looked more quickly at threatening (snakes and angry faces) than non-threatening (flowers and smiling faces) stimuli when they were presented simultaneously (LoBue & DeLoache, 2010).

Compared with positive information, negative information produces more extreme and consistent neurological responses (Cacioppo & Berntson, 1994; Cacioppo et al., 1997; Cunningham, Van Bavel, & Johnsen, 2008). For example, participants in one study (Ito, Larsen, Smith, & Cacioppo, 1998) viewed a large set of neutral pictures that also included two positive (a red Ferrari, people enjoying a roller coaster) and two negative (a mutilated face, a handgun pointed at the camera) images. Brain activity was assessed using event-related brain potentials (ERPs) reflecting changes in electrocortical activity. There was an elevated late positive potential (LPP) when viewing the negative pictures, indicating heightened attention to these stimuli. In another study (Muñoz & Martín-Loeches, 2015), participants made aesthetic judgments of images of men's and women's faces and bodies that, through pretesting, were known to be beautiful, ugly, and neutral. Data showed a heightened response to the ugly images on the P200, an ERP component that has been linked to early attention to valenced material.

People also learn more readily from negative than positive information. This learning asymmetry has been demonstrated in studies using a computerized game called Beanfest (Fazio, Eiser, & Shook, 2004; Fazio, Pietri, Rocklage, & Shook, 2015). In the game, participants try to survive in a virtual world populated with many beans varying in shape (circular, oval, oblong) and the number of surface speckles (1–10). Participants are told to eat beans that increase their energy level and avoid ones that deplete their energy. Because each trial of the game drains their strength by one unit, participants have to learn which beans are beneficial and which are harmful. Some categories of beans (e.g., oval beans with many speckles) produce positive outcomes (+10 points), whereas other beans (e.g., circular beans with only a few speckles) produce a negative result (−10 points). After being given a chance to learn about the beans, participants complete a test phase in which they are asked to indicate which beans produce positive and negative outcomes. Results show that although both positive and negative beans tend to be classified more accurately than chance during the test phase (i.e., participants had learned which beans produced good and bad outcomes), the negative beans are more likely to be judged correctly than the positive beans. In other words, negative associations formed more readily than positive associations.

In sum, negative information is powerful. It draws our attention, produces more extreme responses in our neural systems, and unduly influences learning. Therefore, it is not surprising that negative information is also more likely to be remembered (Ohira, Winton, & Oyama, 1998; Ortony, Turner, & Antos, 1983). This does not mean that positive information is ignored or neglected. Indeed, compared with neutral information, positive information also tends to grab attention and trigger evaluative processes. However, the dominance of negative over positive information produces a variety of consequences in the social domain, as we will later discuss.

FOUNDATIONS OF EVALUATIVE RESPONSES

We now turn to a discussion of fundamental questions: Why is some information positive and other information negative? What in our cognitive and motivational systems leads us to see things as good or bad, right or wrong? These crucial questions do not have simple answers, given that there are multiple factors underlying evaluation. For example: (a) Some evaluative responses, particularly automatic negative reactions to threatening stimuli, appear to be universal and hard-wired, integrated in our cognitive and emotional systems through evolutionary processes (Bargh et al., 2012; Ferguson, 2007); (b) Several characteristics are also universally judged positively (e.g., symmetry), revealing that evolutionary processes can produce preferences not just for stimuli but for specific features; (c) Another set of factors relate to the fact that certain cognitive processes are in themselves hedonically pleasing, with the consequence that certain stimuli can become favored due to the processes used to think about them; and (d) A host of learning factors play crucial roles in determining our preferences. We briefly review several lines of research illustrating the contributions of each of these factors in the development of evaluative responses.

Biological Preparedness

Certain stimuli in the environment provoke extreme, typically negative responses, and these reactions appear to be innate and universal. The tendency for people and animals to demonstrate innate associations between specific stimuli and responses is referred to as *biological preparedness.* Many stimuli are automatically evaluated negatively due to threats they pose to reproductive viability. Both humans and monkeys show more fear of threatening (e.g., predators, snakes, spiders, heights) than non-threatening stimuli (Öhman & Mineka, 2001, 2003). These associations are learned quickly and are difficult to unlearn through counter-conditioning (Öhman, 1986; Olsson, Ebert, Banaji, & Phelps, 2005). They also produce fast responses, with facial muscles responding as quickly as 500 ms after exposure (Dimberg, 1997; Dimberg, Hansson, & Thunberg, 1998).

If evolutionary concerns are at the root of automatic negative evaluation, then any information suggesting a threat to survival might be expected to produce fast and extreme responses. Much research shows that substances or behaviors implying possible exposure to a pathogen or disease-causing agent create immediate and intense negative reactions. Indeed, viewing or thinking of someone consuming rotten meat, licking another person's sores, or eating excrement are all acts that typically produce severe and immediate experiences of disgust (Lieberman & Patrick, 2018; Rozin, Haidt, & McCauley, 2008; Tybur, Lieberman, Kurzban, & DeScioli, 2013). Disgust is viewed as a particularly beneficial emotion as it plays "a key role in motivating behavior that probabilistically reduces exposure to pathogens" (Tybur et al., 2013, p. 66).

However, disgust can also arise in response to objects that have features associated with risk, even if they do not themselves involve any danger. People react as though they believe that properties triggering disgust can pass between entities through physical contact (Huang, Ackerman, & Newman, 2017; Rozin, Millman, & Nemeroff, 1986). They are reluctant to touch a previously neutral item if it had come into contact with disliked peers or members of a disliked group (Rozin et al. 1986; Rozin, Nemeroff, Wane, & Sherrod, 1989). In contrast, people seek contact with items that have been touched by close friends, lovers, or people to whom they are sexually attracted (Nemeroff & Rozin 1994; Rozin et al. 1986, 1989), and they value an item more highly if it has been touched by a celebrity (Newman, Diesendruck, & Bloom, 2011).

Featural Factors

Research indicates that people have intrinsic preferences for particular features. All else being equal, objects and people with certain characteristics are generally better liked, are judged more attractive, and are valued more highly. Several different, but related, features focusing primarily on facial and bodily characteristics have received extensive empirical attention.

Symmetry

There is a general evaluative preference for *bilateral symmetry*, where a pattern of features is mirrored on both sides of a median axis. Symmetry is preferred over non-symmetry in judgments of stimuli, including skin decorations (Cárdenas & Harris, 2006), and graphic patterns (Jacobsen & Höfel, 2003). In social perception, symmetrical faces (see Figure 6.2) (Rhodes, Proffitt, Grady, & Sumich, 1998) and bodies (Brown, Price, Kang, Pound, Zhao, & Yu, 2008) are judged as more beautiful and healthier (Fink, Neave, Manning, & Grammer, 2006). One study examining judgments of identical twins found that the one with higher facial symmetry was typically seen as more attractive (Mealey, Bridgestock, & Townsend, 1999). The preference for symmetry, at least in part, appears to reflect reproductive concerns. For example, women's preferences for symmetrical male faces increase around peak fertility (Little, Jones, Burt, & Perrett, 2007), particularly in short-term mating contexts (e.g., when considering a one-night stand; Little & Jones, 2012).

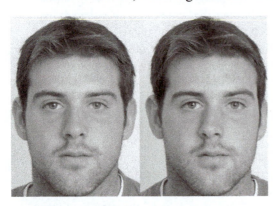

Figure 6.2 Example of a face high (left) and low (right) in bilateral symmetry

Source: From Little, Jones, & DeBruine (2011)

Symmetry detection involves numerous cognitive processes. Symmetry can be detected when stimuli are displayed very briefly (10–100 ms) (Locher & Wagemans, 1993) even when its detection is not required by the task (Wolfe & Friedman-Hill, 1992). Visual attention is drawn to symmetry (Huang, Xue, Spelke, Huang, Zheng, & Peng, 2018; Kootstra, de Boer, & Schomaker, 2011) and symmetric images are better remembered (Attneave, 1955; Kayaert & Wagemans, 2009). Taken together, these findings indicate that symmetrical stimuli are associated with fast and relatively effortless processing (Reber, Schwarz, & Winkielman, 2004).

Typicality

People also prefer exemplars that resemble the prototype or average of a category (e.g., Halberstadt & Rhodes, 2000; Martindale & Moore, 1988). There are again several reasons for this effect. First, such preferences might reflect a perceived association between averageness and mate quality (Lie, Rhodes, & Simmons, 2008; Thornhill & Gangestad, 1993). Second, this preference might reflect the greater likelihood of activation of typical compared with atypical stimuli. This is consistent with the notion that aesthetic preference is in part based on the degree to which the mental representation of a stimulus can be activated from memory (Martindale & Moore, 1988). Finally, prototypical stimuli might be preferred because they seem more familiar, and this sensation produces greater fluency (Reber et al., 2004).

Given the importance of faces in the social domain, much research has focused on facial prototypicality. Compared with atypical faces, faces judged as average for their category are seen as more attractive and better liked. However, because of their low distinctiveness, they can be more difficult to remember (Light, Hollander, & Kayra-Stuart, 1981). Faces naturally vary in the degree that they are prototypical for their category, so combining faces within a category should increase the perceived averageness and enhance evaluative judgments. Research that has presented computer-created composite faces shows this to be the case, with more favorable evaluations of morphs generated from larger sets of faces (Langlois & Roggman, 1990; Langlois, Roggman, & Musselman, 1994).

Sexual Dimorphism

In binary gender terms, men and women differ in several aspects of their appearance and behavior, and people with more extreme secondary sexual characteristics (more feminine for women, more masculine for men) are typically judged as more attractive. The strength of this relationship appears to differ for male and female targets. Feminine female faces are reliably considered beautiful across a variety of cultures (Cunningham, 1986; Jones & Hill, 1993; Perrett et al., 1998). For male faces, some masculine features such as a large jaw enhance judgments of attractiveness in women (Cunningham, Barbee, & Pike, 1990). However, masculine features are also associated with dominance and fear, suggesting why male faces low in masculinity are sometimes judged more attractive (e.g., Rhodes, Hickford, & Jeffery, 2000). Similarly, as we described in Chapter 5, a study using silhouettes of human body shapes whose movements emphasized shoulder "swagger" (a typical masculine walking motion) or hip "sway" (a typical feminine motion) showed the importance of compatibility between perceived gender and body motion. Men who moved in a masculine manner and women who walked in a feminine style were judged more favorably than gender-atypical walkers (Johnson & Tassinary, 2007).

Attractiveness

The *hedonic principle* – that pleasure is liked and pain is disliked – suggests that possession of a desirable feature might trigger a variety of other positive responses, leading to positive evaluations on attributes unrelated to that feature. Conversely, features that are evaluated negatively might produce widespread unfavorable judgments. Research on physical attractiveness provides an example of such overgeneralization in social perception. People with aesthetically pleasing features are also judged favorably on dimensions irrelevant to physical attractiveness (Eagly, Ashmore, Makhijani, & Longo, 1991; Langlois, Kalakanis, Rubenstein, Larson, Hallam, & Smoot, 2000). In other words, in judging people, "what is beautiful is good" (Dion, Berscheid, & Walster, 1972). The preference for attractiveness appears early in life, with infants under one year of age preferring to look longer at attractive compared with unattractive adult faces (Langlois, Ritter, Roggman, & Vaughn, 1991).

Early evidence of the importance of attractiveness in evaluation was provided by a study (Walster, Aronson, Abrahams, & Rottman, 1966) in which college students were randomly paired to date one another (although they were told a computer had performed the pairing). After dancing and talking for a few hours, the students were asked about their perceptions of their date and how much they liked the person. The only significant predictor of the participants' liking of their date was their physical attractiveness. No other characteristics, including the partner's perceived intelligence, were related to liking judgments.

Of course, beliefs about what is attractive can change over time and vary across cultures (Smith, 2018). However, at any given point and in any given culture, a person's possession of attractive features tends to create overgeneralized positive evaluations.

Group-relevant Features

Facial features that are stereotypically associated with a social group can affect evaluations of a person, even if the person is not a group member. One such phenomenon involves the fact that adults' faces vary naturally in terms of their *neonate features* (i.e., infant-like; "babyfaces"). Babies typically have large eyes, a small nose, full cheeks, a small chin, and a round face. Adults vary in the extent that they retain those features or have developed mature faces with fewer such characteristics. Infants with prototypical baby features are seen as "cuter," are evaluated more favorably, are judged less responsible for their actions, and elicit greater motivation for caretaking (Glocker, Langleben, Ruparel, Loughead, Gur, & Sachser, 2009). Adults with a high degree of neonatal features tend to be judged similarly (Keating, Randall, Kendrick, & Gutshall, 2003; Little, 2012; Zebrowitz & McDonald, 1991) despite the seeming irrelevance of infants' features for evaluating adults.

Similar findings have emerged for individuals varying in *Afrocentric facial features* involving the widths of noses and lips, eye color, hair type, and skin tone. Black people with Afrocentric features tend to be evaluated (Livingston & Brewer, 2002) and treated (Kleider-Offutt, Bond, & Hegerty, 2017) more negatively compared with those with fewer such features. Interestingly, these effects tend to occur regardless of a person's race. One study found that both Black and White prison inmates with more pronounced Afrocentric facial features had received harsher sentences (Blair, Judd, & Chapleau, 2004).

Until recently, it was unclear whether skin tone or facial features were responsible for these evaluative differences since they tend to co-occur in the real world. To address this question, researchers (Hagiwara, Kashy, & Cesario, 2012) systematically crossed these two sets of factors in photographs of men so that they depicted persons who had either highly prototypical or low prototypical Afrocentric features and who had either dark or light skin tone. White participants completed a sequential priming task with these stimuli (i.e., judging whether valenced words were good or bad following picture primes) and a self-report measure of liking of the targets. On both measures, the two stimulus factors had independent effects. White participants reacted more negatively toward dark-skinned Black people (regardless of their facial features) and individuals with more prototypical facial features (regardless of the darkness of their skin). Thus, individuals with Afrocentric features are perceived, evaluated, and treated more negatively than are people with weaker Afrocentric features.

Processing Factors

Evaluations also result from the nature of information processing itself. That is, subjective experiences reflecting the familiarity of a stimulus, the general ease of information processing, and whether processing "feels good" – factors about which the perceiver is often unaware – can affect evaluative judgments of the information being processed. Of particular interest is the subjective experience of *fluency*, a factor that is involved in some of the effects we have already discussed (e.g., symmetry and typicality producing higher fluency). Fluent processes entail swift and seamless progress toward stimulus recognition and judgment and are "easy on the mind." In contrast, disfluent processes are slow, effortful, and "hard on the mind" (Winkielman, Halberstadt, Fazendeiro, & Catty, 2006).

High fluency tends to produce positive emotions (Topolinski, Likowski, Weyers, & Strack, 2009; Winkielman, Schwarz, Fazendeiro, & Reber, 2003) and favorable evaluations (Reber et al., 2004; Winkielman & Cacioppo, 2001). The positive feelings from fluency can affect various judgments of the stimulus being processed, even though it arises from processing factors rather than from the stimulus itself. For example, enhanced fluency through repetition has been shown to affect judgments of truth (Bacon, 1979) and fame (Jacoby & Kelley, 1987). In contrast, low fluency prompts negative feelings (Hajcak, 2012; Hajcak & Foti, 2008; Topolinski et al., 2009) and judgments that stimuli are more likely to be false, toxic, or less famous and funny (Topolinski, 2014; Topolinski & Reber, 2010; Topolinski & Strack, 2009). Here, we focus on several independent lines of research demonstrating the general effect of fluency on evaluation through distinct factors.

Familiarity

Greater exposure to a stimulus causes it to be evaluated more favorably, a phenomenon known as the *mere exposure effect* (Zajonc, 1968). Over a century ago, Titchener (1910, p. 408) provided a vivid description of the sense of fluency that arises when one recognizes a familiar stimulus:

> Recognition, as such, seems to be wholly a matter of the feeling. What, then, is this feeling? In experiments upon recognition it is variously reported as a glow of warmth, a sense of ownership, a feeling of intimacy, a sense of being at home, a feeling of ease, a comfortable feeling. It is a feeling in the narrower sense, pleasurable in its affective quality, diffusively organic in its sensory character.

A common example of using familiarity to increase feelings of comfort is "neighbor spoofing" whereby spammers use a person's area code and first three digits to mask the origin of a call. According to the Federal Trade Commission, people are much more likely to respond positively by answering a call with familiar digit strings compared with an entirely unknown number.

Zajonc (1968) provided some of the first experimental evidence of the effect of familiarity on evaluation. In several studies, participants were instructed simply to look at a novel series of stimuli (nonsense syllables, foreign words, Chinese ideographs, photographs of male faces). Unbeknownst to the participants, some of these stimuli occurred frequently, whereas others appeared rarely. Once all the stimuli had been presented, participants evaluated each stimulus using a scale anchored by the terms "bad" and "good." Although participants had little basis for these judgments, stimuli that had appeared more frequently in the set were evaluated more favorably. Later studies (e.g., Moreland & Zajonc, 1977) expanded the evaluative measures to include judgments of liking and valenced adjectives. Across various measures, more frequent stimuli were judged more positively. A meta-analysis of the mere exposure effect (Bornstein, 1989) showed it to be most substantial when stimuli are presented briefly, and the effect plateaus after 10–20 exposures. Liking can decline with additional exposure as repetition and boredom arise. The effect typically does not occur in response to stimuli (both objects and people) that are viewed negatively. Repeated exposure to people we dislike begets even greater antipathy.

Subsequent research (Bornstein & D'Agostino, 1992, 1994) has shown that mere exposure effects are stronger when stimuli are presented subliminally, suggesting that awareness of a stimulus can trigger attempts to discount the influence of repetition. The mere exposure effect shows that what is familiar is good, but the reverse is also true; stimuli that are evaluated positively are also judged as more familiar (Monin, 2003). The mere exposure effect appears to reflect the misattribution of perceptual fluency, enhancing evaluations due to stronger feelings of familiarity (Bornstein & D'Agostino, 1994; Phaf & Roteveel, 2005; Reber et al., 2004).

Processing Ease

Stimuli that are easy to process are typically evaluated more favorably than are stimuli that pose difficulty or challenge (Alter & Oppenheimer, 2009; Forster, Leder, & Ansorge, 2013). Ease of processing has been manipulated in a variety of ways, including high vs. low semantic coherence (Topolinski et al., 2009), matching vs. mismatching prime/target relations (Winkielman & Cacioppo, 2001), high vs. low visual clarity (Reber & Schwarz, 1999), and slow vs. fast presentations (Gerger, Leder, Tinio, & Schacht, 2011). In one study that manipulated presentation durations (Forster, Leder, & Ansorge, 2016), participants viewed a series of degraded line drawings of everyday objects (a tree, a dog). For each image, they were asked to report the fluency of the perception ("How easy was the perception of the image?") and an evaluation ("How positive/negative is the image?"). Processing ease was varied by presenting images for 100, 200, 300, and 400 ms, and each image was displayed four times throughout the experiment (once at each duration speed). Results confirmed that the longer presentation durations produced higher judgments of both fluency and positivity, indicating that fluency influences evaluations of objects.

Fluency has also been tied to social evaluations of individuals and groups (Lick & Johnson, 2015). Laham, Koval, and Alter (2012), for example, showed that people with difficult-to-pronounce names were liked less compared with people whose names were easy to pronounce. Difficulty in determining a person's social category membership can also produce disfluency and negative evaluations. Dislike of members of perceptually ambiguous or concealable categories such as biracial people (Halberstadt & Winkielman, 2014), gay men (Lick & Johnson, 2013), and bisexual individuals (Lick, Johnson, & Rule, 2015) has been linked to disfluency resulting from perceivers' struggle to determine their category.

Disfluency appears to particularly affect judgments of outgroup members, presumably because the influence of fluency increases when expertise in the domain of judgment is low (Ottati & Isbell, 1996; Sedikides, 1995). In one study showing this effect (Pearson, West, Dovidio, Powers, Buck, & Henning, 2008), participants conversed over an audiovisual display with a partner of the same or different race either with or without a one-second delay. The disfluency produced by the slight delay reduced interest in later interacting with the partner, but only when the person was of a different race. Similarly, Pearson and Dovidio (2014) described a study in which White participants read a vignette in a font that was easy or difficult to read. In two different versions of the vignette, the name of the person was changed so that he would be perceived either as White (Jack) or Black (Tyrone). Participants evaluated the Black target more negatively when the font was difficult to read, but ratings of the White target were unaffected.

Regulatory Fit

Fluency can also arise from *regulatory fit* (Higgins, 2000; Motyka et al., 2014), a phenomenon that occurs "when the manner of [people's] engagement in an activity sustains their goal orientation or interests regarding that activity" (Higgins, 2005, p. 209). When people pursue activities that sustain their motivations or use strategies consistent with their motivational concerns, they engage more strongly in the activity and feel better about doing so. The feelings of fluency arising from fit may then influence judgments of an object or person.

Much of the research testing this hypothesis has examined the manner of engagement used under different regulatory foci – either focused on promotion (achieving gains) or prevention (avoiding losses). Eagerness is typically exhibited by people who are attempting to maximize gains, but vigilance serves the motive of avoiding loss. Studies have examined how the fit between motives and strategies affects evaluations. In one study (Higgins, Idson, Freitas, Spiegel, & Molden, 2003), participants' chronic promotion or prevention goals were measured. At the end of the experiment, they were told that they could choose between a coffee mug and a pen as a gift (although pilot testing had indicated that almost everyone would select the mug). Participants were either told to consider what they would gain by choosing the mug (an eager strategy) or what they would lose by not selecting the mug (a vigilant strategy) and then were asked what they would pay to buy one. Participants who were encouraged to think about the item in a way that fit their dominant regulatory concerns (promotion/eager; prevention/vigilant) generated estimates of the mug's value that were approximately 50% higher than in the non-fit conditions (promotion/vigilant; prevention/eager).

Regulatory fit can also affect responses to persuasive messages via fluency. In one study (Lee & Aaker, 2004), participants were presented with advertising taglines framed in terms of gains ("Get Energized!") or losses ("Don't Miss Out on Getting Energized!"). When the ad content was consistent with the frame of the tagline, the product was evaluated more favorably. So, the gain frame combined with promotion information (e.g., that the product increases energy) and the loss frame with prevention information (e.g., that the product reduces cancer risk) produced the highest evaluations. Judgments of ease of processing mirrored these results. Ads that had matching content were judged as easier to process, and these judgments mediated the relation between message matching and evaluative judgments. In other words, the regulatory fit between frames and arguments increased fluency, thereby boosting product evaluations.

Learning Factors

So far, we have discussed people, events, and objects that elicit a high degree of consensus in evaluative responses. Most people hate spiders and love sunsets, but not all preferences are universally shared. Some people like Tesla cars and others prefer Toyotas. People disagree about where they want to vacation, how to spend their free time, what music they enjoy, and political views, to name just a few. Variability in attitudes highlights people's different experiences, demonstrating that preferences also reflect one's upbringing and a lifetime of learning. Much research has examined how people form associations between entities (objects, issues, people) and evaluations (Fazio, 2007). Here we present a brief review of these findings with a focus on the formation of evaluative preferences in the social domain.

Evaluative Conditioning

Attitudes can develop through the pairing of an initially neutral stimulus (the *conditioned stimulus* or CS) with one that is already viewed positively or negatively (the *unconditioned stimulus* or US). The linking of a neutral with a valenced stimulus shifts evaluative responses in the direction of the valenced stimulus (Levey & Martin, 1975; Staats & Staats, 1957). This learning process is called *evaluative conditioning* (De Houwer, Thomas, & Baeyens, 2001; Gawronski &

Bodenhausen, 2018; Hütter & Fiedler, 2016; Jones, Olson, & Fazio, 2010). One common example of attempted evaluative conditioning is when companies use a liked actor in advertisements, hoping that positive evaluations of the person will become associated with the product.

Several hundred studies have provided evidence for evaluative conditioning (see for reviews Corneille & Stahl, 2019; Hofmann, De Houwer, Perugini, Baeyens, & Crombez, 2010). One of the first studies in the social domain (Staats & Staats, 1958) showed that evaluative conditioning could affect attitudes about a person. Participants viewed several male names while speaking aloud words that varied in valence. Most of the names were always paired with neutral words (e.g., chair, twelve), but two names, "Tom" and "Bill," were repeatedly paired with positive (e.g., gift, happy) or negative (e.g., bitter, failure) words. Next, participants were given an unexpected task in which they estimated how pleasant each of the men would be. The results were straightforward, indicating that the pairing of these names with valenced words affected judgments of their pleasantness.

More recently, Walther (2002) showed that evaluative judgments can be generalized beyond the specific targets that have been conditioned. In phase one of the study, participants indicated how much they liked a series of men depicted in photographs. In phase two, these participants were shown pairs of images of men that previously had been judged as neutral; their paired presentation should serve to create a connection between these individuals in memory. In the third phase, a picture of one of the two men who had been judged neutrally was paired with one of the valenced images selected in phase one (which now served as the US). After all phases were complete, participants re-evaluated all of the photographs they had seen. Consistent with previous studies on evaluative conditioning, pairing a previously-neutral man with one who was liked or disliked affected how he was evaluated, being judged more positively when paired with a liked man and more negatively when paired with a disliked man. Importantly, this conditioning effect generalized to a new target person. Judgments of the second neutral face were also affected, even though this target was never directly paired with the US.

Recent evidence suggests that conditioning and generalization processes might occur unconsciously. The issue of conscious awareness has been a matter of much debate, with some theorists claiming that individuals must be consciously aware of the link between the CS and US for evaluative conditioning to occur (Pleyers, Corneille, Luminet, & Yzerbyt, 2007; Stahl, Unkelbach, & Corneille, 2009; Sweldens, Corneille, & Yzerbyt, 2014) and others arguing that conditioning can occur without awareness (Greenwald & De Houwer, 2017; Kawakami, Miura, & Yoshida, 2015; Raio, Carmel, Carrasco, & Phelps, 2012). In one study showing nonconscious effects (Olson & Fazio, 2001), participants viewed several hundred images that appeared rapidly on a computer screen. Their task was to quickly indicate when specific images, one of several Pokémon characters, appeared in the visual stream. Unbeknownst to participants, two of the Pokémon characters that were not targets appeared with either positive words (e.g., "excellent," "awesome") or negative words (e.g., "terrible," "awful") below them. After all of the stimuli were presented, interviews with participants revealed no awareness that these characters had appeared with valenced words. Nonetheless, when they judged the pleasantness of the various stimuli that appeared (including the two Pokémon characters), evaluative conditioning was evident: the Pokémon paired with positive words was judged more favorably than the one paired with negative words. A follow-up study using the same method but with a different dependent variable – performance on an evaluative IAT measure – showed even stronger effects.

Kendrick and Olson (2012) replicated these findings but showed that nonconscious evaluative priming tends to produce evaluations that have different properties than more consciously-derived associations. Attitudes formed implicitly resemble "gut intuitions" that can be overridden when people are uncomfortable relying on intuitive responses. In two studies, participants who were given false feedback that they were "analytical" (rather than "intuitive") or an "expert" (rather than a "non-expert") at judging characters did not show evidence of evaluative conditioning in the Pokémon paradigm. Participants in the other conditions did, indicating their reliance on spontaneous reactions to make explicit judgments.

Operant Conditioning

People like rewards and dislike punishments. When rewards and punishments are received in response to expressed evaluations, principles of *operant conditioning* apply. Rewards increase, and punishments weaken, the strength of evaluative responses, and conditioning processes can influence attitude formation and change.

Research has shown that even subtle social rewards can change intergroup attitudes. Castelli, Carraro, Pavan, Murelli, and Carraro (2012) had participants read a news report to another person (actually a confederate) that depicted Black immigrants in Italy in a negative light. While the participant read the article, the confederate either sat motionless or leaned forward, nodded, and smiled. Later, participants completed both a self-report and an IAT measure of their attitudes toward Black people and answered questions about the confederate. The findings showed that performance on the implicit measure was affected by the nonverbal behavior of the confederate, whereas responses on the self-report measure were not. When the confederate nodded and smiled in agreement with the negative passage, participants inferred that the confederate agreed with the passage, thereby affecting implicit beliefs. These results show that subtle, nonverbal signals of reward can alter implicit attitudes.

Social Learning

For many years it was assumed that learning occurs primarily, if not exclusively, through classical and operant conditioning mechanisms. That view was challenged and broadened by Bandura (1962, 1977), who argued that learning also occurs by observing others. He demonstrated that children's use of aggression in social contexts depended both on the actions of adults they had observed and the responses of others to those actions (Bandura, 1973). Thus, behavioral tendencies can reflect exposure to two sources of information: observations of others' behaviors and the reactions they produce. This is known as *social learning*.

Social learning processes play important roles in the formation and modification of attitudes. We provide two illustrations of this principle, in quite different contexts. Our first example shows that, from observing the behavior of others, even some seemingly "hard-wired" attitudes can be changed. Snake-phobic individuals were recruited for a study (Bandura, Blanchard, & Ritter, 1969) and, not surprisingly, their initial evaluations of snakes were very negative. Participants then were either assigned to a control condition (no therapy) or to receive therapeutic sessions over several weeks where they: (a) imagined snakes while they tried to relax (i.e., desensitization), (b) watched a film depicting people interacting with a snake while they tried to relax (i.e., symbolic modeling), or (c) saw an experimenter interacting with a snake and then joined in the interaction (i.e., live modeling with participation). At the end of the study, attitudes towards snakes improved in all three treatment conditions compared with the control condition. Both modeling treatments improved attitudes to a greater degree than desensitization, and live modeling with participation was most effective in changing attitudes. Both modeling conditions, but particularly the one that involved observing and interacting with a snake under guided conditions, improved attitudes towards an entity that initially had been intensely disliked.

A study in a very different domain (Stout, Dasgupta, Hunsinger, & McManus, 2011) showed that social learning can affect students' attitudes towards science (STEM) fields, disciplines that historically have been highly masculinized. Across several studies, male and female STEM students interacted with a student peer in STEM, read about a successful person in a STEM field, or were taught by instructors in a STEM course who were of the same or opposite gender. Women were strongly affected by exposure to same-sex role models. As depicted in Figure 6.3, women who were taught by a successful female peer later showed stronger implicit identification and more positive implicit attitudes toward STEM on IAT measures. Somewhat surprisingly, role models did not reduce students' implicit or explicit stereotypes of these disciplines as masculine. Therefore, observing role models improved women's attitudes and enhanced their identification with STEM, a social environment still seen as unwelcoming.

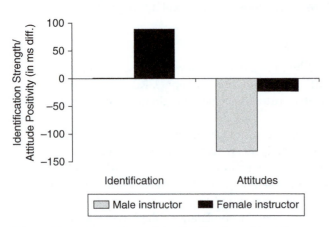

Figure 6.3 Women's implicit identification with and implicit attitudes towards Math as a function of the gender of role models

Source: Adapted from Stout et al. (2011)

Propositional Processes

In Chapter 3, we briefly introduced Gawronski and Bodenhausen's APE model (2006, 2007, 2011, 2014) to illustrate the interplay between automatic and controlled processes. Although this model emphasizes the relation between automatic and controlled processes, it more broadly offers an account of evaluative processes and judgments (APE stands for the Associative–Propositional Evaluation Model). The APE model recognizes the co-existence of both relatively unconscious and conscious evaluative processes. Unconscious processes primarily involve associations that have been formed between concepts and between concepts and valence from various kinds of conditioning and learning processes. As we have discussed, associations determine which mental contents become accessible in response to an object or a person. Importantly, the APE model argues that associations (and the Associative System) are silent about whether the activated links are valid or invalid, true or false. For example, merely having a mental link tying Islamic-sounding names to terrorism (Stroessner, Scholer, Marx, & Weisz, 2015) means that the association might come to mind in any domain where it is relevant, even if the perceiver explicitly rejects the link.

Association-based processes co-exist with propositional processes, which are focused on the validity of information, assessing whether information is accepted as accurate or rejected as false. Propositional processes are involved in monitoring the output generated by the associative system. If a person reacts negatively to a person with an Islamic name because of an association with terrorism, then propositional processes assess the validity of this response by comparing it with other explicit beliefs and values he holds. If, on the one hand, the association is inconsistent with proposition-based beliefs ("I should not fear this Muslim, since virtually no Muslims are terrorists"), then explicit evaluative responses will reflect egalitarian proposition-based beliefs. If, on the other hand, associative and propositional beliefs are consistent ("Being fearful of this Muslim is reasonable since many terrorists are Muslims"), then explicit evaluations will reflect the (uncorrected) content that was spontaneously activated upon encountering the stimulus.

Propositional processes also play a critical role in assessing information intended to change our evaluations (Bodenhausen & Gawronski, 2013; Gawronski & Bodenhausen, 2006). For example, these processes determine whether a persuasive argument is viewed as strong (logical, sound, and supported with evidence) or weak. This determination guides how a perceiver will respond to a persuasive message, particularly if that message contradicts one's current preferences or attitudes. When counterattitudinal information is encountered that is judged as valid and logical ("that's a really good point...I hadn't considered that"), then persuasion tends to occur. Messages judged as weak or invalid tend to produce counterarguments ("what a stupid argument"), yielding either no change in attitude or even a shift against the argument being advocated (i.e., a *boomerang effect*; Hovland, Janis, & Kelley, 1953). Therefore, propositional processes are critical in determining responses to persuasive appeals and, consequently, whether evaluations are altered through such messages. This is the central claim of Greenwald's (1968) *cognitive response theory* of attitude change, which asserts that reactions to messages determine whether evaluation preferences will shift following a persuasive appeal.

Putting it Together: Dual-process Models

We have reviewed a large body of research showing how evaluations are based upon and affected by myriad factors. When we encounter an object (or person), we are inundated with information provided by the object (its identity and specific features), internal associations we have with the object (our associations), and our explicit beliefs about the object (what we believe about it). In addition, any encounter will occur within a particular context that might affect our ability and motivation to process information. Given all these factors, how do people generate coherent evaluative responses to the objects, people, and events they encounter?

Historically, two influential models developed at around the same time delineated how and when various kinds of information are used to make evaluative judgments. They are both *dual-process models* in that they differentiate between two classes of mental processes underlying evaluative judgments, depending on whether they operate automatically or in a controlled fashion. One model, the *elaboration likelihood model* (ELM; Petty & Briñol, 2012; Petty & Cacioppo, 1986), specifies the conditions under which people engage in a thorough, deliberative analysis of information about an object or message (the *central route*) or instead pursue a truncated analysis based on a subset of available information and reliance on cognitive shortcuts (the *peripheral route*). Central route processing does not occur effortlessly; it is a mode of processing that is conscious and deliberate. Two critical factors determine whether people engage in deliberative processing: the perceiver's *ability* and *motivation* to process deliberatively (Fazio & Olson, 2014). For example, when people are tired, overwhelmed, or know little about a topic, it can be challenging to engage in a thorough analysis of arguments. When motivation is low, such as when people care little about a topic, detailed analysis is also unlikely. In sum, attitudes are changed as a result of central route processing primarily when people are both motivated and able to engage in cognitive elaboration and when the information contained in a persuasive message is strong and compelling.

The second model, the *heuristic-systematic model* (HSM) (Chaiken, 1987; Chaiken et al., 1989; Chen & Chaiken, 1999), also describes two basic sets of processes that guide evaluation. *Systematic processing* involves the effortful and deliberate consideration of object-relevant information, and it also requires high levels of motivation and ability. In contrast, *heuristic processing* involves the (often unconscious) use of heuristics and rules of thumb that require few cognitive resources (e.g., "attractive people are trustworthy"). Whether a person engages in systematic processing depends on the *sufficiency principle*, which states that the individual's motivation to engage in systematic processing increases to the degree that the level of confidence falls below a desired level. In other words, people process systematically when they are significantly less confident in their beliefs than they want to be.

In this model, heuristic and systematic processing co-occur, and outputs from each set of processes interact to exert both independent and interdependent effects on evaluations. Systematic processing can completely override the results of heuristic processing when it produces information invalidating persuasion heuristics (Maheswaran & Chaiken, 1991). For example, if a liked source presents an illogical argument, systematic processes help the perceiver resist persuasion that might typically occur under heuristic processing. Heuristic and systematic processing might also work together to affect evaluations in an additive manner, particularly when the two processing modes produce similar responses (Maheswaran, Mackie, & Chaiken, 1992). Finally, heuristic processes can affect systematic processing when the content of a message is ambiguous (Chaiken & Maheswaran, 1994). If a persuasive appeal is mixed in strength, a heuristic cue involving expertise ("I'm not sure those arguments are persuasive, but the speaker is a prominent scientist") might determine whether the message is compelling.

The ELM and HSM differ in one crucial respect. The ELM generally assumes an inverse relationship between central and peripheral processing, but the HSM argues that systematic and heuristic processing coincide. However, both models embrace the notion that two processing systems operate based on qualitatively distinct principles. Both models maintain that evaluations can be changed through central/systematic processing, requiring both capacity and motivation, and through peripheral/heuristic processing that needs little capacity or motivation.

A more recent dual-process model, the APE model, also distinguishes two sets of processes underlying evaluative responses and persuasion. However, the APE model focuses on differences in processes involving links in memory (associational) and judgments of validity (propositional), respectively. Responses on explicit self-report measures (e.g., questionnaires) reflect a blend of associational and propositional processes, but indirect measures (e.g., the IAT, sequential priming tasks) primarily capture associations activated from memory. Because different processes underlie responses to these measures, the degree of agreement in responses to explicit and implicit measures can vary. When activated associations and propositional processes produce a consistent evaluative response, there will generally be consistency in responses assessed by different types of attitudinal measures. However, if automatic associations are inconsistent with activated propositional beliefs, then performance on different evaluative measures might be highly variable.

When perceivers become cognizant of discrepancies between associative and propositional outputs, they typically try to reduce the inconsistencies to minimize aversive feelings of cognitive dissonance (Festinger, 1957). Inconsistency can be attenuated by modifying propositions that contribute to the inconsistency (Gawronski & Strack, 2004). So, for example, if a person who values egalitarianism experiences revulsion toward a homeless person, he might invoke propositions to justify the response ("many homeless are mentally ill and dangerous" or "homeless people are that way by choice").

INTERIM SUMMARY Evaluations arise from numerous processes, some of which are relatively automatic and others that require time, attention, and effort. Some pieces of information can readily be used instead of or in addition to more deliberative processing because they reflect mental associations or simple rules of thumb. Other types of processing require additional effort and intentional activation of mental resources. The original basis of any particular evaluation can vary, and over time many evaluative preferences reflect the influence of more than one factor. For example, your evaluation of a person might initially be based on your responses to his appearance and the associations they brought to mind when you met him. Over time, you might assess the accuracy of these associations as you view his behavior, share experiences with him, and gauge your reactions to him. All of these factors will help determine whether you like or dislike him. As a result, your evaluations are often quite complex. Despite their potential complexity, our evaluations help us determine how to react to objects and people we encounter.

THE NATURE OF EVALUATIVE REPRESENTATIONS IN MEMORY

Given the many factors that contribute to our evaluative preferences, you might wonder how this is all represented in memory. What is the nature of these representations? What are their properties? These questions have been debated for a long time, and there is a voluminous literature on the nature of attitude representation. Although this literature shows some continued disagreements, several consensus views have emerged over time. All models of attitudes agree with the general premise that our mental representations contain information linking evaluations and objects that serve as the basis of evaluative responses to various entities (e.g., people, issues, events, or objects) (Fazio, 1995). How those associations are specifically represented in memory, however, is still a matter of debate.

There is also agreement that attitudes vary in their dynamic qualities. Some representations are relatively stable and enduring and are brought to bear consistently over time, but many are instead time- and context-dependent. The degree of flexibility is also a matter of some debate, with scholars traditionally arguing that attitudes are stable memory structures that are *retrieved* from memory. More recently, others have argued that evaluations are instead akin to states that are *constructed* based on situationally relevant information (Conrey & Smith, 2007; Schwarz & Bohner, 2001). From this point of view, the degree that attitudes appear to be stable depends on the consistency in the underlying bases of evaluative judgments rather than the repeated activation of a unitary, stable evaluative knowledge structure. Finally, all models agree that attitudes vary in several fundamental properties and that these variations have significant consequences for their use. We now discuss several of these issues in greater detail.

Representation of Evaluations

In Chapter 2, we discussed the nature of cognitive representations in detail, focusing on how the knowledge, beliefs, and expectancies about a given content domain are stored in memory. Here we highlight some special considerations regarding the representation of evaluations. There are several accounts of the structure of the mental representation of evaluations, with each account emphasizing different aspects of evaluative responding.

Attitudes as Object-evaluation Associations

Fazio and his colleagues (Fazio, 1989, 1995, 2007; Fazio & Olson, 2003) conceptualize attitudes as associations linking objects and summary evaluations. From this perspective, an attitude can be represented in a semantic network, with one node representing the object and a second node representing the global evaluation of the object. The global evaluation can be based on a variety of information, including beliefs, emotional responses, behavioral history, learning, fluency, or reasoning. Regardless of the source of the evaluation, what is critical is that an attitude object (e.g., a cockroach) is linked in memory to an evaluative response ("disgusting").

In this model, the nature of the link between the object and the summary evaluation is of critical importance. This link indicates the strength of association between the two nodes, ranging from non-attitudes (where there are weak or even nonexistent links with an evaluative response) to strong attitudes (where the link to an evaluative response is robust). In the most extreme case, the link is sufficiently strong that the evaluation is activated from memory upon the observation or mere mention of the attitude object, without intent and even when the person is attempting to engage in another activity. When an evaluation is activated, it can affect attention, interpretation, and behavior regarding the object (Fazio & Olson, 2003). This model emphasizes the efficiency derived from simple object-evaluation associations. When an object is encountered, the perceiver can determine how to respond by consulting the summary evaluation rather than engage in an exhaustive review of the object's features.

Tripartite Models of Attitudes

Fazio's model de-emphasizes the kinds of information that underlie summary evaluations, but several models explicitly emphasize that different types of information underlie evaluations. "Tripartite" models (e.g., Breckler, 1984; Chaiken, Pomerantz, & Giner-Sorolla, 1995; Katz & Stotland, 1959; Ostrom, 1969) share the view that attitudes have distinct cognitive, affective, and behavioral components. The cognitive component reflects our thoughts and beliefs about the attitude object, the affective component represents our feelings and emotions regarding the object, and behavioral information pertains to our past and future intended behaviors toward the object. So, an attitude toward a person might be based on information related to our beliefs ("she is brilliant and funny"), our feelings ("I feel good when I'm with her"), and our behavior ("I hang out with her all the time and intend to do so in the future"). A graphical depiction of a tripartite model is presented in Figure 6.4.

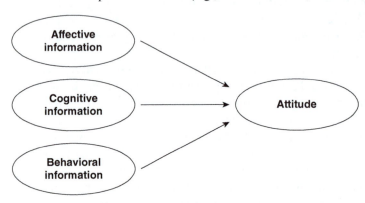

Figure 6.4 A tripartite representation of attitudes

Classic tripartite models highlight the contribution of distinct sources of information in the formation of attitudes. Whereas some accounts point to one source of information as a primary basis of evaluations (e.g., Bem's (1972) emphasis on behavior; Fishbein & Ajzen's (1975) focus on beliefs), tripartite models make clear that evaluations can and often do reflect many aspects of our experiences with attitude objects. Also, the three categories are reasonably exhaustive, in that it is difficult to imagine a basis for an evaluation that cannot be accommodated by at least one of them.

Despite their strengths, these models reflect a set of questionable assumptions (Fazio & Olson, 2003). First, they imply that attitudes are based on all three categories of information. However, attitudes can arise from just one category or various combinations of categories (Zanna & Rempel, 1988). Second, the models imply that all three categories typically will be consistent in their evaluative implications, especially to the degree that attitudes are expected to affect each component causally (e.g., "I like this person – I feel good about her, believe good things about her, and plan to spend time with her") (Eagly & Chaiken, 1998). However, there are often inconsistencies between components, and some research has focused specifically on the processes by which these inconsistencies are resolved (Rosenberg, 1960). Third, the models suggest a relatively direct connection between attitudes and behavior. As we will discuss in a later chapter, knowing a person's attitudes does not allow us to predict subsequent behavior with much confidence. Numerous factors determine when opinions do and not affect actions.

Network Models of Attitudes

Other models (e.g., Bassili & Brown, 2005; Conrey & Smith, 2007; Cunningham, Zelazo, Packer, & Van Bavel, 2007; Judd, Drake, Downing, & Krosnick, 1991; Van Overwalle & Siebler, 2005) depict attitudes as networks containing linked nodes. Some of these nodes represent features ("smile," "sneer") that are themselves valenced ("good," "bad") and connected to other valenced nodes ("kind," "mean"). Evaluative responses to a stimulus (or "input") are based on the pattern of nodes that are activated in response to the input. Different inputs will activate a different body of valenced information because they activate a different set of associations, and the evaluation of any given input will be based on the degree that it activates a coherent set of valenced units. Because the activation pattern depends on the particular features of a given input (which would presumably be unique in every situation) and the strength of associations between units (which can change over time through learning), these models suggest a high degree of potential malleability in evaluative responses.

An example helps to illustrate these points. Imagine meeting a person during an overseas trip. Many factors will affect whether you like him. To name a few, your emotional state ("I am a little anxious in an unfamiliar country") and recent experiences ("what a lovely breakfast we had this morning") and even available sensory information ("what is that smell?") each activate nodes in memory and other nodes associated with them. You also will surely note his physical appearance ("tall," "long hair," "baggy T-shirt"), and each of these features will also activate related nodes in the network. Finally, you might observe the person behave and, by listening to his speech, realize that he comes from your country, activating nodes ("American," "fellow citizen") that would typically lie dormant if you had met him at your local grocery store. This cascade of cognitive activity makes accessible a range of evaluatively or emotionally tinged information, shaping the evaluative judgment of the person. Changing any of these elements – the social context, the surroundings, preceding events, or the person's features – will alter how he is evaluated, even if slightly.

Properties Distinguishing Evaluations and Attitudes

So far, we have been using the terms *evaluations* and *attitudes* interchangeably. Although attitudes and evaluations both involve positive and negative responses to stimuli, they differ in several crucial respects. As is the case with other dichotomies in social cognition (automatic vs. controlled processes, heuristic vs. systematic processing, cognitive vs. affective information), evaluations and attitudes are often viewed as being entirely distinct. However, they can also be discussed in terms of a set of features that distinguish them with the recognition that many evaluative responses can be placed along various continua reflecting differing degrees of these features. Evaluations and attitudes can and have been distinguished in terms of several fundamental, yet related properties.

Activated vs. Constructed Evaluations

Historically, research on attitudes assumed that concepts and associated evaluative information were stored in relatively stable and static representations in memory. Under this view, when a stimulus is encountered that bears a resemblance to a perceiver's existing mental representation, the representation (and the associated attitude) is "activated" to guide subsequent responses. More recent approaches have emphasized the active construction of evaluations, influenced by context, recent experiences, and framing effects. From these perspectives, attitudes are "time-dependent states of the system rather than static 'things' that are 'stored' in memory" (Conrey & Smith, 2007, p. 718).

Views regarding the nature of evaluations (and evaluative responses themselves) range along a continuum between "constructivist" positions (that evaluations are dynamically formed on the spot) and definitions emphasizing retrieval of existing attitudes (that chronic evaluations are stored in and retrieved from memory) (Bohner & Dickel, 2011; Gawronski, 2007; Schwarz, 2007; Schwarz & Bohner, 2001). Issues of representation differentiate these two views. For example, tripartite models suggest that evaluations are relatively consistent because they are typically based on a sizable informational base (one's beliefs, feelings, and behavioral information about an entity). Network models emphasize more dynamic aspects, with some arguing that "representations in the connectionist network do not exist, they occur; they are reconstructed from the unique configuration of inputs each time they come to mind" (Conrey & Smith, 2007, p. 742).

It is important to recognize that both processes occur for any given individual. Some attitudes are potent and can be retrieved when needed ("I like the Republican Party"), whereas other evaluative responses, particularly to novel stimuli, can be generated ("I think I'll like Austria's national dish of Wiener Schnitzel, even though I haven't been able to try it yet"). In most cases, evaluative responses are based on a blend of information reflecting both retrieved evaluative preferences (e.g., political attitudes and prior judgments) and information that has been made accessible through contextual factors (e.g., responses to a particular political candidate of a given party, age, and gender regarding a specific issue framed in a particular manner). Some theories distinguish attitudes from evaluations based on these factors:

> Whereas an attitude is a relatively stable set of representations of a stimulus (only some of which might be active at any time), an evaluation reflects one's current appraisal of the stimulus, including whether it should be approached or avoided. When rendering an evaluation, one draws upon pre-existing attitudes (in particular, those aspects of the attitude that are currently active), together with new information about the stimulus, contextual information, and current goal states. (Cunningham & Zelazo, 2007, p. 736)

Strong vs. Weak Evaluations

Evaluations differ in their *strength* (Howe & Krosnick, 2017; Krosnick & Petty, 1995). Strong evaluations are extreme, clear, and unambivalent (Abelson, 1995; Conner & Armitage, 2008) and held with a high degree of confidence (Rucker, Tormala, Petty, & Briñol, 2014; Tormala & Rucker, 2007). As evaluations increase in strength, they are more likely to be activated upon exposure to a relevant entity (Fazio et al., 1986).

Weak evaluations – referred to as *mere evaluations*, *weak attitudes*, or *nonattitudes* (Converse, 1964; Fazio, 2007) – are low on these properties. Weak attitudes tend to be evaluations that are constructed on the spot when experience with an entity or in a domain is low. In such cases, individuals can generate an evaluative response reflecting their current appraisal of the stimulus. However, this evaluation will tend to be unstable, malleable, unclear, and held with little confidence. Strong evaluations are more likely to affect behavior (Holland, Verplanken, & van Knippenberg, 2002), but even weak evaluations can guide judgments and behavior when expertise is low (e.g., Lev-On & Waismel-Manor, 2016).

Stable vs. Malleable Evaluations

Evaluations vary in the degree that they are fluid or "crystallized" (Converse, 1964). Stable evaluations are those that provide consistent responding across time and context, and stability characterizes evaluations that are regularly activated over time (Fazio, 1995). Stable evaluations are relatively resistant to persuasive appeals (Krosnick & Petty, 1995), and they tend to prevail within attitudinally homogeneous social networks (Visser & Mirabile, 2004).

Evaluations differ in their stability based on whether they are activated or constructed. Judgments constructed based on whatever information is accessible when the evaluation is formed will typically show a high degree of malleability over time, as different situations provide different informational inputs (Conrey & Smith, 2007; Schwarz, 2007). Evaluations also differ in their stability based on genetic heritability (Olson, Vernon, Harris, & Jang, 2001). Evaluative tendencies can be inherited through the presumed influence of genes on psychological characteristics such as temperament and intelligence. Attitudes related to religion, political conservatism, and Right-Wing Authoritarianism show high degrees of heritability (and thus stability) (Bouchard, 2004).

In sum, evaluations differ in several critical respects, and considerations of these differences can help us understand some of the variations in the functioning and consequences of evaluative judgments. Historically, attitudes were viewed as strong and stable evaluative preferences that are retrieved from memory. More recent characterizations emphasize that evaluations are dynamically constructed based on whatever information is triggered by the stimulus and the context in which the stimulus is encountered. Many evaluative judgments likely fall between these extremes, and future research will hopefully clarify the conditions under which evaluations with differing properties shape information processing.

EVALUATION IN UNDERSTANDING THE SELF, PERSONS, AND GROUPS

Evaluative processes are ubiquitous, affecting the processing of various kinds of information we encounter in the social world. Much of our discussion so far has focused on evaluative responses to various stimuli in both social and non-social domains. We now turn to a focused review of how evaluative responses are intrinsically involved in thinking about the self, other individuals, and groups.

Evaluation Processes in Understanding the Self

It is no surprise that people have strong feelings about themselves (Allport, 1943; Markus & Sentis, 1982). In fact, the self can itself be viewed as an attitude object of crucial importance in our lives (Greenwald & Pratkanis, 1984; Meyer & Lieberman, 2018; Rosenberg, 1965). These notions are captured well in a quote from the prominent sociologist, C.H. Cooley (1922, p. 172):

> Since "I" is known to our experience primarily as a feeling, or as a feeling-ingredient in our ideas, it cannot be described or defined without suggesting that feeling…There can be no final test of the self except the way we feel; it is that toward which we have the "my" attitude.

Decades later, Greenwald (1989, p. 438) pithily echoed this argument, stating that "the self is for many people the most important attitude object."

Enhancement in Self-evaluation

As an attitude object, how can self-evaluations be characterized? Much research demonstrates that, with some notable exceptions, people's attitudes about themselves tend to be quite positive. People typically possess high *self-esteem*, maintaining generally positive beliefs and feelings about the self. There is a robust tendency for people to exaggerate their positive qualities (*self-enhancement*) and downplay their negative qualities (*self-protection*) (see Alicke & Sedikides, 2009; Dufner, Gebauer, Sedikides, & Denissen, 2019; Dunning, 2014). They think they are more skilled and moral than other individuals, a phenomenon called the *better-than-average effect* (Brown, 1986, 2012; Zell, Strickhouser, Sedikides, & Alicke, 2020). For example, 94% of college professors say they are better than the average professor, even though this is, of course, statistically impossible (Cross, 1977). This tendency to see oneself in an overly positive light is exhibited even by people who might be expected to attenuate self-flattery: prison inmates judged themselves to be more moral, trustworthy, honest, dependable, compassionate, generous, law-abiding, self-controlled, and kinder than other inmates (Sedikides, Meek, Alicke, & Taylor, 2014). More surprisingly, they also rated themselves as better than people in general (i.e., non-prisoners) on all traits except law-abidingness.

People engage in a variety of actions to build and maintain positive self-evaluations. For example, they tend to affiliate with persons or groups who reflect well on them, and they avoid people who might cast them in a negative light (Cialdini, Borden, Thorne, Walder, Freeman, & Sloan, 1976; Tesser, 1988). Several cognitive processes have also been implicated in self-enhancement. People seek out feedback that accentuates their positive attributes (Gaertner, Sedikides, & Cai, 2012), dismiss feedback suggesting failure (Shepperd, 1993), and diminish the personal relevance of an attribute when receiving negative feedback on it (Tesser, 1988). People typically make self-serving attributions, attributing success to oneself and failure to others or circumstances (Bradley, 1978; Campbell & Sedikides, 1999).

Memory processes can also play a central role in self-enhancement (Sedikides, Green, Saunders, Skowronski, & Zengel, 2016; Skowronski, 2011; Zengel, Wells, & Skowronski, 2018).

Several studies have shown that people tend to forget information that threatens one's positive view of the self, a phenomenon termed *mnemic neglect.* In these experiments, participants read a series of descriptions of either positive or negative behaviors supposedly performed by themselves or by a fictional person. Each behavior is known to imply either a trait that is typically important (kind-unkind) or unimportant (modest-immodest) in people's self-concepts. In later tests of free recall, participants show poorer recall for negative behaviors related to important traits when the self – but not an unknown other – performed those actions (see Figure 6.5). In other words, people selectively forget their failures relating to essential aspects of their self-concepts.

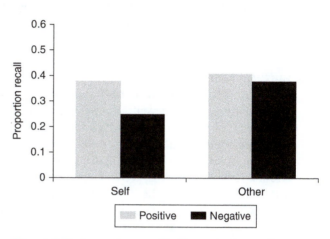

Figure 6.5   Lower free recall of important, negative information about the self compared with another person (i.e., mnemic neglect)

Source: Adapted from Sedikides & Green (2000)

Mnemic neglect is typically manifest on free recall tasks but not on recognition memory measures (Green, Sedikides, & Gregg, 2008). The bias is attenuated when participants have limited time to process each behavioral description (Sedikides & Green, 2000) and when people are instigated to relate threatening information to the self-concept. In one such study (Pinter, Green, Sedikides, & Gregg, 2011), participants were explicitly instructed to integrate some negative behavioral information into the self-concept ("Why *does* this sentence describe you?") and to separate other negative information from the self ("Why *doesn't* this sentence describe you?"). Participants showed lower free recall of the negative information only when they were prompted to negate its relationship to the self. Taken together, these findings indicate that, compared with non-threatening information, self-threatening information is not spontaneously integrated into self-representations in memory.

Moderation of Self-enhancement

Self-enhancement is not ubiquitous. Several factors influence the tendency to engage in self-enhancement processes. Self-enhancement motives are heightened when people perceive a threat to their self-image (Baumeister, Smart, & Boden, 1996; Fein & Spencer, 1997; Gramzow, 2011). Failing at a task increases self-enhancing tendencies (Brown & Gallagher, 1992; Greenberg & Pyszczynski, 1985), particularly when people perceive they have few opportunities for future improvement (Duval & Silvia, 2002). Individual difference variables also moderate self-enhancement tendencies. People high in self-esteem and in promotion focus show high levels of self-enhancement (Campbell, Rudich, & Sedikides, 2002; Hepper, Gramzow, & Sedikides, 2010), as do people high in narcissism (John & Robins, 1994; Morf, Horvath, & Torchetti, 2011). Depressed individuals also show lower levels of self-enhancement and have more accurate views of themselves, a phenomenon labeled depressive realism (Alloy & Abramson, 1988; Moore & Fresco, 2012).

Somewhat ironically, people who chronically underperform on tasks often exhibit the most self-enhancement. In one study (Kruger & Dunning, 1999), students who scored near the bottom on tests of humor, grammar, and logic showed the lowest accuracy of judgments of their abilities, evaluating themselves as above average on these very attributes. This *unskilled but unaware* phenomenon has been shown multiple times (Ehrlinger, Johnson, Banner, Dunning, & Kruger, 2008; Krueger & Mueller, 2002; Schlösser, Dunning, Johnson, & Kruger, 2013).

Cultural Factors

There has been extensive debate about whether self-enhancement is universal, manifesting consistently across different societies, or culturally dependent. A specific focus concerns the prevalence of self-enhancement motives in Western, individualistic cultures compared with more communal cultures of East Asia. Some scholars have argued that self-enhancement is not a common motivation in East Asian cultures, where there is a greater emphasis on relationships (Heine, Lehman, Markus, & Kitayama, 1999; Markus & Kitayama, 1991). In these cultures, self-evaluation reflects the degree that a person has meaningful relationships with other individuals and significant social groups. "Fitting in" is prioritized, and self-focused enhancement may be viewed as unnecessary and even harmful. Several studies have provided evidence of lower levels of self-enhancement in collectivist cultures (Heine et al., 1999; Heine, Kitayama, & Lehman, 2001; Kitayama, Markus, Matsumoto, & Norasakkunkit, 1997). A meta-analysis (Heine & Hamamura, 2007) involving 91 cross-cultural comparisons confirmed that Westerners engage in greater self-enhancement compared with East Asians.

Others have asserted that the self-enhancement motive is universal but manifests itself differently in different cultures (Brown & Kobayashi, 2003; Kurman, 2003; Sedikides, Gaertner, & Cai, 2015; Yamagishi, Hashimoto, & Schug, 2008). Easterners, it is argued, self-enhance strategically and selectively. They privately rate themselves as better than average on traits that are personally important to them (e.g., loyalty or respect) but may publicly state a preference for collectivistic attributes in a strategic attempt to maintain a positive reputation (Yamagishi et al., 2008). On indirect measures of self-esteem (e.g., preferences for letters in one's name or numbers in one's birthday), participants in collectivist and individualist cultures do not differ (Hetts, Sakuma, & Pelham, 1999; Yamaguchi et al., 2007). Similarly, although East Asians tend to show a lesser tendency to endorse positive traits as self-descriptive, they show the equivalent speed as Westerners to make favorable self-descriptive and negative non-self-descriptive trait judgments (Cai, Wu, Shi, Gu, & Sedikides, 2016). Finally, the tendency to self-enhance is positively correlated with psychological health in both Western (Taylor, Lerner, Sherman, Sage, & McDowell, 2003b) and Eastern (Cai, Wu, & Brown, 2009) cultures.

Association with the Self as a Basis of Value

Self-enhancement is also reflected in the tendency to evaluate more favorably and cherish more highly objects that are associated with oneself. People value their own possessions and objects more than do others, a phenomenon called the *endowment effect* (Kahneman, Knetsch, & Thaler, 1991; Morewedge & Giblin, 2015; Thaler, 1980). In one early demonstration of this effect (Knetsch, 1989), students were given a mug, a candy bar, or neither item. Later, they were asked whether they would like to switch what they had for the other item or, for those in the no-item control condition, were asked to indicate which item they would like to own. In the control condition, students' expressed preference for the mug and chocolate was roughly equivalent (56% and 44%, respectively). However, in the two conditions where students were initially given the item and asked if they wanted to switch, very few chose to do so (11% in the mug condition, 10% in the chocolate condition). Once an item was possessed, it appeared to increase in value.

There are several negative consequences of the endowment effect, including restricting the flow of goods and services and encouraging collecting and hoarding behavior. So, for example, "people who own lava lamps demand more to give them up than the people who do not own lava lamps will pay to get them, deals go unmade and storage lockers remain filled with lava lamps that are destined never again to glow" (Morewedge, Shu, Gilbert, & Wilson, 2009, p. 947). Moreover, the endowment effect can present difficulties in negotiations of all types, including negotiations between groups and nations (Ledgerwood, Liviatan, & Carnevale, 2007; Levy, 1992). Getting people to give up what they possess can be notoriously tricky.

The basis of the endowment effect has been a matter of some contention. Initially, the effect was interpreted as reflecting *loss aversion*, that a loss is more painful than an equivalent gain is pleasurable (Kahneman, Knetsch, & Thaler, 1990; Thaler, 1980). Several subsequent accounts provide different bases for the endowment effect (Morewedge & Giblin, 2015). One such account, the *mere ownership* explanation, ties the endowment effect directly to evaluative biases favoring the self. This approach posits that favorable evaluations of the self are transferred to objects that one possesses, thereby increasing their value (Alexopoulos, Šimleša, & Francis, 2015; Beggan, 1992; Morewedge et al., 2009). Several studies have provided evidence consistent with this explanation. For example, providing self-relevant primes before an object is evaluated increases its judged value, creating endowment effects in children as young as three (Hood, Weltzien, Marsh, & Kanngiesser, 2016). Also, merely touching an object (Brasel & Gips, 2014; Peck & Shu, 2009) or imagining that one owns it (Zhang & Aggarwal, 2015) engenders more favorable evaluations and valuations.

There is also evidence directly linking the self to owned objects. Associations form readily between objects and the self for newly-acquired items (LeBarr & Shedden, 2017). Neuroscientific evidence also shows that a brain region involved in self-referential memory (the medial prefrontal cortex; MPFC) shows greater activation while imagining that oneself (rather than another person) owns an object, and the level of MPFC activation predicts more positive evaluations of the object (Hassall, Silver, Turk, & Krigolson, 2016; Kim & Johnson, 2014). In sum, the endowment effect reflects, at least in part, a manifestation of self-enhancement tendencies based on associations that form between the self and objects in the world.

Social Comparison Processes in Self-evaluation

Whether judging ourselves as persons or evaluating our performance on a task, it is often unclear on what basis those evaluations should be made. What criteria can I use in evaluating myself? How well did I do, and how can I know? Such judgments are inherently subjective. Because of these uncertainties, people usually evaluate themselves not against objective standards but by comparing themselves with others. This idea was a central focus of Festinger's (1954) *Social Comparison Theory*. As he noted, "To the extent that objective, non-social means are not available, people evaluate their opinions and abilities by comparison respectively with the opinions and abilities of others" (p. 118)

Festinger realized that in evaluating ourselves against others, we have some flexibility in determining who should serve as the comparison standard ("should I compare myself with a cleric, a classmate, or a criminal?") and what we infer in the process of comparison ("am I similar or dissimilar from this person?"). Festinger's (1954) theory generated a great deal of research focused on social comparison processes. Much of this work has examined when people engage in upward or downward comparison (i.e., comparisons against standards judged as superior or inferior to oneself, respectively, on the dimension in question) and the processes involved in social comparison.

Given the broad tendency for self-enhancement, one might expect people to engage in downward social comparisons when they desire to bolster feelings of self-worth. Indeed, several theorists (Sedikides & Strube, 1997; Wills, 1981; Wood, 1989) have argued that downward comparisons are more likely when people experience failure, negative affect, or chronic low self-esteem. In these cases, downward comparisons might be initiated to restore self-esteem. Despite some supportive evidence for this idea in the literature (e.g., Kruglanski & Mayseless, 1990; Reis, Gerrard, & Gibbons, 1993; Zell, Alicke, & Strickhouser, 2015), a recent meta-analysis (Gerber, Wheeler, & Suls, 2018) revealed some surprising findings. First, there is a tendency for people to engage in upward social comparisons when no threat to the self is involved. However, there is no evidence for a preference for downward comparisons when people feel threatened. In other words, there is no bias favoring downward social comparison when people fail or experience self-relevant threats. Second, for both upward and downward social comparisons, people tend to exhibit contrast effects whereby they distance themselves from the comparison standard. As a consequence, people tend to evaluate themselves more negatively after an upward comparison ("that person's success makes me doubt my abilities") and more positively after a downward comparison ("Compared with that person, I'm a real winner!"). Therefore, although there is no overall bias favoring downward social comparisons under conditions of failure or low self-esteem, people do benefit by comparing themselves against inferior standards.

In some situations, people benefit from upward comparisons, particularly when comparing themselves with superior others who have experienced some misfortune or failure. Fortunately, empathy and sadness are common reactions to the failures of other people and groups. However, there are times when people actually experience pleasure and self-satisfaction when they see or learn of the misfortune, a phenomenon termed *schadenfreude* (a German word meaning "pleasure from the pain of others"). What would lead people to experience pleasure from others' misfortune? Feelings of schadenfreude most typically occur when failure is experienced by a competitor (Cikara & Fiske, 2013) or someone we envy (Van Dijk, Ouwerkerk, Smith, & Cikara, 2015). It also arises when we think failure is deserved (Feather & Sherman, 2002) or when we gain from it (Smith, Eyre, Powell, & Kim, 2006). Schadenfreude produces increases in self-esteem and an enhanced sense of control, a higher sense of belonging, and a belief that one's life is meaningful (Brambilla & Riva, 2017). Thus, schadenfreude yields a variety of benefits that serve to promote self-evaluations through derogating others.

Other Motives in Self-evaluation

Self-enhancement is a fundamental motive in self-evaluation, but it is not people's only motive. People are sometimes motivated to accurately assess their skills, abilities, and characteristics (Gregg, Sedikides, & Gebauer, 2011; Trope, 1986b). However, even when attempting to make accurate evaluations, people tend to make judgments that are overly-positive and overly-confident (Dunning, 2005; Ehrlinger, Mitchum, & Dweck, 2016). At other times, people are motivated toward self-improvement (Cohen & Sherman, 2014; Sedikides & Hepper, 2009). Self-affirming manipulations increase executive functioning (Harris, Harris, & Miles, 2017), allowing people to be more capable and open to learning from information that might otherwise be threatening (Cohen, Garcia, Purdie-Vaughns, Apfel, & Brzustoski, 2009; Sherman & Hartson, 2011).

Finally, *Self-Verification Theory* emphasizes that people often prefer to be seen by others as they see themselves, even if they view themselves negatively (Swann, 2012; Swann, Pelham, & Krull, 1989). However, even self-verification processes can contribute to self-enhancement if self-views are unrealistically positive (as they often are).

In sum, the self is a critical "attitude object" in our lives, and most people tend to view themselves in favorable terms, at least most of the time. Numerous behavioral tendencies and cognitive processes act to create and maintain a positive sense of self. Other motives influence self-evaluation, but even those motives are affected by or complement the tendency for people to self-enhance. Although self-enhancement can create unrealistic beliefs about the self, it also can provide benefits to self-esteem and social functioning.

Evaluation Processes in Understanding Persons

We began this chapter by highlighting the importance, even the automaticity, of evaluative responses to information we encounter. The basic good versus bad distinction seems fundamental. We then discussed that the various elements of the specific information we process have evaluative connotations, and these are all integrated into the process of making overall judgments. Moreover, those pieces of information vary in their importance for the judgment at hand and therefore take on different weights in any given judgment context. It is crucial, therefore, to understand the factors that influence this weighting process. These questions are at the heart of understanding evaluations of persons.

Understanding how people evaluate other persons has been of central interest since Asch's (1946) foundational work on impression formation. As we discussed in Chapter 1, Asch emphasized the active role that perceivers play in the process of forming an impression of another individual. He argued that people actively construct impressions by integrating new information with information already known about the person. As such, impression formation is an active, dynamic cognitive process focused on detecting the consistencies that make individuals both distinct and unique. Many significant findings emerged from Asch's seminal work that continues to shape the study of interpersonal evaluation. Some of these findings speak directly to the question of differential weighting in making judgments.

Asch (1946) tested his ideas with a simple paradigm. Participants were presented with a series of traits describing a person. Impressions of the person were then assessed by having participants write brief descriptions of the person and having them indicate, on a checklist of attributes, other traits descriptive of the person. Several crucial discoveries emerged from this straightforward paradigm (Uleman & Kressel, 2013). Asch's studies were conducted well before the emergence of social cognition in the 1970s, which brought new theoretical frameworks and more developed methodological techniques. More recent research has built upon the groundwork laid by Asch. This research generally has shown these early findings to be robust, but it has provided a deeper understanding of these phenomena and has specified the roles of attentional, memory, and inference processes in evaluation. Here, we highlight research further developing some of Asch's research and elucidating the cognitive underpinnings of these historical findings. We also discuss several topics that have emerged more recently.

The Warm–Cold Effect

Asch recognized that traits varied in the degree that they were consequential for a developing impression (what we have referred to as the weight given to each attribute). In a now-classic study, participants were given seven trait adjectives describing the person and were asked to form an impression of that person. The two conditions of the study differed in only one respect: the middle trait in the sequence was either *warm* or *cold* (the other six were identical). This one difference produced a substantial difference in the attributes checked as also describing the person. Asch referred to warm and cold as *central traits* because of their powerful influence and contrasted them with less important *peripheral traits* (e.g., polite and blunt), which in the same paradigm had far less influence on checklist responses.

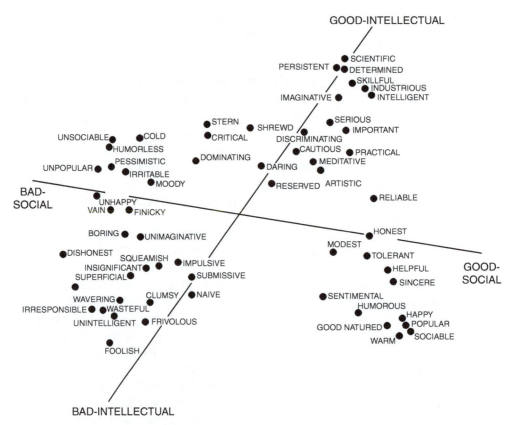

Figure 6.6   Social and intellectual dimensions underlying impressions of persons
Source: From Rosenberg et al. (1968)

Two Fundamental Dimensions

Asch's warm–cold study stimulated much research that has produced new insights into how impressions are formed. One important advance resulted from the development of multi-variate statistical techniques that permitted tests regarding the mental representation of trait information in memory. Using these techniques, Rosenberg, Nelson, and Vivekananthan (1968) identified two dimensions underlying impressions of persons, both with strong evaluative connotations but differing in descriptive content: a good vs. bad social (e.g., warm vs. cold) dimension and a good vs. bad intellectual (e.g., scientific vs. foolish) dimension (see Figure 6.6). These two dimensions (often called *warmth* and *competence*) have been identified as major factors underlying representation and judgment in several domains of research (e.g., Abele, Cuddy, Judd, & Yzerbyt, 2008; Abele & Wojciszke, 2014; Cuddy, Fiske, & Glick, 2008; Fiske et al., 2002; Judd, James-Hawkins, Yzerbyt, & Kashima, 2005; Peeters & Czapinski, 1990; Stroessner, 2020; Wiggins, 1979). Given this consistency, warmth and competence are often referred to as fundamental dimensions of social judgment.

Understanding the "Central Trait" Effect

Rosenberg et al. (1968) proposed that Asch's (1946) findings of central traits could be reinterpreted within this two-dimensional framework. Specifically, they noted that the central traits *warm* and *cold* were located at opposite ends of the social dimension and that the other six attributes all reflected the positive pole of the intellectual dimension. They also observed that the warm–cold manipulation strongly influenced participants' checklist responses for traits on the social dimension but not for traits on the intellectual dimension. The implication was that the apparent "centrality" of warm and cold could be attributed to the fact that (a) they had opposing evaluative implications on the dimension of sociability and (b) they were the *only* traits representing that dimension (whereas the other six traits redundantly represented the intellectual dimension). Thus, warm and cold had a considerable influence on later judgments, but their impact derived from the distinctiveness of the information they provided rather than their inherent centrality in impressions. In other words, unique information receives more weight in judgment than does redundant information.

This possibility was confirmed by a study (Zanna & Hamilton, 1972) replicating and extending Asch's (1946) findings. Again, participants were presented with trait information about a person. In one condition, participants read about a person who was described as either warm or cold embedded in several positive intellectual dimension traits, as in the original warm–cold study. In the other condition, a desirable or undesirable intellectual dimension trait (industrious vs. lazy) was included among several desirable social dimension traits. Participants then indicated the probability that the person possessed other evaluative traits, half of which related to sociability and half to intellectuality. Replicating Asch, the warm–cold variation impacted judgments only for traits representing the social dimension and not the intellectual dimension. In contrast, the industrious–lazy variation impacted trait judgments for intellectual dimension traits, but not social dimension traits. In sum, traits were "central" only to the degree that they provided unique information about one of the two fundamental dimensions of evaluation. The same point was confirmed in a more recent study using a different method (Nunes, Garcia-Marques, Ferreira, & Ramos, 2017).

Relationship Between Dimensions

Asch (and others before him; Newcomb, 1931; Thorndike, 1920; Wells, 1907) provided evidence of a *halo effect* in social judgment, the tendency for global evaluations to affect judgments of individual attributes. In particular, positive judgments on one attribute tend to generalize to favorable judgments on other dimensions, even in the absence of any knowledge of the target on those other attributes. For example, if you know that a person is intelligent, there is no sound reason to assume that the person is also honest. Such halo effects are pervasive in social perception, such that the evaluation of something known about a target tends to color the evaluation of other unknown features and characteristics. In fact, Asch (1946) argued that an overall evaluative impression of a person can color the evaluation of new incoming information about the person, reinforcing and perpetuating the initial evaluation. Much research has extended this finding (Cooper, 1981; Forgas & Laham, 2017; Nisbett & Wilson, 1977b). However, there appear to be constraints on the extent to which halo effects occur. Some interesting possibilities have emerged based on an understanding of the relations between the two fundamental dimensions of social evaluation we have just introduced.

In the analyses by Rosenberg et al. (1968), the two dimensions were not fully independent; the two dimensions were positively correlated, such that a target perceived positively on one dimension (social) would be likely to be judged favorably on the other dimension (intellectual). This, then, reflects a halo effect. However, in our reconsideration of the warm–cold effect, we have seen that generalizations are limited to inferences within each dimension. That is, the warm–cold manipulation influenced checklist responses only about other social attributes (and effects of the industrious-lazy manipulation arose only on the intellectual dimension). So, this two-dimensional structure constrains the extent to which halo effects occur.

The results of other research further complicate the situation. Generalization appears more likely between positive traits (e.g., assuming that a kind person is intelligent) than negative traits (e.g., assuming that an unkind person is unintelligent) (Gräf & Unkelbach, 2016). Generalization from one negative trait to another might be less likely because negative traits and words are more unique and distinct from one another than are similar positive stimuli. In other words, halo effects might be more common because positive traits are more interchangeable than negative traits (Alves, Koch, & Unkelbach, 2017; Koch, Alves, Krüger, & Unkelbach, 2016). As a consequence, generalization effects usually involve halos and not horns.

In some research, judgments on the two dimensions have been uncorrelated while in others they are negatively related (Cuddy, Fiske, & Glick, 2004; Cuddy, Norton, & Fiske, 2005; Glick & Fiske, 2001; Judd et al., 2005; Yzerbyt, Kervyn, & Judd, 2008; Yzerbyt, Provost, & Corneille, 2005). So, there is no simple answer to the question of how the dimensions are related or function together. Several variables could be influential in shaping these disparate outcomes. For example, the targets of judgment are sometimes individuals and other times groups (e.g., ethnic groups, nations). Halo effects are more likely for individual targets and single social groups where an expectation of consistency would be high (c.f., Hamilton, Sherman, et al., 2015). In some cases, the targets persons (or groups) are judged on both dimensions; in other cases, one target is judged on one dimension and compared to another group judged on the other dimension. Any of these (and other) differences can alter the results. There is, however, one intriguing effect that has emerged from these analyses, and it pertains directly to the relationship between dimensions.

The Compensation Effect

In a study examining the evaluation of groups (Judd et al., 2005), participants formed impressions of two anonymous groups that were described by a series of behaviors that varied in warmth and competence. For one group, most behaviors were high on competence and undiagnostic on warmth. For the other group, most behaviors were low on competence and undiagnostic on warmth. Therefore, the two groups were sharply differentiated on competence but were equivalent on warmth. After reading the behaviors, participants rated both groups on traits relating to warmth and competence. The group described as highly competent was, of course, rated as more competent than the other group. However, that group was rated as *less warm* than the low competence group. In a follow-up study, the dimensions were reversed.

The two groups differed in warmth but were neutral and equivalent in competence. In this study, the high warmth group was rated as less competent than the low warmth group. This tendency to evaluate groups lower on a dimension when they are high on the other dimension has been termed the *compensation effect*.

The compensation effect has been replicated several times, and experiments have identified some important contributing factors (Kervyn, Yzerbyt, & Judd, 2010). The original studies concerned groups, but the effect has also been demonstrated in judgments involving two individuals (Judd et al., 2005). The effect does not occur for dimensions other than the two primary dimensions (Yzerbyt et al., 2008), and it requires a comparison between two targets (Judd et al., 2005). The effect is more substantial when the status difference between the groups is large rather than small (Cambon & Yzerbyt, 2017), and the effect is more likely when intergroup relations are cooperative rather than competitive (Cambon, Yzerbyt, & Yakimova, 2015). Evidence suggests that compensation is a means to protect one's ingroup identity by maintaining an advantage on an important dimension, while also recognizing a positive view of the alternative group on a different dimension.

Order Effects in Person Evaluation

Another important finding from Asch's (1946) research was that the evaluative influence (the *weight*) of an attribute depends on where it appears in the sequence of presented information. To some participants, he gave the following traits:

> intelligent, industrious, impulsive, critical, stubborn, envious.

To others, he gave the following:

> envious, stubborn, critical, impulsive, industrious, intelligent.

You likely noticed that the two lists consist of the same traits appearing in the opposite order. Notably, the first list begins with highly desirable attributes and ends with undesirable qualities, whereas the second begins with the undesirable and proceeds to the desirable attributes. Logically, impressions formed in these two conditions should be the same. However, Asch showed that the ordering of attribute information had a considerable influence on evaluative judgments. Impressions formed in the first case were much more favorable than in the second case. In other words, traits early in the sequence received more weight than traits that appeared later in the sequence. This is called a *primacy effect*. Primacy effects in impression formation have been reported in many studies (e.g., Anderson, 1965; Anderson & Barrios, 1961; Belmore, 1987; Eyal et al., 2011; Forgas, 2011; Fourakis & Cone, 2020; Sullivan, 2019). There are certain conditions under which later information is more heavily weighted, a *recency effect*, but primacy effects are much more common in social evaluation.

What explains the primacy effect in evaluation? Two explanations have been proposed. Asch's (1946) *change in meaning* explanation emphasized the evolving nature of impressions. Impressions begin to form immediately based on the first information received, and that initial impression shapes the interpretation of subsequent traits. If the first items are highly desirable, the following terms are construed more favorably, consistent with the emerging impression. The same is true in reverse – initial undesirable information will alter the interpretation of later desirable attributes. So, for example, if you learn that someone is "bright, kind, and clever," what does the attribute "clever" imply about the person? Perhaps it suggests that the person is insightful and can offer new perspectives on problems. If you learn that someone is "selfish, cruel, and clever," what does "clever" mean now? In this case, it may mean that the person is devious and could take advantage of others. Therefore, Asch argued that the same attribute could mean different things based on the informational context in which it is evaluated. Studies supporting this interpretation have shown, for example, that when preceded by favorable traits, the trait *proud* is interpreted as confident. That same trait is more likely to be interpreted as *conceited* when it follows unfavorable attributes (Hamilton & Zanna, 1974; Zanna & Hamilton, 1977).

An alternative explanation, the *attention decrement hypothesis*, posits that primacy effects are due to diminishing attention as the series of items progresses (Stewart, 1965). If attention to later information is reduced, this information is less likely to influence evolving judgments and will be less available in memory if evaluations are based on recall. This interpretation suggests that compelling participants to attend to traits appearing late in a sequence should diminish the primacy effect. Stewart (1965) tested this possibility by manipulating when participants made evaluations. Half of the participants saw an entire sequence of traits before making an evaluative judgment, whereas the other participants made a judgment after each trait (which would maintain attention through the sequence). A primacy effect emerged when participants made an evaluative judgment only after receiving all the information. However, the effect was reversed for participants who provided continuous judgments. For these participants, traits appearing later in the sequence had a more significant impact on evaluations (i.e., they exhibited a *recency effect*). Numerous studies have confirmed that attentional biases favoring initial information contribute to primacy effects (Anderson, 1973; Anderson & Hubert, 1963; Crano, 1977; Morrison, Conway, & Chein, 2014; Yates & Curley, 1986).

It is also possible that both interpretive and attentional mechanisms play a role under different circumstances. For example, manipulations that encourage or discourage impression formation should also moderate the likelihood of primacy effects. This was demonstrated nicely in a study (Lichtenstein & Srull, 1987) in which participants were provided a sequence of 36 descriptions of behaviors supposedly performed by a person. In one condition, participants were told to form a coherent impression of the person. In another condition, participants were told to comprehend the information and to judge how well the descriptions were written. In both conditions, half of the participants received a majority of favorable items toward the beginning of the sequence, whereas the other participants received a majority of unfavorable items at the beginning of the sequence. After reading all of the sentences, participants completed a free recall task and evaluated the likability of the person.

As can be seen in Table 6.2, when participants were forming an impression, their judgments were more positive in the condition where favorable items appeared early in the sequence. In the comprehension condition, however, participants made more positive evaluations when the favorable information appeared near the end. This shows a primacy effect under impression instructions but a recency

Table 6.2 Judgment favorability and correlations of recall and judgment

	Judgment favorability		% Recall (by presentation sequence)			Judgment-recall correlation
Set	Favorable 1st	Unfavorable 1st	First 7	Middle 22	Final 7	
Impression	5.9	5.2	51	48	52	.12
Comprehension	4.3	4.9	11	23	34	.36

Source: Based on data from Lichtenstein & Srull (1987)

effect under comprehension instructions. Analysis of participants' free recall showed that impression instruction participants recalled equivalent amounts of information across the sequence of information. However, participants in the comprehension condition showed a recency effect in their recall. Moreover, correlations between the content of free recall and evaluative judgments showed that participants in the comprehension condition relied on what they could remember to evaluate the person. In contrast, participants who formed an impression showed no relationship between the valence of recalled information and liking judgments. Thus, people's evaluative judgments tend not to be based on what they can recall when they are forming an impression, but they do use recall to form judgments when their goal is to comprehend the information. The differential role of memory in judgment under different processing goals will be discussed in greater detail in Chapter 9.

Negativity Effects

Another important finding to emerge from Asch's (1946) work is a negativity bias: people weigh negative information more heavily than positive information. As we discussed earlier in this chapter, there is a general bias to overweight negative information in various domains of evaluation. The same is true in evaluating persons (Anderson, 1965, 1968; Feldman, 1966; Fiske, 1980; Hamilton & Huffman, 1971; Hamilton & Zanna, 1972; Hodges, 1974; Richey, McClelland, & Shimkunas, 1967).

In one study showing this effect (Richey, Koenigs, Richey, & Fortin, 1975), participants were presented with passages describing favorable and unfavorable behaviors supposedly performed by a person. The balance of favorable and unfavorable behavioral descriptions was manipulated across conditions; participants read five positive or five negative descriptions combined with either one, two, three, four, or five behaviors of the opposing valence. Therefore, there were ten conditions in which the relative amount of desirable and undesirable information varied. The critical measure in the study was an evaluative judgment of the individual (the degree the person was judged better or worse than the average person).

Results revealed the overweighting of negative information in evaluation. In all conditions – even when there were five positive and one negative behavioral description – participants judged the person as being worse than average. In addition, in the negative majority conditions, the amount of positive information affected the evaluation of the person. However, this was not the case in the positive majority conditions. In these conditions, evaluations were not significantly different between conditions where there was one versus five negative behaviors. In other words, a single negative behavior had the same effect as five negative behaviors. Finally, in almost all conditions, participants' judgments were less favorable than was expected based on the average positivity of the behavioral descriptions assessed in pilot testing. All these results attest to the power of negative information to affect evaluations of persons.

Why would people give more weight to negative information? There are several possibilities, one related to the *meaning change* interpretation introduced by Asch (1946). Personality traits are often ambiguous, so their meaning can be influenced by other traits with which they are linked. For example, a "self-confident malicious" person may be judged more malicious than a "shy malicious" person. Negative traits may lead to greater contextual shifts in meaning than positive traits.

Expectancy-contrast theories (e.g., Sherif & Sherif, 1967) suggest that behavioral information is evaluated against standards that are moderate and positive (i.e., that most people are expected to be good and kind people). Information suggesting that a person is unkind or selfish would be surprising and would consequently produce extreme negative judgments.

Another explanation rests on *differential attention* to negative compared to positive information. Fiske (1980) presented subjects with captioned slides depicting people engaged in different activities that varied in likability. The time participants looked at each slide was measured, and after viewing all the slides, they evaluated the likability of each person. Results showed that negative information received more attention and also was disproportionately weighted in evaluative judgments. Therefore, negative information may grab attention when it is encountered, and its undue emphasis in evaluation may be a function of that greater focus.

Another view (Skowronski & Carlston, 1989) emphasizes the *diagnosticity* of information differing across valence and trait domains. Specifically, behaviors or traits are given more weight to the degree they are seen as uniquely informative about the dimension or category of judgment. Because negative behaviors are generally seen as more diagnostic, they have a greater impact on interpersonal evaluation. This account also distinguishes between negativity effects in different trait domains (Reeder & Brewer, 1979). Negativity biases would be expected to be more pronounced in morality domains (because negative behavior is seen as highly diagnostic of moral character; "No good person would ever do that!") than in ability judgments (because poor performance is seen as less diagnostic of ability; "Anyone can have an off day").

Finally, judgments are sometimes based on *information retrieved from memory*. Negative attributes and behaviors are usually more novel and distinctive, making them more accessible in memory. One study found that a week after participants were exposed to positive and negative information about traits and events, they had better recall of negative than positive information (Carlston, 1980). That greater accessibility may result in a more substantial influence of the negative material on judgments.

In sum, negative information is weighted more heavily than positive information in judgments, and several processing mechanisms contribute to this effect.

Interpersonal Evaluation and Similarity

Most historical approaches to interpersonal evaluation focused on the nature and order of trait and behavioral information acquired about others. However, people also receive information about ways that people are similar and different from themselves, and there is extensive evidence that perceived similarity is positively related to interpersonal liking (Gawronski, Walther, & Blank, 2005; Ullrich & Krueger, 2010; for reviews see Byrne, 1971; Eagly & Chaiken, 1993; Montoya, Horton, & Kirchner, 2008).

Does the same principle hold regarding perceptions of similarity within a group of liked individuals? One might reasonably assume that there would be a tendency for people to find many ways that their friends differ from one another compared with disliked individuals. After all, ingroups are typically more differentiated than outgroups (Ostrom & Sedikides, 1992), and people are more likely to interact with and therefore learn more about liked rather than disliked persons (Denrell, 2005). Therefore, it seems plausible that people should see persons they like as being quite diverse compared with people they dislike. However, recent research shows that the opposite is true; social perceivers tend to see their friends as more similar to one another than people they dislike. Why is this the case? Based on past research, it was assumed that people should associate liked persons with predominantly positive characteristics and disliked persons with negative features. Because positive information is denser than negative information, people should see their friends as more similar to one another than people who are not their friends, even though they presumably know more about the former than the latter. This hypothesis has been confirmed in several experiments, illustrating the important role of similarity in producing and maintaining positive interpersonal evaluations (Alves, Koch, & Unkelbach, 2016).

Neural Underpinnings of Evaluation

New insights regarding evaluation have also emerged from recent research using neuroscientific methods. A distinction between the neural regions underlying interpersonal evaluation and other judgments has emerged. In one study examining the independence of these processes (Schiller, Freeman, Mitchell, Uleman, & Phelps, 2009), participants viewed a series of photographs of 20 individuals. On some trials, they simply viewed the photographs. On other trials, they viewed a picture of a person and read information describing his or her behavior (e.g., "He promised not to smoke in his apartment since his roommate was trying to quit"). Finally, participants indicated whether they liked the person. Examination of fMRI data revealed that the dorsomedial prefrontal cortex (dmPFC) was more active when behavioral information accompanied the faces than when they appeared alone. However, activation of the dmPFC did not predict participants' evaluative judgments, but activation of the amygdala and the posterior cingulate cortex (PCC) – regions that underlie emotional and valuation processes (Cunningham et al., 2008) – did. These data and others (Todorov & Engell, 2008) indicate independence between regions responsible for processing highly-valenced information (regulated primarily by the amygdala and the PCC) and regions responsible for inferring and processing less-valenced feature, behavioral, and trait information.

The Spontaneity of Interpersonal Evaluation

One central issue in interpersonal evaluation relates to the degree that evaluative judgments are made spontaneously or require initiation, effort, and resources. It appears that goals or situational factors can readily influence evaluative judgments of individuals. For example, one study (Fitzsimons & Fishbach, 2010) found that participants who had been primed with an achievement goal reported liking their friends with whom they study more than friends with whom they party. This effect was reversed for participants who had been primed with a socialization goal.

Another set of studies directly examined the spontaneity of evaluative judgments of individuals. As we will discuss in the next chapter, there is abundant evidence that people spontaneously form trait inferences (STIs) about individuals and groups. Schneid and colleagues (Schneid, Carlston, and Skowronski, 2015; Schneid, Crawford, Skowronski, Irwin, & Carlston, 2015) tested whether people also form spontaneous evaluative inferences (STEs) when they receive positive or negative information about a person. They used a *savings-in-relearning* paradigm (Carlston & Skowronski, 1994) to assess this question. Participants were first given information describing a person shown in a picture (usually self-descriptive behavioral statements). Some behaviors had clear evaluative connotations (e.g., "When it snows, I shovel the sidewalk in front of my house so pedestrians don't get their feet wet") whereas others did not (e.g., "This morning, when I woke up, I went outside to get the newspaper from my stoop and then went back in the house"). After a delay, those same faces were presented with evaluative words that were or were not implied by the person's original behavior ("good"), and participants learned these face-evaluative pairings. The rationale was that learning of face-evaluative pairings should be easier if that person's behavior had implied the evaluation. In the final stage, participants were again presented with the faces and asked to recall the evaluation that was paired with that face in the second phase. The prediction would be that people would have better recall for evaluations implied by the original behavior than for evaluations that were not implied.

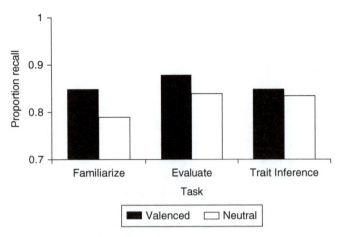

Figure 6.7 Recall of valenced and neutral behavior-target pairings by task

Source: Adapted from Schneid et al. (2015)

Results (displayed in Figure 6.7) showed that participants correctly identified significantly more words on the valenced trials (with implied evaluations) than on the neutral trials. This occurred regardless of whether participants had been asked initially to familiarize themselves with the original stimuli, to make evaluative judgments, or to make trait judgments. These results attest to the spontaneous generation of interpersonal evaluations.

A subsequent study (Schneid et al., 2015) involved participants being exposed to picture-behavioral pairings either under instructions to become familiar with the materials (as in Study 1) or to determine whether the person was lying or telling the truth. Previous work (Crawford, Skowronski, Stiff, & Scherer, 2007) has shown that lie detection disrupts STIs. In this experiment, STIs were eliminated by the lie manipulation but STEs were not. In other words, evaluative judgments formed in both experimental conditions, suggesting that evaluative and trait inferences might reflect independent and separable processes.

Moral Reasoning

Research on moral reasoning – evaluative judgments of right and wrong – has become a central topic in social cognition. Moral judgments appear to rely heavily on emotional responses to stimuli, people, and events, and there is evidence that emotional responses are often automatic (Horberg, Oveis, & Keltner, 2011; Rozin, Haidt, & Fincher, 2009). For example, both adults (Rozin, Haidt, & McCauley, 2000) and children as young as five (Danovitch & Bloom, 2009) agree that moral transgressions (e.g., "Making up mean lies about a good friend") can be appropriately described as "disgusting." Similarly, fMRI research shows heightened amygdala responses to pictorial depictions of behavior associated with disgust (e.g., a person injecting himself with a needle) (Harris & Fiske, 2006). Furthermore, condemnation of moral transgressions increases when judgments are made in a messy room or after exposure to unpleasant odors, and these effects emerge without participants' awareness that their judgments have been affected by these situational factors (Schnall, Haidt, Clore, & Jordan, 2008).

Research has shown that whether a moral judgment is automatic versus controlled depends on the specific kind of judgment being considered (Greene, 2014; Guglielmo, 2015). Rule-based or *deontological* moral judgments (e.g., that harming others is always morally wrong) are relatively automatic whereas *utilitarian* moral judgments (those involving trade-offs between benefits and costs for affected individuals) are resource-dependent. Evidence consistent with this claim includes the finding that manipulations of cognitive load (Greene, Morelli, Lowenberg, Nystrom, & Cohen, 2008) and the time available to make judgments (Suter & Hertwig, 2011) do not affect rule-based judgments but inhibit utilitarian moral judgments.

> **INTERIM SUMMARY** Whereas the early years of social cognition focused primarily on trait judgments of individuals, later work emphasized evaluations of others. Interpersonal evaluation is involved in some of the most crucial aspects of our lives. As William James (1920) argued, "Human beings are born into this little span of life of which the best thing is its friendships and intimacies" (p. 109). Recent research has augmented trait-based understanding of perceptions of persons, emphasizing the essential role of evaluative processes in interpersonal judgment.

Evaluation Processes in Understanding Groups
Cognitive Foundation: Categorization into Groups

Evaluations of groups and their members (i.e., *prejudice*) are of paramount importance in intergroup relations (Molina, Tropp, & Goode, 2016; Tropp & Pettigrew, 2005). Allport's (1954) classic volume, *The Nature of Prejudice*, provided a thorough and prescient analysis of prejudice that foreshadowed many of the research topics that continue through today. A central component of this analysis was an emphasis on the essential role of categorization in social information processing and as a basis for prejudice: "The human mind must think with the aid of categories. Once formed, categories are the basis for normal prejudgment. We cannot possibly avoid this process. Orderly living depends upon it" (Allport, 1954, p. 19).

Tajfel (1969) extended this view and provided some of the earliest and most compelling evidence regarding the consequences of categorization on judgment (Tajfel et al., 1971; Tajfel & Wilkes, 1963). He echoed the argument that categorization processes serve to simplify information processing, stating:

> [Categories] introduce simplicity and order where there is complexity and nearly random variation. They can help us to cope only if fuzzy differences between groups are transmuted into clear ones, or new differences created where none exist. They represent, of course, tendencies towards simplification rather than sharp dichotomies: in other words, in each relevant situation we shall achieve as much stereotyped simplification as we can without doing unnecessary violence to the facts. But there is good evidence that even when facts do turn against us and destroy the useful and comfortable distinctions, we still find ways to preserve the general content of our categories. (Tajfel, 1969, p. 82)

Tajfel's recognition of the cognitive implications of categorization was accompanied by a concern with its evaluative consequences, particularly distinctions between ingroups and outgroups. Dramatic evidence of *ingroup bias* emerged from his research using the *minimal group paradigm* (Tajfel, 1970; Tajfel et al., 1971). This research showed that merely categorizing individuals into ingroups and outgroups, even when based on trivial criteria (e.g., their supposed preference for paintings of one artist versus another), led participants to exaggerate the positive qualities of the ingroup and the negative qualities of the outgroup (see also Dovidio, Gaertner, & Validzic, 1998). When given a chance to allocate rewards, participants favored ingroup over outgroup members (see also Sidanius, Pratto, & Mitchell, 1994). These results emerged consistently even though participants had no prior knowledge of or relationships with the other individuals and could not benefit themselves through the allocation of rewards. The various motivational effects that flowed from the division of the world into ingroups and outgroups became the focus of *Social Identity Theory* (SIT; Tajfel, 1978; Tajfel & Turner, 1979) and, later, *Self-Categorization Theory* (Turner, Hogg, Oakes, Reicher, & Wetherell, 1987).

The cognitive foundation of intergroup prejudice in social categorization is well established (Hamilton & Sherman, 1994; Tajfel & Forgas, 1981). Categorization into ingroup and outgroup produces enhanced perceptions of within-group similarity and between-group differentiation (Corneille & Judd, 1999; Doise, Dechamps, & Meyer, 1978; Rothbart et al., 1997; Tajfel & Wilkes, 1963). This differentiation is fundamental, but it is not enough. By itself, mere categorization cannot completely account for ingroup bias, for which research evidence is pervasive (Brewer, 1979; Gaertner & Insko, 2001; Mullen, Brown, & Smith, 1992). The ingroup inevitably includes the self, and this fact led Tajfel (1978) to define one's *social identity* in both cognitive and evaluative terms; it is part of the self-concept relating to knowledge of one's group memberships together with the value and emotional significance derived from those memberships. Tajfel described a continuum between interpersonal–intergroup situations in which group identities would become more or less salient and relevant. Social identities become particularly crucial in "intergroup contexts," ranging from the mundane (e.g., being a fan of a sports team) to the consequential (e.g., being a citizen of a nation at war). Negative treatment of outgroups serves the motive to protect and enhance the self in intergroup situations (Tajfel & Turner, 1979). However, although social identification often results in negative evaluations and discrimination towards outgroups, these effects reflect ingroup favoritism more strongly than outgroup derogation (Brewer, 1979; Dovidio & Gaertner, 2000; Gaertner, Iuzzini, Witt, & Oriña, 2006; Greenwald, & Pettigrew, 2014; Reynolds, Turner, & Haslam, 2000). Thus, evaluation is at the heart of intergroup judgments and behavior.

Motivational Influences on Ingroup Bias

Given the desire to protect and enhance the self-concept as well as one's social identity, it is reasonable to suspect that threats to one's self-concept or one's group may moderate the degree that people generate and endorse negative evaluations of outgroups. Nonetheless, several studies have empirically confirmed that perceived threats to oneself or one's group increase favoritism toward the ingroup.

Self-threats and Prejudice

When a person receives information that threatens the self-concept, this can lead to higher displays of prejudice as a means for protecting one's self-integrity (Sherman & Cohen, 2006). Conversely, providing opportunities for self-affirmation can reduce the impact of threat on prejudice (Badea & Sherman, 2019). In a study testing these ideas (Fein & Spencer, 1997), participants were given bogus information regarding their performance on an intelligence test: participants were told either that they had scored in the 93rd or the 47th percentile compared with other university students (the latter representing a poor performance amongst these academically successful students). Half of the participants in each group then completed an exercise to affirm their values and self-worth, while the other half did not.

In what was supposedly a separate experiment, participants were then asked to assess the qualifications of a supposed job candidate based on her resume and a video from an interview. The ethnicity of the applicant was manipulated by varying her name, extracurricular activities, sorority affiliation, and jewelry to appear either Italian- or Jewish-American. Based on prevailing stereotypes about "Jewish American Princesses" on campus, the researchers predicted that most students would see the Jewish student as a member of a campus outgroup. After viewing the application materials, participants rated her on her personality and her qualifications for the job.

Results showed that participants who had received negative feedback about their intelligence but who had not received self-affirmation evaluated the candidate more negatively if she was Jewish rather than Italian. In contrast, participants whose intelligence had been affirmed did not differ in their evaluative judgments of the candidate based on her perceived ethnicity. Thus, self-affirmation can reduce the extent to which persons derogate members of stereotyped groups.

Other research has demonstrated another consequence of self-threat for stereotyping (Govorun, Fuegen, & Payne, 2006). For persons who experienced personal threat on an essential element of their self-concept (e.g., intelligence), this concept was activated in a stereotype and then used to derogate others on that attribute. In addition, persons whose group is stereotyped on that attribute (e.g., African Americans) were more likely to be targets of such derogation. This process of perceiving one's undesirable qualities in others (i.e., *projection*) serves a functional role by facilitating motivated self-enhancement.

Group-threats and Prejudice

Since Sherif's (1951; Sherif & Sherif, 1953) research on intergroup relations and the development of *Realistic Conflict Theory* (Campbell, 1965), it has been recognized that negative stereotypes and prejudice can arise from competition between groups for limited resources (Cooper & Fazio, 1986; Stephan & Stephan, 2000; Stephan, Ybarra, & Rios, 2016).

More recent research has shown that adverse economic conditions can constitute such a context for increasing expressions of prejudice, and the mental representation of threatening outgroups plays a critical role in these circumstances. Signals of economic scarcity can affect how non-African American perceivers view Black faces and consequently how they allocate resources (Krosch & Amodio, 2014, 2019; Krosch, Tyler, & Amodio, 2017). In one study (Krosch & Amodio, 2014), participants were asked to express their level of agreement with questions reflecting a zero-sum view of racial economic advancement (e.g., "When Blacks make economic gains, Whites lose out economically"). They then were shown a series of faces that were morphed to vary along a continuum between racially unambiguous extremes (phenotypically White and Black) and indicated for each photograph whether they would consider the person to be White or Black. On average, faces were judged to be Black if they contained 47% or more content from phenotypic Black faces, showing a subtle but systematic deviation from the "correct" judgment of racial equivalence for 50% morphs. Importantly, these results were related to the endorsement of zero-sum economic beliefs. Participants who viewed economic gains for Blacks as harming Whites were more likely to judge morphed faces as Black.

Similar effects emerged from studies where scarcity-related primes preceded the faces and when participants allocated money to individuals based on photographs developed under conditions of scarcity or plenty (Krosch & Amodio, 2014). Subsequent work (Krosch & Amodio, 2019) showed that economic scarcity disrupts the regular encoding of Black faces, accounting for biases in resource allocation. In sum, economic scarcity can increase the ethnic *otherization* of non-White individuals among White Americans, biasing judgments of and treatment toward disadvantaged groups.

Consequences of Prejudice

The studies just reviewed link prejudice to differences in judgments and treatment of outgroups. Several other consequential effects have been tied to prejudicial attitudes.

Prejudice and Attribution

Explanations for stereotype-consistent and stereotype-inconsistent behavior differ based on participants' level of prejudice, with highly prejudiced individuals more likely to attribute expected behaviors to personal dispositions and unexpected behaviors to situational factors (Sekaquaptewa, Espinoza, Thompson, Vargas, & von Hippel, 2003; Sherman, Stroessner, Conrey, & Azam, 2005). Attributions for success and failure also appear to differ based on attitudes. Taylor and Jaggi (1974; see also Khandelwal, Dhillon, Akalamkam, & Papneja, 2014) found that in the context of conflict between Hindus and Muslims in South India, Hindus made more internal attributions for ingroup members for socially desirable acts and external attributions for socially undesirable acts. For outgroups, socially desirable acts were attributed to external causes, whereas their socially undesirable acts were attributed to internal causes. Pettigrew (1979) termed this differential pattern of attributions, shaped in part by prejudice, as the *ultimate attribution error*.

Prejudice and Language

Prejudice can alter the language that is used to describe ingroups and outgroups. In Chapter 5, we introduced research by Maass et al. (1989) on *Linguistic Intergroup Bias* (LIB), the tendency for people to describe positive ingroup actions, and negative outgroup behaviors, using more abstract language. The opposite occurs for negative behaviors, where positive outgroup actions and negative ingroup behaviors are characterized with more specific, context-based terms.

The LIB plays a central role in prejudice. It arises in describing liked versus disliked outgroups (e.g., Canadians vs. Iranians; Hamilton et al., 1992) and increases under group threat (Maass et al., 1996; von Hippel, Sekaquaptewa, & Vargas, 1997). The LIB is also a means by which prejudice can be perpetuated. Ingroup members who demonstrated linguistic biases favoring the ingroup receive higher approval from fellow ingroup members, and such approval has been shown to increase the subsequent frequency of language favoring the ingroup (Assilaméhou-Kunz, Postmes, & Testé, 2019).

Prejudice and Memory

Prejudice can affect what is remembered about the actions of others. Howard and Rothbart (1980) examined memory biases using a minimal group paradigm in which participants were randomly assigned membership in a group based on their supposed accuracy in estimating the number of dots appearing in a rapidly-displayed stimulus ("underestimators" versus "overestimators"). Participants were then presented with two sets of self-descriptive behavioral statements that had supposedly been generated by a group of ingroup and outgroup members. For each group, 48 of the behaviors were positive and 24 were negative. Participants later completed a recognition memory task where previously-presented items had to be differentiated from a similar set of new items. Recognition memory for positive actions was equally accurate for both groups, but participants were more likely to accurately recall negative behaviors performed by members of the outgroup rather than the ingroup.

Prejudice also affects memory for stereotype-relevant information (Pica, Bélanger, Pantaleo, Pierro, & Kruglanski, 2016; Pica, Sciara, Livi, & Pantaleo, 2017). In one study showing this effect (Sherman et al., 2005), students recruited based on their degree of anti-gay bias were presented with behavior descriptions of a gay man that were either consistent ("studied interpretive dance in college") or inconsistent ("watched a football game on Sunday afternoon") with stereotypes. A subsequent recognition-memory test showed that participants low in prejudice showed equivalent memory for both types of information. However, participants high in anti-gay prejudice showed better memory for stereotype-inconsistent than for stereotype-consistent behaviors. Subsequent studies showed that prejudiced individuals paid more attention to stereotype-inconsistent behavior as they attempted to explain away (i.e., make external attributions for) counterstereotypical information.

Prejudice and Policy Preferences

Finally, prejudice has been tied to support for policies favoring the ingroup and opposition to policies favoring the outgroup (Melton, 1989; Spencer, Charbonneau, & Glaser, 2016). However, the effect of prejudice on support for policies is often manifest indirectly rather than directly. For example, people high in prejudice typically do not express the basis of their views bluntly ("I don't support that policy because it benefits people I don't like"). Instead, people typically invoke reasons other than prejudice to justify their policy stances (e.g., "I stand against that policy because it violates my principles") (Federico & Sidanius, 2002; Reyna, Henry, Korfmacher, & Tucker, 2006). Prejudice often combines with prejudicial and stereotypical beliefs to affect positions on policy issues. Public policy issues can spontaneously activate stereotypes and prejudice associated with groups affected by a given policy. Prejudice then can serve as one basis for policy decisions, and stereotypes serve as a second, independent basis in judging social policies (Maurer, Park, & Judd, 1996).

Individual differences on variables strongly related to prejudice also play a central role in policy preferences. For example, individuals high in *Social Dominance Orientation* (SDO; Pratto, Sidanius, Stallworth, & Malle, 1994) – the belief that social groups should be ordered hierarchically and that ingroups should dominate over others – and *Right-Wing Authoritarianism* (RWA; Altemeyer, 1981, 1998, 2004) – people who are conventional, submissive to established authorities, and aggressive when they believe that authorities sanction it – tend to oppose policies such as affirmative action (Haley & Sidanius, 2006) and support the death penalty (McCann, 2008; Stack, 2003) which is disproportionally meted out to men of color.

Implicit and Explicit Prejudice

Traditionally, research on prejudice was almost exclusively based on people's explicit responses to attitudinal measures, an approach that was susceptible to demand characteristics and concerns regarding the desirability of responding. In other words, the validity of self-report measures of prejudice was open to question, particularly as explicit statements of prejudice became outdated and increasingly undesirable. Several methods were developed to increase the veracity of responding to queries about prejudice and other socially undesirable beliefs (e.g., the "bogus pipeline"; Jones & Sigall, 1971), but assessing people's levels of prejudice through self-report had become increasingly challenging over time.

Two related developments emerged in the 1990s that dramatically changed the study of prejudice. First, Devine (1989) argued and provided compelling evidence that many aspects of prejudice operate without conscious awareness, intention, or control. Subsequent studies confirmed that numerous unconscious processes play critical roles in the operation of attitudes about groups and other entities (Eagly & Chaiken, 1993; Fazio et al., 1986; Greenwald & Banaji, 1995; Wilson, Lindsay, et al., 2000). Research on unconscious stereotyping and evaluation of groups and their members, termed *implicit bias* or *implicit prejudice* (Banaji & Greenwald, 1995; Banaji et al., 1993), became a central research topic in social cognition.

Second, this theoretical advance was accompanied by the development of innovative, indirect methods for measuring unconscious processes. Amongst these were Fazio and colleagues' *evaluative priming procedure*, introduced earlier in this chapter (Fazio et al., 1986), modified to assess unconscious prejudice by measuring the speed with which participants categorize valenced words following White and Black male faces (Fazio et al., 1995). The *Implicit Association Test* (IAT; Greenwald et al., 1998) that we have already discussed becomes an indirect measure of attitudes when valenced words must be categorized with group-relevant stimuli such as names and faces. The *Affect Misattribution Procedure* (AMP; Payne, Cheng, et al. 2005) involves the brief display of group-relevant stimuli (e.g., Black and White faces) before the presentation of unfamiliar stimuli (e.g., Chinese pictographs). Participants judge whether any given pictograph is more or less pleasant than average, and these pleasantness ratings reflect the unconscious evaluation of the preceding prime. Each of these tasks allowed the measurement of evaluative responses to groups that people were unwilling or unable to report explicitly.

Based on these parallel developments, research on implicit attitudes became a dominant research topic in social cognition. Here, we briefly highlight some of the significant discoveries that have emerged from this research over the last few decades.

The Relationship Between Implicit and Explicit Prejudice

If implicit evaluative processes are primarily unconscious and uncontrollable, but explicit processes are effortful, deliberative evaluations, one might expect that they function independently and might even be unrelated. There is some evidence that responses to implicit and explicit measures of attitudes are often weakly correlated and sometimes are entirely independent (Boniecki & Jacks, 2002; Dasgupta et al., 2000, Greenwald et al., 1998). However, some studies have found substantial relations between implicit and explicit expressions of attitudes (Cunningham, Preacher, & Banaji, 2001; Wittenbrink, Judd, & Park, 1997).

The lack of independence should not be surprising, given that there is a fair amount of interplay between these systems, with controlled processes monitoring and sometimes overriding outputs from automatic processes (Amodio, Devine, & Harmon-Jones, 2008; Amodio, Harmon-Jones, Devine, Curtin, Hartley, & Covert, 2004; Gawronski & Bodenhausen, 2011). In addition, although there is some independence between implicit and explicit processes, they both occur within an individual with a unique and idiosyncratic set of experiences and learning opportunities. It would be puzzling if a person with a particular set of life experiences developed explicit and implicit evaluations that bore no resemblance to one another.

Indeed, research shows that implicit and explicit evaluations within any individual are usually not strongly correlated but typically are similar in valence. In other words, one can know something about explicit evaluations by assessing implicit judgments (and vice versa). However, responses to explicit and indirect measures are not strongly correlated, and they predict different things and do so to different degrees. For example, one meta-analysis showed that evaluations expressed on explicit measures are more predictive in some domains (consumer behavior, political preferences), whereas performances on implicit measures are more predictive in others (interracial and intergroup behavior) (Greenwald, Poehlman, et al., 2009).

Several factors moderate the magnitude of the relationship between responses to explicit and implicit measures (Nosek, 2005, 2007). One factor appears to be whether concerns about social desirability lead to modification of controlled (i.e., explicit) responses, leading to a divergence in responding to explicit versus implicit measures of attitude. Many people, for example, are reluctant to admit that they have a disdain for people who are overweight, even though implicit bias against heavy people has increased dramatically in recent years (Charlesworth & Banaji, 2019). As such, they might express egalitarian attitudes on self-report scales while harboring anti-fat bias. Indeed, correlations of responses to explicit and implicit measures of this bias are low (approximately +.20; Charlesworth & Banaji, 2019; Nosek, 2007). In a modified bogus pipeline procedure, Nier (2005) showed that responses to explicit and implicit measures regarding another socially sensitive issue (racial prejudice) were significantly correlated only when participants were told that the implicit measure accurately measured racial attitudes and not when it did not reflect prejudice. These findings demonstrate that social desirability concerns contribute to discrepancies in responding to implicit and explicit measures.

Several other factors influence the strength of the relationship between responses on implicit and explicit measures. First, higher personal experience in an attitude domain leads to automatic activation of attitudes (Fazio et al., 1986), helping to account for stronger relationships between implicit and explicit responses following higher levels of intergroup contact (Lemm, 2006). Second, to the degree that attitudinal issues are defined in oppositional terms (pro-choice vs. pro-life, Democrats vs. Republicans), higher implicit-explicit correlations tend to emerge, often over +.70 (Nosek, 2007). Third, responses are more consistent when experimental participants are prompted to focus on their feelings rather than on their thoughts about a group (Smith & Nosek, 2011), highlighting the role of affect in evaluation.

The Relationship Between Prejudice and Stereotyping

The recognition that both conscious and unconscious processes play critical roles in intergroup relations raises questions about the relationships between evaluations (prejudice) and beliefs (stereotyping) at both explicit and implicit levels. Explicit intergroup evaluations and beliefs are generally consistent (Brigham, 1971, 1972; Smith & Clark, 1973), but measures of implicit prejudice and stereotyping are often weakly correlated and even independent. Why might the relationship between beliefs and evaluations differ at explicit versus implicit levels?

There are two distinct possibilities, both of which have received research support. First, and as we have previously discussed, conscious processes are implicated in validation processes (Gawronski & Bodenhausen, 2006; Rydell & McConnell, 2006; Strack & Deutsch, 2004). If inconsistent beliefs and evaluations become automatically activated through the process of social categorization, validation processes can serve to align responses on explicit measures of prejudice and stereotyping. Unconscious processes are more likely to be based upon activated associations that might not be available for validation. As such, the contents of implicit beliefs and evaluations might be more discrepant.

Second, there is evidence that distinct systems underlie implicit memory, with separate neural substrates for affective and semantic memory (Amodio, 2014, 2019; Amodio & Devine, 2006; Amodio & Ratner, 2011). Reflecting research on animals and humans (Lang, Bradley, & Cuthbert, 1990; LeDoux, 2000), Amodio and his colleagues have argued that the amygdala and associated subcortical circuits primarily support the processing of affective information. In this system, evaluative associations can be learned quickly, often after a single presentation, and can be difficult to extinguish. In contrast, semantic information (i.e., information conveyed through language such as stereotypes) is processed in phylogenetically newer neocortical structures that are more prominent in humans than in other species (Gabrieli, 1998; Squire & Zola, 1996). Importantly, these systems are connected to brain regions with distinct primary functions. The amygdala-centered affective system is anatomically and neurochemically linked to regions responsible for responding to reward and punishment and for approach/avoidance responses. In contrast, the semantic system is embedded in the association cortex that is primarily responsible for information integration and higher-order information processing.

Amodio and Devine (2006) examined some implications of these distinct systems in the domain of intergroup judgment. In several studies, participants completed IATs tailored to assess their evaluative and stereotypic associations for Black people compared with White people. The *evaluative IATs* involved the pairing of Black and White faces with valenced words such as "love" and "evil." In contrast, the *stereotyping IATs* measured stereotypes by pairing the same faces with stereotypic words such as "athletic" and "intelligent." Note that each IAT was designed to measure evaluations and stereotypes in an unconfounded fashion (i.e., stereotypes equated on valence and evaluations unrelated to stereotypes).

It was hypothesized that responses to stereotyping and evaluative IATs would correlate with different aspects of judgment and behavior. Performances on the stereotyping IATs were expected to correlate with trait judgments of a Black student essay writer (Study 2) and stereotypic expectations of the student (Study 3), two measures tapping into higher-order reasoning and judgment processes. In contrast, performances on the evaluative IATs were expected to correlate with measures relating to approach/avoidance such as participants' interest in pursuing a friendship (Study 2) or sitting close to the student (Study 3). Importantly, implicit stereotyping was expected to be unrelated to approach/avoidance judgments, and implicit evaluation was expected to be unpredictive of judgments of traits and stereotypic expectations.

As shown in Table 6.3, this is precisely what was found. This *double-dissociation* linking distinct implicit associations with different kinds of judgments provides compelling evidence that affective and semantic information is processed and stored independently. Moreover, these findings highlight that both systems can be the basis of judgments that can have significant consequences for intergroup relations.

Table 6.3 The relationships between implicit stereotyping and implicit evaluations and stereotypical and approach/ avoidance judgments (in *Beta*'s, * = p < .05)

Dependent measures	Measures	
	Stereotyping IATs	Evaluative IATs
Stereotypic traits (Study 2)	+.39*	–.23
Desired friendship (Study 2)	+.01	–.32*
Stereotypic expectations (Study 3)	+.47*	–.25
Seating distance (Study 3)	–.09	+.44*

Source: Adapted from Amodio & Devine (2006)

Reducing Implicit and Explicit Bias

This chapter has discussed some of the main ways that evaluative responses to stimuli form and become available (often automatically) to react and respond efficiently to similar stimuli that are later encountered. Although some automatic associations might prove very useful, such as knowing to avoid things or people that pose a threat, we occasionally learn (often to our chagrin) that we have automatic evaluative responses that violate our personal standards, and that we do not desire (Devine, Monteith, Zuwerink, & Elliot, 1991; Howell, Gaither, & Ratliff, 2015). It can be challenging to resist the influence of activated evaluative associations on later judgments and behavior, particularly since efforts to override them often require motivation and effort (Blair,

2002; Devine et al., 2012; Devine, Plant, Amodio, Harmon-Jones, & Vance, 2002). Fortunately, understanding the processes by which evaluations are learned is useful for designing interventions for preventing their activation.

Reducing Bias through Fluency

One line of research has used an *aftereffects paradigm* to examine how regular exposure to individuals with features that are low in prototypicality (and therefore are evaluated negatively) can reduce prejudice by changing perceptual fluency (Lick & Johnson, 2013, 2015; Lick et al., 2015). Some researchers (Lick & Johnson, 2014) sought to determine whether increasing exposure to atypical female faces would reduce the typical bias favoring feminine faces (Jones & Hill, 1993; Perrett et al., 1998).

Participants in one study selected which face was "most average looking" from a set of computer-generated female faces varying in gender typicality (examples are provided in Figure 6.8). They then viewed pictures of either the most feminine or the most masculine faces in the stimulus set for three seconds each for a total of three minutes. This manipulation was intended to increase the fluency of hyperfeminine or hypermasculine female faces, respectively. Following this manipulation, participants again chose the most average looking face from the original set of faces. Repeated exposure to either hypermasculine or hyperfeminine faces shifted the perceived average; participants selected more masculine and more feminine faces as most typical, respectively, following the fluency manipulation. Subsequent studies showed that judgments on valenced traits were similarly affected, with the selection of more positive attributes shifting in the direction of the type of faces they had been shown repeatedly. A final experiment produced identical results with faces that varied naturally in their gender-typicality. These results raise the possibility that evaluative responses can be shifted through exposure to atypical exemplars and highlight the importance of representation in evaluation.

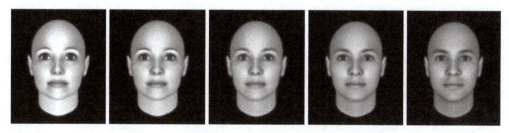

Figure 6.8 Stimuli depicting female faces ranging from feminine (left) to masculine (right) female faces

Source: From Lick & Johnson (2014)

Reducing Bias through Counter-conditioning

Operant and classical conditioning play critical roles in attitude formation, and principles of learning can be used to change them (Olson & Fazio, 2006; Rudman, Ashmore, & Gary, 2001). Extensive practice in *stereotype negation* (e.g., repeatedly responding "No" whenever a Black face appeared with a stereotypical Black word; Boucher & Rydell, 2012; Kawakami et al., 2000), particularly when combined with *counterstereotype affirmation* (responding "Yes!"

when a Black face appeared with a word stereotypically associated with Whites; Gawronski, Deutsch, et al., 2008), reduces the subsequent accessibility of stereotypes.

Other researchers (Johnson, Kopp, & Petty, 2018) tested whether a potent manipulation of negation might by itself lead to the reduction of automatic prejudice. Participants were given instructions in two experimental conditions for responding to Black and White faces paired with stereotype-consistent and stereotype-inconsistent traits. Some participants were told to simply negate specific pairings by hitting the space bar and thinking, "NO!" Other participants were instructed to use a more potent negation response by hitting the space bar and thinking, "THAT'S WRONG!" A second manipulation involved the types of pairings that were to be negated. Some participants were instructed to negate prejudice-consistent pairings (Black and White faces presented with stereotypic traits), and the others were told to negate prejudice-inconsistent pairings (Black and White faces presented with counterstereotypic traits). After completing 200 trials of these judgments, all participants completed an evaluative priming task (Gawronski, Deutsch, et al., 2008) that served as a measure of automatic evaluation of racial prejudice.

Results showed that simple negation (thinking "No!") did not affect automatic evaluation, but the potent negation (thinking "THAT'S WRONG!") did. Specifically, participants in the potent manipulation condition showed *lower* anti-Black evaluative bias when they had negated prejudice-consistent pairings but *higher* bias when they had negated prejudice-inconsistent pairings. These effects were particularly pronounced for participants who were highly motivated to control prejudice (Dunton & Fazio, 1997). These results show that automatic associations acquired through learning can also be unlearned. Although it is unrealistic to expect all people to complete extensive anti-prejudice training, the results indicate that individuals motivated to reduce their automatic negative responses can do so by regularly monitoring and firmly rejecting the activation of stereotypic beliefs.

Reducing Bias by Increasing Associations with the Self

Other less intrusive interventions rely on the prevalent motivation to evaluate the self positively. Several lines of research demonstrate that prejudice can be reduced by facilitating associations between outgroups and oneself or one's valued groups. Consistent with Allport's (1954) analysis, increasing *intergroup contact* has been shown to reduce prejudice (Brown & Hewstone, 2005; Dovidio, Love, Schellhaas, & Hewstone, 2017; Pettigrew & Tropp, 2006, 2011). Positive interactions with outgroup members typically reduce prejudice toward the group, especially when the members are seen as typical of their group and the context emphasizes intergroup considerations (Brown, Vivian, & Hewstone, 1999; Van Oudenhoven, Groenewoud, & Hewstone, 1996). A meta-analysis (Pettigrew & Tropp, 2008) revealed that intergroup contact reduces prejudice through several mechanisms. Contact increases knowledge about the outgroup, but two other factors appear to be even more crucial: reduced anxiety and increased perspective-taking. In other words, increased intergroup contact reduces the perceived danger to oneself and one's group and encourages people to see the world through others' eyes.

Creating positive intergroup contact can be challenging, especially when there is a history of animus, when groups are physically remote, and when a group is numerically rare. In such cases, manipulations of cognitive processes can be used to improve intergroup attitudes. For example, mental simulations of intergroup contact are effective in reducing intergroup bias (Turner & Crisp, 2010). One such study showed that encouraging Chinese students to imagine intergroup contact reduced intergroup attributional biases (Ma, Feng, Lu, Xie, Jiang, & Liu, 2019). Similarly, having participants merely imagine a helping episode involving an outgroup member heightened perspective-taking and increased self-reported intention to help (Gaesser, Shimura, & Cikara, 2020). Mentally simulating an interaction with even a single outgroup member can yield similar effects (Crisp & Turner, 2009), reducing implicit bias toward the outgroup (Vezzali, Capozza, Giovannini, & Stathi, 2012). Moreover, these effects appear to persist over time (Vezzali, Capozza, Stathi, & Giovannini, 2012).

Knowledge of categorization processes can also be used to reduce prejudice. Gaertner and Dovidio's (2000) *Common Ingroup Identity* model argues that intergroup bias can be reduced by encouraging people to recategorize outgroups as members of a more inclusive superordinate group (e.g., thinking of national groups as fellow members of the human race). There is ample evidence that such recategorization can reduce prejudice against a variety of outgroups (Dovidio, Gaertner, Isen, & Lowrance, 1995; Gaertner, Rust, Dovidio, Bachman, & Anastasio, 1994; Riek, Mania, Gaertner, McDonald, & Lamoreaux, 2010).

In one study testing this model (Gaertner, Mann, Murrell, & Dovidio, 1989), small social groups were formed by providing individuals with same-colored nametags, asking them to create a group name, and having them complete a problem-solving exercise. After this group-formation procedure, the group interacted with members of another group under two conditions designed to affect recategorization under a collective ingroup identity. In the one-group condition, people sat interspersed at a single table and created a new name to describe the combined aggregate. In the two-group condition, groups were seated in a segregated fashion and continued to use their group nametags and nickname. Following this interaction, participants completed measures of their conceptual representation of the aggregate (i.e., whether it felt like one or two groups), their liking for the other participants, and judgments of the other participants on valenced traits. As predicted, intergroup bias was lower in the one-group condition compared to the two-group condition. Analyses indicated that the one-group representation reduced bias by increasing the attractiveness of former outgroup members when they shared a social identity with the self.

SUMMARY

Understanding evaluation in its various forms has been one of the most active areas of research in social psychology, broadly, and social cognition, specifically. Research on attitudes began in the 1920s (Thurstone, 1928) and has continued unabated ever since (Briñol & Petty, 2012). Research on interpersonal evaluation began in the 1930s (Asch, 1946; Asch, Block, & Hertzman, 1938), and early work on social cognition focused on how information about individuals is stored in memory and used in trait and evaluative judgment (Hastie, Ostrom, Ebbesen, Wyer, Hamilton, & Carlston, 1980). Similarly, research on evaluative judgments of groups and their members has been an important focus, particularly since Devine's (1989) seminal research on prejudice and the subsequent recognition of implicit bias (Banaji & Greenwald, 1995; Banaji et al., 1993). In this chapter, we have presented the breadth of research on evaluative processes within a single integrative framework to identify principles and processes that cut across content domains.

Evaluative processes infuse and affect social cognition, judgment, and behavior. Judging good and bad, right and wrong, and moral and immoral are among the most ubiquitous and consequential of cognitive processes. We automatically and continuously think of central entities in the world – including objects, events, people, issues, groups, and ourselves – through an evaluative lens. Consequently, understanding evaluation is fundamental to understanding how people make sense of and navigate their world.

FURTHER READING

Hicks, L.L., & McNulty, J.K. (2019). The unbearable automaticity of being...in a close relationship. *Current Directions in Psychological Science*, *28*, 254–259.

Leary, M.R., & Terry, M.L. (2013). Self-evaluation and self-esteem. In D.E. Carlston (Ed.), *The Oxford handbook of social cognition* (pp. 534–547). New York, NY: Oxford University Press.

Ledgerwood, A., Eastwick, P.W., & Smith, L.K. (2018). Toward an integrative framework for studying human evaluation: Attitudes toward objects and attributes. *Personality and Social Psychology Review*, *22*, 378–398.

Mann, T.C., & Ferguson, M.J. (2015). Can we undo our first impressions? The role of reinterpretation in reversing implicit evaluations. *Journal of Personality and Social Psychology*, *108*, 823–849.

Uleman, J.S., & Kressel, L.M. (2013). A brief history of theory and research on impression formation. In D.E. Carlston (Ed.), *The Oxford handbook of social cognition* (pp. 53–73). New York, NY: Oxford University Press.

7
INFERENCE
Going Beyond the Obvious

Tensions were emerging in Europe in September 1938 surrounding governance of the Sudetenland, an area of Czechoslovakia containing a majority of ethnic Germans. Adolf Hitler, the German Chancellor, had been demanding that his country be allowed to annex this territory to stop the supposed persecution of Sudeten Germans. British Prime Minister, Neville Chamberlain, agreed to meet Hitler to discuss this issue in the hope of avoiding war. During their first meeting, Hitler boldly asked if the European powers would allow the Sudetenland simply to be handed over to Germany. Chamberlain said he would have to consult with his Cabinet and allies, but he hoped that they would agree to this proposal in exchange for peace. Chamberlain had observed the Chancellor closely, and he was confident that Hitler could be trusted: "In spite of the hardness and ruthlessness I thought I saw in his face, I got the impression that here was a man who could be relied upon when he had given his word." Several weeks later, an optimistic Chamberlain returned to Germany to inform Hitler that he could have the Sudetenland. "Do I understand that the British, French, and Czech governments have agreed to the transfer of the Sudetenland from Czechoslovakia to Germany?" asked Hitler. "Yes," said the smiling Chamberlain. "I'm awfully sorry," Hitler replied, "but that won't do anymore…this solution is no longer of any use." Hitler now demanded the German occupation of the Sudetenland and the expulsion of all non-Germans living there. These were the terms that Hitler later secured at a conference in Munich, after which Chamberlain declared, "I believe it is peace for our time." This optimism was, of course, unwarranted, and Hitler's armies soon overran almost all of Europe. Acknowledging the error of his initial impression of Hitler, Chamberlain later said, "Hitler is the commonest little swine I have ever encountered" (Buckley, 2017, p. 109).

As we have emphasized, the person is an active participant in the process of comprehending his or her social world. We have already seen in previous chapters that the person plays an essential role in determining what information is attended to and encoded, how that information is interpreted, and the evaluative connotations it takes. We have also discussed how these processes are guided by the cognitive representations that the person brings to the processing of information. In this chapter, we extend this analysis further by focusing on one of the most critical ways in which the perceiver contributes to the process of social comprehension: inference processes.

ELABORATION THROUGH INFERENCE

Inferences involve reasoning to form conclusions based on evidence and knowledge, thereby expanding and elaborating on the information we have acquired. Our encounters with events, with other persons, and with groups provide the raw data of experience. However, these data serve primarily as foundations on which much broader conceptions can be built. Through inference processes, we go beyond that information and infer other features that are assumed to be true. Inferences are assumptions, though they may be entirely plausible assumptions based on our prior knowledge. They also serve as "informal hypotheses" that can be tested in future experiences.

Inferences are distinct from some of the processes discussed in earlier chapters. For example, attention is concerned with what aspects of the stimulus environment are noticed so they enter a person's information processing system. Interpretation concerns how we make sense of what we have attended to by imposing meaning on that information. Both attention and interpretation concern how we confront the information immediately in front of us. Together they determine what aspects of the social environment get encoded into the cognitive processing system.

The cognitive system, however, does not stop once it has selectively attended to and interpreted that stimulus information. It *uses* that information by extending, expanding, and elaborating on it to gain a fuller, more comprehensive understanding and representation of it. We discussed in the last chapter how evaluative processes are used to determine the valence, the goodness or badness, of what we have just learned. Similarly, the inference process elaborates on the encoded information by drawing on our knowledge and beliefs derived from experience to infer what else is likely to be true of this incident, of this person, of this group. In other words, inference processes allow us to "flesh out" the information we have noticed and interpreted.

Why do we make inferences about a person or event from merely observing behavior? The answer is the same one that underlies much of social cognition: As we process information, we want to understand the nature of what we observe so we can anticipate future occurrences. For example, an individual act (of helping, or of aggression) may not, by itself, be terribly informative. However, if we gain some understanding of what the person is like – his dispositions, goals, attitudes, and motives – then we can use that knowledge to predict the person's future actions and reactions. In the narrative that began this chapter, Chamberlain attempted to infer whether or not Hitler was trustworthy. That inference was critical in determining whether to agree to his demands to bring peace or resist his demands and risk war. Chamberlain felt it was essential to meet directly with Hitler so he could develop an accurate sense of Hitler's character. Chamberlain's experience showed that our inferences can be disastrously wrong. However, it also illustrates that we make inferences to increase our ability to anticipate future behavior and, perhaps, the effectiveness of our future interactions.

Types of Inferences

There are several ways in which inference processes can proceed (Beike & Sherman, 1994). Sometimes we use *inductive* or "bottom-up" reasoning to infer more general properties from a specific instance. For example, we are engaged in inductive reasoning when we use knowledge of a person's behavior to make inferences about that person's personality. Such inferences start with observing a specific action and inferring a more general quality (e.g., an attitude, a goal, a personality trait) of the person. Similarly, people use their observations of individual persons to infer the general properties of the groups to which they belong, again moving in a bottom-up direction to infer group-level characteristics from the actions of individual group members. People learn social norms by observing the behaviors of others, for example, inferring the appropriate guidelines governing behavior when one dines in an upscale restaurant. These are examples of inductive inference, using knowledge of specific instances to infer more general properties of persons, groups, or contexts.

Other times we use *deductive* or "top-down" reasoning, applying our knowledge or beliefs to help us understand a single experience. This process uses higher-order generalizations stored in memory to draw conclusions about specific instances. One example of this process is familiar to us all: the use of group stereotypes to make judgments about individual group members. Knowing that a person is a Republican gives one a basis for inferring the person's attitude about gun control, abortion, or taxation. Using a stereotype to judge individuals is a top-down process in which the beliefs associated with the group as a whole are applied to individual group members. A similar deductive process occurs in perceptions of individuals when one's general, pre-existing impression of a person is used to infer what other characteristics the person has or how the person is likely to behave in the future. For example, if a person is friendly, one might presume that the person would introduce herself to new neighbors and provide support for a friend suffering a loss. Deductive reasoning, then, involves using a general representation to infer attributes and properties of specific exemplars.

The importance of deductive reasoning is inherent in two prominent theories (Brewer, 1988; Fiske & Neuberg, 1990), both of which propose that the first step in perceiving others is a categorization based on group membership (initially encoding Crystal as a female, coding Juan as Latino), which activates the stereotypes of the relevant groups. That stereotype is then applied in characterizing Crystal and Juan. This top-down processing is efficient and adaptive in that it quickly and easily allows inferences about these persons and simplifies the task of processing new information about them. Inductive inference based on specific information about the individual will occur when categorization is difficult or when the perceiver is highly motivated to form an accurate impression.

At other times we comprehend a novel, unfamiliar stimulus or experience through *analogical* reasoning in which the properties of the specific instance are inferred from a similar, more familiar case. Our attitudes towards a looming military conflict might depend on whether it seems more similar to World War II or the Iraq War. Another example occurs when we inferentially (and usually unintentionally) transfer known characteristics of one person to another person. Jack, whom you've just met, has a weird sense of humor, which reminds you of Anton's humor, and as a consequence of that similarity, you infer that Jack is also a bit of a loner (another of Anton's attributes).

Induction-Deduction Asymmetry

Perceivers make inferences in all of these ways. One might wonder, then, which kinds of inferences are more common, which are more easily made, and why. Are we more likely to make inductive inferences, inferring traits from behaviors (deciding that a person who donates money to earthquake victims is generous), or deductive inferences, anticipating behaviors from knowledge of a person's traits (concluding that a generous person would donate money to earthquake victims)? Research (Maass, Colombo, Colombo, & Sherman, 2001) indicates that, in our perceptions of others, inductive inferences are made more frequently than deductive inferences. In one experiment demonstrating this finding, participants learned several blocks of information about a stimulus person. Half of the information described the person's traits, and the other half described behaviors that the person had performed. Later, participants were given a recognition test that included a list of some of the traits and behaviors that had been presented, along with new traits and behaviors that had not been shown but were implied by the information given (i.e., traits that were implied by some of the behaviors; behaviors that were implied by some of the traits). Participants' task was to indicate those descriptions (traits and behaviors) that had been presented in the first phase of the study.

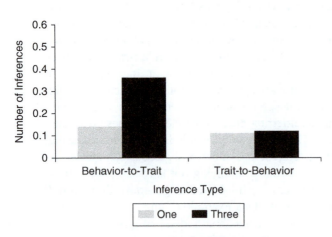

Figure 7.1 Behavior-to-trait and trait-to-behavior inferences as a function of number of behaviors
Source: Based on data from Maass et al. (2001)

Results (depicted in Figure 7.1) showed a systematic bias such that people frequently "misrecognized" traits that were implied by presented behaviors, indicating that they had spontaneously made inductive inferences. Returning to our example, people were likely to say that the word "generous" had been in the sentence about donating to earthquake victims, even though it was not. These recognition errors indicate that the trait had been inferred when the behavior sentence was encoded. In contrast, the opposite effect (deductive inferences of behaviors from traits) was quite infrequent. That is, they were less likely to erroneously infer that "contributing to earthquake victims" had been in the stimulus list if it had not been. Moreover, participants' response times "recognizing" unseen-but-implied traits were as fast as their accurate recognition of actually-presented traits. In contrast, their response times to inferred behaviors were slower than their response times for presented behaviors. This pattern of findings reveals an *induction-deduction asymmetry* (Maass et al., 2001) that is quite robust across many variations in methodology (Maass, Cadinu, Taroni, & Masserini, 2006). Inductive (bottom-up) inferences appear to be made as the information is encoded, whereas deductive (top-down) inferences rely on memory of previously learned information. We appear more inclined to make inductive behavior-to-trait inferences than deductive trait-to-behavior inferences.

There are several possible reasons for this asymmetry. As already noted, the response time data suggest differences in *when* the inferences are made. Inductive inferences appear to occur spontaneously as the information is encoded, whereas deductive trait-to-behavior inferences may need to be triggered and happen in a memory-based fashion (Maass et al., 2001). Another possibility is that this asymmetry may reflect properties of how the information is represented in memory. Specifically, traits may be the organizing units in memory, with various behaviors implied by those traits stored together (e.g., Hamilton, Katz, & Leirer,

1980a, 1980b). A third possibility is that traits dominate because they are seen as lending stability and coherence to the impressions we form of others. If so, then they would have priority both in representation in memory and accessibility. All of these possibilities would account for the asymmetry in the frequency with which people make inductive (behavior → trait) versus deductive (trait → behavior) inferences.

Making inferences is pervasive in our everyday lives and occurs in all contexts. We often make probabilistic inferences about the likelihood of some occurrence ("Will it rain today?"), we infer the causes of behaviors and events that we witness ("Why did she frown at me that way?"), we make predictive inferences about everything from a person's behavior to a group's political leanings ("With us or against us?"), from the performance of the stock market ("Bullish or bearish? Buy or sell?"), to the outcome to today's ball game ("There's no way they can beat us"). In all of these ways, we go beyond the information available to us. Moreover, those inferences influence the information we retain in memory as well as the judgments we make (Sherman, Crawford, Hamilton, & Garcia-Marques, 2003).

Making inferences, then, is one of the crucial ways we elaborate on the actual information we are processing from the social world. How are these inferences made? From where do they come? We have already provided (in Chapter 2) a part of the answer to these questions: inferences are derived from cognitive representations we have developed through a lifetime of experiences. When we learn that a person has volunteered to work on political campaigns for freedom of choice on abortion decisions, for stricter gun control laws, and for more regulations on environmental pollution, we can infer that the person is liberal. When we observe a person telling ethnic jokes, complaining about "welfare moms" living off government programs, and using the "N" word, we can reasonably infer that the person is a racist. Our cognitive structures guide our inferences and enable us to expand on the information we have acquired. However, these examples give us only a glimpse of the processes involved in making inferences about others. In the remainder of this chapter, we discuss in greater depth and detail the processes involved in making inferences.

Trait Inferences and Implicit Personality Theories

Given all the processes involved in making inferences, the ease with which we can do so is impressive. The simplicity of making inferences about others can be illustrated through the following exercise. Think about how you would answer each of the following questions, where your task is to provide a number between "1" and "10", with higher numbers indicating greater likelihood:

If a person is witty, how likely is it that the person is intelligent?

If a person is friendly, how likely is it that the person is honest?

If a person is popular, how likely is it that the person is agreeable?

If a person is extroverted, how likely is it that the person is liberal?

If a person is religious, how likely is it that the person is emotionally stable?

Although you may have had to think about one or two of those questions, you probably could answer them with relative ease.

This task is called a *trait inference task*: if a person has Trait X, how likely is it that he also has Trait Y? The trait inference task was one of the first methods of studying the inferences people make about the personalities of others. Although there may be individual differences in responses to such questions, there is also impressive regularity in people's answers. People share some generalized beliefs about "what goes with what" in the personalities of people. This belief system is called an *implicit personality theory* (IPT) (Bruner & Tagiuri, 1954; Schneider, 1973, 2004). IPTs are cognitive structures that enable us to go beyond the literal information available by allowing us to infer other unobserved features and properties of a person. Witty? Probably also intelligent and talkative. Attractive? Probably also fairly outgoing and funny. These inferences may not always be correct – we've all known witty people who are not talkative ("She's basically quiet, but can be charming") and attractive people that lack a sense of humor – but these associations, which we have learned from our past experiences, may be reasonably accurate across the broad spectrum of people. If so, then such inferences will be quite useful to us in understanding people's personalities and anticipating their behaviors.

TRAIT INFERENCES IN IMPRESSION FORMATION

Asch's Research on Impression Formation

Asch (1946) was among the first researchers to use the trait inference task. He gave his participants a small set of trait terms that described a person and asked them to form an impression of that person. He then gave them a list of trait terms and asked them to check off other attributes that they thought would also describe the person. In other words, Asch asked them to make trait inferences: "If a person is intelligent, skillful, industrious, warm, determined, practical, cautious, then what else is true of him?" Their responses, as recorded in the traits they checked, revealed systematic patterns in the inferences they made. For example, when "warm" and "cold" were included in otherwise identical trait lists, people inferred other attributes that were, in important respects, quite different. As we discussed in the previous chapter, Asch's primacy effect study showed that the valence of early items in the stimulus list guided, to a considerable extent, the evaluative tone of the traits inferred about the target person. In other words, the process of forming an impression of an individual is one that involves expanding on what we learn about a person through making inferences of what else (we believe) is true of him.

Fast Trait Inferences from Faces

Asch's studies revealed the ease with which we make inferences in forming impressions when we have trait-descriptive information available. However, what if we merely see someone's face? We have already discussed how the face is rich in information about others, including their social category memberships and personal identities. The face also allows us to make inferences about what people are like, their traits and characteristics, their emotions and moods (e.g., Cogsdill, Todorov, Spelke, & Banaji, 2014; Rule, Krendl, Ivcevic, & Ambady, 2013; Sutherland, Oldmeadow, Santos, Towler, Michael Burt, & Young, 2013; Zebrowitz, 2017). Willis and Todorov (2006) examined the efficiency of drawing trait inferences from faces. They had participants make personality ratings of a large number of faces on several trait scales (e.g., attractiveness, likability, trustworthiness, competence, aggressiveness). One group of participants rated the photos at a leisurely pace: they could look at each picture and think about their impression before making ratings. Other participants judged the same photos after very brief exposures; each photo was presented for 100, 500, or 1000 ms. In these cases, the face appeared (very briefly!) on a computer screen, followed by a question (e.g., "Is this person competent?"), to which the participant responded (using one computer key or another) "Yes" or "No." These "snap" inferences were then correlated with the ratings made by people who were free to think about each photo as they made their ratings. As the results in Table 7.1 show, even when the faces were exposed for only 100 ms (one-tenth of a second), participants' judgments of the personality attributes were highly correlated with ratings made by the participants whose judgments were not constrained by time pressure. Thus, people were able to extract personality information from very brief exposures that corresponded strongly to the impressions of those same faces formed in a leisurely manner.

Other research reveals that we do not even need to know that we have seen a face to be affected by the trait information it provides. In one experiment (Freeman, Stolier, Ingbretsen, & Hehman, 2014), participants were presented with both real and computer-generated faces that varied in their trustworthiness (determined from pilot ratings) while they were in an fMRI scanner. Each target face was presented for 33 ms (too fast to allow conscious recognition) and then replaced by a neutral face (i.e., a "masking"

Table 7.1 Correlations between time-constrained trait judgments and judgments made in the absence of time constraints

Trait judgment	Exposure time		
	100 ms	500 ms	1000 ms
Trustworthiness	.73	.66	.74
Competence	.52	.67	.59
Likability	.59	.57	.59
Aggressiveness	.52	.56	.59
Attractiveness	.69	.57	.66

Source: Adapted from Willis & Todorov (2006)

stimulus) to halt further visual processing of the target. Since the faces appeared too quickly to be consciously perceived, participants were not expected to be able to report their judgments of trustworthiness verbally. Instead, the researchers examined the activity level of the amygdala, a subcortical region of the brain involved in processing the emotional significance of social stimuli, to faces that differed in trustworthiness. Results revealed that the amygdala showed the highest activation in response to faces that had been judged as low in trustworthiness, and these effects did not differ for the computer-generated and real faces. These findings show that facial characteristics such as trustworthiness may be assessed even before a face can be consciously perceived.

These snap judgments are intriguing, especially in that they correlated highly with more reflective judgments of those same faces. Nevertheless, are these inferences anything more than momentary hunches? Do such quick and easy impressions have any consequences further down the judgmental road? Other research suggests that they do (Olivola, Funk, & Todorov, 2014; Rule & Ambady, 2010; Todorov et al., 2015).

Participants in one study (Todorov et al., 2005) were shown pairs of head-and-shoulder photos of opposing candidates (unfamiliar to the participants) for the U.S. Senate and House of Representatives races during three different election years. Participants rated the competence of each candidate. These ratings, made solely from the face of the candidates with no other information about them, effectively predicted the outcome of the elections. In more than two-thirds of the races, the candidate rated as more competent won the election. Even more remarkably, in another study these pairs of faces were shown for 1000 ms (one second!), and again participants made competency judgments of the candidates that accurately predicted the election outcome in two-thirds of the races. These results show that perceivers can make inferences about others very quickly, and these quick and unreflective judgments, based solely on facial appearance, predicted the outcomes of congressional elections.

There are, however, limitations on this effect. Not surprisingly, we know that physically attractive persons and those described in favorable terms receive higher evaluations than less attractive persons with less desirable personality attributes (Budesheim & DePaola, 1994), and these differences could influence voting decisions (though they did not in Todorov et al.'s 2005 research). For this reason, the attractiveness of candidates is typically statistically controlled in studies of voting preference based on facial features (e.g., Castelli, Carraro, Ghitti, & Pastore, 2009; Todorov et al., 2005). Also, although perceived competence predicted voting outcomes (Todorov et al., 2005), participants' ratings of candidates on other personality dimensions, such as trust (Todorov et al., 2005) and sociability (Castelli et al., 2009), have not predicted election outcomes. Finally, different facial features seem to alter voting preferences in times of war versus times of peace (Little, Burriss, Jones, & Roberts, 2007).

In summary, people can make incredibly fast inferences about the personalities of others just from seeing their faces, and these judgments can be predictive of important outcomes. However, there appear to be constraints on these effects. Additional research is needed to clarify under what conditions, and for which attributes, these fast inferences from faces are accurate and predictive.

Correspondent Inference Theory

The research described so far demonstrates that people make inferences, quickly and easily, from minimal stimulus cues. A single behavior or a face can trigger inference processes. How and why this happens was the focus of an influential theory called *correspondent inference theory* (Jones & Davis, 1965).

From Acts to Dispositions

Jones and Davis were specifically interested in how the perceiver moves from observed acts to inferred dispositions (traits, attitudes, motives, values). Suppose, for example, that you see someone carrying some heavy packages up some stairs for an older woman. You might think, "He is a very helpful person." In doing so, you have made an inference from the person's act (he is helping a person) to a disposition (he is a helpful person). This is referred to as a *correspondent inference* because the inferred disposition corresponds directly to the observed behavior. Similarly, if you observe someone pushing ahead of people in line at a concert, you might infer that he's an aggressive person; his aggressive behavior leads to the correspondent inference that he has the trait of aggressiveness. A correspondent inference has been made when the same term (helpful) can be used to describe the act and the actor. Correspondent inference theory explicitly focused on how and when people make correspondent inferences.

You might be wondering when we *don't* make correspondent inferences. After all, don't we *always* assume that a person's behaviors reflect underlying traits? Research indicates that we do not. Correspondent inferences are less likely to occur when other information is available to suggest that an action should not be interpreted straightforwardly. You might, for example, learn that the person carrying the packages had been hired by the older woman to help her. Inferences about his helpfulness will be tempered by the fact that his act is part of his job. Alternatively, the person's pushing ahead of others in line may have been instigated by a need to get emergency help for someone in pain. In this case, we would probably not infer that he is an aggressive person. So, the question arises, when do we make correspondent inferences?

Jones and Davis (1965; Jones, 1979) identified several factors that should influence the likelihood of making a correspondent inference. For example, if the behavior is highly *normative*, that is, if it's what anyone would do under the circumstances, then it's unlikely a correspondent inference will be made. If you are in the library and see another person who is whispering to a friend, the behavior (speaking very quietly) would not lead you to infer that she necessarily has the corresponding trait (quiet). After all, everyone is (or at least is supposed to be) quiet in the library. Behaviors governed by strong social norms are not informative about any given person, and hence a correspondent inference is not warranted.

Second, *desirable* behaviors provide a less reliable basis for correspondent inference than does undesirable behavior. Most social behavior is at least mildly desirable; our interactions with others are usually positive in value. In contrast, undesirable behavior is less frequent and is typically counter-normative. Therefore, it is seen as more diagnostic of the person's internal properties – her attributes, motives, attitudes, goals – than is desirable behavior. Being thanked by a salesclerk after a purchase is both standard and desirable; we would not likely make a strong correspondent inference about the clerk based on this behavior. If instead, the clerk swore at you and told you never to return to the store, this would probably lead you to generate a highly negative correspondent inference to characterize the person. Thus, a correspondent inference is less likely to follow desirable than undesirable behaviors.

A third variable is the role of *choice*. If the person chooses to perform a behavior, then it is reasonable to infer that it reflects his desires, goals, and dispositions. However, if the behavior was forced or constrained in some way such that he just had to do it, then the behavior should not be seen as informative about his inner nature and should not be a basis for making a correspondent inference. If you see a person giving money to another, you might think it's a generous act and therefore infer (correspondingly) that the person is generous. If it turns out that what you are observing is a person being mugged and the "generous" act of giving money is occurring at gunpoint, then you are unlikely to infer from that behavior that the person is generous.

In sum, according to Correspondent Inference Theory, correspondent inferences are most likely to be made when the behavior observed (a) is not constrained by social norms, (b) is undesirable, and (c) is a result of the person's free choice. In contrast, correspondent inferences should be less likely when the behavior is highly normative, socially desirable, and not a result of choice.

The Correspondence Bias

Correspondent Inference Theory makes much intuitive sense, and it generated a significant amount of research for many years. Ironically, one of the central insights gained from the theory was the result of an unexpected result that deviated from theoretical prediction. Specifically, Jones and Harris (1967) designed a study to test the effect of choice on correspondent inferences. Participants read an essay that either supported or opposed the regime of Fidel Castro in Cuba. At the time of this study, Castro's communist regime in a country only 90 miles from the coast of Florida was seen as posing a significant threat to the United States. Half of the participants in each of those essay conditions were told that the author of the essay (presumably another student) was able to take any position on the topic he wished. However, the other half were told that the author had been assigned to write an essay advocating either the pro- or anti-Castro position. After reading the essay, participants were asked to rate the essay author's real attitude toward Castro.

What would you expect the results to be? If someone writes an essay advocating a particular position, then you would assume that it reflects his opinion and therefore should make a correspondent inference. This would be especially true if you knew that he had free choice in deciding what position to advocate. However, if the author is assigned which position to adopt in the essay, one logically knows nothing at all about what he genuinely thinks or believes. Estimates of his attitude should not differ as a function of whether a pro- or anti- position was advocated in the essay. Hence the arguments advanced in the essay should not be informative about the author's true attitude and, following Jones and Davis' (1965) thinking, should not produce a correspondent inference.

The results of this study are shown in Table 7.2, where higher numbers indicate that the author is seen as holding a more pro-Castro attitude. The top row of the table provides strong support for our first intuition. When the author was supposedly free to choose what to write, he was rated strongly pro-Castro in the pro-Castro condition and strongly anti-Castro in the anti-Castro condition. As seen in the second row of the table, when the author was given no choice regarding the content of the essay, that difference was greatly reduced. Less strong inferences were made about the author in this case. However, something is puzzling in these data: the difference in ratings of the pro- and anti-Castro writers in the No Choice condition was surprisingly large and was not eliminated, as the theory would predict. The author's true attitude was still seen as corresponding (though to a lesser extent) to the position advocated in the essay. This is a surprising outcome since, given that the author was assigned to promote a particular opinion, there was no basis for inferring anything about his actual attitude.

Table 7.2 Mean ratings of essay writer's true attitude

Condition	Essay direction	
	Pro-Castro	Anti-Castro
Choice	59.62	17.38
No choice	44.10	22.87

Source: Adapted from Jones & Harris (1967)

What can we make of this finding? Apparently, perceivers are willing to make correspondent inferences even under conditions where they have clear information indicating that, logically, the person's behavior is *not* informative about his real opinions. Subsequently many other studies have also demonstrated the tendency to make correspondent inferences, even when they are not warranted (for reviews, see Gilbert & Malone, 1995; Jones, 1979, 1990). This tendency is so pervasive that it became known simply as the *correspondence bias*.

Noncorrespondent Dispositional Inferences

The correspondence bias refers to a strong propensity for perceivers to make correspondent inferences, even when logically they shouldn't. Earlier, we briefly mentioned that not all inferences people make about the dispositional qualities of the person represent correspondent inferences. If they are not correspondent inferences, what are they and when do they occur?

A correspondent inference is an inference of some internal disposition (trait, motive, emotion, attitude) that corresponds directly to the manifest qualities of the behavior from which it is inferred. A helpful act implies a helpful person. However, we do not always make such correspondent inferences. Consider again the very plausible inference that, from seeing someone's helpful behavior, the person is indeed a helpful person. You might see that Dr. Bentley has dropped a huge mess of papers on the floor outside a classroom, and you notice that Paul stopped to assist him in picking them up. In many circumstances, you might quickly infer that Paul is a helpful person. If, however, you knew that Paul is a lab assistant who works for Dr. Bentley and is seeking a favorable recommendation letter from him, then you might wonder, "Is Paul really a helpful person (a correspondent inference) or instead, is he an ingratiating person?" Note that both of these inferences are about Paul's personality, and hence both are dispositional inferences. Only the first, however, is a correspondent inference. The second, that Paul's behavior is motivated by a desire to please Dr. Bentley, is a *noncorrespondent* dispositional inference.

This distinction has been studied in research on *suspicion of ulterior motives* (Fein, 1996; Fein, Hilton, & Miller, 1990; Fein, Morgan, Norton, & Sommers, 1997; Hilton, Fein, & Miller, 1993). Fein et al. (1990) had participants read an essay that was either firmly in favor of or opposed to a controversial policy. Some of the participants were told that the essay writer, as part of his job, had been assigned to argue one side or the other of the issue, thereby reproducing the *no choice* condition of Jones and Harris (1967). Other participants were told that the essay writer was free to choose which side he argued. However, from other information it became clear that the person's employer either strongly favored or strongly opposed the policy. This information provided an *ulterior motive* (ingratiation to a person holding power and influence) for the writer's advocacy of the employer's favored position. All participants were then asked to rate the essay writer's real opinion on the issue.

As shown in Figure 7.2, results again revealed the correspondence bias in the no-choice condition. Ratings of the person's true attitude were correspondent with the position advocated in the essay, even though the author had been assigned which side to advocate. In contrast, when participants thought the essay writer was free to argue either side but had an ulterior motive for advocating the chosen position, the correspondence bias was eliminated. In this case, participants did not view the essay as informative about the writer's beliefs. The presence of an ulterior motive blocked the correspondent inference process and instead generated the perception of motivated ingratiation. In other words, participants formed a noncorrespondent dispositional inference.

How can we account for this effect? Further research (Fein, 1996) showed that suspicion of ulterior motives engages a different kind of processing, one that is more analytic and attributional. Suspicion may trigger this more complex, analytic thinking simply as a part of trying to understand the causes of a person's behavior (why did the writer adopt the chosen position?). The perceiver recognizes that the behavior may have multiple possible motivational origins, and consideration of those possibilities may lead to a greater awareness of the situational constraints on the essay writer's behavior. Consideration of and weighing these alternatives would lead to a diminished tendency to make a correspondent inference.

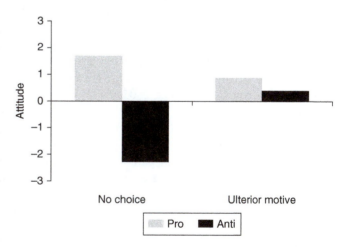

Figure 7.2 Judgments of participants' true attitude as function of position advocated and condition

Source: Adapted from Fein et al. (1990)

In summary, correspondent inferences may be made rather quickly and easily, without much thoughtful analysis, but under some circumstances will be corrected or adjusted in light of other relevant information (such as possible alternate motives). We now turn to a more extended analysis of these two possibilities – the ease with which correspondent inferences are made and the possibility of subsequently revising those inferences.

Spontaneous Trait Inferences

In the correspondence bias, Correspondent Inference Theory uncovered a pervasive tendency of perceivers to infer dispositional attributes from a person's behavior, even when the information available suggests that we should be cautious in doing so. Aside from specifying some conditions that should work against this tendency, the theory was not very precise in delineating the *process* by which these inferences occur. For example, do people consciously consider all of the relevant information (including situational constraints, norms, and choices) *before* making an inference, and do they only make correspondent inferences if those factors do not stop the process? Alternatively, do people make a correspondent inference quickly and then change it later after considering the other information? If so, do people always make the dispositional inference from the behavior? Are people aware that they are doing so? Are they somehow weighing these external constraints as they engage in the inference process? These questions need to be answered if we are to understand how dispositional inferences are made as perceivers observe and comprehend social behavior.

Spontaneous Inferences from Observation

More recent research has shown that people make these dispositional inferences so readily, so quickly, so consistently that they have come to be known as *spontaneous trait inferences*, or STIs. We now know that people move from observing an act to inferring a corresponding disposition simply as a part of comprehending the behavior (Uleman, Saribay, & Gonzalez, 2008). They do so without consciously intending to, and even without their conscious awareness that the inference has been made (Uleman, Newman, & Moskowitz, 1996). How can we know that this occurs? Researchers have devised several ingenious methods for solving this problem (Carlston & Skowronski, 1994; Orghian, Smith, Garcia-Marques, & Heinke, 2017; Todorov & Uleman, 2002, 2003, 2004; Uleman, Hon, Roman, & Moskowitz, 1996; Winter & Uleman, 1984). We will describe one of these paradigms as an illustration. (Another similar method, the savings in relearning paradigm (Carlston & Skowronski, 1994), has also been extensively used.)

The *false recognition* paradigm (Todorov & Uleman, 2002, 2003, 2004) occurs in two stages. In the *learning* phase, participants read a series of stimuli, each of which shows a face of a different person along with a behavior-descriptive sentence (e.g., "Judith picked out the best chocolates before the guests arrived," implying *selfish*). Each behavior implies a different trait. Participants are told this is a memory experiment and are instructed simply to read and remember these sentences. In the *recognition* phase, they are shown the same faces again, each one now accompanied by a trait word. In some cases, that word was implied by the behavior of the person whose face is shown (a "match" trial). In other cases, the probe trait is implied by the behavior of one of the other persons shown during the learning phase (a "mismatch" trial). The participants' task is to indicate whether that word was in the sentence describing the person shown. If the behavior generated an STI about that person, then the inferred trait would be associated with that face, and participants would be more likely to "recognize" (falsely) that the word had been in the sentence about that person. Thus, evidence of having made STIs is manifested in more errors of recognition on the match than on the mismatch trials. This effect has been demonstrated in several studies (Hamilton, Chen, et al., 2015; Olcaysoy Okten &

Moskowitz, 2020; Rim et al., 2009; Shimizu, Lee, & Uleman, 2017; Todorov & Uleman, 2002, 2003, 2004; Uleman et al., 2008).

Research using several paradigms has been valuable in shedding new light on the processes underlying STIs. Results from many studies converge in demonstrating that people spontaneously infer traits of an actor as they comprehend that person's behaviors (e.g., Carlston & Skowronski, 1994; Carlston, Skowronski, & Sparks, 1995; Rim et al., 2009; Wells, Skowronski, Crawford, Scherer, & Carlston, 2011). Moreover, these inferences are about dispositions of the actor (Todorov & Uleman, 2004), are made very quickly (Todorov & Uleman, 2003), and occur as information is encoded, not during retrieval. In most studies, participants are led to believe they are in a memory experiment in order to deflect any natural tendency to form impressions of target persons.

The nature of these STIs is very similar to what Jones and Davis (1965) earlier referred to as correspondent inferences; that is, the inferred disposition corresponds directly to the nature of the behavior observed. Observing an honest behavior (returning a lost wallet) leads to the correspondent inference that the person is honest. In Jones and Davis' theory, these inferences are made consciously, are relatively analytic, and are attenuated by certain other kinds of information (e.g., the behavior is normative, situational factors might have generated the behavior, possible ulterior motives, or lack of choice). However, research on STIs goes a step further and indicates that even when these other considerations are potentially relevant, perceivers nevertheless make the correspondent inference. They do it spontaneously, unintentionally, and even without awareness that they are making that inference. It just happens.

STIs: Downstream Effects

This research on STIs then leads us to another important question. If people make STIs without intending to and without being aware they're doing it, then of what importance are they? If they do not know what they have done, how can those STIs have an important influence on later processes, events, or outcomes?

A critical consequence of this process is that STIs serve as a foundation of the nascent impression of the target person. As noted above, these inferred traits are associated with the person, not merely a summary of behavior. This means that a process that is spontaneous, unintended, and outside of awareness can itself begin to shape an emerging impression of a person about whom one may know little if anything. As we have long known from Asch's (1946) research on impression formation, judgments made early in the impression formation process have an enduring influence on the subsequent interpretation of and inferences about a person.

Another important reason for generating STIs is that we can use them to anticipate future behaviors. McCarthy and Skowronski (2011) demonstrated this benefit by showing participants a series of photos of different persons, each one accompanied by a behavior that implied a different trait. Later, participants were shown those same photos paired with a list of new behaviors, with one of those behaviors matching the trait implied by a behavior in the first task. Participants were then asked to predict which behavior they thought each of the stimulus persons would perform. Analyses showed that they chose behaviors whose trait implication matched the trait implied by the behavior associated with that person in the first phase. This result demonstrates that participants made STIs from a person's behaviors in the first task, and those inferred traits guided the selection of behaviors that the person would likely perform in the future.

These studies establish that STIs lay the foundation for newly emerging impressions of target persons and that those inferred traits are used as a basis for making predictions about the person's likely future behavior. Thus, STIs do have downstream consequences. Later in this chapter, we return to this question when we consider the role of inferred traits in perceptions of groups.

Spontaneous Trait Transference

The research on STIs led to the discovery of a related phenomenon known as *spontaneous trait transference* (STT). As we have seen, an STI occurs when a personality trait is inferred from a person's behavior ("Scott returned the wallet he found" implies *honest*). Now consider a situation in which David tells you that Scott returned the wallet. Somewhat surprisingly, this transaction can lead you to think that David, too, is honest. STT occurs toward a person who is merely describing someone else's behavior. The two are connected only by spatiotemporal continuity (in the same place at the same time), yet the trait attributed to a person is transferred to the communicator as well. Thus, whereas STIs arise from first-hand information (from direct experience), STTs are inferences based on second-hand information (from another person). Both can occur at the same time (both David and Scott are honest). Like STIs, STTs are detected by the same memory and reaction time paradigms and measures and occur without the person's awareness of making them.

The properties of STTs and their relation to STIs have been investigated in several studies (Carlston & Skowronski, 2005; Crawford, Skowronski & Stiff, 2007; Crawford, Skowronski, Stiff, & Leonards, 2008; Mae, Carlston, & Skowronski, 1999; Orghian, Garcia-Marques, Uleman, & Heinke, 2015; Skowronski, Carlston, Mae, & Crawford, 1998). Like STIs, STTs occur reliably, although they are typically half as strong an effect as STIs.

The two effects, having both similarities (spontaneous inferences) and differences (first hand vs. second hand), have raised questions about the mechanisms underlying these phenomena. Do they rest on the same processes or on different mechanisms? That question has been a matter of debate. Some authors (e.g., Carlston & Skowronski, 2005) view STI and STT as reflecting two different processes, with STI requiring an attributional process, whereas STT arises from simple associations. Others (e.g., Brown & Bassili, 2002; Orghian et al., 2015) argue that both of them are based on associative processes. Though the debate is not yet resolved, it is clear that both of these effects reflect spontaneous and involuntary inferences that occur outside of awareness yet contribute to the formation of impressions.

Other Spontaneous Inferences

In most STI experiments, each stimulus item is quite simple: a person performs some trait-implying action. There is no history, no information about the social context, no information about the person's goals, beliefs, group memberships, or any other information we typically acquire when we first meet or learn about someone. The reason for presenting such impoverished information was that it allowed a test of whether people make STIs under the minimal conditions when one intuitively might expect that they would not. The research we have described establishes that they do make those inferences spontaneously, based on minimal information. But what about the role of these other factors? Just as people make inferences about many aspects of social life, so too might different types of spontaneous inferences occur as we attempt to understand the social world. Here we briefly describe several of those spontaneous inferences.

Goals

Our discussion of spontaneous inferences has focused on spontaneous *trait* inferences, which is understandable given the central role of traits in our impressions of others. Another important aspect of understanding the people we see and interact with is knowing something about their goals. Knowing someone's motives and intentions is also helpful in adapting to that person and coordinating one's own behavior in light of his or her objectives. Of course, many times a person's goals are perfectly evident because the person has explicitly indicated the goals she is pursuing, or perhaps the social context and role constraints make clear what anyone's goals in that situation would be. Beyond those contexts, however, evidence indicates that perceivers spontaneously infer goals from people's behavior.

In one such study (Hassin, Aarts, & Ferguson, 2005), participants read short scenarios that either did or did not imply an actor's goal. For example, "Pablo's wife frequently annoys him and he thinks the time has come to call his lawyer," implies that Pablo has a goal of divorcing his wife. Essentially the same words, arranged in a different order – "Pablo calls his lawyer, who tells him that his wife annoys him frequently" – does not carry the same goal implication. Later, in a cued recall task, participants were given cues that were either implied-goal words (divorce) or unrelated words (frequently), and they had to recall as many of the stimulus statements as they could. The cue words that were related to the implied goals facilitated recall of goal-implying sentences more than the goal-unrelated sentences, and the goal-unrelated words (even though they were present in the sentences read by participants) did not facilitate recall. This evidence shows that participants made spontaneous goal inferences as they read the scenarios, even though they were not instructed to think about the actors' goals, they had no intention to infer goals, and (from debriefing) they had no awareness of making those inferences.

Traits and goals are both crucial factors in governing a person's behavior, so it makes great sense that perceivers would be attuned to both of them in making inferences. The question then becomes under what conditions each of them is made (Moskowitz & Olcaysoy Okten, 2016). Traits are dispositions. They are stable properties of the person that lend consistency to behavior. They are also abstract concepts that represent general patterns of a person's behavior, not limited to behavior towards any particular person or group, and not constrained to specific situations. Therefore, behaviors that reflect consistency across time, object, and context should induce trait inferences. Goals, in contrast, are end states that a person is seeking but has not yet attained. They are less general and more concrete than traits, and they are tied to specific contexts in which the goal can be achieved. Behaviors that are linked to specific tasks, objectives, and situations should induce goal inferences. Research findings have provided evidence supporting this distinction (Olcaysoy Okten & Moskowitz, 2017). Both kinds of inferences expand upon and give meaning to the behavior in question, but in different ways and for different reasons.

Other factors can influence the spontaneous use of traits and goals in cognition, and indeed the use of one versus the other can become habitual. For example, some research (e.g., Skitka, Mullen, Griffin, Hutchinson, & Chamberlin, 2002) has found differences between liberals and conservatives in this regard. Specifically, they found that conservatives explain social problems in terms of trait-related attributions. Liberals give higher weight to situational factors. Those differences suggest that conservatives might be more likely to make spontaneous trait inferences, implying stability and consistency. In contrast, liberals would be more likely to make spontaneous goal inferences, reflecting situation dependency and variability. Researchers

(Olcaysoy Okten & Moskowitz, 2020) used the false recognition paradigm to test whether those ideological differences are manifested in the spontaneous inferences of liberals and conservatives. Recall that in this paradigm a false recognition (saying "Yes" that a target word had been in a sentence describing a target person, when in fact it had not been) provides evidence that an inference had spontaneously been made as the sentence was initially encoded. In this study, self-described conservative and liberal participants saw a series of photos, each one with a behavior descriptive sentence. They later saw the same photos, this time with each one being accompanied by a word that was either a trait word or a goal-related word. The results showed that liberals made spontaneous inferences equally for goal and trait words, whereas conservatives made spontaneous inferences only for trait words. Thus, people's ideology can shape one's inferences in understanding behavior. A follow-up study tested the prediction that liberals' goal-related inferences rely on inferences about the situational constraints on the behavior in question. Their results showed liberals' more frequent goal inferences were mediated by their higher situation inferences.

Evaluation

In our desire to understand people, knowing about their traits and goals is undoubtedly very useful. Therefore, it is not surprising that we would develop a ready, spontaneous means for gaining information about them. However, in the last chapter we saw that evaluative reactions to stimuli are fundamental and pervasive, whether it be in response to important social events and political outcomes or to the fragrance of a rose and the beauty of a sunset. We respond evaluatively to virtually all aspects of life, including the people we encounter. Indeed, it's hard to imagine not having an evaluative reaction to people we observe, meet, and interact with. Of course, most of those times, we are quite conscious of our reactions and what we are responding to. Nevertheless, given how basic and widely used the evaluative system is, it seems reasonable that evaluative inferences would come to occur spontaneously.

Using the paradigms developed to study STIs, Schneid and colleagues (Schneid, Carlston, & Skowronski, 2015; Schneid, Crawford, et al., 2015; Olcaysoy Okten, Schneid, & Moskowitz, 2019) have provided evidence for spontaneous evaluative inferences (SEIs). Their findings showed not only that SEIs were spontaneously formed but also that they occurred regardless of processing goal (instructions to "form evaluative impressions" vs. "form trait impressions") and for both positive and negative behaviors. Moreover, STIs and SEIs were comparable in strength, and SEIs were equivalent to STTs (whether the self or another person was described). They did, however, differ in whether a second task interfered with their formation, suggesting that SEIs and STIs are distinct phenomena with somewhat different underlying processes.

Values

Other research has shown that people spontaneously make inferences about the fairness of social situations, particularly when the context makes the situation personally relevant (Ham & van den Bos, 2008). For example, suppose you read a description stating that "You and a colleague do the same work. You make $1000 per month and your colleague makes $1000 per month." That seems fair. However, suppose you read that you both do the same work but that you make $1000 and he makes $3000 per month. That clearly seems unfair. Now let's change things slightly. Imagine that, instead of describing you and a colleague, these scenarios describe two colleagues. Either both of them make $1000, or one makes $1000 while the other makes $3000. Again, the second situation seems less fair than the first. In fact, when people make *explicit* ratings based on these scenarios, in each case the first situation is judged to be fair but the second is not.

However, things are different when people *spontaneously* make inferences about what is just and fair. Such inferences are strongly biased by the personal relevance of the situation. Ham and van den Bos (2008) found that participants spontaneously made more fairness inferences in justice-related (compared to non-justice related) contexts and that this difference was particularly pronounced when the context was personally relevant (i.e., "You and a co-worker do the same work…" vs. "Two co-workers do the same work…"). These findings reveal that we regularly judge the fairness of situations even when we are not prompted to do so. However, we are particularly likely to be affected by unfair situations involving ourselves, even if those judgments might be subconscious and are not able to be reported verbally.

Situational Influences

Perceivers not only infer traits, goals, and values, they also perceive and witness behaviors in a particular situation. Situations can also be the focus of the inferences we make about behavior and events we observe (Ham & Vonk, 2003; Ramos, Garcia-Marques, Hamilton, Ferreira, & Van Acker, 2012; Todd, Molden, Ham, & Vonk, 2011). In one study examining this issue (Lupfer, Clark, & Hutcherson, 1990), participants read sentences describing something that happened to a person ("The electrician gets a promotion and raise"). Before each sentence, a brief capsule of background information provided either a disposition-implying reason for the behavior ("…a diligent, loyal worker…") or a situation-implying reason ("…pay raises are based on seniority; he just completed 10 years…") or, in a control condition, no background information at all. After reading the set of sentences, participants were given a cued recall task in which the cue words reflected either the implied trait (good worker) or the implied situational influence (decade of service). Trait descriptors were very useful cues for retrieving the stimulus sentences when disposition-implying background information preceded them. Similarly, context-related cues were effective in facilitating the recall of sentences when situation-implying background descriptions preceded them. Thus, the contextual information promoted making spontaneous inferences, but their effects were specific, enhancing inferences that are implied by the background information.

Hierarchy of Inferences

Given the variety of inferences people routinely make about others, one might plausibly wonder whether some of these inferences are more likely than others and whether some take priority over others in the inference process. Which come first and which follow later in the course of information processing?

In research investigating these questions (Smith, 1984; Smith & Miller, 1983), participants were presented a large number of sentences, one at a time, on a computer screen, with each one describing a person performing a specific behavior. Immediately following each sentence, a cue word appeared on the screen. The cue words, shown in Table 7.3, correspond to different questions the participants were to answer as they comprehended the behavior described in the sentence. For example, the cue "Intend?" asks whether the person intended to perform the described behavior, whereas the cue "Person?" asked whether something about the person caused him to perform the behavior. On some trials, a trait adjective was presented, and participants were to indicate if that trait described the person. All questions were answered by responding "Yes" or "No" using different response keys. The dependent measure was the amount of time taken to respond to the various items. The rationale of this method was that, if the information necessary to answer the question was accessed during comprehension of the sentence, then response time should be swift; alternatively, if the question was not spontaneously considered during encoding, then response time should be longer. Examining response time differences between different inferences is a means of diagnosing which kinds of inferences were made during comprehension and which were made only in response to the question posed.

Table 7.3 Cue words and associated questions probing different processes

Cue word	Question
REPEAT?	Will the person REPEAT the action described in the sentence?
INTEND?	Did the person INTEND to perform the action described in the sentence?
PERSON?	Did something about the PERSON *cause* the action described in the sentence?
SITUATION?	Did something about the SITUATION *cause* the action described in the sentence?
MALE?	Was the person in the sentence MALE?
LIKE?	Would you LIKE the person in the sentence?
Adjective in lowercase letters	Does this adjective DESCRIBE the person in the sentence?

Source: Adapted from Smith & Miller (1983)

The results of these and other studies using this method (Hamilton, 1988; Malle & Holbrook, 2012) have consistently shown differences in the speed with which various inferences are made. For example, as seen in Table 7.4, participants in one study (Smith & Miller, 1983) were rapid in answering whether the behavior was intended, suggesting that this is a question people spontaneously raise early in comprehending behavior. Response times for other questions, such as whether a trait describes the person or whether the person or the situation was the cause of the behavior, were longer. These differences suggest that trait inferences and attributional inferences may not be as routinely made during initial comprehension of behavior as inferences about goals and intentions. The findings have led to the suggestion that there may be a "hierarchy of social inferences," reflecting priorities in understanding the behaviors we observe in social interaction (Malle & Holbrook, 2012). It is also reasonable to presume that the place of these various inferences within the hierarchy might change, depending on the situational context and its properties and demands.

Table 7.4 Mean response times for responding to different question probes

Question	Mean response time
Gender	2.14
Intend	2.41
Trait	2.48
Like	2.70
Repeat	2.76
Person cause	3.42
Situation cause	3.80

Source: Adapted from Smith & Miller (1983)

Intentional and Spontaneous Inferences

The material presented so far has shown that inferences can be made in a variety of ways. Sometimes they are generated by our conscious thoughts about others based on their behavior. "Alex didn't need to make that remark. He can be a very rude person." "Natalia would do almost anything for a friend. She's a very generous person." This type of conscious, intentional inference process was the focus of the original work on correspondent inferences (e.g., Jones

& Harris, 1967) and in the research on noncorrespondent inferences (e.g., inferences of ulterior motivations; Fein, 1996; Fein et al., 1990). Other research has demonstrated that people spontaneously infer a lot as they comprehend behavior, making inferences of which they may not even be cognizant. These inferences are well exemplified by spontaneous trait inferences (e.g., Carlston & Skowronski, 1994; Todorov & Uleman, 2004; Winter & Uleman, 1984). What features differentiate *intentional* from *spontaneous* inferences?

Uleman (1999) proposed a critical distinction between these inference processes. He argued that intentional inferences occur when one is attending to and processing information about another person with a particular goal in mind. For example, when we are highly motivated to form an impression of a person or to evaluate a person's appropriateness for a job, we are making intentional inferences. In contrast, spontaneous inferences occur simply in the course of observing the behavior of others, without a particular goal in mind. This passive form of inference process happens during what Uleman (p. 146) calls "uneventful people watching."

Intentional and spontaneous inferences differ in several other ways, as summarized in Table 7.5. First, they differ in the types of constructs that guide them. Intentional inferences, being goal-driven, are guided by temporarily-accessible constructs that relate to the relevant goal. Spontaneous inferences are based on constructs (e.g., traits) that are chronically accessible and hence can be easily activated. Second, they differ in the focus of their concern. Being goal-driven, intentional inferences are concerned with the relevance of information to the task at hand. Spontaneous inferences are less focused and hence can be more wide-ranging, responding to stimulus cues and the constructs they activate. Third, they differ in their response to inconsistent information. Intentional inferences are purposive. They are directed at achieving some goal (e.g., evaluating a political candidate). New information, particularly if it is inconsistent with the implications of prior information, needs to be interpreted in a way that either allows it to be integrated with existing inferences or to be dismissed as irrelevant to the goal at hand. Spontaneous inferences, in contrast, arise as information is comprehended. If new information is inconsistent with a prior spontaneous inference, the first inference is simply modified or replaced by the implications of the new information without much consternation. Fourth, they differ in the mechanism by which an inference becomes attached to the actor. Intentional inferences are linked to the actor because one's purpose pertains specifically to understanding that person. In contrast, spontaneous inferences become associated with the actor by their co-occurrence.

Table 7.5 Comparison of intentional and spontaneous inference processes

Intentional	Spontaneous
Inference guided by temporarily accessible constructs related to current goal	Inference based on chronically accessible constructs, easily activated
Focused on relevance of information to operative goal state	Less focused, responsive to salient stimulus cues
Purposive; directed at achieving goal	Not product of conscious intent; occur as information is comprehended
Inconsistent information confronted, either assimilated or dismissed	Inconsistent information activates different construct and new inference, replacing original inference
Inferred trait becomes linked to actor through behavior relevant to perceiver's goal (e.g., impression formation)	Inferred trait becomes associated with actor through co-occurrence
Directs attention to inferred traits, monitors inferential outcomes, allows use in goal attainment (e.g., organizing information in memory, retrieval)	Can later be used in retrieving associated information (e.g., behavior that triggered inference); not easily usable for other purposes

Source: Adapted from Uleman (1999); Ferreira et al. (2012)

Studies also show that intentional and spontaneous inferences result in different memory representations. This possibility was raised by an apparent paradox in findings from research on STIs and research on memory for social information. Specifically, Winter and Uleman (1984) showed that participants spontaneously inferred traits from behavior descriptions, even though they thought they were in a memory experiment. However, Hamilton et al. (1980a) had earlier produced results that seemed inconsistent with this conclusion. In their studies, participants who were about to read a series of behavioral descriptions were asked to form an impression of the person ("Try to form an overall impression of what the person who performed these various actions is like") or to memorize the information ("Try to remember the exact wording of each single description as accurately as you can"). Participants who received impression formation instructions recalled more behaviors and showed more organization in the recalled information (i.e., they clustered behaviors according to implied traits) than did memory condition participants. Together, these studies pose a puzzle: If participants given memory instructions spontaneously infer traits (Winter & Uleman, 1984), then why did Hamilton et al.'s memory condition participants not use those inferred traits to organize behaviors in memory, as did their impression condition counterparts?

Table 7.6 Mean recall and clustering scores as a function of processing task and cue condition

Task	Recall		Clustering	
	No cues	Trait cues	No cues	Trait cues
Impression Formation	10.5	11.1	.22	.24
Memory	7.9	10.1	.02	.11

Source: Adapted from Ferreira et al. (2012)

Ferreira, Garcia-Marques, Hamilton, Ramos, Uleman, and Jeronimo (2012) addressed this question by combining the main features of these two studies into a single experiment. Participants were given either impression formation or memory instructions, read a series of trait-implying behavioral descriptions and were then asked to recall those behaviors either with or without being given the traits as retrieval cues. The number of items recalled and the extent of clustering according to trait categories were analyzed. The results, shown in Table 7.6, reveal several important points. First, on both dependent measures, when not provided trait cues, impression condition participants performed better than memory condition participants, replicating Hamilton et al.'s (1980a) results. Giving trait cues to impression condition participants had no noticeable effect on either measure; presumably, these traits were activated in these participants simply as part of forming an impression, a purposeful, intentional inference task (Uleman, 1999). Second, memory condition participants recalled more behaviors when they were provided with trait cues, paralleling Winter and Uleman's findings of improved memory for behaviors that produced STIs. Third, there was not, however, a significant parallel increase in clustering. These findings indicate that STIs, though useful in retrieving the behaviors that triggered them, were not used in organizing the stimulus behaviors according to those trait themes, as did participants who were asked to form an impression.

Other studies (Ferreira et al., 2012) have shown that: (a) The intentional, goal-driven nature of deliberate impression formation results in an inference monitoring process, in which participants attend to the inferred traits. Those inferred traits are then accessible for use in subsequent tasks, such as organizing behavioral information in memory, as revealed in the clustering by impression participants. (b) Including a cognitive load during behavior encoding disrupts the inference monitoring process that is naturally engaged in impression formation, but it does not disrupt the spontaneous inference process itself. Load inter-feres with monitoring (intentional) but not with STIs (spontaneous). These findings are informative about the properties and functions distinguishing intentional and spontaneous inference processes.

In summary, research on inferences demonstrates that spontaneous inferences occur quickly and automatically as behavioral information is encountered. This early stage may include simultaneously making several kinds of spontaneous inferences (of traits, goals, intentions, and situations) reflecting associations of the behavior with various aspects of the person and context involved. These automatic inferences may then have the status of "candidates" for the ultimate interpretation of the behavior. Intentional inferences, driven by specific processing goals (e.g., evaluating a person, forming an impression), then are made, depending on perceiver goals and on relevant aspects of the information but perhaps also influenced by the quicker, already inferred spontaneous inferences. Finally, any of these inferences (whether spontaneous or intentional) can subsequently be revised or dismissed in light of new information, a topic to which we now turn.

Inferences: Fixed or Changeable?

People quite readily make inferences about the persons and events they witness, both intention-ally and spontaneously, as a part of comprehending those persons and events. These inferences expand their understanding from the literal confines of a single incident to a more general representation of those persons and events. They constitute an essential part of our "first impressions" of other people, and they shape how subsequent information is interpreted. They are important elements in anticipating the future. We know from experience, however, that our earliest inferences about people and events can and do change over time. Our first impressions (as discovered by Neville Chamberlain) can be wrong, but can they be changed? If so, what are the processes by which this occurs?

Research has sought to answer these questions and, in doing so, has broadened our under-standing of inference processes. Yes, many inferences are made spontaneously, but yes, they can be changed. However, to understand the process of inference modification, one must appreciate the prioritization of different cognitive processes and the factors that can influence these processes. Gilbert, Pelham, and Krull (1988) offered a model of inference formation involving three distinct processes: (a) categorization (identifying the behavior), (b) charac-terization (dispositional inference), and (c) correction. The first process involves determining the meaning of the action, which (as we discussed in Chapter 5) is important, particularly when behavioral information is ambiguous. For example, identifying a behavior as a helpful act gives meaning to the action. Once they interpret the information, perceivers make dis-positional inferences (STIs) spontaneously as they encode behavior ("The man carrying the woman's boxes is a helpful person"). This process does not demand much attention, motiva-tion, or cognitive resources but happens nearly automatically. Finally, these inferences can be corrected if additional information is encountered suggesting that the initial inference was unwarranted ("He's being paid to help the woman move"). However, that correction process involves a conscious and effortful analysis of the relevant information. Because the correction process is effortful and requires resources, it is conditional and can be disrupted by other fac-tors. If something interferes with the correction process, then the initial inference will remain. According to this model, these three processes occur in sequence, and they differ in the extent to which they require cognitive resources.

In a study testing these ideas (Gilbert et al., 1988), participants watched a videotape of a woman being interviewed by another person, but the audio portion was turned off. The woman appeared to be quite nervous and fidgety, suggesting that she might be a very anxious person. The topics being discussed were printed at the bottom of the screen. The topics presumably being discussed were varied in two conditions. In one case, these topics supposedly included discussions of her most embarrassing moments, her sexual fantasies, and her personal failures. These are matters that few people enjoy talking about with a stranger, so the fact that the woman appears anxious would be understandable. In the other condition, however, the supposed discussion topics were her favorite hobbies, books, films, and vacations. These are things most people would feel comfortable talking about, and in this case, the woman's apparent unease would probably seem strangely odd and inappropriate; if she's this nervous talking about her favorite vacations, then she must really be an anxious woman!

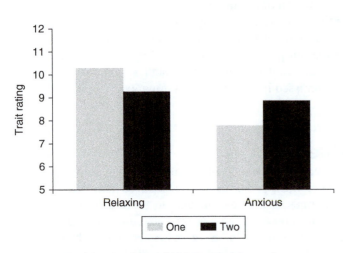

Figure 7.3 Mean ratings of target person's anxiety as a function of discussion topic number of tasks

Source: Based on data from Gilbert et al. (1988)

A second manipulation in the study varied the difficulty of participants' task. In one condition, the study followed the procedure described above. In the other condition, however, participants were given a second task to perform at the same time. Specifically, they were told they would be asked to recall the topics being discussed (as shown at the bottom of the screen). Gilbert et al. (1988) reasoned that this cognitive load manipulation would make a difference in participants' perceptions of the woman. Specifically, they assumed that perceivers would spontaneously infer that she's anxious, based on observing her behavior. However, in the condition where she's discussing very personal topics, her nervousness would be understandable so people would revise their inference that she is a nervous person ("Most people would be anxious talking about their sexual fantasies, so she's not necessarily a highly anxious person"). However, when they were performing two tasks simultaneously, the cognitive load would interfere with their ability to consider the implications of those topics for her behavior. Hence, they would not "correct" or revise their initial inference and instead would continue to think of her as highly anxious.

At the end of this procedure, all participants rated how anxious and nervous the woman is in most situations. The results, shown in Figure 7.3, supported the hypotheses. In the one-task condition, the woman was rated as much more anxious when the topics were relaxing than when they were anxiety-provoking. In contrast, in the two task (cognitive load) condition, she was rated as being highly anxious in both discussion topic conditions. This pattern fits with the view that people inferred the corresponding disposition in all conditions, but they had the cognitive resources to correct that inference only when a second task did not constrain those resources.

INFERENCE PROCESSES IN UNDERSTANDING THE SELF, PERSONS, AND GROUPS

We have described the nature of inference processes and several ways that they influence social perception. We now address the role of these processes in understanding the self, of other persons, and of groups.

Inference Processes in Perceptions of Self

People routinely infer qualities of others based on their behaviors. Do we also make inferences about ourselves? This seems less obvious. After all, if there is anyone on earth we are very familiar with, it is ourselves. Why would we need to make inferences about ourselves? Don't we already know all (or most) of what there is to know?

In fact, the question of self-knowledge (e.g., how we come to know ourselves, how our self-concept develops and changes, how accurate it is) has been the focus of interest for philosophers, theologians, historians, and novelists throughout history. Not surprisingly, social psychologists have also been interested in understanding the answers to these questions.

Self-perception Theory

Much of the research we have talked about in this chapter is driven by the assumption that, if we can make dispositional inferences about persons from their behaviors, then we can increase our understanding of those persons and their internal qualities (their traits, motives, and attitudes). That is, knowledge of other people is gained by inferences we make from observing their behavior. As we discussed in the previous chapter, Bem (1972) argued that the same process is used to acquire self-knowledge. According to his *self-perception theory* (Bem, 1972), each of us comes to understand our own qualities by observing our own behavior and inferring that the characteristics implied by those behaviors are true of us. This idea was revolutionary at the time because it meant both that people often do not have privileged or unique insight into what they are like and that reasoning processes we use to think about other people are also used to think about ourselves.

Consider the question of whether I am a generous person. How do I answer that question? It is, after all, somewhat ambiguous: what constitutes being generous? To answer this question, I might think about behaviors I have engaged in that I think reflect generosity. I make annual contributions to several nonprofit organizations that are doing important work; I donate used household items and clothing to thrift stores which provide them to needy people; I annually write a check to my undergraduate college. Having observed that I do all of these things, I might then infer that I seem to be a generous person. On the other hand, I might also consider that virtually all of these donations are tax-deductible, so perhaps my apparent generosity is driven by self-interest, even greed. And when I compare myself with a deeply religious person who tithes (giving 10% of his income) to his church, then perhaps I'm not very generous after all. In precisely these circumstances, when things are ambiguous, Bem's theory proposed that we arrive at self-perceptions by observing our own actions ("Gee, I donate to a lot of organizations") and the circumstances under which they occur ("Well, I am getting a tax break") and then using that information as a basis for inferring our own qualities ("Yes, on the whole, I'm a generous person").

Bem's theory was influential because it proposed a radically different process compared with other contemporary accounts by which self-perceptions are formed. Eventually, it fell out of favor because it focused too heavily (almost exclusively) on this process as the mechanism underlying our self-perceptions.

The Importance of Thoughts and Feelings

Later research showed that other considerations beyond the knowledge of our own behaviors play important roles in self-understanding. Some authors (Andersen, 1984; Andersen & Ross, 1984) argued that one's internal thoughts and feelings provide more critical and more diagnostic clues to "who we are" than does knowledge of observable behaviors. In one study examining this possibility, participants indicated that they believed that someone would get to know them better if that person had access to their private thoughts and feelings than just from observing their behavior. In another study, an interviewer asked participants about several aspects of their lives having to do with family, friends, education, conflicts, and decisions. In answering these questions, participants in one condition were instructed to focus primarily on their thoughts and feelings. In another condition, the interviewees were told to focus mainly on their behaviors. For example, one woman in the thoughts and feelings focus condition said the following in discussing relationships with close friends:

> The idea of being completely alone and unable to communicate with anyone really frightens me more than anything else. So friends are really important to me. I feel OK, though, about giving up complete honesty, even with friends, if I think it will offend them or hurt them.

Here is an example from another woman, this one in the behavior focus condition, answering the same question:

> I don't make close friends very easily and up until a few years ago I was totally independent and didn't pay much attention to people. I care more now; I sometimes talk for hours with my roommate in the coffeehouse, or we go to a movie. I was very active in high school with lots of acquaintances – I was president of the international relations club…And I ended up going out with one of the AFS students all last year. I also played flute and oboe in the band and piano and recorder for fun.

Afterward, participants rated how informative it was (how well an observer would come to know them, how complete an impression could be formed) from their interviews. At the same time, other participants (observers) watched the interview from an observation room. They also made the same ratings of the interviewee.

As shown in Table 7.7, interviews that emphasized thoughts and feelings were judged to convey more useful information about the interviewee. Both the interviewees and the observers rated the interviews focused on thoughts and feelings as being more informative than the interviews focused on behaviors, and they were seen as providing a better foundation for predicting the person's feelings as well as his or her actions. These findings reveal differences in the types of information that are considered most useful in making inferences about both the self and others.

However, this evidence does not necessarily mean that either the interviewees or the observers are accurate in their belief that thoughts and feelings are more diagnostic than behaviors. Andersen (1984) addressed this question in a follow-up study. Female participants first rated themselves on a variety of personality variables, assessed their anticipated emotional responses to some hypothetical situations, and indicated how they would likely behave in some other hypothetical situations. They then participated in three brief interviews, which were tape-recorded. In one interview, they were given no specific instructions to guide their responses. For the other two interviews, they were instructed either to emphasize their private thoughts and feelings or to focus on their behaviors. Each participant also identified a close same-sex friend who subsequently rated the participant on the same measures on which the participant had rated herself. Finally, a new set of participants listened to the interviews and rated the participants on the identical measures on which both the participant and the close friend had rated the participant.

Table 7.7 Interviewees' and observers' ratings of informativeness as a function of interview focus

	Interview focus	
Measures	Thoughts & feelings	Behavior
Informativeness		
Interviewees	58.0	44.5
Observers	67.8	61.8
Ability to Predict Feelings		
Interviewees	57.5	41.3
Observers	66.3	63.1
Ability to Predict Behavior		
Interviewees	58.8	45.0
Observers	59.6	55.9

Source: Adapted from Andersen & Ross (1984)

The question of interest in this study was the extent to which the participant's self-ratings on the personality, emotion, and behavior prediction measures corresponded to ratings on those same variables made by (a) other participants who listened to the interview tapes and (b) the close friend of the participant, who presumably had extensive knowledge of and familiarity with the participant's personality. Results again showed the usefulness and importance of information about the participant's private experiences. The participants' ratings of themselves were more highly correlated with the ratings made by friends and observers in the thoughts and feelings interview condition than in the behavior focus interview condition. Thus, not only is information about a person's private experiences considered more useful than knowledge of one's behaviors (Andersen & Ross, 1984), but information about one's thoughts and feelings provides more accurate access to knowledge of the person's personality (Andersen, 1984).

Bias Blind Spot

Social cognition research has revealed several ways that people manifest biases in their use of information as they make judgments about themselves and others. For example, people tend to view their performance in academic or job situations in self-serving ways, favorably viewing their own role in their successes but not taking responsibility for failures (Tillman & Carver, 1980); they assimilate new information as fitting with their pre-existing beliefs (Lord et al., 1979); they rate their attributes as more crucial to marital success than characteristics they do not possess (Kunda, 1987); and they possess inflated views of their abilities (Dunning, Meyerowitz, & Holzberg, 1989). Moreover, there are systematic differences in the nature and extent of these and similar biases in judging ourselves versus judging others; that is, these biases tend to be self-serving. Are we cognizant of the biases that plague people's judgments? Are we aware that we too fall prey to these biases? Research designed to answer these questions has shown that people are often aware of these biases in others (Kruger & Gilovich, 1999; Van Boven, Kamada, & Gilovich, 1999), but much less so in themselves (Pronin, Gilovich, & Ross, 2004). This tendency has been called the *bias blind spot* (Pronin, 2007, 2008; Pronin, Lin, & Ross, 2002).

In these studies, participants are given a neutral description of an inferential bias that is well documented in the social cognition literature. For example, in one study (Pronin et al., 2002), participants were told the following:

> Psychologists have claimed that people show a "self-serving" tendency in the way they view their academic or job performance. That is, they tend to take credit for success but deny responsibility for failures; they see their accomplishments as the result of personal qualities, like drive or ability, but their shortcomings as a result of external factors, like unreasonable work environments or inadequate instruction.

They were then asked to rate their own susceptibility to this effect and then to rate the susceptibility of the average person. This procedure was followed for several inferential biases. The results were clear and consistent. For each bias, participants rated themselves as less likely to manifest the bias than would the average person. Thus, people see themselves as less susceptible to bias than others.

Inference Processes in Perceptions of Persons

Much of the material we have already covered in the chapter pertains to inferences about other individuals. Ranging from Asch's (1946) research on impression formation to research on correspondent inferences and biases to research on varieties of spontaneous inferences, the vast majority of what we know about social inference processes comes from research investigating judgments of other persons. In this section, we build on that foundation.

Multiple Simultaneous Spontaneous Inferences

As we have seen, people make several different types of inferences (traits, goals, values) spontaneously as they comprehend people's behaviors. A reasonable next question then is, "When do they do one, and when do they do the other?" In fact, research has shown that people can make multiple inferences simultaneously, and they do so spontaneously, without intention or awareness that they are doing so (Ham & Vonk, 2003). Behavioral information often supports multiple inferences. Suppose, for example, you learn that "John got an A on the test." This fact might lead to an STI that John is smart. It might also lead to the spontaneous situational inference (SSI) that the test was easy. Ham and Vonk proposed that *both* of these inferences can be made at the same time.

Participants in their study read a series of sentences (e.g., "John got an A on the test"), which was immediately followed by a word (e.g., "smart" or "easy"). Participants had to indicate whether or not the word was in the sentence they had just read, and the computer recorded this judgment speed. Sometimes this probe word was implied by the sentence (e.g., "smart," "easy") and sometimes not (e.g., "friendly"), but none of the words had appeared in the sentence. The speed of judgments of the probe words was informative about whether a spontaneous inference had formed. If the participants made an STI or an SSI as they read the sentence, those inferred concepts would be highly accessible in memory. A probe word implicationally related to one of those concepts should create uncertainty about whether the word was or was not in the original sentence, thereby slowing judgment speeds.

There were two important results from this study. First, people had slower response times if the sentence implied the probe word than if it did not, indicating that those probe words had been spontaneously inferred during sentence comprehension. Second, and importantly, the response times were equally slow for probe words that represented STIs and SSIs. In our example, people inferred *both* that John is smart *and* that the test was easy. That is, STIs and SSIs were made concurrently. Later research has shown that these simultaneous inferences are made regardless of cognitive load or instructions to focus on either the actor or the object of the sentence (Todd et al., 2011).

To explain these results, Ham and Vonk (2003) proposed that both STIs and SSIs are made very quickly as information is identified – the first step of the inference process. This is followed by a second stage in which these activated concepts are considered, perhaps more thoughtfully and by relying on what else is known about the person. The consequence is that some of the inferred concepts will be retained, and others will be inhibited (Yes, I know that John is smart; the test probably wasn't all that easy). Finally, because all of this happens very quickly, a third stage can occur in which these quick inferences can be corrected, much like the Gilbert et al. (1988) analysis discussed earlier.

Motives

Much of the research on dispositional inferences involves presenting participants with some behavior information (an essay supporting Castro's government, a statement that John carried some boxes for the retiree) to see which inferences are drawn from those behaviors (the person's real attitude toward Castro, a spontaneous inference that John is helpful). Implicit in this work is the assumption that the perceiver moves directly from acts to dispositions.

This is an oversimplification, and inferences about dispositions based upon observing behavior rest on a set of underlying assumptions. For example, Jones and Davis' (1965) Correspondent Inference Theory – the conceptual origin of much of the work on dispositional inferences – posited that a dispositional inference rests on the assumption that observed behavior is intentional. "The attribution of intentions…is a necessary step in the assignment of more stable characteristics to the actor" (p. 222). More recently, Reeder (2009; Reeder, Kumar, Hesson-McInnis, & Trafimow, 2002; Reeder, Vonk, Ronk, Ham, & Lawrence, 2004) has proposed a *Multiple Inference Model*, positing that perceivers may draw several inferences as a part of forming an impression of a target person. Most importantly, the situational context can be used to infer the motives underlying a given behavior, and the motive inferred can then influence the nature of the disposition that is inferred.

In one study examining this possibility (Reeder et al., 2004), participants watched two videos. All of them saw a tape in which a student named Sara helped a professor move some books and journals onto a cart. They then watched one of three tapes that provided some context for Sara's behavior. In the *Free Choice* tape, it was clear that Sara had some spare time with no obligations, so she was free to help the professor. The *No Choice* tape portrayed Sara as a department employee whose job it was to help the professor. In the *Ulterior Motive* tape, Sara was a candidate for an award, and the professor was a member of the selection committee. After viewing the tapes, participants rated Sara regarding her helpfulness, obedience, and selfishness. Note that inferring her helpfulness would be the (correspondent) dispositional inference of interest here; perceiving her as obedient or selfish would reflect non-correspondent inferences based on motives suggested by the situation tapes.

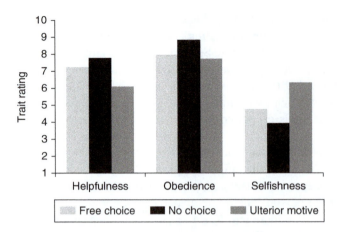

Figure 7.4   Mean traits judgments about helping behavior as a function of condition

Source: Based on data from Reeder et al. (2004)

The results are shown in Figure 7.4. Participants in all conditions viewed Sara as helpful, although those who saw the Ulterior Motive tape rated her as less helpful than in the other two conditions. In the No Choice condition, Sara was rated as more obedient than in the Free Choice and Ulterior Motive conditions. In contrast, she was rated as most selfish in the Ulterior Motive condition. Additional analyses showed that the situational contexts portrayed in the various tapes influenced perceptions of Sara's obedience (in the No Choice condition) and her selfishness (in the Ulterior Motive condition) and that those inferred motives were crucial mediators that influenced perceptions of how helpful she is. Specifically, the content of Sara's inferred motives (selfishness, obedience) played an important role in determining the dispositional inference of helpfulness. These results show that people incorporate information about behavior and the social contexts in which that behavior occurs to understand the implications of that behavior for impression formation.

Social Projection

People often perceive others as having qualities similar to their own – as having similar personality attributes, sharing tastes and preferences, and likely to make the same decisions in choice situations. They may *project* onto others their traits (Holmes, 1968, 1978), emotional reactions (Feschbach & Feschbach, 1963), and drive states (Van Boven & Loewenstein, 2003). As a consequence, people overestimate the similarity between themselves and others. Although this perception of similarity is pervasive, the psychological mechanisms underlying it are less clear. There are several possibilities.

Perhaps the best-known explanation is Freud's concept of *projection*. In his psychoanalytic theory, projection is a defense mechanism that serves an ego-defensive function by protecting the person from the recognition that he or she has an unacceptable characteristic. Knowledge of this attribute would be anxiety-provoking, so the ego represses that knowledge and projects that quality onto another person. The function of projection, then, is the reduction of anxiety generated by repressed material. Through projection, another person is seen as having that attribute, thereby creating an apparent similarity between the two persons. However, an essential element in Freud's account is that the person is not aware that he or she possesses the repressed, projected attribute. Consequently, the person is not cognizant of this similarity between self and other.

Although this concept is widely known in contemporary culture, it seems unlikely that most aspects of Freud's account are viable (Holmes, 1968, 1978). There is little convincing empirical evidence documenting a motivated process in which unacceptable characteristics are repressed below conscious awareness and then projected onto another person. Nevertheless, there is evidence that beliefs about ourselves do regularly affect our judgments of others. People do commonly overestimate their similarities with others (Robbins & Krueger, 2005) and use the self as a basis of judging other people (Krueger, Acevedo, & Robbins, 2005), phenomena referred to as *social projection*. Social projection may rest on a process of generalization, in which people generalize their own attributes to a person being judged or assimilate others to the self, assuming that others share their qualities or engage in similar behaviors.

There are several possible means by which people come to overestimate similarities with others. One possibility would be that people typically seek out and associate with others who are similar to themselves, producing an overestimation of such similarities in general. Another possibility is that knowledge about oneself may be the only (or at least the best) information one has for making inferences about others. In that case, using self-knowledge would, of course, generate perceptions of similarity. A more motivational explanation is that people may have a desire to fit in with others and to seem "normal," therefore exaggerating the extent of similarity they see between others and themselves (Krueger & Clement, 1994b; Ross, Greene, & House, 1977). Finally, people may believe that their perceptions of others and events are veridical, not plagued by bias, and therefore assume that others share their judgments (Gilovich, 1990). If so, then this too might lead people to overestimate the degree of similarity between themselves and others.

Projection does not always dominate in making inferences about others. There are other bases for inference, including the knowledge and expectancies stored in cognitive representations. Ames (2004a, 2004b, 2005; Ames & Mason, 2012; Ames, Weber, & Zou, 2012) has argued that, when information about a target person is ambiguous, the perceived similarity of that person to oneself is an important variable determining whether inferences about that person will be based on (a) the projection of own qualities onto the other when they are seen as similar to the self or (b) stereotypic beliefs based on the person's group membership when they are seen as dissimilar from the self. To test this idea, experimenters led participants in one study (Ames, 2004a) to believe that they were similar or dissimilar to a target person based on their supposed shared preferences (e.g., whether they both liked comedian Adam Sandler). They then read a description of an event involving the target and answered several questions about the person's mental states (thoughts, feelings, reactions). When they believed they were similar to the target person, participants answered these questions by relying on their thoughts of how they themselves would respond in the situation (projecting onto others their own tendencies). If the target person appeared to be dissimilar, however, participants relied on group stereotypes as the basis for inferring the target's feelings and reactions.

Another mechanism influencing inferences about others is *transference* (Andersen & Baum, 1994; Andersen & Cole, 1990; Andersen & Glassman, 1996; Andersen, Glassman, Chen, & Cole, 1995; Chen & Andersen, 1999; Glassman & Andersen, 1999). Imagine that you meet someone who, for some reason, reminds you of someone important to you (a family member, close friend, or former romantic partner) and about whom you, therefore, have a well-developed mental representation. This activation of your representation of a significant other brings to mind the features and attributes of that person and, through spreading activation, those attributes are transferred to the new person. That is, inferences based on the significant other representation are applied to the new person, endowing her with qualities that were not learned about that person. This process can occur at either a conscious (Andersen & Baum, 1994; Andersen & Cole, 1990) or unconscious (Glassman & Andersen, 1999) level.

Inference Processes in Perceptions of Groups

In this chapter, we have extensively discussed the processes involved in inferring dispositional attributes from the observation of a person's behaviors. In everyday life, we also regularly encounter groups and their members. Groups and their members can often be observed engaging in interdependent behavior (e.g., the shared reactions of fans at a sporting event). Also, some individuals, by being categorized as members of salient social groups, are judged through the lens of social stereotypes, even when they are acting alone. This raises intriguing new questions. Are there parallel inference processes in our perceptions of groups, and if so, what drives those processes? Are there special considerations regarding inferences we draw about groups? Also, given that we have stereotypes about groups, how do stereotypes relate to the process of making inferences? In this section, we discuss research addressing these questions.

A Group Inference Error

In Correspondent Inference Theory, a perceiver makes a correspondent dispositional inference about a person from observation of behavior, unless certain constraints (normative behavior, lack of choice, etc.) are present. Do people look at the "behavior" of groups and draw correspondent inferences about the group's "disposition"? It turns out that people do, although there are biases that can produce systematic errors in inferences about groups (Allison, Mackie, & Messick, 1996; Allison & Messick, 1985).

One such case can occur when a group's decision or outcome is used as a basis for inferring something about the attitudes of group members. For example, we might look at the outcome of an election and assume that the result reflected the group's preference. This seems intuitively plausible – a group's decision should, it seems, reflect group members' attitudes. The problem is that a variety of factors can influence group decisions, meaning that outcomes are not always directly reflective of a group's preferences.

The nature of this problem becomes clearer by considering one of Allison and Messick's (1985) studies. Participants in this study read a story about a town in which a recall vote was being held regarding a controversial policy. On election day, either 43% (one condition) or 57% (other condition) of the people voted in favor of the recall. However, according to town ordinances, for a recall to be successful, a specific criterion had to be met. This criterion was also manipulated in three conditions in the study: the vote needed to be 35%, 50%, or 65% in favor of recall to be successful. This means, then, that a 57% vote would fail if 65% were needed for passage, whereas a 43% vote would be successful if the criterion for adoption were 35%.

After reading the scenario, participants were asked to rate the attitude of the typical voter towards the recall, where higher values reflect the perception of being more favorable toward the recall. The average ratings of the participants in the various conditions of the experiment are shown in Table 7.8. The three values in boldface are conditions in which the recall vote would have won; the other three are cases in which the recall vote would have lost. In reality, of course, the best estimate of how the townspeople feel about the issue is represented in the percentage who voted in favor of the recall. However, the data in Table 7.8 make clear that participants' perceptions of the prevailing opinion in the town (as reflected in judgments of the "typical voter") were strongly influenced by the *outcome* of the vote, not merely by the percentage of people who voted for the recall.

Research extending this effect has demonstrated another ironic outcome (Mackie & Allison, 1987). Allison and Messick's study investigated the different inferences made by people who read about different outcomes for a single event (the recall vote). Mackie

Table 7.8 Mean attitude toward recall. Boldface values reflect cases where recall vote passed

Criterion	Percent in favor	
	43%	57%
35%	**4.8**	**5.2**
50%	3.8	**5.1**
65%	3.4	4.2

Source: Adapted from Allison & Messick (1985)

and Allison wondered if the reliance on group outcomes for inferring group attitudes could provide a basis for perceiving a *change* in a group's beliefs over time, when, in fact, there had been none.

As in the previous study, participants read a vignette about a recall election. In this case, however, participants were told that local ordinances stipulated that successful recall required two separate votes on the matter, separated by several months. The percentage of people who voted in favor of the recall was essentially the same on both occasions – 56% or 58% – indicating that the "group attitude" was stable and had not changed during the interim. The variables manipulated in the study were the decision criteria at the time of each election: either 50% or 65% favorable vote was required for passage at the first vote, and 50% or 65% were required for the second vote. In some cases (due to change in criterion from Time 1 to Time 2), the first vote could succeed (fail) and the second vote fail (succeed), even though the percentage of voters in favor of the recall was identical. In two conditions there was such a change in the outcome, whereas in two other conditions the outcomes were the same. Again, after reading the vignettes, participants rated the attitude of the typical voter on the issue. The question was whether participants would use election outcomes to infer a change in group attitudes when voting preferences were stable.

The results are shown in Table 7.9. When the first recall vote succeeded but the second one failed (second row of the table), there was a substantial drop in participants' perceptions of support for the recall, even though the group attitude (56% vs. 58% actual vote) had remained the same. When the first vote failed, but the second suc-

Table 7.9 Mean attitude toward recall as a function of decision criteria at time 1 and time 2 (S = election success, F = election failure)

Criterion T1	Criterion T2	Election		
		First	Second	Difference
50%	50%	4.6 (S)	4.8 (S)	+.2
50%	65%	5.1 (S)	4.3 (F)	−.8
65%	50%	4.4 (F)	4.8 (S)	+.8
65%	65%	4.3 (F)	4.3 (F)	0.0

Source: Adapted from Mackie & Allison (1987)

ceeded (third row of the table), there was a significant increase in perceived support, despite the stability of the group attitude. Thus, participants were strongly influenced by the outcomes (success or failure) when making inferences about the views of the typical voter. The consequence was a perception of change that was illusory.

These results harken back to the correspondence bias, where inferences about an individual's behavior are insufficiently corrected for the social context in which it occurred. Here, inferences about the dominant preferences of a group are misperceived because of a failure to adjust for procedural considerations (Allison & Messick, 1987). In both cases, inferences focus on the actor (an individual or a group) assuming that behavior reflects true intentions, beliefs, and attitudes. It is interesting to consider how these processes might produce distorted perceptions of the beliefs and attitudes of our fellow citizens. For example, when might political practices that work against majority rule (e.g., Gerrymandering, plurality electoral systems with multiple candidates, the Electoral College) lead us to think that minority opinions reflect the general consensus?

Stereotypes

When we think about the perceptions of groups, the concept of stereotypes is paramount. Stereotypes are so central to making inferences about groups that stereotyping has been referred to as "inferencing" (Schneider, 2004).

In Chapter 2, we defined a stereotype as a cognitive representation containing one's knowledge, beliefs, and expectancies about a social group. When a stereotype is activated (by priming, by encountering a group member, by media portrayal), the content of that stereotype becomes accessible to influence our perceptions of the group and its members. Associations between groups and attributes not only are aroused by thinking about a group but also about its members. When I think of Lydia, my 43-year-old neighbor, I may be inclined to think of her as nurturant and good with kids because I have seen her interact many times with her children. I might also know that she is an accomplished artist. My knowledge of her membership in that social group might lead me to infer that she has a variety of other characteristics that I believe are typical of the group (e.g., that she is likely creative, free-spirited, and politically liberal) even though I have never had the opportunity to directly observe behaviors relevant to those traits. Given the stereotype, we infer that the group and its members are likely to have those stereotypic qualities (until we learn otherwise). Thus, stereotyping and inferencing are intimately linked.

Stereotypes and STIs

In this chapter, we have described many studies in which a stimulus person is presented as having performed some behavior to determine the conditions under which an inference about that person is made. In the vast majority of those studies, participants learn very little about the actor. The reason for this approach is that the goal is to study processes in their pure form, controlling for other effects. However, when we perceive others in real life, their membership in certain groups (gender, race, age, occupation) is immediately apparent. Moreover, our stereotypes of those groups can potentially influence the inferences we make. In this section, we consider the relationship between stereotyping and making spontaneous inferences.

The inferences people make about groups and their members can be based on observed behavior or the stereotype about the group observed. In both cases, those inferences can occur automatically, without intention or awareness. What, then, is the relation between these two bases of inferences? And most interestingly, what happens when one type of inference (e.g., a group-based stereotypic inference) conflicts with the other type (e.g., a behavior-based STI)? A series of studies (Stewart, Weeks, & Lupfer, 2003; Wigboldus, Dijksterhuis, & van Knippenberg, 2003; Wigboldus, Sherman, Franzese, & van Knippenberg, 2004) investigating these questions has shown that stereotypes can, under certain conditions, influence the extent to which perceivers spontaneously infer traits from behaviors.

Participants in one study (Wigboldus et al., 2003) were presented with a series of stimulus behaviors e.g., "…won a science quiz") on a computer screen. The subject of the sentence was identified by a group label activating a stereotype that was either consistent ("The professor…") or inconsistent ("The garbage man…") with that behavior. Following each sentence, a probe trait implied by the behavior ("smart") was presented, and participants had to indicate whether the trait word was or was not in the sentence. Participants' response times in responding to these probes were recorded. The logic of the method is as follows. In none of the critically important trials did the probe trait appear in the stimulus sentence, so the correct answer to the test question is always "No." However, if the person's behavior strongly implies the probe trait, and hence would be spontaneously inferred by the participant while encoding the stimulus information, it should increase uncertainty ("Did I really see that word or did I infer it?") and therefore make it more challenging to make that "No" judgment. This uncertainty should slow down the process of making the correct response ("No"), compared to when the behavior does not imply the probe trait.

The central question in this research was whether that effect would differ as a function of whether the actor's occupation was stereotypically consistent or inconsistent with the implications of the behavior. If the stereotype ("professor") also implies the probe trait because the behavior is stereotypically consistent, then this would further enhance the uncertainty because now both the occupation and the behavior imply the same trait ("smart"). In contrast, when the trait implication of the behavior ("smart") is inconsistent with the stereotype activated by the actor's occupational group ("garbage man"), the STI might be diminished. Hence, it would be easier (and quicker) to respond that the probe word was not in the sentence. This is exactly what Wigboldus et al. (2003) found: people took significantly less time to give a "no" response to the probe word ("smart") when the behavior was stereotypically inconsistent (873 ms) than when it was stereotypically consistent (913 ms). Thus, STIs were *less likely* to occur for *stereotype-inconsistent* than for consistent behaviors. Apparently, a stereotype can *inhibit* an STI from occurring when the behavior is inconsistent with the activated stereotype. The stereotype overrides the STI.

Other research (Ramos et al., 2012) has extended this work by examining the influence of contextual information. We have already discussed how perceivers not only spontaneously infer traits of actors (STIs) but also spontaneously recognize the influence of situational factors on behavior (SSIs). Moreover, behaviors can be consistent or inconsistent with stereotypic expectancies. Incorporating both of these factors, Ramos et al. presented behaviors that were consistent or inconsistent with the stereotype of the target person. Those sentences also included an additional phrase that provided a social context that would make the behavior understandable. For example, the action "stepped on his partner's feet while dancing" was consistent when the actor was described as an "old man" but inconsistent when described as a "dancer." Also, in both cases, including the phrase "after a long working day" provided a context-based reason for the behavior (stepping on feet) for both actor conditions. These sentences were then followed by probe words that tapped a trait inference (fumbling) or situation inference (tiredness). Ramos et al. found that STIs (fumbling) were more likely to be made when the behavior (stepping on feet) was consistent with the stereotype of the actor (old man), whereas SSIs (tiredness) were more likely when that behavior was inconsistent with the description of the actor (dancer).

Spontaneous Trait Inferences and Evaluative Ingroup Bias

One of the most pervasive effects in intergroup perception is the ingroup bias, the tendency to see the ingroup as more favorable than the outgroup (Brewer, 1979; Perdue, Dovidio, Gurtman, & Tyler, 1990; Tajfel et al., 1971). These evaluative preferences occur spontaneously and without conscious awareness. Does this mean that spontaneous trait inferences about ingroups and outgroups by themselves foster an evaluative ingroup bias?

In an experiment investigating this question (Otten & Moskowitz, 2000), participants were assigned to groups based on arbitrary and minimal criteria. They then read trait-implying sentences describing behaviors performed by ingroup or outgroup members. Each sentence was followed by a probe trait that was either positive or negative in valence and was either implied or not implied by the preceding sentence. Participants' task was to indicate whether the probe trait had been in the sentence they just read, for which the answer was always "No." Response times to this probe task were recorded, and, following the logic developed above, slower response times reflect that an STI had been made. Analyses showed that response times were significantly longer when positive traits followed sentences describing ingroup members performing behaviors implying the trait. No such differences occurred when negative traits followed ingroup members or when outgroup members were described. These results show that ingroup favoritism (but not outgroup derogation) was manifested in STIs as information about ingroup members was processed. This occurred even when the group distinction was arbitrary, and the inferences were made spontaneously as behavioral information was encoded.

Spontaneous Trait Inferences and Group Impressions

The fact that people spontaneously infer dispositional attributes from an actor's behavior, without even being cognizant of doing so, has been a recurring theme in this chapter. What are the implications of this process for perceptions of groups? If STIs were formed about individuals who belong to the same group, would they influence perceptions of the group as a whole?

Crawford, Sherman, and Hamilton (2002) studied how STIs formed in response to individual group members' behavior are integrated into a group impression and how, once formed, this impression is applied to all group members. Participants read about members of two different groups whose behaviors implied distinct sets of traits. Also, they were given information indicating that the two groups were or were not highly entitative (Hamilton et al., 2002). In a later phase, each group member was shown again, except this time with a trait word. In some cases, the trait had been implied by the behavior originally performed by that target member (e.g., "lazy") and in other cases the trait was implied by the behavior of other members of the same group, not matching the behavior of this particular individual (e.g., "intelligent"). Participants were instructed to learn the person-trait pairings. Finally, the person was shown again, and the participants' task was to report which trait had been previously paired with that person. The key measure was the ease with which participants learned these member-trait pairings. Results showed that participants made spontaneous trait inferences about the group members, regardless of whether the group was high or low in entitativity. However, transferring an inferred trait of one person to the other group members occurred only for high entitativity groups. For the highly entitative groups, the traits inferred from the behaviors of *some* group members had been *spontaneously transferred to all* group members.

These findings are significant for two reasons. First, the STI results demonstrate an important role of spontaneous inferences in group impression formation. Second, the transference results (for high entitativity groups) have important implications for stereotyping. Through this transference, the group members become interchangeable in the sense that the inferred attributes of any member of a highly entitative group come to be associated with all group members. This, then, is a mechanism for spontaneous overgeneralization. Such overgeneralization is the very foundation from which stereotyping can emerge.

Spontaneous Inferences about Groups (STIGs)

In Crawford et al.'s (2002) study, the stimulus items described trait-implying behaviors of *individual members* of the target groups. The next question is, Do perceivers make spontaneous inferences about groups from *group* behaviors? Important aspects of social life occur in groups. Just as we perceive individuals behave in various ways, we also regularly see groups engage in behaviors. If we learn that "The student group raised funds to furnish a shelter for homeless people," or that "The gang members assaulted a member of a rival group," do we spontaneously make group-level dispositional inferences about these groups, parallel to what we do with individual target persons? Do we quickly and without intention infer that the student group is *generous*, that the gang is *aggressive*? Such spontaneous trait inferences about groups (STIGs) would be important in understanding the perceptions of groups. Just as STIs contribute to the emerging impression of an individual, STIGs would contribute to a developing group impression or stereotype of the target group.

Indeed, recent research (Hamilton, Chen, et al., 2015) has shown that people do make spontaneous trait inferences about groups (STIGs); perceivers will, in fact, infer that the student group is generous and that the gang is aggressive. Participants in the study first completed a *learning phase* where they saw a series of photos of a group of four persons along with a behavior-descriptive sentence, each appearing one at a time on a computer screen. In a later *test phase*, each of these photos was presented again, paired with a trait that either (a) was implied by the behavior performed by that group or (b) a trait not implied by that group's behavior but was implied by the behavior of a different group. Participants had to indicate whether the trait word was included in the behavior-descriptive sentence that had been associated with that group in the study phase. A "false recognition" occurs when the participant erroneously indicates the trait word was in the sentence when it was not. The analysis compared the number of false recognitions that occurred when the probe word was an implied vs. an unimplied trait. Results showed that participants made more false recognitions for traits implied by a group's behavior than for traits not implied by the group's behavior. In other words, they made spontaneous trait inferences about groups (STIGs) from the groups' behaviors.

Follow-up studies (Hamilton, Chen, et al., 2015) further substantiated these findings. STIGs occurred both for groups that were high and low in entitativity, suggesting that STIGs occur spontaneously in comprehending behaviors of all groups. Moreover, the STIGs were made even when participants performed this task under cognitive load, indicating that STIGs were made spontaneously and did not require cognitive resources. Having made STIGs, participants made stronger trait ratings about groups on those traits implied by the groups' behaviors than on traits implied by other groups. These results all show that STIGs influenced the impressions perceivers formed of these groups. Finally, another study showed that once they are formed, these spontaneously inferred traits can generalize to new group members. Having completed the experimental procedure to form STIGs, participants were then shown a photo of another person who was a member of a group seen in the learning phase of the study. They rated this person (about whom they had received no information) more highly on traits implied by the group's behavior than on traits not implied by that behavior. The impression spontaneously formed while comprehending a group's behavior was applied to another group member about whom they had learned nothing.

In summary, research on STIs has been important because it shows a spontaneous inference process that begins the formation of impressions, without the perceiver's intent or awareness. A similar process for groups, reflected in STIGs, may constitute the initial impressions of groups based on inferences spontaneously made from the group's behavior. These inferences endow the group with certain qualities that could set the groundwork for stereotype formation.

Stereotypic Inferences from Facial Features

Stereotypes are belief systems that provide a rich basis for inferences about groups. We have already discussed how our knowledge that a person belongs to a social group ("artist" vs. "professor" vs. "gang member") can both serve as a basis for inferences about the person and influence how behavioral information about the person is processed. Might similar effects occur not based on group membership, per se, but based on features that are indicative of group membership? Specifically, might there be facial features that affect inferences about a person directly, without necessarily changing whether a person is seen as a member of a social group? Furthermore, might within-group variation within groups in the extremity of their category-relevant facial features affect inference processes? In this section, we highlight two lines of research that directly tie facial features to inference processes.

Babyfaceness

Human faces have some common elements (eyes, nose, mouth, hair). Those elements can, of course, vary considerably from person to person. For example, some people have a rather small pug nose, whereas others have a large bulbous nose. Some have large, almond-shaped eyes, whereas others have narrow eyes. Moreover, all of these properties can change throughout development. Variation in those features and their patterning (distance between eyes, size of the forehead, the thickness of lips) play essential roles in identifying individual faces and social group memberships.

In the last chapter, we discussed how facial features influence how people are evaluated. Facial features can also affect the inferences that are made about a person or a group possessing certain features. Interestingly, similar inferences can even be made about persons who are not group members but who merely exhibit facial features characteristic of group members. One such phenomenon involves the fact that adults with facial features reminiscent of infants (i.e., adults with "babyfaces") are more likely to be judged as having childlike characteristics and traits than are adults with more mature faces. Babies' faces are differentiated from more mature faces in several ways. Baby faces have large eyes, a small nose, full cheeks, a small chin, and a round face. Of course, babies are also dependent on the protection and guidance of adults as they develop. As adults, people vary to the extent that they retain those babyfaced features or have developed into mature faces with a lesser degree of those features.

People's inferences regarding babyfaced adults reflect attributes associated with children. They are judged to be more naïve, weak and submissive, less strong, less dominant, more honest, warmer, and kinder (Montepare & Zebrowitz, 1998; Zebrowitz, 2017; Zebrowitz & Montepare, 2008; Zebrowitz, Fellous, Mignault, & Andreoletti, 2003). In real-world situations, consumers are less likely to infer that a babyfaced CEO is deceptive during a crisis (Gorn, Jiang, & Johar, 2008), and babyfaced defendants are less likely to be convicted of crimes involving pre-meditation compared with mature-faced adults (Zebrowitz & McDonald, 1991). These perceptions and judgments of babyfaced adults reflect the continuance of responding in ways that were highly appropriate with babies but have continued into adulthood. Facial characteristics themselves have led to the perpetuation of these behavioral and perceptual patterns beyond their origins.

Afrocentric Features

The role of race-related features in race perception and the influence of racial stereotypes on encoding have been studied extensively in recent years, with some intriguing, and at times disturbing, results. What do we mean by race-related facial features? The primary features that differentiate Black faces from White faces are darker skin, full lips, broad nose, and coarse hair. Perceiving those Afrocentric features leads to the categorization of the person as Black. Once that categorization has been made, the perceiver's stereotype of Black people is activated, which can then influence subsequent information processing, perceptions, and behaviors. In other words, the group categorization mediates the relation between perception of Black features of a target person and the perception that that person possesses characteristics stereotypically associated with that group. Throughout this book, we have encountered numerous examples of ways that the activation of a stereotype can guide processing. When the starting point is face perception, perception of those features initiates the process through their influence on categorization.

In addition to this process that is mediated by categorization, Blair and her colleagues (Blair, Judd, & Chapleau, 2004; Blair, Judd, & Fallman, 2004; Blair, Judd, Sadler, & Jenkins, 2002) have proposed that perception of those Afrocentric features can directly and automatically influence perceptions of Black people, independently of the activation of racial stereotypes through categorization. They argued that with repeated activation of the stereotype (through categorization) when race-defining features are perceived, those stereotypical attributes eventually are activated automatically upon exposure to facial features typical of African Americans. The distinction they have drawn is portrayed in Figure 7.5. The two solid arrows represent the traditional thinking of how perceiving certain physical features results in the activation of a social category, which in turn activates stereotypic beliefs associated with that group. The dashed line represents the direct association between physical features and stereotypic attributes, unmediated by the categorization step, as Blair et al. (2002) proposed.

In a series of studies, they have shown that perception of Afrocentric features is directly associated with attributes that have historically been stereotypic of African Americans in American society. In one such study, Blair et al. (2002) provided participants with one of four descriptions of a person who was characterized as a college-aged male African American. Two of the descriptions were favorable and two were unfavorable, and, within each of those sets, one was stereotypic and the other was counterstereotypic. For example, the negative stereotypic person

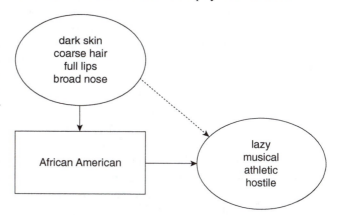

Figure 7.5 Indirect and direct associations between physical features and stereotypic attributes
Source: From Blair et al. (2002)

was raised by his grandmother because his father had disappeared and his mother was frequently in jail for dealing drugs, got into college on a basketball scholarship but doesn't get along with his coach, is doing poorly in his classes, and spends a lot of time hanging out with friends and listening to music. In contrast, the positive stereotypic person was one of eight kids in a very close and religious family, has a part-time job to help pay his college expenses, sings in a church choir, and is career-oriented. The other two descriptions – one positive, one negative – were comparable except they included no mention of stereotypic qualities. After reading one of the descriptions, participants were shown 23 photos of Black males' faces that, based on pretest ratings, were known to vary to the extent they possessed Afrocentric features. For each photo, participants were to estimate the likelihood that the person in the picture was, in fact, the person described in the paragraph they had read. Results showed that whereas Black faces with more Afrocentric features were seen as most likely to be the person in the negative stereotypic description, they were least likely to be judged as the person described in either of the positive descriptions. In other words, the more a Black person had Afrocentric features, the more likely he was perceived as fitting a negative stereotypic description.

However, are these results due solely to the effect of those Afrocentric features? After all, all of the photos were of Black males, so maybe those with more Afrocentric features activated the stereotype more strongly, which was then applied in making judgments. This is a plausible interpretation, one that gives considerable importance to the influence of stereotype activation, which we know can produce biased judgments. However, Blair et al. (2002) argued that the perception of Afrocentric features is also *directly* (without mediation by stereotypes) associated with stereotypic attributes. To further build their case, Blair et al. (2002) did another study that was a replication of the first study in all respects except one. The only difference here was that the photos were all of White males. Given all White faces, the stereotype of African Americans seems unlikely to be activated, ruling out the traditionally-assumed mechanism mediated by category activation. You might be wondering, "how can Afrocentric features vary in White faces?" Although Afrocentric features are used primarily to differentiate Black from White faces in a between-group manner, there is variation *within* both racial groups in the extent to which faces have broad noses, full lips, and darker skin tone. (Indeed, it was that variation among Black faces that predicted differences in judgments in the first study.) The White photos used in this second study had previously been rated on these same features (nose width, skin tone). Again, these photos were presented after participants had read one of the four-person descriptions (with ethnicity no longer mentioned), and participants rated the likelihood that each face was the person described in the material they read. The same pattern of results occurred in this study. White faces with more Afrocentric features were more likely to be associated with the person description that was negative and stereotypic of African Americans, and they were judged less probable to be the person described in the counterstereotypic descriptions.

Blair, Judd, and Chapleau (2004) then studied the implications of this finding in the sentencing of convicted criminals. Photos of Black and White inmates were coded for Afrocentric features, and the researchers determined the extent to which these features were related to the severity of the convict's sentence. After statistically controlling for several variables that are known to influence sentence length (e.g., the seriousness of the offense, the number of prior offenses), more Afrocentric features were associated with longer sentences and, in a similar study, with a higher likelihood of receiving the death penalty in murder cases, particularly when victims were White (Eberhardt, Davies, Purdie-Vaughns, & Johnson, 2006).

In sum, Afrocentric features are associated with attributes stereotypic of African Americans, and those features can influence perceptions of persons. The fact that the same outcomes occurred when the analyses were based on both Black and White faces strongly suggest that these perceptions, based on Afrocentric features, are direct perceptions that are not guided by stereotype activation. Moreover, within-race variation in racialized features also predicted stereotypical trait inferences. In other words, stereotypic inferences can be based directly on perceiving Afrocentric features in faces.

Perceiving Groups of Faces

Social contexts also vary dramatically regarding the frequency that different social categories are represented and, therefore, the kinds of faces and features that we would expect to encounter. If we attend a child's birthday party, we would likely anticipate seeing the faces of similar-aged children. If we entered a bar in the middle of the day, we might expect to encounter a large number of middle-aged men. One question regards whether and how we might make inferences about large groups of faces when they are viewed, even for a brief moment. This question is pursued by researchers who study a phenomenon called *ensemble coding* (Alvarez, 2011; Sweeny & Whitney, 2014).

In one such study (Alt, Goodale, Lick, & Johnson, 2019), participants were presented for 500 ms with pictures of a group of 12 faces. The images varied in their gender composition with 13 different possible ratios of men to women, ranging from 12:0 to 0:12. For each image, participants were asked to judge the number of men in each group and to indicate on several traits the threat posed by the group. Results showed that participants could accurately estimate the gender composition of the groups, even based on this brief exposure. Also, judgments of the threat posed by the group increased linearly with the number of men in the group. Other studies (Goodale, Alt, Lick, & Johnson, 2018) examined other inferences that arise during brief exposure to groups that differ in gender composition. Men and women both agreed that groups with a higher ratio of men would harbor more sexist norms. However, for both men and women, as the number of gender ingroup members increased, inferences that they would fit well in the group also increased. These results show that people can judge the numerical composition of social groups from a mere glimpse and that these judgments underlie a variety of important inferences regarding group norms and social hostility or hospitality.

SUMMARY

As people participate in the continual flow of everyday life, the people and events they encounter provide an immense amount of information to be processed and used in adapting to a complex social environment. Previous chapters have highlighted the critical roles played by people's selective attention to aspects of that information and by their imposing interpretations on it, all guided by their pre-existing knowledge and beliefs. That initial input then lays the foundation for further processing in ways that facilitate comprehension of what has transpired and anticipation of what is likely to occur.

Inference processes go beyond and build upon that foundation in important ways. People routinely make inferences about other persons with whom they interact and whose behavior they observe. These inferences may generate conceptions of the person's personality traits, goals, motives, and attitudes. All of these inferences combine to establish an impression of that person, an impression that the observer will retain and use on future occasions. Similarly, observing and interacting with a group generates inferences about the nature of the group and its goals and functioning. Those inferences contribute to the resulting stereotypes of the group. Also, people make inferences about themselves, adding to and broadening self-understanding and generating self-concepts that represent knowledge of "who we are."

All of these inferences may be the products of a deliberative, thoughtful analysis of the relevant information, or they may be made quickly and spontaneously with minimal conscious thought and consideration. Moreover, whether deliberative or spontaneous, these inference processes are subject to biases that sometimes are quite useful in facilitating this process but also can be prone to error, leading to misjudgment and misunderstanding. Regardless of the focus of these inferences (person, group, self) and the specific processes and mechanisms involved, the resulting inferences are stored in memory as part of people's comprehension of the events they have witnessed. They, therefore, provide invaluable bases for understanding and responding to the social world in which they live.

FURTHER READING

Antonakis, J., & Eubanks, D.L. (2017). Looking leadership in the face. *Current Directions in Psychological Science*, *26*, 270–275.

Hagá, S., Garcia-Marques, L., & Olson, K.R. (2014). Too young to correct: A developmental test of the three-stage model of social inference. *Journal of Personality and Social Psychology*, *107*, 994–1012.

McCarthy, R.J., & Skowronski, J.J. (2011). What will Phil do next? Spontaneously inferred traits influence predictions of behavior. *Journal of Experimental Social Psychology*, *47*, 321–332.

Moskowitz, G.B., & Olcaysoy Okten, I. (2016). Spontaneous goal inference (SGI). *Social and Personality Psychology Compass*, *10*, 64–80.

Zebrowitz, L.A., & Montepare, J.M. (2008). Social psychological face perceptions: Why appearance matters. *Social and Personality Psychology Compass*, *2*, 1497–1517.

8

ATTRIBUTION

Understanding Why Things Happen

In the Fall of 2002, Saddam Hussein, the leader of Iraq, was suspected of possessing weapons of mass destruction that had been forbidden in the wake of the First Gulf War of 1990–1991. The American administration under George W. Bush accused Saddam of hiding these weapons from international inspectors. His press secretary asserted, "If he declares he has none, then we will know that Saddam Hussein is once again misleading the world." The American public proved receptive to the argument that Saddam's lack of cooperation with inspectors meant he had a stockpile of weapons; by the Spring of 2003, polls indicated that about 70% of the American public believed that Saddam Hussein had hidden weapons of mass destruction. Following the subsequent invasion, no such weapons were ever found. However, the question remained: If the Iraqis did not have these weapons, why didn't they cooperate with the inspectors? This question was answered after the CIA analyzed internal Iraqi documents, which revealed that Iraq "prioritized security against Iran above all else." If the destruction of Iraq's entire weapons program during and after the First Gulf War had been revealed to Iran, their longstanding nemesis, it was feared that Iran might consider re-initiating hostilities against their weakened foe. Iraq had resisted the inspectors not because they possessed weapons of mass destruction, but instead because they had feared that their vulnerability would be revealed to a hostile neighbor. A severe misunderstanding of Iraq's behavior played a central role in launching a war that could never meet its stated objectives.

In Chapter 7, we considered the critical role of inference processes in social cognition. Inferences allow the perceiver to elaborate on available information, embellishing actions with meaning so that the perceiver can make sense of the people and events in the social world. We discussed how inferences play an essential role in determining how we think about and respond to other people and groups. In discussing inferences, we intentionally avoided consideration of one type of inference that has received a tremendous amount of attention in the social psychological literature. That inference pertains to the perceived causes of events. Inferences about why an event has occurred are called *causal attributions*, and they are the focus of this chapter.

When people encounter behavior that makes them wonder why it occurred (Why did that man just hit that child? Why was that co-worker so friendly to me when he typically ignores me? Why is Saddam resisting the weapons inspectors?), they attempt to infer its underlying cause or causes. By understanding the roots of behavior, people can better understand the characteristics and motives of the person who acted. Also, causal inferences that people generate to explain events influence how they will react to that event and the people involved. However, just as inferences are subjective judgments that can be systematically biased, so too are attributions. The inference that Saddam Hussein's resistance to inspections indicated that he held weapons of mass destruction, though erroneous, played a critical role in convincing the public and the international community that war was warranted.

You might wonder why an entire chapter is dedicated to attributional processes, given that attributions are merely a particular type of inference. We believe that a detailed examination of attributional processes is warranted for several reasons. First, attribution has been a central topic of interest to social psychologists for many decades. Theorizing about how people explain behavior can be traced to Heider (1944, 1958), who argued that people try to locate the causes of behavior as being due to *internal* or *external* factors. Heider's theorizing, which we develop below, inspired a considerable amount of research examining how people explain their own and others' behavior. Within several years, attribution became one of the most active areas of research in social psychology. The 1970s has been referred to as "the decade of attribution theory in social psychology" (Weiner, 1985a, p. 74).

Second, attribution theories have always been notably focused on cognitive processes. All the theories we discuss in this chapter concern how available information is used to make inferences about the causes of an event. Factors such as selective attention, expectancies, and interpretation play central roles in attributional theories, even though directly studying these factors was difficult. Given the focus of attribution theories on cognitive processes, they inspired and played a critical role in the eventual development of social cognition (Hamilton & Carlston, 2013).

Third, attributions about the causes of events are some of the most critical inferences we make. Attributional thinking is central in many aspects of our lives, ranging from self-regulation ("Why do I overeat?") to impressions of others ("How come he behaves so aggressively at work?"), relationships ("Why is she ignoring me today?"), economic events ("What is causing housing prices to skyrocket?"), political events ("Why is the president so unpopular?"), and, as our opening example attests, even international relations. One could argue that much of our legal system is dedicated to making causal attributions (McGillis, 1978). Decisions about the causes of events have significant consequences for individuals, groups, and institutions.

Fourth, and finally, attribution deserves a distinct focus because the processes used to infer causes are different from those used to infer dispositions (Gawronski, 2004; Hamilton, 1988, 1998; Hilton, Smith, & Kin, 1995; Krull, 2001; Smith & Miller, 1983). Dispositional inferences can influence attributional analyses. However, determining why an event has occurred goes beyond inferring dispositions. Malle (2003, pp. 1–2) succinctly describes some of the differences between trait (dispositional) and explanatory (causal) inferences: "explanations sometimes refer to traits but often do not; trait inferences can be explanatory but usually are not; traits can be inferred from any behavior, whereas explanations are triggered only by surprising or confusing behavior; explanations are answers to why questions, trait inferences are not."

Later, we will return to a more detailed discussion of the differences between dispositional and attributional processes. In the meantime, we offer the following example to illustrate the distinction between dispositional and causal inferences. Imagine that you are a juror in a murder case, and the defendant is a large, fierce-looking man who rides with the Hell's Angels. Based on his appearance and your knowledge of motorcycle gangs, you might spontaneously infer that he is a tough guy, has a short temper, and is prone to violence. However, that dispositional inference says very little about whether he committed this particular crime. To make that causal judgment, you and your fellow jurors will need to consider additional information about this specific event ("How did the victim die?" "What might have motivated the biker to kill this person?"). Dispositional inferences will be of limited value in making a causal determination, which will depend on (among other factors) forensic evidence, eyewitness testimony, and character witnesses. Once you receive all this information, you will engage with other jurors in a laborious process of considering the usefulness of all the evidence to make a causal attribution. This example illustrates that dispositional inferences may play a role in making attributions, but causal reasoning usually requires a broader array of information and more considerable deliberation.

Causal attributions and dispositional inferences are also affected by different factors. Some variables that influence dispositional inferences do not affect attributions and vice versa. These differences are highlighted by some of the questions we will ask to explore attribution. First, when do people consider and analyze the cause of some behavior or event? Do they always engage in attributional analysis, or does this occur only under certain conditions? If so, what are those conditions? Second, what are the properties of attributions? Do the same properties define all attributions, or are there different types of attributions that differ in specific ways? If so, what are the implications of those differences? Third, and perhaps most fundamentally, how are attributions made? Given some behavior or event to be explained, how is that achieved? What are the processes underlying attributional judgments? Attempts to answer this last question have generated several theories aimed at explaining the attribution process.

WHEN DO WE ASK "WHY"?

As we know from the previous chapter, many inferences are made spontaneously, without requiring intent or giving rise to the perceiver's awareness. Inferences often just happen. In contrast, attributional inferences are less likely to occur spontaneously and are more likely to be conditional, occurring in some circumstances but not in others. It would consume significant cognitive resources to consistently ask ourselves why *every* mundane and predictable event occurred ("Why did the mail get delivered today?" "Why did that person say hello?"). Instead, we engage in attributional analysis when identifying the cause of an event is seen as particularly important (such as when a significant event occurs) or useful (such as when we want to develop a detailed impression of a person).

One important factor that triggers attributional processing is the violation of expectations (Gendolla & Koller, 2001; McGill, 1989; Weiner, 1985a). When normal, routine, expected events occur, we rarely are prompted to wonder why they happened. When something unusual, out of the ordinary, or unexpected occurs, it captures our attention, and we seek to explain what caused it to happen. In other words, unexpected events stimulate attributional analysis by prompting us to ask the "Why?" question.

In one study demonstrating this point (Hastie, 1984), participants were asked to form impressions of several individuals based on descriptions of behaviors they had supposedly performed. For each target person, two-thirds of the behaviors implied a specific trait (e.g., "won the chess tournament" implying *intelligence*), and one-third of the behaviors were inconsistent with that trait (e.g., "couldn't remember where he put his wallet"). After participants read all the sentences and formed an impression of each person, they were presented the sentences again and asked to write "continuations" that could be added to each one (e.g., "won the chess tournament _____"). After these continuations were generated, participants were asked to recall as many of the behavioral descriptions as they could.

The primary analyses in the studies focused on the nature of the continuations that were generated for behaviors that were consistent versus inconsistent with the person's dominant trait. To do so, the continuations for each behavior were coded as reflecting *explanations* (Why was the act performed?), *elaborations* (What were the circumstances when the act occurred?), or *temporal successions* (What happened after the act occurred?). For example, a participant might continue the sentence "won the chess tournament" with "because he had spent many hours playing against challenging competition" (a causal explanation), with "in which several dozen people competed" (an elaboration), or by writing "and then went out to celebrate" (a succession). Only the first of these would be considered a causal attribution because it was the only continuation explaining why the behavior (winning the tournament) occurred.

The most common category of continuations by far was elaborations, constituting 69% of the responses to the items. Explanations represented only 24% of the continuations, demonstrating that participants did not spontaneously generate attributions to explain all behaviors. However, and more importantly, the frequency of explanations varied as a function of whether the behavior was expected or unexpected. Participants generally did not try to explain behaviors that were consistent with targets' dominant traits (only 18% of trait-consistent behaviors prompted explanations). In contrast, when the target did something atypical and unexpected, approximately 31% of the continuations were explanations. Not only were these behaviors more likely to trigger attributional responses, but they were also better remembered in free recall. In other words, the same information that prompted the generation of causal explanations was also most likely to be remembered. Other studies have also shown that actions or events that are surprising or inconsistent with general expectations prompt us to explain why they occurred (Clary & Tesser, 1983; Pyszczynski & Greenberg, 1981; Susskind et al., 1999).

Several other factors can promote causal attributions. The experience of success or failure often triggers attributional processing as people try to explain why they experienced an outcome. There is informational value in explaining both achievements and our disappointments (Weiner, 1985b). After a positive achievement, causal explanations allow identification of the reasons we succeeded, allowing us to try to replicate the same conditions in the future. After failure, causal attributions enable us to identify the factors that led to poor performance, allowing us to modify our behavior to reduce the likelihood that we will again fail. Given that the costs of failure often exceed the benefits of success, people are particularly likely to engage in attributional analysis of unfavorable outcomes (Weiner, 1985a). Explanations for results of political elections (Folkes & Morgenstern, 1981), sporting events (Lau, 1984), and business performance (Bettman & Weitz, 1983) all tend to focus more on explaining failure than accounting for success.

Attributional processes are also triggered when we are experiencing a low sense of control. Humans have a fundamental motive to achieve and maintain a sense of mastery and control, and events that make us feel like we have little power prompt analyses to determine why these events are occurring. Understanding the causes of these behaviors and events should help restore a sense of control when it is threatened. As Kelley (1972) succinctly argued, "The purpose of causal analysis – the function that it serves – is effective control" (p. 220).

Several studies provide evidence of increased attributional processing under low control conditions (Burger & Hemans, 1988; Pittman & D'Agostino, 1985). In one study (Pittman & Pittman, 1980), participants completed a series of tasks, and their sense of control was varied by manipulating the feedback they were provided about their performance. Some participants were given no feedback, but others received random, noncontingent feedback. The noncontingent feedback induced a low sense of control, as evidenced in these participants being more distracted and more dejected than participants who received no feedback. Later, participants read an essay on a political issue, after having been told either that the author had been paid a large amount of money to write it or that it was from his personal journal. Presumably, this should affect causal judgments regarding why the essay was written. Participants were later asked questions such as "external influences probably caused him to write this particular essay" and "internal influences due to some dispositions, characteristics, or personal opinions of this particular author caused him to write this particular essay." Participants who had received noncontingent feedback (low control condition) were affected by the information about the writer's motives. Participants who had not been given any feedback (and therefore had a high sense of control) did not differentiate in their attributional judgments of the essay that had been paid for versus one that reflected the writer's private opinion. Thus, depriving people of control increased their desire to learn about others, facilitating causal analysis of others' behavior. This finding was conceptually replicated in a later study in which individual differences in desire for control were measured rather than manipulated (Burger & Hemans, 1988).

Attributional analysis also occurs when an issue is highly involving (e.g., Pittman, Scherrer, & Wright, 1977) or when a person will be directly affected by an event (e.g., Harkness, DeBono, & Borgida, 1985). Whenever personal involvement is high, people strive to have a good understanding of the causes of the events they observe or experience in order to maintain a sense of predictability and control. For example, people are more likely to engage in attributional processes in response to a person with whom we expect to interact in the future (e.g., Harvey, Yarkin, Lightner, & Town, 1980; Knight & Vallacher, 1981; Yarkin-Levin, 1983). Think about when you met your first new friend at college. You probably took close note of her behavior, especially in the early days you spent together, noting her appearance, her preferences, and her words and actions. Acts that you typically might not think much about ("Why does she have so many boxes of pasta?" "Why does she watch sports all the time?") often are the focus of attention, analysis, and speculation. Answering these "why?" questions gives us hope for success in later interactions.

In sum, attributional processes occur quite frequently, but not always. They arise primarily in response to only certain types of events. Unexpected and adverse events trigger a search for causal information. We tend to make causal judgments when we feel like we have little control in a situation or when processing information about an event that affects us directly. In each case, attributional processes help us understand why an event has occurred, providing a sense of predictability and control and allowing us to learn from experience.

PROPERTIES OF CAUSAL ATTRIBUTIONS

"Why did he steal that bread?" "What caused the stock market to drop today?" "Why did the President cancel the meeting with the foreign leader?" These are very different questions from different life domains, and they would generate very different specific causal attributions. Attribution theories do not try to predict the exact attribution used to explain an event ("He stole the bread because his daughter was hungry" vs. "He stole the bread as a prank"). Instead, theories focus on understanding the dimensions along which different causal explanations vary (e.g., is the cause due to an internal or external factor? is the causal factor stable or unstable?). Indeed, some have argued that specific causal judgments are of little importance in themselves; their significance comes from their dimensional properties, which in turn affect subsequent judgments and responses (Weiner, 1985b). Therefore, before considering attribution theories in detail, we first discuss these fundamental properties, with the recognition that each of them can be viewed as a continuum rather than a dichotomy (Passer, Kelley, & Michela, 1978).

Intentionality

Intentionality pertains to whether behavior or events are seen as deliberate or inadvertent. Intentional acts are purposive, done willfully to achieve a particular outcome by implementing behavior that is expected to produce that outcome (Malle, 1999). Consider the following behavior that would unambiguously imply intentionality: "The man pushed the rock, causing it to tumble down the hill." Because the act is intentional, it would raise immediate questions about the man's dispositions and motives that caused him to engage in the behavior. In Heider's view, people explain intentional actions by seeking the "reasons behind the intention" (Heider, 1958, p. 110). In contrast, an action reflects low intentionality when it occurs without human involvement ("the rock tumbled down the hill") or when the event occurred independently of or even in opposition to the wishes of a human actor ("the man leaned on the rock, causing it to tumble down the hill"). The perceived intentionality of an action (which itself can be ambiguous, requiring inference processes) plays a critical role in determining specific causal attributions.

Locus

The locus of causality is one of the most fundamental and salient dimensions underlying causal explanations (Weiner, 2018) and distinguishes between internal and external causes of behavior (Heider, 1958). Internal causes attribute the behavior to the actor's intentions, goals, motives, or dispositions, whereas external cases attribute the behavior to properties of the social context, including another person's behavior and attributes of the event. Consider the following example (Gilbert, 1998, p. 96) showing how numerous pieces of information might be used to explain an at-bat in baseball:

> If a pitcher who wishes to retire a batter (motivation) throws a burning fastball (action) directly into the wind (environmental influence), then the observer should conclude that the pitcher has a particularly strong arm (ability). If a batter tries to hit that ball (motivation) but fails (action), then the observer should conclude that the batter lacked coordination (ability) or was blinded by the sun (environmental influence).

Although people can generate elaborate causal explanations blending internal and external causes of behavior (Kammrath, Mendoza-Denton, & Mischel, 2005), they often do not. Instead, causal explanations generally emphasize one over the other, reflecting people's general preference for simple over complicated explanations (Johnson, Valenti, & Keil, 2019; Lombrozo, 2007). Moreover, people generally prefer internal attributions (Ross, 1977), especially to the degree that the actor (rather than aspects of the situation) grabs the perceiver's attention (McArthur, 1981). With some notable exceptions (discussed later), perceivers generally try to factor out (and may simply be insensitive to) situational influences and instead focus on internal factors (a person's dispositions, goals, or motives) to explain behavior.

Stability

The stability dimension refers to whether causal factors are seen as temporary or permanent (Weiner, 1985b; Weiner, Frieze, Kukla, Reed, Rest, & Rosenbaum, 1972). Both internal and external explanations of events can differ regarding their perceived stability. I might succeed on a Math test due to stable or unstable internal factors – I am good with numbers (i.e., ability, a stable attribution) – or because I studied particularly hard for it (i.e., effort, an internal but unstable attribution). Or my outcome may reflect the influence of external factors – because the teacher always gives easy tests (i.e., task difficulty, stable) – or because this particular test was easy (i.e., luck, unstable). The stability implied by various attributions affects the perceived probability of similar outcomes in the future. If a causal explanation focuses on a stable (internal or external) factor, then consistency might be expected, and things might need to change substantially to overcome that factor. In contrast, temporary factors are less informative about future outcomes.

Controllability

Controllability refers to whether a causal factor is modifiable or cannot be changed. Events caused by controllable factors presumably would not have occurred in the absence of that factor. Hence, attributing blame for adverse events and credit for positive events depends on perceived controllability. If a bridge collapses due to a massive earthquake, it will be viewed as an unavoidable (uncontrollable) tragedy. If that same bridge falls due to poor construction or the negligence of an engineer or builder (controllable factors), it will be judged quite differently, likely producing investigations to establish the liability of responsible parties.

Importantly, controllability is not the same as locus. Although internal causes are often under a person's control, external causes are not necessarily uncontrollable. For example, a student's poor performance might be caused by an ineffective teacher, a factor external to the student. Although the student cannot control the teacher's instructional skills, it is under the control of other entities (e.g., parents, the school board). Consistent with this idea is research that theoretically and empirically distinguished events that are seen as controllable by the self (personal control), by others (external control), and by no one (uncontrollable) (McAuley, Duncan, & Russell, 1992).

In sum, causal attributions differ on a set of fundamental dimensions. Differences on these dimensions will affect how an event is explained and who is held responsible. It will influence how people react emotionally and respond to that event. To return to our earlier example, if your jury concluded that the victim's death resulted from pre-meditated actions of the biker (intentional, internal, stable, and controllable characteristics), then a finding of guilt on a murder charge and a severe sentence would likely result. If that same event was attributed to self-defense (e.g., low intentionality, external, unstable, and uncontrollable cause), the biker might be convicted of a lesser charge or perhaps even be exonerated.

THEORIES OF CAUSAL ATTRIBUTION

Over the last half century, several different theories of attribution have been advanced. These theories differ in the situations where they are applicable (e.g., observations of a single behavior vs. multiple behaviors), the kinds of events they explain (e.g., explanations of behavior vs. outcomes), and the dimensions that are important (e.g., intentionality vs. stability). However, the theories all share a focus on understanding the fundamental aspects of causal judgments, assuming that the properties underlying causal judgments are important for knowing the specific causal attribution that is made. In the following sections, we discuss several major theoretical approaches to attribution, highlighting how they have built upon one another in understanding how people explain the behaviors and events they encounter.

We begin by introducing Heider's (1958) original ideas about *phenomenal causality*, a phrase he used to describe the ways we make subjective judgments about the causes of intentional events. Heider introduced many of the concepts, terms, and distinctions used in subsequent accounts of attribution. We then turn to significant theories of attribution that extended and built upon Heider's formulations, discussing both the domains in which each theory is most directly applicable and the evidence relevant to the claims of each approach.

The Foundation: Heider's Phenomenal Causality

As we discussed in the introductory chapter of this book, Heider (1958) was primarily responsible for introducing the construct of *attribution* into the field of social psychology. He viewed attribution as a process focused on understanding how people make sense of others' behaviors, suggesting that "the ordinary person has a great and profound understanding of himself and of other people" (p. 2). He argued that people derive this knowledge by engaging in "common-sense psychology," using a set of common and interrelated concepts to explain the behavior of the self and others. These intuitive theories (or "lay theories;" Böhm & Pfister, 2015) involve consideration of the roles of several possible causal factors (e.g., ability, effort, task difficulty, and luck) to account for behaviors and events.

Heider was interested in the *naïve psychology* of the everyday person. He viewed people as "intuitive theorists" (Ross, 1977, 2018) who try to understand the regularities in the behaviors of others and themselves. People are motivated to understand these regularities in order to increase their ability to predict the future, to anticipate the behavior of others with whom they interact. Why would perceivers be so motivated? The answer is quite simple. If people can accurately predict how others will act, then they can increase the effectiveness of their interactions by guiding their own behavior accordingly. Therefore, Heider's thinking focused on the ways people seek and identify stable properties ("invariances") in people's behaviors and the environment. Explaining behavior through stable, invariant characteristics lends meaning and order to the large amount of behavioral information confronted in even the simplest social environment. Also, if the stable factors that caused an event can be identified, then people will be better at predicting what might occur in the future. He argued that perceivers make inferences about people's abilities ("can") and about their motives ("want"), and in doing so, they seek to identify the bases of regularity that govern people's behaviors.

Heider proposed that people engage in different attributional processes for intentional and unintentional events. For unintentional behaviors and events, perceivers focus on *impersonal causality*. In explaining an earthquake or a person's sneeze, people will point to factors in the environment that produced the event or the behavior. It would not make sense to attribute these events to characteristics of the actor since they were unintended. Instead, these kinds of events are explained in terms of situational factors that are seen as facilitating the event ("he sneezed because the room was dusty").

However, when behavior is seen as intentional, people engage in *personal causality*. They attempt to identify the cause of the action by focusing on the dispositions, motives, and goals of the person who performed the behavior. The focus begins on the actor because, in Heider's view, people are "action centers" that have abilities, wishes, and sentiments enabling them to affect us. They can benefit or harm us intentionally, and we can benefit or harm them. Heider (1958, p. 21) argued that persons "can act purposefully, and can perceive or watch us." An actor's success or failure in accomplishing an intended action depends upon factors involving the actor (his or her effort or ability in performing the intended action) and factors in the situation that determine whether the action is successful (opportunity or favorable conditions) or unsuccessful (lousy luck or challenging conditions).

An essential part of Heider's naïve psychology concerned how everyday people come to understand the causes of the behaviors they observe. That is, how do people explain why a person engaged in a behavior? As noted earlier, Heider introduced the important distinction between *internal* causes (factors originating within the actor including traits, motives, and abilities) and *external* causes (factors existing outside the actor that allow or inhibit the action) for both intended and unintended events. This distinction continues to be pervasive in virtually all theories of attribution.

Kelley's Covariation Model of Attribution

Harold Kelley (1967) extended Heider's theorizing by developing a formal model accounting for how people decide whether an event was internally or externally caused. Kelly proposed that several different categories of information are typically available that can be used to determine why an event occurred. Specifically, in making causal attributions, people tend to focus on variables that covary with the event that is being explained. In Kelley's words, "the effect is attributed to that condition which is present when the effect is present and which is absent when the effect is absent" (p. 194). Hence Kelley's theory is called the *Covariation Model* of attribution.

In this model, perceivers consider three categories of information in attributing causality for a person's behavior toward a person or object at a given time and circumstance. He referred to these sources of information as *consistency*, *distinctiveness*, and *consensus*. *Consistency* refers to the degree that the observed person (i.e., the actor) behaves in the same way toward the same object or person at other times. For example, if a person behaves in a friendly manner when meeting a new person, is he also friendly when he interacts with that person at a later time? *Distinctiveness* refers to whether the individual behaves similarly toward other objects or persons. If a person is friendly when meeting a new person, is he also friendly when meeting other people or just toward this person? *Consensus* refers to how other people behave toward the object or person in the same situation that is being observed. That is, are other people also being friendly towards this new person, or is he the only one acting that way? In Kelley's model, these three classes of information are integrated to identify whether the *person* (i.e., the *actor*), the *stimulus* (i.e., the *target*), the *situation* (i.e., the *occasion* or *circumstances*), or a combination of the three will be judged as having caused the event.

These ideas may seem complicated in the abstract. However, a simple example can illustrate how different combinations of consistency, distinctiveness, and consensus can point clearly to the cause of a behavior, specifically whether it was due to internal or external factors. Imagine that you are in a large class, listening to a lecture. You notice that your friend, Ivan, sitting next to you has fallen asleep. You wonder, "Why is he snoozing in class?" You can use your knowledge about your friend's history and your observations about others' behavior to answer this question. You would likely think about the consistency of this behavior (Does Ivan always sleep in this class or just today?) and its distinctiveness (Does he also sleep in other classes or just this one?). You would probably look around the room to assess consensus (Is anyone else here asleep or is Ivan the only one?). If consistency is high (he always sleeps in this class), distinctiveness is low (he also sleeps in a lot of his other classes), and consensus is low (no one else is sleeping), it becomes clear that Ivan has a habit of sleeping in his classes. His behavior will be attributed to an internal, stable cause.

What if just one element is altered? If distinctiveness is high rather than low (he doesn't usually sleep in other classes), then that would change the attribution. In this case, you would assume that Ivan finds this particular class to be boring. It will still be an internal attribution because Ivan often sleeps in this class (high consistency), and no one else in the class is sleeping (low consensus) – they appear to find the class interesting, but Ivan does not. What if instead consensus was high so that several other people are also sleeping in class? In that case, you would infer that something about the class is causing this behavior – the lecturer might be boring, the topic might be dull, or perhaps even both might be true. Additional information might be needed to tease apart these two possibilities (is consensus high over time, so that many people regularly sleep through the professor's lectures, or low, suggesting that today's lecture is particularly uninteresting?). It would also be possible that something in the situation itself (say, a hot, stuffy lecture hall) is causing everyone to sleep. However, it would be clear that in such a case, the behavior would be attributed to a cause that is external to the actors.

A strength of this model is that it describes how people can use different pieces of available information to easily identify whether a particular behavior was caused by a characteristic of the actor (the sleeping student), a characteristic of the target (the boring professor), an aspect of the situation (a stuffy room), or a combination of factors. Various combinations of high versus low constancy, distinctiveness, and consensus logically blend to identify the general causes of an event (in the actor, the target, the situation, or combinations thereof) (see Table 8.1). In the first study testing this model (McArthur, 1972), participants were provided with a behavior to be explained (John laughed at the comedian) along with other statements providing high or low consistency, distinctiveness, and consensus information. Participants then indicated whether the behavior was due to something about the actor (an internal cause) or the situation (an external cause). The results provided support for Kelley's model. Consistent with Kelley's

Table 8.1 Covariation and causal attribution from consistency (CIS), distinctiveness (DIS), and consensus (CEN)

CIS	DIS	CEN	Attribution
High	High	High	External (Target)
High	Low	High	Ambiguous
High	Low	Low	Internal (Actor × Target Interaction)
High	Low	Low	Internal (Actor)
Low	High	High	External (Target × Situation Interaction)
Low	Low	High	External (Situation)
Low	High	Low	Internal (Actor × Situation × Target)
Low	Low	Low	Internal (Actor × Situation)

Source: Based on Hewstone & Jaspers (1987)

theorizing, research has shown that modifying information about the consistency, distinctiveness, and consensus of any observed behavior typically produces different causal explanations (Hewstone & Jaspers, 1987).

Despite these strengths, the model is not well equipped to identify what specific causal attribution will be made. For example, if Ivan rarely naps in this class (low consistency), doesn't usually nap in other classes (high distinctiveness), and is the only student napping (low consensus), this suggests that the behavior should be explained with an internal attribution. However, the correct specific internal attribution is unclear. There is something about Ivan that is causing him to sleep today, but it is not completely clear what that might be. Does he not like the specific topic of today's lecture? Did he have a late night last night? Is he not feeling well? All of these internal attributions might explain the behavior, but it is not possible to disambiguate the exact reason why he is napping. Additional information, such as knowing how he has behaved during other lectures on this topic or how late he was up the night before, would be needed to disentangle these possible causal explanations (Cheng & Novick, 1990).

Kelley's (1967) covariation model and McArthur's (1972) experiment testing it stimulated a considerable amount of additional research (e.g., Feldman, Higgins, Karlovac, & Ruble, 1976; Hewstone, 1989; Kelley & Michela, 1980; Orvis, Cunningham, & Kelley, 1975; Ruble & Feldman, 1976; Zuckerman, 1978) providing further tests of the model, identifying its limitations, and generating new theoretical accounts.

Kelley's Causal Schemas

Although Kelley's covariation model described a strategy by which observers could engage in a systematic analysis of covariation to determine causality, he also recognized that critical information is often missing. We might not have the opportunity to observe a person's behavior across situations (limiting access to distinctiveness information), we might see the person behave only once in a given situation (limiting consistency information), or we might see behavior in isolation (reducing consensus information). On these occasions, Kelley (1972) argued that we fill in missing information by using our more general mental representations about how and when specific effects are produced (what he called *causal schemas*). For example, if a person professes to like a rock band in front of someone she knows also loves the group, this provides potentially valuable information about what caused the behavior (i.e., a desire to impress this individual). In making this attribution, we rely on our general beliefs about what accounts for behavior in particular circumstances.

Kelley also proposed that when behavioral information is limited, perceivers rely on two complementary principles: discounting and augmentation. *Discounting* refers to the principle that "the role of a given cause in producing a given effect is discounted if other plausible causes are also present" (Kelley, 1972, p. 8). Kelley labeled this the *multiple sufficient causes schema*. In other words, when several causes would provide sufficient explanations for an event, the influence of any one cause can be reduced due to the presence of the other causes. For example, you would not assume that high intelligence accounted for a student's test score of 90% when the class average was 95% (suggesting that the test was very easy). Because the test appears to have been unchallenging (an external attribution), this should reduce the degree that an internal attribution is warranted. The principle of *augmentation* states, "if for a given effect, both a plausible inhibitory cause and a plausible facilitative cause are present, the role of the facilitative cause in producing the effect will be judged greater" (p. 12). Kelley referred to this as the *multiple necessary causes schema*. To continue the above example, you would likely augment the causal role of a student's intelligence in obtaining 90% if the class average was 45% (suggesting that the test was tough). In this case, the student's success means that she overcame obstacles (the inhibitory influence of test difficulty). Research has confirmed that people do regularly engage in augmentation and discounting in making causal attributions, along with (Van Overwalle & Van Rooy, 2001) or in the absence of (Kruglanski, Schwartz, Maides, & Hamel, 1978) covariation information.

Weiner's Attribution Theory of Achievement Motivation

Bernard Weiner (1979, 1985b) extended Kelley's work in several important respects. First, he examined attributions for people's outcomes rather than their behaviors. Rather than trying to account for judgments of a person's actions ("Why did she ask her out on a date?"), he focused instead on how people explain what subsequently occurred ("Why did she turn her down?"). Second, with this emphasis on outcomes, Weiner focused in particular on how people explain success and failure. Third, given that most people strive for success and hope to avoid failure, his approach allowed important roles for motivational and emotional factors in understanding causal attribution. With these differences in focus, Weiner invoked a new set of considerations that play important roles in causal judgments.

In Weiner's (1985b, 1986) analysis, explanations for success and failure require more than determining their *locus* (i.e., whether the outcome resulted from an internal or external cause). In his view, the value of causal attributions is their ability to help us repeat positive events and avoid negative ones. Therefore, we usually want to know *precisely what it was* in ourselves, another person, or the situation that led to the result we experienced. To do so, people consider two additional dimensions of attribution we discussed earlier: stability and controllability. Simultaneously considering locus (internal versus external), stability (stable versus unstable), and controllability (under one's control versus not under one's control) produces a broad array of more specific reasons for explaining success or failure. In explaining achievement outcomes, the most common perceived causes of success and failure are ability and effort (Cooper & Burger, 1980). That is, success is usually seen as arising from intelligence and/or hard work, whereas failure is generally attributed to low ability and/or a lack of effort. Other attributions that occur less frequently differ in locus, controllability, and stability (e.g., bad luck, a biased referee, an unfair teacher, illness). Table 8.2 shows how these three factors can combine to influence causal attributions for failure.

Table 8.2 Examples of attributions for failure and success based on locus (internal vs. external), stability (stable vs. unstable), and controllability (controllable vs. uncontrollable)

	Internal		External	
	Stable	**Unstable**	**Stable**	**Unstable**
Controllable				
Failure	*Chronic low effort*	*Unusual low effort*	*Biased other*	*Low help*
Success	*Chronic high effort*	*Rare high effort*	*Consistent help*	*Rare help*
Uncontrollable				
Failure	*Innate low ability*	*Bad mood/illness*	*Task difficulty*	*Bad luck*
Success	*Innate high ability*	*Good mood*	*Task ease*	*Good luck*

Source: Based on Weiner (1985b)

The consequences of these different attributions can be profound, and Weiner's model has been used extensively in settings such as schools (Bembenutty, 2015) and organizations (Dasborough, Harvey, & Martinko, 2011). Much of this research has focused on four kinds of attributions that differ in three properties: attributions to ability (an internal, stable, uncontrollable factor), effort (an internal, unstable, controllable factor), task difficulty (an external, stable, uncontrollable factor), and luck (an external, unstable, uncontrollable factor). These attributions are of particular interest because they produce markedly different affective and motivational consequences (Weiner, 1986). For example, research has shown that people's willingness to help an AIDS patient depended on the attributions for and accompanying emotional responses to the person's illness (Badahdah & Alkhder, 2006; Rudolph, Roesch, Greitemeyer, & Weiner, 2004). If the person was not seen as responsible for his condition (e.g., the disease was contracted through a blood transfusion), people responded with pity and a desire to help. However, if the person was seen as responsible for his condition (e.g., he had engaged in unprotected sex), then anger and an unwillingness to help were more common. Thus, attributions of responsibility can have significant repercussions.

Research has also shown that attributions to ability versus effort are critical in determining how people respond to task outcomes (Dweck & Yeager, 2019; Weiner, Heckhausen, & Meyer, 1972). For example, when failure on a task is attributed to low effort, people typically show greater engagement and persistence when they again attempt the task. In contrast, attributing failure to low ability produces anxiety and, since low ability is typically viewed as stable, people expect little possibility of a different outcome if they re-attempt the task. Therefore, under these conditions, people often avoid challenging tasks and, when they do attempt them, persistence decreases. In contrast, attributing failure to external factors can buffer the typical negative affective consequences that usually arise, leaving self-confidence and belief in one's capabilities intact (Norem & Cantor, 1986). Indeed, external attributions for failure are often generated even before a task is attempted, a phenomenon termed *self-handicapping* (Berglas & Jones, 1978; Zuckerman, Kieffer, & Knee, 1998). Doing so allows an unsatisfactory outcome to be pre-explained by an external, unstable, uncontrollable impediment (e.g., "Before I take this test, you should know I got very little sleep last night because of a noisy party next door"). Self-handicapping can also allow a positive outcome to be seen in an especially favorable light since it required overcoming the impediment.

These effects are moderated by beliefs about the nature of traits, however. Dweck and her colleagues (Dweck, 1999, 2006; Dweck & Leggett, 1988; Gunderson, Sorhagen, Gripshover, Dweck, Goldin-Meadow, & Levine, 2018; Heyman & Dweck, 1998) have shown that different attributions can produce divergent responses depending on the person's beliefs, or *implicit theories*, about the nature of ability. Dweck's research differentiates a *fixed mindset* (or *entity theory*) – the idea that traits are stable and unlikely to change – from a *growth mindset* (or *incremental theory*) – the belief that traits can change over time and context. A fixed mindset tends to produce avoidance on tasks where people struggle. For these people, struggle is seen as a signal that one does not possess the ability to do well on the task. Because they believe that intelligence is fixed, they place a high value on success and are concerned that failure, or even having to exert effort to succeed, will be perceived (by themselves and others) as evidence of low ability. Therefore, people operating with a fixed mindset (either due to chronic differences or experimental manipulations) seek out tasks that will allow them to perform well and avoid tasks that might reveal low ability.

In contrast, people operating under a growth mindset, who view intelligence as malleable and unstable, possibly increased through effort and persistence, are more likely to seek out and persist on challenging tasks (Dweck, Chiu, & Hong, 1995). For these individuals, struggle suggests a failure of effort or strategies, implying that success can be achieved if either factor is changed. These students strive for mastery, show greater perseverance on challenging tasks, and seek out challenges that they believe will help them develop intellectually.

The research on implicit theories also highlights the potential benefits of altering the specific attributions described in Weiner's model. If success is attributed to a stable and uncontrollable cause (e.g., innate intelligence), then subsequent challenges that potentially could reveal low ability might be avoided. Alternatively, attributing success to an unstable and controllable characteristic (e.g., high effort) could produce greater persistence when a student is struggling. Mueller and Dweck (1998) demonstrated the consequences of changing attributions for achievement by varying the praise provided to students for success on a task that was challenging but easy enough to complete. One group of students was praised for their intelligence ("You must be smart at this"), a second group received praise for their effort ("You must have worked really hard"), and a third group in a control condition received no feedback.

Students were then asked to choose their next task from a set of options that varied in difficulty. The majority of children who were praised for their intelligence on the previous task selected a task that appeared to be easy. In contrast, most of the students who had been commended for effort chose a challenging task. Thus, the attributions for success in the first task influenced whether children wanted an easy task that would presumably allow them to look intelligent or a task that would provide additional challenges and opportunities for growth.

In a subsequent study, students again completed a task where their success was attributed to ability or effort. In this study, they were given a second task that was much more challenging than the first. Researchers asked the students how much they desired to work on the task (i.e., persistence) and how much they had enjoyed it. As can be seen in Figure 8.1, students who had been praised for intelligence enjoyed the second task less and showed lower persistence and interest than did students who had been praised for effort.

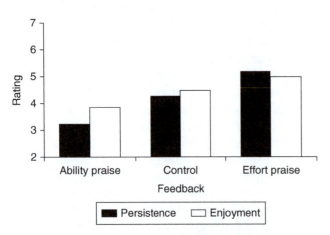

Figure 8.1 Students' average self-reported task persistence and enjoyment as a function of feedback condition
Source: Based on data from Mueller & Dweck (1998)

Another study extended this paradigm further. Students who had been praised for success on a first task were again presented a more challenging second task but were told that they had performed poorly on it. For students who had been praised for ability, this feedback presumably raised questions about their ability to do well on the task being presented. For those students who had initially been praised for effort, this failure feedback was expected to convey information about the need to increase effort or to modify strategies. All students were then given a final task that was as easy as the first. The students whose initial success had been attributed to ability performed poorly on this third task, even though it was just as easy as the first task. In contrast, the students whose success had been attributed to effort performed even better on this task than they had before. The attributions communicated through praise differentially equipped students to succeed in subsequent challenges. These studies illustrate that significant consequences can flow from differing attributions for success and failure (Gunderson et al., 2018).

Malle's Folk-conceptual Theory of Explanation

Bertram Malle's folk-conceptual theory focused on causal explanations for *intended* actions, what Heider (1958) characterized as *personal causality*. In Malle's view, previous theories of attribution had abandoned the critical distinction that Heider drew between intentional and unintentional behavior. He argued, for example, that Kelley's model could account for judgments of unintentional events but not intentional actions (Malle, 2004). Consider a behavior that clearly involves intent: "Adele swore at the sales clerk." Adele chose to engage in this behavior, so some internal attribution would be required. However, Malle argued that although covariation information would implicate the actor (low consensus, low distinctiveness, high consistency), it would provide virtually no information about the precise reason why Adele swore. To generate such an explanation would require the perceiver to gather more information about the intent of the actor, his goals, and his moods and emotions. More generally, Malle has argued that theories of inference and attribution had focused too much on dispositions and traits, neglecting the critical role of mental states that produce intentional actions (Korman & Malle, 2016).

Malle's research has focused on identifying how perceivers use lay theories or "folk concepts" about intentional behavior to generate causal explanations. Malle and Knobe (1997) showed in several studies that people generally agree about the meaning and features of intentional actions. In one study, participants were given descriptions of behaviors and asked to judge the degree of intent behind each action. Half of the participants were given a definition of intentionality before they read the behaviors (intentionality "means that the person had a reason to do what she did and that she chose to do so"), but the other participants were not. In both conditions, there was a high degree of agreement in judgments of perceived intent. Participants agreed that actions such as "Annie watered her plants" showed a high degree of intentionality but that "Annie is sweating" did not.

In another study, participants were asked to name the features of actions that make them appear intentional. These spontaneously-generated features reflected several general themes: (1) A person must show *volition* (referred to as "intent" by Malle & Knobe, 1997) to act, often by suggesting that the person must "decide to do something"; (2) A second feature was *belief*, indicated by comments such as "a person must think about an action and its consequences"; (3) A third commonly mentioned feature was *desire*, as reflected in the comment "does it in hopes of getting some result"; (4) A fourth theme was *awareness* (e.g., "must know what you are doing"); (5) The fifth feature was skill, reflecting the ability to enact the intention. Although perceivers typically use these criteria quite effortlessly in judging causes, they can consider these factors quite systematically and thoroughly in situations involving doubt or dispute, such as a courtroom (Malle & Nelson, 2003).

In these studies, perceivers' causal explanations were assessed by examining the everyday language they use to describe the reasons for others' actions. Research using this approach has shown that people generate both distal and proximate explanations of behavior (Malle, 2011). Distal explanations appeal to background factors, such as a person's upbringing, personality, culture, or unconscious processes. Explaining actions with these distal factors is termed *causal history of reason explanations*. More proximate *reasons* involve inferences about what precisely the person had in mind when deciding to act. Perceivers engage in both forms of causal reasoning. However, reasons are used more than causal history explanations when people try to appear rational (Malle, Knobe, O'Laughlin, Pearce, & Nelson, 2000), when they are explaining the actions of individuals rather than groups (O'Laughlin & Malle, 2002), and when explaining their own actions rather than the actions of others (Malle, Knobe, & Nelson, 2007).

As noted earlier, most attribution studies focus on distinguishing between person and situation attributions. The "person" is represented by the dispositions of the person as she is now, her traits, goals, attitudes. Similarly, the "situation" refers to the immediate context in which the behavior-to-be-explained has occurred (the physical or social context). Malle's *causal history of reasons* concept extends the realm of possible causal factors into the past. A similar concept has been proposed by Gill (Gill & Cerce, 2017; Gill & Getty, 2016; Gill & Ungson, 2018), which he calls *historicist narratives*, in which historical elements can influence the contemporary attribution about a given behavior. Consider a person who does a blameworthy act. According to traditional attribution theories, the observer would seek to determine the locus of causation (person, situation) for that act. A historicist narrative extends into the past and provides an account of how the person's past has shaped the way he is today, in ways that can bear on accounting for the blameworthy behavior. Perhaps, for example, he grew up in a dysfunctional family or suffered a financial crisis or his ethnic group has long been a victim of discrimination. In essence, these historical factors have made him the way he is today.

Historicist understandings can provide a framework for thinking about why he acted in a blameworthy manner. They do not erase the immediate cause or his volitional control, and they do not reduce perceived intentionality (prominent in some other accounts). However, they can reframe the perceiver's perspective on current behavior. For example, studies on the assignment of blame have shown that historicist narratives can diminish blame and corresponding punishment decisions, increasing compassion for the target person. Thus, an understanding of historical elements can influence one's understanding of and attributions for current behavior (see also Costabile, 2016; Costabile & Austin, 2018).

In this section, we have reviewed some of the significant theories of attribution that emerged during the last several decades. In many respects, these accounts have built upon one another, adding complexity and nuance to our understanding of causal attribution. In other respects, these approaches offer distinct portrayals of how people explain the behavior of themselves and others. Although our discussion has highlighted the unique processes contributed by each theoretical analysis, they all share the assumption that people engage in and benefit from the causal attributions they form in making sense of their experiences.

COGNITIVE PROCESSES IN CAUSAL REASONING

These theories stimulated a great deal of research on attribution processes, their origins, and their effects on social judgment and behavior. Because these theories generally pre-dated the development of social cognition, they were neither informed by new theoretical perspectives from cognitive psychology nor were they studied using methodologies allowing direct investigation of cognitive processes. As a consequence, traditional ideas about the processes underlying attribution were mostly speculative. The ability to study them more directly emerged with the development of social cognition (Hamilton & Carlston, 2013).

As the social cognitive perspectives and methods began to be applied to the study of attribution, it became clear that some of these theories were highly *idealized*. That is, to varying degrees, they identified the kinds of information that people *should* seek out and use to determine why an event occurred. Kelley's and Weiner's models, in particular, were highly *prescriptive* and *normative*, delineating both the categories of information and the rules for integrating that information to be used in generating causal explanations. These models reflect the assumption that social perceivers follow logical principles when making causal attributions. Some theorists were quite explicit about this assumption. Heider (1958) referred to social perceivers as *naïve scientists*, and Kelley (1967, 1973) argued that people engage in intuitive statistical techniques (ANOVA) to determine causality.

As research on attribution progressed, it became clear that people often do not utilize information according to these logical prescriptive principles. As is true for many other cognitive processes (e.g., attention, interpretation, inference), people typically do not use all relevant information available to make causal judgments. We often fail to seek out relevant information unless prompted to do so and do not use it effectively, even when it is provided. We engage in shortcuts to minimize the effort necessary to make causal attributions, often truncating our search for information when we generate a causal attribution that is "good enough" to explain an observed behavior (Simon, 1956; Tetlock, 1985). Because of limits in our information processing capacities and in our unwillingness to expend maximal effort, attribution processes can differ substantially from how they are characterized in prescriptive models.

We now turn to a discussion of research examining cognitive processes in causal attribution. In some regards, this research shows that many of the untested assumptions of attribution theories hold up quite well to empirical scrutiny. In other regards, the research evidence highlights the many ways that people differ from the idealized models that pre-dated the cognitive revolution. Even when research confirms the kinds of information used to explain events, it also shows that this information is often used unsystematically, incompletely, and irrationally. Causal determinations can also be influenced by a variety of cognitive and motivational factors, introducing bias into the process. In sum, this evidence shows that traditional attributional theories should be viewed more like descriptions of *what could be* rather than *what is*.

Using Information to Make Attributions

Attribution theories described the *kinds of information* that could be used when making attributions about someone's behavior. However, they did not adequately describe *how* that information is used in making those judgments. For example, Kelly's covariation model pointed to consistency, distinctiveness, and consensus as three relevant sources of information, but the model did not reveal how perceivers use that information. What do people do with the information they receive when they make a judgment regarding causality? Do they integrate the information as attribution theories suggest, giving each piece of information the appropriate weight and emphasis? Alternatively, are there biases favoring certain kinds of information over others? Much research has focused on these questions, revealing that people often do not integrate causal information in the manner described by attribution theories.

One of the most pervasive biases in the way people make attributions is known as the *fundamental attribution error* (Ross, 1977, 2018). As we noted earlier, Heider (1958) had made the central distinction between internal and external attributions, that is, attributing causality to either properties of the person (traits, motives, moods) or to aspects of the situation in which the behavior occurred (social norms, demands of the situation, constraints due to social roles). However, there is substantial bias in this process. Ross (1977, p. 183) defined the fundamental attribution error as the tendency "to underestimate the impact of situational factors and to overestimate the role of dispositional factors in controlling behavior." Perceivers are insensitive to the extent to which the situation drives behavior and, therefore, unduly see the person as cause and ascribe dispositional attributions in accounting for his behavior.

This bias was demonstrated in research based on Milgram's (1963) famous study of obedience to authority. Participants in that study, playing the role of teacher, orally administered a test to a learner (out of sight and actually an experimental confederate). Incorrect answers were punished by the teacher administering electric shocks to the learner. As more errors were made, the experimenter instructed the teacher to increase the voltage of the shock administered to the learner. In many cases, shock levels increased to the point that they clearly were dangerous, and the learner's voice conveyed his experiencing pain. Unbeknownst to the teacher, no actual shock was given. Nevertheless, the teacher, believing he was shocking the learner, became distressed with increasing voltage levels. Nevertheless, a substantial majority of Milgram's participants (teachers) obeyed the experimenter's instructions and continued to increase shock to a dangerous level. The authority of the experimenter was sufficient to induce them to behave in ways that they themselves found objectionable.

When people are provided a detailed description of the Milgram procedure and asked how far people would go in increasing the shock levels in response to the experimenter's instructions, they grossly underestimate the actual level of compliance (Milgram, 1965). When participants in another study were shown an actual reenactment of Milgram's procedure, again they underestimated the compliance manifested by the actual participants (Bierbrauer, 1979). This pervasive tendency to fail to recognize the influence of situational forces (in this case, instructions from an authority figure) has been observed in many studies using a variety of other paradigms (Jones & Harris, 1967; Krull, 2001; McArthur, 1972; Ross, Amabile, & Steinmetz, 1977). Thus, the fundamental attribution error is the pervasive tendency for perceivers to make dispositional attributions over situational attributions, even when the latter provide reasonable accounts for the behavior. Stated another way, perceivers underestimate the vital power of situational influence on behavior.

Another bias in the attribution process is the *underuse of consensus information*. In an early and influential study testing Kelley's covariation model, McArthur (1972) provided participants with descriptions of a series of scenarios in which a person enacted a behavior toward an entity (usually another person), along with consistency, distinctiveness, and consensus information. So, for example, participants might be told that "John laughs at the comedian" and that in the past John has either almost always laughed at the same comedian or almost never laughed at him (consistency information), that he laughs at almost no other comedian or at almost every other comedian (distinctiveness information), and that almost everyone or hardly anyone who hears the comedian laughs at him (consensus information). Participants' responded to questions asking the extent to which they would attribute behaviors to the person (John), the entity (the comedian), the circumstances, or some combination of all three factors. Analyses of these responses showed that both consistency and distinctiveness information strongly influenced causal attributions, but consensus information had much less impact. Other studies have also found that consensus information has relatively little effect on attributions (Nisbett & Borgida, 1975; Nisbett, Borgida, Crandall, & Reed, 1982), although it does exert some influence in some conditions (Kassin, 1979; Ruble & Feldman, 1976). For example, consensus information tends to be used more when people have weak expectations about how a person would typically behave in a social situation, when it provides new or surprising information, and when it is viewed as reflecting a large, representative sample of people.

There may be several reasons for the comparatively minor role of consensus information, but one is noteworthy. Both consistency and distinctiveness information provide additional information about the actor (i.e., the consistency of his behavior across time and the generality of his behavior across different targets). In contrast, consensus information says nothing at all about the actor but relates how other actors behave in a given context. In that case, the actor is not salient at all and therefore gets little weight in attribution judgments. We return to the role of salience shortly.

Attributions are also affected by the temporal sequence with which causal information is received, and the use of consensus information is particularly affected by whether it is received early or late in the processing of behavioral information. In one study (Ruble & Feldman, 1976), participants read behavioral descriptions (e.g., "Jim translates the sentence incorrectly") followed by consensus, distinctiveness, and consistency information. The sequencing of this information was systematically varied, creating six different orderings. Results showed that consensus information had a more significant influence on attributions when it was presented last rather than first. The ordering of the other two types of information did not affect causal judgments.

The temporal sequence of events, particularly events that co-occur in time, can also guide causal conclusions. To some degree, Kelley's covariation model suggested that temporal information is useful in judging causality as perceivers note which of several possible causal factors covary in time with the behavior that is being explained. However, the expression from statistics – "correlation does not imply causation" – also applies to causal attribution. One might repeatedly observe two events co-occur over time and assume that one causes the other. However, it could be that the two events were both caused by another factor and that they have no causal relation. Thus, attributing causality based on covariation may not be entirely warranted as a prescriptive strategy. However, that is what Kelley's theory says perceivers do as they infer causality. Knowing more about the system in question would be helpful for understanding whether the two events are causally related or merely covary in response to some other force.

Heider himself shared this question about Kelley's approach. Weiner (2008, p. 152) conveys an amusing story about a presentation that Heider delivered at a meeting on attribution in which Kelley was in the audience. In discussing Kelley's model, Heider "gently pulled his two ears and followed this by sticking out his tongue. After a few repetitions, he asked the audience if they thought the ear tugging caused the tongue extension." The more general point is that causal inferences often require information beyond whether two events covary.

Another factor that can bias the attribution process is the focus of attention. Historically, studies examining attribution have involved presenting participants with passages or snippets of text that described a behavior that had been performed by a person. Of course, people typically do not receive behavioral information in this fashion. They survey the world around them to determine what is happening, focusing selectively on events and information that seem particularly interesting or relevant. As we have already discussed, the ability to focus on a subset of available information is one of the principal purposes and benefits of attention.

How might selective attention affect causal attributions? In Chapter 4, we reviewed several studies showing that information that is highly salient in the observer's visual field can have a disproportionate influence on judgments. These salience effects can also influence causal attributions (Arkin & Duval, 1975; Lassiter, 2002; Lassiter et al., 2001; Lassiter, Geers, Munhall, et al., 2002; McArthur, 1981; McArthur & Ginsburg, 1981; McArthur & Solomon, 1978; Storms, 1973; Taylor & Fiske, 1978). This research shows that information receiving the perceiver's attention is more likely to influence causal attributions than information that is not.

Information Search

As we noted earlier, many studies of attribution present information to the participants and ask them to make an attribution based on the information provided. For example, in studies stimulated by Weiner's theory of attributions for success and failure, participants experience (or are told about someone who experienced) success or failure on a task, along with information about the task difficulty, past performances, and other relevant information. In many real-life instances, however, that information may not be at hand. A perceiver observes a behavior, wonders why the person did what she did, thereby engaging the attribution process, but often relatively little information is available to aid in that process. Therefore, an important question concerns the kinds of information people seek out when they attempt to explain a behavior. When a cause must be determined, where does attention land? What do people want to know? What do they tend to neglect?

Kelley's covariation theory provides a portrayal of attribution, suggesting that people engage in a thorough information-gathering process seeking to determine the consistency, distinctiveness, and consensus regarding an observed behavior. Although studies show that consistency, distinctiveness, and consensus information conveyed through verbal descriptions provided by an experimenter can be used (Försterling, 1992), people do not gather and utilize all categories of information on their own when merely observing behavior (Fiedler, Walther, & Nickel, 1999). Doing so would take a lot of time and effort and would require awareness of the relevance of each type of information for establishing causality. Also, quite often, some categories of information are unavailable (a fact that Kelley acknowledged, which led to his proposing his causal schemas theory). It therefore becomes important to know how people search for information when they want to make an attributional judgment.

Several studies have examined this question. One approach was to determine the information requested by participants when they had to make a causal attribution (Major, 1980). Participants were provided with a behavioral description such as, "John has been in prison for five years and is now up for parole. Recently, however, he got into a fight with a fellow prisoner, Reggie." Participants were asked to determine what caused the fight by asking for up to 12 pieces of additional information from 3 different categories. These categories pertained to "John's past behavior toward Reggie," "John's behavior toward other prisoners," and "Other prisoners' behavior toward Reggie." Of course, these categories correspond to consistency, distinctiveness, and consensus information, respectively, which are central to Kelley's theory. The amount, sequence, and type of information participants examined before making an attribution were recorded.

The results, displayed in Table 8.3, are informative in several ways. First, participants did not make extensive use of the information available, selecting only about one-third of the available pieces of information. Second, they were most likely to request information about the actor's behavioral consistency and distinctiveness, and consistency information was most likely to be requested first. Third, consensus information was much less likely to be requested than the other two categories, replicating results of other studies we have described (McArthur, 1972; Nisbett & Borgida, 1975). As we noted earlier, consensus is the one information source that does not focus on the actor but instead on the response of other persons to the same entity. In explaining a

Table 8.3 Mean number of items requested and percentage of items requested first

	Number requested	% Requested first
Consistency	4.6	65
Distinctiveness	4.4	20
Consensus	3.8	15

Source: Based on data from Major (1980)

person's behavior, perceivers may have a natural inclination to focus primarily on (in this case, seek information about) the actor and less so on the social context.

Other research has studied the kinds of questions participants spontaneously generate on their own in an attributional context (Ahn, Kalish, Medin, & Gelman, 1995; Lalljee, Lamb, Furnham, & Jaspars, 1984). The results of these studies suggest that people rely less on covariation information (consistency, distinctiveness, consensus) than implied by Kelley's theory. The questions they produced instead reflected participants' attempts to test specific hypotheses they had generated to explain the event (e.g., the actor's motivation or effort in performing a task) or to identify specific mechanisms that would account for the behavior (the actor is nearsighted, which interfered with performance). In sum, the covariation information highlighted by Kelley's theory can be useful in answering attributional questions, and research shows that it is used to some degree. However, people also follow other strategies.

Causal Attributions: Thoughtful and Spontaneous

We have reviewed evidence that attributional processing is conditional, occurring in response to unexpected events or when we are motivated to understand the causes of an event. We also know that, when they are made, causal attributions are relatively slow and effortful. In Chapter 7, we described several studies (Hamilton, 1988; Malle & Holbrook, 2012; Smith, 1984; Smith & Miller, 1983) examining the speed with which people make various social judgments. These studies showed that intentionality judgments were made most quickly, consistent with Heider and Malle's speculations that judgments of intentionality are essential in social inference. In contrast, the slowest judgments were those made in response to questions about causes, and judgments of situational causes were made most slowly. Causal judgments, and particularly judgments of situational causes, appear to be relatively inefficient.

Attributional processes are also resource-dependent. Neuroscientific evidence points to the importance of cognitive resources in making attributional judgments. Spunt and Lieberman (2013) had participants in an fMRI scanner watch a series of silent video clips depicting a man performing a set of everyday actions with his hands. The focus of this study was whether cognitive load would affect the activation of brain regions for each of these goals. The participants viewed the scenes under either a low or high cognitive load – they had to remember either an easy (e.g., 555–5555) or a difficult phone number (e.g., 637–7696) while watching the videos. For any given scene, participants were given one of four goals: to watch passively, to understand what the actor was doing, to understand how the action was performed, or to understand why the action was performed. Of course, only the last goal should prompt attributional judgments. Results showed that cognitive load affected neural activity only when participants were trying to understand why a behavior had been performed. Cortical regions associated with mentalizing (i.e., inferring a person's mental state) – specifically, the dorsomedial prefrontal cortex and the left anterior temporal cortex – showed higher activation under low than high load when participants were asked to make a causal attribution. Thus, high cognitive demands undermined attributional processes because they reduced the activity of brain regions engaged when thinking about the goals, motives, and intentions of other people.

All of the findings discussed so far support the idea that attributions are made deliberatively, with ample thought and cognitive resources. However, other studies suggest that not all attributional judgments are equally resource-dependent. Some research shows that people's attributions for personal failure can occur quite spontaneously. In one study (Sakaki & Murayama, 2013), participants performed a difficult reasoning task and received feedback that they had performed poorly (scoring 28 compared with the average score of 54). After receiving this feedback, half of the participants were placed under a cognitive load, and half were not. All participants (whether or not under cognitive load) then completed a questionnaire asking why they did poorly on the reasoning task. Half of the items on the questionnaire reflected internal (ability) attributions (e.g., "because I'm not smart") and half reflected external (task difficulty) attributions (e.g., "because the test was too advanced"). The degree to which participants agreed with external attributions did not differ based on cognitive load. Agreement with internal attributions did, however. Under high load, participants were quick to attribute their failure to internal factors such as low ability. Under low load, where participants could engage in deliberative processing to consider a broader array of causal factors, internal attributions for failure were reduced. Thus, after failure, people are quick to blame themselves, and they invoke external attributions only when they have the resources to do so. This process is analogous to the findings of Gilbert et al. (1988), who showed that correcting trait inferences in light of situational information also requires cognitive resources.

These results highlight the possibility that, while attributional processes can at times require effort and cognitive resources, they can sometimes occur quite spontaneously, with minimal effort or intent. In fact, Weiner (1985a) argued that attributional activity is spontaneously triggered only under certain conditions, specifically, unexpected events and nonattainment of goals as triggers of attributional processing. However, many of the studies he cited prompted attributional processes through experimental instructions. More convincing evidence of genuinely spontaneous attributions would be provided by studies showing that participants engage in attributional analyses when they are not prompted at all. If this could be done, then determining whether people are aware of making attributions or of the attributional judgment itself might be of tremendous theoretical interest.

Such a study was conducted by Hassin, Bargh, and Uleman (2002). Participants read a set of brief passages and were asked to indicate "how interesting they are." This instruction was included to ensure that participants were not explicitly prompted to engage in causal attribution. Some versions of the passages implied a causal event (e.g., "After spending a day exploring beautiful sights in the crowded streets of New York, Jane discovered that her wallet was missing," suggesting that Jane might have been pickpocketed). In contrast, others were variations that did not imply causality (e.g., "Before leaving home for a day of exploring beautiful sights in the crowded streets of New York, Jane discovered that her wallet was missing"). For each participant, half of the passages implied causality, and half did not. After a delay, participants were given a surprise free recall task and a set of cues that they were told might assist them in recalling what they had read. Half of these cue words were causal factors implied by (but had not appeared in) the passages (causal cues), whereas the other half were words that appeared in a passage but were unrelated to causality (semantic cues). As is shown in Figure 8.2, recall was higher when

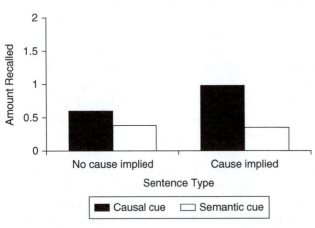

Figure 8.2 Free recall as a function of retrieval cue and sentence type

Source: Adapted from Hassin et al. (2002)

causal cues were provided for passages that implied causality compared with passages that did not. The causal cues would be useful in facilitating recall only if participants had spontaneously inferred the cause as the passages were encoded (i.e., they had made an attribution). Hence, the results show that spontaneously inferring causality facilitated recall.

These results indicate that people spontaneously formed attributions at least some of the time when sentences implied a possible causal event. However, did participants know they were making causal inferences? Were they aware of what they were doing? To answer these questions, the researchers conducted follow-up analyses in which participants were thoroughly interviewed at the end of the study. Their responses revealed little recognition of the focus of the study. In sum, the results of this study show that causal attributions can be made with minimal intent and awareness.

Attributions and Inferences

In Chapter 7, we discussed inference processes, including extensive research on dispositional inferences and recent work on spontaneous trait inferences. In this chapter, we have presented work on attributions, including a bias toward making dispositional attributions. Moreover, we just described a study (Hassin et al., 2002) arguing that attributions too can occur spontaneously. Given these parallels, one might wonder, Are dispositional inferences and dispositional attributions the same or different?

There are several reasons to think they might be the same thing. They both are triggered in response to observed behavior. They both represent ways that the mind elaborates on incoming stimulus information. Both are clearly inferences. Moreover, in most texts, Jones and Davis' (1965) correspondent inference theory is presented as a theory of the attribution process (whereas we have presented it in Chapter 7 as a historically important and conceptually rich theory of dispositional inference processes). In these respects, dispositional and attributional inferences seem the same.

However, Hamilton (1998) has argued that there are qualitative differences between dispositional and attributional inferences. These differences become evident when one considers the nature of inferences in processing behavior that is consistent or inconsistent with prior expectancies. To illustrate, consider the example of when a person makes a rude remark to another person. If the perceiver has an existing impression (expectancy) that the actor is an unfriendly person, then his behavior is expectancy-consistent, it is efficiently processed, and a dispositional inference would confirm the existing impression. On the other hand, if the perceiver's impression is that the actor is a friendly person, then the rude behavior presents an expectancy disconfirmation. Now the perceiver is confronted with a more complicated circumstance, and different processes are invoked. Research has shown that people spend more time processing expectancy-inconsistent than consistent information (Bargh & Thein, 1985; Stern et al., 1984), they retrieve more information from memory while processing inconsistent information (Sherman & Hamilton, 1994), and the expectancy disconfirmation triggers causal thinking ("Why did he do that?") (Hastie, 1984; Susskind et al., 1999). None of these responses occur following expectancy-consistent behaviors.

The essential element underlying this comparison is that attributional analysis is at the heart of those differences. *Dispositional inferences* are spontaneous, quick, and non-analytic. They occur readily following an expectancy-consistent behavior. They do *not* include an analysis of why the person acted that way. On the other hand, *attributions* are most likely to occur precisely when STIs are less likely to be made. Expectancy-inconsistent behaviors trigger them, and they are explicitly aimed at answering why the person acted as he did. These points lead to the conclusion that inferences and attributions are qualitatively different (Gawronski, 2004; Hamilton, 1988, 1998; Krull, 2001).

There is another somewhat ironic relationship between the two, namely, that a dispositional inference, once made, can become the basis for an attribution (Hamilton, 1998). Consider the following. A perceiver observes his friend, Mathias, perform a behavior, such as donating money to charity. The observer makes an STI, quickly and perhaps without intention or awareness, so in the observer's mind, Mathias has a particular trait, say, generous. Later, if the observer is asked by someone else, "Why did Mathias donate the money?" the inferred disposition provides a readily-available causal explanation, namely, "Because he's generous." So, the trait was inferred without any consideration of causal influence, but it becomes a dispositional attribution once it is used to explain Mathias' behavior. Note also that this process, because it began with an STI, is biased toward person rather than situation attributions. Therefore, it can itself contribute to another bias we have discussed, specifically, the fundamental attribution error. This instance provides a further way in which inferences and attributions are not the same things.

In a related vein, it has been argued that trait concepts are inherently causal (Fenker, Waldmann, & Holyoak, 2005; Kressel & Uleman, 2010; Uleman, 2015). Traits are typically thought of as concepts that capture and summarize a category of behaviors, such that someone smart can perform well in a variety of settings. In inferring that an intelligent behavior indicates that a person is intelligent, one is moving to a higher level of generality that would enhance expectations of intelligent behavior on other tasks as well. Kressel and Uleman (2010) posited that the trait itself (intelligent) includes causal potential such that "isolated traits are inherently causes of behaviors" (p. 215). To test this idea, they presented trait-behavior word pairs (e.g., dumb-fail, silly-giggle), sometimes (as in these examples) in the order suggested by causal influence or in the reverse order (giggle-silly). Participants were asked, "whether the concepts described by each word pair are causally related." Response times were recorded. The results showed that people responded faster when the word pair was presented in the order compatible with causal influence than in the opposite order. This difference in response times suggests that traits and behaviors are causally related in semantic memory such that the potential of causing behaviors may be inherent in the meaning of traits.

In sum, the research we reviewed in this section describes some of the ways that people form causal attributions for behavior. These studies highlight that attributional processes often differ significantly and systematically from the normative models of attribution that dominated early theorizing, particularly in the era before the emergence of social cognition. Moreover, the research we have summarized reveals the variety and complexity of processes involved in attributional analysis. We now turn to another important consideration in understanding attribution processes.

CULTURAL DIFFERENCES IN ATTRIBUTIONAL PROCESSES

Attribution research has shown that perceivers readily attribute actions to the internal dispositions of actors rather than to the situations in which behavior occurs (Ross, 1977, 2018). People are viewed as being "action centers" (Heider, 1958) that perceivers study to infer the internal characteristics – motives, goals, and traits – that drive the behavior of those people. Evidence supports this emphasis on internal attributions, which have been shown to occur more readily, quickly, and commonly than situationally-focused attributions. When external attributions are made, they often result from cognitive and motivational biases that serve to counteract this general tendency.

Despite this evidence, research emerging during the last two decades has questioned the assumption that invariably the actor is the central focus of attributional activity. Specifically, we now know that cultural factors "constrain, trigger, or shape the way in which humans think about causal relationships" (Bender, Beller, & Medin, 2017, p. 1). Cultural differences in cognitive processes might reflect differences in the perceived value of various kinds of information in a given cultural context. Such differences might promote specific cognitive processes that, when highly practiced, become automatic and self-perpetuating within a culture (Ishii, 2013; Mason & Morris, 2010). Although identifying the exact basis of these distal cultural factors remains speculative, theories have pointed to factors ranging from differences in supernatural beliefs (Norenzayan & Hansen, 2006), to historical agricultural practices (Talhelm et al., 2014), to essentialist beliefs (Waxman, Medin, & Ross, 2007), to emphases on individuals versus collectives (Nisbett, Peng, Choi, & Norenzayan, 2001), to name a few.

In some of the earliest research demonstrating cultural differences in causal attribution (Miller, 1984), American participants from Chicago, Illinois, and Hindu[1] participants from Mysore, India in four different age groups (8, 11, and 15 years, and adults) were asked to describe four behaviors, two positive and two negative, that they had observed. Specifically, they were to "describe something a person you know well did recently that you considered good for someone else" or "a wrong thing to have done." Immediately after describing each behavior, participants explained why it occurred. These explanations were then coded for the extent they emphasized general dispositions ("He was proud") and contextual factors such as the immediate situation ("His friends were with him") or other persons ("His friend was feeling sick").

Results showed that adult Americans made significantly more dispositional attributions than did adult Hindus, whereas Hindus made significantly more situational attributions. Although there were few significant differences between the American and Hindu children (aged 8 and 11), the samples diverged as the children grew older. Specifically, increases in age were associated with more dispositional explanations in the American sample but more situational attributions in the sample. Miller (1984) argued that these data reflect a stronger emphasis in the United States on individualism, focusing on personal autonomy and responsibility, compared with India's more holistic focus, emphasizing interdependence between persons and their social relationships, role obligations, and situational norms. The age trends suggest that these differing emphases in thinking about people are learned through social development and emerge over the lifespan.

The preference for dispositional over situational attributions in Westerners, and the reverse in East Asians, has also been found in other studies (e.g., Choi, Nisbett, & Norenzayan, 1999; Morris & Peng, 1994; Peng & Knowles, 2003). These results may reflect more general differences between Western versus Asian modes of information processing. Pointing to a divergence between Western thought (influenced by ancient Greece) and Asian thought (influenced by Chinese thought) dating back to at least the 6th century BC, Nisbett and his

---

[1] The study, which took place in Mysore, India, refers to participants in that location as "Hindus" throughout but it does not further classify the American participants. We have followed the study's use of terms in our discussion, though we acknowledge that it is inconsistent to categorize one group by nation and the other by religion.

colleagues (Nisbett et al., 2001; Norenzayan & Nisbett, 2000) echoed Miller (1984) in arguing that Western concepts of the person are predominantly individualistic, promoting the use of rules, logic, and systematic analysis focused on understanding the person. In contrast, East Asians tend to be collectivist, promoting holistic and dialectical analysis of a broader array of available information with little use of formal logic. These cultural differences in social thought have widespread ripple effects influencing attentional processes, the formation of inferences, categorization, and language comprehension (Bender et al., 2017; Ishii, 2013). If differences in these fundamental cognitive processes arise across cultures, it would not be surprising that attributional processes can also be affected.

Much evidence attests to cultural differences in patterns of attentional allocation that facilitate personal and situational attributions. For example, in one study (Masuda & Nisbett, 2001), Japanese and North American participants were shown animated vignettes of underwater scenes and asked to describe their contents. North Americans were more likely to start their descriptions of the scenes by referring to focal elements, whereas Japanese participants were more likely to mention information about the background ("the color of the water was green") and relationships between the focal objects and background information ("a big fish was swimming above the seaweed"). Another study (Chua, Boland, & Nisbett, 2005) tracked eye movements of North American and Chinese participants while they viewed scenes showing an object displayed against a realistic background (e.g., a fighter jet flying in front of a mountainous backdrop). Participants from North America looked at the object sooner and longer than did the Chinese participants, whereas Chinese participants fixated more on the background than did the North Americans. Finally, Masuda and Nisbett (2006) asked American and East Asian students to search for differences between a pair of photographs presented in rapid sequence. American participants were faster to detect changes in salient, focal objects compared with changes in the periphery or context. This was not true for East Asian participants, who attended to the contextual information more than did Americans. Taken together, these studies indicate that cultural differences in causal attribution may reflect differences in attention to focal versus contextual information.

Although there are some consistent differences between North Americans and East Asians in cognitive processes generally, and causal attributions specifically, a few important caveats must be recognized. First, there is variation both within as well as between cultures in these effects, and it is not the case that all Americans and all East Asians manifest the patterns described above. In other words, the differences in patterns of causal attribution are differences in degree rather than in kind (Widlok, 2014). There are substantial differences within cultures in attributional reasoning, particularly in comparing individuals using more scientific approaches versus lay theories or religious beliefs to determine causality (Bender et al., 2017).

Second, these between-group differences can vary over the lifespan and based on experience. Miller's (1984) original work showed that Americans and Hindus did not start making different attributions until the mid-teens. Moreover, other research (Morris & Peng, 1994) found attributional differences between American and Chinese high schoolers but no differences in a sample of older graduate students.

Third, these patterns of attributional judgments can also vary *within* a person depending on one's cultural mindset. For example, one study (Hong, Morris, Chiu, & Benet-Martínez, 2000) investigated causal attributions of people who were bicultural. High school students in Hong Kong typically have had much exposure to both Chinese and Western cultures. In the study, these students were randomly assigned to different priming conditions. In a control condition, participants were shown pictures of landscapes and wrote ten sentences about each one. Participants in the *American culture* priming condition saw pictures of American symbols (e.g., the U.S. Capitol building, the American flag) and then wrote ten sentences about American culture. Participants in the *Chinese culture* priming condition saw Chinese symbols (e.g., a Chinese dragon, the Great Wall) and then wrote ten sentences about Chinese culture. Participants then read a story about an overweight boy who had been advised by a doctor to avoid sugary foods but who, despite this recommendation, had eaten a piece of delicious looking cake while at a buffet dinner with friends. After reading the story, participants

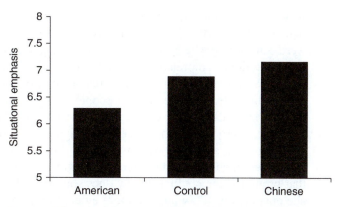

Figure 8.3 Emphasis on situational factors in accounting for behavior in bicultural individuals as a function of exposure to cultural primes

Source: Based on data from Hong et al. (2000)

indicated the extent to which they believed the boy's weight problem was caused by his personality or by the situation. Across the three conditions, participants did not differ in their estimates of the influence of the boy's personality on his behavior. However, as is shown in Figure 8.3, the students who had been primed with American symbols emphasized situational factors to a much lesser degree than did students who had been primed with Chinese symbols. Thus, for these bicultural students, priming one or the other cultural identity influenced the nature of their attributions. These results, of course, parallel the findings of many studies comparing Western and East Asian cultures. However, they highlight the importance of psychological mechanisms (activating different cultural identities) rather than geography, per se, in accounting for those differences.

ATTRIBUTIONAL PROCESSES IN UNDERSTANDING THE SELF, PERSONS, AND GROUPS

We began this chapter by describing a situation in which a judgment about the cause of an ambiguous event (Iraq's possession of weapons of mass destruction) produced severe consequences. We have provided many other examples showing how causal attributions can affect people's understanding of, emotional responses to, and actions following a large variety of social situations. We have also reviewed research investigating how and when attributions are made. As was the case with all of the processes we discussed in previous chapters, much research has focused on how attributions are essential in thinking about ourselves, about other individuals, and about groups. We now turn to a discussion of this research.

Attributional Processes in Understanding the Self

Attributions are made when an observer considers why a person performed a particular behavior. It may seem odd, then, to consider attributions about the self, that is, trying to understand why I did what I just did. Didn't I know my reasons when (or even before) I engaged in a particular behavior? If I do consider why I did something, would the process be the same as if I were considering why another person performed the same behavior? It turns out that answering these questions is more complicated than we might initially think.

There are many reasons to think that attributional processes involving the self would differ from judgments we make of other people. First, we have different information about ourselves than we have about other people. When we engage in behavior, we have access (or at least we think we do) to internal processes that might be responsible for the behavior. For example, if I get into a big argument with my sibling, I might be aware that the dispute was instigated by a comment made a few days ago. My cognitive and emotional responses to a cruel comment that prompted the conflict ("Why does she think she's better than me?…I get outraged when she puts me down") would be more evident to me than it would be to my sister. Second, our attentional systems provide us with different information about ourselves and others. When I see another person's behavior, I see it from an observer's perspective. For my own behavior, however, I cannot assume the role of an observer and "watch myself." Instead, my attention is typically focused outward – on the social context – rather than on the behavior. Third, we generally have different motivations in explaining our own behavior compared with that of others. We usually want to feel good about ourselves and interpret events in a way that preserves positive self-regard. For these reasons, research has shown that we do often make different attributions for our own and others' behavior. However, this research also makes clear that differences in self vs. other attributional processes reflect some complexities.

Actor-Observer Differences

Let us begin with the truism that we have different information about our own compared with other people's behaviors. The fact that we have different perceptual inputs and at least some self-insight led researchers to wonder whether people systematically differ in attributing one's own versus others' behavior to internal versus external factors. Jones and Nisbett (1972) proposed a specific asymmetry in causal explanations, arguing that "there is a pervasive tendency for actors to attribute their actions to situational requirements, whereas observers tend to attribute the same actions to stable personal dispositions" (p. 80). This difference in attributing behavior to internal versus external causes was called the *actor-observer effect*, and it was long viewed as a well-established phenomenon. However, Malle (2006) conducted a meta-analysis (a statistical technique in which data from multiple studies are combined) to assess the strength of support for the effect from 173 tests that had been conducted from 1971–2004. This analysis yielded a striking finding: there was no consistent evidence for the actor-observer asymmetry described by Jones and Nisbett (1972).

The analysis did show that some effects were reliable. For example, the predicted actor-observer effect did occur for negative events (I attribute my failure to external factors, such as evaluator bias, but another person's failure to dispositional causes, such as low ability). However, it was reversed for positive events (My success reflects my ability (internal), but his success reflects the fact that the task was easy (external)). Also, the predicted effect emerged from studies that assessed causal attributions using free-response characterizations. However, studies that used traditional rating scales to measure the contribution of persons versus situational factors showed no actor-observer differences. Finally, several studies suggest that actor-observer differences can arise through mechanisms involving visual attention (Granot, Balcetis, Schneider, & Tyler, 2014; Storms, 1973). One such study (Lassiter & Irvine, 1986) showed that viewers of a videotaped mock police interrogation varied in their judgments of the degree that coercion was responsible for a confession, depending on whether the tape focused on the detective or the suspect. Nevertheless, with these notable exceptions, there is little evidence of widespread actor-observer differences as had been speculated.

Malle (2006; Malle et al., 2007) has argued that the original asymmetry hypothesis was not wrong but that it was simply stated in a too-simplistic form. Specifically, these authors critiqued the simple distinction between attributions to stable dispositions versus the situation. Instead, they argued for distinct forms of actor-observer asymmetries that should affect different, more specific causal attributions. Using Malle's Folk-Conceptual Theory described earlier, they posited that people use qualitatively distinct modes of explanation depending on whether a behavior is seen as intentional or unintentional. An event that is seen to be *unintentional* will be explained by causes that mechanically brought about the event. In explaining a car accident, we might infer that it was caused by poor weather, darkness, or an icy road. In contrast, explanations of *intentional* acts will differ in three respects. First, they will reflect the use of *reasons*, that is, the inferred beliefs and desires that produced the intention ("He worked hard to make more money"), or *causal history explanations*, that is, factors that lie in the background of those reasons ("He worked hard because it's the cultural norm there"). Second, they will differ in their emphasis on *beliefs* ("He thinks exercise is good for his health") or *desires* ("He wants to improve his health"). Third, they will differ in whether they use mental state markers, that is, specific inferences about the actor's reasons ("She bought the chocolate because she thinks it's the best in town") or do not use mental state markers ("She bought the chocolate because it's the best in town").

These three factors were expected to produce explanations for intentional actions that cut across the disposition vs. situation dichotomy and allowed for possible actor-observer differences in attribution. Malle et al. (2007) generated three specific predictions that were tested in nine studies. First, they hypothesized that actors would generate more reason explanations (relative to causal history explanations) than would observers, given their privileged access to their inner thoughts and motivations. Second, they predicted that actors would offer more belief reasons (relative to desire reasons) than observers, again because of privileged access but also because observers can use general social rules and cultural practices to infer desires. Third, they expected that actors would use fewer belief reason markers than would observers, both because actors directly represent the content of their beliefs rather than their own mental states (thinking "I fed the dog because he was hungry" rather than "I fed the dog because I thought he was hungry") and because markers can denote skepticism, which would be used more for observers than actors ("She fed the dog because she thought he was hungry"). The experiments provided consistent support for each hypothesis and no support for the traditional formulation of the actor-observer hypothesis. These results show that people do explain their actions differently from how they explain the actions of others. However, these differences do not reflect the differential use of dispositional compared with situational causes. Differences emerged only when explanations were separated into theoretically meaningful distinctions.

Egocentric Bias

Given that people have different amounts and different kinds of information about their actions and those of others, it is reasonable to ask whether there are biases in the credit that they give for a joint product or activity. Think about deciding whether you or your roommate spends more time cleaning your shared apartment. What information do you have about your own contributions to cleaning? Presumably, you will remember many incidents in which you took time to wash dirty dishes or to put dirty clothes in the hamper. You might also recall a weekend when your roommate was away and you decided to mop the floor, a task that is too-rarely performed. Because you are always "there" when you completed these tasks, it is easy for you to think that you do your "fair share" (or even much more than your share) of the cleaning. What about your roommate's contributions? You would be less likely to have witnessed all of these activities, and you might not even have noticed them. Therefore, your roommate's contributions would probably be less obvious to you. As a result, you might accept more credit for cleaning than your roommate will attribute to you and vice versa. If so, you both would be demonstrating an *egocentric bias* (Ross & Sicoly, 1979; Ross & Ward, 1996).

One of the earliest studies of egocentric bias (Ross & Sicoly, 1979) closely paralleled this example. Married couples were asked to estimate their responsibility for a set of activities (e.g., shopping for groceries, caring for the children) by placing a slash through a line whose endpoints were labeled "primarily wife" and "primarily husband." These dashes were then converted to percentages for analysis purposes (e.g., a slash in the middle of the line would indicate a judgment of 50% responsibility). An "egocentric bias" was determined by summing judgments of each husband and wife couple to determine if they exceeded 100%. For example, if the husband claimed that he contributed 40% to childcare and the wife estimated her contribution at 70%, this would sum to 110%. In such a case, one (or possibly both) of the partners must be overestimating his or her contribution to that shared task. (Of course, it would be impossible to tell who is being inaccurate in making his judgment, as that would require additional information.)

The researchers found that egocentric bias was prevalent in married couples. Amongst these couples, 73% showed some degree of overestimation. Overestimation occurred for 80% of the tasks mentioned in the questionnaire, and these included both positive and negative events (e.g., overestimating contributions to arguments). When asked to recall and write down examples of the contributions they or their spouses had made to each activity, participants provided more examples of their own than of their spouses' contributions, and the difference in the number of items recalled about their own versus their partners' contributions correlated with judgments of responsibility.

Self-serving Bias

We know that people are motivated to feel good about themselves. Does this concern influence the kinds of attributions they make? It does, although there is some complexity in the research findings here as well. In general, as one might expect, research has shown that people tend to make different attributions for positive than for negative events involving the self. Positive events experienced by the self are typically attributed to more internal, stable, and global factors than are attributions for negative events. For example, I might explain my success on a test by invoking my ability or my effort, but failure would be explained by the test being unfair or because I was not feeling well. This attributional pattern is an example of a *self-serving bias* (Miller & Ross, 1975) that is rewarding, motivationally salient, and protective of a positive self-concept. Research evidence confirms this general tendency.

A meta-analysis of the results of 266 studies examining the self-serving attributional bias confirmed that this bias is reliable, observed in nearly all samples. It was moderated, however, by some variables of interest. Children and older adults displayed the most considerable biases, and Asian participants showed less bias than did American and other Western samples.

Psychopathology was associated with a significantly attenuated bias, with the smallest effects for people with depression, anxiety, and attention-deficit/hyperactivity disorder. These findings show that the self-serving attributional bias is pervasive but does vary across age, cultural, and psychopathology groups (Heine et al., 1999; Mezulis, Abramson, Hyde, & Hankin, 2004).

Apparent Mental Causation

It is clear that people both want and need to have some understanding of why the events surrounding their lives happen; therefore, they seek to identify the causes for the behaviors and outcomes they observe and experience. As we have just seen, people are not impartial observers; self-serving biases can influence these attributional analyses. Perhaps we can extend this reasoning one step further: can the perceiver's thinking, driven by self-serving goals, cause specific outcomes to occur? There surely are times when a person really wants something to happen – a desired outcome, another competitor's failure. Can the mind influence behavior to cause such effects?

We cannot answer that question directly, but research has shown that people are quite prone to *believing* that people can cause such outcomes. If certain preconditions exist, then people may experience the feeling of having had causal influence. Specifically, (a) having thoughts in advance of an action (b) that are consistent with the action outcome and (c) there are no apparent causes present can lead a person to believe that he or she actually caused the outcome. This is referred to as *apparent mental causation* (Pronin, Wegner, McCarthy, & Rodriguez, 2006; Wegner, 2003; Wegner, Sparrow, & Winerman, 2004; Wegner & Wheatley, 1999).

Two studies testing these ideas were reported by Pronin et al. (2006). In the first study, people came to believe that their personal thoughts influenced another person's physical health symptoms. In each session, two participants (one of whom was an experimental confederate) arrived for a study investigating physical health symptoms resulting from psychological factors, specifically, from "evil thoughts" such as a voodoo curse. The confederate was trained to act in either a very offensive manner or a neutral manner during an initial encounter. Later, consistent with the alleged purpose of the study, the actual participant was instructed to stick pins in a voodoo doll representing the other participant. After a brief pause, the confederate responded to a physical symptoms interview and indicated that "I have a bit of a headache now." Then, after the victim was taken to another room, the participant completed dependent measures, which included questions about the extent to which the participants thought that he or she had harmed the victim and caused the headache symptoms, and if the practice of voodoo affected the victim's symptoms. Analyses of these responses indicated that participants in the evil thoughts condition, induced to think badly about the victim during the opening encounter, felt they had caused the victim's headache to a greater extent than those in the neutral (control) condition. Thus, these participants, having had prior thoughts consistent with the harm experienced by the victim, believed that their negative thoughts had causally affected another person.

Is apparent mental causation limited to negative effects, or can it be felt about positive outcomes as well? A second study sought to determine if "success" thoughts would lead to the perception of influencing performance in a positive direction. Again, two participants (one of whom was a confederate) reported to the study at a mock basketball court. The confederate was assigned the role of "shooter" and the actual participant to be a "spectator." The shooter's role would be to take a series of eight shots while blindfolded. The spectator participants were given instructions about what to visualize before the shooter took each shot. Some of the spectators were given positive thoughts to visualize, such as the ball leaving the shooter's hand and then going through the basket. The other spectators were instructed to visualize non-basketball-related things, such as the shooter's arm lifting a dumbbell to his shoulder. The blindfolded confederate then made 6 of his 8 shots (made possible by the fact that the blindfold was semi-transparent). After completing the shots, dependent measures asked the participants several questions about the extent to which his/her visualizations influenced the success of the shooter's shots, and had somehow caused the shooter's success. Analyses showed that participants who visualized basketball-related success believed that their visualizations influenced shooting performance (2.4) more than did spectators who visualized non-basketball images (1.6). These spectators viewed themselves as being somewhat responsible for the shooter's success.

In sum, there is a general tendency to highlight oneself in making causal attributions. We invoke different reasons to explain our own behavior compared with others, regularly think we have contributed more to shared tasks than is warranted, and attribute success and failure in a manner that allows us to maintain positive beliefs and feelings about ourselves. Under certain conditions, we even believe our thoughts have influenced another person's outcomes. Although some of these phenomena point to motivational self-protective factors, not all do. Causal judgments involving the self are sometimes biased by the simple fact that we have different information about the self than we do about other people. In addition, motivational and cognitive contributions to attributional processes involving the self are often inextricably intertwined, working together to bias causal attributions (Kunda, 1990; Pyszczynski & Greenberg, 1987).

Attributional Processes in Understanding Persons

Most of the research we have discussed in this chapter has focused on people making attributions for the behavior of other individuals. The catalyst for much of the research on attribution was Heider's (1958) book, *The Psychology of Interpersonal Relations*, which considered not just attributional processes but also "How one person thinks and feels about another person, how he perceives him and what he does to him, what he expects him to do or think, how he reacts to the actions of the other" (p. 1). Given that much of the research we have described dealt with that question, we now know quite a bit about how people explain the actions of other individuals. However, in many studies, those persons are described by verbal characterizations presented on a computer screen. One might wonder, then, about how the attribution process plays out in actual ongoing interactions between persons. In this section, we explore that question by considering research on attributions in two interpersonal contexts: communications between persons and long-term relationships.

Attributions in Interpersonal Interactions

Because causal explanations often occur in the context of communicating with other people, Hilton (1988, 1990) argued that they are constrained by general rules of conversation designed to meet a communication partner's informational needs. In communicating with another person, we decide what causal factor to emphasize based on what we think is already known or important to a communication partner. In doing so, we are following a set of conversational norms to efficiently communicate our understanding of events (Grice, 1975; Schwarz, 1994). These norms state that our communications should be relevant and informative regarding the current purposes of the exchange and that we should not offer more information than is required to answer a partner's query. As such, we often privilege one causal factor over others in discussing the causes of an event, taking into account the interests and knowledge of others.

We generate explanations in anticipation of communicating them to other people (e.g., "What do I tell my parents about why I failed the exam?"). Therefore, understanding how these conversational norms influence causal perceptions becomes a significant concern.

The following example demonstrates how different causal explanations might be generated based on the perceived needs of a conversational partner. Assume you are trying to explain to another person what caused a train accident. Assume further that your attributional analysis revealed that the train crash was due to a combination of several conditions: a bent track rail, the train's speed, and the inattentiveness of the engineer. In deciding what explanation to share with the person, you would take into account what you believe the listener already knows. If the person knows only about the speed of the train and the engineer's inattentiveness, you would likely emphasize the bent rail as *the* cause of the accident. In contrast, if the person knew about the physical aspects of the accident, then your causal explanation would be more likely to focus on the role of the engineer in causing it. In both cases, you, as a communicator, are trying to address a perceived gap in the partner's knowledge, thereby privileging one causal factor over others in explaining an event.

How can we tell what our conversation partner knows? One way to make that determination would be to rely on our beliefs about the person's possible knowledge based on stored cognitive representations. We might assume different expertise between an engineer versus a track maintenance supervisor, for example, leading us to emphasize different causal factors. We can also rely on causal questions to determine what the partner wants to know. If our partner asks, "Was the train following posted speeds?" we would likely provide a very different causal answer than if she asked, "When was the last track inspection?" Both questions are equally valid, but they will elicit responses that will alter the perceived causes of events.

Several studies have provided evidence consistent with the role of conversational norms in generating causal explanations (Kruglanski, Hamel, et al., 1978; Turnbull & Slugoski, 1988). One study (McGill, 1989) showed that changes in the wording used to elicit a causal explanation, in fact, changed the attribution to persons versus situations. There were two manipulations in the experiment. One manipulation involved whether the target was the self or a best friend, and participants were asked to indicate either their own or their friend's college major. A second manipulation varied the focus of a causal explanation through a subtle difference in the wording of a request for information about why that major was selected. Some participants were asked, "Why did you [your best friend] in particular choose this major?" whereas others were asked, "Why did you [your best friend] choose this major in particular?" The wording of the question put the focus on the person in the first case but the situation (specifically, the major) in the second case. In a third group of participants, the question was ambiguous concerning focus: "Why did you [your best friend] choose this major?"

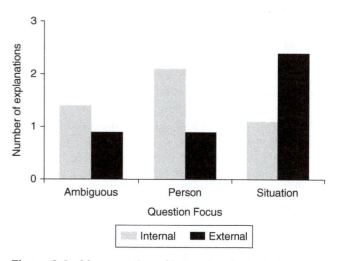

Figure 8.4 Mean number of internal and external explanations generated as a function of question focus
Source: Based on data from McGill (1989)

After being asked one of these questions, participants wrote a paragraph about why the major was chosen, and these explanations were coded as reflecting internal ("I like jobs that are challenging") and external ("finance is very challenging") explanations. Two results were notable. First, there were no differences in the likelihood of generating internal versus external explanations for oneself compared with one's friend. Second, the likelihood of internal versus external explanations varied based on the focus of the question. These results are displayed in Figure 8.4. When the question focused on the person (e.g., "you in particular"), explanations highlighted internal factors such as their preferences, interests, and goals. When the question focused instead on the situation (e.g., "this major in particular"), explanations concerned external factors such as aspects of the major that made it appealing to the actor. These results demonstrate that our causal descriptions of events are affected not only by our perception of the events themselves but also by what we think others want or need to know about those events.

Attributions in Long-term Relationships

In recent years, a considerable amount of research interest has examined attributional processes in close relationships. Therefore, in this section, we move to persons who know each other exceptionally well, especially romantic couples, with a focus on attributions in long-term relationships and marriages. Research has examined how partners' overall evaluation of the relationship (e.g., marital satisfaction) relates to the attributions made in the relationship.

In this literature, it is common to distinguish between causal attributions and those dealing with responsibility for an event (responsibility attributions), that is, attributions that emphasize factors involving intentionality and control. It is also common to compare happy, contented couples with struggling couples on their causal and responsibility attributions for the same behavior or incident. Not surprisingly, attributional patterns differ in struggling versus happy relationships, and these differences highlight many of the properties of attributions we have discussed. For example, partners in distressed couples tend to make more external attributions for their own than for their partner's negative behaviors (Bradbury & Fincham, 1990), and the internal attributions they make for their partner's actions often accentuate their impact. Specifically, they tend to explain relationship problems by pointing to stable and global dispositions of their partner ("He thinks he's always right"). Such attributions imply that partners expect persistent problems in their relationship.

In contrast, healthy couples tend to make attributions that minimize the impact of negative events. When adverse events do occur, they are likely to be attributed to external causes or, if a dispositional attribution is made, to unstable and specific factors ("He was in a bad mood") (Bradbury & Fincham, 1992). Such benign attributions are more likely to produce forgiveness for adverse events in the relationship (Davis & Gold, 2011; Fincham, Paleari, & Regalia, 2002; Kimmes & Durtschi, 2016). In these ways, attributional judgments play a critical role in determining who is satisfied. Indeed, the strength of the association between attributions and satisfaction has been referred to as "arguably the most robust phenomenon in the close-relationship literature" (Fincham, Harold, & Gano-Phillips, 2000, p. 268).

These results raise important questions about the nature and consequences of attributional patterns and the specific mechanisms by which they arise and persist in relationships. We turn to a brief consideration of some of these crucial issues.

Do Negative Attributions Cause Distress?

Evidence that distressed couples make more high-impact negative attributions does not necessarily mean that this attributional tendency itself causes distress. Negative attributions might cause dissatisfaction, but the causal direction could be the other way around; that is, the stress of marital dissatisfaction might create negative attributions. This is an important issue to clarify since some clinical interventions (Baucom, 1987; Baucom & Epstein, 1990) seek to improve marital satisfaction by changing attributions. If attributions are a result of rather than a cause of that distress, this might be ineffective.

Several researchers (Fincham et al., 2000; Fletcher, Fincham, Cramer, & Heron, 1987) have tried to establish whether attributional patterns cause distress in marriages. In one study, (Fincham et al., 2000) couples who had been married for 1–2 years completed measures of marital satisfaction (e.g., agreeing or disagreeing with items such as "We have a good marriage") and made attributional judgments for a series of everyday negative events (e.g., "Your spouse criticizes something you say") using a scale capturing causal locus, stability, and globality. These measures were completed again 18 months later. Approximately halfway between these two testing sessions, couples completed a measure of efficacy to assess the extent to which each spouse believed he or she could resolve conflicts in the marriage. The relations between these responses were assessed, and changes over time were investigated to assess causality.

Several significant findings emerged. First, confirming earlier research, negative attributions (explaining behavior with internal, stable, and global factors) lowered marital satisfaction. Second, analysis of these judgments over time showed that high-impact negative attributions caused later dissatisfaction. Specifically, the relation between previous attributions and later satisfaction was significant for both husbands and wives, whereas the relation between earlier satisfaction and later attributions was not. This pattern indicates that attributions predicted later marital satisfaction but not vice versa. Third, efficacy judgments mediated the relation between attributions and later marital satisfaction. In other words, causal attributions were linked to later satisfaction because they affected the perceived ability to resolve conflicts. Internal, stable, and global attributions for negative behavior produce lower expectations that the behavior will change in the future and, consequently, lowered satisfaction. In sum, these data show that attributions play a crucial causal role in marital satisfaction and stability.

How Do Causal Attributions Affect Behavior?

Attributions can affect behavioral interactions in relationships. For example, in one study, judgments about the controllability of a partner's nonverbal behaviors affected how the person responded. When emotional expressions were seen as controllable, partners responded more engagingly, responding with pleasant gazes and more upright posture to positive nonverbal behaviors (Manusov & Trees, 2002).

Causal attributions also predict whether aggression is present in relationships. Aggressive couples tend to have negative attributional styles (especially when the husbands drink alcohol) (Sillars, Roberts, Leonard, & Dun, 2000). Divergent causal attributions for one another's behavior are common in couples with a high degree of aggression. The husband might state that he engaged in a particular behavior because "I'm trying to get her to talk about it" but assert that his spouse engaged in the same behavior because "She's always got to have her way" (p. 97). Patterns of causal attribution can also contribute to physical aggression. Women who judged adverse marital events as their partner's fault (i.e., they judged their partner's negative behavior as high in intentionality, motivation, and personal responsibility) were more likely to have used violence (e.g., hitting, slapping, throwing objects) against their partner in the previous year. This relationship did not hold for men (Byrne & Arias, 1997).

Evidence of gender differences in the behavioral consequences of attributions has emerged in several studies (Bradbury & Fincham, 1992; Miller & Bradbury, 1995; Sanford, 2005). In one such study (Bradbury, Beach, Fincham & Nelson, 1996), couples engaged in a 10-minute discussion with their partner about an issue that both agreed was a problem in their marriage. These discussions were audiotaped and coded. Analyses of these discussions revealed that women who viewed their partner as more responsible for adverse events in their marriage were less likely to self-disclose, less likely to agree with their partner, and more likely to criticize their partner. Responsibility attributions did not predict men's behaviors. Together, these findings show that attributions affect the behavior of wives to a higher degree than husbands. This difference might indicate that wives feel more invested in their relationships (Worell, 1988) or are more responsive to the immediate context than are husbands (Carels & Baucom, 1999). Both factors might contribute to higher levels of attributional analysis and behavioral consequences for women (Holtzworth-Munroe & Jacobson, 1985).

How Do Attributional Processes Change?

Several studies have tracked heterosexual couples over time to determine the role of attributional processes in relationship development. Karney and Bradbury (2000) assessed marital satisfaction and attributions for partners' hypothetical undesirable behaviors (e.g., "Your spouse does not pay attention to what you are saying") every six months for four years, starting in the first year of marriage. These judgments often changed dynamically and interdependently over time. Specifically, marital satisfaction suffered to the degree that partners began to make more negative attributions for their partner's undesirable behaviors (i.e., attributing behavior to internal, global, stable, intentional, selfish, and blameworthy causes).

Some of the couples had divorced during the study, and two critical differences differentiated couples who were still married and those who divorced. First, couples were more likely to have divorced if wives made negative attributions for their husband's behavior. Men's attributions played little role in predicting divorce. Second, divorced couples showed a more substantial relation between attributions and satisfaction. In other words, the satisfaction of these couples appeared to be more fragile, likely to modulate in response to changes in attributions.

What accounts for the damage caused by negative attributions in marriage over time? This question was the focus of a study (Durtschi, Fincham, Cui, Lorenz, & Conger, 2011) that tracked 280 couples over the first five years of their marriage. Responsibility attributions and marital satisfaction were measured over time, and both self-report and experimenters' observations were used to assess the presence of both warm (e.g., expressing appreciation, showing affection) and hostile behaviors (e.g., criticism, shouting) in interactions between spouses. These data showed that the nature of attributions predicted later behavior and that behavior predicted future marital satisfaction for both spouses. For example, negative attributions increased hostility and decreased behavioral warmth, and these behavioral patterns then decreased marital satisfaction. The relationship between attributions and marital satisfaction was entirely mediated through behavior.

These results illustrate an unfortunate process that occurs in some romantic relationships. In the earliest years of marriage, couples are establishing habitual patterns of explaining their partner's behavior. These attributions are critical in determining how a person behaves toward his or her partner. So, if I attribute my partner forgetting my birthday to his "selfishness" rather than being "distracted by a big project at work," I am much more inclined to respond with anger and hostility than with warmth and affection. These behaviors, in turn, can influence how my spouse behaves towards me, perpetuating a cycle of negative attributions and behavior.

In summary, extensive research has shown the importance of attributions in romantic relationships. The focus thus far has been on marriages between men and women. Research has not yet sufficiently addressed other kinds of meaningful relationships. Some preliminary evidence (Houts & Horne, 2008) indicates that attributions are not as important in predicting satisfaction in gay couples as they are in heterosexual dyads. The lesser importance of attributions in relationships involving gay men may reflect the greater autonomy between partners, compared with heterosexual couples (Kurdek, 2001; Peplau, Veniegas, & Campbell, 1996). A better understanding of the role of attributions in gay and lesbian relationships will be of both theoretical interest and practical importance.

Attributional Processes in Understanding Groups

We began this chapter by describing when an attribution for a group's actions produced consequential (and devastating) results. The inference that Saddam Hussein's regime was resisting inspectors to hide weapons of mass destruction was used to justify, both domestically and internationally, the invasion of Iraq. Attributional judgments play several essential roles in intergroup situations. They can be used in processing stereotype relevant information, in differentially judging the actions of ingroup and outgroup members, and in determining responses to prejudice. We now briefly review research examining each of these issues.

Attributions for Stereotypical Behavior

As we have discussed, information that is unexpected or surprising triggers attributional thinking: Why did that happen? One category of information that prompts attributional analysis is information that contradicts stereotypical expectations. We would be puzzled to encounter a hostile child-care provider, a friendly White supremacist, or an unintelligent physicist. In each case, we would likely try to account for the discrepancy between what we expect for members of these groups and the behavior we have encountered. In general, actions that are consistent with stereotypes are attributed to stable internal causes, whereas stereotype inconsistent actions are attributed to external causes or unstable internal causes (Duncan, 1976; Heyman, 2001; Ramasubramanian, 2011; Yarkin, Town, & Wallston, 1982). Because an identical act might be consistent with expectations for some groups and not for others, people often make different attributions for the same behavior depending on the person's group membership.

One recent study showing such an effect (Salerno & Sanchez, 2020) examined attributions for a police officer's use of force during an encounter with a citizen captured on a dashboard camera. Participants in one condition were shown a minute-long segment of a videotaped interaction where, after a brief discussion, the citizen was thrown to the ground. The resolution of the video was degraded so that the actions were readily apparent, but the officer's gender was vague. Therefore, all elements of the interaction were held constant, but the officer's supposed gender – a dimension for which there are strong and opposing stereotypes regarding dominance and aggression for men and women (Ellemers, 2018; Koenig, Eagly, Mitchell, & Ristikari, 2011; Steinberg & Diekman, 2016) – could be manipulated. This was done by presenting participants with photographs of the officer supposedly in the video (depicting either Black and White men or Black and White women). After viewing the video, participants indicated what they believed caused the officer's actions on measures assessing internal (e.g., emotional volatility, violent tendencies, aggressiveness) and external attributions (e.g., the dangerousness of the situation, the suspect's resistance). They also answered questions about their trust in the officer and the officer's general effectiveness.

Results showed that attributions for the identical behavior depended on the supposed officer's gender but (somewhat surprisingly) not their race. When a male officer used force, participants judged his behavior as more likely to be caused by aspects of his personality and dispositions, and less likely due to situational factors, than when a female officer exhibited the same behavior. Furthermore, participants showed higher levels of trust in the officer and judged the officer as more effective if she were a woman rather than a man. Meditational analyses showed that these differences reflected differences in attributions. The male officer was judged less positively because his actions were attributed internally. In contrast, the female officer's same actions were attributed externally, yielding higher levels of trust and perceived effectiveness. These attributions reflect stereotypes that link men more strongly than women to aggression and dominance.

Stereotypes can also affect attributions of ability and, consequently, predictions for future success. In one study in the United States involving assessment of academic ability (Jackson, Sullivan, & Hodge, 1993), participants were told that their task was to make an admission decision for a student applicant. Half of the participants evaluated an applicant with strong academic credentials (e.g., high GPA), whereas the others viewed a weak application (low GPA). The applicant's race was manipulated by the ethnicity indicated on the application form (White/Caucasian or Black/African American). White participants indicated the importance of ability, effort, luck, and task characteristics in accounting for the applicant's record and also whether they would admit the applicant.

Results showed that strong applications from Black students were more likely attributed to external causes (task ease) or unstable causes (luck) compared with strong applications from White students, whose success was attributed to ability. Analyses of the relationship between attributions and admission decisions also showed racial differences. The only factor that predicted admission decisions for White applicants was their perceived ability. However, effort and task factors also predicted decisions for Black applicants, consistent with the idea that ingroups tend to be judged based on a single criterion. In contrast, the success of outgroups is attributed to multiple factors (Hewstone, Gale, & Purkhardt, 1990). Thus, not only did attributions differ for unexpected versus expected performance, but so did their implications for subsequent judgments.

Intergroup attitudes, including prejudice, can affect attributional judgments for unexpected information. This possibility was tested in one study (Sherman et al., 2005) examining attributions of behaviors supposedly performed by a gay man. Participants who (based on pilot testing) were known to have positive or negative attitudes toward homosexuality read about actions of a gay man. In one condition, the man performed mostly stereotype-consistent actions ("studied interpretive dance in college"). In a second condition, he behaved mostly counter to the stereotype ("watched a football game on Sunday afternoon"). Participants then made trait judgments of the man and were again shown the behavioral descriptions they had read earlier. Like participants in Hastie's (1984) study, they wrote sentence continuations that were then coded as reflecting internal or external attributions (e.g., watching the football game "because he enjoys the sport" or "to be with his male friends").

Participants low in prejudice made trait ratings that were consistent with the man's behavior. He was judged stereotypically, but only when he behaved stereotypically, and was rated nonstereotypically when his behavior indicated he was atypical of gay men. These participants also did not differ in their attributions for behaviors that were consistent or inconsistent with their expectations. In contrast, participants high in prejudice judged the man stereotypically regardless of his behavior, and, as is shown in Figure 8.5, they attributed expectancy-inconsistent behavior to external factors and expectancy-consistent behavior to internal factors. These results demonstrate an important consequence of attributional processes, namely, that they can be used to preserve pre-existing beliefs consistent with one's attitudes towards groups by explaining away behavior that challenges those beliefs. These results and others indicate that attributional processes and stereotyping are linked, suggesting that at least in some circumstances modifying causal attributions might moderate stereotyping (Brandt & Reyna, 2011; Johnston, Bristow, & Love, 2000; Seta, Seta, & McElroy, 2003; Stewart, Latu, Kawakami, & Myers, 2010; Wilder, Simon, & Faith, 1996).

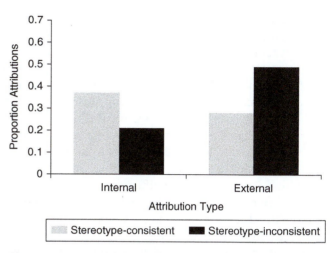

Figure 8.5   Proportion of attributions for stereotype consistent and stereotype inconsistent behavior in individuals with high levels of prejudice
Source: Adapted from Sherman et al. (2005)

Attributions for Ingroups vs. Outgroups

In the studies reviewed so far, expectancies and attitudes of social perceivers were shown to affect attributions for the behavior of outgroup members. How do judgments of ingroups differ from judgments of outgroups? If attributional biases reflect differences in expectations and attitudes, then one might expect to see asymmetries in attributions for actions of ingroups and outgroups. Indeed, that has been found in multiple studies. This was first demonstrated by Taylor and Jaggi (1974) in a study based in South India, who had Hindu participants read descriptions of positive and negative behaviors performed either by another Hindu or by an outgroup member, a Muslim. For each behavior, participants indicated whether it was caused more by internal or external factors. People were more likely to attribute negative ingroup behavior to external factors and positive ingroup behavior to internal factors. The reverse pattern was found for outgroups: positive behavior was explained externally, negative behavior more internally. Thus, attributions for the behavior of individual group members are biased by ingroup vs. outgroup status.

Research has also shown that explanations for the behavior of entire groups can be influenced by one's own group membership (Ariyanto, Hornsey, & Gallois, 2009; Doosje & Branscombe, 2003; Froehlich, Martiny, Deaux, & Mok, 2016). For example, one study examined how instances of interfaith violence in Northern Ireland were explained by Protestant and Catholic students (Hunter, Stringer, & Watson, 1991). These students were shown two videotaped scenes of violence, one showing a Protestant attack on mourners at a funeral and a second showing a Catholic attack on a car containing soldiers. Participants were given three minutes to explain the behaviors depicted in the videos. An examination of these explanations showed that aggressive actions performed by the ingroup were attributed to external factors, whereas outgroup violence was attributed to internal causes. This asymmetry in attributions for ingroup versus outgroup behavior is consistent with a general pattern to make attributions that benefit the ingroup, a phenomenon termed the *ultimate attribution error* (Pettigrew, 1979).

Hewstone (1990) reviewed the evidence for the ultimate attribution error and other attributional asymmetries involving ingroups versus outgroups. From that review, he drew three main conclusions. First, internal attributions for positive actions are stronger for ingroups than for outgroups, whereas the reverse is sometimes true for harmful acts (i.e., stronger internal attributions for outgroups than ingroups). Second, outgroup failure is more likely to be attributed to low ability than ingroup failure. In contrast, outgroup success is more likely to be attributed to good luck, high effort, and task ease than ingroup success. Third, there is a preference to explain group differences by invoking attributions that favor the ingroup. For example, American students explained gender differences in ways that favored their own gender group (Bond, Hewstone, Wan, & Chiu, 1985). When asked to indicate why "women disclose their emotions more often than men," men tended to agree with the notion that "men are more confident than women," whereas women agreed that "women are more open than men." Note that both of these attributions favor one's own group while also perpetuating existing stereotypes.

Attributions to Prejudice in Explaining Outcomes

Like all inferences, attributions are subjective. The reason that any particular event has occurred is not always apparent and, therefore, the social perceiver has some latitude in selecting the causal explanation for any given event. This is particularly true in intergroup domains, where the motives of another person are often ambiguous or in doubt ("Was that person nice to me in order to appear unbiased?") (Kunstman & Fitzpatrick, 2018; Major, Kunstman, Malta, Sawyer, Townsend, & Berry Mendes, 2016; Major, Quinton, & McCoy, 2002). Members of stereotyped and stigmatized groups often operate under *attributional ambiguity*, unsure how to interpret the behavior of outgroup members. Allport (1954) suggested that under these conditions, experiences of prejudice can be attributed *intropunitively*, yielding internal attributions and self-blame, or *extropunatively*, producing external attributions (usually to prejudice) and other-blame.

Crocker and Major (1989) offered an influential, although controversial, view that attributing negative outcomes to prejudice can be beneficial, as it allows adverse personal outcomes and experiences to be explained away due to faults in the perpetrators rather than in the victims of bias. One benefit is that such attributions can be protective of self-esteem. This idea was tested in several experiments where participants from stigmatized groups (e.g., African Americans, women) were asked to perform a task in the laboratory, after which they were provided with bogus negative feedback from an evaluator. The probability that this feedback might reflect prejudice was systematically varied by modifying the extent to which the evaluator could be aware of the participant's group membership (e.g., by leading the participant to believe that group membership information had been shared with the evaluator) or the extent that the evaluator might be prejudiced against the group (e.g., if the participant was led to believe that the person had previously expressed sexist attitudes) (Crocker, Voelkl, Testa, & Major, 1991). Participants whose negative feedback could be attributed to prejudice had higher self-esteem and more positive feelings about the self (Major & Sawyer, 2009). By being able to explain adverse outcomes by invoking prejudice in others, attributions can provide members of oppressed and stigmatized groups with self-protective explanations that can be hard to disprove.

However, external attributions of negative treatment to prejudice might not always be self-protective. People may still feel apprehensive about experiences with prejudice, and these feelings may be exacerbated to the degree that members of oppressed groups have to persistently deal with situations in which they risk feeling rejected (Schmitt & Branscombe, 2002). Consistent with this notion, research has shown that external attributions to prejudice protect against lowered self-esteem but not against anxiety (Major, Kaiser, & McCoy, 2003). A meta-analysis (Schmitt, Branscombe, Postmes, & Garcia, 2014) examined the role of perceived discrimination (a necessary precondition for attributing outcomes to prejudice) in accounting for various aspects of well-being, including self-esteem, anxiety, and life satisfaction. This analysis concluded that perceiving discrimination generally harmed several aspects of psychological well-being, including psychological distress and negative affect, but that effects were weaker on measures of self-esteem, life satisfaction, and positive affect. The finding that self-esteem was only weakly affected by perceived discrimination is consistent with Crocker and Major's (1989) argument that attributing negative outcomes to perceived discrimination can protect self-esteem.

SUMMARY

Causal attributions are inferences about why an event occurred, and attributions are some of the most critical inferences we make. We may often agree with others regarding what occurred but disagree quite strongly regarding why the event occurred. The possibility that people can generate different causal explanations for the same behavior highlights the subjectivity of causal inferences. We use our knowledge, beliefs, prejudices, perspectives, and expectations in making sense of the behavior of others, so it should not be surprising that different people often diverge in their judgments of causal factors and what that judgment says about the person or group being observed. Despite their subjective nature, our answers to causal questions have consequences for our subsequent judgments and behavior. Determining why an event has occurred helps us better understand why things happen, providing information about ourselves, other individuals, and the groups that we encounter in our social world.

FURTHER READING

Malle, B.F. (2011). Time to give up the dogmas of attribution: An alternative theory of behavior explanation. In J.M. Olson & M.P. Zanna (Eds.), *Advances in experimental social psychology* (Vol. 44, pp. 297–352). New York, NY: Academic Press.

Olcaysoy Okten, I., & Moskowitz, G.B. (2018). Goal versus trait explanations: Causal attributions beyond the trait-situation dichotomy. *Journal of Personality and Social Psychology, 114,* 211–229.

Reeder, G.D. (2013). Attribution as a gateway to social cognition. In D.E. Carlston (Ed.), *The Oxford handbook of social cognition* (pp. 95–117). New York, NY: Oxford University Press.

9

JUDGMENT

Reasoning and Decision Making

As soon as questions of will or decision or reason or choice of action arise, human science is at a loss.

Noam Chomsky, 1978 (quoted in Kolatch, 1996)

The essence of ultimate decisions remains impenetrable to the observer – often, indeed the decider himself…There will always be the dark and tangled stretches in the decision-making process – mysterious even to those who may be most intimately involved.

John F. Kennedy (quoted in Sorensen, 1963)

We regularly make decisions about how we should act. Should I smile at that person who seems to recognize me? Should I give money to this charity? Should I follow this person on Twitter? Although these judgments might seem insignificant, we also must decide how to address some of the most critical and consequential questions in our lives. Where should I go to college? Should I keep dating or break up with this person? Should I change my career?

Given the importance of questions like these, social scientists have attempted to understand how people reason and make judgments (see Halpern, 2016; Kahneman, 2011; Lewis, 2016; Van Boven, Travers, Westfall, & McClelland, 2013). Moreover, decision making has developed into an interdisciplinary area of study with contributions from many different fields, including social cognition. The approaches of different disciplines to decision making vary widely. Historians, for example, generally use case studies to analyze critical decisions made by leaders in difficult or uncertain circumstances (e.g., Allison & Zelikow, 1999; Bohn, 2015). Political scientists examine the contributions of legislators, courts, voters, and lobbyists in making decisions within different kinds of governing systems (e.g., Houghton, 2013; Zahariadis, 2003). In medical fields, research focuses on diagnoses and judgments about treatment (Djulbegovic, Elqayam, & Dale, 2018; Trimble & Hamilton, 2016).

Much of the earliest and most influential work on decision making attempted to characterize how individuals make decisions involving money and value. Historically, these economic approaches emphasized the rational nature of judgment and decision making. Adam Smith (1759/1892) famously argued that people's decisions typically serve their self-interests, generally to the benefit of all. Moreover, if a person acts to fulfill his or her objectives and avoids actions that undermine them, the person is seen as behaving rationally (Edwards, 1961). This view rests on several assumptions. It assumes that individuals have a causal role in making choices, that they have extensive information about available actions and also the consequences of these alternatives, that they make choices that maximize self-benefit, and that, given the same information, they exhibit stable and consistent preferences. These assumptions form the basis of a theoretical framework – the *Rational Actor Theory* – that historically dominated the field of economics. This framework served as a *normative model* that *proscribed* how decisions should optimally be made (Simon, 1982).

Psychological research also has focused on decision making at the level of the individual. However, in contrast to the Rational Actor Model, these approaches have historically focused on shortcomings in human decision making. Psychology has emphasized what people *actually do* rather than what they *should do* based on normative models of rationality. This approach has enriched the study of decision making by providing *descriptive* models that characterize how people actually make decisions, emphasizing how people often deviate from rational standards. This chapter will show that many assumptions underlying rational approaches to decision making should be questioned. Psychological research shows that people often have less of a causal role in making decisions than they realize. We often are influenced by forces we neither recognize nor control. We rarely, if ever, have enough information about our options and the consequences of our decisions to ensure that they are optimal. Moreover, we often forego deliberative analysis of available information and instead make snap judgments based on intuition. Our choices often fail to maximize self-benefit, reflecting instead what is merely satisfying, "good enough" to meet our needs. Our preferences are often inconsistent, and our choices can be reversed with slight changes in the way options are described or framed.

Psychological approaches, therefore, reflect the *bounded rationality* of people who are typically limited in the motivation and ability to gather, recall, and fully use available information to make decisions (Gigerenzer & Selten, 2002; Kahneman, 2003; Simon, 1982). The field of *behavioral economics* reflects these limitations, focusing on social, cognitive, and affective factors that characterize decision making in realistic environments (Ariely, 2009; Brafman & Brafman, 2008; Corr & Plagnol, 2019). Findings from behavioral economics have brought about many changes to previously common practices in business, medicine, and government (Benartzi et al., 2017; Roberto & Kawachi, 2016; Thaler & Sunstein, 2008).

Even though judgments and decisions often fall short of logical standards, rational models remain useful in several respects. First, the fact that people do not always act rationally does not mean that they never do. While decision making is sometimes irrational, humans are capable of making logical decisions and regularly make sound (if not perfect) judgments. One critical issue for research is to identify the conditions when decision making is likely to be suboptimal and the factors that affect the quality of judgments.

Second, rational models offer a standard against which the rationality of individual decisions can be judged. For example, human judgments can be compared with optimal standards generated using Bayesian logic, an approach to decision making where knowledge of prior events is used to predict the probability of future outcomes (Oaksford & Chater, 2007, 2009). Recognizing deviations from such a rational standard can be useful in helping people make better decisions in the real world.

Third, even if they are poor at predicting individual behavior, rational models are often quite accurate in accounting for group-level phenomena. For example, financial markets often appear to follow rational rules, even though individual decision-makers in those markets might be highly irrational. Weaknesses in any individual's decision-making processes are often offset by the presence of other decision-makers who can take advantage of those errors. Consequently, decision making involving large groups is often rational despite individual irrationality. However, it is crucial to recognize that although classic economic approaches often accurately account for aggregate-level decision making, psychological approaches recognizing the strengths and weaknesses of individual decision-makers are typically superior in explaining judgments of a single person. Thus, both rational and irrational approaches are important in accounting for human reasoning and decision making. The strength of a psychological approach to judgment lies in its ability to provide a realistic account of individual-level decision making, recognizing several key reasons why decisions sometimes (if not typically) fall short of rational standards.

We began this chapter with two quotes that raise questions about the ability of psychologists (or any scientists, for that matter) to provide useful insights into the nature of human choices and decisions. We think these views are overly pessimistic. Indeed, much has been learned about how people make decisions since Chomsky expressed his doubts. Nonetheless, there is still reason to agree with President Kennedy's view that certain aspects of decision making are impenetrable, at least for the person engaged in the process of making a choice. Indeed, one of the themes of this book (and, more generally, the field of social cognition) is that perceivers have limited insight into their cognitive processes.

The domain of decision making is no exception to this maxim. As we discussed in Chapter 3, people may be aware of and exert control over some aspects of information processing, but many processes can occur without intentional initiation or awareness. A parallel distinction between relatively automatic, effortless, and intuitive processes versus more deliberative, effortful, and rational processes is central in theorizing about judgment. Indeed, recognition of the importance of both intuitive and rational processes was one of the first contributions of psychological approaches to judgment and decision making. Much early research emphasized the importance of intuitive processes, contrasting these effects with predictions made by traditional approaches emphasizing rationality. However, more recent studies have shown how both types of processes co-occur and contribute jointly, sometimes in harmony and sometimes in opposition, to social judgment. We now discuss in some detail the contributions of both types of processes to judgment and decision making. We then turn to a discussion of the role of rationality in judgment, offering descriptions of both optimal decision-making processes and a discussion of factors that lead decision-makers to typically fall short of these standards. We end by discussing research on judgment and decision making involving the self, other individuals, and groups.

INTUITION AND REASONING IN JUDGMENT

Consider how a young woman might go about making an important decision such as where to attend college. On the one extreme, she might begin by gathering extensive information about a large number of colleges and universities. For each one, she might collect data on the size of the student body, the ratio of male to female students, the test scores of incoming first-year students, the curriculum it offers, and the career paths of recent graduates. She might consider the distance from her home, tuition costs, and the quality of specific programs. By gathering and integrating this information for a large number of institutions, she can make comparisons among them in hopes that one option will emerge as her obvious right choice. She will not be able to guarantee that she has made the best choice since much information that will ultimately determine her satisfaction is not yet available (e.g., compatibility with her roommate, peculiarities of her instructors). However, she can at least take comfort that she made her decision using an exhaustive (if also exhausting!) process.

On the other extreme, she might make this decision by immediately limiting her options to a subset of schools, considering only schools within a certain distance from home or focusing only on small colleges. In narrowing her choices further, she might rely on a few handy shortcuts. She could rely on recommendations from family or friends, gauge her enthusiasm as she visits college websites, or take note of successful graduates. Such factors might influence her decision without her awareness, and she might even deny their sway if she were asked how they affected her decision. However, by relying on such intuitive shortcuts, she has spared herself a tremendous amount of effort and exertion.

These processes – one more deliberative and one more intuitive – might have produced different choices, but the student will never know that unless she compares decisions derived through both strategies. Moreover, even if these processes produce different decisions, she will never know which decision was better. Since she will attend only one of these two options, she will never know how happy she would have been at the other school. What is clear is that both approaches can be used to generate a satisfying decision.

This example illustrates two dramatically different styles of decision making. Dating back to William James (1890), it has been recognized that each style of processing exists in each of us. For any given decision, we might engage in one or the other strategy and might even vacillate between the two. Intriguingly, research over the last several decades has revealed that both kinds of judgment can occur in parallel. We can be engaged in deliberative decision making while simultaneously being influenced by intuitive thoughts and responses (De Neys, 2018; Evans, 1984, 2008; Sloman, 1996; Thompson, Prowse Turner, & Pennycook, 2011). When both kinds of processes produce the same decisional outcome, the "correct" decision will seem clear. However, when controlled and intuitive processes produce different preferences, anxiety and uncertainty can prevail. The fact that discrepancies can arise between deliberative versus intuitive processes helps explain why decisions can be inconsistent over time and amenable to reversal.

The recognition of the co-existence of intuitive and rational factors in decision making was one of psychology's first *dual process* models recognizing complementary cognitive processes (Gilovich & Griffin, 2010). Subsequent theorizing about dual processes in reasoning and decision making (Kahneman, 2003; Kahneman & Frederick, 2005; Smith & DeCoster, 2000; Stanovich & West, 2000; Strack & Deutsch, 2004) characterizes intuitive and reasoning systems in ways that roughly correspond to the automatic versus controlled distinction we introduced in Chapter 3. However, the terminology used in decision making has been historically somewhat distinct from the language used in other areas of psychological research. For example, Stanovich and West (2000) coined the terms *System 1* (to describe a set of more automatic processes) and *System 2* (describing more controlled processes). Kahneman (2003, 2011) also embraced these terms in distinguishing intuitive and reasoning systems (see Table 9.1).

Table 9.1 Characteristics of System 1 (intuitive system) and System 2 (reasoning system)

System 1	System 2
Fast	Slow
Automatic	Deliberate
Associative	Rule-based
Effortless	Effortful
Parallel	Serial
Slow-learning	Flexible

Source: Adapted from Kahneman (2003)

In the Kahneman (2003) model, System 1 is the *intuitive system*. It operates quickly and effortlessly, it relies on associations and heuristics ("cognitive shortcuts") developed through experience, and it is difficult to control or modify. People are typically not aware of the processes involved in System 1, though they might become aware of the outcome of such processes (e.g., when a decision is made based on intuition). System 2 is the *reasoning system*. It operates based on rules and algorithms, it works slowly and serially, it requires motivation and effort to instigate and maintain, and it is deliberately controlled. In contrast to System 1 processes, however, reasoning processes are relatively flexible; they can be selected, deployed, and controlled through intention. People are often aware of both the operation and output of processes under System 2 (such as when a decision is made through exhaustive, thoughtful analysis).

System 2 also serves as a check on responses generated by System 1. System 1 "quickly proposes intuitive answers to judgment problems as they arise, and System 2 monitors the quality of these proposals, which it may endorse, correct or override" (Kahneman & Frederick, 2002, p. 51). In other words, if a response provided by System 1 is judged acceptable to System 2, it will be the basis of judgment. If the response raises doubt or is judged to be in error, however, System 2 processes can be invoked to correct or override input from System 1.

Two issues immediately arise from this basic premise. The first issue relates to the conditions that allow for correction of System 1 outputs by System 2. Research shows that variables involving both the judgment context and participants' chronic processing tendencies affect the degree that people can engage in correction of erroneous intuitive judgments. Correction is less likely when people have limited time for deliberation (Bago, Rand, & Pennycook, 2020; Finucane, Alhakami, Slovic, & Johnson, 2000), are operating under a cognitive load (Saini & Thota, 2010; Shiv & Fedorikhin, 1999; Svedholm & Lindeman, 2013), or are in a happy mood (Bless, Clore, Schwarz, Golisano, Rabe, & Wolk, 1996; King, Burton, Hicks, & Drigotas, 2007). Individual differences in intelligence (Stanovich & West, 2000), motivation to reason (Svedholm & Lindeman, 2013), and expertise in statistical reasoning (Agnoli, 1991) also moderate the likelihood of correction. In sum, both motivation and capacity factors allow correction, as has been the case regarding other phenomena we have discussed where controlled processes are required.

A second issue pertains to the factors that trigger System 2 correction of System 1 intuitive responses. Several factors have been shown to initiate System 2 correction processes (Kahneman & Frederick, 2002, 2005). In general, System 2 can be triggered whenever a question arises for which System 1 does not offer an easy answer (Kahneman, 2011). A situation involving financial risk (Epley & Gilovich, 2005) or a task allowing little margin for error (e.g., decisions in emergency medicine; Croskerry, 2008) tends to intensify monitoring processes. System 2 correction is also activated by unexpected or surprising information (Johnston, Lavine, & Woodson, 2015; Meyer, Reisenzein, & Schützwohl, 1997) or when one realizes that an intuitive response has produced an irrational behavior (Risen, 2016). For example. System 2 might reject superstitious beliefs generated by System 1 that are viewed as irrational (e.g., rejecting the automatic, but illogical, anxiety you might have experienced when a black cat crossed your path).

Many triggers of System 2 processes involve *disfluency*, a phenomenon briefly discussed in Chapter 6. As you likely recall, disfluency is experienced when there is a reduction in the speed or efficiency of mental operations. The role of disfluency in initiating System 2 processes is cleverly demonstrated in research showing that reliance on System 1 decreases when subtle manipulation of stimulus features increases disfluency, thereby signaling the need for deliberative processing (Alter, Oppenheimer, Epley, & Eyre, 2007). In one experiment, participants were presented with questions that typically generate intuitive but incorrect responses, requiring correction through deliberative processes. One such question was the following:

A bat and a ball cost $1.10 in total. The bat costs $1.00 more than the ball. How much does the ball cost?

Most people incorrectly conclude that the ball costs $0.10, since $1.10 easily divides into $1.00 and $0.10. That answer is incorrect, of course, since the difference between those amounts is only $0.90. The correct answer is that the ball costs $0.05, and the bat costs $1.05. For most people, deriving the correct answer requires System 2 to override an intuitive but erroneous judgment produced by System 1.

Alter et al. (2007) manipulated the ease with which such questions could be processed by varying the font that was used to present them. The logic of the study was that increasing the difficulty of reading the question should create feelings of disfluency. These feelings should send a signal that System 2 reasoning is required, triggering a more thorough analysis of the question and consequently increasing the likelihood that the problem would be answered correctly. Accordingly, some participants were given the questions printed in a font that was clear and easy to read, but the other participants received the same questions written in a small and difficult to read font. The results showed that the ease of reading the questions influenced the likelihood that they would be answered correctly. When the problems were presented in the easy-to-read font, participants provided an average of 1.9 correct answers out of the three questions. In contrast, when written in the difficult font, the average was 2.45. A full 90% of participants provided at least one incorrect response in the former condition, but only 35% did so in the latter condition. These results illustrate that outputs of the intuitive system are often used by default in making judgments. However, controlled processes can be engaged to override intuitive responses when a signal is received that indicates a possible error, even when that signal arises through factors irrelevant to the difficulty of the problem itself (e.g., type of font). More broadly, these results show that both intuitive and reasoning processes can contribute to effective decision making.

Whereas this research suggests that controlled processes must be initiated in response to intuitive error, there is some evidence showing that intuitive and reasoning processes are both active and available to guide decision making. Evidence of such joint contribution has been provided by a study designed to identify two basic forms of reasoning: relatively automatic intuitive processes and controlled rule-based reasoning processes (Ferreira, Garcia-Marques, Sherman, & Sherman, 2006). Participants in these experiments were given several problems where intuitive responses would likely produce suboptimal decisions. For example, participants were given the following scenario where the number of envelopes containing a prize ticket was manipulated:

Elaine was on a TV show where she had to choose an envelope from one of two sets of envelopes. In the first set, there were 100 envelopes, (*19* or *21*) of which contained a prize ticket of $5,000. In the second set, there were 10 envelopes, 2 of which contained a prize ticket of $5,000.

If you were Elaine, what would you do?

a. I would choose an envelope from the first set of envelopes.
b. I would choose an envelope from the second set of envelopes.

For this problem, intuitive and reasoning processes were expected to produce different choices depending on the condition. When 21 envelopes contained prize tickets, rational and intuitive responses were compatible, with both processes favoring option (a), since a 21% chance of winning is better than a 20% chance. In contrast, when only 19 envelopes contained winning tickets, intuitive and reasoning processes are incompatible. Here, the logical choice is option (b) (a 20% chance is better than a 19% chance), but the intuitive choice continues to be (a). This judgment error occurs because the large number of winning envelopes sometimes leads people to select that option ("19 chances to win, versus only 2!"), even though the probabilities favor the second option. In other words, a higher absolute number of favorable cases makes it more attractive when people are operating intuitively (Kirkpatrick & Epstein, 1992).

The researchers also manipulated the instructions given to participants, indicating how they should approach solving the problems. Half of the participants were told that the study concerned "human intuition" and that they should "base their answers to the problems on their intuition and personal sensitivity." The other participants were told that the study assessed "human rationality" and that they should "behave like scientists and to base their answers on rational and reflective thinking." The logic of this manipulation was that participants would feel more comfortable relying on System 1 responses if they had been encouraged to rely on intuition but would more carefully scrutinize (and correctly respond to) items if they had been encouraged to process rationally.

As is depicted in the left two pairs of bars of Figure 9.1, instructions affected performance on this task. On problems where intuitive and rational processes should both produce correct judgments (compatible problems), the selection of the optimal response was higher when participants were encouraged to act rationally rather than intuitively. In contrast, when intuitive and rational processes are expected to produce different responses (incompatible problems), participants told to act intuitively made a higher proportion of intuitive (but suboptimal) choices. Participants instructed to behave rationally made fewer suboptimal choices.

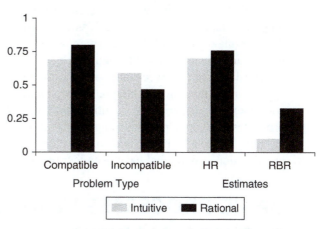

Figure 9.1 Proportion selection of the intuitive options for compatible and incompatible problems (left bars) and estimates of heuristic reasoning (hr) and rule-based reasoning (rbr) (right bars) as a function of instruction condition

Source: Based on data from Ferreira et al. (2006)

The basis of choices was also assessed by calculating estimates of heuristic (intuitive) and rule-based (rational) contributions to judgments using established computational procedures (Jacoby, 1991). As can be seen in the right two pairs of bars in Figure 9.1, these analyses showed that intuition played an influential role in decision making for both groups. The difference in performance was due to a stronger utilization of rational processes by participants who were told to act like scientists. They too had an initial tendency to respond based on their intuitions. However, these responses were overridden by controlled, rational processes focused on avoiding error when intuitions might produce a suboptimal response.

If rational responses reflect controlled processes, they should be more common when cognitive resources are readily available. Conversely, a cognitive load that limits resources should disrupt controlled processes to a greater degree than intuitive processes. Support for this interpretation comes from another experiment (Ferreira et al., 2006) in which some participants made decisions under a cognitive load. As predicted, imposing such a load reduced reasoning processes but did not affect the use of intuition (see also Callan, Sutton, & Dovale, 2010; Conway & Gawronski, 2013). In yet another study (Ferreira et al., 2006), some participants were primed to rely on intuitions by completing several initial problems where heuristics produced the optimal answer. Because System 1 relies on automatic use of associations, repeatedly prompting people to utilize associations to make judgments led to greater use of intuitive processing but no differences in reasoning.

Taken together, these studies show that intuition involves efficient and effortlessly-activated processes, whereas reasoning relies on controlled and resource-consuming cognitive activities. Reasoning and intuitive processes operate independently and in parallel. However, intuitive processes are persistent, whereas reasoning processes depend on having the capacity available to engage in deliberative processes. The relative contribution of the two systems to judgment depends on factors such as the accuracy of the intuitive response, the ability of the decision-maker to think deliberatively about a choice, and the level of motivation required to initiate and to maintain controlled processes.

The distinction between rational and intuitive processes is one crucial contribution of psychology to understanding judgment and decision making. Some processes occur quite effortlessly, and other processes require intention and effort. We have not yet discussed some of the precise processes that vary along this dimension that play central roles in judgment and decision making. We now turn to a more detailed consideration of some of the most critical processes in judgment and decision making that have been identified over the last several decades of research.

BASIC PROCESSES IN JUDGMENT AND DECISION MAKING

The nature of social judgment processes has been a matter of extensive debate (Festinger, 1964; Janis & Mann, 1977; Plous, 1993), but it is clear that multiple factors play essential roles in formulating judgments and decisions. In this section, we first discuss processes involved in *acquiring information* as a person is confronted with a choice or a decision. Where do we look for the information we need to make a decision or judgment? How do we go about gathering that information? How effective are we at gathering useful information? After considering these questions, we then turn to an analysis of how people go about *integrating information* to form a judgment. Given the information gathered, how do we utilize and process this information to derive a judgment? Finally, we end this section by introducing *Prospect Theory* (Kahneman & Tversky, 1979), an influential formal model of decision making that integrates many of the processes we consider in this section. In addressing each of these questions, we also discuss factors that influence the quality of judgments and decisions.

Information Acquisition

The information we use in making judgments and decisions can come from many sources. We might look to other people, including friends, family, or acquaintances as information resources.

We might look to authoritative sources, including textbooks, news stories, databases, or experts. Alternatively, we might derive information from the knowledge and experience that we have stored in memory.

Although we can gather information from many different places, our limited cognitive systems do not allow us to gather all the information that might be relevant to a decision. Several factors constrain our ability to have complete information, and the information that we do gather often is seriously biased by the way it is collected.

In searching for information, we are often guided by preconceptions based on prior knowledge, pre-existing beliefs, impressions, and stereotypes, all of which provide expectancies that we bring to this process. Those expectancies act as hypotheses ("She seems really smart so should be hired for this job" "He seems extremely outgoing, so he might be fun to have at the party") that can then be informally tested in our search for new information. Of course, that search may be biased. Two primary biases have been studied in research. On the one hand, expectancies can orient us toward information consistent with our hypothesis. This might lead us to seek information consistent with it, to ignore information that is inconsistent with it, or to distort or reinterpret inconsistent information in order to preserve our hypothesis. On the other hand, the search may be biased toward disconfirming the hypothesis ("Her grades in her major were not impressive"), a strategy that would avoid making a severe error of judgment (hiring an unqualified person can be costly). Research has produced evidence showing both of these biases, but one is more prevalent than the other. Therefore, it becomes important to know the conditions under which each one is most likely to occur.

Confirmation Bias

In general, our search process is often oriented toward information that confirms our prior expectancies and hypotheses. This tendency is known as *confirmation bias*. People seek information that validates their beliefs and tend not to notice or seek out information that disconfirms what they already believe (or suspect) to be true (Klayman & Ha, 1987; Skov & Sherman, 1986). They seem not to appreciate the importance of seeking information that disconfirms their hunches.

One of the clearest demonstrations of the confirmatory bias is provided in a task developed by Wason (1968). In this task, participants are shown four cards and told that each one has a number on one side and a letter on the other side. Only one side of each card is visible. Participants are then provided with a rule to test: "All cards with a vowel on one side have an even number on the other." They are told to test this rule by turning over the minimum number of cards necessary to determine whether it is true or not. Which of the following cards should you turn over to test the validity of this rule?

A D 2 7

The "A" card should be turned over because the letter on its face is a vowel. If the number on the other side is odd, then the rule would be invalidated. Most people who complete this task correctly turn this card. What about the "D"? Since this letter is a consonant, it does not need to be turned to assess the rule; most people correctly skip this card. Should the "2" be turned? Many people turn over this card, even though doing so offers no information relevant to the rule. The rule states that cards with vowels on one side have even numbers on the other, *not* that if there is an even number on one side, the other side would have a vowel. Since no letter on the other side of the 2 would invalidate the rule, this card should not be turned. Finally, what about the "7"? Most people neglect to turn this card, but they should. Why? If you were to find a vowel on the other side, the rule would be invalidated because 7 is an odd number. Therefore, the "7" and the "A" cards are the only ones that can falsify the rule. While most people do turn over the "A" card (a confirmatory choice), they fail to recognize that the "7" card also represents an opportunity to disconfirm or invalidate the rule. Because of the greater tendency to seek out confirming over disconfirming information, only about 20% of participants in studies using this task correctly pick these two cards (Cosmides, 1989; Evans, 1982).

This tendency to seek out confirmatory information has profound implications in virtually every aspect of our lives (Nickerson, 1998). People are more willing to seek and accept information that confirms prior expectations about themselves, about other people, and about groups. Snyder and Swann (1978) provided an experimental demonstration of the confirmatory bias in social perception. All participants were told that they would interview a woman during the study. Some were told that they should try to determine if she was an extravert (sociable, talkative, outgoing), and the others were told to decide whether she was an introvert (shy, timid, quiet). Participants were given a list of 26 questions from which they were to select 12 that they thought would be most helpful in finding out if the woman was an extravert (or an introvert). Half of the questions asked about behaviors that would likely be true of an extravert ("What would you do if you wanted to liven up a party?" "In what situations are you most talkative?"), the other half being more characteristic of an introvert ("What factors make it hard for you to open up to people?" "What do you dislike about loud parties?"). Participants who were prompted to determine whether the woman was an extravert selected considerably more extraverted-confirming questions, whereas participants prompted to test for introversion selected more of the introvert-confirming questions. The questions they chose would have been difficult to answer in a way that would allow the disconfirmation of the hypothesis that was being tested by the interviewer. These findings have been replicated many times (Davies, 1997, 2003; Snyder, 1981; Snyder & Swann, 1978; Snyder, Campbell, & Preston, 1982).

Despite these findings, important questions have been raised about the methods used in these studies, particularly about the choice of questions used. In particular, it has been argued that the questions are not diagnostic because answers cannot really discriminate between introverts and extraverts (Semin & Strack, 1980; Skov & Sherman, 1986; Trope & Bassok, 1982, 1983). For example, if asked, "What would you do if you wanted to liven up a party?" any reasonable answer would make you appear to be an extravert, even if you are a true introvert.

Other research has documented the confirmatory bias using methods that avoid this weakness. In one study, when participants were presented with strong evidence of a person's introversion or extraversion and selected from a natural set of questions "that would best enable them to learn to know" the person, there was substantial evidence of confirmation bias (Meertens, Koomen, Delpeut, & Hager, 1984). Effects consistent with confirmatory bias have also emerged from studies showing that cognitions tend to be consistent with expectations based on personality descriptions (Davies, 1997, 2003) and that counselors tend to recall expectancy-consistent behaviors performed by clients (Strohmer & Shivy, 1994).

Evidence of confirmation bias has also been shown in various fields including the law (Erard, 2016; Kassin, Dror, & Kukucka, 2013), economics (Aldashev, Carletti, & Righi, 2011; Christandl, Fetchenhauer, & Hoelzl, 2011), and medicine (Cox & Popken, 2008; Coyne & Johansen, 2011). In addition, the confirmation bias has been implicated in the persistence of beliefs in paranormal phenomena such as ESP, psychic ability, astrology, and palm reading (Rudski, 2002; Smith, 2009). Even the sciences are susceptible. Despite the importance of disconfirmation in developing new knowledge (Popper, 1959), accepted scientific wisdom is typically slow to change in response to new claims, even when they are accompanied by strong evidence (Fugelsang, Stein, Green, & Dunbar, 2004; Hergovich, Schott, & Burger, 2010; Hojat, Gonnella, & Caelleigh, 2003).

Although this evidence shows that confirmatory bias is common, research also points to conditions when people seek and value other kinds of information. Specifically, people are especially interested in information that is seen as *diagnostic*, that is, able to accurately shed light on the personality and motives of others. For example, if in selecting a roommate we learned from a mutual friend that a person we thought to be friendly was actually prone to explosive temper tantrums, we would likely seek out additional information before committing to sharing a room. People prefer diagnostic information over information that is nondiagnostic but confirming of our hypotheses (Devine, Hirt, & Gehrke, 1990; Trope & Bassok, 1982; Trope & Liberman, 1996). However, if a wide variety of diagnostic information is available, people also use strategies that elicit hypothesis-confirming information (Skov & Sherman, 1986).

Truncated Search

People often collect less information than is needed to ensure good decisions. We use various strategies and decision rules that minimize the amount of information that we consider, stopping when enough information has been gathered to allow a judgment with sufficient subjective certainty (Bodenhausen & Wyer, 1987; Higgins, 1996; Wyer & Srull, 1989). Think about making a critical decision in your life (Should I go to college? Get married? Have children? Get divorced?). There are many issues to consider. How would you ideally go about considering all the issues and integrating them to make a good decision? You might follow a recommendation Benjamin Franklin (1772/1956) made to a friend, using what he called "Moral or Prudential Algebra" (what is now called a *linear weighted additive strategy*):

> Divide half a Sheet of Paper by a Line into two Columns, writing over the one *Pro*, and over the other *Con*. Then during three or four Days Consideration I put down under the different Heads short Hints of the different Motives that at different Times occur to me for or against the Measure. When I have thus got them all together in one View, I endeavour to estimate their respective Weights; and where I find two, one on each side, that seem equal, I strike them both out: If I find a Reason *pro* equal to some two Reasons *con*, I strike out the three. If I judge some two Reasons *con* equal to some three Reasons *pro*, I strike out the five; and thus proceeding I find at length where the Ballance lies; and if after a Day or two of farther Consideration nothing new that is of Importance occurs on either side, I come to a Determination accordingly.

Note that this procedure requires the identification of many ways in which the options differ from each other and the ability to subjectively weigh the importance of each factor. (It also takes a substantial commitment of time and persistence.)

Because it takes time and effort to complete this process, it should not be surprising that people typically avoid weighted additive approaches in decision making, particularly when they are pressed for time (Edland, 1994). Instead, they consider only a few of the critical factors and use simplifying rules to make decisions (e.g., "if the strongest pro reason is better than the best con reason, do it"). They may consider a subset of the differences between options, they often fail to weigh the importance of each contrast, and they usually do not take the time necessary to properly consider all of the factors involved (see Payne, Bettman, & Johnson, 1988, 1992). These tendencies are illustrated by what a reader named "Lou" posted at a website where Franklin's approach to decision making was being discussed: "This is a lot of effort. This is what coins are for. Just flip it."

Why do people truncate information search? Does this tendency merely reflect cognitive laziness, or might the consideration of too many options itself make decision making more difficult? Research evidence has shown that people often have difficulty making a choice when they are given an excessive number of options (Haynes, 2009; Iyengar & Lepper, 2000; Jacoby, Speller, & Kohn, 1974), a phenomenon called the *overchoice effect*. In one study demonstrating this effect, customers in an upscale food store were invited to sample jams that were displayed on a table. At different times, the table contained either 6 or 24 samples, and the dependent measure in the study was the percentage of customers who purchased one of the jams. For those customers who tasted jams from 6 options, 30% later bought one of them. For those who had sampled from 24 options, only 3% bought jam. In a follow-up experiment, students in a social psychology class were given a chance to write a two-page essay for extra credit. The instructor provided a list of possible topics, and that list contained either 6 or 30 options. A full 74% of students completed the essay in the first condition compared with 60% in the second condition, and the quality of the essays was better in the former than the latter.

Much research has followed these studies, showing negative consequences of having too many choices. These have included both laboratory and field studies in a variety of specific choice domains (ranging from chocolates to pension plans to college choices) (Chernev, 2003; Fasolo, Carmeci, & Misuraca, 2009; Iyengar, Huberman, & Jiang, 2004). These studies show that having too many options can increase the difficulty of decision making. However, a meta-analysis of this literature (Scheibehenne, Greifeneder, & Todd, 2010) showed that the phenomenon is moderated by several variables, including time pressure, the difficulty of trade-offs, and choice justification, each of which can increase, reduce, or even eliminate the overchoice effect.

Although people often express an interest in having "limitless" possibilities, having too many options to choose from can sometimes make it difficult to make and remain satisfied with a choice. Because decision making can be hindered by having too many choices, people might truncate their information search to limit the number of options they must consider.

Integrating Information and Forming a Judgment

The search for relevant information is important, but more cognitive work is required to produce a judgment. Various pieces of information must be combined or integrated in some fashion before a judgment or decision can be made. Much work pre-dating the social cognitive movement focused on integrative processes in decision making. For example, Anderson and his colleagues (1962, 1965, 1971; Anderson & Shanteau, 1970) proposed *information integration theory*, which uses algebraic models to characterize how information from multiple sources is used to formulate judgments. This computational approach has been used to account for a variety of phenomena relating to attitudes, moral judgment, and child development (Anderson, 2013).

In contrast, social cognitive approaches to information integration have emphasized the processes that play important roles in information integration and judgment. In this section, we discuss several areas of research focused on these critical cognitive processes.

On-line vs. Memory-based Judgments

"There ought to be a relationship between memory and judgment," suggested Hastie and Park (1986, p. 258). Intuitively it seems that, in making a judgment, one would retrieve from memory information relevant to a target of judgment and would base the judgment on that retrieved information. If so, then the amount of relevant information recalled should be highly correlated with the strength of the judgment. Sometimes this is true. However, it has long been recognized that the correlation is often very low or near zero (Anderson & Hubert, 1963). This lack of recall-judgment relation suggests that there must be other processes by which judgments are made.

Hastie and Park (1986; see also Hogarth & Einhorn, 1992) distinguished two kinds of judgment processes, which they called *on-line* and *memory-based* judgments, respectively. Memory-based judgments "rely on the retrieval of relatively concrete evidence from long-term memory in order to render a judgment" (p. 261). The items retrieved are integrated and used in making a judgment. This process implies a high correlation between the amount of information recalled and the strength of judgments. In contrast, on-line judgments are formed as decision-makers take in and integrate information in working memory. On-line judgments can be continuously modified and updated as new information is acquired. Once an on-line judgment is made, it is stored in long-term memory and is available for later retrieval. The evidence on which the judgment was based, however, might no longer be available or used at the time the judgment is made. Consequently, the recall-judgment correlation can be quite low. This distinction helps account for a puzzling finding that there is often a weak and sometimes nonexistent relationship between the information that people recall and the content of their judgments.

Hastie and Park (1986) reported several experiments where instructions encouraged on-line or memory-based judgments, thereby affecting the relationship between memory and judgment. In the first experiment, participants judged a man's suitability for a job after hearing a brief conversation between two people. Half of the subjects were told, before hearing the conversation, that they would be asked to make this judgment, ensuring that it would be made on-line. The other half of the participants discovered they would be judging the man's job suitability only after they had listened to the conversation. In both conditions, participants made a job suitability judgment and recalled all the information they could after they heard the conversation. The items recalled were then coded regarding whether they were favorable or unfavorable concerning hiring the man for the position, and the positivity of the most accessible information (i.e., the first five items recalled) and total recall were correlated with the judgment of job suitability. Results (displayed in Table 9.2) showed that the favorability of the material recalled was positively related to the hiring decision only when participants were unaware that they would be making this judgment while listening to the conversation. In contrast, the same correlation was weaker (and, indeed, was negative in sign for total recall) when the judgment was formed on-line. These data reflect that information stored in memory was used to form an unexpected judgment. Memory for the information played a less central role when participants were considering the information in an on-line fashion.

Table 9.2 Correlations between favorability of recalled items (both first five items and total recall) and judgments of job suitability as a function of on-line or memory instructions

	Instructions	
Recall	On-line	Memory
First five items	+.14	+.42
Overall	−.14	+.46

Source: Adapted from Hastie & Park (1986)

This study showed that judgment instructions can prompt either on-line or memory-based judgments. Other research indicates that these different processes can be triggered spontaneously, based on perceivers' expectations. One critical expectation concerns the extent to which one expects the behavior of a social target to be consistent over time. McConnell and colleagues (McConnell et al., 2002; McConnell, Sherman, & Hamilton, 1997) have shown that expectations of high behavioral consistency prompt on-line judgments whereas expectations of low consistency lead to memory-based judgments. Moreover, people expect more or less behavioral consistency for different kinds of social targets, which in turn influences on-line or memory-based judgment processes. Specifically, judgments about the self (where we expect a high degree of consistency) are most likely to be formed on-line, and judgments of groups (for which we expect the lowest consistency) are most likely to be memory-based, with judgments of individuals falling between them. In addition, directly manipulating the expected consistency of behavior within target types produced similar results (McConnell et al., 1997; McGraw & Dolan, 2007) as did measuring individual differences in the expected stability of traits (McConnell, 2001).

Thus, Hastie and Park's (1986) distinction between on-line and memory-based judgments has been useful in understanding how different targets are judged, the contexts when each process occurs, and the mechanisms that underlie those judgments. Moreover, whether judgments are made on-line or in a memory-based fashion affects other important characteristics of judgments. On-line judgments typically can be reported more quickly (Mackie & Asuncion, 1990) and are more stable than memory-based judgments (Hertel & Bless, 2000).

Use of Accessible Information

As we have discussed throughout this book, information that is accessible in memory influences ongoing thought processes. Accessible information can shape both the content and the processes involved in judgment and decision making. Several distinct but related lines of research attest to this influence.

Framing Effects

Decision making is influenced both by the particulars involved in the decision and the other information that is salient when a decision is being made. The concept of *framing* refers to the way a choice is presented or described, and framing can influence the information that is considered as a judgment is being made. Consider a study discussed in Chapter 2 where consumers had to decide between two sofas when the webpage background was varied (Mandel & Johnson, 2002). Information about the sofas was framed in terms of either cost or comfort, and the appearance of either clouds or currency influenced whether consumers preferred a comfortable but expensive or an uncomfortable but inexpensive sofa. There are many similar examples of framing effects affecting consumer decisions (e.g., Khan & Dhar, 2010; Mayer & Tormala, 2010).

Framing effects are also evident in the political sphere, where disagreement about issues often involves contention over the language that should be used to define debates (Lakoff, 2004; Lakoff & Wehling, 2012; Matthes, 2012). For example, referring to a medical procedure as "intact dilation and extraction" (a medical term) or as a "partial-birth abortion" (a term not used by doctors) can significantly affect whether people believe it should be allowed. Other examples from politics in the United States include the use of the terms "tax relief," implying that taxes are oppressive and that citizens need to be liberated from them, and the "death tax" to refer to estate taxes that apply only to inheritances over $11.58 million (as of 2020). Such frames are often selected quite intentionally to advance specific political goals. Table 9.3, for example, presents a series of framing suggestions offered by conservative political consultant Frank Luntz (2005) for assisting Republicans in advancing their desired positions.

Framing can also involve the use of subtle metaphors to invoke features that differentiate a set of choice options. Choices can be changed with surprising ease by altering the metaphor that is used. One study (Landau, Sullivan, & Greenberg, 2009) invoked the metaphor of bacterial infection of the body to discuss the issue of immigration. Participants first read an article about ubiquitous airborne bacteria, describing them either as dangerous to health or as harmless. Participants then read an article about U.S. domestic issues. One of these articles used expressions linking one's country to one's body, whereas the other article avoided this metaphor. For example, the first article contained phrases such as "After the Civil War, the United States experienced an unprecedented growth spurt, and is scurrying to create new laws that will give it a chance to digest the millions of innovations." In contrast, the latter stated, "After the Civil War, the United States experienced an unprecedented period of innovation, and efforts are now underway to create new laws to control the millions of innovations." Later in the study, participants completed questionnaires assessing their attitudes toward immigration and the minimum wage. The combination of describing bacteria as dangerous to the body and associating one's country with one's body reduced support for open immigration but did not affect attitudes regarding the minimum wage. Thus, framing immigration in terms of illness and threat to one's health reduced people's willingness to support open immigration policies (see also Green et al., 2010; Marshall & Shapiro, 2018).

Table 9.3 Recommended words to frame political debate

Issue	Never say	Instead say
Government	Government	Washington
Social Security	Private Accounts	Personal Accounts
Changing Tax Policy	Tax Reform	Tax Simplification
Inheritance	Estate Tax	Death Tax
Globalization	Global Economy	Free Market Economy
Economic Regulation	Outsourcing	Innovation
Immigration Reform	Undocumented Workers	Illegal Immigrants
Trade	Foreign Trade	International Trade
Energy	Drilling for Oil	Exploring for Energy
Legal Reform	Tort Reform	Legal Abuse Reform
Lawyers	Trial Lawyer	Personal Injury Lawyer
Corporations	Corporate Transparency	Corporate Accountability
Education	School Choice	Parental Choice
Healthcare	Healthcare Choice	Right to Choose

Source: Adapted from Luntz (2005)

Judgment Standards

Decisions and judgments, even important ones, often are made using attributes that are subjective and free of context. When someone is described as being "intelligent" or "aggressive," those traits have limited meaning in and of themselves. Instead, those descriptions must be interpreted by understanding the standard against which the person is being compared. If "intelligence" is being used to describe a 3-year-old child, we would not expect her to be an expert at calculus. Instead, we intuitively would understand that she is being compared with other children of the same age, and our judgments of her capabilities would take into account our knowledge of the typical abilities of 3-year-olds. Knowing that such a child is intelligent might lead us to predict that she can already read. In contrast, the same description applied to an 8-year-old child would produce a different inference (e.g., she might be capable of solving intermediate algebra problems).

In this example, the person's category membership (age) provides a frame of reference for judging the person. We can make judgments by comparing her with the other members of a category for which we have general knowledge. However, because our knowledge about social groups (i.e., our stereotypes) is invariably incomplete and frequently inaccurate, judgments can be biased by using category-based standards.

Research by Biernat and her colleagues (see Biernat, 2003, 2005, 2018; Biernat & Manis, 2007; Biernat, Crandall, Young, Kobrynowicz, & Halpin, 1998; Biernat, Manis, & Nelson, 1991; Miron, Branscombe, & Biernat, 2010) has shown that category-specific standards can influence various social judgments. When inherently subjective and relative terms are used, their meaning can vary as a function of the social group membership of an actor. For example, a 6'0" (1.83 m) woman is tall among women but not among men. Because a subjective term is being used to describe her height in comparison with other members of her category, the perceiver would have no basis for judging her height relative to men. Conversely, we would have difficulty knowing how a "short" man compares in height with women. Category-specific standards are most likely to change the meaning of judgments when they involve subjective and comparative dimensions like "aggressiveness," "intelligence," and "friendliness." These are among the most essential attributes in our social lives, yet they are subjective, and their meaning can depend on social standards. Attributes need to be described in objective terms to allow accurate comparisons between categories. For example, by being told that a "tall" woman is 5'11" (1.80 m) we judge whether she might exceed the height of an average man.

An excellent example of such *shifting standards* based on stereotypes is provided by a study (Kobrynowicz & Biernat, 1997) in which participants were given a picture of either an Asian American or an African American man along with several statements he had supposedly made at his 10-year high school reunion. These statements indicated either that he was strong or weak in Math during high school (e.g., remembering either that "Math always came sort of naturally to me" or that "I didn't do too well in Math classes"). After reading these statements, participants estimated the man's Math performance on both objective scales (e.g., estimating his letter grades and ACT scores) and subjective scales (e.g., rating his Math ability and overall academic performance from very poor to very good).

If people use group memberships as comparison standards, then the stereotype of Asian superiority in Math might affect the relative judgments of the two men's Math abilities, even though they described themselves using identical language. Specifically, a man describing himself as "good at math" will be judged as performing better if he were Asian than if he were Black. That is precisely what occurred. On objective indicators of Math ability (e.g., letter grades), participants judged the Asian American man higher than the African American man. However, there were no differences in judgments of the two men on the subjective scales. Ratings of the two men on these scales were equivalent because each of them was presumably compared to a group-referenced standard of high performance. These findings illustrate that stereotypes can serve as standards of comparison, often introducing ambiguity into expressions of judgments.

Assimilation and Contrast in Judgment

Both frames and standards involve using accessible information to make judgments. Although such information can influence judgments, the specific direction of that influence is not always consistent. In some cases, using accessible information to make judgments of a target leads to *assimilation*, that is, judgments indicating that the target and other accessible information (i.e., frames, standards) seem similar. In other cases, comparison leads to *contrast*, reflecting differentiation between pieces of information. For example, if I am comparing how smart my friend is in relation to Albert Einstein, I might either show assimilation in my judgment ("Yeah, he is kind of smart like Einstein") or contrast ("He's an idiot compared with that guy!"). Higgins, Rholes, and Jones' (1977) study on priming (discussed in Chapter 1) provided an early demonstration of an assimilation effect in social judgment. Recall that participants in this study were exposed to words related to *adventurousness* or *recklessness* and subsequently made trait judgments of a character named Donald who had performed a series of ambiguous behaviors that could be construed as reflecting either of those traits. Judgments of Donald were assimilated to the connotations of the prime words. However, soon other studies reported contrast effects in social judgment, in which the target was perceived in opposition to the prime (Herr, Sherman, & Fazio, 1983; Lombardi, Higgins, & Bargh, 1987).

We now know that several factors influence when assimilation and contrast occur in social judgment (Bless & Burger, 2016; Bless & Schwarz, 2010; Mussweiler, 2007). One variable is the *extremity of primed information*. When co-active information differs only minimally (thinking about two people you like or dislike only a little), assimilation tends to occur. However, when differences are substantial (e.g., comparing a person to Adolf Hitler), contrast tends to prevail (Herr, 1986; Manis, Nelson, & Shedler, 1988). A second factor is the *ambiguity of the behavior* of the person being judged (Herr et al., 1983; Lee & Suk, 2010). When the target person's behavior is ambiguous (and therefore open to interpretation), judgments of the person are likely to be assimilated toward that information. When the person's behavior is unambiguous, contrast from that information is more likely (Philippot, Schwarz, Carrera, De Vries, & Van Yperen, 1991). A third factor is whether accessible information involves representations of *concepts or exemplars*. Priming concepts and traits ("intelligence") generally leads to assimilation, whereas providing specific exemplars (Einstein) produces contrast in judgment (Dijksterhuis et al., 2001), especially when they are seen as offering a poor comparison standard (LeBoeuf & Estes, 2004). Activation of stereotypes can produce contrast, however, if comparisons with the self (Schubert & Häfner, 2003) or ingroups (Ledgerwood & Chaiken, 2007) are invoked. A fourth factor is the *motivation and cognitive capacity* of the perceiver. When people are low in motivation or capacity to process thoroughly, assimilation tends to prevail (Dijksterhuis et al., 2001; Martin, Seta, & Crelia, 1990; Newman, Duff, Hedberg, & Blitstein, 1996).

A final moderator is whether the social perceiver is *aware of the possible influence* of accessible information on a judgment. We often use accessible information to judge objects without knowing it or without understanding how such information might influence our judgments. When people are unaware of primed material or of the possible influence of that material on judgment, assimilation is likely (Herr et al., 1983; Loersch & Payne, 2014; Molden, 2014). However, what happens if we become aware of how our judgments might be affected by some extraneous factor? Some interesting research shows that when we are made aware that judgments might be biased by information that is in the forefront of our minds, we often initiate correction processes to "decontaminate" the judgment from the estimated impact of accessible but irrelevant information. Such attempts can lead to contrast effects if the correction is too extreme. One study, for example, showed that during an interview, people whose attention had been drawn to the pleasant weather they were having indicated that they were less happy in their lives compared with people for whom the weather was not mentioned (Schwarz & Clore, 1983). That is, once their attention was drawn to the potentially biasing information (weather), people reduced their estimated happiness in an attempt to "unbias" their judgment.

Several attempts have been made to explain these various effects under a single theoretical framework. Mussweiler (2003, 2007; Crusius & Mussweiler, 2012), for example, offered an interpretation rooted in the confirmation bias in hypothesis testing. As we discussed earlier, people often seek and solicit information that confirms their pre-existing hypotheses and expectations. Mussweiler and colleagues have shown that people typically assume similarity between accessible information and a judgment object unless cues indicate that they should not. Since people tend to assume similarity, they typically search for information that the accessible information and the judgment object have in common. So, for example, in meeting a new co-worker, you might assume similarity with him and ask questions about interests you might share. In such a case, the assumption of similarity would lead the perceiver to test whether the self and other person are similar. Through confirmation bias, evidence of similarity typically will be easy to generate, and assimilation in judgment would naturally follow.

On the other hand, cues indicating dissimilarity can lead to hypothesis-testing about differences between judgment objects. Such a cue might be information clearly indicating an extreme difference between the accessible information and the judgment object. For example, if your classmate's blue hair and pierced tongue lead you to think that he is very different from yourself, the subsequent search for additional information will be biased in favor of identifying ways you are distinct. Looking for evidence of dissimilarity will typically yield information confirming the hypothesis that you are unalike, and your judgments of him will tend to contrast with judgments of yourself.

Mussweiler's theory explains how the factors listed above modulate assimilation and contrast effects in judgment through a common mechanism. Factors that increase the tendency for the perceiver to rely on the default assumption of familiarity – confirmatory or ambiguous initial information, a cognitive load, or a lack of awareness – will increase the search for confirmatory information and will produce assimilation effects in judgment.

Schwarz and Bless (1992, 2007; Bless & Schwarz, 2010) offer an alternative framework, the *inclusion-exclusion model*, proposing that assimilation and contrast effects depend on the construal of targets and the nature of the information accessible at the time of judgment. Assimilation occurs when the target can be included in the category of information that is accessible. Contrast, however, occurs when the target is judged as excluded from the informational category. Thus, similarity between the target and a standard suggests inclusion and produces assimilation, whereas stark differences between the target and a standard suggest exclusion and produce contrast in judgment.

As this brief review shows, whether assimilation or contrast prevails depends on many factors. Although we have presented evidence of some of the major experiments and theories related to this topic, this is an area of research where it can be difficult to predict in advance whether judgments in any given study will show assimilation or contrast. Further research is needed to clarify when and how specific variables, alone or in concert with others, determine the judgment outcomes of comparative processes.

Judgment Heuristics

Most of the processes described so far paint a portrait of people as fairly busy social information processors who actively engage in the integration and comparison of accessible information to make a judgment. These deliberations can be biased, but perceivers are doing their best to disentangle and combine the various sources of information to render a decision. In many contexts and situations, this is an accurate portrayal of the ways we cope with the complexities of information as we make judgments. In many other ways, however, those complexities present severe demands on our cognitive resources. In those cases, judgments become quite simplified through reliance on judgment heuristics. *Heuristics* are "rules of thumb" that provide a quick basis for making complex judgments. The use of heuristics allows social perceivers to truncate the search and integration of information and to rely instead on simple shortcuts to make decisions.

Simon (1956) was the first person to discuss the role of heuristics in decision making. He argued that there are many circumstances where people cannot optimally acquire or integrate all relevant information to identify an optimal solution. In these cases, people will make decisions by *satisficing* (a blend of sufficing and satisfying), settling on a suboptimal decision once an acceptable threshold is met. The idea that decision-makers rely on shortcuts later led Tversky and Kahneman to begin a highly-influential program of research on other heuristics that play central roles in judgment (see Lewis, 2016). In this section, we now turn to a discussion of three of the most important heuristics first explored by Tversky and Kahneman (1974) – the availability heuristic, the representativeness heuristic, and the anchoring and adjustment heuristic – before discussing some others that have been investigated more recently.

The Availability Heuristic

The *availability heuristic* involves using the ease of accessibility of information in memory for judging frequency or commonality. Consider being asked to estimate the number of seven-letter words that have an "n" in the sixth position. Thinking of such words would probably be quite challenging and would produce a relatively low estimate. Now try to think of seven-letter words that end with "ing." It is pretty easy to recall words that have four letters followed by the letters "ing" (reading, running, and playing). Would you estimate that there are more seven-letter words ending in "ing" than merely with an "n" in the sixth position? If you did, you would be making a judgment error, since "ing" words are a subset of the broader category of words with "n" in the sixth position. The existence of a single word with an "n" in the sixth position that does not end in "ing" (e.g., muffins) would mean such an estimate would be incorrect.

People usually make this error because they are using the ease of retrieval to inform frequency estimates. The rule of thumb being relied on is, "if it's easy to think of them, there must be a lot of them." However, this heuristic can lead to error, since frequency is not the only factor that influences ease of retrieval from memory. Retrieval cues also play an important role in determining how much (and how quickly) information can be brought from memory to inform judgment. In our example, the suffix "ing" serves as a better retrieval cue for generating examples than does the single letter "n," and people typically fail to adjust for differences in the effectiveness of retrieval cues (Tversky & Kahneman, 1983).

The availability heuristic also plays a central role in determining satisfaction in relationships. As we mentioned earlier, Ross and Sicoly (1979) had married couples estimate the degree (in percentage terms) that they and their partners perform various household tasks and contribute to everyday events. Logically the percentage estimates from any two partners, on average, should sum to 100% in any given category. However, these sums tended to exceed 100%, occurring for both positive actions (cleaning) and negative actions (starting fights). This finding likely reflects the greater amount of information people possess about themselves compared with their partners. Each person would think about the various things he or she does to contribute to the home, and the tasks they typically perform would be more readily available in memory and hence more accessible in making these estimates. Thus, partners would rely on the greater ease of retrieval for information about themselves to estimate their relative contributions.

Ease-of-Retrieval and the Availability Heuristic

Why does the accessibility of information affect frequency estimates? There are two distinct possibilities. One possibility is that information that is easy to recall produces a greater *quantity* of information to form a judgment. In the example we just discussed, using "ing" as a retrieval cue for seven-letter words with "n" in the sixth position should activate from memory more words fitting the criterion, thereby increasing judgments of their commonality. A second possibility pertains to the *ease* with which information can be recalled. According to this interpretation, the "ing" retrieval cue boosts frequency estimates because it quickly and effortlessly produces numerous examples that fit the rule. According to this view, the *ease of retrieval* provides a meta-cognitive signal indicating that there must a large amount of similar information stored in memory, thereby enhancing estimates of frequency.

These possibilities were tested against one another in studies conducted by Schwarz and his colleagues (Schwarz, Bless, Strack, Klumpp, Rittenauer-Schatka, & Simons, 1991). Participants were asked to recall 6 examples of times they had acted assertively or, in another condition, 12 examples of their assertive behavior. Another set of participants were assigned to the same conditions but were asked to think of times they had acted in an unassertive manner. After a delay, all participants were asked to rate their (un)assertiveness. What predictions would be made by the account focusing on the quantity of information retrieved versus the

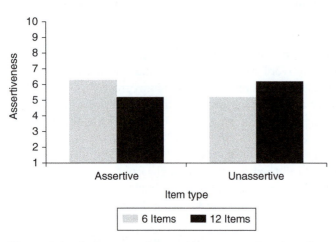

ease-of-retrieval account? If frequency estimates are based on the quantity of content recalled, people who generated 12 instances of assertive behavior would be expected to rate themselves as more assertive than people who generated only 6 examples. However, if frequency estimates are based on the ease of retrieving content, then this pattern might reverse. After all, it is typically easier to remember 6 times you behaved in a certain way than 12 times that you did. The relative ease to recall 6 relevant items might lead you to counterintuitively judge that these behaviors are more common than if you struggled to think of 12 such instances.

Figure 9.2 Judgments of assertiveness as a function of recall of 6 or 12 items and behavior type

Source: Based on data from Schwarz et al. (1991)

This counterintuitive prediction was confirmed. Results (depicted in Figure 9.2) showed that those who recalled 6 instances of their assertive-relevant behaviors rated themselves as higher on the trait in question than did those who were asked to recall 12 such instances. In other words, people who were asked to generate *less* evidence that they possessed a trait judged themselves as *higher* on that trait.

Ease of retrieval has been shown to play an important role in several important spheres of social judgment. For example, it plays a critical role in judging risk. When thinking about taking a trip, people might consider the relative safety of different means of travel. To decide whether to fly or drive, they might rely on the ease with which they can recall different kinds of accidents in order to calculate the relative risk of each type of travel. Given the amount of media attention they generate, airplane fatalities are typically much easier to recall than are deaths from car accidents, despite their far lower frequency (287 airplane deaths globally vs. 38,800 automobile fatalities in the U.S. alone in 2019). Thus, it is quite common for people to think that flying is much more dangerous than driving, even though the reverse is true (Slovic, Fischhoff, & Lichtenstein, 1979, 1982).

The Representativeness Heuristic

The *representativeness heuristic* (Kahneman & Tversky, 1971) refers to using the similarity of an object to its category prototype to judge the likelihood that the object belongs to that category. To gain a sense of this heuristic, consider the following description about Tom, a person enrolled in graduate school (Kahneman & Tversky, 1973):

> Tom W. is of high intelligence, although lacking in true creativity. He has a need for order and clarity, and for neat and tidy systems in which every detail finds its appropriate place. His writing is rather dull and mechanical, occasionally enlivened by somewhat corny puns and by flashes of imagination of the sci-fi type. He has a strong drive for competence. He seems to have little feel and little sympathy for other people and does not enjoy interacting with others. Self-centered, he nonetheless has a deep moral sense.

One group of participants in the study ranked how closely Tom W. resembled the typical student in nine different fields of specialization (e.g., Business, Law, Medicine). A second group ranked the fields in terms of the likelihood that Tom was a student in each. Finally, a control group simply estimated the percentage of all graduate students in the United States in each field (i.e., the base rates for each area of study). Two important findings emerged. First, the rankings were highly similar for estimates of Tom's field and the similarity between Tom and the typical students in each field. Second, neither of these rankings correlated with the estimates of the commonality (base rates) of each field. Judgments of Tom were based almost entirely on his similarity to what was seen as typical in each field. Information about the commonality of each field (i.e., base rates) played nearly no role in making judgments of Tom.

These results attested both to people's use of representativeness to make likelihood judgments and to their general disregard for base rate information when they do so. However, subsequent research has shown that people do not always ignore base rate information. The use of base rate information increases, for example, when it comes from a representative sample (Wells & Harvey, 1977), when it has clear causal implications (Ajzen, 1977), when it has been used recently (Ginossar & Trope, 1987), when it is self-generated (Lick, Johnson, Rule, & Stroessner, 2019), when it is presented after details about the individual (Krosnick, Li, & Lehman, 1990), or when information about a target is not credible or relevant to the judgment (Schwarz, Strack, Hilton, & Naderer, 1991). Thus, base rate information, though often neglected, will be used when it appears to provide a clear and compelling basis for making judgments.

Many real-life judgments require the use of both base rate and individuating information. One of the authors was reminded of the importance of considering both types of information during a recent lecture on the importance of base rate information in medical diagnosis.

Physicians are trained and encouraged to use base rates when they encounter a set of symptoms that might indicate either a common or a rare disorder. The adage in medical decision making, "When you hear hoofbeats, think horses, not zebras," is a reminder that a common disease is more likely to be responsible for a set of symptoms than an obscure disease. During a discussion of this material, one of the students became visibly upset. She furrowed her brow and frowned and even shook her head slowly to indicate disagreement. When the student was approached after class to find out why she was troubled, she said, "Oh, it wasn't the lecture. You're right, doctors do almost always go with the more common disease. In my case, though, they were wrong. I *happen to have* one of those uncommon diseases, and it took years for them to diagnose it properly. Just because a disease is uncommon doesn't mean that it doesn't exist." The lesson of this story is that all kinds of information need to be used in making a judgment. Just as base rates should not be ignored, neither should they be the sole basis of decision making.

In addition to reducing use of base rate information, representativeness can also produce judgments that violate normative rules of logic. Consider a phenomenon termed the *conjunction fallacy* (Tversky & Kahneman, 1982) when people judge that the conjunction of two events is more likely than either of the events alone (Moro, 2009; Stolarz-Fantino, Fantino, Zizzo, & Wen, 2003; Tversky & Kahneman, 1983). When people estimate the probability of any two events co-occurring (e.g., the New York Yankees will win the most games during the regular season *and also* the World Series), that estimate cannot logically exceed the likelihood of either event occurring in isolation. The Yankees may win the most games and not win the World Series. It is also possible that the Yankees do not win the most games and yet win the World Series. Thus, the likelihood of either single outcome must be higher than the likelihood that both outcomes will occur, yet people often judge the conjunction to be more likely. This is the conjunction fallacy.

The representativeness heuristic appears to contribute to this phenomenon. Participants in one study (Tversky & Kahneman, 1983) were given the following personality sketch of a fictitious person named Linda:

> Linda is 31 years old, single, outspoken and very bright. She majored in philosophy. As a student, she was deeply concerned with issues of discrimination and social justice, and also participated in anti-nuclear demonstrations.

After they read this description, participants were asked to rank several statements according to their probability. Three of these statements were:

> Linda is active in the feminist movement.

> Linda is a bank teller.

> Linda is a bank teller and is active in the feminist movement.

Participants typically judged as most likely that Linda was a feminist, followed by Linda being both a bank teller and feminist, and finally that she was a bank teller. Indeed, 85% of participants showed this pattern of probability judgments, reflecting that the conjunction (that Linda is both a banker teller and an active feminist) was seen as more probable than that she was a bank teller alone.

Why is this error so common? There are debates about the cause of the conjunction fallacy (Nilsson, Winman, Juslin, & Hansson, 2009), but Tversky and Kahneman (1983) explained this phenomenon by invoking representativeness. The reason that combined events are judged as more probable than either single event, in their view, is that the characteristics that describe Linda seem very typical for a person who belongs to one of the categories; she has many characteristics that make her appear likely to be a feminist (bright, concerned with social justice, anti-nuclear) so she "fits the profile" (i.e., the stereotype) of a feminist. Therefore, when participants are asked to judge her membership in social categories, her prototypicality as a feminist makes it very easy for perceivers to imagine (and difficult to ignore) that category membership in making probability judgments. Therefore, it seems intuitive that she is more likely a member of two categories than of just one of them.

Such conjunction errors are common. Tversky and Kahneman (1983) found that the conjunction fallacy emerged in samples of undergraduates, graduate students with some background in probability, and doctoral students who had taken several advanced courses in probability. Having this extensive knowledge provided little protection against representativeness producing a violation of fundamental rules of probability. Other studies are more optimistic, showing that incentives, changes in question wording, and information-sharing can reduce the frequency of the conjunction fallacy (Charness, Karni, & Levin, 2010; Mellers, Hertwig, & Kahneman, 2001). Despite the existence of these moderating variables, the conjunction fallacy serves as an example of how typicality can affect perceived probability.

Anchoring and Adjustment Heuristic

Think of a time when you were asked a question about a topic where you knew little (What is the population of India? How many countries elect their leaders?). These kinds of questions require that an estimate be formed with little knowledge, and it is easy to imagine a person trying to answer such a question fishing through memory, searching for some basis for responding. It is also easy to imagine that this search of memory might favor highly accessible information, even if this information clearly has little or no relevance to the question being posed. Tversky and Kahneman (1974) provided several demonstrations that judgments can be biased by the presence of a convenient (but irrelevant) value that is available in the judgment context. When a value is introduced before an individual makes a judgment – even if that value is uninformative about the decision at hand – judgments appear to be "anchored" by that value and then "adjusted" to arrive at a final judgment. Adjustments from the anchor value, however, tend to be excessively conservative (Epley & Gilovich, 2001, 2006), especially when people have limited time to engage in adjustment (Lieder, Griffiths, Huys, & Goodman, 2018). Consequently, judgments end up much closer to the anchor than would be the case had the anchor not been available. This is the *anchoring and adjustment heuristic* (Bahník, Englich, & Strack, 2017). The "anchor" provides a starting point for one's estimate, and the "adjustment" away from it typically is insufficient.

One classic example of the use of this anchoring and adjustment heuristic provided by Tversky and Kahneman (1974) involved experimenters spinning a wheel that yielded an arbitrary number between 0 and 100. After viewing this number, participants were asked to indicate whether the percentage of African countries in the United Nations was higher or lower than that number and to estimate the percentage of African countries in the United Nations. Of course, the number that appeared on the wheel clearly was irrelevant to the question that had been asked. However, participants who had seen larger numbers on the wheel produced higher percentage estimates than those who viewed lower numbers. For example, the median percentage estimates of groups that saw the numbers 10 and 65 were 25% and 45%. The arbitrarily determined number, which was irrelevant to the task, clearly biased responses, presumably because the number served as an anchor for participants' estimates. Apparently, once the number entered the judgment context, it was difficult for the perceiver to ignore it.

In a study showing a real-world implication of anchoring and adjustment (Northcraft & Neale, 1987), real estate agents estimated the value of a house after seeing all the relevant pricing information, inspecting the house, and being provided a list price. Experimenters varied the list price so that it was lower or higher than the value determined by an independent appraiser ($74,900). Even though their livelihoods depended on the accuracy of such judgments, agents' estimates of the house's value shifted dramatically depending on the list price. When the list price was $65,900, the average agents' estimated value was $67,811. When the list price was $83,900, however, the agents produced an average estimated value of $75,190. Again, their adjustment away from the given anchor was insufficient.

Several theoretical accounts have been offered for this phenomenon. One explanation (Mussweiler, 2002; Mussweiler & Strack, 1999, 2000; Strack & Mussweiler, 1997) is that anchoring effects are products of the enhanced accessibility of information consistent with the anchor. When the anchor is manipulated (e.g., "Is the Nile longer or shorter than 5,000 [vs. 800] miles?"), perceivers initiate a search through memory for information consistent with that anchor. Being provided with a high number would lead one to search memory for all the knowledge that might tend to confirm that the Nile is long (e.g., "it appears pretty big on a map") whereas a low anchor would prompt a search for evidence consistent with that anchor (e.g., "I know the Nile ends in Egypt, but I'm not sure how far South it goes"). Because of the confirmation bias in information search, a disproportionate amount of evidence can usually be generated favoring the use of the anchor. Evidence shows that a search for information consistent with an anchor makes that information highly accessible, thereby able to affect subsequent judgments. In one study (Mussweiler & Strack, 2000, Experiment 2), German participants were asked whether the price of an average German car was higher or lower than one of two specific values ("Is the average price for a new car higher or lower than 40,000 [vs. 20,000] German marks?"). In a supposedly unrelated task, they then were presented with a series of letter strings and asked to indicate which of them were words (i.e., a lexical decision task). With a high anchor, participants were faster to identify words associated with expensive cars (Mercedes, limousine) compared with words associated with inexpensive models (Volkswagen, Golf). This pattern reversed with the low anchor, facilitating the speed with which inexpensive brands were identified.

Another explanation for this heuristic is that anchoring works through the activation of semantic content (Oppenheimer, LeBeouf, & Brewer, 2008). Low anchors activate semantic content implying smallness or shortness, whereas high anchors lead to the activation of semantic content associated with large size. One experimental test of this hypothesized mechanism involved asking one group of participants whether the Mississippi River was longer or shorter than 4,800 miles and, in a second group, longer or shorter than 15 miles. Participants were then asked to draw a line equal in length to a toothpick. Participants in the first condition drew longer toothpicks than participants in the second condition. In a subsequent study, participants were exposed to a low or high anchor value and then performed a word fragment completion task. Those participants who received high anchors were more likely to form words connoting bigness (_ONG (LONG), B_G (BIG), _ALL (TALL)) than those exposed to the low anchors.

A third possible mechanism underlying anchoring effects is numeric priming. Providing a number as an anchor might, through spreading activation, increase the accessibility of values close to it, increasing the likelihood that these values will be used in judgment. In a demonstration of this possibility (Wong & Kwong, 2000), two groups of participants were asked to estimate the length of the runway at the Hong Kong International Airport compared with a target number. The two groups received an equivalent number expressed in either small or large units (7.3 km or 7,300 m). Both groups then estimated the cost of an unrelated project. Participants who had been provided an anchor in meters gave higher estimates for the cost of the project than did participants given the same anchor expressed with smaller numbers (kilometers).

The examples we have discussed so far relate to topics of low social relevance because the studies were designed to explore the mechanisms underlying the anchoring and adjustment heuristic. However, there are many studies showing that this heuristic can also affect a variety of judgments in the social domain including judgments of self-efficacy (Cervone and Peake, 1986), attitude inference (Tamir & Mitchell, 2013), and advice-taking (Schultze, Mojzisch, & Schulz-Hardt, 2017). Anchoring and adjustment has also been implicated in real-world domains such as dietary regulation (Marchiori, Papies, & Klein, 2014), economic decisions (Critcher & Gilovich, 2008), negotiation (Galinsky and Mussweiler, 2001), and the law (Englich & Mussweiler, 2001; Englich, Mussweiler, & Strack, 2006).

Other Judgment Heuristics

Numerous other judgment heuristics have been identified since Tversky and Kahneman's (1974) seminal work. We briefly discuss several other heuristics that have broad application to social judgment.

The *fluency heuristic* (Hertwig, Herzog, Schooler, & Reimer, 2008; Whittlesea, 1993) is related to but distinct from the availability heuristic. As we discussed in Chapter 6, fluency can affect evaluations of various stimuli. Research on the fluency heuristic shows that cognitive processes that are relatively swift, effortless, and "easy on the mind" (i.e., are *fluent*) also produce judgments of higher commonality or likelihood than processes that are slow, effortful, or "hard on the mind" (i.e., are *disfluent*) (Winkielman et al., 2006). For example, people judge fluent objects to be more representative of their categories (Lick & Johnson, 2014; Whittlesea & Leboe, 2003), they judge names that have been seen previously (and are therefore fluent) to be more famous than new (nonfluent) names (Jacoby, Woloshyn, & Kelley, 1989), and they judge aphorisms that rhyme to be more valid than those that do not rhyme (McGlone & Tofighbakhsh, 2000). Fluency can also arise from repetition and imagination, with the consequence that imagining an outcome increases its judged likelihood. For example, thinking about what it would be like to have a disease increases estimates that one is likely to get the disease (Sherman, Cialdini, Schwartzman, & Reynolds, 1985). Anything that increases the ease of processing (familiarity, prototypicality, simplicity) can alter judgments through fluency.

The *simulation heuristic* (Kahneman & Tversky, 1982; see also Chambers & Davis, 2012) also involves the ease of imagination. However, in this heuristic people judge the likelihood and impact of an event based on the ease involved in generating a mental simulation of the event. An event with easily imagined alternative outcomes tends to amplify emotional reactions. Participants in one study (Kahneman & Tversky, 1982) read about two men who had missed their scheduled flights because their taxis were delayed in traffic. Both men arrived at the airport 30 minutes after their scheduled departure times. One man's flight left on time, but the other man's flight had been delayed and had left only 5 minutes before he arrived at the airport. Participants expected the latter man to be more upset because it would be easier for him to imagine how he could have arrived on time compared with the man whose flight left on time. The intensity of each man's emotional reaction was expected to be different, reflecting the different ease with which he could generate a counterfactual scenario. (We will revisit the role of simulation in counterfactual thinking in Chapter 11.)

Two related heuristics, the *affect heuristic* (Pachur, Hertwig, & Steinmann, 2012; Slovic, Finucane, Peters, & MacGregor, 2002) and the *"how-do-I-feel-about-it" heuristic* (Schwarz & Clore, 1988), both involve the use of affective reactions to guide judgments and decisions. Both groups of theorists argue that people often make judgments of an object using the affective responses evoked by the object rather than by considering its features in detail. If people feel good when thinking about the object, they infer that they like it and value it. If bad feelings arise, they conclude they neither like nor value it. For instance, suppose you are scanning a menu to decide what you want to eat. You could carefully inspect each item, calculating the nutritional value, caloric content, or noticing the ingredients in each dish. Alternatively, you could scan the menu until a particular item elicits a positive affective response. Reliance on affective information truncates information search and integration, providing a quick, effortless means for making such a decision.

Of course, an affective response might arise from factors extraneous to the judgment object. Your positive feelings might, for instance, occur because of familiarity or even due to the location of the item on the menu (Kershaw, 2009), or perhaps that affect emanates from your enjoyment of or attraction to the person you are dining with. Regardless of the reason they arise, feelings tend to color judgments of an object. However, there are some exceptions to this principle. When there exists a clear standard for judgment (e.g., one dish at the restaurant is deservedly famous), people are less likely to use affective information in judgment (Schwarz, Strack, Kommer, & Wagner, 1987). When the affective response is clearly attributable to an irrelevant source (the picture of only one item on the menu appears in color), people might attempt to discount the affective influence (Schwarz & Clore, 1983). Finally, when people are trying to achieve a goal rather than engage in consummatory behavior, affective information is typically disregarded (Pham, 1998).

Judgments Involving Risk: Prospect Theory

Kahneman and Tversky's research on heuristics and the scholarship it inspired showed that humans often deviate from the rational standards assumed in classic models of decision making. Kahneman and Tversky then turned their research attention to a set of issues central in economics and also of tremendous psychological significance: How do people make decisions involving risk? Do people deviate from rational standards when making judgments involving potential gains and losses? If so, are there regularities in how people make risky decisions? This research yielded a highly-influential paper (Kahneman & Tversky, 1979) that accomplished two things. First, it presented a series of compelling but simple demonstrations that people systematically violate rational standards when making decisions involving risk. Second, it offered a theoretical model that characterized how people make such decisions. This model challenged traditional economic models of decision making and laid the foundation for behavioral economics.

Classic approaches emphasized the importance of several logical axioms in decision making involving risk and judgment more generally. These axioms included *transitivity* (i.e., that a person's choices are consistent across multiple options), *dominance* (i.e., that if one option is better than another, this dominant option should be chosen), and *invariance* (i.e., that different representations of the same mathematically equivalent options should yield the same choices). If people followed these logical principles, then it was possible to predict a person's choices between two (or more) options based on the probability (the likelihood of an outcome) and the utility (the economic value of an outcome) of the options. These ideas were encapsulated in subjective expected utility (SEU) theory (von Neumann & Morgenstern, 1947).

Kahneman and Tversky's (1979) research showed that people regularly violate all three axioms when making decisions involving risk. Changes in the framing of options (e.g., emphasizing losses or gains) regularly reversed choices, even when response options were mathematically identical and when both frames were presented to the same individuals. These reversals showed that people regularly do not make judgments involving risk as described by SEU. In addition, participants' patterns of choice under different conditions were used to formulate a simple but powerful model of *psychological value*, *Prospect Theory*, that differed from traditional economic theorizing.

Prospect Theory departed from SEU in two significant respects. First, in contrast to SEU, it argued that economic value (typically termed "utility") and psychological value are not synonymous. Therefore, changes in psychological value cannot be perfectly predicted from changes in economic value. Second, the theory posits that value is defined not in absolute terms but instead through comparison with a referent point. This implies that psychological value is based on an assessment of gains and losses around a standard, typically the status quo.

Figure 9.3 shows the value curve in Prospect Theory, in which the two principles are illustrated with changes in value shown around a central reference point. A *value function* reflects the psychological consequences of variations around this reference point defined in terms of gains and losses. Classic economic theory posited a perfectly straight line with a slope of +1 running through the reference point. However, research has revealed that the value function is asymmetrically S-shaped, convex in the domain of gains and concave and steeper in the domain of losses. Both the shape and the steepness of the value curve have critical implications for judgment and decision making. For example, for both gains and losses, changes in value are magnified the closer one is to the reference point, and they diminish in importance as one moves further from the reference point. For example, although the gain in wealth from $1 to $2 is the

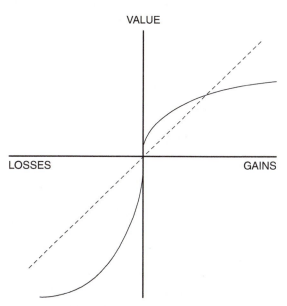

Figure 9.3 Shape of the value curve in Prospect Theory (smooth line) versus classic economic theory (dashed line)

Source: Adapted from Kahneman & Tversky (1979)

same as the gain from $1001 to $1002, the psychological value of the first increase is much higher. The same is true for losses; losing $1 from your pocket will cause more pain than losing a $1 bill from a wad of 50 singles. The fact that the value curve is steeper for losses than for gains means that losses are given more psychological weight than comparable gains. This principle was expressed nicely by professional tennis player Jimmy Connors when he said, "I hate to lose more than I love to win."

The differing shape of the value curve for gains and losses has some significant implications. It implies that people are generally risk-averse for gains and risk-seeking for losses. That is, if you provide an individual with two options, one providing a guaranteed outcome of a specific utility and the other involving a gamble with the same average expected utility, a risk-averse decision-maker will prefer a certain outcome over a gamble. Most people will choose a guaranteed $50 than to be entered in a lottery where they have a 50% chance of receiving $100 and a 50% chance of receiving $0. In contrast, most people (but not all; Scholer, Zou, Fujita, Stroessner, & Higgins, 2010) are risk-averse when they are considering potential losses, preferring to enter a similar lottery in the domain of losses (50% chance of losing $100; 50% of losing $0) than to hand over $50 with certainty.

In Prospect Theory, reference points play a critical role in decisions involving risk. How a problem is framed can change a perceived reference point and, consequently, whether people are risk-seeking or risk-averse. Think about the choices you would make between pairs of options for combating a disease (Tversky & Kahneman, 1981). Half of the participants received the following description:

> Imagine that the U.S. is preparing for the outbreak of an unusual Asian disease, which is expected to kill 600 people. Two alternative programs to combat the disease have been proposed. Assume that the exact scientific estimate of the consequences of the programs are as follows:
>
> a. If Program A is adopted, 200 people will be saved.
>
> b. If Program B is adopted, there is 1/3 probability that 600 people will be saved, and 2/3 probability that no people will be saved.

The remaining participants received the identical description of the scenario but different descriptions of the programs:

> c. If Program C is adopted 400 people will die.
>
> d. If Program D is adopted there is 1/3 probability that nobody will die, and 2/3 probability that 600 people will die.

In each of these choice decisions, which of the two programs would you favor? If you were typical of the experimental participants, you would prefer Program A over Program B (as did 72% vs. 28% in the original study) but Program D over Program C (as did 78% vs. 22%, respectively). If those were your choices, then you might not have noticed that Programs A and C are identical (200 will be saved, and 400 will die) as are Programs B and D (1/3 probability that no one will die and 2/3 probability that 600 people will die).

What accounts for the differing preferences for the two sets of options? The first condition framed the programs in terms of the number of lives that would be saved, emphasizing potential gains relative to the reference point. This emphasis on gains led participants to show risk aversion, choosing the guaranteed gain over the gamble. The second condition, however, framed the programs in terms of losses, and these participants demonstrated risk seeking. They preferred the gamble over a guaranteed loss. Similar effects have been shown in various domains, including medicine (e.g., McNeil, Pauker, Sox, & Tversky, 1982), consumer judgment (e.g., Levin & Gaeth, 1988), and politics (Busby, Flynn, & Druckman, 2018). Thus, the focus on gains versus losses explains why the framing of a problem can produce seemingly-illogical reversals in choice.

Prospect Theory has been hugely influential in a variety of disciplines. It provides an integrative framework that incorporates some of the central psychological processes we have discussed throughout this chapter (e.g., framing, use of standards). It has also proven useful for predicting how people make decisions involving risk when compared with normative theories that prescribe how such choices should be (rather than actually are) made.

Is Reasoning Rational and Intuition Irrational?

Throughout this chapter, we have reviewed research that seemingly implies that reasoning processes are rational and intuitive processes are irrational. This implication seemed quite evident through the various demonstrations showing how decision making can be biased by accessible information, framing, and heuristics. From a historical point of view, this emphasis on the irrationality of intuitive thinking should not be surprising. After all, much of this research was designed to illustrate the shortcomings of the dominant models of rational choice. By demonstrating that decision-makers often rely on intuition rather than reasoning processes, researchers were able to challenge basic assumptions about how people make both trivial and profoundly important decisions in their lives.

One perhaps unintended consequence of the emphasis on errors and biases was that it became common to assert that ordinary people are reliably irrational. Zajonc (1999), for example, reviewed prominent perspectives in social psychology regarding this question. The vast majority of views characterized humans as consistently irrational, guided by unconscious forces that regularly produce biased judgments. This conclusion was somewhat justified, given that decades of research in social psychology explored when and why people deviate from rational standards. However, the research had another more fundamental and important, but perhaps less obvious, goal – to identify the psychological processes that produce both rationality and deviations from it. As Krueger (2012) has argued, "The original promise of the heuristics-and-biases paradigm was not to prove that humans are stupid but to use their failures as a window into the architecture of mind" (p. 61).

Fortunately, recent research has offered a more balanced view of decision making. It has become clear that effort needs to be distinguished from effectiveness. The use of shortcuts or heuristics does not invariably produce suboptimal decisions nor do effortful processes always guarantee logical choices. A person might use a low-effort strategy that generates a perfectly reasonable outcome. In addition, even a motivated individual might make irrational decisions if ability is low in the relevant domain. Consider a person who tries to make a decision requiring knowledge of Calculus he does not possess. In such a case, all the effort in the world will not increase the use of logic. Thus, thinking harder should improve the rationality of decisions only when people know how to think logically in a domain.

Many studies have also highlighted that both intuitive and rational processes are associated with benefits and costs. Some research has emphasized the value of intuitive processes, showing how heuristics can produce judgments that strike a good balance between accuracy and effort. In this view, heuristics can provide judgments that are "good enough," given the substantial additional effort that would be required to improve accuracy. Other research demonstrates that efforts to reason rationally can actually harm the quality of some decisions. This line of research suggests that intuition can produce superior decisions compared with rational analysis, at least in some circumstances. We now discuss both of these viewpoints.

Differing Criteria for Rationality

One problem in assessing the rationality of judgments involves the lack of standards for assessing rationality. Across (and even within) disciplines, multiple definitions of rationality have emerged (Kruglanski & Orehek, 2009). The Rational Actor Model in economics (e.g., Archer & Tritter, 2000; von Neumann and Morgenstern, 1947) assumes that rationality is represented by a person who maximizes utility in making decisions. Thus, in deciding between options, individuals assess the benefits and costs of each option and choose the one that provides the greatest benefit at the lowest cost. Similarly, several psychological approaches share the assumption that rational decisions maximize utility for the decision-maker (Edwards, 1961; Fishbein, 1967; Slovic, 1995). Other definitions, both in economics (Hammond, 1997) and psychology (Dawes, 2001; Kahneman & Tversky, 1984), emphasize *consistency* in defining rationality. If people make contradictory choices over time when given the same set of options, or reverse their decisions based on how options are framed (Tversky & Kahneman, 1981), these inconsistencies constitute evidence of irrationality. Yet others highlight examples in which decisions violate normative rules of rationality, such as transitivity (Tversky, 1969) and rules of probability and statistics (Tversky & Kahneman, 1983).

The existence of multiple definitions for rationality makes it challenging to answer the question, "Are people rational?" By each of these criteria, people do, at times, make decisions in an irrational manner. However, no single decision will likely violate all of these standards for rationality, and decisions can be quite irrational without violating all criteria. Perhaps a more useful way to respond to the existence of varied definitions of rationality is to view these definitions as pertaining to *features* by which one can judge whether a decision is rational or not. A decision to go to your least favorite over your preferred restaurant might be viewed as inconsistent. However, doing so to please one's spouse on her birthday might make the choice rational when viewed through the lens of the Rational Actor Model. Viewing the different criteria as sufficient rather than necessary features allows the analysis of *how and when* choices are irrational and rational.

Moreover, the question "Are people rational?" may be the wrong one to ask. Since decision making quite frequently violates at least a subset of rational criteria, perhaps a better question to ask is, "When and how do people deviate from rational standards?" People might fail to thoughtfully consider all available benefits and costs of a decision if they are distracted or in a good mood. That does not imply, however, that the consistency of choices or the use of probability knowledge will be similarly affected by such factors. Understanding not *if* people are irrational but *how* and *when* they fall short of rational standards might provide a useful way for considering the role of rationality in choice.

Heuristic Thinking as Rational

Kahneman and Tversky and others have provided many demonstrations that intuitive processes often produce judgments that are irrational, as defined by classical axioms. Recently, some theorists have argued that this research "has retained the normative kernel of the classical view. For example, a discrepancy between the dictates of classical rationality and actual reasoning is what defines a *reasoning error* in this program" (Gigerenzer & Goldstein, 1996, p. 650). These researchers argued that intuitively-based judgments can be as accurate as, and often are superior to, judgments that follow traditional definitions of rationality (Gigerenzer, 2007, 2008, 2015; Gigerenzer, Hertwig, & Pachur, 2011; Hertwig & Herzog, 2009). This is particularly true, they argue, in many real-world situations where there are multiple pieces of highly redundant information. In such cases, classic rules of rationality would be nearly impossible to follow, given that many normative approaches require discrete and independent pieces of information. Furthermore, decision quality is not necessarily improved by increases in the amount of information that is utilized. Good decisions often require that some available information be ignored, particularly if it dissuades us from relying on an intuitive but accurate judgment. From this point of view, *fast and frugal* intuitive thinking represents an indispensable psychological tool. In fact, in many circumstances, the product of such thinking can exceed the quality of classic rational approaches while using a fraction of the time and resources required by elaborative reasoning systems.

Gigerenzer (2008, 2015; Raab & Gigerenzer, 2015) and Hertwig (Hertwig & Herzog, 2009; Hertwig & Hoffrage, 2013) provide numerous examples from the *fast and frugal* tradition of heuristics that offer equal or better accounts of judgments compared with models reflecting classic definitions of rationality. Table 9.4 lists some of these heuristics. We discuss two of them here that are particularly relevant to the social domain. One is referred to as the *recognition heuristic* (Filevich, Horn, & Kühn, 2019; Gigerenzer & Goldstein, 2011; Goldstein & Gigerenzer, 2002; Pachur, Todd, Gigerenzer, Schooler, & Goldstein, 2011; Pohl, 2011). This heuristic posits that if one of two alternatives is better recognized, one should infer that it has a higher value on the criterion in question.

Table 9.4 Some fast and frugal heuristics

Heuristic	Definition	Research examples
Recognition	If only one of two alternatives is recognized, infer that it has the higher value on the criterion	Goldstein & Gigerenzer, 2002; Michalkiewicz & Erdfelder, 2016; Pachur & Hartwig, 2006
Default	If there is a default, do nothing	Johnson & Goldstein, 2003; Park, Jun, & MacInnis, 2000
Take the best	To infer which of two alternatives has the higher value, search cues in order of validity, stop the search when a cue discriminates, then choose favored alternative	Graefe & Armstrong, 2012; Gigerenzer & Goldstein, 1996; Newell & Shanks, 2003
Social circle	To infer which of two alternatives has the higher value, search social circles based on proximity. Stop search when instances of one alternative exceed the other, then choose frequent alternative	Pachur, Rieskamp, & Hertwig, 2005; Pachur, Hertwig, & Rieskamp, 2013
Satisficing	Choose from multiple alternatives the first one that exceeds your aspiration level.	Chen & Sun, 2003; Gigerenzer, 2010; Simon, 1955
Equality (1/N)	Allocate resources equally to among N alternatives	DeMiguel, Garlappi, & Uppal, 2009; Hertwig, Davis, & Sulloway, 2002; Messick & Schell, 1992
Fluency	If one of two alternatives is recognized faster, infer that it has the higher value on the criterion	Fukawa & Niedrich, 2015; Jacoby, Woloshyn, & Kelley, 1989; Schooler & Hertwig, 2005
Tit-for-tat	In an interaction, first cooperate then imitate your partner's last behavior	Axelrod & Hamilton, 1981; Duersch, Oechssler, & Schipper, 2014; Pruitt, 1968
Imitate the majority	Imitate the behavior of the majority of people in your peer group	Boyd & Richerson, 2005; Nikolaeva, 2014; Raz & Ert, 2008
Imitate the best	Imitate the behavior of the most successful person in your peer group	Boyd & Richerson, 2005; Duersch, Oechssler, & Schipper, 2012; Garcia-Retamero, Takezawa, & Gigerenzer, 2009
Averaging	Make quantitative predictions by averaging across expert predictions	Mannes, Soll, & Larrick, 2014; Soll & Larrick, 2009
Tallying	To estimate a criterion, count the number of favoring cues rather than estimate their weights	Bonnefon, Dubois, Fargier, & Leblois, 2008; Dawes, 1979; Hogarth & Karelaia, 2006
Regret matching	Stay with current choice if no regret; change if regret	Damjanovic, 2017; Hart, 2005

Source: Adapted from Gigerenzer (2008) & Hertwig & Herzog (2009)

Suppose you were asked to judge whether San Diego or San Antonio had a larger population. How would you go about making this judgment? You might use everything you know about each city (its location, history, number of prominent citizens) to make such an estimate, or you might simply decide whether you had better recognition of one city compared with the other (e.g., you have heard more about it or seen it mentioned more frequently). In either case, you might accurately judge that San Diego is, in fact, a larger city than San Antonio, as do about two-thirds of American participants. However, what if you lived in another country and knew little about either city? In such a case, knowing *less* about each city might actually improve the judgment if the degree of recognition was all that was available to differentiate the options. In fact, nearly all Germans correctly judged that San Diego is the larger city. Conversely, Americans show greater expertise than Germans about the relative size of cities in Germany (Goldstein & Gigerenzer, 2002). When the degree that a stimulus seems familiar correlates with the criterion being judged (bigger, more famous, wealthier), having less information can actually increase the accuracy of judgment.

A second "fast and frugal" heuristic of social importance is termed the *default heuristic* (Johnson & Goldstein, 2003). In many situations, there exist *default practices* such that a person need do nothing more to make a decision. For example, I might discover when I start a new job that 5% of my pay is automatically invested in a retirement fund unless I chose instead to receive the money in my regular pay (an *opt-out default*) or I might find that nothing is contributed to retirement unless I elect to do so (an *opt-in default*). According to this heuristic, people tend to prefer the default action among several possible alternatives. The default hypothesis has been applied to understanding how a host of issues are resolved in which legal or societal norms provide different defaults for handling situations. Consider, for example, the decision of whether an individual is willing to donate his or her organs after death. Some countries have opt-in policies that require an individual to explicitly consent to donate organs, whereas other countries have opt-out defaults that presume consent unless the individual has explicitly indicated an unwillingness to donate.

Differing defaults can produce dramatic differences in choice and behavior. For example, Germany is an "opt-in" country, and only 12% of Germans consent to organ donation. However, in Austria, a neighboring country with an "opt-out" default, 99.98% of Austrians donate their organs. Another study showed that 86% of the employees of one company contributed some of their assets to a fund under an opt-out policy compared with 10% for fellow employees not subject to automatic enrollment (Beshears, Choi, Laibson, & Madrian, 2008). A third study showed that patients who were assigned a flu-shot appointment that they could cancel were three times more likely to be vaccinated compared with patients who were informed that they could schedule an appointment (Chapman, Li, Leventhal, & Leventhal, 2016). These examples show that people tend to follow opt-out defaults and likely recognize their practical and societal benefits. However, the degree of support for opt-out versus opt-in defaults can vary across issues (Azar, 2014). Whereas American survey respondents generally favored opt-in policies for carbon emission offsets, they preferred opt-out approaches for organ donation and retirement savings programs (Yan & Yates, 2019)

The Benefits of Not Thinking?

Most characterizations of System 2 processes portray them as vigilant and ready for conscious activation to correct the error-prone output from System 1. In this view, decisions are improved and errors avoided through the activation of conscious reasoning processes. Some research describes a very different, and counterintuitive, consequence of conscious processing. Proponents of the *Unconscious Thought Theory* (UTT) view of cognition (Dijksterhuis, 2004; Dijksterhuis & Nordgren, 2006; Dijksterhuis, & Strick, 2016; Dijksterhuis & van Olden, 2006; Dijksterhuis, Bos, Nordgren, & von Baaren, 2006; Nordgren & Dijksterhuis, 2009) argue that some decision making can be improved through *withholding* conscious processing. Whereas simple choices, it is argued, benefit through deliberative processes, complex choices are improved through *unconscious thought*. Dijksterhuis and colleagues provide two reasons why unconscious processes might prove better than conscious thought in making complex decisions. First, they argue that the capacity of the unconscious is much larger than the capacity of systems underlying conscious thought. Second, conscious processing can lead to suboptimal weighting of the importance of attributes or features of different choice alternatives. In contrast, unconscious thought is more effective at applying effective weights reflecting the relative importance of different attributes of objects. The provocative notion that unconscious processes may be superior in making complex decisions has been called the *deliberation-without-attention hypothesis*.

What evidence is there that difficult problems are more effectively addressed through non-conscious processes? One early study (Dijksterhuis et al., 2006) showed that people who were distracted while considering their choices made superior decisions compared with people who were not distracted. Participants were asked to imagine that they were deciding what automobile they would purchase from a set of four options. Half of the participants read descriptions providing information about four of the cars' features, whereas the other half of

participants read about 12 features for each car. In both conditions, one car was clearly superior because 75% of its features were desirable, compared with two middling cars (50% desirable attributes) and one poor car (only 25% desirable attributes). Half of the participants in each group were given 4 minutes to think about these options before choosing. The other half were asked to complete a series of anagrams that effectively distracted them from thinking about the cars before making their choice. The dependent measure was the percentage of individuals in each condition who chose the superior car. As predicted, the quality of decision making was a function of both the

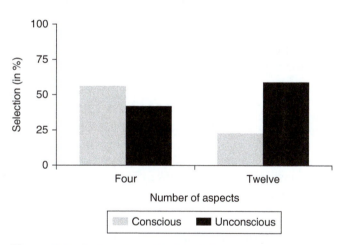

Figure 9.4 Percentage selection of the superior car as a function of decision complexity and conscious involvement

Source: Adapted from Dijksterhuis et al. (2006)

complexity of the decision and the degree of conscious deliberation. As is shown in Figure 9.4, when the choice was simple because information about only four features had been provided, deliberative thinkers performed better than people who had been distracted. For the complex choice, however, distracted individuals selected the superior car at a much higher rate than people who had consciously deliberated about their selection. According to the proponents of this view, people are actively (if unconsciously) deliberating while they are distracted, and such unconscious thinking allows the decision-maker to more clearly differentiate attractive from unattractive choices.

The claim that people can unconsciously deliberate has proved controversial. Critics have identified several boundary conditions for these effects, and alternate interpretations have been proposed (Gonzalez-Vallejo, Lassiter, Bellezza, & Lindberg, 2008; Lassiter, Lindberg, Gonzalez-Vallejo, Bellezza, & Phillips, 2009; Payne, Samper, Bettman, & Luce, 2008). Although one meta-analysis provided evidence consistent with UTT (Strick, Dijksterhuis, Bos, Sjoerdsma, Van Baaren, & Nordgren, 2011), more recent meta-analyses and large-scale replications (Nieuwenstein et al., 2015; Vadillo, Kostopoulou, & Shanks, 2015) have yielded no evidence for the superiority of unconscious thought. Dijksterhuis and Strick (2016) have recently reported evidence consistent with their hypothesis that has emerged from several different laboratories using diverse paradigms. Although these controversies are not yet resolved, this line of research suggests that encouraging engagement and cognitive deliberation might not always improve the quality of decisions.

JUDGMENT AND DECISION MAKING IN UNDERSTANDING THE SELF, PERSONS, AND GROUPS

The research we have discussed so far has explored judgment processes in a variety of domains, ranging from judgments of objects to decisions regarding consumer preferences. As many of our examples illustrate, judgments involving social targets and social situations are also of critical importance. In this section, we consider such judgments in greater detail, focusing on phenomena that are particularly central to judgments involving the self, other individuals, and social groups.

Judgment Processes in Understanding the Self

In earlier chapters, we have seen that self-relevant information draws attention and is evaluated more favorably. There also are a host of biases in inferences and attribution involving the self. Not surprisingly, the self also plays a central role in judgment and decision making. We now consider how people make judgments about the self and how the self influences judgments of others.

Judging the Self

Because we know more about ourselves than about any other person, it would be reasonable to expect that judgments about ourselves would be highly accurate. Given our access to nearly limitless information about our talents, our experiences, and our goals and motivations, we *should* be better able to judge our own abilities, behavior, and future outcomes than those of other people. But is this true? Research suggests that it is not, at least much of the time.

Dunning, Heath, and Suls (2004, 2018) reviewed several ways in which judgments of the self are inaccurate. Judgments of our abilities and traits are often out of line with performance on objective measures of our attributes (Beer, 2014). Estimates of one's own intelligence, for example, rarely correlate with performance on IQ and other academic tests at a level above +.30 (Hansford & Hattie, 1982). One study showed that estimates of one's ability to tell if someone is lying correlated only +.04 with actual performance when faced with a person who might not be telling the truth (DePaulo, Charlton, Cooper, Lindsay, & Muhlenbruck, 1997). Children tend to overestimate their ability to remember pictures (Lipko, Dunlosky, & Merriman, 2009), and consumers overestimate how easy it will be to learn to use new products (Billeter, Kalra, & Loewenstein, 2011). Somewhat ironically, people with the weakest abilities in a domain are likely to show the highest degree of inaccuracy in judging their performance (Kruger & Dunning, 1999). This *unskilled and unaware* phenomenon (a.k.a. the Dunning-Kruger effect) has been shown in many studies (e.g., Bol & Hacker, 2001; Ehrlinger et al., 2008; Williams, Dunning, & Kruger, 2013). In addition, those who are poor in a skill are also among those least likely to pursue opportunities for improvement (Sheldon, Dunning, & Ames, 2014). All of these findings and others suggest that we often do not know ourselves as well as we think we do.

Indeed, other people often can judge us as well as, and sometimes better than, we can judge ourselves. Participants in one study (Borkenau & Liebler, 1993) were able to predict a person's performance on an IQ test almost as well as that person after watching a 90-second videotape of the individual reading a weather report. In another study (Risucci, Torolani, & Ward, 1989), the performance of surgical residents on their medical board exams was predicted more accurately by their supervisors and peers than by themselves. Vazire (2010; Beer & Vazire, 2017; Neubauer, Pribil, Wallner, & Hofer, 2018; Vazire & Mehl, 2008) has proposed the existence of a *self–other knowledge asymmetry*, such that people who observe us are often more accurate in judging ourselves than are we. She argues that the accuracy of one's own compared with others' judgments depends on the observability of the trait being evaluated. Some traits can be readily inferred based on observations of behavior (e.g., one's sociability), but others rely on information more readily available to the self (e.g., one's feelings of nervousness). People should be more accurate in judging themselves on attributes where they have privileged access to information, whereas others may be more accurate in judgments based on observable behavior. In a study testing this idea (Vazire, 2010), participants made ratings of themselves on various traits and were judged on those same traits by a set of friends and strangers. A battery of behavioral measures provided criteria for judging the accuracy of these trait judgments. Results showed that the accuracy of self and other judgments did vary across traits, as predicted. Self-judgments of neuroticism were most accurate compared with judgments of friends and strangers. Friends (who presumably have been able to observe a person's behavior over time) were most accurate at judging intelligence, and all groups were equally accurate in judging the readily observable trait of extraversion.

People also regularly show self-enhancing tendencies in judgment. When people are asked to compare their characteristics with an average person, most people believe themselves to be more intelligent, more attractive, and more moral than others (Alicke & Govorun, 2005; Brown, 2012). This finding, termed the *better-than-average effect*, is so reliable that it has been called one of the "staple findings" in social psychology (Guenther & Alicke, 2010, p. 755). Two independent factors appear to contribute to this effect. First, as we discussed extensively in Chapter 6, people have a fundamental and chronic motive to hold positive views of themselves (Alicke & Sedikides, 2009). Judgments of one's traits or abilities are inflated by a motive to align one's self-views with an image of an ideal or aspirational self. Second, it also appears that in making judgments comparing themselves with others, people anchor on unrealistically favorable self-ratings by focusing selectively on their positive behaviors and then failing to adjust adequately for the positive behaviors of others (Kruger, 1999). Therefore, the better-than-average effect can be viewed as a manifestation of the anchoring and adjustment heuristic (Guenther & Alicke, 2010).

People also assume that their own future is quite rosy compared with that of others (Sharot & Garrett, 2016). For example, college undergraduates estimate that they are more likely than their classmates to live longer than 80 years and are less likely to develop a drinking problem or to suffer a heart attack (Weinstein, 1980). People also tend to be optimistic in predicting their future behavior. In one study (Epley & Dunning, 2000), 90% of undergraduates said they intended to vote in an upcoming presidential election but predicted that only 75% of their peers would. In fact, only 69% of the students ended up actually casting a ballot.

It appears that individuals judge the self, but not others, based on optimistic assumptions and best-case scenarios. There might be more than a little truth to American poet and educator Henry Wadsworth Longfellow's observation that "We judge ourselves by what we feel capable of doing, while others judge us by what we have already done."

Seeing Ourselves in Others

The self also plays a critical role in how we judge others. In Chapter 6, we discussed how people and groups associated with the self are evaluated more favorably than those that are not. In addition, the self can serve as the basis of judging the characteristics of other people and groups. One classic phenomenon showing reliance on the self in judging others is the *false consensus effect* (Aksoy & Weesie, 2012; Gilovich, 1990; Marks & Miller, 1987; Sherman, Chassin, Presson, & Agostinelli, 1984) when people overestimate the extent that others share their attitudes, beliefs, and behaviors. In the original demonstration of this effect (Ross, Greene, & House, 1977), student participants were given descriptions of four situations and had them judge the percentage of their fellow students who would choose each of two courses of action for handling each situation. In one description, for example, participants were asked to judge the percentage of students who would contest a speeding ticket when the police officer's summons contained numerous errors. Later, these same participants were asked which of the two options they themselves would choose for all four situations. Results showed that participants thought that other students would make the same choices as they would (approximately 59% vs. 41%).

The self is also involved in making trait judgments of other people, ranging from close friends and romantic partners (Ashton, Lee, & De Vries, 2014; Cohen, Panter, Turan, Morse, & Kim, 2013) to strangers (Beer & Watson, 2008; Srivastava, Guglielmo, & Beer, 2010). A recent meta-analysis (Thielmann, Hilbig, & Zettler, 2018) showed that the degree of judged similarity in one's own and other individuals' traits varies across the types of traits being judged. The strongest correlations of own and others' traits arose on judgments of sincerity, fairness, avoidance of greed, humility, and openness. The high similarity in these judgments reflects an emphasis on characteristics related to morality, a finding consistent with the claim that "of the many impressions people form of themselves and others, impressions of moral character are likely among the most relevant and consequential" (Barranti, Carlson, & Furr, 2016, p. 806). In addition, the strength of the similarity of trait judgments depended on the closeness of the relationship with the person being judged. Although some had argued that having less information about a person should increase reliance on the self to make trait judgments (Kenny & West, 2010), that was not found. There was a higher degree of similarity between self and other judgments for people who were close compared with strangers on traits related to openness and equivalent similarity on moral judgments. In sum, even individuals with whom people had no familiarity were judged similarly as the self on traits related to morality and openness.

Later research has shown that such *self projection* occurs quite readily and affects a variety of judgments (Krueger, 2007; Robbins & Krueger, 2005). Ames (2004a), for instance, showed that people use the self to make judgments of another person's mental states, but only if the person is similar to the self. In this study, participants were given false feedback about whether another person named "Michael, an investment banker" was or was not similar to them (e.g., if he thought the same jokes were funny and liked the same artists). After receiving this information, they viewed a video clip of Michael engaged in a negotiation with another person and judged whether Michael had various thoughts in mind during the negotiation (he "wanted to win at all costs" or "wanted to joke and have fun"), whether they would have these same thoughts in a similar negotiation, and whether a typical investment banker would have such thoughts. When Michael was described as similar to themselves, participants estimated they would have many of the same thoughts as Michael during the negotiation. When he was described as dissimilar, they judged Michael as having thoughts more similar to those of a typical investment banker than of themselves

The speed with which they made these judgments was informative about the processes underlying them. To interpret these response time data, it is important to take into account a manipulation of the order of the sets of judgments. Half of the participants completed the self judgments first, then the judgments of Michael, and then the judgments of Michael's group (investment bankers). The other participants first judged investment bankers, then Michael, then the self. The logic of this manipulation was that if judgments of Michael were based on the self, then collecting self judgments first should facilitate the speed of making judgments of Michael. That is exactly what was found, but only in the condition when Michael was seen as similar to the self. As shown in Figure 9.5, when Michael had been described as

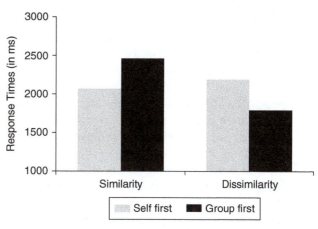

Figure 9.5 Response times as a function of similarity and judgment order

Source: Adapted from Ames (2004a)

similar to the self, judgments of his inner states were made more quickly when participants had just made comparable judgments about the self. When he was described as dissimilar from the self, however, making judgments of an investment banker first facilitated judgments of Michael. Thus, when people see others as similar to themselves, they tend to use the self as a basis for making judgments about those people. In contrast, judging a person who is dissimilar from oneself increases reliance on stereotypes.

Judgment Processes in Understanding Persons

Chapter 6 offered an extensive discussion of Solomon Asch's (1946) research with a focus on evaluative processes in impression formation. Asch was among the first social psychologists to systematically study judgments of individuals, and his theorizing has continued to influence social cognition to this day. Numerous phenomena he explored and developed (e.g., primacy effects, negativity effects, generalization effects across traits, and construal processes) are regularly invoked to account for social judgment. Throughout this text, we have considered much research that followed and built upon this tradition.

Rather than reiterating that research here, in this section we will focus on two issues that are particularly relevant to interpersonal judgment but ask different questions than those posed by traditional research on impression formation. The first question is, "To what degree are people accurate in judging other people?" Two specific research areas have focused on this issue, one examining the accuracy of clinical judgments (i.e., predictions about patients' future outcomes) and a second, more recent, area of research examining the accuracy of trait judgments. The second question is, "given all the information we have available about a person in any given moment (e.g., behavior, categorical, and situational information), how do people integrate that information to make a judgment about the person?" To address this question, we will use Fiske and Neuberg's (1990) continuum model, a dual process model referred to in Chapter 3, as a foundation for discussing how various sources of information are used in interpersonal judgment.

The Accuracy of Interpersonal Judgments

Understanding whether people can accurately judge others' states, traits, and behavioral tendencies is critical because of the importance of prediction in interpersonal interactions. Decisions about approaching or avoiding a person, hiring or passing on a job applicant, or offering or declining an applicant a position in a graduate program, are all based upon judgments of a person's dispositions and likely actions. If these judgments are relatively accurate, then they can be used to guide reactions to and decisions about the people we encounter. If they are not, then we need to understand how interpersonal judgments are inaccurate and the conditions that might improve their accuracy.

Conducting research to address these important issues is challenging for several reasons. Within the traditional literature on impression formation, there is no ability to assess the accuracy of interpersonal judgments since participants are usually tasked with forming impressions of a hypothetical person. Since the target of impression formation does not exist, then there is no basis for knowing whether the "person" will act consistently in the future with participants' predictions. Therefore, controlled studies examining the process of impression formation are not ideal for answering questions about accuracy. Another problem where real persons are involved pertains to the typical absence of objective criteria for assessing accuracy (Biernat, Manis, & Kobrynowicz, 1997; Cronbach & Meehl, 1955; Judd & Park, 1993). If you judge that a person is friendly, how can one test the accuracy of that judgment? The number of times the person smiles? Whether the person helps someone in need? The accuracy of trait judgments is particularly hard to assess, given that trait descriptions compare a person against a standard that can change across contexts (Biernat, 2005).

More fundamentally, although judgment accuracy was a popular topic in the early decades of experimental psychology, critiques regarding the traditional measurement of accuracy raised serious questions about this area of research. Accuracy was typically measured by calculating the amount of agreement between perceiver ratings and self-ratings on a particular attribute. Cronbach (1955; Gage & Cronbach, 1955) showed that scores derived using this technique reflected multiple factors, many of which were irrelevant to what researchers were claiming to study. This critique slowed the advance of research on interpersonal accuracy, making it a topic that for a time was "neither prominent nor prestigious" (Letzring & Funder, 2018, p. 256). Fortunately, these measurement problems were not unsurmountable, and research on accuracy has been an active area of study.

Accuracy of Clinical Judgments

One area of research that has been pursued for decades examines the accuracy of clinical judgments. Meehl (1954) spurred research on this topic by advancing the provocative claim that judgments derived from *actuarial methods* regularly outperform clinical psychologists in predicting patients' outcomes. Meehl argued that even simple algorithms specifying only the relative weights and valence of available evidence (akin to the linear weighted additive strategy advocated by Ben Franklin) produce more accurate predictions (using actual outcomes as the accuracy criterion) than are made by clinical psychologists given identical information (Dawes, 1979; Dawes & Corrigan, 1974). The superiority of the *actuarial* over the *clinical* methods was subsequently replicated in various judgment domains, including teachers' predictions of students' grades, parole boards' judgments about whether prisoners would violate their terms of release, and psychiatrists' estimates of patients' responses to electroshock therapy (Dawes et al., 1989).

Hundreds of studies have examined the relative accuracy of actuarial (i.e., statistical) versus human judgments, and several meta-analyses have emerged in recent years that provide useful summaries of this research. The first such meta-analysis to appear (Grove, Zald, Lebow, Snitz, & Nelson, 2000) examined clinical versus actuarial predictions of a wide variety of behaviors and outcomes, including psychological and medical prognoses and judgments of psychological states and traits. The study found that judgments derived with actuarial methods were approximately 10% more accurate than predictions based on clinical approaches. Actuarial predictions outperformed clinical predictions in around 40% of the studies, and clinical predictions were superior in only about 11% of the studies. Interestingly, clinicians' forecasts were harmed when they were given clinical interview data, the information upon which most diagnoses are made.

Another meta-analysis published several years later (Ægisdóttir et al., 2006) reached similar conclusions. That study showed an overall 13% increase in accuracy when statistical rather than clinical methods were used. Prediction accuracy differed across different behavioral domains; violent behavior and academic performance were predicted much more accurately with statistical techniques, but the necessary length of patients' medical treatments was predicted equally well using both approaches. A third meta-analysis (Spengler et al., 2009) focused on whether the experience of clinicians improved their predictive ability. This study found a small but reliable effect showing that both educational and clinical experience enhance the accuracy of judgments.

The issue of why actuarial methods outperform clinical assessments has been a matter of speculation (Hastie & Dawes, 2010). One clear thing is that formulas are not susceptible to factors that are known to moderate and degrade human decision making. The order in which information is received and the framing of an issue can affect human decision-makers but not regression equations. Variations in humans' levels of distraction and fatigue and the nature of their recent experiences can all affect the quality of clinical decisions. More fundamentally, people have difficulty distinguishing diagnostic from nondiagnostic information and often possess erroneous beliefs about relationships between variables based on implicit theories of personality and stereotypes. In sum, the superiority of statistical over intuitive judgments may reflect various limitations in people's ability to properly integrate information to render accurate judgments about persons.

Accuracy of Personality Judgments

A distinct line of research on the accuracy of interpersonal judgments focuses on whether people can assess the personalities of other people with any precision. Personalities are not always expressed consistently in different contexts (Mischel & Shoda, 1995), but people do tend to behave with at least some regularity across social situations. Can people predict another individual's personality from observing his or her behavior? Here, the accuracy criterion is not in comparison with an actuarial formula but, instead, on whether people can predict personality at a better-than-chance level. In other words, can people exposed to information about a person make personality inferences that are more accurate than if nothing were known? In response to Cronbach's (1955) concerns, self-ratings alone are not typically used as an accuracy criterion. Instead, composite measures are created by averaging self-ratings with ratings provided by one or more people who know the person well (Funder & Colvin, 1988; Kenny, 1991), with ratings made by clinicians following interviews (Letzring, Wells, & Funder, 2006), or with behavioral information (Vazire, 2010). In addition, advanced statistical techniques are now available that successfully deal with some of the measurement challenges that were identified by Cronbach (Kenny & Kashy, 2014).

Much research shows that people can infer personalities based on observing the behavior of other individuals (Letzring & Funder, 2018). Moreover, the research indicates factors that moderate this ability, providing an understanding of the conditions under which personality assessments are more or less accurate. First, the accuracy of personality judgments tends to be superior at higher levels of familiarity. People who have known someone for longer or who have watched longer recorded interactions of the person tend to make more accurate judgments compared with people who have had less exposure to the individual (Connelly & Ones, 2010; Paunonen, 1989). However, the effect of familiarity on accuracy is strongest early in the impression formation process. Accuracy tends to plateau once a solid impression has formed (Kenny, Albright, Malloy, & Kashy, 1994).

As one might expect, the consistency of the person's behavior also affects the accuracy with which their personality can be judged. People who behave consistently are considered *highly judgeable*, and judgeability is typically higher in well-adjusted individuals. One study of the relationship between adjustment and judgeability showed that well-adjusted people more consistently provided cues reflecting their distinctive personalities. As a consequence, perceivers judge such individuals more accurately (Human, Biesanz, Finseth, Pierce, & Le, 2014).

Furthermore, some traits are easier to assess than others, thereby affecting the accuracy of personality judgments. Some aspects of personality are more regularly exhibited in behavior, and this factor affects the visibility or observability of a trait. Internal aspects of personality (e.g., being a remorseful or anxious person) are lower in observability than are outwardly visible dispositions (e.g., extraversion). As a consequence, traits that are manifest internally tend to be judged less accurately than traits that produce multiple external cues (John & Robins, 1993; Paunonen & Kam, 2014).

Although personality is not consistently expressed across situations, people can predict the traits and dispositions of other individuals with some accuracy. Judgments are particularly likely to be accurate when a person is known somewhat well, when she behaves consistently, and when the dominant aspects of her personality produce visible behaviors.

Integration in Judgments of Persons

When we encounter a new person, we typically have an abundance of information that can be used to judge that individual. We receive information about the person's physical features, many of which indicate membership social categories (age, sex, and race) and offer cues about occupations and roles (uniforms, attire). Facial and body information can also serve as a basis of trait judgments. We can see how the person acts; some of those actions will be expected and some will surprise us. We have discussed how people process some of these different kinds of information in isolation (e.g., inferences from behavior, attributions for unexpected actions, evaluations based on features), but we have not yet considered how social perceivers integrate various pieces of information to formulate judgments about people. Here, we briefly discuss how social perceivers "put it all together."

Fiske and Neuberg (1990) offered an influential conceptual framework, the *continuum model*, describing how people integrate various types of available information to form impressions and make judgments of individuals. This model focuses on the relationship between reliance on cognitive structures (e.g., stereotypes) and individual pieces of information about a person's individuating attributes (e.g., behaviors or traits) when forming an impression. The relative weight given to categorical versus individuating information will determine whether a person is judged stereotypically or will be judged using non-stereotypical or even counter-stereotypical attributes (Bodenhausen, Macrae, & Sherman, 1999).

In this model, an impression of a target person begins to form when the perceiver assigns the target person to a social category (e.g., woman, Black, Italian). That social category has expectancies associated with it which are activated, and those expectancies define the initial impression. The perceiver then attends to individual pieces of information about the target (e.g., behaviors), each of which might be consistent or inconsistent with those category-based expectancies. If this specific information is consistent with expectations, then the perceiver moves on to other information, investing attention elsewhere. An impression judgment at this point would be based mainly on those category-based expectancies.

In contrast, if the target information is inconsistent with expectancies, the perceiver continues to attend to the target and tries to recategorize the target ("he's not Italian, perhaps Swiss"), and a judgment made at this point would be based on expectations about the new category. If the recategorization is unsuccessful (e.g., if subsequent information is incompatible with this new category), then the perceiver will continue to attend to new pieces of information to form an individuated impression of the individual (Fiske, Neuberg, Beattie, & Milberg, 1987). In this case, later judgments of the person will be based on the accumulated individual pieces of information, with little if any role of category-based expectancies. The continuum model, then, emphasizes the shifting of emphasis between category-based expectancies and individual-based information in integrating information during impression formation.

Research has supported many aspects of the continuum model (Erber & Fiske, 1984; Fiske & von Hendy, 1992; Neuberg & Fiske, 1987; Pavelchak, 1989; Ruscher, Fiske, Miki, & Van Manen, 1991; see for reviews Fiske, 2012; Fiske, Lin, & Neuberg, 1999). Other prominent models echo the importance of integrating category-based and individual-focused information in impression formation (Brewer, 1988; Brewer & Feinstein, 1999). However, recent research has questioned the dominance of top-down processes, as depicted in the continuum model. Several studies (Crawford, Jussim, Madon, Cain, & Stevens, 2011; Köpetz & Kruglanski, 2008; Monroe, Koenig, Wan, Laine, Gupta, & Ortony, 2018) offer evidence challenging the notion that stereotypes serve as the starting point or default assumption in impression formation and social judgment. Perceivers appear to emphasize whatever information is most useful for making a particular judgment to meet a specific processing goal, regardless of whether that information pertains to stereotypes or attributes. In other words, perceivers' integration processes emphasize whatever information has the highest diagnostic value or relevance for current goals or tasks.

The idea that all available information can be utilized in impression formation is reflected in several models emphasizing dynamic and interactive processes in social judgment (Freeman & Ambady, 2011; Freeman et al., 2020; Kunda & Thagard, 1996; Read & Miller, 1998). These models share the assumption that various kinds of information relevant to person perception are stored as nodes in a connectionist network in memory. Impression formation requires the activation and integration of this information from these networks. For example, Freeman et al.'s (2020; Freeman & Ambady, 2011; Freeman & Johnson, 2016) *Dynamic Interactive Theory* argues that seeing a new face will provide numerous inputs relating to social categories, emotions, and traits. The relative utilization of any particular piece of information will depend on its activation level (reflecting the frequency and recency of activation), how quickly its activation decays, and whether it is being activated by other information.

Patterns of excitation and inhibition will determine the influence of any piece of information in impression formation. Importantly, both bottom-up factors (e.g., facial features linked to categories) and top-down factors (e.g., information processing goals directing attention to particular features) trigger patterns of activation throughout one's network based on connection weights. Because nodes are bidirectionally connected (i.e., each node can affect and be affected by other nodes), activation can flow dynamically between nodes in the system, leading over time to a stable representation that best fits the available inputs. Such models highlight the dynamic relationships between bottom-up sensory cues and top-down social cognitive factors in impression formation.

Judgment Processes in Understanding Groups

Judgments play an important role in determining the nature of interactions between groups and their members. Whether a group is judged as diverse or homogeneous, friendly or hostile, greedy or charitable will greatly influence how the actions of groups and their members are interpreted and evaluated and how people behave in intergroup interactions. Two related aspects of judgment that are particularly consequential in intergroup perception have received significant research attention. One aspect relates to the process of identifying the variability of groups with respect to attributes, including stereotypes. Whether a group is seen as highly homogeneous or diverse can influence whether individuals are treated interchangeably with other group members and in ways consistent with stereotypes. The second aspect pertains to whether stereotypes themselves are applied so that judgments of groups and their members are assimilated to the prevalent social stereotypes. Although stereotypes are readily available and come easily to mind in many contexts, they are not always used in making judgments.

Judging Group Variability

In Chapters 1 and 6, we discussed Tajfel's (1970) seminal research using the minimal group paradigm. In that research, individuals were divided into two social groups, typically based on arbitrary characteristics. A consistent finding from these studies was that group members judged members of their own group differently from members of the other group, even though there were no differences between the groups in the information available. People judged members of groups to which they do not belong (outgroups) as being more similar to one another than members of their own groups (ingroups). The tendency to perceive outgroup members as similar to one another and ingroup members as heterogeneous is called the *outgroup homogeneity effect* (OHE). The OHE is a robust phenomenon that can occur with artificial groups, such as those used in the minimal group paradigm, and also with real groups in naturalistic settings (Ostrom & Sedikides, 1992). Seeing groups as homogeneous ("They all look alike," "If you've seen one, you've seen them all") tends to increase stereotyping (Brauer & Er-rafiy, 2011; Judd, Ryan, & Park, 1991; Park & Judd, 1990; Park & Rothbart, 1982).

The OHE is weakened and can even be reversed (Guinote, 2004). For example, the size of the ingroups and outgroups affects the magnitude of the OHE. Several studies have shown that the OHE is strongest when the ingroup is larger than the outgroup (Mullen & Hu, 1989). In fact, outgroups can seem more heterogeneous than ingroups when the ingroup is a numerically small minority (Simon & Brown, 1987). The effect can also be reversed when the outgroup presents information that is motivationally relevant so that perceivers are motivated to attend closely to the outgroup. In one study (Ackerman et al., 2006), White participants viewed pictures of Black and White faces that were displaying either neutral or angry expressions. Later they showed better recognition memory for ingroup than for outgroup faces when facial expressions were neutral but no memory difference when targets were displaying angry faces. Similarly, perceived threat from the outgroup (e.g., telling participants that "the Hispanic population of the United States will explode in the coming years") can eliminate the typical recognition advantage for ingroup members (Wilson & Hugenberg, 2010). Thus, the OHE can be eliminated when perceivers are motivated to pay close attention to the outgroup.

Several distinct processes likely contribute to the OHE (Hughes, Camp, Gomez, Natu, Grill-Spector, & Eberhardt, 2019; Rubin & Badea, 2012). Linville, Fischer, and Salovey (1989) proposed that the OHE reflects reliance on exemplar information from memory to judge variability. Specifically, they argued that judgments of group variability are computed by retrieving group exemplars (typically, examples of behaviors performed by group members) from memory. Once a variability judgment has been formed (e.g., "That group is quite diverse!"), the judgment itself is stored as an exemplar, available to be retrieved with other behavioral information the next time variability is computed. From this perspective, the OHE occurs because more exemplars are typically available for the ingroup than for the outgroup, reducing the likelihood that extreme exemplars will be available indicating that the outgroup is diverse.

An alternate model (Kraus, Ryan, Judd, Hastie, & Park, 1993; Park & Judd, 1990; Park, Ryan, & Judd, 1992) emphasized the role of on-line processes in judging variability. These authors contend that people form and revise variability judgments automatically as information is received during intergroup interactions or otherwise learn about a group. Like the Linville et al. (1989) model, memory-based processes also play a role in that previously formed variability judgments can be retrieved from memory to influence the processing of available information. However, memory-based processes play a secondary role from this perspective; retrieved information simply serves as additional information that is integrated with new information to determine the perceived variability of the group. Once this determination is made, it is stored in memory as an exemplar, available for later retrieval for blending with any new information that becomes available. From this approach, the OHE arises because of different amounts of exposure to ingroups versus outgroups. The greater exposure one typically has to the ingroup means that a greater variety of people from that group will be encountered. Importantly, a high level of exposure increases the likelihood of meeting extreme members of the group and, therefore, the judged variability of the group as a whole will increase.

These two models differ in their emphasis on on-line versus memory-based processes. Both models likely provide an accurate account of the formation of variability judgments at least in some contexts. We know that people are not always willing or able to engage in on-line processing at all times and, in such cases, rely on retrieving information from memory. When individuals are highly motivated to learn about a group, determining whether it is diverse or homogeneous is of central concern. In such cases, on-line judgments of variability are likely to be made and become available for guiding subsequent judgments and behavior toward the group and its members.

A third approach (Ostrom, Carpenter, Sedikides, & Li, 1993) presented an account of the OHE that involves a different distinction. Unlike the previous two explanations that assume that perceivers make comparisons in the similarity among individual group members, this approach recognizes that information processing can focus on individuation ("What are these persons like?") or on category differentiation ("What are these groups like?"). Ostrom and colleagues argued that information describing the ingroup is processed differently from information about the outgroup. Specifically, ingroup processing involves differentiating unique individuals belonging to one's group, but outgroup information is processed based on stereotypic categories. Several experiments tested this prediction by providing participants with stereotype-consistent information about several fictitious persons, half of whom were ingroup members and the other half outgroup members. In one study focused on gender stereotypes, four individuals were described with four classes of attribute information (e.g., favorite TV show, favorite sport, college major, and personality type). Later, participants recalled all the information they could and indicated the name of the person associated with each piece of information. Analyses of free recall showed that participants clustered ingroup information in terms of person categories (e.g., recalling "Mike's" attributes together) and outgroup information in terms of stereotypic attributes (e.g., recalling information about college majors together). In addition, participants showed fewer name-matching errors for the ingroup than the outgroup. Therefore, a difference in the parsing of ingroup and outgroup information resulted in a greater ability to differentiate individual ingroup compared with outgroup members, the core feature of the OHE.

Using Stereotypes in Group Judgments: When and Why?

Despite their widespread availability, stereotypes are not always used in social judgment. Even though stereotypes might automatically come to mind as a result of social categorization processes, social perceivers can avoid using the stereotype to make judgments of groups and their members. In other words, stereotype *activation* and *application* involve different processes (Kunda & Spencer, 2003; see Burns, Monteith, & Parker, 2017; Rees, Rivers, & Sherman, 2019). Several factors determine whether accessible stereotypes are used or avoided in social judgment.

Perceived Group Variability

We have just discussed group variability as an important aspect of group perception, related to but separate from stereotyping. However, there is a relation between these two aspects, such that the judged variability of a group can influence whether a stereotype is used in judging group members. Ryan, Judd, and Park (1996) collected judgments of stereotypes of several real social groups (e.g., fraternities, Asian American, African Americans) and also the perceived variability of each group around those stereotypes. The variability of groups influenced the use of stereotypes such that people who judged groups as diverse were less likely to hold stereotypes with confidence and were less likely to use stereotypes to judge the behavior of group members. In other words, perceiving homogeneity in groups facilitated stereotyping.

Availability of Individuating Information

Stereotypes are only one possible source of information about people and groups. It is common that in interacting with members of groups, we learn information about what they are like as unique individuals. To the degree that we gain useful information about the unique characteristics of individual group members, we are less likely to use stereotypes to judge the person (Locksley, Hepburn, & Ortiz, 1982). Individuating information is mainly used when an available stereotype is only weakly related to the attribute being judged and when the individuating information is seen as highly diagnostic of the attribute (Krueger & Rothbart, 1988). Stereotypes are more likely to be used as a basis for judgment when stereotypes are seen as relevant to the attribute being judged and when people have little useful information about the individual characteristics of group members (Hilton & Fein, 1989).

Cognitive Capacity

Perceiving a person as an individual and not merely as a group member (and therefore relying on individuating information in judgments) is demanding and resource consuming. Therefore, it should not be surprising that cognitive capacity can influence whether activated stereotypes are used in social judgment. To avoid using stereotypes, one must possess sufficient cognitive resources to attend to and to process idiosyncratic information. As long as the ability to focus is preserved, stereotype application is less likely. Conversely, when capacity is diminished or the ability to maintain focus is exhausted, stereotypes are more likely to be used in judgment. This was demonstrated in an experiment (Pendry & Macrae, 1994) in which participants were asked to make judgments of an older woman either in standard conditions or when they were instructed to simultaneously remember a multidigit number. Participants whose cognitive resources were not burdened with the task of memorizing the number showed lower use of elderly stereotypes compared with participants who had fewer cognitive resources. Stereotype application increased when cognitive resources were scarce. Similarly, Govorun and Payne (2006) demonstrated that people were more likely to utilize stereotypes in judgment when they had just completed a difficult task that demanded deliberate allocation of attention and persistence. In both cases, the use of stereotypes increased when capacity had been diminished, either before or within the judgment context.

Positive Mood

The affective state of the perceiver can also influence whether stereotypes are used in judgment. Several studies have shown that positive moods, in particular, increase the use of stereotypes in making judgments of groups (Bodenhausen, Kramer, & Süsser, 1994; Gold, 2002; Park & Banaji, 2000; Stroessner & Mackie, 1992). Positive moods have been shown to decrease deliberative processing and thereby to increase reliance on stored knowledge structures (Bless, 2001; Krauth-Gruber & Ric, 2000). However, the exact reason why positive moods increase reliance on such structures has been a matter of some disagreement. One explanation highlights the role of reduced cognitive resources, thereby increasing reliance on pre-existing stereotypes (Mackie & Worth, 1989; Stroessner & Mackie, 1992). Other explanations argued that mood produces deficits in the motivation to process deliberatively, either to save cognitive resources (Bodenhausen et al., 1994) or because positive mood is seen as a signal that scrutiny of the environment is unnecessary (Schwarz, 2012).

Self-enhancement

The motivation to maintain positive views of the self has also been implicated in stereotype application. Stereotypes can be applied to other individuals when one's sense of worth has been threatened (Beauregard & Dunning, 1998; Collange, Fiske, & Sanitioso, 2009). In one such study (Fein & Spencer, 1997), participants completed an intelligence test and then were given negative or no feedback regarding their performance. Under the guise of another experiment, they then read a passage about a man who was either gay or straight. The participants who previously had been given negative information about their intelligence judged the man more stereotypically gay when he was gay. Participants who had not been given feedback regarding their intelligence did not differentiate in their judgments of the gay versus straight man. The lowered self-worth of the former group led them to apply a stereotype that they otherwise would have avoided using.

Accuracy

In many contexts, people are motivated to make accurate judgments of others, unbiased by stereotypes and other factors. This motivation may arise from a temporary goal (e.g., to hire the best person for a position) or to consistently avoid prejudiced responses (e.g., to be an egalitarian person). These differing motivations to be accurate both contribute to reducing the application of activated stereotypes. In a study showing the former, participants who were told that they would have to share and explain their judgments of members of occupational groups showed lower use of stereotypes compared with participants whose judgments remained anonymous (Moreno & Bodenhausen, 1999). Interestingly, participants who had to explain their ratings but in whom a cognitive load had been imposed showed higher levels of stereotyping. This result indicates that avoiding the use of stereotypes in judgment can be effortful, requiring cognitive resources. An example of the latter motivation is a study on the suppression of stereotypes. When people are instructed to avoid using stereotypes to judge others, they can succeed in doing so. When they are under a cognitive load or no longer feel that they need to inhibit their stereotypes, however, judgments are colored by stereotypical associations (Macrae, Bodenhausen, et al., 1994; Wyer et al., 1998).

SUMMARY

Research on judgment and decision making has been an interdisciplinary endeavor with contributions from several social sciences and subfields in psychology. Understanding how people make judgments and decisions is also of central interest to social cognition, given the centrality of cognitive processes in human judgment, the critical consequences of judgments and decisions for other processes, and, ultimately, for social behavior. Early demonstrations of the faulty nature of human decision making had a tremendous impact by demonstrating how people differed in their behavior when compared with longstanding assumptions of rationality. During the intervening decades, much research has shed light on the processes that underlie decision making. The processes that have been identified have not typically been unique to judgment phenomena. Indeed, the processes we have considered in this chapter are, in large part, the same factors that we have discussed concerning other aspects of processing. As such, we believe that any consideration of social cognition can benefit from a vigorous consideration of human judgment and decision making. In addition, we believe there are benefits from viewing judgment and reasoning processes as reflective of general social cognitive functioning, despite the historically interdisciplinary nature of this literature.

FURTHER READING

Greifeneder, R., Bless, H., & Pham, M.T. (2011). When do people rely on affective and cognitive feelings in judgment? A review. *Personality and Social Psychology Review, 15*, 107–141.

Hastie, R., & Dawes, R.M. (2010). *Rational choice in an uncertain world: The psychology of judgment and decision making* (2nd ed.). Thousand Oaks, CA: Sage.

Norman, G.R., Monteiro, S.D., Sherbino, J., Ilgen, J.S., Schmidt, H.G., & Mamede, S. (2017). The causes of errors in clinical reasoning: Cognitive biases, knowledge deficits, and dual process thinking. *Academic Medicine: Journal of the Association of American Medical Colleges, 92*, 23–30.

Vohs, K.D., & Luce, M.F. (2019). Judgment and decision making. In E.J. Finkel & R.F. Baumeister (Eds.), *Advanced social psychology: The state of the science* (2nd ed.) (pp. 453–470). New York, NY: Oxford University Press.

10
MEMORY
Storage and Retrieval

Miles Harrison, 49, was an amiable person, a diligent businessman, and a doting, conscientious father until the day last summer – beset by problems at work, making call after call on his cellphone – he forgot to drop his son, Chase, at daycare. The toddler sweltered to death, strapped into a car seat for nearly nine hours in an office parking lot.

Washington Post, March 8, 2009

Remember Terry Howard? He's the University of Louisville guard who had made 28 of 28 free throws before going to the line in the final seconds of the NCAA Final Four game against UCLA in 1974–75. He missed the front end of a one-and-one, letting UCLA off the hook, and Louisville lost in overtime. Asked not long ago if he ever thought about that fateful night, Howard said, "Every day of the week."

Now listen to Abel Kiviat, silver medalist in the Olympic 1,500 meters in 1912 in Stockholm. Kiviat had the race won until Britain's Arnold Jackson came from nowhere to beat him by one-tenth of a second.

Kiviat: "I wake up sometimes and say, 'What the heck happened to me?' It's like a nightmare."

Kiviat is 91 years old.

Los Angeles Times, January 15, 1984

All of us have had the experience of not being able to remember something we "know" that we know well. We struggle to remember the name of a movie, book, or restaurant we enjoyed. While taking an exam, we fail to recall some material we had studied and knew very well the night before. And then there is the uncomfortable experience we have all had when we encounter someone whose face is very familiar, but we cannot come up with his or her name.

These experiences happen with discouraging frequency and are often followed immediately by comments such as "my memory is terrible." Lapses of memory can also have tragic consequences, as illustrated in the heart-wrenching story of a parent forgetting a child in the back seat of the car. In contrast to these experiences, the other quotation opening this chapter provides remarkable examples not of failures to recall but of cases in which memories of long-ago events have proven quite durable and recurring.

Although we often take memory for granted, numerous complex processes work together so that we can effectively utilize information gleaned from our past experiences. A failure in any of these processes can produce memory errors or failures. One critical set of processes involves the *encoding* and *storage* of information into memory. A second set of processes involves the *retrieval* of information from memory. Knowledge is stored in memory so it can be used for our purposes, but we must be able to access knowledge to benefit from it. This chapter focuses on some of these essential considerations for understanding memory and retrieval.

THE NATURE OF MEMORY

Memory serves as the repository of knowledge we have acquired during our lifetime of experiences. We have been processing information all of our lives, and traces of those processes exist in memory. Fortunately, we know that our minds can store an incredibly large amount of information. However, we also know that there are limits in our ability to access everything that has been stored. Therefore, there are certain enigmas involving memory. On the one hand, we might be reminded of the immense capacity of memory when a recent event triggers a distant memory. On the other hand, we might be frustrated by the difficulty we have recalling an event that occurred just in the last few days. Furthermore, sometimes we can remember liking a movie we saw or a novel we read two years ago, even though we can remember only fragments of what transpired in the story. These are experiences all of us have had, and we are sometimes amused (or frustrated) by the seeming contradictions inherent in them. However, when trying to consider what memory is like – what it consists of, how it functions, how experiences are represented and stored, and how those memories are retrieved – these incidences and their apparent contradictions become more than amusing anecdotes. Instead, they become puzzles to be solved by scientifically studying how the mind works.

Cognitive scientists have studied memory for decades. One important task has been to ask fundamental questions concerning how information is *encoded* into memory systems and ultimately *represented* in the mind. Research has identified several different types of memory representations that involve different functions in the storage and use of acquired information. Another important aspect of memory concerns the *processing* of information in memory. This aspect includes understanding factors that influence how, and how much, information is processed and represented in memory.

Scientists have used several metaphors to guide the study of memory and how it functions. These metaphors do not attempt to describe memory processes in detail; instead, they offer conceptual frameworks to facilitate understanding. We have already introduced some of these metaphors. In Chapter 2 on Cognitive Representations, we offered several competing metaphors for describing how the information we encounter – the persons, physical situations, and events we experience – is represented in memory. For example, we discussed how associative networks, hierarchical structures, and distributed connectionist models offer contrasting views of how information might be represented in memory. Other chapters have described ways in which that information is expanded and transformed through processes performed on those initial representations, sometimes using other metaphors to portray this processing. Attention, interpretation, evaluation, inferences, attributions – these processes are both selective (operating on specific aspects of the information available) and elaborative (expanding on the literal information available). In these ways, the initial information encountered has been transformed into something broader, more comprehensive, and more meaningful. That transformed "knowledge" is now represented in memory, along with and sometimes in place of the original information we encountered. As such, our representations may change in significant and consequential ways compared with when the initial information was encountered. The processes that alter our representations can be beneficial in comprehending and understanding the information to which we are exposed. However, they also tend to introduce bias and error into our resulting representations.

Memory Representations

Our memory systems contain traces of specific previous incidences and events; they act as a repository of language, providing us with a "dictionary" of concepts, meanings, and interrelations between semantic information; they contain procedural knowledge, information about how to do things, the steps required for implementing thought and enacting behaviors toward the achievement of goals. As such, memory plays an essential role in almost all aspects of our lives.

Cognitive scientists have differentiated several aspects or components of memory that involve different types of representation and function. Three commonly differentiated types of memory are episodic, semantic, and procedural (see Table 10.1).

Table 10.1 Some differentiated components of memory

	Content	Consciousness	Example
Memory type			
Episodic	Event exemplars	Typically conscious	My last birthday party
Semantic	Verbal knowledge	Conscious & unconscious	Definition of "friend"
Procedural	Routines	Initially conscious	Serving a tennis ball

Episodic Memory

In episodic memory, each experience is represented as an exemplar of a particular previous episode. Taken together, these exemplars constitute a person's memory of all the events he or she has experienced. As such, episodic memory is mainly autobiographical. A 35-year-old American man might have a specific memory of his high school prom – when and where it was, who his date was that evening, what they were wearing, details about the after-prom party. Because episodic memories are exemplars of specific incidents, they typically include representations of time, place, other persons involved, and contextual details. They provide the experience of "reliving" past events and, as such, they include re-experiencing the sights, sounds, and emotions that were part of the original event. Retrieving events from episodic memory is usually a conscious re-experiencing of the past (Tulving, 1993). Our 35-year-old man consciously remembers that prom; it is as if he is "seeing" the evening in his mind. Episodic memory enables us to relive past events mentally.

Semantic Memory

Semantic memory consists of knowledge represented in concepts reflecting the meaning of terms, ideas, and events. You know what a chair is – its properties and functions – without having to think of a specific exemplar. Our 35-year-old man knows what a prom is, even without thinking of his own senior prom. Semantic memory also includes general knowledge of diverse domains like politics, baseball, and music, along with more abstract concepts like peace, freedom, and evil.

From the perspective of an associative network metaphor (introduced in Chapter 2), concepts are the building blocks of semantic memory and are represented in associative networks containing links between related concepts. These links are typically represented as pathways in the network, indicating the existence and strength of interrelations between concepts represented in memory. Each link in the network represents a proposition that connects the two concepts. For example, in thinking of racial stereotypes, the concept of "African Americans" might be associated with specific physical features (dark skin, broad nose), personal attributes (aggressive, athletic, musical), and life conditions (poor, urban). Those features might themselves be linked with other attributes that are not as closely tied to African Americans; for example, jazz might be linked to musical, which is closely associated with African Americans.

When a concept is encountered, it becomes *activated* in memory. Activation is the process of retrieving the concept and accessing its meaning, and it occurs in a graded rather than all-or-none fashion. An essential aspect of this activation is that it spreads along the pathways of the network, thereby activating the other concepts to which it is linked (Collins & Loftus, 1975). Thus, related concepts become more accessible and are more easily retrieved from semantic memory. The extent (strength) of that activation dissipates as it spreads to more remote concepts in the network. In the above example, "jazz" would not be as strongly activated (easily accessible) as "musical" because of the latter's greater proximity to the concept of African Americans. Consequently, more distant concepts are less likely to be activated and retrieved than concepts that are more proximal to the initially-activated concept.

Memory networks vary in the extent to which associative pathways interconnect the concepts represented in them. When few of those concepts have been considered in relation to each other, there will be few pathways linking them; when there are many pathways connecting concepts, the network as a whole is densely interconnected. Therefore, experience in any domain tends to increase the complexity of associative networks. The pathways in a network are used in retrieving information from it, a topic to which we will return later in the chapter.

Procedural Memory

Procedural memory consists of the knowledge of the sequence of actions involved in enacting behaviors. You know how to unlock the front door of your home and how to ride a bicycle. Although these are familiar acts, both of them involve complex routines of behaviors-in-sequence (e.g., get the key, insert the key in the lock, turn the key, then turn the doorknob). In both cases, there are several steps to be followed in achieving one's goal. These production sequences are stored in procedural memory. When one's goal is to unlock the door – or any other purpose to be achieved, task to be performed, or problem to be solved, whether simple or complex – the specific means of implementation are activated from procedural memory.

There are significant differences between these memory systems regarding the role of conscious attention. *Episodic* memory is typically conscious mental activity, the focus of one's attention. When attention is drawn to or refocused on some other topic or event, the contents of episodic memory will be lost. The materials in *semantic* memory are more permanent, and their use may or may not involve conscious activity. When engaged in a conversation about whether a political candidate is liberal or conservative, we are aware of drawing on our semantic knowledge of the meanings of all the terms we use and how well they apply to our understanding of the candidate. In contrast, in previous chapters, we have discussed numerous experiments in which concepts have been primed subliminally, and the influence of their activation on subsequent processes and behaviors is evident. Thus, the use of semantic memory may occur in or out of consciousness. In *procedural* memory, the situation is slightly different. Conscious attention is usually required in learning a procedure (recall the challenges you faced when you first learned to ride a bicycle), but once mastered, the required sequence of actions can be implemented as a well-learned routine that does not require conscious attention. Once a procedure has been routinized, focusing attention on it can actually harm performance (Beilock, Carr, MacMahon, & Starkes, 2002; DeCaro, Thomas, Albert, & Beilock, 2011).

Despite these differences, all of these memories can become associated with other similar representations, as well as with function-related memories. These associations are represented in some form of a memory system, such as an associative network representation or a distributed connectionist representation. Once a particular memory representation – whether episodic, semantic, or procedural – is activated by some internal or external stimulus, that activation spreads through the network and activates those associations as well.

Processes Influencing Memory

We have now introduced several essential principles regarding how information is represented and stored in memory. Several variables can influence the nature of that representation and, in turn, one's ability to recall information. We discuss some of those factors in this section.

Flashbulb Memories

For all of us, certain events from our past stand out, retained indelibly in our memory. The assassinations of President John F. Kennedy, the explosion of the Challenger spacecraft, the 9/11 attack, the death of Osama bin Laden, the election of Donald Trump – depending on your age, at least some of these events are so memorable that they may seem to have occurred quite recently. More interestingly, for such events, you often remember the exact details of *yourself* at the time – where you were when you learned of it, how you learned, who you were with at that moment, what you were doing at the time. These are not aspects of the historic event; they are details of your own experience, yet you can remember them vividly and with high confidence. It is as if someone took a picture of you at that moment, an image that has been vividly preserved in your mind. Brown and Kulik (1977) referred to them as *flashbulb memories* and suggested that they reflect a separate memory system involving detailed encoding and long-term retention.

Flashbulb memories are not memories of the historical event and its details. Those memories – which also can be excellent – are referred to as *event memories* (memories of the flashbulb-inducing event, e.g., the 9/11 attack). In contrast, flashbulb memories are memories for details of the circumstances in which a person first learned of the event, details that objectively are not of crucial importance. Therefore, detailed memory for them over time is puzzling. Brown and Kulik (1977) focused on two properties of flashbulb memories: (1) that they have a high degree of accuracy over extended periods and (2) that they are the product of a particular memory system that is triggered by an event of considerable importance, producing a high level of detailed encoding of information. Their account stimulated many studies (e.g., Conway et al., 1994; Hirst & Phelps, 2016; Hirst et al., 2009, 2015; Kvavilashvili, Mirani, Schlagman,

Foley, & Kornbrot, 2009; McCloskey, Wible, & Cohen, 1988; Neisser, 1982; Neisser & Harsch, 1992; Talarico & Rubin, 2003). One of the most comprehensive studies of flashbulb memories assessed more than 3,000 persons in seven U.S. cities for their memories of the 9/11 attack and re-assessed as many of the same people as possible 1 year, 3 years, and 10 years later (Hirst et al., 2009, 2015). The results of these studies shed light on the nature of this phenomenon and also raised questions about both properties that Brown and Kulik proposed.

The first presumed property is that flashbulb memories are highly accurate. Since the critical event is a one-time occurrence involving details applicable to only one person, it can be challenging to determine the veracity of this assumption. There usually is no way to verify a person's report of where he was, who he was with, and who informed him of the event in question. Moreover, by the time researchers begin posing their questions, time has passed, and some of those specific memories may have been forgotten or altered. To circumvent these problems, researchers have adopted the following strategy: assess the relevant questions as soon as possible after the significant event and then re-ask the same questions at a later time. This plan permits the researcher to determine the *consistency* of the recalled information without having to verify its accuracy. Consistency is not the same as accuracy, but if someone's memories are inconsistent across time, then at least one of them must be inaccurate. Therefore, consistency over time has become a primary measure in most of these studies and is regarded as a (possible) indication of the accuracy of these memories. Typically, participants are also asked to indicate their confidence in each of their recollections.

Although many flashbulb memories may be valid, there are reasons to question the accuracy of any given recollection. Neisser (1982) recounts that he had a clear memory of how he learned about the bombing of Pearl Harbor when he was 13 years old. He vividly remembered listening to a professional baseball game on the radio when it was interrupted for the announcement of the attack. It was not until years later that he realized the fallacy of his memory: professional baseball games are not played in December when the attack occurred.

Many studies have found that changes in memories occur over repeated assessments (again raising questions about the accuracy of these memories), and changes made between Time 1 and Time 2 (e.g., substituting a new memory at Time 2) typically persist in future assessments (Hirst et al., 2009, 2015). Thus, one of the features that Brown and Kulik (1977) assumed to be true of flashbulb memories – high accuracy, even for detailed information, and persisting over time – should be questioned based on these studies.

Nevertheless, the results of several studies reveal a different kind of consistency: participants' confidence in the accuracy of their memories remains consistently high (Hirst et al., 2015). People may have poor memory for where they were and who they were with at the time of a specific event, but they believe their memories to be accurate. That confidence persists across time better than does actual memory consistency. This means that the confidence in their recall does not depend on the consistency of those memories across time. Exactly why people are so confident for so long in the accuracy of their flashbulb memories, even if those memories change over time, remains a puzzle.

The second property of flashbulb memories suggested by Brown and Kulik (1977) was that they reflect the operation of a different memory system than the one that underlies "ordinary" memories. Studies have assessed whether there are distinct systems for storing information about important versus more mundane events that happened in people's lives at approximately the same time. These studies involve asking the same set of questions about both events and comparing those answers and their consistency over time to determine what is "special" about flashbulb memories.

Many factors can influence people's memories for events of all kinds, and several of them are present in the flashbulb situation. These are dramatic events, they are highly salient and distinctive, and they powerfully capture one's attention. Also, these are public events, so there is extensive media coverage, and people talk about what happened (the critical event) and about their own experiences at that time (flashbulb memories), generating high levels of rehearsal that facilitates memory. In many cases, these events are very emotional, and heightened emotion may influence the likelihood of recall. All of these factors can play a role in creating the long-lasting nature of flashbulb memories. However, we know that these same factors also influence memory for more mundane events, and no consistent properties have emerged that distinguish memories for highly salient compared with more mundane events. In other words, flashbulb memories appear to be shaped and guided by the same processes that affect memory in general (Neisser, 1982; Neisser & Harsch, 1992). Therefore, it becomes difficult to maintain that flashbulb memories reflect the operation of a separate memory system.

In sum, research on flashbulb memories shows that there is very little that is unique about them. Their apparent high accuracy is illusory. People do indeed remember details of flashbulb events to an impressive degree, but they also tend to forget some aspects of the incident. Most details seem to be lost within the first year. When some aspect is misremembered, that mis-remembered aspect persists in future recollections.

More broadly, this analysis of flashbulb memories makes several points for understanding fundamental aspects of memory. That people would have a memory for what happened on some significant historical event is not surprising. However, that they (at least sometimes) also have excellent long-term recall for where they were, who they were with, and how they learned about the event, is intriguing. However, although some external factors (novelty, emotional intensity, rehearsal) can make flashbulb memories more memorable, those same factors affect memory more generally. These findings help us realize that, as fascinating as the flashbulb memory phenomenon may be, it reflects the workings of the same memory system that functions to guide, enhance, and bias memory performance in all contexts.

Organizing Knowledge

Memory is limited regarding how much information can be encoded and retained at a given time. This limited capacity was documented in a classic article published in 1956, the title of which was "The Magical Number Seven, Plus or Minus Two: Some Limits on Our Capacity for Processing Information" (Miller, 1956). Miller observed that on numerous tasks assessing information processing (e.g., recalling a long string of numbers or an extensive list of unrelated words) where items need to be later recalled, participants regularly were able to remember approximately seven of them (with some small variation; hence the "plus or minus two" in the title). An illustration of this limit is that people typically can retain in memory, at least for a brief time, a local phone number (7 digits), but they cannot retain a 16-digit credit card number. Thank goodness that our phones allow us to outsource memory for lengthy cell numbers!

If our memory systems allow us only to keep seven items in our heads at any given time, is there a way to overcome this limit? Miller (1956) showed that people could do so, invoking a process he called *chunking* (which is similar to the unitizing process described in Chapter 5 on interpreting a stream of behavior). A chunk is a unit of information that can itself be composed of several items. By grouping several individual elements into a chunk, we increase the amount of information that can be encoded in memory. For example, retaining a string of 39 random letters would be very difficult for most people, well beyond the limits Miller (1956) identified. What if the letters were not random but were instead the following?

FOURSCOREANDSEVENYEARSAGOOURFOREFATHERS

Because these letters can be "chunked" into meaningful subunits (words), retaining them becomes more feasible. In fact, someone already familiar with these words (which, of course, are the first eight words of the familiar Gettysburg Address) can store them as one chunk (Simon, 1974). Such chunking can be extended into larger chunks, thereby increasing further the number of letters (and words, phrases, and sentences) that can be retained in memory.

Chunking can facilitate how information is represented and stored in memory (Bousfield, 1953; Bower, Clark, Lesgold, & Winzenz, 1969; Mandler, 1967; Mathy & Feldman, 2012; Nassar, Helmers, & Frank, 2018; Roenker, Thompson, & Brown, 1971), leaving more storage capacity for processing other information. Moreover, if information gets encoded and stored in terms of meaningful units, later retrieval will be facilitated (Bower et al., 1969; Kahana & Wingfield, 2000; Tulving, 1962). Organizing information into meaningful units is an essential element in the strategies used by "mental athletes" – people who are so effective at processing massive amounts of complex information that they can compete for the title of "world's best mnemonist" (Foer, 2011).

Chunking also applies to the processing of social information. Research has shown that people regularly identify themes that allow them to process and efficiently store behavioral information. One common tendency is for people to infer trait information during social information processing and to use those traits to organize and store information in memory. For example, researchers (Hamilton et al., 1980a) asked participants to form an impression of a target person (we will call him Jeff) based on a series of behavior-descriptive sentences. Jeff's behaviors reflected four recurring themes: friendliness (visited a sick friend, helped a woman move boxes), intelligence (designed a new computer system, made accurate stock predictions), religiosity (attended church, taught Sunday school), and athleticism (jogged, played basketball). Four behaviors reflected each of these themes, but, importantly, the descriptions were presented in random order. However, when participants later recalled these behaviors, the items they remembered were frequently grouped according to these traits. The extent to which this happens is called *clustering* in free recall: items of the same type appear close to one another in the recall list, even though they were not organized this way in the stimulus list. In other words, the participant has imposed an organization on the stimulus items that was not present in the stimulus sequence.

Why does this happen? When we process information about another person, we try to understand the main themes of the person's personality (Asch, 1946). When we learn that Jeff helped design a new computer system for his company, which suggests he is a bright guy, then we recognize the connection between that behavior and other intelligence-implying actions (e.g., he made some accurate stock predictions). In doing so, we organize the information we are acquiring and store it in memory according to the themes (in this case, traits) we discover. In other words, items about each trait become linked with each other as they are represented in memory. This process parallels the chunking mechanisms that Miller (1956) described so that the items, as grouped by trait themes, are stored together in memory.

When participants are asked to recall the items of information, these associations guide the recall process. In this case, recalling one behavior implying that Jeff is smart would then lead to another item that had been interpreted and stored in the same way. When no more intelligent items can be recalled, the search shifts to another trait theme, say, Jeff's athleticism, and then some items describing his athletic behavior would be recalled. In this way, items are recalled from a memory representation that is organized according to the trait themes, clustered in a manner that was not present in the stimulus list (Hamilton et al., 1980b, 1989). Moreover, this organized form of representation facilitates the overall recall of information. That is, the more densely interconnected the items are through these associative connections, the more "routes" there are leading to other items. Therefore, this kind of organization can enhance overall memory for the information as well (Hamilton et al., 1980b).

As this example illustrates, we commonly organize information about individuals in terms of the traits we infer as we attempt to understand their personalities. However, other bases for organization, and hence for cognitive representation, are also used in social information processing. For example, person-descriptive information might be organized in terms of the goals they appear to be pursuing (Hoffman, Mischel, & Mazze, 1981; Loucks et al., 2017) or according to the situational contexts in which the actions occur (Ostrom, Pryor, & Simpson, 1981). Familiarity with the person also can influence the nature and extent of organization (Pryor & Ostrom, 1981). Whatever basis for organization is employed, the principle remains the same: organization of information as it is processed and stored in memory facilitates encoding and later recall of that information.

Processing Goals

The degree that behavioral information is processed thoroughly depends on a perceiver's current cognitive capacities and their motivation. One critical motivational factor is the social perceiver's immediate goal in processing information. Someone might have the goal of forming an impression of a person, or of committing behavioral information to memory, or with the anticipation of later interacting with that person. Research has compared several processing goals in the way information is represented in memory, which in turn affects the amount of that information that can later be recalled. For example, in several studies instructing participants to form an impression of a person led to better recall of information than did instructions to remember the information (Chartrand & Bargh, 1996; Fiedler, Kaczor, Haarmann, Stegmüller, & Maloney, 2009; Hamilton et al., 1980a, 1980b; Srull, 1981, 1983; Srull & Brand, 1983). Also, participants who were led to expect that they would be interacting with the target person recalled more information than did people given memory instructions (Devine, Sedikides, & Furhman, 1989). Different processing goals can focus attention on different aspects of the information and can induce different bases for organizing information, both of which would facilitate retrieval of the items.

There is evidence that distinct neural mechanisms help explain the differences observed under different processing goals. Studies using neuroimaging techniques have shown that distinct brain structures are used to process social information compared with information about inanimate objects (Mitchell, Macrae, & Banaji, 2005). Moreover, different neural structures underlie information processing depending on specific goals (Denny, Kober, Wager, & Ochsner, 2012). Impression formation typically engages the dorsomedial prefrontal cortex, a region distinct from those used to remember the sequencing of behavioral information (Ames & Fiske, 2013; Mitchell, Macrae, & Banaji, 2004). In one study examining this question (Mitchell et al., 2004), the amount of activity in the dorsomedial prefrontal cortex was correlated with the amount of behavioral information recalled when participants were forming an impression of a person but not when they were trying to remember the order in which information was received. This result demonstrates that the goal of impression formation does not merely induce a "deeper" form of processing, as has often been presumed. Instead, the goal of forming an impression invokes brain structures that facilitate the establishment of connections between distinct pieces of behavioral information, thereby increasing later recall and clustering by traits.

Malleability of Memory

The preceding section highlighted some variables that enhance memory. However, we also know from everyday experiences that our memories are not perfect, as we commonly have difficulty remembering even some critical information that we thought we would never forget. Our memories for events can be affected and shaped in significant ways by several factors. In other words, our memories are malleable. In this section, we highlight several examples that illustrate this point.

Leading Questions

We often think that we either remember something or we do not. However, much research shows that memory does not function in such a binary fashion. Memory is often selective and incomplete, a blend of fact, interpretation, and reconstruction. In other words, memory is often a partial replica of what we experienced. This fact is well illustrated in research on *leading questions*, which shows that the way a question is asked can influence the content of what is remembered. In one study examining this issue (Loftus & Palmer, 1974), participants were shown a short film of a traffic accident and then were asked to describe the accident and to answer questions about it. For example, one question focused on the speed of the cars when the accident occurred. One group was asked, "About how fast were the cars going when they hit each other?" For other groups, the verb "hit" was changed to "smashed," "collided," "bumped," or "contacted." Table 10.2 shows the mean estimated miles per hour for the different verb conditions. These estimates varied considerably, ranging from 31.8 mph for cars that "contacted" to 40.8 mph for cars that "smashed." Participants in these different conditions had seen the same car crashes, yet the verb used in asking the question significantly influenced their answers.

Why did this effect occur? One possibility is that, in answering the question, one consults semantic knowledge in understanding key terms. For example, the semantic interpretation of "smashed" versus "hit" may activate different information about the speed of movement and thereby bias participants' answers. Given that the question was posed after seeing the accident, this bias is not the same as the biased interpretation of new information (as discussed in Chapter 5). Instead, it is the reconstruction of information already in memory. (We will return to reconstructive processes in the next chapter.)

Table 10.2 Leading questions: estimated speed as a function of verb condition

Verb	Speed estimate (MPH)
Smashed	40.8
Collided	39.3
Bumped	38.1
Hit	34.0
Contacted	31.8

Source: Adapted from Loftus & Palmer (1974)

However, Loftus and Palmer (1974) proposed an additional possibility, one that suggests more profound implications. They wondered if the leading questions – different forms of asking about car speed – could introduce erroneous information into people's memories. That is, if they were asked about the cars that smashed, would they recall details indicating a more severe accident than they had seen in the film? These researchers again showed a film of a car accident and asked how fast the cars were going when they "smashed," or when they "hit," or no questions about car speed were asked. Again, participants gave higher speed estimates in the "smashed" condition. The new element in this study was that participants returned a week later and, without viewing the accident film again, were asked some additional questions. The critical question was, "Did you see any broken glass?" There was no broken glass in the accident, so responding "Yes" would indicate that the content of memory was biased by how the accident was described the week before. Indeed, a significantly higher number of participants erroneously indicated that they had seen broken glass in the "smashed" than in the "hit" or control conditions. Those participants recalled seeing something that was not there – something suggested by the form of the initial speed estimate. In other words, the "broken glass" had become integrated into the memory representation of the accident. The leading question had produced misleading information in memory.

The Misinformation Effect

A related line of research has demonstrated that changes in one's memory for an event also can occur as a result of being exposed, sometime after the event, to incorrect and misleading information. This phenomenon is called the *misinformation effect*.

In typical experiments on the misinformation effect, people are shown a video or series of images depicting an event (e.g., an accident or a crime). They are then given verbal information and asked questions about the event, which includes new information that is consistent with, misleading, or neutral with the visual depiction. Later, they are asked to make some decisions about what they saw, including the crucial, new information. In one such study (Loftus, Miller, & Burns, 1978), participants were shown a series of colored pictures of events that supposedly preceded an accident in which a car hit a pedestrian at an intersection. They later were given a questionnaire about the incident, and this questionnaire contained information that was either

Table 10.3 Misinformation effect: question type and percent correct responses

Question type	Percent correct
Correct	75
"…stopped at the Yield [Give Way] sign?"	
Misleading	41
"…stopped at the Stop sign?"	

Source: Based on data from Loftus et al. (1978)

consistent with what had been shown in a picture (e.g., "Did another car pass the red Datsun while it was stopped at the Stop sign?") or inconsistent with what they had been shown (e.g., "Did another car pass the red Datsun while it was stopped at the Yield [Give Way] sign?"). Later, people were asked to indicate what they had been shown in the picture set by selecting between pictures that showed a Yield sign or a Stop sign. As shown in Table 10.3, the misleading information produced significantly fewer accurate responses. So, if the questionnaire referred to a Stop sign when a Yield sign was present, a substantial proportion of people showed a false memory for this misinformation.

Many studies have investigated the misinformation effect using several variations of the general paradigm. The effect is quite reliable: misleading post-event information can distort memory under a variety of circumstances (Belli, 1989; Brainerd & Reyna, 2005; Chandler, Gargano, & Holt, 2001; Frenda, Nichols, & Loftus, 2011; Lindsay, Allen, Chan, & Dahl, 2004; Lindsay, Hagan, Read, Wade, & Garry, 2004; Loftus, 2005; Loftus & Hoffman, 1989; Loftus, Schooler, & Wagenaar, 1985; McCloskey & Zaragoza, 1985; Schooler & Tanaka, 1991; Tversky & Tuchin, 1989; Zaragoza & McCloskey, 1989; Zaragoza, Payment, Ackil, Drivdahl, &

Beck, 2001). The magnitude of the effect varies as a function of several variables. For example, misinformation effects are more likely in studies involving young children and the elderly, suggesting an important role of cognitive resources in differentiating accurate from misleading information. Consistent with this view is the fact that misinformation effects are also stronger when attention is limited. In addition, the time interval between viewing the initial information and when the misleading information is presented is important: misinformation effects are greater as the time interval increases, when there has been more time for the initial memory to weaken. Thus, a substantial number of studies have documented the distorting effects of misleading post-event information on memory for information acquired earlier, and much has been learned about the variables that affect this outcome.

Research has also specified several means by which misinformation effects can be reduced and even eliminated. One early study (Dodd & Bradshaw, 1980) showed that the effect was virtually eliminated if participants were informed that the post-event information was offered by a biased source (e.g., a lawyer representing a driver in a car accident). Other studies have examined the effectiveness of a variety of warnings that post-event information might be unreliable or false. Participants in such studies might be instructed that "some of the items mentioned in the questions you answered were not in the slides you saw" (Zaragoza & Lane, 1994) or that "the description of the event was the driver's account in court where she had to explain how and why the accident had happened from her point of view" (Echterhoff, Hirst, & Hussy, 2005). A meta-analysis of 25 studies in which a single warning was provided before a test of recall (Blank & Launay, 2014) found that, on average, the warning reduced the misinformation effect to almost half its typical magnitude compared with control conditions in which no warnings were provided.

The misinformation effect is a real and robust phenomenon. People are likely to assimilate extraneous information into their memories and erroneously to report them as reflecting their experience. This research has enormous implications in the legal context, where the validity of eyewitness testimony not only might be questioned but also can be guided by leading questions and biased by introducing misleading information. Research offers several manipulations for reducing misinformation effects, although these strategies are of little value in real-world situations where misinformation is regularly encountered.

False Memories

The findings presented in the last two sections document that memories can be distorted, massaged, and influenced by various factors. We now turn to a discussion of an even more dramatic phenomenon. Namely, people can sometimes "recall" information they never received and events they never experienced. People may produce what is known as *false memories* (Deese, 1959; Roediger & McDermott, 1995).

Consider the following list of words:

bed	dream	doze	peace	rest
wake	slumber	yawn	awake	snooze
snore	drowsy	tired	blanket	nap

Now get a pencil and paper, and without looking back at the list, write down as many of those words as you can remember. Based on one reading, you likely will be able to recall some, but not all, of these words. One interesting question is whether one particular word appears on your recall list: *sleep*. Research has shown that, when presented with this list of words, people are quite likely to recall the word sleep, even though it was not included in the stimulus list. Similar results have occurred with different lists of words and even when participants have been warned about the nature of the false memory effect (McDermott & Roediger, 1998; Roediger & McDermott, 2000; Roediger, Watson, McDermott, & Gallo, 2001).

Why would people recall an item that had not even been presented? In doing the above exercise, you likely recognized that the list of to-be-learned words all are strongly associated with sleep; indeed, they were selected (based on pretesting) based on that very property. Therefore, when encoding each of those words, other strong associates would be activated so that, at the time of recall, the word sleep would have been activated several times. Hence, that word will be readily accessible for retrieval (Barnhardt, Choi, Gerkens, & Smith, 2006), and this heightened accessibility is mistakenly seen as implying that the word had been on the stimulus list (Johnson, Hashtroudi, & Lindsay, 1993). Another potential contributing factor is that words may not always be encoded simply in terms of their verbatim properties but also in terms of their "gist," which would include associates of a to-be-learned word (Brainerd & Reyna, 2005). In this view, learning includes the broader meaning of the material, which in this case would include notions of sleep.

Other research has extended this work into the domain of social memory (Garcia-Marques, Ferreira, Nunes, Garrido, & Garcia-Marques, 2010; Nunes et al., 2017). In research we described earlier, participants organized behavior-descriptive items into trait-based clusters for storage in memory during impression formation, and those clusters were evident in the way behaviors were grouped in free recall. Those groupings reflect cognitive categories that are used in processing social information. As we have previously discussed, two fundamental dimensions in people's representations of personality are a social dimension (warm, friendly vs. cold, unfriendly) and an intellectual dimension (intelligent, industrious vs. unintelligent, lazy) (Fiske et al., 2002; Judd et al., 2005; Kervyn et al., 2010; Rosenberg, Nelson, & Vivekananthan, 1968). Presumably, items of information in the same category are more strongly associated with one another than are items highly related to the other category. Garcia-Marques et al. (2010) reasoned that those associations could provide the basis for false memories.

To test this hypothesis, researchers asked participants to form an impression of a person who was described by a series of 16 words presented on an audio recording. Ten of those words were traits from one of the four categories (positive or negative exemplars from the social or intellectual dimension) plus six words unrelated to these categories. Each participant's list included traits from only one of the four categories. For example, some participants formed an impression of a person described with socially positive words (e.g., "kind" and "sociable"). After listening to this presentation, participants were shown additional words, some of which had been presented and some had not. As each word was presented, participants indicated whether or not it had appeared in the recording.

Overall, participants performed with high accuracy: they generally could distinguish words they had and had not heard. The crucial result concerns the words reflecting the one trait category included in their presentation. The recognition list included five traits from the category that had not been presented but were strong associates of the presented words (e.g., "friendly" might be presented to participants in the social/positive condition). As predicted, there were more false memories (incorrect "Yes" responses) for the five non-presented words than for any other category of words. These results demonstrate that false memories can arise due to strong associations among items within the broad trait categories used in forming impressions.

In other words, learning some personality-relevant information about a person may lead to the belief that other, strongly associated traits are also true of the person, not as a result of inference processes (as discussed in Chapter 7) but because these associations have generated the (false) "memory" that that information had actually been learned about the person.

In thinking about the research described in this section, you may have thought, "These findings seem rather remote from everyday life." Indeed, in seeking to understand fundamental processes, it sometimes becomes necessary to create seemingly artificial paradigms to maintain experimental precision and control. However, understanding how memory works with somewhat artificial methods is useful in making predictions about a variety of significant problems that occur in real life. We now turn to a discussion of some lines of research demonstrating the real-world importance of several phenomena relating to memory.

Recovery of Repressed Memories

In the 1990s, considerable controversy arose in the scientific study of memory, in the legal system, and indeed in the broader society. The question was whether memories of traumatic experiences that had occurred many years ago, which have been repressed for a long time, can be brought back to consciousness. The issue arose because of several instances in which adults purportedly "recovered" memories of childhood sexual abuse, in many cases leading to legal cases in which the alleged perpetrators (often a parent) faced severe criminal charges, frequently resulting in convictions (Lindsay & Read, 1994; Loftus, 1993; Patihis, Ho, Tingen, Lilienfeld, & Loftus, 2014).

The possibility that repressed memories could be reawakened after lengthy periods of time raised several critical questions. How could the memory of such a traumatic experience be kept from conscious awareness for many years? How could such deeply repressed material become accessible to consciousness after an extended passage of time? What is the status (both scientifically and legally) of such recovered memories? The answers to such questions were not immediately apparent.

There certainly was some receptiveness to the idea that memories might re-emerge after a lengthy period of dormancy. Repression was a central concept in Freud's psychoanalytic theory, and therefore psychotherapists influenced by this tradition would be alert to any signs of repressed memories. From the psychodynamic perspective, uncovering repressed material is essential for understanding unconscious conflict that generates the repressive activity. Hence, repressed memories can unlock the doors hiding the origins of a client's anxieties and interpersonal struggles. Given this understanding, it would seem perfectly natural that a victim of childhood sexual abuse might repress memories of those traumatic events. During the 1990s, some therapists became convinced that many psychological issues concerning interpersonal relations, marital difficulties, and problems in sexual relations may be due (at least in part) to repressed memories of abuse. Their therapeutic strategies, therefore, came to include suggestive probing and even direct suggestions to clients that they had been abused. Several books by therapists aimed at the lay public focused on sexual abuse and the difficulties of recovering those repressed memories.

In a typical therapeutic session aimed at uncovering repressed memories, a trained expert (an authority figure) would interact with a troubled person seeking to understand confusing aspects of his or her life. If the therapist actively provides guidance in charting the client's past, there are plausible reasons that the client would be open to the therapist's suggestions. However, some therapeutic efforts were heavily oriented toward uncovering evidence of such abuse, guided by the therapist's *a priori* beliefs and theoretical assumptions. Because abuse was, to some extent, assumed, therapists often utilized methods that could be characterized (in social psychological terms) as using social influence to produce an expected outcome (i.e., memories of abuse) (Loftus & Davis, 2006). Ultimately, as these cases found their way into courtrooms, judges and juries were faced with the difficult problem of determining whether these recovered memories were real.

There is no easy answer to this question. The events typically occurred decades earlier, and the client (at least initially) had no memory of those events. Moreover, when the abhorrent possibility is raised in therapy, the client often vehemently denies that it happened. However, through therapy, the client comes to believe that it did happen. There is no question that traumatic childhood sexual abuse occurs, and repression of such memories indeed could occur. However, in very few cases are there witnesses who can confirm or deny abuse that might have occurred in the distant past. This means that victims' memories are critical in determining what exactly took place. Unfortunately, in several cases where exonerating evidence did contradict these memories, it became clear that certain clinical practices unintentionally were generating recollections that confirmed the clinician's expectancies but bore little resemblance to reality.

Because of the biased and highly publicized nature of practices by some (but certainly not all) therapists, members of professional communities (including therapists, research psychologists, and those involved in judicial proceedings on such matters) began to examine the many facets of recovered repressed memories and to raise serious questions about their validity. It is now well understood that certain practices can produce false memories of previous abuse (Brainerd & Reyna, 2005; Loftus & Davis, 2006). Nevertheless, some of these practices persist in clinical practice. An extensive survey of people who had sought therapy showed that approximately 9% of them indicated that their therapists raised with them the possibility that they had been abused as a child and had repressed the memory and 5% said they recovered memories of abuse in therapy for which they had no previous memory (Otgaar et al., 2019; Patihis & Pendergrast, 2019). Although the issue is still controversial (Goodman, Gonzalves, & Wolpe, 2019), claims of recovered memories in therapy persist in both the United States (Patihis & Pendergrast, 2019) and Europe (Shaw & Vredeveldt, 2019).

From a theoretical perspective, some critical issues remain. Assume for the moment that the events captured in (at least some of) the recovered memories never occurred. How could such false memories be formed? Is it possible to implant an entirely false memory for an event that never happened? Research shows that this is possible.

In one study demonstrating this possibility (Loftus & Pickrell, 1995), participants thought they were participating in research on memories from childhood and were given brief descriptions of four events that supposedly had occurred between the ages of 4–6. Three of those events were true (as verified by a family member who had been involved); the fourth was a false event manufactured by the researchers describing a plausible event that family members were able to confirm had not happened (e.g., getting separated from mom in a shopping mall, crying, being helped by an older adult, and then being reunited with mom). Participants were interviewed 1–2 weeks after reading these events and then again 1–2 weeks after that. Not surprisingly, participants had a better memory for the true events (68% of those events were remembered in both interviews) than for the false event. However, there was a surprisingly high level of belief in the false event that, of course, had never even taken place. Fully 25% of participants claimed to remember an event that had never happened two weeks after first reading the descriptions. Several other studies have reported similar outcomes (Bernstein & Loftus, 2009; Bernstein, Laney, Morris, & Loftus, 2005a, 2005b; Geraerts, Bernstein, Merckelbach, Linders,

Raymaekers, & Loftus, 2008; Laney, Morris, Bernstein, Wakefield, & Loftus, 2008). These results demonstrate that false memories can be "implanted" under certain conditions, ultimately leading people to "remember" events that never occurred.

Eyewitness Memory

There is one context in which a person's ability to remember information accurately is of crucial importance, namely when that person is testifying in a trial because she was a witness at a crime scene. Many kinds of evidence are introduced during a trial: background information about both the victim and the accused, physical evidence (weapons, objects from the scene, clothing), and photographs of the crime scene. Among the most critical and impactful evidence is eyewitness testimony, the report from a person who was at the crime scene describing what she saw and what happened. As Supreme Court Justice William Brennan stated in a case involving eyewitness testimony, "There is almost nothing more convincing than a live human being who takes the stand, points a finger at the defendant, and says 'That's the one!'" (Watkins vs. Sowders, 1981). The ability to do so, of course, depends entirely on a witness's memory. It is essential, then, that these memories be accurate. Unfortunately, they often are not, and the inaccuracy of an eyewitness's memories can have devastating consequences. One review of eyewitness identification procedures concluded that "cases of proven wrongful convictions of innocent people have consistently shown that mistaken eyewitness identification is responsible for more of these wrongful convictions than all the other causes combined" (Wells, Small, Penrod, Malpass, Fulero, & Brimacombe, 1998, p. 604).

Several factors can reduce the veracity of those memories, such that even the most well-intentioned witness, trying to be cooperative with the justice system's goal of uncovering the truth, may have memories of the event that are biased, incomplete, or inaccurate. When someone describes an incident or a scene to us, we commonly assume that the person has encoded all relevant information to be stored in memory. However, in earlier chapters, we have discussed considerable evidence that people's pre-existing beliefs, based on their past experiences, can influence what they attend to and how it is interpreted. People have scripts (generalized knowledge of what transpires in various situations) that provide expectancies about "who does what" in those situations based on their different roles. People also have general expectancies about members of various groups (stereotypes), which provide expectancies about the likelihood of those group members engaging in various kinds of behaviors. Those expectancies, which the perceiver brings to his perception of the crime incident, can be used in comprehending, interpreting, and understanding the rapidly-occurring events in a situation that does not provide time or opportunity for much thought and analysis. Thus, expectancies can guide processing by filling in gaps and shaping interpretations in schema-consistent ways (Tuckey & Brewer, 2003a, 2003b). Also, the use of leading questions and misleading information can further undermine the accuracy of eyewitness memory. In sum, memories of eyewitnesses are malleable in ways that can influence consequential legal proceedings.

Another important variable is the arousal level of the eyewitness. Crime events are typically emotionally arousing for anyone witnessing them, and this arousal can influence the effectiveness with which observers encode, store, and retrieve relevant information. At higher levels of emotional intensity, people's attention focuses on a narrower range of stimuli. In contrast, under normal stress levels, people attend to a wider variety of aspects of the environment (Easterbrook, 1959). Therefore, in a stressful crime situation, an observer's attention may focus on (and therefore he or she will have a good memory for) certain central aspects of what is happening, such as what the criminal is doing with his hands. However, attention would not be directed at details that might be noticed at normal stress levels, such as the perpetrator's face and clothing.

Many studies have tested the effects of high stress on eyewitness memory, both on memory for eyewitness identification of the perpetrator and on recall of details associated with the crime scene (Deffenbacher, Bornstein, Penrod, & McGorty, 2004; Morgan et al., 2004). The results of these studies provided strong evidence that heightened stress harms the accuracy of both eyewitness identification and eyewitness recall (but see Sauerland et al., 2016)

One final variable to be considered is the confidence with which a witness expresses her testimony. Intuitively, it seems that the more a witness appears confident and sure of herself in providing testimony, the higher the likelihood that she is accurate. In contrast, a witness who seems uncertain about her testimony may not be reliable. Indeed, jurors give much weight to signs of confidence when evaluating eyewitness testimony. This all seems to be common sense. Unfortunately, much of the evidence contradicts these widely-held intuitions (Wells, Lindsay, & Ferguson, 1979; Wells, Olson, & Charman, 2002). When ratings of witness confidence have been correlated with the accuracy of testimony in several studies, the correlations have been discouragingly low. Why would that be so? Several variables can increase the witness's apparent confidence (e.g., knowing that someone else shares the same account; ease of expressing views, which may result from responding to repeated pretrial questioning) that are unrelated to accuracy, thereby limiting the correlation between confidence and accuracy.

The confidence-accuracy correlation can be improved in certain conditions (Juslin, Olsson, & Winman, 1996; Sporer, Penrod, Read, & Cutler, 1995). One review (Wixted & Wells, 2017) concluded that the relationship between confidence and accuracy can be remarkably strong under "pristine" conditions, that is, when optimal procedures are in place to reduce the contamination of eyewitness identification. These conditions include collecting a statement of witness confidence immediately when the identification is first reported, making sure that witnesses interact with people who are unaware of the identity of suspects, and ensuring that witnesses are never provided feedback about the accuracy of their identification. If these recommendations are ignored (and they often have been in practice), then the accuracy of even a highly confident witness could be compromised (Mickes, Clark, & Gronlund, 2017).

Change Blindness

We typically assume that people can detect obvious consistencies and changes in the events they observe. However, as we discussed in Chapter 4, our attentional abilities are limited. Several studies have produced dramatic examples of perceiver's failure to notice easily visible changes in the social environment, thereby harming memory for and recall of events (Davis, Loftus, Vanous, & Cucciare, 2008; Levin, Drivdahl, Momen, & Beck, 2002; Nelson, Laney, Bowman-Fowler, Knowles, Davis, & Loftus 2011; Rensink, 2002; Rensink, O'Regan, & Clark, 1997; Simons & Levin, 1998).

In one study examining the phenomenon of *change blindness* (Simons & Levin, 1998), an experimenter, with a campus map in hand, approached a person walking across campus and asked directions to the library. About 10 seconds later, their conversation was disrupted by two men carrying a door who walked right between them (Figure 10.1). The two men were on the other side of the door from the participant and hence out of view. As they passed, the experimenter (out of sight) took the back of the door from one of the door carriers (another experimenter), a transfer that occurred smoothly within a second or two. The first experimenter then walked away with the door, and the second experimenter replaced him in the conversation, which carried on for a few more minutes. Therefore, the pedestrian interacted with two different persons in one conversation. The two men wore different colored shirts, differed in height by 1½″ (38 mm), and had easily distinguishable voices. After the pedestrian finished giving directions, the experimenter asked if the pedestrian noticed "anything unusual" when the door passed. If they did not, he asked, "Did you notice that I'm not the same person who approached you?" Only 7 of the 15 pedestrians said they had noticed the change of persons. People sometimes fail to notice rather visible changes, even when they are active participants in the ongoing event.

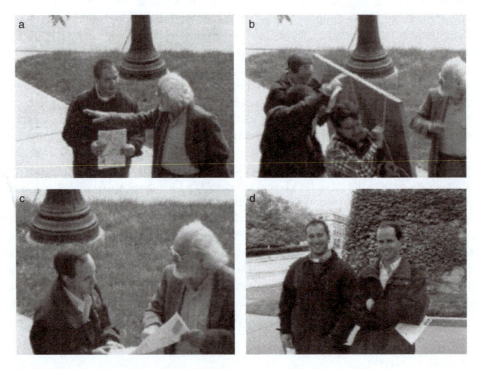

Figure 10.1 Frames from video of a participant in change blindness study
Note: Frames a–c show the sequence of the switch, frame d shows the two experimenters side by side
Source: Simons & Levin (1998)

Change blindness can also result in mistaken eyewitness identification. In an experiment showing this effect (Nelson et al., 2011), participants watched a video showing a student studying at a table in a lounge. When the student got up to leave the table, she put some dollar bills in her book as a bookmark. While she was away, another female student (Actor A) entered and quietly took the money from the book. In the No Change condition, Actor A left the room, turned a corner where she briefly was not visible, and then was seen walking out a door. In the Change condition, the same sequence occurred except that when Actor A turned the corner (temporarily out of sight), she was replaced by another female student of similar appearance (Actor B). Actor B then was seen walking out the door. After the video, participants were shown photos of six females, including Actor A and Actor B, and asked to identify which one stole the money in the video. In the No Change condition, 64% correctly identified Actor A, whereas in the Change condition, only 36% did so. When those in the Change condition were later asked if they noticed anything unusual about the video, only 4.5% detected a change when Actor B replaced Actor A. In other words, 95% of those in the Change condition saw a different person leave the building than the one who stole the money. Nevertheless, they did not notice they were different persons. Thus, change blindness can result in erroneous eyewitness identifications.

COMMENT ON THE MALLEABILITY OF MEMORY In this section, we have discussed research on leading questions, misinformation effects, false memories, repressed memories, and eyewitness testimony. These literatures all show that people regularly fail to recall information from prior experience accurately. However, it would be an overstatement to suggest that memory is inherently unreliable (Neath, 1998). Almost all memories are a combination of our retrieval of episodic information (knowledge of what actually happened) embellished by information from semantic memory, cognitive structures, and stored knowledge from other sources. Thus, memories are the product of a construction process that draws on and integrates different kinds of information. Moreover, the memory system is dynamic and continually changing as new information is acquired and existing knowledge is modified. Therefore, any given memory may be accurate in some respects and inaccurate in others. The scientific study of memory focuses not solely on whether or not it is accurate but also on the processes that lead memories to capture and reflect the realities on which they are based.

RETRIEVAL

Q: Is it common for 60-plus-year-old people to have problems with short term memory storage?

A: Storing memory is not a problem. Retrieving it is the problem.

(from e-mail humor about life for the post-60 set)

The information we process and represent in memory is there for us to use. To use it, it must be retrieved. As Crowder (1976, p. 2) described, retrieval is "the extraction of information when it is needed." How does one gain access to that stored knowledge, and how is it retrieved for use? What principles guide the retrieval process? What kinds of biases influence that process? We address these questions in this section of the chapter.

Information, once represented in memory, presumably persists over at least some period of time. However, research (and everyday experience) tells us that we sometimes cannot retrieve what we have learned and often struggle to recall things we know. The failure to retrieve a piece of information from memory might suggest either that we are having problems accessing it or that it has disappeared over time. It can be challenging to distinguish these two possibilities. One way that we know that many memories persist is that we often are successful in retrieving seemingly forgotten material when we use different retrieval strategies or cues. For example, consider an experience we have all had in which we meet someone who seemed very familiar, but we could not recall when or where we met him. Eventually, some clue reminds us of the previous meeting, and the seemingly lost details again come to mind. The ability for new cues to trigger successful retrieval shows that some memories have persisted, despite an initial difficulty to recall them. Retrieval of those details reflects both the persistence of the initial learning plus the presence of access routes to retrieval.

These observations led Tulving and Pearlstone (1966) to introduce an essential distinction between the *availability* of information in memory and its *accessibility* at any given moment. Information that has been encoded and stored is available in memory and can, in principle, be retrieved. However, any particular piece of information might not be accessible (retrievable) at any given time. Information that exists in memory (i.e., is available) varies in its accessibility. Higgins (1996, p. 134) defined accessibility as "the activation potential of available knowledge." Some information is easily accessed and therefore has a high potential for being activated (retrieved) and used. Other information is less accessible and may require reintroducing appropriate retrieval cues.

What makes available information accessible? There are many factors, several of which we have already discussed: salience, rehearsal, recency of use, time interval since encoding and since last use; the context in which retrieval occurs, including physical context and the affective state of the individual; the nature and availability of retrieval cues. An important general rule underlying the influence of many of these variables is the *encoding specificity principle* (Tulving & Thomson, 1973). This principle states that retrieval is enhanced to the extent that the cues available at retrieval (including contextual as well as semantic cues) are the same as or similar to the cues available at encoding. This idea is reflected in the recommendation that students should study in environments similar to where they will be tested (Smith & Vela, 2001); being in similar contexts during study and testing should facilitate retrieval of information from memory, a phenomenon known as *context-dependent memory*.

Retrieval from Associative Networks

In Chapter 2, we discussed associative network models as one useful way to think about storage of information in memory (Hamilton, 1989; Hamilton & Garcia-Marques, 2003; Hastie, 1980; Hastie & Kumar, 1979; Srull, 1981; Srull et al., 1985; Srull & Wyer, 1989), and this model also has implications for retrieval. As you recall from that chapter (see Figure 2.3), this model posited that a person is represented in memory by a node, and items of information acquired about the person are connected to that node by associative pathways. Items of information (e.g., behaviors by the person) that are *consistent* with one's impression of the person are efficiently processed, and pathways connecting them to the person node are formed. Information *inconsistent* with pre-existing expectancies, however, receives extra processing beyond simple association to the person node. These items also form pathways connecting them with previously-learned behaviors. This aspect of the model describes how person-relevant information is encoded and represented in memory.

The model was also useful because it specified, more precisely than other models at the time, how information is retrieved from memory. The model states that to retrieve information about a person, one enters the network at the person node and proceeds down a pathway to a particular item, which would then be recalled. From there, the model assumes that one would move to recall another item by traversing an interitem pathway, if possible, rather than returning to the person node and starting over again. Because more pathways lead to incongruent than congruent items (because these pathways were formed in encoding the former), people will be able to recall more incongruent than congruent items. This outcome has been documented in numerous studies (Hastie, 1984; Sherman & Hamilton, 1994; Srull, 1981; Srull et al., 1985).

The model also made some nonintuitive predictions about the likely sequence of recall of different types of items. For example, if you recall a congruent item, what is likely to be recalled next? Because all interitem pathways were formed during encoding of incongruent items, all such pathways are connected to incongruent items. Therefore, there never is a pathway directly connecting two congruent items. This leads to the predictions that (a) recall of a congruent item will be followed by an incongruent item, (b) recall of an incongruent item will be followed by either a congruent or an incongruent item, (c) recall of a congruent item should not be followed by recall of another congruent item, and (d) recall of neutral (neither consistent nor inconsistent) items is least likely because they are not linked to other items by associative pathways. When recall protocols are coded to determine the likelihood of these different kinds of recall sequences, the results have supported these predictions (see Table 10.4) (Srull, 1981; Srull et al., 1985). Thus, the model received a substantial amount of empirical support. This analysis of recall sequences rests on the assumption that the differing probabilities of these sequences are diagnostic of the nature of interitem pathways in the associative network. Questions have been raised about this interpretation (Skowronski & Gannon, 2000; Skowronski & Welbourne, 1997). However, other processing measures based on response times in generating recall have provided confirming evidence (Hamilton et al., 1989; Sherman & Hamilton, 1994; Srull et al., 1985).

Table 10.4 Probability of recalling different types of behaviors as a function of the immediately preceding behavior recalled

Previous item recalled	Probability of recall		
	Congruent	Incongruent	Neutral
Congruent	.09	.79	.12
Incongruent	.32	.21	.16
Neutral	.68	.16	.16

Source: Adapted from Srull (1981)

Two Routes for Retrieval

In many studies of memory for person information, participants are given information (typically a series of behavior-descriptive sentences) with the instructions to form an impression of that person. The goal of the research is to assess the participants' memory for that information through free recall. In other studies, participants are presented with similar information, but they are asked to estimate the number of times a particular type of information was presented (e.g., instances in which the person behaved in a friendly manner). Both of these tasks (free recall and frequency estimation) require people to access information from memory to answer the questions that have been posed. These tasks reflect different kinds of questions we often have to answer in the real world. For example, in recommending someone for a job, we might be asked to "tell us about some occasions when the applicant demonstrated exceptional skill?" or, instead, we might be asked, "how often does the applicant demonstrate exceptional skill?" One might think that these essentially equivalent questions would produce similar responses. However, they often do not.

Garcia-Marques and Hamilton (1996) proposed that, to answer these two types of questions, people engage in different retrieval processes in accessing information from the same memory representation. Their analysis rests on the same associative network model we have just described, in which behaviors performed by a person are attached to a node representing the person about whom one already has an initial impression (e.g., that he is friendly). All items are linked directly to the person node. However, expectancy-inconsistent items (in this example, unfriendly behaviors) are also directly linked with other items, due to processes occurring when the inconsistent information is encoded.

In free recall, the pattern of pathways between items within the representation are critical. Because more pathways directly connect expectancy-inconsistent items with other items than connect expectancy-consistent items with other items, more retrieval routes lead to the recall of inconsistent than consistent items. As we have discussed, this difference accounts for why people typically have better recall of expectancy-inconsistent items.

The other retrieval task (frequency estimation) triggers a very different set of processes. In frequency estimation, people are asked to estimate how many items of a particular type (e.g., friendly) were included in the list. To make that estimate, people presumably sample the pathways emanating from the person node, merely noting whether a given behavior was friendly or unfriendly (consistent or inconsistent with expectancies). That sampling process continues until one can gain a sense of whether there are more expectancy consistent or inconsistent items.

These are two fundamentally different strategies for retrieving information from the same memory representation, strategies that are engaged by different retrieval tasks. The two retrieval routes are called *exhaustive retrieval* (for free recall) and *heuristic retrieval* (for frequency estimates), and properties of the two retrieval strategies are shown in Table 10.5. Exhaustive retrieval involves a thorough search of memory to retrieve everything and anything, in any order. This task requires a careful and effortful search of memory; hence, it is resource-demanding. The output of this process would be the generation of a list of specific items recalled. In contrast, heuristic retrieval involves a selective search of memory, seeking items of a particular type (e.g., friendly behaviors). The resulting estimate is based on the ease with which those items of information can be accessed compared with other types of information. The guiding assumption is that if it is easy to generate several items of this type, there must be many of them. This search process is less demanding, and the output of the process is an overall estimate of how many such items were contained in the stimulus list.

Table 10.5 Properties of exhaustive and heuristic retrieval

Exhaustive retrieval	Heuristic retrieval
• Example: Free recall	• Example: Frequency estimates
• Thorough search	• Selective search, focused on specific type of information
• Retrieve anything and everything in any order	• Uses availability to gauge frequency or amount of information
• Resource-consuming	• Less systematic, less demanding
• Output: retrieval of specific items	• Output: summary estimate

For any given representation in memory, information can be retrieved using either strategy. However, the two strategies would be expected to generate different outcomes. Because exhaustive retrieval involves a systematic search through memory, there should be a higher recall of expectancy-inconsistent than of expectancy-consistent items due to their extensive links with other items. In contrast, heuristic retrieval consists of sampling the item-to-person-node pathways in search of a particular type of item (e.g., friendly behaviors), without making use of the direct interitem pathways. Because the pathways linking the person node to consistent items are stronger than those for inconsistent items, more of the expectancy-consistent items should be sampled. The diverging predictions then would be that exhaustive retrieval (free recall) would result in the retrieval of more inconsistent items. In contrast, heuristic retrieval (frequency estimates) would lead to estimates that there were more consistent than inconsistent items.

In a test of these hypotheses (Garcia-Marques & Hamilton, 1996), participants read 18 behavior-descriptive sentences about each of two persons, one a cab driver and the other a computer programmer. Pretesting had shown that people expect cab drivers to be fun but not ambitious, whereas computer programmers are seen as ambitious but boring. For each target person, six of the behaviors were consistent with these occupational expectancies, six were inconsistent with it, and six were neutral. After receiving this information, participants were asked to (1) to write down as many of the behaviors as they could recall (free recall) and (2) to estimate how many ambitious, boring, unambitious, and fun behaviors had been in the stimulus sentences (frequency estimates). The authors made the nonintuitive prediction that, within the same study, people would (a) recall more inconsistent than consistent behaviors and then, on the very next task, (b) estimate that there had been more consistent than inconsistent behaviors.

As is shown in Table 10.6, results supported both hypotheses. Participants recalled more expectancy-inconsistent than consistent behaviors, whereas they estimated there had been more expectancy consistent than inconsistent behaviors. Thus, these two seemingly incompatible outcomes can emerge from the same study, using the same materials, and on immediately successive tasks. The reason that both can happen is that the two tasks (recall, frequency estimation) use different retrieval strategies, accessing information in different

Table 10.6 Exhaustive and heuristic retrieval: mean recall performance and frequency estimates

Recall:	No. of items recalled
Congruent	3.7
Incongruent	4.7
Irrelevant	3.3
Frequency estimates:	**Mean estimate**
Congruent	16.6
Incongruent	13.5

Source: Adapted from Garcia-Marques & Hamilton (1996)

ways. Subsequent research has provided additional support for the model, demonstrating other differences between exhaustive and heuristic retrieval (Garcia-Marques & Garrido, 2015; Garcia-Marques, Hamilton, & Maddox, 2002; Garrido, Garcia-Marques, & Hamilton, 2012a, 2012b).

Retrieval in Connectionist Models

In Chapter 2, we introduced distributed connectionist models as another mode of representation (McClelland, 2000). Such models were developed to account for a variety of phenomena that simpler associative network models could not easily explain. For example, static representations of person nodes connected to behavioral information would have difficulty explaining why our beliefs about a person might shift quite dramatically from context to context (judging Vanessa at a party versus at work) (Conrey & Smith, 2007). Here we consider retrieval processes in such models. In an associative network model, a given concept (e.g., a person) has a particular location (a node) in memory to which various facts, features, attributes, and group memberships become linked by associative connections. When that person node is activated, the associated concepts are activated through spreading activation, thereby generating retrieval of the person and associated concepts. However, in a connectionist representation, there is no single node for a particular person. Instead, memory contains many nodes, all of which are linked to each other by pathways, with weights reflecting their activation potential. Those weights can change over time and context. When a person is encountered, the many concept nodes linked to that person will be activated to varying degrees, depending on the weights associated with the pathways. The extent of activation will determine what information is retrieved (Freeman & Ambady, 2011; Smith, 1996; Smith & DeCoster, 1998; van Overwalle & Labiouse, 2004).

An essential aspect of connectionist models is that the representation system is dynamic, which means that it is forever changing. New information can become a part of the representation, thereby influencing not only the content represented but also by altering the weights associated with the pathways of all concepts linked to all other concepts. These changes thereby influence the likelihood of retrieval of any given content at any given moment.

As an example, suppose you see a person who, based on her physical characteristics, appears to be a Chinese woman. Such a categorization (or her features themselves) would activate concepts associated with your representations of both women and Chinese people and also any unique characteristics representing their intersection. Information related to several aspects of her identity would then be available. The context in which you see this person might also influence the information that becomes accessible. If you see her while visiting Chinatown in San Francisco, nodes (and their associated weights) linked with "Chinese" especially would be activated in this context, whereas if you see her in a group comprised primarily of Chinese men, nodes associated with her gender would receive greater weight and thereby influence the content that is highly likely to be recalled.

Ease of Retrieval and Judgments

The distinction between exhaustive and heuristic retrieval is an example of a more general principle that applies to many contexts in which information is retrieved from memory and used in making judgments. As we briefly discussed in the previous chapter, intuitively, one might think that in making judgments and decisions, one would focus on the content in memory relevant to the judgment task. In deciding which political candidate to vote for, or when buying a car, or in choosing a college to attend, one would gather as much information as possible before deciding. In these cases, one is considering the *relevant content of memory* as a basis for judgment or decision. In addition, however, research has demonstrated the importance of one's subjective experience in retrieving information for those judgments. In particular, the ease or difficulty of retrieval experienced in bringing relevant information to mind has an important effect on judgments, often in surprising ways.

As we described in Chapter 9, Schwarz and his colleagues (Schwarz, Bless, et al., 1991; see also Gabrielcik & Fazio, 1984; Schwarz & Vaughn, 2002) showed that judgments of frequency rely on the ease rather than the content of retrieval. In their experiment, participants rated themselves on a particular trait (e.g., honesty) after they had recalled either a few (6) or many (12) times their behaviors had manifested that trait. Those who recalled a few such occasions rated themselves higher on that trait than those who had recalled many. Why? It is easier to recall a few than a large number of them. Thus, the ease of retrieval influenced participants' ratings.

The *ease-of-retrieval effect* has been demonstrated in many studies, using the few-versus-many task manipulation for numerous kinds of judgments and decisions. These include British students' evaluations of then-Prime Minister Tony Blair (Haddock, 2002), reasons for using (pro) or not using (anti) public transportation (Wänke, Bless, & Biller, 1996), or considering whether oneself is (or is not) socially accepted (Young, Brown, & Hutchins, 2017). Similar effects have also been obtained in other studies in other domains (Caruso, 2006; Dijksterhuis, Macrae, & Haddock, 1999; Ruder & Bless, 2003; Tormala, Falces, Briñol, & Petty, 2007; Winkielman & Schwarz, 2001; Winkielman, Schwarz, & Belli, 1998).

The ease-of-retrieval effect is quite pervasive (Schwarz, 1998, 2004), and a recent meta-analysis of 263 studies confirms that it is a reliable, medium-sized effect (Weingarten & Hutchinson, 2018). Research has, however, identified several variables that influence the extent to which it occurs, and these findings further illuminate underlying processes. For example, if people have strong, pre-established attitudes on a subject, they are less susceptible to the few versus many manipulation than are people with weakly held attitudes (Haddock, 2002). Participants who are asked to read the (few or many) arguments generated by other participants do not show the ease of retrieval effect, indicating that one's own subjective experience of ease versus difficulty in actually generating those arguments from memory is a crucial element underlying the effect (Wänke et al., 1996). The manipulation affects judgments about the self but not about others, indicating that the ease-of-retrieval effect rests on familiarity with the target person being judged (Caruso, 2006).

In sum, we often think that our judgments and decisions are based on consideration of the content relevant to the judgment or decision being made. While this may often be true, research on retrieval processes shows that it is not the entire story. One's ease or difficulty in making a judgment can also influence the decision made, yet we are rarely aware of this influence.

MEMORY PROCESSES IN UNDERSTANDING THE SELF, PERSONS, AND GROUPS

Memory Processes in Understanding the Self

If there is one person in this world about whom you have a rich and extensive storehouse of memories, it is yourself. You might have memories of numerous kinds of events throughout your lifetime, ranging from a favorite vacation trip to winning an award to a party you enjoyed. One's memories are typically not universally pleasant, as they might include the death of a family member or a time you were embarrassed at school. The number and variety of such memories is enormous, they span your lifetime, and they contribute importantly to who you are, or at least how you think about yourself. Therefore, psychologists have long been interested in studying the properties of self-memories, how they are organized in memory, and their characteristics. The study of memories about oneself is called *autobiographical memory*.

Autobiographical Memory

One question that immediately arises concerns how all of these various memories are stored in memory. They would not simply be deposited in memory in some random way; they must be organized somehow.

One prominent theory of autobiographical memory, *Self-Memory System Theory* (Conway, 2005; Conway & Pleydell-Pearce, 2000), explicitly focuses on this question. The theory differentiates three levels of autobiographical memory: event-specific memories, in which individual events are stored in episodic memory (e.g., winning a science award); general events, such as memories of highly similar or recurring events (e.g., being in high school drama productions); and lifetime periods, in which one's past is organized into meaningful, personally defined life periods (e.g., "in high school," "while serving in the Army in Iraq"). These levels of memory are arranged in memory hierarchically, such that specific events are organized together into general events, which are subsumed into cohesive units in lifetime periods.

Recalling autobiographical memories typically begins when prompted by a question ("Have you ever performed in dramatic productions?"), an incident (an event that triggers a memory in one's own life), or another probe. The theory argues that the process of generating autobiographical memories in response to such prompts begins by searching for periods during which the event might have taken place ("high school years"), then proceeds to the level of general event memory ("I was in some plays"), which then leads to identifying a specific autobiographical memory ("I really liked performing in Our Town"). Once again, we see that memory is not merely a matter of reproducing something verbatim from memory but is itself a (re)constructive process.

Once our memories of individual events become organized into event clusters that capture broader themes, those clusters evolve and integrate into broader representations that define and reflect even more significant aspects of the self. Along those lines, some have argued that an essential component of autobiographical memory develops in the form of a narrative (e.g., Conway & Pleydell-Pierce, 2000; McAdams, 1999). The narrative emerges from the episodic and generalized events of autobiographical memory and integrates these aspects in an organized and coherent manner into a life story. It incorporates a person's goals and feelings. It also extends in time (past, present, and perhaps anticipated future) and includes causal relations among its elements. It gives the person's life a sense of unity, purpose, and meaning. In these ways, the narrative provides a view of coherent identity through time (McAdams & Guo, 2015; McAdams & McLean, 2013). Narratives consist not only of memories of one's past but also include an affective component reflecting feelings about those events. A crucial aspect of the narrative is its motivational aspect, specifying important goals that served a guiding function at any given phase of one's life. All of these elements both broaden and lend further organization and coherence to the autobiographical memory (Dunlop, Guo, & McAdams, 2016).

In many respects, the processes we have summarized regarding autobiographical memory are similar to our earlier discussions of memory in general. That is, memory tends to be organized, which in turn facilitates recall, and these processes can be influenced by affective states, goals, and motivations. There are, however, two phenomena relating to autobiographical memory that are unique, to which we now turn.

Childhood Amnesia

Do you remember the party your parents arranged for your third birthday? If you have a younger sibling, what do you remember about the day she/he was born? How old were you at that time?

We opened this section on self-memory by noting that we know more about and have more memories of ourselves than virtually anything else. However, there is one part of our past that we just cannot recall: memories for events that occurred during the first few years of life are virtually nonexistent. People remember almost nothing from the first two years of life, and memories of episodes begin at around age three or four. This near-total lack of memory for our earliest years is called *childhood* or *infantile amnesia*. Note that this term does not refer to poor memory performance by young children. Instead, it relates to the reduced ability of adults to remember events from their early childhood.

This amnesia seems surprising in that we know that young children learn a great many things in the first few years of life. They are continually mastering new words, learning the names of new people, and learning concepts and attaching them to objects – bottle, ball, banana – which are foundational for later emerging of complex language skills. They are also developing skills, learning to walk, and discovering how to grasp and manipulate objects. These early skills primarily relate to semantic and procedural memory and have little to do with episodic memory. What is less well encoded and retained are memories for specific events occurring in specific contexts (i.e., episodic memories), and that is the stuff of autobiographical memory. Adults (and also children) have very poor episodic memory for events that happened during the first few years of life (Akhtar, Justice, Morrison, & Conway, 2018; Bauer, 2015; Gross, Jack, Davis, & Hayne, 2013).

Several theoretical explanations for childhood amnesia have been advanced. Early accounts invoked psychodynamic principles, suggesting that early memories, especially memories of important events, are concealed through the process of repression. Freud argued that "the earliest recollections of a person often seemed to preserve the unimportant and accidental, whereas (frequently though not universally!) not a trace is found in the adult memory of the weighty and affective impressions of this period" (Freud, 1914).

Later accounts (Wetzler & Sweeney, 1986) focused on a variety of cognitive mechanisms that contribute to childhood amnesia, and there are now several explanations that focus on these factors. One possibility is that some *neurological foundations* necessary for developing new memories have not adequately formed in the organism in this period. For example, the hippocampus, an essential structure for creating new memories, is undeveloped at birth and not fully formed for several years. Similarly, the frontal lobe, essential for building associations in memory, is not well developed at this age, and an inability to link different aspects of experience to each other may limit forming autobiographical memories (Newcombe, Drummey, Fox, Lie, & Ottinger-Alberts, 2000). Thus, limited neurological development may contribute to childhood amnesia. A second account, *schema organization theory*, focuses on the undeveloped nature of cognitive structures in very young children, such that some aspects of an experience-in-context are retained but not others. Later, with more developed schemas, the person is unable to retrieve memories formed with an earlier schema. A third view emphasizes the role of language. In the early stages of language acquisition, the cognitive tools for encoding and organizing information are not available. Later, when language has developed, and with the increasing need to share experiences with others (e.g., parents), autobiographical memories can develop (Simcock & Hayne, 2002). Finally, in the *emergent self explanation*, forming autobiographical memories requires the development of a sense of self as an individual entity, which gradually evolves during the first couple of years of life. Once that concept of self has developed, autobiographical memories can be formed and attached to it (Howe & Courage, 1993).

These mechanisms provide multiple explanations rooted in essential aspects of cognitive functioning and development, without needing to invoke motivated processes described in psychoanalytic interpretations of why childhood amnesia occurs and eventually disappears. These cognitive accounts should not be viewed as conflicting interpretations. Instead, they may all be transpiring during this period of early growth, with each of them contributing to childhood amnesia and its ultimate offset. In fact, Nelson and Fivush (2004) have provided a multicomponent account of the emergence of autobiographical memory, incorporating these and other mechanisms.

The Reminiscence Bump

The second puzzling aspect of autobiographical memory is that people consistently show better memory for events that happened during one particular period of their lives, approximately between the ages of 15–25. When people older than 35 are probed for their memories of events in their lives, and if those data are plotted as a function of the respondent's age at the time of the recalled events, there is consistently better memory for events that happened around the age of 20. This effect is referred to as the *reminiscence bump* (Rubin, Rahhal, & Poon, 1998). The effect is quite robust but is most reliable for memories of positive (happy) compared with negative (sad, traumatic) events (Berntsen & Rubin, 2002). Because positive events dominate people's autobiographical memories, the overall effect is the reminiscence bump.

As with childhood amnesia, several mechanisms likely contribute to this phenomenon (Koppel & Rubin, 2016). Neurologically, the age of the reminiscence bump is a time when the neurological system is well developed but has not yet reached the point at which functions begin to decline (starting in the late 20s). Therefore, the system is functioning at its peak for encoding and storing memories of experienced events, producing a better representation of and memory for things that happened in early adulthood. From a cognitive perspective, it is well known that the initial stimuli in a sequence are easier to retrieve than later stimuli in that sequence (a primacy effect). The time of the reminiscence bump – early adulthood – is a phase of life in which one experiences many "firsts" in significant domains – first car, first job, first apartment, first serious romance. These new experiences may engage more significant systematic processing, resulting in better encoding and representation of them. As a consequence, they are easier to later recall than other subsequent instances in those domains. An extension of this view is that people develop a *life script* or *life story* (Berntsen & Rubin, 2004) and that the bump reflects the importance of transition points that occur in early adulthood in one's life script. Similarly, this is an important stage of life when people confront and make decisions about their preferences, values, ideologies, and the like, independently from their parents, which means they are developing their identity of who they are, issues not addressed at earlier ages. All of these factors may contribute to the reminiscence bump, the fact people have an especially good memory for events (particularly positive events) that took place in their late teens and early 20s.

Memory Processes in Understanding Persons

Memory for Faces

The most common and perhaps most crucial form of communication between persons occurs when they are directly interacting in each other's presence. This is known, of course, as face-to-face interaction. People spend an immense amount of time looking at each other's faces; much of social life transpires in such interactions. As a consequence, we become skilled at remembering which face belongs to which person. But not always. We have all had the experience of seeing someone, recognizing the face as familiar, but being unable to remember who it is or how we know the person. Thus, our memory for faces can range from excellent to poor, depending on a variety of factors. Because accurate face memory is crucial for effective social interaction, it is essential to understand the variables that influence face memory.

Face memory is usually studied in research using measures of recognition accuracy. Typically, participants are shown a set of faces with the instruction to study them, and later they are shown those same faces intermixed with an equal number of new faces they have not previously seen. Their task is to indicate, for each face, whether it was in the original set ("old") or not ("new"). Other variables of interest are manipulated to determine if and how they influence the ability to recognize faces. These may include properties of the faces (e.g., half are White, half are Black), the conditions under which they are seen (e.g., the speed of presentation), and perceiver variables (e.g., stress level). Participants' recognition memory in these different conditions can then be assessed and compared.

Each of us has good face memory in some contexts but less accuracy in remembering people in other settings. Also, there is variation among people in their chronic face memory abilities. In fact, there are extreme cases reflecting very poor and excellent face memory.

Prosopagnosia

A small number of people (roughly 2.5%) have very little ability to remember faces at all. This condition is called *prosopagnosia*, also called "face blindness," and is due to a neurological disorder in the fusiform area of the brain. People with this condition have little or no other loss in visual or perceptual functioning, but when they look at the face of a person – even family members – they cannot identify the person. A person with prosopagnosia must learn to use other cues to recognize family members and other close people (e.g., their voice, hair, clothes). When interacting with less-familiar others in social settings, these alternative (to face) cues may not be known, which can make interactions awkward and uncomfortable. Imagine being approached by someone at a social occasion, someone who obviously recognizes you and starts up a conversation. If you have prosopagnosia, you look at her face but, of course, do not know who she is. You then have a choice of stopping the conversation, explaining your impairment, establishing who she is, and then hopefully resuming your conversation or, as people with prosopagnosia often do, faking it. You smile and converse in very generic terms until the conversation moves to a topic that identifies who she is. A woman with prosopagnosia once commented that she does not like to pick up her children at school because of a fear that she would not recognize them. Obviously, this condition presents real challenges that can affect social relationships in many adverse ways.

Super-recognizers

In contrast to the challenges faced by people with prosopagnosia, some people are incredibly good at remembering, and later recognizing, faces they have seen. While some researchers were researching prosopagnosia, a few people casually mentioned to the researchers that their experience was the opposite, that is, they claimed to have excellent face recognition abilities. Consequently, the researchers (Russell, Duchaine, & Nakayama, 2009) tested these people on some standard (and challenging) face recognition tests and compared their performance to that of a control group of college students. In two different studies using different testing procedures, there was a substantial difference between the two groups. Because the recognition ability of the experimental participants greatly exceeded that of the control group, Russell et al. (2009) coined the term *super-recognizers* to refer to them. Similar findings have been reported in subsequent studies (Bobak, Hancock, & Bate, 2016; Robertson, Noyes, Dowsett, Jenkins, & Burton, 2016; Russell, Chatterjee, & Nakayama, 2012).

Super-recognizers have extraordinary face recognition ability for unfamiliar as well as familiar faces and with degraded as well as high-quality images. Having this ability is potentially useful in many contexts. There are many jobs (e.g., airport screening) that require comparing a person's face to a passport photo or driver's license photo, which may not be of the highest quality. Making a "same" versus "different" judgment should be easier for super-recognizers. Also, many aspects of police work require the ability to recognize a suspect from photographic evidence, and the use of super-recognizers in these efforts has proven to be useful (Keefe, 2016; Robertson et al., 2016).

Super-recognizers and people with prosopagnosia are small and atypical groups at opposite ends of a distribution of people in face recognition and face memory ability. On face recognition tests, the two groups perform about 2.5 standard deviations above and below, respectively, the mean performance of control groups (Russell et al., 2009). As these authors commented, their results comparing the two groups on comparable test materials showed that "the super-recognizers are about as good as many prosopagnosics are bad" (Russell et al., 2009, p. 256).

Variables Influencing Face Memory

The performance of most people falls between these two extreme groups, and most research on face memory has studied this broader spectrum of people. This research has revealed numerous insights regarding face memory. The focus on faces begins very early in life. Within the first few minutes of life, infants track faces more than nonface stimuli, and within a few days, they can distinguish their mothers' faces from strangers' faces. Thus, from the outset, faces are extraordinary stimuli (Hugenberg & Wilson, 2013; Riddoch, Johnston, Bracewell, Boutsen, & Humphreys, 2008). Faces grab attention, and what we attend to heavily influences what information gets encoded and represented in memory (Palermo & Rhodes, 2007). Unusual or distinctive features (facial birthmarks, purple hair), intense emotional expressions (fear, anger), and attractive faces all capture attention, resulting in more extended processing of those faces, which in turn increases the likelihood of faces being represented in memory.

Social variables can also play a significant role. In Chapter 5, we introduced construal level theory, in which psychological distance (represented, for example, in physical or temporal distance) can influence one's processing style. According to this theory, greater psychological distance induces global processing, whereas psychological proximity induces more detailed, feature-based processing. Some research has tested whether these processing differences influence memory of faces. For example, in one study (Wyer, Perfect, & Pahl, 2010) participants walking across campus were approached by a confederate, who asked for directions and engaged in conversation for two minutes. After the confederate was gone, the experimenter approached participants and asked if they would answer a few questions for a study. The participants were asked to imagine that they had to give an oral presentation to a group of students, either the next day (near-future) or several weeks later (distant future). After imagining that scenario, they were told that the confederate was a part of the study and asked to identify him from a set of eight photographs. Two-thirds of the participants in the distant-future condition correctly identified the confederate, whereas only one fourth in the near-future condition did. The evidence from this and other studies (Wyer, Hollins, & Pahl, 2015) suggests that a global, abstract processing orientation induces the configural face processing that facilitates face identification and better face memory.

Motivational variables can influence the extent of face processing and hence face memory. For example, we are more motivated to attend to persons of high status than to those of low status (Foulsham, Cheng, Tracy, Henrich, & Kingstone, 2010). Researchers in one study presented faces of persons in high-status occupations (e.g., doctor) and low-status occupations (e.g., mechanic). They found that high status faces captured more attention, were remembered better, and were processed more efficiently (configurally) than were faces of persons in low-status occupations (Ratcliff, Hugenberg, Shriver, & Bernstein, 2011). Interestingly, this effect is reversed when powerful people display threatening facial features; participants avert their gaze from the faces of powerful individuals who appear to be signaling dominance (Holland, Wolf, Looser, & Cuddy, 2017).

Also, we are more motivated to process information about members of our own age group than of other age groups (Anastasi & Rhodes, 2005; Macchi Cassia, Proietti, Gava, & Bricolo, 2015; Rodin, 1987). For example, young and older persons were shown several faces of young and older persons, and eye-tracking and recognition memory were recorded. People in both groups spent more time looking at own-age faces than of other-age faces, and more gaze time led to better recognition memory for the faces (He, Ebner, & Johnson, 2011). Thus, social group memberships can influence attentional processes that consequently determine face memory.

Expectancies and the Incongruency Effect in Person Memory

Expectancies play an essential role in guiding most of the processes we have talked about throughout this book. They influence what we notice and encode into memory, how we interpret that information, the nature of the inferences we draw in expanding on that information, and the nature of the attributions we might make in understanding people and events. Given an expectancy, what transpires will, in most cases, either confirm or disconfirm that expectancy. That distinction has been the focus of a considerable amount of research (Bartholow, Fabiani, Gratton, & Bettencourt, 2001; Hastie, 1981; Skowronski, McCarthy, & Wells, 2013; Stangor & McMillan, 1992) showing pervasive differences in how expectancy-congruent and incongruent information are processed and represented in memory. Understanding the precise reasons for those differences has been a challenge.

Earlier, we presented an associative network model of representation of person information, which argued that incongruent items form more interitem associations than do congruent items, leading to the prediction that incongruent items would be better recalled than congruent items. That prediction has been supported in numerous studies (Dijksterhuis & van Knippenberg, 1996; Hastie & Kumar, 1979; Hemsley & Marmurek, 1982; Srull, 1981; Srull et al., 1985; Srull & Wyer, 1989). These authors reasoned that people seek to reconcile the incongruency and to integrate these discrepant facts into the emerging impression, which leads to the interitem associations that produce better recall of incongruent items (Sherman & Hamilton, 1994).

Although much research has supported this model, there were some questions about the basis for these effects. That is, to what extent does the incongruency effect rest on the differences in interitem associations at the heart of this account? Expectancy violations can have several other consequences. For example, information that does not fit one's expectancies may be salient and distinctive, especially when cognitive capacity is low (Allen, et al., 2009). When expectancy inconsistent information draws one's attention, the resulting extensive processing should enhance its recallability (Heider, Scherer, Skowronski, Wood, Edlund, & Hartnett, 2007; Scherer, Heider, Skowronski, & Edlund, 2012).

Similarly, people may respond to incongruency by developing attributions to explain why the incongruent behavior occurred (Clary & Tesser, 1983; Crocker, Hannah, & Weber, 1983; Hastie, 1984; Sherman et al., 2005; Susskind et al., 1999). None of these processes would necessarily require the formation of more interitem associations for incongruent behaviors. In addition, the incongruency effect can be moderated by several factors, such as motivational variables (Dijksterhuis, van Knippenberg, Kruglanski, & Schaper, 1996; Ruble & Stangor, 1986), cognitive load (Bargh & Thein, 1985; Ehrenberg & Klauer, 2005), and one's intuitive theories about personality traits (Plaks & Halvorson, 2013; Plaks, Stroessner, Dweck, & Sherman, 2001). Many of these factors would promote more extensive processing of expectancy-incongruent information, and such extensive processing by itself can enhance the likelihood of recall of that information.

There is an additional limitation in research on the incongruency effect that is informative about the representation and retrieval of person information. In research testing the associative network model, the information presented about the target person typically pertains to only one trait dimension. That is, participants might learn that the person is friendly, creating a single-trait expectancy, and the stimulus items would describe either friendly (impression-consistent) or unfriendly (impression-inconsistent) behaviors. Earlier in this chapter (in discussing organization by clustering), we described research in which the stimulus behaviors represented several different traits, and recall was clustered by those traits (Hamilton et al., 1980b). In that work, however, no trait-incongruent behaviors were included – only positive exemplars of each trait were presented. If the stimulus items included expectancy-incongruent behaviors, would they again be recalled better than expectancy-congruent behaviors?

In a study examining that question (Hamilton et al., 1989; also see Dijksterhuis & van Knippenberg, 1996), participants formed an impression of a person who, they were told, is friendly, intelligent, and adventurous. They then read a series of behavior-descriptive sentences that included both congruent and incongruent instances for these traits. Following Hamilton et al. (1980b), the researchers predicted that behaviors would be clustered by trait domain and that behaviors (both congruent and incongruent) reflecting the same trait would be interconnected. However, because all items within a trait cluster would be interconnected, there would no longer be more pathways leading to incongruent than to congruent items, which was the presumed basis for the better recall of incongruent traits in the earlier studies. If so, then participants' recall should reveal organization by trait clusters (i.e., sequences of same-trait behaviors recalled together), but incongruent behaviors should not be recalled better than congruent behaviors.

This is precisely what Hamilton et al. (1989) found. For each of the three traits, participants recalled comparable proportions of congruent and incongruent behaviors. Moreover, analyses of the recall sequences were informative. For each type of sequence, the probability of within-trait (friendly → friendly) sequences was twice as high as the between trait (friendly → intelligent) sequences. That is, behaviors were recalled in same-trait clusters. Analyses of response times for recalling different types of sequences confirmed these results. These findings reflect the formation of interitem associations among all items within the same trait cluster and no advantage in the recall of incongruent behaviors.

In sum, expectancies strongly influence the processing of information in ways that can affect what information is recalled and how it is organized. When the information is limited to one domain (e.g., one trait dimension), expectancy-incongruent information stands out. It is processed more thoroughly, generating associations between items that produce an incongruency effect in recall. However, the incongruency itself can have other effects on both the extent of processing and the nature of mental representation, particularly when the information is dimensionally more complex.

Attribution and Memory

At several points, we have observed that variables that affect the extent to which information is processed can impact the representation of that information in memory and, therefore, its accessibility for later retrieval. There is one process that is very important and clearly involves extended processing, namely attribution.

As presented in Chapter 8, attribution is an inference, so it shares many properties with other inference processes (see Chapter 7). However, attribution is a specific type of inference, specifically, an inference about causality. Some kinds of inferences, such as trait inferences and inferences about goals and motives, are made commonly and routinely, even spontaneously. In contrast, attribution only occurs when preconditions trigger a concern with causality. The attribution process involves processing to answer the question, "Why?" Therefore, the process of attribution does not happen all the time. When the "Why" question does arise, it initiates additional processing aimed at answering that question; in other words, people try to determine the cause of the event that triggered the question. Thus, compared with other kinds of inferences, attribution initiates extra processing. The question we consider here is when and how the additional processing of attribution influences memory for attribution-related information.

As we detailed in Chapter 8, several significant theories of attribution appeared in the 1960s (Heider, 1958; Jones & Davis, 1965; Jones & Nisbett, 1972; Kelley, 1967, 1972;

Weiner, Frieze, et al., 1972), which spawned an enormous amount of research in the 1970s and 1980s. Simultaneously, the emergence of social cognition generated a great deal of research on memory for social information (Hastie et al., 1980; Srull & Wyer, 1989). It is perhaps surprising that there has been relatively little research at the intersection of these two literatures. Here we provide an example of research illustrating how a simultaneous consideration of both literatures can be illuminating.

Many studies of attribution have been concerned with the distinction between internal (person) and external (situational) attributions (Heider, 1958; Kelley, 1967) and identifying when people make each kind. A common strategy for studying this question is to present participants with a sentence describing a person's behavior ("Lori yawned during the lecture") along with several context sentences that can be varied to study variables of interest ("Lori was out late the night before"; "The lecturer spoke in a monotone voiced"). The participant's task is to indicate whether the person or the situation caused the behavior. This attribution task can be relatively easy (if most of the context sentences imply the same causal locus), or it can be challenging (if the context sentences have mixed causal implications). If making an attribution is difficult, the relevant information needs to be considered and weighed more extensively compared to the case of a more straightforward attribution. Would that difference in processing influence people's memory for the information?

In a study aimed at answering that question (Hamilton, Grubb, Acorn, Trolier, & Carpenter, 1990), participants were given a series of six attribution problems like the one described above (Lori yawned). Six context sentences accompanied each behavioral description. In the Actor-oriented condition, five of the six context items implied that the person's actions caused the behavior (she was out late the night before). In the Entity-oriented condition, five of the six items implied a situational cause (the lecturer had a monotone voice). In the Mixed condition, three context sentences implied each causal locus. After reading each attribution problem, participants indicated whether they thought the behavior was caused primarily by the actor or the situational context. Participants then returned two days later and completed two recall tasks.

Given that participants were to make causal attributions, each item of context information presumably would be encoded in terms of its implications for allocating responsibility to either the actor or to the situation. Moreover, since this information must be integrated to make a judgment, the context items themselves would be compared with one another, thereby forming associations among them and also with the behavior to be explained. Drawing on our earlier discussion of a network model, this would mean that there would be many more pathways formed between context items in the Mixed condition than in either the Actor-oriented or Entity-oriented condition. If so, then people would have better memory in the Mixed than in the other two conditions. Participants' recall performance (48 hours later) was examined to test these hypotheses. First, participants were asked to recall as many of the six behavior event sentences as they could. Second, they then were given each of those behavior event sentences separately and asked to recall the additional (context) sentences that had accompanied each one. The results supported the hypotheses. First, participants recalled more of the event sentences in the Mixed condition than in the other two conditions. Second, participants recalled significantly more context sentences in the Mixed condition than in either the Actor-oriented or the Entity-oriented condition. Thus, the complexity of the attribution-relevant information influenced the extent to which that information was recalled.

If mixed information requires more extensive processing and complicates attributional judgments, then it should take longer to make those judgments in such conditions. Another study using the same general paradigm directly tested that assumption (Hamilton, 1988). For each stimulus set, the behavior event sentence was presented on a computer screen for four seconds.

Then the six context sentences and the two attribution response options (Lori, the lecture) appeared. The computer recorded how much time passed until the participant's response. Participants took significantly longer to make an attribution when the evidence was mixed compared with the two conditions in which most context sentences favored one attribution (actor) or the other (entity). Thus, the complexity of available relevant information increases the amount of cognitive work needed to form an attribution. This greater effort is then reflected in the representation of that information in memory and in recall performance.

These results are important for a couple of reasons. First, we opened this section with an argument that the attribution process requires more extensive processing than other kinds of inference tasks. The higher recall in the condition with mixed information supports that view and shows that this extra processing impacts people's memory for the information. Second, the research shows that attribution tasks themselves can vary in their complexity and that the difficulty involved in making attributions affects people's memory for attribution-relevant information.

The Group Context: Memory as a Social Product

Memory has traditionally been conceived and studied in terms of systems and processes occurring within an individual person. Memories of one's past experiences are represented in cognitive structures as an outgrowth of the mechanisms engaged (encoding, interpretation, inference) as the information was processed. In this section, we argue that there is more to be considered in understanding memory. Specifically, we highlight the social aspects of these processes, emphasizing that memory is sometimes shared with others. That is, memory is influenced by and can influence the processing and representation of information through social interaction and relationships. In this way, memory can be affected by the nature of one's communication and interactions with others.

Imagine that last summer that you and your friend Chris spent a vacation week hiking in a national park. Both of you were awed by the gorgeous scenery, the diverse animal life, and the stillness that descended as you camped at night – a memorable trip. During an evening with friends months later, you and Chris are asked about the vacation. You describe the day you saw an elk with his impressive full rack of antlers standing by a stream and how majestic he looked. Chris then describes the time you both had seen a small black bear eating berries from a bush. The mention of food reminded you to tell the story about the time you burned the evening meal you were cooking on the camp stove. This then led Chris to reminisce about the pleasure you shared in sitting around a campfire at night, totally relaxed after a strenuous hike during the day. Notice that each experience recalled by one of you brought back new memories in the other. In this way, your friends heard more stories about your vacation than either of you might have generated individually. In this case, then, memory has been a product of a social process in which each person's recalled experience served as a cue to the other person's recall of a different experience. This process has been called *cross-cueing*, and it can lead to the recall of more information than either individual would have been able to recall alone (Harris, Barnier, & Sutton, 2013; Meudell, Hitch, & Boyle, 1995; Meudell, Hitch, & Kirby, 1992).

However, facilitation in retrieval might not always occur. For example, when you recalled seeing that majestic elk by the river, you also visualized the incredible waterfall behind him, cascading down a cliff into the valley. You were about to describe that scene when Chris interjected the story of the bear eating berries with berry juice all over his mouth. When Chris finished that story, you said, "I had something else I was just going to tell you, but now it's gone…maybe I'll remember it later." In this case, Chris's bear anecdote has disrupted your train of thought, with the result that a story about a beautiful waterfall never got told to your friends. Again, the memories shared with your friends are the product of a social process, but, in this case, that process has interfered with the recall of some experiences.

We have all had both of these experiences, times when another person's comment cues our own recall and times when someone's comment disrupts our own retrieval. In this section, we discuss research related to both of these phenomena. At the outset, however, note that there is a fundamental difference between these situations and the kinds of retrieval discussed so far in this chapter. In most research on memory and retrieval, the individual participant is presented with some information and is later asked to retrieve it from memory. In the scenarios just described, you and Chris were together, interactively, retrieving from memory your shared past experiences, and the product (for better or worse) was the result of a social process in which your and Chris's recollections each influenced the other person's retrievals. Memory then becomes the product of a social process. Experiences like these are commonplace, yet relatively limited research attention has focused on social processes in memory.

In thinking about people retrieving information about shared experiences, important questions arise about the processes underlying those effects. Why does this shared experience sometimes have a facilitative effect and sometimes an interference effect? What is the difference in the processes underlying those different outcomes? How can these questions be studied experimentally?

We begin by summarizing research showing the disruptive effect of others' participation, called *collaborative inhibition*. We then turn to instances of the facilitative effects of others, called *transactive memory*. Finally, we highlight the importance of communication in shaping the nature and extent of memory performance. In all of these cases, memory represents a very social phenomenon.

Collaborative Inhibition

Collaborative inhibition occurs when one person's recall interferes with that of another person. To study collaborative inhibition (Garcia-Marques & Garrido, 2015), small groups of three participants participated in each session. All participants were shown the same set of stimulus items and later were asked to recall them. Two experimental conditions differed in the procedure used during the recall phase. In the *collaborative* recall condition, participants took turns recalling items orally; one person recalled aloud an item, then the next person recalled another item, and so forth until no one could remember any more items. In the *nominal* recall condition, each participant recalled items individually by writing them down on paper. The number of items recalled as a group in the collaborative condition was then compared to the number of unique (non-redundant) items recalled by participants in the nominal condition. The results of these studies showed that participants in the collaborative condition recalled fewer items than did people in the nominal group condition. This effect is known as *collaborative inhibition* (Weldon & Bellinger, 1997) because the collaborative process seems to inhibit recall performance. Although this outcome seems counterintuitive, it is highly robust and has been demonstrated under a wide variety of conditions using a variety of different kinds of stimulus items (Kelley, Reysen, Ahlstrand, & Pentz, 2012; Marion & Thorley, 2016; Rajaram & Pereira-Pasarin, 2010; Weldon, Blair, & Huebsch, 2000)

According to a recent meta-analysis, two main factors appear to contribute to collaborative inhibition (Marion & Thorley, 2016). One important factor involves *retrieval disruption*, whereby differences in people's organization of information in memory mean that individuals must often replace an optimal retrieval strategy with a less effective strategy when recalling collaboratively (Basden, Basden, Bryner, & Thomas, 1997). To understand this explanation further, think again about the associative network model discussed earlier. As each participant reads and encodes the stimulus items, those items become represented in memory in a network, with links connecting some items. During retrieval, those links serve as retrieval routes, facilitating recall from one item to the next. However, each person may form a unique representation of the same set of stimuli, with different patterns of connecting links. In collaborative recall, the item recalled by one person may interfere with recall by the subsequent person because it reflects an association pattern (links between items) that differs from the participant whose turn is next.

This is what happened when Chris's recall of the bear disrupted your ability to remember the memory of the elk at the river that was strongly associated (in your mind) with the beautiful waterfall behind it. Thus, the "flow" or sequence of retrieval in one person's memory representation may differ from that of another person, resulting in the disruption of retrieval in the collaborative task. Such disruption does not occur in nominal group conditions where participants simply retrieve and write down items privately. The consequence is that the collaborative process has produced an inhibitory effect on recall.

A second account of collaborative inhibition focuses on *retrieval inhibition* (Barber, Harris, & Rajaram, 2015; Bäuml & Aslan, 2004). From this perspective, collaborative inhibition arises when a recollection expressed by someone leads a person to cognitively inhibit information in his or her own memory to avoid competition for attentional resources. Once a memory representation has been suppressed, it can then be difficult to retrieve it for later expression (Anderson, Bjork, & Bjork, 1994; Nickerson, 1984). For example, when Chris started talking about the bear, you wanted to focus on his story and give him a chance to share his recollection. To do so, you temporarily tried not to think about the elk or other memories of the trip. However, by inhibiting your memories to focus on Chris, it then becomes more challenging to remember what you wanted to say when it comes to your turn to speak.

The *disruption* and *inhibition* accounts make different predictions about the persistence of inhibitory effects. If collaboration harms recall through disruption, then eliminating the disruptive factor (i.e., hearing other's recollections) should improve recall because people can access their memory representation using an optimal strategy. In many studies, people who generate free recall or complete a recognition memory test later when they are alone show better memory performance compared with collaborative recall conditions (Basden & Basden, 1995). However, the inhibition account suggests that there will continue to be recall decrements even after people have left the collaborative recall context. Some studies have shown such continuing deficits, suggesting that people do actively inhibit their memories when engaging in recall in social contexts (Aslan, Bäuml, & Grundgeiger, 2007; Bäuml & Aslan, 2006). Thus, there is support for both accounts, and they both appear to play a role in collaborative inhibition.

So far, we have focused on social processes involving recollections about oneself, but research has extended this work into the realm of person perception. In such studies, participants form an impression of a target person based on a series of behavior-descriptive sentences describing that person. They then recalled these items either individually or in a collaborative, turn-taking manner. Replicating the findings of other studies, collaborative groups recalled fewer items than nominal groups (Garrido, Garcia-Marques, & Hamilton, 2012b; Garrido, Garcia-Marques, Hamilton, & Ferreira, 2012). Thus, the same effect occurs on an impression formation task as well.

According to the retrieval disruption hypothesis, the reason collaborative inhibition occurs is that each of the three members of a collaborative group formed his or her own, distinctive mental representations, organized in different ways, with varying patterns of associations linking the items with each other. These different patterns then result in the three persons having different preferred retrieval paths, which are disrupted by the items recalled by the other group members. The explanation for collaborative inhibition, then, assumes that each group member has a distinctive organization/representation of the stimulus items.

However, what if the group members did not differ in their representations? What if all three of them had encoded the items in the same organized manner? In that case, the pattern of interitem associations – the retrieval paths – would be very similar for all group members. In that case, the sequence of recall by the different participants would be more comparable, and collaborative inhibition (and the poorer recall performance compared to nominal groups) should be significantly reduced (Finlay, Hitch, & Meudell, 2000).

In an experimental test of this hypothesis (Garcia-Marques, Garrido, Hamilton, & Ferreira, 2012), the study followed the same collaborative inhibition paradigm, with one crucial change: the stimulus items either were or were not presented in a meaningfully organized way. Each of the 32 stimulus sentences described one of four people (John, Peter, Louis, Anthony) performing a behavior that reflected one of four traits (intelligent, friendly, ecological, artistic) in one of four settings (home, work, vacation, public holiday). Items were presented in booklets, with one sentence per page. In the organized sequencing condition, items were presented organized by person, by trait, or by setting. For example, in the person-organization sequencing, eight items described each person, and they were organized person by person (e.g., all John items followed by all Peter items). In the trait-organization sequencing, the intelligent behaviors were presented, then the friendly, then the ecological, and then the artistic. In the setting-organization sequencing, behaviors occurring in a given context were presented together. In the nonorganized-sequencing condition, the same items were presented in random order. Following the presentation, participants recalled the stimulus items, either collaboratively (taking turns in sequence) or individually (nominal groups condition).

The mean recall performance for these conditions is shown in Figure 10.2. When the sequence of stimulus items was not organized according to person, trait, or context, the typical collaborative inhibition effect emerged: higher recall in the nominal groups condition than in the collaborative-recall condition. However, when the stimulus presentation was organized according to those themes, participants in collaborative groups recalled almost as many items as those in nominal groups. In other words, by imposing an organizing scheme on the information as it was encoded and represented in memory,

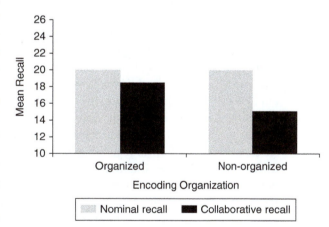

Figure 10.2 Mean recall performance for nominal and collaborative recall conditions as a function of encoding organization

Source: Adapted from Garcia-Marques et al. (2012)

participants engaged in collaborative recall were retrieving items from similar cognitive representations, which thereby minimized the disruptive effect that typically occurs as different participants retrieve items from their idiosyncratic representations. These results show that the collaborative inhibition effect is not due to the social nature of the retrieval process itself but rather is a reflection of the different cognitive representations formed by the different participants. When those cognitive representations of stimulus items are made similar by organizing the stimulus items, the disruptive effect on retrieval, and hence the collaborative inhibition commonly found, disappears.

Transactive Memory

In our story about you and your hiking partner Chris telling friends about your vacation, each memory from one of you brought back another memory from the other. We have just described research showing that such inter-person sequential recall can actually inhibit the total amount of information recalled – unless the organizational scheme of that information was shared among participants. Another line of research has explored the implications of that fact, especially in contexts where different group members possess different aspects of knowledge or expertise.

Consider Elias and Anna, who have been a couple for several years. They enjoy doing cross-word puzzles together and have determined that they make a good team for this task. Anna loves movies and knows a lot about them – the names of movies and their plots, the key actors in each one, which films have won an Oscar. Elias, on the other hand, does not follow movies closely, but he is a big sports fan and has an impressive knowledge of who won what championship in what year and who the star players were. More importantly for our purposes, each of them knows that the other is an expert in one domain but has minimal knowledge in the other. When doing their crossword puzzles, any question about movies is immediately given to Anna, and Elias can ignore it; conversely, Anna can safely ignore sports items. Together, they do well in completing cross-word puzzles, better than either one of them would on their own. As Anna likes to say, "Between the two of us, we have one good brain." This situation often emerges in close relationships. The two persons have a shared knowledge structure in which each of them recognizes their separate areas of knowledge, and both of them can then use it. With this structure in place, the couple has a *transactive memory* that is greater than either of their individual memory structures.

In a study examining this process (Wegner, Erber, & Raymond, 1991), couples were given a memory task that would engage the use of transactive memory. Individuals worked in pairs either with their relationship partner (natural couple) or with a stranger (impromptu couple), and both members of the pair were given factual items of information from various catego-ries of knowledge (e.g., food, science, history). Participants completed a questionnaire that assessed their level of knowledge in each of these areas. Half of the pairs were then placed in the assigned expertise condition, in which each member of the couple was instructed to remem-ber the items in different specific categories that were assigned to them. The other half of the pairs were placed in the nonassigned condition, in which members of the couple were free to focus on topics of their own choosing. Participants were then separated and asked to write down all the information they could remember. The recall performance of each pair was assessed.

The reasoning behind this study was as follows. In the impromptu couple condition, in which members of the pair did not share a transactive memory, assigning members to specific topics should facilitate memory because each person is responsible for only a portion of the overall information. For natural couples, the situation is more complicated. These pairs share a transactive memory that they bring to the experiment based on their experience together. Without assignment to topics, these pairs would naturally rely on their existing knowledge of "who knows what" and benefit from its use. Hence, they should recall more items than impromptu couples in the no assignment condition. However, when assigned to specific topics, members of these pairs may be responsible for topics outside of their typical knowledge domain. This assignment to unfamiliar topics may make encoding of the information difficult or they may revert to their natural implicit organization. Either of these effects would interfere with effective recall. If so, then recall performance by natural couples in the assigned condition may be particularly low. Results shown in Figure 10.3 (and replicated by Hollingshead, 1998a) indicate that the results conformed exactly to these predictions.

Although the first studies of transactive memory focused on couples in close relationships, transactive memory can occur in any context in which group members are aware of the different knowledge and expertise of the individual group members. This differentiation often occurs in committees and task groups. Indeed, these groups are often intentionally composed with those differences specifically in mind, so that the group members bring different domains of knowledge to the group. In that way, the transactive memory of the group includes more and broader knowledge than that possessed by any individual group member. The role of transactive memory in work settings has been of increasing interest (Brandon & Hollingshead, 2004; Lewis & Herndon, 2011; Ren & Argote, 2011). Transactive memory – the shared knowledge of differentiated domains of expertise among group members – can facilitate access to specialized knowledge relevant to the group task (Hollingshead, 1998a, 1998b; Liang, Moreland, & Argote, 1995; Moreland, Argote, & Krishnan, 1996).

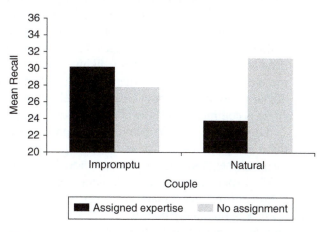

Figure 10.3 Couple recall as a function of couple type (natural vs. impromptu) and assignment (assigned expertise vs. no assignment)

Source: Adapted from Wegner et al. (1991)

Transactive memory depends in crucial ways on effective communication. When people first come together, they may not know about the areas of expertise of other group members, and they must rely on other sources (e.g., gender stereotypes; Hollingshead & Fraidin, 2003) to estimate individuals' areas of knowledge. Over time, increasing interaction and communication (Hollingshead, 1998a, 1998b; Hollingshead & Brandon, 2003) provide increased knowledge of each person's strengths and weaknesses, differences that can then constitute the basis for effective use of that knowledge.

Audience Tuning and the "Saying is Believing" Effect

Communication facilitates the formation and use of transactive memory systems and influences memory in other ways. In many situations, one person communicates to an audience, where an "audience" can range from one listener in a face-to-face interaction to a large number of people listening to a speech. The communicator often knows something about the audience, including its opinions and evaluations on the topic being discussed. Moreover, research has shown that effective communicators typically adjust what they say to make it fit with the opinions of the audience. This habit is well known in effective politicians. For example, President

Ronald Reagan typically emphasized his more conservative positions on issues when speaking to conservative audiences, but, when talking to a liberal group, highlighted other issues where his views were more compatible with this audience. As described by one historian, "He had an instinctive understanding of modern politics which allowed him to sense how to tailor his message to his audience" (De Groot, 2015, p. 266).

The same "tuning" effect happens in everyday conversations as well. Suppose Tamara is telling Beth about her experiences with another person, Irina, and Tamara knows that Beth and Irina are good friends. Tamara is likely to slant her comments about Irina in a favorable light to present views that are congruent with Beth's opinions. However, if Beth doesn't like Irina, then Tamara's comments about Irina are likely to include more negative connotations. This *tuning effect* is commonly observed in social communication (Higgins, 1981).

Of greater interest in the present chapter is evidence showing that this tuning not only shapes the messages communicators transmit to their listeners but also can bias the communicator's own representation of and memory for the message previously delivered (Higgins & Rholes, 1978). In our earlier example, Tamara's comments about Irina would not only reflect Beth's evaluation of Irina, but Tamara's memory of what she said would be biased in that direction as well.

In Higgins and Rholes's (1978) study, participants read an essay describing evaluatively ambiguous behaviors performed by a target person. For example, the person might be described by information ("Michael's contacts with people are limited. He feels he doesn't really need to rely on anyone.") that could be interpreted as suggesting he is either "independent" or "aloof." Participants then prepared a description of the person described, in their own words, and that essay was to be shown to another person who knows Michael and either likes or dislikes him. In line with tuning effects, the participants' (communicators') descriptions were subsequently coded as more positive (negative) if the audience (recipient of the description) likes (dislikes) Michael. Moreover, the effect of tuning on memory was manifested in the fact that the communicators' own memory for the information initially provided to them (the basis for their descriptions) was clearly consistent with the evaluative tone of the audience's views of Michael.

These outcomes have been replicated in other studies (Echterhoff, Higgins, & Groll, 2005; Echterhoff, Higgins, Kopietz, & Groll, 2008; Echterhoff, Kopietz, & Higgins, 2017; Kopietz, Hellmann, Higgins, & Echterhoff, 2010). Thus, both the communication itself and the mental representation of that message have been distorted in the direction of the views held by the recipient of the communication. In this *saying is believing effect*, the act of communication (saying) has generated a biased memory (believing) of the original information.

COMMENT ON MEMORY AS A SOCIAL PRODUCT Throughout the history of psychological research on memory, since the groundbreaking work of Ebbinghaus in the 1880s, investigators have sought to understand how the individual learns, stores, and retrieves information. More than a century of research has produced an immense amount of knowledge informing us of many of the processes that are involved in that everyday task. Furthermore, almost all of it has been focused solely on processes going on in the individual's mind.

Nevertheless, that individual lives in a social world in which she interacts with people all the time, sharing both experiences and memories. In this section, we have discussed research revealing aspects of memory as a social product. Collaborative inhibition, transactive memory, the saying is believing effect – these terms refer to empirical phenomena that occur as people in a social context recall information. They all refer to outcomes that only occur because of the social context in which that individual is placed. Although it has been a relatively recent development in the memory literature, the findings accumulated in this work suggest that there is much more to be learned from considering how this cognitive product – memory – can be influenced by social contexts (see also Echterhoff & Hirst, 2009; Echterhoff, Higgins, & Levine, 2009; Hirst, Coman, & Coman, 2014).

SUMMARY

The people, places, and events that comprise our lives are represented in our memories. Memories are the benefit of our experiences in that they guide our understanding of what has transpired and aid in anticipating the future. Those representations include memories of specific episodes as well as generalized conceptions that summarize and give meaning to those experiences. Memory also includes procedural representations of how actions can be implemented. These individual representations are organized in memory through associations among them and around concepts, which facilitate the activation of related information and make it accessible for retrieval. The representation of information in memory can be biased by cognitive constraints on processing and by the person's motives at the time. However, it is that representation that will be retrieved and used in future processing and in guiding behavior. The use of memory in these ways requires retrieval of those representations.

FURTHER READING

Beike, D.R. (2013). Cherished memories: Autobiographical memory and the self. In D.E. Carlston (Ed.), *The Oxford handbook of social cognition* (pp. 517–533). New York, NY: Oxford University Press.

Loftus, E.F., & Davis, D. (2006). Recovered memories. *Annual Review of Clinical Psychology, 2,* 469–498.

Skowronski, J.J., McCarthy, R.J., & Wells, B. (2013). Person memory: Past, perspectives, and prospects. In D.E. Carlston (Ed.), *The Oxford handbook of social cognition* (pp. 352–374). New York, NY: Oxford University Press.

11
THE TIME DIMENSION

Understanding the Past, Anticipating the Future

On the morning of October 31, 2007, John "Jordan" Lewis entered a Dunkin' Donuts in Philadelphia and pointed his revolver at the head of the store manager with the intent of robbery. Seconds later, Charles Cassidy, a Philadelphia police officer, entered the store dressed in his uniform and stumbled upon the robbery in progress. Officer Cassidy pulled his revolver and crouched down, after which Lewis took two steps towards him, raised his gun, and fired a bullet into his head. Officer Cassidy died instantly. Following his capture, Lewis pleaded guilty to a general charge of murder, and a jury was tasked with deciding his sentence. Crucial evidence considered by the jury was a security video depicting the shooting that was shown to them several times in slow motion. Although Lewis's attorneys argued that he had shot the officer in a surprised, reflexive panic, the jury accepted the prosecution argument that the video depicted premeditated murder and sentenced Lewis to death. Lewis's attorneys appealed the sentence, arguing that the jury's decision had been biased by the playing of the security video in slow motion, unrealistically exaggerating the event and creating a "false impression of premeditation." One of the appellate judges asked Lewis's attorneys, "What can you see in this case only in the slower version that you couldn't see in the fast version?" The judges rejected their suggestion that the slowed video made it seem as though Lewis had more time to form and act on an intention than he did. Lewis's death penalty was upheld.

The chapters in this book have covered a vast territory in considering how the mind functions as it processes and uses information from the social world. We have learned how people's *attention* to stimulus information is selective, processing only a portion of the information available; that people impose some *interpretation* on that information, giving it new meaning; that they respond *evaluatively* to it, guiding not only judgments but also their behavior; that they make *inferences* about the people or events involved and generate *causal attributions* to explain why those events occurred. Information, transformed and elaborated by these processes, then gets stored in *memory*, from which it can be retrieved for later use. For each of these processes, we have identified cognitive and motivational variables that influence how these processes play out, and in every case, we have detailed how biases influence them. Most of these discussions have focused on people's processing of information "in the here and now" – information about people and events that are in the moment.

In this chapter, we explore some quite different questions about processing social information. Specifically, we are concerned with the time dimension. We begin by considering several important issues involved in the perception and experience of time and in the perception of change through time. Recent research has produced fascinating evidence that thinking about the past, present, and future involve different properties and meaning. These differences also have substantial effects on psychological processing (Epstude & Peetz, 2012). We then explore how people understand events (and the people in them, including ourselves) that have occurred in the past. We discuss the flexibility with which people reconstrue the past and use it to serve their current goals and motivations. We then explore how the mind anticipates people and events in times that have not yet arrived, that is, how people look ahead to the future. In all of these cases, the mind goes about these tasks in seemingly reasonable ways. Again, however, some important biases can undermine their effectiveness.

This chapter has a different structure than previous chapters. As just described, there are three major sections of the chapter. Each one introduces several different topic areas and the research related to them. These three sections deal with different aspects of the time dimension and its implications for cognitive processing, integrating theoretical ideas and research findings about temporal factors affecting judgments of the self, persons, and groups.

PSYCHOLOGICAL CONCEPTIONS OF TIME

Time is an abstract concept. We can neither see it nor touch it. We can, of course, mark its passage in measurable, reliable units – hours, days, months, and years. Most people are quite good at tracking the duration of events and the passage of time (Zakay & Block, 1997). We have a general sense of when a lecture should be wrapping up. When we run into an old friend, we intuitively know that it has been years since last seeing her. The units for measuring the past and the future are, of course, the same. For example, if you move into a new apartment, you can easily determine how long you lived in your former residence by consulting a calendar. You can also calculate the date on which you will have lived in your new apartment for the identical period of time as in your previous apartment. In most aspects of everyday life, we rarely need such precision. Consequently, our language is filled with phrases that more casually refer to time periods for looking back and for looking ahead ("That was ages ago…" "It won't be long until…")

In contrast to these actuarial approaches to time, psychological concepts of time are more flexible (Karniol & Ross, 1996; Van Boven & Caruso, 2015; Van Boven, Kane, & McGraw, 2008). Reliable, well-defined units do not bound mental measurements of time. Consequently, one's sense of time in the future may not be equivalent to one's sense of time in the past. Consider the following:

- What occurred in the past is certain; it is done, over, and known (perhaps in detail). What will occur in the future is uncertain; even knowing it will happen in the future, its specific properties and details remain unknown.
- The past cannot be controlled; its nature cannot be influenced. The future, in contrast, has not yet happened, so there remains the possibility that what will transpire can be guided and controlled.
- The notions of moving through time and of distance in time are variable and can differ for the past and the future. For example, because time is an abstract concept, we often adopt the metaphor of physical space to express these concepts (Van Boven & Caruso, 2015), such that an upcoming event is "just around the corner."
- Even the passage of time itself and the duration of events (even short-term events) are amenable to influence from cognitive and affective factors. Arousal and psychological concerns can slow perceived time so that a given length of time feels longer than it was (Moskowitz, Olcaysoy Okten, & Gooch, 2015, 2017).

All of these differences can have interesting implications for mental representations, affect, judgments, and behavior.

Mental Representation of Time

One difference in conceptions of past and future is in the way they are mentally represented (Kane, Van Boven, & McGraw, 2012). Representations of past events are grounded not only in time but also in specific contexts, including locations, persons, and other specifics. Thinking about a day you spent at the beach last summer includes what beach you went to, what you wore, who you were with, how hot it was, what you did together, and any unusual things that may have happened. In contrast, because they have not yet happened, representations of future events are more generic, lacking in historic, episodic details. Thus, the representation of a future event is necessarily more prototypic, containing the main features that would be typical of all such events.

One study (Kane et al., 2012) tested this idea by having participants imagine three homeless people they had met in the last year or would meet in the next year. They then wrote descriptions of them and rated how similar they were to each other and how much they resembled the "average homeless person." In a parallel study, participants wrote descriptions of three different experiences of ordering pizza. Some participants wrote about three such times they ordered pizza in the past, whereas the others wrote about three times they will order pizza in the future. They were then asked to think about the set of three experiences and to rate how similar they were to each other and how characteristic of the typical pizza ordering experience they were. The results of these studies are shown in Table 11.1. In both studies, participants in the "future" condition rated them as more similar to each other than did participants in the "past" condition, consistent with the view that future descriptions were based

Table 11.1 Rated similarity and typicality among imagined instances in past and future conditions

	Condition	
	Past	**Future**
Encounter homeless persons		
Intra-set similarity	3.64	4.38
Resemble "average" person	3.47	4.65
Ordering pizza		
Intra-set similarity	5.43	6.58
Resemble "typical" experience	6.71	7.38

Source: Adapted from Kane et al. (2012)

on a prototypic representation whereas the past descriptions drew on episodic representations of different specific experiences. They also rated the instances as more typical of the average homeless person or pizza experience.

A prototype is a generalized representation of a category, conveying the most typical features of the category without the details that can be a part of any individual instance. If representations of the future are prototypic, they should be abstract rather than concrete characterizations. To test this hypothesis, researchers provided participants with 25 descriptions of everyday activities along with two other phrases, one of which provided a high-level abstract description ("getting organized") and the other a low-level concrete description ("writing things down"). The participants' task was to indicate which of these descriptions best described the event. Half of the participants were told that the event occurred in the past (a year ago), whereas the others were told it would occur in the future. More abstract descriptions were selected for events in the future than in the past (Kane et al., 2012), consistent with the notion that future events are more prototypic than are conceptions of past events.

The findings of other research converge with this conclusion. In Chapter 5, we introduced Construal Level Theory (Trope & Liberman, 2010), which posits that the way people experience events that are not immediately present is by construing them in order to gain psychological meaning. Psychologically distant events (e.g., in time, space) are construed more abstractly than more proximal events. Abstract representations capture features likely to remain invariant over time, whereas concrete representations are more likely to include details of what happened, how it was done, and in what context. For example, in one study, participants read a getting acquainted scenario that had them imagine meeting a person either in the near future (upcoming weekend) or the distant future (six months later). They then rated how familiar the person seemed to be. When the interaction was expected soon, participants rated the person as more familiar. Imagining the event in a more distant future produced a more abstract (less close) representation that diminished the sense of familiarity (Stephan, Liberman, & Trope, 2011).

In a similar vein, the language we use can convey differing degrees of abstractness. The same action described in the present tense (David is walking) versus past tense (David walked) influence perceptions that the action is completed or is still unfolding. These different representations of the same behavior can influence other judgments. For example, paralleling Stephan et al. (2011), research showed that actions and persons described in the past tense were perceived as less familiar than when described in the present tense (Carrera, Muñoz, Caballero, Fernández, Aguilar, & Albarracín, 2014).

Time and Emotional Intensity

People also have different experiences when they think about the past and the future. Thinking about future events tends to produce greater emotional intensity than when thinking retrospectively about past events, and this is true for both positively-valenced and negatively-valenced events. In one study (Van Boven & Ashworth, 2007), participants were asked to think about Thanksgiving Day either two weeks before it occurred or two weeks after the holiday. Later they indicated what emotions they experienced as they contemplated Thanksgiving. Those who anticipated their future Thanksgiving reported feeling happier than did those who thought about their recently-completed holiday. The same asymmetry also occurred in thinking about a future and past negative event. Women were asked to rate their emotional reactions as they contemplated an upcoming or their most recent menstrual period. The anticipation of their next period led women to rate their mood as worse than those who were thinking about their last period. Thus, whether contemplating pleasant or unpleasant experiences, anticipating the future evokes greater emotional intensity than does retrospection of the past (Van Boven & Ashworth, 2007). Similarly, people place a higher value on outcomes they anticipate will happen in the future than on outcomes that happened in the past (Caruso, Gilbert, & Wilson, 2008).

This emotional intensity also influences time perception by reducing psychological distance, making strongly affective experiences seem temporally closer (Van Boven, Kane, McGraw, & Dale, 2010). Participants were asked to describe either their last (past) or their next (future) dentist visit. Some were asked to describe the visit in an involved, empathic manner, conveying feelings of the experience; other participants were told to describe the visit objectively, in an unemotional manner. They then rated temporal distance on rating scales (e.g., "feels very close" to "feels very distant"). The results showed that participants who had been asked to describe the visit to the dentist's office in an emotional manner perceived that visit as less distant than did participants who had described it in an emotionally neutral manner. This effect can be more prevalent in judging the psychological distance of future than of past events that are equally distant from the present (Caruso, Van Boven, Chin, & Ward, 2013). For example, either one week before or one week after Valentine's Day, people were asked to rate the "distance from the present" of the holiday on a scale from "a short time from now" to "a long time from now." Those for whom Valentine's Day was in the future rated it significantly closer than did those for whom it was in an equidistant past.

Time and Intentionality

Temporal factors can also influence the perceived intentionality of behavior. Usually, we experience events as they play out naturally, but thinking about events in the past or future can introduce perturbations in judgments of time that can affect the degree that behavior is seen as purposeful and causal. Michotte (1946) was the first to report on the relationship between timing and perceived causality. He suggested that if an object moves and stops next to a second object, and then the second object moves away within a particular temporal window, people judge that the first object *caused* the second object to move. When the speed of movement is varied, so would observers' judgments of the causal relationship in the shapes' movements.

These speculations led several researchers to investigate whether changes in the speed of observed actions might influence whether they reflect premeditation and intentionality. This idea was tested in studies (Caruso, Burns, & Converse, 2016) where participants viewed a series of video clips of incidents shown either at normal speed or in slow motion. Whether the clips depicted a shooting of a store clerk during a robbery or a violent collision in a football game, participants were more likely to think that actions were intentional when they were seen in slow motion. These effects emerged even when participants were able to view a clock display indicating how much time had elapsed during each incident. Similar effects have also been shown with professional referees who were asked to indicate how they would handle a penalty situation in soccer (with a "yellow card" for reckless conduct or a "red card" indicating excessive force). More red cards were issued when the same action was viewed in slow motion compared with normal speed (Spitz, Moors, Wagemans, & Helsen, 2018). These results provide empirical support for the position argued by Jordan Lewis's lawyers at appeal (in the scenario that opened this chapter). Presenting behavioral evidence in slow motion makes it appear more willful and intentional.

Similarly, when people contemplate an ambiguous event that either has occurred or will occur, future behavior is seen as more intentional than past behavior (Burns, Caruso, & Bartels, 2012). Participants in one study were asked to imagine a scenario in which an older woman gives her husband the wrong medicine, which causes him to have a fatal heart attack.

The scenario included information that made this unfortunate mistake understandable (small print on the medicine label, the woman's poor eyesight) as well as clues that it could have been intentional (poor marital relationship, substantial life insurance gain after his death). Some participants were told that the incident happened a month ago, whereas others were told to imagine that it would happen in a month. After reading the scenario, participants rated their reactions on some rating scales. The results are shown in Table 11.2. Those who placed the action in a future month expressed stronger negative feelings about the event, thought it more likely that the woman intended to kill her husband, and recommended harsher punishment compared to when the action occurred in the previous month. Thus, greater intentionality is perceived if an act is described as occurring in the future rather than the past.

Table 11.2 Mean negative affect, intentionality, and severity of punishment ratings as a function of temporal perspective

	Negative affect	Intentionality	Severity of punishment
Past	5.19	-0.20	2.14
Future	7.03	0.15	3.00

Source: Adapted from Burns et al. (2012)

Earlier, we presented research showing that activating past or present time by use of past or present verbs can influence perceptions of abstractness of representation and familiarity. Other work provides useful evidence of processes underlying those effects, including downstream effects on perceptions of intentionality (Hart & Albarracín, 2011). Participants read sentences describing various behaviors. In one condition, all of the sentences were stated using either present-tense verbs (is reading a book, is playing ball) or past-tense verbs (read a book, played ball). Later they completed a task measuring the accessibility of intention-related words. If the different verb forms differentially affected notions of causality, then words reflecting intentionality would be more accessible. The results revealed that present-tense verbs did lead to greater accessibility of intention-related content. Another study tested whether verb form would influence judgments in a criminal case. Participants read about an argument between two men, which led to one of them shooting the other. The form of the verbs in the passage was manipulated (was pointing the gun vs. pointed the gun). Participants then rated how knowingly and intentionally the shooter acted. Those who read the present-tense version indicated greater criminal intentionality than did those who read past-tense verbs. Thus, the different verb forms can induce more or less abstractness in how the information is represented, and these differences can influence subsequent judgments of intentionality.

Time and Morality

This asymmetry also characterizes judgments of fairness and morality (Caruso, 2010). In 1999, the Coca-Cola Company was developing a vending machine that would automatically charge more for drinks as temperatures increased. News of this plan became known, and the public was outraged by the idea that the same can of soda would cost more on hot days than on chilly days. Given the public reaction, the plan was never implemented. Caruso (2010), however, utilized this episode to test the asymmetry hypothesis. Participants were provided a scenario about a company working on a machine that would automatically change the price of a soda between $1.00 and $3.50 depending on the outside temperature. The temporal location was manipulated by saying that the vending machine was tested last month or would be tested next month. After reading the scenario, participants rated how fair they thought the machine was and also their feelings at the moment (how cheated, angry, outraged they felt). Participants in the future condition rated the machine as less fair than those in the past condition, and this difference was a function of the extent of negative affect experienced by the participants.

Does this effect occur only for unfair or immoral behavior, or are positive behaviors also judged differently if they occurred in the past or will happen in the future? To test this question, researchers told participants about a wealthy man making a large donation for the construction of a homeless shelter in his city (Caruso, 2010). The description indicated that the man either made the donation last month (past condition) or will make it next month (future condition). Participants then rated how generous they thought the donation was. A sizeable future donation was rated as more generous than a large past donation, demonstrating that the past–future asymmetry occurs for positive actions as well.

Another question of central importance is whether this asymmetry generalizes to the intergroup domain. Research has shown that people experience emotions on behalf of their group members, even if they are not involved in the emotion-generating experience (Mackie, Maitner, & Smith, 2009). One instance of this is when group members feel collective guilt based on the actions of other group members, maybe even due to the actions of group members in the distant past (e.g., Americans' historical treatment of slaves). Of course, groups not only have committed actions in the past but also plan future events (e.g., wars). Does the past–future asymmetry occur in group judgments? Do people feel more collective guilt in anticipating their groups' future actions than in retrospections about their groups' past actions? Participants in one study examining this question (Caouette, Wohl, & Peetz, 2012) were Canadian citizens who read a newspaper article describing a harmful action to Aboriginal Canadians. Specifically, they learned about a hydroelectric plant that involved the flooding of some traditional Aboriginal lands. Participants either read that the flooding occurred a month ago or that it would occur in one month. They then indicated the extent the hydro project made them feel guilty, sad, and disgusted. Participants in the future harm condition expressed greater collective guilt than did those in the past harm condition, demonstrating the past–future asymmetry in judgments of group actions.

INTERIM SUMMARY The research reviewed in this section reveals that psychological time is not the same as objective time. It is more elastic, particularly in thinking about the future, and there are numerous asymmetries in the subjective experience of the past compared with what is to come. Future events are psychologically closer, they evoke more intense emotional responses, and they are judged to be more intentional and held to higher moral standards than events that happened an equidistant distance in the past. The mind views events in the past and the future in different terms and judges them by different standards.

Perceiving Continuity and Change Across Time

As participants in the social world, we continually observe other individuals, groups of persons, and even ourselves across many contexts and over time. For each of these entities, we see both continuities and changes over time. Perceiving those continuities and changes can be an essential aspect of adaptation. Observing changes (or lack thereof) over time can provide a richer and more accurate sense of what the self, other individuals, and groups are like, since time allows characteristics, behaviors, and motives to reveal themselves across differing contexts and events (Bem & Allen, 1974; Mischel, Shoda, & Mendoza-Denton, 2002).

We often perceive an impressive amount of consistency in what we observe. Persons seem to us to be essentially the same beings today as they were a week ago, a year ago, five years ago. Perhaps our perception of such consistency is not surprising. After all, people's personalities and attitudes lend consistency to their behavior; the social groups we observe (and belong to) seem broadly consistent; the stereotypes we hold of groups seem to persist; and we typically view ourselves to be substantially stable individuals, adapting to different circumstances but basically the same across time.

One might wonder, though, if these perceptions of consistency in ourselves and others are more apparent than real. People do change over time, they function quite differently in different social contexts, attitudes can and sometimes do change, and even stereotypes can shift over time (consider the U.S. stereotypes of women and African Americans today compared to the 1950s). These considerations lead to some crucial questions: Why and how do we perceive consistency amidst change? How and when do we detect change, and why do we not see it when it is there? Does a social cognition approach shed light on answering these questions? In this section, we explore those questions.

Perceiving Self-continuity

Suppose I ask you to think about what you were like 10 years ago. If you are currently a college student, you would have been a student in junior high or middle school. If you're a thirty-something, you would have been in college or beginning your career. Imagine what you were like and what your life involved at that time and describe it to me. After you have finished your description, I ask you what you are like now, and again to describe yourself to me. Comparing those two descriptions, it seems inevitable that they would look very different. A lot has happened during those 10 years. You have probably experienced profound changes physically, cognitively, emotionally, socially, and in practically every area of your life. Presumably, those changes would be reflected in the differences in your two descriptions. Imagine that I then made the following comment to you: "Gee, as I look at the two descriptions you gave me, I see that they are totally different. There is hardly any overlap between them. Are you really the same person?" After a moment of puzzlement, you might respond, "Yes, of course, I'm the same person." And then I ask you, "Why do you think that?"

The issue posed by this exchange concerns some fundamental questions of consistency and change. All of us change over time, and sometimes (as in changing from pre- to post-adolescence), those changes are fundamental and dramatic. Nevertheless, each of us does not doubt that the same person persists through all those changes. Given the likely dramatic differences in your two self-descriptions, how would you answer the "Why" question? In what sense, and for what reason, do you say you are the same person? What explains that persistence during all these changes?

This precise question was investigated by Chandler (Chandler, 2001; Chandler & Lalonde, 1998; Chandler & Proulx, 2008; Chandler, Lalonde, Sokol, Hallett, & Marcia, 2003) in studies of adolescents in British Columbia. Using a procedure similar to the questions described above, Chandler and colleagues coded the responses these adolescents provided to the "Why" question; that is, they studied the rationales and explanations participants provided for why they saw themselves as persistent across those dynamic changes. They found two prominent strategies that people used to preserve a sense of consistency. One strategy involves emphasizing certain defining elements or essences that remain constant across time. Change may occur, but self-continuity is due to these essential parts of us that remain the same over time. The authors call this the *Essentialist Strategy* to account for consistency. The second strategy, the *Narrative Account*, involves viewing the different slices or phases of one's life as chapters in an ongoing narrative. The sense of continuity is due to the thread of meaning that continues through the distinct, though perhaps quite different, aspects of one's life story.

There are cultural differences in the use of these strategies. Chandler (2001; Chandler et al. 2003) administered their task to a group of adolescents from mainstream urban backgrounds and to an equivalent number from First Nations (indigenous) communities. Respondents from the cultural mainstream primarily used the essentialist rationale in accounting for personal continuity. In contrast, the vast majority of First Nations respondents made use of the narrative strategy to explain the self-continuity question.

Both strategies for explaining self-persistence (and also the persistence of others) can answer the "Why" question, and either version can vary in the level of sophistication or thoroughness with which it is articulated. Regardless of the strategy a person typically uses, Chandler and colleagues found that these adolescents (and presumably all of us) must have considered and answered the question of self-continuity over time. The crucial role of having an accounting for self-persistence was assessed by comparing two groups of hospitalized adolescents, those that were and were not considered suicidal. Compared to the hospitalized but non-suicidal patients, 80% of those who were considered at risk for suicide did not generate any meaningful rationale for their persistence across time in the face of ongoing change. These data clearly indicate that a sense of self-persistence – and also an adequate framework for understanding the persistence of one's life over time in the face of ongoing changes – are essential for one's adaptation and well-being.

Chandler and colleagues (Chandler, 2001; Chandler & Lalonde, 1998) have also shown that one's cultural group can be a source of that continuity. Specifically, cultural continuity can be viewed and can function as a group-level counterpart to developing an individual-level sense of personal persistence. The researchers tested these ideas in British Columbia, where there are some 200 typically small communities or "bands" of First Nations people. Data also clearly document that adolescent suicide rates are much higher in First Nations bands than in culturally mainstream communities (seven times higher in indigenous than in the general youth population). However, First Nations bands vary considerably in the extent to which they are administratively and socially organized and provide cultural continuity for their inhabitants. To assess the importance of cultural continuity in attenuating suicide, the researchers coded each band on six factors reflecting organi-

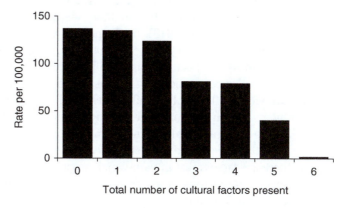

Figure 11.1 Youth suicide rates by number of cultural factors present in the community (1987–1992)

Source: Adapted from Chandler & Lalonde (1998)

zation and administrative factors (e.g., whether the band had self-government; control over health, education, and police services; a cultural center), producing a score of 0 to 6 for each band. The question was whether this variation among bands in the extent to which they have established cultural continuity was related to the suicide rate among adolescents in those communities. The results of the study are shown in Figure 11.1. Among bands that had achieved all six of these markers of cultural continuity, there were no adolescent suicides whatsoever during the five years covered by this analysis. In contrast, in communities that had not achieved such cultural markers, the suicide rate was much higher than the national average.

The research by Chandler and colleagues revealed the importance of self-continuity for adjustment during adolescence. Does this sense of continuity persist in later stages of life, during which other (including significant) changes would likely have occurred? In a study addressing this question in an elderly sample (Troll & Skaff, 1997), researchers interviewed 144 persons aged 85–103 (one-third over 90). The interview included asking, "In what ways have you always been the same?" and "In what ways have you changed over the years?" These open-ended responses were coded for the extent that they reflected "a persistent sense of identity or essential personhood." Most of these elderly respondents (74%) indicated they were essentially the same person they had always been (although they may have changed in some specific attributes). As in the research on adolescents, a sense of self-continuity is fundamental.

In sum, this work demonstrates that achieving some conceptual understanding of continuity through time – at the individual level or cultural level – is vital for maintaining a sense of one's persistence through the life span. This almost existential sense of oneself can be crucial in adjustment and in preventing adverse effects that may occur in the absence of that foundation.

Perspective Effects on Perceived Continuity and Change

All of us, from time to time, think back to events that we experienced in the past. Perhaps it was an event that occurred as recently as last week, and we can easily recall what happened; other times, we think of an incident that happened long ago, yet we can picture the event so vividly that "it seemed like yesterday." An important element of these experiences is the mental imagery with which we re-experience these past events.

Mental images can differ in their visual perspective (Libby & Eibach, 2011; Tausen, Carpenter, & Macrae, 2019). In Chapter 5, we presented research showing that memories can be experienced from a *first-person perspective* or a *third-person perspective.* The difference between these perspectives has significant ramifications for how memories are generated and also for one's understanding of the past and of one's self (Libby & Eibach, 2002; Libby, Eibach, & Gilovich, 2005; Libby et al., 2009; Libby, Schaeffer, Eibach, & Slemmer, 2007; Valenti, Libby, & Eibach, 2011). We return to this topic here because these perspective differences are related to perceptions of continuity and change in self-understanding.

We all use both of these perspectives. However, which perspective is used is not arbitrary, as there are factors that govern which perspective is more likely to be adopted. Moreover, the perspective used is essential because first-person and third-person perspectives differ in their downstream consequences.

Sometimes when we imagine ourselves in some previous time, we almost have the sense that we are looking at a different person, one that has changed so much over time so as to be almost unrecognizable. Experiences such as these led Libby and Eibach (2002) to propose that extensive changes in the self induce a third-person perspective in recalling memories of the past. When we believe that we have changed dramatically over time, the incongruency between the past self and current self prompts the use of a third-person perspective in imagining previous experiences. In one study testing this idea, college students were asked to indicate which aspects (e.g., relationships, religion) of themselves that had *changed the most* and which had *changed the least* since high school. For each aspect, they were instructed to think and write about that aspect for five minutes. They next were asked to think about five specific memories they had about each aspect (e.g., one's bar mitzvah), and to later indicate whether they were using a first-person or third-person perspective for each memory. Participants reported much higher use of third-person perspective for memories corresponding to ways they had changed than to ways they had remained stable.

A mismatch between past and current selves can also result from a change in a social context. For example, in a follow-up experiment (Libby & Eibach, 2002), people were induced to spend a few minutes thinking about what they were typically like when they were with their parents or when they were with their friends. Later they were instructed to recall a specific experience they had had either with their parents or with friends. So the two tasks generate thoughts about two contexts that are the same (parents – parents) or different (parents – friends). The question was whether context-based incompatibility led to greater use of the third-person context. Indeed, it did. In cases in which the primed relationship (parents) was incongruent with the relationship context recalled (friends), 75% of those memories were described from a third-person perspective. In cases of congruency between tasks (friends – friends), only 29% were described using a third-person perspective. Together, these experiments demonstrate that when people think about past events that are incompatible with their current self-concepts, they recall them from a different visual perspective than they use when recalling behaviors and events that are compatible with self-views.

Given that people can (and do) recall events from either perspective, what difference does it make? Research has shown that different perspectives can produce several different downstream effects. One effect is that one's perspective can influence the perceived extremity of change in the self over time (Libby et al., 2005). This finding was identified in people who had participated in psychotherapy (who presumably would both expect change and be motivated to see evidence of change) and were asked to recall their first treatment session. Half of the participants were instructed to visualize that event from the first-person perspective, looking out at the surroundings "through your own eyes." For example, they were asked if they could see the furniture in the room, the wall hangings, who else was in the room. In contrast, other participants were instructed to view the session from a third-person, observer's perspective, "so you can see yourself in the room." They were asked whether they were standing or sitting, what they were wearing, and about their facial expressions. After imaging their first session in one of these ways, participants were asked to rate how much they had changed since their first treatment session. Those who used a third-person perspective judged themselves as having changed more dramatically since their first session than did participants who adopted a first-person perspective.

A second study (Libby et al., 2005) showed that third-person perspectives increased the perceived distance of awkward situations from the past. In this experiment, college students recalled a specific social interaction that occurred in high school when they felt socially awkward. They were instructed to visualize and write about this incident from either the first-person or the third-person perspective. They then were asked to assess their social skills now compared to when they were in high school. Those who visualized the awkward episode from the third-person perspective rated present-day selves as more socially skilled (i.e., they saw more change from the past) compared to participants who used the first-person perspective. Again, adopting a third-person perspective led to higher perceptions of self-change over time.

In both cases, participants were likely motivated to focus on differences between their past and present selves when recalling the event in question. People presumably seek out psychotherapy in the hope that it will help them change and desire to view a previously awkward self as existing in a distant past. Given these presumed motivations, using a third-person perspective helps the perceiver appreciate the degree of personal change over time.

Would shifts in perspective also affect how people behave? This question was addressed by examining how participants in whom either first- or third-person perspectives had been induced interacted with another student, presumably another participant in the study but actually a confederate of the experimenter. The two were left alone for five minutes. Later, after the two were separated, the confederate (who did not know which perspective condition the participant had been in) rated participants in the third-person condition significantly higher on sociability than participants in the first-person condition. Moreover, codings of their conversations revealed that participants in the third-person condition initiated more conversation with the confederate than did those in the first-person condition. Thus, the visual perspective used to recall a past event influenced not only one's subjective feeling of personal change from the past but also influenced one's overt behavior in social interaction (Libby et al., 2005).

Visual perspective can also produce effects that extend into the future. Another study (Libby et al., 2007) had participants imagine themselves, using one of the two perspectives, performing a future behavior (voting in the 2004 U.S. presidential election) and then measured the likelihood that people followed through with that behavior. A few days before election day, participants were given either first-person or third-person visualization instructions and were instructed to use that perspective to picture themselves voting in the election. After the election, the researchers contacted participants to determine whether or not they had voted. Based on the reasoning that actions are considered a reflection of the actor's personality more when seen from a third-person than from a first-person perspective, it was predicted that mentally viewing oneself voting from a third-person perspective would result in higher rates of voting on election day. The results confirmed that prediction: 90% of people in the third-person condition had voted compared with 72% of those in the first-person condition. Thus, inducing people to visualize a behavior using a third-person perspective can increase the likelihood of their performing the behavior.

The research we have summarized has shown several differences between the first- and third-person perspectives about conditions that induce one perspective or the other (congruency or incongruency between past and current self-concepts), perceptions of continuity (first-person) or change (third-person) of self over time, and the nature and likelihood of behavior manifestations. Thus, this distinction between first- and third-person points of view affects the meaning that those actions are perceived to have and affects perceptions of stability and change across time.

Perceiving Change Over Time

In the last two sections, we have reviewed research documenting the importance of maintaining a sense of one's continuity through time and that one's perspective can influence the perception of continuity versus change across time. Recognizing continuities is clearly important. However, it is also true that change is always occurring around us, and we must detect and adapt to it. Consequently, there are important questions regarding how we detect change when it occurs, our sensitivity to it, and the cognitive and motivational processes that affect our perceptions of change over time. In this section, we examine research investigating those questions.

Detecting Change in Performance

Detecting change involves a comparison of current performance with past performance. When we observe a person's or group's performance over time, we can potentially gain a sense of their *average* level of performance as well as of the *variability* of their performance. If our intuitive sense of the level of either past or present performance is inaccurate, then our judgment of the extent to which change has occurred may be erroneous. Therefore, assessing change depends on the accuracy of one's recall of the past, and that recall needs to include both the average performance and the variability of past performance.

Knowledge of the variability of performance is critical for determining how representative any single performance would be. However, research has shown that observers are often insensitive to the variability in performance and have better retention of information about average performance (Silka, 1981). This is particularly true with time when variability information may be lost, and therefore only average performance is retained. When current performance data are compared to recollections of past performance, the loss of variability information may result in overreliance on average performance data. This may make it seem that there has been more change than has occurred (Silka, 1981, 1984; Silka & Albright, 1983).

Evidence consistent with these ideas was provided by a study (Silka, 1981) in which participants were told that they would be given multiple scores about each of three persons (Persons A, B, and C). The values were scores on a psychological test used to diagnose mental illness, with higher scores signifying more significant signs of mental illness. The average of the 12 scores for the three persons differed: Person A = 12, Person B = 47, Person C = 87. Participants' task would be to judge the change in the psychological well-being of Person C. However, half of the participants were instructed to attend to and remember the average score of each person, whereas the other half were told to remember the range of scores for each person. They then read 12 pages, each providing three scores, one for each person. After reading these materials, all participants recalled the information they had been told to focus on – the average or range for each person.

The second part of the study focused on Person C and occurred either immediately or one week later. Participants were told that there was now one additional score for Person C, a value of 76 (lower than his average score). Without access to Person C's original scores, participants were asked to judge the extent to which his mental health had permanently improved. The results are shown in Figure 11.2. Participants in the Immediate condition judged only a minor degree of change, regardless of having focused on the average or range of values. For those in the Delayed condition, those who had attended to the range of scores – knowing that a score of 76 was only modestly lower than previous scores – judged that Person C had changed only slightly. In contrast, participants who had focused on the average of scores were insensitive to the variability of Person C's scores and judged his new

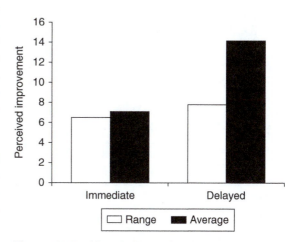

Figure 11.2 Mean ratings of permanence of improvement in psychological health as a function of instructional set and time of recall

Source: Adapted from Silka (1981)

score of 76 to reflect more considerable improvement. Follow-up studies provided further support for this effect (Silka, 1981; Silka & Albright, 1983).

In sum, detecting change over time is not always easy or obvious and requires recognition of both average performance and variability of performance. The results of these studies demonstrate that people's insensitivity to the latter can lead to intuitive judgments of more significant change than are warranted.

Biased Evaluations of Change

Clearly, we are motivated to see ourselves favorably, as having desirable attributes and self-worth. Those judgments are subjective, however, and frequently clear criteria are absent for making such judgments. Therefore, we often compare ourselves to our previous selves – the way we were in the past. Is the current self better than the past self? If so, which past self – our recent past or our distant past? Moreover, on what attributes? Does it matter, and if so, why? These questions are the focus of *Temporal Self-appraisal Theory* (Ross & Wilson, 2003).

The theory begins with the recognition that people are motivated to maintain favorable self-evaluations and that they engage in the comparison process described above. The central notion of the theory is that people can maintain a positive self-appraisal in such comparisons by *devaluing* an earlier self, thereby assuring a positive self-evaluation (by comparison) of the present self. Given the subjectivity of such judgments and the flexibility in selecting comparisons, the outcome of the process is virtually assured. According to Ross and Wilson, that flexibility will guide the comparison process. First, it is more likely that one will compare the present self with a distant, rather than a recent, past self. Recent former selves are probably highly similar to the current self, so devaluing a recent similar self would not provide any benefit of the comparison. Moreover, a short time interval may not include enough passage of time to include improvement, whereas comparing to a more remote past self provides more significant opportunity for improvement to be recognized. Second, a comparison with a former self on an important attribute will not be gratifying, even if the current self-evaluation is better. It would be much more valuable to devalue a past self on an attribute that is important to the current self so the contrast can be maximally beneficial to one's current self-evaluation. Therefore, the theory proposes that both the *psychological closeness of a past self* and the *importance of the attribute* being compared will influence one's retrospective evaluation of the past self.

These hypotheses were tested in a series of studies (Wilson & Ross, 2001). In one study, college students rated themselves on a variety of attributes and social skills for two periods: as they are now (mean age = 20) and also as they had been at age 16. Their ratings were combined into an overall favorability score. The participants' parents were also asked to rate themselves on the same attributes at four different ages: 16, their child's age (20), their current age (mean = 50), and at the age midway between their child's and their own current ages (mean = 35). Temporal Self-appraisal Theory states that people devalue their past selves in order to maintain high current self-regard. The results shown in Table 11.3 document this effect. The students rated themselves significantly more favorably now than they had been when 16 years old. Similarly, their parents rated themselves increasingly more favorably with age

Table 11.3 Mean favorability ratings for past and present selves by student and parent samples

	Rated for age			
	16	20	35	50
Students	5.8	6.3	–	–
Parents	5.8	6.8	7.2	7.5

Source: Adapted from Wilson & Ross (2001)

(particularly on desirable attributes). The data for parents also show that they devalued their distant past selves more than their more recent past self.

The results reported so far support Temporal Self-appraisal Theory, but there is an alternative possibility. It may be that people have a general belief that people improve with age and the progression of time (at least for these periods). If so, then the lower ratings for past selves may not reflect a motivated devaluing of the past but rather an enhancement in the evaluation of the current self. Of course, these processes would not influence perceptions of the past and current selves of other persons, but the notion of general improvement with age would apply to them as well. Therefore, in evaluating others, one process (devaluation) would produce a difference in evaluations of past and present, whereas the other explanation (self-enhancement) would not. An experiment was designed to test these two possibilities. The researchers compared participants' ratings of past and present selves for themselves and for an acquaintance. Participants again rated their current selves more favorably than their past selves, but this difference did not occur in the judgments of the acquaintance. Thus, the results of the previous studies cannot be accounted for by a general belief in self-improvement with time.

Finally, we all believe that some attributes that are characteristic of us are more central to our self-concepts than are others. I may think that my honesty and integrity, as well as my career success, are more important attributes than the fact that I am independent and self-confident. Temporal Self-appraisal Theory predicts that people will devalue past selves most on attributes that are important to their self-regard, compared with attributes that are unimportant and less central to the self-concept. Moreover, this devaluation should occur most strongly for a distant past self, which would highlight self-improvement over time. Consistent with the theory, the results of an experiment testing those hypotheses provided evidence supporting them.

The Best Is Yet to Come

Research on reconstructive memory (Ross, 1989), to be discussed later in this chapter, shows that people's self-based motivations can lead them to revise their memories of their past to create a desired sense of stability or change concerning their present state. We have just seen that they devalue their past selves in order to psychologically enhance their current self-evaluations (Wilson & Ross, 2001). Understanding the past, therefore, seems quite malleable. Of course, the time dimension does not pertain exclusively to the past. People also spend much time thinking about their futures, planning everything from their next vacation to their long-term career paths. Intuitively it seems that people devote considerable importance to their futures and invest much thought and mental energy preparing for it. Are people's conceptions of their futures, like their construals of the past, guided by beliefs, motives, and preconceptions? Also, in their perceptions of others, do people assume that others are similarly consumed with their futures?

The comparisons between the past and present selves, at the heart of Wilson and Ross's (2001) work on temporal appraisal theory, can also be made between current and future selves (Wilson, Buehler, Lawford, Schmidt, & Yong, 2012). Again, this comparison process can be driven by motives for positive self-evaluation. In comparing to past selves, Wilson and Ross (2001) showed that people derogate past selves (especially distant past selves) so that the contrast to the present self is likely to be favorable. In thinking of their futures, however, people are motivated to see self-improvement rather than decline, and in this case, seeing a highly favorable self in the proximal rather than distant future is more beneficial for evaluations of the current self. In a series of studies, participants rated themselves on several desirable attributes both as they are now and as they see themselves in the near (3 months away) or distant (3 years away) future. The results of these studies showed that (a) people rated their future selves more favorably than their present selves, (b) this effect was stronger for proximal than for remote future times, (c) the effect disappears when self-enhancement motives have been satisfied by other means, and (d) participants induced to think of themselves in the near future rated themselves more favorably than those induced to a distant future, showing the more significant benefit of comparison to a proximal than remote future self.

All of these findings suggest that people attach considerable importance to their conceptions of their future selves. Indeed, research has shown that people believe that the future is a centrally important part of their self-definition (Williams & Gilovich, 2008). In one study, college students were instructed to think about how good a student that they have been in the past, are at present, and potentially would be in the future. A parallel study asked participants to think about themselves more generally in those three periods and to rate themselves in each case. In both studies, participants also rated a typical student at their school on the same scales. These self-assessments revealed that participants' beliefs about what they would be like in the future constituted an important part of their conceptions of themselves. For ratings of ability and themselves more generally, the future was judged to be a more significant component of their own identity than of a typical student.

In a follow-up study, participants rated themselves or someone else on a series of scales assessing the extent to which a variety of aspects represent "who I am" (e.g., the traits that describe you; behaviors and activities indicative of your personality; your typical friends and social groups). Three of the scales expressly referred to the future (e.g., the kind of person you will be; how you intend to be in the future). On those future-oriented items (but not on the other scales), participants rated those descriptions as representing who they are more highly than in rating those items for another person. In a final study, the researchers asked participants to think about "life as a journey" with the destination being the point at which they have become the best person they can be. They were then asked to rate themselves as to "How close do you think you are to being the best person you could ever be." They also rated the typical student at their college on the same scale. Participants rated themselves as not being as far along that highway as the typical student. Thus, on this journey of self-improvement, people think they have further to go than the average person toward becoming the person they want to be. Assuming one's continued movement in that direction, the future seems to offer bright prospects for self-improvement. In other words, people seem to believe that "The best is yet to come" (Newby-Clark & Ross, 2003). In sum, in all of these studies, the data indicate that the future is a prominent part of one's self-conception.

Perceiving Continuity and Change in Groups

Like persons, groups are real entities that persist through time and perform certain functions. As perceivers, we become familiar with groups' properties, purposes, priorities, and performances. Therefore, we perceive groups as real and stable entities that persist through time. This perception of continuity is somewhat notable because groups are continually changing in a variety of ways that might seem to undermine their perceived "sameness" over time and across contexts. Consider the following facts that apply to virtually all groups:

- Group membership changes as some members leave and new members join.
- With these membership changes, the group composition may change concerning a variety of characteristics (e.g., age, gender, race, education level, socioeconomic status).

- As the group evolves, the (explicit or implicit) criteria for membership may change – what types of persons does the group seek to attract and perhaps actively recruit.
- Virtually all groups experience changes in leadership over time, as well as changes in how group decisions are made. Such changes can result in altering group goals and activities.
- Moreover, the structural and functional features of a group – its norms, roles, organization, communications patterns, and even its effectiveness and level of performance – may vary as a consequence of these other changes.

Recognizing these facts makes it clear that groups actually are quite fluid entities. How is it, then, that we perceive groups as highly continuous entities?

Perceiving Group Continuity

Several aspects of groups function to create and maintain a sense of group continuity (Hamilton, Levine, & Thurston, 2008). Membership in groups, though changing, is neither random nor arbitrary. Instead, it typically is the result of a process through which existing group members and prospective new members agree that membership will be mutually satisfying (Levine & Moreland, 1994; Levine, Bogart, & Zdaniuk, 1996). Potential group members are "looking for" a group of a particular type, whose members share specific attributes, and a group that is pursuing a particular goal or agenda. Similarly, members of an existing group are typically looking for prospective members that meet specific criteria; that is, they have attributes, skills, and goals that are compatible with those of the existing group. In other words, groups are seeking members who are "like themselves" in critical respects. These two motives converge to produce homogeneous groups. This similarity increases compatibility among group members, and hence the satisfaction members experience in the group. These, in turn, (a) will increase the likelihood that different groups will have different identities as perceived by others, and (b) will serve to perpetuate the group's existence over time.

In addition to this selection process, new members experience a socialization process through which they adopt the group's attitudes, values, and behavioral norms (Levine & Moreland, 1994; Moreland & Levine, 1982). Those who do not conform may be targets of group pressure, be targets of social punishment, and in extreme cases, be rejected from the group (Levine, Moreland, & Hausmann, 2005). These processes further serve to increase and maintain group homogeneity, both in reality and as perceived by others. This socialization process can be an essential mechanism in perpetuating group norms despite other changes that may be occurring in the group.

In addition to these group-based factors that produce the appearance of continuity amid change, there are several cognitive and motivational contributors to this outcome as well. As people encounter groups in complex social contexts, they are exposed to information reflecting both consistency and change. Given people's limited processing capacities, they may not be able to attend to subtle cues indicating change, fostering the appearance of continuity. Moreover, if groups undergo modest change slowly, regularly, and uniformly, those changes (which cumulatively over time may be substantial) may not be sufficiently salient to attract attention, meaning that actual change is not detected.

People may also have expectancies and biases that maintain the appearance of group continuity. As we discussed in Chapter 8, people need to be able to predict events in their world in order to anticipate the behavior of others. Heider (1958) argued that to do so, people identify the "invariances" (continuities) they encounter in others' behaviors. Extending this principle to group perception, people may be predisposed to seek and identify ways that groups remain stable (and hence predictable), thereby overlooking indicators of group change.

In Chandler's (2001) work on the bases for people's beliefs in their own self-continuity, a common way that people justify their continuity is to refer to an inner essence that is continuous and invariant over time. Some authors have argued that people have comparable beliefs about groups, that at least some groups possess an essence that defines the nature of the group (Haslam et al., 2000; Sani, Bowe, & Herrera, 2008; Yzerbyt et al., 1997). If so, then that essence would be unchanging and a basis for believing in a group's continuity over time. Similarly, intuitive beliefs and motives that groups are stable may lead people to reconstruct past events in ways that maintain perceived group homogeneity and persistence across time (Levy, Stroessner, & Dweck, 1998; Ross, 1989).

Finally, membership in groups is closely aligned with group-based motives such as self-esteem (Tajfel & Turner, 1979) and uncertainty reduction (Hogg & Mullin, 1999). To the extent that one's self-identity is derived in part from one's group memberships, then one would be motivated to see those groups as real entities that persist through time (Sani, Todman, & Lunn, 2005; Sherman, Hamilton, & Lewis, 1999).

For all of these reasons, people hold to the appearance of group continuity, even with numerous ongoing changes in those groups. However, despite these forces toward perceiving group continuity, we nevertheless are often aware that groups do change over time. What factors promote the detection of group change?

Perceiving Group Change

Groups can change in a variety of ways that may have differing implications for people's ability to detect such change. Here we discuss some aspects of change and their implications for perceptions of groups.

Although groups are perceived as entities, they are not always seen as *unitary* entities. In Chapter 2, we discussed the fact that differences among members (exemplars) of a category can lead to differentiation in the category structure, establishing subgroups. While still members of the broader category, subsets of members become separately represented. Those subgroups emerge after the observer encounters several exemplars that do not fit well with the overall group prototype. Regarding social categories, subgroups may form in recognition of meaningful differences among different subsets of, say, women, African Americans, political groups, and religious groups.

Sani and colleagues (2005; Sani & Reicher, 1998, 1999; Sani & Todman, 2002) have studied this process in an investigation of a schism that formed in the Church of England, ultimately resulting in the secession of a subgroup from the larger church, triggered by the ordination (for the first time) of female priests (Sani & Reicher 1999). According to Sani's (2005) model, a schism begins when some people believe that emerging changes subvert the group identity (e.g., in policy, ideology). This can lead to negative emotions and decreases in both group identification and perceived entitativity of the group. As these changes progress over time, the intention to initiate a schism increases, resulting in the formation of a distinct subgroup or perhaps a new group utterly distinct from the original.

For those that are involved in this process – both those who remain in the Church and those who leave – it is undoubtedly quite apparent that group change has occurred. However, that change may not be so apparent to those viewing the Church from the outside. From the outsiders' perspective, they see that the religious principles and ideology of the faith remain the same; the sacraments, rituals, and religious holidays observed continue as before, and the church's governance structure has not changed. Thus, depending on the context and extent to which the schism is public, the group change may or may not be apparent for outside observers (Hamilton et al., 2008).

Other factors may influence whether or not group change is detected. For example, basic cognitive-perceptual research on the detection of change indicates that observers are more likely to detect changes in stimuli that involve the addition of new features than the removal of old features (Agostinelli, Sherman, Fazio, & Hearst, 1986). For example, when a man appears with a beard or new glasses, this difference is noticed more than when the man has removed a beard or switched to contact lenses. In the group domain, it may be that, in a group that adopts new appearances, norms, and procedures, change may be more noticeable than in a group that eliminates such features. These differences can affect the perception of group change over time.

> **INTERIM SUMMARY** In this section, we have considered the time dimension and its ramifications for psychological processing. We have discussed differences in conceptions of the past, present, and future. We have reviewed research on the dynamics of perceiving continuity and change between different periods for the self, other persons, and groups. These discussions show that time is a dynamic, not a static, concept.

UNDERSTANDING THE PAST

Being adults, our lives have provided an abundance of experiences. The knowledge of what has happened in our past is an essential repository of our life experiences. That knowledge provides an essential basis for understanding not only those events themselves but also the themes inherent in them. They are important for knowing who we are and for adapting to complex situations. We also can learn from our past experiences. In this section, we consider three different topics, all of which concern aspects of understanding the past. In each case, some biases can potentially limit our ability to benefit from those experiences and can constrain the use of that knowledge to facilitate future performance and adjustment.

As we have seen in the previous chapter, memory can be quite malleable and hence is open to the influence of variables that affect our understanding of and even the reconstruction of our past. We turn now to research that sheds light on how that can happen.

Reconstructing the Past: Implicit Theories of Stability and Change

> Memory is subject to a filtering process that we don't always recognize and can't always control. We remember what we can bear and we block what we cannot. (Grafton, 2015, p. 236)

We often believe that we have a good understanding of "the way we were back then," whether "back then" refers to when we were young children, high school students, or some other earlier era. However, the malleability of memory can influence the conception of our former selves, which in turn can guide our sense of consistency and change over time. In addition, we have intuitive notions of what aspects of our selves are likely to (or should) change over time and which aspects do not (or should not) change. For example, we believe that one's maturity should increase (change) with age, whereas one's native intelligence is a stable property of the person, so it should not change over time. Ross (1989; Ross & McFarland, 1988) calls these notions *implicit theories of stability and change*. These theories of the stability and change of attributes can then bias our recollections of the way we were in the past on any given attribute. The consequence of these biases is that our *memory of the past may be reconstructed* in order to fit with the prescriptions of an intuitive theory.

How does this happen? Ross (1989) has proposed that the long-term recall of personal characteristics is a reconstructive process involving two steps. To judge their prior status on an attribute (e.g., motivation to achieve a particular goal), individuals first assess their present standing on that dimension and then compare that against their prior status on that same attribute. To make this judgment, individuals use their implicit theories regarding the inherent stability of personal attributes and the factors that may produce changes in those characteristics.

If the attribute is one that implies that it could plausibly change over time (due to intervening events), then the person will use an *implicit theory of change* to recall the past, thereby assuming that the present status on that attribute likely differs from the earlier status. In contrast, if the attribute is one that is not expected to change (e.g., intelligence), then an *implicit theory of stability* will be adopted, and the person will assume that the current status on the attribute is similar to one's prior status. From this analysis, the accuracy of people's memory will be a function of the accuracy of the theory being used to recall the past. When the theory does not reflect the degree of change that has taken place over time, systematic biases in memory will occur. In particular, one's reconstruction of the past can be biased to fit with one's theories of stability and change.

These ideas were tested in a study (McFarland, Ross, & Giltrow, 1992) investigating the judgments of older adults regarding changes in psychological and physical attributes over time. The researchers first assessed the beliefs of a group of older adults (mean age = 67) regarding the influence of aging on a variety of dimensions. From these data, they could identify attributes that the sample believed would increase with age (e.g., independence, affection, physical discomforts, emotional intensity), those that would decrease with age (e.g., intellectual quickness, activity, ruggedness), or those they thought would remain stable with age (e.g., political involvement, outgoingness, capability, depression, the importance of attractiveness). Another group of older adults (mean age = 67) were given the same attributes and were asked to indicate their current standing on each and also their standing on each when they were 38 years old. The third group of participants – younger adults (mean age = 38) – indicated their current standing on the same list of attributes. In the absence of longitudinal data, the younger adults' responses served as a proxy for what the older sample was probably like at age 38. The difference between the recall responses of the older adults and the responses of the younger adults constituted a measure of memory bias, and this measure was compared for attributes that (based on the first sample) were expected to increase, to decrease, or to remain stable across the age span.

Results showed that, for attributes expected to increase with age (but that appear to remain stable), older adults recalled that they had a *lower* amount of that trait when they were younger than the younger group possessed; for attributes expected to decrease with age (but appear not to), the older adults recalled themselves as possessing *more* of those attributes than the current younger sample possessed. Similar effects were found for both positive and negative attributes. Thus, people's implicit theories of change guided their recollection of the extent and direction of change over time.

Another study testing this thinking focused on people's implicit theories of menstruation (McFarland, Ross, & DeCourville, 1989). According to widespread beliefs, the onset of menstruation is associated with increases in unpleasant physical and psychological symptoms, including physical pain (e.g., stomach cramps), discomfort due to water retention, and irritability. However, research evidence provides minimal support for these beliefs (Golub & Harrington, 1981; Lahmeyer, Miller, & DeLeon-Jones, 1982; Ruble, 1977; Ruble & Brooks-Gunn, 1979; Slade, 1981, 1984). On average, in comparing responses to daily diary questionnaires collected during versus before menstruation, women reported only minor physical effects and no systematic changes in affective responses (irritability, depression). How can we account for the discrepancy between commonly held beliefs and reality (as manifest in these research findings)? McFarland et al. (1989) reasoned that people's implicit ideas of stability and change could account for these outcomes. When women are menstruating, their ideas of menstrual discomfort may make their premenstrual state seem more positive than it was. In contrast, when not menstruating, these same expectations can lead them to recall their menstrual state as being worse than it was. In both cases, their implicit theories would lead to reconstructions that were discrepant from their actual experiences.

Turning to a different domain, all of us are continually bombarded with promotions for programs aimed at self-improvement. These programs assure us that if we adopt and adhere to them, we can lose weight, quit smoking, or improve study skills. In terms of Ross's (1989) theory, people entering these programs are adopting a theory of change concerning the relevant dimension. That is, the program should result in people having fewer pounds, lower cigarette consumption, or better grades. Unfortunately, most of these programs do not work even though people often report that they did. The paradox, then, is that people believe they are gaining a real benefit even when they are not. How does it happen that they become convinced of their self-improvement? A study by Conway and Ross (1984) showed that adopting an "implicit theory of change" can contribute to this outcome.

College students in a psychology class were offered a limited enrollment study skills program during the course. Half of those who signed up were randomly selected to participate in the course immediately, the other half being placed on a waiting list to take the course later (these participants constituted a control group). The students that had been selected to complete the program then participated in three weekly 1.5-hour sessions, modeled after an actual study skills course offered by another university. The sessions covered several areas, including knowing course requirements, effective listening and note-taking, reading skills, and reviewing materials. In the first session, the students reported their study activities for the preceding week, the amount of time spent studying, and rated their study skills on several scales. At the end of the skills course, they repeated these measures and were also asked to recall the answers they had given on these measures at the beginning of the term (before the skills course began). Students in the control group completed the identical measures at the beginning and the end of the "waiting period" during which they did not have any skills training.

How did the results of these two groups compare? As one would expect, the two groups did not differ in assessments of their study skills taken at the outset, before the study skills course had begun. Later, after the skills training, students who completed the training reported more improvement in study skills and indicated that they expected higher grades on the final exam compared with students in the control group. However, there was no difference in the exam grades received by skills course participants and those of the students on the waiting list. Could the higher expectations of students who completed the skills training reflect an implicit theory of change that they *should* show improvement? Comparisons of the two groups' later recollections of their original study skills indicated that might be the case. Students in the control group accurately recalled their earlier ratings. In contrast, students who had completed the study skills course were biased in recalling their initial ratings in a manner consistent with improvement. Specifically, these students recalled their initial ratings of their study skills as being *weaker than they had actually rated themselves.* As shown in Table 11.4, they achieved apparent improvement by belittling their earlier self-assessment. Their implicit theories of change were confirmed, but their perceived improvement was due to their retrospectively lowering their initial status.

Table 11.4 Mean study skills ratings and later recalled ratings by students in skills program and wait list

| | Skills evaluation | |
Group	Initial	Recall
Skills program	0.11	- 0.19
Wait list	0.01	0.10

Source: Adapted from Conway & Ross (1984)

Over time, people change in certain ways, and, in other ways, they remain the same. Also, people have intuitive theories about when and how those changes occur. This research shows that those theories can influence people's memory for "the way they were" by reconstructing the past to make it fit with their intuitive ideas about stability and change. Those theories and their influence on reconstructive memory reflect a combination of people's cognitive beliefs about attributes that are and are not likely to change and their motives to maintain a sense of stability or to "see" change over time. The interplay between real versus apparent stability or change creates interesting complexities in the ways people come to understand their past and judge their present.

Hindsight Bias

We understand the past by retrieving information from memory about the people and events that comprise our history. As we have seen, those memories are not always accurate portrayals of that past. Our retrieval is selective and incomplete, and the memories we recall can be biased by expectancies and by current motives. Our memories may be reconstructed, distorted to conform to our current beliefs or to fit with what we *want* to remember rather than what actually transpired. In this section, we consider another bias influencing our understanding of events in which our present knowledge sways our judgments of the past.

To illustrate this bias, think back to an election in which an incumbent Senator was in a close race against a political newcomer. Now think back to six months before this election. What would you have predicted? Now that you know the results of that election, can you retrieve your pre-election beliefs about how the election would play out? If the incumbent won, you might remember feeling, "Just what I expected. Incumbents have a big advantage." If the newcomer won, you might remember thinking, "I thought so. That new person was coming on strong at the end." Research has shown that once we know the outcome of some event, we believe that it was likely to happen. As we recollect, we overestimate the probability of that now-known outcome. It is as if we "knew it all along." This is known as the *hindsight bias*.

Fischhoff (1975) provided the first demonstration of this bias. Participants read a passage describing events involving a war in 1814 between British troops in India and the Gurkas in Nepal (an actual historical event, but one that few readers would know of). One group of participants read a version of the passage that omitted information on the outcome of the war. Four other groups were told (through additions to the passage) that there was (a) a British victory, (b) a Gurka victory, (c) a military stalemate with no peace settlement, or (d) a military stalemate with a peace settlement. After reading the passage, all participants were given those four alternative outcomes and asked to estimate the likelihood of each. The results are shown in Table 11.5. Compared with the baseline group that received no outcome information, participants who learned of an outcome estimated that result as having been more likely. The hindsight bias occurred even when people were asked to estimate the likelihood of each outcome as they would have had they not known the result. The fact that the same overestimation occurred under this condition indicates that people are not aware of the effect that knowledge has on their estimates.

Table 11.5   Mean probabilities assigned to each outcome

| | | Outcome evaluated | | | |
| | | British victory | Gurka victory | No peace | Peace settlement |
Group	Provided	(BV)	(GV)	(NPS)	(PS)
Foresight	None	33.8	21.3	32.3	12.3
Hindsight	BV	57.2	14.3	15.3	13.4
Hindsight	GV	30.3	38.4	20.4	10.5
Hindsight	NPS	25.7	17.0	48.0	9.9
Hindsight	PS	33.0	15.8	24.3	27.0

Source: Adapted from Fischhoff (1975)

Moreover, outcome knowledge can even affect participants' recollections of their prior estimates (Fischhoff & Beyth, 1975). Before an important event (President Nixon's historic trip to China in 1972), participants were asked to estimate the probabilities of various outcomes of that trip (e.g., that Nixon would meet with Chairman Mao, that the United States would establish a diplomatic mission in China). Two weeks after the trip, they were asked to recall as accurately as they could the probabilities they had given earlier for each of these outcomes. The probabilities that participants recalled having made previously were biased by their knowledge of what had occurred. That is, they recalled having given higher probabilities than they had for events that they now knew had happened, and they recalled having given lower probabilities for events they now knew had not happened. In other words, their *remembered* predictions were more accurate than were their *actual* predictions. This is why the hindsight bias is sometimes called the *I knew it all along effect* (Fischhoff & Beyth, 1975; Wood, 1978).

The hindsight bias is a general phenomenon not limited to estimates regarding historical events, as originally studied in Fischhoff's groundbreaking work (Fischhoff, 1975; Fischhoff & Beyth, 1975). In fact, hindsight bias is quite common and robust (Hawkins & Hastie, 1990; Roese & Vohs, 2012). It has been demonstrated in studies using diverse populations, ranging from college students to physicians, judges, neuropsychologists, surgeons, anesthesiologists, and members of the general public. It has been found to occur in children under 10 years old and in adults over age 60 (Bayen, Pohl, Erdfelder, & Auer, 2007; Birch & Bernstein, 2007). We illustrate this robustness with examples from three consequential domains of life.

Political Judgments

As we discussed in an earlier example, after an election we often have the feeling that "I was pretty sure he would win." Research has shown, however, that such feelings can reflect a hindsight effect. In one study demonstrating this point (Leary, 1982), either the day before or the day after the 1980 presidential election participants were asked to indicate the percentage of the popular vote they thought each candidate would receive (the "after" group was asked what percentage they would have predicted had they been asked before the election). Those who knew the election outcome (the day after group) predicted an outcome closer to the actual result than did those who made their predictions the day before the election. Knowledge of the outcome led to higher "foresight" estimates than actual estimates made by the "before" group. These findings have been replicated in several other studies of election outcomes using different designs and procedures (Blank, Fischer, & Erdfelder, 2003; Tykocinski, 2001).

Legal Judgments

A second area where the hindsight bias can have insidious effects is in legal judgments (Harley, 2007). In most legal cases, the outcome (a person was assaulted; a bank was robbed) is already known; it is the reason there is even a legal question (guilt, negligence, liability) to be decided. Can that "knowledge of the outcome" influence legal decision making? When police search, say, someone's residence, the precondition of *probable cause* must be met before the search. Would knowledge of whether a search produced the expected evidence affect the judged legitimacy of that search? In one study examining this question (Casper, Benedict, & Kelly, 1988), mock jurors heard arguments from a civil suit in which police were charged with searching a person's apartment without probable cause. The search either had uncovered evidence of illegal drug activity or no incriminating evidence was found. This outcome information influenced the jurors' judgments of the liability of the police officers. In another study (LaBine & LaBine, 1996), participants read about a potentially dangerous mental patient, who then either did or did not become violent. Information about the treatment of the patient indicated that the therapist had provided reasonable and appropriate care. However, participants were asked to judge whether the therapist had been negligent in that treatment. Respondents who learned that the patient later became violent rated that violence as more foreseeable and judged the therapist more negligent than did those in the no violence condition. Similar results demonstrating hindsight effects on judgments of negligence and liability have been reported in other studies (Carli, 1999; Hastie, Schkade, & Payne, 1999; Kamin & Rachlinski, 1995).

Medical Judgments

A third important domain where hindsight effects have been shown is in medical decision making (Arkes, 2013). In one such study (Arkes, Wortmann, Saville, & Harkness, 1981), physicians read an actual case history of a patient with symptoms consistent with four plausible diagnoses. The case history either did or did not include a statement indicating the eventual clinical judgment in the case (i.e., the diagnosis). The participants' task was to indicate the probability of each diagnosis "you would have assigned had you been making the diagnosis." Again, outcome information influenced physicians' judgments: hindsight subjects gave a higher probability that they would have made the diagnosis indicated in the case history.

Now consider the following situation, which is a standard educational procedure in many hospitals. A young physician is given documentation on a case (usually a difficult one), who then studies it, presents it to the medical staff, considers possible diagnoses, and then indicates his or her view of the correct one. The doctor who worked on the case then announces the diagnosis that should have been made and why. Dawson, Arkes, Siciliano, Blinkhorn, Lakshmanan, and Petrelli (1988) studied this process by interrupting the presentations to assess the judgments of two groups of physicians as they heard the case. After the presenter listed possible diagnoses, half of the participants were asked to assign a probability to each one; then, after the doctor announced the actual diagnosis, the other half were asked to assign these probabilities "the way you would have had you been making the initial diagnosis" (i.e., without knowing the actual diagnosis). Comparing judgments of these two groups indicated that hindsight (after) participants estimated higher probabilities that they would have chosen the correct diagnosis than did the foresight (before) group. In essence, the hindsight group mistakenly felt that the diagnostic task was more straightforward than it was (as indicated by the poorer predictions of the foresight group). This study illustrates a consequence of the hindsight bias that is, at minimum, disturbing. By overestimating the likelihood that they would have made the correct diagnosis, physicians inappropriately felt they made the correct decision, reducing the ability to learn from this educational exercise. Thus, the hindsight bias can undermine the potential educational benefit of one's experience (Arkes, Faust, Guilmette, & Hart, 1988).

Explaining Hindsight Bias

In sum, research has demonstrated that knowing the outcome of an event can influence how we understand what has happened. In the hindsight effect, the prior perceived likelihood of an event is altered by knowledge of the outcome. Why and how does it happen? What processes produce this bias? Several mechanisms have been suggested as playing an important role (Hawkins & Hastie, 1990; Roese & Vohs, 2012), which we summarize in this section.

Recollection

One possibility is that, in making judgments after learning the outcome information, people attempt to recall their earlier predictions as a basis for their later judgments (Erdfelder, Brandt, & Bröder, 2007). If one's earlier prediction is recalled, then no hindsight effect (overestimation) would occur. Under many conditions, however, recall of the earlier prediction is not easy, and in fact, knowledge of the outcome could reduce the likelihood of effective recall. In that case, other processes can bias one's recollection in the direction of the outcome knowledge, leading to a hindsight effect.

Assimilation

Fischhoff (1975) proposed that people integrate the new outcome knowledge into what they already know about the event described earlier. They attempt to make sense of all that they have learned, creating a coherent whole or integrated story of the incident in question. This assimilation of new information into existing memory structures reflects the reconstructive nature of memory (Blank & Nestler, 2007). Such integration can be accomplished by creating and activating semantic links between the outcome and more general knowledge representations. In this way, new information strengthens links to information in memory compatible with it, including with the outcome information, making that information more accessible. Thus, the hindsight bias can involve a cognitive reconstruction, that is, a rewriting of the events leading up to the outcome in such a way as to make the outcome seem more plausible. This, in turn, can lead to a higher likelihood estimate of the outcome than what was rendered before knowing the outcome.

This reconstruction can include not only representations of factual information but also beliefs that are stereotypically (and often erroneously) associated with the outcome. In one study (Carli, 1999), participants read a story about a date where, after drinks and dancing at a club, the man then invited the woman to his home, saying he "wanted to stop by his apartment before taking her home." The passage either ended at that point (serving as a control passage) or indicated that that man raped the woman in his apartment. The story had included several aspects that (based on pretesting) people stereotypically associate with incidents of acquaintance rape (e.g., drinking was involved, the woman had dressed in a manner to please her date). After reading the passage, participants were asked to estimate the likelihood of three endings to the story (i.e., the man raped the woman, took her home, or proposed marriage) as if they did not know how the date had ended. Their memory for facts in the story was also assessed. The results revealed a hindsight effect in that participants who had read the passage describing the date ending in rape were more likely to have expected that tragic outcome compared with those who read the control passage. Participants' memory for aspects in the story associated with date rape predicted the hindsight bias. In other words, if the participants knew that the woman had been assaulted, they were more likely to recall particulars from the story that people stereotypically associate with acquaintance rape. This study illustrates one of the potentially damaging consequences of hindsight bias, increasing blame to innocent individuals once their status as victims is known.

Causal Relations

An essential element in the reconstruction process is the role of causal relations. In the typical hindsight study, participants first read a passage about an event and then are asked the likelihood of various possible outcomes (e.g., Fischhoff's classic study describing the British–Gurka war). Participants not only assimilate the outcome to the earlier knowledge they learned and reconstruct the past in light of this new information, but they also seek to establish causal relations between aspects of the case information and the eventual outcome. In one study (Wasserman, Lempert, & Hastie, 1991), participants read the British–Gurka war scenario with slight modification. The outcome alternatives presented in the hindsight condition included a brief phrase that made that outcome (e.g., British victory) seem due to a chance condition (the result of an unexpected monsoon), due to a causally determining factor (discipline of the British troops), or simply described the outcome without explanatory comment. When no causal information was presented, 43% of the participants predicted a British victory, whereas 40% who were given the chance (monsoon) explanation also predicted that victory. In contrast, 57% of those given the deterministic information (disciplined troops) estimated British victory. Thus, the hindsight effect (higher prediction of known outcome) occurred when the information included a causal explanation for the outcome, but not when it appeared due to chance conditions.

Undermining Hindsight Bias

The hindsight bias is pervasive, occurring in many contexts. It can influence both our recollection of what transpired and our reconstruction of what we learned had happened, including what caused the event to occur as it did. It is a bias that can potentially have detrimental effects on judgments and decision making and can undermine new learning. Given these adverse consequences, it becomes crucial to determine how hindsight bias can be diminished or eliminated. Several strategies for *debiasing* (Arkes, 1981; Fischhoff, 1982; Roese & Vohs, 2012) have been studied. Here we highlight two of them, one that has received surprisingly little empirical support and another that has proven to be more effective.

Forewarning

One possibility is that if people were aware of or informed about the hindsight effect, they would be able to avoid its occurrence in their own judgments. This would be particularly useful in legal settings in which jurors and judges typically know the outcome of the crucial incident. It is common for judges to instruct jurors not to be influenced by later knowledge in determining what occurred and why. Several studies have tested this idea, with very mixed results. Two experiments

(Kamin & Rachlinski, 1995; Smith & Greene, 2005) found that such debiasing instructions did not reduce the hindsight effect, whereas two other studies (Clarkson, Emby, & Watt, 2002; Stallard & Worthington, 1998) reported partial reduction (but not elimination) of hindsight bias. As a whole, the results of these studies indicate that forewarning is not always effective.

Considering Alternative Outcomes

To date, the most encouraging findings have come from studies in which, before making hindsight judgments, participants are required to consider alternative outcomes and how they might have come about. For example, in a medical context Arkes et al. (1988) had physicians in a foresight condition read a case history and estimate the probability of three diagnoses. In contrast, those in hindsight conditions were told that one of the diagnoses was correct and were asked to indicate the probability they would have given to each alternative if they were making the original diagnosis. Before making their judgments, half of the participants in each group had to provide one reason why each of the diagnoses may be correct. The results are shown in Table 11.6. In the No Reasons condition, the outcome provided in the case history was, in hindsight, assigned a higher probability than the other diagnoses (the typical hindsight effect). In the Reasons condition, this effect was eliminated. Several other studies have shown that having participants address alternative outcomes either significantly reduced or eliminated the hindsight bias (Anderson, Jennings, Lowe, & Reckers, 1997; Davies, 1987; Herzog & Hertwig, 2009; Hirt & Markman, 1995; Lowe & Reckers, 1994; Mussweiler, Strack, & Pfeiffer, 2000). Why? Learning the outcome focuses one's attention on that fact and, as noted earlier, strengthens associations with other outcome-consistent information in the information initially presented. In contrast, considering alternative outcomes stimulates thinking about other, novel means by which the same outcome might have occurred. In all likelihood, it also generates causal thinking about how those alternatives might occur. The consequence is that the hindsight effect is significantly diminished.

Table 11.6 Mean probabilities assigned to each diagnosis as a function of outcome provided and reasons condition

		Outcome evaluated		
		Alcohol withdrawal	Alzheimer's disease	Brain damage
Group	Provided	(AW)	(AD)	(BD)
No reasons				
Foresight	None	.37	.26	.37
Hindsight	AW	.44	.24	.33
Hindsight	AD	.27	.34	.38
Hindsight	BD	.22	.28	.50
Reasons				
Foresight	None	.33	.32	.34
Hindsight	AW	.29	.34	.36
Hindsight	AD	.22	.39	.39
Hindsight	BD	.22	.38	.39

Source: Adapted from Arkes et al. (1988)

Counterfactual Reasoning

Consider the following incident:

> Mr. Crane and Mr. Tees were scheduled to leave the airport on different flights at the same time. They traveled from town in the same limousine, were caught in

a traffic jam, and arrived at the airport 30 minutes after the scheduled departure time of their flights.

    Mr. Crane is told that his flight left on time.

    Mr. Tees is told that his flight was delayed, and just left five minutes ago.

    Who is more upset, Mr. Crane or Mr. Tees?

Assuming that you are like the vast majority of people who have responded to this question, you believe that Mr. Tees would be more upset. Why, logically, would either person be more upset? The situation is precisely the same for both men. They both have missed their flights, and because of the traffic jam, they both knew they would not get to the airport by the scheduled departure time. They both expected to miss their flights. Why, then, do people generally believe that they would have different emotional reactions to their plight?

The scenario of Mr. Crane and Mr. Tees was used by Kahneman and Tversky (1982) to illustrate a phenomenon people frequently experience in many aspects of their lives. We can understand the difference between Mr. Crane's and Mr. Tees's reactions only by recognizing that they have created different simulations of what might have been, and how things might have been different so that they would have been able to make their flights. For example, they might have left a little earlier, or they would not have been in a traffic jam if they had taken an alternate route. However, it is a lot easier to imagine differences that would have saved 5 versus 30 minutes. Hence, Mr. Tees's simulation (missing flight by 5 minutes) is a lot closer to the experienced reality than is that of Mr. Crane (30 minutes). Given that "closeness," we expect that Mr. Tees would experience more disappointment.

This process of undoing the past and imagining a different sequence of events leading up to a specific outcome is called *counterfactual reasoning*. It involves constructing an alternative reality, one that did not happen, one that is "counter to fact." Similar to the topics already discussed in this chapter, it consists of reconstructing the past. To understand counterfactual reasoning, we need to be able to answer several questions. First, *when* do people construct counterfactuals? They certainly do not do it all the time. What triggers the process? Second, *how* are counterfactuals constructed? They are not random thoughts. There must be rules that guide the process in order to create a compelling alternative version of reality. Third, *why* do people do it? A counterfactual involves generating an alternative sequence of events that would have led to a different outcome. However, that outcome has already happened; it is in the past. Why expend the mental energy to create a different world that would have produced a different outcome? What function does it serve? What benefits does it provide? Answering these questions is a massive and significant undertaking, and there is a large body of research examining counterfactuals (Byrne, 2016; Epstude & Roese, 2008; Kahneman & Miller, 1986; Kahneman & Tversky, 1982; Roese, 1997). What have we learned about counterfactuals from this research?

When Do People Construct Counterfactuals?

Counterfactual thoughts typically occur when unexpected (compared to typical) outcomes occur or when goals are fettered. (Interestingly, these are some of the same conditions that prompt creation of causal attributions, as we discussed in Chapter 8.) Counterfactuals are mental representations of an alternative sequence of events that would have resulted in a different outcome, and they are created to aid in understanding surprising and stymied events. They are thoughts of "what might have been" and usually take the form of "If only I had…" thoughts

("If only I'd studied more, I would've gotten a better grade." "If I'd taken a different route, I wouldn't be stuck in this horrible traffic."). The process, therefore, involves a comparison of an imagined reality with the actual state of affairs in situations where something unusual or undesirable has occurred.

How Do People Construct Counterfactuals?

People develop representations or mental models of events, including the actual event that has happened (Miller, Turnbull, & McFarland, 1990). The process of generating a counterfactual alternative is driven by the *simulation heuristic* (Kahneman & Tversky, 1982) in which the elements of the mental model of the event and what led up to it are considered. In creating a simulation, some of the elements of an event are altered in ways that would change the outcome. These changes are called *mutations*, and they can be achieved by *undoing* an old element that happened (instead of going to a party with friends, I could have used that time to prepare for the exam) or by *inserting* a new element into the counterfactual (the test was easier than I anticipated).

Outcomes vary in the ease or difficulty of generating counterfactual alternatives that would alter the outcome. The typical goal is to mentally alter some element that led up to a negative outcome (causing negative affect) such that the imagined outcome would be an improvement on the actual reality. Norm theory (Kahneman & Miller, 1986) emphasized the desire to maintain "normalcy," so any condition that was "abnormal" would be a likely target of change in generating a counterfactual. For example, deviating from routine (taking an alternate route home) could be regarded as an abnormal condition and, therefore, the likely focus of mutation in a counterfactual. Events that can easily be imagined differently suggest that they are abnormal; the "easily-imagined alternatives" are easily imagined precisely because they are more typical or routine. Returning to "normalcy" would, therefore, inspire mutations of those abnormal conditions.

Because some elements in the mental model are easier to change (are more mutable) than others, the process of generating a counterfactual focuses on elements that are seen as most mutable (Miller et al., 1990). For example:

- An *unusual element* is more likely to be changed than a common element (Gavanski & Wells, 1989). For example, suppose that when she leaves work, Mandy decides to take a scenic route home, even though it takes longer than her regular route. During her drive, she was hit by a truck that ignored a Stop sign, causing considerable injury and damage. In generating a counterfactual, most people would highlight the fact that she used an atypical route and that the accident would likely not have occurred had she followed her usual route home.

- The *distance* (temporal, physical) between the negative outcome and the imagined alternative also affects the counterfactual process (Macrae, Milne, & Griffiths, 1993; Miller & McFarland, 1986). In the example that opened this section of the chapter (Kahneman & Tversky, 1982), Mr. Tees missed his flight by 5 minutes, whereas Mr. Crane had missed his flight by 30 minutes. For Mr. Tees, the "temporal distance" (5 minutes) was smaller than that for Mr. Crane, and hence we think he was more upset. Why? It is easier to construct alternatives in which 5 minutes would have been saved than 30 minutes. Similarly, geographical distance can influence responses. In one study (Miller & McFarland, 1986), participants read about a man who died after a small plane he was in crashed in a remote location. He was injured in the crash but tried to walk to safety. In one condition, he was described as having died when he was 75 miles from the nearest town; in the other condition, he died when he was only ¼ mile from the town. The participants' task was to assign compensation to the victim's family. Although the two versions were otherwise identical, higher compensation was assigned in the ¼-mile condition than in the 75-mile condition. When the negative outcome was almost avoided, the reaction was more robust, resulting in this case in higher compensation.

- Counterfactuals are more likely to involve mutations of *actions* than *inactions* (Feldman & Albarracín, 2017; Kahneman & Tversky, 1982; Landman, 1987). In one study (Kahneman & Tversky, 1982), one man was described as switching invested funds from one stock to another (action), which then lost money. In contrast, a second man considered switching money but did not do so (inaction) and lost an equivalent amount of money. Participants judged that the first man (who had acted) felt more regret than the second man.

- Counterfactuals are likely to change an element that is *controllable* rather than something outside the control of the actor. For example, if Mr. Tees had left his office 10 minutes earlier (a controllable act), he would have arrived at the airport in time for his flight, whereas the fact that there was road construction (not a controllable event) would be less likely to be changed. This point was also dramatically shown in a study concerned with bereaved persons whose spouse or child had been killed in a car accident (Davis, Lehman, Wortman, Silver, & Thompson, 1995). When interviewed several years later, a high percentage of the bereaved still had counterfactual "If only…" thoughts about the event. Remarkably, those counterfactuals always focused on what the bereaved person or the accident victim could have done differently. There was not one case in which the interviewee mentioned thinking of what the other driver (who usually had been negligent) might have done differently.

What Consequences Follow from Counterfactual Thinking?

These comparisons between the real and the imagined often have evaluative overtones (Gleicher, Kost, Baker, Strathman, Richman, & Sherman, 1990; Landman, 1987; Stanley, Parikh, Stewart, & De Brigard, 2017), as the constructed alternative is either better or worse than the actual event. Markman, Gavanski, Sherman, and McMullen (1993; see also Smith, 2000) have differentiated upward counterfactuals from downward counterfactuals regarding the emotional reactions they induce. In *upward counterfactuals*, one compares the current outcome to an alternative that improves on the current outcome (as typified in "If only I'd…" thinking). In *downward counterfactuals*, the comparison is with some worse alternative, producing "At least I didn't…" thinking). These different counterfactuals produce divergent emotional reactions. Upward counterfactuals ("If only I'd…") commonly generate regret, sadness, or disappointment, whereas downward counterfactuals ("At least I didn't…") can produce a feeling of relative well-being and a sense of relief (Landman, 1987; Sweeny & Vohs, 2012).

The effects of generating counterfactuals extend beyond the alleviation of negative affect; they also influence social judgments and behavior (Macrae, 1992; Macrae & Milne, 1992; Macrae et al., 1993; Miller & McFarland, 1986). In one study (Macrae et al., 1993), participants read a vignette about Mike, who, after being at a bar with friends, walked home via either his usual route or a new route. While walking, Mike was mugged, and the mugger was later apprehended and charged. Participants rated the seriousness of the crime, the severity of punishment they recommended for the mugger, and their sympathy for the victim. Harsher judgments were made on all three measures when the incident was preceded by the unusual circumstance than the routine circumstance. Specifically, participants considered the incident to be more serious, endorsed stiffer punishments for the mugger, and reported more considerable sympathy for the victim when Mike was mugged on his atypical route. Similarly, another study (Miller & McFarland, 1986) found that participants recommended higher financial compensation for the victim of a crime when the description of the crime was preceded by abnormal rather than by routine circumstances.

Functions and Benefits of Counterfactual Thinking

We have defined counterfactual reasoning and have illustrated it with many examples and research outcomes. To more fully understand these effects, we need a broader conceptual account of these dynamics. One theoretical framework for understanding counterfactual thinking is known as norm theory (Kahneman & Miller, 1986), which emphasizes the role of mental simulation as a critical component in the production and functioning of counterfactuals. Comparing a simulated mental model against an actual event can reveal places that could be altered in a relatively straightforward manner to change the outcome (e.g., "…if only Mike had taken his normal route home, he wouldn't have been mugged"). This simulation heuristic approach resembles the *heuristics* tradition (availability, representativeness) discussed earlier (Chapter 9) in which a "quick and easy" approach is adopted in preference to a more thorough, detailed, and time-consuming analysis. Like those heuristics, using simulations to generate counterfactuals can be useful and efficient but can also be subject to bias and, therefore, may result in biased judgments (Epstude & Roese, 2008).

Another conceptual approach to counterfactual thinking emphasizes its functional properties (Epstude & Roese, 2008; Roese, 1997). In this view, counterfactual thinking is triggered by an unexpected outcome, typically a negative experience, that produces negative affect. Counterfactuals are generated to create different antecedents that would have changed the outcome and avoided the subsequent negative affect. Although one can imagine counterfactual thoughts occurring after a positive outcome ("What a pleasant surprise! What exactly produced that great outcome?") in hopes of increasing the likelihood of its recurrence, research has clearly shown that counterfactual thinking is much more likely to occur in response to adverse outcomes. In this view, the negative affect one experiences serves as a signal to the person that there is some problem or threat that needs to be confronted and addressed. If Paul tends to talk about himself all the time, he may experience social rejection from others, resulting in him feeling bad. In a counterfactual analysis, he may "undo" his self-focused behavior and replace it with more considerable attention to and interest in others, which might alter the outcome.

In this way, Roese (1997) argues, people can learn from their negative outcomes. Although the past cannot be changed, the benefit of performing a counterfactual analysis is that it can provide insights into what should have been done instead of what actually was done. It, therefore, can suggest more appropriate behaviors and strategies for solving problems. When similar circumstances occur in the future, the counterfactual reconstructions of the past event may provide guidelines for improvement in subsequent performance and lead to more satisfactory outcomes. It is in this way that counterfactual thinking can be highly functional. "Thoughts of what might have been may suggest paths to what might yet be…Short-term negative affect may be offset by inferential benefits that may aid the individual on a longer term basis" (Roese 1997, p. 133).

The benefits of counterfactual thinking may extend well beyond these outcome-specific functions. Consider the mental processes involved in counterfactual analysis. In generating counterfactuals, people examine the various elements of what actually happened and consider numerous alternative possibilities (mutations) that might be substituted. Essentially, this involves generating a causal chain of events in a sequence and identifying an element to mutate in order to alter the outcome. This then creates the counterfactual. The process inherently involves a comparison between reality and an alternative reality of what might have been. In this way, many associations are formed among these elements and their alternatives, including causal associations between events. This has been called a *relational processing style* (Kray, Galinsky, & Wong, 2006) that is set in motion by counterfactual thinking, and it can be a useful means for understanding interconnections between seemingly independent concepts and events.

For example, in several studies some participants have been given a task that would induce counterfactual thinking (e.g., reading a scenario about a person who experiences a negative outcome) and then asked to list the thoughts going through that person's mind (which included counterfactual thoughts); other participants were not induced into this kind of thinking. All participants then completed difficult tasks measuring analytic reasoning, which included identifying relations among concepts, understanding and applying rules, and drawing logical conclusions about complex situations. Those in whom counterfactual thinking had been induced performed better on the analytic reasoning task and other problems requiring relational processing. Thus, considering alternative possibilities in reconstructing an event that has happened – the act of counterfactual thinking – can induce a processing style that facilitates making associations and connections between diverse stimuli (Kray et al., 2006).

Expanding on that conclusion can give it new significance. Seeing new relations between stimuli, between different experiences, between different persons, between different aspects of one's self – all of them broaden one's perspectives and serve to integrate disparate, previously unconnected realms. Making those connections and seeing those relationships can bring new understanding, can offer new cohesion, and can add meaning to one's experience. This suggests that counterfactual reasoning might lead people to see more meaning and value in their choices and actions. This possibility was the focus of a study (Kray, George, Liljenquist, Galinsky, Tetlock, & Roese, 2010) in which students were instructed to think about their decision in choosing a college and how they made that decision. Half of them (counterfactual condition) were then asked to describe all the ways it could have turned out differently; the other half (baseline condition) were not induced to think about those questions. Both groups then completed questions assessing how meaningful their college choice had been ("…has added meaning to my life"; "…defines who I am"; "…has been one of the most significant choices of my life"). Those who had engaged in counterfactual thought rated their college decision as more meaningful than did those in the baseline condition. A parallel study focused people's attention on a close friend. Half of the participants (counterfactual condition) described ways that things "could have turned out differently," whereas those in the factual condition provided a detailed description of how things actually progressed. Again, those in the counterfactual condition rated the relationship as significantly more meaningful than those in the factual condition.

Finally, Kray et al. (2010) recognized that there are turning points in every life, major life transitions that mark milestones along the highway of one's personal history. Turning points may be significant events that are positive in valence (one's wedding, achieving an important goal, starting a great new job) or negative in valence (loss of a loved one, financial setback, personal tragedy). In either case, they seem likely to be times when people "take stock" and consider alternative courses that might have resulted in a different outcome. That is, they may be natural triggers for counterfactual reasoning and hence may be viewed as adding meaning to one's life.

In addition, the authors proposed that counterfactual thinking can strengthen beliefs about these transition points, creating the sense that the event that occurred was inevitable. In other words, the outcome that inspired counterfactual thinking might produce thoughts not only of "what might have been" but also the view that the event "was meant to be." This generates a sense that the event was destined to happen, that the course of events could not have occurred any other way, such that the outcome was inevitable. Why would people come to this conclusion? First, counterfactual thinking (particularly when alternatives are difficult to generate) can enhance the sense that "it always seemed likely to happen." In other words, it increases the hindsight bias. Second, when counterfactuals are easy to generate, there are many reasonable alternatives for how something different might have happened instead of the actual event. In that case, any single alternative (counterfactual) becomes a statistically unlikely outcome. Recognizing this improbability of any single event can make the actual event seem that it was inevitable. That is, something that is so improbable (because of numerous easily-generated alternatives) could not have happened by chance alone, so it must have been due to fate.

To test these ideas Kray et al. (2010) had participants identify and write about a turning point in their life (which they defined as "an episode in which rapid, intense, and clear change occurs, such that the person and his or her life is never the same again"). Half of the participants (counterfactual condition) then had to describe how their lives would now be different if the turning point event had not occurred, and the other half (factual condition) had to describe exactly what happened in that event. Later all participants rated the extent to which the turning point was a product of fate. Consistent with the above reasoning, those who had engaged in counterfactual reflection perceived the event as due to fate significantly more than did those in the factual condition.

Extending this reasoning further, Buffone, Gabriel, and Poulin (2016) proposed that under some conditions, counterfactual thinking can increase people's belief that God plays a role in their lives. They predicted this should occur particularly from downward counterfactuals when people try to generate alternatives for some adverse outcomes. In making sense of this outcome by considering how it might have been otherwise, people may discover an unexpected positive outcome and, in doing so, focus on the influence of a benevolent God. In their study, participants wrote about a significant adverse event they had experienced. Some participants then wrote about how life would have been worse if the event had not happened (downward counterfactuals), and others simply wrote a detailed description of the event (factual condition). All participants then completed measures of religious faith. Those who had written downward counterfactuals rated themselves higher on the religiosity measures than did people who wrote detailed descriptions of the event.

In summary, research on counterfactual reasoning has advanced considerably over the last decades. Initially, counterfactuals were seen merely as a response to a negative outcome that provided a means of coping with the resulting negative affect. Through generating alternative sequences of events that would have produced a more favorable outcome, the person would come to understand (through the simulation heuristic) causal relations that produced the actual outcome and a means to produce a better one. Later research focused on the functional value of counterfactual thinking, showing that such analysis can increase our preparation for similar situations in the future and thereby increase the likelihood of better outcomes. In other words, it provides a learning experience. More recent work has shown that the very act of counterfactual thinking itself can increase mental associations among the elements of both the actual event and of various counterfactual alternatives. These associations can broaden people's understanding of events and increase their meaning for one's life. Finally, when faced with significant turning points in life, counterfactual thinking may lead people to believe that an event may have been destined to occur, and therefore to increase one's belief that fate or other external forces (deity, supernatural powers) may have played a role in the critical event, even increasing one's religious beliefs.

INTERIM SUMMARY The three topics we have covered in this section – reconstructive memory, hindsight bias, and counterfactual thinking – have all focused on looking back, in one way or another, at events that occurred in the past. The value of thinking about the past goes beyond the pleasure people often experience when they reminisce. Instead, each line of research shows a way in which looking back can be functional. This is the reason we call this portion of the chapter "understanding the past." Such understanding goes beyond merely "knowing" the past but includes benefitting from understanding it, even though some of that understanding may include biased reasoning. Each of these ways of understanding the past helps people prepare for and adapt to the future.

We have seen that knowledge of the past is quite malleable and can be construed in a biased manner, often using the past in service of current needs and goals. Psychological conceptions of the future are also malleable and subject to influence by several variables. We turn now to a consideration of ways in which people anticipate the future, and indeed, even shape the future they will encounter.

ANTICIPATING THE FUTURE

> All brains are, in essence, anticipation machines. (Dennett, 1992)

The opening paragraph of this chapter delineated the variety of ways that information is processed, elaborated, and used as it is encountered. These processes have been the foci of the chapters comprising this book: attention, interpretation, inference, attribution, judgment, retrieval. We have emphasized the ways these processes help the person cope with the enormity of information that is encountered in everyday life. However, all of those processes also serve one larger purpose: to be better prepared to anticipate the future.

Although all these processes are useful for facing an unknown future, they all are subject to biases that can undermine accurate anticipation. Sometimes people are good at anticipating that future, and other times they are not. Sometimes our expectancies can actually play a causal role in creating future experiences. In this section, we present research that illustrates aspects of how we anticipate the future.

Affective Forecasting

All of us have experienced significant events or outcomes that, as soon as they occur, we know are "life-changers." Sometimes something genuinely wonderful happens that seems sure to make life better for a long time. Perhaps, for example, you have been accepted (with a scholarship!) by your first choice of college, which means you will receive the education you need for a successful life and career. Or your true love says "Yes" to your marriage proposal, so you'll be able to spend your lives together. When events like these occur, long-term happiness seems guaranteed. At other times we are confronted with tragedies that hit at the very core of our being. A parent, family member, or close friend dies unexpectedly, long before his or her time. A fire or a massive storm destroys your home. You are left feeling a devastating loss, wondering if you will ever recover from the experience. Whether the events that cause these reactions are positive or negative, it seems clear to you that your life will never be the same.

Knowing precisely what the future will be like is impossible. It is, after all, the future – it has not happened yet, so there is inherent uncertainty about what it will be. To expect that our future affective states, and their implications for our lives in general, will continue to be colored by our current feelings and emotions would be risky. Nevertheless, that is what we tend to do. Research on *affective forecasting* (Wilson & Gilbert, 2003, 2005) has shown that people overestimate the intensity and duration of their emotional reactions to events, not only significant life-changing outcomes (e.g., long-term effects on happiness of young faculty who did or did not achieve tenure; Gilbert, Pinel, Wilson, Blumberg, & Wheatley, 1998) but also to less extreme outcomes (e.g., how pleased or displeased students are with the dormitory rooms to which they were randomly assigned; Dunn, Wilson, & Gilbert, 2003). This is known as the *durability bias* or *impact bias* (Gilbert et al., 1998; Gilbert, Driver-Linn, & Wilson, 2002; Wilson, Wheatley, Meyers, Gilbert, & Axsom, 2000) and it has been demonstrated to occur in a variety of contexts (Wilson & Gilbert, 2003). Why would this bias occur? Several factors contribute to its occurrence.

Focalism

One cause of the durability bias is people's natural tendency to overestimate the extent to which they will continue to think about the emotion-arousing event or outcome in the future. This *focalism* results in a failure to consider other factors that might influence their affective states in the future. As time passes, many other events undoubtedly will occur that will influence one's emotional states. Those events – many of them trivial, some of them substantial – will generate their own affective reactions, and those experiences will reshape current feelings. These intervening events distract one's attention from the causal event and therefore diminish the continuing impact of the affect-defining outcome. Because these intervening events are in the future, we are not cognizant of them or of what their role will be in (re)shaping affective experience. The consequence is that our affective forecasting is biased in the direction of the durability bias.

Sensemaking

Dramatic, life-altering events usually come as a complete surprise to us. We typically do not know a life-changing incident is coming and are usually unprepared for it. When this occurs, people are highly motivated to make sense of what has happened. Several processes may be implicated in the sense-making process. People are likely to pay extra attention to such events, they may have strong emotional responses to them, and they may attempt to explain why they happened. In these ways, this new outcome becomes more familiar and less novel, and hence some of its impact is reduced. However, these processes occur rapidly and (often) outside of awareness, so people do not recognize these ways in which the impact of an unexpected outcome will fade. Therefore, they assume that that impact will continue longer than it will.

Immune Neglect

People are particularly likely to engage in these processes when the unexpected outcome is unfavorable (as was discussed earlier in the chapter on attribution), producing negative emotional consequences. People are, of course, generally motivated to avoid negative emotions. In fact, people have a variety of mechanisms to help avoid threats to emotional well-being, and together they constitute a psychological immune system (much like the body's physiological immune system that works against threats to physical health). For example, people often become very skilled at reducing dissonant states that can be troubling, their reasoning processes may be biased in favor of the self, their attributions for events may be biased in a self-serving direction, and they may be inclined to affirm their self-worth in such circumstances. These processes can be quite useful in diminishing the harmful effects of unfavorable outcomes. Moreover, all of these defensive processes generally function outside of awareness, at an unconscious level. So, the individual is not even aware of the operation of these processes and therefore does not recognize that they effectively diminish the duration of the effects of the negative outcome, again leading to overestimations in affective forecasting. Therefore, this system of defenses has been called *immune neglect* (Gilbert et al., 1998).

The rationale underlying this argument is straightforward. People naturally feel bad after experiencing a negative outcome (personal rejection from another person, failing an important exam, negative feedback on job performance), and this negative emotion triggers the psychological immune system. If possible, the immune system works to reduce adverse effects that might typically arise from the experience. For example, a supervisor making an unfavorable decision might be seen as biased, or the criteria for promotion judged to be unfair, such that the negative outcome does not have to be personally accepted. Using such mechanisms to dismiss the negative implications of the outcome should effectively diminish the length of time the negative affective state persists. However, we know that people believe the affect will persist – the durability bias in affective forecasts. Because these mechanisms of the immune system generally operate outside of awareness, the person is not aware of and therefore does not benefit from them. Consequently, the expectation (the *forecast*) that the negative affect will continue – that is, the durability bias – remains. The person has "neglected" the benefits of the immune system. Several experiments have supported these predictions (Gilbert et al., 1998).

Affective forecasting is a common occurrence and can be seen in many domains of life, large and small. For example, students at some universities in California and the Midwest were asked to rate their life satisfaction – both overall satisfaction and satisfaction in several life domains (e.g., job prospects, academic opportunities, social life, cultural opportunities, climate). Some participants rated their own life satisfaction, whereas others rated the life satisfaction of people living in the other region. Among those rating the satisfaction of people living in the *other* region, there was broad consensus among residents of both regions that people living in California experience higher life satisfaction than those living in the Midwest. However, for those who rated their *own* life satisfaction, there was no difference in overall life satisfaction between the two regions (Schkade & Kahneman, 1998). Similarly, students randomly assigned to a desirable or an undesirable dormitory were asked how happy they would be with their living situation. Those assigned to the desirable dormitory predicted that a year later, they would be much happier than those in the undesirable dorm. However, when assessed a year later, there was no difference between residents of the two dorms (Dunn et al., 2003). In another study, people involved in romantic relationships rated their current happiness and also their happiness should the relationship end. Their ratings were compared to the happiness ratings of people who, in fact, had recently experienced the end of a relationship. People anticipated that breaking up would leave them considerably less happy two months later. However, those who had experienced the end of a relationship were no less happy than those who were currently in a relationship (Gilbert et al., 1998).

Affective forecasting is seen in intergroup contexts as well. Most people anticipate (forecast) that if they witness a White person make a racist comment to a Black person, they would shun the person. However, in an experiment where some participants heard a White person make a racial slur, they were as likely to choose that person as a co-worker on a task as did people who heard no racist comment (Kawakami, Dunn, Karmali, & Dovidio, 2009). Moreover, people typically expect that intergroup interactions will be awkward, uneasy, and negative (Crosby, Bromley, & Saxe, 1980; Mallett, Wilson, & Gilbert, 2008; Word, Zanna, & Cooper, 1974).

However, people who experience those interactions typically do not rate them to be as negative as they had expected. In one study (Mallett et al., 2008), White participants were told they would have an interaction with a Black partner (actually an experimental confederate). They exchanged information about their preferences for mundane objects (e.g., "apples or oranges?"), and the participant was always given a set of the partner's preferences that matched 70% of their own. Participants were then asked to write a few paragraphs about the ways they were similar to or different from their partners. After this writing task, participants predicted what the interaction would be like on a series of scales, including their expected emotions (anxious, intimidated, uneasy, secure, relaxed, happy) and the anticipated interaction quality ("the interaction [will] go smoothly," "My partner will feel comfortable," and "I will like my partner"). They then had a five-minute conversation with the confederate on a range of topics and rated the experience using the same scales.

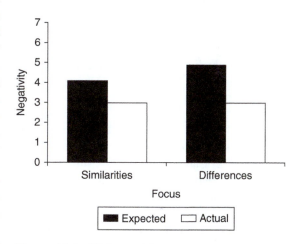

Figure 11.3 White participants' expected versus actual negativity of interracial interaction as a function of focus on interpersonal similarities or differences

Source: Adapted from Mallett et al. (2008)

As shown in Figure 11.3, participants' forecasts were more negative than what was experienced during the interaction. In other words, participants' experiences exceeded their expectations. However, the manipulation of participants' focus did affect the expected quality of the interaction. When participants focused on differences between themselves and their partner, they forecast that the interaction would be more negative. In contrast, participants who had written about their similarities with their partner expected a less negative interaction, although this manipulation did not affect interaction quality. Notably, the interaction experience was negative in both conditions, attesting that interracial interactions can be particularly challenging.

Thus, errors in affective forecasting can occur in many contexts. People not only anticipate affective consequences of events to last longer than they do (the durability effect) but also to have greater intensity than they do (Buehler & McFarland, 2001). The findings summarized here represent errors in judgment and prediction, and, given their pervasiveness, they can have significant consequences. People are continually making decisions based on their forecasts of the future. These decisions can include the seemingly inconsequential (I can get home more quickly by taking city streets rather than contending with freeway traffic), more serious personal crises (He left me for another…I miss him so…will I ever recover?), and involve important plans for the future (My life would be much happier if I lived in Paris.). In some cases, these misjudgments of the future can be costly. Attempts to reduce these errors, primarily by refocusing people's attention, have had some success (Buehler & McFarland, 2001; Mallett et al., 2008; Wilson et al., 2000), but not always (Ubel et al., 2001). However, the tendency for one's attention to be focused on the emotion-inducing event is quite natural, and the elements of the psychological immune system are mainly unconscious, so we typically are not aware of them. Consequently, avoiding these dangers may not be easy.

Although people typically overestimate the impact of events on later emotions, this does not always occur. Some studies have demonstrated conditions when people show underestimation in their affective forecasts (Dunn, Biesanz, Human, & Finn, 2007; Lench, Safer, & Levine, 2011). For example, people underestimate the positive affective benefits of self-presentation with strangers (Dunn et al., 2007). Moreover, the extent that people can forecast the emotional consequences of a triggering event depends on the features of the emotion being assessed: its intensity in response to an event, the frequency with which that emotional response continues to occur, and the effect of the event on one's overall mood state in the future. The conditions under which each of these effects is manifested have been debated and require clarification (Lench et al., 2019; Levine, Lench, Kaplan, & Safer, 2012; Wilson & Gilbert, 2013). There is no doubt, however, that events often have long-lasting emotional ramifications and that people are not always accurate in forecasting those effects.

Expectancies and Self-fulfilling Prophecies

To say that we anticipate the future seems trivial: we obviously care about our futures (both imminent and remote) and want to plan for them. The research on affective forecasting has shown that people are not always adept at foreseeing the future. We now turn to some quite different research showing that we not only anticipate the future but that our expectations some-times play an important role in actually creating that future.

A key element in our ability to anticipate the future is the fact that we have stored knowledge from the past. In Chapter 2, we discussed how that knowledge is stored in cognitive representations, our repositories of knowledge and beliefs gleaned from past experiences. That past knowledge provides expectancies of what will happen when similar events occur in the future. Those expectancies are of crucial importance to our ability to anticipate the future and adapt to it. They are pervasive, ever-present, and influential. They guide all aspects of information processing: what stimuli we attend to and encode (Bargh & Thein, 1985), our interpretations of new information (Darley & Gross, 1983; Jacobs & Eccles, 1992; Sagar & Schofield, 1980), our attributions (Crocker et al., 1983; Hastie, 1984; Weiner, 1985b), and the likelihood and nature of counterfactuals (Johnson & Sherman, 1990; Kahneman & Tversky, 1982).

Expectancies can also be viewed as intuitive hypotheses that people have developed about their social world and how it functions, and those hypotheses can be "tested" in everyday experience, as we discussed in Chapter 9. In testing these hypotheses, people may seek information that would help determine the validity of the hypothesis (Skov & Sherman, 1986; Trope & Bassok, 1982, 1983). For example, when trying to determine if an American is a Democrat or a Republican, one might ask *diagnostic* questions, the answers to which would maximally differ-entiate positions of the two parties. Another strategy is to seek information or ask questions that would support a preferred option, a *confirmatory* strategy. For example, if one "wanted" to see the person as a Democrat, one might ask questions that would likely induce a "Yes" response to questions that would be answered affirmatively by someone of the Democratic persuasion (Skov & Sherman, 1986; Snyder, 1981, 1992; Snyder & Swann, 1978).

Thus, expectancies are used in predicting the future, and they guide behavior. All of these influences are extremely useful, although these effects of expectancies are also open to bias. Expectancies can distort our perceptions of others and their behaviors. Importantly, these biases work mostly in the direction of reinforcing the expectancies that generated them. In other words, expectancies have the effect of maintaining the status quo and of preserving the very expectancies that created these effects. There are excellent and beneficial reasons that we have and use expectancies, but those expectancies have negative downstream consequences as well.

Beyond these biasing influences, expectancies can have another, more far-reaching effect known as a *self-fulfilling prophecy*. Consider the following scenario. Two persons, whom we will call Malik and Harrison, meet and have a conversation. Malik had heard from others that Harrison tends to be unfriendly, so Malik is expecting that Harrison's behavior may manifest some coldness. Given this expectancy, Malik is cautious and somewhat guarded during this interaction, keeping his distance from Harrison. Harrison notices Malik's reticence, and, in response, he is cool toward Malik, behaving in a reserved manner. Thus, Harrison's behavior has confirmed Malik's expectancy about him, and Malik thinks, "Yep, he sure isn't very friendly."

There are three notable points about this interaction. First, Malik's expectancy about Harrison has created a behavioral confirmation of that expectancy. That is, Harrison's reserved behavior is a response to Malik's coolness, which was generated by his own expectancy about Harrison. It is, then, a self-fulfilling prophecy. Second, this is *not* a case of perceptual distortion. Harrison was, in fact, cool in his responses to Malik. Third, in all likelihood, Malik is utterly unaware that his own expectancy and behavior have determined Harrison's behavior. It is truly an insidious effect.

A clever study by Snyder, Tanke, and Berscheid (1977) produced empirical evidence for self-fulfilling prophecies in interpersonal interaction. Two participants, one male and one female, reported to different rooms for the experiment, not seeing each other, presumably to study the get-acquainted process through a phone conversation. At the outset, the man is given a photo supposedly of his female conversation partner. In fact, that photo was the key manipulation of the study and did not depict the woman with whom he would converse. Instead, half of the men were given a photo of a very attractive woman, while the other half received a photo of a woman who (based on pilot testing) was judged to be less attractive. The attractiveness of the woman was manipulated in the study because of well-established stereotypes regarding the presumed traits of attractive people: attractive persons are assumed to possess numerous desirable traits to a greater extent than less attractive persons (Dion et al., 1972). Ratings by the male participants of their female partners based only on these (inaccurate) photographs manifested the stereotype: the attractive female partners were indeed rated more favorably.

The two participants then had a get-acquainted phone conversation, in which each participant's voice was recorded on a separate track of a tape recorder. Later, new participants (raters) listened to one (male) or the other (female) half of the conversations and then rated the person they listened to on several scales. These measures revealed the self-fulfilling prophecy. Specifically, the women whose male partners thought they were attractive were rated as being significantly more confident and animated, enjoying the conversation more, and liking their partners more than did women who interacted with men who had been led to believe that they were unattractive. These raters – who *heard only her half of the conversations* – knew nothing about the attractiveness manipulation nor anything about the purpose of the study.

Yet somehow, they perceived differences between the two sets of female participants based on the attractiveness expectations of their male partners. As Snyder et al. (1977, p. 661) stated, "What had initially been reality in the minds of the men had now become reality in the behavior of the women with whom they had interacted – a behavioral reality discernible even by naïve observer judges, who had access only to tape recordings of the women's contributions to the conversations."

How did this happen? The answer to this question is conveyed by analyses of the judgments made by other raters who *listened only to the male half of these conversations*. Compared to men who interacted with women they thought were unattractive, those who interacted with women they believed to be attractive were rated to be more comfortable, as liking their partners more, as taking the initiative in conversation more often, and as using their voices more effectively. This greater sociability of men while interacting with presumed-to-be attractive women induced comparable sociality in their partners, a pattern that did not occur when men interacted with women they were induced to believe were unattractive.

This process began with the man's expectancy about the attractiveness of the woman, and during the interaction, the woman's behaviors confirmed those expectancies. Thus, it is a self-fulfilling prophecy. However, it seems highly unlikely that the men had any cognizance of their role in inducing those behaviors in their female partners. It is an insidious effect that is difficult to detect.

This study provided a convincing demonstration of a self-fulfilling prophecy in social interaction. Other studies have been useful in breaking down this effect and demonstrating its component parts (Word et al., 1974). Word et al.'s first experiment created a simulated job interview between two college student participants where White interviewers interviewed persons for a job. The interviewees were actually confederates of the experimenter who were trained to enact their role consistently. The confederates were either White or Black. The interactions were videotaped and later coded for the interviewers' nonverbal behaviors. These analyses showed that White interviewers sat further away from Black interviewees, had more speech errors and disfluencies, and conducted shorter interviews than did participants interacting with White interviewees. These findings document the first element in the process of the self-fulling prophecy: race-based expectancies influenced the interviewers' behavior toward the interviewees.

The second experiment was designed to determine if these differences in interviewer behavior would affect the interview performance of the interviewees. Again, White interviewers interviewed job applicants, all of whom were White. The interviewers (again, experimental confederates) were trained to enact the nonverbal behaviors that had been manifested by interviewers in the first study when interacting with White versus Black interviewees. That is, half of them were trained to maintain greater interpersonal distance, to make frequent speech errors, and to terminate the interview sooner (as did interviewers in Experiment 1 when interviewing Black applicants). In contrast, the other half manifested behaviors paralleling Experiment 1's interviewers interacting with White applicants. After the interview, judges viewed the videotapes and rated the adequacy and effectiveness of the applicant's performance and his composure during the interview. These data showed that applicants who were treated the way Black applicants in Experiment 1 had been treated performed more poorly in the interview.

Taken together, these two studies demonstrate the two components of a self-fulfilling prophecy. The interviewers' race-based expectancies resulted in Black applicants being treated differently, in subtle nonverbal ways, than were White applicants (Experiment 1), and those differences, when manifested in an interviewer's behavior, undermined the performance of applicants (Experiment 2).

Self-fulfilling prophecies have been demonstrated in many studies that document expectancy effects in several domains, including the effect of teacher expectations on student performance (Rosenthal & Jacobson, 1968), of race-based expectancies conveyed nonverbally and affecting minority performance (Word et al., 1974), of gender stereotypes (Doyle, Hancock, & Kifer, 1972; Jacobs & Eccles, 1992; Skrypnek & Snyder, 1982; von Baeyer, Sherk, & Zanna, 1981; Zanna & Pack, 1975), and of expectancies based on attractiveness on interpersonal behavior (Snyder et al., 1977). The extent to which these effects occur can be influenced by a variety of factors, including the goals of the perceiver and the extent to which the target person challenges perceiver expectancies (Hilton & Darley, 1985, 1991; Jussim & Fleming, 1996; Miller & Turnbull, 1986; Neuberg, 1994; Snyder, 1981). A self-fulfilling prophecy occurs spontaneously and without recognition of its participants, yet it can influence interpersonal behavior in ways that maintain the expectancies that generated this effect.

SUMMARY

Our lives traverse a considerable period of time during which we have had a wealth of experiences, and we look forward to a rich and varied future. As we think back to those past experiences and our knowledge of past events, our recollections are not verbatim memories but are reconstructions of them. This chapter has highlighted some of the ways that people think about the past. Reconstructive memory distorts recall of past events to make the difference between past and present compatible with current motives, goals, and intuitive theories of stability and change. Hindsight bias alters memories of past events and outcomes to make them fit with what we now know to be the outcomes, generating an exaggerated feeling of "I knew it all along." Counterfactual thinking creates an alternate reality, considering what might have happened instead of what did happen. In all of these ways, our understanding of the past is modified to make it compatible with current expectations, motives, and goals. Similarly, our thinking about the future is shaped by expectancies and motivations, again reflecting biases in looking ahead. Prior expectancies guide anticipations of the future based on past experience and cognitive representations. We are not always effective in forecasting the future, particularly in response to major affective events. On the other hand, expectancies can not only influence interpretations of ongoing events but also can create behavioral confirmation of expectancies through self-fulfilling prophecies. Thus, we know where we have been and where we want to go, but our understanding of that past and of that future can be biased by the way the mind uses prior knowledge and new information.

FURTHER READING

Droit-Volet, S. (2018). Intertwined facets of subjective time. *Current Directions in Psychological Science, 27*, 422–428.

Miloyan, B., & Suddendorf, T. (2015). Feelings of the future. *Trends in Cognitive Sciences, 19*, 196–200.

Roese, N.J., & Epstude, K. (2017). The functional theory of counterfactual thinking: New evidence, new challenges, new insights. In J. Olson (Ed.), *Advances in experimental social psychology* (Vol. 56, pp. 1–79). San Diego, CA: Academic Press.

Smallman, R., & Summerville, A. (2018). Counterfactual thought in reasoning and performance. *Social and Personality Psychology Compass, 40*, e12376.

Urminsky, O. (2017). The role of psychological connectedness to the future self in decisions over time. *Current Directions in Psychological Science, 26*, 34–39.

12

SOCIAL COGNITION AND ACTION

Thinking and Doing

My thinking is first and last and always for the sake of my doing.

William James (1890)

Action is integral to cognitive processes.

Thomas Ostrom (1984)

Throughout this book, we have focused on cognitive processes that occur as people navigate complex social environments. We have discussed how perceivers actively attend to a subset of available information, interpret it, form evaluations, make inferences and attributions, and organize and store information in memory for later use. Our focus on cognitive processes reflects, at least in part, an interest in understanding, explaining, and predicting human behavior. The above quotes by James and Ostrom, made nearly a century apart, both reflect the longstanding assumption that social thought and action are inextricably linked. However, research in the early years of social cognition paid scant attention to the relationship between cognitive processes and behavior. Fiske (1992) highlighted this oversight, arguing that "thinking is for doing." She expressed concern that social cognition had become too focused on internal mental processes and had neglected the link between thought and behavior. Agreeing with the sentiments expressed by James (1890) and Ostrom (1984), Fiske (1992) argued that knowing a person's attitudes and thoughts would allow prediction of how that person would behave and, conversely, that actions would be informative about the person's cognitive processes. Since that call, research on the relationship between cognitive processes and overt behavior has become more common.

The above quotes all suggest that cognitive processes are assumed to play a direct and causal role in determining human action. However, there are good reasons to question this assumption. Yes, you can think of times when your behavior was based on your thoughts, for example, a time you intentionally smiled when you met a new person or deliberated before deciding to vote for a particular political candidate. However, you can probably also think of times when your behavior seemed only loosely tethered to your thoughts, beliefs, or attitudes. You might have been surprised to find yourself chuckling along with friends at a sexist joke, even though you consider yourself to be an unbiased person. You might think of a time you threw away plastic water bottles, even though you consider yourself an environmentalist. Alternatively, you might have developed a pack-a-day cigarette habit, even though you know that smoking is unhealthy and expensive. These examples illustrate that thoughts do not always dictate behavior, and that behavior can be influenced by more than thoughts.

THE INTERFACE BETWEEN COGNITION AND ACTION

There has been a long history of skepticism in social psychology regarding the strength of the relationship between internal states (e.g., attitudes, inferences, traits) and behavior. Dramatic evidence of the independence of thought and action was provided by a classic study examining prejudice and discriminatory behavior in the United States in the 1930s (LaPiere, 1934). At that time, prejudice against Chinese immigrants was commonplace, and public facilities typically denied service to Chinese and most other minority groups. However, Richard LaPiere (a Stanford sociologist) had been traveling extensively with a young Chinese couple and noted that, despite posted policies, they had consistently been served at numerous hotels and restaurants. LaPiere then began to systematically investigate whether this discrepancy between policy and practice was widespread. To do so, he had the couple enter establishments alone to see if they would be given a hotel room or seated in the restaurant. The couple's attire and appearance were varied so that they appeared presentable or sometimes looked tired and dirty. Regardless of their appearance, the couple was welcomed at 66 hotels and 184 restaurants throughout the United States and were refused service only once. A questionnaire was sent to each establishment six months after the couple's visit asking, "Will you accept members of the Chinese race as guests in your establishment?" Of the 128 establishments that replied, 92% of the restaurants and 91% of the hotels stated that they would not. Explicitly stated policies did not predict the treatment of the couple to whom the policies presumably applied.

Growing Evidence of the Independence of Thought and Action

Despite this early demonstration of a striking discrepancy between explicit attitudes and behavior, researchers were slow to appreciate the importance of this and similar findings (e.g., Corey, 1937; Kutner, Wilkins, & Yarrow, 1952; Vroom, 1964). Over time, there developed a recognition that an individual's attitudes do not strongly predict behavior. A review of this literature (Wicker, 1969) found that the relationship between attitudes and behavior rarely produced correlation coefficients exceeding +.3 and frequently produced coefficients close to zero. In other words, knowledge of a person's explicit attitudes typically allowed prediction of less than 10% of the variance in the individual's actions.

Interestingly, similar conclusions were being drawn at about the same time in the field of personality psychology. Several early studies (Dudycha, 1936; Hartshorne & May, 1928; Hartshorne, May, & Shuttleworth, 1930; Newcomb, 1929) found that individuals' personality traits did not, as was commonly assumed, consistently affect behavior across situations. A person viewed as friendly might behave quite inconsistently across situations and over time. Although his actions might typically reflect friendliness, such a person might become more withdrawn as he aged or might be impatient with others when he was pressed for time. Given such situational variability in behavior, Mischel (1968, 1969) argued for a fundamental rejection of an account of behavior based on consistent and stable personality traits. He provided evidence that correlation coefficients reflecting the consistency of behavior across situations usually varied between +.2 and +.3. Because people do not behave with high consistency across social contexts, knowing a person's general dispositions did not provide the predictive power that had previously been assumed.

The critiques that attitudes and personalities do not allow the prediction of behavior raised serious concerns in the fields of social and personality psychology. Indeed, the weak relationship between internal states and external behavior contributed to "crises" in both fields (Carlson, 1971, 1984; Elms, 1975; Epstein & O'Brien, 1985). Some people responded to these crises by calling for an abandonment of traditional constructs. Wicker, for example, stated that "it may be desirable to abandon the attitude concept" (1971, p. 29). Others suggested that major rethinking of theoretical underpinnings should be undertaken, including recognizing the possibility of weak cross-situational consistency of behavior. The idea that "consistency, either in thought or action, does not constitute the normal state of affairs" (Gergen, 1968, pp. 305–306) became more frequent. However, others encouraged a focus on understanding why people expect and perceive such a strong link between internal processes and external behavior. Nisbett and Ross (1980) raised the possibility that the perception of consistent behavior might merely reflect perceivers' expectations: "objectively low or nonexistent covariations (between personality and behavior) can be parlayed into massive perceived covariations through *a priori* theories and assumptions" (p. 109).

It is striking that the same core issue – the supposed strong link between internal processes and observable actions – was sharply critiqued almost simultaneously in two independent literatures. Although research on attitudes and research on personality was generally conducted by different individuals with different measures and methods, both communities were challenged to address evidence that thoughts are not always reflected in actions, and that thinking and acting often can be seemingly disconnected.

A Crisis Averted

Both research communities have successfully responded to these critiques by embracing a more complex view of the relationship between internal processes and behavior. There is now general agreement that personality characteristics and attitudes are of some value in predicting behavior (Sherman & Fazio, 1983). If one wants to know how a person might act in a given situation, knowledge of her internal thoughts, feelings, and processing tendencies can provide at least a tentative prediction regarding how she might behave. However, research has shown that thoughts and actions are not synonymous. Attitudes and personality traits are expressed in behavior only conditionally, under certain social situations, and moderated by numerous factors (Ajzen & Fishbein, 2005; Bizer, Larsen, & Petty, 2011; Cooke & Sheeran, 2004; Dalege, Borsboom, van Harreveld, & van der Maas, 2019; Glasman & Albarracín, 2006; Kaiser & Schultz, 2009; Le, Oh, Robbins, Ilies, Holland, & Westrick, 2011; Mischel & Shoda, 1995). There are conditions under which attitudes and personality dispositions predict behavior, sometimes to a high degree, but there are also many conditions when they do not. Thus, the assumption that internal psychological states go hand in hand with behavior is no longer tenable. The question of "do internal processes direct observable behavior?" has evolved into issues of *when they do* and *how they do*.

In both of these literatures, methodological and theoretical innovations have been developed to understand both *when* and *how* thought and action are linked. However, these advancements have again generally occurred in parallel and in isolation from one another, even when the same underlying causal mechanism produces different effects. In personality research, for example, studies have shown that people can exhibit a high degree of consistency in their behavior if they are observed in similar psychological situations (Fleeson, 2007; Fournier, Moskowitz, & Zuroff, 2008; Mischel, 2004; Mischel & Shoda, 1995; Sherman, Nave, & Funder, 2010). One should not necessarily expect a person who is friendly with peers at work also to be friendly when meeting a stranger. Within each situation, however, people tend to act quite consistently; a person typically might be outgoing with numerous fellow employees but also generally be shy in meeting new people. Similarly, in research on attitudes, the relation between cognitions about an object and behavior concerning that object is increased if an individual has had previous experience with that object (Fazio & Zanna, 1978a; Fazio, Zanna, & Cooper, 1978). If I have tried a new brand of pizza, for example, then my expressed attitude would more accurately predict my likelihood of purchasing that pizza again than if I had only been exposed to advertisements promoting it. In both cases, then, behavior is consistent with internal dispositions, but situational contexts constrain that relation. How does that happen?

What these two seemingly disparate findings have in common is the central role of *accessibility* in moderating the relation between thought and behavior. That is, thoughts that readily come to mind in a situation are more likely to influence how a person behaves in that situation. In Mischel's account of personality, behavior is consistent within situations because similar cognitive structures are activated in similar social contexts through what Mischel and Shoda (1995, 2010) call *if...then contingencies*. In Fazio and colleagues' account of attitude-behavior consistency, experience with an attitude object makes one's evaluations of an object more salient when the person thinks of the object. Evaluations that are prominent in a person's thinking about the object will more likely influence how the person acts in response to the object. Both findings (and others we will review shortly) illustrate that cognitions are more likely to causally affect behavior when they are accessible.

A Preview

This text has highlighted a set of core cognitive processes that are important across content areas. Accordingly, in this chapter we present an analysis of the relation between thoughts and action that cuts across content areas. Interestingly, there is considerable overlap in the factors that govern the relationship between thoughts and behavior across different areas of the field. In addition, a focus on common moderators permits a greater understanding of how other cognitive structures, such as stereotypes, expectancies, and goals, play a role in influencing behavior. Moreover, the influence of implicit and explicit cognition on behavior (and the dynamic relation between them in influencing action) recently has also been a focus of intense interest.

The main body of this chapter is organized into several major sections. First, we consider *when* cognitions guide behavior. We discuss evidence showing that highly accessible cognitions, stable cognitions, and situation-relevant cognitions can direct behavior. Second, we analyze *how* cognitions guide behavior. We show that cognitions can have direct effects on behavior as well as more subtle, indirect influences. Third, we consider the differential role of implicit and explicit processes on behavior. Fourth, we then explore the opposite relation, that is, examining how behavior can guide cognition. Finally, we explore the implications of the relation between thought and action for understanding the self, persons, and groups.

WHEN DO COGNITIONS GUIDE BEHAVIOR?

The recognition that thought and action are frequently independent led to an intense focus on understanding the conditions under which internal cognitions do and do not affect observable behavior. Consequently, there is now much evidence regarding the processes that link thought and action and the conditions that moderate or eliminate that connection.

Accessible Cognitions Direct Behavior

In earlier chapters, we discussed how the accessibility of cognitive representations (concepts, beliefs, stereotypes) affect interpretation, evaluation, inference, attribution, and many other critical psychological processes. Accessibility also plays a vital role in the link between thoughts and actions. Beliefs, attitudes, and experience are most likely to influence behavior when those cognitive representations come to mind in a relevant context (Eitam & Higgins, 2016). Attitudes based on emotion, particularly if the attitude is positive, are especially likely to be accessible in memory (Rocklage & Fazio, 2018). Conversely, behavior is more likely to be influenced by extraneous factors when cognitions are not accessible (Fazio & Towles-Schwen, 1999). Recent research shows that the accessibility of relevant cognitions can predict whether people act consistently with their beliefs in a broad array of domains, including beer consumption (Descheemaeker, Spruyt, & Hermans, 2014) and speeding while driving (Elliott, Lee, Robertson, & Innes, 2015).

Manipulations that increase the accessibility of information tend to enhance its influence on behavior. One way to do so is to ask people about their intentions to engage in a relevant behavior, a phenomenon called the *question-behavior effect* (Rodrigues, O'Brien, French, Glidewell, & Sniehotta, 2015) or the *mere-measurement effect* (Morwitz & Fitzsimons, 2004). In one study examining this phenomenon (Wood, Conner, Sandberg, Godin, & Sheeran, 2014), participants in one condition were asked about their intentions to eat healthily. In two control conditions, participants were either asked about their intention to use the internet or completed an unrelated word unscramble task. The dependent measures in the study included a response latency task to assess the accessibility of attitudes toward healthy food and a behavioral measure indicating whether participants choose a healthy (e.g., a banana) or an unhealthy food (e.g., a chocolate candy bar) as a "gift" for participating in the study. Results showed that inquiring about intentions to eat healthily increased the accessibility of attitudes related to healthy food and increased the consumption of healthy compared with unhealthy foods. Statistical analyses indicated that the accessibility of attitudes towards healthy food accounted for the increase in the consumption of healthy foods.

Direct Experience

Attitudes and beliefs based on direct experience are more likely to be accessible and, consequently, more likely to affect behavior. Consider what your attitude might be toward a product, say, a new candy bar that you see advertised on television. You might form an attitude about the candy bar based on its attributes, such as whether it has milk chocolate (good), nuts (good), or toffee (bad). Based on those attributes, you decide that you will probably like this candy bar. However, this attitude, though it has formed, is based only on information available and not on having tasted it. If, however, you had tried the candy bar and the experience confirmed your expectations, your attitude toward the candy bar might be equally positive compared with not having sampled one, but your attitude would be more accessible. That accessibility will bring your positive feelings to mind when you see the candy in the store. Therefore, the likelihood of your acting consistently with these positive feelings – purchasing a candy bar – will increase.

The increased potency of experience-based attitudes has been repeatedly demonstrated (Fazio & Zanna, 1978a, 1978b; Fazio et al., 1978; Jefferis & Fazio, 2008; see Glasman & Albarracín's (2006) meta-analysis). One study (Regan & Fazio, 1977), for example, was conducted among incoming students at Cornell University, some of whom had been denied housing and were living in temporary quarters. Students' attitudes about the housing issue were assessed with a written survey, and they were also given an opportunity to take several actions in response to the problem (e.g., signing a petition, joining a committee that would investigate the housing problem). Although both students who had and had not been affected by the crisis expressed similarly negative sentiments on the survey, these attitudes significantly predicted behavior only for students who had actually been denied housing. Students affected by the policy were more likely to take action to remedy the housing situation, especially those who held strong opinions about the issue. However, for the students who had not been directly affected, their sentiments did not predict their behavior towards addressing the problem.

Subsequent research (Fazio, 1986; Fazio, Chen, McDonel, & Sherman, 1982; Fazio & Williams, 1986; Millar & Millar, 1996; Vonofakou, Hewstone, & Voci, 2007) has shown that experience-based attitudes affect behavior because they are more accessible in memory compared with attitudes not based on direct experience. To demonstrate this point, Fazio et al. (1982) manipulated the amount of experience individuals had with an intellectual puzzle and measured the speed with which attitudes about the puzzle could be accessed from memory. More accessible attitudes (based on a measure of activation speed) were more powerful determinants of behavior. These results indicate that attitudes based on direct experience are more likely to come easily and quickly to mind in the presence of an attitude object, making them available to influence action in response to that object.

Repeated Expression or Exposure

Attitudes that are accessed repeatedly are also more likely to guide behavior. An attitude or belief might be retrieved frequently from memory for several reasons, and the mere act of repeated retrieval can strengthen the influence of that structure on subsequent judgments and behavior (Descheemaeker, Spruyt, Fazio, & Hermans, 2017; Holland, Verplanken, & van Knippenberg, 2003; Young & Fazio, 2013). If you are highly motivated to hold certain beliefs or if you are prompted to think about your beliefs frequently, your behavior will more likely reflect those beliefs than if you do not hold a belief firmly or think about it rarely. In one study (Powell & Fazio, 1984), individuals who were prompted to express their attitudes more frequently (one, three, or six times) were faster to answer later questions about those attitudes, signifying that repeated expression increases attitude accessibility.

Being repeatedly exposed to a message also serves to increase the intensity of emotional responses to it (Mrkva & Van Boven, 2020) and the correspondence between belief and behavior (Berger, 1992). Berger (1999) showed that individuals are more likely to act consistently with their attitudes when they have been repeatedly exposed to an attitudinally-relevant message. Participants were given written advertisements for five brands of candy bars and were shown simple or complex messages, either one or three times. Later, participants' attitudes toward each candy bar were measured. Although attitudes were correlated with behavioral expressions in all conditions, these correlations were substantially higher in the conditions in which the advertisements had been repeated multiple times. In these conditions, attitudes correlated highly with behavioral intentions. These results illustrate one reason why over $250 billion is spent in the United States per year on advertising; repeating a message increases the likelihood that the recipient of the message will behave consistently with it.

The reason why consistency between attitudes and behavior increases under repeated exposure is a matter of some debate. One straightforward possibility is that repeating a message simply increases its accessibility. However, Berger (1999) conducted mediational analyses showing that repeated viewing of a persuasive message also creates greater consistency between cognitions about the products and attitudes. In other words, seeing a persuasive message on several occasions creates greater consistency in one's thoughts about the object or issue in question. That greater consistency in itself can increase the likelihood of attitude-consistent actions. Another possibility is that repetition increases fluency (Reber & Unkelbach, 2010). Messages that are heard repeatedly might be processed more efficiently, which, in turn, supports positive responses to them (Lee & Labroo, 2004; Reber & Unkelbach, 2010).

High Commitment

Beliefs that are deeply and firmly held are also more likely to become accessible in memory to influence behavior (Maxwell-Smith & Esses, 2012). People who are highly devoted to their attitudes can engage in extreme behavior, exhibiting their commitment through intense emotions and self-sacrifice in pursuit of their beliefs. Consider, for example, the lengths to which an Olympic athlete will sacrifice relationships or forsake personal pleasures for an opportunity to compete for a medal. A recent study (Maxwell-Smith, Conway, Wright, & Olson, 2018) showed that people who are most committed to their beliefs about the environment were most likely to behave consistently with their ideologies.

However, a more fundamental question concerns *when* will an individual demonstrate a strong commitment to an attitude? We all have many beliefs and opinions, but we are not equally committed to and willing to sacrifice for all of them. Higher levels of commitment have been demonstrated for issues that might affect the self (e.g., Millar & Tesser, 1986; Sivacek & Crano, 1982) or relate to one's individual or group values (Blankenship & Wegener, 2008; Cohen, 2003; Honkanen & Verplanken, 2004). Individuals also differ in their ability to process information related to an issue, and these differences can affect the strength of the commitment to attitudes and behavior. For example, individuals high in *need for cognition* (i.e., those who tend to enjoy thinking extensively about issues) are more likely to hold strong attitudes and to behave consistently with them (Barbaro, Pickett, & Parkhill, 2015; Howe & Krosnick, 2017). Researchers in one study (Cacioppo, Petty, Kao, & Rodriguez, 1986) measured the preferences of individuals who were high versus low in need for cognition eight weeks before the 1984 presidential elections and correlated these preferences with voting behavior. Whereas those low in need for cognition showed some degree of consistency between their earlier-expressed attitudes and voting behavior ($r = +.41$), this relation was much stronger for persons high in need for cognition ($r = +.86$), who were more likely to hold extreme attitudes and to report thinking more about those attitudes. Thus, individuals who are chronically motivated and able to think more deeply about issues are likely to have more robust and accessible attitudes available to guide behavior.

Primed Cognitions Direct Behavior

Cognitive structures can be made accessible by cues in the environment that trigger their activation. To the degree that these cues are subtle or undetectable, this influence can occur automatically, without an individual's intent, awareness, or ability to stop it from occurring. Anyone who has found himself behaving with greater caution and suspicion upon exiting a violent movie realizes how difficult it can be to act otherwise. Moreover, Fazio and his colleagues have argued that some attitudes are *chronically primed*, that is, activated spontaneously in the mere presence of an attitude object to produce behavioral consequences without conscious intent. Information made accessible in this way "biases perceptions of the object in the immediate situation, and behavior simply follows from these perceptions without any necessary conscious reasoning process" (Fazio, 1986, p. 237).

Primes and Attitudes

Several lines of research support the notion that primed attitudes are likely to become accessible to influence later behavior. One set of studies (Fazio et al., 1986) involved presenting attitude objects very briefly (200 ms) and showed that these primes affected the speed with which individuals could categorize a subsequent adjective as positive ("delightful") or negative ("awful"). However, this effect occurred only for attitudes where participants had strong evaluative associations; weak attitudes did not produce facilitation in responding to valenced adjectives. In one of the experiments, attitude strength was manipulated by having some participants repeatedly express their attitudes. Again, attitudes made more accessible through repeated expression produced facilitation effects.

Similar results have been obtained for racial attitudes. In an early study assessing the relationship between attitudes and behavior (Fazio et al., 1995), variability in the speed to categorize positive and negative words that followed White and Black faces predicted participants' friendliness toward an African American experimenter they later encountered. A large field study (Hassell & Visalvanich, 2015) produced similar results. In that experiment, participants read a passage discussing a piece of legislation that supposedly would promote hiring by reducing regulatory burdens on businesses. In a baseline condition, participants read an unembellished passage. In two other conditions, phrases were added either emphasizing the high levels of unemployment among construction workers and contractors or emphasizing the same issues regarding racial and ethnic minorities. Participants were then invited to write a letter to their member of Congress advocating support for the legislation. The percentage of people who sent a letter differed by condition and based on participants' level of racial resentment as reflected in their responses to questionnaires given at the end of the study (Kinder & Sanders, 1996). As is shown in Figure 12.1, the willingness to send a letter was not affected by racial resentment in the baseline and construction workers conditions. However, when racial attitudes were

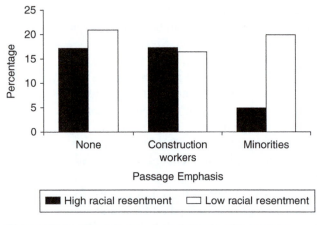

Figure 12.1 Percentage of participants who wrote a supportive letter as a function of passage emphasis and racial resentment

Source: Adapted from Hassell & Visalvanich (2015)

relevant, the degree of resentment strongly affected behavior. This research shows that primed attitudes can affect behavioral responses.

Primes and Norms

Priming can also affect behavior directly without being mediated by attitudes. One such example is provided by research showing the behavioral consequences of activated *norms*, cognitive representations containing information about behavior that is expected in a given social context. Priming a social setting can increase the accessibility of these mental associations, thereby affecting subsequent behavior when people expect to enter a relevant environment. Several studies examining this possibility (Aarts & Dijksterhuis 2003; Aarts, Dijksterhuis, & Custers, 2003) involved presenting participants with pictures of one of two environments (a library or a train station) for which there are strong social norms regarding speaking volume. In contrast to a train station, people are expected to speak in hushed tones in a library. In one experiment, participants viewed a photograph of one of these contexts for 30 seconds. In some conditions, they were told that they would be visiting the site after the experiment. Another set of participants was merely asked to scrutinize the picture of the library. Would showing photos of these two contexts affect how the participants subsequently behaved? The researchers answered this question by measuring how loudly participants spoke as they read aloud ten words during a supposedly separate task immediately following the picture presentation. As is shown in Figure 12.2, participants said these words more quietly if they had viewed a photograph of a library, but only if they thought they were about to visit it.

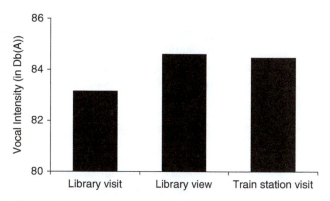

Figure 12.2 Participants' vocal intensity (in decibels; Db(A)) as a function of condition

Source: Based on data from Aarts & Dijksterhuis (2003)

The unconscious influence of activated cognitions on behavior can be particularly pervasive when a person encounters an object for which there exist strong, widely-held semantic associates. This possibility helps explain some classic findings in the literature on aggression that pre-date the emergence of social cognition. Several studies have shown that exposure to stimuli related to violence can produce increases in aggressive behavior. In one study (Berkowitz & LePage, 1967), individuals who were angered by another person gave that person more electric shocks when a rifle and revolver (as compared with badminton racquets) were lying on a nearby table, supposedly left from a previous experiment. This finding was named the *weapons effect*. Subsequent research (Anderson, Benjamin, & Bartholow, 1998; Bartholow, Anderson, Carnagey, & Benjamin, 2005) showed that encountering objects associated with violence leads to greater accessibility of aggression-related thoughts. When people – and particularly non-hunters with less-nuanced mental associations relating to guns – were exposed to pictures of weapons, they were faster to name words related to compared with words unrelated to aggression. People who saw pictures of innocuous objects showed no difference in the speed of naming aggressive versus non-aggressive words. Recent studies raise concerns about possible real-world adverse behavioral consequences of exposure to violent stimuli. For example, violent videogame play in high school students has been linked to heightened aggression and bullying (Dittrick, Beran, Mishna, Hetherington, & Shariff, 2013; Willoughby, Adachi, & Good, 2012).

Several studies offer a more hopeful picture, showing that primed norms can encourage pro-environmental behavior, especially when these norms appear to be changing. Such *dynamic norms* (Loschelder, Siepelmeyer, Fischer, & Rubel, 2019; Sparkman & Walton, 2017, 2019) imply that people are increasingly engaging in sustainable behavior, and these norms can prime behavior that is not yet normative. In one study examining the influence of dynamic norms (Sparkman & Walton, 2017), participants in a campus café line at Stanford University were handed one of two versions of a message regarding the actions of other people, emphasizing either stable [or dynamic] norms (phrases for dynamic norms are in brackets):

> Some people [are starting to] limit how much meat they eat. This is true both nationally and here at Stanford. Specifically, recent research has shown that [over the last 5 years] 30% of Americans [have started to] make an effort to limit their meat consumption. That means that [in recent years] 3 in 10 people [have changed their behavior and begun to] eat less meat than they otherwise would.

Results showed that twice as many individuals given the message emphasizing dynamic norms ordered a meatless meal when they arrived at the counter compared with individuals who received a static norm message. Similar effects have been shown regarding water conservation and cup re-use. Priming people with dynamic norms appears to be a powerful means for promoting prosocial behavior.

A Note on the Reproducibility of Behavioral Priming Effects

In the introductory chapter of this text, we discussed controversies regarding the reproducibility of some phenomena in social psychology that had been previously considered to be reliable. A particularly contentious debate arose around the issue of the effects of exposure to primes on subsequent behavior, an active area of research, particularly following the publication of the study by Bargh, Chen, and Burrows (1996). As several high-profile failures to replicate behavioral priming effects began to emerge over 15 years later (Doyen et al., 2012; Harris, Coburn, Rohrer, & Pashler, 2013; Shanks et al., 2013), concerns were voiced that this research was undermining the credibility of social psychology and, indeed, the entire field of psychology.

Although the debate over behavioral priming effects is not yet settled, some recent developments suggest that confidence in this area of research is warranted. Some researchers have emphasized the importance of identifying the causal mechanisms involved in such effects (Cesario, 2014; Klatzky & Creswell, 2014; Loersch & Payne, 2014; Van Bavel, Mende-Siedlecki, Brady, & Reinero, 2016), providing an understanding of the conditions under which effects will and will not occur. In addition, several independent meta-analyses encapsulating hundreds of studies (including replication failures) have emerged in recent years, agreeing that behavioral priming effects are real and reliable (Cameron, Brown-Iannuzzi, & Payne, 2012; Chen, Latham, Piccolo, & Itzchakov, 2020; Weingarten, Chen, McAdams, Yi, Hepler, & Albarracín, 2016; see also Strack & Schwarz, 2016). Furthermore, these meta-analyses have themselves provided additional insights regarding the conditions under which primes do and do not affect behavior.

Situational Primes of Behavioral Signatures

The principle that situational factors can activate associations from memory to guide behavior also applies to personality. As we discussed earlier, Mischel (1968) critiqued purely traits-based accounts of personality, highlighting that behavior is less stable across social contexts than would be expected if dispositions are the primary basis of behavior. Mischel and his colleagues (e.g., Mischel & Shoda, 1995, 2008, 2010; Shoda et al., 1989, 1994, 2002) later argued that any theory of personality that attempts to predict behavior must recognize the critical role of situational constraints (Wright & Mischel, 1987). Although Mischel's characterization of personality is more complicated than can be considered here, one critical aspect of his view is that situational features activate a set of internal reactions, both cognitive and affective, that reflect a person's experience in those contexts (Mischel, 1973). Therefore, a context can act as a trigger for a set of behavioral tendencies that the person associates with that particular situation. Wright and Mischel (1987) argued that situations activate idiosyncratic *if-then propositions* (e.g., "If a person becomes aggressive, then I will withdraw"), arguing that these mental associations then guide behavior. Consequently, behavior should be relatively consistent in similar psychological situations over time (because similar cognitive-affective reactions arise in situations with similar features) but relatively inconsistent in different psychological situations (because different reactions arise in situations with different features). In contrast with dispositional approaches, Mischel and his colleagues assert their *Cognitive-Affective Personality System* (CAPS) approach will prove superior in accounting for behavior.

Indeed, the CAPS model has been applied successfully to many behavioral phenomena (e.g., Ayduk & Gyurak, 2008; Cain, Meehan, Roche, Clarkin, & De Panfilis, 2019; Mischel, Mendoza-Denton, & Hong, 2009; Roche, Pincus, Conroy, Hyde, & Ram, 2013). In the initial study assessing the utility of this approach, Shoda et al. (1994) conducted an extensive field study involving children at a summer camp facility. Detailed real-time observations of the children's behavior were recorded in five situations, specifically, when they were approached or teased by a peer or when they were praised, warned, or punished by an adult. Observers coded the child's response in terms of five types of behavior, including displaying verbal or physical aggression, babyish behavior, compliance, or talking prosocially. Results showed that children exhibited relatively consistent *behavioral signatures*, that is, patterns of consistent behavior within similar situations but different behavior in differing circumstances. For example, one child might pout when punished by an adult but verbally aggress toward a peer when teased; another child might comply when punished but pout when teased.

In addition, children behaved much more consistently within similar situations than in different situations. Table 12.1 shows the consistency of the five target behaviors within and across the five situations, as reflected in mean correlation coefficients. Only 2 of 24 correlations computed *in different situations* were statistically significant, and no correlation exceeded +.20. (You may note that 24 rather than 25 correlations were tested; fortunately for the counselors, no children ever responded to praise from an adult with physical aggression!) Consistency *in similar situations* was substantially higher, with 14 of 24 statistically significant correlations and some coefficients exceeding +.40. Even though behavior was presumably susceptible to many influences in this real-world study, children behaved quite similarly within similar contexts over time. These results document that situations make accessible specific patterns of thoughts and feelings that increase the predictability of behavior. More broadly, these and similar findings produced a shift in thinking about personality, from explanations of behavior that assumed broad and stable dispositions to accounts recognizing the essential role of situational factors.

Table 12.1   Mean correlations reflecting behavioral consistency in similar versus different situations; significant correlations (*p* < .05) indicated with an *

Behavior and interpersonal situation	In similar situations	In different situations
Verbal aggression		
Peer teased, provoked	.40*	.17
Adult warned	.33*	.16
Adult punished	.36*	.15
Peer positive contact	.25	.07
Adult praised	.03	.09
Physical aggression		
Peer teased, provoked	.16	.12
Adult warned	.22	.11
Adult punished	.30*	.16
Peer positive contact	.03	.01
Adult praised	NA	NA
Whining		
Peer teased, provoked	.45*	.15
Adult warned	.27*	.19*
Adult punished	.25*	.14
Peer positive contact	.25*	.12
Adult praised	.23*	.09
Compliance		
Peer teased, provoked	.39*	.10
Adult warned	.26*	.08
Adult punished	.37*	.04
Peer positive contact	.09	.07
Adult praised	.07	.05
Prosocial talk		
Peer teased, provoked	.02	.16
Adult warned	.21*	.11
Adult punished	.11	.12
Peer positive contact	.35*	.18*
Adult praised	.14	.16

Source: Adapted from Shoda et al. (1994)

In sum, several different lines of research converge on the critical point that cognitions that are accessible in memory are more likely to direct behavior. Cognitions can become accessible for a variety of reasons. Some cues are so clear and semantic associations so strong that people cannot help but experience certain thoughts and feelings when they are encountered. In such cases, behavior is often affected. People's responses can also depend on their experiences so that the thoughts and feelings that are triggered in a given context may differ widely from person to person. In either case, accessible information strongly influences how one acts.

Stable Cognitions Direct Behavior

Accessibility is only one crucial factor in determining the effect of cognition on behavior. Another is the *stability* of cognitions. Stability refers to whether a person thinks similarly about an entity over time and across situations. Presumably, beliefs that you have embraced your entire life should be highly stable. If you have always viewed yourself as a patriotic person who loves his country, then you will likely react and behave consistently concerning your nation. Stability might be lower if you do not value patriotism, tend not to think of events in nationalistic terms, or have ambivalent feelings about your country. Such a person might feel pride in his country if he feels the nation has done something admirable but disappointment or even shame if he feels his nation has acted inappropriately.

Stable beliefs are generally more likely to affect behavior (Cooke & Sheeran, 2004; Dalege et al., 2019; Erber, Hodges, & Wilson, 1995; Glasman & Albarracín, 2006; Kraus, 1995). However, identifying the unique contribution of stability in accounting for behavior can be challenging because many of the same factors that increase the stability of cognitions also increase their accessibility (Eagly, 1992). Stable beliefs also tend to be more accessible than unstable beliefs (Glasman & Albarracín, 2006), and they are more likely to be based on direct experience (Doll & Ajzen, 1992). However, some factors appear to affect stability relatively directly, and they increase attitude-behavior correspondence by making attitudes more potent and not merely more accessible.

Low Ambivalence

One-sided attitudes, that is, evaluations that reflect only positive or negative (but not both) aspects of an object, are more likely to be stable and to produce attitude-consistent behavior (Glasman & Albarracín, 2006; Sipilä, Sundqvist, & Tarkiainen, 2017; van Harreveld, Nohlen, & Schneider, 2015). The behavior of an *ambivalent* person, "inclined to give it [an attitude object] equivalently strong positive or negative evaluations" (Thompson, Zanna, & Griffin, 1995, p. 367), can be difficult to predict (Conner, Sparks, Povey, James, Shepherd, & Armitage, 2002; Hohman, Crano, & Niedbala, 2015). A person who is ambivalent about his country might be highly critical of his nation's foreign policy while, at the same time, feeling great pride in the athletes representing that same nation. Conflicting evaluations might result from incompatibility between accessible cognitive components of attitudes (liking some actions while disliking other actions of your nation) or between cognitive and affective components (McGregor, Newby-Clark, & Zanna, 1999). An example of the latter might be a person who both enjoys the pleasure associated with his first cigarette of the day while also despising the expense and adverse health consequences of smoking. When a person simultaneously holds both positive and negative feelings toward an object or behavior, the stability of the attitude is naturally undermined, and the attitude's impact on behavior also tends to be reduced. Such a smoker might show a high degree of behavioral variability, perhaps resisting cigarettes during work hours but succumbing to their temptations when at a bar with friends (Lipkus, Green, Feaganes, & Sedikides, 2001; Menninga, Dijkstra, & Gebhardt, 2011).

In one study focusing on ambivalence in the social domain (Erickson, Newman, Peterson, & Scarsella, 2015), individuals' views of themselves were measured using scales designed to capture self-ambivalence (Scott, 1966; see also Bonanno, Notarius, Gunzerath, Keltner, &

Horowitz, 1998). Responses to these scales indicate whether one views oneself consistently across traits (e.g., judging oneself as dominant but not submissive) or has ambivalent self-views (e.g., judging oneself as both dominant and submissive). These participants were later recruited for week-long study in which they daily interacted with a different individual in 5-minute "get to know you" sessions. After each interaction, participants characterized their behavior in the session using a checklist assessing actions related to dominance, submissiveness, agreeableness, and quarrelsomeness. Analyses of these ratings indicated that people with higher self-ambivalence (i.e., those with a greater tendency to describe themselves with opposing dispositions) showed higher levels of fluctuation in their behavior when interacting with others.

Confidence

Beliefs held with high certainty and confidence also tend to be more stable and more consistently affect behavior (Rucker et al., 2014; Tormala, 2016). Individuals might have low confidence in an attitude if it is not based on direct experience (Fazio & Zanna, 1978b) but confidence can be increased with heightened exposure to persuasive messages (Berger, 1992; Berger & Mitchell, 1989) or by repeatedly expressing one's beliefs (Einhorn & Hogarth, 1978). Remarkably, merely expressing a belief can produce greater confidence in judgments and can increase its influence on behavior, even when an individual is untruthful about his or her beliefs. Johar and Sengupta (2002) showed American undergraduates advertisements for candy bars from overseas markets with which they would not have been familiar. Students were then asked to indicate their attitudes about each candy bar five times, except some students were asked to indicate their "true attitudes," whereas others were asked to "express the opposite of their true feelings." Another set of students (a control condition) did not report their attitudes. Finally, all students indicated their overall evaluations of each candy bar, their confidence in their evaluations, and which candy sample they would like to receive later. Evaluations were assessed again two days later as a measure of attitude stability.

Students who repeatedly reported their attitudes provided more confident evaluations than did students in the control condition who did not report their attitudes at all. Moreover, repeated evaluations were more stable over time and more strongly predicted participants' choices. This was true whether their stated evaluations were initially genuine or disingenuous. These data provide a strong test of the influence of repeated expression on confidence in and stability of attitudes and, ultimately, on behavior.

Relevant Cognitions Direct Behavior

The work discussed so far highlights several factors that moderate the strength of the relationship between internal states (attitudes, traits) and outward behavior. This research demonstrates that thought and action can be closely related in certain conditions and provides a framework for understanding when this relationship will be weaker. In addition to these substantive insights, the last several decades of research have also produced several theory-based refinements in how this relationship is measured. Through improved methods for measuring the relation between thought and action, it has become clear that they are linked more strongly than many had assumed.

One crucial insight was offered by Fishbein and Ajzen (1974), who suggested that research has chronically underestimated the magnitude of the relation between thought and action because of a poor correspondence in the operationalization of each construct. Many studies that had shown a weak relation between attitudes and behavior had tried to predict specific behaviors (e.g., the likelihood of recycling regularly) from measures of general attitudes (e.g., attitudes toward the environment). Fishbein and Ajzen argued that there is little reason to expect that general attitudes would strongly predict specific actions because any given attitude might manifest itself in many ways. For example, concerns about the environment might be expressed by recycling, by driving a hybrid vehicle, by replacing incandescent with LED bulbs, by becoming a vegetarian, or by donating money to the World Wide Fund for Nature. An environmentally-minded individual might express her beliefs by pursuing some, but probably not all, of these actions. Therefore, general attitudes about environmentalism would not be expected to correlate very highly with any single one of these behaviors.

To accurately assess the relationship between attitudes and behavior, researchers need to embrace the *principle of compatibility*, using measures of attitudes and behavior that equate for the target, the action, the context, and time elements (Ajzen & Fishbein, 1977; Ajzen, Fishbein, Lohmann, & Albarracín, 2019). Fishbein and Ajzen (1974) advocated aggregating across several behaviors when general attitudes are measured. By aggregating behaviors to create measures that correspond in generality to the attitude that is assessed, Fishbein and Ajzen (1974) showed that the strength of correlation between general religious attitudes and religious behavior increased dramatically (from approximately $r = +.15$ to $r = +.80$). In contrast, when specific behaviors are measured, attitudes about those particular actions should be assessed (e.g., "What is your attitude about recycling?"). Davidson and Jaccard's (1979) study on the attitude-behavior relationship

Table 12.2 Increased strength of attitude-behavior relationship with increased behavioral specificity

Attitude toward	r with using birth control in next 2-year period
Birth control	.08
Birth control pills	.32
Using birth control pills	.53
Using birth control pills during the next 2 years	.57

Source: Adapted from Davidson & Jaccard (1979)

regarding birth control showed that questions that increasingly focused on attitudes towards particular behaviors allowed much higher predictive power. As can be seen in Table 12.2, general attitudes towards birth control correlated poorly with the use of oral contraceptives. However, more specific attitudes provided a much stronger basis for predicting behavior.

This line of work has led researchers to be more sensitive about the degree of match between generalities and specifics in measuring both attitudes and actions. For researchers interested in the influence of general attitudes, measures of multiple actions allow aggregation of different behaviors performed in different contexts and different times. For researchers focused on predicting specific consequential behaviors (e.g., condom use to prevent AIDs (Albarracín, Johnson, Fishbein, & Muellerleile, 2001); organ donation (Siegel, Navarro, Tan, & Hyde, 2014), targeted measures of attitudes and behavioral intentions are necessary. As a result of this insight, it is now clear that thoughts can predict behavior to a much higher degree than had been previously appreciated.

Although aggregating across several behaviors solved a methodological problem that undermined the assessment of the relationship between general attitudes and action, this critique also reflected an important theoretical point. This analysis suggested that attempts to measure attitudes might activate in the respondent a cognitive representation not envisioned by the solicitor of the attitude report. In other words, the attitude "object" that is the focus of an attitude measure might bear little resemblance to the respondent's mental representation being used to assess and report their attitude. For example, if you ask a person about her attitude toward hamburgers, she might respond negatively if she had in mind the overcooked, flavorless burger that she had been served the previous evening. If she were then presented an appetizing-looking burger, it would not be surprising if she decided to eat it, even though this action might appear inconsistent with her stated attitude. The apparent hypocrisy is explained by a mismatch between the mental representation of the hamburger she used to assess her attitude and the hamburger she later encountered. When there is a poor fit between the attitude that is being assessed and the respondent's representation used to generate an evaluative response, the individual's actions might appear to be inconsistent with beliefs, even when they are not.

Consider, for example, the proprietors who encountered the Chinese couple that accompanied LaPiere (1934) in his travels across the United States. LaPiere was astounded at the low correspondence between the reported anti-Chinese policies of these establishments and their generous treatment of the couple. One possible way to explain this inconsistency is that the respondents' mental representations of Chinese underlying their policies bore little resemblance to the Chinese couple that appeared and almost always were accommodated. Whereas the "Chinese" imagined by the shopkeepers (given prevailing stereotypes) might have been poor, dirty, and unable to speak English, the couple did not match that representation to any degree. If they had, perhaps they would have been treated consistently with the stated restrictive policies. However, since they did not "fit" that image, they were generally greeted warmly. Attitudes might have guided behavior, but the attitudes that did so might have reflected evaluations of the subtype of "educated, cultured Chinese."

This interpretation is consistent with studies that have examined the role of *typicality* in the attitude-behavior relationship. These studies show that people tend to behave consistently with their attitudes when they correspond to the specific attitude object in question (i.e., when there is a match between the activated representation and the information encountered) (Lord & Lepper, 1999; Lord, Desforges, Fein, Pugh, & Lepper, 1994). This phenomenon was demonstrated nicely in a study (Lord, Lepper, & Mackie, 1984) in which undergraduates were asked whether they would help a transfer student from another college acclimate himself to the university. In the information provided about the student, it was implied that he was gay. Other information indicated that he was, based on common stereotypes from the time, either typical or atypical of gay men. When participants' expressed willingness to help the student was correlated with their previously-assessed attitudes toward gay men, this correlation was significant only when the student was described as being typical of gay male students. When the student was described as atypical of gays, attitudes towards gay men did not predict willingness to help. Thus, attitudes did predict behavior, but only when there was a match between the representations underlying the reported attitudes and the characteristics of the specific attitude "object." As might have been the case in the treatment of LaPiere's student couple, attitudes did not affect behavioral intentions when they were seen as low in relevance to the person(s) being described.

INTERIM SUMMARY In this section, we have reviewed research identifying conditions under which thoughts affect actions. Although *thinking* does not always direct *doing*, certain factors make it more likely that internal cognitive processes will be reflected in observable behavior. Thoughts that are accessible, stable, and held confidently are more likely to affect how a person behaves. Actions can be more consistent with thoughts than it appears if beliefs are measured at the correct level of specificity, and if the actors' memory representations correspond to a specific experience that is later encountered. Because there are conditions under which thinking and doing are quite closely related, social cognitive processes can provide, at least at times, a reasonable basis for predicting how a person might behave.

HOW DO COGNITIONS GUIDE BEHAVIOR?

In the last section, we discussed *when* thoughts guide actions but we did not detail in any depth how they do so. The ways that beliefs are translated into behavior has also received substantial empirical attention, and it is clear that beliefs affect behavior through several distinct mechanisms. The nature of the influence might be relatively direct or indirect. *Direct influence* is involved when a thought becomes accessible in memory and therefore increases the likelihood that thought-consistent behavior occurs without necessarily influencing other cognitive processes. *Indirect influence* refers to the role that active thoughts have on other processes, which themselves might be the basis of behavior. Thoughts can influence action through both routes, and the specific mechanism linking thought and action can vary depending on the nature of influence and the presence of other factors, such as available cognitive capacity, motivation, and prevailing social norms.

Direct Influence
Cognitions as Behavioral Triggers
As we discussed earlier, beliefs can be made accessible by features of the environment, and the accessibility of beliefs alone can produce behavioral consequences quite directly (Bargh & Chartrand, 1999; Dijksterhuis & Bargh, 2001). Examples include stereotype-consistent behavior following activation of social categories (Aarts et al., 2005; Bargh et al., 1996; Cesario, Plaks, Hagiwara, Navarrete, & Higgins, 2010; Chambon, 2009; Follenfant, Légal, Dinard, & Meyer, 2005; but see Doyen et al., 2012), mimicry of interactants' physical behavior (Chartrand & van Baaren, 2009; Paulus, 2014), prosocial behavior following exposure to God concepts (Preston & Ritter, 2013; Shariff & Norenzayan, 2008), and less indulgent, more helpful behavior following subliminal exposure to guilt-inducing adjectives (Zemack-Rugar, Bettman, & Fitzsimons, 2007). Goals and motives can also be activated by situational cues to produce unconscious activation of plans and behavior consistent with those representations (see Chartrand, Dalton, & Cheng, 2008; Gantman, 2017).

These are all examples of behavior being directed merely through the accessibility of thoughts with minimal volitional involvement. The reason for these behavioral effects has been debated. One account has invoked *ideomotor action* as a causal factor (Carpenter, 1852; James, 1890; Prinz, 1987; Shin, Proctor, & Capaldi, 2010). This argument posits that automatic behaviors arise through mental associations between constructs and actions. In such cases, individuals are typically unaware of the instigating stimulus or, if they are aware of the stimulus, deny the possible influence of the stimulus on their subsequent actions. Such behavioral responses require no decision to act in a manner consistent with accessible cognitive representations: "semantic concepts can be directly connected to motor programs" (Strack & Deutsch 2004, p. 224). A similar account, the *auto-motive model*, argues that primes directly activate motivational representations, which consequently activate behaviors appropriate to accomplish the goal (Bargh et al., 2001). Finally, the *active-self account* suggests that primes increase the accessibility of primed and associated constructs that, in turn, alter the active self-concept. For example, primes activating constructs such as meanness or helpfulness will temporarily and dynamically affect a person's view of the self, altering the likelihood of prime-related behaviors (Wheeler, DeMarree, & Petty, 2007, 2014). All accounts agree that action can flow quite directly from perception.

Cognitions as Information

Beliefs can also affect behavior in a relatively direct manner by serving as a source of information. When individuals have accessible and stable beliefs, these stored knowledge structures can simplify complex decisions and allow a perceiver to act without conducting an exhaustive (and, sometimes, exhausting!) analysis of options (Chaiken, 1987; Petty & Cacioppo, 1986). Consider the consumer who is confronted with an aisle in a store offering dozens of different kinds of cereal. They can often seem indistinguishable, and it is often difficult to know what information should be used to make a decision. If the consumer had no existing beliefs about brand preferences, choosing a cereal might prove quite time-consuming and annoying (e.g., Iyengar & Lepper, 2000). (In fact, we have had friends visiting from Europe complain about the overabundance of choices offered in the United States for this very reason.) Fortunately, the ready availability of object-relevant thoughts allows this decision to be made quite easily so that we do not have to exhaust our limited cognitive resources on such mundane decisions. The consumer might miss out on discovering a superior brand because not all information was utilized, but the effort saved might be worth this opportunity cost, particularly if the decision is not particularly important.

However, what about more consequential issues, where one's identity and values come into play, and individuals are motivated to process available information thoroughly? Does the same principle apply? Even in these circumstances, stored attitudes can serve as the basis of behavior in place of deliberative analysis of all relevant information. For example, Cohen (2003; see also Bolsen, Druckman, & Cook, 2014; Kam, 2005) showed that decisions regarding political issues among people with strong political preferences tend to be based primarily on party identification. When information about the position of their party on some issue was unavailable, these individuals based their evaluations of proposals on the details they contained and their consistency with ideological beliefs. However, when information about the position of their party on the issue was available, people sided with their party and acted accordingly, even though they showed no signs of lessened deliberative processing. These are people who are motivated and able to think systematically about the issues presented, but their partisan identities were the primary basis of their decision making and behavior.

Imagination as a Behavioral Trigger

People often imagine or try to explain hypothetical or unknown future events. They wonder about an upcoming sporting event, or election, or social occasion, and as they do so, they often imagine the outcome of that occasion. Several studies have asked participants to estimate the likelihood of a particular outcome. These studies typically find that people overestimate the likelihood of the outcome they imagined (Carroll, 1978; Gregory, Cialdini, & Carpenter, 1982; Hirt & Sherman, 1985; Ross, Lepper, Strack, & Steinmetz, 1977; Sherman et al., 1985). An obvious explanation for this effect draws on the availability heuristic. When imagining an event and its outcome, certain features or images of the scene and action easily come to mind and become readily available in memory. When asked for likelihood judgments, those features are available and can influence participants' probability estimates.

More relevant to the present discussion is the finding that mental imagery also can influence behavior (Gregory et al., 1982; Miles & Crisp, 2014; Sherman, Skov, Hervitz, & Stock, 1981). In several studies examining imagery and behavioral intentions (Gaesser & Schacter, 2014), participants were given 30 stories depicting a person in need, each one shown for 10 seconds. After the stories were presented, participants were asked to complete one of five tasks, each one for one minute: (1) complete a set of Math problems, (2) evaluate the writing style and source of the stories, (3) estimate ways the person in need could be helped, (4) remember an experience of helping a person, or (5) imagine an episode of helping a person depicted in one of the stories. After this task, participants were again presented with the stories and estimated the likelihood that they would assist the people in need. Across the studies, both remembering and imagining helping a person increased behavioral intentions to assist. However, behavioral intentions to help were consistently highest when people engaged in imagery.

Another study (Gaesser et al., 2020) extended this research by examining whether people actually engage in more prosocial behavior following imagery and whether such an increase in helping might reduce ingroup bias. All participants in the studies were asked to report their political identification at the beginning of the experiment. Some participants were then asked to imagine and write about a time when they had helped a person in need, generating as much detail as possible. Other participants were assigned to a control condition where their task did not involve imagination. Following this task, participants then read a series of stories about situations where a person needed assistance. Half of these stories were about Republicans, and half were about Democrats. Participants were asked to indicate the degree they were willing to help each individual and, in some studies, to take action to offer assistance (write a letter of support or make a monetary donation to the victim). Studies showed that imagining a helping episode increased both behavioral intentions and helping behaviors for ingroup and outgroup targets, eliminating a bias favoring the ingroup that emerged in the control condition.

Prediction as a Behavioral Trigger

People imagine not only future events but also predict future behavior and outcomes. Whether it be general ("What will the stock market be like next year?") or specific ("Who will win the next World Series?"), people frequently generate predictions. Furthermore, they often make predictions about their future behavior ("I will definitely vote in the upcoming election"). Does making predictions increase the likelihood of future action?

According to a recent meta-analysis (Wood et al., 2016), it does. In one early demonstration of this tendency (Sherman, 1980), an experimenter called community residents selected randomly from the phone book and asked them to anticipate if they would agree to spend three hours collecting money for the American Cancer Society if they were contacted by someone making this request. Three days later, a different experimenter, posing as a worker for the Cancer Society, called and requested help in collecting neighborhood donations (the Predict-Request condition). In a control condition (the Request-only), a separate set of citizens received a call from the second experimenter who requested help in collecting donations. In the Predict-Request condition, nearly 48% of citizens predicted that they would agree to such a request. When contacted by the Cancer Society, 31% of these participants agreed to volunteer. In the Request-only condition, only 4% of the people consented. Thus, when they had considered what they would do in a possible future situation, people behaved in a way consistent with what they had imagined and predicted.

In a similar study (Greenwald, Carnot, Beach, & Young, 1987), people who had been contacted by telephone were asked to predict whether they would vote in an upcoming election. Half of the participants were first asked if they intended to vote (Predict condition), and the other half were not asked (No Predict condition). Paralleling Sherman's results, the proportion of respondents who predicted that they would vote was much higher than the overall turnout data. Also paralleling the previous study, those who predicted they would vote (virtually all respondents) did so with higher probability than the No Predict control participants who did not predict their behavior.

These studies document a strong effect of thoughts on the enactment of corresponding behavior. As in the studies on imagination, the effect is remarkably simple: asking people to predict whether they will perform a socially desirable action (volunteering, voting) increases the probability that they will perform the behavior.

Indirect Influence

The preceding section focused on the role of activated cognitive representations (including attitudes, stereotypes, and goals) as a direct basis of behavior. In such cases, individuals rely on accessible information to guide action. Now we turn to a discussion of how accessible information can influence behavior *indirectly*. In these cases, accessible thoughts influence other processes that are co-occurring within the actor to affect behavior circuitously.

Cognitions and Biased Information Processing

Beliefs can have an indirect effect on behavior by influencing how information is sought and processed. Beliefs tend to focus attention and bias memory in a manner that favors material that is consistent with one's beliefs and attitudes. Ditto and his colleagues (e.g., Ditto & Lopez, 1992; Ditto et al., 2003, 2019) have provided extensive evidence of biased processing in a variety of domains, including impression formation, politics, and health. People more readily accept the validity of information that is consistent rather than inconsistent with desired beliefs. For example, people judge research findings consistent with their attitudes toward homosexuality as more convincing than findings that challenge their attitudes (Munro & Ditto, 1997). Conversely, people are quite reluctant to accept information that contradicts desired conclusions, and such information tends to be carefully scrutinized (Clark, Wegener, & Fabrigar, 2008; Clark, Wegener, Habashi, & Evans, 2012). Cacioppo and Petty (1979; Petty & Cacioppo, 1979) showed, for example, that individuals exposed to persuasive arguments tended to generate more counterarguments to counterattitudinal compared with proattitudinal messages.

The bias favoring preferred over unpreferred information ultimately can produce substantial consequences for behavior (e.g., Brownstein, 2003; Cha, Najmi, Park, Finn, & Nock, 2010; Meffert, Chung, Joiner, Waks, & Garst, 2006). The tendency to seek out and to believe views we already possess – and to avoid, scrutinize, and readily reject information that challenges our beliefs – means that existing beliefs tend to be self-reinforcing and self-perpetuating. Preferring information that reinforces existing beliefs means that our information processing systems tend to make our beliefs stronger, more consistent, and more accessible over time. Thus, biases in information processing strengthen properties of existing beliefs that we know produce strong relations between thought and action.

Cognitions as the Basis of Intentions

Thoughts also influence behavior indirectly by serving as the basis of *behavioral intentions*, that is, decisions made to act in a particular way. Once formed, intentions become the single most important predictor of actual behavior (Ajzen et al. 2019; Godin & Kok, 1996; Gollwitzer, 1993; Triandis, 1977). Although intentions do not guarantee behavior (Sheeran & Webb, 2016), they nonetheless play a central role in several theories focusing on the link between thought and action.

For example, Ajzen's *Theory of Planned Behavior* (Ajzen, 1991, 2012) argues that the most immediate causes of behavior are not attitudes but intentions to engage in a particular behavior. As displayed in Figure 12.3, intentions arise from the individual's attitudes towards personally engaging in the behavior in question (with positive attitudes increasing intention strength), subjective norms (with supportive norms increasing strength), and perceived behavioral control (with higher control producing stronger intentions).

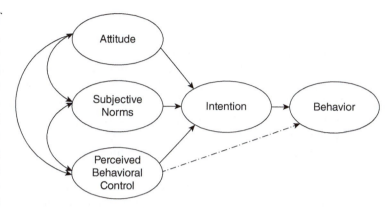

Figure 12.3   Theory of planned behavior
Source: Adapted from Ajzen (1991)

People engage in behavior to the extent they have consciously decided to do so, and this decision process typically reflects the judgment that intended behaviors are likely to have good consequences. We exercise because we enjoy it and think that it will improve our health. We contribute to charities because we think doing so will benefit others, because we can afford it, and because our action will be viewed favorably by others. As these examples illustrate, this perspective on the formation of intentions is most applicable to situations where individuals are motivated to think deliberatively about their actions and are capable of doing so (i.e., have the expertise and ample cognitive capacity). As such, this perspective represents a "pure statement of individual rationality" (Eagly, 1992, p. 694). Under these conditions, this approach has been quite successful in accounting for actions in numerous behavioral domains (e.g., Albarracín et al., 2001; Christian, Armitage, & Abrams, 2007; Yadav & Pathak, 2017; see meta-analyses by Armitage & Conner, 2001; Steinmetz, Knappstein, Ajzen, Schmidt, & Kabst, 2016).

However, intending to do something is not always enough. Gollwitzer and his colleagues (Gollwitzer, 1993, 1996; see summaries by Gollwitzer, 1999; Gollwitzer & Sheeran, 2006; Gollwitzer, Bayer, & McCulloch, 2005; Sheeran, Milne, Webb, & Gollwitzer, 2005) have shown that behavioral intentions alone do not ensure that people will behave consistently with their goals and motives. People must go beyond general intentions ("I want to improve my physical condition") to form *implementation intentions* that specify both the conditions under which intentions are activated and how they will be pursued. Implementation intentions are the mechanism by which general behavioral intentions are turned into action because they delineate specific behaviors that will occur given certain triggering circumstances.

Similar to Mischel's characterization of personality, Gollwitzer argues that implementation intentions exist as "if…then" contingencies ("If I need to go to the grocery store, I will walk instead of drive"). They appear to be effective because they serve as a mental link between the presence of a situational cue and a goal-directed response (Gollwitzer & Sheeran, 2006). Because of the existence of this mental link, the representation of the cue is highly accessible in memory, making it easier for the individual to detect the cue in relevant situations (Aarts, Dijksterhuis & Midden, 1999; Achtziger, Bayer, & Gollwitzer, 2012; Webb & Sheeran, 2004). Once the cue is detected, the response occurs relatively automatically (Brandstätter, Lengfelder, & Gollwitzer, 2001; Gollwitzer & Brandstätter, 1997; Legrand, Bieleke, Gollwitzer, & Mignon, 2017) and potentially interfering thoughts and feelings are inhibited (Achtziger, Gollwitzer, & Sheeran, 2008; Schweiger Gallo, Pfau, & Gollwitzer, 2012). Intentions are most likely to produce behavioral consequences when they are tied to specific actions and readily activated in appropriate contexts.

An impressive body of evidence shows that goals associated with implementation intentions are dramatically more likely to be acted upon than goals alone (Gollwitzer, 1999; Sheeran, Webb, & Gollwitzer, 2005). In one study (Orbell, Hodgkins, & Sheeran, 1997), 100% of women who had the goal of performing a breast self-examination in the next month and had specified where and when they would perform the exam did so. In contrast, only 53% of the women who had the same goal but who had not specified when and where it would occur followed through with the self-examination. Another experiment (Milne, Orbell, & Sheeran, 2002) assessed the efficacy of interventions designed to increase vigorous exercise among college students. One group of students was given a pamphlet containing information about the cardiovascular benefits of regular exercise. In contrast, another group received the pamphlet but were also asked to indicate the day, time, and place that they intended to exercise. Compared with a control group who experienced no intervention, the students who received only the pamphlet were not significantly more likely to have exercised at least once during the subsequent week (38% vs. 35%). However, an astounding 91% of students who also formed implementation intentions did so.

In sum, implementation intentions bind goals to specific contexts and to situational cues that make those intentions accessible and more likely to produce goal-consistent actions. It is interesting to note that just as people are naturally more inclined to behave consistently in situations that trigger similar thoughts and emotions (Mischel & Shoda, 1995), research on implementation intentions shows how people can purposely tie goals to situations in order to trigger desired behavior and consistency in their actions over time.

Cognitions as the Basis of Inaction

So far, our discussion of thought and action has focused exclusively on behaviors that people engage in as they pursue their interests and desires. *Action goals* – general motivations to utilize effortful behaviors to address one's needs – are critical in acquiring essentials such as shelter, food, and safety. Albarracín and her colleagues (Albarracín, Hepler, & Tannenbaum, 2011; Albarracín, Sunderrajan, Dai, & White, 2019; Albarracín, Wang, & McCulloch, 2018) have argued that people also sometimes have *inaction goals*, motivations not to engage in action. People might choose not to act if they are fatigued or overwhelmed. Inaction might also be required to avoid engaging in behaviors about which one is ambivalent (e.g., not eating a piece of chocolate cake when dieting) (Hepler, Albarracín, McCulloch, & Noguchi, 2012).

Once activated, inaction goals produce numerous consequences. For example, studies in which participants were exposed to subliminal or supraliminal primes related to inaction (e.g., "stand," "still," and "calm") showed lowered cognitive and physical activities including exercising, eating, and problem-solving compared with participants primed with activity primes (see Albarracín et al., 2011, for a review). Inaction primes also lead to slower reaction times on memory tasks (Gendolla & Silvestrini, 2010). Inaction goals also affect the processing of persuasive messages. In studies where participants were exposed to inaction (compared with action) primes, these participants were more open to attitude-inconsistent information (Hart & Albarracín, 2012) and showed more considerable attitude change (Albarracín & Handley, 2011). These results show that although action goals often are useful for pursuing one's goals, they also can promote impulsivity. In contrast, inaction goals will decrease various kinds of activity, but they encourage careful and evenhanded deliberation.

IMPLICIT AND EXPLICIT INFLUENCES ON BEHAVIOR

In Chapter 3, we introduced the distinction between explicit and implicit cognition. *Explicit cognition* pertains to processes about which a person usually has some awareness and control. In contrast, *implicit cognition* refers to processes that often occur without the person's awareness and are more difficult to control. Both explicit and implicit processes play essential and complementary roles in many aspects of social functioning, including people's attentional processes, their interpretations and evaluation of events, and their judgments. Research has also demonstrated that the distinction between implicit and explicit processes is important in the domain of behavior (Cameron et al., 2012; Greenwald, Poehlman, et al., 2009; Kurdi et al., 2019; Oswald, Mitchell, Blanton, Jaccard, & Tetlock, 2013, 2015). Although some have questioned the magnitude of implicit influences on real-world behavior (Carlsson & Agerström, 2016; Oswald et al., 2015), implicit attitudes and beliefs have been tied to behavior in a variety of consequential domains. For example, implicit influences on action have been shown in voting (Greenwald, Smith, Sriram, Bar-Anan, & Nosek, 2009; Mo, 2015; Payne, Krosnick, Pasek, Lelkes, Akhtar, & Tompson, 2010), economic decisions and consumer behavior (Perkins & Forehand, 2010; Stanley, Sokol-Hessner, Banaji, & Phelps, 2011; Stepanikova, Triplett, & Simpson, 2011), hiring and employment (Agerström & Rooth, 2011; Ziegert & Hanges, 2005), and health (Wiers, Houben, Roefs, De Jong, Hofmann, & Stacy, 2010).

In this section, we discuss how implicit and explicit beliefs can affect behavior in different ways and can influence different types of behavior. In addition, we consider how the relative dominance of implicit versus explicit effects on behavior depends on several factors. That explicit and implicit cognition influence behavior differently should not be particularly surprising since implicit and explicit attitudes are typically only modestly correlated (Nosek, 2005; Nosek, Smyth, et al., 2007), can arise from distinct cognitive processes (Wilson, Lindsey, & Schooler, 2000), and reflect different kinds of associations in memory (Gawronski & Bodenhausen, 2006).

Even before the recent explosion of research on implicit cognition, Fazio (1990; Fazio & Olson, 2014) proposed that automatically-activated thoughts and attitudes play essential roles in influencing behavior. In his Motivation and Opportunity as Determinants (MODE) model of attitude-behavior relations, Fazio argued that automatically activated attitudes tend to serve as the default influence on behavior unless the individual has both the motivation and the opportunity to override such responses. It is only when the person has sufficient motivation and opportunity to consider the consequences of various actions that explicit attitudes will be the primary basis of responses. As such, one might expect that implicit beliefs will be more likely to affect behaviors that are difficult to control or when the individual is unaware that the opportunity to influence the behavior might exist.

When Do Explicit vs. Implicit Beliefs Direct Behavior?

The fact that implicit and explicit beliefs produce different (and occasionally contradictory) behavioral responses might imply that our behavior is continuously involved in a "tug of war" between our explicit and implicit systems. However, that is typically not the case. There has been some speculation about the ways that behavior is affected by implicit and explicit processes, but there are several ways that they can act in concert to influence behavior (Greenwald & Banaji, 2017; Greenwald & Lai, 2020). First, implicit attitudes might directly affect behavior without conscious involvement, similar to the ideomotor notion introduced earlier. Second, implicit and explicit attitudes might be activated and operate simultaneously on behavior, producing additive effects (Greenwald & Banaji, 1995; Wilson, Lindsey, & Schooler, 2000). Third, implicit attitudes might automatically activate associations that are then used consciously to guide behavior. Although there is currently no empirical basis to differentiate when each of these processes is most likely (Greenwald & Lai, 2020), they each suggest that implicit and explicit processes can influence behavior cooperatively and harmoniously.

The relative influence of implicit and explicit beliefs is moderated by several of the critical social cognitive variables we have been discussing throughout this book. Some of these factors pertain to situation variables, and others relate to individual differences in information processing (Perugini, Richetin, & Zogmaister, 2010).

Situational Moderators

Situational factors that influence the motivation and ability to engage in deliberative processing tend to increase the influence of explicit beliefs on behavior, whereas implicit beliefs tend to prevail when motivation or ability to process is low (Bless & Schwarz, 1999; Fazio & Towles-Schwen, 1999; Friese, Hofmann, & Schmitt, 2008).

For example, cognitive load affects whether implicit or explicit processes drive behavior (Friese, Hofmann, & Wänke, 2008; Hofmann, Rauch, & Gawronski, 2007). Since explicit processes are typically resource-dependent, it should not be surprising that manipulations that temporarily limit perceivers' cognitive capacity increase the influence of implicit processes. This shift from explicit to implicit bases of responding was demonstrated nicely in a study in which implicit and explicit measures of intergroup attitudes were collected from Italian and German citizens (Hofmann, Gschwendner, Castelli, & Schmitt, 2008). These individuals then interacted with an ingroup member (a fellow citizen) or an outgroup member (a citizen from another country). For half of the interview questions, participants' control resources were reduced through manipulation of cognitive load. Implicit attitudes were more predictive of behavior when participants were under a cognitive load than when they were not. Explicit attitudes were somewhat more predictive than implicit attitudes when perceivers had ample cognitive resources. Another study (Czopp, Monteith, Zimmerman, & Lynam, 2004) demonstrated similar findings in the domain of condom use. Explicit attitudes towards condoms predicted intentions to use them when situations prompted people to think carefully (i.e., when environmental cues signaled an increased risk for contracting STDs). However, implicit attitudes predicted intended use when deliberative processing was not encouraged.

Time pressure can influence whether implicit or explicit processes more strongly account for behavior (Pegan & de Luca, 2012). In one study (Friese, Wänke, & Plessner, 2006), participants' explicit and implicit preferences for different food brands were assessed, and they were then asked to make a purchasing decision under time pressure or with no time limit. For participants who had divergent implicit and explicit attitudes towards the products, they were more likely to select the implicitly preferred brand over the explicitly preferred one when decisions were made under time pressure. When they had ample time to make a decision, they were more likely to choose the product for which they had positive explicit attitudes.

Similar, albeit more consequential, effects have been shown by practicing physicians. In one such study (Stepanikova, 2012), family physicians assessed a case involving a patient with chest pain under either low time pressure (having to evaluate a case in three minutes) or high time pressure (evaluating two cases in the same time). Before the presentation of the case, these physicians completed a "concentration exercise" in which they unwittingly were presented with words designed to make accessible the categories of Black, Hispanic, or White. In a control condition, participants were exposed to stimuli unrelated to race. (Results from the control condition were identical with those obtained in the White prime condition.)

Results displayed in Figure 12.4 show that racial primes interacted with time pressure to affect judgments of the patient's condition and physicians' willingness to refer the patient to a specialist. Under low time pressure, there were no differences in the seriousness of the diagnosis or the willingness to make a referral following differing racial primes. In contrast, under high time pressure, diagnoses for the patient were less serious if the physician had been exposed to Black or Hispanic primes compared with the White or control primes. Effects were particularly pronounced for decisions following Black primes under limited time. Although physicians certainly vary in the degree they harbor implicit bias, these results show that such implicit attitudes can affect consequential decisions when judgments must be made quickly.

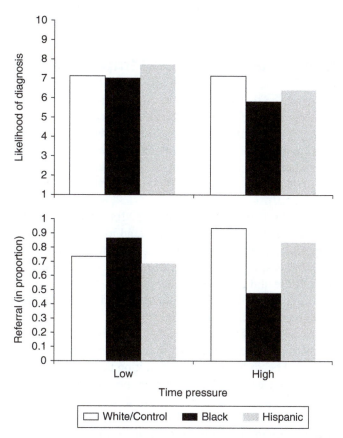

Figure 12.4   Diagnosis of coronary heart disease (top panel) and willingness to refer a patient to a specialist (bottom panel) as a function of racial primes and time pressure

Source: Adapted from Stepanikova (2012)

Individual Differences as Moderators

Individual differences in motivation and ability to process thoroughly also can shift the basis of behavior. People low in need for cognition (Florack, Scarabis & Bless, 2001), who rely on intuition (Hofmann & Baumert, 2010), who are low in motivation to control prejudice (Gabriel, Banse, & Hug, 2007; Olson & Fazio, 2004), and who have low behavioral control (Ellis, Collins, Homish, Parks, & Kiviniemi, 2016) appear particularly reliant on implicit attitudes to guide behavior.

In one study examining drinking behavior (Ostafin & Marlatt, 2008), undergraduate drinkers who were, based on their responses to a questionnaire, low in mindfulness showed a strong relation between implicit alcohol beliefs and the tendency to engage in binge-drinking behaviors. If such a person showed a positive implicit attitude toward alcohol, he was more likely to have consumed at least five drinks during one occasion or to have experienced alcohol-related problems, such as getting hurt or injured in the previous month. In contrast, drinkers high in mindfulness showed no relation between implicit alcohol attitudes and drinking behavior. These people had an apparent ability to regulate their drinking behavior so that it was less likely to reflect the mental associations they held regarding alcohol. These studies converge to suggest that implicit beliefs are most likely to influence behavior when cognitive resources and motivation to process are low.

Different Influence of Explicit and Implicit Beliefs

Studies suggest that implicit beliefs are particularly likely to influence spontaneous and non-verbal behavior (i.e., behavior that is difficult to control or about which people are typically inattentive), whereas explicit beliefs tend to influence behavior that is thoughtfully determined or actions that seemingly can be controlled (Amodio & Devine, 2006; Bessenoff & Sherman, 2000; Dislich, Zinkernagel, Ortner, & Schmitt, 2010; Ferguson, 2007; Gonsalkorale, von Hippel, Sherman, & Klauer, 2009; Hofmann et al., 2008; Huntjens, Rijkeboer, Krakau, & de Jong, 2014; Neumann, Hülsenbeck, & Seibt, 2004; Olson & Fazio, 2007; Rudolph, Schröder-Abè, Riketta, & Schütz, 2010).

McConnell and Leibold (2001; see also Jellison, McConnell, & Gabriel, 2004) provided some of the earliest evidence that implicit attitudes tend to particularly influence spontaneous behavior. In their experiment, White undergraduates completed both a series of self-report measures and an implicit measure (an IAT) of attitudes towards White and Black people while interacting with both a White and Black experimenter. Unbeknownst to the participants, a hidden video camera recorded the actions of the students, and a microphone recorded all verbal exchanges. From these recordings, trained judges (who were unaware of the students' racial attitudes) coded various aspects of the students' behavior, including their overall friendliness, the frequency of laughter, and the curtness of their responses to questions. The judges also systematically noted verbal behavior, including speaking time and the number of speech errors and hesitations. Both explicit and implicit measures predicted experimenters' ratings of the interaction. Specifically, for participants who showed more pro-White bias (on either their self-reported attitudes or the IAT), their overt behavior was seen as more favorable toward the White than the Black experimenter. However, only the implicit (IAT) measure predicted more subtle nonverbal behaviors, such as the length of the conversation, the number of smiles, and the lower frequency of speech errors and hesitations in interactions with the White compared with the Black experimenter.

Similarly, Dovidio, Kawakami, and Gaertner (2002), using different explicit and implicit measures, had students interact with a White or Black confederate in a more structured interaction in which both people responded to common questions about dating relationships. Coders rated the verbal and nonverbal friendliness of the interaction from videotaped recordings. Analyses of those ratings indicated that explicit racial bias was correlated with verbal friendliness, but that implicit bias predicted friendliness as reflected in nonverbal behavior. In addition, explicit attitudes predicted participants' judgments of their friendliness toward White versus Black partners. In contrast, implicit attitudes predicted the bias perceived in the participants' friendliness by the confederates and the observers. Together, these studies show that implicit attitudes predict spontaneous behavior but that explicit attitudes tend to predict deliberative behavior.

Because explicit and implicit beliefs are associated with different behaviors, is it possible for implicit beliefs to predict future behavior that individuals cannot themselves foresee? The answer appears to be that they can, as recently demonstrated in several interesting studies. In one intriguing study of voting behavior (Arcuri, Castelli, Galdi, Zogmaister, & Amadori, 2008), Italians who reported being unsure how they would vote in an upcoming national election completed an IAT examining the strength of their associations between each of two political candidates and evaluative words. Individuals' implicit preferences, as reflected in their IAT performance, significantly predicted their later voting behavior, even though these same individuals were unable to verbally report their preferred candidate at the time they completed the IAT. Implicit beliefs allowed prediction of future behavior even though people could not themselves anticipate how they were going to act.

HOW DOES *BEHAVIOR* GUIDE COGNITIONS?

So far in this chapter, we have examined when and how cognitions have a causal influence on behavior. This review has shown that cognitive processes, both explicit and implicit, often precede and influence behavior. However, much research indicates that this temporal order can be reversed. That is, behavior can causally influence cognitions (Harmon-Jones, Armstrong, & Olson, 2019). Evidence supporting this idea comes from several different lines of research. Some studies emphasize motivated shifts in attitudes following the performance of behaviors that are seen as inconsistent with one's beliefs and values. Other studies have focused on processes that people engage in to infer their attitudes from their actions.

Attitude Change from Performing Attitude Inconsistent Behaviors

Research on cognitive dissonance has shown that people are motivated to reduce discrepancies between attitudes and behavior when their actions violate attitudes they view as important. When such inconsistencies between valued beliefs and behavior are recognized, it creates an aversive state (dissonance) that individuals are motivated to reduce. One way to do so is to change one's cognitions to make them more consistent with one's behavior (see Cooper, 2007).

The ability of behavior to change attitudes was demonstrated in a classic study by Festinger and Carlsmith (1959). In this experiment, participants were paid either $1 or $20 to complete a tedious and boring task. Later, these participants were asked to enthusiastically describe the task to a peer who was about to begin the same experiment. For those participants who had received only $1, this would presumably create a high degree of dissonance; they had misled a peer about the experiment for a small reward. In contrast, participants who were paid $20 could justify their deception by considering the significant compensation they received. To reduce the dissonance caused by telling a peer that a tedious task was actually appealing, individuals might convince themselves that the task was enjoyable. In fact, participants in the $1 condition were more likely to report at the end of the study that the task had been quite enjoyable compared with the participants who had received $20. Beliefs were changed to match behavior when individuals could not invoke situational factors to justify their actions.

Dissonance and attitude change can also result from *hypocrisy*, when one's actions are shown to be inconsistent with one's stated beliefs and values (Aronson, Fried, & Stone, 1991; Priolo, Milhabet, Codou, Fointiat, Lebarbenchon, & Gabarrot, 2016; Stone & Fernandez, 2008; see Priolo, Pelt, Bauzel, Rubens, Voisin, & Fointiat, 2019, for a meta-analysis). In one study examining hypocrisy as a means for behavior change (Stone, Wiegand, Cooper, & Aronson, 1997), participants were asked to videotape a speech for high schoolers emphasizing the importance of condom use in preventing AIDS. In contrast to dissonance paradigms, this message was consistent with the vast majority of college students' values. However, after giving the speech, some participants were asked to "pick out the excuses that have applied to the times in the past when YOU failed to use condoms" (hypocrisy). In other conditions, participants gave the speech but did not consider their past failings (advocacy), prepared a speech but never gave it and listed their previous personal failings in condom use (self reasons), or listed excuses that other people had used for not using condoms in the past (other reasons).

After supposedly completing the experiment, participants were paid several dollars and, as they were about to leave, were approached by a second experimenter. This experimenter provided an opportunity for participants in some conditions to contribute to a program for the homeless or (in other conditions) to purchase condoms. Participants could not both contribute to the homeless and purchase condoms. This manipulation was used to see if people would engage in behaviors unrelated to condom use to restore their positive feelings about themselves (by aiding the homeless) or to specifically act in a manner relating to the behavior that had been the focus of the experiment (condom use). As is shown in Figure 12.5, participants in the hypocrisy condition who admitted their personal failings regarding an advocated desirable behavior engaged in a high level of actions to restore self-worth (when that was the only behavioral response available) or to remediate the hypocrisy (when such an option was available.) Participants in the other conditions showed lower levels of both behaviors and abysmal levels of prosocial behavior in the advocacy condition. This shows that the experience

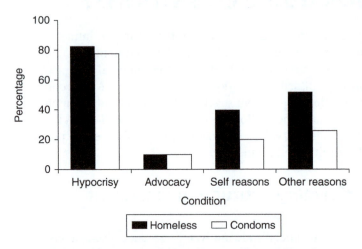

Figure 12.5 Percentage of participants who contributed to feeding the homeless or purchased condoms as a function of condition

Source: Adapted from Stone et al. (1997)

of hypocrisy and not merely advancing a viewpoint about how people should behave was at the root of subsequent changes in attitudes and behavior.

Attitude Change from Behavioral Inferences

Beliefs can follow behavior even in the absence of dissonance and hypocrisy. In Bem's self-perception theory (Bem, 1972), individuals infer their attitudes by observing their behavior. Just as outside observers might assume that we enjoyed a comedy movie because we repeatedly laughed while watching the film, the self functions in the same way. One's own attitudes and beliefs are inferred from noting the way one behaves concerning various situations, objects, and people. Though both cognitive dissonance and self-perception theories suggest that behavior can causally influence beliefs, they differed radically regarding the reasons why this occurs and how they do so.

Research evidence now indicates that the processes described by cognitive dissonance and self-perception both occur but tend to do so in different situations (Fazio, Zanna, & Cooper, 1977). When one's behavior is strongly inconsistent with what is considered acceptable for the self, cognitive dissonance will arise, and beliefs will be modified as a means to reduce dissonance. However, when one's behavior only modestly diverges from one's beliefs, self-perception processes tend to dominate. So, for example, a person might experience dissonance and change her beliefs to reduce it if she found herself enjoying a movie starring a comic who had previously offended her by telling sexist jokes. If she previously did not have strong feelings about the comic, however, then she might readily infer that she believed the comic was talented based on her laughter while watching the film.

A related phenomenon involves attitude change resulting from compliance with social norms. It has been argued that prosocial change (e.g., encouraging pro-environmental, pro-health, anti-bullying, and anti-racist attitudes) might be achieved more effectively by changing relevant social norms rather than attitudes (Crandall, Eshleman, & O'Brien, 2002; Paluck, Shepherd, & Aronow, 2016; Sheeran et al. (2016); Stangor, Sechrist, & Jost, 2001; Tankard & Paluck, 2016; Yamin, Fei, Lahlou, & Levy, 2019). In one recent study examining how perceived changes in social norms affected attitudes (Tankard & Paluck, 2017), participants were presented with brief articles predicting the likely outcome of an upcoming Supreme Court ruling on marriage equality. The articles indicated through their headlines and content that an expert panel either expected that the Supreme Court would or would not rule in favor of gay marriage ("Supreme Court [Un]Likely to Rule in Favor of Gay Marriage"). After reading these articles, participants indicated their

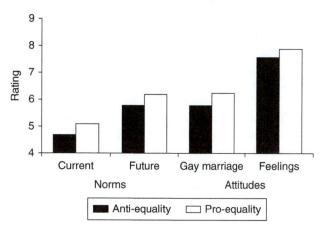

Figure 12.6 Perceived norms and attitudes as a function of expected Supreme Court decision (feeling thermometer ratings converted to 10-point scale)

Source: Adapted from Tankard & Paluck (2017)

perception of current and future norms, their current support for marriage equality, and, using a feeling thermometer, their attitudes toward gay men. Results (depicted in Figure 12.6) showed that participants who had been led to believe that the Supreme Court would support marriage equality reported stronger beliefs in current and future norms supporting same-sex marriage. They also were more likely to express support for marriage equality and showed more positive attitudes on the feeling thermometer. A subsequent large field study following the pro-equality decision showed a similar shift in perceived norms, although there was no evidence that attitudes had changed in response to the new norms. These results show that changes in perceived norms can change attitudes, although such effects might be neither guaranteed nor immediate.

Finally, an extensive interdisciplinary literature on *embodied cognition* (Schwarz & Lee, 2019; Shapiro, 2019) argues that cognitive processes are rooted in interactions between the body and the external world, such that cognition and behavior may occur without the involvement of any internal representations. Although pointed criticism has been directed at this general approach (e.g., Goldinger, Papesh, Barnhart, Hansen, & Hout, 2016; Mahon, 2015), researchers in social cognition have explored whether signals from one's posture or position in space, one's gestures, or one's facial expressions might affect evaluative responses and attitudes. Early evidence consistent with this perspective was provided in a study (Strack, Martin, & Stepper, 1988; see also Noah et al., 2018) in which participants judged the humorousness of a series of cartoons while holding a pen with their lips (producing a frowning expression) or their teeth (producing a smiling expression). Individuals who were induced to smile reported the cartoons as funnier, even though they tended to be oblivious to the possible influence of their facial expressions on their judgments.

A second example of research on embodied cognition focuses on the ways that perceivers' arm movements can influence judgments of stimuli. Pulling arm movements (flexion) are often associated with approaching a desired object and pushing movements (extension) with the avoidance of undesired objects. Some studies (Cacioppo, Priester, & Bernston, 1993; Priester, Cacioppo, & Petty, 1996) have shown that having individuals flex or extend their arms while judging unfamiliar stimuli affected liking judgments. For example, arm flexion increased, but extension decreased, the reported pleasantness of Chinese phonetic symbols. However, other research (Centerbar & Clore, 2006) demonstrates that arm contractions do not bias evaluation in and of themselves. Instead, they facilitate evaluations that are compatible with the movement of the body. Therefore, negative stimuli were judged more positively when arms were extended, but positive stimuli were judged more favorably when arms were flexed.

Still other research indicates that the meaning of arm actions, and not the specific muscles involved, are responsible for these effects (Laham, Kashima, Dix, Wheeler, & Levis, 2014; Markman & Brendl, 2005; Seibt, Neumann, Nussinson, & Strack, 2008). From this perspective, attitudinal inferences are drawn from the conceptual implications of specific movements in terms of approach and avoidance motivations. Importantly, the way a task is framed can reverse the meaning of particular arm motions. Instructions to extend one's arms to "push it away" would activate avoidance, but that same motion would activate approach if it were characterized as "extend your arms towards it." Conversely, pulling one's arms towards oneself could be framed as "drawing it towards you" or "drawing your hands away from it." A recent meta-analysis provided the most substantial support for this account of effects involving arm movements on attitudes (Laham, Kashima, Dix, & Wheeler, 2015).

In sum, these studies show that the causal relationship between social thought and action is bidirectional (Dalege et al., 2019; Holland et al., 2002; Neumann, Förster, & Strack, 2003). Although beliefs and attitudes can direct behavior, a person's actions can also influence how individuals think and make judgments.

SOCIAL COGNITION AND ACTION IN UNDERSTANDING THE SELF, PERSONS, AND GROUPS

We now consider the implications of what we have learned about the relationship between thought and behavior to the three recurring topic areas, self-perception, person perception, and group perception.

Social Cognition and Action in Understanding the Self

The self as a cognitive representation is central to social information processing. For example, self-relevant information draws one's attention (Chapter 4), is interpreted in a manner that favors the self (Chapters 5), is evaluated more favorably (Chapter 6), generates and guides inferences (Chapter 7), and produces biased attributions (Chapter 8). Given the centrality of the self in these processes, it is not surprising that self-relevant cognitions also affect behavior. Several research traditions show that the self can influence behavior in significant ways (see Baumeister, 1999; Carver & Scheier, 1998). However, as we have already discussed, the self-concept we have stored in memory is multi-faceted, containing beliefs about numerous aspects of the self, including one's traits, abilities, motives, beliefs, attitudes, and values (Feng, Yan, Huang, Han, & Ma, 2018; Greenwald et al., 2002; Kihlstrom & Klein, 1994). In addition, different situations and cues in the environment can affect which aspects of the self-concept become accessible in memory (Hartshorne & May, 1928; Mischel & Shoda, 1995), so that the *working self-concept* (the self-concept that is accessible in a given situation; Isbell, McCabe, Burns, & Lair, 2013; Markus & Wurf, 1987; Sim, Goyle, McKedy, Eidelman, & Correll, 2014) is contextually dependent. Another critical factor is the individual's motives in a given situation. People's behavior is influenced by their dominant motives, whether because of chronic individual differences or because the social context invokes them.

Accessible Self-concepts and Behavior

As we have discussed in Chapter 2 on cognitive representations, the accessibility of individuals' self-concepts affects behavior in numerous respects. Individuals differ in the beliefs that are chronically accessible to influence behavior across a variety of contexts (Bargh & Pratto, 1986; Higgins & Brendl, 1995). Markus (1977) referred to individuals who had chronically accessible beliefs about a self-attribute as *self-schematics*, and she classified individuals as self-schematic if they rated an attribute as both self-descriptive and an essential element in understanding "who they are." Importantly, people who are self-schematic process attribute-relevant information differently from individuals who are not self-schematic (see Markus & Sentis, 1982), and this difference can have behavioral implications. So, for example, some individuals believe that they are shy, and such beliefs about the self can affect their actions across a variety of situations.

Other research on accessible self-beliefs and behavior reflects the fact that self-concepts, like other cognitive representations, are amenable to situational priming. Situations can make beliefs accessible that affect an individual's behavior, even if the beliefs are not typically part of the person's self-concept. Consequently, people do not think of themselves in precisely the same terms at all times, and their actions tend to be guided instead by what is called the *working self-concept* (Hinkley & Andersen, 1996; Markus & Wurf, 1987). We now review several aspects of the self-concept that have been tied quite directly to behavior.

Self-efficacy

Self-efficacy is the belief in one's ability to organize and to execute the actions required to produce desired outcomes (Bandura, 1997, 2006). Research has shown that possessing a sense of self-efficacy affects achievement behavior in numerous respects. Individuals who have a high sense of efficacy are more likely to exhibit calm, to effectively self-regulate, and to show strong coping skills when confronting challenges. They are more likely to be productive in work environments (Stajkovic & Luthans, 1998) and are more likely to pursue their goals than are persons low in efficacy.

Although individuals vary naturally in self-efficacy, manipulations can increase or decrease perceived efficacy with predictable consequences. For example, Pham, Taylor, and Seeman (2001) presented undergraduates with information suggesting that they had either little or much control over their lives as students, and both their physiological responses and coping strategies were affected. Students whose control was emphasized had lower blood pressure and heart rate and more evidence of effective planning to meet future goals compared with students who were told they had little control. Behavioral responses were moderated by efficacious beliefs, allowing effective coping and self-regulation under uncertainty when people had a sense of control in their lives.

Rejection Sensitivity

Rejection sensitivity refers to the degree to which an individual anxiously expects to be rejected by others. Individuals who are high in rejection sensitivity tend to show chronic, elevated levels of anxiety and concern about abandonment and also stronger expectations of being rejected by others, compared with individuals who are low in rejection sensitivity. High rejection sensitivity is a risk factor for interpersonal and personal distress, and rejection-sensitive individuals exhibit numerous behaviors indicative of threat. When expecting rejection, individuals high in rejection sensitivity scan the environment in search of rejection cues and show an elevated eyeblink startle response when these cues are detected (Downey, Mougios, Ayduk, London, & Shoda, 2004). They also tend to act in more hostile and aggressive ways in relationships (Downey, Feldman, & Ayduk, 2000; Downey, Freitas, Michaelis, & Khouri, 1998), show avoidance behaviors in domains when identity is threatened (London, Downey, Romero-Canyas, Rattan, & Tyson, 2012), and, when ostracized, are more likely to exhibit aggressive behavior toward the individual who has rejected them (Ayduk, Gyurak, & Luerssen, 2008; Zimmer-Gembeck, Nesdale, Webb, Khatibi, & Downey, 2016).

Implicit Theories

The work reviewed so far in this section has focused on two specific beliefs within the self-concept – efficacy and rejection sensitivity – that have been closely tied to behavior in social environments. Of course, any attribute that is central to the self-concept, either temporarily or chronically, can influence how a person behaves. However, beliefs about the nature of attributes, and not just about the attributes themselves, also influence the relationship between self-concepts and behavior. These beliefs are termed *implicit beliefs* or *mindsets* because they typically are not verbalized. People differ in the extent to which they believe that traits are fixed and stable across time and context or that they are malleable and can change across situations and over time (see Dweck, 1999; Dweck & Grant, 2008). The persistent belief that traits are stable is termed an *entity theory* or a *fixed mindset*. In contrast, a belief in the malleability of traits is referred to as an *incremental theory* or *growth mindset*. Beliefs about the malleability of traits are important in accounting for the behavioral consequences of an accessible attribute.

Entity and incremental beliefs can affect how people go about setting goals and interpreting progress toward achieving those goals (Dweck, 1999). For persons with an entity orientation, behavior in a domain relevant to a self-descriptive trait allows demonstration of competence or ability within that domain. As such, these individuals tend to set performance goals, aiming to exhibit to themselves and others that they possess the trait in question. Individuals with an incremental orientation, in contrast, view trait-relevant activities as opportunities for achieving mastery by finding strategies and levels of effort that are necessary for success. As consumers, people with fixed mindsets are more likely to purchase products to highlight their positive qualities. However, people with a growth mindset seek out products that are useful in pursuing their goals and learning new things (Murphy & Dweck, 2016).

People operating under either orientation deal equally effectively with progress towards goals, but they tend to respond quite differently to failure. Beliefs about failure are particularly important, since these beliefs, communicated from parents to children, determine children's beliefs about whether intelligence is fixed or malleable. Parents who believe failure provides opportunities for enhancement tend to have children who believe they can change their intelligence (Haimovitz & Dweck, 2016). How are mindsets tied to interpretations of failure? Whereas individuals in an entity framework interpret difficulties as being indicative of low ability, an individual in an incremental framework is more likely to interpret challenges in terms of poor strategies or low effort. Consequently, individuals with an entity theory tend to show avoidance behavior when they encounter difficulties, but individuals with an incremental theory respond with increased effort and use of different strategies. In one study (Mueller & Dweck, 1998), children who had been praised for their intelligence placed a higher priority on performance goals and displayed poorer performance when they encountered difficulty, compared with children who had been praised for their effort. Praise for ability has also been shown to lower persistence (Zentall & Morris, 2010) and to increase cheating, presumably because children who receive such praise attempt to uphold their reputations for being smart (Zhao, Heyman, Chen, & Lee, 2017).

These findings show that beliefs about the nature of traits, and not merely their accessibility, can alter the behavioral consequences of the working self-concept.

Motivational Considerations

People pursue different activities and pursue those activities differently based on the self-related motives that are potent in a situation. Among these motivational concerns are needs to obtain accurate information about the self (self-assessment), to confirm one's self-concept (self-verification), and to build and maintain self-esteem (self-enhancement).

Self-assessment

People often want to obtain accurate information about themselves. Beliefs about the self must be at least somewhat accurate, lest we have difficulty calibrating our expectations, aspirations, and, ultimately, our behavior. Because accurate information is important for regulating our current behavior and for planning future actions, we often seek out information that gives us a basis for knowing what we are like compared to others (Festinger, 1954; Trope, 1975). This motivation is particularly strong when we are uncertain about our strengths and weaknesses in a given domain (Försterling & Weiner, 1981; Trope, 1982).

How does accuracy motivation affect social behavior? First, individuals may seek out *diagnostic* tasks to acquire information about their abilities (Skov & Sherman, 1986; Trope & Bassok, 1983). Trope (1980), for example, presented individuals with several tasks that differed in the degree to which success would indicate high ability and failure indicated low ability. Participants were asked to rate the extent to which they thought each task was attractive and their willingness to complete each task. Both judgments increased to the degree that tasks were described as informative about ability, regardless of whether the task was likely to produce success or failure. Thus, participants wanted to complete tasks that would provide accurate information about themselves.

Second, when no objective information regarding ability is available, people tend to seek out opportunities to compare themselves with *similar others* (Festinger, 1954; Tesser, 1988). Particularly if we are uncertain about our abilities and seek accurate information, we are likely to engage in comparison with individuals whom we think are similar to ourselves in other regards. If I want to assess my ability to take up the sport of tennis, I would ask someone to play who is also new to the sport and is similar to me in age, fitness, and body type. If I find someone who is well matched to my level, it will allow the establishment of a potential long-term (and, hopefully, friendly) rivalry (Garcia, Tor, & Schiff, 2013; Kilduff, Elfenbein, & Staw, 2010). It would do me little good to ask a tennis professional or a 10-year-old child to play since such partners would provide virtually no information about my skills. Comparing myself with a more experienced player would likely leave me discouraged and unwilling to expend effort to become a better player. In contrast, comparing myself with someone less capable might provide a temporary boost to the ego, but the information gained would be of limited value for accurate self-assessment.

Self-verification

Assessment motives might prevail when we are uncertain about our attributes in a domain or when the task itself is novel (Seih, Buhrmester, Lin, Huang, & Swann, 2013; Swann, 2012). However, self-verification can become an overriding goal when well-established beliefs about the self are already available (Pelham, 1991). When they are, people seek and value information that confirms the current self-concept. Swann and Read (1981), for example, showed that undergraduate students displayed a clear preference for feedback that confirmed traits that they believed described themselves. Indeed, they were willing to spend more money to have access to information that confirmed than disconfirmed their beliefs about themselves, regardless of whether those beliefs were positive or negative. In addition, people with negative views of themselves were less interested in interacting with a person who evaluates them positively compared with people with positive self-views (Swann, Griffin, Predmore, & Gaines, 1987). This can also affect relationship choices over the longer term. For example, people in long-term relationships are happier to the degree that each partner has similar views of one another, whether positive or negative (Swann, De La Ronde, & Hixon, 1994; Swann, Hixon, & de la Ronde, 1992; Swann & Pelham, 2002).

Self-enhancement

Building and maintaining positive self-esteem is a fundamental human motive (Dufner et al., 2019; Sedikides, Gaertner, & Toguchi, 2003; Wojcik & Ditto, 2014), and individuals often behave in ways that build, preserve, or enhance positive self-regard. However, there are situations where self-enhancement becomes the dominant motive, such as when an individual experiences failure. After failure experiences, individuals tend to seek out information about their assets and abilities rather than about their liabilities and weaknesses (Trope & Pomerantz, 1998).

There are several ways in which a self-enhancement motive affects behavior. One of the most obvious but important ways is by influencing the choice of activities that a person pursues. People tend to pursue activities and engage in behaviors that allow them to demonstrate their strengths and avoid behaviors that reveal their weaknesses. A person who considers himself to be a good athlete but not a good singer would be much more likely to join the community tennis league than the church choir. Avoiding domains in which failure is likely, and seeking out domains where success is likely, helps to maintain a sense of capability and worth.

Another way to self-enhance is to engage in downward social comparisons, evaluating oneself in comparison to an individual who is less (but only slightly less) capable within a domain. If I am feeling poorly about my academic abilities, I might choose to study with a student who tends to perform less well in academic settings. Or if a talented tennis partner has consistently defeated me, I might gain some pleasure by playing someone whom I am likely to defeat. So long as the person with whom I am comparing myself is roughly comparable in ability, I can seek out downward comparisons to restore a sense of accomplishment and ability. I might engage in a similar process when I publicly compare myself with others. One study (Garcia, Song, & Tesser, 2010) showed that people who are successful on a given dimension often show a *social comparison bias*, neglecting to mention people who might surpass them on that dimension when making comparisons.

Self-enhancement can also be achieved through the ironic act of *self-handicapping* (Jones & Berglas, 1978; Schwinger, Wirthwein, Lemmer, & Steinmayr, 2014), wherein an individual actually undermines his or her performance to maintain a positive self-view. How might this occur? Consider a tennis player who expects a tough match with an upcoming opponent. She might prepare for this match by practicing diligently, getting ample rest, and eating a proper diet. If the match went poorly, however, and ended in a loss, the player might experience a loss of confidence in her game and a small (and hopefully temporary) blow to her self-esteem. Self-handicapping is an alternative strategy. When anticipating a match against a formidable foe, she could simply not prepare properly – skipping practice, staying up late, and eating junk food. In that case, self-esteem can be protected because there are a series of causes available to explain her failure unrelated to her ability. In addition, if the poor preparation does not undermine performance and she, in fact, wins the match, the presence of these inhibitory causes actually serves to enhance judgments of one's ability ("I'm better than I thought. I won despite my poor preparation!") (Feick & Rhodewalt, 1997; McCrea & Hirt, 2001).

Finally, there is also evidence that self-enhancement motives can affect even major life choices that individuals make, typically without their being aware of the basis of these choices. Decisions with relatively minor consequences can be affected when stimuli implicate the self, such as when people more favorably evaluate the letters that frequently appear in their name (Koole, Dijksterhuis, & van Knippenberg, 2001; Nuttin, 1985) or elevate the worth of an object they own (Beggan, 1992; Morewedge & Giblin, 2015). Some intriguing studies have shown that similar factors can influence more significant decisions. This phenomenon, termed *implicit egotism*, suggests that the boost in preferences for stimuli associated with the self can give a slight advantage to certain options over others when, for example, deciding where to live, what to pursue as a career, or whom one should marry. Correlational evidence shows that there is a greater-than-chance likelihood that individuals move to places with names similar to their own (e.g., men named Tex who moved to Texas), disproportionally marry partners who share their birthdates, and pursue careers whose titles resemble their last names (Pelham, Carvallo, DeHart, & Jones, 2003; Pelham & Mauricio, 2015; Pelham, Mirenberg, & Jones, 2002).

Experiments provide more direct evidence that these behaviors were caused by implicit egotism. In one series of studies (Jones, Pelham, Carvallo, & Mirenberg, 2004), men were more likely to indicate that they were attracted to a female partner they had just met if she had been assigned an identification number containing the dates in his birthday (e.g., 01–21) rather than a random number. In addition, participants liked other individuals more if they were wearing a jersey with a number that had been previously paired subliminally with their own names. Although the experimental evidence supports the claim that implicit egotism plays a causal role in determining life decisions, it is important to emphasize that such effects tend to be small in the real world. We suspect some women are reading this book named Denise who have no plans to pursue dentistry, marry a man named Dennis, or move to Denver. Nonetheless, the fact that these relationships have emerged at all across a large number of studies with different operationalizations attests to the power and ubiquity of self-enhancement motives.

Social Cognition and Action in Understanding Persons

Although research on person perception has historically focused on judgment processes and how person information is stored in memory, recent work has increasingly studied how people actually behave in dynamic interaction with other individuals. As we all know from experience, behavior involving even just two people is complex and influenced by numerous factors. Some of those influences have to do with the self-concepts that are active in interactants' heads as they perceive, interpret, evaluate, and respond to the actions of a partner. However, situations can also make salient certain traits that influence the way a person acts, even if those features are not typically self-descriptive. In addition, there are also motivational factors to consider.

Accessible Concepts and Interpersonal Behavior

There are times when we behave in ways that are atypical or unusual, given our customary actions. I might usually be a calm, reasonable person but still be capable of showing high stress and anxiety. I might typically be a polite, considerate individual but still behave on occasion like a selfish jerk. Some of the variability in behavior can be attributed to differences in social circumstances. Even a calm person might become anxious on a battlefield, and a polite person might act selfishly if he desperately needed a vital resource. Some of the variation, however, can occur as expectancies, goals, and trait-linked behavioral action tendencies become accessible in memory because of cues in the social context, often without our awareness that they have become accessible or despite our denial that we would be affected by such extraneous signals. Thus, traits, goals, and expectancies can become accessible to influence a person's behavior toward another person even when the attributes are not typically associated with the self.

There is much research evidence that primed cognitive representations influence social perception, judgment, and memory, but priming effects were not tied to interpersonal behavior until more recently. Since the first demonstrations of the behavioral consequences of activated trait concepts (Bargh et al., 1996; Herr, 1986), numerous studies have examined the influence of activated knowledge structures on individuals' behaviors in interactive contexts. Research has shown that primes typically interact with variables including attitudes (Cesario et al., 2006), goals (Shah, 2003), and situational constraints (Cesario et al., 2010) to affect people's actions (see Barsalou, 2016; Eitam & Higgins, 2016; Higgins & Eitam, 2014; Molden, 2014).

One illustrative line of research shows the effect of priming concepts relating to temperature on interpersonal behavior. The idea that friendly and kind people are "warm" and that "cold" people are mean and aloof has a long history in social cognition (cf. Asch, 1946; Fiske, Cuddy, & Glick, 2007). Of course, friendly and unfriendly people do not, in reality, differ in their core body temperatures. Nonetheless, these metaphors are reflected in our semantic representations of trait concepts (Landau, Meier, & Keefer, 2010; Lee, 2016). If terms regarding temperature describe both our sensory experiences and social evaluations, might priming the physical sensations of warmth or coldness affect social judgment and behavior? This would be particularly likely if similar neural processes were involved in temperature perception and interpersonal evaluation. Indeed, similar brain regions (notably the middle-insula) are activated when people are sensing warmth or are thinking about loved ones and friends (Inagaki & Eisenberger, 2013; Inagaki, Hazlett, & Andreescu, 2019), and administering an opioid antagonist (naltrexone) reduced both the physical and social experience of warmth compared with a placebo condition (Inagaki et al., 2019).

Evidence consistent with a link between physical and psychological temperature was provided by an experiment (Williams & Bargh, 2008) in which participants were asked as a favor to a confederate whose hands were full to briefly hold a cup of hot (versus iced) coffee. Participants were then asked to make judgments of a person who was characterized as "intelligent, skillful, industrious, determined, practical, and cautious." Participants who had briefly held the iced coffee judged the person to be colder than did participants who held the warm beverage. The temperature manipulation did not affect judgments related to competence, indicating that the effect was specific to sociability and did not represent a halo effect. A subsequent study showed that participants who had touched a cold therapeutic pad were much more likely to keep their compensation for participation in the study rather than give it to a friend (see Figure 12.7).

This direct effect has been replicated (IJzerman & Semin, 2009; Schilder, IJzerman, & Denissen, 2014), although not all such efforts have been successful (Chabris, Heck, Mandart, Benjamin, & Simons, 2019; but see Bargh & Melnikoff, 2019). Importantly, there have been multiple conceptual replications using various methods demonstrating both direct and indirect effects of temperature on social behavior. For example, in a study in which participants completed a daily diary, reports of their physical warmth covaried with estimates of their interpersonal warmth and agreeableness (Fetterman, Wilkowski, & Robinson, 2018). In experimental studies, manipulations of physical proximity and verbally induced proximity (i.e., having participants generate ways they are similar to a stranger they are communicating with on-line) both increased perceptions of ambient temperature (IJzerman & Semin, 2009). Conversely, temperature manipulations have been shown to affect the extent that people cooperate in dyadic interactions (Storey & Workman, 2013).

The effect of temperature on behavior also appears to be moderated by several factors. The prosocial effects of warm temperatures are more substantial when affiliative motives are high (Fay & Maner, 2018; Shalev, 2015), and the effects of temperature are stronger when social warmth is being used as a means for reducing physical coldness (IJzerman et al., 2018; Zhang

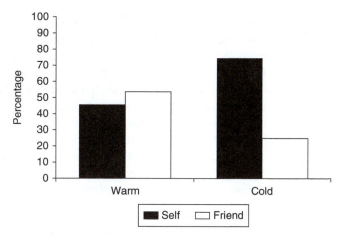

Figure 12.7   Percentage of participants who kept experimental compensation for themselves or gave to a friend as a function of exposure to warm or cold stimuli
Source: Based on data from Williams & Bargh (2008)

& Risen, 2014). Consistent with this argument is the finding that participants in one study who were approached outdoors expressed more substantial interest in engaging in affiliative actions (e.g., "Make social plans with someone," "Try to make a new friend") on cold than on warm days. However, participants who had first tried a heated back wrap (who presumably had met their goal to find heat) were unaffected by the daily temperature (Fay & Maner, 2020). In addition, individual differences in attachment style affected whether children were affected by temperature. Children with secure attachment styles showed greater generosity toward their friends in warm than cold conditions, but children with insecure attachment styles were unaffected by temperature (IJzerman, Karremans, Thomsen, & Schubert, 2013).

In sum, interpersonal interactions are affected in multiple ways by exposure to physical stimuli that invoke metaphors about human traits. Whereas some studies show the direct affect of activated knowledge on behavior, many effects are moderated by individual differences, motives, and goals.

Motivational Considerations

Numerous motivational concerns might arise as one forms an impression of or interacts with another individual. A person might want to be liked and might explore interests or beliefs that she has in common with a new person. Conversely, she might be motivated to differentiate and psychologically distance herself from the other individual if that person appears to have an unattractive personality or beliefs that she finds objectionable. In either case, one's *affiliative motive* plays an important role in guiding behavior during impression formation and interpersonal interactions. Generally, a high level of motivation to affiliate produces assimilative behavior, whereas a low level of affiliative motive produces behavioral contrast and physical distancing from an undesired social partner. This general tendency has been shown in several different but related lines of research.

Affiliative Motives and Behavioral Mimicry

You might occasionally notice that the nonverbal behaviors used by you and your interaction partners can be quite similar. A friend's yawn might produce reciprocal yawning from yourself, or you might notice that placing your hand on your chin soon leads your interaction partner to do the same. When such imitation occurs, it is referred to as *behavioral mimicry* (Chartrand & Bargh, 1999; Chartrand & Lakin, 2013; Lakin & Chartrand, 2013; Leander, Chartrand, & Wood, 2011). Mimicry involves the nonconscious echoing of a partner's postures, mannerisms, facial expressions, or any other behaviors of an interaction partner.

So long as neither partner becomes acutely aware of behavioral mimicry, such an echoing of actions produces several salutatory consequences. Imitation facilitates interpersonal liking and rapport (Ireland, Slatcher, Eastwick, Scissors, Finkel, & Pennebaker, 2011), and individuals with strong motives to affiliate are most likely to engage in mimicry (Lakin & Chartrand, 2003). Mimicry also encourages context-dependent and convergent thought processes (van Baaren, Horgan, Chartrand, & Dijkmans, 2004) and increases prosocial behavior toward the interaction partner (van Baaren, Holland, et al., 2004; van Baaren, Holland, Steenart, & van Knippenberg, 2003). Moreover, *failure* to mimic can incur costs. When people intentionally avoid mimicking their interaction partners, they performed more poorly on later tests requiring self-regulatory control ranging from intellectual puzzles to tasks requiring fine motor skills (Finkel, Campbell, Brunell, Dalton, Scarbeck, & Chartrand, 2006).

Research has also demonstrated similar assimilative phenomena in the use of speech (Bernhold & Giles, 2020; Giles & Coupland 1991) and other communication behavior (Gallois et al., 2005; Ireland et al., 2011). Individuals typically modify communicative behaviors in the direction of interaction partners (known as "speech accommodation") in an attempt to reduce social distance, to signify respect, and to smooth interpersonal functioning. Communicative behaviors can also diverge from an interaction partner if one's communication style signifies possession of a valued attribute, high social status, or membership in an esteemed social group. Such divergence is also used when a person wants to signal disapproval of an interaction partner. The strategic use of accommodation and divergence to send social signals indicates that the affiliative motive is not ubiquitous across social contexts and that individuals can exert some control over their behaviors to send signals of social inclusion or distance.

Affiliative Motives and Social Tuning

Another consequence of the affiliation motive is manifested in people's tendency to assimilate, or *socially tune*, their beliefs and behaviors to the perceived attitudes of others. In these studies, participants either expect to meet or actually interact with a research confederate whose behaviors imply either egalitarian, neutral, or even elitist beliefs. For example, participants in one of these experiments might encounter a person wearing a T-shirt condemning racism or with a race-neutral message (Lun, Sinclair, Whitchurch, & Glenn, 2007; Sinclair, Lowery, Hardin, & Colangelo, 2005). When participants' affiliative motives were high (e.g., when the confederate appeared to be egalitarian), participants converged toward the perceived views of the confederate. When the motive to affiliate was low (e.g., when the confederate wore a neutral T-shirt), participants either did not alter their beliefs or behavior or diverged away from the presumed beliefs of the confederate. These effects emerged on both explicit or implicit measures, and they affected both participants' self-views and their behavior. Importantly, these studies show that the motive to reduce social distance with another individual can lead to a convergence of behavior and expressed beliefs (Jacoby-Senghor, Sinclair, & Smith, 2015; Skorinko & Sinclair, 2018).

Social Cognition and Action in Understanding Groups

Much of the research on behavior within group perception grew out of and paralleled developments (and controversies) in work on interpersonal interaction. Several initial studies demonstrating behavioral consequences from priming social categories (e.g., the elderly (Bargh et al., 1996), professors versus soccer hooligans (Dijksterhuis & van Knippenberg, 1998), and politicians (Dijksterhuis & van Knippenberg, 2000)) were followed by several high-profile failures to replicate and subsequent calls for greater precision in theories and methods (e.g., Dijksterhuis, 2014; Klatzky & Creswell, 2014; Locke, 2015).

As was the case in the literature on priming in interpersonal interaction, there is now increased nuance involving the relationship between intergroup attitudes and behavior. Many studies have shown the effects of exposure to group-relevant primes on behavior (e.g., Bry et al., 2008; Cesario et al., 2010; Hall & Crisp, 2008). However, these effects regularly show that priming effects are conditional and that many factors relating to goals, motivations, attitudes, and situations moderate the effects of primes on behavior.

Nevertheless, there are also larger bodies of research exploring other aspects of the relationship between cognitive representations of groups and behavior. We turn to brief discussions of two meta-analyses that discuss the relationship between beliefs about and attitudes toward groups and their implications for action.

Earlier, we briefly discussed research showing that the activation of age-relevant stereo-types can affect the behavior of older adults. Levy (1996) presented subliminal primes to older persons to make accessible either negative (e.g., decline, dependent) or positive (e.g., wise, enlightened) beliefs about the elderly. Performance on subsequent memory tasks showed that when negative beliefs were made accessible, performance suffered, whereas memory improved following unconscious exposure to positive beliefs about aging. Following the publication of this research, many studies examined the influence of exposure to age-related stereotypes on the behavior of older people. A meta-analysis of this research (Meisner, 2012) showed that elderly-related primes consistently influenced behavior on all of the primary measures used in the research literature: memory, psychomotor skills (gross and fine motor abilities), physio-logical responses (blood pressures, skin conductance, and heart rate), and social evaluations (self- and peer-perceptions). The effects were similar if primes were subliminal or supraliminal. Negative and positive age-related primes influenced behavior in opposing ways, with behav-ioral impairments arising from negative stereotypes and improvements occurring following positive stereotypes. The magnitude of effects for positive and negative primes was asymmet-rical. The effects following negative stereotypical primes were almost three times as large as those that arose after positive primes, compared with control conditions.

A second meta-analysis (Cameron et al., 2012) asked a very different question: Can behav-ior in a variety of domains be predicted by people's performance on tasks designed to assess implicit attitudes? This analysis examined the relationship between performance on numer-ous sequential priming tasks (e.g., Banaji & Hardin, 1996; Fazio et al., 1986; Payne, 2001) and a variety of actions, including behaviors relevant in intergroup contexts. Overall, findings showed that performance on priming tasks assessing prejudice correlated reliably with inter-group behavior ($r = +.28$), an effect size similar to what was obtained involving other domains such as close relationships and impulsivity. This research indicates that there exists a reasonable relationship between implicit attitudes and intergroup action.

Stereotypic Expectancies and Behavior

Behavioral consequences of activated knowledge can have particular resonance when consid-ered in the domain of group perception, where expectancies can lead to stereotype confirmation. Research has identified two different manifestations of these effects in the intergroup domain. Similar processes are involved in both cases, but the actor who provides stereotype-confirming evidence differs. In the first case, an actor in whom the stereotype has been activated and to whom the stereotype can be applied produces evidence in his actions that confirms stereotyp-ical beliefs, often despite intentions to disprove stereotypical beliefs. This phenomenon has been called *stereotype threat*. In the second case, an actor holding the stereotype might act in a fashion that elicits stereotype-confirming behavioral evidence from *others* to whom the ste-reotype might apply. This has been called a *self-fulfilling prophecy* or *behavioral confirmation* of stereotypes.

Stereotype Threat

Members of stereotyped groups are typically well aware of the beliefs held by others about their group. What if a person who is a member of such a group is already aware of the stereotype and the expectations contained in it? Could that knowledge influence the target's behavior, even in the absence of an interaction partner who subscribes to the stereotype?

Research on *stereotype threat* indicates that it can. Stereotype threat refers to the risk of one's behavior confirming, as self-characteristic, a negative stereotype about one's group. Steele and Aronson (1995) raised the possibility that stereotypes suggesting poor performance of certain groups can, when highlighted in a social context, disrupt the performance of a person who identifies with that group. When this occurs, the individual can act in ways that confirm stereotypes, even if the person is highly motivated to disprove stereotypical expectations and if no other person is constraining their behavior. The researchers conducted several studies to test these ideas, assessing whether invoking a self-descriptive stereotype might undermine performance and produce stereotype-confirming behavior. In one experiment, African American and White college students took a difficult verbal exam after being told either that performance on the test was a good indicator of underlying intellectual abilities or that it was non-diagnostic of ability. After statistically controlling for actual ability (as reflected in self-reported SAT scores), African American participants performed less well than their White counterparts in the stereotype threat condition. However, they did as well as Whites in the control condition where the test was described as non-diagnostic of ability. A subsequent study raised stereotype threat in African American students by merely varying when information about racial identity was collected. From half the students, racial information was solicited right before they completed the test items, but the other half provided the information after the test had been completed. Test performance was poorer only among African Americans whose racial identity had been made salient before testing.

Since the Steele and Aronson (1995) studies, research has shown that the behavioral consequences of stereotype threat are quite broad and diverse (Schmader, Hall, & Croft, 2015; Spencer, Logel, & Davies, 2016). Stereotype threat has been shown to produce self-handicapping (Stone, 2002), to undermine learning (Taylor & Walton, 2011), and to reduce the quality of performance with groups in domains as diverse as White men in sports (e.g., Stone, Lynch, Sjomeling, & Darley, 1999), women in Math and science (Beilock, Jellison, Rydell, McConnell, & Carr, 2006; Cheryan, Plaut, Davies, & Steele, 2009), gay men when providing childcare (Bosson, Haymovitz, & Pinel, 2004), and women in driving (Yeung & von Hippel, 2008).

How do these effects come about? Schmader, Johns, and Forbes (2008; Schmader, 2010; see also Pennington, Heim, Levy, & Larkin, 2016) have proposed that performance under stereotype threat can harm performance for three different but interrelated reasons. First, stereotype threat often produces physiological responses that impair prefrontal processing. When an individual recognizes that a group stereotype might apply to her behavior in a situation, she might suddenly experience a surge of adrenaline and other arousing neurotransmitters that can make it challenging to complete difficult tasks. Second, stereotype threat also directs attention to performance monitoring. When a person fears confirming a stereotype, she is more likely to focus on "seeing" her own behavior as an observer would, in order to monitor for failure, instead of focusing on the particulars of the task at hand. Third, stereotype threat can also produce efforts to suppress stereotype-relevant thoughts and emotions, undermining cognitive and executive resources necessary for optimal performance on cognitive and social tasks. Instead of committing full cognitive resources to the problem at hand, the person under stereotype threat might find her thoughts occupied with concerns about struggle, failure, or even anger about the existence of a stereotype. Any one of these factors might be sufficient to harm performance when a person experiences stereotype threat.

Self-fulfilling Prophecy and Behavioral Confirmation of Expectancies

Self-fulfilling prophecies arise when an individual to whom the stereotype does not apply elicits stereotype-conforming behavior from individuals to whom it does apply (e.g., Rosenthal & Jacobson, 1968; Snyder et al., 1977; see Jussim & Harber, 2005; Snyder & Stukas, 1999, for reviews). Some research on self-fulfilling prophecies was introduced in Chapter 11 (Word et al., 1974). Here, we broaden our consideration of this phenomenon, examining how self-fulfilling prophecies can contribute to disparities in academic performance.

Teachers develop expectations regarding students' potential to achieve in the classroom. Inferences about potential are influential in setting educational goals and providing appropriate challenges for students based upon their abilities. These expectations can be formed from several sources of information, such as the student's scores on psychometric tests or performance in previous classes. However, given the prevalence of stereotypes about differences in ability and motivation across social groups, teachers can also be affected by the race, gender, or social-economic status (SES) of a student in setting expectations and goals. Furthermore, these expectations can then affect the behavior of teachers in a manner that leads to their confirmation (Lewis & Cheng, 2006; Riley & Ungerleider, 2012; Rosenthal & Jacobson, 1968). Several studies have shown that teachers regularly underestimate the ability of Black and low SES students (Alvidrez & Weinstein, 1999; Hauser-Cram, Sirin, & Stipek, 2003). The low expectations can then affect how teachers interact directly with students, how students are disciplined, the peer relationships that are encouraged and discouraged, and the tracking of students into programs that ostensibly reflect ability differences (Weinstein, Gregory, & Strambler, 2004). All these differences in treatment limit opportunities for students for whom there exist low expectations. Furthermore, students can detect these differences in treatment, contributing to lower motivation and performance (Babad, Bernieri, & Rosenthal, 1991).

In a large field study on expectancy effects in the classroom, Smith, Jussim, and Eccles (1999) found that while "self-fulfilling prophecies in terms of effect size were relatively small, their presence over time was quite remarkable" (p. 563). They discovered that teachers' initial beliefs about student potential could influence those students for several years after the initial point of contact. Moreover, they also found that students for whom their teachers had high expectations in 7th grade later took a high number of non-remedial high school Math courses compared with students for whom there were lower expectations. This aggregation of benefits for students labeled as "high achieving" has been called the *accumulation expectancy effect*. Thus, the consequences of self-fulfilling prophecies can become magnified over time. Through the processes described here, stereotypes can appear to be valid even though it was the *holder* of the stereotype that acted in a manner that elicited the confirmatory evidence.

Self-regulation in Intergroup Behavior

When interacting with members of a different social group, people are often highly attentive to their own and other people's behavior, and they often exert substantial effort to regulate their actions. Think of the first time you went on a date with someone you found attractive or interacted with a classmate from a different country. Despite our attempts to regulate our behavior to smooth social functioning, we often behave in ways we neither desire nor intend. Part of the reason for these difficulties is that people are typically unaware that activated social categories can direct behavior and that stereotypical beliefs can produce actions that are inconsistent with egalitarian beliefs and values. Similarly, individuals operating under stereotype threat are quite motivated to maintain a high level of performance, but the activation of stereotypical beliefs can make it challenging to do so. Thus, group perception is a domain in which self-regulation of behavior is critical.

Consider the tragic case of Patrick Dorismond in 2000. This African American man was approached by a White undercover police officer who said he wanted to buy drugs from him. Dorismond responded angrily, apparently taking offense at the suggestion that he was a drug dealer because he was Black. Although the officer instigated the interaction, he failed to calm the situation. Instead, he began arguing with Dorismond and, following a physical confrontation, the officer shot and killed him. Failure of self-regulation contributed to this tragic scenario in several respects. First, the officer quite plausibly approached Dorismond for drugs based on racial stereotypes, not realizing that Dorismond himself was an off-duty security officer returning home after an evening of work. Dorismond justifiably responded with anger to what he probably considered to be a racist request by a White person. The officer failed to appreciate why his request produced such a response, and he failed to remain calm in order to diffuse the situation. Moreover, once the conflict became physical, the officer failed to direct and control his behavior to avoid harm.

Although most intergroup interactions do not result in tragedy, they can be fraught with uncertainty and ambiguity. Stereotypical associations are often activated during intergroup interactions. Individuals differ in their motivation to resist these activated beliefs and the time and resources that are available to do so. Even more vexing, actions consistent with stereotypes must sometimes be pursued, even if stereotypes are not the basis of those actions. There are in fact times when a police officer must determine whether a suspect is carrying a threatening weapon or a benign object and is trying not to be affected by the race of the suspect. If an African American suspect actually has a weapon, an officer attempting to act impartially might experience a conflict between his tendency to shoot a suspect with a weapon and his attempt to avoid bias. Conversely, the officer *not* motivated to avoid bias will experience conflict if the suspect does not have a weapon. In such a case, the officer must resist the tendency to shoot based on the association between Blacks and guns.

This exact dilemma has been studied quite extensively, both because of its social importance and because it serves as a useful model for examining self-regulation in intergroup interaction more generally. Correll and his colleagues (Correll, Park, et al., 2002; Correll, Park, Judd, & Wittenbrink, 2007; Correll, Park, Judd, Wittenbrink, Sadler, & Keesee, 2007 Correll, Wittenbrink, Crawford, & Sadler, 2015; Ma & Correll, 2011) conducted a series of experiments in which a White or a Black male was viewed, in a video game, in realistic environments holding either a weapon or a benign object like a cell phone. Participants were instructed to shoot a toy gun if the suspect has a weapon but not to shoot if he does not. Although race should be irrelevant in deciding to shoot or not, the results of these studies consistently showed that participants were more likely to shoot Black targets, and they did so more quickly. They were more likely not to shoot Whites, and they made that decision more quickly. Thus, participants' responses were quicker and more accurate when targets confirmed racial stereotypes but slower and less accurate when targets contradicted stereotypes.

This racial bias arises in the shooting paradigm in part because individuals have a lower response threshold for Black compared with White suspects; it takes less evidence confirming the presence of a gun to make a shooting decision for a Black compared with a White suspect. Moreover, the decision to shoot occurs more quickly for Black than for White suspects. Comparable results have been obtained from both student and police officer samples. However, for the officers, the effect is primarily in the speed with which they make shooting decisions, not whether they shoot. Finally, studies have shown that the accessibility of racial stereotypes (Glaser & Knowles, 2008), the degree of threat perceived in the environment (Kahn & Davies, 2017), and the phenotypicality of facial features (Kahn & Davies, 2011) moderate the degree of shooting bias.

This paradigm is only one of several experimental strategies that have recently been developed for studying self-regulation and the role of racial stereotypes involving threats (see, for example, Greenwald, Oakes, & Hoffman, 2003; Payne, 2001; Vorauer & Sasaki, 2011). Of course, interactions between members of different groups include a much wider variety of groups and stereotypes, and additional complexity will be appreciated as a broader spectrum of interaction types is studied. Moreover, the ability to identify specific processes involved in self-regulation continues to grow (e.g., Conrey et al., 2005; Sherman et al., 2008), allowing greater identification of how people can succeed, but sometimes fail, in interacting with members of different groups.

Identity Fusion and Extreme Pro-group Behavior

At several points in this book, we have seen the critical role played by group identification in aspects of group perception and intergroup behavior, particularly regarding intergroup differentiation. Recent research on *identity fusion* (Swann & Buhrmester, 2015; Swann, Jetten, Gomez, Whitehouse, & Bastian, 2012) extends the notion of group identification to new levels. Identity fusion refers to an extreme connection between the self and a group, a sense of "oneness" to the extent that the borders between self and group become permeable. An essential characteristic of fused groups is that there are potent ties among group members such that the group is seen as a family, and members have a deep concern for the welfare of group members. As a consequence, one who is fused with a group expresses a willingness to engage in extreme prosocial behaviors on behalf of the group, including self-sacrifice and dying for the group. The concept of fusion has been used to understand the extreme self-sacrifice, including a willingness to die for one's group, manifested by the 9/11 bombers and members of other extremist groups who willingly die during the perpetration of an attack. In our attempt in this chapter to explore relations between cognition and behavior, it would seemingly be difficult to study this relation when the ultimate evidence of fusion is one's willingness to die for the group. Experimental tests of that hypothesis are not possible. Nevertheless, several strategies have been devised to test the theory.

A multinational study (Swann et al., 2014) assessed participants' fusion with their country (based on questionnaire items such as "I am one with my country," "I am strong because of my country") and then indicated their degree of endorsement of a series of extreme pro-group behaviors (willingness to fight for one's country, willingness to sacrifice one's life if it saved another country member's life). These measures were administered to participants in 11 countries. Analyses revealed that in every country, there was a significant correlational relationship (ranging from +.37 to +.61) between identity fusion with their country and endorsement of extreme behavior for their country.

A series of studies (Swann, Gomez, Dovidio, Hart, & Jetten, 2010) made use of a moral dilemma problem known as the Trolley Problem. In one version of this problem, participants read about five people who are about to be killed by a runaway trolley. If someone pushes a man off a bridge into the path of the trolley, the five people will be saved, but the man will die. Past research using this problem has shown that most people refuse to push the man and thereby allow the five people to die. In this research, the Trolley Problem was adapted to study the effects of identity fusion. The research was conducted in Spain, where (based on previous research) it was known that Spaniards have a high level of identity fusion with their country (as measured by group identity measures). Participants who had completed measures of identity fusion were sorted into two groups, highly fused with Spain and not fused with Spain. They then read a version of the Trolley Problem in which the choice was between five Spaniards being killed by the runaway trolley or those people being saved by the participant jumping from the bridge into the trolley's path. Among participants not fused with their country, 76.3% chose to let the five ingroup members die, whereas, among those who were highly fused with Spain, 75.0% were willing to sacrifice themselves to save their ingroup members. This basic act of self-sacrifice was replicated in three other experiments employing variations on the Trolley Problem.

Finally, during the revolutionary war in Libya in 2011, researchers gained access to members of the Libyan revolutionary forces. They were allowed to have members of several battalions complete a questionnaire assessing their degree of fusion with several groups (Whitehouse, McQuinn, Buhrmester, & Swann, 2014). Included among the revolutionaries were frontline fighters (who voluntarily served on the frontline with an assault rifle) and battalion nonfighters (logistical and support workers). Nearly all participants indicated high levels of fusion with family, their own battalion, and other battalions. No participants said they felt most fused with other battalions or with ordinary Libyans, who were negatively viewed as free-riders. The bonds among the fighters were strong. Fighters and nonfighters differed in one regard, however. Only 28% of nonfighters reported being more fused with their battalion than with their family, whereas 45% of fighters reported being most fused with their battalion. This latter finding is consistent with the premise that identity fusion entails an extreme sense of "oneness" with the group.

SUMMARY

Historically social cognition has given little recognition to the admonition of William James that the purpose of thinking is ultimately for doing, and focused instead on the processes that occur within the individual. Recently, however, research on attitudes and personality has studied the link between internal processes and behavior, and much has been learned about the conditions under which thoughts influence action, actions impact thoughts, and how they influence each other. Although not all of the principles discovered in the study of attitudes have been applied to other issues in social cognition, we see no *a priori* reason why these relationships will change significantly when considering cognitive structures involving the self, impressions of other individuals, or beliefs about groups. Moreover, the study of behavior within these content areas will likely provide a wealth of knowledge that can be applied to more general issues in social cognition. Discoveries about explicit and implicit influences on behavior, automatic behavioral processes, and self-regulation of behavior, to name a few, should facilitate the study of similar processes involving behavior and its regulation across a diverse range of social phenomena.

FURTHER READING

Anderson, B.A. (2017). Going for it: The economics of automaticity in perception and action. *Current Directions in Psychological Science, 26,* 140–145.

Devine, P.G., Forscher, P.S., Austin, A.J., & Cox, W.T.L. (2012). Long-term reduction in implicit race bias: A prejudice habit-breaking intervention. *Journal of Experimental Social Psychology, 48,* 1267–1278.

Marien, H., Aarts, H., & Custers, R. (2016). How goals control behavior: The role of action-outcome and reward information. In T.S. Braver (Ed.), *Motivation and cognitive control* (pp. 145–163). New York, NY: Routledge.

Wyer, R.S., Shen, H., & Xu, A.J. (2013). The role of procedural knowledge in the generalization of social behavior. In D.E. Carlston (Ed.), *The Oxford handbook of social cognition* (pp. 257–281). New York, NY: Oxford University Press.

REFERENCES

Aarts, H., & Dijksterhuis, A. (2002). Category activation effects in judgment and behaviour: The moderating role of perceived comparability. *British Journal of Social Psychology, 41,* 123–128.

Aarts, H., & Dijksterhuis, A. (2003). The silence of the library: Environment, situational norm, and social behavior. *Journal of Personality and Social Psychology, 84,* 18–28.

Aarts, H., Chartrand, T.L., Custers, R., Danner, U., Dik, G., Jefferis, V.E., & Cheng, C.M. (2005). Social stereotypes and automatic goal pursuit. *Social Cognition, 23,* 465–490.

Aarts, H., Dijksterhuis, A., & Custers, R. (2003). Automatic normative behavior in environments: The moderating role of conformity in activating situational norms. *Social Cognition, 21,* 447–464.

Aarts, H., Dijksterhuis, A., & Midden, C. (1999). To plan or not to plan? Goal achievement or interrupting the performance of mundane behaviors. *European Journal of Social Psychology, 29,* 971–979.

Abdai, J., & Miklosi, A. (2016). The origin of social evaluation, social eavesdropping, reputation formation, image scoring or what you will. *Frontiers in Psychology, 7,* Article 1772.

Abele, A.E., & Wojciszke, B. (2014). Communal and agentic content in social cognition: A dual perspective model. In J.M. Olson & M.P. Zanna (Eds.), *Advances in experimental social psychology* (Vol. 50, pp. 195–255). New York, NY: Academic Press.

Abele, A.E., Cuddy, A.J.C., Judd, C.M., & Yzerbyt, V.Y. (2008). Fundamental dimensions of social judgment. *European Journal of Social Psychology, 38,* 1063–1065.

Abelson, R.P. (1976). Script processing in attitude formation and decision making. In J.S. Carroll & J.W. Payne (Eds.), *Cognition and social behavior* (pp. 33–46). Hillsdale, NJ: Lawrence Erlbaum.

Abelson, R.P. (1981). The psychological status of the script concept. *American Psychologist, 36,* 715–729.

Abelson, R.P. (1995). Attitude extremity. In R.E. Petty & J.A. Krosnick (Eds.), *Attitude strength: Antecedents and consequences* (pp. 25–41). Hillsdale, NJ: Lawrence Erlbaum.

Abrams, D., Vicky, G.T., Masser, B., & Bohner, G. (2003). Perceptions of stranger and acquaintance rape: The role of benevolent and hostile sexism in victim blame and rape proclivity. *Journal of Personality and Social Psychology, 84,* 111–125.

Achtziger, A., Bayer, U.C., & Gollwitzer, P.M. (2012). Committing to implementation intentions: Attention and memory effects for selected situational cues. *Motivation and Emotion, 36,* 287–300.

Achtziger, A., Gollwitzer, P.M., & Sheeran, P. (2008). Implementation intentions and shielding goal striving from unwanted thoughts and feelings. *Personality and Social Psychology Bulletin, 34,* 381–393.

Ackerman, J.M., Shapiro, J.R., Neuberg, S.L., Kenrick, D.T., Vaughn Becker, D., Griskevicius, V., Maner, J.K., & Schaller, M. (2006). They all look the same to me (unless they're angry): From out-group homogeneity to out-group heterogeneity. *Psychological Science, 17,* 836–840.

Acorn, D.A., Hamilton, D.L., & Sherman, S.J. (1988). Generalization of biased perceptions of groups based on illusory correlations. *Social Cognition*, *6*, 345–372.

Adams, F.M., & Osgood, C.E. (1973). A cross-cultural study of the affective meaning of color. *Journal of Cross-Cultural Psychology*, *7*, 135–157.

Adolphs, R. (2008). Fear, faces, and the human amygdala. *Current Opinion in Neurobiology*, *18*, 166–172.

Ægisdóttir, S., White, M.J., Spengler, P.M., Maugherman, A.S., Anderson, L.A., Cook, R.S., Nichols, C.M., Lampropoulos, G.K., Walker, B.S., Cohen, G., & Rush, J.D. (2006). The meta-analysis of clinical judgment project: Fifty-six years of accumulated research on clinical versus statistical prediction. *The Counseling Psychologist*, *34*, 341–382.

Agerström, J., & Rooth, D.O. (2011). The role of automatic obesity stereotypes in real hiring discrimination. *Journal of Applied Psychology*, *96*, 790–805.

Agnoli, F. (1991). Development of judgmental heuristics and logical reasoning: Training counteracts the representativeness heuristic. *Cognitive Development*, *6*, 195–217.

Agostinelli, G., Sherman, S.J., Fazio, R.H., & Hearst, E.S. (1986). Detecting and identifying change: Additions versus deletions. *Journal of Experimental Psychology: Human Perception and Performance*, *12*, 445–454.

Ahn, W., Kalish, C.W., Medin, D.L., & Gelman, S.A. (1995). The role of covariation versus mechanism information in causal attribution. *Cognition*, *54*, 299–352.

Ajzen, I. (1977). Intuitive theories of events and the effects of base-rate information on prediction. *Journal of Personality and Social Psychology*, *35*, 303–314.

Ajzen, I. (1991). The theory of planned behavior. *Organizational Behavior and Human Decision Processes*, *50*, 179–211.

Ajzen, I. (2012). The theory of planned behavior. In P.A.M. Van Lange, A.W. Kruglanski, & E.T. Higgins (Eds.), *Handbook of theories of social psychology* (Vol. 1, pp. 438–459). Thousand Oaks, CA: Sage.

Ajzen, I., & Fishbein, M. (1977). Attitude-behavior relations: A theoretical analysis and review of empirical research. *Psychological Bulletin*, *84*, 888–918.

Ajzen, I., & Fishbein, M. (2005). The influence of attitudes on behavior. In D. Albarracín, B.T. Johnson, & M.P. Zanna (Eds.), *The handbook of attitudes* (pp. 173–221). Mahwah, NJ: Lawrence Erlbaum.

Ajzen, I., Fishbein, M., Lohmann, S., & Albarracín, D. (2019). The influence of attitudes on behavior. In D. Albarracín & B.T. Johnson (Eds.), *The handbook of attitudes: Volume 1: Basic principles* (2nd ed., pp. 197–255). New York, NY: Routledge.

Akhtar, S., Justice, L.V., Morrison, C.M., & Conway, M.A. (2018). Fictional first memories. *Psychological Science*, *29*, 1612–1619.

Aksoy, O., & Weesie, J. (2012). Beliefs about the social orientations of others: A parametric test of the triangle, false consensus, and cone hypotheses. *Journal of Experimental Social Psychology*, *48*, 45–54.

Albarracín, D., & Handley, I.M. (2011). The time for doing is not the time for change: Effects of general action and inaction goals on attitude retrieval and attitude change. *Journal of Personality and Social Psychology*, *100*, 983–998.

Albarracín, D., Hepler, J., & Tannenbaum, M. (2011). General action and inaction goals: Their behavioral, cognitive, and affective origins and influences. *Current Directions in Psychological Science*, *20*, 119–123.

Albarracín, D., Johnson, B.T., Fishbein, M., & Muellerleile, P.A. (2001). Theories of reasoned action and planned behavior as models of condom use: A meta-analysis. *Psychological Bulletin*, *127*, 142–161.

Albarracín, D., Sunderrajan, A., Dai, W., & White, B.X. (2019). The social creation of action and inaction. From concepts to goals to behaviors. In J.M. Olson (Ed.), *Advances in experimental social psychology* (Vol. 60, pp. 223–271). San Diego, CA: Academic Press.

Albarracín, D., Wang, W., & McCulloch, K.C. (2018). Action dominance: The performance effects of multiple action goals and the benefits of an inaction focus. *Personality and Social Psychology Bulletin, 14*, 231–241.

Aldashev, G., Carletti, T., & Righi, S. (2011). Follies subdued: Informational efficiency under adaptive expectations and confirmatory bias. *Journal of Economic Behavior & Organization, 80*, 110–121.

Alexopoulos, T., Muller, D., Ric, F., & Marendaz, C. (2012), I, me, mine: Automatic attentional capture by self-related stimuli. *European Journal of Social Psychology, 42*, 770–779.

Alexopoulos, T., Šimleša, M., & Francis, M. (2015). Good self, bad self: Initial success and failure moderate the endowment effect. *Journal of Economic Psychology, 50*, 32–40.

Alicke, M.D., & Govorun, O. (2005). The better-than-average effect. In M.D. Alicke, D.A. Dunning, & J.I. Krueger (Eds.), *Studies in self and identity* (pp. 85–106). New York, NY: Psychology Press.

Alicke, M.D., & Sedikides, C. (2009). Self-enhancement and self-protection: What they are and what they do. *European Review of Social Psychology, 20*, 1–48.

Alicke, M.D., Klotz, M.L., Breitenbecher, D.L., Yurak, T.J., & Vredenburg, D.S. (1995). Personal contact, individuation and the better than average effect. *Journal of Personality and Social Psychology, 68*, 804–825.

Allen, T.J., & Sherman, J.W. (2011). Ego threat and intergroup bias: A test of motivated-activation versus self-regulatory accounts. *Psychological Science, 22*, 331–333.

Allen, T.J., Sherman, J.W., Conrey, F.R., & Stroessner, S.J. (2009). Stereotype strength and attentional bias: Preference for confirming versus disconfirming information depends on processing capacity. *Journal of Experimental Social Psychology, 45*, 1081–1087.

Allison, G., & Zelikow, P. (1999). *Essence of decision: Explaining the Cuban missile crisis* (2nd ed.). New York, NY: Longman.

Allison, S.T., & Messick, D.M. (1985). The group attribution error. *Journal of Experimental Social Psychology, 21*, 563–579.

Allison, S.T., & Messick, D.M. (1987). From individual inputs to group outputs and back again: Group processes and inferences about members. In C. Hendricks (Ed.), *Review of personality and social psychology* (Vol. 8, pp. 111–143). Beverly Hills, CA: Sage.

Allison, S.T., Mackie, D.M., & Messick, D.M. (1996). Outcome biases in social perception: Implications for dispositional inference, attitude change, stereotyping, and social behavior. In M.P. Zanna (Ed.), *Advances in experimental social psychology* (Vol. 28, pp. 53–93). San Diego, CA: Academic Press.

Allison, S.T., Messick, D.M., & Goethals, G.R. (1989). On being better but not smarter than others: The Muhammad Ali effect. *Social Cognition, 7*, 275–295.

Alloy, L.B., & Abramson, L.Y. (1988). Depressive realism: Four theoretical perspectives. In L.B. Alloy (Ed.), *Cognitive processes in depression* (pp. 223–265). New York, NY: Guilford Press.

Allport, G.W. (1943). The ego in contemporary psychology. *Psychological Review, 50*, 451–478.

Allport, G.W. (1954). *The nature of prejudice.* Cambridge, MA: Addison-Wesley.

Alogna, V.K., Attaya, M.K., Aucoin, P., Bahnik, S., Birch, S., Birt, A.R., ... Zwaan, R.A. (2014). Registered replication report: Schooler and Engstler-Schooler (1990). *Perspectives on Psychological Science, 9*, 556–578.

Alt, N.P., Goodale, B.M., Lick, D.J., & Johnson, K.L. (2019). Threat in the company of men: Ensemble perception and threat evaluations of groups varying in sex ratio. *Social Psychological and Personality Science, 10*, 152–159.

Altemeyer, B. (1981). *Right-wing authoritarianism.* Winnipeg, Canada: University of Manitoba Press.

Altemeyer, B. (1998). The other "authoritarian personality." In M.P. Zanna (Ed.), *Advances in experimental social psychology* (Vol. 30, pp. 85–107). New York, NY: Academic Press.

Altemeyer, B. (2004). Highly dominating, highly authoritarian personalities. *The Journal of Social Psychology*, *144*, 421–447.

Alter, A.L., & Oppenheimer, D.M. (2009). Uniting the tribes of fluency to form a metacognitive nation. *Personality and Social Psychology Review*, *13*, 219–235.

Alter, A.L., Oppenheimer, D.M., Epley, N., & Eyre, R.N. (2007). Overcoming intuition: Metacognitive difficulty activates analytic reasoning. *Journal of Experimental Psychology*, *136*, 569–576.

Alvarez, G.A. (2011). Representing multiple objects as an ensemble enhances visual cognition. *Trends in Cognitive Sciences*, *15*, 122–131.

Alves, H., Koch, A., & Unkelbach, C. (2016). My friends are all alike—the relation between liking and perceived similarity in person perception. *Journal of Experimental Social Psychology*, *62*, 103–117.

Alves, H., Koch, A., & Unkelbach, C. (2017). Why good is more alike than bad: Processing implications. *Trends in Cognitive Sciences*, *21*, 69–79.

Alvidrez, J., & Weinstein, R.S. (1999). Early teacher perceptions and later student academic achievement. *Journal of Educational Psychology*, *91*, 731–746.

Ambady, N., & Rosenthal, R. (1992). Thin slices of expressive behavior as predictors of interpersonal consequences: A meta-analysis. *Psychological Bulletin*, *111*, 256–274.

Ambady, N., & Rosenthal, R. (1993). Half a minute: Predicting teacher evaluations from thin slices of behavior and physical attractiveness. *Journal of Personality and Social Psychology*, *64*, 431–441.

Ambady, N., Bernieri, F., & Richeson, J.A. (2000). Toward a histology of social behavior: Judgmental accuracy from thin slices of behavior. In M.P. Zanna (Ed.), *Advances in experimental social psychology* (Vol. 32, pp. 201–272). San Diego, CA: Academic Press.

Ambady, N., Hallahan, M., & Conner, B. (1999). Accuracy of judgments of sexual orientation from thin slices of behavior. *Journal of Personality and Social Psychology*, *77*, 538–547.

Ambady, N., Koo, J., Rosenthal, R., & Winograd, C. (2002). Physical therapists' nonverbal communication predicts geriatric patients' health outcomes. *Psychology and Aging*, *17*, 443–452.

Ambady, N., LaPlante, D., Nguyen, T., Rosenthal, R., Chaumeton, N., & Levinson, W. (2002). Surgeon's tone of voice: A clue to malpractice history. *Surgery*, *132*, 5–9.

Ames, D.L., & Fiske, S.T. (2013). Outcome dependency alters the neural substrates of impression formation. *NeuroImage*, *83*, 599–608.

Ames, D.R. (2004a). Inside the mind-reader's toolkit: Projection and stereotyping in mental state inference. *Journal of Personality and Social Psychology*, *87*, 340–353.

Ames, D.R. (2004b). Strategies for social inference: A similarity contingency model of projection and stereotyping in attribute prevalence estimates. *Journal of Personality and Social Psychology*, *87*, 573–585.

Ames, D.R. (2005). Everyday solutions to the problem of other minds: Which tools are used when? In B.F. Malle & S.D. Hodges (Eds.), *Other minds: How humans bridge the divide between self and others* (pp. 158–173). New York, NY: Guilford Press.

Ames, D.R., & Mason, M.F. (2012). Mind perception. In S.T. Fiske & C.N. Macrae (Eds.), *The SAGE handbook of social cognition* (pp. 115–137). Thousand Oaks, CA: Sage.

Ames, D.R., Weber, E.U., & Zou, X. (2012). Mind-reading in strategic interaction: The impact of perceived similarity on p erception and stereotyping. *Organizational Behavior and Human Decision Processes*, *117*, 96–110.

Amodio, D.M. (2014). The neuroscience of prejudice and stereotyping. *Nature Reviews Neuroscience*, *15*, 670–682.

Amodio, D.M. (2019). Social cognition 2.0: An interactive memory systems account. *Trends in Cognitive Sciences*, *23*, 21–33.

Amodio, D.M., & Devine, P.G. (2006). Stereotyping and evaluation in implicit race bias: Evidence for independent constructs and unique effects on behavior. *Journal of Personality and Social Psychology, 91,* 652–661.

Amodio, D.M., & Ratner, K.G. (2011). A memory systems model of implicit social cognition. *Current Directions in Psychological Science, 20,* 143–148.

Amodio, D.M., Devine, P.G., & Harmon-Jones, E. (2008). Individual differences in the regulation of intergroup bias: The role of conflict monitoring and neural signals for control. *Journal of Personality and Social Psychology, 94,* 60–74.

Amodio, D.M., Harmon-Jones, E., Devine, P.G., Curtin, J.J., Hartley, S.L., & Covert, A.E. (2004). Neural signals for the detection of unintentional race bias. *Psychological Science, 15,* 88–93.

Anastasi, J.S., & Rhodes, M.G. (2005). An own-age bias in face recognition for children and older adults. *Psychonomic Bulletin & Review, 12,* 1043–1047.

Andersen, S.M. (1984). Self-knowledge and social inference: II. The diagnosticity of cognitive/affective and behavioral data. *Journal of Personality and Social Psychology, 46,* 294–307.

Andersen, S.M., & Baum, A. (1994). Transference in interpersonal relations: Schema-triggered inferences and affect based on significant-other representations. *Journal of Personality, 62,* 459–498.

Andersen, S.M., & Chen, S. (2002). The relational self: An interpersonal social-cognitive theory. *Psychological Review, 109,* 619–645.

Andersen, S.M., & Cole, S. (1990). Do I know you? The role of significant others in general social perception. *Journal of Personality and Social Psychology, 59,* 384–399.

Andersen, S.M., & Glassman, N.S. (1996). Responding to significant others when they are not there: Effects on interpersonal inference, motivation, and affect. In R. Sorrentino & E.T. Higgins (Eds.), *Handbook of motivation and cognition* (Vol. 3, pp. 272–331). New York, NY: Guilford Press.

Andersen, S.M., & Ross, L. (1984). Self-knowledge and social inference: I. The impact of cognitive/affective and behavioral data. *Journal of Personality and Social Psychology, 46,* 280–293.

Andersen, S.M., Glassman, N.S., Chen, S., & Cole, S.W. (1995). Transference in social perception: The role of the chronic accessibility of significant-other representations. *Journal of Personality and Social Psychology, 69,* 41–57.

Andersen, S.M., Tuskeviciute, R., Przybylinski, E., Ahn, J.N., & Xu, J.H. (2016). Contextual variability in personality from significant–other knowledge and relational selves. *Frontiers in Psychology, 6,* Article 1882.

Anderson, C.A., Benjamin, A.J., Jr., & Bartholow, B.D. (1998). Does the gun pull the trigger? Automatic priming effects of weapon pictures and weapon names. *Psychological Science, 9,* 308–314.

Anderson, J.C., Jennings, M.M., Lowe, D.J., & Reckers, P.M. (1997). The mitigation of hindsight bias in judges' evaluation of auditor decisions. *Auditing: A Journal of Practice & Theory, 16,* 20–29.

Anderson, K.O., Green, C.R., & Payne, R. (2009). Racial and ethnic disparities in pain: Causes and consequences of unequal care. *The Journal of Pain, 10,* 1187–1204

Anderson, M.C., Bjork, R.A., & Bjork, E.L. (1994). Remembering can cause forgetting: Retrieval dynamics in long-term memory. *Journal of Experimental Psychology: Learning, Memory, and Cognition, 20,* 1063–1087.

Anderson, N.H. (1962). Application of an additive model to impression formation. *Science, 138,* 817–818.

Anderson, N.H. (1965). Averaging versus adding as a stimulus-combination rule in impression formation. *Journal of Experimental Psychology, 70,* 394–400.

Anderson, N.H. (1968). A simple model for information integration. In R.P. Abelson, E. Aronson, W.J. McGuire, T.M. Newcomb, &

P.H. Tannenbaum (Eds.), *Theories of cognitive consistency: A sourcebook* (pp. 731–743). Chicago, IL: Rand McNally.

Anderson, N.H. (1971). Integration theory and attitude change. *Psychological Review, 78*, 171–206.

Anderson, N.H. (1973). Serial position curves in impression formation. *Journal of Experimental Psychology, 97*, 8–12.

Anderson, N.H. (2013). Unified psychology based on three laws of information integration. *Review of General Psychology, 17*, 125–132.

Anderson, N.H., & Barrios, A.A. (1961). Primacy effects in personality impression formation. *Journal of Abnormal and Social Psychology, 63*, 346–350.

Anderson, N.H., & Hubert, S. (1963). Effects of concomitant verbal recall on order effects in personality impression formation. *Journal of Verbal Learning and Verbal Behavior, 2*, 379–391.

Anderson, N.H., & Shanteau, J.C. (1970). Information integration in risky decision making. *Journal of Experimental Psychology, 84*, 441–451.

Anderson, R.C, & Pichert, J.W. (1978). Recall of previously unrecallable information following a shift in perspective. *Journal of Verbal Learning and Verbal Behavior, 17*, 1–12.

Archer, M., & Tritter, J. (Eds.) (2000). *Rational choice theory*. London: Routledge.

Arcuri, L., Castelli, L., Galdi, S., Zogmaister, C., & Amadori, A. (2008). Predicting the vote: Implicit attitudes as predictors of the future behavior of decided and undecided voters. *Political Psychology, 29*, 369–387.

Ariely, D. (2009). *Predictably irrational: The hidden forces that shape our decisions.* New York, NY: HarperCollins.

Ariyanto, A., Hornsey, M.J., & Gallois, C. (2009). Intergroup attribution bias in the context of extreme intergroup conflict. *Asian Journal of Social Psychology, 12*, 293–299.

Arkes, H.R. (1981). Impediments to accurate clinical judgment and possible ways to minimize their impact. *Journal of Consulting and Clinical Psychology, 49*, 323–350.

Arkes, H.R. (2013). The consequences of the hindsight bias in medical decision making. *Current Directions in Psychological Science, 22*, 356–360.

Arkes, H.R., Faust, D., Guilmette, T.J., & Hart, K. (1988). Eliminating the hindsight bias. *Journal of Applied Psychology, 73*, 305–307.

Arkes, H.R., Wortmann, R.L., Saville, P.D., & Harkness, A.R. (1981). Hindsight bias among physicians weighing the likelihood of diagnoses. *Journal of Applied Psychology, 66*, 252–254.

Arkin, R.M., & Duval, S. (1975). Focus of attention and causal attributions of actors and observers. *Journal of Experimental Social Psychology, 11*, 427–438.

Armitage, C.J., & Conner, M. (2001). Efficacy of the theory of planned behaviour: A meta-analytic review. *British Journal of Social Psychology, 40*, 471–499.

Aronson, E., Fried, C., & Stone, J. (1991). Overcoming denial and increasing the intention to use condoms through the induction of hypocrisy. *American Journal of Public Health, 81*, 1636–1638.

Asch, S.E. (1946). Forming impressions of personality. *Journal of Abnormal and Social Psychology, 41*, 258–290.

Asch, S.E., & Zukier, H. (1984). Thinking about persons. *Journal of Personality and Social Psychology, 46*, 1230–1240.

Asch, S.E., Block, H., & Hertzman, M. (1938). Studies in the principles of judgments and attitudes: I. Two basic principles of judgment. *Journal of Psychology, 5*, 219–251.

Asendorpf, J.B., Banse, R., & Mücke, D. (2002). Double dissociation between implicit and explicit personality self-concept: The case of shy behavior. *Journal of Personality and Social Psychology, 83*, 380–393.

Ashmore, R.D. (1981). Sex stereotypes and implicit personality theory. In D.L. Hamilton (Ed.), *Cognitive processes in stereotyping and intergroup behavior* (pp. 37–81). Hillsdale, NJ: Lawrence Erlbaum.

Ashton, M.C., Lee, K., & De Vries, R.E. (2014). The HEXACO honesty-humility, agreeableness, and emotionality factors: A review of research and theory. *Personality and Social Psychology Review, 18*, 139–152.

Aslan, A., Bäuml, K.H., & Grundgeiger, T. (2007). The role of inhibitory processes in part-list cuing. *Journal of Experimental Psychology: Learning, Memory, and Cognition, 33*, 335–341.

Assilaméhou-Kunz, Y., Postmes, T., & Testé, B. (2019). A normative perspective on the linguistic intergroup bias: How intragroup approval of ingroup members who use the linguistic intergroup bias perpetuates explicit intergroup bias. *European Journal of Social Psychology, 1*, 81–96.

Attneave, F. (1955). Symmetry, information, and memory for patterns. *The American Journal of Psychology, 68*, 209–222.

Axelrod, R., & Hamilton, W.D. (1981). The evolution of cooperation. *Science, 211*, 1390–1396.

Ayduk, O., & Gyurak, A. (2008). Applying the cognitive-affective processing systems approach to conceptualizing rejection sensitivity. *Social and Personality Psychology Compass, 2*, 2016–2033.

Ayduk, O., Gyurak, A., & Luerssen, A. (2008). Individual differences in the rejection-aggression link in the hot sauce paradigm: The case of rejection sensitivity. *Journal of Experimental Social Psychology, 44*, 775–782.

Azar, O.H. (2014). The default heuristic in strategic decision making: When is it optimal to choose the default without investing in information search? *Journal of Business Research, 67*, 1744–1748.

Babad, E., Bernieri, F., & Rosenthal, R. (1991). Students as judges of teachers' verbal and nonverbal behavior. *American Educational Research Journal, 28*, 211–234.

Bacon, F.T. (1979). Credibility of repeated statements: Memory for trivia. *Journal of Experimental Psychology: Human Learning and Memory, 5*, 241–252.

Badahdah, A.M., & Alkhder, O.H. (2006). Helping a friend with AIDS: A test of Weiner's attributional theory in Kuwait. *Illness, Crisis, & Loss, 14*, 43–54.

Badea, C., & Sherman, D.K. (2019). Self-affirmation and prejudice reduction: When and why? *Current Directions in Psychological Science, 28*, 40–46.

Bago, B., Rand, D.G., & Pennycook, G. (2020). Fake news, fast and slow: Deliberation reduces belief in false (but not true) news headlines. *Journal of Experimental Psychology: General, 149*, 1608–1613.

Bahník, Š., Englich, B., & Strack, F. (2017). Anchoring effect. In R.F. Pohl (Ed.), *Cognitive illusions: Intriguing phenomena in thinking, judgment and memory* (2nd ed.) (pp. 223–241). New York, NY: Routledge.

Baillet, S.D., & Keenan, J.M. (1986). The role of encoding and retrieval processes in the recall of text. *Discourse Processes, 9*, 247–268.

Balcetis, E., & Dunning, D. (2006). See what you want to see: Motivational influences on visual perception. *Journal of Personality and Social Psychology, 91*, 612–625.

Balcetis, E., & Dunning, D. (2008). A mile in moccasins: How situational experience reduces dispositionism in social judgment. *Personality and Social Psychology Bulletin, 34*, 102–114.

Baldwin, M.W., Carrell, S.E., & Lopez, D.F. (1990). Priming relationship schemas: My advisor and the Pope are watching me from the back of my mind. *Journal of Experimental Social Psychology, 26*, 435–454.

Ballew, C.C., & Todorov, A. (2007). Predicting political elections from rapid and unreflective face decisions. *Proceedings of the National Academy of Sciences, 104*, 17948–17953.

Banaji, M.R., & Greenwald, A.G. (1995). Implicit gender stereotyping in judgments of fame. *Journal of Personality and Social Psychology, 68*, 181–198.

Banaji, M.R., & Hardin, C.D. (1996). Automatic stereotyping. *Psychological Science, 7*, 136–141.

Banaji, M.R., Hardin, C.D., & Rothman, A.J. (1993). Implicit stereotyping in person judgment. *Journal of Personality and Social Psychology, 65,* 272–281.

Bandura, A. (1962). *Social learning through imitation.* Lincoln, NE: University of Nebraska Press.

Bandura, A. (1973). *Aggression: A social learning analysis.* Englewood Cliffs, NJ: Prentice Hall.

Bandura, A. (1977). *Social learning theory.* Englewood Cliffs, NJ: Prentice Hall.

Bandura, A. (1997). *Self-efficacy: The exercise of control.* New York, NY: W.H. Freeman.

Bandura, A. (2006). Toward a psychology of human agency. *Perspectives on Psychological Science, 1,* 164–180.

Bandura, A., Blanchard, E.B., & Ritter, B. (1969). Relative efficacy of desensitization and modeling approaches for inducing behavioral, affective, and attitudinal changes. *Journal of Personality and Social Psychology, 13,* 173–199.

Bandura, A., Ross, D., & Ross, S.A. (1961). Transmission of aggression through the imitation of aggressive models. *Journal of Abnormal and Social Psychology, 63,* 575–582.

Barbaro, N., Pickett, S.M., & Parkhill, M.R. (2015). Environmental attitudes mediate the link between need for cognition and pro-environmental goal choice. *Personality and Individual Differences, 75,* 220–223.

Barber, S.J., Harris, C.B., & Rajaram, S. (2015). Why two heads apart are better than two heads together: Multiple mechanisms underlie the collaborative inhibition effect in memory. *Journal of Experimental Psychology: Learning, Memory, and Cognition, 41,* 559–566.

Barden, J., Maddux, W.W., Petty, R.E., & Brewer, M.B. (2004). Contextual moderation of racial bias: The impact of social roles on controlled and automatically activated attitudes. *Journal of Personality and Social Psychology, 87,* 5–22.

Bargh, J.A. (1982). Attention and automaticity in the processing of self-relevant information. *Journal of Personality and Social Psychology, 43,* 425–436.

Bargh, J.A. (1994). The four horsemen of automaticity: Awareness, intention, efficiency, and control in social cognition. In R.S. Wyer, Jr. & T.K. Srull (Eds.), *Handbook of social cognition* (2nd ed., Vol. 1, *Basic processes,* pp. 1–40). Hillsdale, NJ: Lawrence Erlbaum.

Bargh, J.A. (1997). The automaticity of everyday life. In R.S. Wyer, Jr. (Ed.), *Advances in social cognition* (Vol. 10, pp. 1–61). Mahwah, NJ: Lawrence Erlbaum.

Bargh, J.A. (2005). Bypassing the will: Toward demystifying the nonconscious control of social behavior. In R.R. Hassin, J.S. Uleman, & J.A. Bargh (Eds.), *The new unconscious* (pp. 37–58). New York, NY: Oxford University Press.

Bargh, J.A., & Chartrand, T.L. (1999). The unbearable automaticity of being. *American Psychologist, 54,* 462–479.

Bargh, J.A., & Ferguson, M.J. (2000). Beyond behaviorism: On the automaticity of higher mental processes. *Psychological Bulletin, 126,* 925–945.

Bargh, J.A., & Melnikoff, D. (2019). Does physical warmth prime social warmth? Reply to Chabris et al. (2019). *Social Psychology, 50,* 207–210.

Bargh, J.A., & Pietromonaco, P. (1982). Automatic information processing and social perception: The influence of trait information presented outside of conscious awareness on impression formation. *Journal of Personality and Social Psychology, 43,* 437–449.

Bargh, J.A., & Pratto, F. (1986). Individual construct accessibility and perceptual selection. *Journal of Experimental Social Psychology, 22,* 293–311.

Bargh, J.A., & Thein, R.D. (1985). Individual construct accessibility, person memory, and the recall-judgment link: The case of information overload. *Journal of Personality and Social Psychology, 49,* 1129–1146.

Bargh, J.A., Bond, R.N., Lombardi, W.J., & Tota, M.E. (1986). The additive nature of chronic and temporary sources of construct accessibility. *Journal of Personality and Social Psychology, 50,* 869–878.

Bargh, J.A., Chen, M., & Burrows, L. (1996). Automaticity of social behavior: Direct effects of trait construct and stereotype activation on action. *Journal of Personality and Social Psychology, 71*, 230–244.

Bargh, J.A., Gollwitzer, P.M., Lee-Chai, A.Y., Barndollar, K., & Trötschel, R. (2001). Bypassing the will: Automatic and controlled self-regulation. *Journal of Personality and Social Psychology, 81*, 1014–1027.

Bargh, J.A., Schwader, K.L., Hailey, S.E., Dyer, R.L., & Boothby, E.J. (2012). Automaticity in social-cognitive processes. *Trends in Cognitive Sciences, 16*, 593–605.

Barnhardt, T.M., Choi, H., Gerkens, D.R., & Smith, S.M. (2006). Output position and word relatedness effects in a DRM paradigm: Support for a dual-retrieval process theory of free recall and false memories. *Journal of Memory and Language, 55*, 213–231.

Barranti, M., Carlson, E.N., & Furr, R.M. (2016). Disagreement about moral character is linked to interpersonal costs. *Social Psychological and Personality Science, 7*, 806–817.

Barsalou, L.W. (1985). Ideals, central tendency, and frequency of instantiation. *Journal of Experimental Psychology: Learning, Memory, and Cognition, 11*, 211–227.

Barsalou, L.W. (2016). Situated conceptualization offers a theoretical account of social priming. *Current Opinion in Psychology, 12*, 6–11.

Bartholow, B.D., Anderson, C.A., Carnagey, N.L., & Benjamin, A.J. (2005). Interactive effects of life experience and situational cues on aggression: The weapons priming effect in hunters and nonhunters. *Journal of Experimental Social Psychology, 41*, 48–60.

Bartholow, B.D., Fabiani, M., Gratton, G., & Bettencourt, B.A. (2001). A psychophysiological examination of cognitive processing of and affective responses to social expectancy violations. *Psychological Science, 12*, 197–204.

Basden, B.H., Basden, D.R., Bryner, S., & Thomas, R.L. (1997). A comparison of group and individual remembering: Does collaboration disrupt retrieval strategies? *Journal of Experimental Psychology: Learning, Memory, and Cognition, 23*, 1176–1189.

Basden, D.R., & Basden, B.H. (1995). Some tests of the strategy disruption interpretation of part-list cuing inhibition. *Journal of Experimental Psychology: Learning, Memory, and Cognition, 21*, 1656–1669.

Bassili, J.N., & Brown, R.D. (2005). Implicit and explicit attitudes: Research, challenges, and theory. In D. Albarracín, B.T. Johnson, & M.P. Zanna (Eds.), *The handbook of attitudes* (pp. 543–574). Mahwah, NJ: Lawrence Erlbaum.

Batchelder, W.H., & Riefer, D.M. (1999). Theoretical and empirical review of multinomial processing tree modeling. *Psychonomic Bulletin & Review, 6*, 57–86.

Batson, C.D., Polycarpou, M.P., Harmon-Jones, E., Imhoff, H.J., Mitchener, E.C., Bednar, L.L., Klein, T.R., & Highberger, L. (1997). Empathy and attitudes: Can feeling for a member of a stigmatized group improve feelings toward the group? *Journal of Personality and Social Psychology, 72*, 105–118.

Baucom, D.H. (1987). Attributions in distressed relations: How can we explain them? In S. Duck & D. Perlman (Eds.), *Intimate relationships: Development, dynamics and deterioration* (pp. 177–206). London: Sage.

Baucom, D.H., & Epstein, N. (1990). *Cognitive-behavioral marital therapy.* New York, NY: Brunner/Mazel.

Bauer, P.J. (2015). A complementary processes account of the development of childhood amnesia and a personal past. *Psychological Review, 122*, 204–231

Baumeister, R.F. (Ed.) (1999). *Key readings in social psychology: The self in social psychology.* New York, NY: Psychology Press.

Baumeister, R.F., & Bargh, J.A. (2014). Conscious and unconscious: Toward an integrative understanding of human mental life and action. In J.W. Sherman, B. Gawronski, & Y. Trope (Eds.), *Dual-process theories of the social mind* (pp. 35–49). New York, NY: Guilford Press.

Baumeister, R.F., & Bushman, B.J. (2008). *Social psychology and human nature.* Belmont, CA: Wadsworth.

Baumeister, R.F., & Leary, M.R. (1995). The need to belong: Desire for interpersonal attachments as a fundamental human motivation. *Psychological Bulletin, 117,* 497–529.

Baumeister, R.F., & Masicampo, E.J. (2010). Conscious thought is for facilitating social and cultural interactions: How simulations serve the animal-culture interface. *Psychological Review, 117,* 945–971.

Baumeister, R.F., Bratslavsky, E., Finkenauer, C., & Vohs, K.D. (2001). Bad is stronger than good. *Review of General Psychology, 5,* 323–370.

Baumeister, R.F., Masicampo, E.J., & Vohs, K.D. (2011). Do conscious thoughts cause behavior? *Annual Review of Psychology, 62,* 331–361.

Baumeister, R.F., Smart, L., & Boden, J.M. (1996). Relation of threatened egotism to violence and aggression: The dark side of high self-esteem. *Psychological Review, 103,* 5–33.

Bäuml, K.H., & Aslan, A. (2004). Part-list cuing as instructed retrieval inhibition. *Memory & Cognition, 32,* 610–617.

Bäuml, K.H., & Aslan, A. (2006). Part-list cuing can be transient and lasting: The role of encoding. *Journal of Experimental Psychology: Learning, Memory, and Cognition, 32,* 33–43.

Bayen, U.J., Pohl, R.F., Erdfelder, E., & Auer, T.-S. (2007). Hindsight bias across the life span. *Social Cognition, 25,* 83–97.

Beauregard, K.S., & Dunning, D. (1998). Turning up the contrast: Self-enhancement motives prompt egocentric contrast effects in social judgments. *Journal of Personality and Social Psychology, 74,* 606–621.

Beer, A., & Vazire, S. (2017). Evaluating the predictive validity of personality trait judgments using a naturalistic behavioral criterion: A preliminary test of the self-other knowledge asymmetry model. *Journal of Research in Personality, 70,* 107–121.

Beer, A., & Watson, D. (2008). Personality judgment at zero acquaintance: Agreement, assumed similarity, and implicit simplicity. *Journal of Personality Assessment, 90,* 250–260.

Beer, J.S. (2014). Exaggerated positivity in self-evaluation: A social neuroscience approach to reconciling the role of self-esteem protection and cognitive bias. *Social & Personality Psychology Compass, 8,* 583–594.

Beggan, J.K. (1992). On the social nature of nonsocial perception: The mere ownership effect. *Journal of Personality and Social Psychology, 62,* 229–237.

Behrmann, M., & Nishimura, M. (2010). Agnosias. *WIREs Cognitive Science, 1,* 203–213.

Beike, D.R., & Sherman, S.J. (1994). Social inference: Inductions, deductions, and analogies. In R.S. Wyer, Jr. & T.K. Srull (Eds.), *Handbook of social cognition* (2nd ed., Vol. 1, pp. 209–285). Hillsdale, NJ: Lawrence Erlbaum.

Beilock, S.L., Carr, T.H., MacMahon, C., & Starkes, J.L. (2002). When paying attention becomes counterproductive: Impact of divided versus skill-focused attention on novice and experienced performance of sensorimotor skills. *Journal of Experimental Psychology: Applied, 8,* 6–16.

Beilock, S.L., Jellison, W.A., Rydell, R.J., McConnell, A.R., & Carr, T.H. (2006). On the causal mechanisms of stereotype threat: Can skills that don't rely heavily on working memory still be threatened? *Personality and Social Psychology Bulletin, 32,* 1059–1071.

Belli, R.F. (1989). Influences of misleading postevent information: Misinformation interference and acceptance. *Journal of Experimental Psychology: General, 118,* 72–85.

Belmore, S.M. (1987). Determinants of attention during impression formation. *Journal of Experimental Psychology: Learning, Memory, and Cognition, 13,* 480–489.

Bem, D.J. (1972). Self-perception theory. In L. Berkowitz (Ed.), *Advances in experimental social psychology* (Vol. 6, pp. 1–62). New York, NY: Academic Press.

Bem, D.J., & Allen, A. (1974). On predicting some of the people some of the time: The search for cross-situational consistencies in behavior. *Psychological Review*, *81*, 506–520.

Bembenutty, H. (2015). *Contemporary pioneers in teaching and learning.* Charlotte, NC: Information Age Publishing.

Benartzi, S., Beshears, J., Milkman, K.L., Sunstein, C.R., Thaler, R.H., Shankar, M., Tucker-Ray, W., Congdon, W.J., & Galing, S. (2017). Should governments invest more in nudging? *Psychological Science*, *28*, 1041–1055.

Bench, S.W., Rivera, G.N., Schlegel, R.J., Hicks, J.A., & Lench, H.C. (2017). Does expertise matter in replication? An examination of the reproducibility project: Psychology. *Journal of Experimental Social Psychology*, *68*, 181–184.

Bender, A., Beller, S., & Medin, D.L. (2017). Causal cognition and culture. In M.R. Waldmann (Ed.), *The Oxford handbook of causal reasoning* (pp. 1–43). New York, NY: Oxford University Press.

Berger, I.E. (1992). The nature of attitude accessibility and attitude confidence: A triangulated experiment. *Journal of Consumer Psychology*, *1*, 103–123.

Berger, I.E. (1999). The influence of advertising frequency on attitude-behavior consistency: A memory based analysis. *Journal of Social Behavior & Personality*, *14*, 547–568.

Berger, I.E., & Mitchell, A.A. (1989). The effect of advertising on attitude accessibility, attitude confidence, and the attitude-behavior relationship. *Journal of Consumer Research*, *16*, 269–279.

Berggren, N., Koster, E.H.W., & Derakshan, N. (2012). The effect of cognitive load in emotional attention and trait anxiety: An eye movement study. *Journal of Cognitive Psychology*, *24*, 79–91.

Berglas, S., & Jones, E.E. (1978). Drug choice as a self-handicapping strategy in response to noncontingent success. *Journal of Personality and Social Psychology*, *36*, 405–417.

Berkowitz, L., & LePage, A. (1967). Weapons as aggression-eliciting stimuli. *Journal of Personality and Social Psychology*, *7*, 202–207.

Berndsen, M., McGarty, C., van-der-Pligt, J., & Spears, R. (2001). Meaning-seeking in the illusory correlation paradigm: The active role of participants in the categorization process. *British Journal of Social Psychology*, *40*, 209–234.

Berne, S.A. (2006). The primitive reflexes: Considerations in the infant. *Optometry & Vision Development*, *37*, 139–145.

Bernhold, Q.S., & Giles, H. (2020). Vocal accommodation and mimicry. *Journal of Nonverbal Behavior*, *44*, 41–62.

Bernstein, D.M., & Loftus, E.F. (2009). The consequences of false memories for food preferences and choices. *Perspectives on Psychological Science*, 4, 135–139.

Bernstein, D.M., Laney, C., Morris, E.K., & Loftus, E.F. (2005a). False memories about food can lead to food avoidance. *Social Cognition*, *23*, 10–33.

Bernstein, D.M., Laney, C., Morris, E.K., & Loftus, E.F. (2005b). False beliefs about fattening foods can have healthy consequences. *Proceedings of the National Academy of Sciences*, *102*, 13724–13731.

Bernstein, M.J., Young, S.G., & Hugenberg, K. (2007). The cross-category effect: Mere social categorization is sufficient to elicit an own-group bias in face recognition. *Psychological Science*, *18*, 706–712.

Berntsen, D., & Rubin, D.C. (2002). Emotionally charged autobiographical memories across the life span: The recall of happy, sad, traumatic, and involuntary memories. *Psychology and Aging*, *17*, 636–652.

Berntsen, D., & Rubin, D.S. (2004). Cultural life scripts structure recall from autobiographical memory. *Memory & Cognition*, *32*, 427–442.

Beshears, J., Choi, J., Laibson, D., & Madrian, B. (2008). The importance of default options for retirement saving outcomes: Evidence from the United States. In S.J. Kay & T. Sinha (Eds.), *Lessons from pension reform in the Americas* (pp. 59–87). New York, NY: Oxford University Press.

Bessenoff, G.R., & Sherman, J.W. (2000). Automatic and controlled components of prejudice toward fat people: Evaluation versus stereotype activation. *Social Cognition, 18*, 329–353.

Bettman, J.R., & Weitz, B.A. (1983). Attributions in the board room: Causal reasoning in corporate annual reports. *Administrative Science Quarterly, 28*, 165–183.

Bierbrauer, G. (1979). Why did he do it? Attribution of obedience and the phenomenon of dispositional bias. *European Journal of Social Psychology, 9*, 67–84.

Biernat, M. (2003). Toward a broader view of social stereotyping. *The American Psychologist, 58*, 1019–1027.

Biernat, M. (2005). *Standards and expectancies: Contrast and assimilation in judgments of self and others.* New York, NY: Psychology Press.

Biernat, M. (2018). Gender stereotyping, prejudice, and shifting standards. In C.B. Travis, J.W. White, A. Rutherford, W.S. Williams, S.L. Cook, & K.F. Wyche (Eds.), *APA handbook of the psychology of women: History, theory, and battlegrounds* (Vol. 1, pp. 343–361). Washington, DC: American Psychological Association.

Biernat, M., & Manis, M. (2007). Stereotypes and shifting standards: Assimilation and contrast in social judgment. In D.A. Stapel & J. Suls (Eds.), *Assimilation and contrast in social psychology* (pp. 75–97). New York, NY: Psychology Press.

Biernat, M., Crandall, C.S., Young, L.V., Kobrynowicz, D., & Halpin, S.M. (1998). All that you can be: Stereotyping of self and others in a military context. *Journal of Personality and Social Psychology, 75*, 301–317.

Biernat, M., Manis, M., & Kobrynowicz, D. (1997). Simultaneous assimilation and contrast effects in judgments of self and others. *Journal of Personality and Social Psychology, 73*, 254–269.

Biernat, M., Manis, M., & Nelson, T.E. (1991). Stereotypes and standards of judgment. *Journal of Personality and Social Psychology, 60*, 485–499.

Billeter, D., Kalra, A., & Loewenstein, G. (2011). Underpredicting learning after initial experience with a product. *Journal of Consumer Research, 37*, 723–736.

Biondi, F., Turrill, J.M., Coleman, J.R., Cooper, J.M., & Strayer, D.L. (2015). Cognitive distraction impairs driver's anticipatory glances: An on-road study. In D.V. McGehee, J.D. Lee, & M. Rizzo (Eds.), *Driving assessment 2015: International symposium on human factors in driver assessment, training, and vehicle design* (pp. 23–29). Iowa City, IA: University of Iowa, Public Policy Center.

Birch, S.A., & Bernstein, D.M. (2007). What can children tell us about hindsight bias: A fundamental constraint on perspective-taking? *Social Cognition, 25*, 98–113.

Bishara, A.J., & Payne, B.K. (2009). Multinomial process tree models of control and automaticity in weapon misidentification. *Journal of Experimental Social Psychology, 45*, 524–534.

Bizer, G.Y., Larsen, J.T., & Petty, R.E. (2011). Exploring the valence-framing effect: Negative framing enhances attitude strength. *Political Psychology, 32*, 59–80.

Bjornsdottir, R.T., & Rule, N.O. (2017). The visibility of social class from facial cues. *Journal of Personality and Social Psychology, 113*, 530–546.

Blair, I.V. (2002). The malleability of automatic stereotypes and prejudice. *Personality and Social Psychology Review, 6*, 242–261.

Blair, I.V., Judd, C.M., & Chapleau, K.M. (2004). The influence of Afrocentric facial features in criminal sentencing. *Psychological Science, 15*, 674–679.

Blair, I.V., Judd, C.M., & Fallman, J.L. (2004). The automaticity of race and Afrocentric facial features in social judgments. *Journal of Personality and Social Psychology, 87*, 763–778.

Blair, I.V., Judd, C.M., Sadler, M.S., & Jenkins, C. (2002). The role of Afrocentric features in person perception: Judging by features and categories. *Journal of Personality and Social Psychology, 83*, 5–25.

Blair, I.V., Ma, J.E., & Lenton, A.P. (2001). Imagining stereotypes away: The moderation of implicit stereotypes through mental imagery. *Journal of Personality and Social Psychology, 81*, 828–841.

Blair, I.V., Steiner, J.F., Hanratty, R., Price, D.W., Fairclough, D.L., Daugherty, S.L., Bronsert, M., Magid, D.J., & Havranek, E.P. (2014). An investigation of associations between clinicians' ethnic or racial bias and hypertension treatment, medication adherence and blood pressure control. *Journal of General Internal Medicine, 29*, 987–995.

Blank, H., & Launay, C. (2014). How to protect eyewitness memory against the misinformation effect: A meta-analysis of post-warning studies. *Journal of Applied Research in Memory and Cognition, 3*, 77–88.

Blank, H., & Nestler, S. (2007). Cognitive process models of hindsight bias. *Social Cognition, 25*, 132–146.

Blank, H., Fischer, V., & Erdfelder, E. (2003). Hindsight bias in political elections. *Memory, 11*, 491–504.

Blankenship, K.L., & Wegener, D.T. (2008). Opening the mind to close it: Considering a message in light of important values increases message processing and later resistance to change. *Journal of Personality and Social Psychology, 94*, 196–213.

Bless, H. (2001). Mood and the use of general knowledge structures. In L.L. Martin & G.L. Clore (Eds.), *Theories of mood and cognition: A user's guidebook* (pp. 9–26). Mahwah, NJ: Lawrence Erlbaum.

Bless, H., & Burger, A.M. (2016). Assimilation and contrast in social priming. *Current Opinion in Psychology, 12*, 26–31.

Bless, H., & Fiedler, K. (2006). Mood and the regulation of information processing and behavior. In J.P. Forgas (Ed.), *Affect in social thinking and behavior* (pp. 65–84). New York, NY: Psychology Press.

Bless, H., & Schwarz, N. (1999). Sufficient and necessary conditions in dual-process models: The case of mood and information processing. In S. Chaiken & Y. Trope (Eds.), *Dual-process theories in social psychology* (pp. 423–440). New York, NY: Guilford Press.

Bless, H., & Schwarz, N. (2010). Mental construal and the emergence of assimilation and contrast effects: The inclusion/exclusion model. In M.P. Zanna (Ed.), *Advances in experimental social psychology* (Vol. 42, pp. 319–373). New York, NY: Academic Press.

Bless, H., Clore, G.L., Schwarz, N., Golisano, V., Rabe, C., & Wolk, M. (1996). Mood and the use of scripts: Does a happy mood really lead to mindlessness? *Journal of Personality and Social Psychology, 71*, 665–679.

Bobak, A.K., Hancock, P.J.B., & Bate, S. (2016). Super-recognizers in action: Evidence from face-matching and face memory tasks. *Applied Cognitive Psychology, 30*, 81–91.

Bodenhausen, G.V. (1988). Stereotypic biases in social decision making and memory: Testing process models of stereotype use. *Journal of Personality and Social Psychology, 55*, 726–737.

Bodenhausen, G.V., & Gawronski, B. (2013). Attitude change. In D. Reisberg (Ed.), *The Oxford handbook of cognitive psychology* (pp. 957–969). New York, NY: Oxford University Press.

Bodenhausen, G.V., & Wyer, R.S., Jr. (1987). Social cognition and social reality: Information acquisition and use in the laboratory and the real world. In H.J. Hippler, N. Schwarz, & S. Sudman (Eds.), *Social information processing and survey methodology* (pp. 6–41). New York, NY: Springer.

Bodenhausen, G.V., Kramer, G., & Süsser, K. (1994). Happiness and stereotypic thinking in social judgment. *Journal of Personality and Social Psychology, 66*, 621–632.

Bodenhausen, G.V., Macrae, C.N., & Sherman, J.W. (1999). On the dialectics of discrimination: Dual processes in social stereotyping. In S. Chaiken & Y. Trope (Eds.), *Dual-process theories in social psychology* (pp. 271–290). New York, NY: Guilford Press.

Bogart, L.M., Catz, S.L., Kelly, J.A., & Benotsch, E.G. (2001). Factors influencing physicians' judgments of adherence and treatment decisions for patients with HIV disease. *Medical Decision Making, 21*, 28–36.

Böhm, G., & Pfister, H.-R. (2015). How people explain their own and others' behavior: A theory of lay causal explanations. *Frontiers in Psychology, 6*, Article 139.

Bohn, M.K. (2015). *Presidents in crisis: Tough decisions inside the White House from Truman to Obama.* New York, NY: Arcade Publishing.

Bohner, G., & Dickel, N. (2011). Attitudes and attitude change. *Annual Review of Psychology, 62*, 391–417.

Bol, L., & Hacker, D. J. (2001). A comparison of the effects of practice tests and traditional review on performance and calibration. *The Journal of Experimental Education, 69*, 133–151.

Bolsen, T., Druckman, J.N., & Cook, F.L. (2014). The influence of partisan motivated reasoning on public opinion. *Political Behavior, 36*, 235–262.

Bonanno, G.A., Notarius, C.I., Gunzerath, L., Keltner, D., & Horowitz, M.J. (1998). Interpersonal ambivalence, perceived relationship adjustment, and conjugal loss. *Journal of Consulting and Clinical Psychology, 66*, 1012–1022.

Bond, M.H., Hewstone, M., Wan, K.-C., & Chiu, C.-K. (1985). Group-serving attributions across intergroup contexts: Cultural differences in the explanation of sex-typed behaviours. *European Journal of Social Psychology, 15*, 435–451.

Boniecki, K.A., & Jacks, J.Z. (2002). The elusive relationship between measures of implicit and explicit prejudice. *Representative Research in Social Psychology, 26*, 1–14.

Bonnefon, J.-F., Dubois, D., Fargier, H., & Leblois, S. (2008). Qualitative heuristics for balancing the pros and cons. *Theory and Decision, 65*, 71–95.

Borkenau, P., & Liebler, A. (1993). Convergence of stranger ratings of personality and intelligence with self-ratings, partner ratings, and measured intelligence. *Journal of Personality and Social Psychology, 65*, 546–553.

Bornstein, R.F. (1989). Exposure and affect: Overview and meta-analysis of research, 1968–1987. *Psychological Bulletin, 106*, 265–289.

Bornstein, R.F., & D'Agostino, P.R. (1992). The attribution and discounting of perceptual fluency: Preliminary tests of a perceptual fluency/attributional model of the mere exposure effect. *Social Cognition, 12*, 103–128.

Bornstein, R.F., & D'Agostino, P.R. (1994). Stimulus recognition and the mere exposure effect. *Journal of Personality and Social Psychology, 63*, 545–552.

Bosson, J.K., Haymovitz, E.L., & Pinel, E.C. (2004). When saying and doing diverge: The effects of stereotype threat on self-reported versus non-verbal anxiety. *Journal of Experimental Social Psychology, 40*, 247–255.

Bouchard, T.J., Jr. (2004). Genetic influence on human psychological traits: A survey. *Current Directions in Psychological Science, 13*, 148–151.

Boucher, K.L., & Rydell, R.J. (2012). Impact of negation salience and cognitive resources on negation during attitude formation. *Personality and Social Psychology Bulletin, 38*, 1329–1342.

Bousfield, W.A. (1953). The occurrence of clustering in the recall of randomly arranged associates. *Journal of General Psychology, 49*, 229–240.

Bower, G.H., Clark, M.C., Lesgold, A.M., & Winzenz, D. (1969). Hierarchical retrieval schemes in recall of categorized word lists. *Journal of Verbal Learning and Verbal Behavior, 8*, 323–343.

Boyd, R., & Richerson, P.J. (2005). *The origin and evolution of cultures.* New York, NY: Oxford University Press.

Bradbury, T.N., & Fincham, F.D. (1990). Attributions in marriage: Review and critique. *Psychological Bulletin, 107*, 3–33.

Bradbury, T.N., & Fincham, F.D. (1992). Attributions and behavior in marital interaction. *Journal of Personality and Social Psychology, 63*, 613–628.

Bradbury, T.N., Beach, S.R.H., Fincham, F.D., & Nelson, G.M. (1996). Attributions and behavior in functional and dysfunctional marriages. *Journal of Consulting and Clinical Psychology, 64*, 569–576.

Bradley, G.W. (1978). Self-serving biases in the attribution process: A reexamination of the fact or fiction question. *Journal of Personality and Social Psychology, 36*, 56–71.

Brafman, O., & Brafman, R. (2008). *Sway: The irresistible pull of irrational behavior.* New York, NY: Random House.

Brainerd, C.J., & Reyna, V.F. (2005). *The science of false memory.* New York, NY: Oxford University Press.

Brambilla, M., & Riva, P. (2017). Self-image and schadenfreude: Pleasure at others' misfortune enhances satisfaction of basic human needs. *European Journal of Social Psychology, 47*, 399–411.

Brandon, D.P., & Hollingshead, A.B. (2004). Transactive memory systems in organizations: Matching tasks, expertise, and people. *Organization Science, 15*, 633–644.

Brandstätter, V., Lengfelder, A., & Gollwitzer, P.M. (2001). Implementation intentions and efficient action initiation. *Journal of Personality and Social Psychology, 81*, 946–960.

Brandt, M.J., & Reyna, C. (2011). Stereotypes as attributions. In E.L. Simon (Ed.), *Psychology of stereotypes* (pp. 47–80). New York, NY: Nova Science.

Bransford, J.D., & Franks, J.J. (1971). The abstraction of linguistic ideas. *Cognitive Psychology, 2*, 331–350.

Bransford, J.D., & Johnson, M.K. (1972). Contextual prerequisites for understanding: Some investigations of comprehension and recall. *Journal of Verbal Learning and Verbal Behavior, 11*, 717–726.

Brasel, S.A., & Gips, J. (2014). Tablets, touchscreens, and touchpads: How varying touch interfaces trigger psychological ownership and endowment. *Journal of Consumer Psychology, 24*, 226–233.

Brauer, M., & Er-rafiy, A. (2011). Increasing perceived variability reduces prejudice and discrimination. *Journal of Experimental Social Psychology, 47*, 871–881.

Breckler, S.J. (1984). Empirical validation of affect, behavior, and cognition as distinct components of attitudes. *Journal of Personality and Social Psychology, 47*, 1191–1205.

Brewer, M.B. (1979). In-group bias in the minimal intergroup situation: A cognitive-motivational analysis. *Psychological Bulletin, 86*, 307–324.

Brewer, M.B. (1988). A dual process model of impression formation. In T.K. Srull & R.S. Wyer, Jr. (Eds.), *Advances in social cognition* (Vol. 1, pp. 1–36). Hillsdale, NJ: Lawrence Erlbaum.

Brewer, M.B. (1991). The social self: On being the same and different at the same time. *Personality and Social Psychology Bulletin, 17*, 475–482.

Brewer, M.B. (2015). Motivated entitativity: When we'd rather see the forest than the trees. In S.J. Stroessner & J.W. Sherman (Eds.), *Social perception from individuals to groups* (pp. 161–176). New York, NY: Psychology Press.

Brewer, M.B., & Feinstein, A.S.H. (1999). Dual processes in the cognitive representation of persons and social categories. In S. Chaiken & Y. Trope (Eds.), *Dual process theories in social psychology* (pp. 255–270). New York, NY: Guilford Press.

Brewer, M.B., & Harasty, A.S. (1996). Seeing groups as entities: The role of perceiver motivation. In R.M. Sorrentino & E.T. Higgins (Eds.), *Handbook of motivation and cognition* (Vol. 3, pp. 347–370). New York, NY: Guilford Press.

Brewer, M.B., Dull, V., & Lui, L. (1981). Perceptions of the elderly: Stereotypes as prototypes. *Journal of Personality and Social Psychology*, *41*, 656–670.

Brigham, J.C. (1971). Ethnic stereotypes. *Psychological Bulletin*, *76*, 15–38.

Brigham, J.C. (1972). Racial stereotypes: Measurement variables and the stereotype-attitude relationship. *Journal of Applied Social Psychology*, *2*, 63–76.

Brigham, J.C., & Barkowitz, P. (1978). Do "they all look alike"? The effect of race, sex, experience, and attitudes on the ability to recognize faces. *Journal of Applied Social Psychology*, *8*, 306–318.

Brigham, J.C., Maass, A., Snyder, L.D., & Spaulding, K. (1982). Accuracy of eyewitness identification in a field setting. *Journal of Personality and Social Psychology*, *42*, 673–681.

Briñol, P., & Petty, R.E. (2012). A history of attitudes and persuasion research. In A.W. Kruglanski & W. Stroebe (Eds.), *Handbook of the history of social psychology* (pp. 283–320). New York, NY: Psychology Press.

Brinsmead-Stockham, K., Johnston, L., Miles, L., & Macrae, C.N. (2008). Female sexual orientation and menstrual influences on person perception. *Journal of Experimental Social Psychology*, *44*, 729–734.

Broadbent, D.E. (1958). *Perception and communication*. London: Pergamon.

Brown, J.D. (1986). Evaluations of self and others: Self-enhancement biases in social judgments. *Social Cognition*, *4*, 353–376.

Brown, J.D. (2012). Understanding the better than average effect: Motives (still) matter. *Personality and Social Psychology Bulletin*, *38*, 209–219.

Brown, J.D., & Gallagher, F.M. (1992). Coming to terms with failure: Private self-enhancement and public self-effacement. *Journal of Experimental Social Psychology*, *28*, 3–22.

Brown, J.D., & Kobayashi, C. (2003). Motivation and manifestation: The cross-cultural expression of the self-enhancement motive. *Asian Journal of Social Psychology*, *6*, 85–88.

Brown, R., & Hewstone, M. (2005). An integrative theory of intergroup contact. In M.P. Zanna (Ed.), *Advances in experimental social psychology* (Vol. 37, pp. 255–343). San Diego, CA: Academic Press.

Brown, R., & Kulik, J. (1977). Flashbulb memories. *Cognition*, *5*, 73–99.

Brown, R., Vivian, J., & Hewstone, M. (1999). Changing attitudes through intergroup contact: The effect of group membership salience. *European Journal of Social Psychology*, *29*, 741–764.

Brown, R.D., & Bassili, J.N. (2002). Spontaneous trait associations and the case of the superstitious banana. *Journal of Experimental Social Psychology*, *38*, 87–92.

Brown, W.M., Price, M.E., Kang, J., Pound, N., Zhao, Y., & Yu, H. (2008). Fluctuating asymmetry and preferences for sex-typical bodily characteristics. *Proceedings of the National Academy of Sciences*, *105*, 12938–12943.

Brown-Iannuzzi, J., Dotsch, R., Cooley, E., & Payne, K. (2017). The relationship between racialized mental representations of welfare recipients and attitudes toward welfare. *Psychological Science*, *28*, 92–103.

Brownstein, A.L. (2003). Biased predecision processing. *Psychological Bulletin*, *129*, 545–568.

Brownstein, M., Madva, A., & Gawronski, B. (2019). What do implicit measures measure? *Wiley Interdisciplinary Reviews. Cognitive Science*, *10*, e1501.

Bruce, V., & Young, A. (1986). Understanding face recognition. *British Journal of Psychology*, *77*, 305–327.

Bruner, J.S. (1957). Going beyond the information given. In H.E. Gruber, K.R. Hammond, & R. Jessor (Eds.), *Contemporary approaches to cognition* (pp. 41–69). Cambridge, MA: Harvard University Press.

Bruner, J.S., & Tagiuri, R. (1954). The perception of people. In G. Lindzey (Ed.), *Handbook of social psychology* (Vol. 2, pp. 634–654). Cambridge, MA: Addison Wesley.

Bruner, J.S., Goodnow, J.J., & Austin, G.A. (1956). *A study of thinking*. Oxford: Wiley.

Bry, C., Follenfant, A., & Meyer, T. (2008). Blonde like me: When self-construals moderate stereotype priming effects on intellectual performance. *Journal of Experimental Social Psychology, 44*, 751–757.

Buchsbaum, B.R., Lemire-Rodger, S., Bondad, A., & Chepesiuk, A. (2015). Recency, repetition, and the multidimensional basis of recognition memory. *The Journal of Neuroscience, 35*, 3544–3554.

Buckley, J., Jr. (2017). *Adolf Hitler*. New York, NY: Simon & Schuster.

Budesheim, T.L., & DePaola, S.J. (1994). Beauty or beast? The effects of appearance, personality, and issue information on evaluations of political candidates. *Personality and Social Psychology Bulletin, 20*, 339–348.

Buehler, R., & McFarland, C. (2001). Intensity bias in affective forecasting: The role of temporal focus. *Personality and Social Psychology Bulletin, 27*, 1480–1493.

Buffone, A., Gabriel, S., & Poulin, M. (2016). There but for the grace of God: Counterfactuals influence religious belief and images of the divine. *Social Psychological and Personality Science, 7*, 256–263.

Burger, J.M., & Hemans, L.T. (1988). Desire for control and the use of attribution processes. *Journal of Personality, 56*, 531–546.

Burnett, R.C., Medin, D.L., Ross, N.O., & Blok, S.V. (2005). Ideal is typical. *Canadian Journal of Experimental Psychology, 59*, 3–10.

Burns, M.D., Monteith, M.J., & Parker, L.R. (2017). Training away bias: The differential effects of counterstereotype training and self-regulation on stereotype activation and application. *Journal of Experimental Social Psychology, 73*, 97–110.

Burns, Z.C., Caruso, E.M., & Bartels, D.M. (2012). Predicting premeditation: Future behavior is seen as more intentional than past behavior. *Journal of Experimental Psychology: General, 141*, 227–232.

Busby, E., Flynn, D.J., & Druckman, J.N. (2018). Studying framing effects on political preferences: Existing research and lingering questions. In P. D'Angelo (Ed.), *Doing news framing analysis II* (pp. 67–90). New York, NY: Routledge.

Byrne, C.A., & Arias, I. (1997). Marital satisfaction and marital violence: Moderating effects of attributional processes. *Journal of Family Violence, 11*, 188–195.

Byrne, D. (1971). *The attraction paradigm.* London: Academic Press.

Byrne, R.M. (2016). Counterfactual thought. *Annual Review of Psychology, 67*, 135–157.

Cacioppo, J.T., & Berntson, G.G. (1994). Relationship between attitudes and evaluative space: A critical review, with emphasis on the separability of positive and negative substrates. *Psychological Bulletin, 115*, 401–423.

Cacioppo, J.T, & Petty, R.E. (1979). Effects of message repetition and position on cognitive response, recall, and persuasion. *Journal of Personality and Social Psychology, 37*, 97–109.

Cacioppo, J.T., Gardner, W.L., & Berntson, G.G. (1997). Beyond bipolar conceptualizations and measures: The case of attitudes and evaluative space. *Personality and Social Psychology Review, 1*, 3–25.

Cacioppo, J.T., Petty, R.E., Kao, C., & Rodriguez, R. (1986). Central and peripheral routes to persuasion: An individual difference perspective. *Journal of Personality and Social Psychology, 51*, 1032–1043.

Cacioppo, J.T., Priester, J.R., & Bernston, G.G. (1993). Rudimentary determination of attitudes: II. Arm flexion and extension have differential effects on attitudes. *Journal of Personality and Social Psychology, 65*, 5–17.

Cai, H., Wu, L., Shi, Y., Gu, R., & Sedikides, C. (2016). Self-enhancement among Westerners and Easterners: A cultural neuroscience approach. *Social Cognitive and Affective Neuroscience, 11*, 1569–1578.

Cai, H., Wu, Q., & Brown, J.D. (2009). Is self-esteem a universal need? Evidence from the People's Republic of China. *Asian Journal of Social Psychology, 12*, 104–120.

Cain, N.M., Meehan, K.B., Roche, M.J., Clarkin, J.F., & De Panfilis, C. (2019). Effortful control and interpersonal behavior in daily life. *Journal of Personality Assessment, 101*, 315–325.

Calanchini, J., Sherman, J.W., Klauer, K.C., & Lai, C.K. (2014). Attitudinal and non-attitudinal components of IAT performance. *Personality and Social Psychology Bulletin, 40,* 1285–1296.

Calder, A.J., Young, A.W., Keane, J., & Dean, M. (2000). Configural information in facial expression perception. *Journal of Experimental Psychology: Human Perception and Performance, 26,* 527–551.

Callan, M.J., Sutton, R.M., & Dovale, C. (2010). When deserving translates into causing: The effect of cognitive load on immanent justice reasoning. *Journal of Experimental Social Psychology, 46,* 1097–1100.

Calvo, M.G., & Esteves, F. (2005). Detection of emotional faces: Low perceptual threshold and wide attentional span. *Visual Cognition, 12,* 13–27.

Calvo, M.G., & Nummenmaa, L. (2007). Processing of unattended emotional visual scenes. *Journal of Experimental Psychology: General, 136,* 347–369.

Cambon, L., & Yzerbyt, V.Y. (2017). Compensation is for real: Evidence from existing groups in the context of actual relations. *Group Processes & Intergroup Relations, 20,* 745–756.

Cambon, L., Yzerbyt, V., & Yakimova, S. (2015). Compensation in intergroup relations: An investigation of its structural and strategic foundations. *British Journal of Social Psychology, 54,* 140–158.

Cameron, C.D., Brown-Iannuzzi, J.L., & Payne, B.K. (2012). Sequential priming measures of implicit social cognition: A meta-analysis of associations with behavior and explicit attitudes. *Personality and Social Psychology Review, 16,* 330–350.

Campbell, D.T. (1950). The indirect assessment of social attitudes. *Psychological Bulletin, 47,* 15–38.

Campbell, D.T. (1958). Common fate, similarity, and other indices of the status of aggregates of persons as social entities. *Behavioral Science, 3,* 14–25.

Campbell, D.T. (1965). Ethnocentric and other altruistic motives. In D. LeVine (Ed.), *Nebraska symposium on motivation* (pp. 283–311). Lincoln, NE: University of Nebraska Press.

Campbell, W.K., & Sedikides, C. (1999). Self-threat magnifies the self-serving bias: A meta-analytic integration. *Review of General Psychology, 3,* 23–43.

Campbell, W.K., Rudich, E., & Sedikides, C. (2002). Narcissism, self-esteem, and the positivity of self-views: Two portraits of self-love. *Personality and Social Psychology Bulletin, 28,* 358–368.

Cantor, N., & Mischel, W. (1979). Prototypes in person perception. In L. Berkowitz (Ed.), *Advances in experimental social psychology* (Vol. 12, pp. 3–52). New York, NY: Academic Press.

Caouette, J., Wohl, M.J., & Peetz, J. (2012). The future weighs heavier than the past: Collective guilt, perceived control and the influence of time. *European Journal of Social Psychology, 42,* 363–371.

Cárdenas, R.A., & Harris, L.J. (2006). Symmetrical decorations enhance the attractiveness of faces and abstract designs. *Evolution & Human Behavior, 27,* 1–18.

Carels, R.A., & Baucom, D.H. (1999). Support in marriage: Factors associated with on-line perceptions of support helpfulness. *Journal of Family Psychology, 13,* 131–144.

Carli, L.L. (1999). Cognitive reconstruction, hindsight, and reactions to victims and perpetrators. *Personality and Social Psychology Bulletin, 25,* 966–979.

Carlson, R. (1971). Where is the person in personality research? *Psychological Bulletin, 75,* 203–219.

Carlson, R. (1984). What's social about social psychology? Where's the person in personality research? *Journal of Personality and Social Psychology, 47,* 1304–1309.

Carlsson, R., & Agerström, J. (2016). A closer look at the discrimination outcomes in the IAT literature. *Scandinavian Journal of Psychology, 57,* 278–287.

Carlston, D.E. (1980). The recall and use of traits and events in social inference processes.

Journal of Experimental Social Psychology, *16*, 303–328.

Carlston, D.E. (2013). On the nature of social cognition: My defining moment. In D.E. Carlston (Ed.), *The Oxford handbook of social cognition* (pp. 3–15). New York, NY: Oxford University Press.

Carlston, D.E., & Skowronski, J.J. (1994). Savings in the relearning of trait information as evidence of spontaneous inference generation. *Journal of Personality and Social Psychology*, *66*, 840–856.

Carlston, D.E., & Skowronski, J.J. (2005). Linking versus thinking: Evidence for the different associative and attributional bases of spontaneous trait inference and spontaneous trait transference. *Journal of Personality and Social Psychology*, *89*, 884–898.

Carlston, D.E., Skowronski, J.J., & Sparks, C. (1995). Savings in relearning: II. On the formation of behavior-based trait associations and transferences. *Journal of Personality and Social Psychology*, *69*, 420–435.

Carnaghi, A., Maass, A., Gresta, S., Bianchi, M., Cadinu, M., & Arcuri, L. (2008). Nomina sunt omina: On the inductive potential of nouns and adjectives in person perception. *Journal of Personality and Social Psychology*, *94*, 839–859.

Carney, D.R., Colvin, C.R., & Hall, J.A. (2007). A thin slice perspective on the accuracy of first impressions. *Journal of Research in Personality*, *41*, 1054–1072.

Carpenter, S., & Trentham, S. (1998). Subtypes of women and men: A new taxonomy and an exploratory categorical analysis. *Journal of Social Behavior and Personality*, *13*, 679–696.

Carpenter, W.B. (1852). On the influence of suggestion in modifying and directing muscular movement, independently of volition. *Royal Institution of Great Britain, Weekly Evening Meeting, Friday, March 12*, 147–153.

Carpinella, C.M., Chen, J.M., Hamilton, D.L., & Johnson, K.L. (2015). Gendered facial cues influence race categorizations. *Personality and Social Psychology Bulletin*, *41*, 405–419.

Carrera, P., Muñoz, D., Caballero, A., Fernández, I., Aguilar, P., & Albarracín, D. (2014). How verb tense affects the construal of action: The simple past tense leads people into an abstract mindset. *Psicologica*, *35*, 209–223.

Carroll, J.S. (1978). The effect of imagining an event on expectations for the event: An interpretation in terms of the availability heuristic. *Journal of Experimental Social Psychology*, *14*, 88–96.

Caruso, E.M. (2006). Use of experienced retrieval ease in self and social judgments. *Journal of Experimental Social Psychology*, *44*, 148–155.

Caruso, E.M. (2010). When the future feels worse than the past: A temporal inconsistency in moral judgment. *Journal of Experimental Psychology: General*, *139*, 610–624.

Caruso, E.M., Burns, Z.C., & Converse, B.A. (2016). Slow motion increases perceived intent. *Proceedings of the National Academy of Sciences*, *113*, 9250–9255.

Caruso, E.M., Gilbert, D.T., & Wilson, T.D. (2008). A wrinkle in time: Asymmetric valuation of past and future events. *Psychological Science*, *19*, 796–801.

Caruso, E.M., Mead, N.L., & Balcetis, E. (2009). Political partisanship influences perception of biracial candidates' skin tone. *Proceedings of the National Academy of Sciences*, *106*, 20168–20173.

Caruso, E.M., Van Boven, L., Chin, M., & Ward, A. (2013). The temporal Doppler effect: When the future feels closer than the past. *Psychological Science*, *24*, 530–536.

Carver, C.S., & Scheier, M.F. (1998). *On the self-regulation of behavior*. New York, NY: Cambridge University Press.

Casper, C., Rothermund, K., & Wentura, D. (2010). Automatic stereotype activation is context dependent. *Social Psychology*, *41*, 131–136.

Casper, J.D., Benedict, K., & Kelly, J.R. (1988). Cognitions, attitudes and decision-making in search and seizure cases. *Journal of Applied Social Psychology, 18,* 93–113.

Castano, E., Yzerbyt, V., Bourguignon, D., & Seron, E. (2002). Who may enter? The impact of ingroup identification on ingroup-outgroup categorization. *Journal of Experimental Social Psychology, 38,* 135–143.

Castelli, L., Carraro, L., Ghitti, C., & Pastore, M. (2009). The effects of perceived competence and sociability on electoral outcomes. *Journal of Experimental Social Psychology, 45,* 1152–1155.

Castelli, L., Carraro, L., Pavan, G., Murelli, E., & Carraro, A. (2012). The power of the unsaid: The influence of nonverbal cues on implicit attitudes. *Journal of Applied Social Psychology, 42,* 1376–1393.

Centerbar, D.B., & Clore, G.L. (2006). Do approach-avoidance actions create attitudes? *Psychological Science, 17,* 22–29.

Cervone, D., & Peake, P.K. (1986). Anchoring, efficacy, and action: The influence of judgmental heuristics on self-efficacy judgments and behavior. *Journal of Personality and Social Psychology, 50,* 492–501.

Cesario, J. (2014). Priming, replication, and the hardest science. *Perspectives on Psychological Science, 9,* 40–48.

Cesario, J., Plaks, J.E., Hagiwara, N., Navarrete, C.D., & Higgins, E.T. (2010). The ecology of automaticity: How situational contingencies shape action semantics and social behavior. *Psychological Science, 21,* 1311–1317.

Cesario, J., Plaks, J.E., & Higgins, E.T. (2006). Automatic social behavior as motivated preparation to interact. *Journal of Personality and Social Psychology, 90,* 893–910.

Cha, C.B., Najmi, S., Park, J.M., Finn, C.T., & Nock, M.K. (2010). Attentional bias toward suicide-related stimuli predicts suicidal behavior. *Journal of Abnormal Psychology, 119,* 616–622.

Chabris, C.F., Heck, P.R., Mandart, J., Benjamin, D.J., & Simons, D.J. (2019). No evidence that experiencing physical warmth promotes interpersonal warmth. *Social Psychology, 50,* 127–132.

Chaiken, S. (1987). The heuristic model of persuasion. In M.P. Zanna, J.M. Olson, & C.P. Herman (Eds.), *Social influence: The Ontario symposium* (Vol. 5, pp. 3–39). Mahwah, NJ: Lawrence Erlbaum.

Chaiken, S., & Maheswaran, D. (1994). Heuristic processing can bias systematic processing: Effects of source credibility, argument ambiguity, and task importance on attitude judgment. *Journal of Personality and Social Psychology, 66,* 460–473.

Chaiken, S., Liberman, A., & Eagly, A.H. (1989). Heuristic and systematic processing within and beyond the persuasion context. In J.S. Uleman & J.A. Bargh (Eds.), *Unintended thought* (pp. 212–252). New York, NY: Guilford Press.

Chaiken, S., Pomerantz, E.M., & Giner-Sorolla, R. (1995). Structural consistency and attitude strength. In R. Petty & J. Krosnick (Eds.), *Attitude strength: Antecedents and consequences* (pp. 387–412). Hillsdale, NJ: Lawrence Erlbaum.

Chambers, J.R., & Davis, M.H. (2012). The role of the self in perspective-taking and empathy: Ease of self-simulation as a heuristic for inferring empathic feelings. *Social Cognition, 30,* 153–180.

Chambon, M. (2009). Embodied perception with others' bodies in mind: Stereotype priming influence on the perception of spatial environment. *Journal of Experimental Social Psychology, 45,* 283–287.

Chandler, C.C., Gargano, G.J., & Holt, B.C. (2001). Witnessing postevents does not change memory traces, but can affect their retrieval. *Applied Cognitive Psychology, 15,* 3–22.

Chandler, M.J. (2001). The time of our lives: Self-continuity in Native and non-Native youth. *Advances in Child Development and Behavior, 28,* 175–221.

Chandler, M.J., & Lalonde, C. (1998). Cultural continuity as a hedge against suicide in Canada's First Nations. *Transcultural Psychiatry, 35,* 191–219.

Chandler, M.J., & Proulx, T. (2008). Personal persistence and persistent peoples:

Continuities in the lives of individual and whole cultural communities. In F. Sani (Ed.), *Self continuity: Individual and collective perspectives* (pp. 213–226). New York, NY: Psychology Press.

Chandler, M.J., Lalonde, C.E., Sokol, B.W., Hallett, D., & Marcia, J.E. (2003). Personal persistence, identity development, and suicide: A study of native and non-native North American adolescents. *Monographs of the Society for Research in Child Development, 2,* 1–138.

Chapman, E.N., Kaatz, A., & Carnes, M. (2013). Physicians and implicit bias: How doctors may unwittingly perpetuate health care disparities. *Journal of General Internal Medicine, 28,* 1504–1510.

Chapman, G.B., Li, M., Leventhal, H., & Leventhal, E.A. (2016). Default clinic appointments promote influenza vaccination uptake without a displacement effect. *Behavioral Science & Policy, 2,* 40–50.

Chapman, L.J. (1967). Illusory correlation in observational report. *Journal of Verbal Learning & Verbal Behavior, 6,* 151–155.

Chapman, L.J., & Chapman, J.P. (1967). Genesis of popular but erroneous psychodiagnostic observations. *Journal of Abnormal Psychology, 72,* 193–204.

Chapman, L.J., & Chapman, J.P. (1969). Illusory correlation as an obstacle to use of valid psychodiagnostic signs. *Journal of Abnormal Psychology, 74,* 271–280.

Charlesworth, T.E.S., & Banaji, M.R. (2019). Patterns of implicit and explicit attitudes: I. Long-term change and stability from 2007 to 2016. *Psychological Science, 30,* 174–192.

Charness, G., Karni, E., & Levin, D. (2010). On the conjunction fallacy in probability judgement: New experimental evidence regarding Linda. *Games and Economic Behavior, 68,* 551–556.

Chartrand, T.L., & Bargh, J.A. (1996). Automatic activation of impression formation and memorization goals: Nonconscious goal priming reproduces effects of explicit task instructions. *Journal of Personality and Social Psychology, 71,* 464–478.

Chartrand, T.L., & Bargh, J.A. (1999). The chameleon effect: The perception–behavior link and social interaction. *Journal of Personality and Social Psychology, 76,* 893–910.

Chartrand, T.L., & Lakin, J. (2013). The antecedents and consequences of human behavioral mimicry. *Annual Review of Psychology, 64,* 285–308.

Chartrand, T.L., & van Baaren, R. (2009). Human mimicry. In M.P. Zanna (Ed.), *Advances in experimental social psychology* (Vol. 41, pp. 219–274). San Diego, CA: Academic Press.

Chartrand, T.L., Dalton, A.N., & Cheng, C.M. (2008). The antecedents and consequences of nonconscious goal pursuit. In J.Y. Shah & W.L. Gardner (Eds.), *Handbook of motivation science* (pp. 342–355). New York, NY: Guilford Press.

Chartrand, T.L., Maddux, W.W., & Lakin, J.L. (2005). Beyond the perception-behavior link: The ubiquitous utility and motivational moderators of nonconscious mimicry. In R.R. Hassin, J.S. Uleman, & J.A. Bargh (Eds.), *The new unconscious* (pp. 334–361). New York, NY: Oxford University Press.

Chen, J.M. (2019). An integrative review of impression formation processes for multiracial individuals. *Social and Personality Psychology Compass, 13,* e12430.

Chen, J.M., & Hamilton, D.L. (2012). Natural ambiguities: Racial categorization of multiracial individuals. *Journal of Experimental Social Psychology, 48,* 152–164.

Chen, J.M., Moons, W.G., Gaither, S.E., Hamilton, D.L., & Sherman, J.W. (2014). Motivation to control prejudice predicts categorization of multiracials. *Personality and Social Psychology Bulletin, 40,* 590–603.

Chen, J.M., Pauker, K., Gaither, S.E., Hamilton, D.L., & Sherman, J.W. (2018). Black + white = not white: A minority bias in categorizations of black-white multiracials. *Journal of Experimental Social Psychology, 78,* 43–54.

Chen, M., & Bargh, J.A. (1997). Nonconscious behavioral confirmation processes: The self-fulfilling consequences of automatic stereotype activation. *Journal of Experimental Social Psychology, 33*, 541–560.

Chen, S., & Andersen, S.M. (1999). Relationships from the past in the present: Significant-other representations and transference in interpersonal life. In M.P. Zanna (Ed.), *Advances in experimental social psychology* (Vol. 31, pp. 123–190). San Diego, CA: Academic Press.

Chen, S., & Chaiken, S. (1999). The heuristic systematic model in its broader context. In S. Chaiken & Y. Trope (Eds.), *Dual-process theories in social psychology* (pp. 73–96). New York, NY: Guilford Press.

Chen, S., Boucher, H., & Kraus, M.W. (2011). The relational self. In S.J. Schwartz, K. Luyckx, & V.L. Vignoles (Eds.), *Handbook of identity theory and research* (pp. 149–175). New York, NY: Springer.

Chen, X., Latham, G.P., Piccolo, R.F., & Itzchakov, G. (2020). An enumerative review and a meta-analysis of primed goal effects on organizational behavior. *Applied Psychology*.

Chen, Y., & Sun, Y. (2003). Age differences in financial decision-making: Using simple heuristics. *Educational Gerontology, 29*, 627–635.

Cheng, P.W., & Novick, L.R. (1990). A probabilistic contrast model of causal induction. *Journal of Personality and Social Psychology, 58*, 545–567.

Chernev, A. (2003). Product assortment and individual decision processes. *Journal of Personality and Social Psychology, 85*, 151–162.

Cherry, E.C. (1953). Some experiments on the recognition of speech with one and two ears. *Journal of the Acoustical Society of America, 25*, 975–979.

Cheryan, S., Plaut, V.C., Davies, P.G., & Steele, C.M. (2009). Ambient belonging: How stereotypical cues impact gender participation in computer science. *Journal of Personality and Social Psychology, 97*, 1045–1060.

Chiroro, P., & Valentine, T. (1995). An investigation of the contact hypothesis of the own-race bias in face recognition. *The Quarterly Journal of Experimental Psychology A: Human Experimental Psychology, 48A*, 879–894.

Choi, I., Nisbett, R.E., & Norenzayan, A. (1999). Causal attribution across cultures: Variation and universality. *Psychological Bulletin, 125*, 47–63.

Chomsky, N. (1959). A review of B.F. Skinner's *Verbal Behavior. Language, 35*, 26–58.

Christandl, F., Fetchenhauer, D., & Hoelzl, E. (2011). Price perception and confirmation bias in the context of a VAT increase. *Journal of Economic Psychology, 32*, 131–141.

Christian, J., Armitage, C.J., & Abrams, D. (2007). Evidence that theory of planned behaviour variables mediate the effects of socio-demographic variables on homeless people's participation in service programmes. *Journal of Health Psychology, 12*, 805–817.

Chua, H.F., Boland, J.E., & Nisbett, R.E. (2005). Cultural variation in eye movements during scene perception. *Proceedings of the National Academy of Sciences, 102*, 12629–12633.

Chun, W., & Lee, H. (1999). Effects of the difference in the amount of group preferential information on illusory correlation. *Personality and Social Psychology Bulletin, 25*, 1463–1475.

Cialdini, R.B., Borden, R.J., Thorne, A., Walder, M.R., Freeman, S., & Sloan, L.R. (1976). Basking in reflected glory: Three (football) field studies. *Journal of Personality and Social Psychology, 34*, 366–375.

Cikara, M., & Fiske, S.T. (2013). Their pain, our pleasure: Stereotype content and schadenfreude. *Annals of the New York Academy of Sciences, 1299*, 52–59.

Clark, J.K., Wegener, D.T., & Fabrigar, L.R. (2008). Attitude accessibility and message processing: The moderating role of message position. *Journal of Experimental Social Psychology, 44*, 354–361.

Clark, J.K., Wegener, D.T., Habashi, M.M., & Evans, A.T. (2012). Source expertise and persuasion: The effects of perceived opposition or support on message scrutiny. *Personality and Social Psychology Bulletin, 38*, 90–100.

Clarkson, P.M., Emby, C., & Watt, V.W.S. (2002). Debiasing the outcome effect: The role of instructions in an audit litigation setting. *Auditing: A Journal of Practice & Theory, 21*, 7–20.

Clary, E.G., & Tesser, A. (1983). Reactions to unexpected events: The naive scientist and interpretive activity. *Personality and Social Psychology Bulletin, 9*, 609–620.

Clausell, E., & Fiske, S.T. (2005). When do subgroup parts add up to the stereotypic whole? Mixed stereotype content for gay male subgroups explains overall ratings. *Social Cognition, 23*, 161–181.

Clerkin, E.M., Fisher, C.R., Sherman, J.W., & Teachman, B.A. (2014). Applying the quadruple process model to evaluate change in implicit attitudinal responses during therapy for panic disorder. *Behaviour Research and Therapy, 52*, 17–25.

Cloutier, J., Mason, M.F., & Macrae, C.N. (2005). The perceptual determinants of person construal: Reopening the social-cognitive toolbox. *Journal of Personality and Social Psychology, 88*, 885–894.

Cogsdill, E.J., Todorov, A., Spelke, E., & Banaji, M.R. (2014). Inferring character from faces: A developmental study. *Psychological Science, 25*, 1132–1139.

Cohen, G.L. (2003). Party over policy: The dominating impact of group influence on political beliefs. *Journal of Personality and Social Psychology, 85*, 808–822.

Cohen, G.L., & Sherman, D.K. (2014). The psychology of change: Self-affirmation and social psychological intervention. *Annual Review of Psychology, 65*, 333–371.

Cohen, G.L., Garcia, J., Purdie-Vaughns, V., Apfel, N., & Brzustoski, P. (2009). Recursive processes in self-affirmation: Intervening to close the minority achievement gap. *Science, 324*, 400–403.

Cohen, T.R., Panter, A.T., Turan, N., Morse, L., & Kim, Y. (2013). Agreement and similarity in self-other perceptions of moral character. *Journal of Research in Personality, 47*, 816–830.

Collange, J., Fiske, S.T., & Sanitioso, R. (2009). Maintaining a positive self-image by stereotyping others: Self-threat and the stereotype content model. *Social Cognition, 27*, 138–149.

Collins, A. (2007). From H = *log sn* to conceptual framework: A short history of information. *History of Psychology, 10*, 44–72.

Collins, A.M., & Loftus, E.F. (1975). A spreading activation theory of semantic processing. *Psychological Review, 82*, 407–428.

Cone, J., & Ferguson, M.J. (2015). He did what? The role of diagnosticity in revising implicit evaluations. *Journal of Personality and Social Psychology, 108*, 37–57.

Cone, J., Flaharty, K., & Ferguson, M.J. (2019). Believability of evidence matters for correcting social impressions. *Proceedings of the National Academy of Sciences, 20*, 9802–9807.

Cone, J., Mann, T.C., & Ferguson, M.J. (2017). Changing our implicit minds: How, when, and why implicit evaluations can be rapidly revised. In J.M. Olson (Ed.), *Advances in experimental social psychology* (Vol. 56, pp. 131–199). New York, NY: Academic Press.

Connelly, B.S., & Ones, D.S. (2010). Another perspective on personality: Meta-analytic integration of observers' accuracy and predictive validity. *Psychological Bulletin, 136*, 1092–1122.

Conner, M., & Armitage, C.J. (2008). Attitudinal ambivalence. In W.D. Crano & R. Prislin (Eds.), *Attitudes and attitude change* (pp. 261–286). New York, NY: Psychology Press.

Conner, M., Sparks, P., Povey, R., James, R., Shepherd, R., & Armitage, C.J. (2002). Moderator effects of attitudinal ambivalence on attitude-behaviour relationships. *European Journal of Social Psychology, 32*, 705–718.

Conrey, F.R., & Smith, E.R. (2007). Attitude representation: Attitudes as patterns in a distributed, connectionist representational system. *Social Cognition, 25*, 718–735.

Conrey, F.R., Sherman, J.W., Gawronski, B., Hugenberg, K., & Groom, C.J. (2005). Separating multiple processes in implicit social cognition: The quad model of implicit task performance. *Journal of Personality and Social Psychology*, *89*, 469–487.

Converse, P.E. (1964). The nature of belief systems in mass publics. In D.E. Apter (Ed.), *Ideology and discontent*. Ann Arbor, MI: University of Michigan Press.

Conway, M., & Ross, M. (1984). Getting what you want by revising what you had. *Journal of Personality and Social Psychology*, *47*, 738–748.

Conway, M.A. (2005). Memory and the self. *Journal of Memory and Language*, *53*, 594–628.

Conway, M.A., & Pleydell-Pearce, C.W. (2000). The construction of autobiographical memories in the self-memory system. *Psychological Review*, *107*, 262–288.

Conway, M.A., Anderson, S.J., Larsen, S.F., Donnelly, C.M., McDaniel, M.A., McClelland, A.G.R., Rawles, R.E., & Logie, R.H. (1994). The formation of flashbulb memories. *Memory & Cognition*, *22*, 326–343.

Conway, P., & Gawronski, B. (2013). Deontological and utilitarian inclinations in moral decision making: A process dissociation approach. *Journal of Personality and Social Psychology*, *104*, 216–235.

Cooke, R., & Sheeran, P. (2004). Moderation of cognition-intention and cognition-behaviour relations: A meta-analysis of properties of variables from the theory of planned behaviour. *British Journal of Social Psychology*, *43*, 159–186.

Cooley, C.H. (1922). *Human nature and the social order*. New York, NY: Scribner.

Cooper, H.M., & Burger, J.M. (1980). How teachers explain students' academic performance: A categorization of free response academic attributions. *American Educational Research Journal*, *17*, 95–109.

Cooper, J. (2007). *Cognitive dissonance: 50 years of a classic theory*. London: Sage.

Cooper, J., & Fazio, R.H. (1986). The formation and persistence of attitudes that support intergroup conflict. In S. Worchel & W. Austin (Eds.), *Psychology of intergroup relations* (pp. 183–195). Chicago, IL: Nelson-Hall.

Cooper, R.M., & Langton, S.R. (2006). Attentional bias to angry faces using the dot-probe task? It depends when you look for it. *Behavior Research and Therapy*, *44*, 1321–1329.

Cooper, W.H. (1981). Ubiquitous halo. *Psychological Bulletin*, *90*, 218–244.

Corey, S.M. (1937). Professional attitudes and actual behavior. *Journal of Educational Psychology*, *28*, 271–280.

Corneille, O., & Hütter, M. (2020). Implicit? What do you mean? A comprehensive review of the delusive implicitness construct in attitude research. *Personality and Social Psychology Review*, *24*, 212–232.

Corneille, O., & Judd, C.M. (1999). Accentuation and sensitization effects in the categorization of multifaceted stimuli. *Journal of Personality and Social Psychology*, *77*, 927–941.

Corneille, O., & Stahl, C. (2019). Associative attitude learning: A closer look at evidence and how it relates to attitude models. *Personality and Social Psychology Review*, *23*, 161–189.

Corneille, O., Huart, J., Becquart E., & Bredart, S. (2004). When memory shifts towards more typical category exemplars: Accentuation effects in the recollection of ethnically ambiguous faces. *Journal of Personality and Social Psychology*, *86*, 236–250.

Corr, P., & Plagnol, A. (2019). *Behavioral economics: The basics*. New York, NY: Routledge.

Correll, J., Guillermo, S., & Vogt, J. (2014). On the flexibility of attention to race. *Journal of Experimental Social Psychology*, *55*, 74–79.

Correll, J., Park, B., Judd, C.M., & Wittenbrink, B. (2002). The police officer's dilemma: Using ethnicity to disambiguate potentially threatening individuals. *Journal of Personality and Social Psychology*, *83*, 1314–1329.

Correll, J., Park, B., Judd, C.M., & Wittenbrink, B. (2007). The influence of stereotypes on decisions to shoot. *European Journal of Social Psychology*, *37*, 1102–1117.

Correll, J., Park, B., Judd, C.M., Wittenbrink, B., Sadler, M.S., & Keesee, T. (2007). Across the thin blue line: Police officers and racial bias in the decision to shoot. *Journal of Personality and Social Psychology*, *92*, 1006–1023.

Correll, J., Wittenbrink, B., Crawford, M., & Sadler, M.S. (2015). Stereotypic vision: How stereotypes disambiguate complex visual stimuli. *Journal of Social & Personality Psychology*, *108*, 219–233.

Cosmides, L. (1989). The logic of social exchange: Has natural selection shaped how humans reason? Studies with the Wason selection task. *Cognition*, *31*, 187–276.

Costabile, K.A. (2016). Narrative construction, social perceptions, and the situation model. *Personality and Social Psychology Bulletin*, *42*, 589–602.

Costabile, K.A., & Austin, A.B. (2018). A riot on campus: The effects of social identity complexity on emotions and reparative attitudes after ingroup-perpetrated violence. *Aggressive Behavior*, *44*, 50–59.

Cox, L.A. Jr., & Popken, D.A. (2008). Overcoming confirmation bias in causal attribution: A case study of antibiotic resistance risks. *Risk Analysis*, *28*, 1155–1172.

Coyne, J.C., & Johansen, C. (2011). Confirmatory bias and the persistent influence of discredited data in interpreting the stress-cancer link: Commentary on Michael et al. (2009). *Health Psychology*, *30*, 374–375.

Crandall, C.S., & Sherman, J.W. (2016). On the scientific superiority of conceptual replications for scientific progress. *Journal of Experimental Social Psychology*, *66*, 93–99.

Crandall, C.S., Eshleman, A., & O'Brien, L. (2002). Social norms and the expression and suppression of prejudice: The struggle for internalization. *Journal of Personality and Social Psychology*, *82*, 359–378.

Crandall, C.S., Silvia, P.J., N'Gbala, A.N., Tsang, J.A., & Dawson, K. (2007). Balance theory, unit relations, and attribution: The underlying integrity of Heiderian theory. *Review of General Psychology*, *11*, 12–30.

Crane, B. (2010, February 5). *Pickles.* Retrieved from: www.thecomicstrips.com/store/add.php?iid=43464 (accessed May 1, 2020).

Crano, W.D. (1977). Primacy versus recency in retention of information and opinion change. *The Journal of Social Psychology*, *101*, 87–96.

Crawford, J.T., Jussim, L., Madon, S., Cain, T.R., & Stevens, S.T. (2011). The use of stereotypes and individuating information in political person perception. *Personality and Social Psychology Bulletin*, *37*, 529–542.

Crawford, M.T., Sherman, S.J., & Hamilton, D.L. (2002). Perceived entitativity, stereotype formation, and the interchangeability of group members. *Journal of Personality and Social Psychology*, *83*, 1076–1094.

Crawford, M.T., Skowronski, J.J., & Stiff, C. (2007). Limiting the spread of spontaneous trait transference. *Journal of Experimental Social Psychology*, *43*, 466–472.

Crawford, M.T., Skowronski, J.J., Stiff, C., & Leonards, U. (2008). Seeing, but not thinking: Limiting the spread of spontaneous trait transference. II. *Journal of Experimental Social Psychology*, *44*, 840–847.

Crawford, M.T., Skowronski, J.J., Stiff, C., & Scherer, C.R. (2007). Interfering with inferential, but not associative, processes underlying spontaneous trait inference. *Personality and Social Psychology Bulletin*, *33*, 677–690.

Crisp, R.J., & Turner, R.N. (2009). Can imagined interactions produce positive perceptions? Reducing prejudice through simulated social contact. *American Psychologist*, *64*, 231–240.

Critcher, C.R., & Gilovich, T. (2008). Incidental environmental anchors. *Journal of Behavioral Decision Making*, *21*, 241–251.

Crocker, J., & Major, B. (1989). Social stigma and self-esteem: The self-protective properties of stigma. *Psychological Review, 96,* 608–630.

Crocker, J., Hannah, D.B., & Weber, R. (1983). Person memory and causal attribution. *Journal of Personality and Social Psychology, 44,* 55–66.

Crocker, J., Voelkl, K., Testa, M., & Major, B. (1991). Social stigma: The affective consequences of attributional ambiguity. *Journal of Personality and Social Psychology, 60,* 218–228.

Cronbach, L.J. (1955). Processes affecting scores on "understanding of others" and "assumed similarity." *Psychological Bulletin, 52,* 177–193

Cronbach, L.J., & Meehl, P.E. (1955). Construct validity in psychological tests. *Psychological Bulletin, 52,* 281–302.

Crosby, F., Bromley, S., & Saxe, L. (1980). Recent unobtrusive studies of black and white discrimination and prejudice: A literature review. *Psychological Bulletin, 87,* 546–563.

Croskerry, P. (2008). Critical thinking and reasoning in emergency medicine. In P. Croskerry, K.S. Cosby, S.M. Schenkel, & R.L. Wears (Eds.), *Patient safety in emergency medicine* (pp. 213–218). Philadelphia, PA: Lippincott Williams & Wilkins.

Cross, P. (1977). Not can but will college teaching be improved? *New Directions for Higher Education, 17,* 1–15.

Crowder, R.G. (1976). *Principles of learning and memory.* Hillsdale, NJ: Lawrence Erlbaum.

Crusius, J., & Mussweiler, T. (2012). To achieve or not to achieve? Comparative mindsets elicit assimilation and contrast in goal priming. *European Journal of Social Psychology, 42,* 780–788.

Cuddy, A.J.C., Fiske, S.T., & Glick, P. (2004). When professionals become mothers, warmth doesn't cut the ice. *Journal of Social Issues, 60,* 701–718.

Cuddy, A.J.C., Fiske, S.T., & Glick, P. (2008). Warmth and competence as universal dimensions of social perception: The stereotype content model and the BIAS map. In M.P. Zanna (Ed.), *Advances in experimental social psychology* (Vol. 40, pp. 61–149). New York, NY: Academic Press.

Cuddy, A.J.C., Norton, M.I., & Fiske, S.T. (2005). This old stereotype: The pervasiveness and persistence of the elderly stereotype. *Journal of Social Issues, 61,* 267–285.

Cuddy, A.J.C., Rock, M.S., & Norton, M.I. (2007). Aid in the aftermath of Hurricane Katrina: Inferences of secondary emotions and intergroup helping. *Group Processes & Intergroup Relations, 10,* 107–118.

Cunningham, M.R. (1986). Measuring the physical in physical attractiveness: Quasi-experiments on the sociobiology of female facial beauty. *Journal of Personality and Social Psychology, 50,* 925–935.

Cunningham, M.R., Barbee, A.P., & Pike, C.L. (1990). What do women want? Facialmetric assessment of multiple motives in the perception of male facial physical attractiveness. *Journal of Personality and Social Psychology, 59,* 61–72.

Cunningham, W.A., & Zelazo, P.D. (2007). Attitudes and evaluations: A social cognitive neuroscience perspective. *Trends in Cognitive Sciences, 11,* 97–104.

Cunningham, W.A., Preacher, K.J., & Banaji, M.R. (2001). Implicit attitude measures: Consistency, stability, and change. *Psychological Science, 12,* 163–170.

Cunningham, W.A., Van Bavel, J.J., & Johnsen, I.R. (2008). Affective flexibility: Evaluative processing goals shape amygdala activity. *Psychological Science, 19,* 152–160.

Cunningham, W.A., Zelazo, P.D., Packer, D.J., & Van Bavel, J.J. (2007). The iterative reprocessing model: A multilevel framework for attitudes and evaluation. *Social Cognition, 25,* 736–760.

Custers, R., & Aarts, H. (2010). The unconscious will: How the pursuit of goals operates outside of conscious awareness. *Science, 329,* 47–50.

Czopp, A.M., Monteith, M.J., Zimmerman, R.S., & Lynam, D.R. (2004). Implicit attitudes as potential protection from risky sex: Predicting condom use with the IAT. *Basic and Applied Social Psychology, 26,* 227–236.

Dalege, J., Borsboom, D., van Harreveld, F., & van der Maas, H.L.J. (2019). A network perspective on attitude strength: Testing the connectivity hypothesis. *Social Psychological and Personality Science, 10,* 746–756.

Damjanovic, V. (2017). Two "little treasure games" driven by unconditional regret. *Economics Letters, 150,* 99–103.

Danovitch, J., & Bloom, P. (2009). Children's extension of disgust to physical and moral events. *Emotion, 9,* 107–112.

Dar-Nimrod, I., & Heine, S.J. (2011). Genetic essentialism: On the deceptive determinism of DNA. *Psychological Bulletin, 137,* 800–818.

Darley, J.M., & Gross, P.H. (1983). A hypothesis-confirming bias in labeling effects. *Journal of Personality and Social Psychology, 44,* 20–33.

Dasborough, M., Harvey, P., & Martinko, M.J. (2011). An introduction to attributional influences in organizations. *Group & Organization Management, 36,* 419–426.

Dasgupta, N. (2009). Mechanisms underlying the malleability of implicit prejudice and stereotypes: The role of automaticity and control. In T.D. Nelson (Ed.), *Handbook of prejudice, stereotyping, and discrimination* (pp. 267–284). New York, NY: Psychology Press.

Dasgupta, N., & Asgari, S. (2004). Seeing is believing: Exposure to counterstereotypic women leaders and its effect on automatic gender stereotyping. *Journal of Experimental Social Psychology, 40,* 642–658.

Dasgupta, N., & Greenwald, A.G. (2001). On the malleability of automatic attitudes: Combating automatic prejudice with images of admired and disliked individuals. *Journal of Personality and Social Psychology, 81,* 800–814.

Dasgupta, N., & Rivera, L.M. (2008). When social context matters: The influence of long-term contact and short-term exposure to admired outgroup members on implicit attitudes and behavioral intentions. *Social Cognition, 26,* 54–56.

Dasgupta, N., McGhee, D.E, Greenwald, A.G., & Banaji, M.R. (2000). Automatic preference for White Americans: Eliminating the familiarity explanation. *Journal of Experimental and Social Psychology, 36,* 316–228.

Davidson, A.R., & Jaccard, J.J. (1979). Variables that moderate the attitude-behavior relation: Results of a longitudinal survey. *Journal of Personality and Social Psychology, 37,* 1364–1376.

Davies, M.F. (1987). Reduction of hindsight bias by restoration of foresight perspective: Effectiveness of foresight-encoding and hindsight-retrieval strategies. *Organizational Behavior and Human Decision Processes, 40,* 50–68.

Davies, M.F. (1997). Positive test strategies and confirmatory retrieval processes in the evaluation of personality feedback. *Journal of Personality and Social Psychology, 73,* 574–583.

Davies, M.F. (2003). Confirmatory bias in the evaluation of personality descriptions: Positive test strategies and output interference. *Journal of Personality and Social Psychology, 85,* 736–744.

Davis, C.G., Lehman, D.R., Wortman, C.B., Silver, R.C., & Thompson, S.C. (1995). The undoing of traumatic life events. *Personality and Social Psychology Bulletin, 21,* 109–124.

Davis, D., Loftus, E.F., Vanous, S., & Cucciare, M. (2008). "Unconscious transference" can be an instance of "change blindness." *Applied Cognitive Psychology, 22,* 605–623.

Davis, J.R., & Gold, G.J. (2011). An examination of emotional empathy, attributions of stability, and the link between perceived remorse and forgiveness. *Personality and Individual Differences, 50,* 392–397.

Davis, M., & Whalen, P.J. (2001). The amygdala: Vigilance and emotion. *Molecular Psychiatry, 6,* 13–34.

Davis, M.H., Conklin, L., Smith, A., & Luce, C. (1996). Effects of perspective-taking on the cognitive representation of persons: A merging of self and other. *Journal of Personality and Social Psychology, 70,* 713–726.

Dawes, R.M. (1979). The robust beauty of improper linear models in decision making. *American Psychologist, 34,* 571–582.

Dawes, R.M. (2001). *Everyday irrationality.* Boulder, CO: Westview Press.

Dawes, R.M., & Corrigan, B. (1974). Linear models in decision making. *Psychological Bulletin, 81,* 95–106.

Dawes, R.M., Faust, D., & Meehl, P.E. (1989). Clinical versus actuarial judgment. *Science, 243,* 1668–1674.

Dawes, R.M., Faust, D., & Meehl, P.E. (1993). Statistical prediction versus clinical prediction: Improving what works. In G. Keren & C. Lewis (Eds.), *A handbook for data analysis in the behavioral sciences: Methodological issues* (pp. 351–367). Hillsdale, NJ: Lawrence Erlbaum.

Dawson, N.V., Arkes, H.R., Siciliano, C., Blinkhorn, R., Lakshmanan, M., & Petrelli, M. (1988). Hindsight bias: An impediment to accurate probability estimation in clinicopathologic conferences. *Medical Decision Making, 8,* 259–264.

De Groot, G.J. (2015). *Selling Ronald Reagan: The emergence of a president.* New York, NY: I.B. Tauris.

De Houwer, J., Teige-Mocigemba, S., Spruyt, A., & Moors, A. (2009). Implicit measures: A normative analysis and review. *Psychological Bulletin, 135,* 347–368.

De Houwer, J., Thomas, S., & Baeyens, F. (2001). Associative learning of likes and dislikes: A review of 25 years of research on human evaluative conditioning. *Psychological Bulletin, 127,* 853–869.

De Neys, W. (Ed.) (2018). *Dual process theory 2.0.* New York, NY: Routledge.

DeCaro, M.S., Thomas, R.D., Albert, N.B., & Beilock, S.L. (2011). Choking under pressure: Multiple routes to skill failure. *Journal of Experimental Psychology: General, 140,* 390–406.

DeCoster, J., & Claypool, H.M. (2004). A meta-analysis of priming effects on impression formation supporting a general model of informational biases. *Personality and Social Psychology Review, 8,* 2–27.

Deese, J. (1959). On the prediction of occurrence of particular verbal intrusions in immediate recall. *Journal of Experimental Psychology, 58,* 17–22.

Deffenbacher, K.A., Bornstein, B.H., Penrod, S.D., & McGorty, E.K. (2004). A meta-analytic review of the effects of high stress on eyewitness memory. *Law and Human Behavior, 28,* 687–706.

Degner, J. (2009). On the (un-)controllability of affective priming: Strategic manipulation is feasible but can possibly be prevented. *Cognition and Emotion, 23,* 327–354.

DeMiguel, V., Garlappi, L., & Uppal, R. (2009). Optimal versus naive diversification: How inefficient is the $1/N$ portfolio strategy? *The Review of Financial Studies, 22,* 1915–1953.

Dennett, D.C. (1992). The self as a center of narrative gravity. In F. Kessel, P. Cole, & D. Johnson (Eds.), *Self and consciousness: Multiple perspectives.* Hillsdale, NJ: Lawrence Erlbaum.

Denny, B., Kober, K., Wager, T., & Ochsner, K. (2012). A meta-analysis of functional neuroimaging studies of self- and other judgments reveals a spatial gradient for mentalizing in medial prefrontal cortex. *Journal of Cognitive Neuroscience, 24,* 1742–1752.

Denrell, J. (2005). Why most people disapprove of me: Experience sampling in impression formation. *Psychological Review, 112,* 951–978.

DePaulo, B.M., Charlton, K., Cooper, H., Lindsay, J.J., & Muhlenbruck, L. (1997). The accuracy-confidence correlation in the detection of deception. *Personality and Social Psychology Review, 1,* 346–357.

Descheemaeker, M., Spruyt, A., Fazio, R.H., & Hermans, D. (2017). On the generalization of attitude accessibility after repeated attitude expression. *European Journal of Social Psychology, 47,* 97–104.

Descheemaeker, M., Spruyt, A., & Hermans, D. (2014). On the relationship between the indirectly measured attitude towards beer and beer consumption: The role of attitude accessibility. *PLOS ONE*, *9*(4).

Deska, J.C., Kunstman, J., Lloyd, E.P., Almaraz, S.M., Bernstein, M.J., Gonzales, J.P, & Hugenberg, K. (2020). Race-based biases in judgments of social pain. *Journal of Experimental Social Psychology*, *88*, 103964.

Deutsch, R., & Strack, F. (2006). Duality models in social psychology: From dual processes to interacting systems. *Psychological Inquiry*, *17*, 166–172.

Devine, P.G. (1989). Stereotypes and prejudice: Their automatic and controlled components. *Journal of Personality and Social Psychology*, *56*, 5–18.

Devine, P.G., & Baker, S.M. (1991). Measurement of racial stereotyping subtyping. *Personality and Social Psychology Bulletin*, *17*, 44–50.

Devine, P.G., & Elliot, A.J. (1995). Are racial stereotypes really fading? The Princeton trilogy revisited. *Personality and Social Psychology Bulletin*, *21*, 1139–1150.

Devine, P.G., & Monteith, M.J. (1993). The role of discrepancy-associated affect in prejudice reduction. In D.M. Mackie & D.L. Hamilton (Eds.), *Affect, cognition, and stereotyping: Interactive processes in group perception* (pp. 317–344). San Diego, CA: Academic Press.

Devine, P.G., & Sharp, L.B. (2009). Automaticity and control in stereotyping and prejudice. In T.D. Nelson (Ed.), *Handbook of prejudice, stereotyping, and discrimination* (pp. 61–87). New York, NY: Psychology Press.

Devine, P.G., Forscher, P.S., Austin, A.J., & Cox, W.T.L. (2012). Long-term reduction in implicit race bias: A prejudice habit-breaking intervention. *Journal of Experimental Social Psychology*, *48*, 1267–1278.

Devine, P.G., Hirt, E.R., & Gehrke, E.M. (1990). Diagnostic and confirmation strategies in trait hypothesis testing. *Journal of Personality and Social Psychology*, *58*, 952–963.

Devine, P.G., Monteith, M.J., Zuwerink, J.R., & Elliot, A.J. (1991). Prejudice with and without compunction. *Journal of Personality and Social Psychology*, *60*, 817–830.

Devine, P.G., Plant, E.A., Amodio, D.M., Harmon-Jones, E., & Vance, S.L. (2002). The regulation of explicit and implicit race bias: The role of motivations to respond without prejudice. *Journal of Personality and Social Psychology*, *82*, 835–848.

Devine, P.G., Sedikides, C., & Furhman, R.W. (1989). Goals in social information processing: The case of anticipated interaction. *Journal of Personality and Social Psychology*, *56*, 680–690.

Devos, T., & Banaji, M.R. (2005). American = white? *Journal of Personality and Social Psychology*, *88*, 447–466.

Devos, T., & Ma, D.S. (2008). Is Kate Winslet more American than Lucy Liu? The impact of construal processes on the implicit ascription of a national identity. *British Journal of Social Psychology*, *47*, 191–215.

Devos, T., & Mohamed, H. (2014). Shades of American identity: Implicit relations between ethnic and national identities. *Social and Personality Psychology Compass*, *8*, 739–754.

DeWall, C.N., Maner, J.K., & Rouby, D.A. (2009). Social exclusion and early-stage interpersonal perception: Selective attention to signs of acceptance. *Journal of Personality and Social Psychology*, *96*, 729–741.

Dijksterhuis, A. (2004). Think different: The merits of unconscious thought in preference development and decision making. *Journal of Personality and Social Psychology*, *87*, 586–598.

Dijksterhuis, A. (2013). Automaticity. In D.E. Carlston (Ed.), *The Oxford handbook of social cognition* (pp. 239–256). New York, NY: Oxford University Press.

Dijksterhuis, A. (2014). Welcome back theory! *Perspectives on Psychological Science*, *9*, 72–75.

Dijksterhuis, A., & Bargh, J.A. (2001). The perception-behavior expressway: Automatic effects of social perception on social behavior. In M.P. Zanna (Ed.), *Advances in experimental social psychology* (Vol. 33, pp. 1–40). San Diego, CA: Academic Press.

Dijksterhuis, A., & Nordgren, L.F. (2006). A theory of unconscious thought. *Perspectives on Psychological Science, 1*, 95–109.

Dijksterhuis, A., & Strick, M. (2016). A case for thinking without consciousness. *Perspectives on Psychological Science, 11*, 117–132.

Dijksterhuis, A., & van Knippenberg, A. (1996). Trait implications as a moderator of recall of stereotype-consistent and stereotype-inconsistent behaviors. *Personality and Social Psychology Bulletin, 22*, 425–432.

Dijksterhuis, A., & van Knippenberg, A. (1998). The relation between perception and behavior, or how to win a game of Trivial Pursuit. *Journal of Personality and Social Psychology, 74*, 865–877.

Dijksterhuis, A., & van Knippenberg, A. (2000). Behavioral indecision: Effects of self-focus on automatic behavior. *Social Cognition, 18*, 55–74.

Dijksterhuis, A., & van Olden, Z. (2006). To think or not to think, or to think unconsciously perhaps? Unconscious thought increases post-choice satisfaction. *Journal of Experimental Social Psychology, 42*, 627–631.

Dijksterhuis, A., Bos, M.W., Nordgren, L.F., & von Baaren, R.B. (2006). On making the right choice: The deliberation-without-attention effect. *Science, 311*, 1005–1007.

Dijksterhuis, A., Macrae, C.N., & Haddock, G. (1999). When recollective experiences matter: Subjective ease of retrieval and stereotyping. *Personality and Social Psychology Bulletin, 25*, 766–774.

Dijksterhuis, A., Spears, R., & Lépinasse, V. (2001). Reflecting and deflecting stereotypes: Assimilation and contrast in impression formation and automatic behavior. *Journal of Experimental Social Psychology, 37*, 286–299.

Dijksterhuis, A., Spears, R., Postmes, T., Stapel, D.A., Koomen, W., van Knippenberg, A., & Scheepers, D. (1998). Seeing one thing and doing another: Contrast effects in automatic

behavior. *Journal of Personality and Social Psychology, 75*, 862–871.

Dijksterhuis, A., van Knippenberg, A., Kruglanski, A.W., & Schaper, C. (1996). Motivated social cognition: Need for closure effects on memory and judgment. *Journal of Experimental Social Psychology, 32*, 254–270.

Dimberg, U. (1997). Facial reactions: Rapidly evoked emotional responses. *Journal of Psychophysiology, 11*, 115–123.

Dimberg, U., Hansson, G., & Thunberg, M. (1998). Fear of snakes and facial reactions: A case of rapid emotional responding. *Scandinavian Journal of Psychology, 39*, 75–80.

Dion, K., Berscheid, E., & Walster, E. (1972). What is beautiful is good. *Journal of Personality and Social Psychology, 24*, 285–290.

Dislich, F.X.R., Zinkernagel, A., Ortner, T.M., & Schmitt, M. (2010). Convergence of direct, indirect, and objective risk taking measures in the domain of gambling: The moderating role of impulsiveness and self-control. *Zeitschrift für Psychologie, 218*, 20–27.

Ditto, P.H., & Lopez, D.F. (1992). Motivated skepticism: Use of differential decision criteria for preferred and nonpreferred conclusions. *Journal of Personality and Social Psychology, 63*, 568–584.

Ditto, P.H., Liu, B.S., Clark, C.J., Wojcik, S.P., Chen, E.E., Grady, R.H., Celniker, J.B., & Zinger, J.F. (2019). At least bias is bipartisan: A meta-analytic comparison of partisan bias in liberals and conservatives. *Perspectives on Psychological Science, 14*, 273–291.

Ditto, P.H., Munro, G.D., Apanovitch, A.M., Scepansky, J.A., & Lockhart, L.K. (2003). Spontaneous skepticism: The interplay of motivation and expectation in responses to favorable and unfavorable medical diagnoses. *Personality and Social Psychology Bulletin, 29*, 1120–1132.

Ditto, P.H., Scepansky, J.A., Munro, G.D., Apanovitch, A.M., & Lockhart, L.K. (1998). Motivated sensitivity to preference-inconsistent information. *Journal of Personality and Social Psychology, 75*, 53–69.

Dittrick, C.J., Beran, T.N., Mishna, F., Hetherington, R., & Shariff, S. (2013). Do children who bully their peers also play violent video games? A Canadian national study. *Journal of School Violence, 12,* 297–318.

Djulbegovic, B., Elqayam, S., & Dale, W. (2018). Rational decision making in medicine: Implications for overuse and underuse. *Journal of Evaluation in Clinical Practice, 24,* 655–665.

Dodd, D.H., & Bradshaw, J.M. (1980). Leading questions and memory: Pragmatic constraints. *Journal of Verbal Learning & Verbal Behavior, 19,* 695–704.

Doise, W., Deschamps, J.C., & Meyer, G. (1978). The accentuation of intra-category similarities. In H. Tajfel (Ed.), *Differentiation between social groups* (pp. 159–168). London: Academic Press.

Doll, J., & Ajzen, I. (1992). Accessibility and stability of predictors in the theory of planned behavior. *Journal of Personality and Social Psychology, 63,* 754–765.

Donders, N.C., Correll, J., & Wittenbrink, B. (2008). Danger stereotypes predict biased attentional allocation. *Journal of Experimental Social Psychology, 44,* 1328–1333.

Doosje, B., & Branscombe, N.R. (2003). Attributions for the negative historical actions of a group. *European Journal of Social Psychology, 33,* 235–248.

Dotsch, R., Wigboldus, D.H.J., Langner, O., & van Knippenberg, A. (2008). Ethnic outgroup faces are biased in the prejudiced mind. *Psychological Science, 19,* 978–980.

Douven, I. (2016). Vagueness, graded membership, and conceptual spaces. *Cognition, 151,* 80–95.

Dovidio, J.F., & Gaertner, S.L. (2000). Aversive racism and selection decisions: 1989 and 1999. *Psychological Science, 11,* 315–319.

Dovidio, J.F., Evans, N., & Tyler, R.B. (1986). Racial stereotypes: The contents of their cognitive representations. *Journal of Experimental Social Psychology, 22,* 22–37.

Dovidio, J.F., Gaertner, S.L., Isen, A.M., & Lowrance, R. (1995). Group representations and intergroup bias: Positive affect, similarity, and group size. *Personality and Social Psychology Bulletin, 21,* 856–865.

Dovidio, J.F., Gaertner, S.L., & Validzic, A. (1998). Intergroup bias: Status, differentiation, and a common in-group identity. *Journal of Personality and Social Psychology, 75,* 109–120.

Dovidio, J.F., Hewstone, M., Glick, P., & Esses, V.M. (Eds.) (2010). *The SAGE handbook of prejudice, stereotyping and discrimination.* Thousand Oaks, CA: Sage.

Dovidio, J.F., Kawakami, K., & Gaertner, S.L. (2002). Implicit and explicit prejudice and interracial interaction. *Journal of Personality and Social Psychology, 82,* 62–68.

Dovidio, J.F., Love, A., Schellhaas, F.M.H., & Hewstone, M. (2017). Reducing intergroup bias through intergroup contact: Twenty years of progress and future directions. *Group Processes & Intergroup Relations, 20,* 606–620.

Dovidio, J.F., Penner, L.A., Albrecht, T.L., Norton, W.E., Gaertner, S.L., & Shelton, J.N. (2008). Disparities and distrust: The implications of psychological processes for understanding racial disparities in health and health care. *Social Science & Medicine, 67,* 478–486.

Dovidio, J.F., ten Vergert, M., Stewart, T.L., Gaertner, S.L., Johnson, J.D., Esses, V.M., Riek, B.M., & Pearson, A.R. (2004). Perspective and prejudice: Antecedents and mediating mechanisms. *Personality and Social Psychology Bulletin, 29,* 1537–1549.

Downey, G., Feldman, S., & Ayduk, O. (2000). Rejection sensitivity and male violence in romantic relationships. *Personal Relationships, 7,* 45–61.

Downey, G., Freitas, A.L., Michaelis, B., & Khouri, H. (1998). The self-fulfilling prophecy in close relationships: Rejection sensitivity and rejection by romantic partners. *Journal of Personality and Social Psychology, 75,* 545–560.

Downey, G., Mougios, V., Ayduk, O., London, B.E., & Shoda, Y. (2004). Rejection sensitivity and the defensive motivational system: Insights from the startle response to rejection cues. *Psychological Science, 15,* 668–673.

Doyen, S., Klein, O., Pichon, C.-L., & Cleeremans, A. (2012). Behavioral priming: It's all in the mind, but whose mind? *PLOS ONE, 7,* e29081.

Doyen, S., Klein, O., Simons, D.J., & Cleeremans, A. (2014). On the other side of the mirror: Priming in cognitive and social psychology. *Social Cognition, 32,* 14–34.

Doyle, W.J., Hancock, G., & Kifer, E. (1972). Teachers' perceptions: Do they make a difference? *Journal of the Association for the Study of Perception, 7,* 21–30.

Dragojevic, M., Sink, A., & Mastro, D. (2017). Evidence of linguistic intergroup bias in U.S. print news coverage of immigration. *Journal of Language and Social Psychology, 36,* 462–472.

Drews, F.A., Pasupathi, M., & Strayer, D.L. (2008). Passenger and cell phone conversations in simulated driving. *Journal of Experimental Psychology: Applied, 14,* 392–400.

Du, S., Tow, Y., & Martinez, A.M. (2014). Compound facial expressions of emotion. *Proceedings of the National Academy of Sciences, 111,* E1454–1462.

Dudycha, G.J. (1936). An objective study of punctuality in relation to personality and achievement. *Archives of Psychology, 204,* 1–53.

Duersch, P., Oechssler, J., & Schipper, B.C. (2012). Unbeatable imitation. *Games and Economic Behavior, 76,* 88–96.

Duersch, P., Oechssler, J. & Schipper, B.C. (2014). When is tit-for-tat unbeatable? *International Journal of Game Theory, 43,* 25–36.

Dufner, M., Gebauer, J.E., Sedikides, C., & Denissen, J.J.A. (2019). Self-enhancement and psychological adjustment: A meta-analytic review. *Personality and Social Psychology Review, 23,* 48–72.

Duncan, B.L. (1976). Differential social perception and attribution of intergroup violence: Testing the lower limits of stereotyping of blacks. *Journal of Personality and Social Psychology, 34,* 590–598.

Dunham, Y., Baron, A.S., & Banaji, M.R. (2008). The development of implicit intergroup cognition. *Trends in Cognitive Sciences, 12,* 248–253.

Dunlop, W.L., Guo, J., & McAdams, D.P. (2016). The autobiographical author through time: Examining the degree of stability and change in redemptive and contaminated personal narratives. *Social Psychological and Personality Science, 7,* 428–436.

Dunn, E.W., Biesanz, J.C., Human, L.J., & Finn, S. (2007). Misunderstanding the affective consequences of everyday social interactions: The hidden benefits of putting one's best face forward. *Journal of Personality and Social Psychology, 92,* 990–1005.

Dunn, E.W., Wilson, T.D., & Gilbert, D.T. (2003). Location, location, location: The misprediction of satisfaction in housing lotteries. *Personality and Social Psychology Bulletin, 29,* 1421–1432.

Dunning, D. (2005). *Self-insight: Roadblocks and detours on the path to knowing thyself.* New York, NY: Psychology Press.

Dunning, D. (2014). Motivated cognition in self and social thought. In M. Mikulincer & P. Shaver (Eds.), *APA handbook of personality and social psychology* (Vol. 1, pp. 777–804). Washington, DC: American Psychological Association.

Dunning, D., & Sherman, D.A. (1997). Stereotypes and tacit inference. *Journal of Personality and Social Psychology, 73,* 459–471.

Dunning, D., Heath, C., & Suls, J.M. (2004). Flawed self-assessment: Implications for health, education, and the workplace. *Psychological Science in the Public Interest, 5,* 69–106.

Dunning, D., Heath, C., & Suls, J.M. (2018). Reflections on self-reflection: Contemplating flawed self-judgments in the clinic, classroom, and office cubicle. *Perspectives on Psychological Science, 13,* 185–189.

Dunning, D., Meyerowitz, J.A., & Holzberg, A.D. (1989). Ambiguity and self-evaluation: The role of idiosyncratic trait definitions in self-serving assessments of ability. *Journal of Personality and Social Psychology, 57,* 1082–1090.

Dunton, B.C., & Fazio, R.H. (1997). An individual difference measure of motivation to control prejudiced reactions. *Personality and Social Psychology Bulletin, 23,* 316–326.

Durtschi, J.A., Fincham, F.D., Cui, M., Lorenz, F.O., & Conger, R.D. (2011). Dyadic processes in early marriage: Attributions, behavior, and marital quality. *Family Relations: An Interdisciplinary Journal of Applied Family Studies, 60,* 421–434.

Duval, T.S., & Silvia, P.J. (2002). Self-awareness, probability of improvement, and the self-serving bias. *Journal of Personality and Social Psychology, 82,* 49–61.

Duval, T.S., & Wicklund, R.A. (1972). *A theory of objective self awareness.* New York, NY: Academic Press.

Dweck, C.S. (1999). *Self-theories: Their role in motivation, personality, and development.* New York, NY: Psychology Press.

Dweck, C.S. (2006). *Mindset: The new psychology of success.* New York, NY: Random House.

Dweck, C.S., & Grant, H. (2008). Self-theories, goals, and meaning. In J.Y. Shah & W.L. Gardner (Eds.), *Handbook of motivation science* (pp. 405–416). New York, NY: Guilford Press.

Dweck, C.S., & Leggett, E.L. (1988). A social-cognitive approach to motivation and personality. *Psychological Review, 95,* 256–273.

Dweck, C.S., & Yeager, D.S. (2019). Mindsets: A view from two eras. *Perspectives on Psychological Science, 14,* 481–496.

Dweck, C.S., Chiu, C.-Y., & Hong, Y.-Y. (1995). Implicit theories and their role in judgments and reactions: A world from two perspectives. *Psychological Inquiry, 6,* 267–285.

Eagly, A.H. (1992). Uneven progress: Social psychology and the study of attitudes. *Journal of Personality and Social Psychology, 63,* 693–710.

Eagly, A.H., & Chaiken, S. (1993). *The psychology of attitudes.* Belmont, CA: Wadsworth.

Eagly, A.H., & Chaiken, S. (1998). Attitude structure and function. In D. Gilbert, S. Fiske, & G. Lindzey (Eds.), *Handbook of social psychology* (4th ed., Vol. 1, pp. 269–322). New York, NY: McGraw-Hill.

Eagly, A.H., & Kite, M.E. (1987). Are stereotypes of nationalities applied to both women and men? *Journal of Personality and Social Psychology, 53,* 451–462.

Eagly, A.H., Ashmore, R.D., Makhijani, M.G., & Longo, L.C. (1991). What is beautiful is good, but...: A meta-analytic review of research on the physical attractiveness stereotype. *Psychological Bulletin, 110,* 109–128.

Easterbrook, J.A. (1959). The effect of emotion on cue utilization and the organization of behavior. *Psychological Review, 66,* 183–201.

Ebbinghaus, H. (1885/1913). *Memory: A contribution to experimental psychology* (H.A. Ruger, & C.E. Bussenius, Trans.). New York, NY: Teachers College, Columbia University.

Eberhardt, J.L., Davies, P.G., Purdie-Vaughns, V.J., & Johnson, S.L. (2006). Looking deathworthy: Perceived stereotypicality of black defendants predicts capital-sentencing outcomes. *Psychological Science, 17,* 383–386.

Eberhardt, J.L., Goff, P.A., Purdie, V.J., & Davies, P.G. (2004). Seeing black: Race, crime, and visual processing. *Journal of Personality and Social Psychology, 87,* 876–893.

Echterhoff, G., & Hirst, W. (2009). Social influence on memory. *Social Psychology, 40,* 106–110.

Echterhoff, G., Higgins, E.T., & Groll, S. (2005). Audience-tuning effects on memory: The role of shared reality. *Journal of Personality and Social Psychology, 89,* 257–276.

Echterhoff, G., Higgins, E.T., Kopietz, R., & Groll, S. (2008). How communication goals determine when audience tuning biases memory. *Journal of Experimental Psychology, 137,* 3–21.

Echterhoff, G., Higgins, E.T., & Levine, J.M. (2009). Shared reality: Experiencing commonality with others' inner states about the world. *Perspectives on Psychological Science, 4,* 496–521.

Echterhoff, G., Hirst, W., & Hussy, W. (2005). How eyewitnesses resist misinformation: Social postwarnings and the monitoring of memory characteristics. *Memory & Cognition, 33,* 770–782.

Echterhoff, G., Kopietz, R., & Higgins, E.T. (2017). Shared reality in intergroup communication: Increasing the epistemic authority of an out-group audience. *Journal of Experimental Psychology: General, 146,* 806–825.

Edland, A. (1994). Time pressure and the application of decision rules: Choices and judgments among multiattribute alternatives. *Scandinavian Journal of Psychology, 35,* 281–291.

Edwards, W. (1961). Behavioral decision theory. *Annual Review of Psychology, 12,* 472–498.

Ehrenberg, K., & Klauer, K.C. (2005). Flexible use of source information: Processing components of the inconsistency effect in person memory. *Journal of Experimental Social Psychology, 41,* 369–387.

Ehrlinger, J., Johnson, K.L., Banner, M., Dunning, D.A., & Kruger, J. (2008). Why the unskilled are unaware: Further explorations of (absent) self-insight among the incompetent. *Organizational Behavior and Human Decision Processes, 105,* 98–121.

Ehrlinger, J., Mitchum, A.L., & Dweck, C.S. (2016). Understanding overconfidence: Theories of intelligence, preferential attention, and distorted self-assessment. *Journal of Experimental Social Psychology, 63,* 94–100.

Einhorn, H.J., & Hogarth, R.M. (1978). Confidence in judgment: Persistence of the illusion of validity. *Psychological Review, 85,* 395–416.

Eitam, B., & Higgins, E.T. (2016). From reaction ('priming') to motivated selection: Changing conceptualizations of accessibility. *Current Opinion in Psychology, 12,* 58–62.

Ejelöv, E., & Luke, T.J. (2020). "Rarely safe to assume": Evaluating the use and interpretation of manipulation checks in experimental social psychology. *Journal of Experimental Social Psychology, 87,* 103937.

Ellemers, N. (2018). Gender stereotypes. *Annual Review of Psychology, 69,* 275–298.

Elliott, M.A., Lee, E., Robertson, J.S., & Innes, R. (2015). Evidence that attitude accessibility augments the relationship between speeding attitudes and speeding behavior: A test of the MODE model in the context of driving. *Accident Analysis and Prevention, 74,* 49–59.

Ellis, E.M., Collins, R.L., Homish, G.G., Parks, K.A., & Kiviniemi, M.T. (2016). Perceived controllability of condom use shifts reliance on implicit versus explicit affect. *Health Psychology, 35,* 842–846.

Elms, A.C. (1975). The crisis of confidence in social psychology. *American Psychologist, 30,* 967–976.

Englich, B., & Mussweiler, T. (2001). Sentencing under uncertainty: Anchoring effects in the courtroom. *Journal of Applied Social Psychology, 31,* 1535–1551.

Englich, B., Mussweiler, T., & Strack, F. (2006). Playing dice with criminal sentences: The influence of irrelevant anchors on experts' judicial decision making. *Personality and Social Psychology Bulletin, 32,* 188–200.

Epley, N., & Dunning, D. (2000). Feeling "holier than thou": Are self-serving assessments produced by errors in self or social prediction? *Journal of Personality and Social Psychology, 79,* 861–875.

Epley, N., & Gilovich, T. (2001). Putting adjustment back into the anchoring and adjustment heuristic: Differential processing of self-generated and experimenter-provided anchors. *Psychological Science, 12,* 391–396.

Epley, N., & Gilovich, T. (2005). When effortful thinking influences judgmental anchoring: Differential effects of forewarning and incentives on self-generated and externally-provided anchors. *Journal of Behavioral Decision Making, 18,* 199–212.

Epley, N., & Gilovich, T. (2006). The anchoring-and-adjustment heuristic: Why the adjustments are insufficient. *Psychological Science, 17*, 311–318.

Epley, N., & Whitchurch, E. (2008). Mirror, mirror on the wall: Enhancement in self-recognition. *Personality and Social Psychology Bulletin, 34*, 1159–1170.

Epstein, S., & O'Brien, E.J. (1985). The person-situation debate in historical and current perspective. *Psychological Bulletin, 98*, 513–537.

Epstude, K., & Peetz, J. (2012). Mental time travel: A conceptual overview of social psychological perspectives on a fundamental human capacity. *European Journal of Social Psychology, 42*, 269–275.

Epstude, K., & Roese, N.J. (2008). The functional theory of counterfactual thinking. *Personality and Social Psychology Review, 12*, 168–192.

Erard, R.E. (2016). If it walks like a duck: A case of confirmatory bias. *Psychological Injury and Law, 9*, 275–277.

Erber, M.W., Hodges, S.D., & Wilson, T.D. (1995). Attitude strength, attitude stability, and the effects of analyzing reasons. In R.E. Petty & J.A. Krosnick (Eds.), *Attitude strength: Antecedents and consequences* (pp. 433–454). Mahwah, NJ: Lawrence Erlbaum.

Erber, R., & Fiske, S.T. (1984). Outcome dependency and attention to inconsistent information. *Journal of Personality and Social Psychology, 47*, 709–726.

Erdfelder, E., Auer, T.-S., Hilbig, B.E., Assfalg, A., Moshagen, M., & Nadarevic, L. (2009). Multinomial processing tree models: A review of the literature. *Journal of Psychology, 217*, 108–124.

Erdfelder, E., Brandt, M., & Bröder, A. (2007). Recollection biases in hindsight judgments. *Social Cognition, 25*, 114–131.

Erdley, C.A., & D'Agostino, P.R. (1988). Cognitive and affective components of automatic priming effects. *Journal of Personality and Social Psychology, 54*, 741–747.

Erickson, T.M., Newman, M.G., Peterson, J., & Scarsella, G. (2015). Ambivalence about interpersonal problems and traits predicts cross-situational variability of social behavior. *Journal of Personality, 83*, 429–440.

Erickson, W.B., Lampinen, J.M., & Leding, J.K. (2014). The weapon focus effect in target-present and target-absent line-ups: The roles of threat, novelty, and timing. *Applied Cognitive Psychology, 28*, 349–359.

Evans, J.S.B.T. (1982). *The psychology of deductive reasoning*. London: Routledge & Kegan Paul.

Evans, J.S.B.T. (1984). Heuristic and analytic processes in reasoning. *British Journal of Psychology, 75*, 451–468.

Evans, J.S.B.T. (2008). Dual-processing accounts of reasoning, judgment, and social cognition. *Annual Review of Psychology, 59*, 255–278.

Evans, J.S.B.T., & Frankish, K. (Eds.) (2009). *In two minds: Dual processes and beyond.* New York, NY: Oxford University Press.

Eyal, T., Hoover, G.M., Fujita, K., & Nussbaum, S. (2011). The effect of distance-dependent construals on schema-driven impression formation. *Journal of Experimental Social Psychology, 47*, 278–281.

Eyal, T., Liberman, N., Trope, Y., & Walther, E. (2004). The pros and cons of temporally near and distant action. *Journal of Personality and Social Psychology, 86*, 781–795.

Fabrigar, L.R., & Wegener, D.T. (2016). Conceptualizing and evaluating the replication of research results. *Journal of Experimental Social Psychology, 66*, 68–80.

Fanselow, M.S., & Pennington, Z.T. (2017). The danger of LeDoux and Pine's two-system framework for fear. *The American Journal of Psychiatry, 174*, 1120–1121.

Fasolo, B., Carmeci, F.A., & Misuraca, R. (2009). The effect of choice complexity on perception of time spent choosing: When choice takes longer but feels shorter. *Psychology & Marketing, 26*, 213–228.

Fawcett, J.M., Peace, K.A., & Greve, A. (2016). Looking down the barrel of a gun: What do we know about the weapon focus effect? *Journal of Applied Research in Memory and Cognition, 5*, 257–263.

Fay, A.J., & Maner, J.K. (20₁,8). Comfortably warm: A momentary lapse of reaffiliation after exclusion. *Journal of Experimental Psychology: General, 147,* 1154–1169.

Fay, A.J., & Maner, J.K. (2020). Interactive effects of tactile warmth and ambient temperature on the search for social affiliation. *Social Psychology, 51,* 199–204.

Fayant, M.-P., Sigall, H., Lemonnier, A., Retsin, E., & Alexopoulos, T. (2017). On the limitations of manipulation checks: An obstacle toward cumulative science. *International Review of Social Psychology, 30,* 125–130.

Fazio, R.H. (1986). How do attitudes guide behavior? In R.M. Sorrentino & E.T. Higgins (Eds.)., *Handbook of motivation and cognition: Foundations of social behavior* (pp. 204–243). New York, NY: Guilford Press.

Fazio, R.H. (1989). On the power and functionality of attitudes: The role of attitude. In A.R. Pratkanis, S.J. Breckler, & A.G. Greenwald (Eds.), *The third Ohio State University volume on attitudes and persuasion: Attitude structure and function* (pp. 153–179). Hillsdale, NJ: Lawrence Erlbaum.

Fazio, R.H. (1990). Multiple processes by which attitudes guide behavior: The MODE model as an integrative framework. In M.P. Zanna (Ed.), *Advances in experimental social psychology* (Vol. 23, pp. 75–109). New York, NY: Academic Press.

Fazio, R.H. (1995). Attitudes as object-evaluation associations: Determinants, consequences, and correlates of attitude accessibility. In R.E. Petty & J.A. Krosnick (Eds.), *Attitude strength: Antecedents and consequences* (pp. 247–282). Hillsdale, NJ: Lawrence Erlbaum

Fazio, R.H. (2001). On the automatic activation of associated evaluations: An overview. *Cognition and Emotion, 15,* 115–141.

Fazio, R.H. (2007). Attitudes as object–evaluation associations of varying strength. *Social Cognition, 25,* 603–637.

Fazio, R.H., & Olson, M.A. (2003). Attitudes: Foundations, functions, and consequences. In M.A. Hogg and J. Cooper (Eds.), *The SAGE handbook of social psychology* (pp. 139–160). London: Sage.

Fazio, R.H., & Olson, M.A. (2014). The MODE model: Attitude-behavior processes as a function of motivation and opportunity. In J.W. Sherman, B. Gawronski, & Y. Trope (Eds.), *Dual process theories of the social mind* (pp. 155–171). New York, NY: Guilford Press.

Fazio, R.H., & Towles-Schwen, T. (1999). The MODE model of attitude-behaviour processes. In S. Chaiken & Y. Trope (Eds.), *Dual-process theories in social psychology* (pp. 97–116). New York, NY: Guilford Press.

Fazio, R.H., & Williams, C.J. (1986). Attitude accessibility as a moderator of the attitude–perception and attitude–behavior relations: An investigation of the 1984 presidential election. *Journal of Personality and Social Psychology, 51,* 505–514.

Fazio, R.H., & Zanna, M.P. (1978a). On the predictive validity of attitudes: The roles of direct experience and confidence. *Journal of Experimental Social Psychology, 46,* 228–243.

Fazio, R.H., & Zanna, M.P. (1978b). Attitudinal qualities relating to the strength of the attitude-behavior relationship. *Journal of Experimental Social Psychology, 14,* 398–408.

Fazio, R.H., Chen, J., McDonel, E.C., & Sherman, S.J. (1982). Attitude accessibility, attitude-behavior consistency, and the strength of the object evaluation association. *Journal of Experimental Social Psychology, 18,* 339–357.

Fazio, R.H., Eiser, J.R., & Shook, N.J. (2004). Attitude formation through exploration: Valence asymmetries. *Journal of Personality and Social Psychology, 87,* 293–311.

Fazio, R.H., Jackson, J.R., Dunton, B.C., & Williams, C.J. (1995). Variability in automatic activation as an unobtrusive measure of racial attitudes: A bona fide pipeline? *Journal of Personality and Social Psychology, 69,* 1013–1027.

Fazio, R.H., Pietri, E.S., Rocklage, M.D., & Shook, N.J. (2015). Positive versus negative valence: Asymmetries in attitude formation and generalization as fundamental individual differences. In J.M. Olson & M.P. Zanna (Eds.), *Advances in experimental social psychology* (Vol. 51, pp. 97–146). New York, NY: Academic Press.

Fazio, R.H., Sanbonmatsu, D.M., Powell, M.C., & Kardes, F.R. (1986). On the automatic activation of attitudes. *Journal of Personality and Social Psychology, 50*, 229–238.

Fazio, R.H., Zanna, M.P., & Cooper, J. (1977). Dissonance and self-perception: An integrative view of each theory's proper domain of application. *Journal of Experimental Social Psychology, 13*, 464–479.

Fazio, R.H., Zanna, M.P., & Cooper, J. (1978). Direct experience and attitude-behavior consistency: An information processing analysis. *Personality and Social Psychology Bulletin, 4*, 48–51.

Feather, N.T., & Sherman, R. (2002). Envy, resentment, schadenfreude, and sympathy: Reactions to deserved and undeserved achievement and subsequent failure. *Personality and Social Psychology Bulletin, 28*, 953–961.

Federico, C. M., & Sidanius, J. (2002). Racism, ideology, and affirmative action revisited: The antecedents and consequences of "principled objections" to affirmative action. *Journal of Personality and Social Psychology, 82*, 488–502.

Feick, D.L., & Rhodewalt, F. (1997). The double-edged sword of self-handicapping: Discounting, augmentation, and the protection and enhancement of self-esteem. *Motivation and Emotion, 21*, 147–163.

Fein, S. (1996). Effects of suspicion on attributional thinking and the correspondence bias. *Journal of Personality and Social Psychology, 70*, 1164–1184.

Fein, S., & Spencer, S.J. (1997). Prejudice as self-image maintenance: Affirming the self through derogating others. *Journal of Personality and Social Psychology, 73*, 31–44.

Fein, S., Hilton, J.L., & Miller, D.T. (1990). Suspicion of ulterior motivation and correspondence bias. *Journal of Personality and Social Psychology, 58*, 753–764.

Fein, S., Morgan, S.J., Norton, M.I., & Sommers, S.R. (1997). Hype or suspicion: The effects of pretrial publicity, race, and suspicion on jurors' verdicts. *Journal of Social Issues, 53*, 487–502.

Feldman, G., & Albarracín, D. (2017). Norm theory and the action-effect: The role of social norms in regret following action and inaction. *Journal of Experimental Social Psychology, 69*, 111–120.

Feldman, N.S., Higgins, E.T., Karlovac, M., & Ruble, D.N. (1976). Use of consensus information in causal attributions as a function of temporal presentation and availability of direct information. *Journal of Personality and Social Psychology, 34*, 694–698.

Feldman, S. (1966). Motivational aspects of attitudinal elements and their place in cognitive interaction. In S. Feldman (Ed.), *Cognitive consistency* (pp. 75–108). New York, NY: Academic Press.

Feng, C., Yan, X., Huang, W., Han, S., & Ma, Y. (2018). Neural representations of the multidimensional self in the cortical midline structures. *NeuroImage, 183*, 291–299.

Fenigstein, A., Scheier, M.F., & Buss, A.H. (1975). Public and private self-consciousness: Assessment and theory. *Journal of Consulting and Clinical Psychology, 43*, 522–527.

Fenker, D.B., Waldmann, M.R., & Holyoak, K.J. (2005). Accessing causal relations in semantic memory. *Memory & Cognition, 33*, 1036–1046.

Ferguson, M.J. (2007). On the automatic evaluation of end-states. *Journal of Personality and Social Psychology, 92*, 596–611.

Ferguson, M.J., & Bargh, J.A. (2004). Liking is for doing: Effects of goal pursuit on automatic evaluation. *Journal of Personality and Social Psychology, 87*, 557–572.

Ferguson, M.J., & Cone, J. (2013). The mind in motivation: A social cognitive perspective on the role of consciousness in goal pursuit.

In D.E. Carlston (Ed.), *The Oxford handbook of social cognition* (pp. 476–496). New York, NY: Oxford University Press.

Ferguson, M.J., & Mann, T.C. (2014). Effects of evaluation: An example of robust "social" priming. *Social Cognition, 32,* 35–48.

Ferguson, M.J., & Zayas, V. (2009). Automatic evaluation. *Current Directions in Psychological Science, 18,* 362–366.

Ferguson, M.J., Mann, T.C., Cone, J., & Shen, X. (2019). When and how implicit first impressions can be updated. *Current Directions in Psychological Science, 28,* 331–336.

Ferreira, M.B., Garcia-Marques, L., Hamilton, D.L., Ramos, T., Uleman, J.S., & Jeronimo, R. (2012). On the relation between spontaneous trait inferences and intentional inferences: An inference monitoring hypothesis. *Journal of Experimental Social Psychology, 48,* 1–12.

Ferreira, M.B., Garcia-Marques, L., Sherman, S.J., & Sherman, J.W. (2006). Automatic and controlled components of judgment and decision making. *Journal of Personality and Social Psychology, 91,* 797–813.

Feschbach, S., & Feschbach, N. (1963). Influence of the stimulus object upon the complementary and supplementary projection of fear. *Journal of Abnormal and Social Psychology, 66,* 498–502.

Festinger, L. (1954). A theory of social comparison processes. *Human Relations, 7,* 117–140.

Festinger, L. (1957). *A theory of cognitive dissonance.* Evanston, IL: Row Peterson.

Festinger, L. (1964). *Conflict, decision, and dissonance.* Stanford, CA: Stanford University Press.

Festinger, L., & Carlsmith, J.M. (1959). Cognitive consequences of forced compliance. *Journal of Abnormal and Social Psychology, 58,* 203–210.

Fetterman, A.K., Wilkowski, B.M., & Robinson, M.D. (2018). On feeling warm and being warm: Daily perceptions of physical warmth fluctuate with interpersonal warmth.

Social Psychological and Personality Science, 9, 560–567.

Fiedler, K. (1991). The tricky nature of skewed frequency tables: An information loss account of distinctiveness-based illusory correlations. *Journal of Personality and Social Psychology, 60,* 24–36.

Fiedler, K., & Bluemka, M. (2005). Faking the IAT: Aided and unaided response control on the Implicit Association Tests. *Basic and Applied Social Psychology, 27,* 307–316.

Fiedler, K., Kaczor, K., Haarmann, S., Stegmüller, M., & Maloney, J. (2009). Impression-formation advantage in memory for faces: When eyewitnesses are interested in targets' likeability, rather than their identity. *European Journal of Social Psychology, 39,* 793–807.

Fiedler, K., Walther, E., & Nickel, S. (1999). Covariation-based attribution: On the ability to assess multiple covariates of an effect. *Personality and Social Psychology Bulletin, 25,* 607–622.

Filevich, E., Horn, S.S., & Kühn, S. (2019). Within-person adaptivity in frugal judgments from memory. *Psychological Research, 83,* 613–630.

Fincham, F.D., Harold, G.T., & Gano-Phillips, S. (2000). The longitudinal association between attributions and marital satisfaction: Direction of effects and role of efficacy expectations. *Journal of Family Psychology, 14,* 267–285.

Fincham, F.D., Paleari, F., & Regalia, C. (2002). Forgiveness in marriage: The role of relationship quality, attributions, and empathy. *Personal Relationships, 9,* 27–37.

Fink, B., Neave, N., Manning, J.T., & Grammer, K. (2006). Facial symmetry and judgements of attractiveness, health and personality. *Personality and Individual Differences, 41,* 491–499.

Finkel, E.J., Campbell, W.K., Brunell, A.B., Dalton, A.N., Scarbeck, S.J., & Chartrand, T.L. (2006). High-maintenance interaction: Inefficient social coordination impairs self-regulation. *Journal of Personality and Social Psychology, 91,* 456–475.

Finlay, F., Hitch, G.J., & Meudell, P.R. (2000). Mutual inhibition in collaborative recall: Evidence for a retrieval-based account. *Journal of Experimental Psychology: Learning, Memory, and Cognition, 26*, 1556–1567.

Finucane, M.L., Alhakami, A., Slovic, P., & Johnson, S.M. (2000). The affect heuristic in judgments of risks and benefits. *Journal of Behavioral Decision Making, 13*, 1–17.

Fiscella, K., & Sanders, M.R. (2016). Racial and ethnic disparities in the quality of health care. *Annual Review of Public Health, 37*, 375–394.

Fischhoff, B. (1975). Hindsight is not equal to foresight: The effect of outcome knowledge on judgment under uncertainty. *Journal of Experimental Psychology: Human Perception and Performance, 1*, 288–299.

Fischhoff, B. (1982). For those condemned to study the past: Heuristics and biases in hindsight. In D. Kahneman, P. Slovic, & A. Tversky (Eds.), *Judgment under uncertainty: Heuristics and biases* (pp. 332–351). New York, NY: Cambridge University Press.

Fischhoff, B., & Beyth, R. (1975). "I knew it would happen": Remembered probabilities of once-future things. *Organizational Behavior and Human Performance, 13*, 1–16.

Fishbein, M. (1967). Attitude and the prediction of behavior. In M. Fishbein (Ed.), *Readings in attitude theory and measurement* (pp. 477–492). New York, NY: Wiley.

Fishbein, M., & Ajzen, I. (1974). Attitudes towards objects as predictors of single and multiple behavioral criteria. *Psychological Review, 81*, 59–74.

Fishbein, M., & Ajzen, I. (1975). *Belief, attitude, intention, and behavior: An introduction to theory and research.* Reading, MA: Addison Wesley.

Fiske, S.T. (1980). Attention and weight in person perception: The impact of negative and extreme behavior. *Journal of Personality and Social Psychology, 38*, 889–906.

Fiske, S.T. (1992). Thinking is for doing: Portraits of social cognition from daguerreotype to laserphoto. *Journal of Personality and Social Psychology, 63*, 877–889.

Fiske, S.T. (1993). Controlling other people: The impact of power on stereotyping. *American Psychologist, 48*, 621–628.

Fiske, S.T. (2012). The continuum model and the stereotype content model. In P.A.M. Van Lange, A.W. Kruglanski, & E.T. Higgins (Eds.), *Handbook of theories of social psychology* (Vol. 1, pp. 267–288). Thousand Oaks, CA: Sage.

Fiske, S.T., & Depret, E. (1996). Control, independence and power: Understanding social cognition in its context. In W. Stroebe & M. Hewstone (Eds.), *European review of social psychology* (Vol. 7, pp. 31–61). Chichester: Wiley.

Fiske, S.T., & Glick, P. (1995). Ambivalence and stereotypes cause sexual harassment: A theory with implications for organizational change. *Journal of Social Issues, 51*, 97–115.

Fiske, S.T., & Neuberg, S.L. (1990). A continuum model of impression formation, from category-based to individuating processes: Influences of information and motivation on attention and interpretation. In M.P. Zanna (Ed.), *Advances in experimental social psychology* (Vol. 23, pp. 1–74). New York, NY: Academic Press.

Fiske, S.T., & von Hendy, H.M. (1992). Personality feedback and situational norms can control stereotyping processes. *Journal of Personality and Social Psychology, 62*, 577–596.

Fiske, S.T., Cuddy, A.J.C., & Glick, P. (2007). Universal dimensions of social cognition: Warmth and competence. *Trends in Cognitive Sciences, 11*, 77–83.

Fiske, S.T., Cuddy, A.J.C., Glick, P., & Xu, J. (2002). A model of (often mixed) stereotype content: Competence and warmth respectively follow from perceived status and competition. *Journal of Personality and Social Psychology, 82*, 878–902.

Fiske, S.T., Lin, M., & Neuberg, S.L. (1999). The continuum model: Ten years later. In S. Chaiken & Y. Trope (Eds.), *Dual process theories in social psychology* (pp. 231–254). New York, NY: Guilford Press.

Fiske, S.T., Neuberg, S.L., Beattie, A.E., & Milberg, S.J. (1987). Category-based and attribute-based reactions to others: Some informational conditions of stereotyping and individuating processes. *Journal of Experimental Social Psychology, 23*, 399–427.

Fitzsimons, G.M., & Bargh, J.A. (2003). Thinking of you: Nonconscious pursuit of interpersonal goals associated with relationship partners. *Journal of Personality and Social Psychology, 84*, 148–164.

Fitzsimons, G.M., & Fishbach, A. (2010). Shifting closeness: Interpersonal effects of personal goal progress. *Journal of Personality and Social Psychology, 98*, 535–549.

Fleeson, W. (2007), Situation-based contingencies underlying trait-content manifestation in behavior. *Journal of Personality, 75*, 825–862.

Fletcher G.J., Fincham, F.D., Cramer L., & Heron, N. (1987). The role of attributions in the development of dating relationships. *Journal of Personality and Social Psychology, 53*, 481–489.

Florack, A., Scarabis, M., & Bless, H. (2001). When do associations matter? The use of automatic associations toward ethnic groups in person judgments. *Journal of Experimental Social Psychology, 37*, 518–524.

Foer, J. (2011). *Moonwalking with Einstein: The art and science of remembering everything*. New York, NY: Penguin.

Folkes, V.S., & Morgenstern, D. (1981). Account-giving and social perception. *Personality and Social Psychology Bulletin, 7*, 451–458.

Follenfant, A., Légal, J-B., Dinard, F.M.D., & Meyer, T. (2005). Effect of stereotypes activation on behavior: An application in a sport setting. *European Journal of Applied Psychology, 55*, 121–129.

Forer, B.R. (1949). The fallacy of personal validation: A classroom demonstration of gullibility. *Journal of Abnormal and Social Psychology, 44*, 118–123.

Forgas, J.P. (2011). Can negative affect eliminate the power of first impressions? Affective influences on primacy and recency effects in impression formation. *Journal of Experimental Social Psychology, 47*, 425–429.

Forgas, J.P., & Laham, S.M. (2017). Halo effects. In R.F. Pohl (Ed.), *Cognitive illusions: Intriguing phenomena in thinking, judgment and memory* (pp. 276–290). New York, NY: Routledge.

Foroni, F., & Rothbart, M. (2011). Category boundaries and category labels: When does a category name influence the perceived similarity of category members? *Social Cognition, 29*, 547–576.

Foroni, F., & Rothbart, M. (2013). Abandoning a label doesn't make it disappear: The perseverance of labeling effects. *Journal of Experimental Social Psychology, 49*, 126–131.

Forster, J., & Jostmann, N.B. (2012). What is automatic self-regulation? *Zeitschrift für Psychologie, 220*, 147–156.

Forster, M., Leder, H., & Ansorge, U. (2013). It felt fluent, and I liked it: Subjective feeling of fluency rather than objective fluency determines liking. *Emotion, 13*, 280–289.

Forster, M., Leder, H., & Ansorge, U. (2016). Exploring the subjective feeling of fluency. *Experimental Psychology, 63*, 45–58.

Försterling, F. (1992). The Kelley model as an analysis of variance analogy: How far can it be taken? *Journal of Experimental Social Psychology, 28*, 475–490.

Försterling, F., & Weiner, B. (1981). Some determinants of task preference and the desire for information about the self. *European Journal of Social Psychology, 11*, 399–407.

Foulsham, T., Cheng, J.T., Tracy, J.L., Henrich, J., & Kingstone, A. (2010). Gaze allocation in a dynamic situation: Effects of social status and speaking. *Cognition, 117*, 319–331.

Fourakis, E., & Cone, J. (2020). Matters order: The role of information order on implicit impression formation. *Social Psychological and Personality Science, 11*, 56–63.

Fournier, M.A., Moskowitz, D.S., & Zuroff, D.C. (2008). Integrating dispositions, signatures, and the interpersonal domain. *Journal of Personality and Social Psychology, 94,* 531–545.

Fox, E., Russo, R., & Dutton, K. (2002). Attentional bias for threat: Evidence for delayed disengagement from emotional faces. *Cognition and Emotion, 16,* 355–379.

Frank, M.G., & Gilovich, T. (1988). The dark side of self- and social perception: Black uniforms and aggression in professional sports. *Journal of Personality and Social Psychology, 54,* 74–85.

Franklin, B. (1772/1956). *Mr. Franklin: A selection from his personal letters.* New Haven, CT: Yale University Press.

Freeman, J.B., & Ambady, N. (2011). A dynamic interactive theory of person construal. *Psychological Review, 118,* 247–249.

Freeman, J.B., & Johnson, K.L. (2016). More than meets the eye: Split-second social perception. *Trends in Cognitive Sciences, 20,* 362–374.

Freeman, J.B., Johnson, K.L., Ambady, N., & Rule, N.O. (2010). Sexual orientation perception involves gendered facial cues. *Personality and Social Psychology Bulletin, 36,* 1318–1331.

Freeman, J.B., Stolier, R.M., & Brooks, J.A. (2020). Dynamic interactive theory as a domain-general account of social perception. In B. Gawronski (Ed.), *Advances in experimental social psychology* (Vol. 61, pp. 237–287). New York, NY: Academic Press.

Freeman, J.B., Stolier, R.M., Ingbretsen, Z.A., & Hehman, E.A. (2014). Amygdala responsivity to high-level social information from unseen faces. *The Journal of Neuroscience, 34,* 10573–10581.

Frenda, S.J., Nichols, R.M., & Loftus, E.F. (2011). Current issues and advances in misinformation research. *Current Directions in Psychological Science, 20,* 20–23.

Freud, S. (1914). *The psychopathology of everyday life* (A.A. Brill, Trans.). New York, NY: Macmillan.

Friese, M., Hofmann, W., & Schmitt, M. (2008). When and why do implicit measures predict behaviour? Empirical evidence for the moderating role of opportunity, motivation, and process reliance. *European Review of Social Psychology, 19,* 285–338.

Friese, M., Hofmann, W., & Wänke, M. (2008). When impulses take over: Moderated predictive validity of explicit and implicit attitude measures in predicting food choice and consumption behaviour. *British Journal of Social Psychology, 47,* 397–419.

Friese, M., Wänke, M., & Plessner, H. (2006). Implicit consumer preferences and their influence on product choice. *Psychology & Marketing, 23,* 727–740.

Froehlich, L., Martiny, S.E., Deaux, K., & Mok, S.Y. (2016). "It's their responsibility, not ours": Stereotypes about competence and causal attributions for immigrants' academic underperformance. *Social Psychology, 47,* 74–86.

Fugelsang, J.A., Stein, C.B., Green, A.E., & Dunbar, K.N. (2004). Theory and data interactions of the scientific mind: Evidence from the molecular and the cognitive laboratory. *Canadian Journal of Experimental Psychology, 58,* 86–95.

Fujita, K., Henderson, M.D., Eng, J., Trope, Y., & Liberman, N. (2006). Spatial distance and mental construal of social events. *Psychological Science, 17,* 278–282.

Fukawa, N., & Niedrich, R.W. (2015). A fluency heuristic account of supraliminal prime effects on product preference. *Psychology & Marketing, 32,* 1061–1078.

Funder, D.C., & Colvin, C.R. (1988). Friends and strangers: Acquaintanceship, agreement, and the accuracy of personality judgment. *Journal of Personality and Social Psychology, 55,* 149–158.

Gabriel, U., Banse, R., & Hug, F. (2007). Predicting private and public helping behaviour by implicit attitudes and the motivation to control prejudiced reactions. *British Journal of Social Psychology, 46,* 365–382.

Gabrielcik, A., & Fazio, R.H. (1984). Priming and frequency estimation: A strict test of the availability heuristic. *Personality and Social Psychology Bulletin, 10,* 85–89.

Gabrieli, J.D. (1998). Cognitive neuroscience of human memory. *Annual Review of Psychology, 49,* 87–115.

Gaertner, L., & Insko, C.A. (2000). Intergroup discrimination in the minimal group paradigm: Categorization, reciprocation, or fear? *Journal of Personality and Social Psychology, 79,* 77–94.

Gaertner, L., Iuzzini, J., Witt, M.G., & Oriña, M.M. (2006). Us without them: Evidence for an intragroup origin of positive in-group regard. *Journal of Personality and Social Psychology, 90,* 426–439.

Gaertner, L., Sedikides, C., & Cai, H. (2012). Wanting to be great and better but not average: On the pancultural desire for self-enhancing and self-improving feedback. *Journal of Cross-Cultural Psychology, 43,* 521–526.

Gaertner, S.L., & Dovidio, J.F. (1986). The aversive form of racism. In J.F. Dovidio & S.L. Gaertner (Eds.), *Prejudice, discrimination, and racism* (pp. 61–89). Orlando, FL: Academic Press.

Gaertner, S.L., & Dovidio, J.F. (2000). *Reducing intergroup bias: The common ingroup identity model.* New York, NY: Psychology Press.

Gaertner, S.L., & McLaughlin, J.P. (1983). Racial stereotypes: Associations and ascriptions of positive and negative characteristics. *Social Psychology Quarterly, 46,* 23–30.

Gaertner, S.L., Mann, J., Murrell, A., & Dovidio, J.F. (1989). Reducing intergroup bias: The benefits of recategorization. *Journal of Personality and Social Psychology, 57,* 239–249.

Gaertner, S.L., Rust, M.C., Dovidio, J.F., Bachman, B.A., & Anastasio, P. (1994). The contact hypothesis: The role of a common ingroup identity on reducing intergroup bias. *Small Groups Research, 25,* 224–249.

Gaesser, B., & Schacter, D.L. (2014). Episodic simulation, memory, and empathy. *Proceedings of the National Academy of Sciences, 111,* 4415–4420.

Gaesser, B., Shimura, Y., & Cikara, M. (2020). Episodic simulation reduces intergroup bias in prosocial intentions and behavior. *Journal of Personality and Social Psychology, 118,* 683–705.

Gage, N.L., & Cronbach, L.J. (1955). Conceptual and methodological problems in interpersonal perception. *Psychological Review, 62,* 411–422.

Gainotti, G. (2007). Different patterns of famous people recognition disorders in patients with right and left anterior temporal lesions: A systematic review. *Neuropsychologia, 45,* 1591–1607.

Gaither, S.E., Pauker, K., Slepian, M.L., & Sommers, S.R. (2016). Social belonging motivates categorization of racially ambiguous faces. *Social Cognition, 34,* 97–118.

Galinsky, A.D., & Moskowitz, G.B. (2000). Perspective-taking: Decreasing stereotype expression, stereotype accessibility, and in-group favoritism. *Journal of Personality and Social Psychology, 78,* 708–724.

Galinsky, A.D., & Mussweiler, T. (2001). First offers as anchors: The role of perspective-taking and negotiator focus. *Journal of Personality and Social Psychology, 81,* 657–669.

Galinsky, A.D., Wang, C.S., & Ku, G. (2008). Perspective takers behave more stereotypically. *Journal of Personality and Social Psychology, 95,* 404–419.

Gallois, C., Ogay, T., & Giles, H. (2005). Communication accommodation theory. In W.B. Gundykunst (Ed.), *Theorizing about intercultural communication* (pp. 121–148). Thousand Oaks, CA: Sage.

Gangestad, S.W., & Haselton, M.G. (2015). Human estrus: Implications for relationship science. *Current Opinion in Psychology, 1,* 45–51.

Gantman, A.P. (2017). Why did I do that? Explaining actions activated outside of awareness. *Psychonomic Bulletin & Review, 24,* 1563–1572.

Garcia, S.M., Song, H., & Tesser, A. (2010). Tainted recommendations: The social comparison bias. *Organizational Behavior and Human Decision Processes, 113*, 97–101.

Garcia, S.M., Tor, A., & Schiff, T.M. (2013). The psychology of competition: A social comparison perspective. *Perspectives on Psychological Science, 8*, 634–650.

Garcia-Marques, L., & Garrido, M.V. (2015). From idiosyncratic impressions to distributed impressions of others: A case for collaborative person memory. In S.J. Stroessner & J.W. Sherman (Eds.), *Social perception from individuals to groups* (pp. 71–89). New York, NY: Psychology Press.

Garcia-Marques, L., & Hamilton, D.L. (1996). Resolving the apparent discrepancy between the incongruency effect and the expectancy-based illusory correlation effect: The TRAP model. *Journal of Personality and Social Psychology, 71*, 845–860.

Garcia-Marques, L., Ferreira, M.B., Nunes, L.D., Garrido, M.V., & Garcia-Marques, T. (2010). False memories and impressions of personality. *Social Cognition, 28*, 556–568.

Garcia-Marques, L., Garrido, M.V., Hamilton, D.L., & Ferreira, M.B. (2012). Effects of correspondence between encoding and retrieval organization in social memory. *Journal of Experimental Social Psychology, 48*, 200–206.

Garcia-Marques, L., Hamilton, D.L., & Maddox, K.B. (2002). Exhaustive and heuristic retrieval processes in person cognition: Further tests of the TRAP Model. *Journal of Personality and Social Psychology, 82*, 193–207.

Garcia-Marques, L., Santos, A.S.C., & Mackie, D.M. (2006). Stereotypes: Static abstractions or dynamic knowledge structures? *Journal of Personality and Social Psychology, 91*, 814–831.

Garcia-Retamero, R., Takezawa, M., & Gigerenzer, G. (2009). Does imitation benefit cue order learning? *Experimental Psychology, 56*, 307–320.

Gardner, H. (1985). *The mind's new science: A history of the cognitive revolution.* New York, NY: Basic Books.

Gardner, W.L., Pickett, C.L., & Brewer, M.B. (2000). Social exclusion and selective memory: How the need to belong influences memory for social events. *Personality and Social Psychology Bulletin, 26*, 486–496.

Garrido, M.V., Garcia-Marques, L., & Hamilton, D.L. (2012a). Enhancing the comparability between part-list cueing and collaborative recall. *Experimental Psychology, 59*, 199–205.

Garrido, M.V., Garcia-Marques, L., & Hamilton, D.L. (2012b). Hard to recall but easy to judge: Retrieval strategies in social information processing. *Social Cognition, 30*, 56–70.

Garrido, M.V., Garcia-Marques, L., Hamilton, D.L., & Ferreira, M.B. (2012). Person memory: A matter of non-collaboration? In N. Payette & B. Hardy-Vallee (Eds.), *Connected minds: Cognition and interaction in the social world* (pp. 134–145). Newcastle: Cambridge Scholars.

Gavanski, I., & Wells, G.L. (1989). Counterfactual processing of normal and exceptional events. *Journal of Experimental Social Psychology, 25*, 314–325.

Gawronski, B. (2004). Theory-based bias correction in dispositional inference: The fundamental attribution error is dead, long live the correspondence bias. *European Review of Social Psychology, 15*, 183–217.

Gawronski, B. (2007). Editorial: Attitudes can be measured! But what is an attitude? *Social Cognition, 25*, 573–581.

Gawronski, B., & Bodenhausen, G.V. (2006). Associative and propositional processes in evaluation: An integrative review of implicit and explicit attitude change. *Psychological Bulletin, 132*, 692–731.

Gawronski, B., & Bodenhausen, G.V. (2007). Unraveling the processes underlying evaluation: Attitudes from the perspective of the APE model. *Social Cognition, 25*, 687–717.

Gawronski, B., & Bodenhausen, G.V. (2011). The associative-propositional evaluation model: Theory, evidence, and open questions. In M.P. Zanna (Ed.), *Advances in experimental social psychology* (Vol. 44, pp. 59–127). New York, NY: Academic Press.

Gawronski, B., & Bodenhausen, G.V. (2014a). Implicit and explicit evaluation: A brief review of the associative-propositional evaluation model. *Social and Personality Psychology Compass, 8,* 448–462.

Gawronski, B., & Bodenhausen, G.V. (2014b). The associative-propositional evaluation model: Operating principles and operating conditions of evaluation. In J.W. Sherman, B. Gawronski, & Y. Trope (Eds.), *Dual process theories of the social mind* (pp. 188–203). New York, NY: Guilford Press.

Gawronski, B., & Bodenhausen, G.V. (2018). Evaluative conditioning from the perspective of the associative-propositional evaluation model. *Social Psychological Bulletin, 13,* 1–33.

Gawronski, B., & Creighton, L.A. (2013). Dual process theories. In D.E. Carlston (Ed.), *The Oxford handbook of social cognition* (pp. 282–312). New York, NY: Oxford University Press.

Gawronski, B., & Hahn, A. (2019). Implicit measures: Procedures, use, and interpretation. In H. Blanton, J.M. LaCroix, & G.D. Webster (Eds.), *Measurement in social psychology* (pp. 29–55). New York, NY: Routledge.

Gawronski, B., & Quinn, K.A. (2013). Guilty by mere similarity: Assimilative effects of facial resemblance on automatic evaluation. *Journal of Experimental Social Psychology, 49,* 120–125.

Gawronski, B., & Strack, F. (2004). On the propositional nature of cognitive consistency: Dissonance changes explicit, but not implicit attitudes. *Journal of Experimental Social Psychology, 40,* 535–542.

Gawronski, B., Deutsch, R., Mbirkou, S., Seibt, B., & Strack, F. (2008). When "just say no" is not enough: Affirmation versus negation training and the reduction of automatic stereotype activation. *Journal of Experimental Social Psychology, 44,* 370–377.

Gawronski, B., Peters, K.R., Brochu, P.M., & Strack, F. (2008). Understanding the relations between different forms of racial prejudice: A cognitive consistency perspective. *Personality and Social Psychology Bulletin, 34,* 648–665.

Gawronski, B., Walther, E., & Blank, H. (2005). Cognitive consistency and the formation of interpersonal attitudes: Cognitive balance affects the encoding of social information. *Journal of Experimental Social Psychology, 41,* 618–626.

Geiger, W., Harwood, J., & Hummert, M.L. (2006). College students' multiple stereotypes of lesbians. *Journal of Homosexuality, 51,* 165–182.

Gelman, S.A. (2003). *The essential child: Origins of essentialism in everyday thought.* New York, NY: Oxford University Press.

Gendolla, G.H.E., & Koller, M. (2001). Surprise and causal search: How are they affected by outcome valence and importance? *Motivation and Emotion, 24,* 237–250.

Gendolla, G.H.E., & Silvestrini, N. (2010). The implicit "go": Masked action cues directly mobilize mental effort. *Psychological Science, 21,* 1389–1393.

Geraerts, E., Bernstein, D.M., Merckelbach, H., Linders, C., Raymaekers, L., & Loftus, E.F. (2008). Lasting false beliefs and their behavioral consequences. *Psychological Science, 19,* 749–753.

Gerber, J.P., Wheeler, L., & Suls, J. (2018). A social comparison theory meta-analysis 60+ years on. *Psychological Bulletin, 144,* 177–197.

Gergen, K.J. (1968). Personal consistency and the presentation of self. In C. Gordon & K.J. Gergen (Eds.), *The self in social interaction* (pp. 299–308). New York, NY: Wiley.

Gerger, G., Leder, H., Tinio, P.P.L., & Schacht, A. (2011). Faces versus patterns: Exploring aesthetic reactions using facial EMG. *Psychology of Aesthetics, Creativity, and the Arts, 5,* 241–250.

Gibson, C.E., Losee, J., & Vitiello, C. (2014). A replication attempt of stereotype susceptibility (Shih, Pittinsky, & Ambady, 1999): Identity salience and shifts in quantitative performance. *Social Psychology, 45,* 194–198.

Gigerenzer, G. (2007). *Gut feelings: The intelligence of the unconscious.* New York, NY: Viking.

Gigerenzer, G. (2008). Why heuristics work. *Perspectives on Psychological Science, 3,* 20–29.

Gigerenzer, G. (2010). Moral satisficing: Rethinking moral behavior as bounded rationality. *Topics in Cognitive Science, 2,* 528–554.

Gigerenzer, G. (2015). *Simply rational: Decision making in the real world.* New York, NY: Oxford University Press.

Gigerenzer, G., & Goldstein, D.G. (1996). Reasoning the fast and frugal way: Models of bounded rationality. *Psychological Review, 103,* 650–669.

Gigerenzer, G., & Goldstein, D.G. (2011). The recognition heuristic: A decade of research. *Judgment and Decision Making, 6,* 100–121.

Gigerenzer, G., & Selten, R. (2002). *Bounded rationality: The adaptive toolbox.* Cambridge, MA: MIT Press.

Gigerenzer, G., Hertwig, R., & Pachur, T. (Eds.) (2011). *Heuristics: The foundations of adaptive behavior.* New York, NY: Oxford University Press.

Gilbert, D.T. (1989). Thinking lightly about others: Automatic components of the social inference process. In J.S. Uleman & J.A. Bargh (Eds.), *Unintended thought* (pp. 189–211). New York, NY: Guilford Press.

Gilbert, D.T. (1998). Ordinary personology. In D.T. Gilbert, S.T., Fiske, & G. Lindzey (Eds.), *The handbook of social psychology* (4th ed., pp. 89–150). New York, NY: McGraw-Hill.

Gilbert, D.T., & Hixon, J.G. (1991). The trouble of thinking: Activation and application of stereotypic beliefs. *Journal of Personality and Social Psychology, 60,* 509–517.

Gilbert, D.T., & Malone, P.S. (1995). The correspondence bias. *Psychological Bulletin, 117,* 21–38.

Gilbert, D.T., Driver-Linn, E., & Wilson, T.D. (2002). The trouble with Vronsky: Impact bias in the forecasting of future affective states. In L.F. Barrett & P. Salovey (Eds.), *The wisdom in feeling: Psychological processes in emotional intelligence* (pp. 114–143). New York, NY: Guilford Press

Gilbert, D.T., Pelham, B.W., & Krull, D.S. (1988). On cognitive busyness: When person perceivers meet persons perceived. *Journal of Personality and Social Psychology, 54,* 733–740.

Gilbert, D.T., Pinel, E.C., Wilson, T.D., Blumberg, S.J., & Wheatley, T.P. (1998). Immune neglect: A source of durability bias in affective forecasting. *Journal of Personality and Social Psychology, 75,* 617–638.

Gilbert, G.M. (1951). Stereotype persistence and change among college students. *Journal of Abnormal and Social Psychology, 46,* 245–254.

Giles, H., & Coupland, N. (1991). *Language: Context and consequences.* Milton Keynes: Open University Press.

Gill, M.J., & Cerce, S.C. (2017). He never willed to have the will he has: Historicist narratives, "civilized" blame, and the need to distinguish two notions of free will. *Journal of Personality and Social Psychology, 112,* 361–382.

Gill, M.J., & Getty, P.D. (2016). On shifting the blame to humanity: Historicist narratives regarding transgressors evoke compassion for the transgressor but disdain for humanity. *British Journal of Social Psychology, 55,* 773–791.

Gill, M.J., & Ungson, N.D. (2018). How much blame does he truly deserve? Historicist narratives engender uncertainty about blameworthiness, facilitating motivated cognition in moral judgment. *Journal of Experimental Social Psychology, 77,* 11–23.

Gilovich, T. (1990). Differential construal and the false consensus effect. *Journal of Personality and Social Psychology, 59,* 623–634.

Gilovich, T. (1991). *How we know what isn't so.* New York, NY: Free Press.

Gilovich, T.D., & Griffin, D.W. (2010). Judgment and decision-making. In S.T. Fiske, D.T. Gilbert, & G. Lindzey (Eds.), *The handbook of social psychology* (5th ed., Vol. 1, pp. 542–580). Hoboken, NJ: Wiley.

Gilovich, T., & Savitsky, K. (1999). The spotlight effect and the illusion of transparency: Egocentric assessments of how we are seen by others. *Current Directions in Psychological Science, 8*, 165–168.

Gilovich, T., Medvec, V.H., & Savitsky, K. (2000). The spotlight effect in social judgment: Bias in estimates of the salience of one's own actions and appearance. *Journal of Personality and Social Psychology, 78*, 211–222.

Gilovich, T., Vallone, R., & Tversky, A. (1985). The hot hand in basketball: On the misperception of random sequences. *Cognitive Psychology, 17*, 295–314.

Ginossar, Z., & Trope, Y. (1987). Problem solving in judgment under uncertainty. *Journal of Personality and Social Psychology, 52*, 464–474.

Glaser, J., & Knowles, E.D. (2008). Implicit motivation to control prejudice. *Journal of Experimental Social Psychology, 44*, 164–172.

Glasman, L.R., & Albarracín, D. (2006). Forming attitudes that predict future behavior: A meta-analysis of the attitude–behavior relation. *Psychological Bulletin, 132*, 778–822.

Glassman, N.S., & Andersen, S.M. (1999). Activating transference without consciousness: Using significant-other representations to go beyond subliminally given information. *Journal of Personality and Social Psychology, 77*, 1146–1162.

Gleicher, F., Kost, K.A., Baker, S.M., Strathman, A.J., Richman, S.A., & Sherman, S.J. (1990). The role of counterfactual thinking in judgments of affect. *Personality and Social Psychology Bulletin, 16*, 284–295.

Glick, P., & Fiske, S.T. (1996). The ambivalent sexism inventory: Differentiating hostile and benevolent sexism. *Journal of Personality and Social Psychology, 70*, 491–512.

Glick, P., & Fiske, S.T. (1997). Hostile and benevolent sexism: Measuring ambivalent sexist attitudes toward women. *Psychology of Women Quarterly, 21*, 119–135.

Glick, P., & Fiske, S.T. (2001). An ambivalent alliance: Hostile and benevolent sexism as complementary justifications for gender inequality. *American Psychologist, 56*, 109–118.

Glick, P., & Fiske, S.T. (2011). Ambivalent sexism revisited. *Psychology of Women Quarterly, 35*, 530–535.

Glocker, M.L., Langleben, D.D., Ruparel, K., Loughead, J.W., Gur, R.C., & Sachser, N. (2009). Baby schema in infant faces induces cuteness perception and motivation for caretaking in adults. *Ethology, 115*, 257–263.

Godin, G., & Kok, G. (1996). The theory of planned behavior: A review of its applications to health-related behaviors. *American Journal of Health Promotion, 11*, 87–98.

Goethals, G.R. (1986). Fabricating and ignoring social reality: Self-serving estimates of consensus. In J.M. Olson, C.P. Herman, & M.P. Zanna (Eds.), *Social comparison and relative deprivation: The Ontario symposium* (Vol. 4, pp. 135–157). Hillsdale, NJ: Lawrence Erlbaum.

Goethals, G.R., Messick, D.M., & Allison, S.T. (1991). The uniqueness bias: Studies of constructive social comparison. In J. Suls & T.A. Wills (Eds.), *Social comparison: Contemporary theory and research* (pp. 149–176). Hillsdale, NJ: Lawrence Erlbaum.

Goff, P.A., Eberhardt, J.L., Williams, M.J., & Jackson, M.C. (2008). Not yet human: Implicit knowledge, historical dehumanization, and contemporary consequences. *Journal of Personality and Social Psychology, 94*, 292–306.

Goff, P.A., Thomas, M.A., & Jackson, M.C. (2008). "Ain't I a woman?": Towards an intersectional approach to person perception and group-based harms. *Sex Roles, 59*, 392–403.

Gold, R.S. (2002). The effects of mood states on the AIDS-related judgements of gay men. *International Journal of STD & AIDS, 13,* 475–481.

Goldinger, S.D., Papesh, M.H., Barnhart, A.S., Hansen, W.A., & Hout, M.C. (2016). The poverty of embodied cognition. *Psychonomic Bulletin & Review, 23,* 959–978.

Goldstein, D.G., & Gigerenzer, G. (2002). Models of ecological rationality: The recognition heuristic. *Psychological Review, 109,* 75–90.

Gollwitzer, P.M. (1993). Goal achievement: The role of intentions. *European Review of Social Psychology, 4,* 141–185.

Gollwitzer, P.M. (1996). The volitional benefits of planning. In P.M. Gollwitzer and J.A. Bargh (Eds.), *The psychology of action: Linking cognition and motivation to behavior* (pp. 287–312). New York, NY: Guilford Press.

Gollwitzer, P.M. (1999). Implementation intentions: Strong effects of simple plans. *American Psychologist, 54,* 493–503.

Gollwitzer, P.M., & Brandstätter, V. (1997). Implementation intentions and effective goal pursuit. *Journal of Personality and Social Psychology, 73,* 186–199.

Gollwitzer, P.M., & Sheeran, P. (2006). Implementation intentions and goal achievement: A meta-analysis of effects and processes. In M.P. Zanna (Ed.), *Advances in experimental social psychology* (Vol. 38, pp. 69–119). New York, NY: Academic Press.

Gollwitzer, P.M., Bayer, U.C., & McCulloch, K.C. (2005) The control of the unwanted. In R.R. Hassin, J.S. Uleman, & J.A. Bargh (Eds.), *The new unconscious* (pp. 485–515). New York, NY: Oxford University Press.

Golub, S., & Harrington, D.M. (1981). Premenstrual and menstrual mood changes in adolescent women. *Journal of Personality and Social Psychology, 41,* 961–965.

Gonsalkorale, K., Sherman, J.W., Allen, T.J., Klauer, K.C., & Amodio, D.M. (2011). Accounting for successful control of implicit racial bias: The roles of association activation, response monitoring, and overcoming bias. *Personality and Social Psychology Bulletin, 37,* 1534–1545.

Gonsalkorale, K., von Hippel, W., Sherman, J.W., & Klauer, K.C. (2009). Bias and regulation of bias in intergroup interactions: Implicit attitudes toward Muslims and interaction quality. *Journal of Experimental Social Psychology, 45,* 161–166.

Gonzalez-Vallejo, C., Lassiter, G.D., Bellezza, F.S., & Lindberg, M.J. (2008). "Save angels perhaps": A critical examination of unconscious thought theory and the deliberation-without-attention effect. *Review of General Psychology, 12,* 282–296.

Goodale, B.M., Alt, N.P., Lick, D.J., & Johnson, K.L. (2018). Groups at a glance: Perceivers infer social belonging in a group based on perceptual summaries of sex ratio. *Journal of Experimental Psychology: General, 147,* 1660–1676.

Goodman, G.S., Gonzalves, L., & Wolpe, S. (2019). False memories and true memories of childhood trauma: Balancing the risks. *Clinical Psychological Science, 7,* 29–31.

Goodwin, S.A., Gubin, A., Fiske, S.T., & Yzerbyt, V.Y. (2000). Power can bias impression processes: Stereotyping subordinates by default and by design. *Group Processes and Intergroup Relations, 3,* 227–256.

Goren, C.C., Sarty, M., & Wu, P.Y.K. (1975). Visual following and pattern discrimination of face-like stimuli by newborn infants. *Pediatrics, 56,* 544–549.

Gorn, G.J, Jiang, Y., & Johar, G.V. (2008). Babyfaces, trait inferences, and company evaluations in a public relations crisis. *Journal of Consumer Research, 35,* 36–49.

Govorun, O., & Payne, B.K. (2006). Ego-depletion and prejudice: Separating automatic and controlled components. *Social Cognition, 24,* 111–136.

Govorun, O., Fuegen, K., & Payne, B.K. (2006). Stereotypes focus defensive projection. *Personality and Social Psychology Bulletin, 32,* 781–793.

Graefe, A., & Armstrong, J.S. (2012). Predicting elections from the most important issue: A test of the take-the-best heuristic. *Journal of Behavioral Decision Making, 25,* 41–48.

Gräf, M., & Unkelbach, C. (2016). Halo effects in trait assessment depend on information valence: Why being honest makes you industrious, but lying does not make you lazy. *Personality and Social Psychology Bulletin, 42,* 290–310.

Graf, P., & Schacter, D.L. (1985). Implicit and explicit memory for new associations in normal and amnesic subjects. *Journal of Experimental Psychology: Learning, Memory, and Cognition, 11,* 501–518.

Grafton, S. (2015). *X.* New York, NY: G.P. Putnam.

Gramzow, R.H. (2011). Academic exaggeration: Pushing self-enhancement boundaries. In M.D. Alicke & C. Sedikides (Eds.), *Handbook of self-enhancement and self-protection* (pp. 455–471). New York, NY: Guilford Press.

Granot, Y., Balcetis, E., Schneider, K.E., & Tyler, T.R. (2014). Justice is not blind: Visual attention exaggerates effects of group identification on legal punishment. *Journal of Experimental Psychology: General, 143,* 2196–2208.

Gray, H.M., Ambady, N., Lowenthal, W.T., & Deldin, P. (2004). P300 as an index of attention to self-relevant stimuli. *Journal of Experimental Social Psychology, 40,* 216–224.

Green, A.R., Carney, D.R., Palin, D.J., Ngo, L.H., Raymond, K.L., Iezzoni, L.I., & Banaji, M.R. (2007). Implicit bias among physicians and its prediction of thrombolysis decisions for black and white patients. *Journal of General Internal Medicine, 22,* 1231–1238.

Green, E.G.T., Krings, F., Staerklé, C., Bangerter, A., Clémence, A., Wagner-Egger, P., & Bornand, T. (2010). Keeping the vermin out: Perceived disease threat and ideological orientations as predictors of exclusionary immigration attitudes. *Journal of Community & Applied Social Psychology, 20,* 299–316.

Green, J.D., Sedikides, C., & Gregg, A.P. (2008). Forgotten but not gone: The recall and recognition of self-threatening memories.

Journal of Experimental Social Psychology, 44, 547–561.

Greenberg, J., & Pyszczynski, T. (1985). Compensatory self-inflation: A response to the threat to self-regard of public failure. *Journal of Personality and Social Psychology, 49,* 273–280.

Greene, J.D. (2014). The cognitive neuroscience of moral judgment and decision making. In M.S. Gazzaniga & G.R. Mangun (Eds.), *The cognitive neurosciences* (pp. 1013–1023). Cambridge, MA: MIT Press.

Greene, J.D., Morelli, S.A., Lowenberg, K., Nystrom, L.E., & Cohen, J.D. (2008). Cognitive load selectively interferes with utilitarian moral judgment. *Cognition, 107,* 1144–1154.

Greenwald, A.G. (1968). Cognitive learning, cognitive response to persuasion, and attitude change. In A.G. Greenwald, T.C. Brock, & T.M. Ostrom (Eds.), *Psychological foundations of attitudes* (pp. 147–170). New York, NY: Academic Press.

Greenwald, A.G. (1976). An editorial. *Journal of Personality and Social Psychology, 33,* 1–7.

Greenwald, A.G. (1989). Why attitudes are important: Defining attitude and attitude theory 20 years later. In A.R. Pratkanis, S.J. Breckler, & A.G. Greenwald (Eds.), *The third Ohio State University volume on attitudes and persuasion: Attitude structure and function* (pp. 429–440). Hillsdale, NJ: Lawrence Erlbaum.

Greenwald, A.G., & Banaji, M.R. (1995). Implicit social cognition: Attitudes, self-esteem, and stereotypes. *Psychological Review, 102,* 4–27.

Greenwald, A.G., & Banaji, M.R. (2017). The implicit revolution: Reconceiving the relation between conscious and unconscious. *American Psychologist, 72,* 861–871.

Greenwald, A.G., & De Houwer, J. (2017). Unconscious conditioning: Demonstration of existence and difference from conscious conditioning. *Journal of Experimental Psychology: General, 146,* 1705–1721.

Greenwald, A.G., & Lai, C.K. (2020). Implicit social cognition. *Annual Review of Psychology, 71*, 419–445.

Greenwald, A.G., & Pettigrew, T.F. (2014). With malice toward none and charity for some: Ingroup favoritism enables discrimination. *American Psychologist, 69*, 669–684.

Greenwald, A.G., & Pratkanis, A.R. (1984). The self. In R.S. Wyer, Jr. & T.K. Srull (Eds.), *Handbook of social cognition* (Vol. 3, pp. 129–178). Mahwah, NJ: Lawrence Erlbaum.

Greenwald, A.G., Banaji, M.R., Rudman, L.A., Farnham, S.D., Nosek, B.A., & Mellot, D.S. (2002). A unified theory of implicit attitudes, stereotypes, self-esteem, and self-concept. *Psychological Review, 109*, 3–25.

Greenwald, A.G., Carnot, C.G., Beach, R., & Young, B. (1987). Increasing voting behavior by asking people if they expect to vote. *Journal of Applied Psychology, 72*, 315–318.

Greenwald, A.G., McGhee, D.E., & Schwartz, J.L.K. (1998). Measuring individual differences in implicit cognition: The Implicit Association Test. *Journal of Personality and Social Psychology, 74*, 1464–1480.

Greenwald, A.G., Oakes, M.A., & Hoffman, H.G. (2003). Targets of discrimination: Effects of race on responses to weapons holders. *Journal of Experimental Social Psychology, 39*, 399–405.

Greenwald, A.G., Poehlman, T.A., Uhlmann, E., & Banaji, M.R. (2009). Understanding and using the Implicit Association Test: III. Meta-analysis of predictive validity. *Journal of Personality and Social Psychology, 97*, 17–41.

Greenwald, A.G., Smith, C.T., Sriram, N., Bar-Anan, Y., & Nosek, B.A. (2009). Implicit race attitudes predicted vote in the 2008 U.S. presidential election. *Analyses of Social Issues and Public Policy, 9*, 341–253.

Gregg, A.P., Sedikides, C., & Gebauer, J.E. (2011). Dynamics of identity: Between self-enhancement and self-assessment. In S. Schwartz, K. Luyckx, & V. Vignoles (Eds.), *Handbook of identity theory and research* (pp. 305–327). New York, NY: Springer.

Gregory, W.L., Cialdini, R.B., & Carpenter, K.M. (1982). Self-relevant scenarios as mediators of likelihood estimates and compliance: Does imagining make it so? *Journal of Personality and Social Psychology, 43*, 89–99.

Grice, H.P. (1975). Logic and conversation. In P. Cole & J.L. Morgan (Eds.), *Syntax and semantics 3: Speech acts* (pp. 41–58). New York, NY: Academic Press.

Gross, J., Jack, F., Davis, N., & Hayne, H. (2013). Do children recall the birth of a younger sibling? Implications for the study of childhood amnesia. *Memory, 21*, 336–346.

Grove, W.M., Zald, D.H., Lebow, B.S., Snitz, B.E., & Nelson, C. (2000). Clinical versus mechanical prediction: A meta-analysis. *Psychological Assessment, 12*, 19–30.

Guenther, C.L., & Alicke, M.D. (2010). Deconstructing the better-than-average effect. *Journal of Personality and Social Psychology, 99*, 755–770.

Guglielmo, S. (2015). Moral judgment as information processing: An integrative review. *Frontiers in Psychology, 6*, 1637.

Guinote, A. (2004). Group size, outcome dependency, and power: Effects on perceived and objective group variability. In V. Yzerbyt, C.M. Judd, & O. Corneille (Eds.), *The psychology of group perception: Perceived variability, entitativity, and essentialism* (pp. 221–236). New York, NY: Psychology Press.

Guinote, A. (2007). Power affects basic cognition: Increased attentional inhibition and flexibility. *Journal of Experimental and Social Psychology, 43*, 685–697.

Gunderson, E.A., Sorhagen, N.S., Gripshover, S.J., Dweck, C.S., Goldin-Meadow, S., & Levine, S.C. (2018). Parent praise to toddlers predicts fourth grade academic achievement via children's incremental mindsets. *Developmental Psychology, 54*, 397–409.

Haddock, G. (2002). It's easy to like or dislike: Accessibility experiences and the favourability of attitude judgments. *British Journal of Psychology*, *93*, 257–267.

Hagiwara, N., Kashy, D.A., & Cesario, J. (2012). The independent effects of skin tone and facial features on Whites' affective reactions to Blacks. *Journal of Experimental Social Psychology*, *48*, 892–898.

Hahn, A., & Gawronski, B. (2018). Implicit social cognition. In J.T. Wixted (Ed.), *The Stevens' handbook of experimental psychology and cognitive neuroscience*, Vol. 4 (pp. 395–427). New York, NY: Wiley.

Haidt, J. (2001). The emotional dog and its rational tail: A social intuitionist approach to moral judgment. *Psychological Review*, *108*, 814–834.

Haimovitz, K., & Dweck, C.S. (2016). Parents' views of failure predict children's fixed and growth intelligence mind-sets. *Psychological Science*, *27*, 859–869.

Hajcak, G. (2012). What we've learned from mistakes: Insights from error-related brain activity. *Current Directions in Psychological Science*, *21*, 101–106.

Hajcak, G., & Foti, D. (2008). Errors are aversive: Defensive motivation and the error-related negativity. *Psychological Science*, *19*, 103–108.

Hajibayova, L. (2013). Basic-level categories: A review. *Journal of Information Science*, *39*, 676–687.

Halberstadt, J., & Rhodes, G. (2000). The attractiveness of nonface averages: Implications for an evolutionary explanation of the attractiveness of average faces. *Psychological Science*, *4*, 285–289.

Halberstadt, J., & Winkielman, P. (2014). Easy on the eyes, or hard to categorize: Classification difficulty decreases the appeal of facial blends. *Journal of Experimental Social Psychology*, *50*, 175–183.

Halberstadt, J., Sherman, S.J., & Sherman, J.W. (2011). Why Barack Obama is black: A cognitive account of hypodescent. *Psychological Science*, *22*, 29–33.

Haley, H., & Sidanius, J. (2006). The positive and negative framing of affirmative action: A group dominance perspective. *Personality and Social Psychology Bulletin*, *32*, 656–668.

Hall, E.V., & Livingston, R.W. (2012). The hubris penalty: Biased responses to "celebration" displays of black football players. *Journal of Experimental Social Psychology*, *48*, 899–904.

Hall, N.R., & Crisp, R.J. (2008). Assimilation and contrast to group primes: The moderating role of ingroup identification. *Journal of Experimental Social Psychology*, *44*, 344–353.

Halpern, D. (2016). *Inside the nudge unit: How small changes can make a big difference.* New York, NY: Random House.

Ham, J., & van den Bos, K. (2008). Not fair for me! The influence of personal relevance on social justice inferences. *Journal of Experimental Social Psychology*, *44*, 699–705.

Ham, J., & Vonk, R. (2003). Smart and easy: Co-occurring activation of spontaneous trait inferences and spontaneous situational inferences. *Journal of Experimental Social Psychology*, *39*, 434–447.

Hamilton, D.L. (Ed.) (1981). *Cognitive processes in stereotyping and intergroup behavior.* Hillsdale, NJ: Lawrence Erlbaum.

Hamilton, D.L. (1988). Causal attribution viewed from an information processing perspective. In D. Bar-Tal & A.W. Kruglanski (Eds.), *The social psychology of knowledge* (pp. 359–385). New York, NY: Cambridge University Press.

Hamilton, D.L. (1989). Understanding impression formation: What has memory research contributed? In P.R. Solomon, G.R. Goethals, C.M. Kelley, & B.R. Stephens (Eds.), *Memory: Interdisciplinary approaches* (pp. 221–242). New York, NY: Springer.

Hamilton, D.L. (1998). Dispositional and attributional inferences in person perception. In J.M. Darley & J. Cooper (Eds.), *Attribution and social interaction: The legacy of Edward E. Jones.* Washington, DC: American Psychological Association.

Hamilton, D.L. (2007). Understanding the complexities of group perception: Broadening the domain. *European Journal of Social Psychology*, *37*, 1077–1101.

Hamilton, D.L., & Carlston, D.E. (2013). The emergence of social cognition. In D.E. Carlston (Ed.), *The Oxford handbook of social cognition* (pp. 16–32). New York, NY: Oxford University Press.

Hamilton, D.L., & Garcia-Marques, L. (2003). The effects of expectancies on the representation, retrieval and use of social information. In G.V. Bodenhausen & A.J. Lambert (Eds.), *Foundations of social cognition: A festschrift in honor of Robert S. Wyer, Jr.* (pp. 25–50). Hillsdale, NJ: Lawrence Erlbaum.

Hamilton, D.L., & Gifford, R.K. (1976). Illusory correlation in interpersonal perception: A cognitive basis of stereotypic judgments. *Journal of Experimental Social Psychology*, *12*, 392–407.

Hamilton, D.L., & Huffman, L.J. (1971). Generality of impression-formation processes for evaluative and nonevaluative judgments. *Journal of Personality and Social Psychology*, *20*, 200–207.

Hamilton, D.L., & Rose, T.L. (1980). Illusory correlation and the maintenance of stereotypic beliefs. *Journal of Personality and Social Psychology*, *39*, 832–845.

Hamilton, D.L., & Sherman, J.W. (1994). Stereotypes. In R.S. Wyer, Jr. & T.K. Srull (Eds.), *Handbook of social cognition* (2nd ed., Vol. 2, pp. 1–68). Mahwah, NJ: Lawrence Erlbaum.

Hamilton, D.L., & Sherman, S.J. (1996). Perceiving persons and groups. *Psychological Review*, *103*, 336–355.

Hamilton, D.L., & Trolier, T.K. (1986). Stereotypes and stereotyping: An overview of the cognitive approach. In S.L. Gaertner & J.F. Dovidio (Eds.), *Prejudice, discrimination, and stereotyping* (pp. 127–157). New York, NY: Academic Press.

Hamilton, D.L., & Zanna, M.P. (1972). Differential weighting of favorable and unfavorable attributes in impressions of personality.

Journal of Experimental Research in Personality, *6*, 204–212.

Hamilton, D.L., & Zanna, M.P. (1974). Context effects in impression formation: Changes in connotative meaning. *Journal of Personality and Social Psychology*, *29*, 649–654.

Hamilton, D.L., Chen, J.M., Ko, D., Winczewski, L., Banerji, I., & Thurston, J.A. (2015). Sowing the seeds of stereotypes: Spontaneous inferences about groups. *Journal of Personality and Social Psychology*, *109*, 569–588.

Hamilton, D.L., Chen, J.M., & Way, N. (2011). Dynamic aspects of entitativity: From group perception to social interaction. In R.M. Kramer, G.J. Leonardelli, & R.W. Livingston (Eds.), *Social cognition, social identity, and intergroup relations: A festschrift in honor of Marilynn Brewer* (pp. 27–52). New York, NY: Psychology Press.

Hamilton, D.L., Driscoll, D.M., & Worth, L.T. (1989). Cognitive organization of impressions: Effects of incongruency in complex representations. *Journal of Personality and Social Psychology*, *57*, 925–939.

Hamilton, D.L., Dugan, P.M., & Trolier, T.K. (1985). The formation of stereotypic beliefs: Further evidence for distinctiveness-based illusory correlations. *Journal of Personality and Social Psychology*, *48*, 5–17.

Hamilton, D.L., Gibbons, P., Stroessner, S.J., & Sherman, J.W. (1992). Stereotypes and language use. In G.R. Semin & K. Fiedler (Eds.), *Language and social cognition* (pp. 102–128). London: Sage.

Hamilton, D.L., Grubb, P.D., Acorn, D.A., Trolier, T.K., & Carpenter, S. (1990). Attribution difficulty and memory for attribution-relevant information. *Journal of Personality and Social Psychology*, *59*, 891–898.

Hamilton, D.L., Katz, L.B., & Leirer, V.O. (1980a). Cognitive representation of personality impressions: Organizational processes in first impression formation. *Journal of Personality and Social Psychology*, *39*, 1050–1063.

Hamilton, D.L., Katz, L.B., & Leirer, V.O. (1980b). Organizational processes in impression formation. In R. Hastie, T.M. Ostrom,

E.B. Ebbesen, R.S. Wyer, Jr., D.L. Hamilton, & D.E. Carlston (Eds.), *Person memory: The cognitive basis of social perception* (pp. 121–153). Hillsdale, NJ: Lawrence Erlbaum.

Hamilton, D.L., Levine, J.M., & Thurston, J.A. (2008). Perceiving continuity and change in groups. In F. Sani (Ed.), *Self continuity: Individual and collective perspectives* (pp. 117–130). New York, NY: Psychology Press.

Hamilton, D.L., Sherman, S.J., & Castelli, L. (2002). A group by any other name: The role of entitativity in group perception. In W. Stroebe & M. Hewstone (Eds.), *European review of social psychology* (Vol. 12, pp. 139–166). Chichester: Wiley.

Hamilton, D.L., Sherman, S.J., & Rodgers, J.S. (2004). Perceiving the groupness of groups: Entitativity, homogeneity, essentialism, and stereotypes. In V. Yzerbyt, C.M. Judd, & O. Corneille (Eds.), T*he psychology of group perception: Perceived variability, entitativity, and essentialism* (pp. 39–60). New York, NY: Psychology Press.

Hamilton, D.L., Sherman, S.J., Way, N., & Percy, E.J. (2015). Convergence and divergence in perceptions of persons and groups. In M. Mikulincer, P.R. Shaver (Eds.), J.F. Dovidio, & Simpson, J.A. (Assoc. Eds.), *APA handbook of personality and social psychology: Vol. 2. Group processes* (pp. 229–261). Washington, DC: American Psychological Association.

Hamilton, D.L., Stroessner, S.J., & Driscoll, D.M. (1994). Social cognition and the study of stereotyping. In P.G. Devine, D.L. Hamilton, & T.M. Ostrom (Eds.), *Social cognition: Impact on social psychology* (pp. 291–321). San Diego, CA: Academic Press.

Hammond, P.J. (1997). Rationality in economics. *Rivista Internazionale di Scienze Sociali, Anno CV*, 247–288.

Hampson, S.E., John, O.P., & Goldberg, L.R. (1986). Category breadth and hierarchical structure in personality: Studies of asymmetries in judgments of trait implications. *Journal of Personality and Social Psychology, 51*, 37–54.

Handley, I.M., & Lassiter, G.D. (2002). Mood and information processing: When happy and sad look the same. *Motivation and Emotion, 26*, 223–255.

Hansen, C.H., & Hansen, R.D. (1988). Finding the face in the crowd: An anger superiority effect. *Journal of Personality and Social Psychology, 54*, 917–924.

Hansen, J., & Wänke, M. (2009). Think of capable others and you can make it! Self-efficacy mediates the effect of stereotype activation on behavior. *Social Cognition, 27*, 76–88.

Hansford, B.C., & Hattie, J.A. (1982). The relationship between self and achievement/performance measures. *Review of Educational Research, 52*, 123–142.

Harkness, A.R., DeBono, K.G., & Borgida, E. (1985). Personal involvement and strategies for making contingency judgments: A stake in the dating game makes a difference. *Journal of Personality and Social Psychology, 49*, 22–32.

Harley, E.M. (2007). Hindsight bias in legal decision making. *Social Cognition, 25*, 48–63.

Harmon-Jones, E., Armstrong, J., & Olson, J.M. (2019). The influence of behavior on attitudes. In D. Albarracín & B.T. Johnson (Eds.), *The handbook of attitudes: Volume 1: Basic principles* (2nd ed., pp. 404–449). New York, NY: Routledge.

Harris, C.B., Barnier, A.J., & Sutton, J. (2013). Shared encoding and the costs and benefits of collaborative recall. *Journal of Experimental Psychology: Learning, Memory, and Cognition, 39*, 183–195.

Harris, C.R., Coburn, N., Rohrer, D., & Pashler, H. (2013). Two failures to replicate high-performance-goal priming effects. *PLOS ONE, 8*, e72467.

Harris, L.T., & Fiske, S.T. (2006). Dehumanizing the lowest of the low: Neuro-imaging responses to extreme outgroups. *Psychological Science, 17*, 847–853.

Harris, P.S., Harris, P.R., & Miles, E. (2017). Self-affirmation improves performance on tasks related to executive functioning. *Journal of Experimental Social Psychology, 70*, 281–285.

Hart, S. (2005). Adaptive heuristics. *Econometrica, 73*, 1401–1430.

Hart, W., & Albarracín, D. (2011). Learning about what others were doing: Verb aspect and attributions of mundane and criminal intent for past actions. *Psychological Science, 22*, 261–266.

Hart, W., & Albarracín, D. (2012). Craving activity and losing objectivity: Effects of general action concepts on approach to decision-consistent information. *Social Psychological and Personality Science, 3*, 55–62.

Hartshorne, H., & May, M.A. (1928). *Studies in the nature of character: I. Studies in deceit.* New York, NY: Macmillan.

Hartshorne, H., May, M.A., & Shuttleworth, F.K. (1930). *Studies in the nature of character: Vol. 3. Studies in the organization of character.* New York, NY: Macmillan.

Harvey, J.H., Yarkin, K.L., Lightner, J.M., & Town, J.P. (1980). Unsolicited interpretation and recall of interpersonal events. *Journal of Personality and Social Psychology, 38*, 551–568.

Haselton, M. (2018). *Hormonal: The hidden intelligence of hormones – How they drive desire, shape relationships, influence our choices, and make us wiser.* New York, NY: Little, Brown.

Haselton, M.G., & Gangestad, S.W. (2006). Conditional expression of women's desires and male mate retention efforts across the ovulatory cycle. *Hormones and Behavior, 49*, 509–518.

Hasher, L., & Zacks, R.T. (1979). Automatic and effortful processes in memory. *Journal of Experimental Psychology: General, 108*, 356–388.

Hasher, L., & Zacks, R.T. (1984). Automatic processing of fundamental information: The case of frequency of occurrence. *American Psychologist, 39*, 1372–1388.

Haslam, N. (2017). The origins of lay theories: The case of essentialist beliefs. In C.M. Zedelius, B.C.N. Müller, & J.W. Schooler (Eds.), *The science of lay theories: How beliefs shape our cognition, behavior, and health* (pp. 3–16). New York, NY: Springer.

Haslam, N., Rothschild, L., & Ernst, D. (2000). Essentialist beliefs about social categories. *British Journal of Social Psychology, 39*, 113–127.

Haslam, N., Rothschild, L., & Ernst, D. (2002). Are essentialist beliefs associated with prejudice? *British Journal of Social Psychology, 41*, 87–100

Haslam, N., Rothschild, L., & Ernst, D. (2004). Essentialism and entitativity: Structures of beliefs about the ontology of social categories. In V. Yzerbyt, C.M. Judd, & O. Corneille (Eds.), *The psychology of group perception: Perceived variability, entitativity, and essentialism* (pp. 61–78). New York, NY: Psychology Press.

Hassall, C.D., Silver, A., Turk, D.J., & Krigolson, O.E. (2016). We are more selfish than we think: The endowment effect and reward processing within the human medial-frontal cortex. *Quarterly Journal of Experimental Psychology, 69*, 1676–1686.

Hassell, H.J.G., & Visalvanich, N. (2015). Call to (in)action: The effects of racial priming on grassroots mobilization. *Political Behavior, 37*, 911–932.

Hassin, R.R. (2013). Yes it can: On the functional abilities of the human unconscious. *Perspectives on Psychological Science, 8*, 195–207.

Hassin, R.R., & Sklar, A.Y. (2014). The human unconscious: A functional perspective. In J.W. Sherman, B. Gawronski, & Y. Trope (Eds.), *Dual-process theories of the social mind* (pp. 299–313). New York, NY: Guilford Press.

Hassin, R.R., Aarts, H., & Ferguson, M.J. (Eds.) (2005). Automatic goal inferences. *Journal of Experimental Social Psychology, 41*, 129–140.

Hassin, R.R., Bargh, J.A., & Uleman, J.S. (2002). Spontaneous causal inferences. *Journal of Experimental Social Psychology, 38*, 515–522.

Hassin, R.R., Bargh, J.A., & Zimerman, S. (2009). Automatic and flexible: The case of nonconscious goal pursuit. *Social Cognition, 27*, 20–36.

Hassin, R.R., Uleman, J.S., & Bargh, J.A. (Eds.) (2005). *The new unconscious.* New York, NY: Oxford University Press.

Hastie, R. (1980). Memory for behavioral information that confirms or contradicts a personality impression. In R. Hastie, T.M. Ostrom, E.B. Ebbesen, R.S. Wyer, Jr., D.L. Hamilton, & D.E. Carlston (Eds.), *Person memory: The cognitive basis of social perception* (pp. 155–177). Hillsdale, NJ: Lawrence Erlbaum.

Hastie, R. (1981). Schematic principles in human memory. In E.T. Higgins, C.P. Herman, & M.P. Zanna (Eds.), *Social cognition: The Ontario symposium*. Hillsdale, NJ: Lawrence Erlbaum.

Hastie, R. (1984). Causes and effects of causal attribution. *Journal of Personality and Social Psychology, 46,* 44–56.

Hastie, R., & Dawes, R.M. (2010). *Rational choice in an uncertain world: The psychology of judgment and decision making* (2nd ed.). Thousand Oaks, CA: Sage.

Hastie, R., & Kumar, P.A. (1979). Person memory: Personality traits as organizing principles in memory for behaviors. *Journal of Personality and Social Psychology, 37,* 25–38.

Hastie, R., & Park, B. (1986). The relationship between memory and judgment depends on whether the judgment task is memory-based or on-line. *Psychological Review, 93,* 258–268.

Hastie, R., Ostrom, T.M., Ebbesen, E.B., Wyer, R.S., Jr., Hamilton, D.L., & Carlston, D.E. (Eds.) (1980). *Person memory: The cognitive basis of social perception.* Hillsdale, NJ: Lawrence Erlbaum.

Hastie, R., Schkade, D.A., & Payne, J.W. (1999). Juror judgments in civil cases: Effects of plaintiff's requests and plaintiff's identity on punitive damage awards. *Law and Human Behavior, 23,* 445–470.

Hastorf, A.H., & Cantril, H. (1954). They saw a game: A case study. *Journal of Abnormal and Social Psychology, 49,* 129–134.

Hauser-Cram, P., Sirin, S.R., & Stipek, D. (2003). When teachers' and parents' values differ: Teachers' ratings of academic competence in children from low-income families. *Journal of Educational Psychology, 95,* 813–820.

Hawkins, S.A., & Hastie, R. (1990). Hindsight: Biased judgments of past events after the outcomes are known. *Psychological Bulletin, 107,* 311–327.

Haynes, G.A. (2009). Investigating the dynamics of choice overload. *Psychology and Marketing, 26,* 204–212.

He, Y., Ebner, N.C., & Johnson, M.K. (2011). What predicts the own-age bias in face recognition memory? *Social Cognition, 1,* 97–109.

Heider, F. (1944). Social perception and phenomenal causality. *Psychological Review, 6,* 358–374.

Heider, F. (1946). Attitudes and cognitive organization. *Journal of Psychology, 21,* 107–112.

Heider, F. (1958). *The psychology of interpersonal relations.* New York, NY: Wiley.

Heider, J.D., Scherer, C.R., Skowronski, J.J., Wood, S.E., Edlund, J.E., & Hartnett, J.L. (2007). Trait expectancies and stereotype expectancies have the same effect on person memory. *Journal of Experimental Social Psychology, 43,* 265–272.

Heine, S.J., & Hamamura, T. (2007). In search of East Asian self-enhancement. *Personality and Social Psychology Review, 11,* 4–27.

Heine, S.J., Kitayama, S., & Lehman, D.R. (2001). Cultural differences in self-evaluation: Japanese readily accept negative self-relevant information. *Journal of Cross-Cultural Psychology, 32,* 434–443.

Heine, S.J., Lehman, D.R., Markus, H.R., & Kitayama, S. (1999). Is there a universal need for positive self-regard? *Psychological Review, 106,* 766–794.

Heine, S.J., Proulx, T., & Vohs, K.D. (2006). The meaning maintenance model: On the coherence of social motivations. *Personality and Social Psychology Review, 10,* 88–110.

Hemsley, G.D., & Marmurek, H.H.C. (1982). Person memory: The processing of consistent and inconsistent person information. *Personality and Social Psychology Bulletin, 8,* 433–438.

Henderson, J.M., Williams, C.C., & Falk, R.J. (2005). Eye movements are functional during face learning. *Memory & Cognition, 33*, 98–106.

Henderson, M.D., Fujita, K., Trope, Y., & Liberman, N. (2006). The effect of spatial distance on social judgment. *Journal of Personality and Social Psychology, 91*, 845–856.

Hepler, J., Albarracín, D., McCulloch, K.C., & Noguchi, K. (2012). Being active and impulsive: The role of goals for action and inaction in self-control. *Motivation and Emotion, 36*, 416–424.

Hepper, E.G., Gramzow, R.H., & Sedikides, C. (2010). Individual differences in self-enhancement and self-protection strategies: An integrative analysis. *Journal of Personality, 78*, 781–814.

Hergovich, A., Schott, R., & Burger, C. (2010). Biased evaluation of abstracts depending on topic and conclusion: Further evidence of a confirmation bias within scientific psychology. *Current Psychology, 29*, 188–209.

Hermans, D., De Houwer, J., & Eelen, P. (2001). A time course analysis of the affective priming effect. *Cognition and Emotion, 15*, 143–165.

Herr, P.M. (1986). Consequences of priming: Judgment and behavior. *Journal of Personality and Social Psychology, 51*, 1106–1115.

Herr, P.M., Sherman, S.J., & Fazio, R.H. (1983). On the consequences of priming: Assimilation and contrast effects. *Journal of Experimental Social Psychology, 19*, 323–340.

Herring, D.R., White, K.R., Jabeen, L.N., Hinojos, M., Terrazas, G., Reyes, S.M., Taylor, J.H., & Crites, S.L., Jr. (2013). On the automatic activation of attitudes: A quarter century of evaluative priming research. *Psychological Bulletin, 139*, 1062–1089.

Hershler, O., & Hochstein, S. (2005). At first sight: A high-level pop out effect for faces. *Vision Research, 45*, 1707–1724.

Hertel, G., & Bless, H. (2000). "On-line" versus memory-based judgments: Triggering conditions and empirical methods for differentiation. *Psychologische Rundschau, 51*, 19–28.

Hertwig, R., & Herzog, S.M. (2009). Fast and frugal heuristics: Tools of social rationality. *Social Cognition, 27*, 661–698.

Hertwig, R., & Hoffrage, U. (Eds.) (2013). *Simple heuristics in a social world.* New York, NY: Oxford University Press.

Hertwig, R., Davis, J.N., & Sulloway, F.J. (2002). Parental investment: How an equity motive can produce inequality. *Psychological Bulletin, 128*, 728–745.

Hertwig, R., Herzog, S.M., Schooler, L.J., & Reimer, T. (2008). Fluency heuristic: A model of how the mind exploits a by-product of information retrieval. *Journal of Experimental Psychology: Learning, Memory, and Cognition, 34*, 1191–1206.

Herzog, S.M., & Hertwig, R. (2009). The wisdom of many in one mind: Improving individual judgments with dialectical bootstrapping. *Psychological Science, 20*, 231–237.

Hetts, J.J., Sakuma, M., & Pelham, B.W. (1999). Two roads to positive regard: Implicit and explicit self-evaluation and culture. *Journal of Experimental Social Psychology, 35*, 512–559.

Hewstone, M. (1989). Changing stereotypes with disconfirming information. In D. Bar-Tal, C.F. Graumann, A.W. Kruglanski, & W. Stroebe (Eds.), *Stereotyping and prejudice* (pp. 207–223). New York, NY: Springer.

Hewstone, M. (1990). The ultimate attribution error? A review of the literature on intergroup causal attribution. *European Journal of Social Psychology, 20*, 311–335.

Hewstone, M., & Jaspars, J. (1987). Covariation and causal attribution: A logical model of the intuitive analysis of variance. *Journal of Personality and Social Psychology, 53*, 663–672.

Hewstone, M., Gale, L., & Purkhardt, N. (1990). Intergroup attributions for success and failure: Group-serving bias and group-serving causal schemata. *European Bulletin of Cognitive Psychology, 10*, 23–44.

Heyman, G.D. (2001). Children's interpretation of ambiguous behavior: Evidence for a 'boys are bad' bias. *Social Development, 10*, 230–247.

Heyman, G.D., & Dweck, C.S. (1998). Children's thinking about traits: Implications for judgments of the self and others. *Child Development*, *69*, 391–403.

Higgins, E.T. (1981). The "communication game": Implications for social and cognition and persuasion. In E.T. Higgins, C.P. Herman, & M.P. Zanna (Eds.), *Social cognition: The Ontario symposium* (Vol. 1. pp. 343–392). Hillsdale, NJ: Lawrence Erlbaum.

Higgins, E.T. (1996). Knowledge activation: Accessibility, applicability, and salience. In E.T. Higgins & A.W. Kruglanski (Eds.), *Social psychology: Handbook of basic principles* (pp. 133–168). New York, NY: Guilford Press.

Higgins, E.T. (1998). Promotion and prevention: Regulatory focus as a motivational principle. In M.P. Zanna (Ed.), *Advances in experimental social psychology* (Vol. 30, pp. 1–46). New York, NY: Academic Press.

Higgins, E.T. (2000). Making a good decision: Value from fit. *American Psychologist*, *55*, 1217–1230.

Higgins, E.T. (2005). Value from regulatory fit. *Current Directions in Psychological Science*, *14*, 209–213.

Higgins, E.T. (2012). Accessibility theory. In P.A.M. Van Lange, A.W. Kruglanski, & E.T. Higgins (Eds.), *Handbook of theories of social psychology* (Vol. 1, pp. 75–96). Thousand Oaks, CA: Sage.

Higgins, E.T., & Brendl, C.M. (1995). Accessibility and applicability: Some "activation rules" influencing judgment. *Journal of Experimental Social Psychology*, *31*, 218–243.

Higgins, E.T., & Eitam, B. (2014). Priming... Shmiming: It's about knowing when and why stimulated memory representations become active. *Social Cognition*, *32*, 234–251.

Higgins, E.T., & Rholes, W.S. (1978). "Saying is believing": Effects of message modification on memory and liking for the person described. *Journal of Experimental Social Psychology*, *14*, 363–378.

Higgins, E.T., Idson, L.C., Freitas, A.L., Spiegel, S., & Molden, D.C. (2003). Transfer of value from fit. *Journal of Personality and Social Psychology*, *84*, 1140–1153.

Higgins, E.T., King, G.A., & Mavin, G.H. (1982). Individual construct accessibility and subjective impressions and recall. *Journal of Personality and Social Psychology*, *43*, 35–47.

Higgins, E.T., Rholes, W.S., & Jones, C.R. (1977). Category accessibility and impression formation. *Journal of Experimental Social Psychology*, *13*, 141–154.

Hikosaka, O., & Isoda, M. (2010). Switching from automatic to controlled behavior: Cortico-basal ganglia mechanisms. *Trends in Cognitive Sciences*, *14*, 154–161.

Hilton, D.J. (1988). Logic and causal attribution. In D.J. Hilton (Ed.), *Contemporary science and natural explanation: Commonsense conceptions of causality* (pp. 33–65). Brighton: Harvester Press.

Hilton, D.J. (1990). Conversational processes and causal explanation. *Psychological Bulletin*, *107*, 65–81.

Hilton, D.J., Smith, R.H., & Kin, S.H. (1995). Processes of causal explanation and dispositional attribution. *Journal of Personality and Social Psychology*, *68*, 377–387.

Hilton, J.L., & Darley, J.M. (1985). Constructing other persons: A limit on the effect. *Journal of experimental social psychology*, *21*, 1–18.

Hilton, J.L., & Darley, J.M. (1991). The effects of interaction goals on person perception. In L. Berkowitz (Ed.), *Advances in experimental social psychology* (Vol. 24, pp. 235–267). San Diego, CA: Academic Press.

Hilton, J.L., & Fein, S. (1989). The role of typical diagnosticity in stereotype-based judgments. *Journal of Personality and Social Psychology*, *57*, 201–211.

Hilton, J.L., Fein, S., & Miller, D.T. (1993). Suspicion and dispositional inference. *Personality and Social Psychology Bulletin*, *19*, 501–512.

Hilton, J.L., Klein, J.G., & von Hippel, W. (1991). Attention allocation and impression formation. *Personality and Social Psychology Bulletin*, *17*, 548–559.

Hinkley, K., & Andersen, S.M. (1996). The working self-concept in transference: Significant-other activation and self change. *Journal of Personality and Social Psychology*, *71*, 1279–1295.

Hinzman, L., & Maddox, K.B. (2017). Conceptual and visual representations of racial categories: Distinguishing subtypes from subgroups. *Journal of Experimental Social Psychology*, *70*, 95–109.

Hirst, W., & Phelps, E.A. (2016). Flashbulb memories. *Current Directions in Psychological Science*, *25*, 36–41.

Hirst, W., Coman, A., & Coman, D. (2014). Putting the social back into human memory. In T.J. Perfect & D.S. Lindsay (Eds.), *The SAGE handbook of applied memory*. London: Sage.

Hirst, W., Phelps, E.A., Buckner, R.L., Budson, A.E., Cuc, A., Gabrielli, J.D.E., & Vaidya, C.J. (2009). Long-term memory for the terrorist attack of September 11: Flashbulb memories, event memories, and the factors that influence their retention. *Journal of Experimental Psychology: General*, *138*, 161–176.

Hirst, W., Phelps, E.A., Meskin, R., Vaidya, C.J., Johnson, M.K., Mitchell, K.J., ... Olsson, A. (2015). A ten-year follow-up of a study of memory for the attack of September 11, 2001: Flashbulb memories and memories for flashbulb events. *Journal of Experimental Psychology: General*, *144*, 604–623.

Hirt, E.R., & Markman, K.D. (1995). Multiple explanation: A consider-an-alternative strategy for debiasing judgments. *Journal of Personality and Social Psychology*, *69*, 1069–1086.

Hirt, E.R., & Sherman, S.J. (1985). The role of prior knowledge in explaining hypothetical events. *Journal of Experimental Social Psychology*, *21*, 519–543.

Ho, A.K., Roberts, S.O., & Gelman, S.A. (2015). Essentialism and racial bias jointly contribute to the categorization of multiracial individuals. *Psychological Science*, *26*, 1639–1645.

Ho, A.K., Sidanius, J., Cuddy, A.J.C., & Banaji, M.R. (2013). Status boundary enforcement and the categorization of black–white biracials. *Journal of Experimental Social Psychology*, *49*, 940–943.

Ho, A.K., Sidanius, J., Levin, D.T., & Banaji, M.R. (2011). Evidence for hypodescent and racial hierarchy in the categorization and perception of biracial individuals. *Journal of Personality and Social Psychology*, *100*, 492–506.

Hodges, B.H. (1974). Effect of valence on relative weighting in impression formation. *Journal of Personality and Social Psychology*, *30*, 378–381.

Hoffman, C., Mischel, W., & Mazze, K. (1981). The role of purpose in the organization of information about behavior: Trait-based versus goal-based categories in person cognition. *Journal of Personality and Social Psychology*, *40*, 211–225.

Hoffman, K.M., Trawalter, S., Axt, J.R., & Oliver, M.N. (2016). Racial bias in pain assessment and treatment recommendations, and false beliefs about biological differences between Blacks and Whites. *Proceedings of the National Academy of Sciences*, *113*, 4296–4301.

Hofmann, W., & Baumert, A. (2010). Immediate affect as a basis for intuitive moral judgment: An adaptation of the affect misattribution procedure. *Cognition and Emotion*, *24*, 522–535.

Hofmann, W., & Wilson, T.D. (2010). Consciousness, introspection, and the adaptive unconscious. In B.G. Gawronski & B.K. Payne (Eds.), *Handbook of implicit social cognition: Measurement, theory, and application* (pp. 197–215). New York, NY: Guilford Press.

Hofmann, W., De Houwer, J., Perugini, M., Baeyens, F., & Crombez, G. (2010). Evaluative conditioning in humans: A meta-analysis. *Psychological Bulletin*, *136*, 390–421.

Hofmann, W., Friese, M., & Strack, F. (2009). Impulse and self-control from a dual-systems perspective. *Perspectives on Psychological Science*, *4*, 162–176.

Hofmann, W., Gschwendner, T., Castelli, L., & Schmitt, M. (2008). Implicit and explicit attitudes and interracial interaction: The moderating role of situationally available control resources. *Group Processes & Intergroup Relations, 11*, 69–87.

Hofmann, W., Gschwendner, T., Nosek, B.A., & Schmitt, M. (2005) What moderates implicit–explicit consistency? *European Review of Social Psychology, 16*, 335–390.

Hofmann, W., Rauch, W., & Gawronski, B. (2007). And deplete us not into temptation: Automatic attitudes, dietary restraint, and self-regulatory resources as determinants of eating behavior. *Journal of Experimental Social Psychology, 43*, 497–504.

Hogarth, R.M., & Einhorn, H.J. (1992). Order effects in belief updating: The belief-adjustment model. *Cognitive Psychology, 24*, 1–55.

Hogarth, R.M., & Karelaia, N. (2006). "Take-the-best" and other simple strategies: Why and when they work "well" with binary cues. *Theory and Decision, 61*, 205–249.

Hogg, M.A., & Mullin, B.A. (1999). Joining groups to reduce uncertainty: Subjective uncertainty reduction and group identification. In D. Abrams & M.A. Hogg (Eds.), *Social identity and social cognition* (pp. 249–279). Oxford: Blackwell.

Hohman, Z.P., Crano, W.D., & Niedbala, E.M. (2015). Attitude ambivalence, social norms, and behavioral intentions: Developing effective antitobacco persuasive communications. *Psychology of Addictive Behaviors, 30*, 209–219.

Hojat, M., Gonnella, J.S., & Caelleigh, A.S. (2003). Impartial judgment by the "gate-keepers" of science: Fallibility and accountability in the peer review process. *Advances in Health Sciences Education, 8*, 75–96.

Holland, E., Wolf, E.B., Looser, C., & Cuddy, A. (2017). Visual attention to powerful postures: People avert their gaze from nonverbal dominance displays. *Journal of Experimental Social Psychology, 68*, 60–67.

Holland, R.W., Verplanken, B., & van Knippenberg, A. (2002). On the nature of attitude-behavior relations: The strong guide, the weak follow. *European Journal of Social Psychology, 32*, 869–876.

Holland, R.W., Verplanken, B., & van Knippenberg, A. (2003). From repetition to conviction: Attitude accessibility as a determinant of attitude certainty. *Journal of Experimental Social Psychology, 39*, 594–601.

Holleran, S.E., Mehl, M.R., & Levitt, S. (2009). Eavesdropping on social life: The accuracy of stranger ratings of daily behavior from thin slices of natural conversations. *Journal of Research in Personality, 43*, 660–672.

Hollingshead, A.B. (1998a). Retrieval processes in transactive memory systems. *Journal of Personality and Social Psychology, 74*, 659–671.

Hollingshead, A.B. (1998b). Communication, learning, and retrieval in transactive memory systems. *Journal of Experimental Social Psychology, 34*, 423–442.

Hollingshead, A.B., & Brandon, D.P. (2003). Potential benefits of communication in transactive memory systems. *Human Communication Research, 29*, 607–615.

Hollingshead, A.B., & Fraidin, S.N. (2003). Gender stereotypes and assumptions about expertise in transactive memory. *Journal of Experimental Social Psychology, 39*, 355–363.

Holmes, D.S. (1968). Dimensions of projection. *Psychological Bulletin, 69*, 248–268.

Holmes, D.S. (1978). Projection as a defense mechanism. *Psychological Bulletin, 85*, 677–688.

Holtz, P., & Wagner, W. (2009). Essentialism and attribution of monstrosity in racist discourse: Right-wing internet postings about Africans and Jews. *Journal of Community & Applied Social Psychology, 19*, 411–425.

Holtzworth-Munroe, A., & Jacobson, N.S. (1985). Causal attributions of married couples: When do they search for causes? What do they conclude when they do? *Journal of Personality and Social Psychology, 48*, 1398–1412.

Hong, Y.-Y., Morris, M.W., Chiu, C.-Y., & Benet-Martínez, V. (2000). Multicultural minds: A dynamic constructivist approach to culture and cognition. *American Psychologist, 55,* 709–720.

Honkanen, P., & Verplanken, B. (2004). Understanding attitudes towards genetically modified food: The role of values and attitude strength. *Journal of Consumer Policy, 27,* 401–420.

Hood, B., Weltzien, S., Marsh, L., & Kanngiesser, P. (2016). Picture yourself: Self-focus and the endowment effect in preschool children. *Cognition, 152,* 70–77.

Horberg, E.J., Oveis, C., & Keltner, D. (2011). Emotions as moral amplifiers: An appraisal tendency approach to the influences of distinct emotions upon moral judgment. *Emotion Review, 3,* 237–244.

Horrey, W.J., & Wickens, C.D. (2006). Examining the impact of cell phone conversations on driving using meta-analytic techniques. *Human Factors, 48,* 196–205.

Houghton, D.P. (2013). *The decision point: 6 cases in US foreign policy decision making.* New York, NY: Oxford University Press.

Houts, C.R., & Horne, S.G. (2008). The role of relationship attributions in relationship satisfaction among cohabiting gay men. *The Family Journal, 16,* 240–248.

Hovland, C.I., Janis, I.L., & Kelley, H.H. (1953). *Communication and persuasion.* New Haven, CT: Yale University Press.

Howard, J.W., & Rothbart, M. (1980). Social categorization and memory for in-group and out-group behavior. *Journal of Personality and Social Psychology, 38,* 301–310.

Howe, L.C., & Krosnick, J.A. (2017). Attitude strength. *Annual Review of Psychology, 68,* 327–351.

Howe, M.L., & Courage, M.L. (1993). On resolving the enigma of infantile amnesia. *Psychological Bulletin, 113,* 305–326.

Howell, J.L., Gaither, S.E., & Ratliff, K.A. (2015). Caught in the middle: Defensive responses to IAT feedback among Whites, Blacks, and biracial Black/Whites. *Social Psychological and Personality Science, 6,* 373–381.

Huang, L.M., & Sherman, J.W. (2018). Attentional processes in social perception. In J.M. Olson (Ed.), *Advances in experimental social psychology* (Vol. 58, pp. 199–241). New York, NY: Academic Press.

Huang, J.Y., Ackerman, J.M., & Newman, G.E. (2017). Catching (up with) magical contagion: A review of contagion effects in consumer contexts. *Journal of the Association for Consumer Research, 2,* 430–443.

Huang, Y., Xue, X., Spelke, E., Huang, L., Zheng, W., & Peng, K. (2018). The aesthetic preference for symmetry dissociates from early-emerging attention to symmetry. *Scientific Reports, 8,* 6263.

Huart, J., Corneille, O., & Becquart, E. (2005). Face-based categorization, context-based categorization, and distortions in the recollection of gender ambiguous faces. *Journal of Experimental Social Psychology, 41,* 598–608.

Hugenberg, K., & Wilson, J.P. (2013). Faces are central to social cognition. In D.E. Carlston (Ed.), *The Oxford handbook of social cognition* (pp. 167–193). New York, NY: Oxford University Press.

Hugenberg, K., Miller, J., & Claypool, H.M. (2007). Categorization and individuation in the cross-race recognition deficit: Toward a solution to an insidious problem. *Journal of Experimental Social Psychology, 43,* 334–340.

Hugenberg, K., Young, S.G., Bernstein, M.J., & Sacco, D.F. (2010). The categorization-individuation model: An integrative account of the other-race recognition deficit. *Psychological Review, 117,* 1168–1187.

Hughes, B.L., Camp, N.P., Gomez, J., Natu, V.S., Grill-Spector, K., & Eberhardt, J.L. (2019). Neural adaptation to faces reveals racial outgroup homogeneity effects in early perception. *Proceedings of the National Academy of Sciences, 116,* 14532–14537.

Hull, C.L. (1943). *Principles of behavior: An introduction to behavior theory.* Oxford: Appleton-Century.

Human, L.J., Biesanz, J.C., Finseth, S.M., Pierce, B., & Le, M. (2014). To thine own self be true: Psychological adjustment promotes judgeability via personality-behavior congruence. *Journal of Personality and Social Psychology, 106,* 286–303.

Hunter, J.A., Stringer, M., & Watson, R.P. (1991). Intergroup violence and intergroup attributions. *British Journal of Social Psychology, 30,* 261–266.

Huntjens, R.J.C., Rijkeboer, M.M., Krakau, A., & de Jong, P.J. (2014). Implicit versus explicit measures of self-concept of self-control and their differential predictive power for spontaneous trait-relevant behaviors. *Journal of Behavior Therapy and Experimental Psychiatry, 45,* 1–7.

Hütter, M., & Fiedler, K. (2016). Conceptual, theoretical, and methodological challenges in evaluative conditioning research. *Social Cognition, 34,* 343–356.

IJzerman, H., & Semin, G.R. (2009). The thermometer of social relations: Mapping social proximity on temperature. *Psychological Science, 20,* 1214–1220.

IJzerman, H., Karremans, J.C., Thomsen, L., & Schubert, T.W. (2013). Caring for sharing: How attachment styles modulate communal cues of physical warmth. *Social Psychology, 44,* 160–166.

IJzerman, H., Lindenberg, S., Dalğar, I., Weissgerber, S.S.C., Vergara, R.C., Cairo, A.H., ... Zickfeld, J.H. (2018). The Human Penguin Project: Climate, social integration, and core body temperature. *Collabra: Psychology, 4,* 37.

Inagaki, T.K., & Eisenberger, N.I. (2013). Shared neural mechanisms underlying social warmth and physical warmth. *Psychological Science, 24,* 2272–2280.

Inagaki, T.K., Hazlett, L.I., & Andreescu, C. (2019). Naltrexone alters responses to social and physical warmth: Implications for social bonding. *Social Cognitive and Affective Neuroscience, 14,* 471–479.

Ireland, M.E., Slatcher, R.B., Eastwick, P.W., Scissors, L.E., Finkel, E.J., & Pennebaker, J.W. (2011). Language style matching predicts relationship initiation and stability. *Psychological Science, 22,* 39–44.

Isbell, L.M., McCabe, J., Burns, K.C., & Lair, E.C. (2013). Who am I?: The influence of affect on the working self-concept. *Cognition and Emotion, 27,* 1073–1090.

Ishigami, Y., & Klein, R.M. (2009). Is a hands free phone safer than a hand-held phone? *Journal of Safety Research, 40,* 157–164.

Ishii, K. (2013). Culture and the mode of thought: A review. *Asian Journal of Social Psychology, 16,* 123–132.

Itier, R.J., & Taylor, M.J. (2004). N170 or N1? Spatiotemporal differences between object and face processing using ERPs. *Cerebral Cortex, 14,* 132–142.

Ito, T.A., Friedman, N.P., Bartholow, B.D., Correll, J., Loersch, C., Altamirano, L.J., & Miyake, A. (2015). Toward a comprehensive understanding of executive cognitive function in implicit racial bias. *Journal of Personality and Social Psychology, 108,* 187–218.

Ito, T.A., Larsen, J.T., Smith, N.K., & Cacioppo, J.T. (1998). Negative information weighs more heavily on the brain: The negativity bias in evaluative categorizations. *Journal of Personality and Social Psychology, 75,* 887–900.

Iyengar, S.S., & Lepper, M.R. (2000). When choice is demotivating: Can one desire too much of a good thing? *Journal of Personality and Social Psychology, 79,* 995–1006.

Iyengar, S.S., Huberman, G., & Jiang, W. (2004). How much choice is too much? Contributions to 401(k) retirement plans. In O.S. Mitchell & S. Utkus (Eds.), *Pension design and structure: New lessons from behavioral finance* (pp. 83–95). Oxford: Oxford University Press.

Jackson, L.A., Sullivan, L.A., & Hodge, C.N. (1993). Stereotype effects of attributions, predictions, and evaluations: No two social judgments are quite alike. *Journal of Personality and Social Psychology, 65,* 69–84.

Jacobs, J.E., & Eccles, J.S. (1992). The impact of mothers' gender-role stereotypic beliefs on mothers' and children's ability perceptions. *Journal of Personality and Social Psychology, 63,* 932–944.

Jacobsen, T., & Höfel, L. (2003). Descriptive and evaluative judgment processes: Behavioral and electrophysiological indices of processing symmetry and aesthetics. *Cognitive, Affective, & Behavioral Neuroscience, 3,* 289–299.

Jacoby-Senghor, D.S., Sinclair, S., & Smith, C.T. (2015). When bias binds: Effect of implicit outgroup bias on ingroup affiliation. *Journal of Personality and Social Psychology, 109,* 415–433.

Jacoby, J., Speller, D.E., & Kohn, C.A. (1974). Brand choice behavior as a function of information load. *Journal of Marketing Research, 11,* 63–69.

Jacoby, L.L. (1991). A process dissociation framework: Separating automatic from intentional uses of memory. *Journal of Memory and Language, 30,* 513–541.

Jacoby, L.L., & Kelley, C.M. (1987). Unconscious influences of memory for a prior event. *Personality and Social Psychology Bulletin, 13,* 314–336.

Jacoby, L.L., Woloshyn, V., & Kelley, C. (1989). Becoming famous without being recognized: Unconscious influences of memory produced by dividing attention. *Journal of Experimental Psychology: General, 118,* 115–125.

James, W. (1920). *The letters of William James, Volume 2.* H. James (Ed.). Boston, MA: Atlantic Monthly Press.

James, W.H. (1890). *The principles of psychology.* New York, NY: Henry Holt.

Janis, I.L., & Mann, L. (1977). *Decision making: A psychological analysis of conflict, choice, and commitment.* New York, NY: Free Press.

Jefferis, V.E., & Fazio, R.H. (2008). Accessibility as input: The use of construct accessibility as information to guide behavior. *Journal of Experimental Social Psychology, 44,* 1144–1150.

Jellison, W.A., McConnell, A.R., & Gabriel, S. (2004). Implicit and explicit measures of sexual orientation attitudes: In-group preferences and related behaviors and beliefs among gay and straight men. *Personality and Social Psychology Bulletin, 30,* 629–642.

Johar, G.V., & Sengupta, J. (2002). The effects of dissimulation on the accessibility and predictive power of weakly held attitudes. *Social Cognition, 20,* 257–293.

John, O.P., & Robins, R.W. (1993). Determinants of interjudge agreement on personality traits: The Big Five domains, observability, evaluativeness, and the unique perspective of the self. *Journal of Personality, 61,* 521–551.

John, O.P., & Robins, R.W. (1994). Accuracy and bias in self-perception: Individual differences in self-enhancement and the role of narcissism. *Journal of Personality and Social Psychology, 66,* 206–219.

Johnson, A.L., Crawford, M.T., Sherman, S.J., Rutchick, A.M., Hamilton, D.L., Ferreira, M., & Petrocelli, J. (2006). A functional perspective on group memberships: Differential need fulfillment in a group typology. *Journal of Experimental Social Psychology, 42,* 707–719.

Johnson, C., & Mullen, B. (1994). Evidence for the accessibility of paired distinctiveness in distinctiveness-based illusory correlation in stereotyping. *Personality and Social Psychology Bulletin, 20,* 65–70.

Johnson, C., Mullen, B., Carlson, D., & Southwick, S. (2001). The affective and memorial components of distinctiveness-based illusory correlations. *British Journal of Social Psychology, 40,* 337–358.

Johnson, D.J., Cheung, F., & Donnellan, M.B. (2014). Does cleanliness influence moral judgments? A direct replication of Schnall, Benton, and Harvey (2008). *Social Psychology, 45,* 209–215.

Johnson, E.J., & Goldstein, D.G. (2003). Do defaults save lives? *Science, 302,* 1338–1339.

Johnson, I.R., Kopp, B.M., & Petty, R.E. (2018). Just say no! (and mean it): Meaningful negation as a tool to modify automatic racial attitudes. *Group Processes & Intergroup Relations, 21,* 88–110.

Johnson, K.L., & Freeman, J.B. (2010). A new look at person construal: Seeing beyond dominance and discreteness. In E. Balcetis & D. Lassiter (Eds.), *The social psychology of visual perception* (pp. 253–272). New York, NY: Psychology Press.

Johnson, K.L., & Tassinary, L.G. (2005). Perceiving sex directly and indirectly: Meaning in motion and morphology. *Psychological Science, 16,* 890–897.

Johnson, K.L., & Tassinary, L.G. (2007). Compatibility of basic social perceptions determines perceived attractiveness. *Proceedings of the National Academy of Sciences, 104,* 5246–5251.

Johnson, K.L., Freeman, J.B., & Pauker, K. (2012). Race is gendered: How covarying phenotypes and stereotypes bias sex categorization. *Journal of Personality and Social Psychology, 102,* 116–131.

Johnson, K.L., Gill, S., Reichman, V., & Tassinary, L.G. (2007). Swagger, sway, and sexuality: Judging sexual orientation from body motion and morphology. *Journal of Personality and Social Psychology, 93,* 321–334.

Johnson, K.L., Pollick, F.E., & McKay, L. (2010). Social constraints on the visual perception of biological motion. In R.B. Adams, N. Ambady, K. Nakayama, & S. Shimojo (Eds.), *Social vision* (pp. 264–277). New York, NY: Oxford University Press.

Johnson, M.H., Dziurawiec, S., Ellis, H.D., & Morton, J. (1991). Newborns' preferential tracking of faces and its subsequent decline. *Cognition, 40,* 1–19.

Johnson, M.K., & Sherman, S.J. (1990). Constructing and reconstructing the past and the future in the present. In E.T. Higgins & R.M. Sorrentino (Eds.), *Handbook of motivation and cognition: Foundations of social behavior* (Vol. 2, pp. 482–526). New York, NY: Guilford Press.

Johnson, M.K., Hashtroudi, S., & Lindsay, S. (1993). Source monitoring. *Psychological Bulletin, 114,* 3–28.

Johnson, S.G.B., Valenti, J.J., & Keil, F.C. (2019). Simplicity and complexity preferences in causal explanation: An opponent heuristic account. *Cognitive Psychology, 113,* Article 101222.

Johnston, C.D., Lavine, H., & Woodson, B. (2015). Emotion and political judgment: Expectancy violation and affective intelligence. *Political Research Quarterly, 68,* 474–492.

Johnston, L., Arden, K., Macrae, C.N., & Grace, R.C. (2003). The need for speed: The menstrual cycle and personal construal. *Social Cognition, 21,* 89–100.

Johnston, L., Bristow, M., & Love, N. (2000). An investigation of the link between attributional judgments and stereotype-based judgments. *European Journal of Social Psychology, 30,* 551–568.

Jones, A.L., Tree, J., & Ward, R. (2019). Personality in faces: Implicit associations between appearance and personality. *European Journal of Social Psychology, 49,* 658–669.

Jones, B.C., Little, A.C., Burt, D.M., & Perrett D.I. (2004). When facial attractiveness is only skin deep. *Perception, 33,* 569–576.

Jones, C.R, Olson, M.A., & Fazio, R.H. (2010). Evaluative conditioning: The "how" question. In M.P. Zanna & J.M. Olson (Eds.), *Advances in experimental social psychology* (Vol. 43, pp. 205–255). San Diego, CA: Academic Press.

Jones, D., & Hill, K. (1993). Criteria of facial attractiveness in five populations. *Human Nature, 4,* 271–296.

Jones, E.E. (1979). The rocky road from acts to dispositions. *American Psychologist, 34,* 107–117.

Jones, E.E. (1990). Correspondence bias. In E.E. Jones (Ed.), *Interpersonal perception* (pp. 139–166). New York, NY: W.H. Freeman.

Jones, E.E., & Berglas, S. (1978). Control of attributions about the self through self-handicapping strategies: The appeal of alcohol and the role of underachievement. *Personality and Social Psychology Bulletin, 4,* 200–206.

Jones, E.E., & Davis, K.E. (1965). From acts to dispositions: The attribution process in person perceptions. In L. Berkowitz (Ed.), *Advances in experimental social psychology* (Vol. 2, pp. 219–266). New York, NY: Academic Press.

Jones, E.E., & Harris, V.A. (1967). The attribution of attitudes. *Journal of Experimental Social Psychology, 3,* 1–24.

Jones, E.E., & Nisbett, R.E. (1972). The actor and the observer: Divergent perceptions of the causes of behavior. In E.E. Jones, D. Kanouse, H.H. Kelley, R.E. Nisbett, S. Valins, & B. Weiner (Eds.), *Attribution: Perceiving the causes of behavior* (pp. 79–94). Morristown, NJ: General Learning Press.

Jones, E.E., & Sigall, H. (1971). The bogus pipeline: A new paradigm for measuring affect and attitude. *Psychological Bulletin, 76,* 349–364.

Jones, J.T., Pelham, B.W., Carvallo, M., & Mirenberg, M.C. (2004). How do I love thee? Let me count the Js: Implicit egotism and interpersonal attraction. *Journal of Personality and Social Psychology, 87,* 665–683.

Jost, J.T., & Banaji, M.R. (1994). The role of stereotyping in system-justification and the production of false consciousness. *British Journal of Social Psychology, 33,* 1–27.

Judd, C.M., & Park, B. (1993). Definition and assessment of accuracy in social stereotypes. *Psychological Review, 100,* 109–128.

Judd, C.M., Drake, R.A., Downing, J.W., & Krosnick, J.A. (1991). Some dynamic properties of attitude structures: Context-induced response facilitation and polarization. *Journal of Personality and Social Psychology, 60,* 193–202.

Judd, C.M., James-Hawkins, L., Yzerbyt, V., & Kashima, Y. (2005). Fundamental dimensions of social judgment: Understanding the relations between judgments of competence and warmth. *Journal of Personality and Social Psychology, 89,* 899–913.

Judd, C.M., Ryan, C.S., & Park, B. (1991). Accuracy in the judgment of in-group and out-group variability. *Journal of Personality and Social Psychology, 61,* 366–379.

Juslin, P., Olsson, N., & Winman, A. (1996). Calibration and diagnosticity of confidence in eyewitness identification: Comments on what can be inferred from the low confidence-accuracy correlation. *Journal of Experimental Psychology: Learning, Memory, and Cognition, 22,* 1304–1316.

Jussim, L., & Fleming, C. (1996). Self-fulfilling prophecies and the maintenance of social stereotypes: The role of dyadic interactions and social forces. In C.N. Macrae, C. Stangor, & M. Hewstone (Eds.), *Stereotypes and stereotyping* (pp. 161–192). New York, NY: Guilford Press.

Jussim, L., & Harber, K.D. (2005). Teacher expectations and self-fulfilling prophecies: Knowns and unknowns, resolved and unresolved controversies. *Personality and Social Psychology Review, 9,* 131–155.

Kahana, M.J., & Wingfield, A. (2000). A functional relation between learning and organization in free recall. *Psychonomic Bulletin & Review, 7,* 516–521.

Kahn, K.B., & Davies, P.G. (2011). Differentially dangerous? Phenotypic racial stereotypicality increases implicit bias among ingroup and outgroup members. *Group Processes & Intergroup Relations, 14,* 569–580.

Kahn, K.B., & Davies, P.G. (2017). What influences shooter bias? The effects of suspect race, neighborhood, and clothing on decisions to shoot. *Journal of Social Issues, 73,* 723–743.

Kahneman, D. (1973). *Attention & effort.* Englewood Cliffs, NJ: Prentice Hall.

Kahneman, D. (2003). A perspective on judgment and choice: Mapping bounded rationality. *American Psychologist, 58,* 697–720.

Kahneman, D. (2011). *Thinking, fast slow.* New York, NY: Farrar, Straus & Giroux.

Kahneman, D., & Frederick, S. (2002). Representativeness revisited. In T. Gilovich, D.W. Griffin, & D. Kahneman (Eds.), *Heuristics and biases* (pp. 49–81). New York, NY: Cambridge University Press.

Kahneman, D., & Frederick, S. (2005). A model of heuristic judgment. In K.J. Holyoak & R.G.

Morrison (Eds.), *The Cambridge handbook of thinking and reasoning* (pp. 267–293). New York, NY: Cambridge University Press.

Kahneman, D., & Miller, D.T. (1986). Norm theory: Comparing reality to its alternatives. *Psychological Review, 93,* 136–153.

Kahneman, D., & Treisman, A. (1984). Changing views of attention and automaticity. In R. Parasuraman & D.R. Davies (Eds.), *Varieties of attention* (pp. 29–61). Orlando, FL: Academic Press.

Kahneman, D., & Tversky, A. (1971). Subjective probability: A judgment of representativeness. *Cognitive Psychology, 3,* 430–454.

Kahneman, D., & Tversky, A. (1973). On the psychology of prediction. *Psychological Review, 80,* 237–251.

Kahneman, D., & Tversky, A. (1979). Prospect theory: An analysis of decision under risk. *Econometrica, 47,* 263–291.

Kahneman, D., & Tversky, A. (1982). The simulation heuristic. In D. Kahneman, P. Slovic, & A. Tversky (Eds.), *Judgment under uncertainty: Heuristics and biases* (pp. 201–208). New York, NY: Cambridge University Press.

Kahneman, D., & Tversky, A. (1984). Choices, values, and frames. *American Psychologist, 39,* 341–350.

Kahneman, D., Knetsch, J.L., & Thaler, R.H. (1990). Experimental tests of the endowment effect and the Coase theorem. *Journal of Political Economy, 98,* 1325–1348.

Kahneman, D., Knetsch, J.L., & Thaler, R.H. (1991). Anomalies: The endowment effect, loss aversion, and status quo bias. *Journal of Economic Perspectives, 5,* 193–206.

Kaiser, F.G., & Schultz, P.W. (2009). The attitude-behavior relationship: A test of three models of the moderating role of behavioral difficulty. *Journal of Applied Social Psychology, 39,* 186–207.

Kam, C.D. (2005). Who toes the party line? Cues, values, and individual differences. *Political Behavior, 27,* 163–182.

Kamin, K.A., & Rachlinski, J.J. (1995). Ex post ≠ ex ante. *Law and Human Behavior, 19,* 89–104.

Kammrath, L.K., Mendoza-Denton, R., & Mischel, W. (2005). Incorporating if… then…personality signatures in person perception: Beyond the person-situation dichotomy. *Journal of Personality and Social Psychology, 88,* 605–618.

Kane, J., Van Boven, L., & McGraw, A.P. (2012). Prototypical prospection: Future events are more prototypically represented and simulated than past events. *European Journal of Social Psychology, 42,* 354–362.

Kang, S.K., Plaks, J.E., & Remedios, J.D. (2015). Folk beliefs about genetic variation predict avoidance of biracial individuals. *Frontiers in Psychology, 6,* Article 357.

Karlins, M., Coffman, T.L., & Walters, G. (1969). On the fading of social stereotypes: Studies in three generations of college students. *Journal of Personality and Social Psychology, 13,* 1–16.

Karney, B.R., & Bradbury, T.N. (2000). Attributions in marriage: State or trait? A growth curve analysis. *Journal of Personality and Social Psychology, 78,* 295–309.

Karniol, R., & Ross, M. (1996). The motivational impact of temporal focus: Thinking about the future and the past. *Annual Review of Psychology, 47,* 593–620.

Kassin, S.M. (1979). Consensus information, prediction, and causal attribution: A review of the literature and issues. *Journal of Personality and Social Psychology, 37,* 1966–1981.

Kassin, S.M., Dror, I.E., & Kukucka, J. (2013). The forensic confirmation bias: Problems, perspectives, and proposed solutions. *Journal of Applied Research in Memory and Cognition, 2,* 42–52.

Katz, D., & Braly, K. (1933). Racial stereotypes in one hundred college students. *Journal of Abnormal and Social Psychology, 28,* 280–290.

Katz, D., & Stotland, E. (1959). A preliminary statement to a theory of attitude structure and change. In S. Koch (Ed.), *Psychology: A study of a science* (Vol. 3, pp. 423–475). New York, NY: McGraw-Hill.

Kawakami, K., Dovidio, J.F., Moll, J., Hermsen, S., & Russin, A. (2000). Just say no (to stereotyping): Effects of training in the negation of stereotype associations on stereotype activation. *Journal of Personality and Social Psychology, 78*, 871–888.

Kawakami, K., Dunn, E., Karmali, F., & Dovidio, J. F. (2009). Mispredicting affective and behavioral responses to racism. *Science, 323*, 276–278.

Kawakami, K., Williams, A., Sidhu, D., Choma, B.L., Rodriguez-Bailon, R., Canadas, E., Chunch, D., & Hugenberg, K. (2014). An eye for the I: Preferential attention to the eyes of ingroup members. *Journal of Personality and Social Psychology, 107*, 1–20.

Kawakami, K., Young, H., & Dovidio, J.F. (2002). Automatic stereotyping: Category, trait, and behavioral activations. *Personality and Social Psychology Bulletin, 28*, 3–15.

Kawakami, N., Miura, E., & Yoshida, F. (2015). Conscious and unconscious processes are sensitive to different types of information. *Evolution, Mind and Behaviour, 13*, 37–46.

Kayaert, G., & Wagemans, J. (2009). Delayed shape matching benefits from simplicity and symmetry. *Vision Research, 49*, 708–717.

Keating, C.F., Randall, D.W., Kendrick, T., & Gutshall, K.A. (2003). Do babyfaced adults receive more help? The (cross-cultural) case of the lost resume. *Journal of Nonverbal Behavior, 27*, 89–109.

Keefe, P.R. (2016). Total recall. *The New Yorker*, August 22, pp. 48–57.

Kelley, H.H. (1967). Attribution theory in social psychology. In D. Levine (Ed.), *Nebraska symposium on motivation* (Vol. 15, pp. 192–238). Lincoln, NE: University of Nebraska Press.

Kelley, H.H. (1972). Causal schemata and the attribution process. In E.E. Jones, D.E. Kanouse, H.H. Kelley, R.E. Nisbett, S. Valins, & B. Weiner (Eds.), *Attribution: Perceiving the causes of behavior* (pp. 151–174). Morristown, NJ: General Learning Press.

Kelley, H.H. (1973). The process of causal attribution. *American Psychologist, 28*, 107–128.

Kelley, H.H., & Michela, J.L. (1980). Attribution theory and research. *Annual Review of Psychology, 31*, 457–501.

Kelley, M.R., Reysen, M.B., Ahlstrand, K.M., & Pentz, C.J. (2012). Collaborative inhibition persists following social processing. *Journal of Cognitive Psychology, 24*, 727–734.

Kendrick, R.V., & Olson, M.A. (2012). When feeling right leads to being right in the reporting of implicitly-formed attitudes, or how I learned to stop worrying and trust my gut. *Journal of Experimental Social Psychology, 48*, 1316–1321.

Kenny, D.A. (1991). A general model of consensus and accuracy in interpersonal perception. *Psychological Review, 98*, 155–163.

Kenny, D.A., & Judd, C.M. (2019). The unappreciated heterogeneity of effect sizes: Implications for power, precision, the planning of research, and replication. *Psychological Methods, 24*, 578–589.

Kenny, D.A., & Kashy, D.A. (2014). The design and analysis of data from dyads and groups. In H.T. Reis, C.M. Judd, H.T. Reis, & C.M. Judd (Eds.), *Handbook of research methods in social and personality psychology* (2nd ed., pp. 589–607). New York, NY: Cambridge University Press.

Kenny, D.A., & West, T.V. (2010). Similarity and agreement in self- and other perception: A meta-analysis. *Personality and Social Psychology Review, 14*, 196–213.

Kenny, D.A., Albright, L., Malloy, T.E., & Kashy, D.A. (1994). Consensus in interpersonal perception: Acquaintance and the Big Five. *Psychological Bulletin, 116*, 245–258.

Kenski, H.C., Aylor, B., & Kenski, K. (2002). Explaining the vote in a divided country: The Presidential election of 2000. In R. E. Denton, Jr. (Ed.), *The 2000 Presidential campaign: A communication perspective* (pp. 225–263). Westport, CT: Praeger.

Kershaw, S. (2009). Using menu psychology to entice diners. *New York Times*, D1, December 22.

Kervyn, N., Yzerbyt, V., & Judd, C.M. (2010). Compensation between warmth and competence: Antecedents and consequences of a negative relation between the two fundamental dimensions of social perception. *European Review of Social Psychology, 21,* 155–187.

Khan, U., & Dhar, R. (2010). Price-framing effects on the purchase of hedonic and utilitarian bundles. *Journal of Marketing Research, 47,* 1090–1099.

Khandelwal, K., Dhillon, M., Akalamkam, K., & Papneja, D. (2014). The ultimate attribution error: Does it transcend conflict? The case of Muslim adolescents in Kashmir and Delhi. *Psychological Studies, 59,* 427–435.

Kihlstrom, J.F. (2008). The psychological unconscious. In O.P. John, R.W. Robins, & L.A. Pervin (Eds.), *Handbook of personality: Theory and research* (3rd ed., pp. 583–602). New York, NY: Guilford Press.

Kihlstrom, J.F., & Klein, S.B. (1994). The self as a knowledge structure. In R.S. Wyer, Jr. & T.K. Srull (Eds.), *Handbook of social cognition, Vol. 2: Applications* (pp. 153–208). Mahwah, NJ: Lawrence Erlbaum.

Kilduff, G.J., Elfenbein, H.A., & Staw, B.M. (2010). The psychology of rivalry: A relationally-dependent analysis of competition. *Academy of Management Journal, 53,* 943–969.

Kim, D. (2003). Voluntary controllability of the Implicit Association Test (IAT). *Social Psychology Quarterly, 66,* 83–96.

Kim, K., & Johnson, M.K. (2014). Extended self: Spontaneous activation of medial prefrontal cortex by objects that are "mine." *Social Cognitive and Affective Neuroscience, 9,* 1006–1012.

Kimmes, J.G., & Durtschi, J.A. (2016). Forgiveness in romantic relationships: The roles of attachment, empathy, and attributions. *Journal of Marital and Family Therapy, 42,* 645–658.

Kinder, D.R. & Sanders, L.M. (1996). *Divided by color: Racial politics and democratic ideals.* Chicago, IL: University of Chicago Press.

King, L.A., Burton, C.M., Hicks, J.A., & Drigotas, S.M. (2007). Ghosts, UFOs, and magic: Positive affect and the experiential system. *Journal of Personality and Social Psychology, 92,* 905–919.

Kirkpatrick, L.A., & Epstein, S. (1992). Cognitive–experiential self-theory and subjective probability: Further evidence for two conceptual systems. *Journal of Personality and Social Psychology, 63,* 534–544.

Kitayama, S., Markus, H.R., Matsumoto, H., & Norasakkunkit, V. (1997). Individual and collective processes in the construction of the self: Self-enhancement in the United States and self-criticism in Japan. *Journal of Personality and Social Psychology, 72,* 1245–1267.

Klatzky, R.L., & Creswell, J.D. (2014). An intersensory interaction account of priming effects—and their absence. *Perspectives on Psychological Science, 9,* 49–58.

Klayman, J., & Ha, Y.-W. (1987). Confirmation, disconfirmation, and information in hypothesis testing. *Psychological Review, 94,* 211–228.

Kleider-Offutt, H.M., Bond, A.D., & Hegerty, S.E.A. (2017). Black stereotypical features: When a face type can get you in trouble. *Current Directions in Psychological Science, 26,* 28–33.

Klein, N., & Epley, N. (2016). Maybe holier, but definitely less evil, than you: Bounded self-righteousness in social judgment. *Journal of Personality and Social Psychology, 110,* 660–674.

Klein, R.A., Ratliff, K.A., Vianello, M., Adams, R.G., Bahnik, S., Bernstein, M.J.,... Nosek, B.A. (2014). Investigating variation in replicability: A "many labs" replication report. *Social Psychology, 45,* 142–152.

Klein, S.B., & Loftus, J. (1988). The nature of self-referent encoding: The contributions of elaborative and organizational processes. *Journal of Personality and Social Psychology, 55,* 5–11.

Klein, S.B., & Loftus, J. (1993). The mental representation of trait and autobiographical knowledge about the self. In T.K. Srull & R.S. Wyer, Jr. (Eds.), *Advances in social cognition* (Vol. 5, pp. 1–49). Hillsdale, NJ: Lawrence Erlbaum.

Klein, S.B., Chan, R.L., & Loftus, J. (1999). Independence of episodic and semantic self-knowledge: The case of autism. *Social Cognition, 17*, 413–436.

Klein, S.B., Loftus, J., & Burton, H.A. (1989). Two self-reference effects: The importance of distinguishing between self-descriptiveness judgments and autobiographical retrieval in self-referent encoding. *Journal of Personality and Social Psychology, 56*, 853–865.

Klein, S.B., Loftus, J., Trafton, J.G., & Fuhrman, R.W. (1992). Use of exemplars and abstractions in trait judgments: A model of trait knowledge about self and others. *Journal of Personality and Social Psychology, 63*, 739–753.

Knetsch, J.L. (1989). The endowment effect and evidence of nonreversible indifference curves. *American Economic Review, 79*, 1277–1284.

Knight, J.A., & Vallacher, R.R. (1981). Interpersonal engagement in social perception: The consequences of getting into the action. *Journal of Personality and Social Psychology, 40*, 990–999.

Kobrynowicz, D., & Biernat, M. (1997). Decoding subjective evaluations: How stereotypes provide shifting standards. *Journal of Experimental Social Psychology, 33*, 579–601.

Koch, A., Alves, H., Krüger, T., & Unkelbach, C. (2016). A general valence asymmetry in similarity: Good is more alike than bad. *Journal of Experimental Psychology: Learning, Memory, and Cognition, 42*, 1171–1192.

Koenig, A.M., Eagly, A.H., Mitchell, A.A., & Ristikari, T. (2011). Are leader stereotypes masculine? A meta-analysis of three research paradigms. *Psychological Bulletin, 137*, 616–642.

Kolatch, A.J. (1996). *Great Jewish quotations.* New York, NY: Jonathan David.

Koole, S.L., Dijksterhuis, A., & van Knippenberg, A. (2001). What's in a name: Implicit self-esteem and the automatic self. *Journal of Personality and Social Psychology, 80*, 669–685.

Kootstra, G., de Boer, B., & Schomaker, L.R.B. (2011). Predicting eye fixations on complex visual stimuli using local symmetry. *Cognitive Computation, 3*, 223–240.

Köpetz, C., & Kruglanski, A.W. (2008). Effects of accessibility and subjective relevance on the use of piecemeal and category information in impression formation. *Personality and Social Psychology Bulletin, 34*, 692–705.

Kopietz, R., Hellmann, J.H., Higgins, E.T., & Echterhoff, G. (2010). Shared-reality effects on memory: Communicating to fulfill epistemic needs. *Social Cognition, 28*, 353–378.

Koppel, J., & Rubin, D.C. (2016). Recent advances in understanding the reminiscence bump: The importance of cues in guiding recall from autobiographical memory. *Current Directions in Psychological Science, 25*, 135–140.

Korman, J., & Malle, B.F. (2016). Grasping for traits or reasons? How people grapple with puzzling social behaviors. *Personality and Social Psychology Bulletin, 11*, 1451–1465.

Kozak, M.N., Marsh, A.A., & Wegner, D.M. (2006). What do I think you're doing? Action identification and mind attribution. *Journal of Personality and Social Psychology, 90*, 543–555.

Kramer, T.H., Buckhout, R., & Eugenio, P. (1990). Weapon focus, arousal and eyewitness memory. *Law and Human Behavior, 14*, 167–184.

Kraus, M.W., & Chen, S. (2009). Striving to be known by significant others: Automatic activation of self-verification goals in relationship contexts. *Journal of Personality and Social Psychology, 97*, 58–73.

Kraus, S., Ryan, C.S., Judd, C.M., Hastie, R., & Park, B. (1993). Use of mental frequency distributions to represent variability among members of social categories. *Social Cognition, 11*, 22–43.

Kraus, S.J. (1995). Attitudes and the prediction of behavior: A meta-analysis of the empirical literature. *Personality and Social Psychology Bulletin, 21*, 58–75.

Krauth-Gruber, S., & Ric, F. (2000). Affect and stereotypic thinking: A test of the mood-and-general-knowledge model. *Personality and Social Psychology Bulletin, 26*, 1587–1597.

Kravitz, D.A., & Martin, B. (1986). Ringelmann rediscovered: The original article. *Journal of Personality and Social Psychology, 50*, 936–941.

Kray, L.J., Galinsky, A.D., & Wong, E.M. (2006). Thinking within the box: The relational processing style elicited by counterfactual mind-sets. *Journal of Personality and Social Psychology, 91*, 33–48.

Kray, L.J., George, L.G., Liljenquist, K.A., Galinsky, A.D., Tetlock, P.E., & Roese, N.J. (2010). From what might have been to what must have been: Counterfactual thinking creates meaning. *Journal of Personality and Social Psychology, 98*, 106–118.

Kressel, L.M., & Uleman, J.S. (2010). Personality traits function as causal concepts. *Journal of Experimental Social Psychology, 46*, 213–216.

Krieglmeyer, R., & Sherman, J.W. (2012). Disentangling stereotype activation and stereotype application in the stereotype misperception task. *Journal of Personality and Social Psychology, 103*, 205–224.

Krosch, A.R., & Amodio, D.M. (2014). Economic scarcity alters the perception of race. *Proceedings of the National Academy of Sciences, 111*, 9079–9084.

Krosch, A.R., & Amodio, D.M. (2019). Scarcity disrupts the neural encoding of Black faces: A socioperceptual pathway to discrimination. *Journal of Personality and Social Psychology, 117*, 859–875.

Krosch, A.R., Berntsen, L., Amodio, D.M., Jost, J.T., & Van Bavel, J.J. (2013). On the ideology of hypodescent: Political conservatism predicts categorization of racially ambiguous faces as Black. *Journal of Experimental Social Psychology, 49*, 1196–1203.

Krosch, A.R., Tyler, T.R., & Amodio, D.M. (2017). Race and recession: Effects of economic scarcity on racial discrimination. *Journal of Personality and Social Psychology, 113*, 892–909.

Krosnick, J.A., & Petty, R.E. (1995). Attitude strength: An overview. In R.E. Petty & J.A. Krosnick (Eds.), *Ohio State University series on attitudes and persuasion, Vol. 4. Attitude strength: Antecedents and consequences* (pp. 1–24). Mahwah, NJ: Lawrence Erlbaum.

Krosnick, J.A., Li, F., & Lehman, D.R. (1990). Conversational conventions, order of information acquisition, and the effect of base rates and individuating information on social judgments. *Journal of Personality and Social Psychology, 59*, 1140–1152.

Krueger, J. (2007). From social projection to social behaviour. *European Review of Social Psychology, 18*, 1–35.

Krueger, J. (Ed.) (2012). *Social judgment and decision making.* New York, NY: Psychology Press.

Krueger, J., & Clement, R.W. (1994a). Memory-based judgments about multiple categories: A revision and extension of Tajfel's accentuation theory. *Journal of Personality and Social Psychology, 67*, 35–47.

Krueger, J., & Clement, R.W. (1994b). The truly false consensus effect: An eradicable and egocentric bias in social perception. *Journal of Personality and Social Psychology, 67*, 596–610.

Krueger, J., & Mueller, R.A. (2002). Unskilled, unaware, or both? The better-than-average heuristic and statistical regression predict errors in estimates of own performance. *Journal of Personality and Social Psychology, 82*, 180–188.

Krueger, J., & Rothbart, M. (1988). Use of categorical and individuating information in making inferences about personality. *Journal of Personality and Social Psychology, 55*, 187–195.

Krueger, J., & Rothbart, M. (1990). Contrast and accentuation effects in category learning. *Journal of Personality and Social Psychology*, *59*, 651–663.

Krueger, J., Acevedo, M., & Robbins, J.M. (2005). Self as sample. In K. Fiedler & P. Juslin (Eds.), *Information sampling and adaptive cognition* (pp. 353–377). New York, NY: Cambridge University Press.

Kruger, J. (1999). Lake Wobegon, be gone! The "below-average effect" and the egocentric nature of comparative ability judgments. *Journal of Personality and Social Psychology*, *77*, 221–232.

Kruger, J., & Dunning, D. (1999). Unskilled and unaware of it: How difficulties in recognizing one's own incompetence lead to inflated self-assessments. *Journal of Personality and Social Psychology*, *77*, 1121–1134.

Kruger, J., & Gilovich, T. (1999). "Naïve cynicism" in everyday theories of responsibility assessment: On biased assumptions of bias. *Journal of Personality and Social Psychology*, *76*, 743–753.

Kruglanski, A.W., & Mayseless, O. (1990). Classic and current social comparison research: Expanding the perspective. *Psychological Bulletin*, *108*, 195–208.

Kruglanski, A.W., & Orehek, E. (2009). Toward a relativity theory of rationality. *Social Cognition*, *5*, 639–660.

Kruglanski, A.W., Hamel, I.Z., Maides, S.A., & Schwartz, J.M. (1978). Attribution theory as a special case of lay epistemology. In J.H. Harvey, W. Ickes, & R.F. Kidd (Eds.), *New directions in attribution research* (Vol. 2, pp. 299–333). Hillsdale, NJ: Lawrence Erlbaum.

Kruglanski, A.W., Schwartz, J.M., Maides, S., & Hamel, I.Z. (1978). Covariation, discounting, and augmentation: Towards a clarification of attributional principles. *Journal of Personality*, *46*, 176–189.

Krull, D.S. (2001). On partitioning the fundamental attribution error: Dispositionalism and the correspondence bias. In G.B. Moskowitz (Ed.), *Cognitive social psychology* (pp. 211–227). Mahwah, NJ: Lawrence Erlbaum.

Kruschke, J.K. (1996). Base rates in category learning. *Journal of Experimental Psychology: Learning, Memory, and Cognition*, *22*, 3–26.

Kruschke, J.K. (2003). Attention in learning. *Current Directions in Psychological Science*, *12*, 171–175.

Kruschke, J.K. (2011). Models of attentional learning. In E.M. Pothos & A.J. Wills (Eds.), *Formal approaches in categorization* (pp. 120–152). New York, NY: Cambridge University Press.

Ku, G., Wang, C.S., & Galinsky, A.D. (2010). Perception through a perspective-taking lens: Differential effects on judgments and behavior. *Journal of Experimental Social Psychology*, *46*, 792–798.

Kunda, Z. (1987). Motivated inference: Self-serving generation and evaluation of causal theories. *Journal of Personality and Social Psychology*, *53*, 636–647.

Kunda, Z. (1990). The case for motivated reasoning. *Psychological Bulletin*, *108*, 480–498.

Kunda, Z., & Spencer, S.J. (2003). When do stereotypes come to mind and when do they color judgment? A goal-based theoretical framework for stereotype activation and application. *Psychological Bulletin*, *129*, 522–544.

Kunda, Z., & Thagard, P. (1996). Forming impressions from stereotypes, traits, and behaviors: A parallel-constraint-satisfaction theory. *Psychological Review*, *103*, 284–308.

Kunda, Z., Sinclair, L., & Griffin, D. (1997). Equal ratings, but separate meanings: Stereotypes and the construal of traits. *Journal of Personality and Social Psychology*, *72*, 720–734.

Kunstman, J.W., & Fitzpatrick, C.B. (2018). Why are they being so nice to us? Social identity threat and the suspicion of Whites' motives. *Self and Identity*, *17*, 432–442.

Kurdek, L.A. (2001). Differences between heterosexual-nonparent couples and gay, lesbian, and heterosexual-parent couples. *Journal of Family Issues*, *22*, 728–755.

Kurdi, B., Seitchik, A.E., Axt, J.R., Carroll, T.J., Karapetyan, A., Kaushik, N., Tomezsko, D., Greenwald, A.G., & Banaji, M.R. (2019). Relationship between the implicit association test and intergroup behavior: A meta-analysis. *American Psychologist, 74,* 569–586.

Kurman, J. (2003). Why is self-enhancement low in certain collectivist cultures? An investigation of two competing explanations. *Journal of Cross-Cultural Psychology, 34,* 496–510.

Kutlaca, M., Becker, J., & Radke, H. (2020). A hero for the outgroup, a black sheep for the ingroup: Societal perceptions of those who confront discrimination. *Journal of Experimental Social Psychology, 88,* Article 103832.

Kutner, B., Wilkins, C., & Yarrow, P.R. (1952). Verbal attitudes and overt behavior involving racial prejudice. *Journal of Abnormal and Social Psychology, 47,* 649–652.

Kvavilashvili, L., Mirani, J., Schlagman, S., Foley, K., & Kornbrot, D.E. (2009). Consistency of flashbulb memories of September 11 over long delays: Implications for consolidation and wrong time slice hypotheses. *Journal of Memory and Language, 61,* 556–572.

LaBine, S.J., & LaBine, G. (1996). Determinations of negligence and the hindsight bias. *Law and Human Behavior, 20,* 501–516.

Labov, W. (1973). The boundaries of words and their meanings. In C.-J.N. Bailey & R.W. Shuy (Eds.), *New ways of analyzing variations in English* (pp. 340–373). Washington, DC: Georgetown University Press.

Laham, S.M., Kashima, Y., Dix, J., & Wheeler, M. (2015). A meta-analysis of the facilitation of arm flexion and extension movements as a function of stimulus valence. *Cognition and Emotion, 29,* 1069–1090.

Laham, S.M., Kashima, Y., Dix, J., Wheeler, M., & Levis, B. (2014). Elaborated contextual framing is necessary for action-based attitude acquisition. *Cognition and Emotion, 28,* 1119–1126.

Laham, S.M., Koval, P., & Alter, A.L. (2012). The name-pronunciation effect: Why people like Mr. Smith more than Mr. Colquhoun. *Journal of Experimental Social Psychology, 48,* 752–756.

Lahmeyer, H.W., Miller, M., & DeLeon-Jones, F. (1982). Anxiety and mood fluctuation during the normal menstrual cycle. *Psychosomatic Medicine, 44,* 183–194.

Lai, C.K., Marini, M., Lehr, S.A., Cerruti, C., Shin, J.L., Joy-Gaba, J.A., … Nosek, B.A. (2014). Reducing implicit racial preferences: I. A comparative investigation of 17 interventions. *Journal of Experimental Psychology: General, 143,* 1765–1785.

Lai, C.K., Skinner, A.L., Cooley, E., Murrar, S., Brauer, M., Devos, T., … Nosek, B.A. (2016). Reducing implicit racial preferences: II. Intervention effectiveness across time. *Journal of Experimental Psychology: General, 145,* 1001–1016.

Laidlaw, K.E.W., Risko, E.F., & Kingstone, A. (2012). A new look at social attention: Orienting the eyes is not (entirely) under volitional control. *Journal of Experimental Psychology: Human Perception and Performance, 38,* 1132–1143.

Lakin, J.L., & Chartrand, T.L. (2003). Using nonconscious behavioral mimicry to create affiliation and rapport. *Psychological Science, 14,* 334–339.

Lakoff, G.P. (2004). *Don't think of an elephant!* White River Junction, VT: Chelsea Green.

Lakoff, G.P., & Wehling, E. (2012). *The little blue book: The essential guide to thinking and talking Democratic.* New York, NY: Free Press.

Lalljee, M., Lamb, R., Furnham, A.F., & Jaspars, J. (1984). Explanations and information search: Inductive and hypothesis-testing approaches to arriving at an explanation. *British Journal of Social Psychology, 23,* 201–212.

Landau, M.J., Meier, B.P., & Keefer, L.A. (2010). A metaphor-enriched social cognition. *Psychological Bulletin, 136,* 1045–1067.

Landau, M.J., Sullivan, D., & Greenberg, J. (2009). Evidence that self-relevant motives and metaphoric framing interact to influence political and social attitudes. *Psychological Science, 20*, 1421–1427.

Landman, J. (1987). Regret and elation following action and inaction: Affective responses to positive versus negative outcomes. *Personality and Social Psychology Bulletin, 13*, 524–536.

Laney, C., Morris, E.K., Bernstein, D.M., Wakefield, B.M., & Loftus, E.F. (2008). Asparagus, a love story: Healthier eating could be just a false memory away. *Experimental Psychology, 55*, 291–300.

Lang, P.J., Bradley, M.M., & Cuthbert, B.N. (1990). Emotion, attention, and the startle reflex. *Psychological Review, 97*, 377–395.

Langer, E.J. (1978). Rethinking the role of thought in social interaction. In J.H. Harvey, W.I. Ickes, & R.F. Kidd (Eds.), *New directions in attribution research* (Vol. 2, pp. 35–58). Hillsdale, NJ: Lawrence Erlbaum.

Langer, E.J. (2014). Mindfulness forward and back. In A. Ie, C.T. Ngnoumen, & E.J. Langer (Eds.), *The Wiley Blackwell handbook of mindfulness* (pp. 7–20). New York, NY: Wiley Blackwell.

Langer, E.J., & Imber, L. (1980). Role of mindlessness in the perception of deviance. *Journal of Personality and Social Psychology, 39*, 360–367.

Langer, E.J., Blank, A., & Chanowitz, B. (1978). The mindlessness of ostensibly thoughtful action: The role of "placebo" information in interpersonal interaction. *Journal of Personality and Social Psychology, 36*, 635–642.

Langer, E.J., Pirson, M., & Delizonna, L. (2010). The mindlessness of social comparisons. *Psychology of Aesthetics, Creativity, and the Arts, 4*, 68–74.

Langer, G. (2004). Poll: Viewers divided on debate winner. *ABC News*, October 9.

Langeslag, S.J.E., & van Strien, J.W. (2018). Early visual processing of snakes and angry faces: An ERP study. *Brain Research, 1678*, 297–303.

Langlois, J.H., & Roggman, L.A. (1990). Attractive faces are only average. *Psychological Science, 1*, 115–121.

Langlois, J.H., Kalakanis, L., Rubenstein, A.J., Larson, A., Hallam, M., & Smoot, M. (2000). Maxims or myths of beauty? A meta-analytic and theoretical review. *Psychological Bulletin, 126*, 390–423.

Langlois, J.H., Ritter, J.M., Roggman, L.A., & Vaughn, L.S. (1991). Facial diversity and infant preferences for attractive faces. *Developmental Psychology, 27*, 79–84.

Langlois, J.H., Roggman, L.A., & Musselman L. (1994). What is average and what is not average about attractive faces. *Psychological Science, 5*, 214–220.

LaPiere, R.T. (1934). Attitudes versus actions. *Social Forces, 13*, 230–237.

Larkin, J.L., & Chartrand, T.L. (2003). Using nonconscious behavioral mimicry to create affiliation and rapport. *Psychological Science, 14*, 334–339.

Lassiter, G.D. (2002). Illusory causation in the courtroom. *Current Directions in Psychological Science, 11*, 204–208.

Lassiter, G.D., & Irvine, A.A. (1986). Videotaped confessions: The impact of camera point of view on judgments of coercion. *Journal of Applied Social Psychology, 16*, 268–276.

Lassiter, G.D., Geers, A.L., Apple, K.J., & Beers, M.J. (2000). Observational goals and behavior unitization: A reexamination. *Journal of Experimental Social Psychology, 36*, 649–659.

Lassiter, G.D., Geers, A.L., Handley, I.M., Weiland, P.E., & Munhall, P.J. (2002). Videotaped interrogations and confessions: A simple change in camera perspective alters verdicts in simulated trials. *Journal of Applied Psychology, 87*, 867–874.

Lassiter, G.D., Geers, A.L., Munhall, P.J., Handley, I.M., & Beers, M.J. (2001). Videotaped confessions. Is guilt in the eye of the camera? In M.P. Zanna (Ed.), *Advances in experimental social psychology* (Vol. 33, pp. 189–254). New York, NY: Academic Press.

Lassiter, G.D., Geers, A.L., Munhall, P.J., Ploutz-Snyder, R.J., & Breitenbecher, D.L. (2002). Illusory causation: Why it occurs. *Psychological Science, 13*, 299–305.

Lassiter, G.D., Lindberg, M.J., Gonzalez-Vallejo, C., Bellezza, F.S., & Phillips, N.D. (2009). The deliberation-without-attention effect: Evidence for an artifactual interpretation. *Psychological Science, 20,* 671–675.

Latane, B., & Darley, J.M. (1970). *The unresponsive bystander: Why doesn't he help?* New York, NY: Appleton-Century-Crofts.

Lau, R.R. (1984). Dynamics of the attribution process. *Journal of Personality and Social Psychology, 46,* 1017–1028.

Le, H., Oh, I.-S., Robbins, S.B., Ilies, R., Holland, E., & Westrick, P. (2011). Too much of a good thing: Curvilinear relationships between personality traits and job performance. *Journal of Applied Psychology, 96,* 113–133.

Le Bon, G. (1897). *The crowd: A study of the popular mind.* New York, NY: Macmillan.

Leander, N.P., Chartrand, T.L., & Wood, W. (2011). Mind your mannerisms: Behavioral mimicry elicits stereotype conformity. *Journal of Experimental Social Psychology, 47,* 195–201.

Leary, M.R. (1982). Hindsight distortion and the 1980 presidential election. *Personality and Social Psychology Bulletin, 8,* 257–263.

LeBarr, A.N., & Shedden, J.M. (2017). Psychological ownership: The implicit association between self and already-owned versus newly-owned objects. *Consciousness and Cognition, 48,* 190–197.

LeBoeuf, R.A., & Estes, Z. (2004). "Fortunately, I'm no Einstein": Comparison relevance as a determinant of behavioral assimilation and contrast. *Social Cognition, 22,* 607–636.

Lebrecht, S., Pierce, L.J., Tarr, M., & Tanaka, J.W. (2009). Perceptual other-race training reduces implicit racial bias. *PLOS ONE, 4,* 1–7.

Ledgerwood, A., & Boydstun, A.E. (2014). Sticky prospects: Loss frames are cognitively stickier than gain frames. *Journal of Experimental Psychology: General, 143,* 376–385.

Ledgerwood, A., & Chaiken, S. (2007). Priming us and them: Automatic assimilation and contrast in group attitudes. *Journal of Personality and Social Psychology, 93,* 940–956.

Ledgerwood, A., Liviatan, I., & Carnevale, P.J. (2007). Group-identity completion and the symbolic value of property. *Psychological Science, 18,* 873–878.

Ledgerwood, A., Wakslak, C.J., & Wang, M.K. (2010). Differential information use for near and distant decisions. *Journal of Experimental Social Psychology, 46,* 638–642.

LeDoux, J.E. (1995). Emotion: Clues from the brain. *Annual Review of Psychology, 46,* 209–235.

LeDoux, J.E. (1996). *The emotional brain.* New York, NY: Simon & Schuster.

LeDoux, J.E. (2000). Emotion circuits in the brain. *Annual Review of Neuroscience, 23,* 155–184.

LeDoux, J.E., & Pine, D.S. (2016). Using neuroscience to help understand fear and anxiety: A two-system framework. *American Journal of Psychiatry, 173,* 1083–1093.

Lee, A.Y., & Aaker, J.L. (2004). Bringing the frame into focus: The influence of regulatory fit on processing fluency and persuasion. *Journal of Personality and Social Psychology, 86,* 205–218.

Lee, A.Y., & Labroo, A.A. (2004). The effect of conceptual and perceptual fluency on brand evaluation. *Journal of Marketing Research, 41,* 151–165.

Lee, M.P., & Suk, K. (2010). Disambiguating the role of ambiguity in perceptual assimilation and contrast effects. *Journal of Consumer Research, 36,* 890–897.

Lee, S.W.S. (2016). Multimodal priming of abstract constructs. *Current Opinion in Psychology, 12,* 37–44.

Lee, T.L., Fiske, S.T., & Glick, P. (2010). Next gen ambivalent sexism: Converging correlates, causality in context, and converse causality, an introduction to the special issue. *Sex Roles: A Journal of Research, 62,* 395–404.

Legrand, E., Bieleke, M., Gollwitzer, P.M., & Mignon, A. (2017). Nothing will stop me?

Flexibly tenacious goal striving with implementation intentions. *Motivation Science, 3,* 101–118.

Lemm, K.M. (2006). Positive associations among interpersonal contact, motivation, and implicit and explicit attitudes toward gay men. *Journal of Homosexuality, 51,* 79–99.

Lench, H.C., & Ditto, P.H. (2008). Automatic optimism: Biased use of base rate information for positive and negative events. *Journal of Experimental Social Psychology, 44,* 631–639.

Lench, H.C., Levine, L.J., Perez, K., Carpenter, Z.K., Carlson, S.J., Bench, S.W., & Wan, Y. (2019). When and why people misestimate future feelings: Identifying strengths and weaknesses in affective forecasting. *Journal of Personality and Social Psychology, 116,* 724–742.

Lench, H.C., Safer, M.A., & Levine, L.J. (2011). Focalism and the underestimation of future emotion: When it's worse than imagined. *Emotion, 11,* 278–285.

Letzring, T.D., & Funder, D.C. (2018). Interpersonal accuracy in trait judgments. In V. Zeigler-Hill & T.K. Shackelford (Eds.), *The SAGE handbook of personality and individual differences: Applications of personality and individual differences* (pp. 253–282). Thousand Oaks, CA: Sage.

Letzring, T.D., Wells, S.M., & Funder, D.C. (2006). Information quantity and quality affect the realistic accuracy of personality judgment. *Journal of Personality and Social Psychology, 91,* 111–123.

Lev-On, A., & Waismel-Manor, I. (2016). Looks that matter: The effect of physical attractiveness in low- and high-information elections. *American Behavioral Scientist, 60,* 1756–1771.

Levey, A.B., & Martin, I. (1975). Classical conditioning of human 'evaluative' responses. *Behaviour Research and Therapy, 4,* 205–207.

Levin, D.T. (2000). Race as a visual feature: Using visual search and perceptual discrimination tasks to understand face categories and the cross-race recognition deficit. *Journal of Experimental Psychology: General, 129,* 559–574.

Levin, D.T., Drivdahl, S.B., Momen, N., & Beck, M.R. (2002). False predictions about the detectability of visual changes: The role of beliefs about attention, memory, and the continuity of attended objects in causing change blindness blindness. *Consciousness and Cognition: An International Journal, 11,* 507–527.

Levin, I.P., & Gaeth, G.J. (1988). Framing of attribute information before and after consuming the product. *Journal of Consumer Research, 15,* 374–378.

Levine, J.M., & Moreland, R.L. (1994). Group socialization: Theory and research. In W. Stroebe & M. Hewstone (Eds.), *European review of social psychology* (Vol. 5, pp. 305–336). Chichester: Wiley.

Levine, J.M., Bogart, L.M., & Zdaniuk, B. (1996). Impact of anticipated group membership on cognition. In R.M. Sorrentino & E.T. Higgins (Eds.), *Handbook of motivation and cognition* (Vol. 3, pp. 531–569). New York, NY: Guilford Press.

Levine, J.M., Moreland, R.L., & Hausmann, L.R.M. (2005). Managing group composition: Inclusive and exclusive role transitions. In D. Abrams, M.A. Hogg, & J.M. Marques (Eds.), *The social psychology of inclusion and exclusion* (pp. 139–160). New York, NY: Psychology Press.

Levine, L.J., Lench, H.C., Kaplan, R.L., & Safer, M. (2012). Accuracy and artifact: Reexamining the intensity bias in affective forecasting. *Journal of Personality and Social Psychology, 103,* 584–605.

Levy, B. (1996). Improving memory in old age through implicit self-stereotyping. *Journal of Personality and Social Psychology, 71,* 1092–1107.

Levy, B., Ashman, O., & Dror, I. (2000). To be or not to be: The effects of aging stereotypes on the will to live. *Omega, 40,* 409–420.

Levy, B.R., Hausdorff, J.M., Hencke, R., & Wei, J.Y. (2000). Reducing cardiovascular stress with positive self-stereotypes of aging. *Journals of Gerontology, Series B:*

Psychological Sciences & Social Sciences, *55,* 205–213.

Levy, B.R., Pilver, C., Chung, P.H., & Slade, M.D. (2014). Subliminal strengthening: Improving older individuals' physical function over time with an implicit-age-stereotype intervention. *Psychological Science, 25,* 2127–2135.

Levy, J.S. (1992). Prospect theory and international relations: Theoretical applications and analytical problems. *Political Psychology, 13,* 283–310.

Levy, S.R., Stroessner, S.J., & Dweck, C.S. (1998). Stereotype formation and endorsement: The role of implicit theories. *Journal of Personality and Social Psychology, 74,* 1421–1436.

Lewin, K. (1935). *A dynamic theory of personality.* New York, NY: McGraw-Hill.

Lewis, K., & Herndon, B. (2011). Transactive memory systems: Current issues and future research directions. *Organization Science, 22,* 1254–1265.

Lewis, M. (2016). *The undoing project: A friendship that changed our minds.* New York, NY: Norton.

Lewis, T., & Cheng, S.-Y. (2006). Tracking, expectations, and the transformation of vocational education. *American Journal of Education, 113,* 67–99.

Leyens, J.-P., & Yzerbyt, V.Y. (1992). The ingroup overexclusion effect: The impact of valence and confirmation on information search. *European Journal of Social Psychology, 22,* 549–569.

Liang, D.W., Moreland, R.L., & Argote, L. (1995). Group versus individual training and group performance: The mediating role of transactive memory. *Personality and Social Psychology Bulletin, 21,* 384–393.

Libby, L.K., & Eibach, R.P. (2002). Looking back in time: Self-concept change affects visual perspective in autobiographical memory. *Journal of Personality and Social Psychology, 82,* 167–179.

Libby, L.K., & Eibach, R.P. (2011). Visual perspective in mental imagery: A representational tool that functions in judgment, emotion, and self-insight. In M.P. Zanna & J.M. Olson (Eds.), *Advances in experimental social psychology* (Vol. 44, pp. 185–245). San Diego, CA: Academic Press.

Libby, L.K., Eibach, R.P., & Gilovich, T. (2005). Here's looking at me: The effect of memory perspective on assessments of personal change. *Journal of Personality and Social Psychology, 88,* 50–62.

Libby, L.K., Shaeffer, E.M., & Eibach, R.P. (2009). Seeing meaning in action: A bidirectional link between visual perspective and action identification level. *Journal of Experimental Psychology: General, 138,* 503–516.

Libby, L.K., Shaeffer, E.M., Eibach, R.P., & Slemmer, J.A. (2007). Picture yourself at the polls: Visual perspective in mental imagery affects self-perception and behavior. *Psychological Science, 18,* 199–203.

Lichtenstein, M., & Srull, T.K. (1987). Processing objectives as a determinant of the relationship between recall and judgment. *Journal of Experimental Social Psychology, 23,* 93–118.

Lick, D.J., & Johnson, K.L. (2013). Fluency of visual processing explains prejudiced evaluations following categorization of concealable identities. *Journal of Experimental Social Psychology, 49,* 419–425.

Lick, D.J., & Johnson, K.L. (2014). Recalibrating gender perception: Face aftereffects and the perceptual underpinnings of gender-related biases. *Journal of Experimental Psychology: General, 143,* 1259–1276.

Lick, D.J., & Johnson, K.L. (2015). The interpersonal consequences of processing ease: Fluency as a metacognitive foundation for prejudice. *Current Directions in Psychological Science, 24,* 143–148.

Lick, D.J., Johnson, K.L., & Gill, S.V. (2013). Deliberate changes to gendered body motion influence basic social perceptions. *Social Cognition, 31,* 656–671.

Lick, D.J., Johnson, K.L., & Rule, N.O. (2015). Disfluent processing helps to explain anti-bisexual prejudice. *Journal of Nonverbal Behavior, 39,* 257–288.

Lick, D.J., Johnson, K.L., Rule, N.O., & Stroessner, S.J. (2019). Perceivers infer base rates from social context to judge perceptually ambiguous social identities. *Social Cognition, 37*, 596–623.

Lickel, B., Hamilton, D.L., Wieczorkowska, G., Lewis, A., Sherman, S.J., & Uhles, A.N. (2000). Varieties of groups and the perception of group entitativity. *Journal of Personality and Social Psychology, 78*, 223–246.

Lie, H.C., Rhodes, G., & Simmons L.W. (2008). Genetic diversity revealed in human faces. *Evolution, 62*, 2473–2486.

Lieberman, D., & Patrick, C. (2018). *Objection: Disgust, morality, and the law.* New York, NY: Oxford University Press.

Lieberman, M.D. (2003). Reflective and reflexive judgment processes: A social cognitive neuroscience approach. In J.P. Forgas, K.R. Williams, & W. von Hippel (Eds.), *Social judgments: Explicit and implicit processes* (pp. 44–67). New York, NY: Cambridge University Press.

Lieberman, M.D. (2013). *Social: Why our brains are wired to connect.* New York, NY: Crown.

Lieder, F., Griffiths, T.L., Huys, Q.J.M., & Goodman, N.D. (2018). Empirical evidence for resource-rational anchoring and adjustment. *Psychonomic Bulletin & Review, 25*, 775–784.

Light, L.L., Hollander, S., & Kayra-Stuart, F. (1981). Why attractive people are harder to remember. *Personality and Social Psychology Bulletin, 7*, 269–276.

Lin, M.-Y., & Kressin, N.R. (2015). Race/ethnicity and Americans' experiences with treatment decision making. *Patient Education and Counseling, 98*, 1636–1642.

Lindsay, D.S., & Read, J.D. (1994). Psychotherapy and memories of childhood sexual abuse: A cognitive perspective. *Applied Cognitive Psychology, 8*, 281–338.

Lindsay, D.S., Allen, B.P., Chan, J.C.K., & Dahl, L.C. (2004). Eyewitness suggestibility and source similarity: Intrusions of details from one event into memory reports of another event. *Journal of Memory and Language, 7*, 1–19.

Lindsay, D.S., Hagen, L., Read, J.D., Wade, K.A., & Garry, M. (2004). True photographs and false memories. *Psychological Science, 15*, 149–154.

Linville, P.W., Fischer, G.W., & Salovey, P. (1989). Perceived distributions of the characteristics of in-group and out-group members: Empirical evidence and a computer simulation. *Journal of Personality and Social Psychology, 57*, 165–188.

Lipko, A.R., Dunlosky, J., & Merriman, W.E. (2009). Persistent overconfidence despite practice: The role of task experience in preschoolers' recall predictions. *Journal of Experimental Child Psychology, 103*, 152–166.

Lipkus, I.M., Green, J.D., Feaganes, J.R., & Sedikides, C. (2001). The relationship between attitudinal ambivalence and desire to quit smoking among college smokers. *Journal of Applied Social Psychology, 31*, 113–133.

Little, A.C. (2012). Manipulation of infant-like traits affects perceived cuteness of infant, adult and cat faces. *Ethology, 118*, 775–782.

Little, A.C., & Jones, B.C. (2012). Variation in facial masculinity and symmetry preferences across the menstrual cycle is moderated by relationship context. *Psychoneuroendocrinology, 37*, 999–1008.

Little, A.C., Burriss, R.P., Jones, B.C., & Roberts, S.C. (2007). Facial appearance affects voting decisions. *Evolution and Human Behavior, 28*, 18–27.

Little, A.C., Jones, B.C., Burt, D.M., & Perrett, D.I. (2007). Preferences for symmetry in faces change across the menstrual cycle. *Biological Psychology, 76*, 209–216.

Little, A.C., Jones, B.C., & DeBruine, L.M. (2011). Facial attractiveness: Evolutionary based research. *Philosophical Transactions of the Royal Society, 366*, 1638–1659.

Liu, L., Ioannides, A.A., & Streit, M. (1999). Single trial analysis of neurophysiological correlates of the recognition of complex objects and facial expressions of emotion. *Brain Topography, 11*, 291–303.

Liviatan, I., Trope, Y., & Liberman, N. (2008). Interpersonal similarity as a social distance dimension: Implications for perceiving others' actions. *Journal of Experimental Social Psychology*, *44*, 1256–1269.

Livingston, R.W., & Brewer, M.B. (2002). What are we really priming? Cue-based versus category-based processing of facial stimuli. *Journal of Personality and Social Psychology*, *82*, 5–18.

LoBue, V., & DeLoache, J.S. (2010). Superior detection of threat-relevant stimuli in infancy. *Developmental Science*, *13*, 221–228.

Locher, P.J., & Wagemans, J. (1993). The effects of element type and spatial grouping on symmetry detection. *Perception*, *22*, 565–587.

Locke, E.A. (2015). Theory building, replication, and behavioral priming: Where do we need to go from here? *Perspectives on Psychological Science*, *10*, 408–414.

Locksley, A., Hepburn, C., & Ortiz, V. (1982). Social stereotypes and judgments of individuals: An instance of the base-rate fallacy. *Journal of Experimental Social Psychology*, *18*, 23–42.

Loersch, C., & Payne, B.K. (2014). Situated inferences and the what, who, and where of priming. *Social Cognition*, *32*, 142–156.

Loftus, E.F. (1993). The reality of repressed memories. *American Psychologist*, *48*, 518–537.

Loftus, E.F. (2005). Planting misinformation in the human mind: A 30-year investigation of the malleability of memory. *Learning & Memory*, *12*, 361–366.

Loftus, E.F., & Davis, D. (2006). Recovered memories. *Annual Review of Clinical Psychology*, *2*, 469–498.

Loftus, E.F., & Hoffman, H.G. (1989). Misinformation and memory: The creation of memory. *Journal of Experimental Psychology: General*, 118, 100–104.

Loftus, E.F., & Palmer, J.C. (1974). Reconstruction of automobile destruction: An example of the interaction between language and memory. *Journal of Verbal Learning and Verbal Behavior*, *13*, 585–589.

Loftus, E.F., & Pickrell, J.E. (1995). The formation of false memories. *Psychiatric Annals*, *25*, 720–725.

Loftus, E.F., Loftus, G.R., & Messo, J. (1987). Some facts about "weapon focus." *Law and Human Behavior*, *11*, 55–62.

Loftus, E.F., Miller, D.G., & Burns, H.J. (1978). Semantic integration of verbal information into a visual memory. *Journal of Experimental Psychology: Human Learning and Memory*, *4*, 19–31.

Loftus, E.F., Schooler, J.W., & Wagenaar, W.A. (1985). The fate of memory. Comment on McCloskey & Zaragoza. *Journal of Experimental Psychology: General*, *114*, 375–380.

Lombardi, W.J., Higgins, E.T., & Bargh, J.A. (1987). The role of consciousness in priming effects on categorization: Assimilation versus contrast as a function of awareness of the priming task. *Personality and Social Psychology Bulletin*, *13*, 411–429.

Lombrozo, T. (2007). Simplicity and probability in causal explanation. *Cognitive Psychology*, *55*, 232–257.

London, B., Downey, G., Romero-Canyas, R., Rattan, A., & Tyson, D. (2012). Gender-based rejection sensitivity and academic self-silencing in women. *Journal of Personality and Social Psychology*, *102*, 961–979.

Lord, C.G., & Lepper, M.R. (1999). Attitude representation theory. In M.P. Zanna (Ed.), *Advances in experimental social psychology* (Vol. 31, pp. 265–343). San Diego, CA: Academic Press.

Lord, C.G., & Saenz, D.S. (1985). Memory deficits and memory surfeits: Differential cognitive consequences of tokenism for tokens and observers. *Journal of Personality and Social Psychology*, *49*, 918–926.

Lord, C.G., Desforges, D.M., Fein, S., Pugh, M.A., & Lepper, M.R. (1994). Typicality effects in attitudes toward social policies: A concept-mapping approach. *Journal of Personality and Social Psychology*, *66*, 658–673.

Lord, C.G., Lepper, M.R., & Mackie, D. (1984). Attitude prototypes as determinants of attitude-behavior consistency. *Journal of Personality and Social Psychology, 46,* 1254–1266.

Lord, C.G., Ross, L., & Lepper, M.R. (1979). Biased assimilation and attitude polarization: The effects of prior theories on subsequently considered evidence. *Journal of Personality and Social Psychology, 37,* 2098–2109.

Loschelder, D.D., Siepelmeyer, H., Fischer, D., & Rubel, J.A. (2019). Dynamic norms drive sustainable consumption: Norm-based nudging helps café customers to avoid disposable to-go-cups. *Journal of Economic Psychology, 75* (Part A), 102146.

Loucks, J., Mutschler, C., & Meltzoff, A.N. (2017). Children's representation and imitation of events: How goal organization influences 3-year-old children's memory for action sequences. *Cognitive Science, 41,* 1904–1933.

Lowe, D.J., & Reckers, P.M. (1994). The effects of hindsight bias on jurors' evaluations of auditor decisions. *Decision Sciences, 25,* 401–426.

Lowery, B.S., Eisenberger, N.I., Hardin, C.D., & Sinclair, S. (2007). Long-term effects of subliminal priming on academic performance. *Basic and Applied Social Psychology, 29,* 151–157.

Lun, J., Sinclair, S., Whitchurch, E.R., & Glenn, C. (2007). (Why) do I think what you think? Epistemic social tuning and implicit prejudice. *Journal of Personality and Social Psychology, 93,* 957–972.

Luntz, F.I. (2005). *Frank Luntz Republican playbook for 2006.* Alexandria, VA: Luntz Research.

Lupfer, M.B., Clark, L.F., & Hutcherson, H.W. (1990). Impact of context on spontaneous trait and situational attributions. *Journal of Personality and Social Psychology, 58,* 239–249.

Ma, D.S., & Correll, J. (2011). Target prototypicality moderates racial bias in the decision to shoot. *Journal of Experimental Social Psychology, 47,* 391–396.

Ma, D.S., Correll, J., & Wittenbrink, B. (2015). The Chicago Face database: A free stimulus set of faces and norming data. *Behavior Research Methods, 47,* 1122–1135.

Ma, W., Feng, R., Lu, B., Xie, Q., Jiang, L., & Liu, X. (2019). The reducing effect of positive imagined intergroup contact on intergroup attributional bias. *Journal of Applied Social Psychology, 49,* 168–177.

Maass, A. (1999). Linguistic intergroup bias: Stereotype perpetuation through language. In M.P. Zanna (Ed.), *Advances in experimental social psychology* (Vol. 31, pp. 79–121). San Diego, CA: Academic Press.

Maass, A., & Arcuri, L. (1992). The role of language in the persistence of stereotypes. In G.R. Semin & K. Fiedler (Eds.), *Language, interaction and social cognition* (pp. 129–143). Newbury Park, CA: Sage.

Maass, A., & Arcuri, L. (1996). Language and stereotyping. In C.N. Macrae, C. Stangor, & M. Hewstone (Eds.), *Stereotypes and stereotyping* (pp. 193–226). New York, NY: Guilford Press.

Maass, A., & Kohnken, G. (1989). Eyewitness identification: Simulating the "weapon effect." *Law and Human Behavior, 13,* 397–408.

Maass, A., Cadinu, M., Taroni, M., & Masserini, M. (2006). The induction-deduction asymmetry: Fact or artifact? *Social Cognition, 24,* 74–109.

Maass, A., Ceccarelli, R., & Rudin, S. (1996). Linguistic intergroup bias: Evidence for in-group-protective motivation. *Journal of Personality and Social Psychology, 71,* 512–526.

Maass, A., Colombo, A., Colombo, A., & Sherman, S.J. (2001). Inferring traits from behaviors versus behaviors from traits: The induction-deduction asymmetry. *Journal of Personality versus Social Psychology, 81,* 391–404.

Maass, A., Salvi, D., Arcuri, L., & Semin, G. (1989). Language use in intergroup contexts: The linguistic intergroup bias. *Journal of Personality and Social Psychology, 57,* 981–993.

Macchi Cassia, V., Proietti, V., Gava, L., & Bricolo, E. (2015). Searching for faces of different ages: Evidence for an experienced-based own-age detection advantage in adults. *Journal of Experimental Psychology: Human Perception and Performance, 41,* 1037–1048.

Mack, M.L., Wong, C.A.N., Gauthier, I., Tanaka, J.W., & Palmeri, T.J. (2009). Time course of visual object categorization: Fastest does not necessarily mean first. *Vision Research, 49,* 1961–1968.

Mackie, D.M., & Allison, S.T. (1987). Group attribution errors and the illusion of group attitude change. *Journal of Experimental Social Psychology, 23,* 460–480.

Mackie, D.M., & Asuncion A.G. (1990). On-line and memory-based modification of attitudes: Determinants of message recall–attitude change correspondence. *Journal of Personality and Social Psychology, 59,* 5–16.

Mackie, D.M., & Worth, L.T. (1989). Cognitive deficits and the mediation of positive affect in persuasion. *Journal of Personality and Social Psychology, 57,* 27–40.

Mackie, D.M., Maitner, A.T., & Smith, E.R. (2009). Intergroup emotion theory. In T.D. Nelson (Ed.), *Handbook of prejudice, stereotyping, and discrimination* (pp. 285–308). New York, NY: Psychology Press.

Mackworth, N.H. (1948). The breakdown of vigilance during prolonged visual search. *Quarterly Journal of Experimental Psychology, 1,* 6–21.

MacLin, O.H., & Malpass, R.S. (2001). Racial categorization of faces: The ambiguous race face effect. *Psychology, Public Policy, and Law, 7,* 98–118.

Macrae, C.N. (1992). A tale of two curries: Counterfactual thinking and accident-related judgments. *Personality and Social Psychology Bulletin, 18,* 84–87.

Macrae, C.N., & Milne, A.B. (1992). A curry for your thoughts: Empathic effects on counterfactual thinking. *Personality and Social Psychology Bulletin, 18,* 625–630.

Macrae, C.N., Alnwick, K.A., Milne, A.B., & Schloerscheidt, A.M. (2002). Person perception across the menstrual cycle: Hormonal influences on social-cognitive functioning. *Psychological Science, 13,* 532–536.

Macrae, C.N., Bodenhausen, G.V., & Milne, A.B. (1995). The dissection of selection in person perception: Inhibitory processes in social stereotyping. *Journal of Personality and Social Psychology, 69,* 397–407.

Macrae, C.N., Bodenhausen, G.V., Milne, A.B., & Jetten, J. (1994). Out of mind but back in sight: Stereotypes on the rebound. *Journal of Personality and Social Psychology, 67,* 808–817.

Macrae, C.N., Milne, A.B., & Bodenhausen, G.V. (1994). Stereotypes as energy-saving devices: A peek inside the cognitive toolbox. *Journal of Personality and Social Psychology, 66,* 37–47.

Macrae, C.N., Milne, A.B., & Griffiths, R.J. (1993). Counterfactual thinking and the perception of criminal behaviour. *British Journal of Psychology, 84,* 221–226.

Macrae, C.N., Mitchell, J.P., McNamara, D.L., Golubickis, M., Andreou, K., Moller, S., Peytcheva, K., Falben, J., & Christian, B.M. (2016). Noticing future me: Reducing egocentrism through mental imagery. *Personality and Social Psychology Bulletin, 42,* 855–863.

Maddox, K.B. (2004). Perspectives on racial phenotypicality bias. *Personality and Social Psychology Review, 8,* 383–401.

Madon, S., Guyll, M., Aboufadel, K., Montiel, E., Smith, A., Palumbo, P., & Jussim, L. (2001). Ethnic and national stereotypes: The Princeton Trilogy revisited and revised. *Personality and Social Psychology Bulletin, 27,* 996–1010.

Mae, L., Carlston, D.E., & Skowronski, J.J. (1999). Spontaneous trait transfer to familiar communicators: Is a little knowledge a dangerous thing? *Journal of Personality and Social Psychology, 77,* 233–246.

Maheswaran, D., & Chaiken, S. (1991). Promoting systematic processing in low-motivation settings: Effect of incongruent information on processing and judgment. *Journal of Personality and Social Psychology, 61,* 13–25.

Maheswaran, D., Mackie, D.M., & Chaiken, S. (1992). Brand name as a heuristic cue: The effects of task importance and expectancy confirmation on consumer judgments. *Journal of Consumer Psychology, 1*, 317–336.

Mahon, B.Z. (2015). The burden of embodied cognition. *Canadian Journal of Experimental Psychology, 69*, 172–178.

Major, B. (1980). Information acquisition and attribution processes. *Journal of Personality and Social Psychology, 39*, 1010–1023.

Major, B., & Sawyer, P.J. (2009). Attributions to discrimination: Antecedents and consequences. In T.D. Nelson (Ed.), *Handbook of prejudice and discrimination* (pp. 89–110). New York, NY: Psychology Press.

Major, B., Kaiser, C.R., & McCoy, S.K. (2003). It's not my fault: When and why attributions to prejudice protect self-esteem. *Personality and Social Psychology Bulletin, 29*, 772–781.

Major, B., Kunstman, J.W., Malta, B.D., Sawyer, P.J., Townsend, S.S.M., & Berry Mendes, W. (2016). Suspicion of motives predicts minorities' responses to positive feedback in interracial interactions. *Journal of Experimental Social Psychology, 62*, 75–88.

Major, B., Quinton, W.J., & McCoy, S.K. (2002). Antecedents and consequences of attributions to discrimination: Theoretical and empirical advances. In M.P. Zanna (Ed.), *Advances in experimental social psychology* (Vol. 34, pp. 251–330). San Diego, CA: Academic Press.

Malle, B.F. (1999). How people explain behavior: A new theoretical framework. *Personality and Social Psychology Review, 3*, 23–48.

Malle, B.F. (2003). Attributions as behavior explanations: Toward a new theory. Unpublished manuscript, University of Oregon.

Malle, B.F. (2004). *How the mind explains behavior.* Cambridge, MA: MIT Press.

Malle, B.F. (2006). The actor–observer asymmetry in causal attribution: A (surprising) meta-analysis. *Psychological Bulletin, 132*, 895–919.

Malle, B.F. (2011). Attribution theories: How people make sense of behavior. In D. Chadee (Ed.), *Theories in social psychology* (pp. 72–95). New York, NY: Wiley Blackwell.

Malle, B.F., & Holbrook, J. (2012). Is there a hierarchy of social inferences? The likelihood and speed of inferring intentionality, mind, and personality. *Journal of Personality and Social Psychology, 102*, 661–684.

Malle, B.F., & Knobe, J. (1997). The folk concept of intentionality. *Journal of Experimental Social Psychology, 33*, 101–121.

Malle, B.F., & Nelson, S.E. (2003). Judging *mens rea*: The tension between folk concepts and legal concepts of intentionality. *Behavioral Sciences and the Law, 21*, 563–580.

Malle, B.F., Knobe, J., & Nelson, S. (2007). Actor-observer asymmetries in behavior explanations: New answers to an old question. *Journal of Personality and Social Psychology, 93*, 491–514.

Malle, B.F., Knobe, J., O'Laughlin, M.J., Pearce, G.E, & Nelson, S.E. (2000). Conceptual structure and social functions of behavior explanations: Beyond person-situation attributions. *Journal of Personality and Social Psychology, 79*, 309–326.

Mallett, R.K., Wilson, T.D., & Gilbert, D.T. (2008). Expect the unexpected: Failure to anticipate similarities leads to an intergroup forecasting error. *Journal of Personality and Social Psychology, 94*, 265–277.

Malpass, R.S., & Kravitz, J. (1969). Recognition for faces of own and other "race." *Journal of Personality and Social Psychology, 13*, 330–334.

Malt, B.C., & Smith, E.E. (1984). Correlated properties in natural categories. *Journal of Verbal Learning and Verbal Behavior, 23*, 250–269.

Mandel, N., & Johnson, E.J. (2002). When web pages influence choice: Effects of visual primes on experts and novices. *Journal of Consumer Research, 2*, 235–245.

Mandler, G. (1967). Organization and memory. In K.W. Spence & J.T. Spence (Eds.), *The psychology of learning and motivation: Advances in research and theory* (Vol. 1, pp. 328–372). New York, NY: Academic Press.

Mandler, J.M. (1984). *Stories, scripts, scenes: Aspects of schema theory.* Hillsdale, NJ: Lawrence Erlbaum.

Manis, M., Nelson, T. E., & Shedler, J. (1988). Stereotypes and social judgment: Extremity, assimilation, and contrast. *Journal of Personality and Social Psychology, 55,* 28–36.

Mann, T.C., & Ferguson, M.J. (2015). Can we undo our first impressions? The role of reinterpretation in reversing implicit evaluations. *Journal of Personality and Social Psychology, 108,* 823–849.

Mann, T.C., & Ferguson, M.J. (2017). Reversing implicit first impressions through reinterpretation after a two-day delay. *Journal of Experimental Social Psychology, 68,* 122–127.

Mannes, A.E., Soll, J.B., & Larrick, R.P. (2014). The wisdom of select crowds. *Journal of Personality and Social Psychology, 107,* 276–299.

Manusov, V., & Trees, A.R. (2002). "Are you kidding me?" The role of nonverbal cues in the verbal accounting process. *Journal of Communication, 52,* 640–656.

Marchiori, D., Papies, E.K., & Klein, O. (2014). The portion size effect on food intake: An anchoring and adjustment process? *Appetite, 81,* 108–115.

Marien, H., Custers, R., Hassin, R.R., & Aarts, H. (2012). Unconscious goal activation and the hijacking of the executive function. *Journal of Personality and Social Psychology, 103,* 399–415.

Marion, S.B., & Thorley, C. (2016). A meta-analytic review of collaborative inhibition and postcollaborative memory: Testing the predictions of the retrieval strategy disruption hypothesis. *Psychological Bulletin, 142,* 1141–1164.

Markman, A.B., & Brendl, C.M. (2005). Constraining theories of embodied cognition. *Psychological Science, 16,* 6–10.

Markman, K.D., Gavanski, I., Sherman, S.J., & McMullen, M.N. (1993). The mental simulation of better and worse possible worlds. *Journal of Experimental Social Psychology, 29,* 87–109.

Marks, G., & Miller, N. (1987). Ten years of research on the false-consensus effect: An empirical and theoretical review. *Psychological Bulletin, 102,* 72–90.

Markus, H. (1977). Self-schemata and processing information about the self. *Journal of Personality and Social Psychology, 35,* 63–78.

Markus, H.R., & Kitayama, S. (1991). Culture and the self: Implications for cognition, emotion, and motivation. *Psychological Review, 98,* 224–253.

Markus, H., & Kunda, Z. (1986). Stability and malleability of the self-concept. *Journal of Personality and Social Psychology, 51,* 858–866.

Markus, H., & Sentis, K. (1982). The self in social information processing. In J. Suls (Ed.), *Social psychological perspectives on the self* (pp. 41–70). Mahwah, NJ: Lawrence Erlbaum.

Markus, H., & Wurf, E. (1987). The dynamic self-concept: A social psychological perspective. *Annual Review of Psychology, 38,* 299–337.

Markus, H., Smith, J., & Moreland, R.L. (1985). Role of the self-concept in the perception of others. *Journal of Personality and Social Psychology, 49,* 1494–1512.

Marques, J.M., & Paez, D. (1994). The "black sheep effect": Social categorization, rejection of ingroup deviates and perception of group variability. In W. Stroebe & M. Hewstone (Eds.), *European review of social psychology* (Vol. 5, pp. 37–68). Chichester: Wiley.

Marques, J.M., & Yzerbyt, V.Y. (1988). The black sheep effect: Judgment extremity towards ingroup members in inter- and intragroup situations. *European Journal of Social Psychology, 18,* 287–292.

Marques, J.M., Yzerbyt, V.Y., & Leyens, J.-P. (1988). The "black sheep effect": Extremity of judgments towards ingroup members as a function of group identification. *European Journal of Social Psychology, 18,* 1–16.

Marsh, A.A., Kozak, M.N., Wegner, D.M., Reid, M.E., Yu, H.H., & Blair, R.J.R. (2010). The neural substrates of action identification. *Social Cognitive and Affective Neuroscience, 5,* 392–403.

Marshall, M.A., & Brown, J.D. (2007). On the psychological benefits of self-enhancement. In E. Chang (Ed.), *Self-enhancement and self-criticism: Theory, research, and clinical implications* (pp. 19–35). New York, NY: American Psychological Association.

Marshall, S.R., & Shapiro, J.R. (2018). When "scurry" vs. "hurry" makes the difference: Vermin metaphors, disgust, and anti-immigrant attitudes. *Journal of Social Issues, 74,* 774–789.

Martin, L.L., Seta, J.J., & Crelia, R.A. (1990). Assimilation and contrast as a function of people's willingness and ability to expend effort in forming an impression. *Journal of Personality and Social Psychology, 59,* 27–37.

Martindale, C., & Moore, K. (1988). Priming, prototypicality, and preference. *Journal of Experimental Psychology: Human Perception and Performance, 14,* 661–670.

Masicampo, E.J., & Baumeister, R.F. (2011). Consider it done! Plan making can eliminate the cognitive effects of unfulfilled goals. *Journal of Personality and Social Psychology, 101,* 667–683.

Mason, M.F., & Morris, M.W. (2010). Culture, attribution and automaticity: A social cognitive neuroscience view. *Social Cognitive and Affective Neuroscience, 5,* 292–306.

Mastro, D., Tukachinsky, R., Behm-Morawitz, E., & Blecha, E. (2014). News coverage of immigration: The influence of exposure to linguistic bias in the news on consumer's racial/ethnic cognitions. *Communication Quarterly, 62,* 135–154.

Masuda, T., & Nisbett, R.E. (2001). Attending holistically versus analytically: Comparing the context sensitivity of Japanese and Americans. *Journal of Personality and Social Psychology, 81,* 922–934.

Masuda, T., & Nisbett, R.E. (2006). Culture and change blindness. *Cognitive Science, 30,* 381–399.

Mathy, F., & Feldman, J. (2012). What's magic about magic numbers? Chunking and data compression in short-term memory. *Cognition, 122,* 346–362.

Matthes, J. (2012). Framing politics: An integrative approach. *American Behavioral Scientist, 56,* 247–259.

Maurer, D., LeGrand, R., & Mondloch, C.J. (2002). The many faces of configural processing. *Trends in Cognitive Sciences, 6,* 255–260.

Maurer, K.L., Park, B., & Judd, C.M. (1996). Stereotypes, prejudice, and judgments of group members: The mediating role of public policy decisions. *Journal of Experimental Social Psychology, 32,* 411–436.

Maxwell, S.E. (2004). The persistence of underpowered studies in psychological research: Causes, consequences, and remedies. *Psychological Methods, 9,* 147–163.

Maxwell, S.E., Lau, M.Y., & Howard, G.S. (2015). Is psychology suffering from a replication crisis? What does "failure to replicate" really mean? *American Psychologist, 70,* 487–498.

Maxwell-Smith, M.A., & Esses, V.M. (2012). Assessing individual differences in the degree to which people are committed to following their beliefs. *Journal of Research in Personality, 46,* 195–209.

Maxwell-Smith, M.A., Conway, P.J., Wright, J.D., & Olson, J.M. (2018). Translating environmental ideologies into action: The amplifying role of commitment to beliefs. *Journal of Business Ethics, 153,* 839–858.

Mayer, N.D., & Tormala, Z. L. (2010). "Think" versus "feel" framing effects in persuasion. *Personality and Social Psychology Bulletin, 36,* 443–454.

McAdams, D.P. (1999). Personal narratives and the life story. In L. Pervin & O. John (Eds.), *Handbook of personality: Theory and research* (2nd ed., pp. 478–500). New York, NY: Guilford Press.

McAdams, D.P., & Guo, J. (2015). Narrating the generative life. *Psychological Science, 26,* 475–483.

McAdams, D.P., & McLean, K.C. (2013). Narrative identity. *Current Directions in Psychological Science, 22,* 233–238.

McArthur, L.Z. (1972). The how and what of why: Some determinants and consequences of causal attribution. *Journal of Personality and Social Psychology, 22,* 171–193.

McArthur, L.Z. (1981). What grabs you? The role of attention in impression formation and causal attribution. In E.T. Higgins, C.P. Herman, & M.P. Zanna (Eds.), *Social cognition: The Ontario symposium* (Vol. 1, pp. 201–246). Hillsdale, NJ: Lawrence Erlbaum.

McArthur, L.Z., & Ginsburg, E. (1981). Causal attribution to salient stimuli: An investigation of visual fixation mediators. *Personality and Social Psychology Bulletin, 7,* 547–553.

McArthur, L.Z., & Post, D.L. (1977). Figural emphasis and person perception. *Journal of Experimental Social Psychology, 13,* 520–535.

McArthur, L.Z., & Solomon, L.K. (1978). Perceptions of an aggressive encounter as a function of the victim's salience and the perceiver's arousal. *Journal of Personality and Social Psychology, 36,* 1278–1290.

McAuley, E., Duncan, T.E., & Russell, E.W. (1992). Measuring causal attributions: The revised causal dimension scale (CDSII). *Personality and Social Psychology Bulletin, 18,* 566–573.

McCann, S.J.H. (2008). Societal threat, authoritarianism, conservatism, and U.S. state death penalty sentencing (1977–2004). *Journal of Personality and Social Psychology, 94,* 913–923.

McCarthy, R.J., & Skowronski, J.J. (2011). What will Phil do next? Spontaneously inferred traits influence predictions of behavior. *Journal of Experimental Social Psychology, 47,* 321–332.

McCarthy, R.J., Skowronski, J.J., Verschuere, B., Meijer, E.H., Jim, A., Hoogesteyn, K. ... Yildiz, E. (2018). Registered replication report on Srull and Wyer (1979). *Advances in Methods and Practices in Psychological Science, 1,* 321–336.

McClelland, J.L. (1991). Stochastic interactive processes and the effect of context on perception. *Cognitive Psychology, 23,* 1–44.

McClelland, J.L. (2000). Connectionist models of memory. In E. Tulving & F.I.M. Craik (Eds.), *The Oxford handbook of memory* (pp. 583–596). New York, NY: Oxford University Press.

McClelland, J.S. (1989). *The crowd and the mob: From Plato to Canetti.* New York, NY: Routledge.

McCloskey, M., & Zaragoza, M. (1985). Misleading postevent information and memory for events: Arguments and evidence against memory impairment hypotheses. *Journal of Experimental Psychology: General, 114,* 1–16.

McCloskey, M., Wible, C.G., & Cohen, N.J. (1988). Is there a special flashbulb-memory mechanism? *Journal of Experimental Psychology: General, 117,* 171–181.

McConnell, A.R. (2001). Implicit theories: Consequences for social judgments of individuals. *Journal of Experimental Social Psychology, 37,* 215–227

McConnell, A.R. (2011). The multiple self-aspects framework: Self-concept representation and its implications. *Personality and Social Psychology Review, 15,* 3–27.

McConnell, A.R., & Leibold, J.M. (2001). Relations among the Implicit Association Test, discriminatory behavior, and explicit measures of racial attitudes. *Journal of Experimental Social Psychology, 37,* 435–442.

McConnell, A.R., & Rydell, R.J. (2014). The systems of evaluation model: A dual-systems approach to attitudes. In J.W. Sherman, B. Gawronski, & Y. Trope (Eds.), *Dual process theories of the social mind* (pp. 204–217). New York, NY: Guilford Press.

McConnell, A.R., Rydell, R.J., & Leibold, J.M. (2002). Expectations of consistency about the self: Consequences for self-concept formation. *Journal of Experimental Social Psychology, 38,* 569–585.

McConnell, A.R., Rydell, R.J., Strain, L.M., & Mackie, D.M. (2008). Forming implicit and explicit attitudes toward individuals: Social group association cues. *Journal of Personality and Social Psychology, 94,* 792–807.

McConnell, A.R., Sherman, S.J., & Hamilton, D.L. (1997). Target entitativity: Implications for social information processing. *Journal of Personality and Social Psychology, 72,* 750–762.

McCrea, S.M., & Hirt, E.R. (2001). The role of ability judgments in self-handicapping. *Personality and Social Psychology Bulletin, 27,* 1378–1389.

McCulloch, K.C., Ferguson, M.J., Kawada, C.C.K., & Bargh, J.A. (2008). Taking a closer look: On the operation of nonconscious impression formation. *Journal of Experimental Social Psychology, 44,* 614–623.

McDermott, K.B., & Roediger, H.L. III. (1998). Attempting to avoid illusory memories: Robust false recognition of associates persists under conditions of explicit warnings and immediate testing. *Journal of Memory and Language, 39,* 508–520.

McEvoy, S.P., Stevenson, M.R., McCartt, A.T., Woodward, M., Haworth, C., Palamara, P., & Cercarelli, R. (2005). Role of mobile phones in motor vehicle crashes resulting in hospital attendance. *British Medical Journal, 331,* 428–433.

McFarland, C., Ross, M., & DeCourville, N. (1989). Women's theories of menstruation and biases in recall of menstrual symptoms. *Journal of Personality and Social Psychology, 57,* 522–531.

McFarland, C., Ross, M., & Giltrow, M. (1992). Biased recollections in older adults: The role of implicit theories of aging. *Journal of Personality and Social Psychology, 5,* 837–850.

McGarty, C., Haslam, S.A., Turner, J.C., & Oakes, P.J. (1993). Illusory correlation as accentuation of actual intercategory difference: Evidence for the effect with minimal stimulus information. *European Journal of Social Psychology, 23,* 391–410.

McGill, A.L. (1989). Context effects in causal judgment. *Journal of Personality and Social Psychology, 57,* 189–200.

McGillis, D. (1978). Attribution and the law: Convergences between legal and psychological concepts. *Law and Human Behavior, 2,* 289–300.

McGlone, M.S., & Tofighbakhsh, J. (2000). Birds of a feather flock conjointly(?): Rhyme as reason in aphorisms. *Psychological Science, 11,* 424–428.

McGraw, K.M. and Dolan, T.M. (2007). Personifying the state: Consequences for attitude formation. *Political Psychology, 28,* 299–327.

McGregor, I., Newby-Clark, I.R., & Zanna, M.P. (1999). "Remembering" dissonance: Simultaneous accessibility of inconsistent cognitive elements moderates epistemic discomfort. In E. Harmon-Jones & J. Mills (Eds.), *Cognitive dissonance: Progress on a pivotal theory in social psychology* (pp. 325–353). Washington, DC: American Psychological Association.

McNeil, B.J., Pauker, S.G., Sox, H.C., & Tversky, A. (1982). On the elicitation of preferences for alternative therapies. *New England Journal of Medicine, 21,* 1259–1262.

Mealey, L., Bridgestock, R., & Townsend, G.C. (1999). Symmetry and perceived facial attractiveness: A monozygotic co-twin comparison. *Journal of Personality and Social Psychology, 76,* 151–158.

Medin, D.L., & Ortony, A. (1989). Psychological essentialism. In S. Vosnaidou & A. Ortony (Eds.), *Similarity and analogical reasoning* (pp. 179–195). New York, NY: Cambridge University Press.

Medin, D.L. (1989). Concepts and conceptual structure. *American Psychologist, 44,* 1469–1481.

Meehl, P.E. (1954). *Clinical versus statistical prediction: A theoretical analysis and a review of the evidence.* Minneapolis, MN: University of Minnesota Press.

Meertens, R.W., Koomen, W., Delpeut, A.P., & Hager, G.A. (1984). Effects of hypothesis and assigned task on question selection strategies. *European Journal of Social Psychology, 14,* 369–378.

Meffert, M.F., Chung, S., Joiner, A.J., Waks, L., & Garst, J. (2006). The effects of negativity and motivated information processing during a political campaign. *Journal of Communication, 56*, 27–51.

Meisner, B.A. (2012). A meta-analysis of positive and negative age stereotype priming effects on behavior among older adults. *The Journals of Gerontology: Series B, 67B*, 13–17.

Meissner, C.A., & Brigham, J.C. (2001). Thirty years of investigating the own-race bias in memory for faces: A meta-analytic review. *Psychology, Public Policy, and Law, 7*, 3–35.

Mekawi, Y., Bresin, K., & Hunter, C.D. (2016). White fear, dehumanization, and low empathy: Lethal combinations for shooting biases. *Cultural Diversity and Ethnic Minority Psychology, 22*, 322–332.

Mellers, B., Hertwig, R., & Kahneman, D. (2001). Do frequency representations eliminate conjunction effects? An exercise in adversarial collaboration. *Psychological Science, 12*, 269–275.

Melton, G.B. (1989). Public policy and private prejudice: Psychology and law on gay rights. *American Psychologist, 44*, 933–940.

Mende-Siedlecki, P., Qu-Lee, J., Backer, R., & Van Bavel, J.J. (2019). Perceptual contributions to racial bias in pain recognition. *Journal of Experimental Psychology: General, 148*, 863–889.

Menninga, K.M., Dijkstra, A., & Gebhardt, W.A. (2011). Mixed feelings: Ambivalence as a predictor of relapse in ex-smokers. *British Journal of Health Psychology, 16*, 580–591.

Messick, D.M., & Schell, T. (1992). Evidence for an equality heuristic in social decision making. *Acta Psychologica, 80*, 311–323.

Messick, D.M., Bloom, S., Boldizar, J.P., & Samuelson, C.D. (1985). Why we are fairer than others. *Journal of Experimental Social Psychology, 21*, 480–500.

Meudell, P.R., Hitch, G.J., & Boyle, M.M. (1995). Collaboration in recall: Do pairs of people cross-cue each other to produce new memories? *The Quarterly Journal of Experimental Psychology, 48A*, 141–152.

Meudell, P.R., Hitch, G.J., & Kirby, P. (1992). Are two heads better than one? Experimental investigations of the social facilitation of memory. *Applied Cognitive Psychology, 6*, 525–543.

Meyer, M.L., & Lieberman, M.D. (2018). Why people are always thinking about themselves: Medial prefrontal cortex activity during rest primes self-referential processing. *Journal of Cognitive Neuroscience, 30*, 714–721.

Meyer, W.U., Reisenzein, R., & Schützwohl, A. (1997). Towards a process analysis of emotions: The case of surprise. *Motivation & Emotion, 21*, 251–274.

Mezulis, A.H., Abramson, L.Y., Hyde, J.S., & Hankin, B.L. (2004). Is there a universal positivity bias in attributions? A meta-analytic review of individual, developmental, and cultural differences in the self-serving attributional bias. *Psychological Bulletin, 130*, 711–747.

Michalkiewicz, M., & Erdfelder, E. (2016). Individual differences in use of the recognition heuristic are stable across time, choice objects, domains, and presentation formats. *Memory & Cognition, 44*, 454–468.

Michotte, A. (1946). *The perception of causality.* New York, NY: Basic Books.

Mickes, L., Clark, S.E., & Gronlund, S.D. (2017). Distilling the confidence-accuracy message: A comment on Wixted and Wells (2017). *Psychological Science in the Public Interest, 18*, 6–9.

Miles, E., & Crisp, R.J. (2014). A meta-analytic test of the imagined contact hypothesis. *Group Processes & Intergroup Relations, 17*, 3–26.

Milgram, S. (1963). Behavioral study of obedience. *Journal of Abnormal and Social Psychology, 67*, 371–378.

Milgram, S. (1965). Liberating effects of group pressure. *Journal of Personality and Social Psychology, 1*, 127–134.

Millar, M.G., & Millar, K.U. (1996). The effects of direct and indirect experience on affective and cognitive responses and the attitude–behavior relation. *Journal of Experimental Social Psychology, 32,* 561–579.

Millar, M.G., & Tesser, A. (1986). Effects of affective and cognitive focus on the attitude–behavior relation. *Journal of Personality and Social Psychology, 51,* 270–276.

Miller, D.T., & McFarland, C. (1986). Counterfactual thinking and victim compensation: A test of norm theory. *Personality and Social Psychology Bulletin, 12,* 513–519.

Miller, D.T., & Prentice, D.A. (1999). Some consequences of a belief in group essence: The category divide hypothesis. In D.A. Prentice & D.T. Miller (Eds.), *Cultural divides: Understanding and overcoming group conflict* (pp. 213–238). New York, NY: Russell Sage Foundation.

Miller, D.T., & Ross, M. (1975). Self-serving biases in the attribution of causality: Fact or fiction? *Psychological Bulletin, 82,* 213–225.

Miller, D.T., & Turnbull, W. (1986). Expectancies and interpersonal processes. *Annual Review of Psychology, 37,* 233–256.

Miller, D.T., Turnbull, W., & McFarland, C. (1990). Counterfactual thinking and social perception: Thinking about what might have been. In M.P. Zanna (Ed.), *Advances in experimental social psychology* (Vol. 23, pp. 305–331). New York, NY: Academic Press.

Miller, G.A. (1951). *Language and communication.* New York, NY: McGraw-Hill.

Miller, G.A. (1956). The magical number seven, plus or minus two: Some limits on our capacity for processing information. *Psychological Review, 63,* 81–97.

Miller, G.A., & Frick, F.C. (1949). Statistical behavioristics and sequences of responses. *Psychological Review, 56,* 311–324.

Miller, G.E., & Bradbury, T.N. (1995). Refining the association between attributions and behavior in marital interaction. *Journal of Family Psychology, 9,* 196–208.

Miller, J.G. (1984). Culture and the development of everyday social explanation. *Journal of Personality and Social Psychology, 46,* 961–978.

Millon, T., Krueger, R.F., & Simonsen, E. (Eds.) (2011). *Contemporary directions in psychopathology. Scientific foundations of the DSM-V and ICD-11.* New York, NY: Guilford Press.

Milne, S., Orbell, S., & Sheeran, P. (2002). Combining motivational and volitional interventions to promote exercise participation: Protection motivation theory and implementation intentions. *British Journal of Health Psychology, 7,* 163–184.

Minda, J.P., & Smith, J.D. (2011). Prototype models of categorization: Basic formulation, predictions, and limitations. In E.M. Pothos & A.J. Wills (Eds.), *Formal approaches in categorization* (pp. 40–64). New York, NY: Cambridge University Press.

Mineka, S., & Öhman, A. (2002). Phobias and preparedness: The selective, automatic, and encapsulated nature of fear. *Biological Psychiatry, 52,* 927–937.

Miron, A.M., Branscombe, N.R., & Biernat, M. (2010). Motivated shifting of justice standards. *Personality and Social Psychology Bulletin, 36,* 768–779.

Mischel, W. (1968). *Personality and assessment.* New York, NY: Wiley.

Mischel, W. (1969). Continuity and change in personality. *American Psychologist, 24,* 1012–1018.

Mischel, W. (1973). Toward a cognitive social learning reconceptualization of personality. *Psychological Review, 80,* 252–283.

Mischel, W. (2004). Toward an integrative science of the person. *Annual Review of Psychology, 55,* 1–22.

Mischel, W., & Shoda, Y. (1995). A cognitive-affective system theory of personality: Reconceptualizing situations, dispositions, dynamics, and invariance in personality structure. *Psychological Review, 102,* 246–268.

Mischel, W., & Shoda, Y. (2008). Toward a unified theory of personality: Integrating dispositions and processing dynamics within the cognitive-affective processing system.

In O.P. John, R.W. Robins, & L.A. Pervin (Eds.), *Handbook of personality* (3rd ed., pp. 208–241). New York, NY: Guilford Press.

Mischel, W., & Shoda, Y. (2010). The situated person. In B. Mesquita, L.F. Barrett, & E.R. Smith (Eds.), *The mind in context* (pp. 149–173). New York, NY: Guilford Press.

Mischel, W., Mendoza-Denton, R., & Hong, Y.-Y. (2009). Toward an integrative CAPS approach to racial/ethnic relations. *Journal of Personality*, *77*, 1365–1379.

Mischel, W., Shoda, Y., & Mendoza-Denton, R. (2002). Situation-behavior profiles as a locus of consistency in personality. *Current Directions in Psychological Science*, *11*, 50–54.

Mitchell, J.P., Heatherton, T.F., & Macrae, C.N. (2002). Distinct neural systems subserve person and object knowledge. *Proceedings of the National Academy of Sciences*, *99*, 15238–15243.

Mitchell, J.P., Macrae, C.N., & Banaji, M.R. (2004). Encoding-specific effects of social cognition on the neural correlates of subsequent memory. *Journal of Neuroscience*, *24*, 4912–4917.

Mitchell, J.P., Macrae, C.N., & Banaji, M.R. (2005). Forming impressions of people versus inanimate objects: Social-cognitive processing in the medial prefrontal cortex. *NeuroImage*, *26*, 251–257.

Mitchell, K.J., Livosky, M., & Mather, M. (1998). The weapon focus effect revisited: The role of novelty. *Legal and Criminological Psychology*, *3*, 287–304.

Mo, C.H. (2015). The consequences of explicit and implicit gender attitudes and candidate quality in the calculations of voters. *Political Behavior*, 37, 357–395.

Mogg, K., & Bradley, B.P. (1999). Orienting of attention to threatening facial expressions presented under conditions of restricted awareness. *Cognition and Emotion*, *13*, 713–740.

Molden, D.C. (2014). Understanding priming effects in social psychology: What is "social priming" and how does it occur? *Social Cognition*, *32*, 1–11.

Molina, L.E., Tropp, L.R., & Goode, C. (2016). Reflections on prejudice and intergroup rela-

tions. *Current Opinion in Psychology*, *11*, 120–124.

Mondloch, C.J., Elms, N., Maurer, D., Rhodes, G., Hayward, W.G., Tanaka, J.W., & Zhou, G. (2010). Processes underlying the cross-race effect: An investigation of holistic, featural, and relational processing of own-race versus other-race faces. *Perception*, *39*, 1065–1085.

Monin, B. (2003). The warm glow heuristic: When liking leads to familiarity. *Journal of Personality and Social Psychology*, *85*, 1035–1048.

Monroe, B.M., Koenig, B.L., Wan, K.S., Laine, T., Gupta, S., & Ortony, A. (2018). Re-examining dominance of categories in impression formation: A test of dual-process models. *Journal of Personality and Social Psychology*, *115*, 1–30.

Monteith, M.J. (1993). Self-regulation of prejudiced responses: Implications for progress in prejudice-reduction efforts. *Journal of Personality and Social Psychology*, *65*, 469–485.

Monteith, M.J., & Mark, A.Y. (2005). Changing one's prejudiced ways: Awareness, affect, and self-regulation. *European Review of Social Psychology*, *16*, 113–154.

Monteith, M.J., & Voils, C.I. (1998). Proneness to prejudiced responses: Towards understanding the authenticity of self-reported discrepancies. *Journal of Personality and Social Psychology*, *75*, 901–916.

Monteith, M.J., Ashburn-Nardo, L., Voils, C.I., & Czopp, A.M. (2002). Putting the brakes on prejudice: On the development and operation of cues for control. *Journal of Personality and Social Psychology*, *83*, 1029–1050.

Monteith, M.J., Sherman, J.W., & Devine, P.G. (1998). Suppression as a stereotype control strategy. *Personality and Social Psychology Review*, *2*, 63–82.

Monteith, M.J., Woodcock, A., & Gulker, J.E. (2013). Automaticity and control in stereotyping and prejudice: The revolutionary role of social cognition across three decades of research. In D.E. Carlston (Ed.), *The Oxford handbook of social cognition* (pp. 74–94). New York, NY: Oxford University Press.

Montoya, R.M., Horton, R.S., & Kirchner, J. (2008). Is actual similarity necessary for attraction? A meta-analysis of actual and perceived similarity. *Journal of Social and Personal Relationships, 25*, 889–922.

Montepare, J.M., & Zebrowitz, L.A. (1998). Person perception comes of age: The salience and significance of age in social judgments. In M.P. Zanna (Ed.), *Advances in experimental social psychology* (Vol. 30, pp. 93–163). San Diego, CA: Academic Press.

Moore, M.T., & Fresco, D.M. (2012). Depressive realism: A meta-analytic review. *Clinical Psychology Review, 32*, 496–509.

Moors, A. (2016). Automaticity: Componential, causal, and mechanistic explanations. *Annual Review of Psychology, 67*, 263–287.

Moors, A., & De Houwer, J. (2007). What is automaticity? An analysis of its component features and their interrelations. In J.A. Bargh (Ed.), *Social psychology and the unconscious: The automaticity of higher mental processes* (pp. 11–50). New York, NY: Psychology Press.

Moradi, Z., Najlerahim, A., Macrae, C.N., & Humphreys, G.W. (2020). Attentional saliency and ingroup biases: From society to the brain. *Social Neuroscience Online*, January.

Moray, N. (1959). Attention in dichotic listening: Affective cues and the influence of instructions. *Quarterly Journal of Experimental Psychology, 11*, 56–50.

Moreland, R.L., & Levine, J.M. (1982). Socialization in small groups: Temporal changes in individual-group relations. In L. Berkowitz (Ed.), *Advances in experimental social psychology* (Vol. 15, pp. 137–192). New York, NY: Academic Press.

Moreland, R.L., & Zajonc, R.B. (1977). Is stimulus recognition a necessary condition for the occurrence of exposure effects? *Journal of Personality and Social Psychology, 35*, 191–199.

Moreland, R.L., Argote, L., & Krishnan, R. (1996). Socially shared cognition at work: Transactive memory and group performance. In J.L. Nye & A.M. Brower (Eds.), *What's new about social cognition? Research on socially shared cognition in small groups* (pp. 57–84). Thousand Oaks, CA: Sage.

Moreno, K.N., & Bodenhausen, G.V. (1999). Resisting stereotype change: The role of motivation and attentional capacity in defending social beliefs. *Group Processes & Intergroup Relations, 2*, 5–16.

Morewedge, C.K., & Giblin, C.E. (2015). Explanations of the endowment effect: An integrative review. *Trends in Cognitive Sciences, 19*, 339–348.

Morewedge, C.K., Shu, L.L., Gilbert, D.T., & Wilson, T.D. (2009). Bad riddance or good rubbish? Ownership and not loss aversion causes the endowment effect. *Journal of Experimental Social Psychology, 45*, 947–951.

Morf, C.C., Horvath, S., & Torchetti, L. (2011). Narcissistic self-enhancement: Tales of (successful?) self-portrayal. In M.D. Alicke & C. Sedikides (Eds.), *Handbook of self-enhancement and self-protection* (pp. 399–424). New York, NY: Guilford Press.

Morgan, C.A., Hazlett, G., Doran, A., Garrett, S., Hoyt, G., Thomas, P., Baranoski, M., & Southwick, S.M. (2004). Accuracy of eyewitness memory for persons encountered during exposure to highly intense stress. *International Journal of Law and Psychiatry, 27*, 265–279.

Moro, R. (2009). On the nature of the conjunction fallacy. *Synthese, 171*, 1–24.

Morris, M.W., & Peng, K. (1994). Culture and cause: American and Chinese attributions for social and physical events. *Journal of Personality and Social Psychology, 67*, 949–971.

Morrison, A., Conway, A., & Chein, J.M. (2014). Primacy and recency effects as indices of the focus of attention. *Frontiers in Human Neuroscience, 8*, 1–6.

Morton, J., & Johnson, M.H. (1991). CONSPEC and CONLERN: A two-process theory of infant face recognition. *Psychological Review, 98*, 164–181.

Morwitz, V.G., & Fitzsimons, G.J. (2004). The mere-measurement effect: Why does measuring intentions change actual behavior? *Journal of Consumer Psychology, 14*, 64–74.

Moskowitz, G.B., & Ignarri, C. (2009). Implicit volition and stereotype control. *European Review of Social Psychology, 20,* 97–145.

Moskowitz, G.B., & Olcaysoy Okten, I. (2016). Spontaneous goal inference (SGI). *Social and Personality Compass, 10,* 64–80.

Moskowitz, G.B., Gollwitzer, P.M., Wasel, W., & Schaal, B. (1999). Preconscious control of stereotype activation through chronic egalitarian goals. *Journal of Personality and Social Psychology, 77,* 167–184.

Moskowitz, G.B., Olcaysoy Okten, I., & Gooch, C.M. (2015). On race and time. *Psychological Science, 26,* 1783–1794.

Moskowitz, G.B., Olcaysoy Okten, I., & Gooch, C.M. (2017). Distortion in time perception as a result of concern about appearing biased. *PLOS ONE, 12,* e0182241.

Moskowitz, G.B., Salomon, A.R., & Taylor, C.M. (2000). Preconsciously controlling stereotyping: Implicitly activated egalitarian goals prevent the activation of stereotypes. *Social Cognition, 18,* 151–177.

Mossey, J.M. (2011). Defining racial and ethnic disparities in pain management. *Clinical Orthopaedics and Related Research, 469,* 1859–1870.

Motyka, S., Grewal, D., Puccinelli, N.M., Roggeveen, A.L., Avnet, T., Daryanto, A., de Ruyter, K., & Wetzels, M. (2014). Regulatory fit: A meta-analytic synthesis. *Journal of Consumer Psychology, 24,* 394–410.

Mrkva, K., & Van Boven, L. (2020). Salience theory of mere exposure: Relative exposure increases liking, extremity, and emotional intensity. *Journal of Personality and Social Psychology, 6,* 1118–1145.

Mueller, C.M., & Dweck, C.S. (1998). Praise for intelligence can undermine children's motivation and performance. *Journal of Personality and Social Psychology, 75,* 33–52.

Mullen, B., & Hu, L. (1989). Perceptions of in-group and out-group variability: A meta-analytic integration. *Basic and Applied Social Psychology, 10,* 233–252.

Mullen, B., Brown, R., & Smith, C. (1992). Ingroup bias as a function of salience, relevance, and status: An integration. *European Journal of Social Psychology, 22,* 103–122.

Mummendey, A. (2012). Scientific misconduct in social psychology: Towards a currency reform in science. *European Bulletin of Social Psychology, 24,* 4–7.

Muñoz, F., & Martín-Loeches, M. (2015). Electrophysiological brain dynamics during the esthetic judgment of human bodies and faces. *Brain Research, 1594,* 154–164.

Munro, G.D., &, Ditto, P.H. (1997). Biased assimilation, attitude polarization, and affect in reactions to stereotyped-relevant scientific information. *Personality and Social Psychology Bulletin, 23,* 636–653.

Muraven, M. (2005). Self-focused attention and the self-regulation of attention: Implications for personality and pathology. *Journal of Social and Clinical Psychology, 24,* 382–400.

Murphy, M.C., & Dweck, C.S. (2016). Mindsets shape consumer behavior. *Journal of Consumer Psychology, 26,* 127–136.

Murphy, S.T., & Zajonc, R.B. (1993). Affect, cognition, and awareness: Affective priming with optimal and suboptimal stimulus exposures. *Journal of Personality and Social Psychology, 64,* 723–739.

Mussweiler, T. (2002). The malleability of anchoring effects. *Experimental Psychology, 49,* 67–72.

Mussweiler, T. (2003). Comparison processes in social judgment: Mechanisms and consequences. *Psychological Review, 110,* 472–489.

Mussweiler, T. (2007). Assimilation and contrast as comparison effects: A selective accessibility model. In D.A. Stapel & J. Suls (Eds.), *Assimilation and contrast in social psychology* (pp. 165–185). New York, NY: Psychology Press.

Mussweiler, T., & Strack, F. (1999). Hypothesis-consistent testing and semantic priming in the anchoring paradigm: A selective accessibility model. *Journal of Experimental Social Psychology, 35,* 136–164.

Mussweiler, T., & Strack, F. (2000). The use of category and exemplar knowledge in the solution of anchoring tasks. *Journal of Personality and Social Psychology, 78,* 1038–1052.

Mussweiler, T., Strack, F., & Pfeiffer, T. (2000). Overcoming the inevitable anchoring effect: Considering the opposite compensates for selective accessibility. *Personality and Social Psychology Bulletin, 26,* 1142–1150.

Nassar, M.R., Helmers, J.C., & Frank, M.J. (2018). Chunking as a rational strategy for lossy data compression in visual working memory. *Psychological Review, 125,* 486–511.

Neath, I. (1998). *Human memory: An introduction to research, data, and theory.* Pacific Grove, CA: Brooks/Cole.

Neisser, U. (1967). *Cognitive psychology.* New York, NY: Appleton-Century-Crofts.

Neisser, U. (1982). Snapshots or benchmarks? In U. Neisser (Ed.), *Memory observed: Remembering in natural contexts* (pp. 43–48). San Francisco, CA: W.H. Freeman.

Neisser, U., & Harsch, N. (1992). Phantom flashbulbs: False recollections of hearing the news about Challenger. In E. Winograd & U. Neisser (Eds.), *Emory symposia in cognition, 4. Affect and accuracy in recall: Studies of "flashbulb" memories* (pp. 9–31). New York, NY: Cambridge University Press.

Nelson, K., & Fivush, R. (2004). The emergence of autobiographical memory: A social cultural developmental theory. *Psychological Review, 111,* 486–511.

Nelson, K.J., Laney, C., Bowman-Fowler, N., Knowles, E., Davis, D., & Loftus, E.F. (2011). Change blindness can cause mistaken eyewitness identification. *Legal and Criminological Psychology, 16,* 62–74.

Nelson, T.D. (Ed.) (2016). *The handbook of prejudice, stereotyping, and discrimination* (2nd ed.). New York, NY: Psychology Press.

Nemeroff, C.J., & Rozin, P. (1994). The contagion concept in adult thinking in the United States: Transmission of germs and of interpersonal influence. *Ethos: Journal of the Society for Psychological Anthropology, 22,* 158–186.

Neubauer, A.C., Pribil, A., Wallner, A.O., & Hofer, G. (2018). The self–other knowledge asymmetry in cognitive intelligence, emotional intelligence, and creativity. *Heliyon, 4,* e01061.

Neuberg, S.L. (1994). Expectancy-confirmation processes in stereotype-tinged social encounters: The moderating role of social goals. In M.P. Zanna & J.M. Olson (Eds.), *The psychology of prejudice: The Ontario symposium* (Vol. 7, pp. 103–130). Hillsdale, NJ: Lawrence Erlbaum.

Neuberg, S.L., & Fiske, S.T. (1987). Motivational influences on impression formation: Outcome dependency, accuracy-driven attention, and individuating processes. *Journal of Personality and Social Psychology, 53,* 431–444.

Neugarten, B.L. (1974). Age groups in American society and the rise of the young-old. *The Annals of the American Academy of Political and Social Science, 415,* 187–198.

Neumann, R., Förster, J., & Strack, F. (2003). Motor compatibility: The bidirectional link between behavior and evaluation. In J. Musch & K.C. Klauer (Eds.), *The psychology of evaluation: Affective processes in cognition and emotion* (pp. 371–391). Mahwah, NJ: Lawrence Erlbaum.

Neumann, R., Hülsenbeck, K., & Seibt, B. (2004). Attitudes towards people with AIDS and avoidance behavior: Automatic and reflective bases of behavior. *Journal of Experimental Social Psychology, 40,* 543–550.

New, J., Cosmides, L., & Tooby, J. (2007). Category-specific attention for animals reflects ancestral priorities, not expertise. *Proceedings of the National Academy of Sciences, 104,* 16598–16603.

Newby-Clark, I.R., & Ross, M. (2003). Conceiving the past and future. *Personality and Social Psychology Bulletin, 29,* 807–818.

Newcomb, T. (1931). An experiment designed to test the validity of a rating technique.

Journal of Educational Psychology, 22, 279–289.

Newcomb, T.M. (1929). *Consistency of certain extrovert-introvert behavior patterns in 51 problem boys.* New York, NY: Columbia University, Teachers College, Bureau of Publications.

Newcombe, N.S., Drummey, A.B., Fox, N.A., Lie, E., & Ottinger-Alberts, W. (2000). Remembering early childhood: How much, how, and why (or why not). *Current Directions in Psychological Science, 9,* 55–58.

Newell, A., & Simon, H.A. (1972). *Human problem solving* (Vol. 104, No. 9). Englewood Cliffs, NJ: Prentice Hall.

Newell, B.R., & Shanks, D. R. (2003). Take the best or look at the rest? Factors influencing "one-reason" decision making. *Journal of Experimental Psychology: Learning, Memory, and Cognition, 29,* 53–65.

Newman, G.E., Diesendruck, G., & Bloom, P. (2011). Celebrity contagion and the value of objects. *Journal of Consumer Research, 38,* 215–228.

Newman, L.S., Duff, K.J., Hedberg, D.A., & Blitstein, J. (1996). Rebound effects in impression formation: Assimilation and contrast effects following thought suppression. *Journal of Experimental Social Psychology, 32,* 460–483.

Newtson, D. (1973). Attribution and the unit of perception of ongoing behavior. *Journal of Personality and Social Psychology, 28,* 28–38.

Newtson, D. (1976). Foundations of attribution: The perception of ongoing behavior. In J.H. Harvey, W.J. Ickes, & R.F. Kidd (Eds.), *New directions in attribution research* (Vol. 1, pp. 223–248). Hillsdale, NJ: Lawrence Erlbaum.

Newtson, D., & Enquist, G. (1976). The perceptual organization of ongoing behavior. *Journal of Experimental Social Psychology, 12,* 436–450.

Ng, W.-J., & Lindsay, R.C.L. (1994). Cross-race facial recognition: Failure of the contact hypothesis. *Journal of Cross-Cultural Psychology, 25,* 217–232.

Nickerson, R.S. (1984). Retrieval inhibition from part-set cuing: A persisting enigma in memory research. *Memory & Cognition, 12,* 531–552.

Nickerson, R.S. (1998). Confirmation bias: A ubiquitous phenomenon in many guises. *Review of General Psychology, 2,* 175–220.

Nicolas, G., de la Fuente, M., & Fiske, S.T. (2017). Mind the overlap in multiple categorization: A review of crossed categorization, intersectionality, and multiracial perception. *Group Processes & Intergroup Relations, 20,* 621–631.

Nicolas, S., Collins, T., Gounden, Y., & Roediger, H.L. III (2011). The influence of suggestibility on memory. *Consciousness and Cognition, 20,* 399–400.

Niedenthal, P.M. (1990). Implicit perception of affective information. *Journal of Experimental Social Psychology, 26,* 505–527.

Nier, J.A. (2005). How dissociated are implicit and explicit racial attitudes? A bogus pipeline approach. *Group Processes & Intergroup Relations, 8,* 39–52

Nieuwenstein, M., Wierenga, T., Morey, R.D., Wicherts, J.M., Blom, T.N., Wagenmakers, E.-J., & Van Rijn, H. (2015). On making the right choice: A meta-analysis and large-scale replication attempt of the unconscious thought advantage. *Judgment and Decision Making, 10,* 1–17.

Nigro, G., & Neisser, U. (1983). Point of view in personal memories. *Cognitive Psychology, 15,* 467–482.

Nikolaeva, R. (2014). Interorganizational imitation heuristics arising from cognitive frames. *Journal of Business Research, 67,* 1758–1765.

Nilsson, H., Winman, A., Juslin, P., & Hansson, G. (2009). Linda is not a bearded lady: Configural weighting and adding as the cause of extension errors. *Journal of Experimental Psychology: General, 138,* 517–534.

Nisbett, R.E., & Borgida, E. (1975). Attribution and the psychology of prediction. *Journal of Personality and Social Psychology, 32,* 932–943.

Nisbett, R.E., & Ross, L.D. (1980). *Human inference: Strategies and shortcomings of social judgment*. New York, NY: Prentice Hall.

Nisbett, R.E., & Wilson, T.D. (1977a). Telling more than we can know: Verbal reports on mental processes. *Psychological Review, 84,* 231–259.

Nisbett, R.E., & Wilson, T.D. (1977b). The halo effect: Evidence for unconscious alteration of judgments. *Journal of Personality and Social Psychology, 35,* 250–256.

Nisbett, R.E., Borgida, E., Crandall, R., & Reed, H. (1982). Popular induction: Information is not necessarily informative. In D. Kahneman, P. Slovic, & A. Tversky (Eds.), *Judgment under uncertainty: Heuristics and biases* (pp. 101–116). New York, NY: Cambridge University Press.

Nisbett, R.E., Peng, K., Choi, I., & Norenzayan, A. (2001). Culture and systems of thought: Holistic vs. analytic cognition. *Psychological Review, 108,* 291–310.

Noah, T., Schul, Y., & Mayo, R. (2018). When both the original study and its failed replication are correct: Feeling observed eliminates the facial-feedback effect. *Journal of Personality and Social Psychology, 114,* 657–664.

Nordgren, L.F., & Dijksterhuis, A. (2009). The devil is in the deliberation: Thinking too much reduces preference consistency. *Journal of Consumer Research, 36,* 39–46.

Norem, J., & Cantor, N. (1986). Anticipatory and post hoc cushionary strategies: Optimism and defensive pessimism in "risky" situations. *Cognitive Therapy and Research, 10,* 347–362.

Norenzayan, A., & Hansen, I.G. (2006). Belief in supernatural agents in the face of death. *Personality and Social Psychology Bulletin, 32,* 174–187.

Norenzayan, A., & Nisbett, R.E. (2000). Culture and causal cognition. *Current Directions in Psychological Science, 9,* 132–135.

Northcraft, G.B., & Neale, M.A. (1987). Experts, amateurs, and real estate: An anchoring-and-adjustment perspective on property pricing decisions. *Organizational Behavior and Human Decision Processes, 39,* 84–97.

Nosek, B.A. (2005). Moderators of the relationship between implicit and explicit evaluation. *Journal of Experimental Psychology: General, 134,* 565–584.

Nosek, B.A. (2007). Implicit-explicit relations. *Current Directions in Psychological Science, 16,* 65–69.

Nosek, B.A., & Lakens, D.D. (2014). Registered reports: A method to increase the credibility of published results. *Social Psychology, 45,* 137–141.

Nosek, B.A., & Smyth, F.L. (2007). A multi-trait-multimethod validation of the Implicit Association Test: Implicit and explicit attitudes are related but distinct constructs. *Experimental Psychology, 54,* 14–29.

Nosek, B.A., Greenwald, A.G., & Banaji, M.R. (2007). The Implicit Association Test at age 7: A methodological and conceptual review. In J.A. Bargh (Ed.), *Automatic processes in social thinking and behavior* (pp. 265–292). New York, NY: Psychology Press.

Nosek, B.A., Hawkins, C.B., & Frazier, R.S. (2011). Implicit social cognition: From measures to mechanisms. *Trends in Cognitive Science, 15,* 152–159.

Nosek, B.A., Smyth, F.L., Hansen, J.J., Devos, T., Lindner, N.M., Ranganath, K.A., Smith, C.T., Olson, K.R., Chugh, D., Greenwald, A.G., & Banaji, M.R. (2007). Pervasiveness and correlates of implicit attitudes and stereotypes. *European Review of Social Psychology, 18,* 36–88.

Nunes, L.D., Garcia-Marques, L., Ferreira, M.B., & Ramos, T. (2017). Inferential costs of trait centrality in impression formation: Organization in memory and misremembering. *Frontiers in Psychology, 8,* Article 1408.

Nussbaum, S., Liberman, N., & Trope, Y. (2006). Predicting the near and distant future. *Journal of Experimental Psychology: General, 135,* 152–161.

Nussbaum, S., Trope, Y., & Liberman, N. (2003). Creeping dispositionism: The temporal dynamics of behavior prediction. *Journal of Personality and Social Psychology, 84,* 485–497.

Nussinson, R., Seibt, B., Häfner, M., & Strack, F. (2010). Come a bit closer: Approach motor actions lead to feeling similar and behavioral assimilation. *Social Cognition, 28*, 40–58.

Nuttin, J.M. (1985). Narcissism beyond Gestalt and awareness: The name letter effect. *European Journal of Social Psychology, 15*, 353–361.

O'Donnell, M., Nelson, L.D., Ackermann, E., Aczel, B., Akhtar, A., Aldrovandi, S., ... Zrubka, M. (2018). Registered replication report: Dijksterhuis and van Knippenberg (1998). *Perspectives on Psychological Science, 13*, 268–294.

O'Laughlin, M.J., & Malle, B.F. (2002). How people explain actions performed by groups and individuals. *Journal of Personality and Social Psychology, 82*, 33–48.

Oaksford, M., & Chater, N. (2007). *Bayesian rationality: The probabilistic approach to human reasoning.* Oxford: Oxford University Press.

Oaksford, M., & Chater, N. (2009). Précis of Bayesian rationality: The probabilistic approach to human reasoning. *Behavioral & Brain Sciences, 32*, 69–84.

Ohira, H., Winton, W.M., & Oyama, M. (1998). Effects of stimulus valence on recognition memory and endogenous eyeblinks: Further evidence for positive-negative asymmetry. *Personality and Social Psychology Bulletin, 24*, 986–993.

Öhman, A. (1986). Face the beast and fear the face: Animal and social fears as prototypes for evolutionary analyses of emotion. *Psychophysiology, 23*, 123–145.

Öhman, A., & Mineka, S. (2001). Fears, phobias, and preparedness: Toward an evolved module of fear and fear learning. *Psychological Review, 108*, 483–522.

Öhman, A., & Mineka, S. (2003). The malicious serpent: Snakes as a prototypical stimulus for an evolved module of fear. *Current Directions in Psychological Science, 12*, 5–9.

Öhman, A., Flykt, A., & Esteves, F. (2001). Emotion drives attention: Detecting the snake in the grass. *Journal of Experimental Psychology: General, 130*, 466–478.

Olcaysoy Okten, I., & Moskowitz, G.B. (2017). Goal versus trait explanations: Causal attributions beyond the trait-situation dichotomy. *Journal of Personality and Social Psychology, 114*, 211–229.

Olcaysoy Okten, I., & Moskowitz, G.B. (2020). Spontaneous goal versus spontaneous trait inferences: How ideology shapes attributions and explanations. *European Journal of Social Psychology, 50*, 177–188.

Olcaysoy Okten, I., Schneid, E.D., & Moskowitz, G.B. (2019). On the updating of spontaneous impressions. *Journal of Personality and Social Psychology, 117*, 1–25.

Olivola, C.Y., Funk, F., & Todorov, A. (2014). Social attributions from faces bias human choices. *Trends in Cognitive Sciences, 18*, 566–570.

Olson, J.M., Roese, N.J., & Zanna, M.P. (1996). Expectancies. In E.T. Higgins & A.W. Kruglanski (Eds.), *Social psychology: Handbook of basic principles* (pp. 211–238). New York, NY: Guilford Press.

Olson, J.M., Vernon, P.A., Harris, J.A., & Jang, K.L. (2001). The heritability of attitudes: A study of twins. *Journal of Personality and Social Psychology, 80*, 845–860.

Olson, M.A., & Fazio, R.H. (2001). Implicit attitude formation through classical conditioning. *Psychological Science, 12*, 413–417.

Olson, M.A., & Fazio, R.H. (2004). Trait inferences as a function of automatically activated racial attitudes and motivation to control prejudiced reactions. *Basic and Applied Social Psychology, 26*, 1–11.

Olson, M.A., & Fazio, R.H. (2006). Reducing automatically activated racial prejudice through implicit evaluative conditioning. *Personality and Social Psychology Bulletin, 32*, 421–433.

Olson, M.A., & Fazio, R.H. (2007). Discordant evaluations of Blacks affect nonverbal behavior. *Personality and Social Psychology Bulletin, 33*, 1214–1224.

Olson, M.A., Fazio, R.H., & Hermann, A.D. (2007). Reporting tendencies underlie discrepancies between implicit and explicit measures of self-esteem. *Psychological Science, 18,* 287–291.

Olsson, A., Ebert, J.P., Banaji, M.R., & Phelps, E.A. (2005). The role of social groups in the persistence of learned fear. *Science, 309,* 785–787.

Oosterhof, N.N., & Todorov, A. (2008). The functional basis of face evaluation. *Proceedings of the National Academy of Sciences, 105,* 11087–11092.

Open Science Collaboration (2012). An open, large-scale, collaborative effort to estimate the reproducibility of psychological science. *Perspectives on Psychological Science, 7,* 657–660.

Open Science Collaboration (2015). Estimating the reproducibility of psychological science. *Science, 6251,* aac4716.

Oppenheimer, D.M., LeBoeuf, R.A., & Brewer, N.T. (2008). Anchors aweigh: A demonstration of cross-modality anchoring. *Cognition, 206,* 13–26.

Orbell, S., Hodgkins, S., & Sheeran, P. (1997). Implementation intentions and the theory of planned behavior. *Personality and Social Psychology Bulletin, 23,* 945–954.

Orghian, D., Garcia-Marques, L., Uleman, J.S., & Heinke, D. (2015). A connectionist model of spontaneous trait inference and spontaneous trait transference: Do they have the same underlying processes? *Social Cognition, 33,* 20–66.

Orghian, D., Smith, A., Garcia-Marques, L., & Heinke, D. (2017). Capturing spontaneous trait inferences with the modified free association paradigm. *Journal of Experimental Social Psychology, 73,* 243–257.

Ortony, A., Turner, T.J., & Antos, S.J. (1983). A puzzle about affect and recognition memory. *Journal of Experimental Psychology: Learning, Memory, and Cognition, 9,* 725–729.

Orvis, B.R., Cunningham, J.D., & Kelley, H.H. (1975). A closer examination of causal inference: The roles of consensus, distinctiveness, and consistency information. *Journal of Personality and Social Psychology, 32,* 605–615.

Ostafin, B.D., & Marlatt, G.A. (2008). Surfing the urge: Experiential acceptance moderates the relation between automatic alcohol motivation and hazardous drinking. *Journal of Social & Clinical Psychology, 27,* 404–418.

Ostrom, T.M. (1969). The relationship between affective, behavioral, and cognitive components of attitude. *Journal of Experimental Social Psychology, 5,* 12–30.

Ostrom, T.M. (1984). The sovereignty of social cognition. In R.S. Wyer, Jr., & T.K. Srull (Eds.), *Handbook of social cognition* (Vol. 1, pp. 1–38). Mahwah, NJ: Lawrence Erlbaum.

Ostrom, T.M., & Sedikides, C. (1992). Outgroup homogeneity effects in natural and minimal groups. *Psychological Bulletin, 112,* 536–552.

Ostrom, T.M., Carpenter, S.L., Sedikides, C., & Li, F. (1993). Differential processing of in-group and out-group information. *Journal of Personality and Social Psychology, 64,* 21–34.

Ostrom, T.M., Pryor, J.B., & Simpson, D.D. (1981). The organization of social information. In E.T. Higgins, C.P. Herman, & M.P. Zanna (Eds.), *Social cognition: The Ontario symposium* (Vol. 1, pp. 3–38). Hillsdale, NJ: Lawrence Erlbaum.

Oswald, F.L., Mitchell, G., Blanton, H., Jaccard, J., & Tetlock, P E. (2013). Predicting ethnic and racial discrimination: A meta-analysis of IAT criterion studies. *Journal of Personality and Social Psychology, 105,* 171–192.

Oswald, F.L., Mitchell, G., Blanton, H., Jaccard, J., & Tetlock, P.E. (2015). Using the IAT to predict ethnic and racial discrimination: Small effect sizes of unknown societal significance. *Journal of Personality and Social Psychology, 108,* 562–571.

Otgaar, H., Howe, M.L., Patihis, L., Merckelbach, H., Lynn, S.J., Lilienfeld, S.O., & Loftus, E.F. (2019). The return of the repressed: The persistent and problematic claims of long-forgotten trauma. *Perspectives on Psychological Science, 14,* 1072–1095.

Ottati, V., & Isbell, L.M. (1996). Effects of mood during exposure to target information on subsequently reported judgments: An on-line model of misattribution and correction. *Journal of Personality and Social Psychology, 71*, 39–53.

Otten, S., & Moskowitz, G.B. (2000). Evidence for implicit evaluative in-group bias: Affect-biased spontaneous trait inference in a minimal group paradigm. *Journal of Experimental Social Psychology, 36*, 77–89.

Overbeck, J.R., & Park, B. (2001). When power does not corrupt: Superior individuation processes among powerful perceivers. *Journal of Personality and Social Psychology, 81*, 549–565.

Overbeck, J.R., & Park, B. (2006). Powerful perceivers, powerless objects: Flexibility of powerholders' social attention. *Organizational Behavior and Human Decision Processes, 99*, 227–243.

Pachur, T., & Hertwig, R. (2006). On the psychology of the recognition heuristic: Retrieval primacy as a key determinant of its use. *Journal of Experimental Psychology: Learning, Memory, and Cognition, 32*, 983–1002.

Pachur, T., Hertwig, R., & Rieskamp, J. (2013). Intuitive judgments of social statistics: How exhaustive does sampling need to be? *Journal of Experimental Social Psychology, 49*, 1059–1077.

Pachur, T., Hertwig, R., & Steinmann, F. (2012). How do people judge risks: Availability heuristic, affect heuristic, or both? *Journal of Experimental Psychology: Applied, 18*, 314–330.

Pachur, T., Rieskamp, J., & Hertwig, R. (2005). The social circle heuristic: Fast and frugal decisions based on small samples. In K. Forbus, D. Gentner, & T. Regier (Eds.), *Proceedings of the 26th annual conference of the Cognitive Science Society* (pp. 1077–1082). Mahwah, NJ: Lawrence Erlbaum.

Pachur, T., Todd, P.M., Gigerenzer, G., Schooler, L.J., & Goldstein, D.G. (2011). The recognition heuristic: A review of theory and tests. *Frontiers in Psychology, 2*, Article 147.

Palermo, R., & Rhodes, G. (2002). The influence of divided attention on holistic face perception. *Cognition, 82*, 225–257.

Palermo, R., & Rhodes, G. (2007). Are you always on my mind? A review of how face perception and attention interact. *Neuropsychologia, 45*, 75–92.

Palfai, T. (2004). Automatic processes in self-regulation: Implications for alcohol interventions. *Cognitive and Behavior Practice, 11*, 190–201.

Paluck, E.L., Shepherd, H., & Aronow, P.M. (2016). Changing climates of conflict. *Proceedings of the National Academy of Sciences, 113*, 566–571.

Park, B., & Judd, C.M. (1990). Measures and models of perceived group variability. *Journal of Personality and Social Psychology, 59*, 173–191.

Park, B., & Rothbart, M. (1982). Perception of out-group homogeneity and levels of social categorization: Memory for the subordinate attributes of in-group and out-group members. *Journal of Personality and Social Psychology, 42*, 1051–1068.

Park, B., Ryan, C.S., & Judd, C.M. (1992). Role of meaningful subgroups in explaining differences in perceived variability for in-groups and out-groups. *Journal of Personality and Social Psychology, 63*, 553–567.

Park, C.W., Jun, S.Y., & MacInnis, D.J. (2000). Choosing what I want versus rejecting what I do not want: An application of decision framing to product option choice decisions. *Journal of Marketing Research, 37*, 187–202.

Park, J., & Banaji, M.R. (2000). Mood and heuristics: The influence of happy and sad states on sensitivity and bias in stereotyping. *Journal of Personality and Social Psychology, 78*, 1005–1023.

Parks-Stamm, E.J., Oettingen, G., & Gollwitzer, P.M. (2010). Making sense of one's actions in an explanatory vacuum: The interpretation of nonconscious goal striving. *Journal of Experimental Social Psychology, 46*, 531–542.

Pascalis, O., de Martin de Viviés, X., Anzures, G., Quinn, P.C., Slater, A.M., Tanaka, J.W., & Lee, K. (2011). Development of face processing. *Wiley Interdisciplinary Reviews. Cognitive Science, 2,* 666–675.

Pashler, H., & Harris, C.R. (2012). Is the replicability crisis overblown? Three arguments examined. *Perspectives on Psychological Science, 7,* 531–536.

Pashler, H., & Wagenmakers, E.-J. (2012). Editors' introduction to the special section on replicability in psychological science: A crisis of confidence? *Perspectives on Psychological Science, 7,* 528–530.

Passer, M.W., Kelley, H.H., & Michela, J.L. (1978). Multidimensional scaling of the causes for negative interpersonal behavior. *Journal of Personality and Social Psychology, 36,* 951–962.

Patihis, L., & Pendergrast, M.H. (2019). Reports of recovered memories of abuse in therapy in a large age-representative U.S. national sample: Therapy type and decade comparisons. *Clinical Psychological Science, 7,* 3–21.

Patihis, L., Ho, L.Y., Tingen, I.W., Lilienfeld, S.O., & Loftus, E.F. (2014). Are the "memory wars" over? A scientist-practitioner gap in beliefs about repressed memory. *Psychological Science, 25,* 519–530.

Patten, C.J.D., Kircher, A., Östlund, J., & Nilsson, L. (2004). Using mobile telephones: Cognitive workload and attention resource allocation. *Accident Analysis &Prevention, 36,* 341–350.

Pauker, K., Weisbuch, M., Ambady, N., Sommers, S.R., Adams, R.B., & Ivcevic, Z. (2009). Not so black and white: Memory for ambiguous group members. *Journal of Personality and Social Psychology, 96,* 795–810.

Paul, E.S., Pope, S.A.J., Fennell, J.G., & Mendl, M.T. (2012). Social anxiety modulates subliminal affective priming. *PLOS ONE, 7,* e37011.

Paulus, M. (2014). The ideomotor approach to imitative learning (IMAIL) in infancy:
Challenges and future perspectives. *European Journal of Developmental Psychology, 11,* 662–673.

Paunonen, S.V. (1989). Consensus in personality judgments: Moderating effects of target-rater acquaintance and behavior observability. *Journal of Personality and Social Psychology, 56,* 823–833.

Paunonen, S.V., & Kam, C. (2014). The accuracy of roommate ratings of behaviors versus beliefs. *Journal of Research in Personality, 52,* 55–67.

Pavelchak, M.A. (1989). Piecemeal and category-based evaluation: An idiographic analysis. *Journal of Personality and Social Psychology, 56,* 354–363.

Paxton, J.M., Ungar, L., & Greene, J.D. (2012). Reflection and reasoning in moral judgment. *Cognitive Science, 36,* 163–177.

Payne, B.K. (2001). Prejudice and perception: The role of automatic and controlled processes in misperceiving a weapon. *Journal of Personality and Social Psychology, 81,* 181–192.

Payne, B.K. (2012). Control, awareness, and other things we might learn to live without. In S.T. Fiske & C.N. Macrae (Eds.), *The SAGE handbook of social cognition* (pp. 12–30). London: Sage.

Payne, B.K., & Gawronski, B. (2010). A history of implicit social cognition: Where is it coming from? Where is it now? Where is it going? In B.G. Gawronski & B.K. Payne (Eds.), *Handbook of implicit social cognition: Measurement, theory, and application* (pp. 1–15). New York, NY: Guilford Press.

Payne, B.K., Brown-Iannuzzi, J.L., & Loersch, C. (2016). Replicable effects of primes on human behavior. *Journal of Experimental Psychology. General, 145,* 1269–1279.

Payne, B.K., Cheng, C.M., Govorun, O., & Stewart, B.D. (2005). An inkblot for attitudes: Affect misattribution as implicit measurement. *Journal of Personality and Social Psychology, 89,* 277–293.

Payne, B.K., Krosnick, J.A., Pasek, J., Lelkes, Y., Akhtar, O., & Tompson, T. (2010).

Implicit and explicit prejudice in the 2008 American presidential election. *Journal of Experimental Social Psychology*, *46*, 367–374.

Payne, B.K., Shimizu, Y., & Jacoby, L.L. (2005). Mental control and visual illusions: Toward explaining race-biased weapon misidentifications. *Journal of Experimental Social Psychology*, *41*, 36–47.

Payne, J.W., Bettman, J.R., & Johnson, E.J. (1988). Adaptive strategy selection in decision making. *Journal of Experimental Psychology: Learning, Memory, and Cognition*, *14*, 534–552.

Payne, J.W., Bettman, J.R., & Johnson, E.J. (1992). Behavioral decision research: A constructive processing perspective. *Annual Reviews of Psychology*, *43*, 87–131.

Payne, J.W., Samper, A., Bettman, J.R., & Luce, M.F. (2008). Boundary conditions on unconscious thought in complex decision making. *Psychological Science*, *19*, 1118–1123.

Pearson, A.R., & Dovidio, J.F. (2014). Intergroup fluency: How processing experiences shape intergroup cognition and communication. In J.P. Forgas, J. Laszlo, & O. Vincze (Eds.), *Social cognition and communication* (pp. 101–120). New York, NY: Psychology Press.

Pearson, A.R., West, T.V., Dovidio, J.F., Powers, S.R., Buck, R., & Henning, R. (2008). The fragility of intergroup relations: Divergent effects of delayed audiovisual feedback in intergroup and intragroup interaction. *Psychological Science*, *19*, 1272–1279.

Peck, J., & Shu, S.B. (2009). The effect of mere touch on perceived ownership. *Journal of Consumer Research*, *36*, 434–447.

Peery, D., & Bodenhausen, G.V. (2008). Black + White = Black: Hypodescent in reflexive categorization of racially ambiguous faces. *Psychological Science*, *19*, 973–977.

Peeters, G., & Czapinski, J. (1990). Positive-negative asymmetry in evaluations: The distinction between affective and informational negativity effects. *European Review of Social Psychology*, *1*, 33–60.

Pegan, G., & de Luca, P. (2012). Can implicit and explicit attitudes predict green product choice under time pressure? An experimental research. *Journal of Management and World Business Research*, *9*, 21–36.

Pegna, A.J., Khateb, A., Michel, C.M., & Landis, T. (2004). Visual recognition of faces, objects, and words using degraded stimuli: Where and when it occurs. *Human Brain Mapping*, *22*, 300–311.

Pelham, B., & Mauricio, C. (2015) When Tex and Tess Carpenter build houses in Texas: Moderators of implicit egotism. *Self and Identity*, *14*, 692–723.

Pelham, B.W. (1991). On confidence and consequence: The certainty and importance of self-knowledge. *Journal of Personality and Social Psychology*, *60*, 518–530.

Pelham, B.W., Carvallo, M., DeHart, T., & Jones, J.T. (2003). Assessing the validity of implicit egotism: A reply to Gallucci (2003). *Journal of Personality and Social Psychology*, *85*, 800–807.

Pelham, B.W., Mirenberg, M.C., & Jones, J.T. (2002). Why Susie sells seashells by the seashore: Implicit egotism and major life decisions. *Journal of Personality and Social Psychology*, *82*, 469–487.

Pendry, L.F., & Macrae, C.N. (1994). Stereotypes and mental life: The case of the motivated but thwarted tactician. *Journal of Experimental Social Psychology*, *30*, 303–325.

Peng, K., & Knowles, E. (2003). Culture, ethnicity and the attribution of physical causality. *Personality and Social Psychology Bulletin*, *29*, 1272–1284.

Pennington, C.R., Heim, D., Levy, A.R., & Larkin, D.T. (2016). Twenty years of stereotype threat research: A review of psychological mediators. *PLOS ONE*, *11*, e0146487.

Penton-Voak, I.S., & Perret, D.I. (2000). Female preference for male faces changes cyclically: Further evidence. *Evolution and Human Behavior*, *21*, 39–48.

Penton-Voak, I.S., Perrett, D.I., Castles, D.L., Kobayashi, T., Burt, D.M., Murray, L.K., &

Minamisawa, R. (1999). Menstrual cycle alters face perception. *Nature, 399*, 741–742.

Peplau, L.A., Veniegas, R.C., & Campbell, S.M. (1996). Gay and lesbian relationships. In R.C. Savin-Williams & K.M. Cohen (Eds.), *The lives of lesbians, gays, to adults* (pp. 250–273). Fort Worth, TX: Harcourt Brace.

Perdue, C.W., & Gurtman, M.B. (1990). Evidence for automatic ageism. *Journal of Experimental Social Psychology, 26*, 199–216.

Perdue, C.W., Dovidio, J.F., Gurtman, M.B., & Tyler, R.B. (1990). Us and them: Social categorization and the process of intergroup bias. *Journal of Personality and Social Psychology, 59*, 475–486.

Perkins, A., & Forehand, M. (2010). Implicit social cognition and indirect measures in consumer behavior. In B. Gawronski & B.K. Payne (Eds.), *Handbook of implicit social cognition: Measurement, theory, and applications* (pp. 535–547). New York, NY: Guilford Press.

Perrett, D.I., Lee, K.J., Penton-Voak, I.S., Rowland, D.R., Yoshikawa, S., Burt, D.M., Henzi, S.P., Castles, D.L., & Akamatsu, S. (1998). Effects of sexual dimorphism on facial attractiveness. *Nature, 394*, 884–887.

Perugini, M., Richetin, J., & Zogmaister, C. (2010). Prediction of behavior. In B. Gawronski & B.K. Payne (Eds.), *Handbook of implicit social cognition: Measurement, theory, and applications* (pp. 255–277). New York, NY: Guilford Press.

Peters, K.R., & Gawronski, B. (2011). Mutual influences between the implicit and explicit self-concepts: The role of memory activation and motivated reasoning. *Journal of Experimental Social Psychology, 47*, 436–442.

Pettigrew, T.F. (1979). The ultimate attribution error: Extending Allport's cognitive analysis of prejudice. *Personality and Social Psychology Bulletin, 5*, 461–476.

Pettigrew, T.F., & Tropp, L.R. (2006). A meta-analytic test of intergroup contact theory. *Journal of Personality and Social Psychology, 90*, 751–783.

Pettigrew, T.F., & Tropp, L.R. (2008). How does intergroup contact reduce prejudice? Meta-analytic tests of three mediators. *European Journal of Social Psychology, 38*, 922–934.

Pettigrew, T.F., & Tropp, L.R. (2011). *When groups meet: The dynamics of intergroup contact.* New York, NY: Psychology Press.

Petty, R.E., & Briñol, P. (2012). The elaboration likelihood model. In P.A.M. Van Lange, A.W. Kruglanski, & E.T. Higgins (Eds.), *Handbook of theories in social psychology* (Vol. 1, pp. 224–245). London: Sage.

Petty, R.E., & Cacioppo, J.T. (1979). Issue involvement can increase or decrease persuasion by enhancing message-relevant cognitive responses. *Journal of Personality and Social Psychology, 37*, 1915–1926.

Petty, R.E., & Cacioppo, J.T. (1986). The elaboration likelihood model of persuasion. In L. Berkowitz (Ed.), *Advances in experimental social psychology* (Vol. 19, pp. 123–205). San Diego, CA: Academic Press.

Petty, R.E., Tormala, Z.L., Briñol, P., & Jarvis, W.B.G. (2006). Implicit ambivalence from attitude change: An exploration of the PAST model. *Journal of Personality and Social Psychology, 90*, 21–41.

Pfister, R., Pohl, C., Kiesel, A., & Kunde, W. (2012). Your unconscious knows your name. *PLOS ONE, 7*, e32402.

Phaf, R.H., & Rotveel, M. (2005). Affective modulation of recognition bias. *Emotion, 5*, 309–318.

Pham, L.B., Taylor, S.E., & Seeman, T.E. (2001). Effects of environmental predictability and personal mastery on self-regulatory and physiological processes. *Personality and Social Psychology Bulletin, 27*, 611–620.

Pham, M.T. (1998). Representativeness, relevance, and the use of feelings in decision making. *Journal of Consumer Research, 25*, 144–159.

Phelps, E.A. (2006). Emotion and cognition: Insights from studies of the human amygdala. *Annual Review of Psychology, 57*, 27–53.

Philippot, P., Schwarz, N., Carrera, P., De Vries, N., & Van Yperen, N.W. (1991). Differential effects of priming at the encoding and judgment stage. *European Journal of Social Psychology, 21*, 293–302.

Phillips, W.A., & Baddeley, A.D. (1971). Reaction time and short-term visual memory. *Psychonomic Science, 22*, 73–74.

Pica, G., Bélanger, J.J., Pantaleo, G., Pierro, A., & Kruglanski, A.W. (2016). Prejudice in person memory: Self-threat biases memories of stigmatized group members. *European Journal of Social Psychology, 46*, 124–131.

Pica, G., Sciara, S., Livi, S., & Pantaleo, G. (2017). Ethnic prejudice in person memory. Lessened retrieval-induced forgetting of negative traits ascribed to an African-American target. *Psicologia Sociale, 3*, 351–362.

Pichert, J.W., & Anderson, R.C. (1977). Taking different perspectives on story. *Journal of Educational Psychology, 69*, 309–315.

Pickel, K.L. (1998). Unusualness and threat as possible causes of "weapon focus." *Memory, 6*, 277–295.

Pickel, K.L. (1999). The influence of context on the "weapon focus" effect. *Law and Human Behavior, 23*, 299–311.

Pickel, K.L. (2009). The weapon focus effect on memory for female versus male perpetrators. *Memory, 17*, 664–678.

Pickel, K.L., French, T., & Betts, J. (2003). A cross-modal weapon focus effect: The influence of a weapon's presence on memory for auditory information. *Memory, 11*, 277–292.

Pinter, B., Green, J.D., Sedikides, C., & Gregg, A.P. (2011). Self-protective memory: Separation/integration as a mechanism for mnemic neglect. *Social Cognition, 29*, 612–624.

Pittman, T.S., & D'Agostino, P.R. (1985). Motivation and attribution: The effects of control deprivation of subsequent information processing. In J.H. Harvey & G. Weary (Eds.), *Attribution: Basic issues and applications* (pp. 117–142). New York, NY: Academic Press.

Pittman, T.S., & Pittman, N.L. (1980). Deprivation of control and the attribution process. *Journal of Personality and Social Psychology, 39*, 377–389.

Pittman, T.S., Scherrer, F.W., & Wright, J.B. (1977). The effect of commitment on information utilization in the attribution process. *Personality and Social Psychology Bulletin, 3*, 276–279.

Plaks, J.E., & Halvorson, H.G. (2013). Does accountability attenuate or amplify stereotyping? The role of implicit theories. *Social Cognition, 31*, 543–561.

Plaks, J.E., Stroessner, S.J., Dweck, C.S., & Sherman, J.W. (2001). Person theories and attention allocation: Preferences for stereotypic vs. counterstereotypic information. *Journal of Personality and Social Psychology, 80*, 876–893.

Pleyers, G., Corneille, O., Luminet, O., & Yzerbyt, V. (2007). Aware and (dis)liking: Item-based analyses reveal that valence acquisition via evaluative conditioning emerges only when there is contingency awareness. *Journal of Experimental Psychology: Learning, Memory, and Cognition, 33*, 130–144.

Plous, S. (1993). *The psychology of judgment and decision making.* New York, NY: McGraw-Hill.

Pohl, R.F. (2011). On the use of recognition in inferential decision making: An overview of the debate. *Judgment and Decision Making, 6*, 423–438.

Popper, K. (1959). *The logic of scientific discovery.* New York, NY: Basic Books.

Posner, M.I., & Keele, S.W. (1968). On the genesis of abstract ideas. *Journal of Experimental Psychology, 77*, 155–158.

Posner, M.I., & Keele, S.W. (1970). Retention of abstract ideas. *Journal of Experimental Psychology, 83*, 304–308.

Posner, M.I., & Snyder, C.R.R. (1975). Attention and cognitive control. In R.L. Solso (Ed.), *Information processing and cognition: The Loyola symposium* (pp. 55–85). Hillsdale, NJ: Lawrence Erlbaum.

Powell, M.C., & Fazio, R.H. (1984). Attitude accessibility as a function of repeated attitudinal expression. *Personality and Social Psychology Bulletin, 10*, 139–148.

Pratto, F., & John, O.P. (1991). Automatic vigilance: The attention-grabbing power of negative social information. *Journal of Personality and Social Psychology, 61*, 380–391.

Pratto, F., Sidanius, J., Stallworth, L.M., & Malle, B.F. (1994). Social dominance orientation: A personality variable predicting social and political attitudes. *Journal of Personality and Social Psychology, 67*, 741–763.

Preston, J.L., & Ritter, R.S. (2013). Different effects of religion and God on prosociality with the ingroup and outgroup. *Personality and Social Psychology Bulletin, 39*, 1471–1483.

Priester, J.R., Cacioppo, J.T., & Petty, R.E. (1996). The influence of motor processes on attitudes toward novel versus familiar semantic stimuli. *Personality and Social Psychology Bulletin, 22*, 442–447.

Primi, C., & Agnoli, F. (2002). Children correlate infrequent behaviors with minority groups: A case of illusory correlation. *Cognitive Development, 85*, 1–27.

Prinz, W. (1987). Ideo-motor action. In H. Heuer & A.F. Sanders (Eds.), *Perspectives on perception and action* (pp. 47–76). Hillsdale, NJ: Lawrence Erlbaum.

Priolo, D., Milhabet, I., Codou, O., Fointiat, V., Lebarbenchon, E., & Gabarrot, F. (2016). Encouraging ecological behaviour through induced hypocrisy and inconsistency. *Journal of Environmental Psychology, 47*, 166–180.

Priolo, D., Pelt, A., Bauzel, R.S., Rubens, L., Voisin, D., & Fointiat, V. (2019). Three decades of research on induced hypocrisy: A meta-analysis. *Personality and Social Psychology Bulletin, 45*, 1681–1701.

Pronin, E. (2007). Perception and misperception of bias in human judgment. *Trends in Cognitive Science, 11*, 37–43.

Pronin, E. (2008). How we see ourselves and how we see others. *Science, 320*, 1177–1180.

Pronin, E., Gilovich, T., & Ross, L. (2004). Objectivity in the eye of the beholder: Divergent perceptions of bias in self versus others. *Psychological Review, 111*, 781–799.

Pronin, E., Lin, D.Y., & Ross, L. (2002). The bias blind spot: Perceptions of bias in self versus others. *Personality and Social Psychology Bulletin, 28*, 369–381.

Pronin, E., Wegner, D.M., McCarthy, K., & Rodriguez, S. (2006). Everyday magical powers: The role of apparent mental causation in the overestimation of personal influence. *Journal of Personality and Social Psychology, 91*, 218–231.

Pruitt, D.G. (1968). Reciprocity and credit building in a laboratory dyad. *Journal of Personality and Social Psychology, 8*, 143–147.

Pryor, J.B., & Ostrom, T.M. (1981). The cognitive organization of social information: A converging-operations approach. *Journal of Personality and Social Psychology, 41*, 628–641.

Pryor, J.B., Geidd, J.L., & Williams, K.B. (1995). A social-psychological model for predicting sexual harassment. *Journal of Social Issues, 51*, 69–84.

Purdie-Vaughns, V., & Eibach, R.P. (2008). Intersectional invisibility: The distinctive advantages and disadvantages of multiple subordinate-group identities. *Sex Roles, 59*, 377–391.

Pyszczynski, T.A., & Greenberg, J. (1981). Role of disconfirmed expectancies in the instigation of attributional processing. *Journal of Personality and Social Psychology, 40*, 31–38.

Pyszczynski, T.A., & Greenberg, J. (1987). Toward an integration of cognitive and motivational perspectives on social inference: A biased hypothesis-testing model. In L. Berkowitz (Ed.), *Advances in experimental social psychology* (Vol. 20, pp. 297–340). San Diego, CA: Academic Press.

Raab, M., & Gigerenzer, G. (2015). The power of simplicity: A fast-and-frugal heuristics approach to performance science. *Frontiers in Psychology, 6*, Article 1672.

Raio, C.M., Carmel, D., Carrasco, M., & Phelps, E.A. (2012). Nonconscious fear is quickly acquired but swiftly forgotten. *Current Biology, 22*, R477–R479.

Rajaram, S., & Pereira-Pasarin, L.P. (2010). Collaborative memory: Cognitive research and theory. *Perspectives on Psychological Science, 5*, 649–663.

Rakison, D.H., & Derringer, J. (2008). Do infants possess an evolved spider-detection mechanism? *Cognition, 107*, 381–393.

Ramasubramanian, S. (2011). The impact of stereotypical versus counterstereotypical media exemplars on racial attitudes, causal attributions, and support for affirmative action. *Communication Research, 38*, 497–516.

Ramos, T., Garcia-Marques, L., Hamilton, D.L., Ferreira, M.B., & Van Acker, K. (2012). What I infer depends on who you are: The influence of stereotypes on trait and situational spontaneous inferences. *Journal of Experimental Social Psychology, 48*, 1247–1256.

Ramsey, S.L., Lord, C.G., Wallace, D.S., & Pugh, M.A. (1994). The role of subtypes in attitudes towards superordinate social categories. *British Journal of Social Psychology, 33*, 387–403.

Rangel, U., & Keller, J. (2011). Essentialism goes social: Belief in social determinism as a component of psychological essentialism. *Journal of Personality and Social Psychology, 100*, 1056–1078.

Ratcliff, N., Hugenberg, K., Shriver, E.R, & Bernstein, M.J. (2011). The allure of status: High-status targets are privileged in face processing and memory. *Personality and Social Psychology Bulletin, 37*, 1003–1015.

Ratner, K.G., Dotsch, R., Wigboldus, D.H.J., van Knippenberg, A., & Amodio, D.M. (2014). Visualizing minimal ingroup and outgroup faces: Implications for impressions, attitudes, and behavior. *Journal of Personality and Social Psychology, 106*, 897–911.

Raz, O., & Ert, E. (2008). "Size counts": The effect of queue length on choice between similar restaurants. In A.Y. Lee & D. Soman (Eds.), *Advances in consumer research* (Vol. 35, pp. 803–804). Duluth, MN: Association for Consumer Research.

Read, S.J., & Miller, L.C. (1998). On the dynamic construction of meaning: An interactive activation and competition model of social perception. In S.J. Read & L.C. Miller (Eds.), *Connectionist models of social reasoning and social behavior* (pp. 27–68). Mahwah, NJ: Lawrence Erlbaum.

Reber, R., & Schwarz, N. (1999). Effects of perceptual fluency on judgments of truth. *Consciousness and Cognition, 8*, 338–342.

Reber, R., & Unkelbach, C. (2010). The epistemic status of processing fluency as source for judgments of truth. *Review of Philosophy and Psychology, 1*, 563–581.

Reber, R., Schwarz, N., & Winkielman, P. (2004). Processing fluency and aesthetic pleasure: Is beauty in the perceiver's processing experience? *Personality and Social Psychology Review, 8*, 364–382.

Redelmeier, D.A., & Tibshirani, R.J. (1997). Association between cellular-telephone calls and motor vehicle collisions. *New England Journal of Medicine, 336*, 453–458.

Redelmeier, D.A., & Tversky, A. (1996). On the belief that arthritis pain is related to the weather. *Proceedings of the National Academy of Sciences, 93*, 2895–2896.

Reeder, G.D. (2009). Mindreading: Judgments about intentionality and motives in dispositional inference. *Psychological Inquiry, 20*, 1–18.

Reeder, G.D., & Brewer, M.B. (1979). A schematic model of dispositional attribution in interpersonal perception. *Psychological Review, 86*, 61–79.

Reeder, G.D., Kumar, S., Hesson-McInnis, M.S., & Trafimow, D. (2002). Inferences about the morality of an aggressor: The role of perceived motive. *Journal of Personality and Social Psychology, 83*, 789–803.

Reeder, G.D., Vonk, R., Ronk, M.J., Ham, J., & Lawrence, M. (2004). Dispositional attribution: Multiple inferences about motive-related traits. *Journal of Personality and Social Psychology*, *86*, 530–544.

Rees, H.R., Rivers, A.M., & Sherman, J.W. (2019). Implementation intentions reduce implicit stereotype activation and application. *Personality and Social Psychology Bulletin*, *45*, 37–53.

Regan, D.T., & Fazio, R.H. (1977). On the consistency between attitudes and behavior: Look to the method of attitude formation. *Journal of Experimental Social Psychology*, *13*, 28–45.

Reis, T.L, Gerrard, M., & Gibbons, F.X. (1993). Social comparison and the pill: Reactions to upward and downward comparison of contraceptive behavior. *Personality and Social Psychology Bulletin*, *19*, 13–20.

Remedios, J.D., & Snyder, S.H. (2018). Intersectional oppression: Multiple stigmatized identities and perceptions of invisibility, discrimination, and stereotyping. *Journal of Social Issues*, *74*, 265–281.

Ren, Y., & Argote, L. (2011). Transactive memory systems 1985–2010: An integrative framework of key dimensions, antecedents, and consequences. *The Academy of Management Annals*, *5*, 189–229.

Rensink, R.A. (2002). Change detection. *Annual Review of Psychology*, *53*, 245–277.

Rensink, R.A., O'Regan, J.K., & Clark, J.J. (1997). To see or not to see: The need for attention to perceive changes in scenes. *Psychological Science*, *8*, 368–373.

Reyna, C., Henry, P.J., Korfmacher, W., & Tucker, A. (2006). Examining the principles in principled conservatism: The role of responsibility stereotypes as cues for deservingness in racial policy decisions. *Journal of Personality and Social Psychology*, *90*, 109–128.

Reynolds, K.J., Turner, J.C., & Haslam, S.A. (2000). When are we better than them and they worse than us? A closer look at social discrimination in positive and negative domains. *Journal of Personality and Social Psychology*, *78*, 64–80.

Rhodes, G., Hickford, C., & Jeffery, L. (2000). Sex-typicality and attractiveness: Are super-male and superfemale faces super-attractive? *British Journal of Psychology*, *91*, 125–140.

Rhodes, G., Proffitt, F., Grady, J.M., & Sumich, A. (1998). Facial symmetry and the perception of beauty. *Psychonomic Bulletin & Review*, *5*, 659–669.

Rhodes, M., Leslie, S.-J., Saunders, K., Dunham, Y., & Cimpian, A. (2018). How does social essentialism affect the development of inter-group relations? *Developmental Science*, *1*, e12509.

Richards, Z., & Hewstone, M. (2001). Subtyping and subgrouping: Processes for the prevention and promotion of stereotype change. *Personality and Social Psychology Review*, *5*, 52–73.

Richey, M.H., Koenigs, R.J., Richey, H.W., & Fortin, R. (1975). Negative salience in impressions of character: Effects of unequal proportions of positive and negative information. *The Journal of Social Psychology*, *97*, 233–241.

Richey, M.H., McClelland, L., & Shimkunas, A.M. (1967). Relative influence of positive and negative information in impression formation and persistence. *Journal of Personality and Social Psychology*, *6*, 322–327.

Richtel, M. (2009). In study, texting lifts crash risk by large margin. *New York Times*, July 28.

Riddoch, M.J., Johnston, R.A., Bracewell, R.M., Boutsen, L., & Humphreys, G.W. (2008). Are faces special? A case of pure prosopagnosia. *Cognitive Neuropsychology*, *25*, 3–26.

Riek, B.M., Mania, E.W., Gaertner, S.L., McDonald, S.A., & Lamoreaux, M.J. (2010). Does a common ingroup identity reduce intergroup threat? *Group Processes & Intergroup Relations*, *13*, 403–423.

Riley, T., & Ungerleider, C. (2012). Self-fulfilling prophecy: How teachers' attributions, expectations, and stereotypes influence the learning opportunities afforded Aboriginal students. *Canadian Journal of Education*, *35*, 303–333.

Rim, S., Uleman, J.S., & Trope, Y. (2009). Spontaneous trait inference and construal level theory: Psychological distance increases non-conscious trait thinking. *Journal of Experimental Social Psychology, 45,* 1088–1097.

Rips, L.J. (1975). Inductive judgments about natural categories. *Journal of Verbal Learning and Verbal Behavior, 14,* 665–681.

Risen, J.L. (2016). Believing what we do not believe: Acquiescence to superstitious beliefs and other powerful intuitions. *Psychological Review, 123,* 182–207.

Risucci, D.A., Torolani, A.J., & Ward, R.J. (1989). Ratings of surgical residents by self, supervisors and peers. *Surgical Gynecology and Obstetrics, 169,* 519–526.

Ritchie, K.L., Palermo, R., & Rhodes, G. (2017). Forming impressions of facial attractiveness is mandatory. *Scientific Reports, 7,* 469.

Robbins, J.M., & Krueger, J.I. (2005). Social projection to ingroups and outgroups: A review and meta-analysis. *Personality and Social Psychology Review, 9,* 32–47.

Roberto, C.A., & Kawachi, I. (2016). *Behavioral economics & public health.* New York, NY: Oxford University Press.

Robertson, D.J., Noyes, E., Dowsett, A.J., Jenkins, R., & Burton, A.M. (2016). Face recognition by metropolitan police super-recognisers. *PLOS ONE, 11,* 1–8.

Roche, M.J., Pincus, A.L., Conroy, D.E., Hyde, A.L., & Ram, N. (2013). Pathological narcissism and interpersonal behavior in daily life. *Personality Disorders: Theory, Research, and Treatment, 4,* 315–323.

Rocklage, M.D., & Fazio, R.H. (2018). Attitude accessibility as a function of emotionality. *Personality and Social Psychology Bulletin, 44,* 508–520.

Rodin, M.J. (1987). Who is memorable to whom? A study of cognitive disregard. *Social Cognition, 5,* 144–165.

Rodrigues, A.M., O'Brien, N., French, D.P., Glidewell, L., & Sniehotta, F.F. (2015). The question–behavior effect: Genuine effect or spurious phenomenon? A systematic review of randomized controlled trials with meta-analyses. *Health Psychology, 34,* 61–78.

Roediger, H.L. III, & McDermott, K.B. (1995). Creating false memories: Remembering words not presented in lists. *Journal of Experimental Psychology: Learning, Memory, and Cognition, 21,* 803–814.

Roediger, H.L., & McDermott, K.B. (2000). Tricks of memory. *Current Directions in Psychological Science, 9,* 123–127.

Roediger, H.L. III, Watson, J.M., McDermott, K.B., & Gallo, D.A. (2001). Factors that determine false recall: A multiple regression analysis. *Psychonomic Bulletin & Review, 8,* 385–407.

Roenker, D.L., Thompson, C.P., & Brown, S.C. (1971). Comparison of measures for the estimation of clustering in free recall. *Psychological Bulletin, 76,* 45–48.

Roese, N.J. (1997). Counterfactual thinking. *Psychological Bulletin, 121,* 133–148

Roese, N.J., & Vohs, K.D. (2012). Hindsight bias. *Perspectives on Psychological Science, 7,* 411–426.

Rogers, T.B., Kuiper, N.A., & Kirker, W.S. (1977). Self-reference and the encoding of personal information. *Journal of Personality and Social Psychology, 35,* 677–688.

Röhner, J., & Thoss, P. (2018). EZ: An easy way to conduct a more fine-grained analysis of faked and nonfaked implicit association test (IAT) data. *The Quantitative Methods for Psychology, 14,* 17–37.

Rolison, J.J., Evans, J.S.B.T., Dennis, I., & Walsh, C.R. (2012). Dual-processes in learning and judgment: Evidence from the multiple cue probability learning paradigm. *Organizational Behavior and Human Decision Processes, 118,* 189–202.

Rosch, E. (1973). Natural categories. *Cognitive Psychology, 4,* 328–350.

Rosch, E. (1977). Human categorization. In N. Warren (Ed.), *Advances in cross-cultural psychology* (Vol. 1. pp. 1–72). London: Academic Press.

Rosch, E. (1978). Principles of categorization. In E. Rosch & B.B. Lloyd (Eds.), *Cognition and categorization* (pp. 27–48). Hillsdale, NJ: Lawrence Erlbaum.

Rosch, E., & Lloyd, B.B. (Eds.) (1978). *Cognition and categorization*. Hillsdale, NJ: Lawrence Erlbaum.

Rosch, E., & Mervis, C.B. (1975). Family resemblances: Studies in the internal structure of categories. *Cognitive Psychology, 7*, 573–605.

Rosch, E., Mervis, C.B., Gray, W.D., Johnson, D.M., & Boyes-Braem, P. (1976). Basic objects in natural categories. *Cognitive Psychology, 8*, 382–439.

Rosch, E., Simpson, C., & Miller, R.S. (1976). Structural bases of typicality effects. *Journal of Experimental Psychology: Human Perception and Performance, 2*, 491–502.

Rosenberg, M. (1965). *Society and the adolescent self image*. Princeton, NJ: Princeton University Press.

Rosenberg, M.J. (1960). A structural theory of attitude dynamics. *Public Opinion Quarterly, 24*, 319–340.

Rosenberg, S., Nelson, C., & Vivekananthan, P.S. (1968). A multidimensional approach to the structure of personality impressions. *Journal of Personality and Social Psychology, 9*, 283–294.

Rosenthal, R., & Jacobson, L. (1968). *Pygmalion in the classroom: Teacher expectations and student intellectual development*. New York, NY: Holt, Rinehart, & Winston.

Ross, L. (1977). The intuitive psychologist and his shortcomings: Distortions in the attribution process. In L. Berkowitz (Ed.), *Advances in experimental social psychology* (Vol. 10, pp. 173–220). New York, NY: Academic Press.

Ross, L. (2018). From the fundamental attribution error to the truly fundamental attribution error and beyond: My research journey. *Perspectives on Psychological Science, 13*, 750–769.

Ross, L., & Ward, A. (1996). Naive realism in everyday life: Implications for social conflict and misunderstanding. In T. Brown, E. Reed, & E. Turiel (Eds.), *Values and knowledge*. Hillsdale, NJ: Lawrence Erlbaum.

Ross, L., Greene, D., & House, P. (1977). The false consensus effect: An egocentric bias and social perception and attribu-

tion processes. *Journal of Experimental Social Psychology, 13*, 279–301.

Ross, L., Lepper, M.R., Strack, F., & Steinmetz, J. (1977). Social explanation and social expectation: Effects of real and hypothetical explanations on subjective likelihood. *Journal of Personality and Social Psychology, 35*, 817–829.

Ross, L.D., Amabile, T.M., & Steinmetz, J.L. (1977). Social roles, social control, and biases in social-perception processes. *Journal of Personality and Social Psychology, 35*, 485–494.

Ross, M. (1989). Relation of implicit theories to the construction of personal histories. *Psychological Review, 96*, 341–357.

Ross, M., & McFarland, C. (1988). Constructing the past: Biases in personal memories. In D. Bar-Tal & A. Kruglanski (Eds.), *Social psychology of knowledge* (pp. 299–314). New York, NY: Cambridge University Press.

Ross, M., & Sicoly, F. (1979). Egocentric biases in availability and attribution. *Journal of Personality and Social Psychology, 32*, 880–892.

Ross, M., & Wilson, A.E. (2003). Autobiographical memory and conceptions of self: Getting better all the time. *Current Directions in Psychological Science, 12*, 66–69.

Rothbart, M. (1981). Memory processes and social beliefs. In D.L. Hamilton (Ed.), *Cognitive processes in stereotyping and intergroup behavior* (pp. 145–181). Mahwah, NJ: Lawrence Erlbaum.

Rothbart, M., & John, O.P. (1985). Social categorization and behavioral episodes: A cognitive analysis of the effects of intergroup contact. *Journal of Social Issues, 41*, 81–104.

Rothbart, M., & Taylor, M. (1992). Category labels and social reality: Do we view social categories as natural kinds? In G.R. Semin & K. Fiedler (Eds.), *Language, interaction, and social cognition* (pp. 11–36). London: Sage.

Rothbart, M., Davis-Stitt, C., & Hill, J. (1997). Effects of arbitrarily based category boundaries on similarity judgments. *Journal of Experimental Social Psychology, 33*, 122–145.

Rozin, P., & Royzman, E.B. (2001). Negativity bias, negativity dominance, and contagion. *Personality and Social Psychology Review*, *5*, 296–320.

Rozin, P., Haidt, J., & Fincher, K. (2009). From oral to moral. *Science*, *323*, 1179–1180.

Rozin, P., Haidt, J., & McCauley, C.R. (2000). Disgust. In M. Lewis & J.M. Haviland-Jones (Eds.), *Handbook of emotions* (2nd ed., pp. 637–653). New York, NY: Guilford Press.

Rozin, P., Haidt, J., & McCauley, C.R. (2008). Disgust. In M. Lewis, J.M. Haviland-Jones, & L.F. Barrett (Eds.), *Handbook of emotions* (3rd ed., pp. 757–776). New York, NY: Guilford Press.

Rozin, P., Millman, L., & Nemeroff, C.J. (1986). Operation of the laws of sympathetic magic in disgust and other domains. *Journal of Personality and Social Psychology*, *50*, 703–712.

Rozin, P., Nemeroff, C.J., Wane, M., & Sherrod, A. (1989). Operation of the sympathetic magical law of contagion in interpersonal attitudes among Americans. *Bulletin of the Psychonomic Society*, *27*, 367–370.

Rubin, D.C., Rahhal, T.A., & Poon, L.W. (1998). Things learned in early adulthood are remembered best. *Memory & Cognition*, *26*, 3–19.

Rubin, M., & Badea, C. (2012). They're all the same!...But for several different reasons: A review of the multicausal nature of perceived group variability. *Current Directions in Psychological Science*, *21*, 367–372.

Rubin, M., Paolini, S., & Crisp, R.J. (2013). Linguistic description moderates the evaluations of counterstereotypical people. *Social Psychology*, *44*, 289–298.

Ruble, D.N. (1977). Premenstrual symptoms: A reinterpretation. *Science*, *197*, 291–292.

Ruble, D.N., & Brooks-Gunn, J. (1979). Menstrual symptoms: A social cognition analysis. *Journal of Behavioral Medicine*, *2*, 171–194.

Ruble, D.N., & Feldman, N.S. (1976). Order of consensus, distinctiveness, and consistency information and causal attributions. *Journal of Personality and Social Psychology*, *34*, 930–937.

Ruble, D.N., & Stangor, C. (1986). Stalking the elusive schema: Insights from developmental and social psychological analysis of gender schemas. *Social Cognition*, *4*, 227–261.

Rucker, D.D., Tormala, Z.L., Petty, R.E., & Briñol, P. (2014). Consumer conviction and commitment: An appraisal-based framework for attitude certainty. *Journal of Consumer Psychology*, *24*, 119–136.

Ruder, M., & Bless, H. (2003). Mood and the reliance on the ease of retrieval heuristic. *Journal of Personality and Social Psychology*, *85*, 20–32.

Rudman, L.A. (2004). Sources of implicit attitudes. *Current Directions in Psychological Science*, *13*, 79–82.

Rudman, L.A., Ashmore, R.D., & Gary, M.L. (2001). "Unlearning" automatic biases: The malleability of implicit prejudice and stereotypes. *Journal of Personality and Social Psychology*, *81*, 856–868.

Rudman, L.A., Phelan, J.E., & Heppen, J.B. (2007). Developmental sources of implicit attitudes. *Personality and Social Psychology Bulletin*, *33*, 1700–1713.

Rudolph, A., Schröder-Abè, M., Riketta, M., & Schütz, A. (2010). Easier when done than said! Implicit self-esteem predicts observed or spontaneous behavior, but not self-reported or controlled behavior. *Zeitschrift für Psychologie*, *218*, 12–19.

Rudolph, U., Roesch, S.C., Greitemeyer, T., & Weiner, B. (2004). A meta-analytic review of help-giving and aggression from an attributional perspective: Contributions to a general theory of motivation. *Cognition and Emotion*, *18*, 815–848.

Rudski, J.M. (2002). Hindsight and confirmation biases in an exercise in telepathy. *Psychological Reports*, *91*, 899–906.

Rule, N.O. (2017). Perceptions of sexual orientation from minimal cues. *Archives of Sexual Behavior*, *46*, 129–139.

Rule, N.O., & Ambady, N. (2008). Brief exposures: Male sexual orientation is accurately perceived at 50-ms. *Journal of Experimental Social Psychology, 44,* 1100–1105.

Rule, N.O., & Ambady, N. (2010). First impressions of the face: Predicting success. *Social and Personality Psychology Compass, 4,* 506–516.

Rule, N.O., Ambady, N., Adams, R.B., Jr., & Macrae, C.N. (2007). Us and them: Memory advantages in perceptually ambiguous groups. *Psychonomic Bulletin & Review, 14,* 687–692.

Rule, N.O., Ambady, N., Adams, R.B. Jr., & Macrae, C.N. (2008). Accuracy and awareness in the perception and categorization of male sexual orientation. *Journal of Personality and Social Psychology, 95,* 1019–1028.

Rule, N.O., Ambady, N., & Hallett, K.C. (2009). Female sexual orientation is perceived accurately, rapidly, and automatically from the face and its features. *Journal of Experimental Social Psychology, 45,* 1245–1251.

Rule, N.O., Krendl, A.C., Ivcevic, Z., & Ambady, N. (2013). Accuracy and consensus in judgments of trustworthiness from faces: Behavioral and neural correlates. *Journal of Personality and Social Psychology, 104,* 409–426.

Rule, N.O., Macrae, C.N., & Ambady, N. (2009). Ambiguous group membership is extracted automatically from faces. *Psychological Science, 20,* 441–443.

Rumelhart, D.E. (1984). Schemata and the cognitive system. In R.S. Wyer, Jr. & T.K. Srull (Eds.), *Handbook of social cognition* (Vol. 1, pp. 161–188). Mahwah, NJ: Lawrence Erlbaum.

Ruscher, J.B., Fiske, S.T., Miki, H., & Van Manen, S. (1991). Individuating processes in competition: Interpersonal versus intergroup. *Personality and Social Psychology Bulletin, 17,* 595–605.

Russell, R., Chatterjee, G., & Nakayama, K. (2012). Developmental prosopagnosia and super-recognition: No special role for surface reflectance processing. *Neuropsychologia, 50,* 334–340.

Russell, R., Duchaine, B., & Nakayama, K. (2009). Super-recognizers: People with extraordinary face recognition ability. *Psychonomic Bulletin & Review, 16,* 252–257.

Ryan, C.S., Judd, C.M., & Park, B. (1996). Effects of racial stereotypes on judgments of individuals: The moderating role of perceived group variability. *Journal of Experimental Social Psychology, 32,* 71–103.

Rydell, R.J., & McConnell, A.R. (2006). Understanding implicit and explicit attitude change: A systems of reasoning analysis. *Journal of Personality and Social Psychology, 91,* 995–1008.

Rydell, R.J., Hamilton, D.L., & Devos, T. (2010). Now they are American, now they are not: Valence as a determinant of the inclusion of African Americans in the American identity. *Social Cognition, 28,* 161–179.

Rydell, R.J., McConnell, A.R., Mackie, D.M., & Strain, L.M. (2006). Of two minds: Forming and changing valence-inconsistent implicit and explicit attitudes. *Psychological Science, 17,* 954–958.

Sagar, H.A., & Schofield, J.W. (1980). Racial and behavioral cues in Black and White children's perceptions of ambiguously aggressive acts. *Journal of Personality and Social Psychology, 39,* 590–598.

Saini, R., & Thota, S.C. (2010). The psychological underpinnings of relative thinking in price comparisons. *Journal of Consumer Psychology, 20,* 185–192.

Sakaki, M., & Murayama K. (2013). Automatic ability attribution after failure: A dual process view of achievement attribution. *PLOS ONE, 8,* e63066.

Salerno, J.M., & Sanchez, J. (2020). Subjective interpretation of "objective" video evidence: Perceptions of male versus female police officers' use-of-force. *Law and Human Behavior, 2,* 97–112.

Sanbonmatsu, D.M., Sherman, S.J., & Hamilton, D.L. (1987). Illusory correlation in the perception of individuals and groups. *Social Cognition, 5,* 1–25.

Sanbonmatsu, D.M., Strayer, D.L., Behrends, A.A., Ward, N., & Watson, J.M. (2016). Why drivers use cellphones and support legislation to restrict this practice. *Accident Analysis & Prevention, 92*, 22–33.

Sanbonmatsu, D.M., Strayer, D.L., Biondi, F., Behrends, A.A., & Moore, S.M. (2016). Cell-phone use diminishes self-awareness of impaired driving. *Psychonomic Bulletin & Review, 23*, 617–623.

Sanford, K. (2005). Attributions and anger in early marriage: Wives are event-dependent and husbands are schematic. *Journal of Family Psychology, 19*, 180–188.

Sani, F. (2005). When groups secede: Extending and refining the social psychological model of schism in groups. *Personality and Social Psychology Bulletin, 31*, 1074–1086.

Sani, F., & Reicher, S. (1998). When consensus fails: An analysis of the schism within the Italian Communist Party (1991). *European Journal of Social Psychology, 28*, 623–645.

Sani, F., & Reicher, S. (1999). Identity, argument and schism: Two longitudinal studies of the split in the Church of England over the ordination of women to the priesthood. *Group Process and Intergroup Relations, 2*, 279–300.

Sani, F., & Todman, J. (2002). Should we stay or should we go? A social psychological model of schisms in groups. *Personality and Social Psychology Bulletin, 28*, 1647–1655.

Sani, F., Bowe, M., & Herrera, M. (2008). Perceived collective continuity: Seeing groups as temporally enduring entities. In F. Sani (Ed.), *Self continuity: Individual and collective perspectives* (pp. 159–172). New York, NY: Psychology Press.

Sani, F., Todman, J. & Lunn, J. (2005). The fundamentality of group principles and perceived group entitativity. *Journal of Experimental Social Psychology, 41*, 567–573.

Satpute, A.B., & Lieberman, M.D. (2006). Integrating automatic and controlled processes into neurocognitive models of social cognition. *Brain Research, 1079*, 86–97.

Sauerland, M., Raymaekers, L.H.C., Otgaar, H., Memon, A., Waltjen, T.T., Nivo, M., Slegers, C., Broers, N.J., & Smeets, T. (2016). Stress, stress-induced cortisol responses, and eyewitness identification performance. *Behavioral Sciences & the Law, 34*, 580–594.

Saunders, D. (2007). Blame Gandhi and Churchill for a split that poisoned the world. *Globe & Mail*, July 14.

Schacter, D.L. (1987). Implicit memory: History and current status. *Journal of Experimental Psychology: Learning, Memory, and Cognition, 11*, 501–518.

Schaller, M., & Maass, A. (1989). Illusory correlation and social categorization: Toward an integration of motivational and cognitive factors in stereotype formation. *Journal of Personality and Social Psychology, 18*, 776–785.

Schank, R.C., & Abelson, R.P. (1977). *Scripts, plans, goals and understanding: An inquiry into human knowledge structures.* Hillsdale, NJ: Lawrence Erlbaum.

Scheibehenne, B., Greifeneder, R., & Todd, P.M. (2010). Can there ever be too many options? A meta-analytic review of choice overload. *Journal of Consumer Research, 37*, 409–425.

Scherer, C.R., Heider, J.D., Skowronski, J.J., & Edlund, J.E. (2012). Trait expectancies and stereotype expectancies affect person memory similarly in a jury context. *The Journal of Social Psychology, 152*, 613–622.

Schilder, J.D., IJzerman, H., & Denissen, J.J.A. (2014). Physical warmth and perceptual focus: A replication of IJzerman and Semin (2009). *PLOS ONE, 9*, Article e112772.

Schiller, D., Freeman, J.B., Mitchell, J.P., Uleman, J.S., & Phelps, E.A. (2009). A neural mechanism of first impressions. *Nature Neuroscience, 12*, 508–514.

Schkade, D.A., & Kahneman, D. (1998). Does living in California make people happy? A focusing illusion in judgments of life satisfaction. *Psychological Science, 9*, 340–346.

Schlösser, T., Dunning, D., Johnson, K.L., & Kruger, J. (2013). How unaware are the unskilled? Empirical tests of the "signal extraction" counterexplanation for the Dunning-Kruger effect in self-evaluation of performance. *Journal of Economic Psychology, 39*, 85–100.

Schmader, T. (2010). Stereotype threat deconstructed. *Current Directions in Psychological Science, 19*, 14–18.

Schmader, T., Hall, W., & Croft, A. (2015). Stereotype threat in intergroup relations. In M. Mikulincer, P.R. Shaver (Eds.), J.F. Dovidio, & J.A. Simpson (Assoc. Eds.), *APA handbook of personality and social psychology: Vol. 2. Group processes* (pp. 447–471). Washington, DC: American Psychological Association.

Schmader, T., Johns, M., & Forbes, C. (2008). An integrated process model of stereotype threat effects on performance. *Psychological Review, 115*, 336–356.

Schmidt, D.F., & Boland, S.M. (1986). Structure of perceptions of older adults: Evidence for multiple stereotypes. *Psychology and Aging, 1*, 255–260.

Schmitt, M.T., & Branscombe, N.R. (2002). The meaning and consequences of perceived discrimination in disadvantaged and privileged social groups. *European Review of Social Psychology, 12*, 167–199.

Schmitt, M.T., Branscombe, N.R., Postmes, T., & Garcia, A. (2014). The consequences of perceived discrimination for psychological well-being: A meta-analytic review. *Psychological Bulletin, 140*, 921–948.

Schnall, S., Haidt, J., Clore, G.L., & Jordan, A. H. (2008). Disgust as embodied moral judgment. *Personality and Social Psychology Bulletin, 34*, 1096–1109.

Schneid, E.D., Carlston, D.E., & Skowronski, J.J. (2015). Spontaneous evaluative inferences and their relationship to spontaneous trait inferences. *Journal of Personality and Social Psychology, 108*, 681–696.

Schneid, E.D., Crawford, M.T., Skowronski, J.J., Irwin, L.M., & Carlston, D.E. (2015). Thinking about other people: Spontaneous trait inferences and spontaneous evaluations. *Social Psychology, 46*, 24–35.

Schneider, D.J. (1973). Implicit personality theory: A review. *Psychological Bulletin, 79*, 294–309.

Schneider, D.J. (2004). *The psychology of stereotyping*. New York, NY: Guilford Press.

Schneider, W., & Chein, J.M. (2003). Controlled & automatic processing: Behavior, theory, and biological mechanisms. *Cognitive Science, 27*, 525–559.

Schneider, W., & Shiffrin, R.M. (1977). Controlled and automatic human information processing. I. Detection, search, and attention. *Psychological Review, 84*, 1–66.

Scholer, A.A., & Higgins, E.T. (2010). Regulatory focus in a demanding world. In R.H. Hoyle (Ed.), *Handbook of personality and self-regulation* (pp. 291–314). New York, NY: Wiley Blackwell.

Scholer, A.A., & Higgins, E.T. (2011). Promotion and prevention systems: Regulatory focus dynamics within self-regulatory hierarchies. In K.D. Vohs & R.F. Baumeister (Eds.), *Handbook of self-regulation: Research, theory, and applications* (pp. 143–161). New York, NY: Guilford Press.

Scholer, A.A., Zou, X., Fujita, K., Stroessner, S.J., & Higgins, E.T. (2010). When risk seeking becomes a motivational necessity. *Journal of Personality and Social Psychology, 99*, 215–231.

Schooler, J.W., & Tanaka, J.W. (1991). Composites, compromises, and CHARM: What is the evidence for blend memory representations? *Journal of Experimental Psychology: General, 120*, 96–100.

Schooler, J.W., Mrazek, M.D., Baird, B., & Winkielman, P. (2015). Minding the mind: The value of distinguishing among unconscious, conscious, and metaconscious processes. In M. Mikulincer & P.R. Shaver (Eds.), *APA handbook of personality and social psychology* (Vol. 1, *Attitudes and social cognition*, pp. 179–202). Washington, DC: American Psychological Association.

Schooler, L.J., & Hertwig, R. (2005). How forgetting aids heuristic inference. *Psychological Review, 112*, 610–628.

Schubert, T.W., & Häfner, M. (2003). Contrast from social stereotypes in automatic behavior.

Journal of Experimental Social Psychology, *39*, 577–584.

Schultze, T., Mojzisch, A., & Schulz-Hardt, S. (2017). On the inability to ignore useless advice: A case for anchoring in the judge-advisor-system. *Experimental Psychology*, *64*, 170–183.

Schwarz, N. (1994). Judgment in a social context: Biases, shortcomings, and the logic of conversation. In M.P. Zanna (Ed.), *Advances in experimental social psychology* (Vol. 26, pp. 23–62). New York, NY: Academic Press.

Schwarz, N. (1998). Accessible content and accessibility experiences: The interplay of declarative and experiential information in judgment. *Personality and Social Psychology Review*, *2*, 87–99.

Schwarz, N. (2004). Metacognitive experiences in consumer judgment and decision making. *Journal of Consumer Psychology*, *14*, 332–348.

Schwarz, N. (2007). Attitude construction: Evaluation in context. *Social Cognition*, *25*, 638–656.

Schwarz, N. (2012). Feelings-as-information theory. In P.A.M. Van Lange, A.W. Kruglanski, & E.T. Higgins (Eds.), *Handbook of theories of social psychology* (Vol. 1, pp. 289–308). Thousand Oaks, CA: Sage.

Schwarz, N., & Bless, H. (1992). Constructing reality and its alternatives: An inclusion/exclusion model of assimilation and contrast effects in social judgment. In L. Martin & A. Tesser (Eds.), *The construction of social judgment* (pp. 217–245). Hillsdale, NJ: Lawrence Erlbaum.

Schwarz, N., & Bless, H. (2007). Mental construal processes: The inclusion/exclusion model. In D.A. Stapel & J. Suls (Eds.), *Assimilation and contrast in social psychology* (pp. 119–142). New York, NY: Psychology Press.

Schwarz, N., & Bohner, G. (2001). The construction of attitudes. In A. Tesser & N. Schwarz (Eds.), *Blackwell handbook of social psychology, Vol. 1: Intraindividual processes* (pp. 436–457). Oxford: Blackwell.

Schwarz, N., & Clore, G.L. (1983). Mood, misattribution, and judgments of well-being: Informative and directive functions of affective states. *Journal of Personality and Social Psychology*, *45*, 513–523.

Schwarz, N., & Clore, G.L. (1988). How do I feel about it? The information function of affective states. In K. Fiedler & J.P. Forgas (Eds.), *Affect, cognition and social behavior: New evidence and integrative attempts* (pp. 44–63). Toronto: C.J. Hogrefe.

Schwarz, N., & Lee, S.W.S. (2019). Embodied cognition and the construction of attitudes. In D. Albarracín & B.T. Johnson (Eds.), *The handbook of attitudes: Volume 1: Basic principles* (2nd ed., pp. 450–480). New York, NY: Routledge.

Schwarz, N., & Vaughn, L.A. (2002). The availability heuristic revisited: Ease of recall and content of recall as distinct sources of information. In T. Gilovich, D.W. Griffin, & D. Kahneman (Eds.), *Heuristics and biases: The psychology of intuitive judgment* (pp. 103–119). New York, NY: Cambridge University Press.

Schwarz, N., Bless, H., Strack, F., Klumpp, G., Rittenauer-Schatka, H., & Simons, A. (1991). Ease of retrieval as information: Another look at the availability heuristic. *Journal of Personality and Social Psychology*, *61*, 195–202.

Schwarz, N., Strack, F., Hilton, D.J., & Naderer, G. (1991). Base rates, representativeness, and the logic of conversation: The contextual relevance of "irrelevant" information. *Social Cognition*, *9*, 67–84.

Schwarz, N., Strack, F., Kommer, D., & Wagner, D. (1987). Soccer rooms and the quality of your life: Mood effects on judgments of the satisfaction with life in general and with specific life-domains. *European Journal of Social Psychology*, *17*, 69–79.

Schweiger Gallo, I., Pfau, F., & Gollwitzer, P.M. (2012). Furnishing hypnotic instructions with implementation intentions enhances hypnotic responsiveness. *Consciousness and Cognition*, *21*, 1023–1030.

Schweinsberg, M., Madan, N., Vianello, M., Sommer, S.A., Jordan, J., Tierney, W. ... Uhlmann, E.L. (2016). The pipeline project: Pre-publication independent replications of a single laboratory's research pipeline. *Journal of Experimental Social Psychology, 66*, 55–67.

Schwinger, M., Wirthwein, L., Lemmer, G., & Steinmayr, R. (2014). Academic self-handicapping and achievement: A meta-analysis. *Journal of Educational Psychology, 106*, 744–761.

Scott, W.A. (1966). Brief report: Measures of cognitive structure. *Multivariate Behavioral Research, 1*, 391–395.

Sedikides, C. (1995). Central and peripheral self-conceptions are differentially influenced by mood: Tests of the differential sensitivity hypothesis. *Journal of Personality and Social Psychology, 69*, 759–777.

Sedikides, C., & Green, J.D. (2000). On the self-protective nature of inconsistency-negativity management: Using the person memory paradigm to examine self-referent memory. *Journal of Personality and Social Psychology, 79*, 906–922.

Sedikides, C., & Hepper, E.G.D. (2009). Self-improvement. *Social and Personality Psychology Compass, 3*, 899–917.

Sedikides, C., & Strube, M.J. (1997). Self evaluation: To thine own self be good, to thine own self be sure, to thine own self be true, and to thine own self be better. In M.P. Zanna (Ed.), *Advances in experimental social psychology* (Vol. 29, pp. 209–269). New York, NY: Academic Press.

Sedikides, C., Gaertner, L., & Cai, H. (2015). On the panculturality of self-enhancement and self-protection motivation: The case for the universality of self-esteem. In A.J. Elliot (Ed.), *Advances in motivation science* (Vol. 2, pp. 185–241). New York, NY: Academic Press.

Sedikides, C., Gaertner, L., & Toguchi, Y. (2003). Pancultural self-enhancement. *Journal of Personality and Social Psychology, 84*, 60–79.

Sedikides, C., Green, J.D., Saunders, J., Skowronski, J.J., & Zengel, B. (2016). Mnemic neglect: Selective amnesia of one's faults. *European Review of Social Psychology, 27*, 1–62.

Sedikides, C., Meek, R., Alicke, M.D., & Taylor, S. (2014). Behind bars but above the bar: Prisoners consider themselves more prosocial than non-prisoners. *British Journal of Social Psychology, 53*, 396–403.

Seibt, B., Neumann, R., Nussinson, R., & Strack, F. (2008). Movement direction or change in distance? Self- and object-related approach-avoidance motions. *Journal of Experimental Social Psychology, 44*, 713–720.

Seih, Y., Buhrmester, M.D., Lin, Y., Huang, C., & Swann, W.B., Jr. (2013). Do people want to be flattered or understood? The cross-cultural universality of self-verification. *Journal of Experimental Social Psychology, 49*, 169–172.

Sekaquaptewa, D., Espinoza, P., Thompson, M., Vargas, P., & von Hippel, W. (2003). Stereotypic explanatory bias: Implicit stereotyping as a predictor of discrimination. *Journal of Experimental Social Psychology, 39*, 75–82.

Semin, G.R., & Fiedler, K. (1988). The cognitive functions of linguistic categories in describing persons: Social cognition and language. *Journal of Personality and Social Psychology, 54*, 558–568.

Semin, G.R., & Fiedler, K. (1992). The inferential properties of interpersonal verbs. In G.R. Semin & K. Fiedler (Eds.), *Language, interaction, and social cognition* (pp. 58–78). London: Sage.

Semin, G.R., & Strack, F. (1980). The plausibility of the implausible: A critique of Snyder and Swann (1978). *European Journal of Social Psychology, 10*, 379–388.

Seta, J.J., Seta, C.E., & McElroy, T. (2003). Attributional biases in the service of stereotype maintenance: A schema-maintenance through compensation analysis. *Personality and Social Psychology Bulletin, 29*, 151–163.

Shah, J. (2003). Automatic for the people: How representations of significant others implicitly affect goal pursuit. *Journal of Personality and Social Psychology*, *84*, 661–681.

Shah, J.Y., Friedman, R., & Kruglanski, A.W. (2002). Forgetting all else: On the antecedents and consequences of goal shielding. *Journal of Personality and Social Psychology*, *83*, 1261–1280.

Shalev, I. (2015). The architecture of embodied cue integration: Insight from the "motivation as cognition" perspective. *Frontiers in Psychology*, *6*, 658.

Shanks, D.R., Newell, B.R., Lee, E.H., Balakrishnan, D. Ekelund, L., Cenac, Z. & Kavvadia, F. (2013). Priming intelligent behavior: An elusive phenomenon. *PLOS ONE*, *8*, e56515.

Shapiro, L. (2019). *Embodied cognition* (2nd ed.). New York, NY: Routledge.

Shariff, A.F., & Norenzayan, A. (2008). God is watching you: Priming God concepts increases prosocial behavior in an anonymous economic game. *Psychological Science*, *18*, 803–809.

Sharot, T., & Garrett, N. (2016). Forming beliefs: Why valence matters. *Trends in Cognitive Sciences*, *20*, 25–33.

Shavitt, S., Sanbonmatsu, D.M., Smittipatana, S., & Posavac, S. (1999). Broadening the conditions for illusory correlation formation: Implications for judging minority groups. *Basic and Applied Social Psychology*, *21*, 263–279.

Shaw, J., & Vredeveldt, A. (2019). The recovered memory debate continues in Europe: Evidence from the United Kingdom, the Netherlands, France, and Germany. *Clinical Psychological Science*, *7*, 27–28.

Sheeran, P., & Webb, T.L. (2016). The intention–behavior gap. *Social and Personality Psychology Compass*, *10*, 503–518.

Sheeran, P., Maki, A., Montanaro, E., Avishai-Yitshak, A., Bryan, A., Klein, W.M.P., Miles, E., & Rothman, A.J. (2016). The impact of changing attitudes, norms, and self-efficacy on health-related intentions and behavior: A meta-analysis. *Health Psychology*, *35*, 1178–1188.

Sheeran, P., Milne, S.E., Webb, T.L., & Gollwitzer, P.M. (2005). Implementation intentions. In M. Conner & P. Norman (Eds.), *Predicting health behavior* (2nd ed., pp. 276–323). Milton Keynes: Open University Press.

Sheeran, P., Webb, T.L., & Gollwitzer, P.M. (2005). The interplay between goal intentions and implementation intentions. *Personality and Social Psychology Bulletin*, *31*, 87–98.

Sheldon, S., Dunning, D., & Ames, D.R. (2014). Emotionally unskilled, unaware, and uninterested in learning more: Biased self-assessments of emotional intelligence. *Journal of Applied Psychology*, *99*, 125–137.

Shen, X., Mann, T.C., & Ferguson, M.J. (2020). Beware a dishonest face? Updating face-based implicit impressions using diagnostic behavioral information. *Journal of Experimental Social Psychology*, *86*, 103888.

Shepperd, J.A. (1993). Student derogation of the scholastic aptitude test: Biases in perceptions and presentations of college board scores. *Basic and Applied Social Psychology*, *14*, 455–473.

Sherif, M. (1935). A study of some social factors in perception. *Archives of Psychology*, *187*, 5–61.

Sherif, M. (1951). A preliminary study of intergroup relations. In J.H. Rohrer & M. Sherif (Eds.), *Social psychology at the crossroads: The University of Oklahoma lectures in social psychology* (pp. 388–424). New York, NY: Harper.

Sherif, M., & Sherif, C.W. (1953). *Groups in harmony and tension: An integration of studies of intergroup relations*. New York, NY: Harper.

Sherif, M., & Sherif, C.W. (1967). Attitudes as the individual's own categories: The social judgment approach to attitude change. In C.W. Sherif & M. Sherif (Eds.), *Attitude, ego involvement, and change* (pp. 105–139). New York, NY: Wiley.

Sherman, D.K., & Cohen, G.L. (2006). The psychology of self-defense: Self-affirmation theory. In M.P. Zanna (Ed.), *Advances in experimental social psychology* (Vol. 38, pp. 183–242). San Diego, CA: Academic Press.

Sherman, D.K., & Hartson, K.A. (2011). Reconciling self-protection with self-improvement: Self-affirmation theory. In M.D. Alicke & C. Sedikides (Eds.), *Handbook of self-enhancement and self-protection* (pp. 128–151). New York, NY: Guilford Press.

Sherman, J.W. (1996). Development and mental representation of stereotypes. *Journal of Personality and Social Psychology*, *70*, 1126–1141.

Sherman, J.W. (2001). The dynamic relationship between stereotype efficiency and mental representation. In G.B. Moskowitz (Ed.), *Cognitive social psychology* (pp. 177–190). Mahwah, NJ: Lawrence Erlbaum.

Sherman, J.W. (2006). On building a better process model: It's not only how many, but which ones and by which means. *Psychological Inquiry*, *17*, 173–184.

Sherman, J.W. (2008). Controlled influences on implicit measures: Confronting the myth of process-purity and taming the cognitive monster. In R.E. Petty, R.H. Fazio, & P. Briñol (Eds.), *Attitudes: Insights from the new implicit measures* (pp. 391–426). New York, NY: Psychology Press.

Sherman, J.W., & Frost, L.A. (2000). On the encoding of stereotype-relevant information under cognitive load. *Personality and Social Psychology Bulletin*, *26*, 26–34.

Sherman, J.W., & Hamilton, D.L. (1994). On the formation of interitem associative links in person memory. *Journal of Experimental Social Psychology*, *30*, 203–217.

Sherman, J.W., & Klein, S.B. (1994). Development and representation of personality impressions. *Journal of Personality and Social Psychology*, *67*, 972–983.

Sherman, J.W., Conrey, F.R., & Groom, C.J. (2004). Encoding flexibility revisited: Evidence for enhanced encoding of stereotype-inconsistent information under cognitive load. *Social Cognition*, *32*, 214–232.

Sherman, J.W., Gawronski, B., Gonsalkorale, K., Hugenberg, K., Allen, T.J., & Groom, C.J. (2008). The self-regulation of automatic associations and behavioral impulses. *Psychological Review*, *115*, 314–335.

Sherman, J.W., Gawronski, B., & Trope, Y. (Eds.) (2014). *Dual process theories of the social mind*. New York, NY: Guilford Press.

Sherman, J.W., Huang, L.M., & Sacchi, D.L.M. (2015). Variations on a theme: Attentional processes in group and individual perception. In S.J. Stroessner & J.W. Sherman (Eds.), *Social perception from individuals to groups* (pp. 125–140). New York: Psychology Press.

Sherman, J.W., Klauer, K.C., & Allen, T.J. (2010). Mathematical modeling of implicit social cognition: The machine in the ghost. In B. Gawronski & B.K. Payne (Eds.), *Handbook of implicit social cognition: Measurement, theory, and applications* (pp. 156–174). New York, NY: Guilford Press.

Sherman, J.W., Kruschke, J.K., Sherman, S.J., Percy, E.J., Petrocelli, J.V., & Conrey, F.R. (2009). Attentional processes in stereotype formation: A common model for category accentuation and illusory correlation. *Journal of Personality and Social Psychology*, *96*, 305–323.

Sherman, J.W., Lee, A.Y., Bessenoff, G.R., & Frost, L.A. (1998). Stereotype efficiency reconsidered: Encoding flexibility under cognitive load. *Journal of Personality and Social Psychology*, *75*, 589–606.

Sherman, J.W., Stroessner, S.J., Conrey, F.R., & Azam, O.A. (2005). Prejudice and stereotype maintenance processes: Attention, attribution, and individuation. *Journal of Personality and Social Psychology*, *89*, 607–622.

Sherman, R.A., Nave, C.S., & Funder, D.C. (2010). Situational similarity and personality predict behavioral consistency. *Journal of Personality and Social Psychology*, *99*, 330–343.

Sherman, S.J. (1980). On the self-erasing nature of errors of prediction. *Journal of Personality and Social Psychology*, *39*, 211–221.

Sherman, S.J., & Fazio, R.H. (1983) Parallels between attitudes and traits as predictors of behavior. *Journal of Personality*, *51*, 308–345.

Sherman, S.J., Castelli, L., & Hamilton, D.L. (2002). The spontaneous use of a group typology as an organizing principle in memory. *Journal of Personality and Social Psychology*, *82*, 328–342.

Sherman, S.J., Chassin, L., Presson, C.C., & Agostinelli, G. (1984). The role of the evaluation and similarity principles in the false consensus effect. *Journal of Personality and Social Psychology*, *47*, 1244–1262.

Sherman, S.J., Cialdini, R.B., Schwartzman, D.F., & Reynolds, K.D. (1985). Imagining can heighten or lower the perceived likelihood of contracting a disease: The mediating effect of ease of imagery. *Personality and Social Psychology Bulletin*, *11*, 118–127.

Sherman, S.J., Crawford, M.T., Hamilton, D.L., & Garcia-Marques, L. (2003). Social inference and social memory: The interplay between systems. In M.A. Hogg & J. Cooper (Eds.), *The SAGE handbook of social psychology* (pp. 65–86). London: Sage.

Sherman, S.J., Hamilton, D.L., & Lewis, A.C. (1999). Perceived entitativity and the social identity value of group memberships. In D. Abrams & M.A. Hogg (Eds.), *Social identity and social cognition* (pp. 80–110). Oxford: Blackwell.

Sherman, S.J., Skov, R.B., Hervitz, E.F., & Stock, C.B. (1981). The effects of explaining hypothetical future events: From possibility to probability to actuality and beyond. *Journal of Experimental Social Psychology*, *17*, 142–158.

Shiffrin, R.M., & Schneider, W. (1977). Controlled and automatic human information processing: II. Perceptual learning, automatic attending and a general theory. *Psychological Review*, *84*, 127–190.

Shiffrin, R.M., & Schneider, W. (1984). Automatic and controlled processing revisited. *Psychological Review*, *91*, 269–276.

Shimizu, Y., Lee, H., & Uleman, J.S. (2017). Culture as automatic processes for making meaning: Spontaneous trait inferences. *Journal of Experimental Social Psychology*, *69*, 79–85.

Shin, Y.K., Proctor, R.W., & Capaldi, E.J. (2010). A review of contemporary ideomotor theory. *Psychological Bulletin*, *136*, 943–974.

Shiv, B., & Fedorikhin, A. (1999). Heart and mind in conflict: The interplay of affect and cognition in consumer decision making. *Journal of Consumer Research*, *26*, 278–292.

Shoda, T.M., McConnell, A.R., & Rydell, R.J. (2014). Implicit consistency processes in social cognition: Explicit-implicit discrepancies across systems of evaluation. *Social and Personality Psychology Compass*, *8*, 135–146.

Shoda, Y., & Mischel, W. (2006). Applying meta-theory to achieve generalisability and precision in personality science. *Applied Psychology: An International Review*, *55*, 439–452.

Shoda, Y., LeeTiernan, S., & Mischel, W. (2002). Personality as a dynamical system: Emergence of stability and constancy from intra- and inter-personal interactions. *Personality and Social Psychology Review*, *6*, 316–325.

Shoda, Y., Mischel, W., & Wright, J.C. (1989). Intuitive interactionism in person perception: Effects of situation-behavior relations on dispositional judgments. *Journal of Personality and Social Psychology*, *56*, 41–53.

Shoda, Y., Mischel, W., & Wright, J.C. (1994). Intraindividual stability in the organization and patterning of behavior: Incorporating psychological situations into the idiographic analysis of personality. *Journal of Personality and Social Psychology*, *67*, 674–687.

Shriver, E.R., Young, S.G., Hugenberg, K., Bernstein, M.J., & Lanter, J.R. (2008). Class, race, and the face: Social context modulates the cross-race effect in face recognition. *Personality and Social Psychology Bulletin*, *34*, 260–274.

Shrout, P.E., & Rodgers, J.L. (2018). Psychology, science, and knowledge construction: Broadening perspectives from the replication crisis. *Annual Review of Psychology, 69,* 487–510.

Sidanius, J., & Pratto, F. (1999). *Social dominance: An intergroup theory of hierarchy and oppression.* New York, NY: Cambridge University Press.

Sidanius, J., Pratto, F., & Mitchell, M. (1994). Ingroup identification, social dominance orientation, and differential intergroup social allocation. *Journal of Social Psychology, 134,* 151–167.

Siegel, J.T., Navarro, M.A., Tan, C.N., & Hyde, M.K. (2014). Attitude–behavior consistency, the principle of compatibility, and organ donation: A classic innovation. *Health Psychology, 33,* 1084–1091.

Silka, L. (1981). Effects of limited recall of variability on intuitive judgments of change. *Journal of Personality and Social Psychology, 40,* 1010–1016.

Silka, L. (1984). Intuitive perceptions of change: An overlooked phenomenon in person perception? *Personality and Social Psychology Bulletin, 10,* 180–190.

Silka, L., & Albright, L. (1983). Intuitive judgments of rate change: The case of teenage pregnancies. *Basic and Applied Social Psychology, 4,* 337–352.

Sillars, A., Roberts, L.J., Leonard, K.E., & Dun, T. (2000). Cognition during marital conflict: The relationship of thought and talk. *Journal of Social and Personal Relationships, 17,* 479–502.

Silvia, P.J., & Duval, T.S. (2001). Objective self awareness theory: Recent progress and enduring problems. *Personality and Social Psychology Review, 5,* 230–241.

Silvia, P.J., & Phillips, A.G. (2013). Self-awareness without awareness? Implicit self-focused attention and behavioral self-regulation. *Self and Identity, 12,* 114–127.

Sim, J.J., Goyle, A., McKedy, W., Eidelman, S., & Correll, J. (2014). How social identity shapes the working self-concept. *Journal of Experimental Social Psychology, 55,* 271–277.

Simcock, G., & Hayne, H. (2002). Breaking the barrier? Children fail to translate their pre-verbal memories into language. *Psychological Science, 13,* 225–231.

Simon, B., & Brown, R. (1987). Perceived intragroup homogeneity in minority-majority contexts. *Journal of Personality and Social Psychology, 53,* 703–711.

Simon, H.A. (1955). A behavioral model of rational choice. *Quarterly Journal of Economics, 69,* 99–118.

Simon, H.A. (1956). Rational choice and the structure of the environment. *Psychological Review, 63,* 261–273.

Simon, H.A. (1974). The organization of complex systems. In H.H. Pattee (Ed.), *Hierarchy theory: The challenge of complex systems* (pp. 3–27). New York, NY: Braziller.

Simon, H.A. (1982). *Models of bounded rationality* (Vols. 1 and 2). Cambridge, MA: MIT Press.

Simons, D.J. (2000). Attentional capture and inattentional blindness. *Trends in Cognitive Sciences, 4,* 147–155.

Simons, D.J. (2014). The value of direct replication. *Perspectives on Psychological Science, 9,* 76–80.

Simons, D.J., & Chabris, C.F. (1999). Gorillas in our midst: Sustained inattentional blindness for dynamic events. *Perception, 28,* 1059–1074.

Simons, D.J., & Levin, D.T. (1998). Failure to detect changes to people during a real-world interaction. *Psychonomic Bulletin & Review, 5,* 644–649.

Sinclair, S., Lowery, B.S., Hardin, C.D., & Colangelo, A. (2005). Social tuning of automatic racial attitudes: The role of affiliative motivation. *Journal of Personality and Social Psychology, 89,* 583–592.

Sipilä, J., Sundqvist, S., & Tarkiainen, A. (2017). Winding paths: Ambivalence in consumers' buying processes. *Journal of Consumer Behaviour, 16,* e93–e112.

Sivacek, J., & Crano, W.D. (1982). Vested interest as a moderator of attitude–behavior consistency. *Journal of Personality and Social Psychology, 43,* 210–221.

Skinner, B.F. (1938). *The behavior of organisms: An experimental analysis.* Oxford: Appleton-Century.

Skitka, L.J., Mullen, E., Griffin, T., Hutchinson, S., & Chamberlin, B. (2002). Dispositions, scripts, or motivated correction? Understanding ideological differences in explanation for social problems. *Journal of Personality and Social Psychology, 83,* 470–487.

Skorinko, J.L., & Sinclair, S. (2018). Shared reality through social tuning of implicit prejudice. *Current Opinion in Psychology, 23,* 109–112.

Skov, R.B., & Sherman, S.J. (1986). Information-gathering processes: Diagnosticity, hypothesis-confirmatory strategies, and perceived hypothesis confirmation. *Journal of Experimental Social Psychology, 22,* 93–121.

Skowronski, J.J. (2011). The positivity bias and the fading affect bias in autobiographical memory: A self-motives perspective. In C. Sedikides & M. Alicke (Eds.), *The handbook of self-enhancement and self-protection* (pp. 211–231). New York, NY: Guilford Press.

Skowronski, J.J., & Carlston, D.E. (1989). Negativity and extremity biases in impression formation: A review of explanations. *Psychological Bulletin, 105,* 131–142.

Skowronski, J.J., & Gannon, K. (2000). Raw conditional probabilities are a flawed index of associative strength: Evidence from a single expectancy paradigm. *Basic and Applied Social Psychology, 22,* 9-18.

Skowronski, J.J., & Welbourne, J. (1997). Conditional probability may be a flawed measure of associative strength. *Social Cognition, 15*(1), 1–12.

Skowronski, J.J., Carlston, D.E., Mae, L., & Crawford, M.T. (1998). Spontaneous trait transference: Communicators take on the qualities they describe in others. *Journal of Personality and Social Psychology, 74,* 837–848.

Skowronski, J.J., McCarthy, R.J., & Wells, B.M. (2013). Person memory: Past, perspectives, and prospects. In D.E. Carlston (Ed.), *The Oxford handbook of social cognition* (pp. 352–374). New York, NY: Oxford University Press.

Skrypnek, B.J., & Snyder, M. (1982). On the self-perpetuating nature of stereotypes about men and women. *Journal of Experimental Social Psychology, 18,* 277–291.

Slade, P. (1981). Menstrual cycle symptoms in infertile and control subjects: A re-evaluation of the evidence for psychological changes. *Journal of Psychosomatic Research, 25,* 175–181.

Slade, P. (1984). Premenstrual emotional changes in normal women: Fact or fiction? *Journal of Psychosomatic Research, 28,* 1–7.

Sloman, S.A. (1996). The empirical case for two systems of reasoning. *Psychological Bulletin, 119,* 3–22.

Sloman, S.A., & Malt, B.C. (2003). Artifacts are not ascribed essences, nor are they treated as belonging to kinds. *Language and Cognitive Processes, 18,* 563–582.

Slovic, P. (1995). The construction of preference. *American Psychologist, 50,* 364–371.

Slovic, P., Finucane, M., Peters, E., & MacGregor, D.G. (2002). The affect heuristic. In T. Gilovich, D.W. Griffin, & D. Kahneman (Eds.), *Heuristics and biases: The psychology of intuitive judgment* (pp. 397–420). New York, NY: Cambridge University Press.

Slovic, P., Fischhoff, B., & Lichtenstein, S. (1979). Rating the risks. *Environment, 21,* 14–20, 36–39.

Slovic, P., Fischhoff, B., & Lichtenstein, S. (1982). Facts versus fears: Understanding perceived risk. In D. Kahneman, P. Slovic, & A. Tversky (Eds.), *Judgment under uncertainty: Heuristics and biases* (pp. 463–492). New York, NY: Cambridge University Press.

Smith, A. (1759/1892). *The theory of moral sentiments.* New York, NY: Prometheus.

Smith, A.C., & Greene, E. (2005). Conduct and its consequences: Attempts at debiasing jury judgments. *Law and Human Behavior, 29,* 505–526.

Smith, A.E., Jussim, L., & Eccles, J. (1999). Do self-fulfilling prophecies accumulate, dissipate, or remain stable over time? *Journal of Personality and Social Psychology, 77,* 548–565.

Smith, A.J., & Clark, R.D. (1973). The relationship between attitudes and beliefs. *Journal of Personality and Social Psychology, 26,* 321–326.

Smith, C.T., & Nosek, B.A. (2011). Affective focus increases the concordance between implicit and explicit attitudes. *Social Psychology, 42,* 300–313.

Smith, E.E., Shoben, E.J., & Rips, L.J. (1974). Structure and process in semantic memory: A featural model for semantic decisions. *Psychological Review, 81,* 214–241.

Smith, E.R. (1984). Attributions and other inferences: Processing information about the self versus others. *Journal of Experimental Social Psychology, 20,* 97–115.

Smith, E.R. (1990). Content and process specificity in the effects of prior experiences. In T.K. Srull & R.S. Wyer, Jr. (Eds.), *Advances in social cognition* (Vol. 3, pp. 1–59). Hillsdale, NJ: Lawrence Erlbaum.

Smith, E.R. (1991). Illusory correlation in a simulated exemplar-based memory. *Journal of Experimental Social Psychology, 27,* 107–123.

Smith, E.R. (1996). What do connectionism and social psychology offer each other? *Journal of Personality and Social Psychology, 70,* 893–912.

Smith, E.R., & DeCoster, J. (1998). Knowledge acquisition, accessibility, and use in person perception and stereotyping: Simulation with a recurrent connectionist network. *Journal of Personality and Social Psychology, 74,* 21–35.

Smith, E.R., & DeCoster, J. (2000). Dual-process models in social and cognitive psychology: Conceptual integration and links to underlying memory systems. *Personality and Social Psychology Review, 4,* 108–131.

Smith, E.R., & Lerner, M. (1986). Development of automatism in social judgments. *Journal of Personality and Social Psychology, 50,* 246–259.

Smith, E.R., & Miller, F.D. (1983). Mediation among attributional inferences and comprehension processes: Initial findings and a general method. *Journal of Personality and Social Psychology, 44,* 492–505.

Smith, J.C. (2009). *Pseudoscience and extraordinary claims of the paranormal: A critical thinker's toolkit.* New York, NY: Wiley.

Smith, P.K., & Trope, Y. (2006). You focus on the forest when you're in charge of the trees: Power priming and abstract information processing. *Journal of Personality and Social Psychology, 90,* 578–596.

Smith, P.K., Jostmann, N.B., Galinsky, A.D., & van Dijk, W.W. (2008). Lacking power impairs executive functions. *Psychological Science, 19,* 441–447.

Smith, R.H. (2000). Assimilative and contrastive emotional reactions to upward and downward social comparisons. In J. Suls & L. Wheeler (Eds.), *Handbook of social comparison: Theory and research* (pp. 173–200). New York, NY: Kluwer.

Smith, R.H., Eyre, H.L., Powell, C.A., & Kim, S.H. (2006). Relativistic origins of emotional reactions to events happening to others and to ourselves. *British Journal of Social Psychology, 45,* 357–371.

Smith, R.M. (2018). *The biology of beauty: The science behind human attractiveness.* Santa Barbara, CA: Praeger/ABC-CLIO.

Smith, S.M., & Vela, E. (2001). Environmental context-dependent memory: A review and meta-analysis. *Psychonomic Bulletin & Review, 8,* 203–220.

Snyder, M. (1981). On the self-perpetuating nature of social stereotypes. In D.L. Hamilton (Ed.), *Cognitive processes in stereotyping and intergroup behavior* (pp. 183–212). Hillsdale, NJ: Lawrence Erlbaum.

Snyder, M. (1992). Motivational foundations of behavioral confirmation. In M.P. Zanna (Ed.), *Advances in experimental social psychology* (Vol. 25, pp. 67–114). San Diego, CA: Academic Press.

Snyder, M., & Stukas, A.A., Jr. (1999). Interpersonal processes: The interplay of cognitive, motivational, and behavioral activities in social interaction. *Annual Review of Psychology, 50,* 273–303.

Snyder, M., & Swann, W.B., Jr. (1978). Hypothesis-testing processes in social interaction. *Journal of Personality and Social Psychology, 36,* 1202–1212.

Snyder, M., Campbell, B.H., & Preston, E. (1982). Testing hypotheses about human nature: Assessing the accuracy of social stereotypes. *Social Cognition, 1,* 256–272.

Snyder, M., Tanke, E.D., & Berscheid, E. (1977). Social perception and interpersonal behavior: On the self-fulfilling nature of social stereotypes. *Journal of Personality and Social Psychology, 35,* 656–666.

Soll, J.B., & Larrick, R.P. (2009). Strategies for revising judgment: How (and how well) people use others' opinions. *Journal of Experimental Psychology: Learning, Memory, and Cognition, 35,* 780–805.

Sorensen, T.C. (1963). *Decision making in the White House: The olive branch or the arrows.* New York, NY: Columbia University Press.

Sparkman, G., & Walton, G.M. (2017). Dynamic norms promote sustainable behavior, even if it is counternormative. *Psychological Science, 28,* 1663–1674.

Sparkman, G., & Walton, G.M. (2019). Witnessing change: Dynamic norms help resolve diverse barriers to personal change. *Journal of Experimental Social Psychology, 82,* 238–252.

Spencer-Rodgers, J., Hamilton, D.L., & Sherman, S.J. (2007). The central role of entitativity in stereotypes of social categories and task groups. *Journal of Personality and Social Psychology, 92,* 369–388.

Spencer, K.B., Charbonneau, A.K., & Glaser, J. (2016). Implicit bias and policing. *Social and Personality Psychology Compass, 10,* 50–63.

Spencer, S.J., Logel, C., & Davies, P.G. (2016). Stereotype threat. *Annual Review of Psychology, 67,* 415–437.

Spengler, P.M., White, M.J., Ægisdóttir, S., Maugherman, A.S., Anderson, L.A., Cook, R.S., … Rush, J.D. (2009). The meta-analysis of clinical judgment project: Effects of experience on judgment accuracy. *The Counseling Psychologist, 37,* 350–399.

Spitz, J., Moors, P., Wagemans, J., & Helsen, W.F. (2018). The impact of video speed on the decision-making process of sports officials. *Cognitive Research: Principles and Implications, 3,* 1–10.

Sporer, S.L., Penrod, S., Read, D., & Cutler, B. (1995). Choosing, confidence, and accuracy: A meta-analysis of the confidence–accuracy relation in eyewitness identification studies. *Psychological Bulletin, 118,* 315–327.

Spruyt, A., Tibboel, H., De Schryver, M., & De Houwer, J. (2018). Automatic stimulus evaluation depends on goal relevance. *Emotion, 18,* 332–341.

Spunt, R.P., & Lieberman, M.D. (2013). The busy social brain: Evidence for automaticity and control in the neural systems supporting social cognition and action understanding. *Psychological Science, 24,* 80–86.

Squire, L.R., & Zola, S.M. (1996). Structure and function of declarative and nondeclarative memory systems. *Proceedings of the National Academy of Sciences, 93,* 13515–13522.

Srivastava, S., Guglielmo, S., & Beer, J.S. (2010). Perceiving others' personalities: Examining the dimensionality, assumed similarity to the self, and stability of perceiver effects. *Journal of Personality and Social Psychology, 98,* 520–534.

Srull, T.K. (1981). Person memory: Some tests of associative storage and retrieval models. *Journal of Experimental Psychology: Human Learning & Memory, 7,* 440–463.

Srull, T.K. (1983). Organizational and retrieval processes in person memory: An examination of processing objectives, presentation format, and the possible role of self-generated retrieval cues. *Journal of Personality and Social Psychology, 44,* 1157–1170.

Srull, T.K., & Brand, J.F. (1983). Memory for information about persons: The effect of encoding operations on subsequent retrieval. *Journal of Verbal Learning & Verbal Behavior, 22,* 219–230.

Srull, T.K., & Wyer, R.S., Jr. (1979). The role of category accessibility in the interpretation of information about persons: Some determinants and implications. *Journal of Personality and Social Psychology, 37,* 1660–1672.

Srull, T.K., & Wyer, R.S., Jr. (1989). Person memory and judgment. *Psychological Review, 96*, 58–83.

Srull, T.K., Lichtenstein, M., & Rothbart, M. (1985). Associative storage and retrieval processes in person memory. *Journal of Experimental Psychology: Learning, Memory, and Cognition, 11*, 316–345.

Staats, A.W., & Staats, C.K. (1958). Attitudes established by classical conditioning. *Journal of Abnormal and Social Psychology, 57*, 37–40.

Staats, C.K., & Staats, A.W. (1957). Meaning established by classical conditioning. *Journal of Experimental Psychology, 54*, 74–80.

Stack, S. (2003). Authoritarianism and support for the death penalty: A multivariate analysis. *Sociological Focus, 36*, 333–352.

Stahl, C., Unkelbach, C., & Corneille, O. (2009). On the respective contributions of awareness of US valence and US identity in valence acquisition through evaluative conditioning. *Journal of Personality and Social Psychology, 97*, 404–420.

Stajkovic, A., & Luthans, F. (1998). Self-efficacy and work-related performance: A meta-analysis. *Psychological Bulletin, 124*, 240–261.

Stallard, M.J., & Worthington, D.L. (1998). Reducing the hindsight bias utilizing attorney closing arguments. *Law and Human Behavior, 22*, 671–682.

Stangor, C. (1990). Arousal, accessibility of trait constructs, and person perception. *Journal of Experimental Social Psychology, 26*, 305–321.

Stangor, C., & McMillan, D. (1992). Memory for expectancy-congruent and expectancy-incongruent information: A review of the social and social-developmental literatures. *Psychological Bulletin, 111*, 42–61.

Stangor, C., Sechrist, G.B., & Jost, J.T. (2001). Changing racial beliefs by providing consensus information. *Personality and Social Psychology Bulletin, 27*, 486–496.

Stanley, D.A., Sokol-Hessner, P., Banaji, M.R., & Phelps, E.A. (2011). Implicit race attitudes predict trustworthiness judgments and economic trust decisions. *Proceedings of the National Academy of Sciences, 108*, 7710–7715.

Stanley, M.L., Parikh, N., Stewart, G.W., & De Brigard, F. (2017). Emotional intensity in episodic autobiographical memory and counterfactual thinking. *Consciousness and Cognition: An International Journal, 48*, 283–291.

Stanovich, K.E., & West, R.F. (2000). Individual differences in reasoning: Implications for the rationality debate. *Behavioral and Brain Sciences, 23*, 645–665.

Steblay, N.M. (1992). A meta-analytic review of the weapon focus effect. *Law and Human Behavior, 16*, 413–424.

Steele, C.M., & Aronson, J. (1995). Stereotype threat and the intellectual test performance of African-Americans. *Journal of Personality and Social Psychology, 69*, 797–811.

Steinberg, M., & Diekman, A.B. (2016). The double-edged sword of stereotypes of men. In Y.J. Wong & S.R. Wester (Eds.), *APA handbook of men and masculinities* (pp. 433–456). Washington, DC: American Psychological Association.

Steinmetz, H., Knappstein, M., Ajzen, I., Schmidt, P., & Kabst, R. (2016). How effective are behavior change interventions based on the theory of planned behavior? A three-level meta-analysis. *Zeitschrift für Psychologie, 224*, 216–233.

Stelzl, M., Janes, L., & Seligman, C. (2008). Champ or chump: Strategic utilization of dual social identities of others. *European Journal of Social Psychology, 38*, 128–138.

Stepanikova, I. (2012). Racial-ethnic biases, time pressure, and medical decisions. *Journal of Health and Social Behavior, 53*, 329–343.

Stepanikova, I., Triplett, J., & Simpson, B. (2011). Implicit racial bias and prosocial behavior. *Social Science Research, 40*, 1186–1195.

Stephan, E., Liberman, N., & Trope, Y. (2010). Politeness and psychological distance: A construal level perspective. *Journal of Personality and Social Psychology, 98*, 268–280.

Stephan, E., Liberman, N., & Trope, Y. (2011). The effects of time perspective and level of construal on social distance. *Journal of Experimental Social Psychology*, *47*, 397–402.

Stephan, W.G., & Stephan, C.W. (2000). An integrated threat theory of prejudice. In S. Oskamp (Ed.), *Reducing prejudice and discrimination* (pp. 23–45). Mahwah, NJ: Lawrence Erlbaum.

Stephan, W.G., Ybarra, O., & Rios, K. (2016). Intergroup threat theory. In T.D. Nelson (Ed.), *Handbook of prejudice, stereotyping, and discrimination* (pp. 255–278). New York, NY: Psychology Press.

Stern, C., Balcetis, E., Cole, S., West, T.V., & Caruso, E.M. (2016). Government instability shifts skin tone representations of and intentions to vote for political candidates. *Journal of Personality and Social Psychology*, *110*, 76–95.

Stern, L.D., Marrs, S., Millar, M.G., & Cole, E. (1984). Processing time and the recall of inconsistent and consistent behaviors of individuals and groups. *Journal of Personality and Social Psychology*, *47*, 253–262.

Stevenson, H.W. (1954). Latent learning in children. *Journal of Experimental Psychology*, *47*, 17–21.

Stewart, R.H. (1965). Effect of continuous responding on the order effect in personality impression formation. *Journal of Personality and Social Psychology*, *1*, 161–165.

Stewart, T.L., Latu, I.M., Kawakami, K., & Myers, A.C. (2010). Consider the situation: Reducing automatic stereotyping through situational attribution training. *Journal of Experimental Social Psychology*, *46*, 221–225.

Stewart, T.L., Weeks, M., & Lupfer, M.B. (2003). Spontaneous stereotyping: A matter of prejudice? *Social Cognition*, *21*, 263–298.

Stolarz-Fantino, S., Fantino, E., Zizzo, D.J., & Wen, J. (2003). The conjunction effect: New evidence for robustness. *American Journal of Psychology*, 116, 15–34.

Stolier, R.M., Hehman, E., Keller, M.D., Walker, M., & Freeman, J.B. (2018). The conceptual structure of face impressions. *Proceedings of the National Academy of Sciences*, *115*, 9210–9215.

Stone, J. (2002). Battling doubt by avoiding practice: The effect of stereotype threat on self-handicapping in white athletes. *Personality and Social Psychology Bulletin*, *28*, 1667–1678.

Stone, J., & Fernandez, N.C. (2008). To practice what we preach: The use of hypocrisy and cognitive dissonance to motivate behavior change. *Social and Personality Psychology Compass*, *2*, 1024–1051.

Stone, J., Lynch, C.I., Sjomeling, M., & Darley, J.M. (1999). Stereotype threat effects on black and white athletic performance. *Journal of Personality and Social Psychology*, *77*, 1213–1227.

Stone, J., Wiegand, A.W., Cooper, J., Aronson, E. (1997). When exemplification fails: Hypocrisy and the motive for self-integrity. *Journal of Personality and Social Psychology*, *72*, 54–65.

Storbeck, J., & Clore, G.L. (2007). On the interdependence of cognition and emotion. *Cognition and Emotion*, *21*, 1212–1237.

Storey, S., & Workman, L. (2013). The effects of temperature priming on cooperation in the iterated prisoner's dilemma. *Evolutionary Psychology*, *11*, 52–67.

Storms, M. (1973). Videotape and the attribution process: Reversing actors' and observers' points of view. *Journal of Personality and Social Psychology*, *27*, 165–175.

Stout, J.G., Dasgupta, N., Hunsinger, M., & McManus, M. (2011). STEMing the tide: Using ingroup experts to inoculate women's self-concept and professional goals in science, technology, engineering, and mathematics (STEM). *Journal of Personality and Social Psychology*, *100*, 255–270.

Strack, F., & Deutsch, R. (2004). Reflective and impulsive determinants of social behavior. *Personality and Social Psychology Review*, *8*, 220–247.

Strack, F., & Mussweiler, T. (1997). Explaining the enigmatic anchoring effect: Mechanisms of selective accessibility. *Journal of Personality and Social Psychology, 73*, 437–446.

Strack, F., & Schwarz, N. (Eds.) (2016). Social priming. *Current Opinion in Psychology, 12*, 1–100.

Strack, F., Martin, L.L., & Stepper, S. (1988). Inhibiting and facilitating conditions of the human smile. *Journal of Personality and Social Psychology, 54*, 768–777.

Strayer, D.L., & Drews, F.A. (2007). Cellphone-induced driver distraction. *Current Directions in Psychological Science, 16*, 128–131.

Strayer, D.L., & Johnston, W.A. (2001). Driven to distraction: Dual-task studies of simulated driving and conversing on a cellular phone. *Psychological Science, 12*, 462–466.

Strayer, D.L., Drews, F.A., & Crouch, D.J. (2006). A comparison of the cell phone driver and the drunk driver. *Human Factors, 48*, 381–391.

Strayer, D.L., Turrill, J., Cooper, J.M., Coleman, J.R., Medeiros-Ward, N., & Biondi, F. (2015). Assessing cognitive distraction in the automobile. *Human Factors, 53*, 1300–1324.

Strick, M., Dijksterhuis, A., Bos, M.W., Sjoerdsma, A., Van Baaren, R.B., & Nordgren, L.F. (2011). A meta-analysis on unconscious thought effects. *Social Cognition, 29*, 738–763.

Stroebe, W. (2016). Are most published social psychological findings false? *Journal of Experimental Social Psychology, 66*, 134–144.

Stroebe, W., & Strack, F. (2014). The alleged crisis and the illusion of exact replication. *Perspectives on Psychological Science, 9*, 59–71.

Stroessner, S.J. (1996). Social categorization by race or sex: Effects of perceived non-normalcy on response times. *Social Cognition, 14*, 247–276.

Stroessner, S.J. (2020). On the social perception of robots: Measurement, moderation, and implications. In R. Pak, E. de Visser, & E. Rovira (Eds.), *Living with robots: Emerging issues on the psychological and social implications of robots* (pp. 21–47). San Diego, CA: Academic Press.

Stroessner, S.J., & Dweck, C.S. (2015). Inferring group traits and group goals: A unified approach to social perception. In S.J. Stroessner & J.W. Sherman (Eds.), *Social perception from individuals to groups* (pp. 177–196). New York, NY: Psychology Press.

Stroessner, S.J., & Heuer, L.B. (1996). Cognitive bias in procedural justice: Formation and implications of illusory correlations in perceived intergroup fairness. *Journal of Personality and Social Psychology, 71*, 717–728.

Stroessner, S.J., & Mackie, D.M. (1992). The impact of induced affect on the perception of variability in social groups. *Personality and Social Psychology Bulletin, 18*, 546–554.

Stroessner, S.J., & Plaks, J.E. (2001). Illusory correlation and stereotype formation: Tracing the arc of research over a quarter century. In G.B. Moskowitz (Ed.), *Cognitive social psychology* (pp. 247–259). Mahwah, NJ: Lawrence Erlbaum.

Stroessner, S.J., Hamilton, D.L., & Mackie, D.M. (1992). Affect and stereotyping: Effect of induced mood on distinctiveness-based illusory correlations. *Journal of Personality and Social Psychology, 62*, 564–576.

Stroessner, S.J., Scholer, A.A., Marx, D.M., & Weisz, B.M. (2015). When threat matters: Self-regulation, threat salience, and stereotyping. *Journal of Experimental Social Psychology, 59*, 77–89.

Strohmer, D.C., & Shivy, V.A. (1994). Bias in counselor hypothesis testing: Testing the robustness of counselor confirmatory bias. *Journal of Counseling & Development, 73*, 191–197.

Stroop, J.R. (1935). Studies of interference in serial verbal reactions. *Journal of Experimental Psychology, 18*, 643–662.

Sullivan, J. (2019). The primacy effect in impression formation: Some replications and extensions. *Social Psychological and Personality Science, 10*, 432–439.

Suslow, T., Kugel, H., Ohrmann, P., Stuhrmann, A., Grotegerd, D., Redlich, R., Bauer, J., & Dannlowski, U. (2013). Neural correlates of affective priming effects based on masked facial emotion: An fMRI study. *Psychiatry Research: Neuroimaging, 211*, 239–245.

Susskind, J., Maurer, K., Thakkar, V., Hamilton, D.L., & Sherman, J.W. (1999). Perceiving individuals and groups: Expectancies, dispositional inferences, and causal attributions. *Journal of Personality and Social Psychology, 76*, 181–191.

Suter, R.S., & Hertwig, R. (2011). Time and moral judgment. *Cognition, 119*, 454–458.

Sutherland, C.A.M., Oldmeadow, J.A., Santos, I.M., Towler, J., Michael Burt, D., & Young, A.W. (2013). Social inferences from faces: Ambient images generate a three-dimensional model. *Cognition, 127*, 105–118.

Sutin, A.R., & Robins, R.W. (2008). When the "I" looks at the "Me": Autobiographical memory, visual perspective, and the self. *Consciousness and Cognition, 17*, 1386–1397.

Svedholm, A.M., & Lindeman, M. (2013). The separate roles of the reflective mind and involuntary inhibitory control in gatekeeping paranormal beliefs and the underlying intuitive confusions. *British Journal of Psychology, 104*, 303–319.

Swann, W.B., Jr. (2012). Self-verification theory. In P.A.M. Van Lange, A.W. Kruglanski, & E.T. Higgins (Eds.), *Handbook of theories of social psychology* (Vol. 2, pp. 23–42). London: Sage.

Swann, W.B., Jr., & Buhrmester, M.D. (2015). Identity fusion. *Current Directions in Psychological Science, 24*, 52–57.

Swann, W.B., Jr., & Pelham, B.W. (2002). Who wants out when the going gets good? Psychological investment and preference for self-verifying college roommates. *Journal of Self and Identity, 1*, 219–233.

Swann, W.B., Jr., & Read, S.J. (1981). Acquiring self-knowledge: The search for feedback that fits. *Journal of Personality and Social Psychology, 41*, 1119–1128.

Swann, W.B., Jr., Buhrmester, M.D., Gomez, A., Jetten, J., Bastian, B., Vasquez, A.,... Zhang, A. (2014). What makes a group worth dying for? Identity fusion fosters perception of familial ties, promoting self-sacrifice. *Journal of Personality and Social Psychology, 106*, 912–926.

Swann, W.B., Jr., de la Ronde, C., & Hixon, J.G. (1994). Authenticity and positivity strivings in marriage and courtship. *Journal of Personality and Social Psychology, 66*, 857–869.

Swann, W.B., Jr., Gomez, A., Dovidio, J.F., Hart, S., & Jetten, J. (2010). Dying and killing for one's group: Identity fusion moderates responses to intergroup versions of the trolley problem. *Psychological Science, 21*, 1176–1183.

Swann, W.B., Jr., Griffin, J.J., Predmore, S.C., & Gaines, B. (1987). The cognitive-affective crossfire: When self-consistency confronts self-enhancement. *Journal of Personality and Social Psychology, 52*, 881–889.

Swann, W.B., Jr., Hixon, J.G., & de la Ronde, C. (1992). Embracing the bitter "truth": Negative self-concepts and marital commitment. *Psychological Science, 3*, 118–121.

Swann, W.B., Jr., Jetten, J., Gomez, A., Whitehouse, H., & Bastian, B. (2012). When group membership gets personal: A theory of identity fusion. *Psychological Review, 119*, 441–456.

Swann, W.B., Jr., Pelham, B.W., & Krull, D.S. (1989). Agreeable fancy or disagreeable truth? Reconciling self-enhancement and self-verification. *Journal of Personality and Social Psychology, 57*, 782–791.

Sweeny, K., & Vohs, K.D. (2012). On near misses and completed tasks: The nature of relief. *Psychological Science, 23*, 464–468.

Sweeny, T.D., & Whitney, D. (2014). Perceiving crowd attention: Ensemble perception of a crowd's gaze. *Psychological Science, 25*, 1903–1913.

Sweldens, S.T.L.R., Corneille, O., & Yzerbyt, V. (2014). The role of awareness in attitude formation through evaluative conditioning.

Personality and Social Psychology Review, 18, 187–209.

Syrek, C.J., Weigelt, O., Peifer, C., & Antoni, C.H. (2017). Zeigarnik's sleepless nights: How unfinished tasks at the end of the week impair employee sleep on the weekend through rumination. *Journal of Occupational Health Psychology, 22*, 225–238.

Szucs, D., & Ioannidis, J.P. (2017). Empirical assessment of published effect sizes and power in the recent cognitive neuroscience and psychology literature. *PLOS Biology, 15*, e2000797.

Tait, R.C., & Chibnall, J.T. (2014). Racial/ethnic disparities in the assessment and treatment of pain: Psychosocial perspectives. *American Psychologist, 69*, 131–141.

Tajfel, H. (1969). Cognitive aspects of prejudice. *Journal of Social Issues, 25*, 79–97.

Tajfel, H. (1970). Experiments in intergroup discrimination. *Scientific American, 223*, 96–102.

Tajfel, H. (1978). The achievement of intergroup differentiation. In H. Tajfel (Ed.), *Differentiation between social groups* (pp. 77–100). London: Academic Press

Tajfel, H., & Forgas, J.P. (1981). Social categorization: Cognitions, values and groups. In J.P. Forgas (Ed.), *Social cognition: Perspectives in everyday understanding* (pp. 113–140). London: Academic Press.

Tajfel, H., & Turner, J.C. (1979). An integrative theory of intergroup conflict. In W.G. Austin & S. Worchel (Eds.), *The social psychology of intergroup relations* (pp. 33–47). Monterey, CA: Brooks/Cole.

Tajfel, H., & Wilkes, A.L. (1963). Classification and quantitative judgment. *British Journal of Social Psychology, 54*, 101–114.

Tajfel, H., Billig, M.G., Bundy, R.P., & Flament, C. (1971). Social categorization and intergroup behaviour. *European Journal of Social Psychology, 1*, 149–177.

Talarico, J.M., & Rubin, D.C. (2003). Confidence, not consistency, characterizes flashbulb memories. *Psychological Science, 14*, 455–461.

Talhelm, T., Zhang, X., Oishi, S., Shimin, C., Duan, D., Lan, X., & Kitayama, S. (2014). Large-scale psychological differences within China explained by rice versus wheat agriculture. *Science, 344*, 603–608.

Tamir, D.I., & Mitchell, J.P. (2013). Anchoring and adjustment during social inferences. *Journal of Experimental Psychology: General, 142*, 151–162.

Tanaka, J.W., & Sengco, J.A. (1997). Features and their configuration in face perception. *Memory and Cognition, 25*, 583–592.

Tanaka, J.W., & Taylor, M. (1991). Object categories and expertise: Is the basic level in the eye of the beholder? *Cognitive Psychology, 23*, 457–482.

Tankard, M.E., & Paluck, E.L. (2016). Norm perception as a vehicle for social change. *Social Issues and Policy Review, 10*, 181–211.

Tankard, M.E., & Paluck, E.L. (2017). The effect of a Supreme Court decision regarding gay marriage on social norms and personal attitudes. *Psychological Science, 28*, 1334–1344.

Tarde, G. (1898). *L'opinion et la foule*. Paris: Presses Universitaires de France.

Tarde, G. (1903). *The laws of imitation* (E. Parsons, Trans.; French ed., 1880). New York, NY: Henry Holt.

Tausen, B.M., Carpenter, S., & Macrae, C.N. (2019). Just another variant of psychological distance? The role of visual perspective in mental simulation. *Psychology of Consciousness: Theory, Research, and Practice.*

Taylor, D.M., & Jaggi, V. (1974). Ethnocentrism and causal attribution in a South Indian context. *Journal of Cross-Cultural Psychology, 5*, 162–171.

Taylor, S.E., & Fiske, S.T. (1975). Point-of-view and perceptions of causality. *Journal of Personality and Social Psychology, 32*, 439–445.

Taylor, S.E., & Fiske, S.T. (1978). Salience, attention, and attribution: Top of the head phenomena. In L. Berkowitz (Ed.), *Advances in experimental social psychology* (Vol. 11, pp. 249–288). New York, NY: Academic Press.

Taylor, S.E., Fiske, S.T., Etcoff, N.L., & Ruderman, A.J. (1978). Categorical and contextual bases of person memory and stereotyping. *Journal of Personality and Social Psychology, 36*, 778–793.

Taylor, S.E., Lerner, J.S., Sherman, D.K., Sage, R.M., & McDowell, N.K. (2003a). Portrait of the self-enhancer: Well-adjusted and well-liked or maladjusted and friendless? *Journal of Personality and Social Psychology, 84*, 165–176.

Taylor, S.E., Lerner, J.S., Sherman, D.K., Sage, R.M., & McDowell, N.K. (2003b). Are self-enhancing cognitions associated with healthy or unhealthy biological profiles? *Journal of Personality and Social Psychology, 85*, 605–615.

Taylor, V.J., & Walton, G.M. (2011). Stereotype threat undermines academic learning. *Personality and Social Psychology Bulletin, 37*, 1055–1067.

Tesser, A. (1988). Toward a self-evaluation maintenance model of social behavior. In L. Berkowitz (Ed.)., *Advances in experimental social psychology* (Vol. 21, pp. 181–227). New York, NY: Academic Press.

Tetlock, P.E. (1985). Toward an intuitive politician model of attribution processes. In B.R. Schlenker (Ed.), *The self and social life* (pp. 203–234). New York, NY: McGraw-Hill.

Thaler, R.H. (1980). Toward a positive theory of consumer choice. *Journal of Economic Behavior and Organization, 1*, 39–60.

Thaler, R.H., & Sunstein, C.R. (2008). *Nudge: Improving decisions about health, wealth, and happiness.* New Haven, CT: Yale University Press.

Thielmann, I., Hilbig, B.E., & Zettler, I. (2018). Seeing me, seeing you: Testing competing accounts of assumed similarity in personality judgments. *Journal of Personality and Social Psychology.* Advance online publication.

Thompson, M.M., Zanna, M.P., & Griffin, D.W. (1995). Let's not be indifferent about (attitudinal) ambivalence. In R.E. Petty & J.A. Krosnick (Eds.), *Attitude strength: Antecedents and consequences* (pp. 361–386). Mahwah, NJ: Lawrence Erlbaum.

Thompson, V.A., Prowse Turner, J.A., & Pennycook, G. (2011). Intuition, reason, and metacognition. *Cognitive Psychology, 63*, 107–140.

Thorndike, E.L. (1920). A constant error in psychological ratings. *Journal of Applied Psychology, 4*, 25–29.

Thornhill, R., & Gangestad, S.W. (1993). Human facial beauty: Averageness, symmetry, and parasite resistance. *Human Nature, 4*, 237–269.

Thurstone, L.L. (1928). Attitudes can be measured. *American Journal of Sociology, 33*, 529–554.

Tillman, W.S., & Carver, C.S. (1980). Actors' and observers' attributions for success and failure: A comparative test of predictions from Kelley's cube, self-serving bias, and positivity bias formulations. *Journal of Experimental Social Psychology, 16*, 18–32.

Titchener, E.B. (1910). *A textbook of psychology.* New York, NY: Macmillan.

Todd, A.R., & Burgmer, P. (2013). Perspective taking and automatic intergroup evaluation change: Testing an associative self-anchoring account. *Journal of Personality and Social Psychology, 104*, 786–802.

Todd, A.R., & Galinsky, A.D. (2014). Perspective-taking as a strategy for improving intergroup relations: Evidence, mechanisms, & qualifications. *Social and Personality Psychology Compass, 8*, 374–387.

Todd, A.R., Bodenhausen, G.V., & Galinsky, A.D. (2012). Perspective taking combats the denial of intergroup discrimination. *Journal of Experimental Social Psychology, 48*, 738–745.

Todd, A.R., Molden, D.C., Ham, Y., & Vonk, R. (2011). The automatic and co-occurring activation of multiple social inferences. *Journal of Experimental Social Psychology, 47*, 37–49.

Todorov, A., & Engell, A.D. (2008). The role of the amygdala in implicit evaluation of emotionally neutral faces. *Social Cognitive and Affective Neuroscience, 3*, 303–312.

Todorov, A., & Uleman, J.S. (2002). Spontaneous trait inferences are bound to actors' faces: Evidence from a false recognition paradigm. *Journal of Personality and Social Psychology, 83*, 1051–1065.

Todorov, A., & Uleman, J.S. (2003). The efficiency of binding spontaneous trait inferences to actors' faces. *Journal of Experimental Social Psychology, 39*, 549–562.

Todorov, A., & Uleman, J.S. (2004). The person reference process in spontaneous trait inferences. *Journal of Personality and Social Psychology, 87*, 482–493.

Todorov, A., Mandisodza, A.N., Goren, A., & Hall, C.C. (2005). Inferences of competence from faces predict election outcomes. *Science, 308*, 1623–1626.

Todorov, A., Olivola, C.Y., Dotsch, R., & Mende-Siedlecki, P. (2015). Social attributions from faces: Determinants, consequences, accuracy, and functional significance. *Annual Review of Psychology, 66*, 519–545.

Topolinski, S. (2014). A processing fluency-account of funniness: Running gags and spoiling punchlines. *Cognition and Emotion, 28*, 811–820.

Topolinski, S., & Reber, R. (2010). Immediate truth—temporal contiguity between a cognitive problem and its solution determines experienced veracity of the solution. *Cognition, 114*, 117–122.

Topolinski, S., & Strack, F. (2009). The architecture of intuition: Fluency and affect determine intuitive judgments of semantic and visual coherence, and of grammaticality in artificial grammar learning. *Journal of Experimental Psychology: General, 138*, 39–63.

Topolinski, S., Likowski, K., Weyers, P., & Strack, F. (2009). The face of fluency: Semantic coherence automatically elicits a specific pattern of facial muscle reactions. *Cognition and Emotion, 23*, 260–271.

Tormala, Z.L. (2016). The role of certainty (and uncertainty) in attitudes and persuasion. *Current Opinion in Psychology, 10*, 6–11.

Tormala, Z.L., & Rucker, D.D. (2007). Attitude certainty: A review of past findings and emerging perspectives. *Social and Personality Psychology Compass, 1*, 469–492.

Tormala, Z.L., Falces, C., Briñol, P., & Petty, R.E. (2007). Ease of retrieval effects in social judgment: The role of unrequested cognitions. *Journal of Personality and Social Psychology, 93*, 143–157.

Törnros, J., & Bolling, A. (2006). Mobile phone use: Effects of conversation on mental workload and driving speed in rural and urban environments. *Transportation Research Part F: Traffic Psychology and Behaviour, 9*, 298–306.

Trawalter, S., & Hoffman, K.M. (2015). Got pain? Racial bias in perceptions of pain. *Social and Personality Psychology Compass, 9*, 146–157.

Trawalter, S., Hoffman, K.M., & Waytz, A. (2012). Racial bias in perceptions of others' pain. *PLOS ONE, 7*, e48546.

Trawalter, S., Todd, A.R., Baird, A.A., & Richeson, J.A. (2008). Attending to threat: Race-based patterns of selective attention. *Journal of Experimental Social Psychology, 44*, 1322–1327.

Treisman, A.M. (1964). Selective attention in man. *British Medical Bulletin, 20*, 12–16.

Treisman, A.M. (1969). Strategies and models of selective attention. *Psychological Review, 76*, 282–299.

Treisman, A.M. (1991). Search, similarity, and integration of features between and within dimensions. *Journal of Experimental Psychology: Human Perception & Performance, 17*, 652–676.

Treisman, A.M., & Gormican, S. (1988). Feature analysis in early vision: Evidence from search asymmetries. *Psychological Review, 95*, 15–48.

Triandis, H.C. (1977). *Interpersonal behavior.* Monterey, CA: Brooks/Cole.

Trimble, M., & Hamilton, P. (2016). The thinking doctor: Clinical decision making in contemporary medicine. *Clinical Medicine, 16*, 343–346.

Triplett, N. (1898). The dynamogenic factors in pacemaking and competition. *The American Journal of Psychology, 9*, 507–533.

Troll, L.E., & Skaff, M.M. (1997). Perceived continuity of self in very old age. *Psychology and Aging, 12*, 162–169.

Trope, Y. (1975). Seeking information about one's ability as a determinant of choice among tasks. *Journal of Personality and Social Psychology, 32*, 1004–1013.

Trope, Y. (1980). Self-assessment, self-enhancement, and task preference. *Journal of Experimental Social Psychology, 16*, 116–129.

Trope, Y. (1982). Self-assessment and task performance. *Journal of Experimental Social Psychology, 18*, 201–215.

Trope, Y. (1986a). Identification and inferential processes in dispositional attribution. *Psychological Review, 93*, 239–257.

Trope, Y. (1986b). Self-enhancement and self-assessment in achievement behavior. In R.M. Sorrentino & E.T. Higgins (Eds.), *Handbook of motivation and cognition: Foundations of social behavior* (pp. 350–378). New York, NY: Guilford Press.

Trope, Y., & Bassok, M. (1982). Confirmatory and diagnosing strategies in social information gathering. *Journal of Personality and Social Psychology, 43*, 22–34.

Trope, Y., & Bassok, M. (1983). Information-gathering strategies in hypothesis-testing. *Journal of Experimental Social Psychology, 19*, 560–576.

Trope, Y., & Liberman, A. (1996). Social hypothesis testing: Cognitive and motivational mechanisms. In E.T. Higgins & A.W. Kruglanski (Eds.), *Social psychology: Handbook of basic principles* (pp. 239–270). New York, NY: Guilford Press.

Trope, Y., & Liberman, N. (2010). Construal level theory of psychological distance. *Psychological Review, 117*, 440–463.

Trope, Y., & Pomerantz, E.M. (1998). Resolving conflicts among self-evaluative motives: Positive experiences as a resource for overcoming defensiveness. *Motivation and Emotion, 22*, 53–72.

Tropp, L.R., & Pettigrew, T.F. (2005). Differential relationships between intergroup contact and affective and cognitive dimensions of prejudice. *Personality and Social Psychology Bulletin, 31*, 1145–1158.

Tskhay, K.O., & Rule, N.O. (2013). Accuracy in categorizing perceptually ambiguous groups: A review and meta-analysis. *Personality and Social Psychology Review, 17*, 72–86

Tsukamoto, S., Enright, J., & Karasawa, M. (2013). Psychological essentialism and nationalism as determinants of interethnic bias. *The Journal of Social Psychology, 153*, 515–519.

Tuckey, M.R., & Brewer, N. (2003a). How schemas affect eyewitness memory over repeated retrieval attempts. *Applied Cognitive Psychology, 7*, 785–800.

Tuckey, M.R., & Brewer, N. (2003b). The influence of schemas, stimulus ambiguity, and interview schedule on eyewitness memory over time. *Journal of Experimental Psychology: Applied, 9*, 101–118.

Tulving, E. (1962). Subjective organization in free recall of "unrelated" words. *Psychological Review, 69*, 344–354.

Tulving, E. (1993). What is episodic memory? *Current Directions in Psychological Science, 3*, 67–70.

Tulving, E., & Pearlstone, Z. (1966). Availability versus accessibility of information in memory for words. *Journal of Verbal Learning and Verbal Behavior, 5*, 381–391.

Tulving, E., & Thomson, D.M. (1973). Encoding specificity and retrieval processes in episodic memory. *Psychological Bulletin, 80*, 352–373.

Turnbull, W., & Slugoski, B.R. (1988). Conversational and linguistic processes in causal attribution. In D.J. Hilton (Ed.), *Contemporary science and natural explanation: Commonsense conceptions of causality* (pp. 66–93). Brighton: Harvester Press.

Turner, J.C., Hogg, M., Oakes, P.J., Reicher, S., & Wetherell, M. (1987). *Rediscovering the social group: A self-categorization theory.* Oxford: Blackwell.

Turner, R.N., & Crisp, R.J. (2010). Imagining intergroup contact reduces implicit prejudice. *British Journal of Social Psychology, 49,* 129–142.

Tversky, A. (1969). Intransitivity of preferences. *Psychological Review, 76,* 31–48.

Tversky, A., & Kahneman, D. (1971). Belief in the law of small numbers. *Psychological Bulletin, 76,* 105–110.

Tversky, A., & Kahneman, D. (1973). Availability: A heuristic for judging frequency and probability. *Cognitive Psychology, 5,* 207–232.

Tversky, A., & Kahneman, D. (1974). Judgment under uncertainty: Heuristics and biases. *Science, 185,* 1124–1130.

Tversky, A., & Kahneman, D. (1981). The framing of decisions and the psychology of choice. *Science, 211,* 453–458.

Tversky, A., & Kahneman, D. (1982). Judgments of and by representativeness. In D. Kahneman, P. Slovic, & A. Tversky (Eds.), *Judgment under uncertainty: Heuristics and biases* (pp. 84–98). New York, NY: Cambridge University Press.

Tversky, A., & Kahneman, D. (1983). Extensional versus intuitive reasoning: The conjunction fallacy in probability judgment. *Psychological Review, 90,* 293–315.

Tversky, B., & Tuchin, M. (1989). A reconciliation of the evidence on eyewitness testimony: Comments on McCloskey and Zaragoza (1985). *Journal of Experimental Psychology: General, 118,* 86–91.

Tybur, J.M., Lieberman, D., Kurzban, R., & DeScioli, P. (2013). Disgust: Evolved function and structure. *Psychological Review, 120,* 65–84.

Tykocinski, O.E. (2001). I never had a chance: Using hindsight tactics to mitigate disappointments. *Personality and Social Psychology Bulletin, 27,* 376–382.

Ubel, P.A., Lowenstein, G., Hershey, J., Baron, J., Mohr, T., Asch, D., & Jepson, C. (2001). Do nonpatients underestimate the quality of life associated with chronic health conditions because of a focusing illusion? *Medical Decision Making, 21,* 190–199.

Uleman, J.S. (1999). Spontaneous versus intentional inferences in impression formation. In S. Chaiken & Y. Trope (Eds.), *Dual-process theories in social psychology* (pp. 141–160). New York, NY: Guilford Press.

Uleman, J.S. (2005). Introduction: Becoming aware of the new unconscious. In R.R. Hassin, J.S. Uleman, & J.A. Bargh (Eds.), *The new unconscious* (pp. 3–15). New York, NY: Oxford University Press.

Uleman, J.S. (2015). Causes and causal attributions: Questions raised by Dave Hamilton and spontaneous trait inferences. In S.J. Stroessner & J.W. Sherman (Eds.), *Social perception from individuals to groups* (pp. 52–70). New York, NY: Psychology Press.

Uleman, J.S., & Kressel, L.M. (2013). A brief history of theory and research on impression formation. In D.E. Carlston (Ed.), *The Oxford handbook of social cognition* (p. 53–73). New York, NY: Oxford University Press.

Uleman, J.S., Blader, S.L., & Todorov, A. (2005). Implicit impressions. In R.R. Hassin, J.S. Uleman, & J.A. Bargh (Eds.), *The new unconscious* (pp. 362–392). New York, NY: Oxford University Press.

Uleman, J.S., Hon, A., Roman, R., & Moskowitz, G.B. (1996). On-line evidence for spontaneous trait inferences at encoding. *Personality and Social Psychology Bulletin, 22,* 377–394.

Uleman, J.S., Newman, L.S., & Moskowitz, G.B. (1996). People as flexible interpreters: Evidence and issues from spontaneous trait inference. In M.P. Zanna (Ed.), *Advances in experimental social psychology* (Vol. 28, pp. 211–279). San Diego CA: Academic Press.

Uleman, J.S., Saribay, S.D., & Gonzalez, C.M. (2008). Spontaneous inferences, implicit impressions, and implicit theories. *Annual Review of Psychology, 59,* 329–360.

Ullrich, J., & Krueger, J.I. (2010). Interpersonal liking from bivariate attitude similarity.

Social Psychological and Personality Science, *1*, 214–221.

Unkelbach, C., Fiedler, K., Bayer, M., Steg-müller, M., & Danner, D. (2008). Why positive information is processed faster: The density hypothesis. *Journal of Personality and Social Psychology, 95*, 36–49.

Vadillo, M.A., Kostopoulou, O., & Shanks, D.R. (2015). A critical review and meta-analysis of the unconscious thought effect in medical decision making. *Frontiers in Psychology, 6*, Article 636.

Valenti, G., Libby, L.K., & Eibach, R.P. (2011). Looking back with regret: Visual perspective in memory images differentially affects regret for actions and inactions. *Journal of Experimental Social Psychology, 47*, 730–737.

Vallacher, R.R., & Wegner, D.M. (1985). *A theory of action identification.* Hillsdale, NJ: Lawrence Erlbaum.

Vallacher, R.R., & Wegner, D.M. (1987). What do people think they're doing? Action identification and human behavior. *Psychological Review, 94*, 3–15.

Vallacher, R.R., & Wegner, D.M. (1989). Levels of personal agency: Individual variation in action identification. *Journal of Personality and Social Psychology, 57*, 660–671.

van Baaren, R.B., Holland, R.W., Kawakami, K., & van Knippenberg, A. (2004). Mimicry and prosocial behavior. *Psychological Science, 15*, 71–74.

van Baaren, R.B., Holland, R.W., Steenart, B., & van Knippenberg, A. (2003). Mimicry for money: Behavioural consequences of imitation. *Journal of Experimental Social Psychology, 39*, 393–398.

van Baaren, R.B., Horgan, T.G., Chartrand, T.L., & Dijkmans, M. (2004). The forest, the trees, and the chameleon: Context dependence and mimicry. *Journal of Personality and Social Psychology, 86*, 453–459.

Van Bavel, J.J., Mende-Siedlecki, P., Brady, W.J., & Reinero, D.A. (2016). Contextual sensitivity in scientific reproducibility. *Proceedings of the National Academy of Sciences, 113*, 6454–6459.

Van Boven, L., & Ashworth, L. (2007). Looking forward, looking back: Anticipation is more evocative than retrospection. *Journal of Experimental Psychology: General, 136*, 289–300.

Van Boven, L., & Caruso, E.M. (2015). The tripartite foundations of temporal psychological distance: Metaphors, ecology, and teleology. *Social and Personality Psychology Compass, 9*, 593–605.

Van Boven, L., & Loewenstein, G. (2003). Projection of transient drive states. *Personality and Social Psychology Bulletin, 29*, 1159–1168.

Van Boven, L., Kamada, A., & Gilovich, T. (1999). The perceiver as perceived: Everyday intuitions about the correspondence bias. *Journal of Personality and Social Psychology, 77*, 1188–1199.

Van Boven, L., Kane, J., & McGraw, A.P. (2008). Temporally asymmetric constraints on mental simulation: Retrospection is more constrained than prospection. In L. Van Boven, J. Kane, A. P. McGraw, K.D. Markman, W. Klein, & J.A. Suhr (Eds.), *The handbook of imagination and mental simulation* (pp. 131–147). New York, NY: Psychology Press.

Van Boven, L., Kane, J., McGraw, A.P., & Dale, J. (2010). Feeling close: Emotional intensity reduces perceived psychological distance. *Journal of Personality and Social Psychology, 98*, 872–885.

Van Boven, L., Travers, M., Westfall, J., & McClelland, G. (2013). Judgment and decision making. In D.E. Carlston (Ed.), *The Oxford handbook of social cognition* (pp. 375–401). New York, NY: Oxford University Press.

Van de Vondervoort, J.W., & Hamlin, J.K. (2018). The early emergence of sociomoral evaluation: Infants prefer prosocial others. *Current Opinion in Psychology, 20*, 77–81.

Van Dijk, W.W., Ouwerkerk, J.W., Smith, R.H., & Cikara, M. (2015). The role of self-evaluation and envy in schadenfreude. *European Review of Social Psychology, 26*, 247–282.

van Harreveld, F., Nohlen, H.U., & Schneider, I.K. (2015). The ABC of ambivalence: Affective, behavioral, and cognitive consequences of attitudinal conflict. In M.P. Zanna & J. Olson (Eds.), *Advances in experimental social psychology* (Vol. 52, pp. 285–324). New York, NY: Academic Press.

van Honk, J., Tuiten, A., de Haan, E., van den Hout, M., & Stam, H. (2001). Attentional biases for angry faces: Relationships to trait anger and anxiety. *Cognition and Emotion, 15*, 279–297.

Van Lange, P.A.M. (1991). Being better but not smarter than others: The Muhammad Ali effect at work in interpersonal situations. *Personality and Social Psychology Bulletin, 17*, 689–693.

Van Oudenhoven, J.P., Groenewoud, J.T., & Hewstone, M. (1996). Cooperation, ethnic salience and generalization of interethnic attitudes. *European Journal of Social Psychology, 26*, 649–661.

Van Overwalle, F., & Labiouse, C. (2004). A recurrent connectionist model of person impression formation. *Personality and Social Psychology Review, 8*, 28–61.

Van Overwalle, F., & Siebler, F. (2005). A connectionist model of attitude formation and change. *Personality & Social Psychology Review, 9*, 231–274.

Van Overwalle, F., & Van Rooy, D. (2001). How one cause discounts or augments another: A connectionist account of causal competition. *Personality and Social Psychology Bulletin, 27*, 1613–1626.

Van Overwalle, F., De Coninck, S., Heleven, E., Perrotta, G., Taib, N.O.B., Manto, M., & Mariën, P. (2019). The role of the cerebellum in reconstructing social action sequences: A pilot study. *Social Cognitive and Affective Neuroscience, 14*, 549–558.

Van Ryn, M., & Fu, S.S. (2003). Paved with good intentions: Do public health and human service providers contribute to racial/ethnic disparities in health? *American Journal of Public Health, 93*, 248–255.

Vazire, S. (2010). Who knows what about a person? The self–other knowledge asymmetry (SOKA) model. *Journal of Personality and Social Psychology, 98*, 281–300.

Vazire, S., & Mehl, M.R. (2008). Knowing me, knowing you: The accuracy and unique predictive validity of self-ratings and other-ratings of daily behavior. *Journal of Personality and Social Psychology, 95*, 1202–1216.

Verheyen, S., & Égré, P. (2018). Typicality and graded membership in dimensional adjectives. *Cognitive Science, 42*, 2250–2286.

Vezzali, L., Capozza, D., Giovannini, D., & Stathi, S. (2012). Improving implicit and explicit intergroup attitudes using imagined contact: An experimental intervention with elementary school children. *Group Processes and Intergroup Relations, 15*, 203–212.

Vezzali, L., Capozza, D., Stathi, S., & Giovannini, D. (2012). Increasing outgroup trust, reducing infrahumanization, and enhancing future contact intentions via imagined intergroup contact. *Journal of Experimental Social Psychology, 48*, 437–440.

Visser, P.S., & Mirabile, R.R. (2004). Attitudes in the social context: The impact of social network composition on individual-level attitude strength. *Journal of Personality and Social Psychology, 87*, 779–795.

von Baeyer, C.L., Sherk, D.L., & Zanna, M.P. (1981). Impression management in the job interview: When the female applicant meets the male (chauvinist) interviewer. *Personality and Social Psychology Bulletin, 7*, 45–51.

von Hippel, W., Sekaquaptewa, D., & Vargas, P. (1997). The linguistic intergroup bias as an implicit indicator of prejudice. *Journal of Experimental Social Psychology, 33*, 490–509.

von Neumann, J., & Morgenstern, O. (1947). *Theory of games and economic behavior* (2nd ed.). Princeton, NJ: Princeton University Press.

Vonk, R. (1998). The slime effect: Suspicion and dislike of likable behavior toward superiors. *Journal of Personality and Social Psychology, 74*, 849–864.

Vonk, R., & Ashmore, R.D. (2003). Thinking about gender types: Cognitive organization of female and male types. *British Journal of Social Psychology, 42*, 257–280.

Vonfakou, C., Hewstone, M., & Voci, A. (2007). Contact with out-group friends as a predictor of meta-attitudinal strength and accessibility of attitudes toward gay men. *Journal of Personality and Social Psychology, 92*, 804–820.

Vorauer, J.D., & Sasaki, S.J. (2011). In the worst rather than the best of times: Effects of salient intergroup ideology in threatening intergroup interactions. *Journal of Personality and Social Psychology, 101*, 307–320.

Vroom, V.H. (1964). *Work and motivation.* New York, NY: Wiley.

Wagenmakers, E.-J., Beek, T., Dijkhoff, L., Gronau, Q.F., Acosta, A., Adams, R.B. ... Zwaan, R.A. (2016). Registered replication report: Strack, Martin, & Stepper (1988). *Perspectives on Psychological Science, 11*, 917–928.

Wakslak, C.J., Nussbaum, S., Liberman, N., & Trope, Y. (2008). Representations of the self in the near and distant future. *Journal of Personality and Social Psychology, 95*, 757–773.

Walster, E., Aronson, V., Abrahams, D., & Rottman, L. (1966). Importance of physical attractiveness in dating behavior. *Journal of Personality and Social Psychology, 4*, 508–516.

Walther, E. (2002). Guilty by mere association: Evaluative conditioning and the spreading attitude effect. *Journal of Personality and Social Psychology, 82*, 919–934.

Wänke, M., Bless, H., & Biller, B. (1996). Subjective experience versus content of information in the construction of attitude judgments. *Personality and Social Psychology Bulletin, 22*, 1105–1113.

Wason, P.C. (1968). Reasoning about a rule. *Quarterly Journal of Experimental Psychology, 20*, 273–281.

Wasserman, D., Lempert, R.O., & Hastie, R. (1991). Hindsight and causality. *Personality and Social Psychology Bulletin, 17*, 30–35.

Watkins v. Sowders, 449 U.S. *341*, 1981.

Watson, J.B. (1913). Psychology as the behaviorist views it. *Psychological Review, 20*, 158–177.

Watson, J.B. (1928). Behaviorism: The modern note in psychology. In J.B. Watson & W. McDougall (Eds.), *The battle of behaviorism* (pp. 7–41). London: Kegan Paul, Trench, Trubner & Co.

Waxman, S., Medin, D.L., & Ross, N.O. (2007). Folkbiological reasoning from a cross-cultural developmental perspective: Early essentialist notions are shaped by cultural beliefs. *Developmental Psychology, 43*, 294–308.

Waxman, S.R., & Gelman, S.A. (2009). Early word-learning entails reference, not merely associations. *Trends in Cognitive Sciences, 13*, 258–263.

Webb, T.L., & Sheeran, P. (2004). Identifying good opportunities to act: Implementation intentions and cue discrimination. *European Journal of Social Psychology, 34*, 407–419.

Weber, R., & Crocker, J. (1983). Cognitive processes in the revision of stereotypic beliefs. *Journal of Personality and Social Psychology, 45*, 961–977.

Wegner, D.M. (1994). Ironic processes of mental control. *Psychological Review, 101*, 34–52.

Wegner D.M. (2003). The mind's best trick: How we experience conscious will. *Trends in Cognitive Science, 7*, 65–69.

Wegner, D.M. (2005). Who is the controlled of controlled processes? In R.R. Hassin, J.S. Uleman, & J.A. Bargh (Eds.), *The new unconscious* (pp. 19–36). New York, NY: Oxford University Press.

Wegner, D.M., & Erber, R. (1992). The hyperaccessibility of suppressed thoughts. *Journal of Personality and Social Psychology, 63*, 903–912.

Wegner, D.M., & Wheatley, T. (1999). Apparent mental causation: Sources of the experience of will. *American Psychologist, 54*, 480–492.

Wegner, D.M., Erber, R., & Raymond, P. (1991). Transactive memory in close relationships. *Journal of Personality and Social Psychology*, *61*, 923–929.

Wegner, D.M., Schneider, D.J., Carter, S., & White, T. (1987). Paradoxical effects of thought suppression. *Journal of Personality and Social Psychology*, *53*, 5–13.

Wegner, D.M., Sparrow, B., & Winerman, L. (2004). Vicarious agency: Experiencing control over the movements of others. *Journal of Personality and Social Psychology*, *86*, 838–848.

Weiner, B. (1979). A theory of motivation for some classroom experiences. *Journal of Educational Psychology*, *71*, 3–25.

Weiner, B. (1985a). "Spontaneous" causal thinking. *Psychological Bulletin*, *97*, 74–84.

Weiner, B. (1985b). An attributional theory of achievement motivation and emotion. *Psychological Review*, *92*, 548–573.

Weiner, B. (1986). Attribution, emotion, and action. In R.M. Sorrentino & E.T. Higgins (Eds.), *Handbook of motivation and cognition: Foundations of social behavior* (pp. 281–312). New York, NY: Guilford Press.

Weiner, B. (2008). Reflections on the history of attribution theory and research: People, personalities, publications, problems. *Social Psychology*, *39*, 151–156.

Weiner, B. (2018). The legacy of an attribution approach to motivation and emotion: A no-crisis zone. *Motivation Science*, *4*, 4–14.

Weiner, B., Frieze, I., Kukla, A., Reed, L., Rest, S., & Rosenbaum, R.M. (1972). Perceiving the causes of success and failure. In E.E. Jones, D.E. Kanouse, H.H. Kelley, R.E. Nisbett, S. Valins, & B. Weiner (Eds.), *Attribution: Perceiving the causes of behavior* (pp. 95–120). Morristown, NJ: General Learning Press.

Weiner, B., Heckhausen, H., & Meyer, W.-U. (1972). Causal ascriptions and achievement behavior: A conceptual analysis of effort and reanalysis of locus of control. *Journal of Personality and Social Psychology*, *21*, 239–248.

Weingarten, E., & Hutchinson, J.W. (2018). Does ease mediate the ease-of-retrieval effect? *Psychological Bulletin*, *144*, 227–283.

Weingarten, E., Chen, Q., McAdams, M., Yi, J., Hepler, J., & Albarracín, D. (2016). From primed concepts to action: A meta-analysis of the behavioral effects of incidentally presented words. *Psychological Bulletin*, *142*, 472–497.

Weinstein, N.D. (1980). Unrealistic optimism about future life events. *Journal of Personality and Social Psychology*, *58*, 806–820.

Weinstein, R.S., Gregory, A., & Strambler, M.J. (2004). Intractable self-fulfilling prophecies fifty years after Brown v Board of Education. *American Psychologist*, *59*, 511–520.

Weinstock, M.B., & Neides, D.M. (Eds.) (2009). *The resident's guide to ambulatory care: Frequently encountered and commonly confused clinical conditions* (6th ed.). Columbus, OH: Anadem.

Weldon, M.S., & Bellinger, K.D. (1997). Collective memory: Collaborative and individual processes in remembering. *Journal of Experimental Psychology: Learning, Memory, and Cognition*, *23*, 1160–1175.

Weldon, M.S., Blair, C., & Huebsch, P.D. (2000). Group remembering: Does social loafing underlie collaborative inhibition? *Journal of Experimental Psychology: Learning, Memory, and Cognition*, *26*, 1568–1577.

Wells, B.M., Skowronski, J.J., Crawford, M.T., Scherer, C.R., & Carlston, D.E. (2011). Inference making and linking both require thinking: Spontaneous trait inference and spontaneous trait transference both rely on working memory capacity. *Journal of Experimental Social Psychology*, *47*, 1116–1126.

Wells, D.C. (1907). Social Darwinism. *American Journal of Sociology*, *12*, 695–716.

Wells, G.L., & Harvey, J.H. (1977). Do people use consensus information in making causal attributions? *Journal of Personality and Social Psychology*, *35*, 279–293.

Wells, G.L., Lindsay, R.C.L., & Ferguson, T.J. (1979). Accuracy, confidence, and juror perceptions in eyewitness identification. *Journal of Applied Psychology, 64,* 440–448.

Wells, G.L., Olson, E.A., & Charman, S.D. (2002). The confidence of eyewitnesses in their identifications from lineups. *Current Directions in Psychological Science, 11,* 151–154.

Wells, G.L., Small, M., Penrod, S., Malpass, R.S., Fulero, S.M., & Brimacombe, C.A.E. (1998). Eyewitness identification procedures: Recommendations for lineups and photospreads. *Law and Human Behavior, 22,* 603–647.

Wetzler, S.E., & Sweeney, J.A. (1986). Childhood amnesia: A conceptualization in cognitive-psychological terms. *Journal of the American Psychoanalytic Association, 34,* 663–685.

Whalen, P.J., Kagan, J., Cook, R.G., Davis, F.C., Kim, H., Polis, S., McLarin, D.G., Somerville, L.H., McLean, A.A., Maxwell, J.S., & Johnstone, T. (2004). Human amygdala responsivity to masked fearful eye whites. *Science, 306,* 2061.

Whalen, P.J., Rauch, S.L., Etcoff, N.L., McInerney, S.C., Lee, M.B., & Jenike, M.A. (1998). Masked presentations of emotional facial expressions modulate amygdala activity without explicit knowledge. *Journal of Neuroscience, 18,* 411–418.

Wheeler, S.C., DeMarree, K.G., & Petty, R.E. (2007). Understanding the role of the self in prime-to-behavior effects: The active-self account. *Personality and Social Psychology Review, 11,* 234–261.

Wheeler, S.C., DeMarree, K.G., & Petty, R.E. (2014). Understanding prime-to-behavior effects: Insights from the active-self account. *Social Cognition, 32,* 109–123.

White, J.D., & Carlston, D.E. (1983). Consequences of schemata for attention, impressions, and recall in complex social interactions. *Journal of Personality and Social Psychology, 45,* 538–549.

Whitehouse, H., McQuinn, B., Buhrmester, M., & Swann, W.B., Jr. (2014). Brothers in arms: Libyan revolutionaries bond like family.

Proceedings of the National Academy of Sciences, 111, 17783–17785.

Whittlesea, B.W.A. (1993). Illusions of familiarity. *Journal of Experimental Psychology: Learning, Memory, and Cognition, 19,* 1235–1253.

Whittlesea, B.W.A., & Leboe, J.P. (2003). Two fluency heuristics (and how to tell them apart). *Journal of Memory and Language, 49,* 62–79.

Wicker, A.W. (1969). Attitudes versus actions: The relationship of verbal and overt behavioral responses to attitude objects. *Journal of Social Issues, 4,* 41–78.

Wicker, A.W. (1971). An examination of the "other variables" explanation of attitude-behavior inconsistency. *Journal of Personality and Social Psychology, 19,* 18–30.

Widlok, T. (2014). Agency, time and causality. *Frontiers in Psychology, 5,* 1264.

Wiers, R.W., Houben, K., Roefs, A., de Jong, P., Hofmann, W., & Stacy, A. (2010). Implicit cognition in health psychology: Why common sense goes out of the window. In B. Gawronski & B.K. Payne (Eds.), *Handbook of implicit social cognition: Measurement, theory, and applications* (pp. 463–488). New York, NY: Guilford Press.

Wigboldus, D.H.J., Dijksterhuis, A., & van Knippenberg, A. (2003). When stereotypes get in the way: Stereotypes obstruct stereotype-inconsistent trait inferences. *Journal of Personality and Social Psychology, 84,* 470–484.

Wigboldus, D.H.J., Sherman, J.W., Franzese, H.L., & van Knippenberg, A. (2004). Capacity and comprehension: Spontaneous stereotyping under cognitive load. *Social Cognition, 22,* 292–309.

Wiggins, J.S. (1979). A psychological taxonomy of trait-descriptive terms: The interpersonal domain. *Journal of Personality and Social Psychology, 37,* 395–412.

Wilder, D.A., Simon, A.F., & Faith, M. (1996). Enhancing the impact of counterstereotypic information: Dispositional attributions for deviance. *Journal of Personality and Social Psychology, 71,* 276–287.

Williams, E.F., & Gilovich, T. (2008). Conceptions of the self and others across time. *Personality and Social Psychology, 34,* 1037–1046.

Williams, E.F., Dunning, D., & Kruger, J. (2013). The hobgoblin of consistency: Algorithmic judgment strategies underlie inflated self-assessments of performance. *Journal of Personality and Social Psychology, 104,* 976–994.

Williams, J.E., & McMurtry, C.A. (1970). Color connotations among Caucasian seventh graders and college students. *Perceptual and Motor Skills, 30,* 707–713.

Williams, L.E., & Bargh, J.A. (2008). Experiencing physical warmth influences interpersonal warmth. *Science, 322,* 606–607.

Willis, J., & Todorov, A. (2006). First impressions: Making up your mind after a 100-ms exposure to a face. *Psychological Science, 17,* 592–598.

Willoughby, T., Adachi, P.J.C., & Good, M. (2012). A longitudinal study of the association between violent video game play and aggression among adolescents. *Developmental Psychology, 48,* 1044–1057.

Wills, T.A. (1981). Downward comparison principles in social psychology. *Psychological Bulletin, 90,* 245–271.

Wilson, A.E., & Ross, M. (2001). From chump to champ: People's appraisals of their earlier and present selves. *Journal of Personality and Social Psychology, 80,* 572–584.

Wilson, A.E., Buehler, R., Lawford, H., Schmidt, C., & Yong, A.G. (2012). Basking in projected glory: The role of subjective temporal appraisal in future self-appraisal. *European Journal of Social Psychology, 42,* 342–353.

Wilson, J.P., & Hugenberg, K. (2010). When under threat, we all look the same: Distinctiveness threat induces ingroup homogeneity in face memory. *Journal of Experimental Social Psychology, 46,* 1004–1010.

Wilson, J.P., Hugenberg, K., & Rule, N.O. (2017). Racial bias in judgments of physical size and formidability: From size to threat. *Journal of Personality and Social Psychology, 113,* 59–80.

Wilson, T.D. (2002). *Strangers to ourselves.* Cambridge, MA: Harvard University Press.

Wilson, T.D. (2003). Knowing when to ask: Introspection and the adaptive unconscious. *Journal of Consciousness Studies, 10,* 131–140.

Wilson, T.D., & Gilbert, D.T. (2003). Affective forecasting. In M.P. Zanna (Ed.), *Advances in experimental social psychology* (Vol. 35, pp. 345–411). San Diego, CA: Academic Press.

Wilson, T.D., & Gilbert, D.T. (2005). Affective forecasting: Knowing what to want. *Current Directions in Psychological Science, 14,* 131–134.

Wilson, T.D., & Gilbert, D.T. (2013). The impact bias is alive and well. *Journal of Personality and Social Psychology, 105,* 740–748.

Wilson, T.D., Lindsey S., & Schooler T.Y. (2000). A model of dual attitudes. *Psychological Review, 107,* 101–126.

Wilson, T.D., Wheatley, T., Meyers, J.M., Gilbert, D.T., & Axsom, D. (2000). Focalism: A source of durability bias in affective forecasting. *Journal of Personality and Social Psychology, 78,* 821–836.

Winkielman, P., & Cacioppo, J.T. (2001). Mind at ease puts a smile on the face: Psychophysiological evidence that processing facilitation increases positive affect. *Journal of Personality and Social Psychology, 81,* 989–1000.

Winkielman, P., & Schwarz, N. (2001). How pleasant was your childhood? Beliefs about memory shape inferences from experienced difficulty of recall. *Psychological Science, 12,* 176–179.

Winkielman, P., Halberstadt, J., Fazendeiro, T., & Catty, S. (2006). Prototypes are attractive because they are easy on the mind. *Psychological Science, 17,* 799–806.

Winkielman, P., Schwarz, N., & Belli, R.F. (1998). The role of ease of retrieval and attribution in memory judgments: Judging your memory as worse despite recalling more events. *Psychological Science, 9,* 124–126.

Winkielman, P., Schwarz, N., Fazendeiro, T., & Reber, R. (2003). The hedonic marking of processing fluency: Implications for evaluative judgment. In J. Musch & K.C. Klauer (Eds.), *The psychology of evaluation: Affective processes in cognition and emotion* (pp. 189–217). Mahwah, NJ: Lawrence Erlbaum.

Winter, L., & Uleman, J.S. (1984). When are social judgments made? Evidence for the spontaneousness of trait inferences. *Journal of Personality and Social Psychology, 47,* 237–252.

Wittenbrink, B., Gist, P.L., & Hilton, J.L. (1997). Structural properties of stereotypic knowledge and their influences on the construal of social situations. *Journal of Personality and Social Psychology, 47,* 526–543.

Wittenbrink, B., Judd, C.M., & Park, B. (1997). Evidence for racial prejudice at the implicit level and its relationships with questionnaire measures. *Journal of Personality and Social Psychology, 72,* 262–274.

Wittenbrink, B., Judd, C.M., & Park, B. (2001). Spontaneous prejudice in context: Variability in automatically activated attitudes. *Journal of Personality and Social Psychology, 81,* 815–827.

Wixted, J.T., & Wells, G.L. (2017). The relationship between eyewitness confidence and identification accuracy: A new synthesis. *Psychological Science in the Public Interest, 18,* 10–65.

Wojcik, S.P. & Ditto, P.H. (2014). Motivated happiness: Self-enhancement inflates self-reported subjective well-being. *Social Psychological and Personality Science, 5,* 185–194.

Wolfe, J.M., & Friedman-Hill, S.R. (1992). On the role of symmetry in visual search. *Psychological Science, 3,* 194–198.

Wong, K.F.E., & Kwong, J.Y.Y. (2000). Is 7300 m equal to 7.3 km? Same semantics but different anchoring effects. *Organizational Behavior & Human Decision Processes, 82,* 314–333.

Wood, C., Conner, M., Miles, E., Sandberg, T., Taylor, N., Godin, G., & Sheeran, P. (2016). The impact of asking intention or self-prediction questions on subsequent behavior: A meta-analysis. *Personality and Social Psychology Review, 20,* 245–268.

Wood, C., Conner, M., Sandberg, T., Godin, G., & Sheeran, P. (2014). Why does asking questions change health behaviours? The mediating role of attitude accessibility. *Psychology & Health, 29,* 390–404.

Wood, G. (1978). The knew-it-all-along effect. *Journal of Experimental Psychology: Human Perception and Performance, 4,* 345–353.

Wood, J.V. (1989). Theory and research concerning social comparisons of personal attributes. *Psychological Bulletin, 106,* 231–248.

Wood, N.L., & Cowan, N. (1995a). The cocktail party phenomenon revisited: Attention and memory in the classic selective listening procedure of Cherry (1953). *Journal of Experimental Psychology: General, 124,* 243–262.

Wood, N.L., & Cowan, N. (1995b). The cocktail party phenomenon revisited: How frequent are attention shifts to one's name in an irrelevant auditory channel? *Journal of Experimental Psychology: Learning, Memory, and Cognition, 21,* 255–260.

Wooden, J. (1997). *Wooden: A lifetime of observations and reflections on and off the court.* New York, NY: McGraw-Hill.

Woodward, A.L. (2009). Infants' grasp of others' intentions. *Current Directions in Psychological Science, 18,* 53–57.

Word, C.O., Zanna, M.P., & Cooper, J. (1974). The nonverbal mediation of self-fulfilling prophecies in interracial interaction. *Journal of Experimental Social Psychology, 10,* 109–120.

Worell, J. (1988). Women's satisfaction in close relationships. *Clinical Psychology Review, 8,* 477–498.

Wright, J.C., & Mischel, W. (1987). A conditional approach to dispositional constructs:

The local predictability of social behavior. *Journal of Personality and Social Psychology*, *53*, 1159–1177.

Wyer, N.A. (2007). Motivational influences on compliance with and consequences of instructions to suppress stereotypes. *Journal of Experimental Social Psychology*, *43*, 417–424.

Wyer, N.A. (2010). You never get a second chance to make a first (implicit) impression: The role of elaboration in the formation and revision of implicit impressions. *Social Cognition*, *28*, 1–19.

Wyer, N.A., Hollins, T.J., & Pahl, S. (2015). The hows and whys of face processing: Level of construal influences the holistic processing of human faces. *Journal of Experimental Psychology: General*, *144*, 1037–1041.

Wyer, N.A., Perfect, T.J., & Pahl, S. (2010). Temporal distance and person memory: Thinking about the future changes memory for the past. *Personality and Social Psychology Bulletin*, *36*, 805–816.

Wyer, N.A., Sherman, J.W., & Stroessner, S.J. (1998). The spontaneous suppression of racial stereotypes. *Social Cognition*, *16*, 340–352.

Wyer, N.A., Sherman, J.W., & Stroessner, S.J. (2000). The roles of motivation and ability in controlling the consequences of stereotype suppression. *Personality and Social Psychology Bulletin*, *26*, 13–25.

Wyer, R.S., Jr., & Srull, T.K. (1989). *Memory and social cognition in its social context.* Hillsdale, NJ: Lawrence Erlbaum.

Yadav, R., & Pathak, G.S. (2017). Determinants of consumers' green purchase behavior in a developing nation: Applying and extending the theory of planned behavior. *Ecological Economics*, *134*, 114–122.

Yamagishi, T., Hashimoto, H., & Schug, J. (2008). Preferences versus strategies as explanations for culture-specific behavior. *Psychological Science*, *19*, 579–584.

Yamaguchi, S., Greenwald, A.G., Banaji, M.R., Murakami, F., Chen, D., Shiomura, K., Kobayashi, C., Cai, H., & Krendl, A. (2007). Apparent universality of positive implicit self-esteem. *Psychological Science*, *18*, 498–500.

Yamin, P., Fei, M., Lahlou, S., & Levy, S. (2019). Using social norms to change behavior and increase sustainability in the real world: A systematic review of the literature. *Sustainability*, *11*, 5847.

Yan, H., & Yates, J.F. (2019). Improving acceptability of nudges: Learning from attitudes towards opt-in and opt-out policies. *Judgment and Decision Making*, *14*, 26–39.

Yarkin-Levin, K. (1983). Anticipated interaction, attribution, and social interaction. *Social Psychology Quarterly*, *46*, 302–311.

Yarkin, K.L., Town, J.P., & Wallston, B.S. (1982). Blacks and women must try harder: Stimulus persons' race and sex attributions of causality. *Personality and Social Psychology Bulletin*, *8*, 21–24.

Yates, J.F., & Curley, S.P. (1986). Contingency judgment: Primacy effects and attention decrement. *Acta Psychologica*, *62*, 293–302.

Yeung, N.C.J., & von Hippel, C. (2008). Stereotype threat increases the likelihood that female drivers in a simulator run over jaywalkers. *Accident Analysis & Prevention*, *40*, 667–674.

Yin, R.K. (1969). Looking at upside-down faces. *Journal of Experimental Psychology*, *81*, 141–145.

York, B. (2009, April 27). The black-white divide in Obama's popularity. Retrieved from www.washingtonexaminer.com/the-black-white-divide-in-obamas-popularity.

Young, A.I., & Fazio, R.H. (2013). Attitude accessibility as a determinant of object construal and evaluation. *Journal of Experimental Social Psychology*, *49*, 404–418.

Young, S.G., & Hugenberg, K. (2010). Mere social categorization modulates identification of facial expressions of emotion. *Journal of Personality and Social Psychology*, *99*, 964–977.

Young, S.G., Brown, C.M., & Hutchins, B. (2017). Ease-of-retrieval provides meta-cognitive information about social affiliation. *Social Cognition*, *35*, 54–65.

Young, S.G., Hugenberg, K., Bernstein, M.J., & Sacco, D.F. (2009). Interracial contexts debilitate same-race face recognition. *Journal of Experimental Social Psychology, 45*, 1123–1126.

Young, S.G., Hugenberg, K., Bernstein, M.J., & Sacco, D.F. (2012). Perception and motivation in face recognition: A critical review of theories of the cross-race effect. *Personality and Social Psychology Review, 16*, 116–142.

Yu, F., Ye, R., Sun, S., Carretié, L., Zhang, L., Dong, Y., Zhu, C., Luo, Y., & Wang, K. (2014). Dissociation of neural substrates of response inhibition to negative information between implicit and explicit facial Go/Nogo tasks: Evidence from an electrophysiological study. *PLOS ONE, 9*, 1–10.

Yudell, M., Roberts, D., DeSalle, R, & Tishkoff, S. (2016). Taking race out of human genetics. *Science, 351*, 564–565.

Yzerbyt, V., Corneille, O., & Estrada, C. (2001). The interplay of subjective essentialism and entitativity in the formation of stereotypes. *Personality and Social Psychology Review, 5*, 141–155.

Yzerbyt, V.Y., Kervyn, N., & Judd, C.M. (2008). Compensation versus halo: The unique relations between the fundamental dimensions of social judgment. *Personality and Social Psychology Bulletin, 34*, 1110–1123.

Yzerbyt, V., Provost, V., Corneille, O. (2005). Not so competent but warm . . . Really? Compensatory stereotypes in the French-speaking world. *Group Processes & Intergroup Relations, 8*, 291–308.

Yzerbyt, V., Rocher, S., & Schadron, G. (1997). Stereotypes as explanations: A subjective essentialist view of group perception. In R. Spears, P.J. Oakes, N. Ellemers, & S.A. Haslam (Eds.), *The social psychology of stereotyping and group life* (pp. 20–50). Oxford: Blackwell.

Zacks, J.M. (2004). Using movement and intentions to understand simple events. *Cognitive Science, 28*, 979–1008.

Zacks, J.M., & Swallow, K.M. (2007). Event segmentation. *Current Directions in Psychological Science, 16*, 80–84.

Zacks, J.M., Tversky, B., & Iyer, G. (2001). Perceiving, remembering, and communicating structure in events. *Journal of Experimental Psychology: General, 130*, 29–58.

Zadeh, L.A. (1965). Fuzzy sets. *Information and Control, 8*, 338–353.

Zadny, J., & Gerard, H.B. (1974). Attributed intentions and informational selectivity. *Journal of Experimental Social Psychology, 10*, 34–52.

Zafeiriou, D.I. (2004). Primitive reflexes and postural reactions in the neurodevelopmental examination. *Pediatric Neurology, 31*, 1–8.

Zahariadis, N. (2003). *Ambiguity and choice in public policy: Political decision making in modern democracies.* Washington, DC: Georgetown University Press.

Zajonc, R.B. (1968). Attitudinal effects of mere exposure. *Journal of Personality and Social Psychology Monograph Supplement, 9*, 1–27.

Zajonc, R.B. (1980a). Cognition and social cognition: A historical perspective. In L. Festinger (Ed.), *Retrospectives on social psychology* (pp. 180–204). New York, NY: Oxford University Press.

Zajonc, R.B. (1980b). Feelings and thinking: Preferences need no inferences. *American Psychologist, 35*, 151–175.

Zajonc, R.B. (1984). On the primacy of affect. *American Psychologist, 39*, 117–123.

Zajonc, R.B. (1999). One hundred years of rationality assumptions in social psychology. In A. Rodrigues & R.V. Levine (Eds.), *Reflections on 100 years of experimental social psychology* (pp. 200–214). New York, NY: Basic Books.

Zakay, D., & Block, R.A. (1997). Temporal cognition. *Current Directions in Psychological Science, 6*, 12–16.

Zanna, M.P., & Hamilton, D.L. (1972). Attribute dimensions and patterns of trait inferences. *Psychonomic Science, 27*, 353–354.

Zanna, M.P., & Hamilton, D.L. (1977). Further evidence for meaning change in impression formation. *Journal of Experimental Social Psychology, 13*, 224–238.

Zanna, M.P., & Pack, S.J. (1975). On the self-ful-filling nature of apparent sex differences in behavior. *Journal of Experimental Social Psychology, 11*, 583–591.

Zanna, M.P., & Rempel, J.K. (1988). Attitudes: A new look at an old concept. In D. Bar-Tal & A.W. Kruglanski (Eds.), *The social psychology of knowledge* (pp. 315–334). New York, NY: Cambridge University Press.

Zaragoza, M.S., & Lane, S.M. (1994). Source misattributions and the suggestibility of eyewitness memory. *Journal of Experimental Psychology: Learning, Memory, and Cognition, 20*, 934–945.

Zaragoza, M.S., & McCloskey, M. (1989). Misleading postevent information and the memory impairment hypothesis: Comment on Belli and reply to Tversky and Tuchin. *Journal of Experimental Psychology: General, 118*, 92–99.

Zaragoza, M.S., Payment, K.E., Ackil, J.K., Drivdahl, S.B., & Beck, M. (2001). Interviewing witnesses: Forced confabulation and confirmatory feedback increase false memories. *Psychological Science, 12*, 473–477.

Zárate, M.A., & Smith, E.R. (1990). Person categorization and stereotyping. *Social Cognition, 8*, 161–185.

Zebrowitz, L.A. (2017). First impressions from faces. *Current Directions in Psychological Science, 26*, 237–242.

Zebrowitz, L.A., & Collins, M.A. (1997). Accurate social perception at zero acquaintance: The affordances of a Gibsonian approach. *Personality and Social Psychology Review, 1*, 204–233.

Zebrowitz, L.A., & McDonald, S.M. (1991). The impact of litigants' baby-facedness and attractiveness on adjudications in small claims courts. *Law and Human Behavior, 15*, 603–623.

Zebrowitz, L.A., & Montepare, J.M. (2008). Social psychological face perception: Why appearance matters. *Social and Personality Psychology Compass, 2*, 1497–1517.

Zebrowitz, L.A., Fellous, J.M., Mignault, A., & Andreoletti, C. (2003). Trait impressions as overgeneralized responses to adaptively significant facial qualities: Evidence from connectionist modeling. *Personality and Social Psychology Review, 7*, 194–215.

Zeigarnik, B. (1927). Uber das Behalten von erledigten und unerledigten Handlungen [On the retention of completed and uncompleted transactions]. *Psychologische Forschung, 9*, 1–85.

Zell, E., Alicke, M.D., & Strickhouser, J.E. (2015). Referent status neglect: Winners evaluate themselves favorably even when the competitor is incompetent. *Journal of Experimental Social Psychology, 56*, 18–23.

Zell, E., Strickhouser, J.E., Sedikides, C., & Alicke, M.D. (2020). The better-than-average effect in comparative self-evaluation: A comprehensive review and meta-analysis. *Psychological Bulletin, 146*, 118–149.

Zemack-Rugar, Y., Bettman, J.R., & Fitzsimons, G.J. (2007). The effects of non-consciously priming emotion concepts on behavior. *Journal of Personality and Social Psychology, 93*, 927–939.

Zengel, B., Wells, B.M., & Skowronski, J.J. (2018). The waxing and waning of mnemic neglect. *Journal of Personality and Social Psychology, 114*, 719–734.

Zentall, S.R., & Morris, B.J. (2010). "Good job, you're so smart": The effects of inconsistency of praise type on young children's motivation. *Journal of Experimental Child Psychology, 107*, 155–163.

Zhang, M., & Aggarwal, P. (2015). Looking ahead or looking back: Current evaluations and the effect of psychological connectedness to a temporal self. *Journal of Consumer Psychology, 25*, 512–518.

Zhang, Y., & Risen, J.L. (2014). Embodied motivation: Using a goal systems framework to understand the preference for social and physical warmth. *Journal of Personality and Social Psychology, 107*, 965–977.

Zhao, L., Heyman, G.D., Chen, L., & Lee, K. (2017). Praising young children for being smart promotes cheating. *Psychological Science, 28*, 1868–1870.

Ziegert, J.C., & Hanges, P.J. (2005). Employment discrimination: The role of implicit attitudes, motivation and a climate for racial bias. *Journal of Applied Psychology, 90,* 553–562.

Zimmer-Gembeck, M.J., Nesdale, D., Webb, H.J., Khatibi, M., & Downey, G. (2016). A longitudinal rejection sensitivity model of depression and aggression: Unique roles of anxiety, anger, blame, withdrawal and retribution. *Journal of Abnormal Child Psychology, 44,* 1291–1307.

Zouhri, B., & Rateau, P. (2015). Social representation and social identity in the black sheep effect. *European Journal of Social Psychology, 45,* 669–677.

Zuckerman, M. (1978). Actions and occurrences in Kelley's cube. *Journal of Personality and Social Psychology, 36,* 647–656.

Zuckerman, M., Kieffer, S.C., & Knee, C.R. (1998). Consequences of self-handicapping: Effects on coping, academic performance, and adjustment. *Journal of Personality and Social Psychology, 74,* 1619–1628.

AUTHOR INDEX

Page numbers in *italics* refer to figures; page numbers in **bold** refer to tables.

Fointiat, V., 478
Foley, K., 371–372
Folkes, V.S., 280
Follenfant, A., 99, 467, 489
Forbes, C., 491
Forehand, M., 473
Forer, B.R., 162
Forgas, J.P., 218, 219, 226
Foroni, F., 50
Forscher, P.S., 101, 105–106, 232–233
Forster, J., 93, 94
Forster, M., 198
Försterling, F., 296, 483
Fortin, R., 221
Foti, D., 197
Foulsham, T., 396
Fourakis, E., 219
Fournier, M.A., 454
Fox, E., 124
Fox, N.A., 393
Fraidin, S.N., 405
Francis, M., 213
Frank, M.G., 165–166
Frank, M.J., 374
Frankish, K., 84
Franklin, B., 329–330
Franks, J.J., 10
Franzese, H.L., 268
Frazier, R.S., 81
Frederick, S., 322, 323
Freeman, J.B., 37, 40, 54, 159, 160, 176, 223, 243, 360, 389
Freeman, S., 210
Freitas, A.L., 199, 482
French, D.P., 455
French, T., 126
Frenda, S.J., 377–378
Fresco, D.M., 211
Freud, S., 68–69, 264–265, 380, 393
Frick, F.C., 9
Fried, C., 478
Friedman-Hill, S.R., 194
Friedman, R., 93–94
Friese, M., 84, 474
Frieze, I., 283
Froehlich, L., 315
Frost, L.A., 120–121
Fu, S.S., 80
Fuegen, K., 227
Fugelsang, J.A., 329
Fugita, K., 157–158, 219
Fuhrman, R.W., 59–60
Fujita, K., 157–158, 346
Fukawa, N., **349**
Fulero, S.M., 382
Funder, D.C., 356, 358, 454
Funk, F., 243
Furhman, R.W., 375

Furnham, A.F., 297
Furr, R.M., 354

Gabarrot, F., 478
Gabriel, S., 441, 476
Gabriel, U., 476
Gabrielcik, A., 390
Gabrieli, J.D., 231–232
Gaertner, L., 210, 212, 226, 477, 484
Gaertner, S.L., 80, 84, 97, 225, 226, 235
Gaesser, B., 234–235, 468–469
Gaeth, G.J., 346
Gage, N.L., 356
Gaines, B., 484
Gainotti, G., 28
Gaither, S.E., 183–185, 232
Galdi, S., 477
Gale, L., 314
Galinsky, A.D., 99, 103–104, 132, 343, 440–441
Gallagher, F.M., 211
Gallo, D.A., 379
Gallois, C., 79, 315, 489
Gangestad, S.W., 195, 123
Gannon, K., 387
Gano-Phillips, S., 310
Gantman, A.P., 467
Garcia, A., 317
Garcia, J., 214
Garcia-Marques, L., 41, 217, 241, 248, 250, 253, 256–257, 324, 379, 386, 387–389, 401, 402, 403
Garcia-Marques, T., 379
Garcia-Retamero, R., **349**
Garcia, S.M., 484, 485
Gardner, H., 9
Gardner, W.L., 121–122, 191–192
Gargano, G.J., 377–378
Garlappi, L., **349**
Garrett, N., 354
Garrido, M.V., 379, 389, 401, 402, 403
Garry, M., 377–378
Garst, J., 470
Gary, M.L., 233
Gauthier, I., 32
Gava, L., 396
Gavanski, I., 437, 438
Gawronski, B., 70, 71, 72, 82, 83, 84, 85, 86, 89, 95, 199–200, 202–203, 204, 208, 222, 230, 231, 233–234, 278, 300, 326, 473, 474, 494
Gebauer, J.E., 210, 214, 484
Gebhardt, W.A., 463
Geers, A.L., 139–140, 150, 295
Gehrke, E.M., 329
Geidd, J.L., 60–61

Geiger, W., 32–33
Gelman, S.A., 35, 183–184, 297
Gendolla, G.H.E., 279, 472
George, L.G., 440–441
Geraerts, E., 381–382
Gerard, H.B., 183
Gerber, J.P., 214
Gergen, K.J., 453
Gerger, G., 198
Gerkens, D.R., 379
Gerrard, M., 214
Getty, P.D., 292
Ghitti, C., 244
Gibbons, F.X., 214
Gibbons, P., 155
Giblin, C.E., 212, 213, 485
Gibson, C.E., 23
Gifford, R.K., 12, 128, 140–141, 163
Gigerenzer, G., 320, 348–349, **349**
Gilbert, D.T., 84, 98, 213, 246, 257, 258, 282, 298, 413, 443, 444–445, 446
Gilbert, G.M., 60, 61, 97
Giles, H., 79, 489
Gill, M.J., 292
Gill, S.V., 159
Gilman, S.A., 34
Gilovich, T., 10, 135–136, 162, 165–166, 261–262, 265, 322, 323, 341, 343, 354, 418–420, 424
Giltrow, M., 428
Giner-Sorolla, R., 206
Ginossar, Z., 339
Ginsburg, E., 125, 295
Giovannini, D., 235
Gips, J., 213
Gist, P.L., 34
Glaser, J., 180, 493–494
Glasman, L.R., 453, 456, 463
Glassman, N.S., 265
Gleicher, F., 438
Glenn, C., 489
Glick, P., 37, 60–61, 216–217, 218, 379, 486–487
Glidewell, L., 455
Glocker, M.L., 196
Godin, G., 455, 470
Goethals, G.R., 173
Goff, P.A., 54, 143–145, 166
Gold, G.J., 310
Gold, R.S., 363
Goldberg, L.R., 156
Goldin-Meadow, S., 289
Goldinger, S.D., 480
Goldstein, D.G., 348, 349, **349**, 350
Golisano, V., 323
Gollwitzer, P.M., 77–78, 104, 467, 470, 471–472
Golub, S., 429
Gomez, A., 494–495

Hartnett, J.L., 397
Hartshorne, H., 453, 481
Hartson, K.A., 214
Harvey, J.H., 281, 339
Harvey, P., 288–289
Harwood, J., 32–33
Haselton, M.G., 122, 123
Hasher, L., 73
Hashimoto, H., 212
Hashtroudi, S., 379
Haslam, N., 34, 35, 426
Haslam, S.A., 129, 226
Hassall, C.D., 213
Hassell, H.J.G., 458
Hassin, R.R., 68, 70, 77, 78, 90, 91,
    251, 298–299
Hastie, R., 12–13, 37, 56, 120, 235,
    280, 299, 314, 331–332, 357,
    361, 386, 397, 399, 431, 432,
    433, 434, 446
Hastorf, A.H., 168
Hattie, J.A., 352
Hausdorff, J.M., 100
Hauser-Cram, P., 492
Haussman, L.R.M., 425
Hawkins, C.B., 81
Hawkins, S.A., 431, 433
Haymovitz, E.L., 491
Hayne, H., 392, 393
Haynes, G.A., 330
Hazlett, L.I., 487
He, Y., 396
Hearst, E.S., 427
Heath, C., 352
Heatherton, T.F., 14
Heck, P.R., 487
Heckhausen, H., 289
Hedberg, D.A., 335
Hegerty, S.E.A., 196
Hehman, E.A., 37, 243
Heider, F., 6–8, 10, 13, 278, 282,
    284–285, 291, 293, 295, 297,
    300–301, 308, 398–399, 425
Heider, J.D., 397
Heim, D., 491
Heine, S.J., 35, 162, 212, 307
Heinke, D., 248, 250
Hellmann, J.H., 406
Helmers, J.C., 374
Helsen, W.F., 413
Hemans, L.T., 281
Hemsley, G.D., 397
Hencke, R., 100
Henderson, J.M., 137
Henderson, M.D., 157–158
Henning, R., 198
Henri, V., 5
Henrich, J., 396
Henry, P.J., 229

Hepburn, C., 363
Hepler, J., 460, 472
Heppen, J.B., 40
Hepper, E.G., 211, 214
Hergovich, A., 329
Hermann, A.D., 83
Hermans, D., 76, 455, 456
Hermsen, S., 100, 233
Herndon, B., 405
Heron, N., 311
Herr, P.M., 335, 486
Herrera, M., 426
Herring, D.R., 76, 189
Hershler, O., 74
Hertel, G., 332
Hertwig, R., 224, 341, 343, 344, 348,
    349, **349**, 435
Hertzman, M., 235
Hervitz, E.F., 468
Herzog, S.M., 343, 348, 349, 435
Hesson-McInnis, M.S., 263
Hetherington, R., 459–460
Hetts, J.J., 212
Heuer, L.B., 129
Hewstone, M., 60, 61, 234, 286–287,
    314, 316, 456
Heyman, G.D., 289, 313, 483
Hickford, C., 195
Hicks, J.A., 24, 323
Higgins, E.T., 11–12, 43–44, 45–46,
    57, 75, 99, 148, 149, 164, 198–199,
    287, 329, 335, 346, 386, 406–407,
    455, 467, 481, 486
Hikosaka, O., 86
Hilbig, B.E., 87, 354
Hill, J., 50, 226
Hill, K., 195, 233
Hilton, D.J., 278, 308, 339
Hilton, J.L., 34, 119, 247, 363, 449
Hinkley, K., 482
Hinzman, L., 32–33
Hirst, W., 371–372, 378, 406–407
Hirt, E.R., 329, 435, 468, 485
Hitch, G.J., 400, 403
Hixon, J.G., 98, 484
Ho, A.K., 183–184
Ho, L.Y., 380
Hochstein, S., 74
Hodge, C.N., 314
Hodges, B.H., 221
Hodges, S.D., 463
Hodgkins, S., 472
Hoelzl, E., 328
Höfel, L., 194
Hofer, G., 353
Hoffman, C., 375
Hoffman, H.G., 377–378, 494
Hoffman, K.M., 166
Hoffrage, U., 349

Hofmann, W., 69, 83, 84, 90, 200,
    473, 474, 476
Hogarth, R.M., 331, **349**, 464
Hogg, M.A., 225, 426
Hohman, Z.P., 463
Hojat, M., 329
Holbrook, J., 254, 297
Holland, E., 396, 453
Holland, R.W., 80, 209, 456, 480, 488
Hollander, S., 195
Holleran, S.E., 175
Hollingshead, A.B., 405
Hollins, T.J., 396
Holmes, D.S., 264
Holt, B.C., 377–378
Holtz, P., 35
Holtzworth-Munroe, A., 312
Holyoak, K.J., 300
Holzberg, A.D., 261
Homish, G.G., 476
Hon, A., 248
Hong, Y.-Y., 289, 302–303, 461
Honkanen, P., 457
Hood, B., 213
Hoover, G.M., 157–158, 219
Horberg, E.J., 224
Horgan, T.G., 488
Horn, S.S., 349
Horne, S.G., 313
Hornsey, M.J., 315
Horowitz, M.J., 463–464
Horrey, W.J., 116
Horton, R.S., 222
Horvath, S., 211
Houben, K., 473
Houghton, D.P., 319
House, P., 265, 354
Hout, M.C., 480
Houts, C.R., 313
Hovland, C.I., 203
Howard, G.S., 24
Howard, J.W., 228
Howe, L.C., 209, 457
Howe, M.L., 393
Howell, J.L., 232
Hu, L., 361
Huang, C., 484
Huang, J.Y., 193–194
Huang, L., 140, 194
Huang, L.M., 140, 194
Huang, W., 481
Huang, Y., 194
Huart, J., 142
Huberman, G., 330
Hubert, S., 220, 331
Huebsch, P.D., 401
Huffman, L.J., 221
Hug, F., 476
Hugenberg, K., 72, 124, 137–138,
    141, 142, 361, 396, 494

SUBJECT INDEX